Human Resource Management

First Canadian Edition

Human Resource Management

First Canadian Edition

Robert L. Mathis
University of Nebraska at Omaha

John H. Jackson
University of Wyoming

Deborah M. Zinni
Brock University

Australia Canada Mexico Singapore Spain United Kingdom United States

Human Resource Management
First Canadian Edition

by Robert L. Mathis, John H. Jackson, and Deborah M. Zinni

Associate Vice President, Editorial Director:
Evelyn Veitch

Publisher:
Veronica Visentin

Acquisitions Editor:
Shannon White

Senior Developmental Editor:
Karina Hope

Photo Researcher/Permissions Coordinator:
Kristiina Bowering

Content Production Manager:
Wendy Yano

Copy Editor/Proofreader:
Erin Moore

Indexer:
Edwin Durbin

Senior Production Coordinator:
Ferial Suleman

Design Director:
Ken Phipps

Interior Design:
Jack Steiner

Cover Design:
Montage Studio

Cover Images:
Top: Tipp Howell/Taxi/Getty Images; Middle left: © Royalty-Free/Corbis; Middle: © Don Mason/Corbis; Middle right: Andreas Kindler/Johner Images/Getty Images; Bottom: Photodisc Blue/Getty Images. Part Opener Image: © Royalty-Free/Corbis.

Compositor:
Integra

Printer:
Thomson/West

Printed and bound in the United States
1 2 3 4 10 09 08 07

For more information contact Nelson, 1120 Birchmount Road, Toronto, Ontario, M1K 5G4. Or you can visit our Internet site at http://www.nelson.com

Library and Archives Canada Cataloguing in Publication

Mathis, Robert L., 1944–
Human resource management / Robert L. Mathis, John H. Jackson, Deborah M. Zinni.
—1st Canadian ed.

Includes bibliographical references and index.
ISBN-13: 978-0-17-625144-4
ISBN-10: 0-17-625144-8

1. Personnel management. I. Jackson, John Harold II. Zinni, Deborah M., 1956– III. Title.

HF5549.M3348 2007 658.3
C2006-905971-3

TO

Jo Ann Mathis
who manages me

R. D. and M. M. Jackson
who were successful managers of people for many years

Joe, Michael, and Ozzie
who know how to keep me balanced

Contents in Brief

Contents

PART 4

COMPENSATING HUMAN RESOURCES 359

Preface

Welcome to *Human Resource Management*, First Canadian Edition! In today's competitive business environment, the study of human resource management has never been more important. It is through people that organizations gain their competitive advantage. It is through the *management* of people that organizations can sustain it. With dynamic changing environments, human resource professionals need to ensure that they have the necessary knowledge, skills, and abilities to meet the needs of their organizations, and *Human Resource Management,* First Canadian Edition will provide you with the tools you need to be successful. The authors bring to you their multiple years of practical experience in the field in addition to their academic training, and provide many real-world examples throughout the textbook.

Human Resource Management was written to address a wide range of challenges. One of the more pressing issues for human resources today is being a strategic player. As such, each of the chapters ensures that HR professionals are well equipped to consider the strategic challenges that they may face. In today's fast and dynamic environments, it is becoming increasingly important for human resource professionals to understand the effects of globalization, technology, and more importantly, the role that strategy plays in the delivery of programs. This book also addresses a wide range of audiences. Whether you are a manager who needs to deal with human resource issues, a small business owner who needs to know the basics of HR, a senior manager who needs a general understanding of the topic, an instructor who needs to teach students the elements required for certification of their CHRP, or a new graduate who may be seeking employment in human resources, this book will be an invaluable resource. With both global and strategic perspectives, this book will aid the HR professional to be ready to meet the needs of both the organization and, more importantly, its people, without whom there would be no need for such a text.

The First Canadian Edition

Human Resource Management, First Canadian Edition has been written to reflect the challenges facing HR management as they evolve. As well as the research content, this edition has other useful features that are worth noting, as follows:

HR Metrics

The value of HR management activities increasingly has to be justified to executives in organizations by using financial and other data. To identify ways to respond to these pressures, *Human Resource Management* includes a feature in most chapters called "HR Metrics" that identifies how different HR management activities are being measured. By incorporating "HR Metrics" into each chapter, the student will be able to practice the metric as it relates directly to the HR topic matter, and thus gain a better understanding of its application. A special metrics icon is used to identify this content.

Global Coverage

Rather than having a separate chapter on global HR management, the coverage of global issues has been integrated throughout the various chapters. This integration is a reflection of the current business environment, in which most organizations face global competition. Consequently, HR issues and practices are becoming more transnational in nature. In the chapters, global material is indicated with a small global icon and highlighted in the HR Globally boxed feature where applicable.

HR Headline

An HR Headline opens every chapter. This feature contains an example of a contemporary HR problem, situation, or practice to more fully illustrate a concept presented in the chapter.

Learning Objectives

Learning Objectives are listed at the beginning of each chapter to provide the basis for the Integrated Learning System. These help to keep the students focused on key areas within a particular HR subject matter, which in turn helps the student to break down the learning into interrelated components. Icons that identify the learning objectives appear throughout the text and all ancillaries.

Integrated Learning System

The Integrated Learning System uses each chapter's learning objectives to give structure and coherence to the text and instructor's ancillaries, all of which are keyed to these objectives. Learning Objectives at the beginning of each chapter outline the goals for study. These objectives are reinforced throughout each chapter, in the Chapter Summary, and again throughout the ancillaries. Each piece of the integrated learning system reinforces the other components to help students learn quickly and to ease lecture preparation.

Technology Transforming HR

Technology Transforming HR boxes focus on how technology is being used to change how HR activities are performed. This feature is found in most of the chapters and serves as both a preview of how HR will be changing and a source of information on specific approaches currently being used. Critical Thinking Questions follow every box.

HR Perspective

Each chapter contains at least one HR Perspective, a feature that highlights HR management examples, ethical issues, and research studies. Critical Thinking Questions follow every box.

HR Practice

Many chapters contain HR Practice boxes. This feature presents suggestions on how to handle specific HR issues or situations. Critical Thinking Questions follow every box.

Logging On

This feature provides website links to content beyond what is found in the text.

Key Terms

Key terms appear in boldface and are defined in margin notes next to the text discussion. The same as the learning objectives, these help the student to focus on important elements within a given HR subject matter. The key terms are also listed at the end of the chapter and appear in the glossary at the end of the text.

Figures

An abundance of graphic materials and flowcharts provides a visual, dynamic presentation of concepts and HR activities.

Summary

Each chapter includes a paragraph or two for each learning objective, providing a brief and focused review of the chapter.

Review and Application Questions

These questions provide critical thinking queries. A question for each Learning Objective in the chapter is included.

Experiential Exercises

These exercises, representing many real-world examples, have been carefully selected as skill building exercises to help students gain practical experience when dealing with human resource issues such as compensation, training, and benefits.

Learning Review

A selection of multiple-choice questions grouped by Learning Objective is included at the end of each chapter for quick student self-testing of key concepts.

Case

An end-of-chapter case has been selected to focus on each chapter's concepts. Through the case, students apply their knowledge of the chapter material and think more critically about the themes of the chapter.

Video Cases

Video cases are found at the end of each part. The video clips have been selected to support the themes of the book and to broaden students' understanding of the material.

Reference Notes

The Reference notes cite sources used in the chapter, with particular attention given to the inclusion of the most current references and research possible. This text represents the most up-to-date references, making this book the most current HR text available.

Organization of the First Canadian Edition

The following overview highlights some of the significant content.

HR's Strategic Contribution to Organizational Effectiveness

This text stresses how HR professionals and the activities they direct contribute to the strategic business success of organizations. The first chapter looks at the roles of HR management, particularly the importance of the *strategic* role of HR management, and how it is being affected by HR technology. The competencies for careers in HR also are discussed. Chapter 2 addresses the strategic factors affecting HR, strategic HR planning, and how to evaluate the effectiveness of HR management. In the competitive world of today, organizations need individuals who perform well and remain as employees. No other general HR text provides comparable in-depth coverage of retention, which is fast becoming the most important concern for employers.

Staffing the Organization

Chapter 3 introduces the legal framework including the Canadian Charter of Rights and Freedom, employment standards, and other relevant legislation. Diversity is also incorporated into this framework. Because the issues of diversity and equal employment are so closely linked, various aspects of implementing equal employment opportunities, such as employment and pay equity, sexual harassment, discrimination, and other issues, are also included. The prohibited grounds of discrimination have been highlighted with specific court cases that have appropriately addressed each of the issues. Nepotism and workplace romances have been thoroughly discussed—making these unique topics not extensively discussed in other texts. The chapter concludes with an extensive discussion of diversity and the importance of managing diversity as a critical part of HR management.

Chapter 4 describes job design issues that have an impact on organizations and the people working in them. Based on job design, the chapter then provides useful coverage of job analysis and various approaches to and methods of job analysis.

Chapter 5 focuses on recruiting in various labour markets. It discusses the difficulties of recruiting employees with rare skills—and new methods to attract individuals with rare skills. The chapter contains considerable content on Internet recruiting and the evaluation of recruiting efforts. Chapter 6 encompasses the selection strategy choices that management must make, including the importance of reliability and validity. The discussion of psychological testing and interviewing approaches and techniques reflects current research and practices in HR management.

Training and Developing Human Resources

Chapter 7 discusses the strategic role training plays in organizations and how training must be linked to business strategies and organizational competitiveness. Specific content on adult learning and newer training design and delivery means is provided. As the text addresses the growing use of *e-learning,* it discusses both the contributions and problems associated with Web-based training.

Chapter 8 on Careers and HR development looks at the means organizations use to expand the capabilities of their human resources. The unique issues associated with the designated groups and career barriers are extensively discussed. The chapter contains content on succession planning and why it is a growing focus of HR management.

Chapter 9 expands the material on identifying and measuring employee performance, including additional information on the numerous approaches used. The chapter emphasizes performance management and the role of the performance appraisal process in enhancing the performance of human resources in organizations.

Compensating Human Resources

Compensation of human resources covers pay, incentives, and benefits. Chapters 10 and 11 include information on approaches such as broadbanding and competency-based pay to augment the well-regarded coverage of base compensation, pay-for-performance, and variable-pay programs already in those chapters.

Chapter 12 highlights the growing concerns of the cost of benefits, which face HR professionals and organizations, with specific new content that discusses consumer-driven health-care programs.

Employee Relations

The discussion of employee relations addresses several areas, including health, safety, and security. The coverage in Chapter 13 identifies current health and safety issues and compliance requirements. Young workers are highlighted, given their propensity to incur higher than average accident rates in the workplace. Ergonomics is also discussed extensively as are hazards in the workplace. Emotional/mental health issues focuses on the key job stressors that can affect workplace productivity and individual health. The chapter also provides new content on the prevention of workplace violence and the importance of workplace security, as well as issues concerning pandemics in light of global issues.

The various issues associated with employee rights and discipline, such as privacy rights, wrongful dismissal, and substance abuse, are discussed in Chapter 14. Employment contracts highlight issues that employers should consider, as well as non-disclosure and non-competition agreements. It also looks at such emerging issues as electronic monitoring, privacy, e-mail, and other employee-rights issues affected by technology. Landmark cases provide examples of these issues. Whistleblowing discusses the inherent problems employees may face, and the legal protection available to them. The chapter ends with a discussion of how HR should handle matters concerning discipline.

The changing role of unions in the Canadian economy is discussed in Chapter 15. In addition to covering the basic laws and regulations governing union-management relations in Canada, the chapter discusses reasons for the declining percentage of workers in unions and the challenges facing both unions and management. It concludes with coverage of collective bargaining and grievance management.

Supplements

Instructor's Manual with Video Guide

The instructor's manual represents one of the most exciting and useful instructor's aids available. Comprehensive teaching materials, including chapter overviews, chapter outlines, instructor's notes, and suggested answers to end-of-chapter Review and Application Questions and Case Studies. The video guide describes the content in the video segments that is available to help integrate chapter content through current, interesting examples. The Instructor's Manual is available on both the Instructor's Resource CD and on a password protected Instructor's website.

Test Bank

The test bank contains more than 1500 test questions. Multiple-choice, true/false, and essay questions are provided for every chapter. Answers are cross-referenced to pages within the text so that it is easy to pinpoint where relevant material is found. When the answer to a true/false question is "false," feedback is provided to underscore the reason why. Questions are identified by type, such as definition and related to learning objectives from the chapter. The test bank is available on the Instructor's Resource CD.

ExamView

ExamView contains all of the questions in the printed test bank. This program is an easy-to-use test creation software compatible with Microsoft Windows. Instructors can add or edit questions, instructions, and answers. Questions may be selected by previewing them on screen, selecting them randomly, or selecting them by number. Instructors can also create quizzes online whether over the Internet, a local area network (LAN), or a wide area network (WAN). The ExamView test bank is available on the Instructor's Resource CD.

PowerPoint Slide Presentation

PowerPoint slides are available on both the Instructor's Resource CD and on a password protected Instructor's website. Approximately 400 slides are included.

Instructor's Resource CD (0-17-644167-0)

The Instructor's Resource CD includes the instructor's manual, test bank, PowerPoints, and ExamView.

JoinIn on TurningPoint

JoinIn on TurningPoint is simply the easiest, most powerful, completely interactive Microsoft PowerPoint tool on the market today. This unique tool transforms PowerPoint presentation files into an easy-to-use, graphically enhanced system for delivering interactive content in the classroom. By using JoinIn on TurningPoint, instructors can pose questions to a large group, gather results, compare percentages to the class average, and display them in the class in "real time" while using PowerPoint presentation slides. Ask your Thomson Nelson sales rep about JoinIn on TurningPoint!

Video (0-17-644175-1)

The video collection features companies and/or particular individuals with a relevant HR issue. All video content is closely tied to concepts within the text.

Website

At the website dedicated to the First Canadian Edition of *Human Resource Management*, instructors and students will find useful tools and additional resources to enrich and extend textbook presentations. Instructors will find downloadable ancillary materials. Students and other readers can locate other resources, such as quick links to a number of useful items. The website is found at www.mathis.nelson.com. Some of the items included on the website are Test Yourself questions, chapter Web links, study resources, listings of HR literature, supplemental cases, Professional Practice in Human Resources (RPCs), and more.

Acknowledgments

Deepest thanks go to the reviewers who helped to shape the First Canadian Edition of *Human Resource Management*. They include:

D. Robert Bagg
Mount Saint Vincent University

Kathryne Dupré
Memorial University of Newfoundland

Linda Eligh
University of Western Ontario

Suzanne Kavanagh
George Brown College

Elizabeth Kelley
Dalhousie University

Beverly Linnell
Southern Alberta Institute of Technology

Barbara Lipton
Seneca College of Applied Arts & Technology

Aaron Schat
McMaster University

Piers Steel
University of Calgary

Chantal Westgate
McGill University

I am deeply indebted to Roseanne Ida who has worked with me relentlessly throughout this entire process. As well, both Leah Smyth and Michelle Leece offered much needed assistance. All three of these individuals answered the call at ridiculous hours and met demanding timelines. Without their efforts this book would not have met the highest standards we all aimed to achieve. I am also thankful to my good friend Michelle who kept reminding me of fast approaching deadlines. Each one of them played a pivotal role in the completion of this text.

Thanks also go to Karina Hope, Senior Developmental Editor; Mary Stangolis, Editorial Assistant; Kristriina Bowering, Permissions Coordinator; Wendy Yano, Content Production Manager; Erin Moore, Copyeditor; and Veronica Visentin, Publisher. Particular thanks go to Karina, Kristriina, Mary, and Erin who were always there to provide excellent advice. Their professionalism, coupled with their witty sense of humour has made this monumental task achievable. They truly set an example of how teams are supposed to operate to be successful.

The authors feel confident that this edition will set a high standard for the HR field. We believe it offers a relevant and interesting look at HR management, and we are optimistic that those who use the book will agree.

Deborah M. Zinni, CHRP
Mississauga, Ontario

John H. Jackson
Laramie, Wyoming

Robert L. Mathis, SPHR
Omaha, Nebraska

About the Authors

Dr. Robert L. Mathis

Dr. Robert Mathis is Professor of Management at the University of Nebraska at Omaha (UNO). Born and raised in Texas, he received a B.B.A. and M.B.A. from Texas Tech University and a Ph.D. in Management and Organization from the University of Colorado. At UNO he has received the University's "Excellence in Teaching" award.

Dr. Mathis has co-authored several books and has published numerous articles covering a variety of topics over the last 25 years. Dr. Mathis also has held numerous national offices in the Society for Human Resource Management and in other professional organizations, including the Academy of Management. He has served as President of the Human Resource Certification Institute (HRCI) and is certified as a Senior Professional in Human Resources (SPHR) by HRCI.

He has had extensive consulting experiences with organizations of all sizes and in a variety of areas. Firms assisted have been in telecommunications, telemarketing, financial, manufacturing, retail, health-care, and utility industries. He has extensive specialized consulting experience in establishing or revising compensation plans for small- and medium-sized firms. Internationally, Dr. Mathis has consulting and training experience with organizations in Australia, Lithuania, Romania, Moldova, and Taiwan.

Dr. John H. Jackson

Dr. John H. Jackson is Professor of Management at the University of Wyoming. Born in Alaska, he received his B.B.A. and M.B.A. from Texas Tech University. He then worked in the telecommunications industry in human resources management for several years. After leaving that industry, he completed his doctoral studies at the University of Colorado and received his Ph.D. in Management and Organization.

During his academic career, Dr. Jackson has authored four other college texts and over 50 articles and papers, including those appearing in *Academy of Management Review, Journal of Management, Human Resources Management,* and *Human Resources Planning*. He has consulted widely with a variety of organizations on HR and management development matters. During the past several years, Dr. Jackson has served as an expert witness in a number of HR-related cases.

At the University of Wyoming, he has served three terms as Department Head in the Department of Management and Marketing. Dr. Jackson has received the top teaching award at Wyoming and was one of the first to work with two-way interactive television for MBA students in the state. He has served on the boards of directors of the Wyoming Business Council and the Wyoming Workforce Development Council. In addition to teaching, Dr. Jackson is president of Silverwood Ranches, Inc.

Dr. Deborah M. Zinni

Dr. Deborah Zinni is a Professor in the Faculty of Business at Brock University in St. Catharines, Ontario. Born in Northern Ontario, she received her post secondary education in Southern Ontario. Deborah received her Bachelor of Business Administration from York University, as well as her M.B.A. from Schulich School of Business at York, and her Ph.D. in Human Resources and Industrial Relations from McMaster University.

Dr. Zinni brings with her over 20 years of senior human resource management experience in various industries, having worked at companies such as NEC Canada Inc., Nissan Canada Inc., and Proctor & Redfern. Her combined academic and professional experiences allow her the advantage of bringing real-world examples, both in the classroom and in her written work. She also possesses extensive consulting experience.

She has authored several articles pertaining to industrial relations, specifically the union organizing of graduate students in the U.S. and in Canada, the participation decisions of union members and striker replacement workers. Additionally, she researches and writes papers on the retention of Aboriginal workers in Canada, as well as the duty to consult with respect to employment equity.

Dr. Zinni has sat on several committees at the Human Resources Professional Association of Ontario (HRPAO) pertaining to professional standards and educational standards. She also holds a Certified Human Resources Professional designation (CHRP).

An avid hockey fan, you can find her at a rink most evenings. She is the one with the lap top or marking papers with a blanket wrapped around her, raising her head now and again to cheer on her son whilst calming down her husband at the same time! A multi-tasker to be sure!

Features

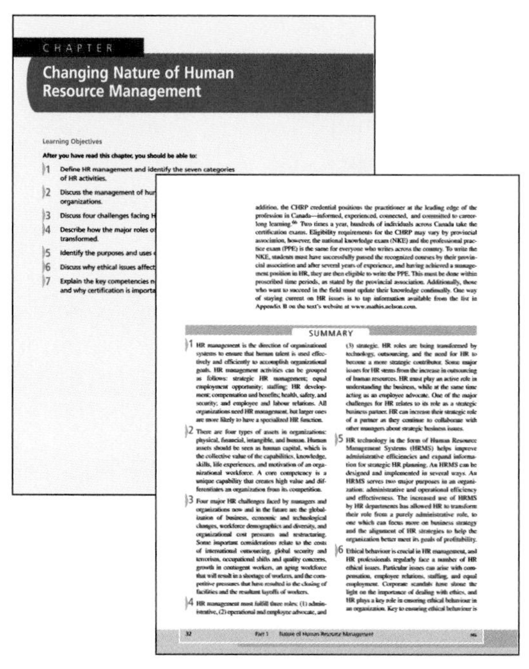
CHAPTER

Changing Nature of Human Resource Management

Learning Objectives

SUMMARY

The Integrated Learning System uses each chapter's learning objectives to give structure and coherence to the text and instructor's ancillaries, all of which are keyed to these objectives. Learning Objectives at the beginning of each chapter outline the goals for study. These objectives are reinforced throughout each chapter, in the Chapter Summary, and again throughout the ancillaries. Each piece of the integrated learning system reinforces the other components to help students learn quickly and to simplify lecture preparation.

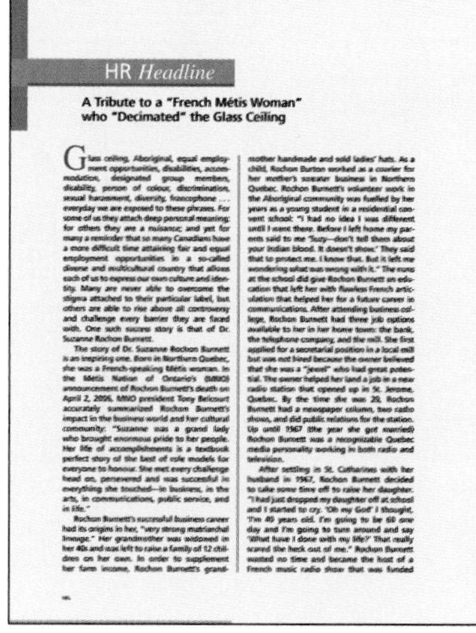
HR *Headline*

A Tribute to a "French Métis Woman" who "Decimated" the Glass Ceiling

An HR Headline opens every chapter. This feature contains an example of a contemporary HR problem, situation, or practice to more fully illustrate a concept presented in the chapter.

Technology Transforming HR

Telework and Technology

Technology Transforming HR boxes focus on how technology is being used to change how HR activities are performed. This feature is found in every chapter and serves as both a preview of how HR will be changing and a source of information on specific approaches currently being used. Critical Thinking Questions follow every box.

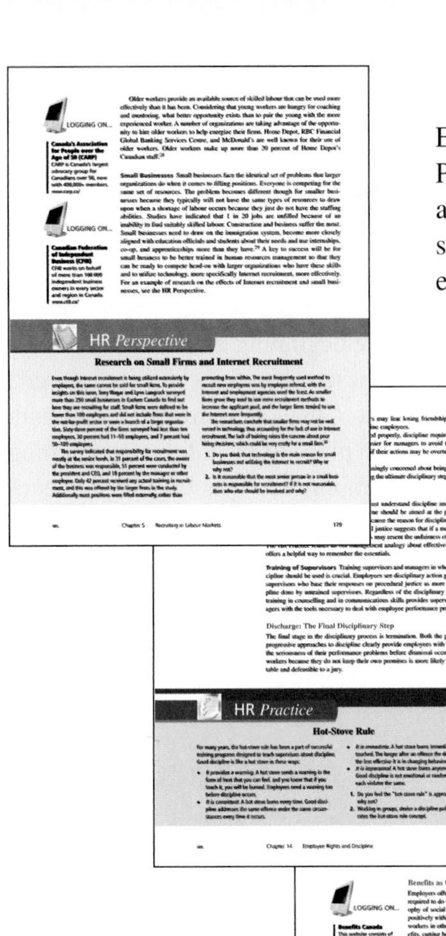
HR Perspective

Research on Small Firms and Internet Recruitment

Each chapter contains at least one HR Perspective, a feature that highlights HR management examples, ethical issues, and research studies. Critical Thinking Questions follow every box.

Many chapters contain HR Practice boxes. This feature presents suggestions on how to handle specific HR issues or situations. Critical Thinking Questions follow every box.

This Logging On feature provides website links to content beyond what is found in the text.

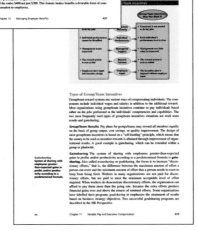

Key terms appear in boldface and are defined in margin notes next to the text discussion. The key terms are also listed at the end of the chapter and appear in the glossary at the end of the text.

The value of HR management activities increasingly has to be justified to executives in organizations by using financial and other data. To identify ways to respond to these pressures, *Human Resource Management* includes a feature in most chapters called "HR Metrics" that identifies how different HR management activities are being measured.

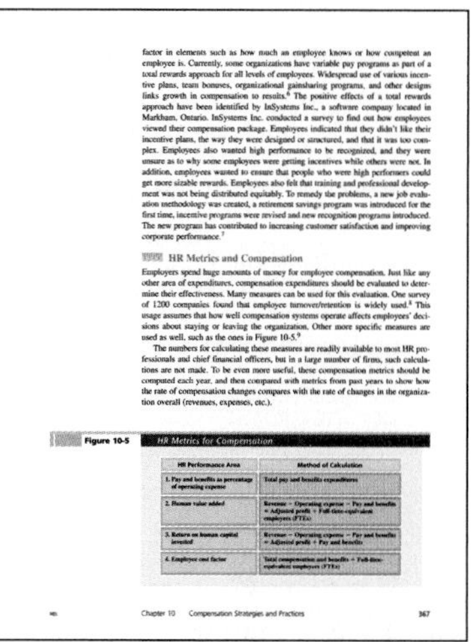

factor in elements such as how much an employee knows or how competent an employee is. Currently, some organizations have variable pay programs as part of a total rewards approach for all levels of employees. Widespread use of various incentive plans, team bonuses, organizational gainsharing programs, and other designs links growth in compensation to results.[6] The positive effects of a total rewards approach have been identified by InSystems Inc., a software company located in Markham, Ontario. InSystems Inc. conducted a survey to find out how employees viewed their compensation package. Employees indicated that they didn't like their incentive plans, the way they were designed or structured, and that it was too complex. Employees also wanted high performance to be recognized, and they were unsure as to why some employees were getting incentives while others were not. In addition, employees wanted to ensure that people who were high performers could get more sizable rewards. Employees also felt that training and professional development was not being distributed equitably. To remedy the problems, a new job evaluation methodology was created, a retirement savings program was introduced for the first time, incentive programs were revised and new recognition programs introduced. The new program has contributed to increasing customer satisfaction and improving corporate performance.[7]

HR Metrics and Compensation

Employers spend huge amounts of money for employee compensation. Just like any other area of expenditures, compensation expenditures should be evaluated to determine their effectiveness. Many measures can be used for this evaluation. One survey of 1200 companies found that employee turnover/retention is widely used.[8] This usage assumes that how well compensation systems operate affects employees' decisions about staying or leaving the organization. Other more specific measures are used as well, such as the ones in Figure 10-5.[9]

The numbers for calculating these measures are readily available to most HR professionals and chief financial officers, but in a large number of firms, such calculations are not made. To be even more useful, these compensation metrics should be computed each year, and then compared with metrics from past years to show how the rate of compensation changes compares with the rate of changes in the organization overall (revenues, expenses, etc.).

Figure 10-5 HR Metrics for Compensation

HR Performance Area	Method of Calculation
1. Pay and benefits as percentage of operating expense	Total pay and benefits expenditures [illegible]
2. Human value added	Revenue − Operating expense − Pay and benefits = Adjusted profit ÷ Full-time-equivalent employees (FTEs)
3. Return on human capital invested	Revenue − Operating expense − Pay and benefits = Adjusted profit ÷ Pay and benefits
4. Employee cost factor	Total compensation and benefits ÷ Full-time-equivalent employees (FTEs)

NEL Chapter 10 Compensation Strategies and Practices 367

Nature of Human Resource Management

1 As a field, human resource (HR) management is undergoing significant transformation. **Human resource (HR) management** is defined as the policies, practices, and systems that influence employee's behaviour, attitude, and performance in the attainment of organizational goals. Whether employees are in a large company with 10 000 positions or a small non-profit agency with ten positions, those employees must be recruited, selected, trained, and managed. They also must be compensated, and many will be given benefits of some type, which means that an appropriate and legal compensation system is needed. In an environment in which the workforce keeps changing, laws and the needs of employers may change too. Therefore, HR management activities continue to change and evolve.

Human resource (HR) management The policies, practices, and systems that influence employee's behaviour, attitude, and performance in the attainment of organizational goals.

HR Activities

HR management is composed of seven interlinked activities taking place within organizations, as depicted in Figure 1-1. Additionally, external forces—legal, economic, technological, global, environmental, cultural/geographic, political, and social—significantly affect HR activities and affect how they are designed, managed, and changed.

Global Forces and HR Management HR management truly is becoming transnational as organizations compete globally. For instance, in the past few years, the international outsourcing of Canadian jobs to India, the Philippines, China, and other countries has become a significant political concern. However, Canada is also in a unique position to reap the benefits of receiving jobs outsourced from the U.S., which leads the world in outsourcing jobs. Also, the worldwide growth of global firms such as Toyota and SAP means that management must consider transnational concerns in all HR activities. In this book, global content is integrated throughout all the chapters, rather than being isolated into a separate chapter. The global content is highlighted by a special global icon as the following seven HR activities are discussed.

Strategic HR Management Strategic HR management is the process of linking the HR function with the strategic objectives of the organization in order to improve performance. To anticipate and respond to the HR changes facing organizations, strategic HR management has grown in importance. As part of maintaining organizational competitiveness, *HR effectiveness* must be increased through the use of *HR metrics*. **HR metrics** are specific measures tied to HR performance indicators. One key to increasing HR effectiveness is using *HR technology*. Many organizations have *HR management systems (HRMSs)*, which use information technology to provide managers and employees with more accurate and timely information on HR programs and activities. Through *HR planning*, managers attempt to anticipate forces that will influence the future supply of and demand for employees. In light of our aging population and impending skill shortages, an important issue in HR planning is the retention of employees. All of these topics are discussed in Chapter 2.

Strategic HR management Process of linking the HR function with the strategic objectives of the organization in order to improve performance.

HR metrics Specific measures tied to HR performance indicators.

Equal Employment Opportunity *Compliance* with providing equal employment opportunities and its relevant laws and regulations affects all other HR activities and

4 Part 1 Nature of Human Resource Management NEL

Rather than having a separate chapter on global HR management, the coverage of global issues has been integrated throughout the various chapters. This integration is a reflection of the current business environment, in which most organizations face global competition. Consequently, HR issues and practices are becoming more transnational in nature. In the chapters, global material is indicated with a small global icon and highlighted in the HR Globally boxed feature where applicable.

These questions provide critical thinking queries. A question for each Learning Objective in the chapter is included.

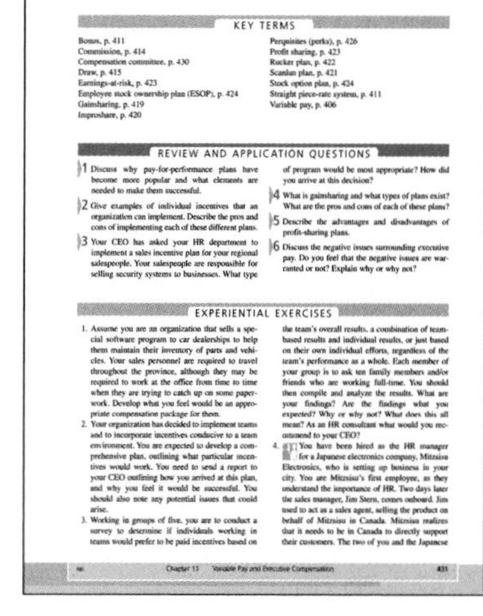

KEY TERMS

Bonus, p. 411
Commission, p. 414
Compensation committee, p. 430
Draw, p. 415
Earnings-at-risk, p. 423
Employee stock ownership plan (ESOP), p. 424
Gainsharing, p. 419
Improshare, p. 420
Perquisites (perks), p. 426
Profit sharing, p. 423
Rucker plan, p. 422
Scanlan plan, p. 421
Stock option plan, p. 424
Straight piece-rate system, p. 411
Variable pay, p. 406

REVIEW AND APPLICATION QUESTIONS

1 Discuss why pay-for-performance plans have become more popular and what elements are needed to make them successful.

2 Give examples of individual incentives that an organization can implement. Describe the pros and cons of implementing each of these different plans.

3 Your CEO has asked your HR department to implement a sales incentive plan for your regional salespeople. Your salespeople are responsible for selling security systems to businesses. What type of program would be most appropriate? How did you arrive at this decision?

4 What is gainsharing and what types of plans exist? What are the pros and cons of each of these plans?

5 Describe the advantages and disadvantages of profit-sharing plans.

6 Discuss the negative issues surrounding executive pay. Do you feel that the negative issues are warranted or not? Explain why or why not?

EXPERIENTIAL EXERCISES

1. Assume you are an organization that sells a special software program to car dealerships to help them maintain their inventory of parts and vehicles. Your sales personnel are required to travel throughout the province, although they may be required to work at the office from time to time when they are trying to catch up on some paperwork. Develop what you feel would be an appropriate compensation package for them.
2. Your organization has decided to implement teams and to incorporate incentives conducive to a team environment. You are expected to develop a comprehensive plan, outlining what particular incentives would work. You need to send a report to your CEO outlining how you arrived at this plan, and why you feel it would be successful. You should also note any potential issues that could arise.
3. Working in groups of five, you are to conduct a survey to determine if individuals working in teams would prefer to be paid incentives based on the team's overall results, a combination of team-based results and individual results, or just based on their own individual efforts, regardless of the team's performance as a whole. Each member of your group is to ask ten family members and/or friends who are working full-time. You should then compile and analyze the results. What are your findings? Are the findings what you expected? Why or why not? What does this all mean? As an HR consultant what would you recommend to your CEO?
4. You have been hired as the HR manager for a Japanese electronics company, Mitzsisu Electronics, who is setting up business in your city. You are Mitzsisu's first employee, as they understand the importance of HR. Two days later the sales manager, Jim Stern, comes onboard. Jim used to act as a sales agent, selling the product on behalf of Mitzsisu in Canada. Mitzsisu realizes that it needs to be in Canada to directly support their customers. The two of you and the Japanese

NEL Chapter 11 Variable Pay and Executive Compensation 431

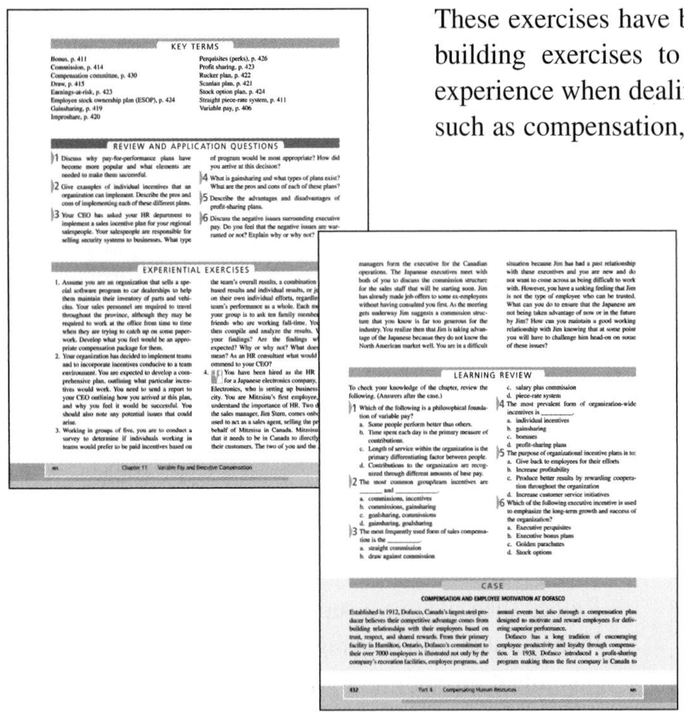

KEY TERMS

REVIEW AND APPLICATION QUESTIONS

EXPERIENTIAL EXERCISES

LEARNING REVIEW

CASE

These exercises have been carefully selected as skill building exercises to help students gain practical experience when dealing with human resource issues such as compensation, training, and benefits.

A selection of multiple-choice questions grouped by Learning Objective are included at the end of each chapter for quick student self-testing of key concepts.

End-of-chapter cases have been selected to focus on each chapter's concepts. Through the case, students apply their knowledge of the chapter material and think more critically about the themes of the chapter.

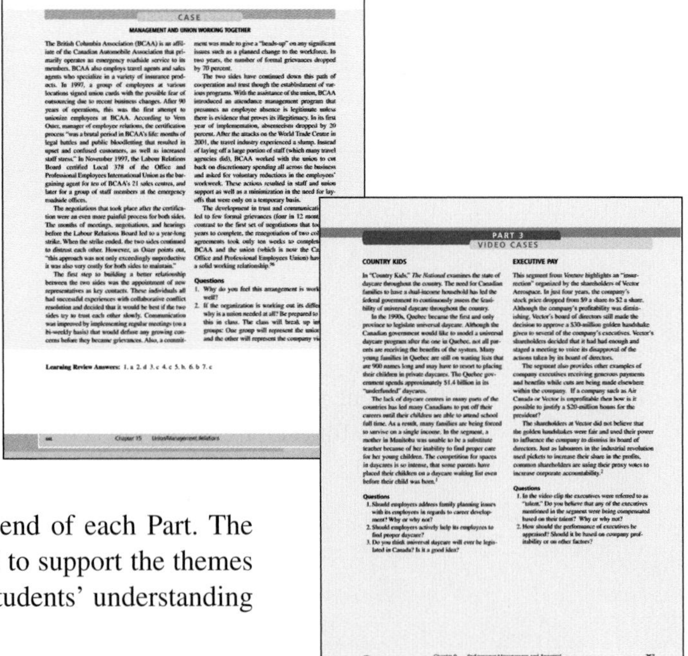

CASE

MANAGEMENT AND UNION WORKING TOGETHER

PART 3
VIDEO CASES

COUNTRY KIDS

EXECUTIVE PAY

Video cases are found at the end of each Part. The video clips have been selected to support the themes of the book and to broaden students' understanding of the material.

PART 1

Nature of Human Resource Management

CHAPTER

Changing Nature of Human Resource Management

Learning Objectives

After you have read this chapter, you should be able to:

1 Define HR management and identify the seven categories of HR activities.

2 Discuss the management of human capital in organizations.

3 Discuss four challenges facing HR today.

4 Describe how the major roles of HR management are being transformed.

5 Identify the purposes and uses of HR technology.

6 Discuss why ethical issues affect HR management.

7 Explain the key competencies needed by HR professionals and why certification is important.

HR *Headline*

What Do HR Managers Do?

The reality of what HR managers do on a weekly basis varies significantly from what is typically reported in academic and media sources. Here is some of what an HR manager in a 700-employee firm dealt with during one week:

- Resolved an employee complaint about "offensive" pictures being shown by a co-worker
- Met with the CEO to plan compensation budgets for the following year
- Met with an outside lawyer regarding a sexual harassment complaint by a former employee who had been terminated because of performance problems
- Negotiated with the provider of health-care insurance benefits to bring a projected 22-percent increase in premiums down to a 14-percent increase
- Reviewed an employee performance appraisal with a supervisor and discussed how to communicate both positive feedback and problem areas
- Advised an executive on the process for terminating a sales manager whose sales performance and management efforts were significantly below the sales goals set
- Addressed a manager's report of an employee's accessing of pornographic websites on his company computer
- Chaired an employee recognition luncheon
- Discussed an employee succession plan for the customer operations division, consisting of 400 employees
- Discussed with the other members of the executive leadership team (the CEO, the CFO, and division heads) an employee staffing plan for the following year and ways to reduce employee turnover

Many other topics were part of this HR manager's job that week. However, that list illustrates one fact: "there are a wide range of issues that are part of the regular work in HR management."

"It's very obvious to the CEO whether you get it or not. If you only understand the HR part of the business, there won't be much rapport."

—Nancy Anderson

Nature of Human Resource Management

Human resource (HR) management
The policies, practices, and systems that influence employee's behaviour, attitude, and performance in the attainment of organizational goals.

1 As a field, human resource (HR) management is undergoing significant transformation. **Human resource (HR) management** is defined as the policies, practices, and systems that influence employee's behaviour, attitude, and performance in the attainment of organizational goals. Whether employees are in a large company with 10 000 positions or a small non-profit agency with ten positions, those employees must be recruited, selected, trained, and managed. They also must be compensated, and many will be given benefits of some type, which means that an appropriate and legal compensation system is needed. In an environment in which the workforce keeps changing, laws and the needs of employers may change too. Therefore, HR management activities continue to change and evolve.

HR Activities

HR management is composed of seven interlinked activities taking place within organizations, as depicted in Figure 1-1. Additionally, external forces—legal, economic, technological, global, environmental, cultural/geographic, political, and social—significantly affect HR activities and affect how they are designed, managed, and changed.

Global Forces and HR Management HR management truly is becoming transnational as organizations compete globally. For instance, in the past few years, the international outsourcing of Canadian jobs to India, the Philippines, China, and other countries has become a significant political concern. However, Canada is also in a unique position to reap the benefits of receiving jobs outsourced from the U.S., which leads the world in outsourcing jobs. Also, the worldwide growth of global firms such as Toyota and SAP means that management must consider transnational concerns in all HR activities. In this book, global content is integrated throughout all the chapters, rather than being isolated into a separate chapter. The global content is highlighted by a special global icon as the following seven HR activities are discussed.

Strategic HR management
Process of linking the HR function with the strategic objectives of the organization in order to improve performance.

HR metrics
Specific measures tied to HR performance indicators.

Strategic HR Management **Strategic HR management** is the process of linking the HR function with the strategic objectives of the organization in order to improve performance. To anticipate and respond to the HR changes facing organizations, strategic HR management has grown in importance. As part of maintaining organizational competitiveness, *HR effectiveness* must be increased through the use of *HR metrics.* **HR metrics** are specific measures tied to HR performance indicators. One key to increasing HR effectiveness is using *HR technology.* Many organizations have *HR management systems (HRMSs*), which use information technology to provide managers and employees with more accurate and timely information on HR programs and activities. Through *HR planning,* managers attempt to anticipate forces that will influence the future supply of and demand for employees. In light of our aging population and impending skill shortages, an important issue in HR planning is the retention of employees. All of these topics are discussed in Chapter 2.

Equal Employment Opportunity *Compliance* with providing equal employment opportunities and its relevant laws and regulations affects all other HR activities and

Figure 1-1 *HR Management Activities*

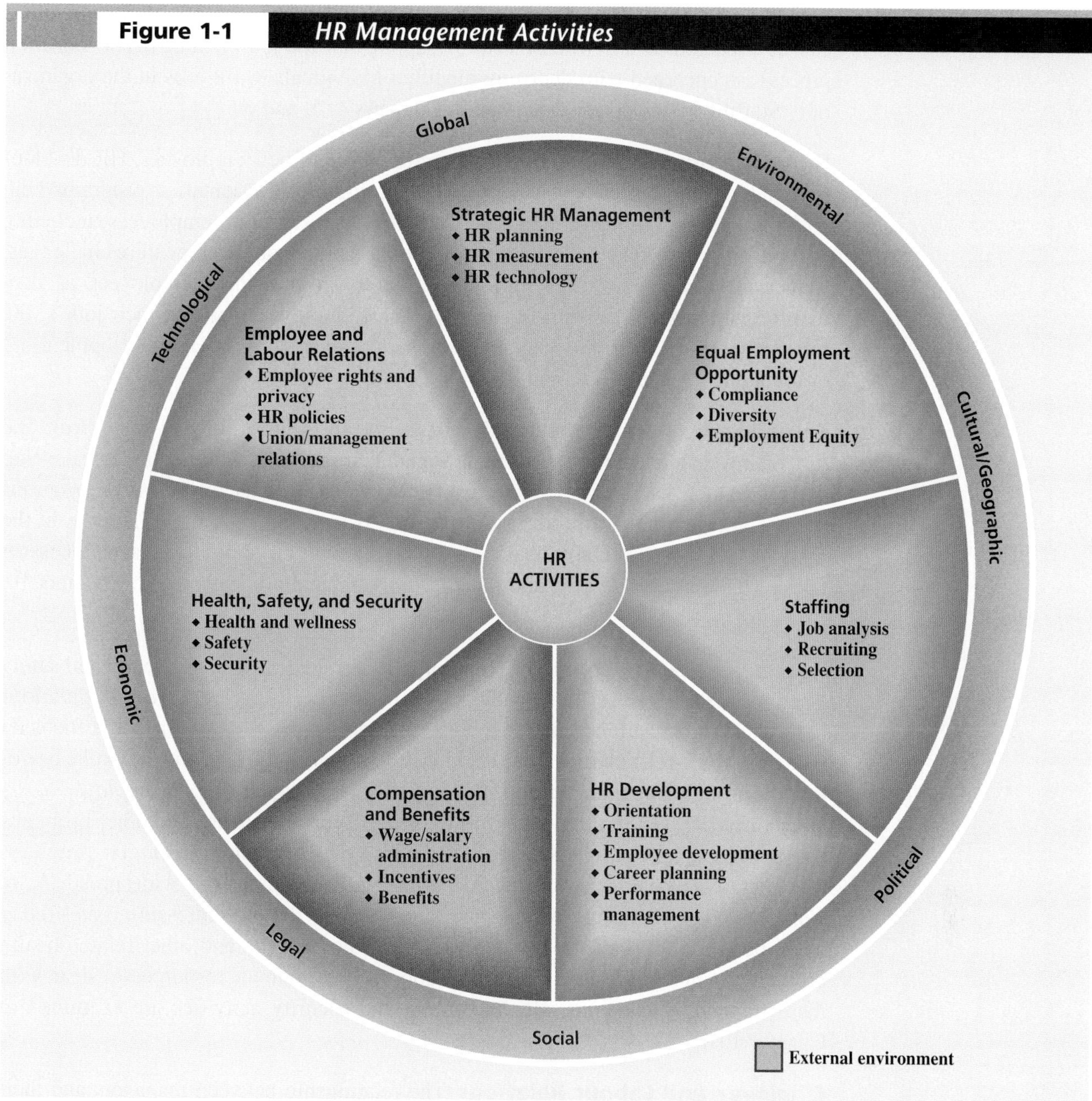

is integral to HR management. The *diversity* of a multicultural and global workforce is creating more challenges for HR professionals and all managers. For instance, strategic HR plans must ensure sufficient availability of employees who represent the "designated groups" (women, Aboriginal peoples, persons with disabilities, members of visible minorities) as determined by *Employment Equity legislation*. Human rights legislation is integral to fair and equal treatment of all Canadians. The nature of employment equity and diversity management in the context of equal opportunities in employment is discussed in Chapter 3.

Staffing The aim of staffing is to provide an adequate supply of qualified individuals to fill jobs in an organization. By studying what workers do, *job analysis* lays the foundation for the staffing function. Then both *job descriptions* and *job specifications* can be prepared to use when *recruiting* applicants for job openings. The *selection* process is concerned with choosing qualified individuals to fill jobs in the organization. Staffing activities are discussed in Chapters 4, 5, and 6.

HR Development Beginning with the *orientation* of new employees, HR development includes different types of *job-skill training*. Solid orientation programs help with the retention of key employees. Also, *development* of all employees, including supervisors and managers, is necessary to prepare organizations for future challenges. Career planning identifies paths and activities for individual employees as they develop within the organization. Assessing how employees perform their jobs is the focus of *performance management*. Activities associated with HR development are examined in Chapters 7, 8, and 9.

Compensation and Benefits Compensation in the form of *pay, incentives,* and *benefits* rewards people for performing organizational work. Employers must develop and refine their basic *wage and salary* systems. Also, the use of *incentive programs* such as gainsharing and productivity rewards is growing. The rapid increase in the costs of benefits, especially health-care benefits, will continue to be a major issue. Compensation, variable pay, and benefits activities are all discussed in Chapters 10, 11, and 12.

Health, Safety, and Security Ensuring the physical and mental health and safety of employees is vital. The Canadian Occupational Health and Safety Regulations have made organizations more responsive to concerns for *safety* through a focus on reducing work-related illnesses, accidents, injuries, bullying, and workplace violence. Through a broader focus on *health*, HR management can use *employee assistance programs (EAPs)* to help employees with substance abuse and other problems and thereby retain otherwise satisfactory employees. *Health promotion* programs that encourage healthy employee lifestyles are becoming more widespread. Also, workplace *security* has grown in importance. One of the more pressing issues today is the potential for pandemics, such as SARS, the bird flu, and other related health problems, which calls for a proactive approach by human resources to deal with these impending concerns. Health, safety, and security activities are examined in Chapter 13.

Employee and Labour Relations The relationship between managers and their employees must be handled effectively if both the employees and the organization are to prosper together. Whether or not some of the employees are represented by a union, *employee rights* must be addressed. It is important to develop, communicate, and update HR *policies and procedures* so that managers and employees alike know what is expected. In some organizations, *union/management relations* must be addressed as well. Activities associated with employee and labour/management relations are discussed in Chapters 14 and 15.

HR in Organizations

In a real sense, *every* manager in an organization is an HR manager. Sales managers, head nurses, drafting supervisors, project managers, and accounting supervisors all engage in HR management, and their effectiveness depends in part on the success of organizational HR systems. However, it is unrealistic to expect a nursing supervisor or an engineering manager to know about the nuances of equal employment legislation, or how to design and administer a compensation and benefits system. For that reason, larger organizations frequently have people in an HR department who specialize in these activities.

Smaller Organizations and HR Management In Canada and worldwide, the number of small businesses continues to grow. The term "small business" is generally understood to include businesses with fewer than 100 employees in manufacturing and fewer than 50 employees in other sectors, while "medium-sized" business are those with 100 to 500 employees. According to data from Statistics Canada, small businesses employ 49 percent of all private-sector employees and generate 50 percent to 59 percent of all net new jobs each year.[1]

In surveys conducted by the Canadian Federation of Independent Business (CFIB), the issues identified as the greatest concerns in small organizations are consistently: (1) shortages of qualified workers, (2) increasing costs such as energy and benefits, (3) legislative changes that do not necessarily consider the special needs of small business, (4) increased wage pressures, and (5) increasing competition.[2]

As a result, for many smaller organizations HR issues are often significant. But not every organization is able to maintain an HR department. In a company with an owner and only three employees, the owner usually takes care of HR issues. As an organization grows, often a clerical employee is added to handle payroll, benefits, and required HR recordkeeping. If new employees are hired, supervisors and managers usually do the recruiting, selecting, and training. These HR activities reduce the time that supervisors and managers have to focus on operations, sales and marketing, accounting, and other business areas. At 80 to 100 employees, an organization typically needs to designate a person to specialize in HR management. Other HR jobs are added as the company gets even larger.

Small business owners face many of the same HR issues as larger organizations, but have a more difficult time since many of these organizations do not possess HR expertise to solve the problems that do arise.

Source: © 2006 JupiterImages and its Licensors. All Rights Reserved.

Cooperation of HR with Operating Managers Cooperation between operating managers, such as those in sales and manufacturing, and HR staff is necessary for HR efforts to succeed. In many cases, the HR professionals and staff members design processes and systems that the operating managers must help implement. The exact division of labour between HR and other departments varies from organization to organization. For example, one organization may have the human resources department handle all orientation of new employees, whereas another organization may have the orientation of new employees handled by both human resources and the employee's supervisor.

Throughout this book, figures titled "Typical Division of HR Responsibilities" illustrate how HR responsibilities in various areas are usually divided

Figure 1-2 Typical Division of HR Responsibilities: Training

HR Unit	Managers
• Prepares skill-training materials • Coordinates training efforts • Conducts or arranges for off-the-job training • Coordinates career plans and employee development efforts • Provides input and expertise for organizational development	• Provide technical information • Monitor training needs • Conduct and monitor continuing on-the-job training • Continually discuss employees' growth and future potential • Participate in organizational change

in organizations having specialized HR departments. Figure 1-2 shows how the responsibilities for training might be divided between the HR department and operating managers in an organization.

Management of Human Capital in Organizations

2 Organizations must manage four types of assets:

- *Physical:* Buildings, land, furniture, computers, vehicles, equipment, etc.
- *Financial:* Cash, financial resources, stocks, financial securities, etc.
- *Intangible:* Specialized research capabilities, patents, information systems, designs, operating processes, etc.
- *Human:* Individuals with talents, capabilities, experience, professional expertise, relationships, etc.

All these assets are crucial in varying degrees. However, the human assets are the "glue" that holds all the other assets together and guides their use to achieve organizational goals and results.[3] Certainly, the cashiers, stockers, supervisors, and other employees at Home Depot or the doctors, nurses, receptionists, technical professionals, and other employees at a hospital allow all the other assets of their organization to be used to provide customer or patient services. By recognizing the importance of human assets, organizations are increasingly emphasizing human capital.

Human Capital and HR

Human capital
The collective value of the capabilities, knowledge, skills, life experiences, and motivation of an organizational workforce.

Human capital is not the people in organizations—it is what those people bring and contribute to organizational success.[4] **Human capital** is the collective value of the capabilities, knowledge, skills, life experiences, and motivation of an organizational workforce.

Sometimes it is called *intellectual capital* to reflect the thinking, knowledge, creativity, and decision making that people in organizations contribute. For example, firms with high intellectual capital may have technical and research employees who create new biomedical devices, formulate pharmaceuticals that can be patented, and develop new software for specialized uses. All these organizational contributions indicate the value of human capital.

Measuring the Value of Human Capital The value of human resources in organizations can be seen in various ways. One is sheer costs. In some industries, such as the hospitality industry, employee costs exceed 60 percent of total operating costs. Various studies have found that an average of 60 percent to 70 percent of total company expenditures are related to human resources today, compared with about 38 percent in 1992.[5]

Increasingly, organizations are recognizing the strategic value of their human assets.[6] With that recognition comes an increasing need to measure how the value of their human capital is changing.[7] This focus on human capital, much like that on other capital resources such as finances, has led to greater interactions between HR leaders and chief financial officers (CFOs). One study by Mercer, a global consulting firm, found that most CFOs see human capital as a key factor in creating value for shareholders. However, only 16 percent have calculated the return on human capital investments.[8] The measurement of human capital is discussed more in Chapter 2.

Human Resources as a Core Competency

The development and implementation of specific organizational strategies must be based on the areas of strength in an organization. Referred to as *core competencies,* those strengths are the foundation for creating a competitive advantage for an organization. A **core competency** is a unique capability that creates high value and differentiates an organization from its competition.

Core competency
A unique capability that creates high value and differentiates an organization from its competition.

Certainly, many organizations have stated that their human resources differentiate them from their competitors and are a key determinant of competitive advantage.[9] Studies also have documented that HR practices help create competitive advantages.[10] Organizations as widely diverse as the Royal Bank and Rogers Communications have focused on human resources as having special strategic value for the organization.

Some ways that organizations make human resources a core competency are attracting and retaining employees with unique professional and technical capabilities, investing in the training and development of those employees, and compensating them in ways that retain them and keep them competitive with their counterparts in other organizations. For example, organizations such as Loblaws have made it easier for their customers with one-stop shopping for items such as prescriptions, dry cleaning, clothing, household items, mortgages, and a host of other services, in addition to their groceries. This offers their employees a wide variety of opportunities for employment. The focus is on developing their human resources to give them a competitive advantage as they face significant HR challenges.

HR Management Challenges

3 The environment faced by organizations and their managers is a challenging one. A force affecting the management of human resources is the *globalization of business,* as shown in such areas as international outsourcing and global competitive pressures. Significant changes in *economic forces* and the rapid growth in *technology* have changed how people work. *Changing demographics* in the workforce are significantly affecting HR management, particularly with the increase in the diversity of employees and the aging of the workforce in many countries. All of these factors are combining to put more *cost pressures* on organizations. Consequently, employers in many industries have reduced the number of jobs and employees as part of *organizational restructuring.* A look at some of these challenges follows.

Globalization of Business

The internationalization of business has proceeded at a rapid pace. Many Canadian firms, both large and small, receive a substantial portion of their profits and sales from other countries. The U.S. continues to be a major trading partner for Canada. The U.S. share of Canadian exports has climbed by 10 percent to 85 percent over the past decade. At the same time, Canada has become less dependent on the U.S. for imports and has increased trading with many other countries. In particular, there has been an increase in trade activity with China, as well as with other Asian nations.[11] Bombardier is an example of a Canadian organization that has taken advantage of the global market, with over 95 percent of its revenues being earned outside of the Canadian market.[12] Conversely, a number of Japanese conglomerates such as Toyota, Honda, and Nikon have invested in Canada. Canada is now about the 15th largest recipient of Japanese foreign direct investment behind the United Kingdom, Australia, Brazil, and others.[13]

The globalization of business has shifted from trade and investment to the integration of global operations, management, and strategic alliances, which has significantly affected the management of human resources. The United States have taken the lead in international outsourcing. However, the outsourcing of jobs remains a dilemma for many—while companies and investors can reap rewards from reduced payroll costs and customers from cheaper goods and services, workers can lose their jobs. Whenever international outsourcing occurs, HR management should be involved to ensure the appropriate consideration of various laws, cultural factors, and other issues.[14]

Outsourcing
Business strategy that companies implement to focus on core functions in order to reduce costs.

Offshoring
Moving of work that would typically have been done domestically, to another country.

Outsourcing Outsourcing is a business strategy that many large Canadian and multinational companies implement to focus on core functions in order to reduce costs. **Outsourcing** involves two major concepts: IT outsourcing and/or business process outsourcing. Meta Group Canada is forecasting 15 percent to 20 percent annual growth in IT outsourcing in Canada over the next few years. That will see an increase from $6.8 billion in 2003 to $8.9 billion in 2007.[15] Canadian information technology will be radically transformed by 2010 as more IT services are outsourced offshore. **Offshoring** occurs when work that could be performed domestically, is moved to another country. The work could still be performed by your company, called "*captive offshoring*" or a third party could perform the work, which is referred to as "*offshore outsourcing*." As many as 75 000 Canadian IT jobs, or 1 in 7, are projected to disappear as a result of offshore outsourcing. However, Canada still lags many other countries such as the U.S. and the U.K. in the amount of offshore outsourcing.[16]

The primary reason for these shifts is to save on labour costs. A Java computer programmer with a university degree is paid about $5,000 a year in India, but $60,000 a year in Canada. The average yearly pay of financial analysts who have MBAs and are fluent in English is $15,000 to $20,000 in Bulgaria, Argentina, and India, compared with $100,000 or more in Canada. Less-skilled, English-speaking employees of customer call centres average $150 a month in China, whereas comparable Canadian employees make about $2,500 a month.

Canada currently leads the G7 countries for low business costs, with a cost advantage of 5.5 percent over the U.S.[17] Even though India is a popular choice for outsourcing, they have recognized Canada's cost advantage and all five of the major Indian-based outsourcers have opened up development facilities in Canada, as have major U.S.-based outsourcers.[18] Call centre work, though not IT-intensive, has been a major form of offshore work that has gravitated to Canada, particularly from the U.S. A study conducted for HRDC estimates that 500 000 Canadians are employed in call centre work.[19]

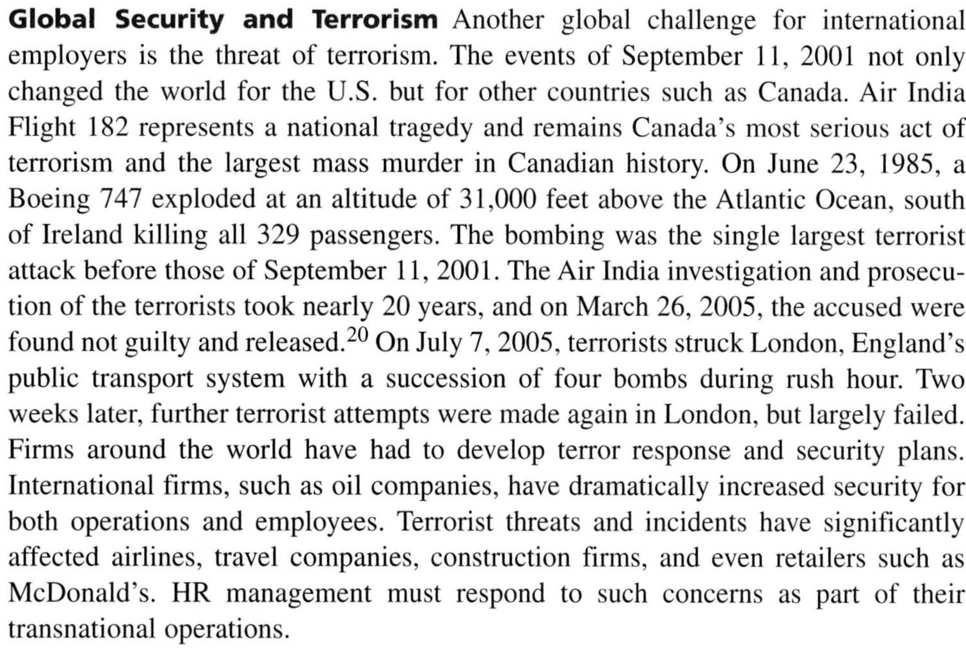

Global Security and Terrorism Another global challenge for international employers is the threat of terrorism. The events of September 11, 2001 not only changed the world for the U.S. but for other countries such as Canada. Air India Flight 182 represents a national tragedy and remains Canada's most serious act of terrorism and the largest mass murder in Canadian history. On June 23, 1985, a Boeing 747 exploded at an altitude of 31,000 feet above the Atlantic Ocean, south of Ireland killing all 329 passengers. The bombing was the single largest terrorist attack before those of September 11, 2001. The Air India investigation and prosecution of the terrorists took nearly 20 years, and on March 26, 2005, the accused were found not guilty and released.[20] On July 7, 2005, terrorists struck London, England's public transport system with a succession of four bombs during rush hour. Two weeks later, further terrorist attempts were made again in London, but largely failed. Firms around the world have had to develop terror response and security plans. International firms, such as oil companies, have dramatically increased security for both operations and employees. Terrorist threats and incidents have significantly affected airlines, travel companies, construction firms, and even retailers such as McDonald's. HR management must respond to such concerns as part of their transnational operations.

Statistics Canada
This website contains data on Canadian workforce composition and trends.
www.statscan.ca

Economic and Technological Changes

Economic and technological changes have altered several occupational and employment patterns in Canada. Several of these changes are discussed next.

Occupational Shifts A major change is the shift of jobs from manufacturing and agriculture to service and telecommunications. In general, the Canadian economy has become predominately a service economy, and that shift is expected to continue. Over 80 percent of Canadian jobs are in service industries, and most new jobs created by the year 2010 will also be in services.[21] Over the last decade, engineering, health professions, biotechnology, education, law, business, and computer science have been among the fastest growing occupations. While these occupations accounted for less than 20 percent of all employment, they accounted for more than 40 percent of job growth. Most of the fastest-growing occupations percentage-wise are related to information technology and health care. The anticipated increase in technology jobs is due to the rapid growth of information technology, such as databases, systems design and analysis, and desktop publishing, while the growth in health-care jobs is due to the demands of an aging population. The shift to a knowledge economy is projected to create even more jobs in these sectors with 30 percent to 70 percent of the employees in these occupations being university graduates. The knowledge economy also requires people with "soft skills," defined by the Conference Board of Canada in *Employability Skills 2000+* as a wide range of abilities including managing information, the ability to communicate effectively, problem-solving skills, analytical and critical thinking leadership skills, flexibility, and adaptability to change. High-technology companies are looking for employees not just with technical skills, but also those who have demonstrated an ability to think logically and analytically, to communicate the results of their work in a multitude of settings, to work both independently and in groups, and to be real problem-solvers.[22]

Workforce Availability and Quality Concerns Many parts of Canada face significant workforce shortages that exist due to an inadequate supply of workers with the skills needed to perform the jobs being added. It is not that there are too few

High tech employees require not only technical skills, but must also be able to think logically, analytically, and possess adequate communication skills, work independently, and be problem-solvers.

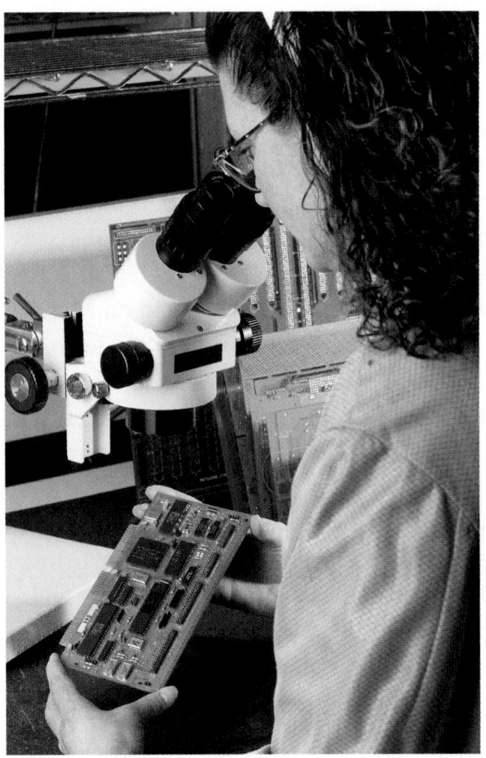

Source: © 2006 JupiterImages and its Licensors. All Rights Reserved.

people—only that there are too few with the skills being demanded. For instance, the 2001 Canadian Census revealed that the aging population will provide problems for many occupations including the health sector. The demand for health care will grow as the population ages and to further complicate the anticipated shortage, the average age of medical specialists and general practitioners is 45.6. This means that many health-care workers will be retiring as the demand for health care increases.[23]

Labour

Even though more Canadians are graduating from high school (83 percent between the ages of 25 and 64 have high school diplomas and 39 percent of 25 to 64-year-olds, including an increased proportion of at-risk groups, possess a post-secondary credential), employers are concerned about the preparation and specific skills of new graduates. Additionally, there is a shortage of tradespeople in Canada, and it is expected to worsen in the next few years. Comparisons of international test results show that students in Canada perform slightly above average in math and science, but *behind* students in some other directly competitive nations.[24] Also, graduates with degrees in computers, engineering, and the health sciences remain in short supply relative to demand. That is another reason why international outsourcing has grown. Unless major improvements are made to Canadian educational systems, Canadian employers will be unable to find enough qualified workers for the growing number of skilled jobs of all types. Early in the 1990s senior executives from corporate Canada, represented by companies such as Noranda Forest Inc., CP Rail, Bell Canada, and Inco Limited, put their heads together and came up with an outline of the ideal job applicant. It was the basis of a report from the Conference Board titled, "The Employability Skills Profile: What Are Employers Looking For?" The profile was updated in 2000. The goal of the profile is to cut across all occupations and fields to define a set of universal skills that make people trainable, and to allow them to develop and grow. Figure 1-3 defines the employability skills in detail. This document is used widely by government agencies, educators, and consultants to assist Canadians in better understanding the needed skills to succeed in the workplace.

Employee Retention With impending shortages of skilled and non-skilled workers looming, it is imperative that organizations try to maintain their employment levels in order to remain competitive. One of the major challenges for employers will be retention of employees. Employers will need to become more vigilant in understanding why their employees are leaving, and to try and address organization shortcomings in order to keep these employees. Employee retention is discussed in more detail in Chapter 2.

Figure 1-3 ***Employability Skills***

Fundamental Skills

The skills needed as a base for further development

You will be better prepared to progress in the world of work when you can:

Communicate

- read and understand information presented in a variety of forms (e.g., words, graphs, charts, diagrams)
- write and speak so others pay attention and understand
- listen and ask questions to understand and appreciate the points of view of others
- share information using a range of information and communications technologies (e.g., voice, e-mail, computers)
- use relevant scientific, technological, and mathematical knowledge and skills to explain or clarify ideas

Manage Information

- locate, gather and organize information using appropriate technology and information systems
- access, analyze, and apply knowledge and skills from various disciplines (e.g., the arts, languages, science, technology, mathematics, social sciences, and the humanities)

Use Numbers

- decide what needs to be measured or calculated
- observe and record data using appropriate methods, tools, and technology
- make estimates and verify calculations

Think & Solve Problems

- assess situations and identify problems

Personal Management Skills

The personal skills, attitudes, and behaviours that drive one's potential for growth

You will be able to offer yourself greater possibilities for achievement when you can:

Demonstrate Positive Attitudes & Behaviours

- feel good about yourself and be confident
- deal with people, problems, and situations with honesty, integrity, and personal ethics
- recognize your own and other people's good efforts
- take care of your personal health
- show interest, initiative, and effort

Be Responsible

- set goals and priorities balancing work and personal life
- plan and manage time, money, and other resources to achieve goals
- assess, weigh, and manage risk
- be accountable for your actions and the actions of your group
- be socially responsible and contribute to your community

Be Adaptable

- work independently or as a part of a team
- carry out multiple tasks or projects
- be innovative and resourceful: identify and suggest alternative ways to achieve goals and get the job done
- be open and respond constructively to change
- learn from your mistakes and accept feedback
- cope with uncertainty

Learn Continuously

- be willing to continuously learn and grow

Teamwork Skills

The skills and attributes needed to contribute productively

You will be better prepared to add value to the outcomes of a task, project, or team when you can:

Work with Others

- understand and work within the dynamics of a group
- ensure that a team's purpose and objectives are clear
- be flexible: respect, be open to and supportive of the thoughts, opinions, and contributions of others in a group
- recognize and respect people's diversity, individual differences, and perspectives
- accept and provide feedback in a constructive and considerate manner
- contribute to a team by sharing information and expertise
- lead or support when appropriate, motivating a group for high performance
- understand the role of conflict in a group to reach solutions
- manage and resolve conflict when appropriate

Participate in Projects & Tasks

- plan, design, or carry out a project or task from start to finish with well-defined objectives and outcomes
- develop a plan, seek feedback, test, revise, and implement
- work to agreed quality standards and specifications
- select and use appropriate tools and technology for a task or project
- adapt to changing requirements and information

(continued)

Figure 1-3 continued		
• seek different points of view and evaluate them based on facts • recognize the human, interpersonal, technical, scientific, and mathematical dimensions of a problem • identify the root cause of a problem • be creative and innovative in exploring possible solutions • readily use science, technology, and mathematics as ways to think, gain, and share knowledge, solve problems, and make decisions • evaluate solutions to make recommendations or decisions • implement solutions • check to see if a solution works, and act on opportunities for improvement	• assess personal strengths and areas for development • set your own learning goals • identify and access learning sources and opportunities • plan for and achieve your learning goals *Work Safely* • be aware of personal and group health and safety practices and procedures, and act in accordance with these	• continuously monitor the success of a project or task and identify ways to improve

Source: Employability Skills 2000+ Brochure 2000 E/F (Ottawa: The Conference Board of Canada, 2000). Reprinted by permission.

Growth in Contingent Workforce "Contingent workers" (temporary workers, independent contractors, leased employees, and part-timers) can represent up to one-third of the Canadian workforce. Many employers operate with a core group of regular employees who have critical skills, and then expand and shrink the workforce through the use of contingent workers.

The use of contingent workers has grown for many reasons. One reason is that many contingent workers are paid less and/or receive fewer benefits than regular employees. Omitting contingent workers from health-care benefits saves some firms 20 percent to 40 percent in labour costs. Another reason for the increased use of contingent workers is that doing so may reduce legal liability for employers. As more and more employment-related lawsuits are filed, some employers have become more wary about adding regular full-time employees. By using contract workers, employers feel that they can reduce the number of legal issues they face regarding selection, discrimination, benefits, discipline, and termination.

Technological Shifts and the Internet Globalization and economic shifts have been accelerated by technological changes, with the Internet being a primary driver. The explosive growth in information technology and in the use of the Internet has driven changes in jobs and organizations of all sizes. For employees and managers, technology means always being "available." Cellphones, wireless networks for laptop computers, and personal digital organizers, BlackBerries, and other similar devices allow many workers to be always "on call." Technology is also enabling more people to work from home, at nights and on weekends, resulting in more weekly hours worked and more stress on balancing work and personal lives.

Organizations have had to deal with the management of "virtual employees," who may not be working on-site, and of employees and vendors in other countries. They have also had to develop HR policies regarding electronic sexual harassment and inappropriate Internet usage, among other day-to-day issues introduced by technology. But organizations have taken advantage of technology to establish e-learning programs whereby employees can access training programs through Web-based systems. Many HR management practices, such as employee benefits enrollment, performance appraisal documentation, job posting, and recruiting, have become Web-based. These and many other examples illustrate how technological advances and the Internet are changing how HR management activities are performed.

Workforce Demographics and Diversity

Multiculturalism
Ensures that all citizens can keep their identities, can take pride in their ancestry, and have a sense of belonging.

Canada is hailed as a model in managing diversity as the first and only country that has established multiculturalism as its official policy. **Multiculturalism** ensures that all citizens can keep their identities, can take pride in their ancestry, and have a sense of belonging.[25] Canada is also one of the few countries in the Western world that is actively looking for immigrants who are highly qualified. Canada's immigration policy is meant to achieve a number of national objectives including the need for economic growth as well as to offset the aging of the population and the increasing proportion of retired persons to workers.[26]

One of the results of a concerted immigration policy is that the Canadian workforce has become more diverse racially and ethnically. There are also more women in the workforce than ever before, and the average age of its members is now considerably older. As a result of these demographic shifts, HR management in organizations has had to adapt to a more varied labour force both externally and internally.

Visible Minorities and Diversity As a result of Canada's immigration policy, visible minorities account for a growing percentage of the overall labour force. According to Statistics Canada, 20 percent of Canada's labour force was born outside of the country.[27] The influx of immigrants will continue to expand that growth. Canada's experience with diversity distinguishes it from most other countries. Thirty million inhabitants reflect a cultural, ethnic, and linguistic makeup found nowhere else on earth. Approximately 200 000 immigrants a year from all parts of the globe continue to choose Canada, drawn by its quality of life and its reputation as an open, peaceful, and caring society that welcomes newcomers and values diversity.[28]

Canada's concept of what constitutes diversity is expanding. Diversity is moving beyond language, ethnicity, race, and religion, to include cross-cutting characteristics such as gender, sexual orientation, and range of ability and age. The same approaches that have helped Canadians develop into a bilingual, multicultural society are now also helping to bring down other barriers that prevent individuals from reaching their full potential. For example, global events since 2001 have increased employers' attention to individuals who are Muslim, and more awareness and accommodation for Islamic religious beliefs and practices have become a common concern.

Women in the Workforce Women constitute about 47 percent of the workforce in Canada and 43 percent in Europe.[29] Many women workers are single, separated, divorced, or widowed, and therefore are "primary" income earners. Many women who are married have spouses who are also employed. A growing number of households in Canada include "domestic partners," who are committed to each other though not married and who may be of the same or the opposite sex.

For many workers in Canada, balancing the demands of family and work is a significant challenge. Although that balancing has always been a concern, the increased number of working women and dual-career couples has resulted in greater tensions for many workers, both male and female. Employers have had to respond to

The implementation of flexible hours, job sharing, child-care referral services, onsite child-care facilities, elder-care programs, and more flexible leave programs are helping families balance both work and family.

Source: Dave J Anthony/Photodisc/Getty Images

work/family concerns in order to retain employees. Responses have included greater use of flexible hours, job sharing, the establishment of child-care referral services or on-site child-care facilities, elder-care programs, and more flexible leave programs.

Aging Workforce In many economically developed countries, there is occuring a significantly aging workforce.[30] For example, in 2006, approximately 9.8 million baby boomers will turn 60 in Canada.[31] In Canada, over the next decade, a significant number of experienced employees will be retiring, changing to part-time, or otherwise shifting their employment. Replacing the experience and talents of longer-service workers is a growing challenge facing employers in all industries.

Overall, the growing diversity and aging of the workforce are creating more tensions and a greater likelihood of individuals filing employment discrimination complaints against employers. Therefore employers are devoting more time and effort to ensuring that non-discriminatory policies and practices are followed. Training on diversity issues and the effective management of diversity issues in organizations are getting more attention.

Organizational Cost Pressures and Restructuring

An overriding theme facing managers and organizations is to operate in a "cost-less" mode, which means continually looking for ways to reduce costs of all types—financial, operations, equipment, and labour. Pressures from global competitors have forced many Canadian firms to close facilities, use international outsourcing, adapt their management practices, increase productivity, and decrease labour costs in order to become more competitive. The growth of information technology, particularly that linked to the Internet, has influenced the number, location, and required capabilities of employees.

One familiar example is Wal-Mart, the giant retailer, whose corporate philosophy is providing the lowest prices to customers. Consequently, Wal-Mart has driven its vendors and suppliers to reduce their costs. One result has been for suppliers to manufacture their goods overseas by using cheaper labour rates. Another consequence has been for many suppliers to cut jobs and close factories that were not as cost-efficient and productive as foreign competitors. So while Wal-Mart has grown, and Wal-Mart's customers have gotten lower prices, many suppliers and other retailers have had to follow the "cost-less" strategy.[32]

To respond to the cost pressures, many organizations have restructured to become more competitive. Also, firms in the same industries have completed mergers and acquisitions (M&As) to ensure greater global competitiveness.

As part of organizational changes, many organizations have "rightsized" by: (1) eliminating layers of managers, (2) closing facilities, (3) merging with other organizations, and (4) displacing workers. To improve productivity, quality, and service while also reducing costs, they are redesigning jobs and affecting people. One of the challenges that HR management faces with organizational restructuring is dealing with the human consequences of change. The human cost associated with downsizing has been much discussed in the popular press: increased workloads and a "survivor's mentality" for those who remain; loss of employee and customer loyalty; unmet cost-savings; and ultimately, increased turnover of the remaining employees.

These organizational shifts have caused some organizations to reduce the number of employees, while at the same time scrambling to attract and retain employees with different capabilities than were previously needed. To respond to organizational cost pressures and restructurings, as well as the other HR challenges it faces, HR management has had to transform the roles it plays in organizations.

HR Management Roles

4 Several roles can be fulfilled by HR management. The nature and extent of these roles depends on both what upper management wants HR management to do and what competencies the HR staff have demonstrated. Three roles are typically identified for HR:

- *Administrative:* Focusing on HR clerical administration and recordkeeping
- *Operational and Employee Advocate:* Managing most HR activities and serving as employee "champion"
- *Strategic:* Becoming a contributor to organizational results and the "keeper" of organizational ethics

The administrative role has been the dominant part of HR. However, as Figure 1-4 indicates, a significant transformation in HR is occurring. The HR pyramid has had to be turned upside down, so that significantly less HR time and fewer HR staff are used for clerical administration. Notice in Figure 1-4 that the percentage of emphasis on the operational and employee advocate role remains constant. The greatest shift is for HR to devote more emphasis to strategic HR management. A study by Towers-Perrin, a large consulting firm, found that HR is being pressured to change because of four critical business issues identified by senior HR managers: cost-reduction pressures, business restructuring, broad scale downsizing/layoffs, and globalization of business.[33] A look at each of the roles of HR and how they are being transformed follows.

Administrative Role of HR

The administrative role of HR management has been heavily oriented to processing and recordkeeping. However, this role has given HR management in some organizations the reputation of being staffed by paper shufflers who primarily tell managers and employees what cannot be done. If limited to the administrative role, HR staff is

Figure 1-4 *Changing Roles of HR Management*

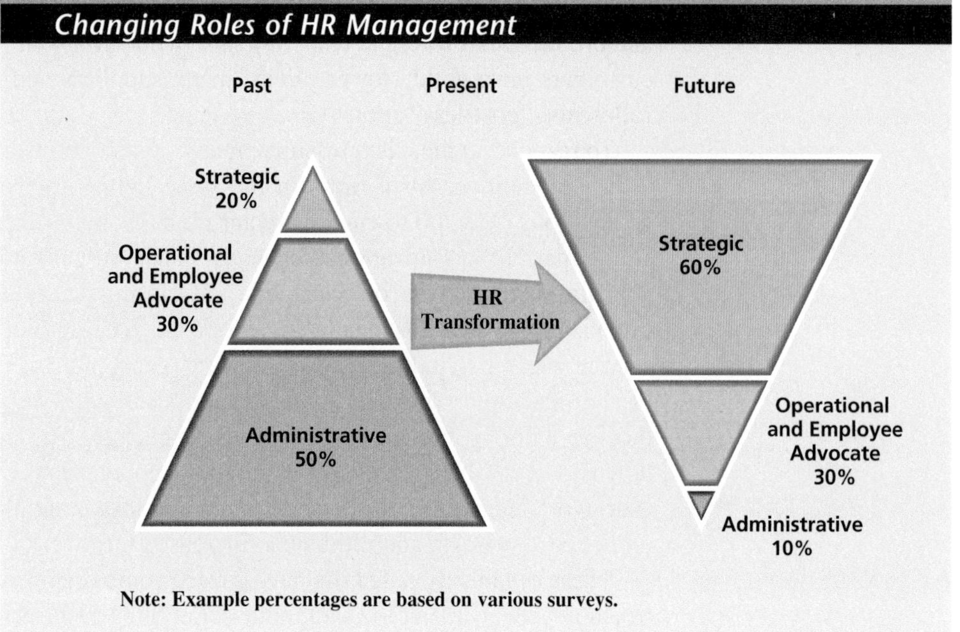

then perceived primarily as clerical and lower-level administrative contributors to the organization. Two major shifts driving the transformation of the administrative role are greater use of technology and outsourcing.

Technology Transforming HR To improve the administrative efficiency of HR and responsiveness of HR to employees and managers, more HR functions are becoming available electronically or are being performed on the Internet. Web-based technology is reducing the amount of HR administrative time and staff needed. Technology is being used in all HR activities, from employment application and employee benefits enrollment to e-learning using Internet-based resources. Later in this chapter there is more discussion on the nature, types, and uses of HR technology.

Outsourcing of HR Increasingly, many HR administrative functions are being outsourced. A recent survey found that about 50 percent of all HR work is being outsourced, and HR outsourcing revenues for vendors have jumped $15 billion in just two years. According to various surveys by outsourcing firms, the areas most commonly outsourced are employee assistance/counselling, pension/retirement planning, benefits administration, training, and payroll services.[34] CIBC and Hamilton Health Sciences recently outsourced their entire HR departments. Some view this tactic as detrimental to the survival of HR, but there are others who find that their exposure to more business processes only enhances their ability to deal at senior levels. A survey conducted by the Chartered Institute of Personnel and Development in the United Kingdom found that of the 1800 surveyed, 40 percent felt that the outsourcing of HR had a negative impact on HR careers, in contrast to 16 percent who felt HR call centres and shared services offered good HR career opportunities.[35]

The primary reasons why HR functions are outsourced is to save money on HR staffing, to take advantage of specialized vendor expertise and technology, and to be able to focus on more strategic HR activities. As a result, it is forecasted that up to 65 percent of all HR administrative staff jobs are or will be eliminated in the next few years. These jobs are being outsourced to firms both in North America and worldwide. Canadian companies are also looking to slash costs by contracting out their

HR departments as part of the newest trend in outsourcing. A recent Aon Consulting study found that among 260 top HR decision makers across Canada, about 31 percent said their firm has outsourced its HR work and most expect to move at least part of their HR division outside the company.[36] Estimates are that outsourcing arrangements will save employers 30 percent or more on labour costs.[37]

Employee Advocate and Operational Role for HR

Traditionally, HR has been viewed as the "employee advocate" in organizations. As the voice for employee concerns, HR professionals traditionally have been seen as "company morale officers" who do not understand the business realities of the organizations and do not contribute measurably to the strategic success of the business. Despite this view, someone must be the "champion" for employees and employee issues.

HR professionals spend considerable time on HR "crisis management" dealing with employee problems that are both work and non-work related. Employee advocacy helps ensure fair and equitable treatment for employees regardless of personal background or circumstances. Sometimes the HR advocate role may create conflict with operating managers. However, that role is important to make the organization a better place to work. In addition, without the advocate role, employers would face even more lawsuits and regulatory complaints than they do now.

The operational role requires HR professionals to identify and implement needed programs and policies in the organization, in cooperation with operating managers. This role traditionally includes many of the HR activities mentioned earlier in the chapter. HR implements plans suggested by or developed with other managers, as well as those identified by HR professionals. Even though priorities may change as labour markets and economic shifts occur, the operational HR role emphasizes support for executives, managers, and employees when addressing and resolving HR problems and issues.

Operational activities are tactical in nature. Compliance with equal employment opportunity and other laws are ensured, employment applications are processed, current openings are filled through interviews, supervisors are trained, safety problems are resolved, and wages and salaries are administered. These efforts require coordinating the management of HR activities with actions of managers and supervisors throughout organizations.

Managers' and employees' impressions of HR are driven directly by how those individuals experience the benefits and services that HR provides. Unfortunately, operating managers hold a less positive view of HR than might be desired. In a survey by Watson Wyatt, about one-third of managers rated HR as performing well, while 24 percent rated HR as performing poorly. The remaining managers rated HR as "average" in meeting managerial needs.[38]

Strategic Role for HR

Differences between the operational and strategic approaches in a number of HR areas exist.[39] As shown in Figure 1-5, the strategic HR role requires that HR professionals be pro-active in addressing business realities and focus on future HR needs, such as workforce planning, compensation strategies, and demonstrating the value of HR to top management.

Many executives, managers, and HR professionals increasingly see the need for HR management to become a greater strategic contributor to the "business" success of organizations. Even organizations that are not-for-profit, such as governmental and social service entities, must manage their human resources in a "business-oriented" manner.

Figure 1-5 Operational to Strategic Transformation of HR

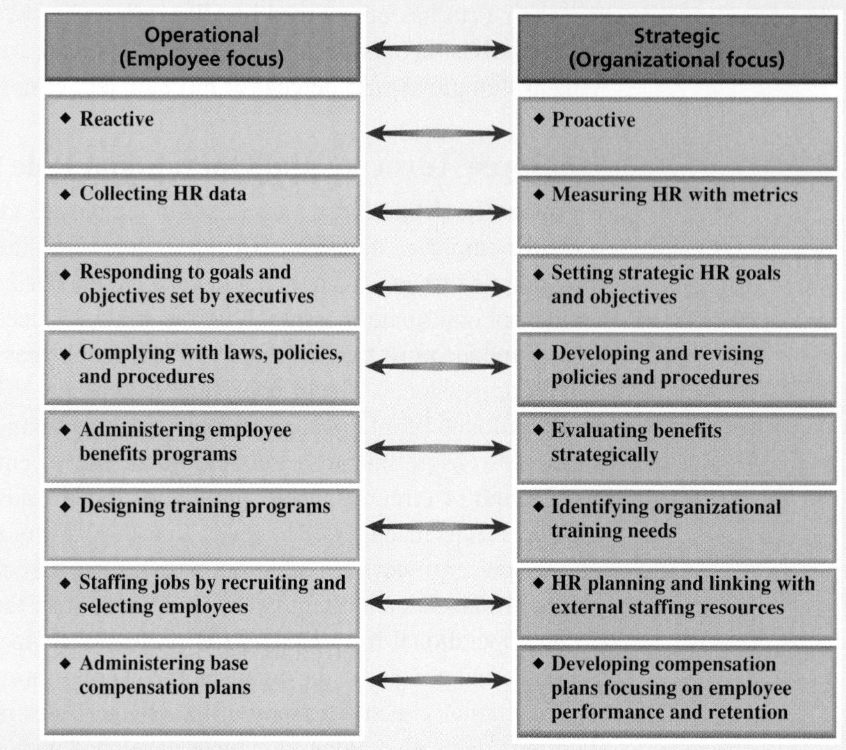

Operational (Employee focus)
Strategic (Organizational focus)
◆ Reactive
◆ Proactive
◆ Collecting HR data
◆ Measuring HR with metrics
◆ Responding to goals and objectives set by executives
◆ Setting strategic HR goals and objectives
◆ Complying with laws, policies, and procedures
◆ Developing and revising policies and procedures
◆ Administering employee benefits programs
◆ Evaluating benefits strategically
◆ Designing training programs
◆ Identifying organizational training needs
◆ Staffing jobs by recruiting and selecting employees
◆ HR planning and linking with external staffing resources
◆ Administering base compensation plans
◆ Developing compensation plans focusing on employee performance and retention

Employers are implementing many programs, including fitness, to help maintain high levels of performance.

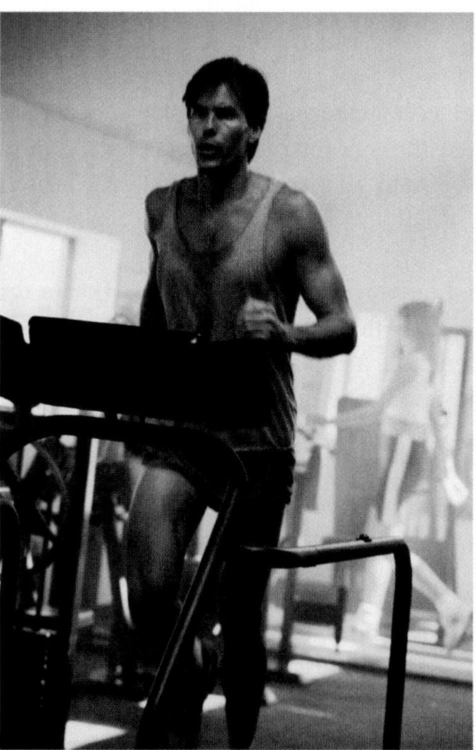

Source: © 2006 JupiterImages and its Licensors.

"Contributing at the Table" The role of HR as a *strategic business partner* is often described as "having a seat at the table," and contributing to the strategic directions and success of the organization. This role means partnering with the chief financial officers (CFOs) and meeting the expectations of the chief executive officer (CEO). For instance, at Wal-Mart, the major retailer, HR is accountable for workforce planning, staffing, and employee retention, all of which affect customer service in Wal-Mart stores.[40]

Other examples illustrate how HR is playing a significant strategic role. At BASF, a global chemical firm with 89 000 employees, HR is in charge of a corporate restructuring plan to save $250 million annually and reduce staffing costs by 30 percent over a four-year period.[41] At Huskey Injection Molding Systems Ltd., they have infused a strategic initiative that has instituted investments in facilities and programs such as child care, wellness, and fitness in order to allow their employees to maintain high standards of performance, which translate into benefits that can be clearly measured. Their return is a lower rate of turnover compared to others in the global marketplace.[42] However, as described in the HR Perspective, even though this role of HR is recognized, many organizations still need to make significant progress toward fulfilling it. Some examples of areas of strategic contributions by HR are as follows:

- Evaluating mergers and acquisitions for organizational "compatibility," structural changes, and staffing needs
- Conducting workforce planning to anticipate the retirement of employees at all levels and workforce expansion identified in organizational strategic plans
- Leading site selection efforts for new facilities, or transferring operations to international outsourcing locations
- Instituting HR management systems to reduce administrative time and staff
- Working with executives to develop a revised sales compensation and incentives plan as new products/services are rolled out to customers.

Collaborative HR The process whereby HR professionals from several different organizations work jointly to address shared business problems.

Collaborative HR Increasingly organizations are implementing new approaches to improve the efficiency and effectiveness of HR management. **Collaborative HR,** the process whereby HR professionals from several different organizations work jointly to address shared business problems, is becoming more prevalent. In this approach, a number of different firms from various industries collaborate on sharing HR resources with other firms in a collaborative group.

Usually these firms are from different industries, so that no competitive conflicts arise. The employers in the group participate in research related to employee

HR *Perspective*

Research on HR as a Strategic Partner

Significant attention has been given to HR becoming a strategic partner in organizations. However, the extent to which that transition is occurring has been questioned. Research by Lawler and Mohrman published in *Human Resource Planning* provides some perspectives. Beginning in 1995 and continuing every three years, the researchers have surveyed senior HR executives in large U.S. firms, most of which have global operations.

The focus of the tri-annual surveys is to determine to what extent the role of HR as a strategic business partner has been changing. However, somewhat discouragingly, from 1995 to the latest survey, HR spent only about 23 percent of its time on its strategic role. The operational role as a service provider has remained relatively constant at about one-third of time spent. Rather surprisingly, the administrative role has declined only slightly over the same time period. About 40 percent of the HR respondents indicated that they function as full strategic business partners, up from 29 percent in 1995. Most of the remaining responses indicated some strategic HR involvement.

To provide further insights, Lawler and Mohrman compared how HR contributes to organizations where it is a full strategic partner and where it is not. As would be expected, the "strategic players" place more emphasis on planning, organizational design, and other broader HR activities. Also, their firms have made much greater use of technology and HR information systems.

Overall, this study illustrates that HR is moving toward being more strategic. But the movement is occurring somewhat more slowly than might be expected, despite a large number of articles and seminars on the need for HR to become a strategic partner.[43]

1. Why do you think HR is moving slowly towards being more strategic than might be expected?
2. Is becoming a strategic partner really that important? Why or why not?

engagement and turnover issues. This sharing of information and programs allows each firm to benefit from the expertise of other firms, without having the time and expense of developing some of their own HR practices. For example, 13 British Columbia retailers (including Safeway, Sears, and Home Depot) have taken a collaborative approach in order to exchange information and ideas related to reducing workplace accidents. The organizations have contributed their best safety practices in the *Health and Safety Guide for New Retail Workers*.[44]

HR Technology

5 The use of information technology of all types is transforming the various roles of HR management. Over the past decade, firms have developed and implemented information systems to simplify use of vast amounts of HR data.

Human resource management system (HRMS)
An integrated system providing information used by HR management, in conjunction with other managers in decision making.

Greater use of technology has led to organizational use of a **human resource management system (HRMS),** which is an integrated system providing information used by HR management, in conjunction with other managers in decision making. The HRMS terminology emphasizes that making HR decisions, not just building databases, is the primary reason for compiling data in an information system. The use of HR technology has grown rapidly in the past decade as "workforce technologies" are used to transform the way HR delivers its activities.[45]

Purposes of an HRMS

An HRMS serves two major purposes in organizations. One relates to administrative and operational efficiency, the other to effectiveness. The first purpose of an HRMS is to improve the efficiency with which data on employees and HR activities are compiled. Many HR activities can be performed more efficiently and more quickly and with less paperwork if automated. One survey of about 200 companies found a 60-percent decline in HR administrative work when employees were given self-service access to HR through Web-based systems.[46]

The second purpose of an HRMS is more strategic and is related to HR planning. Having accessible data enables HR planning and managerial decision making to be based to a greater degree on information rather than relying on managerial perceptions and intuition. One study found that 47 percent of the surveyed firms use HR technology to help with strategic HR planning and particularly with attracting and retaining human resource talent.[47] The Technology Transforming HR discussion on the next page illustrates why an HRMS at Greyhound Lines Inc. will be beneficial to the organization.

The final stage of implementing an HRMS is *HR work flow.* In this stage, not only can the users access information and input changes, the system will now guide the users through all the steps of the transaction. An increasing number of firms have HRMSs that offer employees access to pension benefits information, allowing employees and managers to make changes to their own data without the assistance of an HR professional.

Uses of an HRMS

An HRMS has many uses in an organization. The most basic is the automation of payroll and benefits activities. Another common use of HRMS is tracking employment equity activities. Beyond those basic applications, the use of Web-based information systems has allowed the HR unit in organizations to become more

Technology Transforming HR

Greyhound Lines Inc.

Organizations of all sizes are using HR technology to transform how HR activities are performed. One example is Greyhound Lines Inc. which is a blending of GLI, Greyhound Canada Transportation Corporation, and its subsidiaries. Until recently, there were 58 different sources of data within the Greyhound system. As the company grew, different departments purchased and used their own software solutions. A problem resulted because of these numerous databases: "With information residing in so many places, updating becomes a difficult task. Which database is correct?"

The EIMS Project Core Team developed three alternatives and came to the conclusion that the best solution was to implement an integrated HRMS system with the following benefits:

- provide benefits to all Greyhound employees
- provide a management tool to executives
- provide the technology tool to improve manual and cumbersome processes
- simplify IT system infrastructure by eliminating many multiple data sources and outdated systems within Greyhound
- provide a means to identify safety solutions and effectively manage the driver workforce.[48]

1. What are other possible benefits of implementing an integrated HRMS system?
2. Do you feel there are any drawbacks to implementing an integrative HRMS system? If so, what are they?

administratively efficient and to deal with more strategic and longer-term HR planning issues. Figure 1-6 highlights what is included in Web-based systems.

The greater use of HRMS technologies is affecting how HR activities are performed in many ways. To illustrate, Coca-Cola has a Web-based employee self-service program for its worldwide staff in over 200 countries. Employees can go online to access and change their personal data, enroll in or change benefits programs, and prepare for performance reviews. The employee self-service system is available in various languages, and reflects country and cultural differences.[49] Self-service HRMS such as these are estimated to reduce HR administrative transaction costs by 43 percent.[50] Additional examples of how various HR activities are being transformed by technology will be presented throughout the chapters of this text.

Figure 1-6 ***Web-Based Systems***

- ***Bulletin boards:*** **Information on personnel policies, job postings, and training materials can be accessed by employees globally.**
- ***Data access:*** **Linked to databases, an extranet or an intranet allows employees to access benefits information such as sick leave usage. This frees up time for HR staff members who previously spent considerable time answering routine employee inquiries.**
- ***Employee self-service:*** **Many HR technology uses enable employees to access and update their own personnel records, change or enroll in employee benefits plans, and respond to employment opportunities in other locations. Obviously, maintaining security is critical when the employee self-service option is available.**
- ***Extended linkage:*** **Integrating an HRMS allows the databases of vendors of HR services and an employer to be linked so that data can be exchanged electronically. Also, employees can communicate directly from throughout the world to submit and retrieve personnel details, take online training courses, and provide complete career planning data.**

Ethics and HR Management

6 Closely linked with the strategic role of HR is the way HR management professionals influence the organizational ethics practised by executives, managers, and employees. On the strategic level, organizations with high ethical standards are more likely to meet long-term strategic objectives and profit goals. Organizations that are seen as operating with integrity are viewed more positively by individuals in the community and throughout industry, as well as by consumers and employees.[51] These positive views often translate into bottom-line financial results and the ability to attract and retain human resources.

The need for greater attention to ethics has grown in the past few years in Canada, as evidenced by the corporate scandal at Nortel, the federal sponsorship scandal, the Bre-X gold scandal, etc. Ethical problems at Parmalat (an Italian-based food company), Credit Lyonnais (a French financial firm), and other companies illustrate that ethical lapses are not problems just in Canada.

Ethics and Global Differences

Differences in legal, political, and cultural values and practices in different countries often raise ethical issues for global employers. Those employers also must comply with their home-country laws. Canada, the U.S., and some Western European countries have laws regarding the conduct of firms based domestically. For example, the Corruption of Foreign Public Officials Act prohibits Canadian firms from engaging in bribery and other practices in foreign countries that would be illegal in Canada. Internationally, Canada has actively participated in anti-corruption initiatives in various international forums, including the Organisation for Economic Co-operation and Development (OECD), the Organization of American States, the Council of Europe, the United Nations, the Commonwealth, and within the G-8.[52] However, competing firms from certain other countries are not bound by similar restrictions, which may create competitive disadvantages for firms in Canada, the U.S., and Europe.[53]

The impact of those laws often requires global managers to draw some fine ethical distinctions between bribery and gift-giving, particularly given differences in business practices in various Asian and Eastern European countries.[54] Two examples illustrate typical ethical dilemmas:

- Many global firms have found that establishing or expanding operations in some Asian, African, and Latin American countries is much easier if the global firm arranges for the children of key government officials to be admitted to and receive scholarships from colleges and universities in Canada or Great Britain. Without this "sponsorship," the global firms often face endless delays in obtaining the necessary government agency approvals for its operations.
- In some Eastern European and Asian countries, obtaining a new telephone line in less than three months requires making a cash payment, referred to as an "expediting charge," to the local manager of the telephone office. All parties to the deal know that the manager personally will retain the cash, but a telephone is essential for doing business internationally.

These and other situations reflect how different legal, political, and cultural factors in other countries can lead to ethical conflicts for global managers. Some global firms have established guidelines and policies to reduce the payments of bribes, but even those efforts do not provide detailed guidance on handling the situations that can arise.

HR's Role in Organizational Ethics

Organizations that are seen as ethical in the way they operate have longer-term success. Because people in organizations are ones making ethical decisions on a daily basis, HR management plays a key role as the "keeper and voice" of organizational ethics. All managers, including HR managers, must deal with ethical issues and be sensitive to how they interplay with HR activities.[55] To help HR professionals deal with standards of behaviour relating to fairness, justice, truthfulness, and social responsibility issues, the Canadian Council of Human Resources Association (CCHRA) has developed a code of ethics for its members. Figure 1-7 highlights the

Figure 1-7 ***CCHRA CHRP National Code of Ethics***

1. **Preamble**

   As HR practitioners in the following categories—

   - **Certified Human Resources Professionals,**
   - **CHRP Candidates, or**
   - **CHRP Exam Registrants,**

   we commit to abide by all requirements of the Code of Ethics of the Canadian Council of Human Resources Associations (CCHRA), as listed in this document. (Where provincial codes are legislated, those will prevail.)

2. **Competence**

   - **Maintain competence in carrying out professional responsibilities and provide services in an honest and diligent manner.**
   - **Ensure that activities engaged in are within the limits of one's knowledge, experience and skill.**
   - **When providing services outside one's level of competence, or the profession, the necessary assistance must be sought so as not to compromise professional responsibility.**

3. **Legal Requirements**

   - **Adhere to any statutory acts, regulation or by-laws which relate to the field of Human Resources Management, as well as all civil and criminal laws, regulations and statutes that apply in one's jurisdiction.**
   - **Not knowingly or otherwise engage in or condone any activity or attempt to circumvent the clear intention of the law.**

4. **Dignity in the Workplace**

   - **Support, promote, and apply the principles of human rights, equity, dignity, and respect in the workplace, within the profession, and in society as a whole.**

5. **Balancing Interests**

   - **Strive to balance organizational and employee needs and interests in the practice of the profession.**

6. **Confidentiality**

   - **Hold in strict confidence all confidential information acquired in the course of the performance of one's duties, and not divulge confidential information unless required by law and/or where serious harm is imminent.**

7. **Conflict of Interest**

   - **Either avoid or disclose a potential conflict of interest that might influence or might be perceived to influence personal actions or judgments.**

8. **Professional Growth and Support of Other Professionals**

   - **Maintain personal and professional growth in Human Resources Management by engaging in activities that enhance the credibility and value of the profession.**

9. **Enforcement**

   - **The Canadian Council of Human Resources Associations works collaboratively with its member associations to develop and enforce high standards of ethical practice among all its members.**

Source: "Code of Ethics," Canadian Council of Human Resources Association, www.cchra-ccarh.ca/parc/en/default.asp. Reprinted by permission.

code of ethics HR professionals are expected to abide by. There are a number of different views about the importance of HR in ensuring that ethical practices, justice, and fairness are present throughout HR practices.[56] Figure 1-8 identifies some of the most frequent areas of ethical misconduct involving HR activities.[57]

Ethical issues pose fundamental questions about fairness, justice, truthfulness, and social responsibility. Ethics deal with what "ought" to be done. Just complying with the laws does not guarantee ethical behaviour. Laws and regulations cannot cover every situation that executives, managers, and employees will face. Instead of relying on laws, people must be guided by values and personal behaviour "codes," including the following two questions:

- Does the behaviour or result meet all applicable *laws, regulations, and government codes*?
- Does the behaviour or result meet both *organizational standards* and *professional standards* of ethical behaviour?

Organizational culture
The shared values and beliefs in an organization.

Ethical Behaviour and Organizational Culture Numerous writers on business ethics consistently stress that the primary determinant of ethical behaviour is **organizational culture,** which is the shared values and beliefs in an organization. Basically, organizational culture is "how things are done here." Every organization has a culture, and that culture influences how executives, managers, and employees act in making organizational decisions. For example, the more common it is for employees to lie about why they missed work in order to use sick leave, the more likely it is that employees will adopt that behaviour. Or, if meeting objectives and financial targets is stressed, regardless of how the desired results are obtained, then it should not be a surprise when executives and managers fudge numbers or falsify cost records. The financial scandals in many firms in recent years illustrate the consequences of an "anything goes" organizational culture. However, a positive ethical culture exists in many organizations, as the HR Perspective describes.

HR plays a key role in ensuring ethical behaviour in organizations. One survey revealed that the number of employees reporting ethical misconduct has grown in the past

Figure 1-8 *Examples of Ethical Misconduct in HR Activities*

Types of Misconduct	Examples of Employee, Supervisor, and Managerial Behaviour
Compensation	• **Misrepresenting hours and time worked** • **Falsifying expense reports** • **Personal bias in performance appraisals and pay increases** • **Inappropriate overtime classifications**
Employee Relations	• **Employees lying to supervisors** • **Executives/managers providing false information to public, customers, and vendors** • **Personal gains/gifts from vendors** • **Misusing/stealing organizational assets and supplies** • **Intentionally violating safety/health regulations**
Staffing and Equal Employment	• **Favouritism in hiring and promotion** • **Sexual harassment** • **Sex, race, and age discrimination in hiring, discipline, and termination**

Source: "Survey Examines Relationship Between HR and Ethics," *HR News,* www.shrm.org/hrnews; other surveys; and personal interviews with selected HR professionals.

How UPS Delivers Ethics and Corporate Integrity

With all the reports of corporate scandals in the past several years, one company whose name has not appeared in them is UPS, a transportation and logistics firm. The "Big Brown" company, as UPS is also called, sees ethics as a primary part of achieving competitive advantage with customers, as well as an aid in attracting and retaining employees at all levels. Lea Soupta, senior vice president of HR and her staff are key in ensuring that UPS has ethical practices throughout the firm's worldwide operations. The company has underscored the importance of HR by placing Soupta on its board of directors.

UPS has taken a number of actions to, as it says, "lead with integrity." A detailed code-of-conduct manual is given to and reviewed with all employees. The manual includes specific examples of ethical situations that employees may face and how to respond to them. The manual itself is updated regularly, and the code of conduct is reinforced annually through training sessions and communications.

Additionally, UPS contracts with an external firm to provide a hotline for receiving confidential calls on ethical problems. The vendor notes the information and sends it to a special compliance department at UPS where investigations and follow-ups are handled. Regular summaries of the hotline reports are presented to department managers and senior executives. Annually, managers complete a "conduct code" report that asks specific questions about ethical problems that have arisen during the year. In summary, an emphasis on ensuring corporate integrity and ethical behaviour permeates UPS, and HR plays both strategic and operational roles in delivering on ethics at UPS.[58]

1. How does HR specifically play a strategic and operational role with regards to corporate ethics at UPS?
2. How does abiding by a corporate ethics culture result in an increased competitive advantage for UPS?

few years, primarily because of the corporate scandals from several years earlier.[59] When the following four elements of ethics programs exist, ethical behaviour is likely to occur:[60]

- A written code of ethics and standards of conduct
- Training on ethical behaviour for all executives, managers, and employees
- Means for employees to obtain advice on ethical situations they face, often provided by HR
- Systems for confidential reporting of ethical misconduct or questionable behaviour

Yet, having all those elements may not prevent individual managers or executives from engaging in or failing to report unethical behaviour. Even HR staff members may be reluctant to report ethics concerns, primarily because of fears that doing so may affect their current and future employment. Specific ethical issues that have created difficulty in the HR area include the following:

- How much information on a problem employee should be given to or withheld from another potential employer?
- Should an employment manager check credit agency or law enforcement records on applicants without informing them?
- What obligations are owed a long-term employee who has become an ineffective performer because of changes in the job skills required?
- What impact should an employee's off-the-job lifestyle have on promotion decisions if on-the-job work performance has been satisfactory?
- Should employees who smoke be forced to stop smoking on breaks when new no-smoking restrictions are implemented by the employer? Also, should an employer be allowed to reject a job applicant solely on the basis of off-the-job smoking?
- Should an otherwise qualified applicant be refused employment because the applicant's dependent child has major health problems that would significantly raise the employer's insurance costs?

Canadian Council of Human Resources Associations (CCHRA)
A forum of human resources associations from across Canada representing the profession nationally and internationally.
www.cchra-ccarh.ca/en

- How should co-workers' "right to know" be balanced with individual privacy rights when a worker discloses he or she has AIDS, hepatitis C, or other serious communicable diseases?

A broad study of ethics is philosophical, complex, and beyond the scope of this book. The intent here is to highlight ethical aspects of HR management. Various ethical issues in HR management are highlighted throughout the text as well.

HR Management Competencies and Careers

7 As HR management becomes more complex, greater demands are placed on individuals who make HR their career specialty. Even readers of this book who do not become HR managers and professionals will find it useful to know about the competencies required for effective HR management.

HR Competencies

The transformation of HR toward being more strategic has implications for the competencies needed by HR professionals. According to a recent study conducted jointly by the University of Michigan (UM) and the Society for Human Resources Management (SHRM), five areas of HR competencies have been summarized from information collected from 7000 HR professionals and other executives and managers.[61] The competencies are described as follows:

- *Strategic contribution:* The key competency that HR needs to fulfill its strategic role is the ability to be a strategic contributor to organizational success. That means that HR must focus on the long-term implications of HR issues.
- *Business knowledge:* HR professionals must have business knowledge of the organization and its strategies if they are to contribute strategically. They must understand the financial, technological, and other facets of the industry and the organization.[62]
- *HR delivery:* The HR activities must be delivered effectively and efficiently in ways that meet the needs of both the organization and its employees.
- *HR technology:* Technology, particularly information systems and Web-based resources, have become a significant part of HR management today. HR professionals must develop the abilities needed to work effectively with various dimensions of an HRMS.
- *Personal credibility:* HR professionals must have credibility personally and professionally. That means they must develop effective internal relationships with individual executives, employees, managers, and supervisors. Also, HR professionals must establish personal and professional credibility in various external relationships.

The Canadian Council of Human Resource Associations (CCHRA) is the national "umbrella" organization for several provincial (e.g., HRPAO in Ontario) and specialist human resources (HR) groups in Canada. With over 30 000 HR professionals in Canada, the CCHRA is responsible for developing and administering key policies for the national designation. In October 1997, the CCHRA, in partnership with Human Resources Development Canada (HRDC), began a major initiative called the Human Resources Professional Capabilities Project (HRPCP). The ultimate goal was to create national certification standards for the HR profession in Canada. The national certification standards are both knowledge and capabilities based.[63]

A broad range of capabilities is required for the HR professional. The exact mix of capabilities that an HR professional must bring to a business problem is often determined by the size and nature of the organization. In developing this profile for the Canadian HR profession, required professional capabilities (RPCs) have been broken into seven functional areas of practice, and an additional cross-functional area referred to as Professional Practice in Human Resources. Some of the capabilities are very specific to a functional area, while others are widely shared across several functional areas. A list of RPCs are found in Appendix A and are available on the text's website at www.mathis.nelson.com. The HR profession is characterized by the interrelationships of these eight functional areas, and the crossover use of capabilities is itself a defining characteristic of HR practice.[64] Figure 1-9 shows the broad range of capabilities required.

HR Management as a Career Field

HR generalist A person who has responsibility for performing a variety of HR activities.

HR specialist A person who has in-depth knowledge and expertise in a limited area of HR.

There are a variety of jobs within the HR career field, ranging from executive to clerical. As an employer grows large enough to need someone to focus primarily on HR activities, the role of the **HR generalist** emerges—that is, a person who has responsibility for performing a variety of HR activities. Further growth leads to the addition of **HR specialists,** or individuals who have in-depth knowledge and expertise in limited areas of HR.

Human resources professionals are generally employed in medium to large-sized organizations that have formal human resources departments. Graduates are qualified to assume a wide variety of management-oriented positions in the diversified field of human resources services.

Common entry-level positions include:

- Human Resources Assistant
- Staff Recruiter
- Compensation Analyst
- Pension and Benefit Adviser

Figure 1-9 *Human Resources Professional Capabilities Profile*

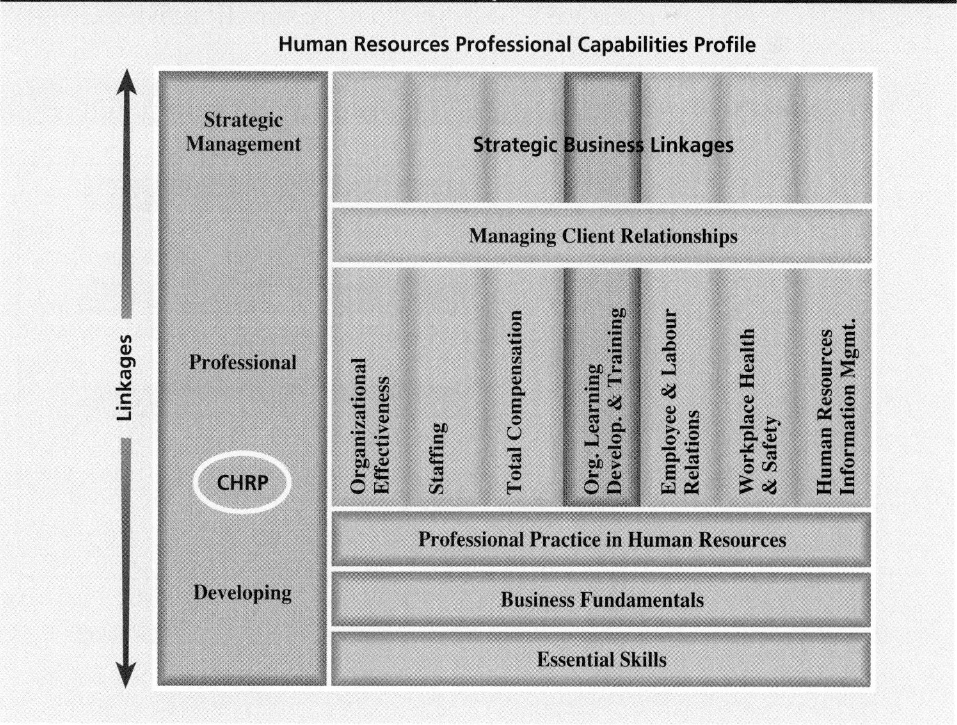

Source: Canadian Council of Human Resources Practitioners (CCHRA), Phase I Report, Introduction, CCHRA Required Capabilities Profile. Reprinted by permission.

National Occupational Classification (NOC)
The National Occupational Classification system continues to be the authoritative resource on occupational information in Canada.
www23.hrdc-drhc.gc.ca/2001/e/generic/welcome.shtml

- Labour Relations Officer
- Occupational Health and Safety Coordinator
- Wage and Salary Administrator
- Employment and Pay Equity Officer
- Training and Development Coordinator.

Compensation and Career Outlook Compensation levels for HR jobs vary by industry, company size, and geography. As would be expected, pay generally increases with company size although it may vary significantly due to differences in job responsibilities in small, medium, and large firms. Many HR executives and managers are eligible for short- and long-term incentives.[65]

The earnings level for an HR manager tends to be above average when compared to all other occupations. Logically, younger, less experienced individuals will not earn as much as the older, and more experienced individuals. However, after several years of experience the earnings level can increase. Figure 1-10 presents the expected earnings by age for an HR manager as noted by the federal government's Job Futures program.

Regarding career outlook, positions for human resources professionals is considered to be a promising field as reflected in the number of opportunities that have become available. The highest concentration (per 10 000 people) of specialists in human resources are found in Ontario, Quebec, and Prince Edward Island while the lowest concentrations are in Newfoundland and Saskatchewan. Figure 1-11 highlights the 2007 career prospects for HR. These highlights are updated regularly to reflect the trends.

HR Professionalism and Certification

The idea that "liking to work with people" is the major qualification necessary for success in HR is one of the greatest myths about the field. Depending on the job, HR professionals may need considerable knowledge about employment regulations, finance, tax law, statistics, and information systems. In most cases, they also need extensive knowledge about specific HR activities.

Figure 1-10 *Expected Earnings by Age for HR Manager*

Average Hourly Earnings ($/hour)

Age	This Occupation	All Occupations
All	$29.89	$16.91
55+	$30.21	$18.25
25–54	$29.83	$18.46
20–24	$3.57	$11.09

- Hourly wages ($29.89) are above the national average ($16.91).
- These earnings are above average for occupations in the business, finance, and administration sectors and are close to the average for all managerial occupations.
- These wages grew at a significantly above-average rate from 1999 to 2001.

Source: Service Canada, Job Futures, National Edition. Human Resources and Skills Development Canada. Reproduced with the permission of Her Majesty the Queen in Right of Canada 2006.

Figure 1-11 *Career Outlook for Human Resource Managers (NOC 0112)*

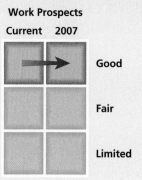

Current Conditions

Work prospects are rated GOOD because:

- Demand is increasing because employers are placing greater emphasis on human resources issues such as recruitment/training, creative compensation/benefit packages, and employee relations.
- Hourly wages ($29.89) are above average ($16.91), and the rate of wage growth has been almost three times the average.
- The unemployment rate (2.9%) is below average (5%).
- The number of job openings exceeds the number of job seekers, mostly people moving up the ranks.

Work Prospects	Current	2007
Good	■ →	■
Fair		
Limited		

Outlook to 2007

Work prospects will continue to be rated GOOD because:

- The employment growth rate will likely be significantly above average because of the ongoing emphasis on human resources issues.
- The retirement rate will likely be about average, and the number of retiring workers should contribute to job openings.
- The number of job openings will likely exceed the number of job seekers, mostly people moving up the ranks.

Preparing for the Competition

- You're more likely to succeed if you have skills in technology/information systems.
- You'll need to learn about different processes for resolving disputes.

Source: Service Canada, Job Futures, National Edition. Human Resources and Skills Development Canada. Reproduced with the permission of Her Majesty the Queen in Right of Canada 2006.

HRPAO
HRPAO is the professional association for human resource management in Ontario. This site lists information on the CHRP certification process.
www.hrpao.org

Professional Involvement and Development The broad range of issues faced by HR professionals has made involvement in professional associations and organizations important. For HR generalists, most provinces across Canada have a human resources association. For example, in Ontario, HRPAO is the largest with over 14 000 members. HR professionals in Nova Scotia would join the HRANS, in Manitoba the HRMAM, and in British Columbia the BCHRA. Public-sector HR professionals tend to be concentrated in the Canadian Public Personnel Management Association (IPMA). Other major specialized HR organizations include the International Association for Human Resource Information Management (IHRIM), the World at Work Association (formerly the Canadian Compensation Association), and the Canadian Society for Training and Development (CSTD).

One of the characteristics of a professional field is having a means to certify the knowledge and competence of members of the profession. The CPA for accountants and the CLU for life insurance underwriters are examples. The most well-known certification programs for HR generalists are administered by the CCHRA in partnership with the provincial human resources associations.

CHRP Certification The Certified Human Resources Professional Designation (CHRP) is a nationally recognized level of achievement within the field of human resources. There are a number of reasons why human resources professionals should achieve their professional designation. The achievement of the designation reflects a conviction that the professional practice of human resources management can safeguard the interest of employers, employees, and the general public. The designation represents continuing recognition of the bearer's outstanding professionalism. In addition, the CHRP credential positions the practitioner at the leading edge of the profession in Canada—informed, experienced, connected, and committed to career-long learning.[66] Two times a year, hundreds of individuals across Canada take the certification exams. Eligibility requirements for the CHRP may vary by provincial association, however, the national knowledge exam (NKE) and the professional practice exam (PPE) is the same for everyone who writes across the country. To write the NKE, students must have successfully passed the recognized courses by their provincial association and after several years of experience, and having achieved a management position in HR, they are then eligible to write the PPE. This must be done within proscribed time periods, as stated by the provincial association. Additionally, those who want to succeed in the field must update their knowledge continually. One way of staying current on HR issues is to tap information available from the list in Appendix B on the text's website at www.mathis.nelson.com.

SUMMARY

1 HR management is the direction of organizational systems to ensure that human talent is used effectively and efficiently to accomplish organizational goals. HR management activities can be grouped as follows: strategic HR management; equal employment opportunity; staffing; HR development; compensation and benefits; health, safety, and security; and employee and labour relations. All organizations need HR management, but larger ones are more likely to have a specialized HR function.

2 There are four types of assets in organizations: physical, financial, intangible, and human. Human assets should be seen as human capital, which is the collective value of the capabilities, knowledge, skills, life experiences, and motivation of an organizational workforce. A core competency is a unique capability that creates high value and differentiates an organization from its competition.

3 Four major HR challenges faced by managers and organizations now and in the future are the globalization of business, economic and technological changes, workforce demographics and diversity, and organizational cost pressures and restructuring. Some important considerations relate to the costs of international outsourcing, global security and terrorism, occupational shifts and quality concerns, growth in contingent workers, an aging workforce that will result in a shortage of workers, and the competitive pressures that have resulted in the closing of facilities and the resultant layoffs of workers.

4 HR management must fulfill three roles: (1) administrative, (2) operational and employee advocate, and (3) strategic. HR roles are being transformed by technology, outsourcing, and the need for HR to become a more strategic contributor. Some major issues for HR stems from the increase in outsourcing of human resources. HR must play an active role in understanding the business, while at the same time acting as an employee advocate. One of the major challenges for HR relates to its role as a strategic business partner. HR can increase their strategic role of a partner as they continue to collaborate with other managers about strategic business issues.

5 HR technology in the form of Human Resource Management Systems (HRMS) helps improve administrative efficiencies and expand information for strategic HR planning. An HRMS can be designed and implemented in several ways. An HRMS serves two major purposes in an organization: administrative and operational efficiency and effectiveness. The increased use of HRMS by HR departments has allowed HR to transform their role from a purely administrative role, to one which can focus more on business strategy and the alignment of HR strategies to help the organization better meet its goals of profitability.

6 Ethical behaviour is crucial in HR management, and HR professionals regularly face a number of HR ethical issues. Particular issues can arise with compensation, employee relations, staffing, and equal employment. Corporate scandals have shone the light on the importance of dealing with ethics, and HR plays a key role in ensuring ethical behaviour in an organization. Key to ensuring ethical behaviour is

to have a written code of conduct, training for all employees, mechanism to deal with issues or questions, and confidential reporting.

7 The five areas of competencies needed by HR professionals are strategic contribution, business knowledge, HR delivery, HR technology, and personal credibility. Current knowledge about HR management is required for professionals in the HR career field, and professional certification has grown in importance for HR generalists and specialists. Human resources is recognized as a professional field, and as such, an accredited designation known as the CHRP (Certified Human Resources Professional) exists in Canada. The national certification standards are both knowledge and capabilities based.

KEY TERMS

Collaborative HR, p. 21
Core competency, p. 9
HR generalist, p. 29
HR metrics, p. 4
HR specialist, p. 29
Human capital, p. 8
Human resource (HR) management, p. 4
Human resource management system (HRMS), p. 22
Multiculturalism, p. 15
Offshoring, p. 10
Organizational culture, p. 26
Outsourcing, p. 10
Strategic HR management, p. 4

REVIEW AND APPLICATION QUESTIONS

1 Why is it important for HR to work cooperatively with operating managers?

2 In which way does an organization's human resources differentiate them from their competitors?

3 Describe how economic and workforce changes are affecting organizations in which you have worked, and give specific examples of how these changes should be addressed.

4 Why is it important for HR management to transform from being primarily administrative and operational to becoming a more strategic contributor?

5 How has technology transformed HR?

6 With increased globalization, how has ethics become a concern for organizations?

7 Discuss the five competencies required for HR, and provide specific examples of how these would be achieved?

EXPERIENTIAL EXERCISES

1. Using the "Employability Skills Profile" discussed in the chapter, determine what specific skills are required for the following positions:
   a. Customer Service Representative—Individual works in an automotive parts manufacturing facility. They take phone orders and enter the orders into a computerized system. They may have to deal with irate customers and check on missing orders. They must also handle returns.
   b. Recruitment Specialist—Individual works for a software developer, employing over 1000 employees with a turnover of IT specialists of 30 percent, which is above the industry average. The market for these individuals is very scarce. The RS works with managers to ensure up-to-date job descriptions and prepares ads for recruitment. They are responsible for all types of recruitment from placing ads in newsprint, job boards, and/or college/university recruitment.
   c. University Professor—Working in a business faculty, conducts qualitative and quantitative research. Writes journal articles for submission to journals and/or conferences. Also prepares and delivers lectures to students. Will prepare and give assignments and mark student submissions. Meets with students as required. May need to deal with issues surrounding academic dishonesty.

2. Working in groups of five, discuss the work/family balance issues that you have witnessed in your own families, or in your own personal experiences. Have the employers that you or your families worked for provided flexibility in work schedules? What type of family-friendly policies were implemented? Based on your own needs at this time, what policies would you find important now and in the future?
3. Assume you are an HR director with a staff of seven people. A departmental objective is for all staff members to become professionally certified within a year. Using Internet resources of associations listed in Appendix B, develop a table that identifies four to six certifications that could be obtained by your staff members, and show the following details for each certification:
   - Name of sponsoring organization
   - Name and types of certification
   - Addresses for relevant websites containing more information
   - Experience and education requirements
   - Nature of certification process
4. You are a newly appointed HR specialist, having moved from the sales department several months ago. You've kept your friendships with the employees from the sales department, and continue to go out on pub crawls with them after your weekly volleyball games. On one of your regular outings, your closest friend starts to discuss his compensation concerns with you. He discloses to you that he tries to make up short falls in pay by padding his expense reports. You don't say anything, but you realize that he could be reprimanded severely for his actions since he is going against company policy. However, you know that this is a practice that a lot of employees engage in, and that many managers are aware of it, but overlook such discretions. You don't want to alienate yourself from your friends, but you also want to do what is right. What would you do in this situation?

LEARNING REVIEW

To check your knowledge of the chapter, review the following. (Answers after the case.)

1 As part of maintaining organizational competitiveness, HR effectiveness must be increased through the use of:

a. strategic planning
b. HR metrics
c. EAPs
d. HR development

2 The aim of ____________________ is to provide an adequate supply of appropriately qualified individuals to fill jobs in an organization.

a. diversity assessment and training
b. staffing
c. HR planning and analysis
d. human resource development

3 Approximately ______ percent of Canadian jobs are in the service industry.

a. 60
b. 70
c. 80
d. 90

4 Recruiting and selecting employees for current openings is an example of the ______________ role of human resource management activities.

a. operational
b. administrative
c. global
d. strategic

5 Employee self-service will have what effect on HR administrative transaction costs?

a. no effect since this feature is not used often
b. a substantial effect because of the huge savings to HR
c. a less than desirable effect because employees don't want to help themselves
d. a very weak effect—there are some savings but they are not great

6 Numerous writers on business ethics consistently stress that the primary determinant of ethical behaviour is:

a. strategic planning
b. a written code of ethics and standards of conduct
c. organizational culture
d. strict enforcement made against those who go against policies

7 For HR generalists, the largest professional HR organization is the:

a. International Personnel Management Association (IPMA)
b. Canadian Society for Training and Development (CSTD)
c. Human Resources Professionals Association of Ontario (HRPAO)
d. Canadian Council of Human Resources Associations (CCHRA)

CASE

HR CONTRIBUTES AT SYSCO

Many people in Canada are not familiar with SYSCO, but they see its results because SYSCO is the largest food services and distribution company with almost $24 billion in annual sales. SYSCO Canada employs over 4000 employees and runs a fleet of 500 trucks. SYSCO supplies food products to customers in restaurants, hotels, supermarkets, hospitals, and other companies. In a firm the size of SYSCO with over 40 000 employees worldwide, HR management is making significant contributions to organizational success. As an indication of this success, SYSCO received the Optimas award for general HR Excellence from *Workforce Magazine.*

Beginning several years ago, the need to revitalize HR activities was recognized by both executives and senior HR staff members. At the time, the SYSCO operating regions had administered many of their own HR practices. To bring change to HR corporate-wide, while preserving the entrepreneurial independence of the regions, a "market-driven" HR approach was developed. In this approach, corporate HR identified ways it could assist regional operations, and then developed programs and services that met regional needs. However, unlike in many other corporations where corporate HR programs would be "mandated" to operating units, SYSCO took a different approach. Key to market-driven HR is that managers in the regional operations must be convinced to "buy" the corporate HR services. For example, if a supervisory training program is developed by corporate HR, regional managers decide if they want to use the program for supervisory training in their regions.

Another part of creating HR as market driven was the establishment by corporate HR of a Virtual Resource Centre (VRC) to provide services to managers and employees. A key aspect of the VRC is use of HR technology to gather extensive data on HR activities and provide that data to operating managers. One source of data is workplace climate surveys of employees. Using the survey data, HR developed initiatives to increase safety, which reduced workers' compensation claims by 30 percent, resulting in savings of $10 million per year.

Another problem that SYSCO had was high turnover rates of night shift warehouse workers. Recruiting these workers has been a constant challenge for SYSCO and other distribution firms. By implementing a variety of programs and services, based on employee and managerial input from the surveys, the retention rate for these warehouse employees has been increased by 20 percent, resulting in savings of $15 million per year. These savings are due to reduced time and money spent recruiting, selecting, and training new employees. Also, employees with more experience are more productive and more knowledgeable about SYSCO operations and products.

Another area where HR has contributed is with truck and delivery drivers. Data gathered through the VRC has been used to revise base pay and incentive programs, increase driver retention rates, and improve driver safety records. Additionally, customer satisfaction rates increased and delivery expenses declined.

All of these changes illustrate that HR efforts at SYSCO have been paying off for the company, managers, and employees. But as the value of HR efforts is recognized by more managers, HR's role at SYSCO is likely to continue growing and changing.[67]

Questions

1. How does the market-driven approach illustrate that HR has strategic, operational, and administrative roles at SYSCO?
2. Discuss what types of HR changes could have affected reductions in workers' compensation expenses, employee turnover, and increases in customer satisfaction.

Learning Review Answers: 1. b 2. b 3. a 4. b 5. c 6. b 7. d

CHAPTER

Strategic HR Management and Planning

Learning Objectives

After you have read this chapter, you should be able to:

1 Explain strategic HR management and how it is linked to organizational strategies.

2 Define HR planning and outline the HR planning process including the importance of scanning the external environment and assessing the internal workforce including jobs and skills audit and organizational capabilities inventory.

3 Describe the process for forecasting HR supply and demand including forecasting methods.

4 Discuss the importance surrounding the retention of employees.

5 Describe the process of developing and using a strategic HR plan including the action to be taken when there is a surplus of employees, or a shortage.

6 Identify why HR metrics must consider both strategic and operational HR measures.

HR *Headline*

Measurement of HR Is Crucial to Strategic Success

Many executives and operating managers recognize the importance of HR but have concerns about the lack of quantifiable measures of HR efforts. Various surveys have found that over half of executives and 80 percent of operating managers see HR management as critical to their organizations. However, those surveyed indicate that HR activities are not being evaluated adequately, using specific quantifiable measures similar to those used for activities performed in other departments.

The greatest way of showing that HR management is strategic is to present better data on the financial effects of HR programs. HR expenses represent about 60 percent or more of the total expenses in many firms. But justification for those expenditures and documentation of the value added by HR is lacking.

Fortunately, a growing number of HR professionals have responded to these concerns and are developing HR metrics to provide hard data on the strategic and operational contributions of HR management. One example of how HR measurement has been helpful is seen at Royal & SunAlliance Canada, one of the largest property and casualty insurance firms operating in Canada. Royal & SunAlliance measures a variety of metrics to assess the practices instituted by HR including staff, customer satisfaction, and revenue. This organization looks at things such as productivity, age ratios, performance management ratios, the number of new hires, the amount of staff turnover, customer feedback, growth in revenues, and annual employee surveys. These evaluation efforts continue to give Royal & SunAlliance a better understanding of the cost/benefit payoffs of its HR efforts, and how well these efforts contribute to attainment of Royal & SunAlliance's strategic and operational goals. Rowan Saunders, president and CEO of Royal & SunAlliance stated, "HR plays a critical role in the organization. It deserves a seat at the top table. You need to have the human resource element at the top table to be a successful organization that's helping to drive and shape strategy and then of course support that afterwards."[1]

> *"If you don't measure, you're not going to know how much progress you're making."*
>
> —*Rowan Saunders*

Effective management of all resources, including human resources, is significant in determining longer-term organizational success. The extent to which organizations reach established strategic goals and objectives results in organizational effectiveness. Many organizations are becoming increasingly aware that human resources often contribute to a competitive advantage.

Nature of Strategic HR Management

Strategic HR management (SHRM) Process of linking the HR function with the strategic objectives of the organization in order to improve performance.

1 **Strategic HR management (SHRM)** is defined as the process of linking the HR function with the strategic objectives of the organization in order to improve performance. SHRM links human resources vertically and horizontally. Vertical linkages require connecting HR practices with the strategic management process of the organization, while horizontal linkages involve the coordination of various practices within HR through a patterned or planned action. HR strategies are linked to organizational plans, anticipated HR needs, and to HR programs that will be implemented to meet those needs. SHRM involves multiple HR processes, such as recruiting, selection, performance management, employee and career development, succession planning, retirement, and termination. Each of these can be linked to an organization's strategic objectives.[2] For example, a planned expansion and upgrade of an organization's manufacturing facility could be supported by strategic development of employees, which will require extensive training of personnel and strategic recruitment and selection of personnel for the increased number of positions. Figure 2-1 shows the factors that affect strategic HR management.

HR should be involved in implementing strategies that affect and are affected by human resources. Even though it is reported that 75 percent of Canadian businesses

Figure 2-1 *Strategic HR Management Process*

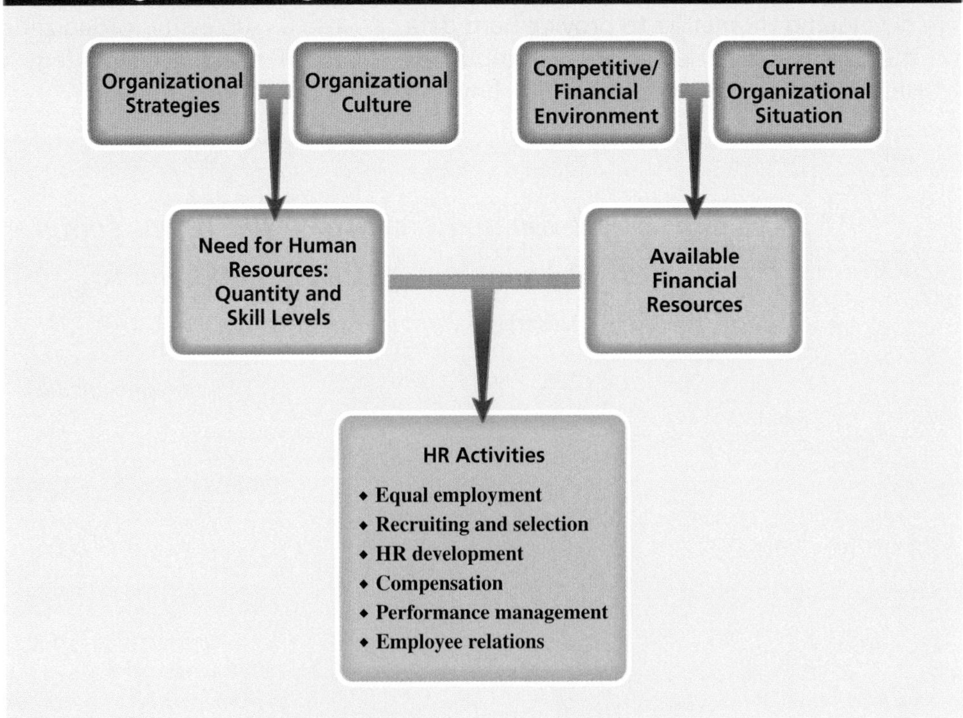

view HR management as a critical part of the overall business strategy[3] the findings of a survey conducted by PricewaterhouseCoopers indicate that only 1 in 3 companies (37 percent) have developed a formal HR strategy.[4]

As an example, the organizational success of Windsor Family Credit Union (WFCU) is strongly linked to strategic use of human resources by the firm. A financial services institution operating in Windsor, Ontario, WFCU has established its HR strategy in a matrix form and developed specific strategic objectives for each element within this matrix. The categories within the matrix include recruitment, orientation, staffing, training and development, benefits, salaries, performance management, records management, legislative compliance, HR management, employee relations, and exit process. This organization is committed to attracting the brightest and the most talented individuals for employment opportunities. WFCU is also devoted to developing employees by putting new employees through rigorous training and testing. Another challenge that WFCU faces is to understand the values of its younger workforce while aligning the systems and the culture to reflect these. The CEO is committed to engaging the workforce in determining gaps and areas of improvement by establishing a CEO advisory committee that meets quarterly. The organization has become ISO-9001:2000 certified, which allows it to achieve a more focused strategic direction. Marty Komsa, CEO and president of WFCU states, "Rather you have to understand their values and make sure the organizational structure will allow them sufficient room to grow, to learn their expertise. If you do that, it's easier to have them buy into organizational goals that you want to accomplish."[5]

Linkage of Organizational and HR Strategies

There should be a close relationship between organizational strategy and HR strategy. While there are many ways that this strategic relationship can be explained, two popular typologies used are Porter's Competitive Strategies[6] and Miles and Snow's Strategy Typology.[7] Using either of these approaches can help in determining which HR strategies best fit with an organization's overall business strategy. Competitiveness can be achieved through strategic choices.

Organizational strategy
The pattern of decisions in a company that determines and reveals its objectives, purposes, or goals, produces the principle policies, and plans for achieving those goals.

Organizational strategy is the pattern of decisions in a company that determines and reveals its objectives, purposes, or goals, produces the principle policies and plans for achieving those goals. It also defines the range of business the company is to pursue, the kind of economic and human organization it intends to be, and the nature of the economic and non-economic contribution it intends to make to its shareholders, employees, customers, and communities.[8] Organizational strategy must also be competitive to be effective. A competitive strategy is about deliberately choosing a different set of activities to deliver a unique mix of value to the customer. Competitive advantage arises from the fit across activities. If there is no fit among the activities, then there is no distinctive strategy and little sustainability.[9] Research suggests that individual policies or practices have limited ability to generate competitive advantage in isolation but in combination they can enable a firm to realize its full competitive advantage.[10] What is important is the appropriate fit between the organizational strategy and the HR strategy, regardless of the type of typology an organization might adopt. The relationship is reciprocal since each type of strategy will be ineffective without consideration for the other. The best strategy for a given firm is ultimately a unique construction reflecting its particular circumstance.[11]

Porter's Strategic Models At the broadest level Porter has identified three internally consistent generic strategies for creating a defendable position and outperforming competitors in an industry. These consist of overall cost leadership, differentiation, and focus. Depending on what strategy is selected, will determine what particular HR strategy would fit best. A company like WestJet or The Real Canadian Superstore follows a cost-leadership strategy, and firms like Intel or Microsoft follow a differentiation strategy.

Cost-leadership strategy
Strategy that approaches competition on the basis of low price and high quality of product or service

A **cost-leadership strategy** approaches competition on the basis of low price and high quality of product or service. It may require an organization to "build" its own employees to fit its specialized needs. This approach needs a longer HR-planning horizon. When specific skills are necessary for a new market or product, it may be more difficult to develop them quickly internally. Typically, if an organization chooses this strategy, they may employ a high number of contract and part-time employees, use tightly defined job descriptions, use employee referrals as opposed to placing recruitment ads, pay below market, offer little to no training, have more rules, and focus on supervisory-based control measures. However, to ensure a higher quality of product or service, the organization may have to offer more training.

Differentiation strategy
Strategy is more appropriate in a dynamic environment characterized by rapid change, and requires continually finding new products and new markets.

A **differentiation strategy** is more appropriate in a more dynamic environment characterized by rapid change, and requires continually finding new products and new markets. Since this strategy is more responsive, HR planning is likely to have a shorter time frame. Also, this type of approach makes greater use of external sources, such as the acquisition of another company with specialized employees to staff the organization. With the globalization of business, many organizations must succeed throughout the world. To work in this organization, employers would need to hire more full-time employees, with formal succession plans, use loosely defined jobs, attract highly skilled labour, scientists, or creative people, use structured interviewing, team-based rewards, and pay above market, with average or better training opportunities, little supervisory control, and open levels of communication.

Focused strategy
Occurs when a firm concentrates its efforts on serving a distinctively defined market segment, which may include some combination of a portion of a product line, particular customer segment, limited geographic area, or particular distribution channel.

A **focused strategy** occurs when a firm concentrates its efforts on serving a distinctively defined market segment, which may include some combination of a portion of a product line, particular customer segment, limited geographic area, or particular distribution channel. As such they attempt to achieve either a cost advantage or differentiation. Porsche is an example of a focused company, which competes against General Motors in the sports car segment of the car market but not in other segments. An organization may need to adopt a mixture of approaches to effectively implement HR strategies to meet the needs of a focused strategy.

Miles and Snow's Strategy Typology Miles and Snow's typology (1978) has been used extensively in literature on the alignment of organizational and HR strategy. Their view of organizations are as a complete and integrative system in dynamic interaction with its environments.[12] According to Miles and Snow, competing firms within a single industry can be categorized into four basic types on the basis of their general strategic orientation: defenders, prospectors, analyzers, and reactors.

Defenders are companies with limited product lines that focus on improving the efficiency of their existing operations. As such, there is centralized authority and tight cost control that leads to low overhead. There is little employee empowerment with very close supervision. Lincoln Electric is an example of a defender. This is similar to a cost leadership strategy.

Prospectors are organizations with fairly broad products lines that focus on product innovation and search for new market opportunities. Organizations will have a learning orientation that is flexible, fluid, and decentralized in structure. There is a strong capability in research, and creativity is valued, as are risk-taking and innovation. Rubbermaid and 3M are examples of a prospector as they continually seek out new innovations. This is similar to a differentiation strategy.

Analyzers are organizations that operate in at least two different product-market areas, where one is stable and one is variable. In stable areas, efficiency is emphasized. In the variable areas, innovation and risk-taking are emphasized. Multidivisional firms, such as IBM and Procter & Gamble, are examples of analyzers.

A *reactor* is an organization that lacks a consistent strategy, structure, or culture relationship. There is no clear organizational approach. Design characteristics may shift abruptly depending on the current needs. Airlines, such as Air Canada, are organizations that can be classified as reactors because they have had to react by cutting costs in order to respond to new entrants to the market.[13]

Because business strategies affect HR plans and policies, consideration of human resource issues should be part of the strategy formulation process. Strategies sometimes need to be more flexible to adapt to ever-changing conditions. It may be important to identify competitive advantage opportunities that fit the existing employees or to assess strategic alternatives given the current capabilities of organizational human resources. HR managers should be scanning the environment to pinpoint what workforce skills are and are not available. HR professionals also should be able to estimate lead times for adjusting to labour shortages or surpluses.

Human Resource Planning

Human resource planning (HRP)
The process of analyzing and identifying the need for and availability of human resources so that the organization can meets its objectives.

2 The competitive strategies and objectives of an organization are the foundation for **human resource planning (HRP),** which is the process of analyzing and identifying the need for and availability of human resources so that the organization can meet its objectives. HR plans must be "linked" effectively with strategic plans for human resources to be a "core competency" that provides competitive advantage for the organization. For instance, both FedEx and Dofasco have identified their human resources as being important to achieving their organizational strategic goals. Even though they are competitors, both firms have emphasized HR efforts as key to organizational success. However, the unique nature of each organization and its culture has led to differing HR strategies and plans.

Industry Canada
This site offers business information on all aspects of HR Planning.
http://strategis.ic.gc.ca

Purpose of Strategic HR Planning

The focus of HR planning, as shown in Figure 2-2, is to have the *right number of human resources,* with the *right capabilities,* at the *right times,* and in the *right places.* In HR planning, an organization must consider the availability of and allocation of people to jobs over long periods of time, not just for the next month or even the next year.

This level of planning requires knowledge of strategic expansions or reductions in operations and any technological changes that may affect the organization. Sometimes specific professions can result in a shortage of skilled workers. One such example in Canada exists for physicians. With many physicians approaching retirement age, the situation is getting worse, considering our aging population. With funding from the Canadian government and a partnership with other medical organizations, efforts continue to resolve the physician shortage. A three-stage plan began with Task Force One seeing an increase in undergraduate positions in medical

Figure 2-2 *Purpose of Human Resource Planning (HRP)*

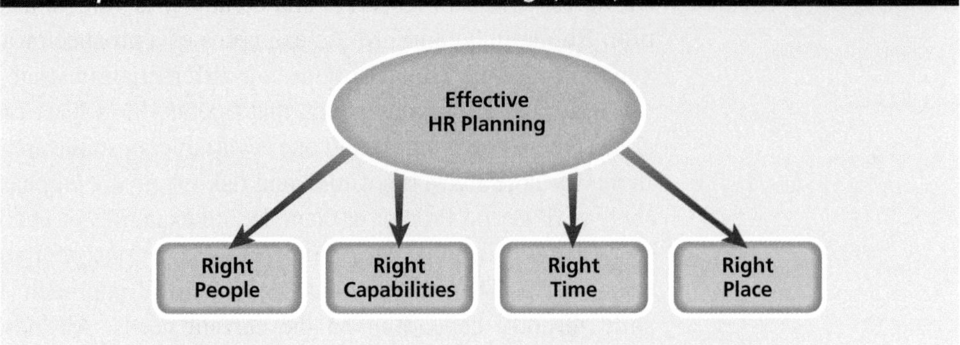

schools. Task Force Two is mandated to undertake a comprehensive examination of the labour market for physicians and to develop options for a long-term physician human resource strategy that is sensitive to Canada's provinces and territorial realities. During Task Force Two, practice models suited for the future will be assessed. During Task Force Three, a human resources strategy for physicians will be defined.[14]

HR planning must identify the knowledge, skills, abilities, experience, and other characteristics affecting the capabilities of employees for current and future jobs. It must consider changes in those capabilities as well. For instance, many large Canadian cities such as Toronto and Vancouver increasingly need multilingual police and fire officers to meet the needs of the growing number of citizens who are Chinese, South Asian, Filipino, and other ethnic groups for whom English may not be widely used. Forecasting specific language capabilities and identifying means for enhancing the language skills of existing police and fire officers, as well as hiring a more diverse workforce, are part of successful HR planning for those cities.

Additionally, as part of analyses, HR plans can be made for shifting employees within the organization, laying off employees or otherwise cutting back the number of employees, retraining present employees, or increasing the number of employees in certain areas. Factors to consider include the current employees' knowledge, skills, and abilities in the organization and the expected vacancies resulting from retirements, promotions, transfers, and discharges. In summary, doing HR planning right requires significant time and effort by HR professionals working with executives and managers.

LOGGING ON...

Strategic Capability Network
Formerly the Canadian Human Resources Planning Association, this organization helps leaders through organizations achieve competitive strength through people.
www.scnetwork.ca

HR Planning Responsibilities

In most organizations that carry out HR planning, the top HR executive and subordinate staff specialists have most of the responsibilities for this planning. However, as Figure 2-3 indicates, other managers must provide information for the HR specialists to analyze. In turn, those other managers need to receive data from the HR unit. Because top managers are responsible for overall strategic planning, they usually ask the HR unit to project the human resources needed to implement overall organizational goals.

Small Businesses and HR Planning

The need for HR planning in larger organizations is clear because if some formal adjustments to changes are not made, people or even entire divisions might be working at cross-purposes with the rest of the company. In a smaller business, even

Figure 2-3 Typical Division of HR Responsibilities: HR Planning

HR Unit	Managers
• Participates in strategic planning process for entire organization • Identifies HR strategies • Designs data systems for HR planning • Compiles and analyzes data from managers on staffing needs • Implements HR plan as approved by top management	• Identify supply-and-demand needs for each division/department • Review/discuss HR planning information with HR specialists • Integrate HR plan with departmental plans • Monitor HR plan to identify changes needed • Review employee succession plans associated with HR plan

though the owner/manager knows on a daily basis what is happening and what should be done, planning is still important. Perhaps the most difficult area for HR planning in small businesses is family matters and succession.[15]

Particular difficulties arise when a growing business is passed from one generation to another, resulting in a mix of family and non-family employees. Key to a successful transition is having a clear HR plan. In small businesses, such a plan includes incorporating key non-family members in HR planning efforts, because non-family members often have important capabilities and expertise that family members do not possess.[16] Planning for the attraction and retention of these "outsiders" may be vital to the future success of smaller organizations.[17] Small businesses, depending on how small they are, may use the HR planning process that follows, but in very small organizations, the process is much more intuitive and is often done entirely by the top executives, who often are family members. Foley Coating Inc., a small family-run business in Ajax, Ontario, indicates that planning for future human resource needs are difficult to formalize and rely on intuition and wide knowledge of the business.

HR Planning Process

The steps in the HR planning process are shown in Figure 2-4. Notice that the HR planning process begins with considering the organizational objectives and strategies. Then HR needs and supply sources must be analyzed both externally and internally, and forecasts must be developed. Key to assessing internal human resources is having solid information accessible through a **human resource management system (HRMS).** An HRMS is a system that lets you keep track of all your employees and information about them. It is usually done in a database or, more often, in a series of inter-related databases.

Human resource management system (HRMS)
A system that lets you keep track of all your employees and information about them. It is usually done in a database or, more often, in a series of inter-related databases.

Once the assessments are complete, forecasts must be developed to identify the relationship between supply and demand for human resources. Management then formulates HR strategies and plans to address imbalances, both short term and long term.

HR strategies are means used to anticipate and manage the supply of and demand for human resources. These strategies provide overall direction for the ways HR activities will be designed and managed. Finally, specific HR plans are developed to provide more specific direction for the management of HR activities. The most telling evidence of successful HR planning is a consistent alignment of the availabilities and capabilities of human resources with the needs of the organization over a period of time.

HR strategies
Means used to anticipate and manage the supply of and demand for human resources.

Figure 2-4 HR Planning Process

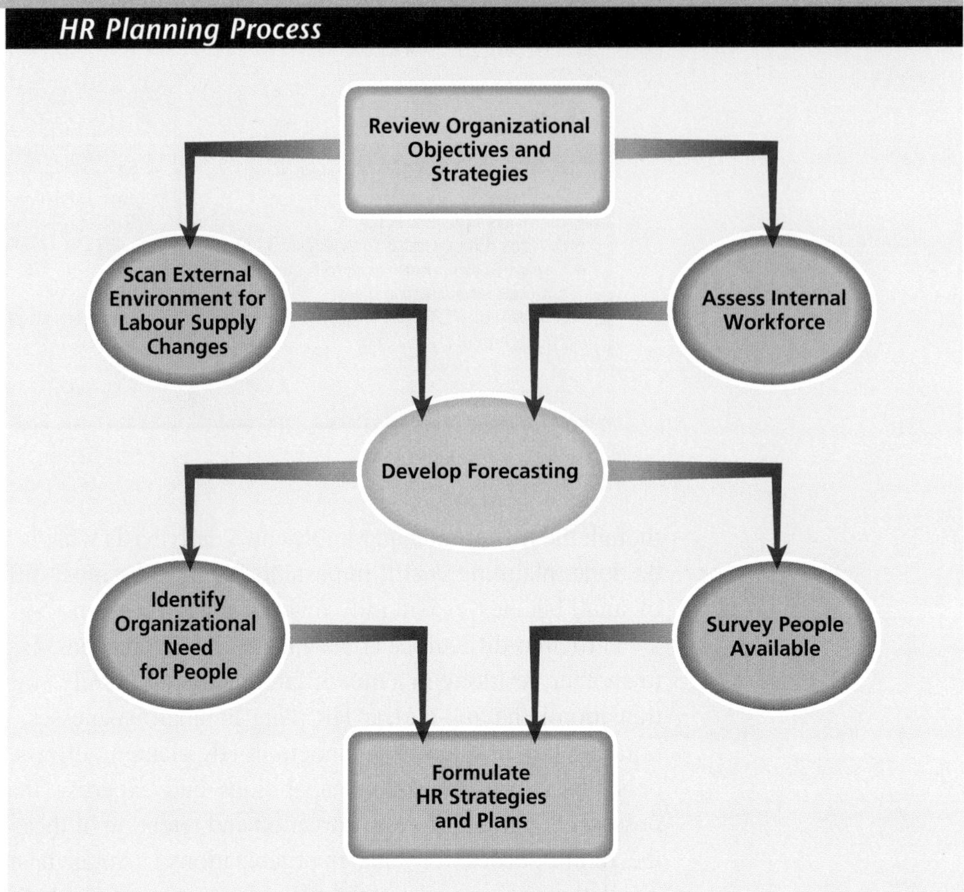

Scanning the External Environment

Environmental scanning
Process of studying the environment of the organization to pinpoint opportunities and threats.

At the heart of strategic planning is environmental scanning, a process of studying the environment of the organization to pinpoint opportunities and threats. The external environment especially affects HR planning because each organization must draw from the same labour market that supplies all other employers. Indeed, one measure of organizational effectiveness is the ability of an organization to compete for a sufficient supply of human resources with the appropriate capabilities. All elements of the external environment—government influences, economic conditions, geographic and competition issues, and workforce changes—must be part of the scanning process.

Government Influences

An expanding and often bewildering array of government regulations affect the labour supply and therefore, HR planning. As a result, HR planning must be performed by individuals who understand the legal requirements of various government regulations. For example, firms operating globally may need to know that in France, the government has changed the length of the workweek from 39 to 35 hours. Also, the European Union has the Working Time Directive, which states that European workers should be limited to a maximum of 48 hours a week.

In Canada and other countries, tax legislation at provincial and federal levels also affects HR planning. Pension legislation may change retirement patterns and funding options. Elimination or expansion of tax benefits for job-training expenses might alter some job-training activities associated with workforce expansions. Employee benefits may be affected significantly by tax law changes. Tax credits for employee day care and financial aid for education may influence employer practices in recruiting and retaining certain workers. Legislation such as employment equity and pay equity has had a profound impact on a number of organizations, as have changes in occupational health and safety. In summary, an organization must consider a wide variety of government policies, regulations, and laws during the HR planning process.

Economic Conditions

The general business cycle of economic recessions and economic booms also affects HR planning. Factors such as interest rates, inflation, and economic growth affect the availability of workers and should figure into organizational and HR plans and objectives. There is a considerable difference between finding qualified applicants in a 3-percent unemployment market and in a 7-percent unemployment market. In the 3-percent unemployment market, significantly fewer qualified applicants are likely to be available for any kind of position, which can be described as a tight labour market. Applicants who are available may be less employable because they are less educated, less skilled, or unwilling to work. As the unemployment rate rises, the number of qualified people looking for work increases, making it easier to fill jobs, which is described as a loose labour market.

Geographic and Competitive Concerns

In making HR plans, employers must consider a number of geographic and competitive concerns. The *net migration* into a particular region is important. For example, in the past decade, the populations of Ontario, British Columbia, and Alberta have steadily increased and provided a ready source of labour. However, provinces such as New Brunswick and Saskatchewan have had declining populations.

Within the last decade, many workers, especially those with working spouses, have expressed an increasing reluctance to accept *geographic relocation* as a precondition of moving up in organizations. This trend has forced organizations to change their employee development policies and practices as well as their HR plans.

Direct competitors are another important external force in HR planning. Failure to consider the competitive labour market and to offer pay scales and benefits competitive with those of organizations in the same general industry and geographic location may cost a company dearly in the long run. Underpaying or "undercompeting" may result in a much lower-quality workforce. Also, *other employers* in a geographic region can greatly expand or diminish the labour supply. For instance, if a new Wal-Mart or a Canadian Tire store opens in a suburban location, other retail employers in the area may see greater turnover and face greater difficulty in recruiting new employees.

HR for Employers
This government site provides information on government and non-government sources.
www.hrmanagement.gc.ca

Finally, the impact of *international competition* must be considered as part of environmental scanning. Global competition for labour intensifies as global competitors shift jobs and workers around the world, as illustrated by the outsourcing of jobs from North America to countries with cheaper labour.

Workforce Composition

Changes in the composition of the workforce, combined with the use of different work patterns, have created workplaces and organizations that are notably different from those of a decade ago. Many organizations face major concerns about having

Workplaces are becoming much more diverse with people of different cultural backgrounds.

Source: Philip Date/ShutterStock

sufficient workers with the necessary capabilities. When scanning the workforce, it is important to consider a number of variables, including these, as were discussed in Chapter 1:

- Aging of the workforce
- Growing diversity of workers
- Women workers and work/life balancing
- Availability of "contingent workers"
- Outsourcing possibilities

When considering these factors, it is important to analyze how they affect the current and future availability of workers with specific capabilities and experience. For instance, in Canada, the median age of engineers is about 43, and there is anticipated to be more jobs than job seekers in the near future due to retirements, and emerging new fields in engineering where trained engineers may be scarce.[18]

Assessing the Internal Workforce

Analyzing the jobs that will need to be done and the skills of people who are currently available in the organization to do them is the next part of HR planning. The needs of the organization must be compared against the labour supply available inside the organization.

Jobs and Skills Audit

The starting point for evaluating internal strengths and weaknesses is an audit of the jobs being done in the organization. A comprehensive analysis of all current jobs provides a basis for forecasting what jobs will need to be performed in the future. Much of the data to answer the questions in the audit should be available from existing staffing and organizational databases. The following questions are addressed during the internal assessment:

- What jobs exist now?
- How many individuals are performing each job?
- What are the reporting relationships of jobs?
- How essential is each job?
- What jobs will be needed to implement future organizational strategies?
- What are the characteristics of anticipated jobs?

Organizational Capabilities Inventory

As HR planners gain an understanding of the current and future jobs that will be necessary to carry out organizational plans, they can make a detailed audit of current employees and their capabilities. The basic source of data on employees is the HR records in the organization. Different HR information databases can be used to identify the knowledge, skills, and abilities (KSAs) of employees. Planners can use KSA inventories to determine future needs for recruiting, selection, and HR development. The information in those inventories can also provide a basis for determining what additional capabilities will be needed in the future workforce.

Using Organizational Capability Inventory Data An inventory of organizational capabilities may consider a number of elements, including the following:

- Individual employee demographics (age, length of service in the organization, time in present job)
- Individual career progression (jobs held, time in each job, promotions or other job changes, pay rates)
- Individual performance data (work accomplishment, growth in skills)

All the details on an individual employee's skills that go into a data bank may affect the employee's career. Therefore, the data and their use must meet the same standards of job-relatedness and non-discrimination as when the employee was initially hired. Furthermore, security measures must ensure that sensitive information is available only to those who have specific use for it.

Managers and HR staff members can gather data on individual employees and aggregate details into a profile of the current organizational workforce. This profile may reveal many of the current strengths and deficiencies. If some specialized expertise, such as advanced computer skills, is absent, the organization may find it difficult to take advantage of new technological developments. Or if a large group of experienced employees are in the same age bracket, their eventual retirements around the same time might lead to future "gaps" in the organization.

Forecasting HR Supply and Demand

Forecasting
Using information from the past and the present to identify expected future conditions.

3 The information gathered from scanning the external environment and assessing internal strengths and weaknesses is used to predict HR supply and demand in light of organizational objectives and strategies. **Forecasting** uses information from the past and the present to identify expected future conditions. Figure 2-5 shows the role of HR forecasting in the HR planning process. Projections for the future are, of course, subject to error. Usually, though, experienced people are able to forecast with enough accuracy to benefit long-range organizational planning.

Figure 2-5 *HR Forecasting*

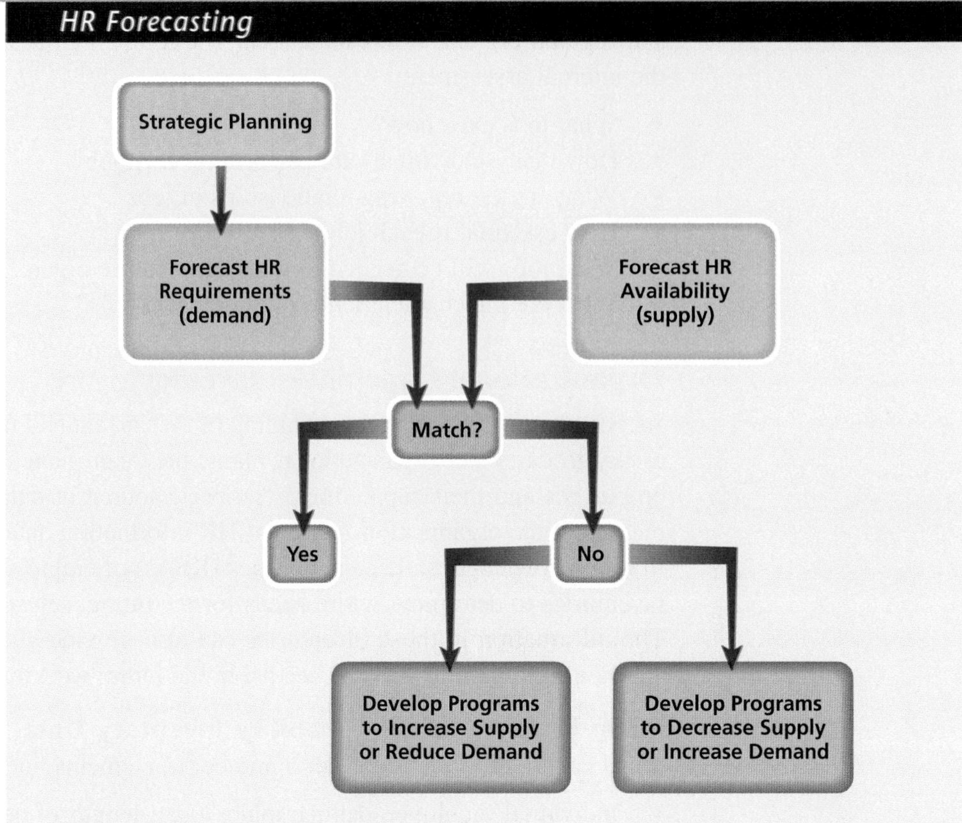

Forecasting Methods

Forecasting methods may be either quantitative (mathematical) or qualitative (judgmental). Methods for forecasting human resources range from a manager's best guess to a rigorous and complex computer simulation. Despite the availability of sophisticated mathematical models and techniques, forecasting is still a combination of quantitative and qualitative methods. The facts must be evaluated and weighed by knowledgeable individuals, such as managers or HR planners, who use the mathematical models as tools and make judgments to arrive at decisions.

Forecasting Periods

HR forecasting should be completed over three planning periods: short-range, intermediate-range, and long-range. The most commonly used planning period of six months to one year focuses on *short-range* forecasts for the immediate HR needs of an organization. Intermediate and long-range forecasting are much more difficult processes. *Intermediate-range* plans usually project one to five years into the future, and *long-range* plans extend beyond five years.

Forecasting the Demand for Human Resources

The forecast for employees is not an exact science as there are a number of variables that may impact on the final outcome. For example, if an organization determined that they would need to upgrade their production facilities to increase production because of the increased demand for their product, they may decide that 50 new production employees would be required. If interest rates were low enough, then it may be feasible to expand the operation. What would happen though, if the economy took a bit of a downturn, thus pushing down demand for the product, and then banks raised their interest rates? Obviously an organization would have to rethink the need to upgrade their facilities, and the eventual hire of 50 new employees. In this case, the better way would probably be to hire some temporary employees until things settled down and a proper determination of what employees were actually needed could be made.

The demand for employees can be calculated for an entire organization and/or for individual units in the organization. For example, a forecast might indicate that a firm needs 125 new employees next year, or that it needs 25 new people in sales and customer service, 45 in production, 20 in accounting and information systems, two in HR, and 33 in the warehouse. The unit breakdown obviously allows HR planners to better pinpoint the specific skills needed than the aggregate method does.

Demand for human resources can be forecast by considering specific openings that are likely to occur. The openings (or demands) are created when employees leave positions because of promotions, transfers, and terminations. The analysis always begins with the top positions in the organization, because from there no promotions to a higher level are possible.

This analysis is used to develop decision rules (or "fill rates") for each job or level. For example, a decision rule for a financial institution might state that 50 percent of branch supervisor openings will be filled through promotions from customer service tellers, 25 percent through promotions from personal bankers, and 25 percent from new hires. Forecasters must be aware of chain effects throughout the organization, because as people are promoted, their previous positions become available. Continuing our example, forecasts for the need for customer service tellers and personal bankers would also have to be developed. The overall purpose of the forecast is to identify the needs for human resources by number and type for the forecasting period.

Quantitative Approaches to Forecasting Demand There are a number of ways in which forecasting could take place in an organization. Much will depend on the size of the organization, and the amount of sophistication the organization chooses to use. Larger organizations are more likely to use *quantitative* approaches such as trend or ratio analysis, the scatter plot, regression analysis, and simulation models. Technology is often employed to perform the calculations.

A *trend analysis* is a study of an organization's past employment needs over a period of years to predict future needs. For example, you might find that you needed one sales representative for every $600,000 in sales for the past three years. If you predict $60,000,000 in sales, then you would need 60,000,000/600,000 = 100 sales representatives. The assumption is that a historical ratio will predict future staffing needs. The problem here is that only one factor is being considered when other factors such as productivity and the economy can affect your employment numbers.

A *ratio analysis* could be related to factors such as productivity. Productivity would be determined by dividing the average number of units produced per employee. The number would then be applied to sales forecasts to determine the number of employees required. Another ratio could be staffing to estimate indirect labour. For example, if the organization used one sales administrator for every ten salespeople, that ratio would be useful to determine the number of administrators required.

A *scatter plot* is a graphical method used to help identify the relationship between two variables. For example, consider a car dealership that employs mechanics to service cars. The relationship could be between the number of working bays available versus the number of vehicles sold.

Regression analysis makes a statistical comparison of past relationships among a number of factors. For example, a statistical relationship might be found between various gross sales and number of salespersons between sales regions. Depending on how certain regions are doing, using regression analysis may determine the number of employees needed.

Simulation models are representations of real situations in abstract form. They may include available economic models. These will be used in very sophisticated circumstances. For example, an aerospace program may very well run simulation models to determine possible outcomes of a project.

Qualitative Approaches to Forecasting Demand Both the qualitative and quantitative methods are useful when engaging in HR planning. The qualitative methods utilized are management forecasts, the Delphi technique, and the nominal group technique.

Management forecasts occur when managers use their experiences to make projections and judgments about the needs of their operations. Since managers and supervisors have direct knowledge of the job and the industry, they are in the best position to offer advice on what to do in the future.

The *Delphi* technique was originally developed as a means to obtain the opinion of experts without having them meet face-to-face. In this technique, input from a group of experts is sought by administering separate questionnaires to be filled out anonymously on what forecasted situations will be. These expert opinions are then aggregated and returned to the experts for a second anonymous opinion. This process continues through several rounds until the experts essentially agree on a judgment. The Delphi technique has been shown to produce better one-year forecasts as compared to linear regression analysis, but it does have some limitations. Difficulties can arise in integrating the expert's opinions. This particular technique, however, appears to be particularly useful in generating insights in highly unstructured or undeveloped subject areas, such as human resource planning.

In the *nominal group technique*, participants are brought together for a discussion session led by a moderator. After the topic has been presented to session participants and they have had an opportunity to ask questions or briefly discuss the scope of the topic, they are asked to take a few minutes to think about and write down their responses. The session moderator will then ask each participant to read, and elaborate on, one of their responses. These are noted on a flipchart. Once everyone has given a response, participants will be asked for a second or third response, until all of their answers have been noted on flipchart sheets posted around the room. Once duplications are eliminated, each response is assigned a letter or number. Session participants are then asked to choose up to ten responses that they feel are the most important and rank them according to their relative importance. These rankings are collected from all participants, and aggregated.

Forecasting the Supply of Human Resources

Once human resources needs have been forecast, then availability of human resources must be identified. Forecasting the availability of human resources considers both *external* and *internal* supplies. Although the internal supply may be easier to calculate, it is important to calculate the external supply as accurately as possible.

External Supply The external supply of potential employees available to the organization needs to be identified. Extensive use of government estimates of labour force populations, trends in the industry, and many more complex and interrelated factors must be considered. National labour market information can be obtained through the Department of Human Resources and Social Development (HRSDC). Job Futures is a product of the Canadian Occupational Projection System (COPS), a labour supply-and-demand information and data bank designed by HRSDC. The information is constantly updated and each province has information regarding their regions. In addition, industry associations are another excellent source to gain valuable information on current labour market supply conditions within a particular industry. As well, such information is often available from regional economic development offices, including information on:

- Net migration into and out of the area
- Individuals entering and leaving the workforce
- Individuals graduating from schools and colleges/universities
- Changing workforce composition and patterns
- Economic forecasts for the next few years
- Technological developments and shifts
- Actions of competing employers
- Government regulations and pressures
- Circumstances affecting persons entering and leaving the workforce

Internal Supply When employees are sought internally, there are several places from which to determine if the necessary knowledge, skills, and abilities (KSAs) exist within the organization. Usually the first stage is to review any *skills inventories* that may exist. These may be manual or computerized. This information will identify internal candidates who may be ready for promotion or for transfer. It may also summarize the employee's education, experience, interests, skills, previous training, and performance record.

Another useful way to source employees for potential movement in an organization is to look at *organizational charts or staffing tables*. This will clearly demonstrate the reporting relationships between employees and the movement that can be achieved within an organization.

A *Markov analysis* can also be utilized. This is a statistical analysis that predicts needs based on probabilities determined by the pattern of movement through the various jobs. The analysis shows the number of people who remain in their job from one year to the next (e.g., 2006–2007), and the proportion of those who have been promoted, remain in their position, or who have left. It requires a large sample size and is insensitive to multiple moves in a time period. For example, it would be difficult to determine if a person had been promoted and then demoted, or had even left the organization after a short while in the new job. It also does not consider underlying causes or changes, and therefore to be effective, other methods should also be employed to understand why the movement is occurring. Figure 2-6 is an example of a Markov analysis.

Data from *replacement charts* can also be used to project potential personnel changes, identify possible backup candidates, and keep track of attrition (resignations, retirements, etc.) for each department in an organization. Replacement charts are often used for executive positions, however, with the impending skill shortages that will occur in the near future, it may be necessary for organizations to consider a replacement chart for a wider range of positions. Replacement charts usually include age, present performance rating, and their potential promotability status. Figure 2-7 depicts an example of an executive replacement chart.

Succession planning
Process of identifying a longer-term plan for the orderly replacement of key employees.

Succession planning is the process of identifying a longer-term plan for the orderly replacement of key employees. In larger organizations, such as the federal

Figure 2-6 **Markov Analysis for a Hypothetical Sales Office**

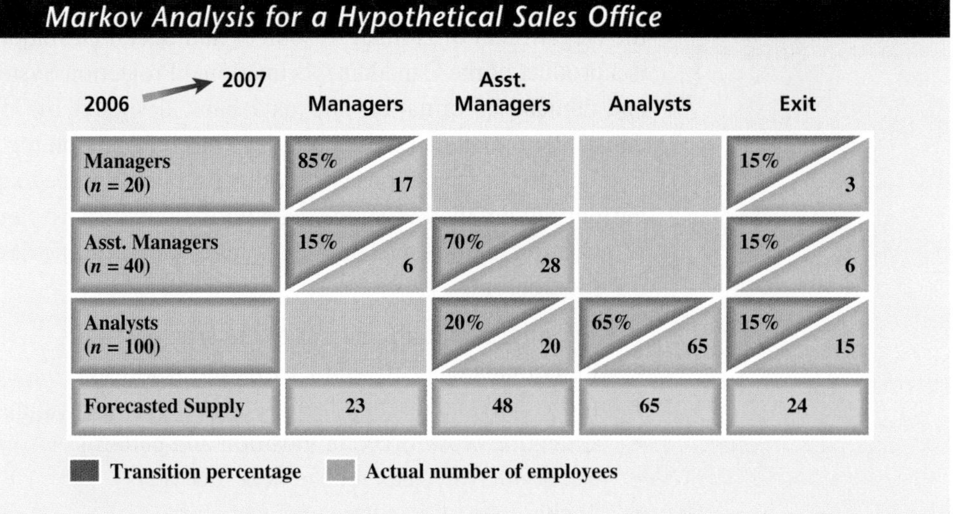

2006 → 2007	Managers	Asst. Managers	Analysts	Exit
Managers (n = 20)	85% 17			15% 3
Asst. Managers (n = 40)	15% 6	70% 28		15% 6
Analysts (n = 100)		20% 20	65% 65	15% 15
Forecasted Supply	23	48	65	24

government, the aging of the workforce has significant implications for HR planning and succession planning. In terms of small to medium-sized employers, which make up the largest component of Canada's employers, the implications for succession planning are paramount. The aging population in North America has reached epidemic proportions. In the coming decades, Canada's population is expected to age more rapidly than that of other industrialized countries. Over the next four decades, growth of the seniors' population will account for close to half the growth of the overall Canadian population. Canada's population growth will stagnate and may even decline by 2026 if our immigration rates do not increase significantly. Succession planning has never been more important than it is at this moment. The HR Perspective highlights the concerns of many employers.

As with executive replacement summaries, one common flaw in succession planning is that too often it is limited to key executives. It may be just as critical to replace several experienced mechanical engineers or specialized nurses as to plan for replacing the CEO.

Figure 2-7 **Executive Replacement Chart for Hypothetical Company**

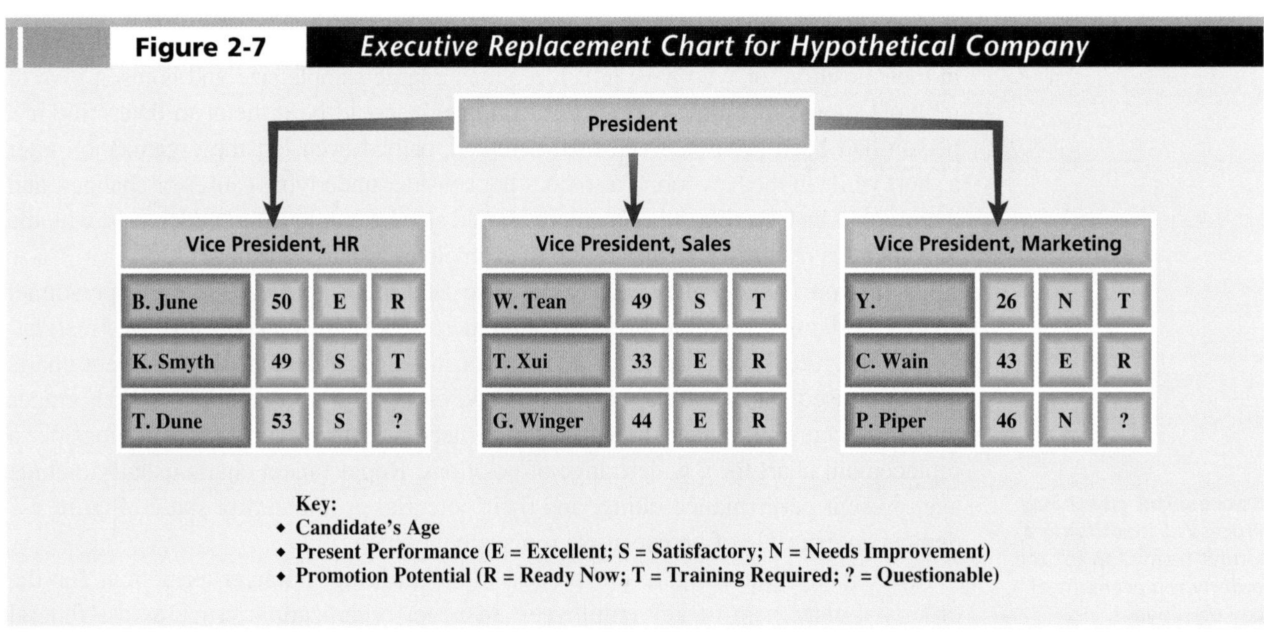

Canadian Employers Face Workforce Retirements

The overall aging of the Canadian population raises many questions for the different levels of government across the country because of the repercussions that an aging population has in such areas as health care and old age pensions. Notably, one area of the economy that is beginning to feel the implications of this aging population is the labour market. Indeed, the upcoming retirements of the baby boomers, which still form the largest segment of the Canadian population, will leave serious gaps in the workforce considering the diminishing number of youths entering this workforce. Nowhere will these gaps be more evident than in the upper ranks of the Canadian federal public service. In fact, over the next ten years forecasts show that approximately 5 percent of public service executives will retire each year in addition to the 2.5 percent that are expected to leave the Public Service for reasons other than retirement. Examples of department's that fall under the public service are Justice Canada, HRSDC, Health Canada, Transport Canada, and Statistics Canada.

Another key organization is the Royal Canadian Mounted Police (RCMP), as well as other police forces across Canada. Each of these organizations will endure excessive amounts of retirement, but with few people to replace them. The RCMP depends on a mixture of internal and external hires to fill replacements for key positions. The external hires come from other police forces across the country. However, with impending shortages in those agencies, recruitment will be difficult. Both the RCMP and the police agencies expect to lose 25 percent of their workforce in the next few years.

More than 40 percent of the owners of Canadian small to medium-sized businesses—about 400 000 people—plan to retire in the next five years, and less than a third have formal succession plans. These often family-run businesses make up almost half of the Canadian economy and the changes could disrupt two million jobs across the country.

This retirement situation among all of these stakeholders illustrates two key points. First, general numbers projecting retirements may be interesting, but HR planning must focus on specific organizations and on occupational groups in those organizations. Second, identifying sources for potential replacements and developing "replacement charts" to ensure that the organizations continue to staff all their jobs, especially those requiring highly specialized education, experience, and qualifications, is a crucial part of strategic HR management.[19]

1. Do you feel that the impending shortage of skilled workers and an aging population will truly impact small to medium-sized businesses in Canada? Why?
2. How do you think HR planning can be effective when there are no people to fill jobs? Should organizations even bother?

Figure 2-8 shows in general terms how the internal supply can be calculated for a specific employer. Estimating internal supply considers that employees move from their current jobs into others through promotions, lateral moves, and terminations. It also considers that the internal supply is influenced by training and development programs, transfer and promotion policies, and retirement policies, among other factors. As the internal supply of employees becomes increasingly more difficult to maintain, the retention of employees is increasingly becoming one of HR's main concerns. The following discussion on retention highlights the importance of this challenge.

Retention of Human Resources

4 One of the most important contemporary management issues today is the retention of talent. Retention must be viewed as a strategic business issue. Until a few years ago, turnover was a routine HR matter requiring records and reports, but top management did not get involved. Today, there are now fewer qualified and productive people in the workforce, and the good ones are even more in demand. Companies are being forced to study why employees leave and why they stay. While experts can (and do)

A number of professions are going to be facing skills shortages in the near future. One field that has had difficulty with skill shortages is the medical profession.

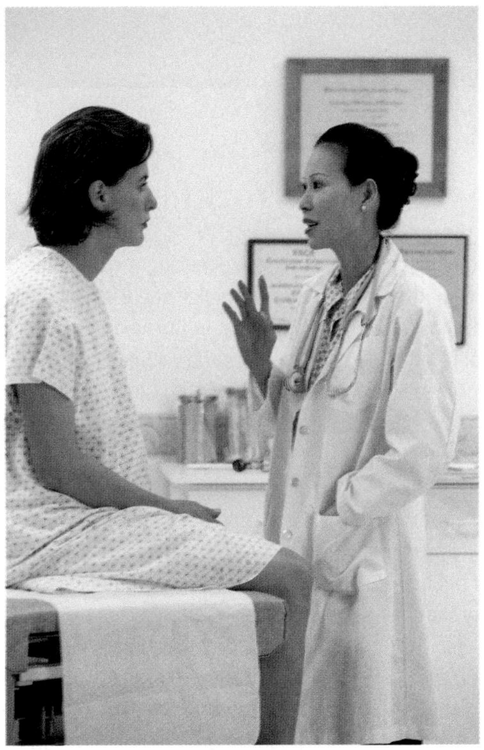

Source: © Royalty-Free/Corbis

make some observations, each organization must determine the causes for its own specific retention situation.

Conventional wisdom says that employees leave if they are dissatisfied, and that money will make them stay. That greatly oversimplifies the issue.[20] People often leave jobs for reasons that have nothing to do with the jobs themselves. Mergers, unsolicited job offers, family responsibilities, a spouse's relocation, a poor performance appraisal, and administrative changes are all "shocks" that can bring on serious thoughts of leaving, even when people are not dissatisfied with their jobs. Further, people sometimes stay with jobs for non-work reasons. Some factors that limit individuals' willingness to leave the jobs are *links* between themselves and others; compatibility, or *"fit,"* with the job/organization/community; and potential *sacrifice,* or what they would have to give up if they left the job.

Those characteristics of the "stay or go" decision are personal and not entirely within the control of an employer. However, there are factors related to those individual decisions that an employer *can* control. Figure 2-9 shows those factors, and also indicates that they are "drivers" of retention, or forces that an employer can manage to improve retention.[21]

Figure 2-8 Estimating Internal Labour Supply for a Given Unit

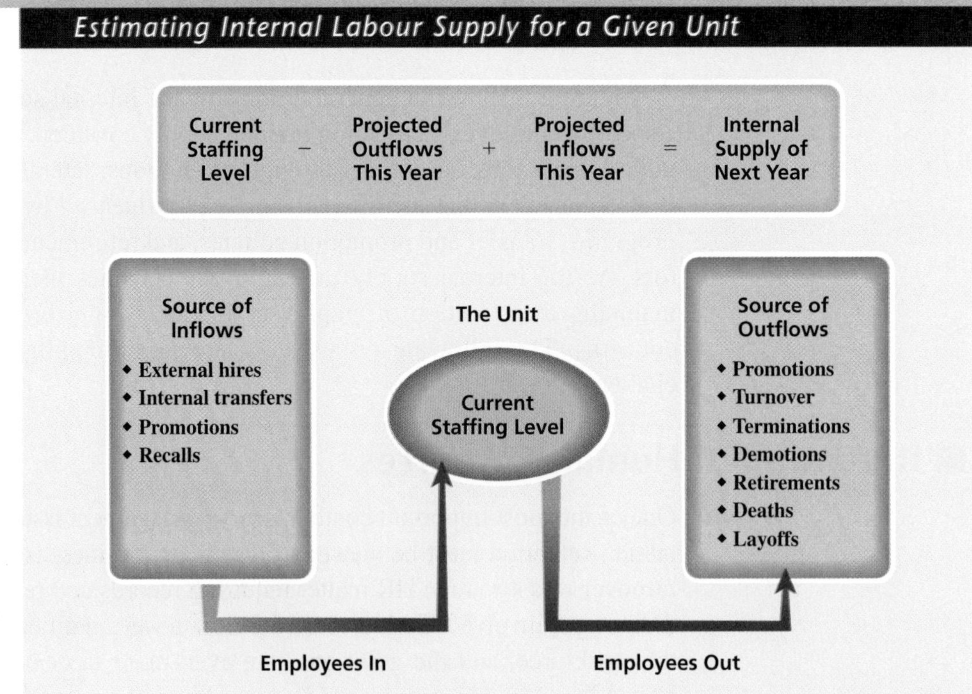

Figure 2-9 Drivers of Retention

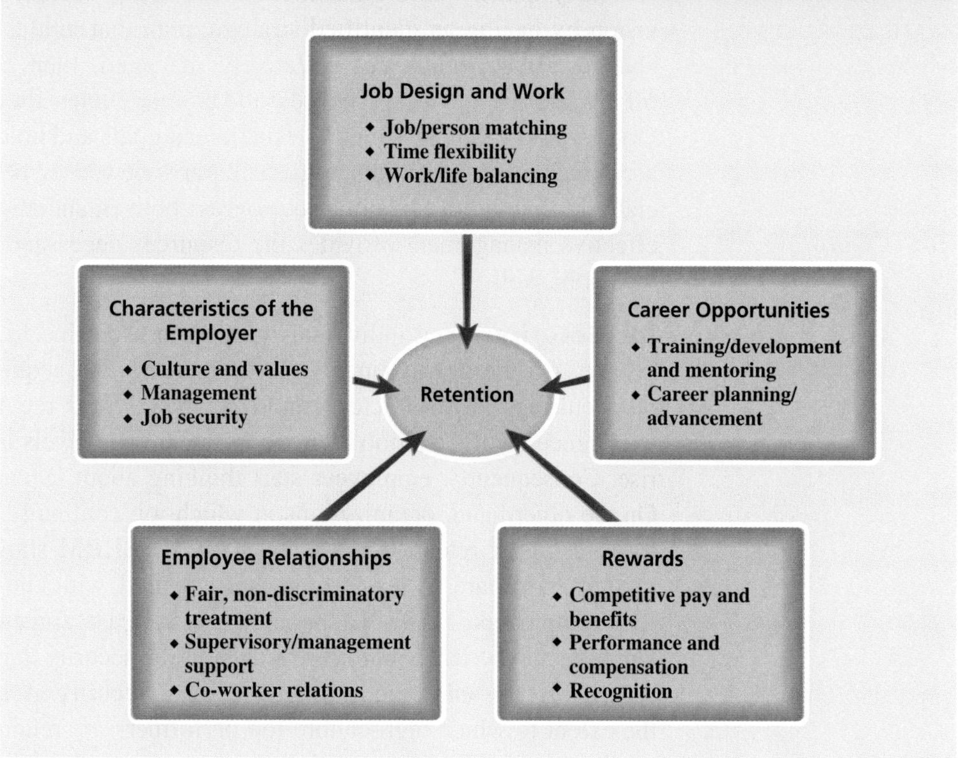

If employees choose to leave an organization for family reasons—because a spouse is transferring, to raise children, etc.—there are a limited number of actions the employer can take. However, there *are* significant actions that an employer *can* do to retain employees.

Characteristics of the Employer and Retention

A number of organizational characteristics influence individuals in their decisions to stay with or leave their employers. Organizations experience less turnover when they have positive, distinctive cultures; effective management; and recognizable job security.

Organizational culture
The shared values and beliefs of a workforce.

Culture and Values **Organizational culture** is a pattern of shared values and beliefs of a workforce. Those items provide organizational members with meaning and rules for behaviour.

One firm that uses culture and values to retain employees is Starbucks, which considers providing a "great work environment" as number one on its six-point mission statement. The "100 Best Companies to Work For" have somewhat different cultures and values, yet their commitment to treating their employees well is a constant in good times and bad.[22]

Management and Retention Other organizational components that affect employee retention are related to the management of the organization. Some organizations see external events as threatening, whereas others see changes as challenges requiring responses. The latter approach can be a source of competitive advantage, especially if an organization is in a growing, dynamic industry. The attitudes and approaches of management are the key.

Another factor affecting how employees view their organizations is the *visionary quality* of organizational leadership. Often, leaders demonstrate their vision by having an identified strategic plan that guides how the firm responds to changes. If a firm is not effectively managed, then employees may be turned off by the ineffective responses and inefficiencies they deal with in their jobs. Organizations that have clearly established goals and hold managers and employees accountable for accomplishing results are viewed as better places to work, especially by individuals wishing to progress both financially and career-wise. Further, effective management provides the resources necessary for employees to perform their jobs well.

Job Security Many individuals have seen a decline in job security over the past decade. All the downsizings, layoffs, mergers and acquisitions, and organizational restructurings have affected employee loyalty and retention. Also, as co-workers experience layoffs and job reductions, the anxiety levels of the remaining employees rise. Consequently, employees start thinking about leaving before they too get cut. On the other hand, organizations in which job continuity and security are high tend to have higher retention rates. A survey by SHRM showed that about 75 percent of employees are at least somewhat satisfied with the job security provided by their employers, while 13 percent are at least somewhat dissatisfied. Younger employees experience more concern about job security than do older workers. But job security is not solely about one's personal security. A major issue in retention is the extent to which high-calibre top performers are retained by the company. Other employees view high turnover in this group and the company as a negative in the retention equation.[23]

Job Design/Work and Retention

Some jobs are considered "good" and others are thought to be "bad." People vary considerably in their preferences for particular job features. That is fortunate, because it means there are people willing to do most jobs.

Job/Person Match Matching people with jobs they like and fit can be a challenge. If people do not fit their jobs well, they are more likely to look for other employment, so retention is affected by the *selection process.* A number of organizations have found that high turnover rates in the first few months of employment are often linked to inadequate selection screening efforts.

Once individuals have been placed in jobs, several job/work factors affect retention. Because individuals spend significant time on the job, they expect to have modern equipment, technology, and *good working conditions,* given the nature of the work. Physical and environmental factors such as space, lighting, temperature, noise, and layout affect retention of employees.

Additionally, workers want a *safe work environment,* where risks of accidents and injuries have been addressed. That is especially true for employees in such industries as manufacturing, agriculture, utilities, and transportation, which have higher safety risks than do many service industries and office environments.

Time Flexibility Flexibility in work schedules has grown in importance. Workload pressures have increased because of downsizing. On average, employees work 41.2 hours a week at their main jobs, but would prefer to work 34.5 hours a week. That discrepancy leads to 44 percent of employees working more than they want to and feeling overworked.[24] Further, with more North Americans living longer, the need for

Healthy Workplace Resources
One of the resources available at this site is a search option on work/life balance that links to other useful sites and resources.
www.nqi.ca/hwr

elder care is increasing. Dual-income couples in the "sandwich generation," caring for children *and* aged parents, may find flexible scheduling options very desirable. B.C. BioMedical Laboratories Ltd., named one of the 50 best employers in Canada, are committed to adopting family-friendly practices by offering employees job-sharing opportunities.[25]

Work/Life Balancing Balancing the demands of work with the responsibilities of life, including family and personal responsibilities, is a challenge; some may say it is an impossibility. Work/life balancing programs commonly used include:

- Different work arrangements
- Leave for children's school functions
- Compressed workweek
- Job sharing
- On-site child/adult care
- Telecommuting
- Employee assistance plans
- On-site health services
- Wellness programs
- Fitness facility

An increasing number of organizations are offering employees services that address the work/life balance issues that many individuals face. These services help to make employees lives more manageable and less stressful. For example, Wyeth Pharmaceuticals, based in Markham, Ontario, offers flexible schedules to improve work/life balance of employees, Ceridan Canada Ltd., located in Toronto, provides on-site flu immunization and cardiovascular screening for employees, and Pfizer Global Pharmaceuticals Group Canada, in Kirkland, Quebec, offers its employees a service for car maintenance.[26]

A recent survey conducted by CareerBuilder.com indicates that 4-in-10 working dads say they would stay at home and assume the role of Mr. Mom if their spouse or partner earned enough to support their families. When comparing the work situations of men and women, the survey shows that working dads experience less flexibility with their employers than working moms. Forty percent of working dads say their companies offer flexible work arrangements, compared to 53 percent of working moms. The importance associated with balance of family may no longer be relegated to the female role, but seems to be now extended to the male role as well.[27]

The value of work/life programs has been documented by a number of employers. One large manufacturer worked to reduce absenteeism and increase employee commitment to the firm. A revised time-off program and more flexible work arrangements have reduced absenteeism and unscheduled time off, and increased employee satisfaction with the company.

Career Opportunities and Retention

Surveys of workers in all types of jobs consistently indicate that organizational efforts to aid career development can significantly affect employee retention. Such surveys have found that *opportunities for personal growth* lead the list of reasons why individuals took their current jobs and why they stay there. That component is even more essential for technical professionals and those under age 35, for whom opportunities to develop skills and obtain promotions rank above compensation as a retention concern. Envision Financial, a financial services company based in Langley, B.C., has established a career planning program for its employees.

Training/Development and Mentoring Organizations address training and development in a number of ways. Tuition aid programs, typically offered as a benefit by many employers, allow employees to pursue additional educational and training opportunities. For example, Sleep Country Canada in Toronto, offers its employees a tuition reimbursement program to compensate for courses taken in addition to their working responsibilities.[28] These programs often contribute to higher employee retention rates. However, just offering such programs is not sufficient. Employers must also identify ways to use employees' new knowledge and capabilities inside the organization. Otherwise, employees are likely to feel that their increased "value" is not being recognized. Overall, training and development efforts are designed to meet many employees' expectations that their employers are committed to keeping their knowledge, skills, and abilities current. Orientation of new employees that is well administered may increase employee retention rates by as much as 25 percent.[29] Mentoring, formal or informal, can also increase retention, as it provides both career opportunities and development. As the number of contacts grows through mentors or others, it turns into a career networking system, either inside the organization or outside, or perhaps both. For example, mentoring programs are offered to employees by Delta Hotels Canada based in Toronto. Another interesting example of a mentoring program is "Mentor Match," which has been developed and introduced by Bell Canada in the fall of 2002. Bell Canada offers its employees an online mentoring program available to employees in all business levels. The program was implemented due to the aging workforce, a unique opportunity to develop employees, improve communications as well as the increase in competition as a result of deregulation. The online mentoring system allows employees to create a profile, which matches them to other registered employees based on the criteria entered. One major benefit of the mentoring system is the resulting culture of cooperation and helping fellow colleagues to achieve organizational goals.[30]

Career Planning/Advancement Organizations also increase employee retention through formal career planning efforts. Employees discuss with their managers career opportunities within the organization and career development activities that will help the employees grow. Career development and planning efforts may include formal mentoring programs. Also, companies can reduce attrition by showing employees that they are serious about promoting from within. In very large companies, it is not always easy to know who might be qualified for an open job. Research suggests that when people have been promoted, they are less likely to leave the organization.[31] By staying with an organization, costs of training, recruiting, and turnover are reduced.

Rewards and Retention

The tangible rewards that people receive for working come in the form of pay, incentives, and benefits. Numerous surveys and experiences of HR professionals reveal that one key to retention is having *competitive compensation practices.* Many managers believe that money is the prime retention factor. Often, employees cite better pay or higher compensation as a reason for leaving one employer for another. However, the reality is a bit more complex.

Competitive Pay and Benefits Pay and benefits *must be competitive,* which means they must be close to what other employers are providing and what individuals believe to be consistent with their capabilities, experience, and performance. If compensation is less than what other employees are paid, often defined as within 10 percent of the "market" rate, then turnover is likely to be higher. This is especially true for individuals making less than $25,000 to $30,000 annually. On the other hand, for more highly paid individuals, especially those earning $60,000 and more, retention is less affected by how close compensation is to the market rate. Other considerations are more likely to enter into their decisions to stay or leave. In fact, money may be why some people leave a job, but other factors may be why many stay. Offering health insurance, pension plan, tuition assistance, and other benefits commonly provided by competing employers often is vital to retention, as are more exotic benefits such as dry cleaning pick up and drop off, car maintenance at work, or onsite ATM machines. By offering special benefits and perks, employers hope to be seen by employees more favourably, which may increase retention rates.[32] Prospera Credit Union & Insurance Agencies in B.C. offers a benefit program that allows employees to spend flex dollars on healthcare, RRSPs, vacations, or taxable cash. This flexibility allows employees the opportunity to dictate the allocation amounts for their benefits.

Performance and Compensation Many individuals expect their rewards to be differentiated from those of others based on performance. That means, for instance, that if an employee receives about the same pay increase and overall pay as others who produce less, are absent more, and work fewer hours, then that person may feel that the situation is "unfair." This may prompt the individual to look for another job where compensation recognizes performance differences. Generally individuals are more satisfied with the actual levels of their pay than with the processes used to determine pay. That is why the performance management systems and performance appraisal processes in organizations must be designed so they are linked to compensation increases. One travel company, Flight Centre North America in Vancouver, B.C., has developed its performance appraisal system linked to the employee compensation. At this company, employees are granted travel rewards based on sales performance.

Recognition Employee recognition as a form of reward can be either tangible or intangible. Tangible recognition comes in many forms, such as "employee of the month" plaques and perfect-attendance certificates. Intangible and psychological recognition includes feedback from managers and supervisors that acknowledges extra effort and performance, even if monetary rewards are not given.

Employee Relationships and Retention

A final set of factors found to affect retention is based on the relationships that employees have in organizations. Such areas as the reasonableness of HR policies, the fairness of disciplinary actions, and the means used to decide work assignments and opportunities all affect employee retention. If individuals feel that policies are unreasonably restrictive or are applied inconsistently, then they may be more likely to look at jobs offered by other employers.[33] Abbott Canada in St-Laurent, Quebec, a pharmaceutical company involves employees in developing HR policies that likely lead to improved employment relationships.[34]

The organizational commitment and job satisfaction of ethnically diverse individuals are affected by perceived discriminatory treatment. A number of firms have recognized that proactive management of diversity issues results in greater retention of individuals of all backgrounds.

Other relationships that affect employee retention are *supervisory/management support* and *co-worker relations.* A supervisor or manager builds positive relationships and aids retention by being fair and non-discriminatory, allowing work flexibility and work/family balancing, giving feedback that recognizes employee efforts and performance, and supporting career planning and development. Many individuals build close relationships with co-workers. Such friendships do not appear on employee records, but research suggests that they can be an important signal that a workplace is positive.[35]

Managing Retention

The foregoing section summarized the results of many studies and HR practices to identify factors that can cause retention difficulties. Now the focus turns to what a manager can do about retention issues. Figure 2-10 shows the keys to managing retention.

Retention Measurement and Assessment

To ensure that appropriate actions are taken to enhance retention, management decisions require data and analyses rather than subjective impressions, anecdotes of selected individual situations, or panic reactions to the loss of key people. Having several *absence and turnover measurements* to analyze is important. Two other sources of information might be useful before analysis is done: employee surveys and exit interviews.

Employee Surveys Employee surveys can be used to diagnose specific problem areas, identify employee needs or preferences, and reveal areas in which HR activities are well received or are viewed negatively. For example, questionnaires may be sent to employees to collect ideas for revising a performance appraisal system or to determine how satisfied employees are with their benefits programs. Regardless of the topic of a survey, obtaining employee input provides managers and HR professionals with data on the "retention climate" in an organization.

Figure 2-10 Keys to Managing Retention

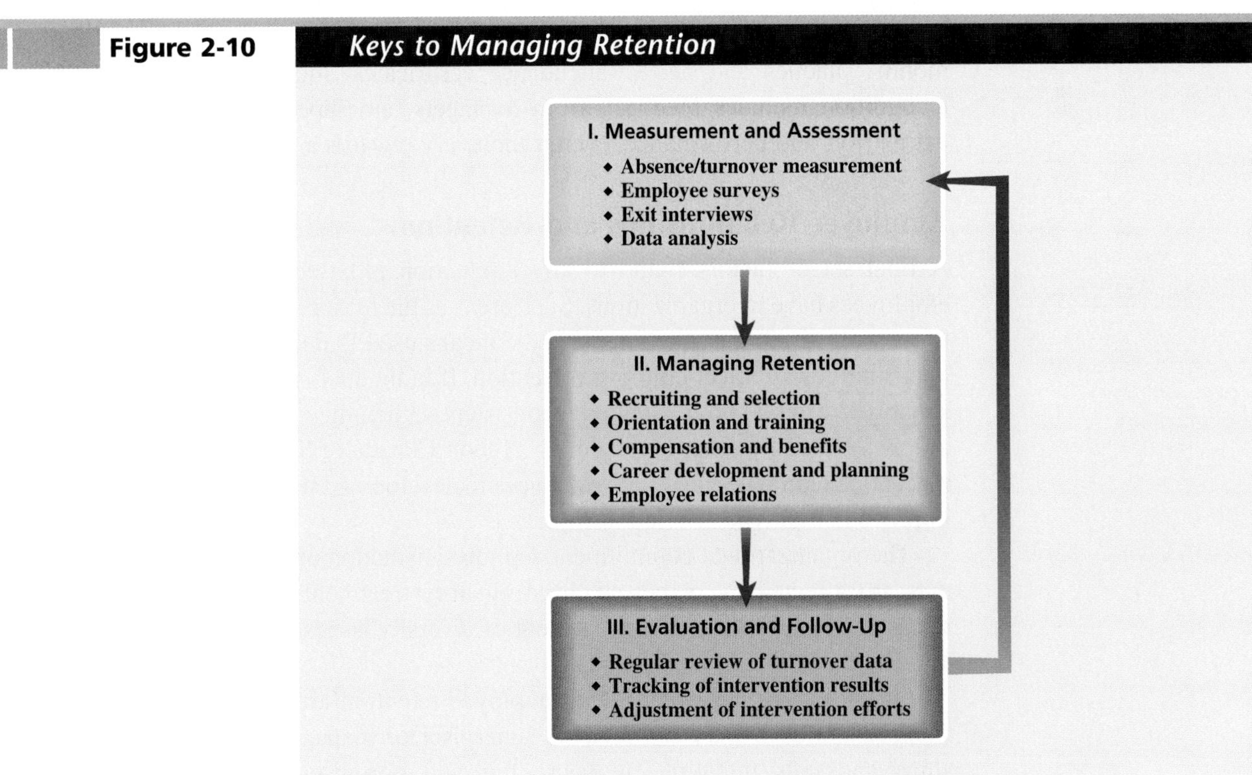

Attitude survey
A survey that focuses on employees' feelings and beliefs about their jobs and the organization.

Attitude Survey One specific type of survey used by many organizations is an **attitude survey** that focuses on employees' feelings and beliefs about their jobs and the organization. By obtaining data on how employees view their jobs, their supervisors, their co-workers, and organizational policies and practices, these surveys can be starting points for reducing turnover and increasing the length of time that employees are retained. Some employers conduct attitude surveys regularly (such as every year), while others do so intermittently. As the use of the Internet has spread, more organizations have begun conducting attitude surveys electronically.[36]

Engagement survey
Engagement is defined as the degree to which workers identify with, are motivated by, and are willing to expend extra effort for their employer.

Engagement Survey Another employee survey is called an **engagement survey.** An engagement survey measures the degree to which workers identify with, are motivated by, and are willing to expend extra effort for their employer. Organizations that fail to engage their people fail to achieve their full potential. Engaged employees reduce costs, work harder, and create more satisfied customers. In a recent survey conducted by ISR, an international employee research and consulting firm, 70 percent of Canadians were engaged, compared with 75 percent in the U.S. and Brazil, which ranked highest, and 59 percent in France, the lowest-ranked country. Canadian employees are most likely to connect to their companies through an emotional attachment. The most important workplace issue affecting employee engagement in Canada is the availability of opportunities for personal growth and development.[37] Companies such as FedEx, ADP Canada, and B.C. Medical Laboratories all emphasize employee engagement in order to be successful.[38]

Attitude and engagement surveys are developed by consulting firms, academicians, and others. They can also be custom designed to address specific issues and concerns in an organization. Regardless of their type, only surveys that are valid and reliable can measure attitudes accurately. Often a "research" survey developed in-house is poorly structured, asks questions in a confusing manner, or leads employees to respond in ways that will give "favourable" results.[39]

By asking employees to respond candidly to an employee survey, management is building up employees' expectations that action will be taken on the concerns identified. Therefore, a crucial part of conducting any type of employee survey is providing feedback to those who participated in it. It is especially important that even negative survey results be communicated, to avoid fostering the appearance of hiding the results or placing blame.

Exit interview
An interview in which individuals are asked to give their reasons for leaving the organization.

Exit Interviews One widely used type of interview is the **exit interview,** in which individuals are asked to give their reasons for leaving the organization. In one survey of employers, 87 percent of them claimed to conduct exit interviews, and more than half used the information gathered to make changes to aid retention. A wide range of issues can be examined in exit interviews, as described in the HR Practice on conducting them.

Determining Retention Management Actions

The analysis of data mined from turnover and absenteeism records, surveys of employees, and exit interviews is an attempt to get at the cause of retention problems. Analysis should recognize that turnover and absenteeism are symptoms of other factors that may be causing problems. When the causes are treated, the symptoms will go away. Some of the first areas to consider when analyzing data for retention include the work, pay/benefits, supervision, and management systems.

HR Practice

Conducting Exit Interviews

One task commonly performed by HR staff members in organizations with significant turnover is conducting exit interviews. HR specialists, rather than department managers or supervisors, usually conduct these interviews. One reason for that is because a skilled HR interviewer may be able to gain useful information that departing employees may not wish to share with managers and supervisors, particularly if it pertains to problems and issues with those managers and supervisors. Departing employees may be reluctant to divulge their real reasons for leaving because they may wish to return to the company someday. Also, they may fear that candid responses will hinder their chances of receiving favourable references.

The following suggestions may be useful when conducting exit interviews:

- Decide who will conduct the exit interviews and when the discussions will occur. Usually, they are done on the last day of a departing individual's employment.
- Develop a checklist or a set of standard questions so that the information can be summarized. Typical areas covered include reasons for leaving, supervision, pay, training, best- and least-liked aspects of the job, and organization to which the employee is moving.
- Emphasize that the information provided by departing employees will be treated confidentially, and will be summarized to use for making future improvements and changes in the organization.
- Regularly summarize the data by reasons for leaving, department, length of service, etc., to provide data for improving company retention efforts.
- If possible, contact departed employees a month or so after they leave. The "real reasons" for departure may be voiced at that time. One major reason employees commonly give for leaving their jobs is that they got an offer for more pay elsewhere; however, the pay increase may not be the only reason.
- Recognize that former employees may be more willing to provide information on questionnaires mailed to their homes or in telephone conversations conducted some time after they have left the organization.[40]

1. Do you think that if a departing employee were to leave the organization that they would be willing to share their true feelings about leaving? Why or why not?
2. If this is truly an area of strategic concern, does it make sense that the HR administrator should be conducting the exit interview? Why or why not?

Creative Organizational Design
This organization offers design and analysis of employee surveys and exit interviews.
www.creativeorgdesign.com

There are numerous actions management might take to deal with retention issues. The choice of a particular action depends on the analysis of the turnover and retention problems in a particular organization and should be custom-tailored for that organization.

Retention Evaluation and Follow-Up

Once appropriate management actions have been implemented, it is important that they be evaluated and that appropriate follow-up be conducted and adjustments made. *Regular review of turnover data* can identify when turnover increases or decreases among different employee groups classified by length of service, education, department, and gender, etc.

Tracking of intervention results and *adjustment of intervention efforts* also should be part of evaluation efforts. Some firms may use pilot programs to see how changes affect turnover before extending them to the entire organization. For instance, to test the effect of flextime scheduling on employee turnover, a firm might try flexible scheduling in one department. If the turnover rate in that department drops in comparison with the turnover rates in other departments still working set schedules, then the experimental project may indicate that flexible scheduling can reduce turnover. Next, the firm might extend the use of flexible scheduling to other departments.

Developing and Using a Strategic HR Plan

5 With all the data collected and forecasts completed, an organizational plan can be developed. Such a plan can be extremely sophisticated or rather rudimentary. Regardless of the degree of complexity, the ultimate purpose of the plan is to enable managers in the organization to match the available supply of labour with the demand that is expected given the strategies of the organization. If the necessary skill levels do not exist in the present workforce, the organization can train employees in the new skills or undertake outside recruiting. If the plan reveals that the firm employs too many people for its needs, a human resource surplus exists.

Managing a Human Resources Surplus

HR planning is of little value if no subsequent action is taken. The action taken depends on the likelihood of a human resources surplus or shortage. A surplus of workers can be managed within an HR plan in a variety of ways. Regardless of the means, the actions are difficult because workforce reductions are ultimately necessary.

Workforce Reductions and Legislation In this era of mergers, acquisitions, and downsizing, many workers have been laid off or had their jobs eliminated due to the closing of selected offices, plants, and operations. Each of the provinces and territories' Employment Standards Acts, as well as federal legislation stated under the Canada Labour Code, provide employees with sufficient notice of such losses. These standards require employers to give sufficient notice before implementing a layoff or facility closing that involves more than 50 people. Canadian labour legislation requires that part-timers and seasonal employees be given the same notification period as full-time employees.

Workforce Downsizing It has been given many names, including *downsizing, rightsizing,* and *reduction in force (RIF),* but it almost always means cutting employees. Focusing on trimming underperforming units or employees as part of a plan that is based on sound organizational strategies may make sense. After a decade of many examples and studies, it is clear that downsizing has worked for some firms. However, it does not generate additional revenue, and it only generates lower costs in the short term. When companies cannibalize the human resources needed to grow and innovate, disruption follows for some time. Also, downsizing can hurt productivity by leaving "surviving" employees overburdened and demoralized.

A common myth is that those who are still around after downsizing are so glad to have a job that they pose no problems to the organization. However, some observers draw an analogy between those who survive downsizing and those who survive wartime battles. They may experience guilt because they were spared while their friends were not. Bitterness, anger, disbelief, and shock all are common reactions. For those who survive workforce cuts, the culture and image of the firm as a "lifetime" employer often is gone forever.

Downsizing may adversely affect the performance of the survivors and communications throughout the organization. Survivors need information about why the actions had to be taken, and what the future holds for them personally. The more that employees are involved in the restructuring, the more likely the transition is to be smoother.[41] HR professionals and managers, too, find downsizing situations stressful and may react negatively to having to be the bearers of bad news.

The need for downsizing has inspired various innovative ways of removing people from the payroll, sometimes on a massive scale. Several different methods can be used when downsizing must occur: attrition, early retirement buyouts, and layoffs are the most common.

Attrition and Hiring Freezes *Attrition* occurs when individuals quit, die, or retire and are not replaced. By use of attrition, no one is cut out of a job, but those who remain must handle the same workload with fewer people. Unless turnover is high, attrition will eliminate only a relatively small number of employees in the short run. Therefore, employers may combine attrition with a freeze on hiring. Employees usually understand this approach better than they do other downsizing methods.

Voluntary Separation Programs Organizations can downsize while also reducing legal liabilities if employees volunteer to leave. Often firms entice employees to volunteer by offering them additional severance and benefit payments.

Early retirement buyouts are widely used to encourage more senior workers to leave organizations early. As an incentive, employers make additional payments to employees so that they will not be penalized too much economically until their pensions and Old Age Security benefits take effect. These buyouts are widely viewed as ways to accomplish workforce reduction without resorting to layoffs and individual firings. Ford offered retirement buyouts to its assembly line workers at its Windsor, Ontario, plant. These early retirements will have a positive impact. Approximately 325 employees took the buyout retirement incentive of $70,000.[42]

Volunteer separation programs appeal to employers because they can reduce payroll costs significantly over time. Although the organization faces some up-front costs, it does not incur as many continuing payroll costs. Using such programs is also viewed as a more humane way to reduce staff than terminating long-service, loyal employees. In addition, as long as buyouts are truly voluntary, the organization offering them is less exposed to age discrimination suits. One drawback is that some employees the company wishes would stay, as well as those it wishes would leave, can take advantage of a buyout. Also, employers must comply with Employment Standards Acts and other legislation.

Layoffs Layoffs occur when employees are put on unpaid leaves of absence. If business improves for the employer, then employees can be called back to work. Layoffs may be an appropriate downsizing strategy during a temporary economic downturn in an industry. Nevertheless, careful planning of layoffs is essential. Care must be taken to ensure that age and other types of discrimination do not occur. In a union environment, layoffs often occur on a seniority basis (last in, first out). Some organizations are now asking the more senior employees to take temporary layoffs so that the younger and newer employees can continue to work and build their seniority.

Under provincial and federal legislation, employees cannot be laid off indefinitely. There are two types of layoffs—temporary and permanent. Every jurisdiction has requirements as to how long a temporary layoff is permitted. If at the end of the temporary layoff period the employer has determined that the layoff should be extended beyond what is considered to be temporary by law, then a termination of the employee would have to take effect and the appropriate notice periods and/or severances would apply. Employers need to ensure that if an employee is returned to work after a temporary layoff and then laid off again, that it is within the specified period of time.

Terminations Sometimes it is necessary to reduce staff by terminating those employees whose positions are no longer required. Employment Standards Acts and the Canada Labour Code both require that a certain amount of notice be provided to the employee(s) who are being terminated from their employment and depending on their years of service with the organization, severance may also have to be paid. The amount of notice and severance differs across the federal and provincial jurisdictions. Sometimes employees are not happy with their settlements and choose to sue their employers. In this case, the courts would judge the amount of settlement based on what has happened in the past in other similar situations. In this case, common law would apply. The amounts applied against common law, may exceed the employment standards amounts. An employee needs to weigh the cost of suing an organization versus what they might expect to gain by taking such action. The courts will usually consider the employee's length of service, their age, and their position at the time of the termination. Other factors may also determine a settlement such as how the employee was treated during their tenure, or how the termination was handled.

Reducing Hours Another option is to reduce an employee's hours until such time that things can get back to normal. Someone who wants to take reduced hours may only work three or four days per week instead of five. Additionally, two employees may decide to share the job over a four-day period. Other means to reduce hours may be to have those who wish to work part-time, change their status. Incentives such as keeping the employee's benefits intact, with no loss in hourly wage may be a way to entice employees to take this option.

Outplacement Services

Outplacement is a group of services provided to give displaced employees support and assistance. It is most often used with those involuntarily removed because of performance problems or job elimination. Outplacement services typically include personal career counselling, résumé preparation and typing services, interviewing workshops, and referral assistance. Such services are generally provided by outside firms that specialize in outplacement assistance and whose fees usually are paid by the employer. It is important that outplacement be viewed as part of strategic HR planning.[43] Figure 2-11 shows that it is only one of five factors that should be considered to make downsizing more effective. Aviva Canada made a decision to open a call centre in Montreal in a different location than the head office. The employees who were unable to move to the new location were offered positions in the head office location. In addition, Aviva Canada developed a severance package formula, as well as outplacement support including counselling, résumé writing, and job techniques to employees who were deemed unnecessary by the company.[44]

KWA Partners
This is a national network of entrepreneurial career management professionals.
www.kwapartners.com

HR Planning in Mergers and Acquisitions

Another cause for downsizing has been the proliferation of mergers and acquisitions in many industries. One has only to look at the financial or telecommunications industry to see massive consolidation in the number of firms. A common result of most mergers and acquisitions (M&As) is an excess of employees once the firms have been combined, due to redundant departments, plants, and people. Because much of the rationale for combinations is financial, eliminating employees with overlapping responsibilities is a primary concern. However, studies of numerous M&As reveal that a majority do not achieve their financial and strategic objectives.[45] Numerous

Figure 2-11 *Making Downsizing More Effective*

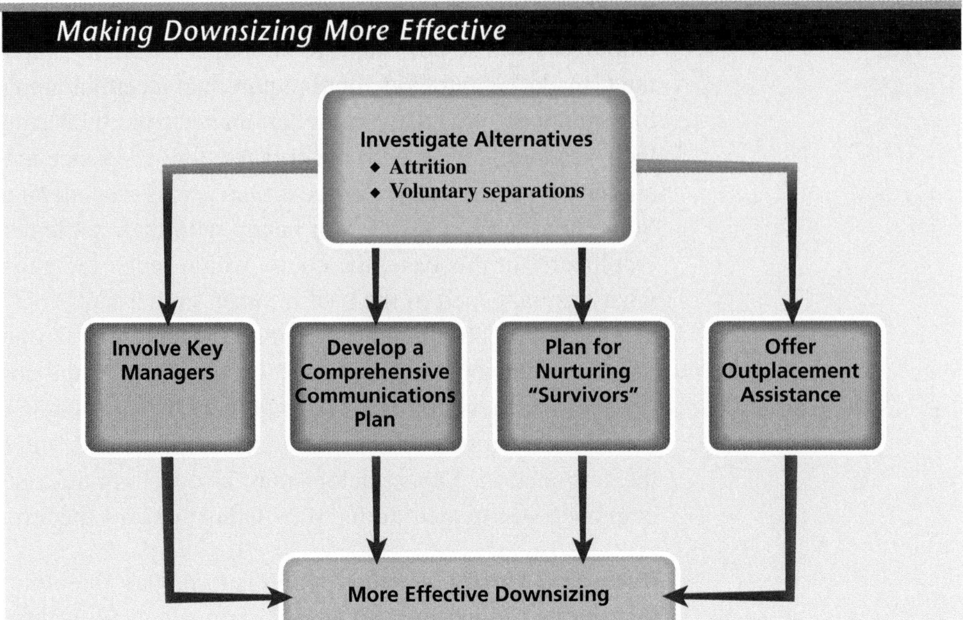

studies have found that HR issues play a significant role in the success or failure of M&As, with the meshing of organizational cultures being crucial.[46] HR management can contribute to the success of mergers and acquisitions.

Experience with the failures shows clearly that for M&As to succeed, organizations have to ensure that different organizational cultures mesh. *Cultural compatibility* is the extent to which such factors as decision-making styles, levels of teamwork, information-sharing philosophies, and the formality of the two organizations are similar. To address organizational culture concerns, HR professionals should be involved before, during, and after M&As.[47] Significant time must be spent identifying the cultural differences, how they are to be addressed, and ways to integrate managers and employees from both entities.[48]

Communicating Decisions The failures of M&As are often attributed to the incompatibility of the different organizational cultures involved. What changes will be made to the organization structure, how employee benefits will be meshed, what jobs and locations will get more or less staff, and many other issues must be decided and communicated. The longer such issues are left unanswered, the greater employee anxiety will be, and the more rumours will proliferate.[49]

Revising the Organization Structure A crucial part of HR is being sure that employee downsizing is handled legally and effectively. Also, critical is the impact of job elimination on the remaining employees. Often, employee morale declines in the short term, and some firms see longer-term declines in employee morale after downsizing. Additionally, resignations and employee turnover may increase substantially in the year following downsizing if the HR issues are mismanaged.

Merging HR Activities Another key role played by HR in mergers and acquisitions is melding together the HR activities in each organization.[50] Compensation, benefits, performance appraisal systems, and employee relations policies all require significant attention by HR staff in both organizations. Who will head HR, and which employees will and will not have jobs in the new HR function, must be addressed. Compatibility of databases and information systems must be considered. Ultimately, how HR contributes to various aspects of mergers and acquisitions likely affects the overall effectiveness of the newly combined organizations

In 2000, Toronto Dominion Bank and Canada Trust merged its operations together including 1500 branches, 44 000 employees, 10 million customers, and $265 billion in assets. A key success factor of the merger of these two large companies was the integration of the employees from two distinct cultures. The change management team insisted that "plaiding" was key to success, which put the critical supports in place to allow employees to learn and support each other through this change process. "Plaiding" has been described to be the process of integrating existing TD "green" employees and Canada Trust "red" employees in branches across Canada. This was a major challenge of the merger and was essential to the outcomes of this change process.[51]

Managing Shortages of Labour

With an aging population, and a lack of skills, Canada will face more instances of labour shortages than they will about having excess employees. Some jobs will be harder to fill than others. It is anticipated that more senior roles will be difficult to fill as the baby boomers begin their exit from the workforce. Strategies to overcome this obstacle are being dealt with through public policy. The Ontario government abolished the mandatory retirement age of 65 to help deal with the shortage of skilled workers. Additionally, the Ontario government is also trying to pass legislation that would keep children in school up to age 18 rather than the current age of 16. This will help to ensure that students have acquired the basic skills to help them in the workplace. The federal government is considering allowing workers to come into Canada on visas that will allow them to work temporarily. A number of strategies that could be used to deal with labour shortages include offering overtime, hiring temporary employees, subcontracting work, external recruitment, transfers, and promotions.

Overtime Whenever organizations need extra work completed, they will often ask employees to work late, work on weekends, or even on holidays. Some employees do not mind earning the extra money, but others do not want to work past their deadlines. As younger workers are hired, their attitudes and values towards work are different as they value quality of life. Therefore, as a long-term strategy, overtime is not always the most effective or efficient way to deal with the problem of labour shortages.

Hiring Temporary Employees When an organization can determine that workers will be needed for a short period of time they may seek the help of temporary employees. The assignment may be to cover for someone who will be away on vacation, away sick for a short period of time, or a seasonal time when business is very busy. New employees have been increasingly offered temporary jobs. Of all women newly hired in 2004, 23 percent held temporary jobs, over twice the rate of 11 percent in 1989. Among their male counterparts, 20 percent held temporary jobs in 2004 compared with only 12 percent in 1989.[52] Temporary employees can be hired by calling a temporary agency or by using the same methods for hiring full-time employees. While temporary employees can resolve a problem in the short term, these employees could become demotivated when they realize how much more the full-time workers are earning compared to them, yet they are doing the same job. Some temporary employees are often hopeful that they will get a full-time job with the employer and will work

Some provinces in Canada require specialized workers to fill positions with significant pay opportunities.

Source: Ingvar Tjostheim/ShutterStock

diligently to prove themselves. After time though, if there is no chance for a full-time position, their interest may begin to wane, as will their effort. There is also a cost to using these types of employees because of continuous training.

At certain times, there may be a temporary opening for a position that can be filled by an individual internally. This offers a good opportunity to someone who may want to try something different. If the position is one that can be easily learned, then transfers of employees will occur until the most junior position is left open. These are usually easier to fill with a temporary person outside the organization.

External Recruitment Although recruitment will be discussed in detail in Chapter 5, it should be noted that when there are labour shortages, particularly for key positions, external recruitment may be required. This will be a continuous effort that will always be utilized. External recruitment could arise because someone has been promoted to a vacant position, thus leaving that employee's position to be filled, or it could be that someone has left the organization and an external recruitment effort is required. The Alberta civil service is currently experiencing skills shortages due to Alberta employers from the private sector luring talent with significant pay opportunities to address the labour shortages they are experiencing.[53]

Measuring HR Effectiveness Using HR Metrics

6 A longstanding myth perpetuates the notion that one cannot really measure what the HR function does. That myth has hurt HR departments in some cases, because it suggests that any value added by HR efforts is somehow "mystical." That notion is, of course, untrue; HR—like marketing, operations, or finance—must be evaluated by considering the results of its actions and the value it adds to the organization.

Other departments, managers, and employees are the main "customers" for HR services. If HR services are lacking, too expensive, or of poor quality, then HR loses some credibility in the organization. Unfortunately, the perceptions of managers and employees in many organizations is mixed because HR often has not measured and documented its contributions, or communicated those results to executives, managers, and employees.

During the past several years, the importance of measuring HR effectiveness has grown. A number of writers have stressed that HR cannot be a strategic business contributor without focusing on measuring its programs, its services, and its contributions to organizational success. It is through the development and use of metrics that HR can better demonstrate its value and track its performance.

Developing and Using HR Metrics

HR metrics
Specific measures tied to HR performance indicators.

HR metrics are specific measures tied to HR performance indicators. A metric can be developed using costs, quantity, quality, timeliness, and other designated goals. One pioneer in developing HR measurements, Jac Fitz-Enz, has identified a wide range of HR metrics.[54] Some examples are shown in Figure 2-12. Other statistics can be tracked when technology is used. Technology Transforming HR provides an example of one organization that tracks statistics of internal promotions.

Whether determining the cost of turnover, the average time needed to fill job openings, scores on employee satisfaction surveys, or the ratio of payroll expenditures to revenues, metrics provide specific data to track HR performance. Characteristics of good HR metrics include the following:

- Accurate data can be collected.
- Measures are linked to strategic and operational objectives.
- Calculations can be clearly understood.
- Measures provide information expected by executives.
- Results can be compared both externally and internally.
- Measurement data drives HR management efforts.

Metrics that meet all these characteristics give HR a better foundation for explaining and justifying its costs. Gathering and analyzing HR data and then using them for decision making is at the heart of measuring HR effectiveness. Data to evaluate performance can come from several sources. Some of those sources are already available in most organizations, but some data may have to be collected from existing HR records or HR research. For example, HR data can

Figure 2-12 *Examples of Strategic and Operational HR Metrics*

Strategic	Operational
• Revenue generated per FTE*	• Annual turnover rate
• Net income before taxes per FTE	• Benefits costs as percentage of payroll
• Ratio of managers to non-managers	• Training expenditures per FTE
• Labour costs as percentage of total operating costs	• Average time to fill openings
• ROI of human capital expenditures	• Workers' compensation costs per FTE
• HR department expenses as percentage of total expenses	• Number of applicants per opening
• Payroll/benefits costs as percentage of revenues	• Absenteeism by employee level/department

**FTE—Full-Time Equivalent*

Technology Transforming HR

Retention and Technology

Some companies are using Web-based solutions to help them identify internal talent for promotion. By taking an electronic look within the company, the firms not only save money, but also aid the prospects for retention of current employees because people see possible opportunities to move up.

Fireman's Fund Insurance is a California-based casualty and property insurer, with offices in Canada, which has implemented an electronic system for internal recruiting. By logging on to the company intranet, an employee can create a personal profile including career objectives, education, skills, and salary expectations. When a job opens up, the program automatically looks in the company database for matches. Then appropriate candidates are notified by e-mail, and they can choose to go through the regular hiring process.

Using a "click and drag" technology, employees can register a profile easily and quickly. Previously, the task took employees 15–30 minutes to complete. It was so cumbersome that only 2000 of its 7000 employees submitted information to be considered for transfers or promotions. Statistics show that, by using the Web-based system, in one year 38 percent of the positions at Fireman's Fund were filled internally, compared with 5 percent in the previous year.[55]

1. What kind of training should companies be offering to ensure that everyone is comfortable with using this type of technology?
2. Is so much internal hiring really a good thing and why or why is it not?

Saratoga Institute
This organization is well-known for its HR benchmarking data and studies.
www.saratogainstitute.com

identify units with high turnover or an unusual number of disciplinary problems. Or HR records on training can be compared with subsequent employee performance to determine if additional training expenditures are justified. Much of what has typically been measured by HR has focused on internal HR expenditures and effectiveness. A broader strategic perspective in measuring HR effectiveness is also needed.[56]

Fortunately in many organizations the growth in HR technology has made useful HR metric data much more available and its compilation much less time-consuming.

Measures of Strategic HR Effectiveness

For HR to fulfill its role as a strategic business partner, HR metrics that reflect organizational strategies and goods must be used. Some of the more prevalent measures compare *full-time equivalents* (FTEs) with organizational measures. An FTE is a measure equal to one person working full-time for a year. For instance, two employees each working half-time would count as one FTE.

Return on investment (ROI)
Calculation showing the value of expenditures for HR activities.

Return on Investment (ROI) A widely used financial measure that can be applied to measure the contribution and cost of HR activities is **return on investment (ROI),** which is a calculation showing the value of expenditures for HR activities. It can also be used to show how long it will take for the activities to pay for themselves. The following formula can be used to calculate the potential ROI for a new HR activity:

$$\text{ROI} = C / A + B$$

where:

A = Operating costs for a new or enhanced system for the time period
B = One-time cost of acquisition and implementation
C = Value of gains from productivity improvements for the time period

ROI is stressed because it is used in most other parts of organizations. It also is the "language" used by CFOs, CEOs, and boards of directors. To conduct ROI analyses, firms complete three stages:[57]

- Identify all potential/actual costs
- Determine the potential/actual benefits
- Calculate the ROI

Although it is recommended that ROI be calculated before programs are implemented, the reality is that such calculations often occur after the fact. This is counter to what would be typical in other parts of the organization, where the ROI of establishing a new plant or store would often be calculated before ever beginning the project. For instance, assume that a bank spent $100,000 on a customer service incentive program for employees to sell new services, and sales of the new services produced net revenues of $110,000. The ROI was $110,000/$100,000 or 10 percent, which was below the threshold ROI of 20 percent that the CFO used for other company expenditures. Although the incentive program was successful in adding revenues, looking at the ROI indicates that it could not be judged as successful using normal financial measures. Though data for this example could be easily tracked, trying to determine the ROI for overall employee benefits costs or for management development and training programs is much more difficult. Often, *utility analyses* or *cost/benefit analyses* are part of efforts to compute the ROI of HR efforts.

Economic value added (EVA)
Net operating profit of a firm after the cost of capital is deducted.

Economic Value Added (EVA) Another measure used is **economic value added (EVA),** which is the net operating profit of a firm after the cost of capital is deducted. Cost of capital is the minimum rate of return demanded by shareholders. When a company is making more than the cost of capital, it is creating wealth for shareholders. An EVA approach requires that all policies, procedures, measures, and methods use cost of capital as a benchmark against which their return is judged. Human resource decisions can be subjected to the same analyses.

HR and the Balanced Scorecard One effective approach to the measurement of the strategic performance of organizations, including their HR departments, is the *balanced scorecard.* Use of the balanced scorecard stresses measuring the strategic performance of organizations on four perspectives:[58]

- Financial
- Internal business processes
- Customer
- Learning and growth

Organizational measures in each of these areas are calculated to determine if the organization is progressing toward its strategic objectives. For example, some firms have noticed that when survey results show a decline in employee satisfaction, several months later there is a decline in customer loyalty and repeat customer sales. Or expenditures in employee leadership development training can be linked to lower employee turnover and reduced time to hire managers from outside the organization.

Using the balanced scorecard requires spending considerable time and effort to identify the appropriate HR measures in each of the four areas and how they tie to strategic organization success.[59] Both large companies, as diverse as AT&T Canada Long Distance, Ontario Hospital, and Carleton University, and smaller firms are using the balanced scorecard to ensure better alignment of HR measurement efforts and strategic goals.[60] However, regardless of the time and effort spent trying to develop and utilize objective measures in the balanced scorecard, subjectivity in what is selected and how the measures are interpreted can still occur.[61] In this book, HR metrics sections will be highlighted throughout the discussion of the various HR activities, using the special HR metrics icon that appears at the beginning of this section.

Measures of Operational HR Effectiveness

As indicated in Figure 2-12, there are a number of operational HR metrics that must also be utilized so that HR can determine that specific policies and procedures are working effectively and the organization is running effectively and efficiently. Two specific measures that an organization could track would be absenteeism and turnover. A major step in reducing the expense of absenteeism and turnover is to decide how the organization is going to record those events and what calculations are necessary to maintain and benchmark their rates. A number of considerations are required.

Measuring Absenteeism Controlling or reducing absenteeism must begin with continuous monitoring of the absenteeism statistics in work units. Such monitoring helps managers pinpoint employees who are frequently absent and departments that have excessive absenteeism. Various methods of measuring or computing absenteeism exist. For example, one formula is as follows:

$$\frac{\text{Number of person-days lost through job absence during period}}{(\text{Average number of employees}) \times (\text{Number of workdays})} \times 100$$

(This rate also can be based on number of hours instead of number of days.)

Wayne Cascio has prepared one source of extremely detailed information on absenteeism and turnover calculation. He suggests calculating the employee hours lost each month (or some other period) and the cost of those hours (including benefits), then calculating the cost of supervisory time lost to the management of absenteeism problems. The combination of the two costs is the cost of absenteeism for that period.[62] Sometimes it takes a six-or seven-figure cost number to get the attention of management to address absenteeism levels. Calculations of the costs of absenteeism should usually include these variables:

- Lost wages
- Benefits
- Overstaffing necessary to cover absences
- Fees for temporary employees, if incurred
- Supervisor's time
- Substandard production
- Overtime for replacements

Additional information can be gained by separating absenteeism data into long- and short-term categories. Different problems are caused by employees who are absent for one day ten times during a year, and employees who are absent one time for ten days. Other useful measures of absenteeism might include:

- *Incidence rate:* The number of absences per 100 employees each day
- *Inactivity rate:* The percentage of time lost to absenteeism
- *Severity rate:* The average time lost per absent employee during a specified period of time (a month or a year)

Measuring Turnover It has been estimated that the cost of replacing a lower-level employee is one-third of the new hire's annual salary. Using only $7 an hour for an example, that equals \$4,853 for each departing employee. Professional and managerial replacement rates are higher—perhaps as much as 2 or 2.5 times the new hire's annual salary.[63]

The turnover rate for an organization can be computed in different ways. The following formula is widely used; in it, *separations* mean departures from the organization.

$$\frac{\text{Number of employee separations during the month}}{\text{Total number of employees at midmonth}} \times 100$$

Common turnover rates range from almost 0 percent to more than 100 percent a year and vary among industries. Often a part of HR management systems, turnover data can be gathered and analyzed in a number of different ways, including the following categories:

- Job and job level
- Demographic characteristics
- Department, unit, and location
- Education and training
- Reason for leaving
- Knowledge, skills, and abilities
- Length of service
- Performance ratings/levels

Two examples illustrate why detailed analyses of turnover are important. One manufacturing organization had a company-wide turnover rate that was not severe, but 80 percent of the turnover occurred within one department. That imbalance indicated that some action was needed to resolve problems in that unit. A health-care institution found that its greatest turnover in registered nurses occurred 24–36 months after hire, so the firm instituted a two-year employee recognition program and expanded the career development and training activities for employees with at least two years' service. For these employers, the targeted turnover rates declined as a result of the actions taken in response to the turnover analyses that were done.

Determining Turnover Costs Determining turnover costs can be relatively simple or very complex, depending on the nature of the efforts and data used. Figure 2-13 shows a simplified costing model. In this model, if a job pays \$20,000 (A) and benefits

Figure 2-13 *Simplified Turnover Costing Model*

Job Title: ____________________

A. Typical annual pay for this job	______
B. Percentage of pay for benefits multiplied by annual pay	______
C. Total employee annual cost (add A + B)	______
D. Number of employees who voluntarily quit the job in the past 12 months	______
E. Number of months it takes for one employee to become fully productive	______
F. Per person turnover cost (multiply [E ÷ 12] × C × 50%*)	______
G. Annual turnover cost for this job (multiply F × D)	______

**Assumes 50-percent productivity throughout the learning period (E).*

cost 40 percent (B), then the total annual cost for one employee is $28,000. Assuming that 20 employees quit in the previous year (D) and that it takes three months for one employee to be fully productive, the calculation in (F) results in a per person turnover cost of $3,500. Overall, the annual turnover costs would be $70,000 for the 20 individuals who left. In spite of its conservative and simple nature, this model makes the point that turnover is costly. For instance, if the job is that of a teller in a large bank where more than 150 people leave in a year, the conservative model produces turnover costs of more than $500,000 a year. More detailed and sophisticated turnover costing models consider a number of factors. Some of the most common areas considered include the following:

- *Separation costs:* Includes HR staff and supervisor time and salaries to prevent separations, exit interview time, unemployment expenses, legal fees for separations challenged, accrued vacation, continued benefits, etc.
- *Replacement costs:* Includes recruiting and advertising expenses, search fees, HR interviewer and staff time and salaries, employee referral fees, relocation and moving costs, supervisor and managerial time and salaries, employment testing costs, reference checking fees, pre-employment medical expenses, etc.
- *Training costs:* Includes paid orientation time, training staff time and salaries, costs of training materials, supervisors' and managers' time and salaries, co-worker "coaching" time and salaries, etc.
- *Hidden costs:* Includes costs not obvious but that affect lost productivity, decreased customer service, other employee turnover, missed deadlines, etc.

Competent employees who are satisfied with their employers, who know what is expected, and who have minimal absenteeism and reduced turnover potential are assets to the organization. But just as individuals in an organization can be a competitive advantage, they can also be a liability. When few employees know how to do their jobs, when people are constantly leaving, and when the employees who do remain work ineffectively, human resources are a problem that puts the organization at a competitive disadvantage. Individual performance, motivation, and employee retention are key for organizations to maximize the effectiveness of individual human resources.

HR Measurement and Benchmarking

Benchmarking
Comparing specific measures of performance against data on those measures in other organizations.

One approach to assessing HR effectiveness is **benchmarking,** which compares specific measures of performance against data on those measures in other organizations. HR professionals interested in benchmarking compare their measurement data with those from outside sources, including individual companies, industry sources, and professional associations.

Some diagnostic measures can be used to check the effectiveness of the HR function. HR expenditures by workforce size vary significantly. As might be expected, the total number of staff needed to serve 1000 employees is not significantly different from the number needed to serve 2500 employees. But the cost per employee of having an HR department is greater in organizations with fewer than 250 employees.

Using benchmarking, HR effectiveness is best determined by comparing ratios and measures from year to year. But it is crucial that the benchmarking look at the strategic contributions HR makes to the organization, not just the operating efficiency measures.

A report completed in late 1999 demonstrates the value of e-HR, where employees are able to take care of their personal information, thus eliminating the need for someone in HR to perform this administrative and costly duty. Figure 2-14 shows how much money was saved.

Figure 2-14 *Performance Benchmarking*

Task	Manual Cost	Self Service Cost	% Saved
View benefit profile	$6.00	$0.50	92%
Access policy handbook	$4.00	$1.00	75%
Change home address	$10.00	$2.00	80%
View paycheque	$3.00	$0.50	83%
Job posting	$8.00	$0.50	94%
View skill profile	$1.50	$0.50	67%
Employee change action	$12.00	$4.00	67%

Source: 1998–1999 Human Resources Self-Service Survey, The Hunter Group, Baltimore, 1999. Used by permission of CedarCrestone, Inc.

HR Audit

HR audit
Formal research effort that evaluates the current state of HR management in an organization.

One general means for assessing HR is through an **HR audit,** which is similar to a financial audit. An HR audit is a formal research effort that evaluates the current state of HR management in an organization. This audit attempts to evaluate how well HR activities in each of the HR areas (staffing, compensation, health and safety, etc.) have been performed, so that management can identify areas for improvement. An HR audit often helps smaller organizations without a formal HR professional identify issues associated with legal compliance, administrative processes and recordkeeping, employee retention, etc.

Regardless of the time and effort placed on HR measurement and HR metrics, the most important consideration is that HR effectiveness and efficiency must be measured regularly for HR staff and other managers to know how HR is contributing to organizational success.

SUMMARY

1 Organizations doing business internationally may evolve from organizations engaged in importing and exporting to multinational enterprises, to global organizations. Porter's strategy model of cost leadership, differentiation, and focus and Miles and Snow's typologies can explain the competitive advantages that exist when organizational strategy and HR strategy are appropriately aligned.

2 HR planning involves analyzing and identifying the need for and availability of human resources so that the organization can meet its objectives. The HR unit has major responsibilities in HR planning, but managers must provide supportive information and input.

Assessing internal strengths and weaknesses as a part of HR planning requires auditing and inventorying current jobs and employee capabilities. When developing HR plans, it is important for managers to scan the external environment to identify the effects of government influences, economic conditions, geographic and competitive concerns, and workforce composition changes.

3 The supply and demand for human resources can be forecast with a variety of methods and for differing periods of time. Both quantitative and qualitative methods of forecasting are necessary. Quantitative methods include such tools as ratio analysis, regression analysis and simulation models. Qualitative methods include management forecast, the Delphi technique and nominal group technique. A combination of the two methods is most appropriate. When examining internal supply, useful methods include a review of organizational charts, staffing tables, Markov analysis, replacement charts, and succession planning.

4 With the impending shortage of skilled workers, and the demand for qualified employees, retention has become a strategic business issue. Organizations

must have a clearer understanding of why people stay or leave organizations and an understanding of the drivers of retention such as characteristics of an employer, job design and work, career opportunities, rewards, and employee relationships. Employers need to continually monitor their turnover and absenteeism rates to determine the type of problems that may exist in their organizations. To gauge how employees feel about their organizations, employee surveys, such as attitude or engagement, should be conducted. Exit interviews must be conducted on all employees who leave the organization.

5 Once all data are collected and forecasts complete, an organizational plan can be developed. Management must decide what to do about HR surpluses and labour shortages. Management of HR surpluses may require downsizing through use of attrition and hiring freezes, early retirement buyouts, layoffs, terminations, reduction of hours, and outplacement assistance. Management of labour shortages can be dealt with overtime, the use of temporary employees, and effective external recruitment. HR plays a crucial role in mergers and acquisitions, particularly in dealing with organizational culture issues.

6 HR effectiveness must be measured using HR metrics that consider both strategic and operational effectiveness. The ROI of human capital and the balanced scorecard are two common means for strategic HR measurement. Operational HR metrics would always include absenteeism and turnover measures. Benchmarking allows an organization to compare its practices against "best practices" in different organizations, and HR audits can be used to get a comprehensive overview on HR activities.

KEY TERMS

Attitude survey, p. 61
Benchmarking, p. 74
Cost-leadership strategy, p. 40
Differentiation strategy, p. 40
Economic value added (EVA), p. 71
Engagement survey, p. 61
Environmental scanning, p. 44
Exit interview, p. 61
Focused strategy, p. 40
Forecasting, p. 47
HR audit, p. 75
HR metrics, p. 69
HR strategies, p. 43
Human resource management system (HRMS), p. 43
Human resource planning (HRP), p. 41
Organizational culture, p. 55
Organizational strategy, p. 39
Return on investment (ROI), p. 70
Strategic HR management (SHRM), p. 38
Succession planning, p. 51

REVIEW AND APPLICATION QUESTIONS

1 What is the difference between an organization following a cost-leadership strategy and a differentiation strategy? What are the implications for human resources?

2 What is the HR planning process and the role of HR strategies in the overall process?

3 Describe the various methods for forecasting supply and demand of employees.

4 Describe three drivers of retention that are personally important to you, and explain why they are important to you.

5 Unfortunately organizations are forced to downsize their operations from time to time. What options are available to an organization when a downsizing decision has to be made? Is downsizing always a negative event? Can it be positive, and if so why?

6 What steps can HR professionals take to overcome the view that what HR accomplishes is not measurable?

EXPERIENTIAL EXERCISES

1. Working in groups of five identify three organizations and determine whether they fall under a defender or a prospector strategy as stated by Miles and Snow's typology. What specific HR strategies would be most appropriate for these organizations given their defender or prospector strategy with respect to staffing, performance appraisal, training, and compensation? Do not select the same organizations that were discussed in this section of the text.
2. The CEO has approached you and indicated that a major competitor has just announced a new and innovative product that will have a direct impact on your sales. As such, she has indicated that you will need to begin downsizing 20 percent of your organization, which currently sits at 700. She anticipates that the downsizing will need to begin in the next month and take place over the next three months. How should you go about planning for this downsizing? How will you deal with the surplus of employees?
3. As a newly hired HR manager for a medical clinic with 20 physicians and 100 employees, you want to identify and develop some HR metrics. Using the metrics discussed at www.saratogainstitute.com and other Web sources that you find, identify five specific metrics and discuss why those measures could be useful.
4. You are to determine some organizations that would ideally be comparable to your organization for the purposes of benchmarking. Your CEO has asked you to consider the names of some organizations that you know do not compare to yours, and would undoubtedly, when compared, make your organization look like they are doing things quite well, when in fact you know this would not be true, and would be misleading to both shareholders and employees. What should you do in light of your CEO's request to embellish on the accomplishments of your organization's success? What are some of the factors that need to be considered when selecting benchmark companies to ensure a fair comparison?

LEARNING REVIEW

To check your knowledge of the chapter, review the following. (Answers after the case.)

1 The differentiation strategy is more appropriate in:
   a. stable environments
   b. dynamic environments
   c. stagnant environments
   d. global environments

2 The HR planning process begins with:
   a. considering the objectives and strategies of the organization
   b. auditing the jobs currently being done in the organization
   c. analyzing the internal inventory of HR capabilities
   d. developing HR forecasts

3 Once all data is collected and forecasts completed, a(n) ________ can be developed:
   a. strategic plan
   b, data collection
   c. skill analysis
   d. organizational plan

4 Drivers of retention include all the following except:
   a. Job design and work
   b. Characteristics of the employer
   c. Career opportunities
   d. Union affiliation

5 One strategy used to downsize employees that is considered to be more humane than many others is:
   a. volunteer separation programs
   b. attrition
   c. temporary layoffs
   d. terminations

6 One approach to assessing HR effectiveness is __________, which is comparing specific measures of performance against data on those measures in other organizations.
   a. benchmarking
   b. compa-valuation
   c. HR appraisal
   d. HR imitation

CASE

RETENTION OF EMPLOYEES AT BAYTECH PLASTICS

Baytech Plastics designs and delivers high quality custom-moulded plastic components and assemblies to North American and overseas customers. Since 1953, it has experienced considerable success and has responded well to changing market conditions. Employing 260 people, Baytech manufactures from two facilities in Midland, Ontario. Baytech employs a high ratio of engineering support staff relative to its competition. In fact, Baytech's emphasis on skills means employee retention and knowledge transfer are key elements in their business strategy of pursuing higher value-added niche markets.

Retaining employees and managing skills is critical to Baytech's developing business model. Baytech pays close attention to the kinds of skills it needs within its organization, and the kind of business and human resource practices that help it to effectively manage skill requirements, including practices aimed at employee retention and knowledge transfer.

Turnover runs at a rate of around 1.2 to 1.3 percent, and is not a problem for the company. Management attributes this turnover performance to a number of factors, including the nature of their work environment, their location within a smaller community, and their corporate philosophy of treating employees well. The company has no need of a formally defined retention policy or program, but has in place a number of practices that keep employee retention high.

According to a long-term employee of Baytech, she accords the success of the organization with practices that include competitive wages and benefits including a *pension plan, open communications, healthy union-management relations*, characterized by open communications, trust, and employee involvement through committees, *feedback from the company on performance*, *good work environment and safe workplace, job satisfaction,* and *training opportunities*.

Baytech's commitment to communications is at the centre of its approach to employee retention. For Anton Mudde, CEO of Baytech, there are three words that sum up that approach: *"fairness, communication, and recognition."* Baytech may not have a formalized employee retention strategy, but its human resource practices are always guided by these principles.[64]

Questions

1. Baytech states that it does not have a formalized employee retention strategy, but that its human resources are guided by the principles of fairness, communication, and recognition. Is a written policy required? Why or why not?
2. Compare the list of retention drivers that aids Baytech in maintaining low turnover, with the drivers of retention discussed in the chapter? Are any elements missing from Baytech's strategy? If so, what should be included or changed if anything?

Learning Review Answers: 1. b 2. a 3. d 4. d 5. a 6. a

KEEPING THEM

A low unemployment rate in Canada will lead to an increase in voluntary staff turnover for many Canadian firms. A large turnover can be detrimental to a firm because it increases training and recruitment costs and results in a loss of productivity. The video clip from *Venture* examines ways in which a handful of Canadian firms have attempted to prevent turnover and simultaneously create employee loyalty.

An important question that has been raised by firms such as LGS and Labatt's is: "What do employees want?" The most obvious answer is that employees want greater financial security. However, through workplace polls it has been discovered that although money is important, employees also greatly value non-monetary benefits such as career development, flexibility, child daycare and "casual dress." The ultimate goal for firms looking to inspire employee loyalty should be to create a work environment that is, "too good to leave."

As the unemployment rate decreases, the power of employees increases, which will give them a greater opportunity to move to another company. A high turnover can impede a company's growth as it did at LGS, which managed to resolve its problem by focusing on career development for its employees. To create a positive work environment, employers should always keep communication open with their employees in order to find out what will keep them satisfied at work.[1]

Questions

1. What do you believe makes a work environment, "too good to leave?"
2. Would you take a pay cut to have a more casual work environment?

PART 2

Staffing the Organization

CHAPTER 3

Legal Environment of Equal Employment and Diversity

Learning Objectives

After you have read this chapter, you should be able to:

1 Introduce Canada's legal environment and discuss the Canadian Charter of Rights and Freedoms.

2 Identify the Canadian Human Rights Acts in various jurisdictions and direct and indirect discrimination on prohibited grounds.

3 Explain the meaning of several prohibited grounds with examples of court challenges.

4 Describe the two types of sexual harassment and how employers should respond to sexual harassment complaints.

5 Discuss the employment standards acts, labour relations legislation, and occupational health and safety, and the requirements of each jurisdiction.

6 Outline the issues surrounding employment equity and pay equity.

7 Define diversity management and discuss why it is important.

HR *Headline*

A Tribute to a "French Métis Woman" who "Decimated" the Glass Ceiling

Glass ceiling, Aboriginal, equal employment opportunities, disabilities, accommodation, designated group members, disability, person of colour, discrimination, sexual harassment, diversity, francophone . . . everyday we are exposed to these phrases. For some of us they attach deep personal meaning; for others they are a nuisance; and yet for many a reminder that so many Canadians have a more difficult time attaining fair and equal employment opportunities in a so-called diverse and multicultural country that allows each of us to express our own culture and identity. Many are never able to overcome the stigma attached to their particular label, but others are able to rise above all controversy and challenge every barrier they are faced with. One such success story is that of Dr. Suzanne Rochon Burnett.

The story of Dr. Suzanne Rochon Burnett is an inspiring one. Born in Northern Quebec, she was a French-speaking Métis woman. In the Métis Nation of Ontario's (MNO) announcement of Rochon Burnett's death on April 2, 2006, MNO president Tony Belcourt accurately summarized Rochon Burnett's impact in the business world and her cultural community: "Suzanne was a grand lady who brought enormous pride to her people. Her life of accomplishments is a textbook perfect story of the best of role models for everyone to honour. She met every challenge head on, persevered and was successful in everything she touched—in business, in the arts, in communications, public service, and in life."

Rochon Burnett's successful business career had its origins in her, "very strong matriarchal lineage." Her grandmother was widowed in her 40s and was left to raise a family of 12 children on her own. In order to supplement her farm income, Rochon Burnett's grandmother handmade and sold ladies' hats. As a child, Rochon Burton worked as a courier for her mother's sweater business in Northern Quebec. Rochon Burnett's volunteer work in the Aboriginal community was fuelled by her years as a young student in a residential convent school: "I had no idea I was different until I went there. Before I left home my parents said to me 'Suzy—don't tell them about your Indian blood. It doesn't show.' They said that to protect me. I know that. But it left me wondering what was wrong with it." The nuns at the school did give Rochon Burnett an education that left her with flawless French articulation that helped her for a future career in communications. After attending business college, Rochon Burnett had three job options available to her in her home town: the bank, the telephone company, and the mill. She first applied for a secretarial position in a local mill but was not hired because the owner believed that she was a "jewel" who had great potential. The owner helped her land a job in a new radio station that opened up in St. Jerome, Quebec. By the time she was 20, Rochon Burnett had a newspaper column, two radio shows, and did public relations for the station. Up until 1967 (the year she got married) Rochon Burnett was a recognizable Quebec media personality working in both radio and television.

After settling in St. Catharines with her husband in 1967, Rochon Burnett decided to take some time off to raise her daughter. "I had just dropped my daughter off at school and I started to cry. 'Oh my God' I thought, 'I'm 40 years old. I'm going to be 60 one day and I'm going to turn around and say 'What have I done with my life?' That really scared the heck out of me." Rochon Burnett wasted no time and became the host of a French music radio show that was funded

Suzanne Rochon Burnett became the first Aboriginal woman to be inducted to the Canadian Aboriginal Business Hall of Fame.

Source: Photo courtesy Canada Council for the Arts/Photo Features

by the Ministry of Culture and broadcast throughout Ontario. In the 1980s, she began to work on several international, national, and provincial boards including the Canadian Native Foundation for the Arts, TVO, MNO, Brock University, and the Canada Council for the Arts. In 1995, her husband's radio station had failed and she was called to revitalize the station and ultimately make it profitable. She brought the station back to solvency and was granted a rare FM licence from the CRTC. Spirit 91.7 was marketed as a country radio station with an Aboriginal soul. The station was successful in both southern Ontario and in North-Western New York. It was during this time that she was diagnosed with an incurable respiratory disease that she decided to sell the business.

In February 2006, Suzanne Rochon Burnett became the first Aboriginal woman to be inducted to the Canadian Aboriginal Business Hall of Fame. Rochon Burnett has been named to both the Order of Ontario and the Order of Canada. She has also received a Governor General's Medal, a Women of Distinction Award (for arts and culture), a Royal Bank Initiative of the Year Award, an Eagle Feather from the Aboriginal Community, an Honourary Doctorate from Brock University, and a Lifetime Achievement award by the National Aboriginal Achievement Foundation.

Rochon Burnett exemplifies the true spirit of diversity. She has worked hard at every juncture. Barriers were not barriers—they were challenges to be embraced. To have known her would have been a privilege and an honour. To know of her is inspiring nonetheless.[1]

"Don't be afraid to move forward despite challenges. Look at them as opportunities to grow and learn. You must move forward. After all, even if you fall flat on your face, you're still moving forward!"

—Suzanne Rochon Burnett

Canadians today reflect a vast diversity of cultural heritages and racial groups. This multicultural diversity is a result of centuries of immigration. Multiculturalism has been described as preserving a "cultural mosaic" of separate ethnic groups, and is contrasted to a "melting pot" that mixes them. The concept of diversity recognizes that there are differences among people and that those differences provide both opportunities and challenges for employers.

As the opening HR Headline points out, various groups in society have been disadvantaged in employment and barriers have made it difficult for some individuals to attain their goals because of prejudices they may face in employment. For others, such as Suzanne Rochon Burnett, barriers have been overcome with determination. Yet so many others in our society have a difficult time breaking past the barriers. As such, a legal framework is needed to guide how people of different backgrounds should be treated in employment so that opportunities are presented, and challenges overcome.

Canada's Legal Framework

1 Canada has a complex set of legislation governing how individuals are to be treated in the workplace and in society. What is distinct in Canada is that two sets of laws govern the equal employment opportunity of workers in either the federal or the provincial and territorial sectors of the country.

The Canada Labour Code and the Canadian Human Rights Act governs the federal sector that applies to about 10 percent of the Canadian workforce. The federally regulated sector of the labour force includes interprovincial and international services such as railways, telephone, telegraph and cables services, highway transport, pipelines, ferries, tunnels and bridges, and many others. Also included are radio and television broadcasting, air transport, banks, and Crown corporations. Other pieces of legislation important to the federal sector include employment equity and pay equity. The Canada Labour Code also includes provisions for health and safety and labour relations.

The remaining 90 percent of the workforce are covered under provincial and territorial labour legislation. For example, employment standards legislation and human rights acts for each of the provinces and territories mandates minimal standards of treatment for employees. Various provinces have also established employment equity, pay equity, health and safety, and labour relations legislation. While there are similarities between the federal and provincial and territorial jurisdictions, there are subtle differences that HR professionals and managers should be familiar with in order to effectively manage the issues that can arise. A problem that occurs in Nova Scotia may be dealt with differently in Manitoba. The various pieces of legislation will be briefly discussed next. Throughout the textbook, each chapter will address, in more detail, the respective pieces of legislation as it pertains to the particular subject matter.

Canadian Charter of Rights and Freedoms
Federal law enacted in 1982, guaranteeing fundamental rights and freedoms to all Canadians.

The Canadian Charter of Rights and Freedoms

The **Canadian Charter of Rights and Freedoms** is one part of the Canadian Constitution, established on April 17, 1982. The Constitution is a set of laws containing the basic rules about how our country operates. For example, it contains the powers of the federal and provincial governments in Canada. The Constitution is

The Constitution Act 1982
This website contains the Constitution Act 1982, as well as the Charter of Rights and Freedoms.
http://laws.justice.gc.ca/en/const/annex_e.html

the supreme law of Canada and it can override any laws that are inconsistent with its provisions. Any challenges to the charter or constitution are handled by the courts.

The basic premise of the Charter is that it "*guarantees the rights and freedoms*" of individuals. These rights are guaranteed but can also be limited by Section 1 of the Charter, and can be temporarily invalidated by the notwithstanding clause of the Charter. Everyone has the following fundamental freedoms:[2]

(a) freedom of conscience and religion;
(b) freedom of thought, belief, opinion and expression, including freedom of the press and other media of communication;
(c) freedom of peaceful assembly; and
(d) freedom of association.

Other rights under the Charter include mobility rights (e.g., the right to live anywhere in Canada), legal rights (e.g., the right to life, liberty, and security of the person) and equality rights, and recognizes the multicultural heritage of Canadians. It also protects official language and minority language education rights. In addition, the provisions of Section 25 guarantee the rights of Aboriginal peoples of Canada.

The Charter has had a major impact on the promotion and protection of human rights in Canada. With regard to equality rights, it has led to the recognition and enforcement of the rights of a number of minority and disadvantaged groups.

Under Section 1 of the Charter, there may be limitations on the rights and freedoms so long as those laws are reasonable and justified in a free and democratic society. So, a law that limits a Charter right is nevertheless valid if it conforms to Section 1. For example, employment equity, which will be discussed, allows for different treatment of designated group members in order to right the wrongs of the past.

It is also possible for governments to pass laws that take away some rights under the Charter. Under Section 33 of the Charter (sometimes called the "notwithstanding clause"), Parliament or a legislature can make a particular law exempt from certain sections of the Charter: the fundamental freedoms (in Section 2), the legal rights (in Sections 7 to 14), and the equality rights (in Section 15). However, a law that limits Charter rights under the notwithstanding clause expires after five years. This clause is used very rarely. One of its few uses occurred when the Quebec government passed a law requiring signs to be in French only.

The most controversial right for unions has been the freedom of association. Freedom of association includes the right to join a trade union. In the late 1980s, the Supreme Court of Canada ruled that collective bargaining was not Charter protected. Unions continue to fight this ruling stating that, "collective bargaining goes to the core of the purpose of Section 2(d) of the Charter by importing principles of democracy into the workplace."[3]

A more controversial issue has recently arisen in British Columbia with Bill 29, the Health and Social Services Delivery Improvement Act. Bill 29 removes significant impediments to and restrictions on reorganization that have been negotiated into collective agreements. It also aims to prevent the Labour Relations Board (LRB) or an arbitrator from making decisions that could frustrate the provisions of the Health and Social Services bill. Unions feel freedom of association will be breached in two ways: it voids existing collective agreement provisions agreed to by both the unions and employers that are currently in force, and it prohibits indefinitely the renegotiation of those provisions. The B.C. Supreme Court ruled that Bill 29 was not in violation of any charter rights, thus impacting existing collective bargaining agreements. An appeal was filed with the Supreme Court of Canada, which at the time of writing this book, had not yet been finalized.[4]

Human Rights

Canadian Human Rights Act
This website contains information regarding the Canadian Human Rights Acts and related regulations.
http://laws.justice.gc.ca/en/H-6/Index.html

Provincial and territorial human rights legislation
All provinces and territories have their own human rights laws and commissions prohibiting discrimination in employment.

Canadian Human Rights Act
A federal law prohibiting discrimination in employment under various prohibited grounds.

Direct discrimination
An adverse distinction based on a prohibited ground.

2 There are many other laws that protect human rights in Canada. The federal and provincial and territorial governments have adopted legislation (human rights acts or codes) prohibiting discrimination on various grounds in relation to employment, the provision of goods, services and facilities customarily available to the public, and accommodation. This legislation differs in its application from the Charter's Section 15 on equality rights in that it provides protection against discrimination by individuals in the private sector, as well as by governments.

Canada's federal, **provincial and territorial human rights legislation** prohibits discriminatory acts and practices on the grounds of race, colour, religion, national or ethnic origin, age, sex, sexual orientation, marital status, family status, disability, or conviction for an offence for which a pardon has not been granted. Federally regulated employees are covered under the **Canadian Human Rights Act,** while provincial and territorial human rights laws cover the remainder of employees under the respective human rights acts. Federally regulated employers, made up of 10 percent of the Canadian workforce, are defined as railways, airlines, banks, grain elevators, shipping, telephone, broadcasting, and trucking companies, where their operations have an interprovincial/international component. While there are many similarities between the jurisdictions, the terminology used can be slightly different. A list of the prohibited grounds is found in Figure 3-1.

What is Discrimination

According to the New Brunswick Human Rights Commission, discrimination is defined as:

> Discrimination is any practice or standard that, intentionally or not, has the effect of limiting the opportunities available to certain individuals or groups because of shared personal characteristics such as race or colour, in a way that perpetuates the view that they are less capable, or are less worthy of recognition or value.[5]

Essentially, discrimination means treating people differently, negatively or adversely without a good reason. As used in human rights laws, discrimination means making a distinction between certain individuals or groups based on a prohibited ground. Canadian courts have recognized two types of illegal discrimination: (1) direct discrimination and (2) adverse effect discrimination (also called indirect discrimination, constructive or systemic discrimination).

Direct Discrimination **Direct discrimination** occurs when people are treated differently (usually less favourably), that is, there is an adverse distinction based on a prohibited ground. For example, an organization will only hire men for a job they consider to be "man's work." This is discriminatory to women because it specifically denies them an employment opportunity.

Figure 3-1 *Prohibited Grounds of Discrimination in Employment*

Jurisdiction	Fed	Alta	BC	Man	NB	Nfld	NS	Ont	PEI	Que	Sask	NWT	Yukon
Race or colour	*	*	*	*	*	*	*	*	*	*	*	*	*
Religion[a]	*	*	*	*	*	*	*	*	*	*	*	*	*
Physical or mental disability[b]	*	*	*	*	*	*	*	*	*	*	*	*	*
Dependence on alcohol or drugs[c]	*	*	*	*	*	*	*	*	*	*	*		
Age[d]	*	*	*	*	*	*	*	*	*	*	*	*	*
Sex (includes pregnancy and childbirth)[e]	*	*	*	*	*	*	*	*	*	*	*	*	*
Marital status[f]	*	*	*	*	*	*	*	*	*	*	*	*	*
Family status[g]	*	*	*	*			*	*	*	*	*	*	*
Sexual orientation	*	*	*	*	*	*	*	*	*	*	*	*	*
National or ethnic origin (including linguistic background)[h]	*			*	*	*	*	*	*	*	*	*	*
Ancestry or place of origin		*	*	*	*			*			*	*	*
Language								*		*			*
Social condition or origin					*	*				*		*	
Source of income		*		*			*		*	*	*		
Assignment, attachment, or seizure of pay					*	*	*					*	
Association[i]				*	*		*	*	*			*	*
Political belief			*	*	*	*	*		*	*			*
Record of criminal conviction										*			*
Pardon conviction	*											*	*

[a]Yukon's Act reads "religion or creed, or religious belief, religious association or religious activity"

[b]Quebec uses the phrase "handicap or use of any means to palliate a handicap" in physical or mental disability

[c]Included in "handicap" ground in Quebec; Previous dependence only in New Brunswick

[d]British Columbia includes breast feeding; Alberta uses the term "gender"; Manitoba includes gender-determined characteristics; Ontario recognizes the protection of transgendered persons and accepts complaints related to "gender identity"; Ontario accepts complaints related to female genital mutilation; In Quebec, pregnancy as such is considered a ground of discrimination

[e]Quebec uses the term "civil status"

[f]Saskatchewan defines as being in a parent-child relationship; Quebec uses the term "civil status"

[g]Saskatchewan and Northwest Territories use the term "nationality"; Ontario's Code includes both "ethnic origin" and "citizenship"

[h]Northwest Territories has prohibition on basis of "political association"

Source: "Prohibited Grounds of Discrimination in Canada," www.chrc-ccdp.ca/publications/prohibitedgrounds-en.asp. Canadian Human Rights Commission. Reproduced with the permission of the Ministry of Public Works and Government Services, 2006.

Bona fide occupational requirement (BFOR)
A justifiable reason for discriminating against a member of a designated group.

There are situations where employers are allowed to discriminate for justifiable business reasons. This legal discrimination is known as a **bona fide occupational requirement (BFOR),** or bona fide occupational qualification (BFOQ). For example, age is often a BFOR when screening actors for a particular role. Multilingualism is a BFOR if an organization such as a legal aid clinic serving an ethnically diverse population wants to know what languages a candidate speaks.

To be considered a BFOR, a job requirement that is being challenged must pass the three-part test set out by the Supreme Court of Canada in *British Columbia (Public Service Employees Relations Commission) v. BCGSEU* (the *Meiorin* case). *Meiorin* involved a female firefighter who, after three successful years on the job, was terminated when she failed to meet one aspect of a new physical fitness test imposed by the employer. In this particular case she was not able to pass the aerobic part of the test. BCGSEU challenged that female's aerobic capacity is less than a man's and therefore, there has to be some accommodation made for the differences in female and male aerobic capacity. The test requires employers to consider accommodation before an employment rule is adopted and allows exemptions only when reasonably necessary. Referred to as the "Meiorin Test," it provides a simpler approach in determining whether an employment rule is justified:[6]

1. First, the employer must show that it adopted the standard for a purpose *rationally* connected to the performance of the job. The focus at the first step is not on the validity of the particular standard, but rather on the validity of its more general purpose.
2. Second, the employer must establish that it adopted the particular standard in an honest and good faith belief that it was necessary to the fulfillment of that legitimate work-related purpose.
3. Third, the employer must establish that the standard is reasonably necessary to the accomplishment of that legitimate work-related purpose. To show that the standard is reasonably necessary, it must be demonstrated that it is impossible to accommodate individual employees sharing the characteristics of the claimant without imposing **undue hardship** on the employer.

Undue hardship
Undue hardship pertains to the significant difficulty or expense imposed on an employer in making an accommodation for individuals with disabilities.

Systemic (or constructive) discrimination
Systemic (or constructive) discrimination occurs when a seemingly neutral policy or practice results in unintentional discrimination.

Indirect or Adverse Effect Discrimination Also referred to as **systemic (or constructive) discrimination,** a seemingly neutral policy or practice results in unintentional discrimination. Policies are applied equally to all people without distinction on a prohibited ground, but which nonetheless have an adverse effect based on a prohibited ground. For example, a supervisor insists on holding his team meeting to review the week's performance between 11:30 a.m. and 12:30 p.m. on a Friday. The meeting regularly lasts beyond 12:30 p.m. Such a practice could disadvantage Muslim employees who attach particular importance to Friday mid-day prayers. It could, therefore, be discriminatory if it cannot be justified. To avoid a complaint on a prohibited grounds, an employer would be required to prove two things:

- that there was a rational connection between the job and the standard or policy; and
- that it was not possible to accommodate the specific complainant without incurring undue hardship.

If the employer was unable to prove the rational connection element, the standard or policy would fall. If, however, the employer succeeded in establishing the rational connection element, the standard would remain intact and the focus would shift to individual accommodation.

There are numerous examples of employment criteria that have an adverse impact on designated group members and which have been challenged in the courts. Some of these are as follows:

- Implementing minimum height and weight standards would exclude women, persons of Asian descent, or persons belonging to indigenous population groups from Latin America who are, on average, of smaller physical stature than the majority population group in Canada.[7]
- Word-of-mouth hiring that excludes many designated group members from hearing about employment opportunities.
- When cognitive ability tests are used in selection decisions as part of a top-down hiring process, majority/minority group differences in test scores invariably lead to lower job selection rates for minority groups because they score lower on average than majority group members.[8]
- Workplace policies that use seniority-based systems for promotions and layoffs tend to affect designated group members who have less seniority and would therefore be disproportionately affected by layoffs.[9]
- Selection processes that do not focus on particular accommodation needs.

Duty to accommodate
An employer's legal duty to take reasonable steps, in policies or conditions of work, to accommodate an employee's individual needs.

Duty to Accommodate The Supreme Court of Canada has ruled that an employer has a legal duty to take reasonable steps, in policies or conditions of work, to accommodate an employee's individual needs. This duty applies to all prohibited grounds of discrimination. For example, a person may be unable to work on a particular day because it conflicts with his or her religious beliefs. In such cases, the employer must try to resolve the conflict in a way that is agreeable to both parties. However, this legal duty does not apply if the only way to resolve the problem will cause the employer undue hardship. Other human rights codes in Canada also have similar stipulations.

The Supreme Court of Canada has ruled that the employer's hardship must be "substantial in nature." For instance, a physically disabled employee, as part of his or her job duties, may be required to carry boxes up a flight of stairs. If the business has no elevator, it may be deemed an undue hardship to expect the employer to install an elevator to accommodate the employee. However, it may be possible to have another employee do that task. In exchange, the disabled person could assume one or more of that employee's regular tasks.

Figure 3-2 contains a list of the prohibited grounds that were challenged at the Canadian Human Rights Commission by federally regulated employees for the years 2002 to 2005. The most challenged prohibited rights pertain to disability and sex and the least are marital status and pardoned conviction. Further analysis of information obtained from the Canadian Human Rights Commission affirms Ontario has the highest number of claims, and PEI rarely files any claims. One of the concerns with filing human rights claims has been the length of time for cases to be resolved.[10] Only a few years ago it could take up to 25 months to resolve a claim. That number has now been reduced to about ten months. A review of Ontario's complaints, the most active of all provinces, shows that racism and harassment are amongst the highest claims processed. The next section discusses and provides examples of court rulings on many of the prohibited grounds.

Figure 3-2 ***Grounds of Discrimination Cited in Complaints****

	2002		2003		2004		2005	
	#	%	#	%	#	%	#	%
Disability	438	44	495	37	389	39	429	50
Sex	188	19	204	16	165	17	102**	12
National or ethnic origin	94	9	141	11	109	11	73	8
Race	71	7	146	11	105	11	74	8
Family status	30	3	38	3	61	6	45	5
Age	65	7	159	12	60	6	51	6
Religion	30	3	35	3	34	3	40	5
Colour	30	3	59	4	26	3	14	2
Sexual orientation	31	3	27	2	21	2	23	3
Marital status	14	2	15	1	14	2	13	1
Pardon	3	—	1	—	5	—	2	—
Total	994	100	1320	100	989	100	66	100

*** Total number of grounds cited exceeds the total number of complaints signed because some complaints dealt with more than one ground.**

**** The Commission accepted a group of 594 related complaints that are counted as one.**

Source: "Grounds of Discrimination Cited in Complaints," www.chrc-ccdp.ca/publications/ar_2005_ra/page8.asp. Canadian Human Rights Commission. Reproduced with the permission of the Ministry of Public Works and Government Services, 2006.

Prohibited Grounds

3 Race or Colour

Public opinion research suggests that racism remains a serious problem. Racial discrimination means any distinction, exclusion, restriction, or preference based on race, colour, descent, or national or ethnic origin that has the purpose or effect of nullifying or impairing the recognition, enjoyment or exercise, on an equal footing, of human rights and fundamental freedoms in the political, economic, social, cultural, or any other field of public life.[11]

The findings in a 2003 Ipsos-Reid survey confirmed that 74 percent of respondents expressed the view that there is still considerable racism in Canada. Other research, including the Ethnic Diversity Survey and Statistics Canada census data, identifies a number of concerns:[12]

- 36 percent of visible minorities feel they have experienced discrimination and unfair treatment because of ethno-cultural characteristics.
- nearly 50 percent of Blacks reported discrimination or unfair treatment. By contrast, 33 percent of South Asian and Chinese respondents reported discrimination or unfair treatment.
- when broken down by gender, there is a slight increase in reports of discrimination by Black men (53 percent compared to 47 percent for women). There is a similar increase reported by South Asian men (38 percent compared to 27 percent for women).
- according to a 2003 Ekos survey, 46 percent of Aboriginal people living off-reserve reported being a victim of racism or discrimination at least once over the previous two years.
- research by Ipsos-Reid (2002) suggested that more than six-out-of-ten Canadians (61 percent) think that racism separates Aboriginal peoples from the rest of society.

- roughly the same proportion (59 percent) felt that Aboriginal peoples are discriminated against by other Canadians.

After working for the same company for many years, a Métis man was transferred to a new location. He claimed that his new co-workers made offensive comments about "Natives," which continued until he was again transferred. At the next site, he alleged that he was called a racist name every time he went into the social room. He also became the target of crude jokes and remarks about Natives. A resolution was reached through conciliation, including a financial settlement, changes to company policy, and an apology.[13]

Religion and Creed

The Canadian Human Rights Act prohibits discrimination on the basis of "religion." The Ontario Human Rights Code, on the other hand, prohibits discrimination on the basis of "creed." For the purposes of Canadian human rights legislation, these two terms are virtually synonymous.

In many cases involving discrimination on the basis of religion or creed, the discrimination in question is usually indirect discrimination. For example, an employer may require its salesclerks to work on Saturdays but does not realize that one or more of those clerks belong to a religion that recognizes Saturday as the Sabbath. If the individual is let go from their job, docked a day's pay, or suffers some other disadvantage, this could amount to discrimination based on religion or creed. The employer would need to provide accommodation to the salesclerks because of their religious affiliation.

The Supreme Court of Canada has made it very clear, in a number of cases, that there is a very real duty imposed on employers to "reasonably accommodate" an employee's right to freedom of religion or creed, short of "undue hardship." There will be very few, if any, cases in which an employer will be successful in establishing undue hardship.

Mr. Renaud, a school custodian was a Seventh Day Adventist. His religion prevented him from working from sundown Friday to sundown Saturday. The work schedule, which required him to work a Friday shift from 3 p.m. to 11 p.m. was set out in the collective agreement between the Okanagan School Board and C.U.P.E., Local 523. Accommodating Mr. Renaud's religious beliefs would have required allowing him to work hours different than those specified. The respondent school board and union could not agree on a means of accommodating Mr. Renaud and as a result he was dismissed from his job. The B.C. Council of Human Rights found that though it was a *bona fide* requirement that a custodian be present in the schools, it was not a *bona fide* requirement that a custodian in Mr. Renaud's school work the 3 p.m. to 11 p.m. shift on Fridays. The Council concluded that Mr. Renaud should have been accommodated and that both the employer and the union were liable for the failure to do so.[14]

In a more recent case involving religious rights, *Multani v. Commission scolaire Marguerite-Bourgeoys,* the courts found in favour of Multani ruling that his religious rights had been infringed. Multani, a 12-year old Khalsa Sikh student in Montreal, had been forbidden from wearing his ceremonial kirpan dagger to school due to a "no weapons" policy. The board of education alleged that the kirpan presented safety issues, while Multani's family argued that banning the kirpan violated his religious rights. The Supreme Court allowed the Ontario Human Rights Commission to intervene in this case, agreeing that Ontario had an interest in the outcome, and that the Commission had unique arguments to offer. Ontario had ruled 15 years earlier in a similar case of *Pandori v. Peel Board of Education*. The Commission argued that justifying the denial of religious accommodation calls for proof of undue hardship, rather than "what if" speculation about what might happen. In *Pandori*, a human rights tribunal and the Ontario Divisional Court agreed that staff, students, and teachers should be allowed to wear a kirpan as long as it is a reasonable size, worn under the clothing, and secured with a stitched flap so that it cannot be removed from its sheath. Since the time of that decision, there have been no incidents of misuse of a kirpan in Ontario schools. In its decision, Canada's highest court stated that "Religious tolerance is a very important value of Canadian society. . . . By disregarding the right to freedom of religion, and by invoking the safety of the school community without considering the possibility of a solution that posed little or no risk, the school board made an unreasonable decision."[15]

Age

Agism is an attitude that makes assumptions about older persons and their abilities and puts labels on them. Agism is also a tendency to view and design society on the basis that everyone is young. Age discrimination is a consequence of agist attitudes.[16]

Some people have stereotypical views about older workers, considering them to be less productive, less flexible, unable or unwilling to adapt to new technologies or to upgrade their skills, prone to absenteeism, and less capable of engaging in physically demanding or stressful work. Several studies have demonstrated that such generalizations are quite inaccurate and certainly do not reflect the working capacity of older workers.[17] Figure 3-3 shows what two studies identified as the advantages and disadvantages of retaining older workers. It also lists what those studies say are consequences that employers may face with those employees.[18] Some firms also rehire their retirees as part-time workers, independent contractors, or consultants. One survey found that more than 60 percent of surveyed organizations are using such means.[19] Retirees are often employed at organizations such as McDonald's and Wal-Mart.

Agism is not only associated with older workers. In a recent survey of 500 IT workers conducted in 2005, the results indicate that age discrimination is a problem for not only the older IT worker, but also for the younger worker. Young workers felt that their managers did not take them seriously, and that their lower pay was justified because of being younger and having less responsibility than older people doing the same job. As well, managers indicated that they felt younger workers were less reliable.[20] Another study reported that younger workers are bringing with them different values and attitudes about work than previous generations. Young workers are not as willing to sacrifice their lives for work and they reject older models of authority and leadership.[21]

Mandatory retirement has been the subject of several unsuccessful challenges under the Canadian Charter of Rights and Freedoms. The Supreme Court of Canada has found that mandatory retirement does discriminate on the basis of age but that it is a reasonable limit on the equality rights of older persons. In *McKinney v. University of Guelph,*

Figure 3-3 *HR Managers' Views of Older Workers*

Advantages	Disadvantages	Consequences
Are willing to work different schedules	**Are weak on new technology**	**Health-care usage**
Serve as mentors	**Cause expenses to rise**	**Health-care costs**
Have invaluable experience	**Are less flexible**	**More training/retraining**
Have strong work ethic		**Employee stress**
Are more reliable		

and *Harrison v. University of British Columbia*, the Supreme Court of Canada found that a public sector mandatory retirement policy was not justifiable.[22] Based on these decisions, many speculate that Canada may soon see an end to mandatory retirement.[23]

Sex

Discrimination based on sex and on the basis of pregnancy is prohibited across Canada. The right to equal treatment without discrimination or harassment because of sex extends to all persons.

There are many examples where women, because of their gender, have been discriminated against. Discrimination based on sex has more far-reaching effects. In a unanimous decision, the Supreme Court of Canada ruled that sexual harassment is sex discrimination, thereby overturning a decision of the Manitoba Court of Appeal, which found that sexual harassment was not sex discrimination within the meaning of Subsection 6(1) of the 1974 Manitoba Human Rights Act.[24] Two female waitresses had been sexually harassed by the male cook, and it was deemed to be sex discrimination. The owners were also found liable. The reason sexual harassment applied in this instance was because only the women were the targets of discrimination and not the males.

In a landmark decision, the Supreme Court of Canada, in *Brooks v. Canada Safeway Ltd.* (1989), 59 D.L.R. 321, explained the rationale for describing discrimination because of pregnancy as sex discrimination. It stated:[25]

> In retrospect, one can only ask—how could pregnancy discrimination be *anything other than sex* discrimination? The disfavoured treatment accorded Mrs. Brooks, Mrs. Allen and Mrs. Dixon flowed entirely from their state of pregnancy, a condition unique to women. They were pregnant because of their sex. Discrimination on the basis of pregnancy is a form of sex discrimination because of the basic biological fact that only women have the capacity to become pregnant.

Sexual Orientation

Over the past 20 years, the legal rights of lesbians and gay men in Canada have been the subject of considerable judicial, political, and legislative activity. All Canadian jurisdictions prohibit discriminatory treatment based on sexual orientation, and the introduction of the Canadian Charter of Rights and Freedoms significantly altered the legal framework in matters of equality rights for lesbians and gay men. Generally speaking, legal issues relating to sexual orientation have arisen in two contexts:

- the prohibition of discrimination, primarily to ensure that individual lesbians and gay men are not discriminated against; and
- the recognition of same-sex relationships, and the extension to homosexual partners of the benefits and rights that are accorded to unmarried heterosexual partners

One specific issue that some employers have had to address is that of individuals who have had or are undergoing sex-change surgery and therapy. The B.C. Supreme Court concluded in *Vancouver Rape Relief Society v. British Columbia (Human Rights Commission)* that the use of the word "sex" in human rights legislation include protection for transsexual persons.[26] Sexual orientation or sex-change issues that arise at work include:

- *Clarification of HR policies:* Access to company benefits plans must be clarified. Also, the "restroom issue" is often the most sensitive. At some firms, the policy is that whatever restroom the individual wishes to use, that is the one that is acceptable.

- *Reactions of co-workers:* It is crucial to ensure that co-workers understand that the employer will not tolerate snide remarks or harassment of individuals over these issues.
- *Continuing acceptance:* If an employer believes that it is important to retain every worker who is performing satisfactorily, then keeping an employee who is in a same-sex relationship or is transgendered is just as important as retaining any other employee. Managers and supervisors must ensure that such an individual is evaluated fairly and not discriminated against in work assignments, raises, training, or promotions.

Marital Status

Marital status is not defined in the Code. The term is defined in some other jurisdictions. The Ontario Human Rights Act states that "Marital status means the status of being married, single, widowed, divorced or separated and includes the status of living with a person in a conjugal relationship outside marriage."[27]

An individual's marital status should have no bearing on employment decisions. In *Saskatchewan (Human Rights Commission) v. Prince Albert Elks Club Inc.* (2002), 20 CCEL (3d) 98 (Sask. CA), the employee was hired as the manager of a private club, many of whose members were correctional officers at Saskatchewan Penitentiary. She was dismissed approximately two weeks later, after the club learned she was married to a convicted murderer who was an inmate at the penitentiary. The club perceived that there was a security risk for its members in employing her. The employee filed a human rights complaint claiming discrimination on grounds of marital status. The court determined that the employer had not judged the employee on her own merits but had made stereotypical assumptions about her relationship with her husband and about her husband as well, without doing any factual investigation into the situation. The court therefore concluded that she was a victim of prejudice and discrimination.[28]

Family Status

The Code currently prohibits discrimination on the basis of family status in the areas of employment, housing, contracts, vocational and professional associations, and services, goods, and facilities. An employer may give preference in summer employment to children of employees. However, it is important to note that this exception does not allow for the dismissal of employees once they are hired. Nor does it appear to allow for different employment conditions outside of hiring or promotion. For example, family members could not be paid more than others in the same job.[29]

Nepotism
Practice of allowing relatives to work for the same employer.

Many employers have policies that restrict or prohibit **nepotism,** the practice of allowing relatives to work for the same employer. Other firms require only that relatives not work directly for or with each other or not be placed in positions where collusion or conflict could occur. The policies most frequently cover spouses, brothers, sisters, mothers, fathers, sons, and daughters. Generally, employer anti-nepotism policies have been upheld by courts, in spite of the concern that they tend to discriminate against women more than men (because women tend to be denied employment or to leave employers more often as a result of marriage to other employees).

The City of Toronto came under attack in the wake of a city hiring scandal. Top officials were found to be hiring relatives, close friends, and family members of politicians for senior positions. The Integrity Chief has proposed a ban on hiring close family members (spouses, children, and parents) from top jobs such as city manager, clerk, or solicitor. Currently the City of Toronto lacks clear policies on hiring councillors' relatives and no policies on councillors' providing job references.[30] The legitimate concern in such cases has to do with the conflict of interest that can arise when someone holds power. The HR Perspective demonstrates that such anti-nepotism policies must allow for such exceptions.

Disability

LOGGING ON...

The Office for Disability Issues (ODI)
The Office for Disability Issues (ODI) is the focal point within the Government of Canada for key partners working to promote the full participation of Canadians with disabilities in learning, work, and community life.
www.sdc.gc.ca/en/gateways/nav/top_nav/program/odi.shtml

Disabilities are defined under the Canadian Human Rights Code as either being physical or mental, or previous or existing; and including dependence on alcohol or a drug. A disability can be either permanent (e.g., a visual or mobility impairment) or temporary (e.g., a treatable illness or temporary impairment that is the result of an accident).

At the heart of employing individuals with disabilities is for employers to make reasonable accommodations in several areas. First, architectural barriers should not prohibit disabled individuals' access to work areas or restrooms. Second, appropriate work tasks must be assigned. Satisfying this requirement may mean modifying jobs, work area layouts, or work schedules, or providing special equipment. All reasonable accommodation must be conducted up to the point of undue hardship to the employer.

Both drugs and alcohol as disabilities are perhaps the most controversial of all disabilities. Two landmark cases are used as the basis for deciding on cases of alcohol and drug concerns in employment.

In *Entrop v. Imperial Oil,* Mr. Entrop was required to disclose past drug and alcohol addiction to his employer as a result of a new drug and alcohol policy. Mr. Entrop disclosed to his employer that he was an alcoholic but had not had a drink since February 1984. Imperial Oil immediately removed him from his

HR *Perspective*

Anti-Nepotism Policy Considerations

Line Laurin applied for a position as a lifeguard for the town of Brossard. Her mother was already employed as a secretary in the local police station. The Town of Brossard's policy was to refuse to hire members of the immediate family of town councillors and existing staff in order to avoid nepotism or favouritism or any appearance thereof in the hiring practices of the municipality.

The Supreme Court of Canada understood that the Town wanted to ensure that there were no real or potential conflicts of interest in the employment of municipal staff and that the goal of the Town was to avoid conflicts of interest. This was a qualification rationally connected to employment with the Town. However, the court found that the Town's no-relative rule was overboard since it operated as a blanket policy and did not allow exceptions, nor was it tailored to apply to those positions in which real or potential conflicts of interest could arise. Line Laurin's mother was not in a position to influence the hiring of her daughter, and there was no reason to expect that she could influence it. The Court found that the Town's anti-nepotism policy could not be justified as a bona fide qualification for employment.[31]

1. What should an organization do if a manager marries their subordinate? What are the major considerations to be addressed?
2. Develop a policy on anti-nepotism to be presented to the class. Be prepared to justify the content of your policy.

"safety sensitive" position but after a brief period recognizing that he was not a risk, reinstated him to his old position. But in order to be reinstated Mr. Entrop had to agree to submitting to unannounced alcohol tests. The Supreme Court of Canada upheld the board's finding that Imperial Oil discriminated against Entrop. The reinstatement process was lengthy and demeaning and caused Entrop stress and anxiety that was unnecessary in light of Entrop's work record and years of sobriety. Experts testified that drug testing is not effective to determine whether a person is capable of performing the essential requirements of their job since it is virtually impossible to predict with any specificity the degree of impairment that will result from drug use. As well neither blood nor urine tests are sufficiently accurate to indicate impairment from drugs. On the other hand, random alcohol testing for safety sensitive positions though discriminatory can be justified providing the sanctions for a positive test are individually tailored since a breathalyzer can be used to determine impairment.[32]

The Toronto Dominion Bank established a policy requiring employees to submit to a urine drug test. The bank would pay for rehabilitation programs for employees who had positive results. The Canadian Human Rights Tribunal designated to hear the initial complaint found that the policy was not discriminatory. However, on appeal by the Human Rights Commission, the Federal Court of Canada, Trial Division, set aside the decision ruling that the policy constituted indirect discrimination. Although the bank had made extraordinary efforts to accommodate drug users discovered through the testing process, the court found that the testing policy itself was not rationally related to job performance concerns. Without a performance-related justification, the policy could not be justified, regardless of how well the bank treated drug-abusing employees. The bank then appealed the decision to the Canadian Court of Appeal. Two of the three Court of Appeal judges classified the bank's work rule as indirect discrimination. The bank's rationale for implementing its policy is that it was concerned with the effect drugs have on work performance as well as on employee responsibility. The court said the bank's policy was under-inclusive. If the bank were truly concerned with the correlation between drug use and employee job performance and responsibility it would have adopted a rule for random testing that applies to all employees including those at the senior levels.[33]

Employers should only ask about criminal records if it applies directly to the job, and only if legislation in the particular jurisdiction allows it.

Source: Lou Oates/ShutterStock

Record of Criminal Conviction and Pardoned Conviction

Employers should only ask criminal record related questions if it directly impacts the job. Further, under the Criminal Records Act, a federal government job application cannot ask questions that could expose a conviction for which a pardon has been granted. If an employer wishes to obtain information about a person's criminal record history, the question should be phrased: "Have you ever been convicted of an offence for which you have not received a pardon?" In this case the individual can answer "No." If the question is not asked in a manner that recognizes the possibility of a pardon, the individual can respond one of two ways:

1. If the question arises in an interview situation, the employee can answer "Yes, I had a criminal record, but I have received a pardon."
2. If the question is found on an application form related to federal jurisdiction (e.g., if the employer is the federal government or a bank), the person can ask for a copy of the application and forward it to the Canadian Human Rights Commission. The Commission will then advise the employer that the question is inappropriate.

For example, where a person applies for work at a mine and has a conviction related to child molestation, it is unlikely the employer would be able to legally deny employment based on this conviction as no children are allowed on the employer's worksite. However if the same applicant were applying for work with children, the hiring decision could be influenced by this conviction without violating the *Code*.

Filing a Complaint

Each jurisdiction has its own procedures for filing a complaint, although there are similarities. For example, in Alberta, a person who thinks his or her human rights have been violated can file a complaint with the Human Rights and Citizenship Commission. There is no fee for filing a complaint and it is not necessary to hire a lawyer to file a complaint. The individual has the right to appoint someone to assist or represent in filing a complaint. The same options apply if a complaint has been filed against the individual. The Commission will keep all the parties informed of the steps that are being taken, and the Commission welcomes questions at any time during the process. Figure 3-4 outlines the steps in the complaint process for Alberta.[34]

The Canadian Human Rights Commission tries to resolve complaints of discrimination filed against federally regulated employers, unions, and service providers. If a complaint cannot be resolved, the Commission may investigate the case further, and may ultimately request that the Canadian Human Rights Tribunal hear the case. To file a complaint with the Canadian Human Rights Commission, an inquiries questionnaire can be completed, or direct contact by telephone, e-mail, fax, or mail can be made. The Commission will contact the individual to provide basic information about the Commission and the *Canadian Human Rights Act,* and to advise if a complaint can be filed with the Commission. If so, the officer will send a kit so that a complaint form can be filed. If not, staff will try to suggest another alternative or organization that can help.[35]

Harassment

4 Under the Canadian Human Rights code harassment is defined as "any unwanted physical or verbal conduct that offends or humiliates you. Such conduct can interfere with your ability to do a job or obtain a service." Harassment is a type of discrimination. It can take many forms, such as:[36]

- threats, intimidation, or verbal abuse;
- unwelcome remarks or jokes about subjects like your race, religion, disability, sex, or age;
- displaying sexist, racist, or other offensive pictures or posters;
- sexually suggestive remarks or gestures;
- inappropriate physical contact, such as touching, patting, pinching, or punching;

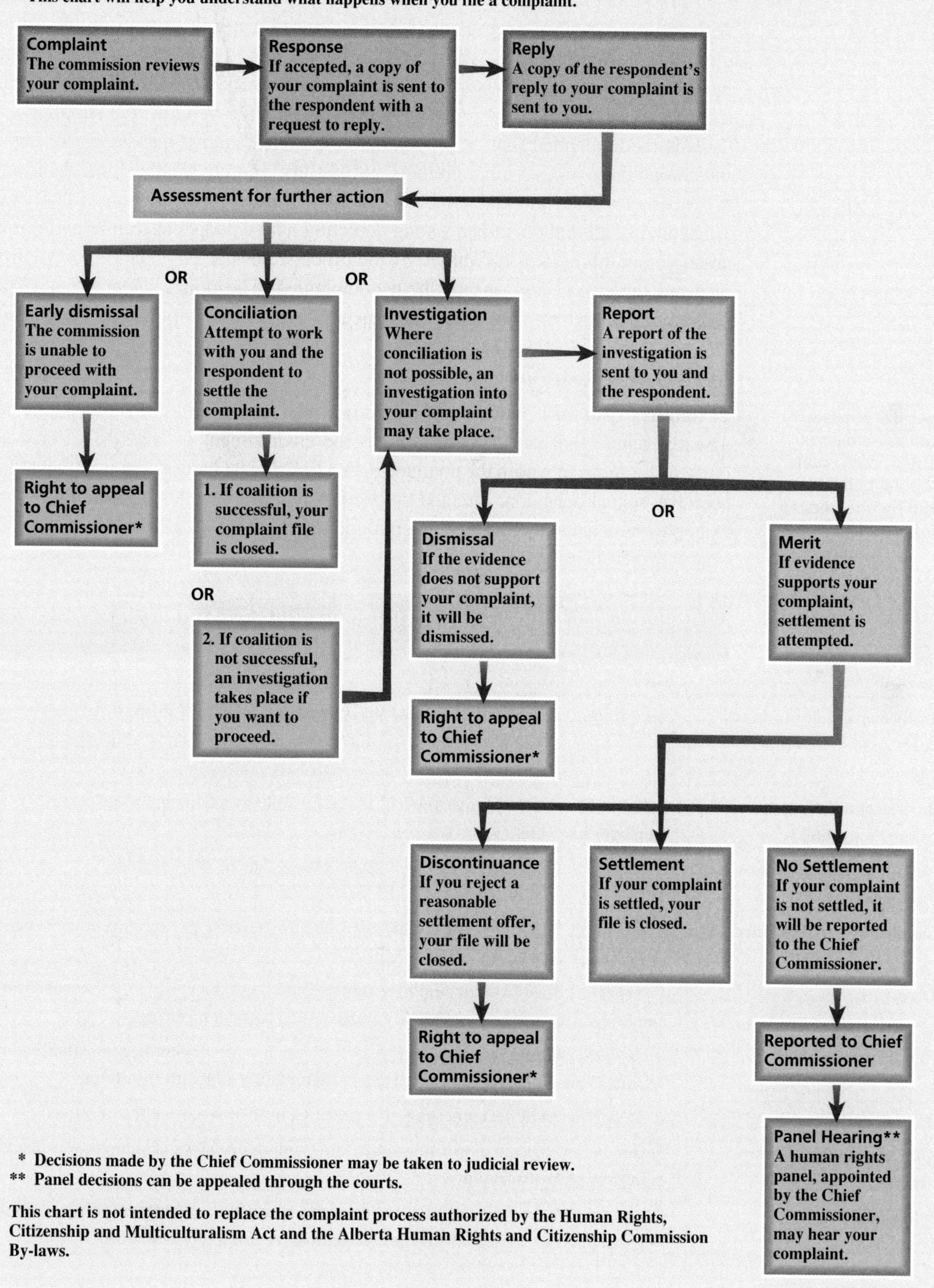

Source: "Complaint Process," Alberta Human Rights Commission, 2006. Reprinted by permission.

- leering or whistling;
- outright demands for sexual favours;
- physical assault, including sexual assault.

Harassment can create a negative or hostile work environment that can interfere with job performance and result in being refused a job, a promotion, or a training opportunity. The harasser, who could be of the same or opposite sex as the person harassed, may be a supervisor, a co-worker, or someone providing a service, such as a bank officer or a clerk in a government department, a vendor, or a supplier.

It is recommended that employers adopt policies against harassment of any type, including ethnic jokes, vulgar epithets, racial slurs, and physical actions. A recent case in Ontario involved the discipline of five RCMP officers for passing a racist e-mail. An audio e-mail that contained a song depicting native people as drunks and criminals, among other things, was forwarded by the officers. Several First Nation RCMP officers received the e-mail and one of them complained. The police agency has a specific policy against such transmission. The officers were to be disciplined for their actions.[37]

Sexual Harassment

Sexual harassment
Sexual harassment is unwanted, often coercive, sexual behaviour directed by one person towards another.

Sexual harassment is one type of harassment and is defined as unwelcome conduct of a sexual nature that detrimentally affects the environment or leads to adverse consequences for those to whom the conduct is directed. Sexual harassment is unwanted, often coercive, sexual behaviour directed by one person towards another. Figure 3-5 provides examples of behaviours that have been found to constitute sexual harassment in Canada.

Figure 3-5 *Behaviours Found to Constitute Sexual Harassment in Canadian Legal Cases*

Behaviour	Example
Sexually degrading words or remarks used to describe an individual or group.	A co-worker made insulting sexual jokes or remarks about women.
Inquiries/comments about an individual's sex life.	A co-worker made an employee feel uncomfortable by asking questions about employee's sex life.
Sexual flirtations, advances, and propositions.	A co-worker repeatedly asked an employee for a date or relationship.
Demands for sexual favours.	A co-worker hinted that the employee could have a better job or some other benefit in exchange for a sexual relationship.
Leering.	Co-worker leaned over an employee unnecessarily, got too close, and/or cornered the employee. A co-worker consistently stared at the body of a colleague.
Verbal threats or abuse.	A co-worker hinted that the employee could lose her job or that her job situation might be hurt if the employee did not have a sexual relationship with the abuser.
Unwanted gestures.	A co-worker made sexually suggestive gestures in the presence of a colleague.
Display of sexually offensive material.	Sexual material, such as pornography or degrading drawings of women, was displayed in or around the workplace.
Sexual assault.	Co-worker touched suggestively, intentionally brushed up against employee, patted, hugged, pinched, kissed, or grabbed the employee using physical force.

Source: Adapted from D. Crocker and V. Kalemba, "The Incidence and Impact of Women's Experiences of Sexual Harassment in Canadian Workplaces," *Canadian Review of Sociology and Anthropology*, vol. 36, no. 4, 1999, p. 556. Used by permission.

Sexual harassment can be emotionally abusive and creates an unhealthy, unproductive atmosphere in the workplace. It is one of the most frequent complaints received by human rights agencies, and the most costly for employers who fail to have effective policies, or when an employer fails to treat such complaints from their employees or customers and clients seriously.[38]

As more women have entered the workforce, more men and women work together in teams and on projects. Consequently, more employers are becoming concerned about the close personal relationships that develop at work. Some of these can eventually lead to sexual harassment.

Consensual Relationships and Workplace Romances

When work-based friendships lead to romance and off-the-job sexual relationships, managers and employers face a dilemma: Should they "monitor" these relationships to protect the firm from potential legal complaints, thereby "meddling" in employees' private, off-the-job lives? Or do they simply ignore these relationships and the potential problems they present?

According to one survey, 63 percent of Canadians have had a workplace romance and another reported that 59 percent of American respondents had also breached this taboo. Studies conducted by Sydney University indicate that at any given time, 11 percent of the Australian workforce is involved in an office liaison and the IRS Employment Review found that in this "long hours" work culture, half of UK workers meet their partners on the job.[39] Of special concern is what will happen if or when the office romance turns into sexual harassment.

Different actions may be taken if a relationship is clearly consensual than if it involves a supervisor-subordinate relationship. The greatest concerns are romantic relationships between supervisors and subordinates, because the harassment of subordinates by supervisors is the most frequent type of sexual harassment. Some employers have addressed the issue of workplace romances by establishing policies dealing with them. Employers need to be mindful that a consensual romance between a manager and subordinate can lead to a case of sexual harassment when the relationship ends.

Workplace romances can complicate matters at work for both the employer and the employees, particularly when supervisor-subordinate relationships exist.

Source: © 2006 JupiterImages and its Licensors. All Rights Reserved.

In *Simpson v. Consumers' Association of Canada* in 2001, Mr. Simpson was fired for a number of sexually related interactions with his subordinates that occurred outside the workplace. The interactions were, for the most part, consensual. However, the Court of Appeal found that consensual conduct is not the same as welcome conduct. Because of the power imbalance inherent in a relationship between a supervisor and his subordinates, a subordinate may simply go along with the sexual conduct of the supervisor because of the perceived consequences to objecting to it. In that regard, even apparently consensual relationships may constitute harassment. Furthermore, relying on one of its previous decisions, the court found that management has two positive duties: the first to protect its employees from offensive conduct, and the second to protect the corporation against lawsuits at the hands of individual complainants.[40]

Nature of Sexual Harassment

Sexual harassment is a significant concern in many organizations and can occur in a variety of workplace relationships. For example, both customer service representatives and food servers have won sexual harassment complaints because their employers refused to protect them from regular sexual harassment by aggressive customers.

Most frequently, sexual harassment occurs when a male in a supervisory or managerial position harasses women within his "power structure." However, women managers have been found guilty of sexually harassing male employees. Also, same-sex harassment has occurred. Court decisions have held that a person's sexual orientation neither provides nor precludes a claim of sexual harassment. It is enough that the harasser engaged in pervasive and unwelcome conduct of a sexual nature.[41] As computer and Internet technology has spread, the number of electronic sexual harassment cases has grown, as the Technology Transforming HR describes.

Types of Sexual Harassment Two basic types of sexual harassment have been defined as follows:

Quid pro quo
Sexual harassment in which employment outcomes are linked to the individual granting sexual favours.

Hostile environment
Sexual harassment in which an individual's work performance or psychological well-being is unreasonably affected by intimidating or offensive working conditions.

1. **Quid pro quo** is harassment in which employment outcomes are linked to the individual granting sexual favours.
2. **Hostile environment** harassment exists when an individual's work performance or psychological well-being is unreasonably affected by intimidating or offensive working conditions.

In quid pro quo harassment, an employee may be promised a promotion, a special raise, or a desirable work assignment, but only if the employee grants some sexual favours to the supervisor. Unfortunately, hostile environment harassment is much more prevalent, partially because the standards and consequences are more varied. This is sometimes more prevalent for females when they work in male-dominated environments. Female firefighters in British Columbia are currently battling against "widespread sexual harassment" from their male colleagues. The following is a list of some of the issues they have had to endure:[42]

- Jeanette Moznik went to the B.C. Supreme Court with harassment allegations against her male counterparts. Moznik claimed that they had harassed her by committing lewd and pornographic acts towards her. She alleges that they had placed human waste in her articles of clothing and would often display explicit pornography whenever she was in their company. Moznik believes that some of their actions, including cutting off her hose's water supply that she was using to put out a blaze, had put her life in danger.
- Sandra Jansen made the decision to file a discrimination complaint with the B.C. Human Rights Tribunal after she began to feel that her workplace was no longer a safe place for her to be in.

Technology Transforming HR

Electronic Sexual Harassment

Much has been made of the advantages of the Internet and its positive effects on HR management. However, electronic information technology is creating new problems for HR managers as well, because sexual harassment occurs in e-mails and Internet access systems.

Cyber sexual harassment is a growing concern because it occurs in a variety of forms. It may be an employee forwarding an e-mail joke with sexual content received from a friend outside the company. Or it may be an employee repeatedly sending e-mails asking another employee to meet for lunch or a date.

Another more troublesome form is employees accessing pornographic websites at work, and then sharing some content with other employees. Even something such as an employee having a screen saver of his wife in a revealing outfit or an actress dressed in a bikini has led to complaints by other employees.

Many employers have developed policies addressing the inappropriate use of e-mail and company computer systems. Most employers have policies on electronic technology usage, and many of those policies have "zero tolerance," whereby disciplinary action occurs regardless of the proclaimed innocence of the employee.

More serious situations have led to employee terminations, as evidenced by some examples. Dow Chemical disciplined more than 200 employees and fired 50 of them for having e-mailed pornographic images and other inappropriate materials using the company information system. A well-publicized case occurred at the New York Times, where 20 employees were fired for sending offensive and inappropriate e-mails—many of the individuals repeatedly doing so. At the University of British Columbia, a worker was fired for viewing porn, after having been reprimanded previously for repeated offences.

HR managers are handling cyber sexual harassment in a number of ways. First, having a policy is important, but it is even more crucial to train all employees on sexual harassment and electronic usage policies. Additionally, many employers have equipped their e-mail systems and websites with scanners that screen for inappropriate words and images. Offending employees receive the warnings and disciplinary actions associated with "flagged" items. As with all sexual harassment situations, HR professionals should document the incidents, their investigative efforts, and the actions taken to prevent further cyber sexual harassment.[43]

1. How can employer's realistically control the use of technology in the workplace?
2. How is this different from employees using the telephone at work for personal reasons? If it is different, shouldn't phone calls be monitored as well? Be prepared to justify your decision.

- Female fire captain in Richmond, Jocelyn Roberts, allegedly committed suicide over her working environment. The chief stated that Roberts did not have an easy time as one of the first females to supervise male employees in the department.
- Burnaby fire captain Boni Prokopetz reached a settlement with her fire department after claiming that her male peers had harassed her for 11 years.
- Two of the male firefighters who had backed Prokopetz's claims filed their own complaints because of the threats and retaliation coming from their co-workers for supporting Prokopetz . One of the firefighters had even been told that it would be difficult for him to receive a promotion.

A number of court cases have emphasized that commenting on appearance or attire, telling jokes that are suggestive or sexual in nature, allowing revealing photos and posters to be on display, or making continual requests to get together after work can lead to the creation of a hostile work environment.

Regardless of the type of sexual harassment, it is apparent that sexual harassment has significant consequences on the organization, other employees, and especially those harassed. Follow-up interviews and research with victims of sexual harassment reveal that the harassment has both job-related and psychological effects. Also, harassment even has a ripple effect on others who fear being harassed or view their employer more negatively if prompt, remedial actions do not occur. Thus, how employers respond to sexual harassment complaints is crucial for both legal reasons and employee morale.

Legal Standards on Sexual Harassment

One survey found that 90 percent of all women working outside of the home will experience sexual harassment at some point in their working lives. Forty-nine percent of women in the workforce have experienced at least one type of unwanted sexual attention.[44] Only four of every ten Canadian women who suffer sexual harassment at work take any formal action. Only one out of every two women believe that a complaint would be taken seriously in their workplace. If the workplace culture fosters harassment, and policies and practices do not inhibit harassment, an employer is wise to re-evaluate and solve the problem before lawsuits follow.[45]

Only if the employer can produce evidence that they took reasonable care to prohibit sexual harassment does the employer have the possibility of avoiding liability. The landmark case highlighted in HR Perspective demonstrates the costs to an organization and its employees when complaints are not taken seriously. To avoid such incidents critical components of ensuring reasonable care include the following:

- Establishing a sexual harassment policy
- Communicating the policy regularly
- Training employees and managers on avoiding sexual harassment
- Investigating and taking action when complaints are voiced

HR *Perspective*

Sexual Harassment

Carol Shaw was harassed over a period of 14 years by a co-worker who constantly criticized her work, denigrated her sexuality, and degraded her as a woman. The Board of Inquiry in this case found that the most common understanding of sexual harassment is conduct such as making passes, soliciting sexual favours, sexual touching, and the like. However, it finds that conduct that denigrates a woman's sexuality or vexatious conduct, which is directed at a woman because of her sex, also constitutes sexual harassment.

In this case, Carol Shaw was subjected to constant negative comment on her person and her performance by a co-worker. Herb Robertson made fun of the way Ms. Shaw walked and of her figure by saying "waddle, waddle" when she walked by, or "swish, swish" to imitate the sound of her nylons rubbing against each other. He called her a "fat cow" to another employee and made remarks indicating that he believed women should be at home looking after their children, as his wife was.

The Board of Inquiry found that Carol Shaw brought Herb Robertson's behaviour to the attention of Roger Levac, who was in charge of operations for the company, on a number of occasions over the course of her employment. Mr. Levac did nothing effective to stop it and Ms. Shaw left her employment with Levac Supply.

The board found that Herb Robertson, Roger Levac, and Levac Supply Ltd. were jointly and severally liable for the losses arising from Ms. Shaw's harassment. The respondents were ordered to pay Ms. Shaw $43,273 in compensation for lost wages, as well as $5,000 in general damages. At that time, it was the largest settlement ever offered to a complainant.[46]

1. What could the organization have done to ensure that this type of behaviour was avoided?
2. Do you consider the punishment appropriate for the behaviour of the individuals? Would you do anything differently? Why or why not?

Other Legislation

5 In addition to the Charter of Rights and Freedom and Human Rights legislation that governs how citizens and employees are to be treated, there are several other pieces of legislation that are also important for the fair and equitable treatment of employees. The Canada Labour Code governs the workplace for industries within federal jurisdiction, and regulates labour standards and occupational health and safety. Employment standards, occupational health and safety, and labour relations are covered under separate pieces of legislation for provincial and territorial employees.

Employment Standards

Employment standards are designed to protect workers from possible exploitation through unregulated labour markets. Standards may be set out in legislation, in collective bargaining agreements, or through voluntary codes of conduct. These are the minimum standards required by law. Employers therefore cannot negotiate anything less than what is established under employment standards legislation with their employees.

The following are some examples of standards typically governed under the Canada Labour Code or an Employment Standards Act:

- Hours of work
- Minimum wages
- Termination notice and pay
- Rest periods
- Vacation time and pay
- Overtime pay
- Leaves of absences

Most Employment Standards Acts require employers to display a poster in the workplace describing the highlights of the Act. Figure 3-6 provides an example of a posting from the Ontario's Employment Standards Act. Throughout each of the chapters, the specific standards will be explained as they apply to the topic area. Chapter 10, Compensation Strategies and Practices, provides information with respect to wages, overtime hours, and minimum working age; Chapter 12, Managing Employee Benefits, will review leaves of absence; and Chapter 14, Employee Rights and Discipline, will discuss wrongful terminations.

Occupational Health and Safety

Occupational health and safety (OH&S) legislation in Canada outlines the general rights and responsibilities of the employer, the supervisor, and the worker. Each of the ten provinces, three territories, and the federal government has its own OH&S legislation.

All employees have three basic rights with respect to occupational health and safety:

- The Right to Know
- The Right to Participate
- The Right to Refuse Dangerous Work

Chapter 13 discusses occupational health and safety in more detail.

Figure 3-6 ***Employment Standards Act, 2000 Poster***

What You Should Know

About The Ontario Employment Standards Act

The Employment Standards Act, 2000, known as the ESA, is a law that sets minimum standards for fair workplace practices in Ontario. If you work in Ontario, you are probably protected by the ESA. It does not cover employees in federal jurisdiction and persons in a few other special categories. There are exceptions and special rules for some employees.

Your Rights and Responsibilities at Work

Employers cannot intimidate, fire, suspend, or otherwise punish an employee, or threaten any of these actions because the employee asks for or asks about their ESA rights. If an employee thinks that an employer is not following the ESA law, he or she can contact the Ministry of Labour for help.

Note: Unionized employees should talk to their union representative before contacting the Ministry of Labour if they think their rights have been violated.

Hours of Work – Generally, employees cannot be forced to work more than

- Daily Limit: 8 hours a day – or the number of hours in a regular work day, if it's more than 8. Employees may work more than the daily limit if requirements for obtaining their written agreement are met.
- Weekly Limit: 48 hours a week. Employees may work more than 48 hours in a week if requirements for obtaining their written agreement are met and the employer has an approval from the Director of Employment Standards. (In certain cases and subject to restrictions, where an approval application has been pending for at least thirty days, employees may work a limited number of excess weekly hours.)

Rest Periods - Generally, employees must have at least

- 11 consecutive hours off work each day.
- 24 consecutive hours off work each week or 48 consecutive hours off work in every 2-week period.

Overtime Pay – Most employees must be paid overtime pay after 44 hours of work each week.
The overtime rate must be at least 1½ times the regular rate of pay.

Minimum Wage – Most employees are entitled to be paid at least the minimum wage.

February 1, 2004	February 1, 2005	February 1, 2006	February 1, 2007
$7.15 per hour	$7.45 per hour	$7.75 per hour	$8.00 per hour

Note: The minimum wage is different for students, liquor servers, homeworkers, and hunting and fishing guides.

Payday – Employees must be paid on a regular, recurring payday and given a statement showing their wages and deductions for that pay period.

Vacation Time and Pay – Most employees earn at least 2 weeks of vacation time after every 12 months. Employees are entitled to be paid at least 4 per cent of their total wages earned as vacation pay.

Public Holidays - Ontario has 8 public holidays every year. Most employees take these days off work, with public holiday pay.

Leaves of Absence – Eligible employees are entitled to these unpaid, job-protected leaves:

- 17 weeks of pregnancy leave
- 35 or 37 weeks of parental leave
- 10 days each calendar year of emergency leave for personal illness, injury or medical emergency, or for the death, illness, injury, medical emergency or urgent matter of certain family members
- 8 weeks in a 26-week period of family medical leave to care for or support certain family members who have a serious illness with a significant risk of dying within a period of 26 weeks.

Termination Notice and Pay – Generally, if an employee has been working for 3 months or more and his or her job is terminated, the employer must give the employee advance written notice, or termination pay instead of notice, or a combination of both.

Young Workers - ***For more information on your rights and responsibilities at work, please visit: www.labour.gov.on.ca/english/site/youngworkers.html***

There are other ESA rights not covered on this poster and not all employees qualify for all ESA rights.

Contact the Ministry of Labour for More Information

Call 416-326-7160, toll-free 1-800-531-5551 or Hearing Impaired TTY 1-866-567-8893

Visit www.labour.gov.on.ca for more information and to contact the Ministry by e-mail.

Employment Standards publications and forms can be obtained by visiting a ServiceOntario Centre. To locate the nearest centre, call 1-800-267-8097.

Version 3.0

ISBN 1-4249-1018-8 (Print)
ISBN 1-4249-1019-6 (HTML)
ISBN 1-4249-1020-X (PDF)

Source: "What You Should Know about the Employment Standards Act," Ministry of Labour, Queen's Printer for Ontario.

Labour Relations Legislation

Labour legislation governs collective bargaining and industrial relations among employers, their unionized employees, and trade unions. In most provinces these matters are covered in separate statutes. The Canada Labour Code and each of the provincial statutes protects the right of employees to join the union of their choice. Employers are not allowed to discriminate against employees for joining a trade union or participating in any of its lawful activities. Any discrimination could be deemed to be an unfair labour practice. The employer is required by law to bargain in good faith with the union chosen as bargaining agent by a majority of his or her employees.

In addition to the legislation there are regulations, practices, countless decisions by labour boards, and many court judgments that make up the labour law governing unfair labour practices, union certification, and the duty to bargain in good faith. The process of labour relations and related legislation is discussed in more detail in Chapter 15.

Employment Equity and Pay Equity

6 Both employment equity and pay equity legislation are concerned with aspects of discrimination in employment. Employment equity addresses discrimination in employment, particularly where **designated group members** are concerned. Pay equity addresses the historical wage gap that exists between females and males doing the same or comparable work. There are many reasons for pay inequity, but one of the reasons most cited is that jobs typically held by females have been undervalued compared to men's work. It is important to understand that employment equity and pay equity are separate pieces of legislation that deal with discrimination in employment in different ways. Both are important to ensuring fair and equitable treatment of employees in different aspects of employment.

Designated group members
Those most disadvantaged in employment opportunities: women, Aboriginal people, visible minorities, and persons with disabilities.

Employment Equity

A Royal Commission was established in 1983 to study equal employment opportunities of employees in the federal government. This Commission, chaired by Judge Rosalie Abella, tabled a report, "Equality in Employment," in November 1984. Her report, in which she coined the term and concept of "employment equity," advocated a new strategy for reducing barriers in employment faced by designated groups: women, Aboriginal people, visible minorities, and persons with disabilities. Judge Abella coined the term "employment equity" to distinguish the Canadian initiative from American affirmative action programs, which had been associated with quotas.[47] Employment equity (EE) is defined as "a program, practice or legislation intended to provide access to employment for people in designated groups who have been the object of some form of discrimination."[48]

In 1986 the Employment Equity Act was passed in response to the findings of the commission. Its purpose as defined under Section 2 was to:[49]

> achieve equality in the workplace so that no person shall be denied employment opportunities or benefits for reasons unrelated to ability and, in the fulfillment of the goals, to correct the conditions of disadvantage in employment experienced by women, Aboriginal peoples, persons with disabilities, and visible minority people by giving effect to the principle that employment equity means more than treating persons in the same way but also requires special measures and the accommodation of differences.

Major highlights of the 1986 legislation included:

- Legislated Employment Equity Program (LEEP) became fully operational in 1988. Employers received two years to set up their employment equity processes.
- Federal Contractors Program (FCP) became fully operational in 1988 and was established by government policy, not legislation.

Following a parliamentary review in 1995, a new act came into force in October 1996. The act covers private sector employers under federal jurisdiction as well as almost all employees of the federal government. The 1996 act improved upon its 1986 model and was strengthened in the following areas:[50]

- The federal public service was now included.
- The Canadian Human Rights Commission was given authority to conduct on-site audits to verify and gain compliance, and, where necessary, provide final enforcement through an employment equity review tribunal, which was empowered to hear disputes and issue orders.
- Mandatory consultation with employees and/or employee groups such as unions.
- Federal Crown corporation employment equity requirements were made equivalent to those of the private sector employers covered under the Act.
- Federal Contractors Program responsibilities stated in the legislation.
- A mandatory parliamentary review of the legislation every five years was assured.

Goal of Employment Equity To achieve the objectives of achieving equality in the workplace based on the 1986 and 1995 acts, employers are required to identify and remove barriers to employment that adversely affect designated group members. Employers are also required to implement special measures and make reasonable accommodations when necessary to achieve and maintain a representative workplace.

Legislated Programs

Federal Legislated Employment Equity Program (LEEP) Under the LEEP, the following employers are subject to the *Employment Equity Act:*

- All federally regulated employers with 100 or more employees, including organizations in industries such as banking, communications, and international and interprovincial transportation.
- Other parts of the public service, including the Canadian Forces and the Royal Canadian Mounted Police may be specified by order of the Governor in Council, on the recommendation of the Treasury Board, as being required to comply with the Employment Equity Act.

Federal Contractors Program (FCP) Under the FCP, provincially regulated employers (contractors) with 100 or more employees who have secured a federal goods or services contract of $200,000 or more are required to sign a certificate of commitment to fulfill their mandated goal of implementing employment equity in their workplace. Contractors who refuse to honour their commitment to employment equity and are found in non-compliance with program criteria may lose the right to bid on further federal government contracts.[51]

Provincial Employment Equity Legislation At this time, the only province that has enacted EE legislation is British Columbia in the public service sector. Six other provinces have committed to an EE policy (Manitoba, Saskatchewan, Quebec, Nova Scotia, New Brunswick, and Prince Edward Island). All of the policies, except for Quebec's, applies to the public service sector. Employment equity policy may be limited to specific programs of the government, or applicable to certain sectors of the government. Policy packages may or may not be subject to detailed systems of reporting and accountability. Also, policy packages are not subject to a process of legislative review, debate, and passage into law.[52]

Provinces who have made no commitment to employment equity are Newfoundland, Alberta, and Ontario. In Newfoundland, the discussion has been limited to a discussion of gender equity. Employment equity has been actively debated in Alberta, but legislation has never been enacted. In Ontario, employment equity was implemented when the NDP government were in power, and later repealed under the Conservative reign of Mike Harris.[53]

Human Resources and Social Development Canada (HRSDC)
The HRSDC Workplace Equity website provides general information on equal pay and employment equity programs or access tools and resources for the implementation of employment equity.
www.sdc.gc.ca/asp/gateway.asp?hr=en/lp/lo/lswe/we/ee_tools/reports/annual/index-we.shtml&hs=wzp

Employer Requirements

Employers are required to develop and implement employment equity plans and programs, and to report annually (by June 1) to the Labour Program, Department of Human Resources and Social Development Canada (HRSDC) on their progress in achieving a representative workforce for the four designated groups.

The reports submitted by the employers to HRSDC describe the employment situation of the four designated groups and the progress made toward achieving an equitable workforce during the preceding calendar year. Under the *Employment Equity Act,* the Canadian Human Rights Commission is responsible for ensuring compliance with the act. The Commission conducts audits to determine whether employers meet the statutory requirements of the act. As required by the act, the Minister of Labour's annual Report to Parliament consolidates and analyzes employer reports.

Advantages of Employment Equity A report conducted by the Conference Board of Canada found that a number of organizations were starting to recognize employment equity as a key element for corporate success. Its effectiveness is enhanced when it is linked to business strategy. By tying it to business strategy it becomes an integral part of the organization. In addition, employment equity is now recognized worldwide as a uniquely Canadian tool for efficient use of scarce skilled human resources and is increasingly being borrowed by many advanced industrialized countries.[54]

According to the Conference Board survey, a number of advantages had become evident because of the implementation of the Employment Equity Act. Organizations had improved their economic competitiveness and their ability to maximize human potential. Almost two in ten surveyed employees noted that employment equity had helped them to enhance innovation in their organizations and had improved their access to new markets. Another 12 percent felt that employment equity practices helped them to improve the effectiveness of their international business dealings. In addition, respondents found that employment equity had assisted them to create work cultures tolerant of diversity, and had improved their corporate image. Employers believed that employment equity enhanced their recruitment efforts and increased the level of employee commitment in their firms.[55]

The following are the top ten benefits that can come from employment equity:[56]

1. Removing the barriers facing 70 percent of Canada's labour force.
2. Supporting the government's inclusion agenda.
3. Accessing the pool of human capital for a knowledge-based economy.
4. Confronting the double whammy of brain drain and brain waste.
5. Replenishing the declining stock of human capital.
6. Improving Canada's international economic competitiveness.
7. Assuring Canada's standing as a world leader.
8. Creating a business case for private businesses.
9. Improved human resources management for better performance.
10. Confirming the new thinking that equity and efficiency go together.

Establishing an Employment Equity Plan

Section 12 of the Employment Equity Act requires that an employer's employment equity plan will lead to reasonable progress. Reasonable progress is defined both as achieving the plan's annual hiring and promotion goals and demonstrating progress in line with the representation goals. There are a number of activities that organizations must undertake in order to demonstrate that a reasonable effort has been made to effectively establish an employment equity plan.[57]

Developing the Organizational Commitment and Structure for an Employment Equity (EE) Program This includes getting the commitment of the chief executive officer, assigning responsibility for the program to a senior executive, making an announcement to all staff about the program, and appointing staff to undertake the administrative functions of the program. One way to ensure commitment from managers is to make employment equity part of their overall goals to be assessed as part of performance management. EE must be made part of the overall organizational strategies and embedded in the culture. The Bank of Montreal has an office dedicated to overseeing equity issues—Office of Workplace Equality. Many other organizations have made this commitment as well.

Developing a Mechanism to Consult and Collaborate with Employee Representatives This can be achieved through the establishment of an employment equity committee or by other means appropriate to the organization. Consultation and collaboration is an ongoing process, and is essential for an effective employment equity program. A recent study found that consultation with employee groups does not always occur until after decisions have been made. Particularly where union groups are involved, the unions may not have a vested interest in pursuing representation because its membership does not have many designated group members, or because there is no one assigned the responsibility to EE. Employers may be reluctant to have others involved. Employees need advocates to help with this process, and it is important that they be involved at the initial stages rather than at the completion of the project.[58]

Conducting a Workforce Survey Employer must survey employees and ask whether or not they are members of the designated groups. Through self-identification, it is important to have employees answer honestly about their designated group status. Some of the issues surrounding the workforce survey is that not all employees will complete their survey, nor will they complete it accurately, and the true composition of the workforce will not be known. An organization must ensure it is obtaining accurate information, and that as many employees as possible complete the survey. First confidentiality of the information must be maintained. Many employees are concerned about confidentiality and might not be willing to disclose personal information if they perceive it might be used against them. For example employees with disabilities that are not visible such as a heart problem or epilepsy may not want their employer to know about their disabilities. Other strategies are to ensure that everyone is provided with a survey and each one is returned, whether the survey is completed or not. Even if it is obvious that someone is a designated group member and does not indicate so on the survey, no one is allowed to change the information except for the self-identifying employee.

Undertaking a Workforce Analysis Employers must analyze the representation of designated group members in the employer's workforce and compare it to the representation in the appropriate segments of the Canadian workforce (e.g., geographic location from which the employer draws their labour force). This is done to determine if equitable representation exists within the employer's workforce. Self-identification becomes important because an organization needs to know how representative they are, and without having accurate information obtained through the self-identification process, a true representation of the workforce will be unknown.

Undertaking an Employment Systems Review (Only When Underrepresentation Occurs) All human resource policies and practices need to be examined to determine if any barriers exist that prohibit the full participation of designated group members within the employer's workforce. This review includes examining policies and practices as they relate to the special needs of members of designated groups. Systemic discrimination is responsible for most of the inequities that exists for designated group members. Word-of-mouth hiring is an example of systemic discrimination. Employers offer incentives for employees to recommend their friends for hire, but if the organization is primarily White, then employees will probably recommend their White friends, and so the composition of the workforce remains White. Such actions can lead to **disparate impact** on designated group members (underrepresentation of designated group members).

Disparate impact
Occurs when designated group members are substantially underrepresented in employment decisions.

Developing and Implementing an Employment Equity Plan to Address the Inequities Discovered Through the Workforce Analysis and Employment Systems Review Different strategies to meet the needs of the various designated groups will be required. The plan must include the following:

- Positive policies and practices to accelerate the integration of designated group members in employers' workforces. For example, an organization could ensure that all designated group members be given first opportunity for training to make them more qualified for senior positions. Organizations might also demonstrate full commitment to hiring only designated group members. However, this type of commitment might not be viewed positively by White males. Recently, the deputy minister in the Public Works department circulated an e-mail instructing all managers to hire only designated group members so that they could achieve their EE goals. Permission to hire able-bodied White males would require written permission from their superiors.[59] Canada's Charter of Rights and Freedoms permits some discrimination to assist groups identified by the government as disadvantaged, but the form it usually takes is through programs that promote recruitment and hiring of qualified people from those groups—not by banning members of a non-minority class. Therefore, positive policies and practices need to take into consideration all members of the organization.
- Elimination of employment barriers pinpointed during the employment systems review. The plan must specify the measures the employer intends to take in the next one to three years to eliminate any barriers that have been identified in the employment systems review. Systemic discrimination is usually hidden in the way employment systems work. Employment barriers are located in the almost invisible and seemingly neutral practices entrenched "in the way we do things around here." As a result, formal and informal employment policies and practices may unintentionally exclude people for reasons that are unrelated to the job or to ability. Systemic discrimination creates employment barriers, a major cause of the underrepresentation of designated groups in organizations or in specific occupations.[60] Employers are obligated

to remove systemic barriers in all aspects of employment: staffing; pay and benefits; job evaluation; working conditions and employee relations; training and development; and workplace safety and health.

Barriers that designated group members could be faced with are: attitudinal barriers in terms of bias and stereotypes; credential barriers where foreign credentials are undervalued; cultural barriers; employment experience barriers; information barriers; physical barriers marked by inaccessibility to buildings and workstation design and tools that cannot be used by disabled persons; and social barriers that make balancing the needs of family and work difficult. Brock University has made a concerted effort to change the attitudes of how persons with disabilities are perceived. They have embarked on a poster campaign, highlighting various disabilities of students and faculty to gain awareness.

- A timetable for implementation.
  - Short-term numerical goals. The plan must contain short-term numerical goals for the hiring and promotion of designated group members. The purpose of the goals must be to increase the representation of designated group members in each occupational group in the employer's workforce where underrepresentation has been identified.
  - Longer-term goals. The plan must contain longer-term goals for increasing the representation of designated groups in the employer's workforce. It must also contain a strategy for achieving these goals. These goals do not have to be numerical, although they may be.

Monitoring the Implementation of the Plan and Reviewing and Revising It as Necessary The employer must make all reasonable efforts to implement the plan. The employer must also monitor the plan to ensure that reasonable progress is being made and it must review and revise its plan, in consultation with, and with the collaboration of, employee representatives.

Progress for Designated Group Members

Annually employers are required to file employment equity reports disclosing their progress to the Canadian Human Rights Commission. The reports are posted on the Commission's website, as well as an EE report card to indicate how well organizations are meeting their plans. Figure 3-7 is an example of an EE report card, rated from A (superior performance) to D (poor performance). In this particular example, it is evident that visible minorities, rated at a C (average to less average performance), are not highly representative in many of the organizations.

The most recent report on the private sector, which includes banking, communications, and transportation, and other sectors such as mining, museums, grain companies, and nuclear power corporations, indicates that over half the available hires went to designated group members in 2004. However, only visible minorities received hires in line with their availability as determined by the 2001 Census. Persons with disabilities continue to benefit the least. In the public service, there were encouraging signs of progress for all groups except visible minorities who continue to be severely underutilized. According the 2005 Annual Employment Equity Report, the following briefly outlines the progress of the designated groups.[61]

Aboriginal Peoples The Employment Equity Act defines Aboriginals as North American Indian or a member of a First Nation, Métis, or Inuit. North American

Figure 3-7 *EE Report Card*

Organization	Total employees	Women	Aboriginal peoples	Persons with disabilities	Visible minorities
Scotiabank	27 098	A	A	C	A
Royal Bank	36 325	A	B	C	A
TD Bank	24 331	A	A	C	A
CIBC	34 245	A	B	C	B
Air Canada	24 633	A	A	C	C
CN Rail	17 012	C	C	C	C
Greyhound Canada	1836	C	A	C	C
AT&T Canada	4477	A	A	C	A
Bell Canada	27 191	A	B	D	C
Canada Post	56 468	A	A	C	A
CBC	6620	A	A	C	C
CHUM Limited	1898	A	C	C	D
FedEx Canada	4503	A	B	C	A
Purolator Courier	12 184	C	A	C	A
Canadian Museum of Civilization	394	A	A	D	A

Source: "2005 Annual Employment Equity Report," Canadian Human Rights Commission, May 3, 2006. Reproduced with the permission of the Minister of Public Works and Government Services Canada, 2006.

Aboriginal peoples
Defined by the Employment Equity Act as a North American Indian or a member of a First Nation, Métis, or Inuit. North American Indians or members of a First Nation include status, treaty, or registered Indians, as well as non-status and non-registered Indians

Indians or members of a First Nation include status, treaty, or registered Indians, as well as non-status and non-registered Indians. In the private sector, **Aboriginal peoples** have increased their share of jobs from 1.3 percent in 2003 to 1.7 percent in 2004. However, their share of jobs is still lower than the 2.6 percent availability that was determined by the 2001 Census.

Aboriginals have greater representation in the public sector where their share of jobs has increased every year since 1997 from 2.7 percent to 4.2 percent in March 2005. Aboriginals' share of hires was greater than the benchmarks established by the census in all occupational categories with the exception of the executive category where they received 1.7 percent. Although the Department of Indian Affairs and Northern Development (DIAND) employs 17.2 percent of Aboriginal employees in the federal public service, without the inclusion of the DIAND, the representation of Aboriginals is 3.5 percent, which is still higher than the public service availability of 2.5 percent.

Persons with disabilities
Defined by the Employment Equity Act as persons who have a long-term or recurring physical, mental, sensory, psychiatric, or learning implement.

Persons with Disabilities **"Persons with disabilities"** are defined by the Employment Equity Act as persons who have a long-term or recurring physical, mental, sensory, psychiatric or learning implement. The persons have to either "consider themselves to be disadvantaged in employment by reason of that impairment" or "believe that an employer or potential employer is likely to consider them to be disadvantaged in employment by reason of that impairment." Persons with disabilities also include disadvantaged employees who have been accommodated in their current job or workplace. Approximately one in eight Canadians live with disabilities.

Of the four designated groups, persons with disabilities have benefited the least from employment equity. The group's representation in all private sectors is consistently lower than the 2001 Census availability of 5.3 percent. Their representation has increased slightly from 2.3 percent in 1997 to 2.5 percent in 2004. There have been improvements made in the banking sector where their traditionally low representation increased from 2.2 percent in 2003 to 2.8 percent in 2004.

In the public sector, the presence of persons with disabilities has increased each year from 3.9 percent in 1997 to 5.8 percent in 2005, which is higher than the public service availability of 3.6 percent. In the executive category, persons with disabilities occupied only 5.5 percent of the available positions. From 2000 to 2004, persons with disabilities only received 3.1 percent of all hires, which suggests that the rise in representation may be due to an increase in self-identification instead of hires.

Visible minorities Persons (other than Aboriginal peoples) who are non-Caucasian in race or non-White in colour.

Members of Visible Minorities The Employment Equity Act defines "members of **visible minorities**" as persons (other than Aboriginal peoples) who are non-Caucasian in race or non-White in colour. This designated group's share of jobs in the private sector has increased from 9.7 percent in 1997 to 13.3 percent in 2004, which is higher than the 2001 Census availability of 12.6 percent. The percentage of hires in 2004 was 14.2 percent and has been higher than availability since 1997. For senior management positions, there has been an increase in the group's share of positions from 2.8 percent in 1997 to 4.4 percent in 2004. However, the availability for this category is 8.2 percent. Visible minorities are best represented in the banking sector where their share of jobs grew from 15.0 percent in 1997 to 21.8 percent in 2004. This designated group holds 7.4 percent of all positions in senior management (up from 4.3 percent in 1997), 15.4 percent in middle management (9.3 percent in 1997), and 24.9 percent of all professional occupations (18.3 percent in 1997).

In public service, the overall representation of visible minorities increased from 7.8 percent in 2003 to 8.1 percent in 2004. However, this share is still lower than the public service availability figure of 10.4 percent. In the executive category, the visible minorities' share of hires fell from 13.3 percent in 2003 to 6.7 percent in 2004. Only 15 of the 73 federal departments were able to meet the 10.4 percent benchmark given for visible minorities in the public service.

Women In the last couple of years, women have managed to make gains in the private sector, particularly in senior management roles. Women held 43.4 percent of all jobs in 2004, down slightly from the 44.6 percent in 1997, and below the overall census availability for the private sector of 47.3 percent. Their share of senior management positions increased to 20.9 percent from 14.8 percent in 1997, but remains lower than the availability of 25.1 percent for these jobs. Women continue to hold most of the jobs in the banking sector, mainly because of the large number of clerical jobs. Their representation dropped slightly from 73.6 percent to 69.6 percent between 1997 and 2004.

In the public sector, women's share of jobs was 53.5 percent in 2004, which is consistent with the census availability of 52.2 percent. Women's share of positions in the executive category has increased from 25.1 percent in 1997 to 37.2 percent in 2004. Their presence in the scientific and professional category has also increased from 32.2 percent to 42.3 percent since 1997. Three out of ten women work in the administrative support category.

Women do have a greater share of part-time and temporary work than men. In 2004, 23.4 percent of women and 10.8 percent of men held part-time and temporary work positions. Women with disabilities and visible minority women did hold more part-time and temporary jobs than men in 2004 but it was most significant among Aboriginal women who held 25.7 percent of these types of jobs.

Glass ceiling
Discriminatory practices that have prevented women and other protected-class members from advancing to executive-level jobs.

Glass Ceiling For years, women's groups have alleged that women in workplaces encounter a **glass ceiling,** which refers to discriminatory practices that have prevented women and other designated group members from advancing to executive-level jobs. Women in Canada are making some progress. There has also been a long-term increase in the share of women employed in managerial positions. In 2004, 37 percent of all those employed in managerial positions were women, up from 30 percent in 1987. However, while these figures have increased, most of the increases incurred between 1987 and 1996, but has declined somewhat since 1996.[62] This success is also short-lived since among managers, women tend to be better represented in lower-level positions as opposed to those at more senior levels.

Nevertheless, women held only 14.4 percent of the highest-ranking executive management jobs in Fortune 500 companies in Canada and 14.7 percent in the U.S.[63] In another global study conducted by Corporate Women Directors International (CWDI) that looked at Global 200 companies, they reported that U.S. women held 17.5 percent of the highest ranking-executive positions, compared to 9.1 percent for Canada, 0.7 percent for Japan, 1.8 percent for Italy, 12.5 percent for the U.K., 10.3 percent for Germany, and 7.2 percent for France.[64]

LOGGING ON...

Catalyst Organization
This nonprofit research and advisory organization is dedicated to advancing women in business.
www.catalystwomen.org

Glass walls/glass elevators
Practice of advancing women to senior management in positions that pay less compared to other jobs.

"Glass Walls" and "Glass Elevators" A related problem is that women have tended to advance to senior management in a limited number of support or staff areas, such as HR and corporate communications. Because executive jobs in these "supporting" areas tend to pay less than jobs in sales, marketing, operations, or finance, the overall impact is to reduce women's career progression and income. Limits that keep women from progressing only in certain fields have been referred to as **"glass walls"** or **"glass elevators."**

"Breaking the Glass" A number of employers have recognized that "breaking the glass," whether ceilings, walls, or elevators, is good business for all designated group members. The HR Perspective shows the results of a study on both. Some of the most common means used to "break the glass" are as follows:

- Establishing formal mentoring programs for women and members of designated group members.
- Providing opportunities for career rotation into operations, marketing, and sales for individuals who have shown talent in accounting, human resources, and other areas.
- Increasing the memberships of top management and boards of directors to include women and individuals of colour.[65]
- Establishing clear goals for retention and progression of designated group members and holding managers accountable for achieving these goals.
- Allowing for alternative work arrangements for employees, particularly those balancing work/family responsibilities.

Debate on Employment Equity

Reverse discrimination
When a person is denied an opportunity because of preferences given to designated group members who may be less qualified.

Supporters offer many reasons why employment equity is important, while opponents argue firmly against it. When employment equity was first introduced in 1986, there was a backlash from White males, as well as from some of the designated group members. White males felt that EE promoted **reverse discrimination,** while some designated group members wanted to earn their promotions on their own merit. Many designated group members are also concerned that others will view their promotions and hires as something that was given to them rather than being earned.

The incident discussed earlier where the Department of Public Works announced that they would not hire White males without written permission, has only added to the "backlash" effect and actually impinges on the intent of EE. The point of EE is to ensure that equal opportunity in employment is extended to everyone and that the most qualified individual should be hired or promoted into an open position. It is these types of anomalies that lead to a "backlash" effect, and are fortunately rare.

The debate most frequently proposed by both sides is highlighted in the HR Perspective. Readers can examine the points of both sides in the debate and compare them with their personal views of EE. The authors of this text believe that whether one supports or opposes EE, it is important to understand why its supporters believe that it is needed and why its opponents believe it should be discontinued.

Pay Equity

Pay equity
Right to equal pay for work of equal value. The value of the job is based on the levels of skill, effort, responsibility and working conditions involved in doing the work.

Pay equity is the right to equal pay for work of equal value. The value of the job is based on the levels of skill, effort, responsibility, and working conditions involved in doing the work. Equal pay for work of equal value is not a new idea. The United Nations Convention on the "Elimination of All Forms of Discrimination Against Women" addresses this issue, as does the International Labour Organization Convention 100 on Equal Remuneration. Canada ratified Convention 100 in 1972 and currently there are laws addressing equal pay in every jurisdiction in Canada. Despite ratified conventions, pay inequities for females continue to exist.

Pay equity legislation was enacted in Canada in 1987 to address the historical wage gap that exists between men and women. The current wage gap between women and men is reported to be about 71 percent.[66] That number widens when race and ethnic background are considered. Pay equity is governed by the Canadian Human Rights Act and the Equal Wages Guideline. The Pay Equity Act requires that jobs be evaluated and work mostly or traditionally performed by women be compared to work mostly or traditionally performed by men. If jobs are of comparable value, then female jobs must be paid at least the same as male jobs. For example, librarian, child care worker, nurse, or administrative assistant are jobs held mostly or traditionally performed by women. Truck driver, firefighter, longshoreman, or shipper/receiver are examples of jobs held mostly or traditionally performed by men.

There are three important, but different concepts that explain pay equity. They are:

- Equal Pay for Equal Work—address the more overt form of discrimination in wages on the basis of gender. It involves direct comparison of jobs occupied by the opposite genders where the job is the same or basically the same.
- Equal Pay for Work of Equal Value—provides for reducing the wage gap by comparing jobs of a different nature that are considered "male" or "female" jobs.
- Pay Equity Laws—refers to legislated programs that aim to achieve equity in pay in an organized manner. Pay equity laws are most often proactive in that they don't require a complaint to be filed in order to achieve their goal. They use specific targets and deadlines and the collective bargaining process to achieve their aims.

Provisions on equal pay are found in three types of laws: human rights legislation, employment standards legislation, and pay equity legislation. Canada's 13 jurisdictions provide for some type of equal pay in their human rights legislation although it

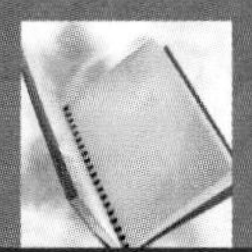

HR *Perspective*

Employment Equity Is Still Needed

1. Employment equity is needed to overcome past injustices or to eliminate the effects of those injustices. Proponents of employment equity believe that it is necessary because women and visible minorities historically have been subjected to unfair and illegal employment treatment by being relegated to lower positions (such as clerical and low-paying jobs), being discriminated against for promotions, and being disciplined more often. Without employment equity, the inequities will continue to exist for individuals who are not White males.
2. Employment equity creates more equality for all persons, even if temporary injustice to some individuals may result. White males, in particular, may be disadvantaged temporarily in order for employment equity to create broader opportunities for all. Proponents argue for programs to enable women, visible minorities, Aboriginal peoples, and persons with disabilities to be competitive with White males. Otherwise, they will never "catch up" and have appropriate opportunities.
3. Raising the employment level of designated group members will benefit Canada in the long run. As employment assists people in these groups, it addresses socioeconomic disparities. Without employment equity, proponents argue that many in Canadian will be permanently economically disadvantaged. When economic levels are low, other social ills proliferate, such as crime, drug use, and disparities in educational opportunities.
4. Properly used, employment equity does not discriminate against White males. An employment equity plan should include a deadline for accomplishing long-term goals, but in the short term, case by case, individuals must meet the basic qualifications for jobs. Once all the criteria for jobs are established, *designated group members* should be chosen, only if they are the most qualified or all things are equal between the candidates. Then, those not selected are discriminated against only in the sense that they did not get the jobs.
5. Goals indicate progress needed, not quotas. The proponents of employment equity stress that employment equity involves *goals,* not *quotas.* The difference is that quotas are specific, required numbers, whereas goals are targets for "good faith" efforts to ensure that members of protected classes truly are given consideration in employment-related decisions.

Employment Equity Is No Longer Needed

1. Employment equity penalizes individuals (White males) even though they have not been guilty of practising discrimination. Opponents argue that employment equity is unfair to "innocent victims"—White males. These individuals had nothing to do with past discrimination or disparate impact, and were not even present at the time those occurred. Thus, opponents of employment equity wonder why these individuals should have to pay for the remediation of past discriminatory actions.
2. Creating preferences of certain groups results in reverse discrimination. Those opposed to employment equity believe that discriminating *for* someone means discriminating *against* someone else. If equality is the ultimate aim, then it is wrong to discriminate for or against anyone on any basis other than the knowledge, skills, and abilities needed to perform a job. Thus, discrimination in reverse is counter to creating a truly equal society.
3. Employment equity results in greater polarization and separatism along gender and racial lines. The opponents of employment equity believe that it establishes two groups: (1) designated group members, and (2) White males. For any job, a person will clearly fall into one group or the other. Thus, employment equity affects White males negatively because of their gender or other inherent characteristics. Consequently, they become bitter against designated group members, and their bitterness leads to greater racism, prejudice, and societal conflicts.
4. Employment equity stigmatizes those it is designed to help. Because employment equity is viewed by some people as placing unqualified members from designated members in jobs, it reinforces the belief held by some persons that designated group members would not have succeeded on their own efforts. This belief leads to the conclusion that designated group members in responsible positions are there only because of who they are, not because of what they can do and have done. Additionally, when members of designated groups perform poorly in jobs because they do not have the knowledge, skills, and abilities needed, the result is to reinforce gender or racial/ethnic stereotypes.
5. Goals become quotas by forcing employers to "play by the numbers." Opponents of employment equity state that regardless of the language used, when goals or targets are set, they become quotas to be met. If they are not met, employers are subjected to legal actions and condemnation.

1. What perspective do you support? The class should be broken into two groups in order to debate the position that "employment equity is needed to provide equal employment opportunities to designated group members."
2. Are White males disadvantaged by this process? Why or why not?

may only refer generally to job discrimination rather than specifically to equity in wages. In six jurisdictions, there are equality of pay provisions under the employment standards law and six have pay equity laws. Most jurisdictions have more than one law that deals with equal pay.

Pay equity laws provide a systematic and mandatory approach to eliminating systematic discrimination in wages in female-dominated occupations compared to male-dominated occupations. Some of these laws apply to both the public and private sector, while in some jurisdictions they apply only to the public sector. What it fails to address, however, is the undervaluation of jobs performed by other designated group members.

Effective job evaluation methods are required to appropriately evaluate the value of the jobs based on the four factors: skill, effort, responsibility, and working conditions. Chapter 10 provides further explanation on pay equity and job evaluation.

Managing Diversity

7 As the foregoing examples have shown, the Canadian workforce has become quite diverse, and employment equity legislation has encouraged and protected that diversity. Figure 3-8 shows the tangible indicators of diversity that employers must consider.

By 2017, more than half of the people living in Toronto and Vancouver will likely be members of a visible minority. More than half of Canada's South Asians and about 40 percent of Canada's Chinese will be living in Toronto. Nearly one-half will be Chinese. The visible minority population of Montreal would continue to be quite different than that of Toronto or Vancouver because of the higher proportion of Blacks and Arabs. By 2017, Blacks could represent 27 percent of Montreal's visible minority population and Arabs 19 percent.[67]

Figure 3-8 *Indicators of Diversity*

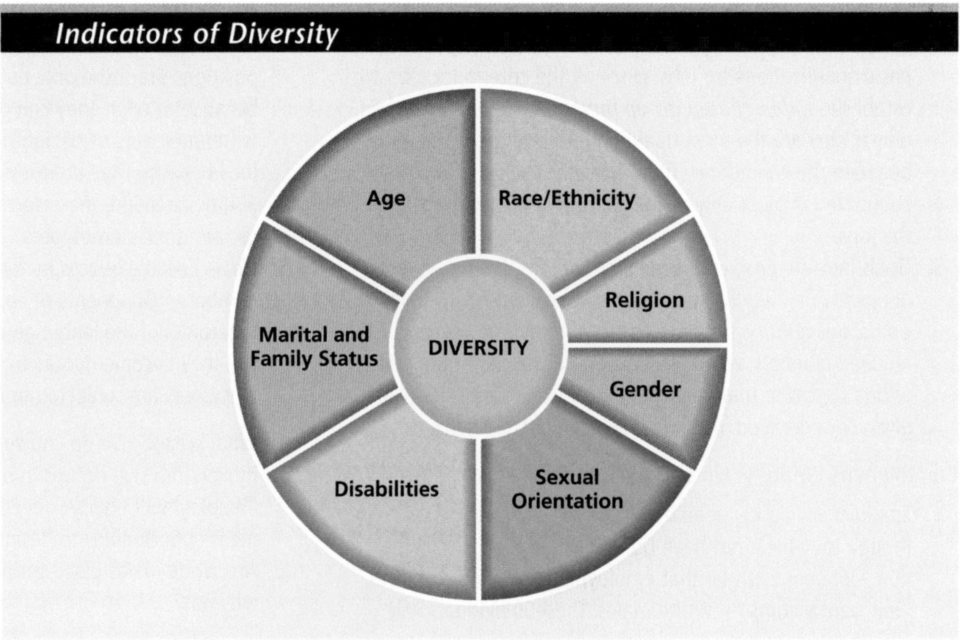

With 47 percent of the population reporting ethnic origins other than Canadian, British, or French and more than 200 different ethnic origins reported in the 2001 Census, Canada is one of the most ethnically and linguistically diverse countries in the world. A recent study suggested that when Canada celebrates its 150th anniversary in 2017, one out of five people (between 19 percent and 23 percent of the population) could be a member of a visible minority.[68] These increases in minority proportions suggest that in some cases, the company without a diversity plan may not have sufficient employees.[69] Many organizations have already begun to deal with the diversity challenge, but others have yet to begin.[70]

Different organizations approach the management of diversity from several perspectives. As Figure 3-9 shows, the continuum can run from resistance to creation of an inclusive diversity culture. The increasing diversity of the available workforce, combined with growing shortages of workers in many occupations and industries, has forced more employers to recognize that diversity must be managed.

Diversity: The Business Case

Diversity can be justified on the basis of social justice, but does it make business sense? The answer is mixed. The "business case" for diversity can be argued based on the following points:

- Diversity allows new talent and new ideas from employees of different backgrounds.
- Diversity helps recruiting and retention, as people tend to prefer to work with others "like" themselves.

Figure 3-9 *Various Approaches to Diversity and Their Results*

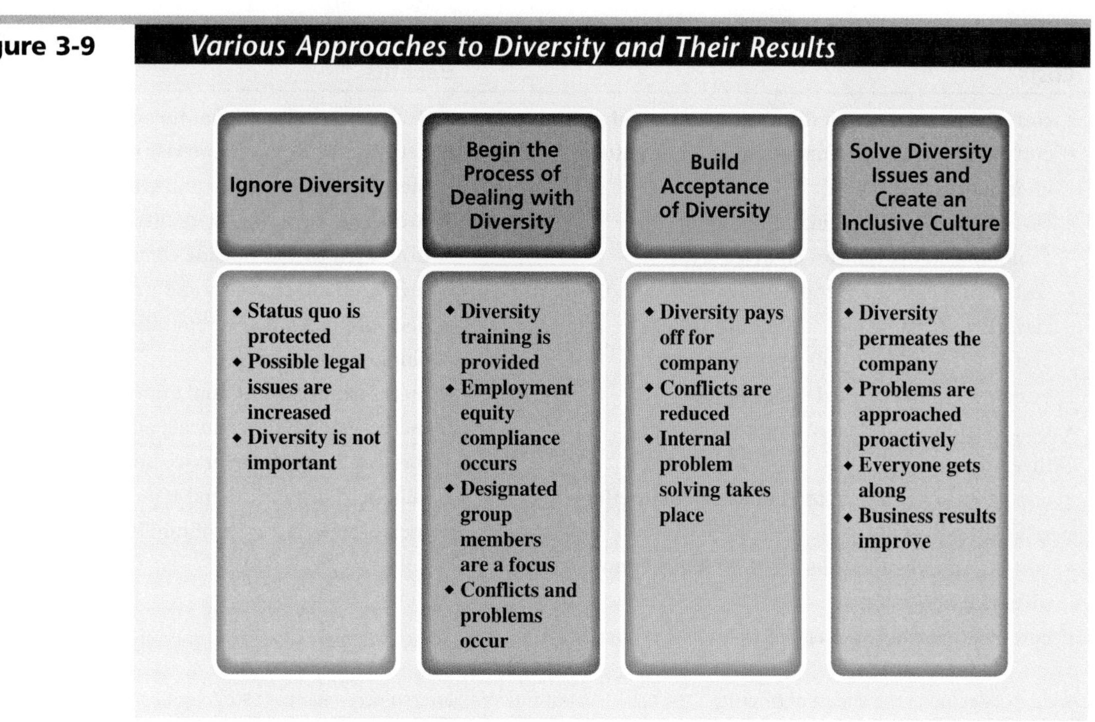

Ignore Diversity
Begin the Process of Dealing with Diversity
Build Acceptance of Diversity
Solve Diversity Issues and Create an Inclusive Culture
• Status quo is protected
• Possible legal issues are increased
• Diversity is not important
• Diversity training is provided
• Employment equity compliance occurs
• Designated group members are a focus
• Conflicts and problems occur
• Diversity pays off for company
• Conflicts are reduced
• Internal problem solving takes place
• Diversity permeates the company
• Problems are approached proactively
• Everyone gets along
• Business results improve

- Diversity allows for an increase of market share, as customers tend to prefer to buy from people of the same race or ethnic background.
- Diversity leads to lower costs because there may be fewer lawsuits.

Many "experts" have significant interests in diversity efforts.[71] It should be noted that an estimated $8-billion industry in North America has developed around diversity: consultants, diversity officers, scorecards, benchmarks, best practices, training, and conferences to deal with it.[72] Whether or not the money spent by employers is producing results has not been clearly documented. Figure 3-10 highlights costs and benefits of instituting a diversity management system.

Diversity Management Programs and Activities

A wide variety of programs and activities have been used in organizations as part of diversity management efforts. Figure 3-11 shows common components of diversity management efforts. For diversity to succeed, the most crucial component is seeing it as a commitment throughout the organization, beginning with top management. Diversity results must be measured, and management accountability for achieving these results must be emphasized and rewarded. Once management accountability for diversity results has been established, then a number of different activities can be implemented as part of a diversity management program, including diversity training.

LOGGING ON...

Diversity at Work
This site provides news, resources, and other commentary on the role of diversity in corporations.
www.diversityatwork.com/sponsorship.html

Diversity Training

There are a number of different goals for traditional diversity training. One prevalent goal is to minimize discrimination and harassment lawsuits. Other goals focus on improving acceptance and understanding of people with different backgrounds, experiences, capabilities, and lifestyles.

Figure 3-10 *Selected Costs and Benefits of Instituting a Diversity Management System*

Costs	Benefits
• cost of time to establish diversity policies and procedures • cost of developing and maintaining an inventory of organizational skills • cost of developing and maintaining internal communications vehicles on diversity • cost of developing appropriate evaluation and reward systems • cost of executing the policies, procedures, evaluations, and reward systems • cost of training and education to entrench diversity values • cost of image building and public relations efforts related to diversity • cost of expanded benefits systems that acknowledge diverse needs • cost of preparing supplement to annual report	• decreased dysfunctional turnover cost • decreased cost of absenteeism • increased productivity and efficiency of employees • decreased cost of poor quality goods and services • decreased cost of outside consultants • increased effectiveness and productivity of teams • decrease in legal and reputation costs of diversity-related employee grievances • increased organizational innovation • increased employee morale and job satisfaction • increased customer service and satisfaction • enhanced organizational reputation • increased long-run profitability and financial health

Source: "Measuring the Impact of Diversity," The Canadian Institute of Chartered Accountants, 1996, Toronto, Canada. Used by permission.

Figure 3-11 *Common Diversity Management Components*

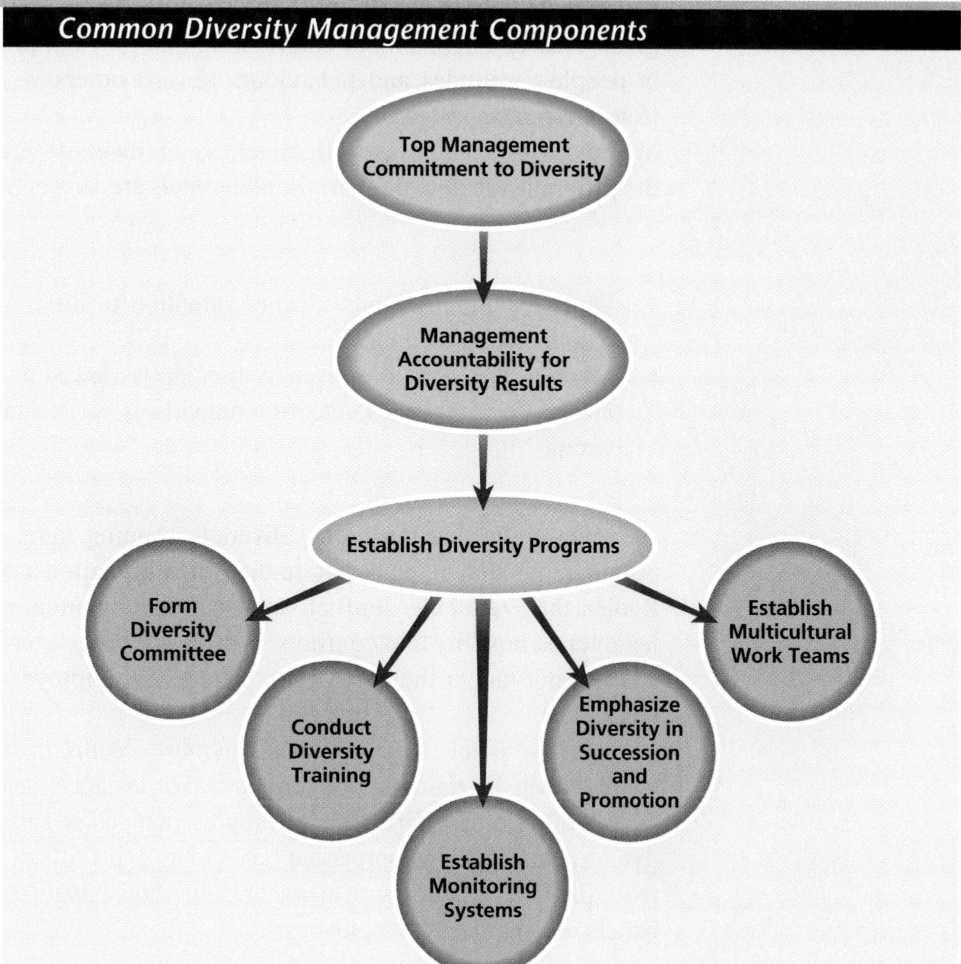

Components of Traditional Diversity Training Approaches to diversity training vary, but often include at least three components. *Legal awareness* is the first and most common component. Here, the training focuses on the legal implications of discrimination. A limited approach to diversity training stops with these legal "do's and don'ts."

By introducing *cultural awareness,* employers hope to build greater understanding of the differences among people. Cultural awareness training helps all participants to see and accept the differences in people with widely varying cultural backgrounds.

The third component of diversity training—*sensitivity training*—is more difficult. The aim here is to "sensitize" people to the differences among them and how their words and behaviours are seen by others. Some diversity training includes exercises containing examples of harassment and other behaviours.

Effects of Diversity Training The effects of diversity training are viewed as mixed by both organizations and participants. Relatively few studies have been done on the effectiveness of diversity training expenditures, other than asking participants how they felt about the training. There is some concern that the programs may be interesting or entertaining, but may not produce longer-term changes in people's attitudes and behaviours toward others with characteristics different from their own.

Mixed reviews about the effectiveness of diversity training suggest that either the programs or how they are implemented are suspect. Two common complaints are:

- Diversity training tends to draw attention to differences, building walls rather than breaking them down.
- Much of the content in diversity training is viewed as "politically correct," which means that it blames majority individuals, particularly White males, for past wrongs.

Some argue that traditional diversity training more often than not has failed, pointing out that it does not reduce discrimination and harassment complaints. Rather than reducing conflict, in a number of situations, diversity training has heightened hostility and conflicts.[73] In some firms, it has produced divisive effects, and has not taught the behaviours needed for employees to get along in a diverse workplace.

This last point, focusing on behaviours, seems to hold the most promise for making diversity training more effective. For instance, dealing with cultural diversity as part of training efforts for sales representatives and managers has produced positive results. Teaching appropriate behaviours and skills in relationships with others is more likely to produce satisfactory results rather than focusing just on attitudes and beliefs among diverse employees.

Backlash Against Diversity Efforts

The negative consequences of diversity training manifest themselves more broadly in a backlash against diversity efforts. This backlash takes two main forms. First, and somewhat surprisingly, the individuals in designated groups, such as women and visible minorities, sometimes see the diversity efforts as inadequate and nothing but "corporate public relations." Thus, it appears that by establishing diversity programs, employers are raising the expectation levels of designated group members, but the programs are not meeting the expectations. This failure can result in further disillusionment and more negativity toward the organization by those who would initially appear to benefit the most from such programs.

On the other side, a number of individuals who are not in designated groups, primarily White males, believe that the emphasis on diversity sets them up as scapegoats for the societal problems created by increasing diversity. Surveys of White males frequently show hostility and anger at diversity efforts. Those programs are widely perceived as benefiting only women and minorities and taking away opportunities for men and non-minorities.[74] This resentment and hostility is usually directed at employment equity programs that employers have instituted.

Managing diversity training, and indeed diversity itself, is more than assuming that "good intentions cannot hurt." Programs must be well thought out and implemented. Diversity is a reality for employers today, and effective diversity management is crucial to HR management.

SUMMARY

1 Canada has two sets of laws that govern the equal employment opportunity for workers in federal or provincial and territorial sectors. The Canada Labour Code and the Canadian Human Rights Act govern the federal sector that is responsible for about 10 percent of the working population. Provincial and territories enforce employment standards legislation and human rights acts. Employment equity and pay equity, occupational health and safety, and labour relations are also integral to the fair employment of workers. The Charter of Rights and Freedoms guarantees certain fundamental rights to workers.

2 Human rights legislation prohibits discrimination on various grounds in relation to employment. Prohibited grounds are race, colour, religion, national or ethnic origin, age, sex, sexual orientation, marital and family status, disability, or conviction for an offence for which a pardon has not been granted. Federally regulated employees are covered under Canadian Human Rights Codes, while provinces and territories each have their own human rights commissions. Two types of discrimination are direct and adverse effect (also referred to as systemic or constructive discrimination). Employers may be allowed to discriminate for justifiable reasons known as BFOR. BFOR must be challenged under the three-part test set out by the Supreme Court of Canada case known as the *Meiorin* case. Employers have a duty to accommodate in certain situations, where undue hardship can be avoided.

3 This section discusses the various prohibited grounds and introduces landmark cases, and more recent decisions, that will become very important in employment decisions. Racism continues to be a problem in employment. Employers are under a very real duty to reasonably accommodate an employee's right to freedom of religion or creed, short of undue hardship. Agism continues to be a problem with many stereotypes associated with older workers. Canada may soon see an end to mandatory retirement with court challenges striking down mandatory retirement policies in the public sector. It is becoming clear that organizations need to be tolerant where issues of sexual orientation arise. Sexual orientation or sex-change issues are being brought to the forefront. Policies that restrict or prohibit nepotism are being successfully challenged, particularly in cases where employees cannot influence one another. Disabilities do not only refer to physical or mental conditions, but also to dependence on alcohol or drugs. Employers need to accommodate where possible. In cases of criminal convictions and pardoned convictions, employers can only ask criminal record related questions if it directly impacts on the job.

4 As more women have entered the workforce, sex/gender issues in equal employment have included discrimination in jobs and careers, as well as sexual harassment in its two forms, quid pro quo and hostile environment. Employers should develop policies on sexual harassment, have identifiable complaint procedures, train all employees on what constitutes sexual harassment, promptly investigate complaints, and take action when sexual harassment is found to have occurred. Consensual relationships that lead to workplace romances can become problematic when there is a manager-subordinate relationship. Organizations need to have policies to address this type of behaviour. Courts have made awards to subordinates because managers hold power over their subordinates. Electronic sexual harassment is becoming more problematic for employers, and for those who are targeted.

5 Employment standards act, labour relations legislation, and occupational health and safety are also important for fair and equitable treatment of employees. The Canada Labour Code governs the workplace for industries within federal jurisdiction, and regulates labour standards and OH&S. Employment standards, labour relations, and OH&S are covered under separate pieces of legislation for provincial and territorial employees. Employment standards are minimum standards required by law and include, for example, hours of work, overtime pay, minimum wages, vacation time and pay, and termination notice and pay. OH&S is concerned with fundamental rights for workers: right to know, right to participate, and right to refuse unsafe work without fear of reprisal. Labour relations govern such things as collective bargaining, applications for bargaining unit, disputes, arbitration, and unfair labour practices. Labour boards are established in each of the provinces.

6 Employment equity addresses discrimination in employment for designated group members: women, visible minorities, Aboriginal peoples, and people with disabilities. These four groups have been undervalued and underutilized in employment. Pay equity addresses the historical wage gap that exists between females and males doing the same or comparable work. The goal of employment equity is to identify and remove barriers to employment that adversely affect designated group members and that leads to disparate impact. Pay equity differs from employment equity because it deals only with wage differences between males and females, and does not consider other aspects of employment. There are many advantages to both programs.

7 Diversity management is concerned with organizational efforts to ensure that all people are valued regardless of their differences. The "business case" for diversity is built on its ability to allow new talent and ideas, aid in employee attraction and retention, allow for an increase in market share, and lead to lower costs. However, results are mixed. Diversity training has had limited success, possibly because it too often has focused on beliefs rather than behaviours.

KEY TERMS

Aboriginal peoples, p. 113
Bona fide occupational requirement (BFOR), p. 89
Canadian Charter of Rights and Freedoms, p. 85
Canadian Human Rights Act, p. 87
Designated group members, p. 107
Direct discrimination, p. 87
Disparate impact, p. 111
Duty to accommodate, p. 90
Glass ceiling, p. 115
Glass walls/glass elevators, p. 115
Hostile environment, p. 102
Nepotism, p. 95
Pay equity, p. 116
Persons with disabilities, p. 113
Provincial and territorial human rights legislation, p. 87
Quid pro quo, p. 102
Reverse discrimination, p. 115
Sexual harassment, p. 100
Systemic (or constructive) discrimination, p. 89
Undue hardship, p. 89
Visible minorities, p. 114

REVIEW AND APPLICATION QUESTIONS

1 What is meant by the "notwithstanding clause" as stated under the Charter of Rights and Freedoms?

2 What is discrimination? Provide examples to explain your response.

3 What is meant by the three-part step? How would the three-part step be used in the Imperial Oil and Toronto Dominion cases?

4 From your own experience or that of someone you know, give specific examples of two types of sexual harassment.

5 Why are employment standards important to employees? Provide examples to explain your answer.

6 As an HR manager you are to implement an employment equity program. Explain what you would do at each of the steps in the process.

7 Explain why you agree or disagree with this statement: "Employers in Canada must learn to adjust to diversity if they are to be effective in the future."

EXPERIENTIAL EXERCISES

1. You need to convince senior management of the usefulness of a company-wide diversity program. How will you define diversity and what arguments can be made for doing so? Be prepared to present a five-minute Power Point presentation to senior management (the class).
2. You are to develop a policy on sexual harassment for presentation to your manager (your professor) at a boardroom meeting (in-class presentation). You are to access the course website at www.mathis.nelson.com and view the document "Developing Policies and Procedures." Using the information provided, develop your policy. It should be one to two pages in length.
3. Your organization is sorely lacking in persons with disabilities. In order to increase your hires for this designated group, you will need to ensure that your organization is appropriately equipped to meet their needs. What are the different types of disabilities that you may need to address, and what accommodation will be required in your workplace? Assume you have no accessibility at the moment. You will need to visit a number of websites to learn more about disabilities and accessibility. What are the costs associated with your remedies assuming that you are hiring a great number of disabled persons.
4. As discussed in the text, the Department of Public Works recently implemented a plan that would ensure only designated group members would be targeted for hire, and that White males would not be eligible for hire without special written permission. What, if any, are the ethical issues associated with such a decision? What would you do if you were the HR manager who was given this mandate?

LEARNING REVIEW

To check your knowledge of the chapter, review the following. (Answers after the case.)

1 The most controversial right for unions has been:
   a. mobility rights
   b. freedom of association
   c. freedom of religion
   d. freedom of speech

2 Adverse effect discrimination is also known as:
   a. direct discrimination
   b. prohibited ground discrimination
   c. systemic discrimination
   d. perpetual discrimination

3 In *Multani v. Commission scolaire Marguerite-Bourgeoys*, one of the reasons that the courts awarded in favour of Multani was because:
   a. undue hardship was required
   b. of the "what if" speculation about what might happen
   c. a kirpan is not really that sharp
   d. a kirpan is not really a weapon in the true sense of the word

4 Sexual harassment in which employment outcomes are linked to the individual granting sexual favours is referred to as:
   a. poisoned environment
   b. hostile environment
   c. disparate outcome
   d. quid pro quo

5 The Canada Labour Code takes responsibility for all the following except:
   a. occupational health and safety
   b. labour standards
   c. federally regulated employees
   d. provincially regulated employees

6 What is the particular barrier to employment and advancement that individuals with disabilities face?

a. lack of experience
b. cost of supervision
c. lack of requisite skills and training
d. attitudes or stereotypes

7 Which of the following is a reason why organizations should be proactively addressing their diversity issues?

a. There is a shortage of workers in many occupations and industries.
b. It is "politically correct."
c. Diversity creates conflict and problems.
d. Doing so is the legal responsibility of organizations.

CASE

BROCK RAISES AWARENESS OF ACCESSIBILITY FOR ALL PEOPLE

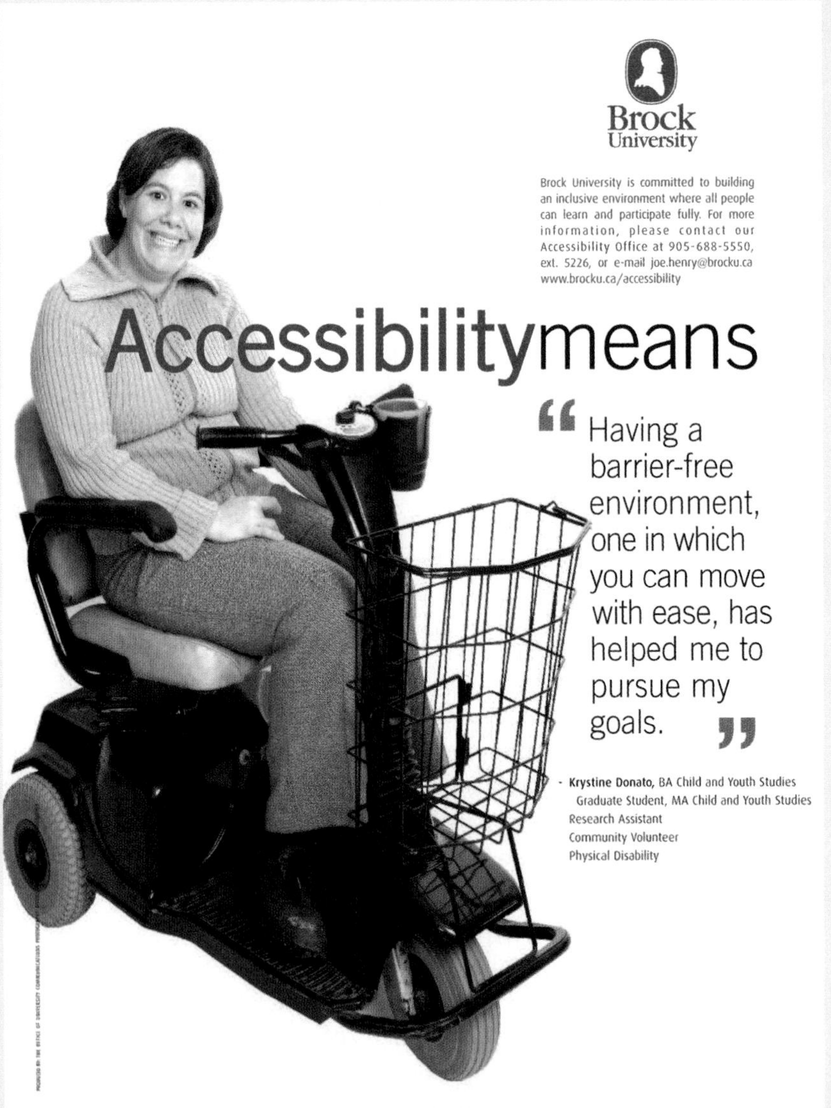

Brock University
Brock University is committed to building an inclusive environment where all people can learn and participate fully. For more information, please contact our Accessibility Office at 905-688-5550, ext. 5226, or e-mail joe.henry@brocku.ca
www.brocku.ca/accessibility
Accessibilitymeans
"Having a barrier-free environment, one in which you can move with ease, has helped me to pursue my goals."
- Krystine Donato, BA Child and Youth Studies
Graduate Student, MA Child and Youth Studies
Research Assistant
Community Volunteer
Physical Disability

Brock University has made a concerted effort to change the attitudes of how persons with disabilities are perceived by embarking on a poster campaign, highlighting various disabilities of students and faculty to gain awareness.

Source: Courtesy of Brock University

Brock University took a unique step of being the first university in Ontario to establish a full-time Accessibility Office. Brock is an example of an organization that, like all other public institutions, has thousands of people entering its premises throughout the year. Many of these people possess disabilities that make it difficult to move about the facility. Others attending classes may have other types of invisible disabilities, e.g., learning disabilities, that may impede on their learning or performing their jobs at work. To deal with these challenges, the university employs an accessibility coordinator, Joe Henry.

To gain recognition of the services offered, Henry has undertaken two important projects. First, he has gathered a group of students and staff members who are featured on a new poster campaign at the university to raise accessibility for all people. As well, Brock is undergoing an accessibility audit of its environment as part of the university's commitment to build an inclusive community in which faculty, staff, students, and visitors can learn and participate fully.

According to Henry, "By sharing the personal stories of people in our community, the poster campaign has been very effective in creating a greater understanding of the meaning of accessibility. The audit is important to our accessibility initiatives as it will evaluate the university's strengths and weaknesses in terms of removing barriers of all kinds. It will identify better practices to ensure that there is equal opportunity for everyone to participate in the academic, cultural and recreational activities of the university."

A committee made up of several departments from around the university work with Henry to ensure the success of meeting legislative and university standards. The committee meets several times over the year. A strategic plan is established at the beginning of each year that highlights goals and action plans. Training is also offered to anyone who requires it, a complaint procedure is in place for those who have accessibility concerns, staff is assigned in areas where student's disability needs can be appropriately addressed, workshops to raise awareness of disabilities, and a host of other initiatives.[75]

Questions

1. As the HR manager, how would you begin development of a diversity effort for your organization?
2. Working in groups of five, you are to conduct a survey of the organizations in your area to determine how many of those organizations are dealing with accessibility in a concerted effort such as Brock? What do these organizations do for accessibility? You can review Brock's website at www.brocku.ca/accessibility to assess what questions to ask of others.

Learning Review Answers: 1. b 2. c 3. b 4. d 5. d 6. d 7. a

CHAPTER

Redefining Jobs and Job Analysis

Learning Objectives

After you have read this chapter, you should be able to:

1 Discuss workflow analysis and business process re-engineering as approaches to organizational work, as well as defining job design and the importance of using teams.

2 Explain how work schedules and telework are affecting jobs and work.

3 Describe job analysis, and the stages in and methods used in the job analysis process.

4 Indicate how job analysis has behavioural aspects.

5 Identify the components of job descriptions and job specifications.

HR *Headline*

Dramatic Changes Occurring in Work and Jobs

Work and jobs in organizations throughout the world are changing dramatically. Globalization and technology are primary drivers. Consider how some jobs have shifted from North America and Europe to China, India, Romania, Mexico, the Philippines, and other lower-wage countries.

Changes in work and jobs are being reported daily on television, on the Internet, and in other media. According to a recent study by RAND Corporation, key factors that will be affecting the jobs in many organizations are the following:[1]

- *Globalization of workers,* whereby much work can be done regardless of time zones and physical locations.
- *Organization of production,* in which firms are decentralizing work and using information technology (IT) to network with employees, contractors, co-workers in various other countries, and "e-lancers" (freelance contributors who use IT).
- *Changes in work and job skill requirements,* where jobs are increasingly falling into two tiers, requiring either highly skilled technical and professional workers or lower-skilled service employees.

The interplay of these factors, along with the demographic shifts occurring in many countries, will dramatically change how work is done, where work is done, and the number of jobs. The aging of the workforce and subsequent retirements of many experienced workers will provide employers with opportunities to restructure or eliminate jobs. Information technology is being incorporated more extensively into jobs, which means more pressures on HR training efforts.

These are just two illustrations of how HR management is being affected by changes in jobs and work. How HR professionals deal with these pressures will significantly affect how HR is viewed by executives and managers.

"That is not in my job description."

—A disgruntled employee

Work
Effort directed toward accomplishing results.

Job
Grouping of tasks, duties, and responsibilities that constitute the total work assignment for employees.

Position
The group of tasks, duties, and responsibilities performed by an individual employee.

One way to visualize an organization is as an entity that takes inputs from the surrounding environment and then, through some kind of "work," turns those inputs into goods or services. **Work** is effort directed toward accomplishing results. The work may be done by humans, machines, or both. But the entire amount of work to be done must be divided into jobs so that it can be coordinated in some logical way. A **job** is a grouping of tasks, duties, and responsibilities that constitutes the total work assignment for employees. Tasks are related activities associated with a job. A **position** is a grouping of tasks, duties, and responsibilities performed by an individual employee. Most jobs in organizations have more than one position. For example, an airline service company can have several positions for the job of mechanic or a car dealership may have 20 positions for the job of salesperson. One might expect all the tasks, duties, and responsibilities for each position to be very similar, however, there may be some subtle differences that will need to be determined. For example, the job of a salesperson could be misleading if it assumed that all salespersons in an organization handle only selling as one of their tasks. A salesperson who works in a smaller region of an organization may have to take on other duties in addition to sales—whereas a salesperson in a larger region with more support may have a narrower scope of duties. These tasks, duties, and responsibilities may change over time, and therefore the job may change. Ideally, when all the jobs in an organization are added together, they should equal the amount of work that the organization needs to have done—no more, no less. The degree to which this ideal is met drives differences in organizational productivity.

Changing Nature of Work and HR Management

1 During the past ten years, domestic increases in organizational productivity in many industries have resulted in significant changes in work and jobs. A focus on productivity has led to replacing employees with technology, international outsourcing of work to lower-wage countries, and more flexibility in how and when work is done.

Jobs that are "routinized," meaning jobs whose work can be divided into step-by-step tasks with little variation daily and weekly, are being affected the most. Routinization occurs in jobs ranging from assembling products on a manufacturing line, to doing repetitive computer programming, to handling simple customer service inquiries, to processing mortgage loan applications. Use of information and communications technologies has allowed the "knowledge" to perform these tasks to be built into computer programs and databases, so that individuals with less training and fewer skills can perform the work by just "following the programs." Jobs and work that cannot be routinized and that require significant communication or managerial capability are less likely to be affected by job losses.[2] Undoubtedly the nature of jobs and work will continue to be affected as the drive for productivity and global competitiveness continue.

As Figure 4-1 indicates, organizational values and strategies linked to customer needs, affect the nature of work, which in turn influences the relationship of jobs, people, and HR management activities. For WestJet, organizational values and strategies are tied to having involved employees working in an enjoyable culture that delivers dependable service at low fares. Thus, WestJet has a high degree of flexibility in how its employees perform the work, even to the point that pilots may help clean planes if the workload demands it. Other airlines, such as Air Canada have higher fares, more service amenities, but employees who have more narrowly defined jobs. The way work is done and jobs are designed and performed vary significantly under the two approaches, and the differences impact the number of jobs and people needed.

Figure 4-1 Influences Affecting Jobs, People, and Related HR Policies

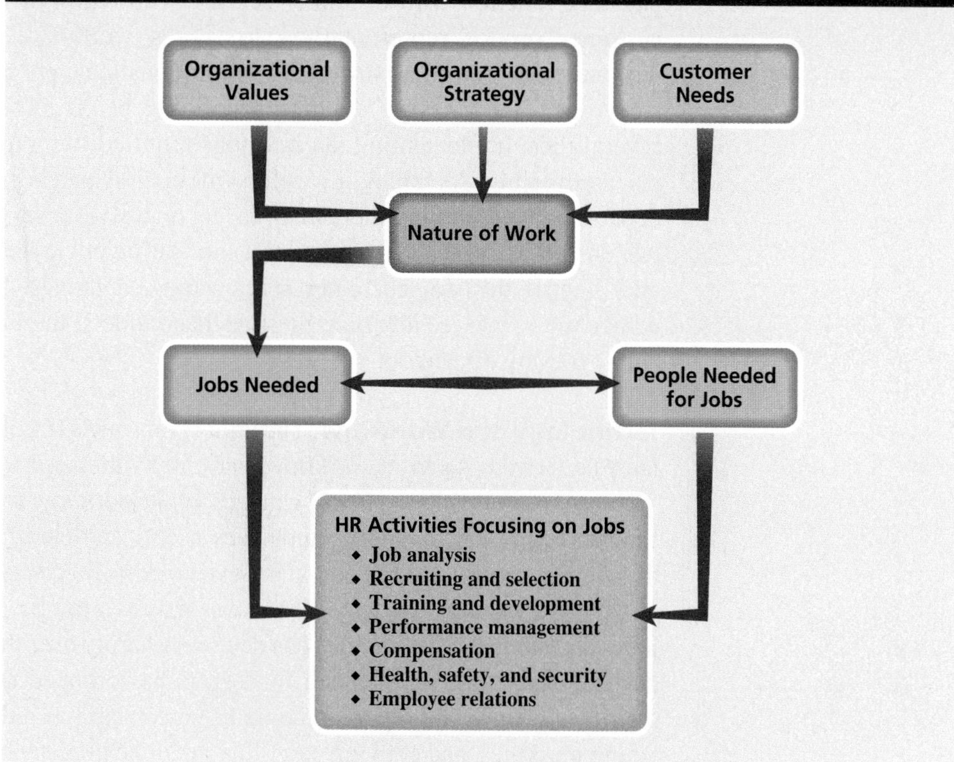

In HR management, the most important activities associated with jobs are:

- *Workflow analysis:* Examining how work flows through the organization, in order to improve operating efficiency
- *Re-engineering:* Improving productivity by changing the jobs themselves
- *Job design:* Dividing up organizational work into jobs in order to utilize employee capabilities effectively
- *Job analysis:* Analyzing what people do in jobs currently
- *Job descriptions and job specifications:* Identifying the tasks, duties, and responsibilities in jobs, and the capabilities needed for people to perform jobs well

Workflow Analysis

Workflow analysis Study of the way work (inputs, activities, and outputs) moves through an organization.

Workflow analysis is the study of the way work moves through an organization. Usually, it begins with an examination of the quantity and quality of the desired and actual *outputs* (goods and services). Then, the *activities* (tasks and jobs) that lead to the outputs are evaluated to see if they are achieving the desired outputs. Finally, the *inputs* (people, material, information, data, equipment, etc.) must be assessed to determine if they make the outputs and activities more efficient and better.

Several years ago, at an electric utility company, if a customer called with a service outage problem, a customer service representative typically took the information and entered it into a database. Then, in the operations department, a dispatcher accessed the database to schedule a line technician to repair the problem. Then, someone else called to tell the customer when the repair would be done. The line technician also received instructions from a supervisor, who got information on workload and locations from the dispatcher. A workflow analysis showed that there were too many steps involving too many different jobs in this process. Therefore, the utility implemented a new customer information system and combined the dispatching function with customer service. The redesign in workflow permitted the customer service representatives to access workload information and schedule the line technicians as part of the initial consumer phone calls, except in unusual situations. The redesign required redefining tasks, duties, and responsibilities of several jobs. Implementing the new jobs required training the customer service representatives in dispatching, as well as moving dispatchers into the customer service department and training them in all facets of customer service. The result was a more responsive workflow for customers, more efficient scheduling of line technicians, and broader jobs for customer service representatives. Ultimately, through retirements and employee attrition, the firm has reduced the number of customer service employees by 20 percent.

Technology and Workflow The utility company example illustrates how technology must be viewed as part of workflow analysis. With the rapid growth of the Internet and Web-based information systems, changes in the workflow are occurring in many organizations. For instance, having employees access and change their benefits information themselves has reduced HR administrative work by 60 percent, according to one survey.[3]

Another example of why workflow analysis may be helpful involves secretarial jobs. The number of secretaries has declined sharply over the last decade as technology has changed. Also, the demand for typists has dropped as more managers compose their own memos and reports on e-mail. Voice mail has reduced the need for someone taking messages, and copying and filing are done in many organizations through office service centres, not by individual secretaries. On the other hand, current office support functions require greater responsibility and entail more coordination and authority.[4] The job title today is more likely to be "administrative coordinator" or "administrative assistant" to reflect these changes, and organizations are doing workflow analysis to make adjustments.

Business Process Re-engineering

Business process re-engineering (BPR) Measures for improving such activities as product development, customer service, and service delivery.

After workflow analysis provides an understanding of how work is being done, re-engineering generates the needed changes in the operations. The purpose of **business process re-engineering (BPR)** is to improve such activities as product development, customer service, and service delivery. BPR consists of three phases:

1. *Re-think:* Examine how the current organization of work and jobs affects customer satisfaction and service.
2. *Re-design:* Analyze how jobs are put together, the workflow, and how results are achieved; then redesign the process as necessary.
3. *Re-tool:* Look at new technologies (equipment, computers, software, etc.) as opportunities to improve productivity, service quality, and customer satisfaction.

In the past, HR has been excluded from BPR in many organizations because the focus of BPR has been in operations areas. However, because of the desire to improve HR efficiency and effectiveness, BPR is increasingly being applied to HR management.[5] Organizations such as CIBC and Nortel have engaged in re-engineering and restructuring their HR departments. Key to successful BPR of HR or other organizational areas is providing effective and continuous communication, doing detailed planning, and training managers on the BPR processes. Without these efforts, the success rates of BPR are low, around 30 percent.[6]

Job Design

Job design
Organizing tasks, duties, and responsibilities into a productive unit of work.

Job design refers to organizing tasks, duties, and responsibilities into a productive unit of work. It addresses the content of jobs and the effect of jobs on employees. Identifying the components of a given job is an integral part of job design. Currently, job design is receiving greater attention for three major reasons:

- Job design can influence *performance* in certain jobs, especially those where employee motivation can make a substantial difference. Lower costs resulting from reduced turnover and absenteeism also are related to the effective design of jobs.
- Job design can affect *job satisfaction.* Because people are more satisfied with certain job configurations than with others, identifying what makes a "good" job becomes critical.
- Job design can affect both *physical* and *mental health.* Problems such as hearing loss, backache, and leg pain sometimes can be traced directly to job design, as can stress, high blood pressure, and heart disease.

Person/job fit
Matching characteristics of people with characteristics of jobs.

Not everyone would enjoy being an HR manager, an engineer, a nurse, or a drill-press operator. But various people like and do well at each of these jobs. The **person/job fit** is a simple but important concept of matching characteristics of people with characteristics of jobs. Figure 4-2 depicts some of the personal factors and job functions that must mesh. If a person does not fit a job, either the person can be changed or replaced, or the job can be altered. In the past, it was much more common to try to make the "round" person fit the "square" job.

But, it is hard to successfully reshape people. By re-designing jobs, the person/job fit may be improved more easily. Improving the person/job fit may affect individual responses to jobs because a job may be motivating to one person but not to someone else. Also, depending on how jobs are designed, they may provide more or less opportunity for employees to satisfy their job-related needs. For example, a sales job may furnish a good opportunity to satisfy social needs, whereas a training assignment may satisfy a need to expand expertise in a specific area. A job that gives little autonomy may not satisfy a need to be creative or innovative.

When jobs are inadequately designed, employees can often feel stressed, which can affect their ability to perform their jobs adequately.

Source: © JupiterImages and its Licensors. All Rights Reserved.

Nature of Job Design

One tactic for designing or re-designing jobs is to simplify the job tasks and responsibilities. Job simplification may be appropriate for jobs that are to be staffed with entry-level employees. However, making jobs too simple may result in boring jobs that appeal to few people, causing high turnover. Several different approaches are useful as part of job design.

Figure 4-2 *Person/Job Fit*

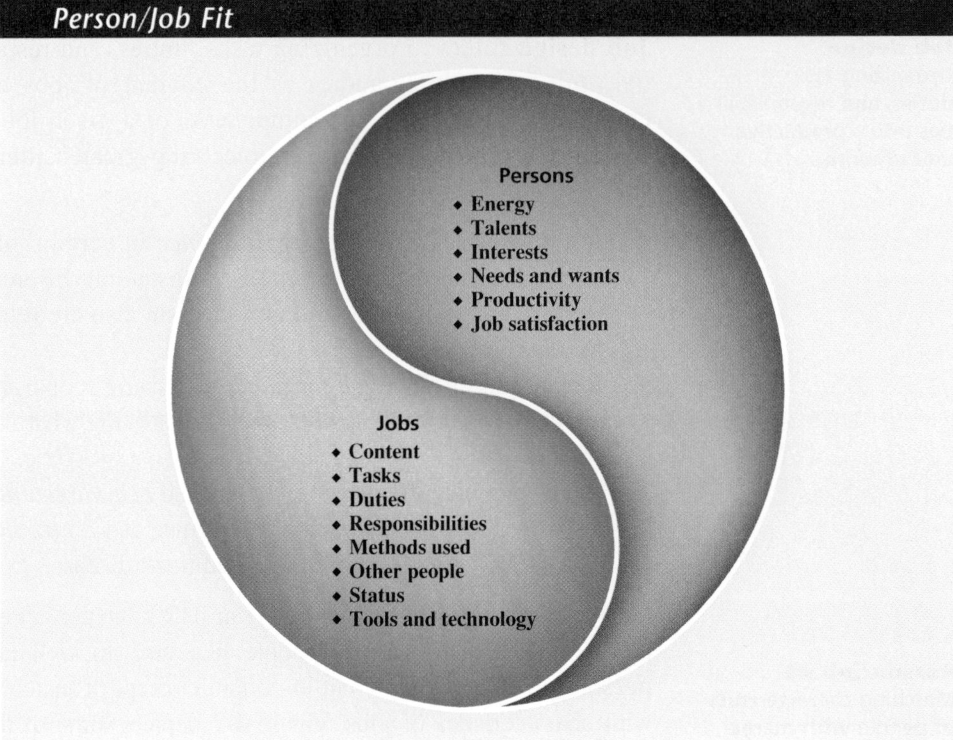

Job enlargement
Broadening the scope of a job by expanding the number of different tasks to be performed.

Job enrichment
Increasing the depth of a job by adding responsibility for planning, organizing, controlling, or evaluating the job.

Job Enlargement and Job Enrichment Attempts to alleviate some of the problems encountered in excessive job simplification fall under the general headings of job enlargement and job enrichment. **Job enlargement** involves broadening the scope of a job by expanding the number of different tasks to be performed. **Job enrichment** is increasing the depth of a job by adding responsibility for planning, organizing, controlling, or evaluating the job. A manager might enrich a job by promoting variety, requiring more skill and responsibility, providing more autonomy, and adding opportunities for personal growth. Giving an employee more responsibility for planning and controlling the tasks to be done also enriches a job. However, simply adding more similar tasks actually does not enrich a job. Some examples of job enrichment are:

- Giving the employee an entire job rather than just a piece of the work
- Giving more freedom and authority so that the employee can perform the job as he or she sees fit
- Increasing the employee's accountability for work by reducing external control
- Expanding assignments so that the employee can learn to do new tasks and develop new areas of expertise
- Giving feedback reports directly to the employee rather than only to management

Job rotation
Process of shifting a person from job to job.

Job Rotation One technique that can break the monotony of an otherwise simple, routine job is **job rotation,** which is the process of shifting a person from job to job. Some argue that job rotation does little in the long run—that although rotating a person from one boring job to another may help somewhat initially, the jobs are still perceived as boring. The advantage of job rotation is that it develops an employee's capabilities for doing several different jobs.

Characteristics of Jobs

A model developed by Hackman and Oldham identifies five important design characteristics of jobs. Figure 4-3 shows that *skill variety, task identity,* and *task significance* affect the meaningfulness of work; *autonomy* stimulates responsibility; and *feedback* provides knowledge of results. Each aspect can make a job better for the jobholder to the degree that each is present.

Skill variety
Extent to which the work requires several different activities for successful completion.

Skill Variety The extent to which the work requires several different activities for successful completion indicates its **skill variety.** For example, lower skill variety exists when an assembly-line worker performs the same two tasks repetitively. The more skills involved, the more meaningful the work becomes. Skill variety is not to be confused with *multi-tasking,* which is doing several tasks at the same time with computers, telephones, personal organizers, and other gadgets. The price of multi-tasking may be never getting away from the job—not a "better" outcome for everyone.

Task identity
Extent to which the job includes a "whole" identifiable unit of work that is carried out from start to finish and that results in a visible outcome.

Task Identity The extent to which the job includes a "whole" identifiable unit of work that is carried out from start to finish and that results in a visible outcome is its **task identity.** For example, in the utility company mentioned previously, now, when a customer calls with a problem, one employee, called a customer care advocate, handles problems from maintenance to repair. As a result, more than 40 percent of customer problems are resolved by one person while the customer is still on the line. Previously fewer than 1 percent of customer problems were resolved immediately because the customer service representative had to complete paperwork and forward it to operations, which then followed a number of separate steps using different people to resolve problems. In the current system, the customer care advocate generally follows the problem from start to finish, solving the whole problem, not just a part of it, which makes the job more meaningful to the employees involved.

Task significance
Impact the job has on other people.

Task Significance The impact the job has on other people indicates its **task significance.** A job is more meaningful if it is important to other people for some reason. For instance, soldiers may experience more fulfillment when defending their country from a real threat than when merely training to stay ready in case a threat arises.

Figure 4-3 *Job Characteristics Model*

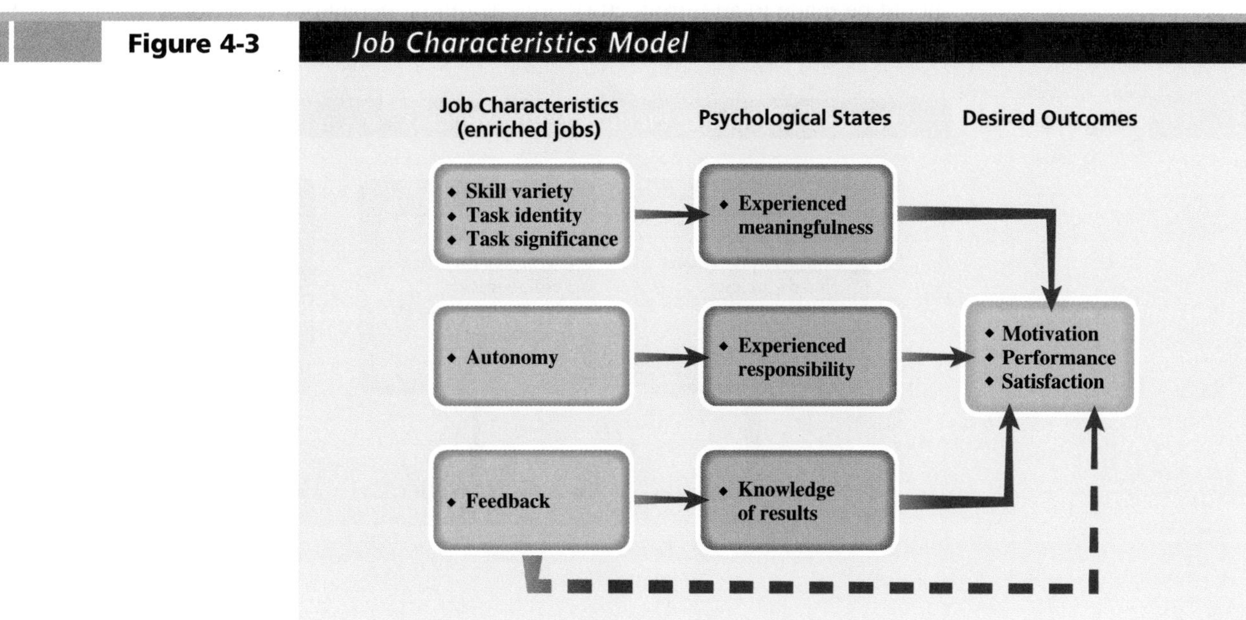

Autonomy
Extent of individual freedom and discretion in the work and its scheduling.

Feedback
Amount of information employees receive about how well or how poorly they have performed.

Autonomy The extent of individual freedom and discretion in the work and its scheduling indicates **autonomy.** More autonomy leads to a greater feeling of personal responsibility for the work.

Feedback The amount of information employees receive about how well or how poorly they have performed is **feedback.** The advantage of feedback is that it helps employees to understand the effectiveness of their performance and contributes to their overall knowledge about the work. At one firm, feedback reports from customers who contact the company with problems are given directly to the employees who handle the customers' complaints, instead of being given only to the department manager.

Consequences of Job Design

Jobs designed to take advantage of these important job characteristics are more likely to be positively received by employees. Job characteristics can help distinguish between "good" and "bad" jobs. Many approaches to enhancing productivity and quality reflect efforts to expand one or more of the job characteristics. Because of the effects of job design on performance, employee satisfaction, health, and other factors, changing the design of some jobs may be beneficial.

Using Teams in Jobs

Typically, a job is thought of as something done by one person. However, where it is appropriate jobs may be designed for teams. In an attempt to make jobs more meaningful and to take advantage of the increased productivity and commitment that can follow such a change, more organizations are assigning jobs to teams of employees instead of individuals. Some firms have gone as far as dropping such terms as *workers* and *employees,* replacing them with *teammates, crew members, associates,* and other titles that emphasize teamwork. There are several types of teams that exist: special-purpose teams, self-directed teams, global virtual teams, and virtual teams. Virtual teams are used by such firms as Hewlett-Packard, IBM, Ford, Toyota, and Johnson & Johnson.[7] Research by the Center for the Study of Work Teams indicates that the success of virtual work teams depends on a number of factors.[8] Some of the key factors are depicted in Figure 4-4. For a more thorough discussion on teams, reference should be made to an introductory organizational behaviour textbook.

Figure 4-4 *Factors Affecting Virtual Team Success*

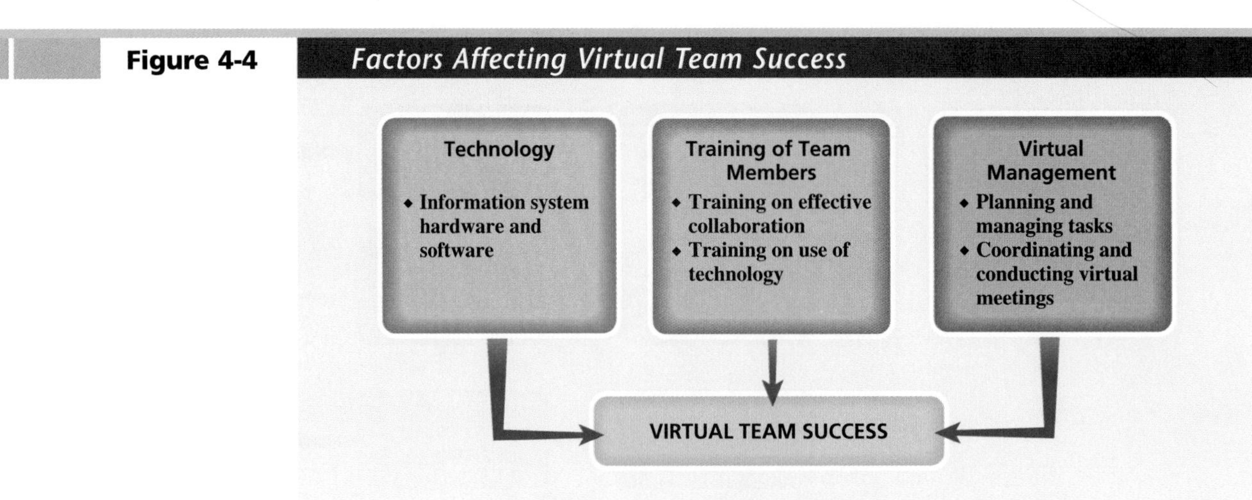

No matter how employees conduct their work, it is difficult to complete work assignments without involvement of other employees. Teams are therefore evident throughout most organizations in some form or another.

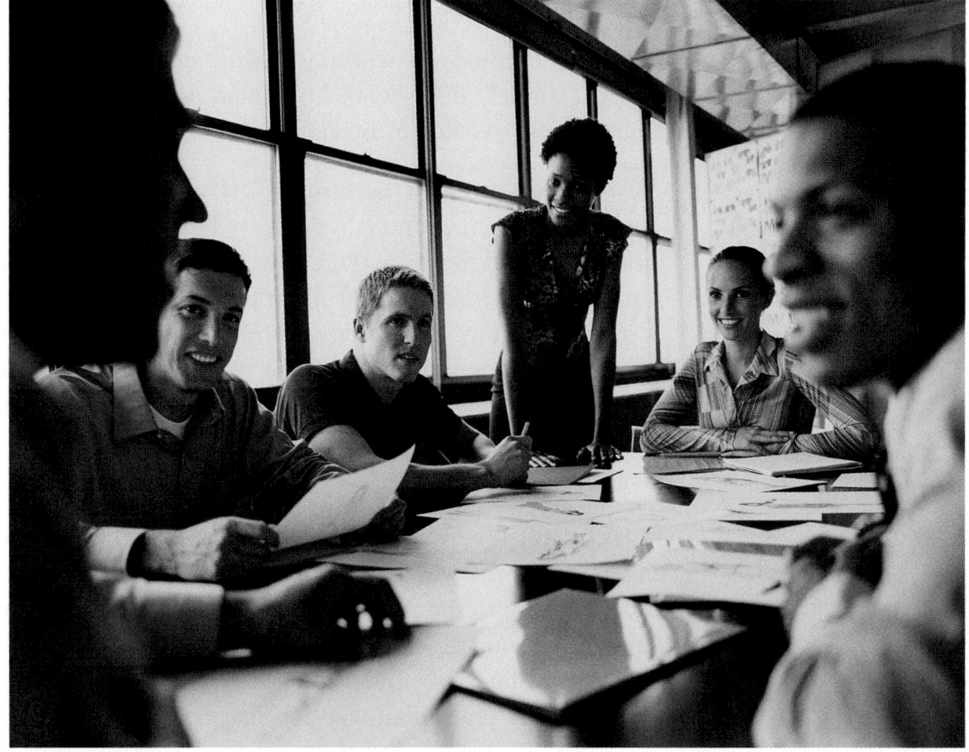

Source: BJ Formento/Digital Vision/Getty Images

Job Design, Work Schedules, and Telework

2 A job consists of the tasks an employee does, the relationships required on the job, the tools the employee works with, and many other elements. Considerations that increasingly affect job design for both employers and employees are the time during which work is scheduled and the location of employees when working.

The pressures of employees' lives, coupled with the demands of their jobs, can lead to emotional imbalances that are collectively labelled *stress*. The main causes of job-related stress appear to be time pressures, fears of losing a job, deadlines, and fragmented work. The increasing use of technology means that many employees are "always on call" and can "burn out" on work. How employees view the demands of work have been identified in several opinion polls conducted by www.workplace.ca, which found the following:[9]

- Two thirds (66 percent) of respondents would work for less pay just to be able to get a break.
- In a poll regarding work/life balance, all respondents rated the importance of work/life balance as being high with a rating of at least 7 out of 10 (10 being extremely important).
- Seventy-one percent of respondents to a poll about stress rated their stress levels as being high.

To respond to stress and other concerns, employers are using different work schedule alternatives, flexible scheduling, and telework.

Work Schedules

The work schedules associated with different jobs vary. Some jobs must be performed during "normal" daily work hours and workdays, and some jobs require working nights, weekends, and extended hours.

Global Work Schedule Differences The number of work hours in a week varies from country to country. For instance, the European Union (EU) has issued the Working Time Directive, which states that employees in EU countries should work a maximum of 48 hours a week. However, EU workers can opt out of the maximum, and over one-third of British workers have such opt-outs.[10] France has a law limiting working hours to 35 hours a week, but because various exceptions are made, the weekly average is lower than 35. Workers in Canada average significantly more work hours than do workers in many other developed countries.[11]

Work Schedule Alternatives The traditional work schedule in Canada, in which employees work eight hours a day, five days a week at the employer's place of operation, is in transition. Throughout many organizations, many different work scheduling arrangements are being used, including the four-day, 40-hour week; the four-day, 32-hour week; the three-day week; shift work and the compressed workweek; flexible scheduling; and job sharing.

Shift Work and the Compressed Workweek *Shift work* is a commonly used work schedule design. Many organizations need 24-hour coverage and therefore schedule three 8-hour shifts each day. Many employers provide some form of additional pay, called a *shift differential,* for working the evening or night shift. Shift work has been found to increase the number of workplace accidents, with employees who work the "graveyard" shift (11 p.m. to 7 a.m.) having 20 percent more accidents and five times as many work-related mistakes.[12] Also, shift work has long been known to cause difficulties for many employees with families. Twelve-hour shifts, which some employees choose, often involve significant life changes. Nevertheless, many employers must have 24-hour, seven-day coverage, so shift work is likely to continue to be an HR concern.

Compressed workweek
Schedule in which a full week's work is accomplished in fewer than five 8-hour days.

One type of shift work is the **compressed workweek,** in which a full week's work is accomplished in fewer than five 8-hour days. Compression simply alters the number of hours an employee works each day, usually resulting in more work hours each day and fewer workdays each week. The use of the compressed workweek illustrates how greater flexibility in work schedules is occurring.

Flextime
Scheduling arrangement in which employees work a set number of hours a day but vary starting and ending times.

Flexible Scheduling Flexible work schedules allow organizations to make better use of workers by matching work demands to work hours. One type of flexible scheduling is **flextime,** in which employees work a set number of hours a day but vary starting and ending times. In another variation, employees work 30 minutes longer Monday through Thursday, take short lunch breaks, and leave work at 1 p.m. or 2 p.m. on Friday. Some firms allow employees to work reduced schedules and receive proportional wages/salaries. Certain levels of hours are worked weekly or monthly.

Flexible scheduling allows management to relax some of the traditional "time clock" control of employees, while still covering workloads. According to a report by HRSDC, more than 30 percent of Canadian workers have said that flextime is available to them.[13]

Job sharing
Scheduling arrangement in which two employees perform the work of one full-time job.

Job Sharing Another alternative used to add flexibility and more work/life balancing is **job sharing,** in which two employees perform the work of one full-time job. For instance, a hospital allows two radiological technicians to fill one job, whereby each individual works every other week. Such arrangements are beneficial for employees who may not want to or be able to work full-time because of family, school, or other reasons. Job sharing also can be effective because each person can substitute for the other when illness, vacation, or other circumstances occur. The key to successful job sharing is that both "job sharers" work effectively together and each is competent in meeting the job requirements.[14]

LOGGING ON...

Innovisions Canada and the Canadian Telework Association
This website gives information about telework in Canada, which promotes the use of telework practices in Canadian organizations.
www.ivc.ca/

Telework

The developments in information and communications technology mean that employees can work anywhere and anytime. As a result, a growing number of employers are allowing employees to work from widely varied locations. Some employees work partly at home and partly at an office, while others share office space with other "office nomads."

Some employees *telecommute,* which means they work via electronic computing and telecommunications equipment. Many Canadian employers have employees who telecommute one or more days a week, and who may work from home, a client's facility, an airport conference room, a work suite in a hotel resort, a business-class seat on an international airline flight, or even a vacation condominium. Telecommuting allows employees to work from home when bad weather or family illness prevents them from coming to office facilities.[15] Canadians are somewhat behind worldwide trends in telecommuting, although it is anticipated that Canada will meet the global averages by 2008. While the trend in Canada is not as widespread, those Canadians who do telework tend to do so for a greater proportion of their working week compared with those teleworking in the United States and parts of Western Europe.[16]

HR Management of Teleworkers A number of HR management issues and employee concerns must be addressed with teleworkers, as Figure 4-5 indicates. Because managers have less direct supervision of teleworkers, there is more self-scheduling by employees. Thus, employees have to be evaluated more on producing

Figure 4-5 *Telework Concerns of Management and Employees*

Management Concerns	Employee Concerns
• Loss of control over staff • Employee perceptions of unequal treatment when only certain employees are permitted to telecommute • Security, especially with information systems • Diminished interaction with staff, and team-building problems • Employees' spending time on non-work-related activities (e.g., child care) • Telecommuters' straying from the culture and values of the organization	• Overworking and failing to create a distinction between work and home • Trouble with self-motivation and time management • Difficulty working among home distractions • Isolation and diminished interaction with colleagues • Negative impact on career development from less interaction with supervisors • Inadequate equipment or technology support

Source: Adapted from: *HR Department Benchmarks and Analysis Survey 2004.* (Washington, DC: Bureau of National Affairs, 2004) 131, 140. To purchase this publication and find out more about other BNA HR solutions visit http://hrcenter.bna.com or call 800-372–1033. Used with permission.

Many employers are offering telework as one of the flexible work options available to employees.

Source: Ryan McVay/Photodisc/Getty Images

results and less on "putting in time."[17] HR must develop policies regarding teleworkers and must train supervisors and managers on how to "lead" employees who may not be physically present much of the time."[18] Technology Transforming HR discusses how one organization is able to use technology to increase flexibility and productivity.

Another concern comes from evidence that telecommuting employees may not advance as quickly as office-based executives, because of an "out-of-sight, out-of-mind" framework of some managers.[19] This is especially a concern for global employees, whose working hours may not be consistent with Canadian working times. For instance, the 16-hour time zone difference between Canada and some Asian countries may make it difficult for global employees to participate in conference calls. Despite these concerns, telework is likely to continue to increase, which may add to employee stress.

Technology Transforming HR

Telework and Technology

With the changing nature of work and an increased demand from employees for more flexibility in work schedules, organizations are finding innovative ways of balancing flexibility with retaining productivity and efficiency targets in order to remain competitive. The following example shows how one organization is using technology to increase flexibility and productivity.

Based in Brampton, Ontario, Nortel Networks, an international information technology company, implemented a telework program called HOMEbase. When HOMEbase was first introduced in 1995 the program had only 230 users. Today, Canadian workers represent about 40 percent of the 20 000 Nortel teleworkers worldwide.

Nortel uses the latest technology to keep teleworkers connected to the organization whether they choose to work at home or the office. With voice over Internet protocol (VoIP) teleworkers can make calls just like they would at the office and a "find me-follow me" feature allows colleagues and customers to reach them no matter where they are working. Instant messaging and other Internet features allow workers to easily set up video and teleconferences with colleagues, while electronic white board and other application sharing programs support team communication and collaboration.

The benefits of the HOMEbase program are significant. Since implementing the program, Nortel has seen a 24-percent improvement in productivity and a savings of $22 million from a decreased need for office space. With 99 percent of teleworkers wanting to stay in the program, employees have also seen the benefits of telework. In response to the success of the HOMEbase program, employee satisfaction increased 10 percent and Nortel has seen a 24-percent reduction in employee turnover.[20]

1. Based on Nortel's experience, do you think that telework can work as well for small organizations? Why or why not?
2. How do you think the increased use of telework will affect the nature of how jobs are designed and performed in organizations?

Nature of Job Analysis

3 Job design attempts to develop jobs that fit effectively into the flow of the organizational work that needs to be done. The more narrow focus of job analysis centres on using a formal system to gather data about what people do in their jobs. This data is used to generate job descriptions and job specifications. An overview of job analysis is depicted in Figure 4-6.

Job analysis Systematic way of gathering and analyzing information about the content, context, and human requirements of jobs.

The most basic building block of HR management, **job analysis,** is a systematic way of gathering and analyzing information about the content, context, and human requirements of jobs. Using job analysis to document HR activities is important because the legal defensibility of an employer's recruiting and selection procedures, performance appraisal system, employee disciplinary actions, and pay practices rests in part on the foundation of job analysis.

Various methods and sources of data can be used to conduct job analyses. The real value of job analysis begins as the information is compiled into job descriptions and job specifications for use in virtually all HR activities. To justify HR actions as job related for human rights matters, accurate details on job requirements are needed. To be effective, HR planning, recruiting, and selection all must be based on job requirements and the capabilities of individuals.[21] Additionally compensation, training, and employee performance appraisals all should be based on the specific needs of the job. Job analysis also is useful in identifying job factors and duties that may contribute to workplace health and safety issues. For instance, one study used job analysis to identify physical demands causing work-related injuries, and the steps to be taken to reduce those injuries.[22] Finally, job analysis plays a key role in employee/labour relations issues.

Figure 4-6 *Job Analysis in Perspective*

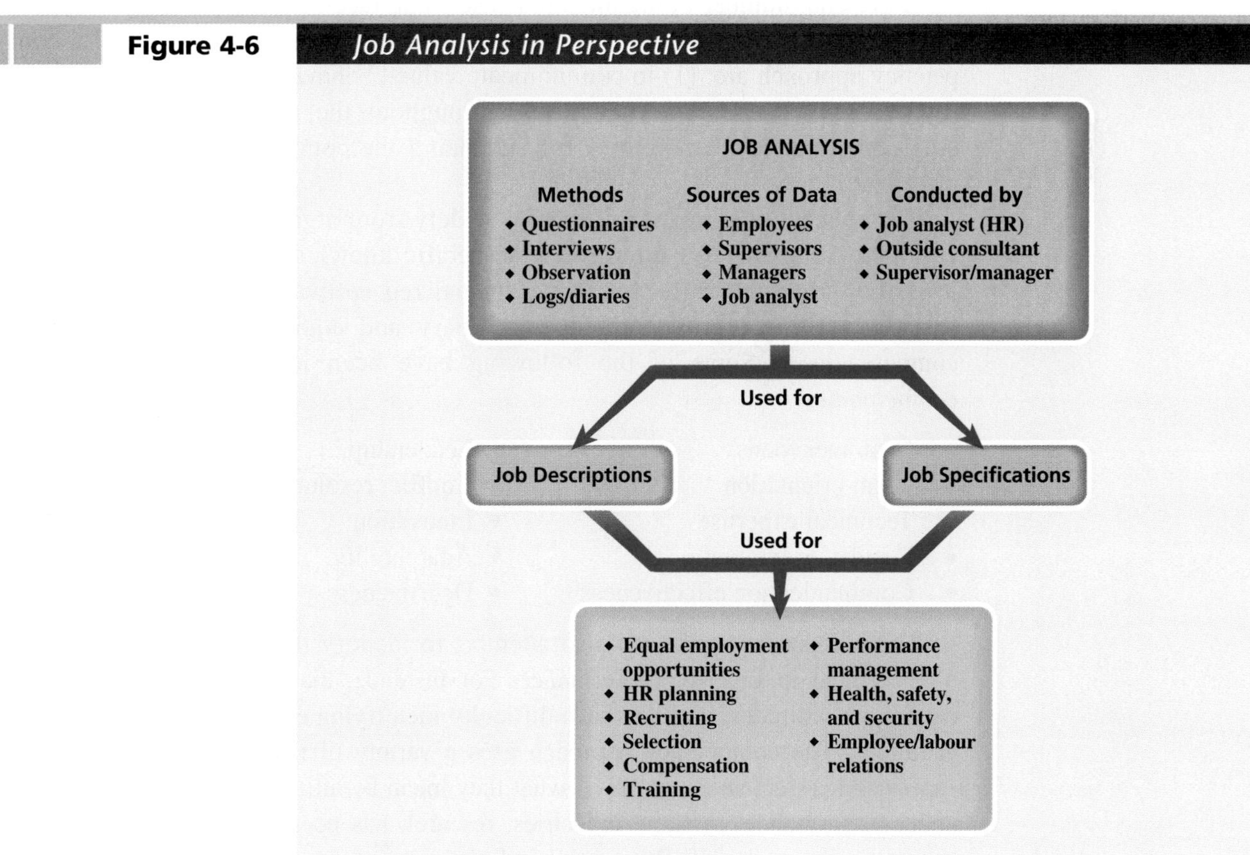

Job analysis involves collecting information on the characteristics of a job that differentiate it from other jobs. The information generated by job analysis may be useful in redesigning jobs, but its primary purpose is to capture a clear understanding of what is done on a job and what capabilities are needed to do it as designed. There are two approaches to job analysis, one focusing on tasks performed in the job, the other on competencies needed for job performance. It is important to be aware that job analysis is not about the incumbent's qualifications, but concerned only with the job in which the incumbent holds.

Task-Based Job Analysis

Task
Distinct, identifiable work activity composed of motions.

Duty
Larger work segment composed of several tasks that are performed by an individual.

Responsibilities
Obligations to perform certain tasks and duties.

Competencies
Individual capabilities that can be linked to enhanced performance by individuals or teams.

Task-based job analysis is the most common form and focuses on the tasks, duties, and responsibilities performed in a job. A **task** is a distinct, identifiable work activity composed of motions, whereas a **duty** is a larger work segment composed of several tasks that are performed by an individual. Because both tasks and duties describe activities, it is not always easy or necessary to distinguish between the two. For example, if one of the employment supervisor's duties is to interview applicants, one task associated with that duty would be asking questions. **Responsibilities** are obligations to perform certain tasks and duties.

Competency-Based Job Analysis

Unlike the traditional approach to analyzing jobs, which identifies the tasks, duties, knowledge, and skills associated with a job, the competency approach considers how the knowledge and skills are used. **Competencies** are individual capabilities that can be linked to enhanced performance by individuals or teams.

A growing number of organizations use some facets of competency analysis in various HR activities.[23] The three primary reasons that organizations use a competency approach are: (1) to communicate valued behaviours within the organization; (2) to raise competency levels throughout the organization; and (3) to emphasize people's capabilities for enhancing the competitive advantage of the organization.

The concept of competencies varies widely from organization to organization. *Technical competencies* often refer to specific knowledge and skills employees have. For example, skills for using specialized software to design Web pages or for operating highly complex machinery and equipment may be cited as competencies.[24] Some of the following have been identified as *behavioural competencies:*

- Customer focus
- Team orientation
- Technical expertise
- Results orientation
- Communication effectiveness
- Leadership
- Conflict resolution
- Innovation
- Adaptability
- Decisiveness

The competency approach also attempts to identify the hidden factors that are often critical to superior performance. For instance, many supervisors talk about employees' attitudes, but they have difficulty identifying exactly what they mean by "attitude." The competency approach uses a variety of methodologies to help the supervisors articulate examples of what they mean by attitude and how those factors affect performance. In some industries, research has been done to identify critical competencies, as the HR Perspective indicates.

Competencies Needed in Hotels

In the last several years, significant attention in HR has been focused on identifying competencies needed in jobs. Studies conducted in various industries on the types of competencies have been helpful. To extend the understanding of competencies needed by middle managers in hotels, Brophy and Kiely focused on identification of managerial competencies in two departments common in many hotels: rooms management and food/beverage operations. The results of their study were published in the *Journal of European Industrial Training* and contained several interesting insights.

The study was conducted on 42 three-star hotels in Ireland and used input from both general managers and lower-level managers in the hotels. Data were gathered using interviews, task analyses, and critical incident documentation. The results of the study identified the following managerial competency areas as important in the two hotel departments:

- Providing customer care
- Maintaining quality and standards
- Managing staff
- Achieving profitability
- Growing the business

Within each of these areas, specific competencies were identified. In customer care, some competencies were: having good relations with hotel customers, handling dissatisfied customers, resolving complaints, and tracking customer satisfaction. In the area of strategic-business, competencies included financial awareness and strategic thinking, among others. Though the competencies identified in this study are specific to the hotel industry, similar competencies may be needed in a number of other industries.[25]

1. Managerial competencies were identified for two hotel departments. Considering non-management staff such as front desk and housekeeping, what competencies do you think should be considered for these types of jobs?
2. Do you feel that the competencies described in this research can be applied across the board to all managers, or will it be industry specific? Why or why not?

Choosing a Job Analysis Approach

Whether to use the task-based or competency-based approach to job analysis is affected by the nature of jobs and how work is changing. In some high-technology industries, employees work in cross-functional project teams and shift from project to project. Organizations in these industries focus less on performing specific tasks and duties, and more on competencies needed to attain results. For example, a project team of eight employees in different countries who are developing software that will allow various credit cards to be used with ATMs worldwide will work on many different tasks and use various competencies, some individually and some with other team members. When that project is finished, those employees will move to other projects, possibly with other employees. Such shifts may happen several times a year. Therefore, the basis for recruiting, selecting, and compensating these individuals is their competencies and capabilities, not just the tasks they perform.

However, in many industries, traditional jobs will continue to exist. Studying these jobs and their work consequences is relatively easy because of the repetitiveness of the work and the limited number of tasks each worker performs, so the task-based approach to job analysis is appropriate. Studying different types of jobs—lower-skilled ones or more varied, highly technical ones—requires different approaches to job analysis. Some important considerations include how job analysis is done, who provides data, and who conducts and uses the data so that job descriptions and job specifications can be prepared and reviewed. Focusing on the competencies that individuals need in order to perform complete jobs, rather than on the tasks, duties, and responsibilities that compose a job, emphasizes how significantly people's capabilities influence organizational performance.

Job Analysis vs. Competencies

Traditional task-based job analysis can provide a defensible basis for such activities as compensation, selection, and training, all of which may be the subject of legal action by employees if they believe they are being wronged in some way. The traditional job analysis approach has been used successfully to substantiate employment decisions. Currently, there is little legal precedent regarding competency analysis, which leaves it open to legal challenge as not being documented as well as the traditional approach. For that reason, task-based job analysis is more widely used, and it is the primary focus of the rest of this chapter.

Job Analysis Responsibilities

Job analysis requires a high degree of coordination and cooperation between the HR unit and operating managers. Figure 4-7 shows a typical division of responsibilities in organizations with an HR unit. The assignment of responsibility for job analysis depends on who can best perform various aspects of the process. In large companies, the HR unit supervises the process to maintain its integrity, and writes the job descriptions and specifications for uniformity. The managers review the efforts of the HR unit to ensure accuracy and completeness. They also may request new job analyses when jobs change significantly. In small organizations, managers may perform all the job analysis responsibilities.

Stages in the Job Analysis Process

Psychometric practices
Practices concerned with the design, administration, and interpretation of quantitative tests for the measurement of psychological variables such as intelligence, aptitude, and personality traits.

The process of job analysis must be conducted in a logical manner, following appropriate management and professional psychometric practices. **Psychometric practices** are concerned with the design, administration, and interpretation of quantitative tests for the measurement of psychological variables such as intelligence, aptitude, and personality traits. Therefore, analysts usually follow a multistage process, regardless of the specific job analysis methods used.[26] The stages for a typical job analysis, as outlined in Figure 4-8, may vary somewhat with the number of jobs included.

Planning the Job Analysis

A crucial aspect of the job analysis process is the planning done before gathering data from managers and employees. Probably the most important consideration is to identify the objectives of the job analysis, from just updating job descriptions to

Figure 4-7 *Typical Division of HR Responsibilities: Job Analysis*

HR Unit	Managers
• Coordinates job analysis • Writes job descriptions and specifications for review by managers • Periodically reviews job descriptions and specifications • Reviews managerial input to ensure accuracy • May seek assistance from outside experts for difficult or unusual analyses	• Complete or help complete job analysis information • Review job descriptions and specifications and maintain their accuracy • Request new analysis as jobs change • Use job analysis information to identify performance standards • Provide information to outside experts

Figure 4-8 Stages in the Job Analysis Process

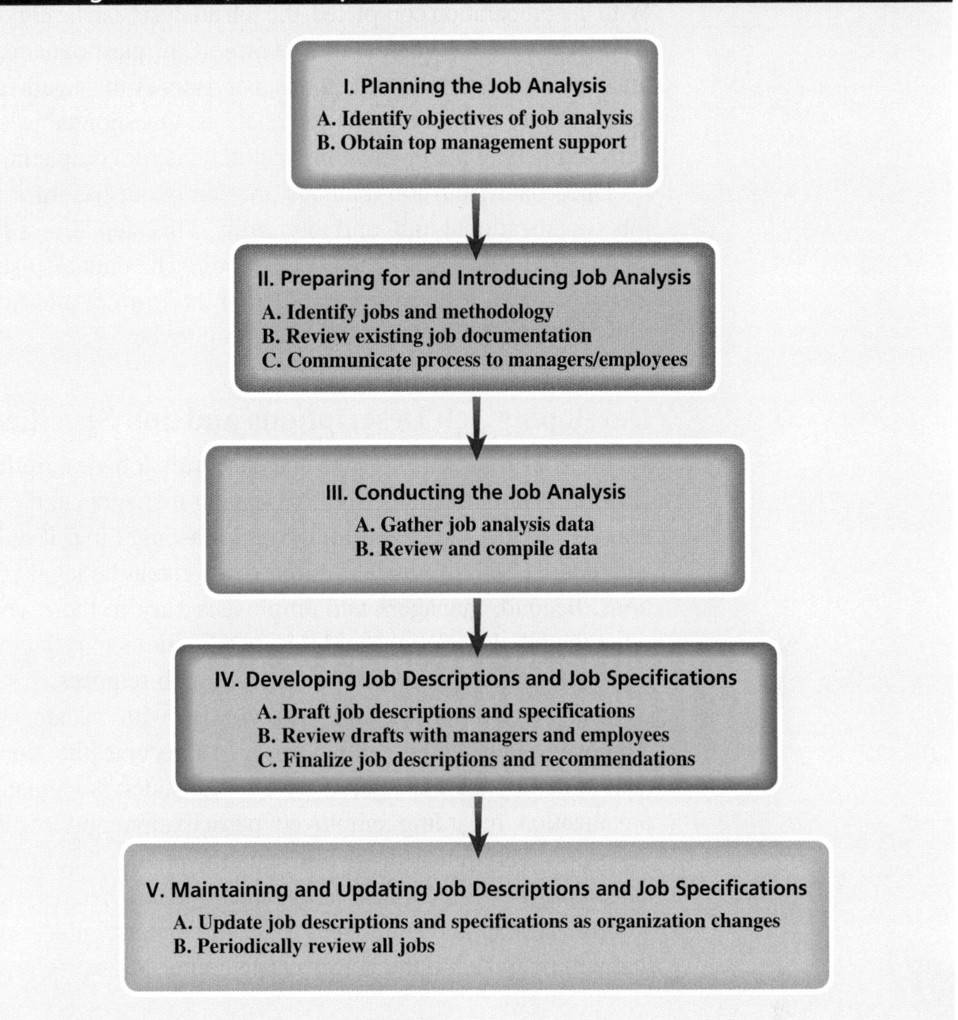

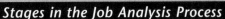

revising the compensation programs in the organization. Whatever the purpose identified, it is vital to obtain the support of top management.

Preparing for and Introducing the Job Analysis

Preparation for job analysis begins with the identification of the jobs under review. For example, are the jobs to be analyzed hourly jobs, clerical jobs, all jobs in one division, or all jobs in the entire organization? Reviewing existing job descriptions, organization charts, previous job analysis information, and other industry-related resources is part of the planning.

This phase identifies those who will be involved in conducting the job analysis and the methods to be used. A crucial step is communicating and explaining the process to managers, affected employees, and other concerned people, such as union stewards. Explanations should address the natural concerns and anxieties people have when someone closely scrutinizes their jobs. When employees are represented by a union, it is essential that union representatives be included in reviewing the job descriptions and specifications, to lessen the possibility of future conflicts.

Conducting the Job Analysis

With the preparation completed, the job analysis can be conducted. The methods selected will determine the timeline for the project. If questionnaires are used, it is often helpful to have employees return them to supervisors or managers for review before giving them back to those conducting the job analysis. Questionnaires should be accompanied by a letter explaining the process and instructions for completing and returning them.

Once data from job analysis are compiled, the information should be sorted by job, organizational unit, and job family. This step allows for comparison of data from similar jobs throughout the organization. The data also should be reviewed for completeness, with follow-up as needed in the form of additional interviews or questions to be answered by managers and/or employees.

Developing Job Descriptions and Job Specifications

At the fourth stage, the job analysts draft job descriptions and job specifications. Generally, organizations find that having managers and employees write job descriptions is not recommended for several reasons. First, it reduces consistency in format and details, both of which are important given the legal consequences of job descriptions. Second, managers and employees vary in their writing skills. Also, they may write the job descriptions and job specifications to reflect what they do and what their personal qualifications are, not what the job requires.

Completed drafts should be reviewed with managers and supervisors. Whether employees review the drafts or wait to receive the final job descriptions is often determined by the managerial style of the supervisors/managers and the culture of the organization regarding employee participation and communication. When the job descriptions are finished, the HR department distributes them to managers, supervisors, and employees. Supervisors or managers should then review the completed descriptions with the appropriate employees to ensure understanding and agreement on the content that will be linked to the performance appraisals, as well as to all other HR activities.

LOGGING ON...

Job-Analysis.NETwork
This website has resources for conducting a job analysis, including different types of methods, questionnaires, and job descriptions.
www.job-analysis.net

Maintaining and Updating Job Descriptions and Job Specifications

Once job descriptions and specifications have been completed and reviewed by all appropriate individuals, a system must be developed for keeping them current. One effective way to ensure that appropriate reviews occur is to use job descriptions and job specifications in other HR activities. For example, each time a vacancy occurs, the job description and specifications should be reviewed and revised as necessary *before* recruiting and selection efforts begin. Similarly, in some organizations, managers and employees review their job descriptions during each performance appraisal interview.

Job Analysis Methods

Job analysis information about what people are doing in their jobs can be gathered in a variety of ways. One consideration is who is to conduct the job analysis. Most frequently, a member of the HR staff coordinates this effort. Depending on which of the methods discussed next is used, others who often participate are managers, supervisors, and employees doing the jobs. For more complex analyses, industrial engineers may conduct time-and-motion studies.

Another consideration is the method to be used. Whatever method is chosen, it should be content based and should not reflect rater bias.[27] Common methods are observation, interviewing, questionnaires, and computerized systems. The use of a combination of these approaches depends on the situation and the organization.[28] Each of these methods is discussed next.

Observation

With the observation method, a manager, job analyst, or industrial engineer observes the individual performing the job and takes notes to describe the tasks and duties performed. Use of the observation method is limited because many jobs do not have complete and easily observable job duties or complete job cycles. Thus, observation may be more useful for repetitive jobs and in conjunction with other methods.

Work Sampling One type of observation, work sampling, does not require attention to each detailed action throughout an entire work cycle. This method allows a manager to determine the content and pace of a typical workday through statistical sampling of certain actions rather than through continuous observation and timing of all actions. Work sampling is particularly useful for routine and repetitive jobs.

Employee Diary/Log Another method requires employees to "observe" their own performances by keeping a diary/log of their job duties, noting how frequently those duties are performed and the time required for each one. Although this approach sometimes generates useful information, it may be burdensome for employees to compile an accurate log. Also, employees sometimes perceive this approach as creating needless documentation that detracts from the performance of their work.

Interviewing

The interview method of gathering information requires a manager or an HR specialist to visit each job site and talk with the employees performing each job. A standardized interview form is used most often to record the information. Frequently, both the employee and the employee's supervisor must be interviewed to obtain a complete understanding of the job.

Sometimes, group or panel interviews are used. A team of "subject matter experts" (SMEs) who have varying insights about a group of jobs is assembled to provide job analysis information.[29] This option may be particularly useful for highly technical jobs and others for which a range of individuals can provide input.

The interview method can be quite time-consuming, especially if the interviewer talks with two or three employees doing each job. Professional and managerial jobs are often more complicated to analyze and usually require longer interviews. For these reasons, combining the interview method with one of the other methods is suggested.

Questionnaires

The questionnaire is a widely used method of gathering data on jobs. A survey instrument is developed and given to employees and managers to complete. The typical job questionnaire often covers the areas shown in Figure 4-9.

The questionnaire method offers a major advantage in that information on a large number of jobs can be collected inexpensively in a relatively short period of time. However, the questionnaire method assumes that employees can accurately analyze and communicate information about their jobs. Employees may vary in their perceptions of the jobs, and even in their literacy. Using interviewing and observation in combination with the questionnaire method allows analysts to clarify and verify the information gathered in questionnaires.

Figure 4-9 **Typical Areas Covered in a Job Analysis Questionnaire**

Duties and Percentage of Time Spent on Each	Contact with Other People
• **Regular duties**	• **Internal contacts**
• **Special duties performed less frequently**	• **External contacts**
Supervision	Physical Dimensions
• **Supervision given to others**	• **Physical demands**
• **Supervision received from others**	• **Working conditions**
Decisions Made	Jobholder Characteristics
• **Records and reports prepared**	• **Knowledge**
• **Materials and equipment used**	• **Skills**
• **Financial/budget responsibilities**	• **Abilities**
	• **Training needed**

Position Analysis Questionnaire (PAQ) The Position Analysis Questionnaire (PAQ) is a specialized instrument incorporating checklists. Each job is analyzed on 27 dimensions composed of 187 "elements." The PAQ has a number of divisions, each containing numerous job elements. The divisions include:

- *Information input:* Where and how does the worker get information to do the job?
- *Mental process:* What levels of reasoning are necessary on the job?
- *Work output:* What physical activities are performed on the job?
- *Relationships with others:* What relationships are required while performing the job?
- *Job context:* What working conditions and social contexts are involved in the job?
- *Other:* What else is relevant to the job?

LOGGING ON...

PAQ Services, Inc.
This site provides information on position analysis questionnaires for management and administrative positions.
www.paq.com

The PAQ focuses on "worker-oriented" elements that describe behaviours necessary to do the job, rather than on "job-oriented" elements that describe the technical aspects of the work. Although its complexity may deter many potential users, the PAQ is easily quantified and can be used to conduct validity studies on selection tests. It also may contribute to internal pay fairness because it considers the varying demands of different jobs.

Functional Job Analysis (FJA) Functional Job Analysis (FJA) is a task analysis technique that distinguishes between what gets done on a job and what workers do to get the job done.[30] For example, what a bus driver actually does (starting bus, steering bus etc.) rather than task accomplishment of transporting kids to school. A functional definition of what is done in a job can be generated by examining the following three components of *data, people,* and *things:*

- *Data*—Extent to which cognitive resources are needed to handle info, facts, ideas
- *People*—Extent to which interpersonal resources are needed
- *Things*—Extent to which physical resources are needed (strength, speed, etc.)

The levels of these components are used to identify and compare important elements of jobs. The Public Safety Communication Operators in British Columbia utilize the FJA. The federal government incorporates the FJA into their compilation of occupational information.

The most recent version of FJA uses seven scales to describe what workers do in jobs: (1) Things, (2) Data, (3) People, (4) Worker Instructions, (5) Reasoning, (6) Math, and (7) Language. Each scale has several levels that are anchored with specific behavioural statements and illustrative tasks. Like other job analysis instruments, FJA is a methodology for collecting job information.

There are a number of steps involved in conducting the FJA:

1. Identify the job to be analyzed.
2. Break the job into tasks—Evaluate data, who they communicate with (clients, peers, supervisors, agencies, colleagues).
3. Write task statements—Indicate the task performer, what actions are performed by the performer using action verbs, the reason for the action, tools, equipment, or work aids that are used by the performer and describe expected output.
4. Classify each task on the worker function scale—Classify each task according to the interaction of the worker with data, people, and things. Specify the level of the activity of the worker involving data, people, and things using the standard terminology of FJA. For example, in the case of data, you must determine whether this task involves comparing data (level 1), copying data (level 2), computing data (level 3), and so forth.
5. Identify the proportion of time in each area—Sum will be 100 percent of time spent on people, data, and things
6. Specify the related requirements—Specify the instructional level for each task
7. Record this information on a standardized form.

The FJA provides concise task descriptions, permits comparison of tasks across jobs, provides precision in identifying worker activities, attends to detailed activities of workers, and provides a standardized vocabulary for describing jobs. Some of the disadvantages of FJA are that it imposes a restrictive approach to defining work and conceptualizing tasks, it is time consuming; since the degree of specificity requires in-depth analysis of jobs, it is a relatively inflexible procedure and it forces all activity into a small number of categories.[31]

Managerial Job Analysis Questionnaire Because managerial jobs differ in character from jobs with clearly observable routines and procedures, some specialized methods have evolved for their analysis. One well-known and widely used method is the Management Position Description Questionnaire (MPDQ). Composed of more than 200 statements, the MPDQ examines a variety of managerial dimensions, including decision making and supervising.

Computerized Systems

With the expansion of information technology, computerized job analysis systems have been developed. These systems all have several common characteristics, including the way they are administered. First, analysts compose task statements that relate to all jobs. Then, those statements are listed in questionnaires, which are distributed to employees. Next, employees respond on computer-scannable documents, which are fed into computer-based services capable of scoring, recording, analyzing, and reporting thousands of pieces of information about any job.

An important feature of computerized job analysis is the specificity of data that can be gathered. All this specific data is compiled into a job analysis database. As a result, a computerized job analysis system can often reduce the time and effort involved in writing job descriptions. These systems often store banks of job duty statements that relate to each of the task and scope statements of the questionnaires. Interestingly, a study found little variation in the results of job analysis data obtained by paper questionnaires and by computerized methods.[32] Thus, the use of computerized methods will likely grow.

National Occupational Classification 2001 (NOC)
This website describes duties, skills, interests, aptitudes, education requirements, and work settings for occupations in the Canadian labour market.
www23.hrdc-drhc.gc.ca/2001/e/generic/welcome.shtml

The National Occupational Classification (NOC) 2001 NOC is compiled by the federal government and it contains the classification structure and descriptions of 520 occupational unit groups and includes over 30 000 occupational titles. It also features an intuitive search engine to help you find the information you need. An online training tutorial is available to assist new users and NOC trainers. The NOC code numbers facilitate the exchange of statistical information about jobs and are useful in reporting research in the HR area, in vocational counselling and in charting career paths through job transfers and/or advancement.

A chart called the NOC *Matrix* shows the major and the minor groups, and the relationship between skill types and skill levels. This provides an overview of the entire classification structure. The skill types are represented in the columns while the skill levels are found in rows. Managerial occupations are found in the top portion of the chart, indicating the presence of management across all segments of the labour market. While the matrix can be helpful in identifying *major* and *minor groups*, it does not identify *unit groups*. Figure 4-11 highlights the *Matrix* (see pages 152–53).

The *Career Handbook* is the counselling component of the National Occupational Classification (NOC) system. The *Career Handbook* provides global ratings assigned to occupations to further define skills, worker characteristics, and other indicators related to occupations that are important for career exploration and informed career decision making. This counselling resource is used by a wide range of professionals for many applications, and by individuals engaged in self-directed career planning. The *Career Handbook* provides 923 occupational profiles for counselling based on NOC 2001 occupations and maintains the original descriptor scales, factors, and presentation format. It includes information on aptitudes, interests, involvement with data/people/things, physical activities, environmental conditions, education/training indicators, career progression, and work settings. It is important to note that the second edition of the *Career Handbook* should be used in conjunction with the 2001 version of the NOC.

Figure 4-10 is an example of a job description with the national classification code for human resources managers. Note that the NOC code for the position is 0112. All positions classified under NOC are coded with a 4-digit number.

Combination Methods

There are a number of different ways to obtain and analyze information about a job. Therefore, in dealing with issues that may end up in court, HR specialists and others doing job analysis must carefully document all the steps taken. Each method has strengths and weaknesses, and a combination of methods generally may be more appropriate than one method alone. Regardless of the methods used, in its most fundamental form job analysis provides the information necessary to develop job descriptions and job specifications.

Behavioural Influences on Job Analysis

4 Job analysis involves determining what the "core" job is. A detailed examination of jobs, although necessary, sometimes can be a demanding and disruptive experience for both managers and employees, in part because job analysis can identify the difference between what currently is being performed in a job and what *should* be done. Consequently, a number of behavioural factors can affect job analysis, some of which are discussed next.

Figure 4-10 *Job Description for Human Resources Managers, NOC Code 0112*

0112 Human Resources Managers

Human resources managers plan, organize, direct, control, and evaluate the operations of human resources and personnel departments, and develop and implement policies, programs, and procedures regarding human resource planning, recruitment, collective bargaining, training and development, occupation classification, and pay and benefit administration. They represent management and participate actively on various joint committees to maintain ongoing relations between management and employees. Human resources managers are employed throughout the private and public sectors.

Example Titles

administrator, human resources
manager, employer-employee relations
manager, employment equity–human resources
manager, human resources
manager, industrial relations
manager, occupational health and safety
manager, pay and benefits
manager, personnel
manager, personnel services
manager, personnel training and development
manager, recruiting
manager, staff relations

Main duties

Human resources managers perform some or all of the following duties:

- **Plan, organize, direct, control, and evaluate the operations of human resources or personnel departments**
- **Plan human resource requirements in conjunction with other departmental managers**
- **Coordinate internal and external training and recruitment activities**
- **Develop and implement labour relations policies and procedures and negotiate collective agreements**
- **Administer employee development, language training, and health and safety programs**
- **Advise and assist other departmental managers on interpretation and administration of personnel policies and programs**
- **Oversee the classification and rating of occupations**
- **Organize and conduct employee information meetings on employment policy, benefits and compensation, and participate actively on various joint committees**
- **Direct the organization's quality management program**
- **Ensure compliance with legislation such as the Pay Equity Act.**

Employment requirements

- **A bachelor's degree in a field related to personnel management, such as business administration, industrial relations, commerce, or psychology**

  or
- **Completion of a professional development program in personnel administration is required.**
- **Several years of experience as a personnel officer or human resource specialist are required.**

Additional information

- **Progression to senior management positions is possible with experience.**
- **Other joint committees led by human resources managers may focus on issues such as alcohol or drug addiction.**

Classified elsewhere

- **Specialists in Human Resources (1121)**

Classification Structure - 0

Source: National Occupational Classification Matrix 2001, Human Resources and Skills Development Canada. Reproduced with the permission of the Minister of Public Works and Government Services Canada, 2006.

Figure 4-11 ***National Occupational Classification Matrix 2001***

	1 BUSINESS, FINANCE AND ADMINISTRATION OCCUPATIONS	2 NATURAL AND APPLIED SCIENCES AND RELATED OCCUPATIONS	3 HEALTH OCCUPATIONS	4 OCCUPATIONS IN SOCIAL SCIENCE EDUCATION, GOVERNMENT SERVICE AND RELIGION
0 **Management Occupations**	011 Administrative Services Managers 012 Managers in Financial and Business Services 013 Managers in Communication (Except Broadcasting)	021 Managers in Engineering, Architecture, Science and Information Systems	031 Managers in Health, Education, Social and Community Services 041 Managers in Public Administration	
SKILL LEVEL A Occupations usually require university education	**Major Group 11** PROFESSIONAL OCCUPATIONS IN BUSINESS AND FINANCE 111 Auditors, Accountants and Investment Professionals 112 Human Resources and Business Service Professionals	**Major Group 21** PROFESSIONAL OCCUPATIONS IN NATURAL AND APPLIED SCIENCES 211 Physical Science Professionals 212 Life Science Professionals 213 Civil, Mechanical, Electrical and Chemical Engineers 214 Other Engineers 215 Architects, Urban Planners and Land Surveyors 216 Mathematicians, Statisticians and Actuaries 217 Computer and Information Systems Professionals	**Major Group 31** PROFESSIONAL OCCUPATIONS IN HEALTH 311 Physicians, Dentists and Veterinarians 312 Optometrists, Chiropractors and Other Health Diagnosing and Treating Professionals 313 Pharmacists, Dietitians and Nutritionists 314 Therapy and Assessment Professionals 315 Nurse Supervisors and Registered Nurses	**Major Group 41** PROFESSIONAL OCCUPATIONS IN SOCIAL SCIENCE, EDUCATION, GOVERNMENT SERVICES AND RELIGION 411 Judges, Lawyers and Quebec Notaries 412 University Professors and Assistants 413 College and Other Vocational Instructors 414 Secondary and Elementary School Teachers and Educational Counsellors 415 Psychologists, Social Workers, Counsellors, Clergy and Probation Officers 416 Policy and Program Officers, Researchers and Consultants
SKILL LEVEL B Occupations usually require college education or apprenticeship training	**Major Group 12** SKILLED ADMINISTRATIVE AND BUSINESS OCCUPATIONS 121 Clerical Supervisors 122 Administrative and Regulatory Occupations 123 Finance and Insurance Administrative Occupations 124 Secretaries, Recorders and Transcriptionists	**Major Group 22** TECHNICAL OCCUPATIONS RELATED TO NATURAL AND APPLIED SCIENCES 221 Technical Occupations in Physical Sciences 222 Technical Occupations in Life Sciences 223 Technical Occupations in Civil, Mechanical and Industrial Engineering 224 Technical Occupations in Electronics and Electrical Engineering 225 Technical Occupations in Architecture, Drafting, Surveying and Mapping 226 Other Technical Inspectors and Regulatory Officers 227 Transportation Officers and Controllers 228 Technical Occupations in Computer and Information Systems	**Major Group 32** TECHNICAL AND SKILLED OCCUPATIONS IN HEALTH 321 Medical Technologists and Technicians (Except Dental Health) 322 Technical Occupations in Dental Health Care 323 Other Technical Occupations in Health Care (Except Dental)	**Major Group 42** PARAPROFESSIONAL OCCUPATIONS IN LAW, SOCIAL SERVICES, EDUCATION AND RELIGION 421 Paralegals, Social Services Workers and Occupations in Education and Religion, n.e.c.
SKILL LEVEL C Occupations usually require secondary school and/or occupation-specific training	**Major Group 14** CLERICAL OCCUPATIONS 141 Clerical Occupations, General Office Skills 142 Office Equipment Operators 143 Finance and Insurance Clerks 144 Administrative Support Clerks 145 Library, Correspondence and Related Information Clerks 146 Mail and Message Distribution Occupations 147 Recording, Scheduling and Distributing Occupations		**Major Group 34** ASSISTING OCCUPATIONS IN SUPPORT OF HEALTH SERVICES 341 Assisting Occupations in Support of Health Services	
SKILL LEVEL D On-the-job training is usually provided for occupations				

Source: National Occupational Classification Matrix 2001, Human Resources and Skills Development Canada. Reproduced with the permission of the Minister of Public Works and Government Services Canada, 2006.

5 OCCUPATIONS IN ART, CULTURE, RECREATION AND SPORT	6 SALES AND SERVICE OCCUPATIONS	7 TRADE, TRANSPORT AND EQUIPMENT OPERATORS AND RELATED OCCUPATIONS	8 OCCUPATIONS UNIQUE TO PRIMARY INDUSTRY	9 OCCUPATIONS UNIQUE TO PROCESSING, MANUFACTURING AND UTILITIES
Major Group 00 SENIOR MANAGEMENT OCCUPATIONS 001 Legislators and Senior Management	→	→	→	→
051 Managers in Art, Culture, Recreation and Sport	061 Sales, Marketing and Advertising Managers 062 Managers in Retail Trade 063 Managers in Food Service and Accommodation 064 Managers in Protective Service 065 Managers in Other Services	071 Managers in Construction and Transportation 072 Facility Operation and Maintenance Managers	081 Managers in Primary Production (Except Agriculture)	091 Managers in Manufacturing and Utilities
Major Group 51 PROFESSIONAL OCCUPATIONS IN ART AND CULTURE 511 Librarians, Archivists, Conservators and Curators 512 Writing, Translating and Public Relations Professionals 513 Creative and Performing Artists				
Major Group 52 TECHNICAL AND SKILLED OCCUPATIONS IN ART, CULTURE, RECREATION AND SPORT 521 Technical Occupations in Libraries, Archives, Museums and Art Galleries 522 Photographers, Graphic Arts Technicians and Technical and Co-ordinating Occupations in Motion Pictures, Broadcasting and the Performing Arts 523 Announcers and Other Performers 524 Creative Designers and Craftpersons 525 Athletes, Coaches, Referees and Related Occupations	**Major Group 62** SKILLED SALES AND SERVICE OCCUPATIONS 621 Sales and Service Supervisors 622 Technical Sales Specialists, Wholesale Trade 623 Insurance and Real Estate Sales Occupations and Buyers 624 Chefs and Cooks 625 Butchers and Bakers 626 Police Officers and Firefighters 627 Technical Occupations in Personal Service	**Major Group 72/73** TRADES AND SKILLED TRANSPORT AND EQUIPMENT OPERATORS 721 Contractors and Supervisors, Trades and Related Workers 722 Supervisors, Railway and Motor Transportation Occupations 723 Machinists and Related Occupations 724 Electrical Trades and Telecommunication Occupations 725 Plumbers, Pipefitters and Gas Fitters 726 Metal Forming, Shaping and Erecting Trades 727 Carpenters and Cabinetmakers 728 Masonry and Plastering Trades 729 Other Construction Trades 731 Machinery and Transportation Equipment Mechanics (Except Motor Vehicle) 732 Automotive Service Technicians 733 Other Mechanics 734 Upholsterers, Tailors, Shoe Repairers, Jewellers and Related Occupations 735 Stationary Engineers and Power Station and System Operators 736 Train Crew Operating Occupations 737 Crane Operators, Drillers and Blasters 738 Printing Press Operators, Commercial Divers and Other Trades and Related Occupations, n.e.c.	**Major Group 82** SKILLED OCCUPATIONS IN PRIMARY INDUSTRY 821 Supervisors, Logging and Forestry 822 Supervisors, Mining, Oil and Gas 823 Underground Miners, Oil and Gas Drillers and Related Workers 824 Logging Machinery Operators 825 Contractors, Operators and Supervisors in Agriculture, Horticulture and Aquaculture 826 Fishing Vessel Masters and Skippers and Fishermen/women	**Major Group 92** PROCESSING, MANUFACTURING AND UTILITIES SUPERVISORS AND SKILLED OPERATORS 921 Supervisors, Processing Occupations 922 Supervisors, Assembly and Fabrication 923 Central Control and Process Operators in Manufacturing and Processing
	Major Group 64 INTERMEDIATE SALES AND SERVICE OCCUPATIONS 641 Sales Representatives, Wholesale Trade 642 Retail Salespersons and Sales Clerks 643 Occupations in Travel and Accommodation 644 Tour and Recreational Guides and Casino Occupations 645 Occupations in Food and Beverage Service 646 Other Occupations in Protective Service 647 Childcare and Home Support Workers 648 Other Occupations in Personal Service	**Major Group 74** INTERMEDIATE OCCUPATIONS IN TRANSPORT, EQUIPMENT OPERATION, INSTALLATION AND MAINTENANCE 741 Motor Vehicle and Transit Drivers 742 Heavy Equipment Operators 743 Other Transport Equipment Operators and Related Workers 744 Other Installers, Repairers and Servicers 745 Longshore Workers and Material Handlers	**Major Group 84** INTERMEDIATE OCCUPATIONS IN PRIMARY INDUSTRY 841 Mine Service Workers and Operators in Oil and Gas Drilling 842 Logging and Forestry Workers 843 Agriculture and Horticulture Workers 844 Other Fishing and Trapping Occupations	**Major Group 94/95** PROCESSING AND MANUFACTURING MACHINE OPERATORS AND ASSEMBLERS 941 Machine Operators and Related Workers in Metal and Mineral Products Processing 942 Machine Operators and Related Workers in Chemical, Plastic and Rubber Processing 943 Machine Operators and Related Workers in Pulp and Paper Production and Wood Processing 944 Machine Operators and Related Workers in Textile Processing 945 Machine Operators and Related Workers in Fabric, Fur and Leather Products Manufacturing 946 Machine Operators and Related Workers in Food, Beverage and Tobacco Processing 947 Printing Machine Operators and Related Occupations 948 Mechanical, Electrical and Electronics Assemblers 949 Other Assembly and Related Occupations 951 Machining, Metalworking, Woodworking and Related Machine Operators
	Major Group 66 ELEMENTAL SALES AND SERVICE OCCUPATIONS 661 Cashiers 662 Other Sales and Related Occupations 664 Food Counter Attendants, Kitchen Helpers and Related Occupations 665 Security Guards and Related Occupations 666 Cleaners 667 Other Occupations in Travel, Accommodation, Amusement and Recreation 668 Other Elemental Service Occupations	**Major Group 76** TRADES HELPERS, CONSTRUCTION LABOURERS AND RELATED OCCUPATIONS 761 Trades Helpers and Labourers 762 Public Works and Other Labourers, n.e.c.	**Major Group 86** LABOURERS IN PRIMARY INDUSTRY 861 Primary Production Labourers	**Major Group 96** LABOURERS IN PROCESSING, MANUFACTURING AND UTILITIES 961 Labourers in Processing, Manufacturing and Utilities

"Inflation" of Jobs and Job Titles

Employees and managers have some tendency to inflate the importance and significance of their jobs. Because job analysis information is used for compensation purposes, both managers and employees hope that "puffing up" jobs will result in higher pay levels and greater "status" for résumés and more possible promotion opportunities.

Titles of jobs often get inflated too.[33] Some firms give fancy titles in place of pay raises, and others do it to keep well-paid employees from leaving for "status" reasons. For instance, many organizations will use the term "engineer" to try and build up the status of a position. Positions in maintenance, sales, or field technicians are sometimes called an engineer. However, there are rules against the improper use of the engineer title in Canada if the individual is not a professionally trained engineer. As the HR Globally identifies, the problem of job titles is not limited to Canadian firms.

Employee and Managerial Anxieties

Both managers and employees have concerns about job analysis. Through the information developed in a job analysis, the job description is ideally supposed to identify the nature of a job. However, it is difficult to capture all facets of a job, particularly for jobs in which employees perform a variety of duties and operate with a high degree of independence.

Managerial Straitjacket One primary concern of managers and supervisors is that the job analysis and job descriptions will unrealistically limit managerial flexibility. As workloads and demands change rapidly, managers and supervisors want to be able to move duties to other employees, cross-train employees, and have more dynamic, flexible ways to get work accomplished. If job descriptions are written restrictively, some employees may use an omission to limit

HR *Globally*

Japanese Job Titles and Global Competitiveness

The culture of Japan has long included extensive use of *keigo,* an honourific language that has traditionally been taught to children and continued throughout the society. Central to *keigo* is the formalization of how individuals are addressed. The formalization often includes language to honour older people, organizational managers, and others.

However, the global economic changes facing many Japanese companies has led a growing number of employers to issue policy directives to discontinue the use of job titles and such high formalization when addressing other employees and managers. For example, Elpida, a senior conductor manufacturer, issued a policy statement that employees should add *san* to their names, as in Tyuka-san, but discontinue addressing each other by additional formal job titles, such as Department Chief Tyuka-san. Another factor contributing to the decline in formal language use by younger Japanese is that many of them have had education and travel experiences outside of Japan, and they use just first names or first and last names without any formalities.

Numerous older Japanese have resisted the changes, and Japanese schools have had to change educational curriculums to de-emphasize formalization. Thus HR professionals and managers from throughout the world who deal with Japanese companies, employees, and customers must be aware of the changes in job titling in Japan.[34]

1. Has our culture become too casual or do you feel that more formalization is required in the workplace?
2. Does an organization have a right to dictate how formalized employees are to be with each other?

managerial flexibility. The resulting attitude, "It's not in my job description," puts a straitjacket on a manager. In some organizations with unionized workforces, very restrictive job descriptions exist. Because of such difficulties, the final statement in many job descriptions is a *miscellaneous clause,* which consists of a phrase similar to "Performs other duties as needed upon request by immediate supervisor." This statement covers unusual situations that may occur in an employee's job.

Employee Fears One fear that employees may have concerns the purpose of a detailed investigation of their job. Perhaps they feel that such a detailed look means someone thinks they have done something wrong. The attitude behind such a fear might be, "As long as no one knows precisely what I am supposed to be doing, I am safe."

Often the content of a job may reflect the desires and skills of the incumbent employee. For example, in one firm, an employee promoted to customer service supervisor continued to spend considerable time answering customer calls, rather than supervising employees taking the calls. As part of job analysis discussions, the customer service manager and the supervisor discussed the need for the supervisor to train his employees on handling special customer requests and to delegate more routine duties to the customer service representatives.

Also, some employees may fear that an analysis of their jobs will put a straitjacket on them, limiting their creativity and flexibility by formalizing their duties. However, analyzing a job does not necessarily limit job scope or depth. In fact, having a well-written, well-communicated job description can assist employees by clarifying their roles and the expectations within those roles.[35] One effective way to handle anxieties is to involve the employees in the revision process.

Current Incumbent Emphasis

As illustrated by the example of the customer service supervisor, a job analysis and the resulting job description and job specifications should not describe just what the person currently doing the job does or his or her personal qualifications. The incumbent may have unique capabilities and the ability to expand the scope of the job to assume more responsibilities. The company would have difficulty finding someone exactly like that individual if he or she left. Consequently, it is useful to focus on *core* duties and *necessary* knowledge, skills, and abilities (KSAs) by determining what the jobs would be if the incumbents quit or were no longer available to do the jobs.

Marginal job functions
Duties that are part of a job but are incidental or ancillary to the purpose and nature of the job.

Marginal job functions are duties that are part of a job but are incidental or ancillary to the purpose and nature of the job. Figure 4-12 shows three major considerations used in determining essential functions and marginal functions. Job analysts, HR staff members, and operating managers must evaluate and make decisions when information on the three considerations is not clear.

Job analysis also can identify the physical demands of jobs.[36] An understanding of the skills and capabilities used on a job is critical. For example, a warehouse worker must be able to lift a certain amount of weight. However, lifting may be less essential for an administrative assistant working in an office environment.

An important part of job analysis is obtaining information about what duties are being performed and what percentage of time is devoted to each duty. The percentage of time spent on a duty generally indicates its relative importance. Also, if duties are regularly performed daily, weekly, and/or monthly, they are more likely

Figure 4-12 *Determining Essential and Marginal Job Functions*

Considerations	Essential Functions	Marginal Functions
Percentage of time spent on task	Significant percentage of time, often 20 percent or more, is spent on task.	Generally less than 10 percent of time is spent on task.
Frequency of task	Task is performed regularly: daily, weekly, or monthly.	Task is performed infrequently or when substituting in part of another job.
Importance of task	Task affects other parts of job and other jobs.	Task is unrelated to job, and there are few consequences if not performed.

to be seen as essential. In contrast, a task performed only infrequently or when helping another worker on a totally unrelated job more likely falls in the marginal category.[37]

Another consideration is the ease or difficulty of assigning a duty to be performed by someone else, or in a different job. For instance, assume an assembler of electronic components places the completed parts in a bin next to the work area. At the end of each day, the bin of completed parts must be carried to another room for use in the final assembly of a product. Carrying the bin to the other room probably would be defined as a marginal task, because assigning someone else to carry it would not likely create major workflow problems with other jobs and workers.

Job Descriptions and Job Specifications

5 The output from the analysis of a job is used to develop a job description and its job specifications. Together, these summarize job analysis information in a readable format and provide the basis for defensible job-related actions. They also identify individual jobs for employees by providing documentation from management.

In most cases, the job description and job specifications are combined into one document that contains several sections. A **job description** identifies the tasks, duties, and responsibilities of a job. It describes what is done, why it is done, where it is done, and, briefly, how it is done. **Performance standards** flow directly from a job description, and indicate what the job accomplishes and how performance is measured in key areas of the job description.

Job description
Identification of the tasks, duties, and responsibilities of a job.

Performance standards
Indicators of what the job accomplishes and how performance is measured in key areas of the job description.

Performance Standards

The reason for establishing performance standards linked to job descriptions and job responsibilities is clear. If employees know what is expected and how performance is to be measured, they have a much better chance of performing satisfactorily. Figure 4-13 shows job duty statements and some performance standards used for a customer response representative in a telecommunications firm.

Unfortunately, performance standards are often not developed as supplemental items from job descriptions. Even if performance standards have been identified and matched to job descriptions, they may not be communicated to employees if the job descriptions are not provided to employees but are used only as tools. Such an approach limits the value of job descriptions.

Figure 4-13 *Sample Job Duty Statements and Performance Standards*

Job Title: Customer Response Representative

Supervisor: Customer Response Supervisor

Duty	Performance Standards
Discusses non-payment of bills with customers and notifies them of non-payment disconnecting of service	• **Flags accounts, within two days, which are not to be disconnected according to discussions with local manager** • **Mails notices to cable television customers to be received at least five days before disconnection date** • **Uses prior payment history to determine which accounts require credit deposit** • **Calmly discusses with customers the non-payment status of accounts, along with options for reconnection** • **Disconnects and reconnects long-distance calling cards for non-payment, with 100-percent accuracy**
Receives and records trouble reports from customers and dispatches reports to appropriate personnel	• **Completes all required trouble information on the trouble-reporting system accurately, with no more than five errors annually** • **Dispatches trouble ticket information to voice mail with 100-percent accuracy** • **Tests line if needed or as requested by technician for telephone troubles**

Job Specifications

Job specifications The knowledge, skills, and abilities (KSAs) an individual needs to perform a job satisfactorily.

While the job description describes activities to be done, the **job specifications** list the knowledge, skills, and abilities (KSAs) an individual needs to perform a job satisfactorily. KSAs include education, experience, work skill requirements, personal abilities, and mental and physical requirements. It is important to note that accurate job specifications identify what KSAs a person needs to do the job, not necessarily the current employee's qualifications. The job specifications of a particular job also include working conditions of particular positions in organizations. Job specifications are helpful in determining ergonomic concerns or constraints for particular positions. For example, how a person sits in front a computer and where the tools are in relation to the seating would be reviewed and possible adjustments made to ensure that the work is designed in such a way as to minimize risk or injury. The chair may need to be adjusted and the mouse located at the appropriate height, a small stool under foot to protect the back, short breaks after many hours of working, etc.

Job Description Components

A typical job description contains several major parts. The HR Practice provides some suggestions for writing job descriptions. Overviews of the most common components are presented next.

Identification Figure 4-14 shows a sample job description and also contains job specifications. The first part of the job description is the identification section, in

HR *Practice*

Writing Job Descriptions

Although not the most exciting part of HR management, developing and maintaining current job descriptions is important. Some key suggestions for writing the essential functions and duties of a job follow:

- Compose specific duty statements that contain most of the following elements:
  - a precise action verb
  - an object of the verb
  - the expected outcome
  - the tools, equipment, aids, and processes to be used
  - the frequency of the duties
- Be logical: Make the job description easy for the reader to understand. If the job is repetitive, describe the tasks as they occur in the workcycle. For varied jobs, list the major tasks first, and follow those with the less frequent and/or less important tasks in order.
- Use proper detail: Make sure the description covers all the meaningful duties of the job, but recognize that excessive detail only makes the description difficult to read and use in other HR activities.
- Use the active voice: Start each statement with a functional verb in the present tense (third-person singular)—for instance, "Bends," "Approves," or "Analyzes." Avoid "Is responsible for" because each duty is already assumed to be a responsibility.
- Eliminate unnecessary words: Do not use personal pronouns, because they do not add to the description and the gender of the jobholder is irrelevant.
- Quantify: For example, instead of saying, "Lifts heavy packages," say, "Frequently lifts heavy packages weighing up to 22 kilograms (50 pounds)."
- Describe, do not prescribe: Say, "Operates electronic imaging machine," not, "Must know how to operate electronic image machine." (The latter is a job specification, not a job description.)
- Be specific: Specify what is done by the employee. Do not say, "Does clerical computations"; better, say, "Computes sales frequency percentages."
- Avoid vague terms: Avoid terms like prepares, handles, maintains, and processes. Substitute active, action verbs like checks and reviews.
- Be consistent: Define terms like may, occasionally, and periodically. For example, say, "May is used to describe tasks that only some of the employees in a job perform; occasionally can describe tasks performed once in a while and not by a particular employee on a job."
- Prepare a miscellaneous clause: This clause allows flexibility, and may be phrased such as "Performs other related duties as assigned by supervisory personnel."

1. Are job descriptions really required for all positions in an organization?
2. What are the advantages and disadvantages to the employee and to the employer for having the miscellaneous clause added to the description?

which the job title, department, reporting relationships, location, and date of analysis may be given. Usually, it is advisable to note other information that is useful in tracking jobs and employees through HR systems. Additional items commonly noted in the identification section are: job code, pay grade, and the NOC classification, particularly if the organization is subject to employment equity legislation.

General Summary The second part, the general summary, is a concise statement of the general responsibilities and components that make the job different from others. One HR specialist has characterized the general summary statement as follows: "In 30 words or less, describe the essence of the job." It is generally recommended that the summary be written after all other sections are completed, so that a more complete overview is prepared.

Figure 4-14 *Sample Job Description*

Identification Section:

Position Title: Human Resource Manager **Department: Human Resources** **Reports to: President**

General Summary: Directs HR activities of the firm to ensure compliance with laws and policies, and assists president with overall HR planning

Essential Job Functions:

1. **Manages compensation and benefits programs for all employees, resolves compensation and benefits questions from employees, and negotiates with benefits carriers (20 percent)**
2. **Ensures compliance with both internal policies and applicable federal and provincial legislation, including pay equity, employment equity, and OH&SA (20 percent)**
3. **Identifies HR planning issues and suggested approaches to president and other senior managers (15 percent)**
4. **Assists managers and supervisors to create, plan, and conduct training and various development programs for new and existing employees (15 percent)**
5. **Recruits candidates for employment over telephone and in person. Interviews and selects internal and external candidates for open positions (10 percent)**
6. **Reviews and updates job descriptions, assisted by department supervisors, and coordinates performance appraisal process to ensure timely reviews are completed for all employees (10 percent)**
7. **Administers various HR policies and procedures and helps managers resolve employee performance and policy issues (10 percent)**
8. **Performs other duties as needed and directed by president**

Knowledge, Skills, and Abilities:

- **Knowledge of HR policies, HR practices, and HR-related laws and regulations**
- **Knowledge of company products and services and policies and procedures**
- **Knowledge of management principles and practices**
- **Skill in operating equipment, such as personal computer, software, and IT systems**
- **Skill in oral and written communication**
- **Ability to communicate with employees and various business contacts in a professional and courteous manner**
- **Ability to organize multiple work assignments and establish priorities**
- **Ability to negotiate with others and resolve conflicts, particularly in sensitive situations**
- **Ability to pay close attention to detail and to ensure accuracy of reports and data**
- **Ability to make sound decisions using available information while maintaining confidentiality**
- **Ability to create a team environment and sustain employee commitment**

Education and Experience: Bachelor's degree in HR management or equivalent, plus 3–5 years' experience

Physical Requirements:	**Percentage of Work Time Spent on Activity**			
	0%–24%	**25%–49%**	**50%–74%**	**75%–100%**
Seeing: **Must be able to read computer screen and various reports**				**X**
Hearing: **Must be able to hear well enough to communicate with employees and others**				**X**
Standing/walking	**X**			
Climbing/stooping/kneeling	**X**			
Lifting/pulling/pushing	**X**			
Fingering/grasping/feeling: **Must be able to write, type, and use phone system**				**X**

Working Conditions: Good working conditions with the absence of disagreeable conditions

Note: The statements herein are intended to describe the general nature and level of work performed by employees, but are not a complete list of responsibilities, duties, and skills required of personnel so classified. Furthermore, they do not establish a contract for employment and are subject to change at the discretion of the employer.

Essential Functions and Duties The third part of the typical job description lists the essential functions and duties. It contains clear, precise statements on the major tasks, duties, and responsibilities performed. Writing this section is the most time-consuming aspect of preparing job descriptions.

Job Specifications The next portion of the job description gives the qualifications needed to perform the job satisfactorily. The job specifications typically are stated as: (1) knowledge, skills, and abilities, (2) education and experience, and (3) physical requirements and/or working conditions.

Disclaimer and Approvals The final section on many job descriptions contains approval signatures by appropriate managers and a legal disclaimer. This disclaimer allows employers to change employees' job duties or to request employees to perform duties not listed, so that the job description is not viewed as a contract between the employer and the employee.

SUMMARY

1 Work is organized into jobs for people to do. Both workflow analysis and business process re-engineering are approaches used to check how well this has been done. Job design involves developing jobs that people like to do. It may include simplification, enlargement, enrichment, or rotation. Designing jobs so that they incorporate skill variety, task identity and significance, autonomy, and feedback is important for both employers and employees. There is a growing use of teams in jobs, especially with self-directed work and virtual teams.

2 Greater flexibility in work schedules and the use of telework has affected the design of many jobs. Flexibility may include work schedule alternatives, shift work, compressed workweek, flexible scheduling, and job sharing. It is evident that the pressures from employees' lives and demands from employers lead to emotional imbalances that place pressure on employers to develop policies and practices that take all of these into consideration through flexible working arrangements. These flexible work arrangements allow employees to achieve a better work/life balance that can be accomplished with telework opportunities.

3 Job analysis is a systematic investigation of the content, context, and human requirements of a job. Task-based job analysis focuses on the tasks, duties, and responsibilities associated with jobs. Competency-based job analysis focuses on basic characteristics that can be linked to enhanced performance, such as technical and behavioural competencies. The job analysis process has five stages, beginning with planning and ending with maintaining and updating job descriptions and job specifications. A number of methods of job analysis are used, with interviews and questionnaires being the most popular. NOC 2001, developed by the federal government contains over 30 000 job descriptions available for public use.

4 The behavioural reactions of employees and managers must be considered as part of job analysis. Jobs may sometimes be inflated, as well as job titles. Employees and managers may feel anxious that not all information is being captured. A job description needs to be flexible enough so that managers have freedom to assign tasks, and employees do not feel that they are restricted in performing duties. The focus has to be on the job, not the person. Another way to describe job analysis is that jobs are evaluated based on behavioural aspects of how jobs are completed and not on personal aspects of individuals in a job.

5 The end products of job analysis are job descriptions, which identify the tasks, duties, and responsibilities of jobs, and job specifications, which list the knowledge, skills, and abilities needed to perform a job satisfactorily.

KEY TERMS

Autonomy, p. 136
Business process re-engineering (BPR), p. 132
Competencies, p. 142
Compressed workweek, p. 138
Duty, p. 142
Feedback, p. 136
Flextime, p. 138
Job, p. 130
Job analysis, p. 141
Job description, p. 156
Job design, p. 133
Job enlargement, p. 134
Job enrichment, p. 134
Job rotation, p. 134
Job sharing, p. 139
Job specifications, p. 157
Marginal job functions, p. 155
Performance standards, p. 156
Person/job fit, p. 133
Position, p. 130
Psychometric practices, p. 144
Responsibilities, p. 142
Skill variety, p. 135
Task, p. 142
Task identity, p. 135
Task significance, p. 135
Work, p. 130
Workflow analysis, p. 131

REVIEW AND APPLICATION QUESTIONS

1 For many individuals, the nature of work and jobs is changing. Describe some reasons for the changes and how they are affecting HR management and organizations.

2 Describe the type of organizations and the type of people that would best suit telework? What are the pros and cons of telework?

3 Explain how you would conduct a job analysis in a company that had never had job descriptions.

4 What are the behavioural factors that can affect job analysis? How do they affect job analysis?

5 Describe the elements of a job description.

EXPERIENTIAL EXERCISES

1. Working in pairs, one person will conduct a job analysis using the interview method. Select a job you are currently doing, or one that you have performed in the past. You are then to prepare a job description based on the example presented in Figure 4-14. Refer to the HR Practice tool (on p. 158) on how to write job descriptions.
2. As an HR specialist, you have been asked to develop job descriptions for a *computer support specialist* who assists with LAN/WAN networks. Using the NOC 2001 system, (www23.hrdc-drhc.gc.ca/2001/e/groups/0112.shtml), job boards, and other Web-based resources, locate the details needed and prepare a job description using the format shown in Figure 4-13.
3. Develop a minimum of five behavioural competencies for the following positions:
   - Sales Associate
   - Cashier
   - Bartender
   - Machine Operator
   - Professor
4. Your organization has recently undertaken the task of writing up job descriptions for all jobs in the company. You therefore need to conduct a job analysis on each of the jobs in the organization. You are told by your manager to write one job description per job. You believe that this would be wrong because you know that although many of the individuals hold what is

believed to be the same job, there are differences among many of the positions. For example, the job of IT specialist has about ten positions, but you know that in the regions there are at least two IT specialists that also perform some of the clerical duties because they are so small, yet the other eight specialists have a purely IT-specialist role. The same is evident for many of the administrative and marketing assistants' positions throughout your five regions, and a host of other positions. What are the implications if you don't do this correctly? How will you resolve this issue? Is it realistic to expect that you can resolve this if your manager has given you a direct order?

LEARNING REVIEW

To check your knowledge of the chapter, review the following. (Answers after the case.)

1 A __________ is a grouping of tasks, duties, and responsibilities that constitutes the total work assignment for employees.
   a. job
   b. essential function
   c. job specification
   d. job design

2 One type of shift work is:
   a. shift differential
   b. compressed workweek
   c. job sharing
   d. flextime

3 The most basic building block of HR management is:
   a. essential job functions
   b. knowledge, skills, and abilities
   c. job analysis
   d. job specifications

4 One primary concern of managers and supervisors is that the job analysis and job descriptions will unrealistically:
   a. inflate job specifications
   b. limit flexibility
   c. limit employee growth
   d. inflate employee's job titles

5 The essential functions and duties section of a job description should contain clear and precise statements on the:
   a. tasks, duties, and responsibilities performed
   b. qualifications needed to do the job satisfactorily
   c. conditions in which the work is performed
   d. mental and physical requirements of the job

CASE

PHYSICAL DEMANDS AND JOBS AT PUROLATOR

In a dynamic economy, organizations are constantly striving for inventive ways to decrease costs in order to remain competitive. Job analysis provides one way for organizations to reduce costs and increase efficiency. The following example illustrates what happens when job analysis positively links workers capabilities and productivity.

Purolator, Canada's largest courier company, uses over 12 000 workers across Canada to process 275 million packages a year. In response to $13 million in workers' compensation costs, Purolator hired occupational nurses and workers' compensation specialists to design a return-to-work program that increased coordination between managers, human resources, unions, and physicians. The use of physical demands analysis helped Purolator classify 25 high-risk jobs that accounted for 95 percent of their injury and lost-time cases. Purolator also used the physical demands analysis to identify transitional positions that would best match injured workers' skills and physical capabilities, keeping them productive instead of recovering at home alone. To ensure the success of this program, Purolator linked key accommodation targets to managers' compensation and focused on building stronger relationships with doctors to increase the opportunities to bring people back to work.

With staff at work with lighter duties, Purolator believes that employees seem to show better healing time. As a result, in 2005 Purolator has reduced the total number of days lost by 3000 and the number of modified days by over 5000. As an additional bonus of focusing on matching workers with modified duties, Purolator has increased productivity year after year.[38]

Questions

1. Discuss what job analysis methods you think Purolator used to assess the physical demands of their 25 most high-risk jobs?
2. Identify examples of how job analysis has changed productivity where you have worked and what HR activities were effective and ineffective?

Learning Review Answers: 1. a 2. b 3. c 4. b 5. a

CHAPTER

Recruiting in Labour Markets

Learning Objectives

After you have read this chapter you should be able to:

1 Identify different ways that labour markets can be identified and approached.

2 Discuss the advantages and disadvantages of internal and external recruiting.

3 Specify three internal sources for recruiting and issues associated with their use.

4 List and briefly discuss five external recruiting sources.

5 Explain why Internet recruiting has grown and how employers are conducting it.

6 Discuss three factors to consider when evaluating recruiting efforts.

HR *Headline*

Employment "Branding" Can Help Recruiting

To become an "employer of choice" for excellent job candidates, companies find that it is advantageous to have a recognized "brand" or identity. Organizations viewed as desirable employers are better able to attract more qualified applicants than are organizations with poor reputations. For example, one firm had good pay and benefits, but its work demands were seen as excessive, and frequent downsizings had resulted in some terminations and transfers. The result was high turnover and a low rate of individuals interested in applying for employment at the company.

Companies spend considerable effort and money establishing brand images for their products. Firms that regularly appear in the "100 Best Companies to Work For in Canada" as designated by *The Financial Post*, like Golder & Associates, WestJet, Cisco Systems, EllisDon Corporation, and Dofasco, have achieved success in establishing a brand image that helps their recruiting. An executive in one firm noted that the reason people come to work for them is because of their focus on career development, including bursaries for full and part-time studies, as well as the opportunity to become owners of the firm.

Not only can the brand help generate more recruits, but it can also help with applicant self-selection. For example, EllisDon Corporation, a construction industry services company, recognized as one of the 50 best employers in Canada, is known for progressive compensation and comprehensive benefits package, entrepreneurial environment, and investment in its people. Its mystique does not require mass marketing, because they are an equal opportunity employer and the brightest and best apply.

This marriage between marketing, public relations, and HR is not always easy, or may not be possible in some firms. But when it has occurred, indicators that branding has indeed worked include the following:

- The employer experiences positive name recognition because both individuals inside and outside the company discuss it favourably.
- The employer is a top choice for high performers because they see the firm as a prestigious place that invests in their future.
- If individuals quit, they are more likely to return once they discover that another employer is not as desirable a place to work.
- The employer's sign-up lists at job fairs, colleges, and universities are longer than other employers', which aids both recruiting and enhances the employer's reputation with other potential candidates.[1]

"Ability will never catch up with the demand for it."

—Malcolm Forbes

Recruiting Process of generating a pool of qualified applicants for organizational jobs.

The staffing process matches people with jobs through recruiting and selection. This chapter examines recruiting, and the next examines selection. **Recruiting** is the process of generating a pool of qualified applicants for organizational jobs. If the number of available candidates only equals the number of people to be hired, no real selection is required—the choice has already been made. The organization must either leave some openings unfilled or take all the candidates.

Recruiting is about finding qualified applicants, and doing that often requires much more than just running an ad in a newspaper. For example, simply acquiring the human capital necessary to replace normal attrition and provide for growth probably will require an employer to:[2]

- Know the business and industry to successfully recruit qualified employees
- Identify keys to success in the labour market, including ways to deal with competitors' recruiting efforts
- Cultivate networks and relationships with sources of prospective employees
- Promote the company brand so that the organization becomes known as a good place to work
- Create recruiting metrics in order to measure the effectiveness of recruiting efforts

Without significant HR attention recruiting can become just a set of administrative functions: coordinating internal openings, handling the flow of candidate data, dealing with regulatory reporting, and moving candidates through the system. These steps are important, but more important is tying the employer's business strategy to its recruiting strategy.[3]

Strategic Approach to Recruiting

1 A strategic approach to recruiting becomes more important as labour markets shift and become more competitive. Strategic HR planning helps to align HR strategies with organizational goals and plans. For example, at one time the Canadian airforce never had to look for pilots. People who wanted to fly would always apply to the airforce. However, in the mid 1990s the airforce had too many pilots and stopped accepting applications. At the same time, pilots were being released from the military with buyout packages. By 2003 the airforce had to ramp up its recruitment program in order to attract pilots. With a downturn in the airline industry because of the 9/11 terrorist attacks, a dark cloud was cast on the aviation occupation. This left many spots open with no available candidates to draw upon to fill the gaps when new recruits were needed.[4] The military had not counted on the sharp downturn in the airline industry, and had a false sense that there would always be available recruits. Therefore, it is important that recruiting be a part of strategic HR planning that considers the worst-case scenarios and how to be ready should they arise.

Strategy is a general framework that provides guidance for actions. If a company is driven by technology, recruiting must determine how to bring in the best technologists. If the strategy of a company is based on marketing, the focus should be on where the company will look to find the best marketing candidates. Certainly, cost is an issue, and some employers are quite concerned about cost per hire. However, if an HR strategy focuses on *quality,* a company might choose to hire only from the top 15 percent of candidates for critical jobs, and from the top 30 percent of candidates for all other important positions.[5] This approach likely would improve workforce quality, but it would cost more per hire.

Strategic recruiting may sometimes need to go beyond just filling empty positions. It can focus on discovering talent *before* it is needed, capitalizing on windfall opportunities

Figure 5-1 Strategic Recruiting Stages

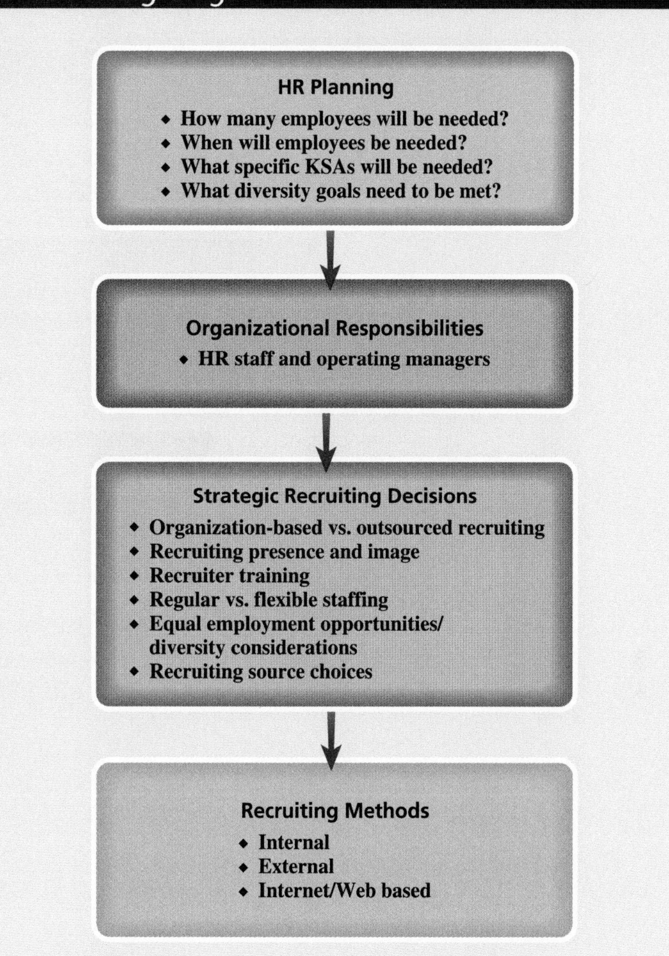

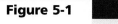

when there is an abundance of highly qualified people, or perhaps developing strong Internet recruiting abilities.[6] Generally, the recruiting decisions dictate not only the kinds and numbers of applicants, but also how difficult or successful recruiting efforts may be. Figure 5-1 shows an overview of the strategic recruiting stages.

Even during periods of reduced hiring, implementing long-range plans means keeping in contact with outside recruiting sources to maintain visibility, while also maintaining employee recruiting channels inside the organization. These efforts allow management to match recruiting activity with organizational and human resource plans.

Employers have faced shortages of workers who have the appropriate knowledge, skills, and abilities. Further, as business cycles fluctuate, demand for labour changes and the number of people looking for work changes.

Labour Markets

Labour markets External supply pool from which organizations attract employees.

Because staffing takes place in such variable labour markets, learning some basics about labour markets aids in understanding recruiting. **Labour markets** are the external supply pool from which employers attract employees. To understand where recruiting takes place, one can think of the sources of employees as a funnel, in which the broad scope of labour markets narrows progressively to the point of selection and job offers (see Figure 5-2). Of course, if the selected candidate rejects the offer, then

Figure 5-2 Labour Market Components

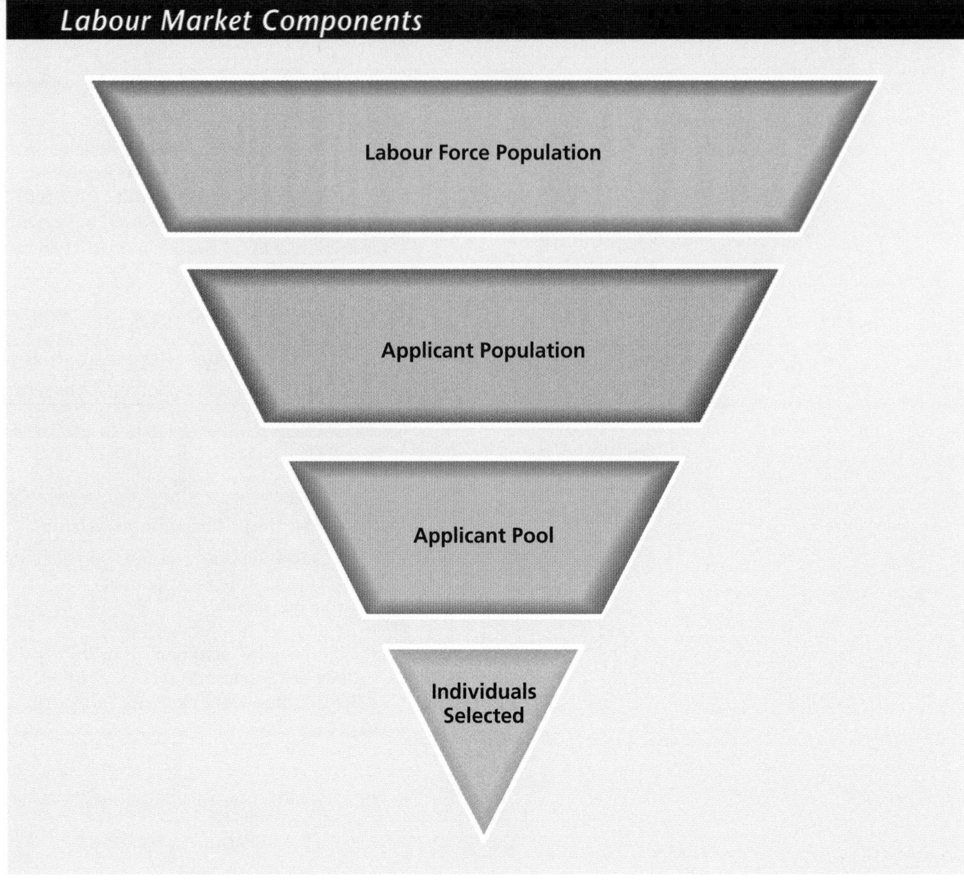

HR staff members must move back up the funnel to the applicant pool for other candidates and in extreme cases to re-open the recruiting process. It is important for recruiting efforts to address a number of specific issues that affect employers in today's labour markets.

Labour Market Components

Labour force population
All individuals who are available for selection if all possible recruitment strategies are used.

Applicant population
A subset of the labour force population that is available for selection using a particular recruiting approach.

The broadest labour market component and measure is the **labour force population,** which is made up of all individuals who are available if all possible recruitment strategies are used. This large number of potential applicants may be reached using many different recruiting methods—for example, newspaper ads, Internet sites, campus job fairs, and word of mouth. Each recruiting method will reach different segments of the labour force population.

The **applicant population** is a subset of the labour force population that is available for selection if a particular recruiting approach is used. For example, an organization might limit its recruiting for management trainees to MBA graduates from major universities. This recruiting method results in a different group of applicants from those who might apply if the employer advertises openings for management trainees in the local newspaper or posts a listing on an Internet job board. At least four recruiting decisions affect reaching the applicant population:

- *Recruiting method:* Advertising medium chosen, including use of employment agencies
- *Recruiting message:* What is said about the job and how it is said

- *Applicant qualifications required:* Education level and amount of experience necessary, for example
- *Administrative procedures:* When recruiting is done, applicant follow-up, and use of previous applicant files

In tight labour markets, many employers try to expand the applicant population in a number of ways. One method that employers have used to expand the applicant population is to consider *ex-convicts*. In fact, in the oil industry, where it is difficult to hire people willing to work in remote locations, recruiters stand outside prisons and approach the released prisoners about working for them at these sites. Care is needed in evaluating the individuals and ensuring appropriate placements given their criminal backgrounds. But giving individuals a second chance has paid off in some situations and not in others, for both small and large employers.

Applicant pool
All persons who are actually evaluated for selection.

The **applicant pool** consists of all persons who are actually evaluated for selection. Many factors can affect the size of the applicant pool, including the reputation of the organization and industry as a place to work, the screening efforts of the organization, the job specifications, and the information available. If a suitable candidate can be found, the organization then selects the individual and makes the job offer.

LOGGING ON...

Job Futures
Job Futures is a career tool that provides useful information about 226 occupational groups and describes the work experiences of recent graduates from 155 programs of study.
http://jobfutures.ca/

Labour Markets and Recruiting

The supply of workers in various labour markets substantially affects staffing. An organization can recruit in a number of labour markets, including geographic, industry and occupational, and educational and technical. The labour markets can be viewed in several ways to provide information that is useful for recruiting. Looking at projections for the labour force by age, participation rates, annual rates of labour force growth, and growth in employment in certain occupations will help alert recruiters to trends in the labour markets.

Geographic Labour Markets One common way to classify labour markets is based on geographic location. Some markets are local, some are regional, some national, and others international. Local and area labour markets vary significantly in terms of workforce availability and quality. For instance, in rural areas such as Northwestern Ontario, it is a major challenge to recruit and retain physicians. As a result, the Northwestern Ontario Medical Programme (NOMP) was established in 1972 in order to encourage both undergraduate and graduate medical students to take a placement in an area that has difficulties recruiting physicians. A study found that NOMP placements were significantly associated with physician recruitment to the area with 217 participants (out of 1982) deciding to establish a practice in Northwestern Ontario.[7]

Changes in a geographic labour market may force changes in recruiting efforts. If a new major employer locates in a regional labour market, then other employers may see a decline in their numbers of applicants. In B.C., five or six foundries have closed in the last ten years. Vulnerable companies were owned by larger companies that were unionized, i.e., high cost and inflexible. Survivors are small, with low debt, low overhead, often family-owned, and flexible. To deal competitively with the problem, quality of products has been sacrificed by buying product overseas and selling it at a fraction of the cost, in addition to the loss of jobs in the larger firms.[8]

Attempting to recruit locally or in a limited geographic area for a job market that is really national will likely result in disappointing applicant rates. For example, a catalogue retailer will likely not be able to recruit a senior merchandising manager from only the small town where the firm is located. Conversely, it may not need to recruit nationally for workers to fill administrative support jobs.

Global Labour Markets North American employers tap global labour markets when necessary and export work to overseas labour markets when doing so is advantageous. Scores of Western firms have farmed out software development and back-office work to India and other countries with lower wages. The migration of work overseas has been controversial. While many decry the loss of North American jobs, some employers respond that they cannot be competitive in a global market if they fail to take advantage of labour savings.

Fortunately Canada has been one of the benefactors of the U.S. outsourcing panacea, particularly with respect to call centres. The turnover rate in U.S. call centres ranges from 50 percent to 70 percent, whereas in Canada, the turnover rate is about 15 percent to 25 percent. In Canada, those pursuing call centres for employment view it as a career, which may be one of the reasons the turnover rate is so much lower. Additionally, wage rates are about 30 percent lower in Canada, although that may change as the U.S. rate of inflation increases, and Canada's dollar strengthens. An advantage for Canada is that our education systems are similar to some extent, and clients in the U.S. want to speak with English-speaking individuals. Our proximity is also an attractive enticement. Approximately 150 000 employees work in Canada's call centres nationally, half of which comes from U.S. outsourcing. It is expected that this industry will grow considerably over the next five to ten years.[9]

Recruiting employees for global assignments requires approaches and understanding different from those used for typical recruiting efforts in the home country. The recruiting processes must consider differences in culture, laws, and language. For instance, in Eastern Europe, potential recruits like to work for European and North American firms, so recruiters emphasize the "Western" image. In Hong Kong, recruiting ads often stress success factors by showing "typical employees" of a firm wearing expensive watches and stylish clothes.

Dealing with foreign labour markets can present challenges. In China, for example, recruiting is regulated and generally requires the approval of local personnel or labour authorities. Article 8 of the Labor Market Regulations sets out the specific channels that may be used for recruiting. Recruitment agencies, employment fairs, mass media, and the Internet are allowable. Unfortunately, two government bureaucracies, with different rules, have overlapping authority in recruiting, and the result is bureaucratic confusion as to what recruiting can be done.[10]

The growth of the Internet has made global recruiting much more accessible, particularly for individuals in search of professional management jobs. Those individuals and more technologically knowledgeable candidates can be reached using Internet advertising. Global search firms also can be used to locate specialized global managerial talent.

Industry and Occupational Labour Markets Labour markets also can be classified by industry and occupation. The demand for truck drivers, hotel workers, nurses, teachers, and others has been strong, creating tight labour markets in the industries served by those occupations.

Occupational labour markets are based on the knowledge, skills, and abilities (KSAs) required for the jobs. These markets include physical therapists, HR managers, engineers, accountants, welders, and bank tellers. One occupational area of extreme volatility in the past several years is the *information technology* (IT) labour market, which has fluctuated from being extremely tight several years ago, to rather soft after many dot-coms failed and employers began exporting software work.

Educational and Technical Labour Markets Another way to look at labour markets is by considering educational and technical qualifications to define the people being recruited. Employers may need individuals with specific licences, certifications, or educational backgrounds. For instance, a shortage of business professors with Ph.D.s is forecasted to affect many colleges and universities in the next few years due to the retirement of many baby boomers from faculty positions. Other examples include shortages of certified auto mechanics, heating and air-conditioning technicians, and network-certified computer specialists.

Unemployment Rate and Labour Markets

When the unemployment rate is high in a given market, many applicants are looking for jobs. Such a candidate glut is a mixed blessing, as a down economy generates more unqualified candidates (who simply apply for anything) to sift through—but the big volume of applicants can mean more qualified people as well.[11] When the unemployment rate is low, there are few applicants. Of course, unemployment rates vary with the business cycle and present very different challenges for recruiting. For instance, at the end of 2004, the tourism sector in Banff Alberta was experiencing an employee shortage due to the low unemployment rate (around 2 percent) between Jasper, Alberta, and the American border. Erin Langevin who is the director of recruitment at the Rimrock Resort Hotel in Banff says that she doesn't see many résumés and is recruiting from a small labour pool that is transient and shrinking. As a result, the community of Banff got together to create www.banfflife.com to promote Banff as not only a place for university students or transient students but also as a permanent place of residence.[12]

Strategic Recruiting Decisions

2 An employer must make a number of recruiting decisions based on the recruiting needs identified as part of HR planning. Important ones are discussed next.

Organization-Based vs. Outsourced Recruiting

An initial and basic decision is whether the recruiting will be done by the employer or outsourced. This decision need not be an "either-or" decision, with all recruiting done by organizational staff or else external resources used exclusively.

In most organizations, HR staff members handle the bulk of recruiting efforts. The distribution of recruiting responsibilities between the HR department and operating managers shown in Figure 5-3 is typical for all but the smallest organizations.

Because recruiting can be a time-consuming process, given all the other responsibilities of HR staff and other managers in organizations, outsourcing it is a way

Figure 5-3 *Typical Division of HR Responsibilities: Recruiting*

HR Unit	Managers
• Forecasts recruiting needs • Prepares copy for recruiting ads and campaigns • Plans and conducts recruiting efforts • Audits and evaluates all recruiting activities	• Anticipate needs for employees to fill vacancies • Determine KSAs needed from applicants • Assist in recruiting efforts with information about job requirements • Review success/failure of recruiting activities

to both decrease the number of HR staff needed and free up time for HR staff members. Recruiting can be outsourced in a number of ways. For example, some large employers outsource such functions as placement of advertisements, initial screening of résumés, and initial phone contacts with potential applicants. Once those activities are done, then the employer's HR staff take over the rest of the recruiting activities.

A common means of outsourcing is retaining search firms and employment agencies to recruit candidates. Currently, about 10 percent of all firms outsource large parts of recruiting operations, and about 58 percent plan to increase outsourcing at some point.[13] For example, Kellogg, with 14 000 employees worldwide, outsources the hiring of all but hourly employees. Outsourcing gives the firm more flexibility: when 200 salespeople were needed quickly, the vendor was able to fill those positions faster and cheaper ($3,800 per hire vs. $6,000 per hire) than inhouse recruiters could have.[14]

Moen, a large manufacturer of plumbing fixtures with 3500 employees, works with only one outsource recruiter. On any day, between 175 and 200 temporary workers are provided by the recruiting firm, which keeps two of its own full-time employees on-site to oversee HR issues with the temps, who are rated and receive points. All full-time employees are hired from those individuals with the highest scores in the temp pool.[15]

Professional Employer Organizations (PEOs) and Employee Leasing

A specific type of outsourcing uses professional employer organizations (PEOs) and employee leasing. This approach has grown rapidly in recent years. Some sources estimate that about 3 million individuals are employed by PEOs doing employee leasing.[16]

The employee leasing process is simple: An employer signs an agreement with the PEO, after which the existing staff is hired by the leasing firm and leased back to the company. For a fee, a small-business owner or operator turns the staff over to the leasing company, which then writes the paycheques, pays the taxes, prepares and implements HR policies, and keeps all the required records.

PEOs and employment agencies are different entities. An *employment agency* provides a "workfinding" service for job seekers and supplies employers with applicants they may then hire. A PEO has its own workforce, which it supplies by contract to employers with jobs. Small-business owners do not always know how to comply with employment standards and other requirements. Using a PEO can be an advantage because the PEO handles the HR complexities.[17] There are, however, some legal and tax-related issues that must be considered when using a PEO, so employers should consult outside experts before shifting to PEOs for staffing.[18]

OI Group of Companies
OI is an employee leasing company representing First Nations People.
www.oigroup.ca/

One advantage for employees of leasing companies is that they may receive better benefits than they otherwise would get in many small businesses. All this service comes at a cost. Leasing companies often charge employers between 4 percent and 6 percent of employees' monthly salaries. Thus, while leasing may save employers money on benefits and HR administration, it may also increase total costs of payroll.

An example of an employee leasing company in Canada is the OI Group of Companies, which represents First Nations People. OI provides over 1000 leased employees to a variety of not-for-profit organizations (friendship centres, health organizations, cultural centres, housing groups), band councils, government departments, and private businesses allowing them to focus their valuable energy, time, and resources to their core mission.

Recruiting Presence and Image

Recruiting efforts may be viewed as either continuous or intensive. *Continuous* efforts to recruit offer the advantage of keeping the employer in the recruiting market. For example, with campus recruiting, some organizations may find it advantageous to have a recruiter on a given campus each year. Employers that visit a campus only occasionally are less likely to build a following in that school over time.

Intensive recruiting may take the form of a vigorous recruiting campaign aimed at hiring a given number of employees, usually within a short period of time. Such efforts may be the result of failure in the HR planning system to identify needs in advance or to recognize drastic changes in workforce needs due to unexpected workloads.

As noted in the chapter opener, a factor related to recruiting is portraying a positive image of the employer. The way the "employment brand" of the organization is viewed by both employees and outsiders is crucial to attracting applicants and retaining employees, who also may describe the organization in positive or negative terms to others.

Additionally, the recruiting image of an industry and an employer can significantly affect whether individuals ever consider a firm and submit applications. For example, in the fast-food industry, the product image and reputation of a firm affects the attractiveness of the firm as a potential employer of teenagers and retirees. Recruiting should be seen as part of organizational marketing efforts and linked to the overall image and reputation of the organization and its industry.

Training of Recruiters

Another important strategic issue is how much training will be given to recruiters. In addition to being trained on interviewing techniques, communications skills, and knowledge of the jobs being filled, it is crucial that recruiters learn the types of actions that violate human rights and how to be sensitive to diversity issues with applicants. Training in those areas often includes interview do's and don'ts and appropriate language to use with applicants. Racist, sexist, and other inappropriate remarks hurt the image of the employer and may result in legal complaints. For instance, a male campus recruiter regularly asked female candidates about their marital status, and if they were single and attractive, he later called applicants and asked them for dates. Only after two students complained to the university placement office did the employer learn of the recruiter's misconduct.

Incidents such as this one reinforce the importance of employers' monitoring recruiters' behaviours and actions. Some employers send interviewees follow-up surveys asking about the effectiveness of the recruiters and the image the candidates have of the employers as a result of their recruiting contacts.

Regular vs. Flexible Staffing

Another strategic decision affects how much recruiting will be done to fill staffing needs with regular full-time and part-time employees. Decisions as to who should be recruited hinge on whether to seek traditional employees or to use more flexible approaches, which might include temporaries or independent contractors. A number of employers feel that the cost of keeping a regular workforce has become excessive and grows worse due to increasing government-mandated costs. However, not just the money is at issue. The number of governmental regulations also constrains the employment relationship, making many employers reluctant to hire new employees.

Flexible staffing
Use of workers who are not traditional employees.

Flexible staffing uses workers who are not traditional employees. Using flexible staffing arrangements allows an employer to avoid some of the cost of full-time benefits such as vacation pay and pension plans, as well as to recruit in a somewhat different market. These arrangements provide temporary workers, independent contractors, and employee leasing.

Temporary Workers Employers who use temporary employees can hire their own temporary staff members or contract with agencies supplying temporary workers on a rate-per-day or rate-per-week basis. Originally developed to provide clerical and office workers to employers, such agencies now provide workers in many other areas. The use of temporary workers may make sense for an organization if its work is subject to seasonal or other fluctuations. Hiring regular employees to meet peak employment needs would require that the employer find some tasks to keep employees busy during less active periods or resort to layoffs.[19]

Some employers hire temporary workers as a way for individuals to move into full-time, regular employment. Better-performing workers may move to regular positions when they become available. This "try before you buy" approach is potentially beneficial to both employers and employees. However, most temporary service firms bill client companies a placement charge if a temporary worker is hired full-time within a certain time period—usually 90 days.

Independent contractors
Workers who perform specific services on a contract basis.

Independent Contractors Some firms employ **independent contractors,** who are workers that perform specific services on a contract basis. Independent contractors are used in a number of areas, including building maintenance, security, advertising, and others. One major reason for use of independent contractors is that some employers get significant savings by using independent contractors because benefits do not have to be provided to those individuals. Some employers, in their angst to cut costs, have hired employees as independent contractors so that they would not be responsible for government remittances such as Canada Pension, employment insurance, or workers' compensation. However, a Supreme Court ruling in *671122 Ontario v. Sagaz Industries Canada Inc.* (2001) clearly spells out the differences.

Organizations hire independent contractors when special skills are required for specific projects for defined periods of time.

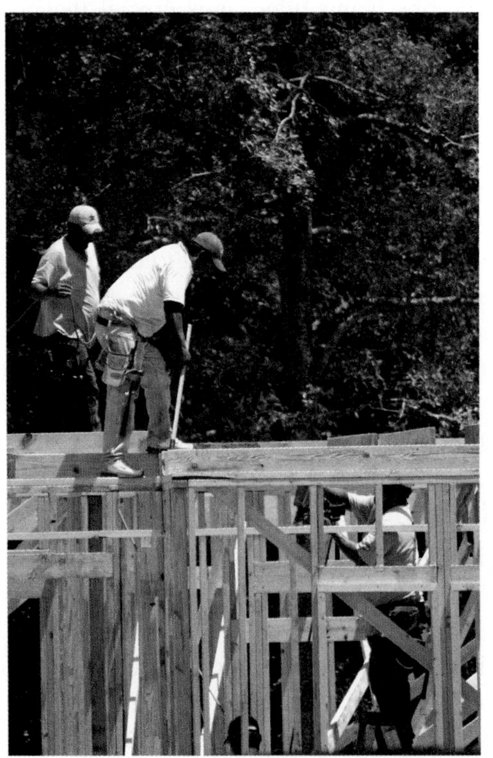

Source: Jason Smith/ShutterStock

A non-exhaustive list of factors to consider includes: whether the person performs services as a business on his or her own account; the level of control held over the worker's activities; whether the worker provides the equipment and hires helpers; the degree of financial risk taken by the worker as well as the degree or responsibility for investment and management held by the worker; and the worker's opportunity for profit. The consequences of incorrectly characterizing a working relationship as an independent contractor arrangement are dire. They include: penalties, interest, and liability under the Income Tax Act; liability under the Employment Insurance Act as a result of an organization's failure to withhold and remit employment insurance premiums; liability for Canada Pension Plan contributions; and liability under the Workplace Safety and Insurance Act.[20]

Recruiting and Diversity Considerations

As Figure 5-4 indicates, a number of factors go into ensuring that recruiting decisions meet diversity considerations. Recruiting as a key employment-related activity is subject to various legal considerations, especially human rights legislation. All applicants must be given the same consideration. For employers with employment equity plans, a concerted effort has to be made to reach designated group members so that they have equal opportunity to apply for positions. The determination of who should proceed in the recruitment process must be made on the valid credentials of the applicant and the requirements of the job without regard for issues pertaining to gender, marital status, nationality, ethnicity, religion, physical ability, or any other discriminatory considerations.

Employment Advertising Employers must exercise care when preparing employment advertisements. The federal and provincial human rights commissions provide guidelines that state no direct or indirect references implying gender or age are permitted. Some examples of impermissible terminology are: "young and enthusiastic," "single," "male or female," "Christian values," and "journeyman lineman." The position must also state requirements that match the job. For example, the ad cannot state that a driver's licence would be required, if there was no need for the individual to drive as part of their normal duties; or asking for ten years of experience, when no experience is really required. The requirements must be for the minimal requirements of the job. Figure 5-5 demonstrates unacceptable job advertisements that employers must avoid in terms of discriminating on many of the prohibited grounds.[21]

Figure 5-4 *Recruiting and Diversity Considerations*

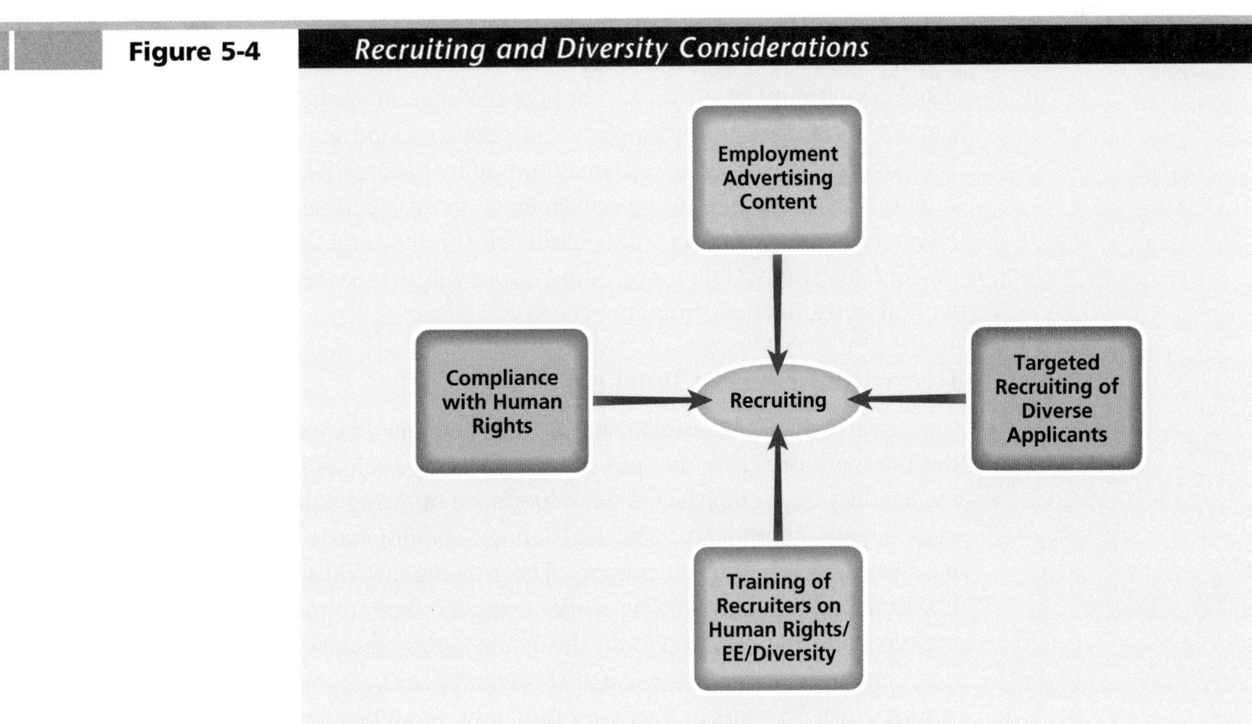

Figure 5-5 ***Unacceptable Job Advertisements***

Example 1

Applicants must be young and energetic and possess superior customer relations skills. Applicants who are selected would be required to stand for long periods of time and to lift 9 to 13 kilograms (20 to 30 pounds).

Example 2

Position for a person seeking to supplement pension. Part-time position available for service counter position in small cafe from 9:00 a.m.–2:00 p.m., Monday–Thursday. Responsibilities include serving customers, maintaining dishwasher, cleaning tables, and handling transactions. Retired persons preferred.

Example 3

Young-thinking, "new wave" progressive advertising firm has openings for entry-level position for graphic artists with no more than three years' experience. We specialize in music videos and broadcast productions for a youthful audience. Our main focus is in the area of animation. Our clients include famous rock stars. If you have fresh, innovative ideas and can relate to our audience, send your résumé.

Example 4

Experienced slender models between 18 and 30 for upcoming summer collection of Beachwear wanted. Applicants must bring a portfolio and references to our Vancouver office. Only those persons in the specified age category need apply.

Example 5

***Wanted*: Individuals of all ages. Day and evening hours available. Full-time and part-time positions. All inquiries welcomed. Excellent secondary source of income for students and retired persons.**

Additionally, employment advertisements should indicate that the employer is an equal opportunity employer to send the message to applicants that they will be considered on merit and fair employment practices, and not on discriminatory factors. Employers demonstrate inclusive recruiting by having diverse individuals represented in company materials, in advertisements, and as recruiters. Ernest & Young, RBC Financial, Family Service Association of Toronto, and other firms have found that making diversity visible in recruiting efforts has helped them recruit more individuals with more varied backgrounds.[22]

Recruiting Diverse Workers

Since the early 1990s, organizations have become aware of the need to hire a more diverse workforce. Various pieces of legislation such as human rights and employment equity have emphasized the importance of hiring a more diverse workforce that goes beyond compliance with legislation. The emphasis now is on the survival of business in a more global economy. The growing difficulty that many employers have had in attracting and retaining workers has led them to recruit workers from diverse backgrounds.[23] In addition to the designated group members (women, visible minorities, persons with disabilities, and Aboriginal peoples), another target group are older workers over 55 years of age. Unfortunately, small businesses will face the most difficulty in recruiting workers.

Designated Group Members Employers that do business with the federal government must have employment equity plans, as discussed in Chapter 3. Consequently, those employers may face pressures to increase proportionately the number of employees who are women, visible minorities, persons with disabilities, or Aboriginal peoples. These pressures often are stronger for managerial, professional, and technical jobs than for unskilled, clerical, and blue-collar jobs. A popular misconception about hiring for employment equity reasons is that a designated group member must always be selected above other qualified candidates. This is not the case. The most qualified individual must be hired. If, all things being equal, that is, the designated group member has the same qualifications as the White male, and there is a need to fulfill an employment equity obligation to hire more designated group members, then the designated group member would have the first opportunity. If the White male were the most qualified candidate, then he would be given the employment opportunity first. These groups have been protected due to historical treatment including high unemployment rates, lower wages and occupying lower job status positions.

Women Women represent 47 percent or the workforce, yet their employment is relegated to the lower levels. There are very few women holding senior positions in Canada, particularly at the CEO level. According to a study conducted by Catalyst Canada, women held 14.4 percent of corporate officer positions in Canada in 2004.[24] The need to be aware of the disparity in recruitment must also be addressed in terms of promotional opportunities that will help women gain the training needed for senior roles. Breaking the "glass ceiling" remains a major problem in the recruitment of senior women. Another problem area for women is in engineering, science, technology, and trade. The Canadian Coalition of Women in Engineering, Science, Technology and Trade continues to work with industry, government, and education to increase the opportunities for women in these technical professions.[25]

Visible Minorities Visible minorities represent enormous opportunities to fulfill employment gaps in a number of professions. New immigrants to Canada must have substantial credentials in order to obtain working visas in Canada. However, once they are here, we do little to help them succeed, particularly professionals. Many of them are trained health-care workers, such as doctors, IT professionals, accountants, tool-and-die makers, and scientists. Their new jobs in Canada are delivering pizzas, driving taxis, working in low-paying jobs that don't make use of their skills. Many others are volunteering so that they can gain Canadian experience.

Lynne Sullivan, president of Lynne Sullivan & Associates Inc., specializes in diversity and employment equity and recommends the following to ensure that we capture the necessary skills and experience of these professionals entering Canada:[26]

1. Relax the Canadian experience requirement—The requirement for Canadian experience could be viewed as systemic barrier to gaining access to employment, unless it is a bona fide occupational requirement. A person's accent is often regarded negatively, with assumptions that the individual does not understand you. This is discriminatory in its own right.
2. Facilitate access to that first job—Participate in internship and bridging programs, such as Career Bridge, offered through educational institutions and community agencies to give newcomers the experience they need to land on their feet. To qualify for Career Bridge, the résumé must be assessed by World Education Service (WES) for Canadian equivalency.
3. Make employee orientation more supportive—One way for new Canadians to become acclimatized to the way we conduct business is to have them attend a program at a local community college that teaches them business-language training,

Career Bridge
Career Bridge is a not-for-profit internship program set up to help foreign professionals find work in their fields.
www.careerbridge.ca

teamwork, presentations, social functions, and legal environment for employment. One such program exists at George Brown College in Toronto for IT professionals.

4. Make it someone's job to help the newcomer succeed—It is important to assign a coach or mentor to the newcomer. The role of the coach or mentor is to explain how things are done in the organization such as procedures, rules, dress code, or accepted behaviour, to name just a few.
5. Make sure your people are cross-culturally savvy—Everyone needs to be educated on cross-cultural differences.
6. Support the community that's helping you—Organizations should become involved in programs for internationally trained professionals to help them get started and contribute to our organizations.

LOGGING ON...

Disability Weblinks
This site provides individuals with links to the different agencies across Canada.
www.disabilityweblinks.ca/

Persons with Disabilities Persons with disabilities provide a potential pool of recruits. Jobs must be such that accommodation can be made for people with disabilities. Not every disability lends itself to every job for accommodation. However, in many cases, changes in job duties, work stations, and equipment might result in a job that a person with a disability can do—and do well. For example, at Rogers Communications, special monitors and software are used by visually impaired individuals who take customer calls. Recruitment for these individuals can be enhanced by sourcing the various community groups that can help bridge the organization with the qualified individuals.

LOGGING ON...

Aboriginal Canada Portal
This site offers Canadian Aboriginal peoples online resources to listings of Aboriginal associations, businesses, organizations, bands, communities, groups, news, and peoples.
www.aboriginalcanada.gc.ca/

Aboriginal Peoples Aboriginal peoples are the fastest growing segment of the population and offer an available resource for employers, yet organizations do not appear to be making a lot of progress on this front. A number of reasons have been cited for this failure to capture this labour market. The Aboriginal workforce participation is 47 percent while the non-Aboriginal participation rate is 78 percent, and the vast majority of Aboriginal workers earn far below the poverty line. Some reasons for this failure to attract the Aboriginal labour force relates to a lack of succession planning, word-of-mouth hiring that excludes Aboriginals, a failure to connect with the agencies that help find employment for Aboriginals, better alliance with educational systems to ensure that the proper skills are being taught, and lack of role models because there are so few Aboriginals in many of the organizations. A consideration of some of these issues should lead to a better understanding of how to work with Aboriginal groups.[27]

Older Workers When discussing the recruitment of older workers, the first task is to identify which individuals are included in this group. Senior and experienced individuals may include the following:

- *Mid-life career changers:* Those who are burned out in their jobs and career fields and leave voluntarily to try new fields
- *Displaced older workers:* Those who have worked but have been displaced, often involuntarily, through job reductions or plant closings
- *Retirees:* Those who took early retirement buyouts or formally retired from prior jobs

Employees with disabilities are able to perform jobs, sometimes with only minor accommodation. Perhaps one of the largest barriers to successful employment are stereotypical views that disabled persons are not capable employees.

Source: Stockbyte

LOGGING ON...

Canada's Association for People over the Age of 50 (CARP)
CARP is Canada's largest advocacy group for Canadians over 50, now with 400,000+ members.
www.carp.ca/

LOGGING ON...

Canadian Federation of Independent Business (CFIB)
CFIB works on behalf of more than 100 000 independent business owners in every sector and region in Canada.
www.cfib.ca/

Older workers provide an available source of skilled labour that can be used more effectively than it has been. Considering that young workers are hungry for coaching and mentoring, what better opportunity exists than to pair the young with the more experienced worker. A number of organizations are taking advantage of the opportunity to hire older workers to help energize their firms. Home Depot, RBC Financial Global Banking Services Centre, and McDonald's are well known for their use of older workers. Older workers make up more than 20 percent of Home Depot's Canadian staff.[28]

Small Businesses Small businesses face the identical set of problems that larger organizations do when it comes to filling positions. Everyone is competing for the same set of resources. The problem becomes different though for smaller businesses because they typically will not have the same types of resources to draw upon when a shortage of labour occurs because they just do not have the staffing abilities. Studies have indicated that 1 in 20 jobs are unfilled because of an inability to find suitably skilled labour. Construction and business suffer the most. Small businesses need to draw on the immigration system, become more closely aligned with education officials and students about their needs and use internships, co-op, and apprenticeships more than they have.[29] A key to success will be for small business to be better trained in human resources management so that they can be ready to compete head-on with larger organizations who have these skills and to utilize technology, more specifically Internet recruitment, more effectively. For an example of research on the effects of Internet recruitment and small businesses, see the HR Perspective.

HR *Perspective*

Research on Small Firms and Internet Recruitment

Even though Internet recruitment is being utilized extensively by employers, the same cannot be said for small firms. To provide insights on this issue, Terry Wagar and Lynn Langrock surveyed more than 350 small businesses in Eastern Canada to find out how they are recruiting for staff. Small firms were defined to be fewer than 100 employees and did not include firms that were in the not-for-profit sector or were a branch of a larger organization. Sixty-three percent of the firms surveyed had less than ten employees, 30 percent had 11–50 employees, and 7 percent had 50–100 employees.

The survey indicated that responsibility for recruitment was mostly at the senior levels. In 31 percent of the cases, the owner of the business was responsible, 51 percent were conducted by the president and CEO, and 18 percent by the manager or other employee. Only 42 percent received any actual training in recruitment, and this was offered by the larger firms in the study. Additionally most positions were filled externally, rather than promoting from within. The most frequently used method to recruit new employees was by employee referral, with the Internet and employment agencies used the least. As smaller firms grow they tend to use more recruitment methods to increase the applicant pool, and the larger firms tended to use the Internet more frequently.

The researchers conclude that smaller firms may not be well versed in technology, thus accounting for the lack of use in Internet recruitment. The lack of training raises the concern about poor hiring decisions, which could be very costly for a small firm.[30]

1. Do you think that technology is the main reason for small businesses not utilizing the Internet to recruit? Why or why not?
2. Is it reasonable that the most senior person in a small business is responsible for recruitment? If it is not reasonable, then who else should be involved and why?

Figure 5-6 Advantages and Disadvantages of Internal and External Recruiting Sources

Recruiting Source	Advantages	Disadvantages
Internal	• The morale of the promotee is usually high. • The firm can better assess a candidate's abilities. • Recruiting costs are lower for some jobs. • The process is a motivator for good performance. • The process causes a succession of promotions. • The firm has to hire only at entry level.	• "Inbreeding" results. • Those not promoted may experience morale problems. • Employees may engage in "political" infighting for promotions. • A management development program is needed.
External	• New "blood" brings new perspectives. • Training new hires is cheaper and faster because of prior external experience. • The new hire has no group of "political supporters" in the organization. • The new hire may bring new industry insights.	• The firm may not select someone who will fit the job or the organization. • The process may cause morale problems for internal candidates not selected. • The new employee may require a longer adjustment or orientation time.

Recruiting Source Choices: Internal vs. External

Recruiting strategy and policy decisions entail identifying where to recruit, whom to recruit, and how to recruit. One of the first decisions determines the extent to which internal or external sources and methods will be used. Both promoting from within the organization (internal recruitment) and hiring from outside the organization (external recruitment) come with advantages and disadvantages. Figure 5-6 shows some of the major pluses and minuses of each.

Most employers combine the use of internal and external methods. Organizations that face rapidly changing competitive environments and conditions may need to place a heavier emphasis on external sources in addition to developing internal sources. However, for organizations existing in environments that change slowly, promotion from within may be more suitable. Once the various recruiting policy decisions have been addressed, then the actual recruiting methods can be identified and used. These include internal and external sources, as well as Internet/Web-based approaches.

Internal Recruiting

3 Pursuing internal recruiting with the advantages mentioned earlier means using various sources developed and managed inside the organization. The most common internal recruiting methods include: organizational databases, job postings, promotions and transfers, current-employee referrals, and re-recruiting of former employees and applicants.

Internal Recruiting Processes

Within the organization, tapping into databases, job postings, promotions, and transfers provides ways for current employees to move to other jobs. Filling openings internally may add motivation for employees to stay and grow in the organization rather than pursuing career opportunities elsewhere.

Organizational Databases The increased use of HR management systems allows HR staff members to maintain background and KSA information on existing employees. As openings arise, HR employment specialists can access databases by entering job requirements and then get a listing of current employees meeting those requirements. Various types of employment software sort employee data by occupational fields, education, areas of career interests, previous work histories, and other variables. For instance, if a firm has an opening for someone with an MBA and marketing experience, the key words *MBA* and *marketing* can be entered in a search field, and the program displays a list of all current employees with these two items identified in their employee profiles.

The advantage of such databases is that they can be linked to other HR activities. Opportunities for career development and advancement are major reasons why individuals stay or leave their employers. With databases, internal opportunities for individuals can be identified. Employee profiles are continually updated to include such items as additional training or education completed, special projects worked on, and career plans and desires noted during performance appraisal and career mentoring discussions.

Job posting
System in which the employer provides notices of job openings and employees respond by applying.

Job Posting The major means for recruiting employees for other jobs within the organization is **job posting,** a system in which the employer provides notices of job openings and employees respond by applying for specific openings. Without some sort of job posting system, it is difficult for many employees to find out what jobs are open elsewhere in the organization. The organization can notify employees of job vacancies in a number of ways, including posting notices on the company intranet and website, using employee newsletters, and sending out e-mails to managers and employees.

In a unionized organization, job posting and bidding can be quite formal because the procedures are often spelled out in labour agreements. Seniority lists may be used by organizations that make promotions based strictly on seniority, so candidates are considered for promotions in the order of seniority. In other cases, even though a job posting is to be used, a "ringer" or "shoe-in" candidate may exist. This of course causes concern for the integrity and intent of a job posting systems. What some organizations do to bring the issue to the forefront is to add a qualifier to the job posting that indicates a "strong internal candidate exists but you are still encouraged to apply." This qualifier helps to eliminate resentment or low morale. It also helps management to identify future promotional material and/or select someone if the strong candidate decides, at the last minute not apply.

Regardless of the means used, the purpose of the job posting system is to provide employees with more opportunities to move within the organization. When establishing and managing a job posting system, a number of answers to many potential questions must be addressed:

- What happens if no qualified candidates respond to postings?
- Must employees inform their supervisors that they are applying for another job?
- Are there restrictions on how long an employee must stay in a job before applying for another one?
- How much notice should an employee be required to give before transferring to a new department?
- What types of or levels of jobs will not be posted?

Job posting systems can be ineffective if handled improperly. Jobs generally are posted before any external recruiting is done. The organization must allow a reasonable period of time for present employees to check notices of available jobs before it considers external applicants. When employees' bids are turned down, they should discuss with their supervisors or someone in the HR area the knowledge, skills, and abilities they need in order to improve their opportunities in the future.

Some organizations use automated systems that combine elements of databases and job postings. The Technology Transforming HR presents examples of such systems.

Promotions and Transfers Many organizations choose to fill vacancies through promotions or transfers from within whenever possible. Although promotions and transfers from within are usually successful, there can also be some drawbacks as well. A person's performance on one job may not be a good predictor of performance on another, because different skills may be required on the new job. For example, not every high-performing worker makes a successful supervisor. In most supervisory jobs, an ability to accomplish the work through others requires skills in influencing and dealing with people, and those skills may not have been a factor in non-supervisory jobs.

As employees transfer or are promoted to other jobs, individuals must be recruited to fill their vacated jobs. Planning on how to fill those openings should occur before the job transfers or promotions, not afterward. It is clear that people in organizations with fewer levels may have less frequent chances for promotion. Also,

Technology Transforming HR

Automated Job Posting

A number of vendors offer systems that allow large companies to match existing employees with new job openings. Taking a close look at their own employees saves firms money and helps loyalty. It has been noted that "if you are not recruiting your own employees, someone else will," and that if employees have no internal opportunities to advance, the best performers will look outside.

Most companies have had some kind of job posting systems for internal jobs; now more use pro-active efforts to get employees to apply through Web-based systems. For example, a typical job posting system works like this: Employees log on to the company intranet and create personal profiles including career objectives, education, skill sets, and salary expectations. They may also attach a résumé. When a job opens, the placement program automatically mines the database for matches. Candidates are notified by e-mail and go through the regular hiring cycle.

Thomson Legal and Regulatory, a legal publishing firm with 17 000 employees worldwide, uses a similar system. After logging on to the intranet and creating profiles, applicants respond to a series of questions about their experiences, skills, and professional qualifications. These responses are scored and ranked automatically. If an applicant fits criteria set by a hiring manager, then a face-to-face interview can be scheduled.

At Whirlpool, 68 000 employees can use a somewhat similar system, making it simpler for employees to access job openings. They can go online to retrieve a list of jobs that match their backgrounds and to apply for jobs. Further, managers can enter job criteria and instantly receive names of internal and external candidates who fit them. More than half of the people Whirlpool hired in 2003 were internal candidates. The company estimates that it saved $1 million with the system that year.

These examples illustrate how automated job posting is paying off for employers. Use of such systems is expected to grow in the future.[31]

1. Do you feel that a system where you keep your profile up-to-date, as well as your résumé is fair to all employees in recruitment scenarios? Explain your answer?
2. Is it reasonable for a current employee to go through a pre-screening when the managers already know who you are? Why or why not?

in most organizations, promotions may not be an effective way to speed the movement of designated-group individuals up through the organization if doing that is an organizational concern. Some promotions and transfers may require employee relocation as well.[32]

Employee-Focused Recruiting

One reliable source of potential recruits is suggestions from current or former employees. Because current and former employees are familiar with the employer, most employees usually do not refer individuals who are likely to be unqualified or to make the employees look bad. Also, follow-up with former employers is likely to be done only with persons who were solid employees previously.

Current-Employee Referrals A reliable source of people to fill vacancies is composed of acquaintances, friends, and family members of employees. The current employees can acquaint potential applicants with the advantages of a job with the company, furnish letters of introduction, and encourage candidates to apply. However, using only word-of-mouth or current employee referrals can lead to cases of systemic discrimination because of the belief that our friends are just like us. Therefore, some external recruiting might be necessary to avoid potential human rights issues in this area unless it can be proven that a diverse group of applicants have been referred using this method.

Utilizing this source is usually one of the most effective methods of recruiting because many qualified people can be reached at a low cost. In an organization with numerous employees, this approach can develop quite a large pool of potential employees. Some studies have found that new workers recruited through current-employee referrals have longer tenure with organizations than do those recruited through other sources. According to a study, referral programs cost an average of $500 per salaried employee hired and $70 per hourly employee hired, whereas print advertising costs $2,884 per salaried employee hired and $726 per hourly employee hired.[33]

Tight labour markets in many geographic areas and certain occupational fields prompted many employers to establish employee referral incentive programs. Mid-sized and larger employers are much more likely to use employee referral bonuses. Some referral programs provide different amounts for hard-to-fill jobs compared with common openings.

Re-recruiting of Former Employees and Applicants Former employees and former applicants represent another source for recruitment. Both groups offer a time-saving advantage because something is already known about them. Seeking them out as candidates is known as re-recruiting because they were successfully recruited previously.

Former employees are considered an internal source in the sense that they have ties to the employer, and may be called "boomerangers" because they left and came back. Individuals who left for other jobs might be willing to return because the other jobs and employers turned out to be less attractive than initially thought. For example, Accenture, a consulting firm, attracted more than 100 people who had left in the prior two years by contacting them and offering them "loyalty grants." Firms such as Microsoft, and others have established "alumni reunions" to keep in touch with individuals who have left, and also to allow them to re-recruit individuals as appropriate openings arise.[34] Key issues in the decision to re-recruit someone include the reasons why the individual left originally and whether or not the individual's performance and capabilities were good.

Another potential source of applicants is former applicants. Although these are not entirely an internal source, information about them can be found in the organizational files or an applicant database. Re-contacting those who have previously applied for jobs can be a quick and inexpensive way to fill unexpected openings. For instance, one firm that needed two cost accountants immediately contacted qualified previous applicants and was able to hire individuals who were disenchanted with their current jobs at other companies.

Re-recruiting has another meaning as well. The idea is to treat the best current employees as if they were top recruits. For example, if a company is giving signing bonuses to top recruits, perhaps it should give retention bonuses to top existing staff members. As one manager put it: "Think of your best staff member. What would you do or say if he or she was leaving? Do these things anyway."[35]

External Recruiting Sources

4 Many external sources are available for recruiting. In some tight labour markets, multiple sources and methods may be used to attract candidates for the variety of jobs available in organizations. Some of the more prominent methods are highlighted next.

Campus Recruiting

College and university students are a significant source for entry-level professional and technical employees. Most colleges and universities maintain career placement offices in which employers and applicants can meet. A number of considerations affect an employer's selection of colleges and universities at which to conduct interviews. The major determinants are:

- Current and anticipated job openings
- Reputations of the colleges and universities
- Experiences with placement offices and previous graduates
- Organizational budget constraints
- Market competition for graduates
- Cost of available talent and typical salaries

Campus recruiting can be expensive; therefore, an organization should determine if the jobs it is trying to fill really require persons with diplomas or degrees. A great many jobs do not, yet many employers often insist on filling them with graduates. The result may be employees who must be paid more and who are likely to leave if the jobs are not sufficiently challenging.

There is a great deal of competition for the top students in many college and university programs, and less competition for students with less impressive records. Attributes that recruiters seem to value most highly in graduates—poise, oral and written communication skills, personality, and appearance—all are typically mentioned ahead of grade point average (GPA). However, for many employers, a high GPA is a major criterion for considering candidates for jobs during on-campus interviews. Research suggests that recruiters use GPA decision rules in a variety of ways to initially screen applicants in college and university recruiting. These include setting minimum GPA requirements to screen large applicant pools, not considering GPA at all, and screening out students with *high* GPA.[36]

A number of factors determine success in campus recruiting. Some employers actively build continuing relationships with individual faculty members and career staff at designated colleges and universities. Maintaining a presence on campus by providing guest speakers to classes and student groups increases the contacts for an employer.

The important point is that employers that show continuing presence and support on a campus are more likely to see better college recruiting results. For instance, Shell Oil has concentrated its campus recruiting to only 26 schools. Formerly, the company recruited at 84 colleges and universities. As a result, recruiting costs have dropped, time-to-hire has dropped, and the acceptance rate for job offers has gone up.[37]

Another example is GE, which stresses internships in its campus recruiting. About 65 percent of the 1400 students it hires annually have had an internship or a type of cooperative experience. The company achieves better retention using internship and cooperative programs.[38] PricewaterhouseCoopers uses internships, focusing on early identification of potential candidates through contacts with professors and others. Ford uses an interactive assessment program posted on a website, and a weekend leadership conference that includes an interview. When the weekend is over, successful candidates know if they got a job, what the salary is, and when they start.[39]

As these examples illustrate, well-planned internships can be excellent sources for talented job candidates. For successful internship suggestions, see the HR Practice.

School Recruiting

High schools or vocational/technical schools may be good sources of new employees for some organizations. Many schools have a centralized guidance or placement office. Promotional brochures that acquaint students with starting jobs and career opportunities can be distributed to counsellors, librarians, or others. Participating in career days and giving company tours to school groups are other ways of maintaining good contact with school sources. Cooperative programs in which students work part-time and

HR *Practice*

Making Internships Work

Internships have the potential for being good situations for both the individual student intern and an employer. The student gets an opportunity to see if the employer and its culture fit, and the employer gets the equivalent of a 90-day interview instead of a 30-minute one. But not all internships actually are good situations for either party. Some basic guidelines for the employer can help improve the odds that internships will be rewarding:

- *Decide what the company needs.* A specific project is more challenging for the student and a better predictor of future employment capabilities for the company than just providing a job.
- *Require meaningful work.* Challenging assignments are best. Using interns as clerical replacements is usually not the best way to impress them.
- *Pay well.* Competitive wages help attract talent. In the past there were many unpaid internships, but most interns today are paid. Average pay of $3,000–$4,000 for a summer or $9–$10 per hour is typical.
- *Treat the intern like a new employee.* Interns need workspace, appropriate tools for the job, Internet access, a telephone, training feedback, and someone to provide guidance when needed.
- *Look at several candidates.* Use a broad internship description to increase the chances of finding a talented person with appropriate capabilities.

1. Even though you are getting an opportunity to be on an internship program, do you feel that you are compensated fairly compared to the other employees you are working with?
2. What are some potential problems with internships?

receive some school credits also may be useful in generating qualified future applicants for full-time positions.

Until recently, students not going on to college or university received little guidance or training on finding jobs after high school. However, the number of "partnerships" with schools through "school to work" programs has grown. Companies are entering the classroom not only to recruit, but to tutor students in skills such as the reading and math needed for work. Internships during the summer and work/school programs also are widely used.[40]

Employers recognize that they may need to begin attracting students with capabilities while those students are in high school. For example, GE, Lucent Technologies, and other corporations fund programs to encourage students with science and math skills to participate in engineering internships during summers. These and other employers specifically target talented designated group members in high schools and provide them with career encouragement, summer internships, and mentoring programs. In addition to fulfilling some social responsibilities and aiding in workforce diversity, the organizations hope to generate employment interest from the students they assist, and that that interest may help fill future openings.

Another consideration is at elementary school as grades 7 and 8 students gear up for high school. Many schools hold career days so that students can learn about the potential occupations they might want to consider. One of the authors of this textbook took part in a career day at her child's school. Parents and their families volunteered to come and speak about the education and training required for their profession, what they actually did in their jobs, and the range of money that could be earned. Students were required to select five professions that they would like to hear about, and then they rotated throughout the day to the sessions of their choice.

A common belief exists that if young people are exposed to a variety of experiences, they will be encouraged to explore potential career related interests. Students therefore need to be exposed to opportunities at an early age in order to encourage inner city students to become hooked on learning. In a pilot project targeting Aboriginal students at an inner school in Winnipeg, Manitoba, six students from grades 5, 6, and 7 were partnered with organizations such as Bison Transport, the Canadian Armed Forces, and other organizations, where they had to apply for a position with a prepared résumé, were interviewed, filled out the required employee paper work, and then job shadowed an employee, participating in some aspects of the job on the first day. They were provided with a small "take back" so that they could speak about their experience in a presentation to their class and partnering organizations. For example, one student was extremely excited when he returned to school with a part of a broken aircraft propeller. On the second day, the students actively participated in a work activity and given another take back, along with a paycheque for $10. Each student was taught how to open a bank account so they could deposit their earnings. The end result was that students demonstrated loyalty back to their partnering organization. Since the beginning of the project, it has received a national "Best Practice" recognition from the Aboriginal Human Resource Development Council of Canada, and has been featured in several national newscasts. Future goals are for 200 more Aboriginal students to participate in the program.[41]

Labour Unions

Labour unions are a good source of certain types of workers. In such industries as electrical and construction, unions have traditionally supplied workers to employers. A labour pool is generally available through a union, and workers can be dispatched from it to particular jobs to meet the needs of the employers.

In some instances, the union can control or influence recruiting and staffing needs. An organization with a strong union may have less flexibility than a non-union company in deciding who will be hired and where that person will be placed. Unions can also benefit employers through apprenticeship and cooperative staffing programs, as they do in the building and printing industries.

Employment Agencies and Headhunters

The Department of Human Resources and Social Development Canada (HRSDC) has offices across Canada that help provide the tools needed for career development. There are no fees charged to either the applicants who may be looking for a job, or for the employer who wants to place a job posting.

Private employment agencies also operate in most cities. For a fee collected from either the employee or the employer, these agencies do some preliminary screening and put the organization in touch with applicants. Private employment agencies differ considerably in the levels of service, costs, policies, and types of applicants they provide. Employers can reduce the range of possible problems from these sources by giving complete descriptions and specifications for jobs to be filled.

Some employment agencies focus their efforts on executive, managerial, and professional positions. These executive search firms are split into two groups: (1) contingency firms that charge a fee only after a candidate has been hired by a client company, and (2) retainer firms that charge a client a set fee whether or not the contracted search is successful. Most of the larger firms work on a retainer basis. The fee charged by executive search firms may be 30 percent or more of the employee's first-year salary. For placing someone in a high-level executive job, a search firm may receive $300,000 or more, counting travel expenses and the placement fee.[42] The size of the fees and the aggressiveness with which some firms pursue candidates for openings have led to such firms being called *headhunters*. However, search firms are ethically bound in Canada not to approach employees of client companies in their search for job candidates for another employer.[43]

Competitive Sources

Other sources for recruiting include professional and trade associations, trade publications, and competitors. Many professional societies and trade associations publish newsletters or magazines and have websites containing job ads. Such sources may be useful for recruiting specialized professionals needed in an industry.

Some employers have extended recruiting to customers. Retailers such as Home Depot and Best Buy have aggressive programs to recruit employees in stores. Customers at these firms can receive applications blanks, apply online using kiosks, or schedule interviews with managers or HR staff members, all while in the stores. Other firms have included employment announcements when sending out customer bills or newsletters.

Media Sources

Media sources such as newspapers, trade journals, television, radio, and billboards are widely used. Some firms have used direct mail with purchased lists of individuals in certain fields or industries. Whatever medium is used, it should be tied to the relevant labour market and should provide sufficient information on the company and the job. Figure 5-7 highlights some pros and cons of using some of the media sources mentioned above.

Figure 5-7 *Pros and Cons of Various Media Sources*

Newspapers	
Pros	***Cons***
• Job seekers traditionally look here for job openings • Low cost in terms of how many people they reach	• Not the most efficient means to advertise positions • Increased number of individuals using online sources to search for job opportunities
Trade Journals	
Pros	***Cons***
• Targets specialized audience of technical and professional employees with a unique set of skills • Overall costs relatively modest	• Feedback on job postings is delayed due to the publications being published • Cost per viewer high
Television	
Pros	***Cons***
• Effective at increasing brand recognition of the employer • Creative way to attract people to the organization	• High costs due to production and airtime of the advertisement • Difficult to target specific group (i.e., job seekers)
Radio	
Pros	***Cons***
• Can reach a large number of potential candidates in a short period of time • Less costly than television advertisements • Captive audience since most people listen to the radio in their vehicles or in their homes	• Not as effective as other forms of advertising mediums

How to Prepare an Effective Job Advertisement

A helpful acronym to remember when creating job advertisements is AIDA—Attention, Interest, Desire, and Action. The elements of AIDA should be used in every job advertisement in order to develop effective job advertisements.

Attention: The lead into the advertisement needs to catch attention.

Interest: Inform the reader about the job and your firm; include "must have" skills.

Desire: Explain how the job will benefit the job seeker; "sell" them on working for you.

Action: This is the contact information you provide for the applicant to take action.

Figure 5-8 shows information that a good recruiting advertisement should include. Notice that details about the job and the application process, desired candidate qualifications, and an overview of the organization are all important.

Figures 5-9 and 5-10 represent two ads. One is an ineffective ad and the other is a more acceptable ad. However, it should be noted, that the larger the ad, the more

Figure 5-8 What to Include in an Effective Recruiting Ad

Information on the Job and on the Application Process

- Job title and responsibilities
- Location of job
- Starting pay range
- Closing date for application
- Whether or not to submit a résumé and a cover letter
- Whether or not calls are invited
- Where to mail application or résumé

Desired Candidate Qualifications

- Years of experience
- Three to five key characteristics of successful candidates

Information on the Organization

- That it is an equal employment opportunity employer
- Its primary business

Figure 5-9 Example of an Ineffective Ad

Tunnelstone Visions Computers Inc.

Job Type: Full Time

Location: Calgary, Alberta

Job Category: Engineering, Computer

Industry: Recruitment/Staffing

Company URL: http://www.tunnelstonevisions.org

Year(s) of Experience: 2

Number of Positions: 2

Date Posted: June 30, 2007

Contact E-mail: ozzie@tunnelstonevisions.com

Our firm, a manufacturer of large computer robotics, currently requires Robot programmers to set up and execute welding routines for calibration applications. The individuals must have minimum 2 years Newton Robot or Inkster Robot specific experience. People skills would be a great asset.

This is a 3–6 month contract with a good chance of extension.

If you are interested, please forward your résumé to ozzie@tunnelstonevisions.com or by fax to 1-403-121-7717

Source: Adapted from Workopolis.

Figure 5-10 *Example of an Effective Ad*

It's the experience of a

lifetime

opportunities • training • advancement • recognition

Shoppers Drug Mart is one of the most recognized and trusted names in Canadian retailing. The Company is the licensor of full-service retail drug stores operating under the name Shoppers Drug Mart (Pharmaprix in Québec). With more than 960 Shoppers Drug Mart and Pharmaprix stores operating in prime locations in each province and two territories, the Company is one of the most convenient retailers in Canada.

At Shoppers Drug Mart, we have always remained true to our belief that the root of our success lies with our people. We pride ourselves on the quality and commitment of our employees who thrive on exciting challenges.

Embark upon the experience of a lifetime in our finance department as a…

FINANCIAL ANALYST (PERMANENT FULL-TIME)

Summary

Reporting to the Senior V.P. Finance, the Financial Analyst – Capital Investment, will be responsible for working on strategic and financial issues and creating financial models in support of Shoppers Drug Mart's capital investment plan as well as project analysis. Project analysis includes the assessment of investments in doctors' clinics, dispositions, development and enhancement of pro forma's and models, and assessment of the financial impact of planned transactions and performance of specific business lines and associated investments.

Essential Responsibilities and Duties

- Responsible for preparing comprehensive analysis of the financial performance of the Company's capital investment portfolio, both on an ongoing and ad hoc basis, to support the information and decision needs of both senior management and the Company's Board of Directors.
- Required to develop models and financial analysis (IRRs), including the underpinning evaluation criteria and assumptions as to ongoing operating performance, to support the initial investment decisions with respect to Shoppers Drug Mart capital projects including providing thorough analysis and financial conclusions on all new stores, relocations and expansions.
- Required to seek out and research all appropriate financial information from various departments to create the return of investment projections which involves the ongoing review and critique of assumptions vis-à-vis actual performance.
  Responsible for the detailed post-investment analysis on sales including variance analysis between the actual financials and the return of investment projections and provide conclusions/recommendations for future analysis and development.
- Provide detailed analysis for the EBITDA and sales on weekly and period basis for all capital projects and when necessary, provide conclusions on results and recommendations to improve the financials.

Source: Reprinted by permission of Shoppers Drug Mart.

- Prepare and interpret all internal rate of return analysis for capital projects including the analysis of relocations, the closure of stores and potential future business practices and the way they will affect the internal rate of return.
- Take a lead role in the co-ordination and preparation of annual capital plan with respect to new, relocated and expanded stores.
- Analyse the impact on existing Shoppers stores due to new capital investments and suggest proposals for future capital investments.
- Update and modify performance reports and projection templates for senior management to reflect ongoing changes in the business or operating model.

Experience

- Minimum of 5 years of financial analysis experience is required.
- Experience in a financial environment with exposure to various approaches to financial analysis and modeling.
- Accounting/finance designation (CA, CMA, CGA, CFA); MBA an asset.
- Ability to apply concepts from the fields of finance, strategy, accounting, real estate and economics in completing projects.
- Strong interpersonal and communication skills.
- Advanced knowledge of Excel.
- Experience with LAWSON & SPAM would be an asset.

Please forward a cover letter and resume to resumes@shoppersdrugmart.ca.
State the position of interest in the subject heading of your email and salary expectations in your cover letter.

We thank all interested applicants, however only qualified candidates will be contacted for an interview. For more information about our organization, please visit our website at www.shoppersdrugmart.ca

expensive will be the costs if placed in a newspaper, industry journal, or other type of media. Online advertisements are usually less expensive. Can you identify why each ad is effective or ineffective?

Evaluating Ads HR recruiters should measure the responses they generate in order to evaluate the effectiveness of various media. The easiest way to track responses to ads is to use different contact names, e-mail addresses, or phone number codes in each ad. Then the employer can note which advertisement prompted each applicant response that is received.

Although the total number of responses to each ad should be tracked, judging the success of an ad only by this number is a mistake. For example, it is better to have ten responses with two qualified applicants than 30 responses with only one qualified applicant. Therefore, after the individuals are hired, follow-up should be done to see which sources produced employees who stayed longer and performed better.

Canada Career Consortium
Canada Career Consortium lists career fairs that are taking place in Canada.
www.careerccc.org

Job Fairs and Special Events

Employers in tight labour markets or needing to fill a large number of jobs quickly have used job fairs and special recruiting events. Employers will collect résumés of qualified candidates at a job fair. Job fairs also have been held by economic development entities, employer associations, HR associations, and other community groups to help bring employers and potential job candidates together. Some employers at job fairs may see current employees "shopping" for jobs at other employers.

Another cautionary note: "General" job fairs are likely to attract many people including more unemployed (and unemployable) attendees. Industry- or skill-specific events offer more satisfactory candidates. For example, Canadianretail.com hosts an online job fair with the latest information on retail job fairs and new store openings. There are other "targeted" job fairs for positions such as financial professionals or "diversity" events for specific designated group members. Such job fairs can attract employed candidates who are looking casually but may not put their résumés out on the Internet.[44]

Creative Recruiting Methods

In labour markets that are tight and in industries with significant shortages of qualified applicants, employers turn to more creative recruiting methods. Regardless of the methods used, the goal is to generate a pool of qualified applicants so that the jobs in organizations are filled in a timely manner. Some methods may be more effective at recruiting for certain jobs than others. To illustrate, here are some examples:

- Using a plane towing an advertising banner over beach areas
- Advertising jobs on local movie theatre screens as pre-show entertainment
- Holding raffles for employees who refer candidates, with cars and trips being used as prizes
- Offering free rock concert tickets to the first 20 applicants hired
- Setting up recruiting tables at bowling alleys, minor-league baseball games, or stock car races
- Recruiting younger technical employees at video game parlours
- Arranging partnerships with downsizing firms to interview those being laid off
- Connecting with outplacement firms to find out about individuals who have lost their jobs
- Offering tuition assistance for those willing to work their way through school
- Sponsoring book fairs to recruit publishing company sales representatives

- Interviewing two hours a week even if the organization does not have any openings—and maintaining good files on those interviewed
- Parking motor homes—all set up for interviews, testing, and hiring—in parking lots at malls, with signs saying, "Want a job? Apply here."

Internet Recruiting

5 The Internet has become the primary means for many employers to search for job candidates and for applicants to look for jobs. The explosive growth in general Internet use is a key reason. Internet users tap the Internet to search for jobs almost as frequently as they read classified ads in newspapers. Many of them also post or submit résumés on the Internet.

Global Internet Recruiting

The percentage of Global 500 companies that use websites for recruiting has jumped to 88 percent. Use of the Internet has increased around the globe. The Internet is used for recruiting most widely in North America: 36.1 percent of Internet users in the Canada visited a website from home for recruitment in 2003, while only 7.3 percent of Internet users in Europe did so.[45] The explosive growth of Internet recruiting can overwhelm HR professionals in breadth and scope.

E-Recruiting Methods

e-recruiting methods Electronic method for recruiting, including Internet job boards, professional/career websites, and employer websites.

Several **e-recruiting methods** are used on the Internet. The most common ones are Internet job boards, professional/career websites, and employer websites.

Internet Job Boards Numerous Internet job boards, such as Monster.ca, Yahoo.ca, and Workopolis.ca provide places for employers to post jobs or search for candidates. Another prevalent one is through HRSDC. A unique job board is CanadaPartTime.com, which is Canada's leading part-time Internet recruitment company. Another group is careeredge.ca for recent graduates, abilityedge.ca for graduates with disabilities, and careerbridge.ca for international professionals.

Workopolis
This website contains a database of job opportunities, searchable by job category and location.
www.workopolis.ca

Job boards provide access to numerous candidates. However, many individuals accessing the sites are "job lookers" who are not serious about changing jobs, but are checking out compensation levels and job availability in their areas of interest. Various estimates are that about one-third of all visitors to job boards are just browsing, not seriously considering changing employment. Despite these concerns, HR recruiters find general job boards useful for generating applicant responses. In order to maintain recruiting competitiveness, a recruiter for a firm can pretend to be an applicant in order to check out what other employers are looking for in similar job candidates and offering as compensation.

Professional/Career Websites Many professional associations have employment sections at their websites. As illustration, for HR jobs in Ontario see the HRPAO website, which has another site for its members called "The Hire Authority" at www.hrpao.org, or for HR Planners, visit The Strategic Capabilities Network (SCNetwork) at www.scnetwork.ca. A number of private corporations maintain specialized career or industry websites to focus on IT, telecommunications, engineering, physician, or other areas. Using these more targeted websites limits somewhat the recruiters' search time and efforts. Also, posting jobs on such websites is likely to target applicants specifically interested in the job field and may reduce the number of less-qualified applicants who actually apply.

Internet recruitment is fast becoming the means by which employers search for candidates, and the way that people search for jobs.

Source: Photodisc/Getty Images

Employer Websites Despite the popularity of job boards and association job sites, many employers have found their own websites to be more effective and efficient when recruiting candidates. See the HR Practice for advice on designing an effective careers or employment section for a website.

Numerous employers have included employment and career information on their sites. Many company websites have a tab labelled "Careers" or "Employment." This is the place that recruiting (internal and external) is often conducted. On many of these sites, job seekers are encouraged to e-mail résumés or complete online applications. According to one survey, about 16 percent of hires come through a company website—a much higher proportion than résumés received from online job boards.[46]

A good website can also help reach "passive" job seekers, who have a good job and are not really looking to change, but might consider a better opportunity if it were presented. These individuals often are not usually listed on job boards, but they might visit a company website for other reasons and check out the careers or employment section. A well-designed corporate website can help stimulate interest in some passive job seekers, as well as other potential candidates.

It is important that the recruiting and employment portions of an employer website be seen as part of the marketing efforts of the firm. Therefore, the employment section of an organizational website must be shaped to market jobs and careers effectively. Also, a company website should market the employer by outlining information on the organization, its products and services, organizational and industry growth potential, and organizational operations.

LOGGING ON...

Recruit Canada
This website is for both recruiters and job applicants. The recruiters can find assistance on Web recruiting, while applicants can find help using the Web to search for jobs.
www.recruitcanada.com

Advantages of Internet Recruiting

Employers have found a number of advantages in using Internet recruiting. A primary one is that many employers have saved money using Internet recruiting versus other recruiting methods such as newspaper advertising, employment agencies, and search firms.

Effective Recruiting Through a Company Website

Using a company website for effective recruiting includes a number of suggestions. The primary ones are:

- Make the site easy to navigate. The "Careers" button should be on the home page and clearly labelled. Job information should be no more than three clicks away.
- Build a strong image for the company and the job. One company lists open positions and also describes the kind of work people would be doing in those positions, shows pictures of facilities and the people who work there, and describes the company climate and location.
- Make it easy to apply for a job. There should be a résumé builder, or a place to paste an existing résumé. Online applications are important too.
- Use qualifying categories (location, job function, skills, keyword search, etc.) to help candidates find the jobs for which they are eligible. Using such categories saves time, especially in a big company.
- Use self-assessment checklists to ask candidates about experience and interests and to direct them to the jobs that fit them the best.
- Include items people care about. Describe the company, its products and services, careers, and other unique advantages of working for the company.
- Link the site to a database. Doing this provides recruiters with a way to post jobs, search for résumés and applications, and screen applicants. Without this necessary step, it is impossible to manage a busy website.
- Collect metrics on the site. To determine how effective the site is, gather information such as the numbers of visitors, hits from ads, and actual hires.

1. Visit some organizations and determine if their website navigation tools work fairly easily when you are looking for a job opportunity.
2. Visit Best Buy at www.recruitingsite.com/csbsites/bestbuy careers/careers.asp and try to apply for a position online. How long did it take to apply? Was it fairly easy?

Internet recruiting can also save considerable *time*. Applicants can respond quickly to job postings by sending e-mails, rather than using "snail mail." Recruiters can respond to qualified candidates more quickly, and establish times for interviews or request additional candidate information.

An expanded pool of applicants can be generated using Internet recruiting. In fact, a large number of candidates may see any given job listing, although exposure depends on which Internet sources are used. One side benefit of the Internet is that jobs literally are posted globally, so potential applicants in other geographic areas and countries can view job openings posted on the Internet. The Internet also improves the ability to target specific audiences through the use of categories, information, and other variables.[47]

Disadvantages of Internet Recruiting

The positives associated with Internet recruiting come with a number of disadvantages. In getting broader exposure, employers also may get more unqualified applicants. HR recruiters find that Internet recruiting creates additional work for HR staff members. More résumés must be reviewed, more e-mails need to be dealt with, and expensive specialized software may be needed to track the increased number of applicants resulting from many Internet recruiting efforts. A related concern is that many individuals who access job sites are just browsers who may submit résumés just to see what happens but are not seriously looking for new jobs.

Another issue with Internet recruiting is that some applicants may have limited Internet access, especially individuals from lower socio-economic groups. A "digital divide" separates those who have Internet access from those who do not. Consequently, employers using Internet recruiting may not be reaching as diverse a recruitment pool as might be desired.

Privacy is another potential disadvantage with Internet recruiting. Sharing information gleaned from people who apply to job boards or even company websites has become common. But information sharing is being done in ways that might violate human rights and privacy legislation.

Legal Issues in Internet Recruiting

With Internet recruiting new legal concerns arise. Several of the concerns have ethical and moral implications, as well as legal ones. For example:[48]

- When companies use screening software to avoid looking at each of the thousands of résumés they receive, are rejections really based on the qualifications needed for the job?
- Are the designated group members and older employees being excluded from the process?
- Who are real applicants? Is someone who sent an e-mail asking if the employer has a job open really an applicant?
- General informality online can lead to discussions or information that might be improper if the person does not get the job.

Recruiting Evaluation and Metrics

6 To determine how effective various recruiting sources and methods have been, it is important to evaluate recruiting efforts. The primary way to find out whether recruiting efforts are cost-effective is to conduct formal analyses as part of recruiting evaluation. Several areas *can* be measured when trying to analyze recruiting effectiveness; five specific areas that *need* to be considered include: quantity of recruits, quality of recruits, time available for filling empty positions, cost per recruit, and satisfaction of parties involved. Metrics that look at the quality of the selection decisions made will be included here.

Evaluating Recruiting Quantity and Quality

As one means of evaluating recruiting, organizations can see how their recruiting efforts compare with past patterns and with the recruiting performance of other organizations. Certain measures of recruiting effectiveness are quite useful in indicating whether sufficient numbers of the targeted applicant population group are being attracted. Information on job performance, absenteeism, cost of training, and turnover by recruiting source also help adjust future recruiting. For example, some companies find that recruiting at certain colleges or universities furnishes stable, high performers, whereas recruiting at other schools provides employees who are more prone to leave the organization. General metrics for evaluating quantity and quality of recruiting include the following variables:

- *Quantity of applicants:* Because the goal of a good recruiting program is to generate a large pool of applicants from which to choose, quantity is a natural place to begin evaluation. The basic measure here considers whether the quantity of recruits is sufficient to fill job vacancies. A related question is: Does recruiting provide enough qualified applicants with an appropriate mix of designated group members?

- *Quality of applicants:* In addition to quantity, a key issue is whether or not the qualifications of the applicant pool are sufficient to fill the job openings. Do the applicants meet job specifications, and do they perform the jobs well after hire? What is the failure rate for new hires for each recruiter? Measures that can be used include items such as performance appraisal scores, months until promotion, output, and sales volume for each hire.

Evaluating the Time Required to Fill Openings

Looking at the length of time it takes to fill openings is a common means of evaluating recruiting efforts. If openings are not filled quickly with qualified candidates, the work and productivity of the organization will likely suffer. If it takes 75 days to fill empty positions, managers who need those employees will be unhappy. Generally, it is useful to calculate the average amount of time it takes from contact to hire for each source of applicants, because some sources may produce recruits faster than others. For example, one firm calculated the following averages:

Source	Average Time from Contact to Hire
Agencies	**25 days**
Walk-ins	**7 days**
Internet	**12 days**

These data reveal that use of agencies takes significantly longer to fill openings than relying on other means. Therefore, it suggests matching the use of sources to the time available.

Evaluating the Cost of Recruiting

The major number for measuring cost is calculating recruiting expenses for the year divided by the number of hires for the year:

$$\frac{\text{Recruiting expenses}}{\text{Number of recruits hired}}$$

The problem with this approach is accurately identifying what should be included in the recruiting expenses. Should expenses for testing, background checks, relocations, or signing bonuses be included, or are they more properly excluded?

If those questions are answered, then the costs might be allocated to various sources to determine how much each hire from each source costs. The costs also can be sorted by type of job—costs for hiring managers, secretaries, bookkeepers, and sales personnel will all be different.

Evaluating Recruiting Satisfaction

The satisfaction of two groups is useful in evaluating recruiting. Certainly the views of managers with openings to fill are important, because they are "customers" in a very real sense. But also the applicants (those hired and those not hired) are an important part of the process and can provide useful input.

Managers can respond to questions about the quality of the applicant pool, the recruiter's service, the timeliness of the process, and any problems that they see. Applicants might provide input on how they were treated, their perceptions of the company, and the length of the recruiting process.

General Recruiting Process Metrics

Because recruiting activities are important, the costs and benefits associated with them should be analyzed. A cost-benefit analysis of recruiting efforts may include both direct costs (advertising, recruiters' salaries, travel, agency fees, etc.) and indirect costs (involvement of operating managers, public relations, image, etc.). Cost-benefit information on each recruiting source can be calculated. Comparing the length of time that applicants hired from each source stay in the organization with the cost of hiring from that source also offers a useful perspective.

Yield ratios Comparisons of the number of applicants at one stage of the recruiting process with the number at the next stage.

Yield Ratios One means for evaluating recruiting efforts is **yield ratios,** which compare the number of applicants at one stage of the recruiting process with the number at another stage. The result is a tool for approximating the necessary size of the initial applicant pool. It is useful to visualize yield ratios as a pyramid, in which the employer starts with a broad base of applicants that progressively narrows. As Figure 5-11 depicts, to end up with five hires for the job in question, a sample company must begin with 100 applicants in the pool, as long as yield ratios remain as shown.

Figure 5-11 *Sample Recruiting Evaluation Pyramid*

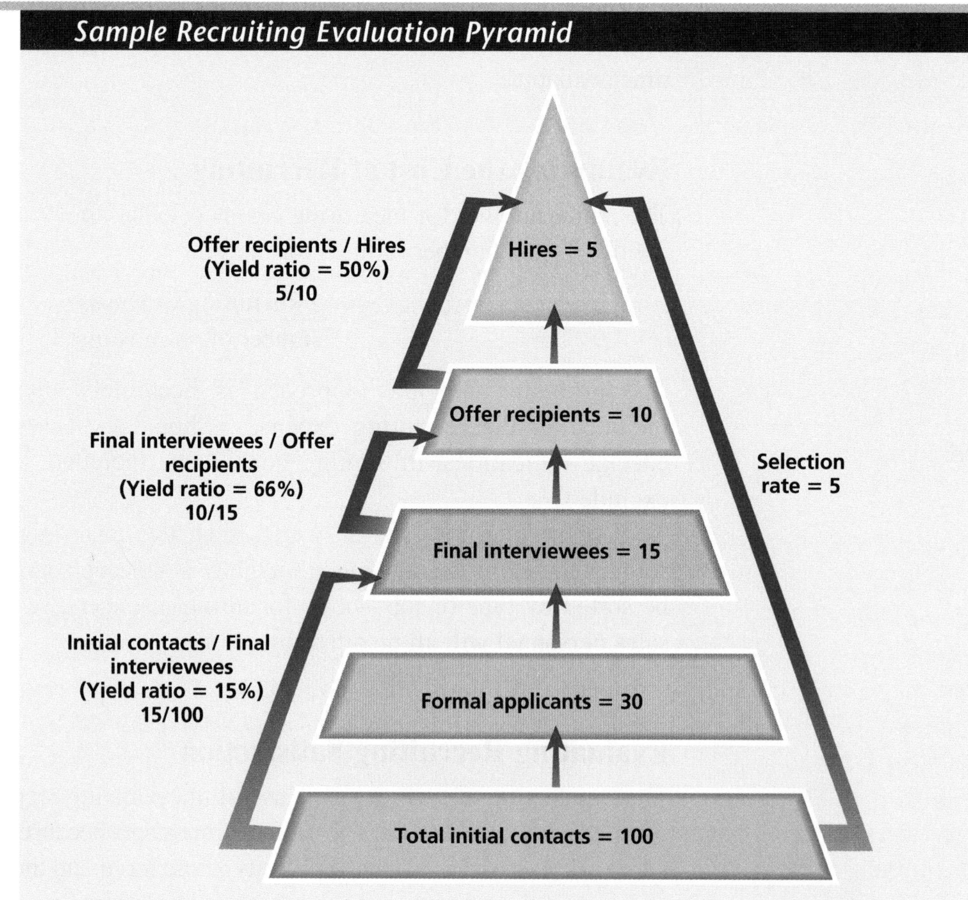

A different approach to using yield ratios suggests that over time, organizations can develop ranges for crucial ratios. When a given indicator ratio falls outside that range, it may indicate problems in the recruiting process. For example, in university recruiting, the following ratios might be useful:

$$\frac{\text{University candidates given second interview}}{\text{Total number of seniors interviewed}} = \text{Range of 30\%–50\%}$$

$$\frac{\text{Number who accept offer}}{\text{Number invited to the company to visit}} = \text{Range of 50\%–70\%}$$

$$\frac{\text{Number hired}}{\text{Number offered a job}} = \text{Range of 70\%–80\%}$$

$$\frac{\text{Number finally hired}}{\text{Total number interviewed on campus}} = \text{Range of 10\%–20\%}$$

Selection rate
Percentage hired from a given group of candidates.

Selection Rate Another useful calculation is the **selection rate,** which is the percentage hired from a given group of candidates. It equals the number hired divided by the number of applicants; for example, a rate of 30 percent indicates that three out of ten applicants were hired. The selection rate is also affected by the validity of the selection process. A relatively unsophisticated selection program might pick eight out of ten applicants for the job. Four of those might turn out to be good employees. A more valid selection process might pick five out of ten applicants but all perform well. Selection rate measures not just recruiting but selection issues as well. So do acceptance rate and success base rate.

Acceptance rate
Percent of applicants hired divided by total number of applicants.

Acceptance Rate Calculating the acceptance rate helps identify how successful the organization is at hiring candidates to employ. The **acceptance rate** is the percent of applicants hired divided by the total number of applicants. After the company goes through all the effort to screen, interview, and make job offers, hopefully, most candidates accept job offers. If they do not, then HR might want to look at reasons why managers and HR staff cannot "close the deal." It is common for HR staff members to track the reasons candidates turn down job offers, which help explain the rejection rate, in order to learn how competitive the employer is compared with other employers and what factors are causing candidates to choose employment elsewhere.

Success Base Rate A longer-term measure of recruiting effectiveness is the success rate of applicants. The *success base rate* can be determined by comparing the number of past applicants who have become successful employees against the number of applicants they competed against for their jobs, using historical data within the organization. Also, the success base rate can be compared with the success rates of other employers in the area or industry, using benchmarking data. This rate indicates whether the quality of the employees hired results in employees who perform well and have low turnover. For example, assume that if ten people were hired at random, one would expect four of them to be good employees. Thus, a successful recruiting program should be aimed at attracting the four in ten who are capable of doing well on this particular job. Realistically, no recruiting program will attract only the four in ten who will succeed. However, efforts to make the recruiting program attract the largest proportion of those in the base rate group can make recruiting efforts more effective.

Increasing Recruiting Effectiveness

The efforts to evaluate recruiting should be used to make recruiting activities more effective. Using the data to target different applicant pools, tap broader labour markets, use different recruiting methods, improve internal handling and interviewing of applicants, and train recruiters and managers all can increase recruiting effectiveness.

Another way to increase recruiting effectiveness rests on the recruiters themselves. Those involved in the recruiting process can turn off recruits or create excitement among them. Recruiters who are knowledgeable about the jobs and their employers and who treat applicants with respect and enthusiasm are viewed more positively. A positive image is more likely to result in more applicants pursuing employment opportunities with an employer.

SUMMARY

1 Recruiting is the process of generating a pool of qualified applicants for organizational jobs through a series of activities. Recruiting must be viewed strategically, and discussions should be held about the relevant labour markets in which to recruit. A strategic approach to recruiting begins with human resource planning and decisions about organizational recruiting responsibilities. The components of labour markets are labour force population, applicant population, and applicant pool. Labour markets can be categorized by geographic area, industry, occupation, qualifications, and other characteristics.

2 Employers must make decisions about organization-based versus outsourced recruiting, regular versus flexible staffing, and other strategic aspects of recruiting. Efforts should be made to recruit a diverse workforce including the designated group members and older workers. Small business owners are also competing for the same resources as larger organizations and need more training in recruitment and the use of technology, specifically Internet recruitment. The decision to use internal or external sources should consider both the advantages and disadvantages of each source.

3 The most common methods of internal recruiting include organizational databases, job postings, promotions and transfers, current-employee referrals, and re-recruiting of former employees and applicants. Some challenges include individuals must be recruited to fill jobs vacated from promotions, costs, technology, communication and systemic discrimination.

4 The most common external recruiting sources include colleges and universities, schools, labour unions, employment agencies and headhunters, competitive sources, media sources, job fairs and special events, and creative methods. External recruiting sources should be evaluated to determine if they make sense for particular types of businesses or industries. One way to achieve this is for HR recruiters to measure the responses they generate in order to evaluate the effectiveness of various media.

5 Internet recruiting has grown in use through job boards and various websites. Internet recruiting can save costs and time, but they also can generate more unqualified applicants and frequently may not reach certain groups of potential applicants. Recruiting efforts should be evaluated to assess how effective they are. Although Internet recruiting may appear to have many advantages including cost, time, and expanded pool of applicants the disadvantages must be considered. The disadvantages of using the Internet to recruit potential candidates may result in an increase in unqualified candidates, applicants may not have access to the Internet and privacy concerns may arise.

6 Recruiting evaluation typically includes evaluating recruiting quantity and quality, tracking the time to fill openings, and examining the costs and benefits of various recruiting sources. A cost-benefit analysis of recruiting efforts may include both direct costs and indirect costs. Yield ratios and selections rates are two examples of metrics that help to explain the valued sources of recruitment.

KEY TERMS

Acceptance rate, p. 199
Applicant pool, p. 169
Applicant population, p. 168
e-recruiting methods, p. 193
Flexible staffing, p. 174
Independent contractors, p. 174
Job posting, p. 181
Labour force population, p. 168
Labour markets, p. 167
Recruiting, p. 166
Selection rate, p. 199
Yield ratios, p. 198

REVIEW AND APPLICATION QUESTIONS

1 What labour markets should be considered when recruiting to fill an opening for a sales representative for a pharmaceutical manufacturer?

2 What can an organization do to recruit designated group members? Should the same methods be used for each of the groups?

3 Discuss the various methods of recruitment that could be used to hire in small or large organizations.

4 What types of recruitment should be utilized for a sales administrator, a marketing manager, and a VP of operations?

5 Discuss ways a bank could effectively use the Internet to recruit management trainees.

6 Explain the difference between a yield ratio and a selection rate. Use a numerical example to explain how these metrics are calculated.

EXPERIENTIAL EXERCICES

1. Go to www.recruitcanada.com or www.recruitusa.com, and other sites to get ideas on evaluating recruiting efforts and then prepare a report for review.
2. In groups of five, contact ten local businesses and try to determine to what extent they are using the Internet for recruitment. Ask them their size, who handles the recruitment (level), is training provided, and if they hire all positions internally or externally, or a combination, and what their turnover rate is for the year. You will draw up a chart to consolidate your answers. The professor will collect and compile the results of what is occurring in your area with respect to the use of the Internet for small and larger sized organizations.
3. For each designated group, you are to locate five agencies that offer assistance in recruitment of these individuals. What are the names of the agencies or companies that organizations can call upon when they are trying to hire for these designated group members, and what area does each of these agencies address (e.g., disabilities such as hearing impaired). Are their fees for using these services?
4. Your organization is a federally regulated company that has recently announced its commitment to an employment equity plan. A recent audit indicates that you must begin to hire a more diverse group of employees, particularly more visible minorities and Aboriginal peoples. Additionally, there are very few women in senior positions. Currently there are two senior positions that you are recruiting for, and several junior positions. You realize that this would be an ideal opportunity to start off the employment equity program in a positive way. Ideally you could promote some women, and hire some junior positions, utilizing a number of agencies that can supply you with contacts. Unfortunately, you are working with three senior managers who are known to be racist, and also have continuously made rude comments about women, suggesting that women do not belong in corporate boardrooms, and that the kitchen was a better place of employment for them. You have spoken with your manager about the dilemma, and have come to realize that his views may also be somewhat biased. He is suggesting that you should listen to the senior managers, because they are your customer and you have to do what's best for them. Utilizing the Internet, research how you would resolve this dilemma?

LEARNING REVIEW

To check your knowledge of the chapter, review the following. (Answers after the case.)

1 One of the advantages for the employees of employee leasing companies is that:
   a. they usually receive many interesting assignments in a variety of start-up businesses
   b. they may receive better benefits than they would otherwise get in many small businesses
   c. they do not require Canada Pension, employment insurance, or workers' compensation contributions
   d. they can be regarded as self-employed for CRA purposes

2 Which of the following is given as an advantage of external recruiting?
   a. It allows for better assessment of abilities.
   b. It involves a shorter adjustment or orientation time.
   c. The new hire may bring new industry insights.
   d. The company has to hire only at entry level.

3 Which of the following statements regarding job posting and bidding is *false*?
   a. It gives each employee an opportunity to move to a better job within the organization.
   b. It makes it difficult for supervisors to develop employees over the long term.
   c. Jobs are generally posted before any external recruiting is done.
   d. In a unionized organization, job posting and bidding often is spelled out in the labour agreement.

4 A number of considerations affect an employer's selection of college or university, except:
   a. cost of available talent and typical salary
   b. budget constraints
   c. location of school
   d. reputation of the schools

5 The Internet has become the primary means for many employers to search for candidates, except:
   a. large organizations
   b. small businesses
   c. employment agencies
   d. professionals

6 Evaluating the success of recruiting efforts is important because it:
   a. provides input to the compensation system of the HR unit
   b. is one way to measure the reputation of the firm on campuses
   c. indicates how the employer measures up against competitors
   d. is the primary way to find out whether or not the efforts are cost effective

CASE

ENTERPRISE RECRUITING

Enterprise Rent-A-Car, with more than 340 locations across Canada was ranked 35th of the 50 Best Employers in Canada. Many customers use Enterprise Rent-A-Car each year, and it is bigger than its competitors Hertz, Avis, and National. In ten years Enterprise has doubled the number of cars in its fleet and increased its workforce over 30 percent, to 54 000 employees. What may not be widely known is that Enterprise recruits large numbers of university graduates each year for its management training program and other jobs. About 6000 university graduates have been hired annually, so that Enterprise can staff its expanding number of offices. Enterprise is committed to its employees through developing promotion from within policies, providing employees with extensive training opportunities, and rewarding employees for taking initiative and being entrepreneurial.

Several innovative means are being used in addition to the typical recruiting approaches. On the company's website the online game called "Give Me the Business" gets many hits. The game is not directly related to renting cars, but it lets people experience the challenges of a customer-service business. The hidden message is its "virtual marketing" of Enterprise and its fun culture.

Another creative approach used was sponsoring *My Personal Enterprise* on MTV, in which candidates for a job at Enterprise were viewed during two rounds of behavioural interviews. The candidates were asked questions, and they were "judged" on their answers. But unlike other TV reality shows where only one person wins, three of the four candidates were offered jobs. *My Personal Enterprise* is a theme of all of Enterprise's recruiting materials, advertisements, website, and other recruiting efforts. The main focus of *My Personal Enterprise* is to convince university graduates that there are career opportunities in the rental car firm, and that jobs in the company can be fun and fulfilling.

The online games and the TV show were attention-getters, but the greatest source of Enterprise recruits comes from employee referrals. Enterprise employees who refer candidates who are hired and remain with the firm can receive incentives of $500 to $1,500 each. Often, referrals check out Enterprise or its website and mention the firm to others, which expands the pool of potential recruits.

Enterprise is somewhat unusual as an employer because it uses both traditional and creative recruiting means. The wide range of activities has helped Enterprise recruit more effectively, which aids its strategic goal of establishing its "employment brand."[49]

Questions

1. How does having multiple recruiting means help Enterprise establish its brand?
2. Go to the Enterprise website (www.enterprise.com) and check out the game, career opportunities, and other components. Then evaluate how effective you feel the website is as an employment branding and recruiting resource.

Learning Review Answers: 1. b 2. c 3. b 4. c 5. b 6. d

CHAPTER

Selection of Human Resources

Learning Objectives

After you have read this chapter, you should be able to:

1 Describe the relationship between criteria, predictors, job performance, and selection

2 Diagram the sequence of a typical selection process.

3 Identify several types of selection tests and legal concerns about their uses.

4 Discuss the different types of selection interviews and some key considerations in conducting these interviews.

5 Explain how legal concerns affect background investigations of applicants and use of medical examinations in the selection process.

6 Describe the major issues to be considered when selecting candidates for global assignments.

HR *Headline*

Better Recruiting, Screening, and Testing Cuts Turnover

The use of call centres is on the rise, as is the struggle to find and retain qualified staff. Turnover in this industry is a concern with between 15 percent to 25 percent turnover reported as an industry average compared to 18 percent in other types of businesses. As stated by one consultant, "the biggest reason for turnover is that companies hire people that don't fit."

A study conducted by Olsten Forum on Human Resources found that few call centre managers looked beyond a customer service background. Less than one-third of interviewers seek previous inbound or outbound call centre experience, and only one-quarter require product knowledge. Managers tend to look for a positive attitude, strong work ethic, command of the English language, the ability to get along with others, and a commitment to scheduled hours.

Jack Green, president of Entretel Inc., a call centre consulting firm headquartered in Oakville, Ontario, says that extensive screening, including valid testing devices, is essential to limiting turnover. Green suggests that the focus needs to be on individual characteristics that can be trained versus the skills necessary when starting the job. Applicants must go through an extensive process that begins with an interactive voice response screening process. Often they screen themselves out of the process once they are provided with further information on the job. Applicants are then ranked on the information they provide electronically. The electronic interview is followed by a personal telephone-based interview where skills such as listening, questioning, and other factors, including voice quality and a second language, if applicable, can be monitored. Next, applicants under serious consideration are given a hands-on test of basic skills that could include typing, software knowledge, and talk/type capabilities. Before hiring, a personality profile is developed analyzing the desirable personal qualities required for the work. Once the right individual is hired, the next task is about retaining that employee. Retention can be achieved by following a regimen of respecting staff members as individuals, identifying the benefits of growing skill sets, providing career paths, and making the work environment stimulating.[1]

"Selecting qualified employees is like putting money in the bank."

—John Boudreau

Selection decisions are an important part of successful HR management. Some even would argue that they are the *most* important part. Improvement in organizational performance may come from many sources—but unless the employer begins by having the necessary people with the appropriate capabilities in place, positive organization results are less likely to occur.

Selection and Placement

Selection
Process of choosing individuals with qualifications needed to fill jobs in an organization.

1 **Selection** is the process of choosing individuals with qualifications needed to fill jobs in an organization. Without qualified employees, an organization is less likely to succeed. Perhaps the best perspective on selection and placement comes from two HR "truisms" that clearly identify the importance of an effective selection process:

- *"Hire hard, manage easy."* The amount of time and effort spent selecting the right people for jobs may make managing them as employees much less difficult because more problems will be eliminated.
- *"Good training will not make up for bad selection."* When the right people with the appropriate capabilities are not selected for jobs, employers have difficulty later adequately training those individuals who are selected.

Selection Responsibilities

Organizations vary in how they allocate selection responsibilities between HR specialists and operating managers. The need to meet human rights requirements and employment standards has forced many organizations to better plan their selection efforts. Still, in some organizations, each department screens and hires its own employees. Many managers insist on selecting their own people because they are sure no one else can choose employees for them as well as they can themselves. This practice is particularly prevalent in smaller firms. But the validity and effectiveness of this approach may be questionable.

Other organizations have the HR unit do the initial screening of the candidates, and managers or supervisors make the final selection from a qualified group of individuals. As a rule, the higher the position being filled, the greater the likelihood that the ultimate hiring decisions will be made by operating managers rather than HR specialists. Typical selection responsibilities are shown in Figure 6-1.

Selection responsibilities are affected by the existence of a central employment office, which usually is part of an HR department. In smaller organizations, especially in those with fewer than 100 employees, a full-time employment specialist or unit may be impractical. But for larger employers, centralizing employment within one unit may be appropriate.

The employment function in any organization may be concerned with some or all of the following activities: (1) receiving applications, (2) interviewing applicants, (3) administering tests to applicants, (4) conducting background investigations, (5) arranging for physical examinations, (6) placing and assigning new employees, (7) coordinating follow-up of these employees, (8) conducting exit interviews with departing employees, and (9) maintaining appropriate records and reports.

Placement

Placement
Fitting a person to the right job.

The ultimate purpose of selection is **placement,** or fitting a person to the right job. Placement of human resources should be seen as primarily a matching process. How well an employee is matched to a job affects the amount and quality of the employee's

Figure 6-1 *Typical Division of HR Responsibilities: Selection*

HR Unit	Managers
• Provides initial reception for applicants • Conducts initial screening interview • Administers appropriate employment tests • Obtains background and reference information and arranges for the employment physical examination, if used • Refers top candidates to managers for final selection • Evaluates success of selection process	• Requisition employees with specific qualifications to fill jobs • Participate in selection process as appropriate • Interview final candidates • Make final selection decision, subject to advice of HR specialist • Provide follow-up information on the suitability of selected individuals

work. This matching also directly affects training and operating costs. Individuals who are unable to produce the expected amount and quality of work can cost an organization a great deal of money and time.

Person/job fit
Match between individual KSAs and demands of the job or the needs/desires of an individual and what is provided by the job

Person-organization fit
The congruence between individuals and organizational factors.

Selection and placement activities typically focus on applicants' knowledge, skills, and abilities (KSAs). The **person/job fit** is a simple but important concept that involves a match between individual KSAs and demands of the job or the needs/desires of an individual and what is provided by the job. People already in jobs can help identify the most important KSAs for success, as part of job analysis.

In addition to matching individuals to jobs, employers also increasingly try to determine the congruence between individuals and organizational factors to achieve **person-organization fit.** Person-organization fit is important when general factors of job success are as important as specific KSAs.

Criteria, Predictors, and Job Performance

Whether an employer uses specific KSAs or a more general approach, effective selection of employees involves using criteria and predictors of job performance. At the heart of an effective selection system must be knowledge of what constitutes appropriate job performance and what employee characteristics are associated with that performance. First, an employer defines successful employee performance; then, using that definition as a basis, the employer determines the employee KSAs required to achieve that success. A **selection criterion** is a characteristic that a person must have to do that specific job successfully. Figure 6-2 shows that ability, motivation, intelligence, conscientiousness, appropriate risk, and permanence might be good selection criteria for many jobs.

Selection criterion
Characteristic that a person must have to do a job successfully.

Predictors
Measurable or visible indicators of a selection criterion.

To determine whether or not candidates might have a certain selection criterion (such as ability or motivation), employers try to identify **predictors** that are measurable or visible indicators—of that criterion. For example, in Figure 6-2, three good predictors of performance might be individual interests, salary requirements, and tenure on previous jobs.

The information gathered about an applicant through predictors should be focused on the likelihood that the applicant will be able to perform the job well. Predictors can take many forms (for example, application form, test, interview, education requirements, or years of experience required), but they should be used only if they are valid predictors of job performance. Using invalid predictors can result in selecting the "wrong" candidate and rejecting the "right" one.

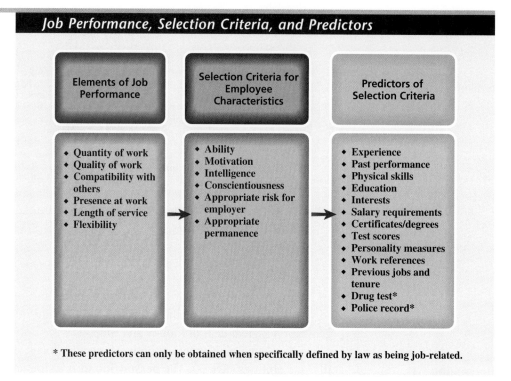

Figure 6-2 ***Job Performance, Selection Criteria, and Predictors***

To illustrate how criteria and predictors can be beneficial, Maple Leaf Sports & Entertainment Ltd. (MLSEL), the owner of the Toronto Maple Leafs, the Toronto Raptors, and the Air Canada Centre (ACC), decided to use a unique interviewing method when hiring for part-time positions such as hotdog vendors and ushers for the ACC. The candidates were placed into groups and asked to demonstrate their performance skills in singing, dancing, and acting for the hiring managers. Marci Walker, the vice-president of people at MLSEL believes that this type of interviewing method would be a good predictor of the type of service these candidates would provide: "These are our front-line staff dealing with our fans at every single event, so you have to have a certain amount of comfort level being outgoing with people and not afraid to talk to strangers." MLSEL no longer uses this method for several reasons including the fact that the ACC is fully staffed and has a low turnover.[2]

Reliability and Validity

Employment "test" Any employment procedure used as the basis for making an employment-related decision.

When we are selecting employees, the decisions we make about the applicants are based on a number of factors including the job interview and any other employment tests we may administer. An **employment test** is any employment procedure used as the basis for making an employment-related decision. As such, we must ensure that the employment tests we are using are appropriate and are job-related to ensure compliance with federal or provincial legislation. Any employment test used must consider the following:

- The test measures what it claims to measure consistently or reliably. This means that if a person were to take the test again, the person would get a *similar* test score.
- The test measures what it claims to measure. For example, a test of mental ability does in fact measure mental ability, and not some other characteristic.

- The test is job-relevant. In other words, the test measures one or more characteristics that are important to the job.
- By using the test, more effective employment decisions can be made about individuals. For example, an arithmetic test may help you to select qualified workers for a job that requires knowledge of arithmetic operations.[3]

The degree to which a test has these qualities is indicated by two technical properties: *reliability* and *validity*.

Reliability
Consistency of your measurement, or the degree to which an instrument measures the same way each time it is used under the same condition with the same subjects.

Reliability **Reliability** refers to consistency of your measurement, or the degree to which an instrument measures the same way each time it is used under the same condition with the same subjects. For a test to be reliable, an individual's score should be about the same every time the individual takes the test (allowing for the effects of practice). Unless a test measures a factor consistently (reliably), it is of little value in predicting job performance. Reliability can be measured by several statistical methodologies. The ones used most frequently are test-retest, alternate forms, and internal-consistency estimates. A *test-retest* simply means a group of people is tested twice, using the same tests, and the two sets of scores obtained are correlated. *Alternate forms* is the degree to which two versions of a test produce similar results. For example, a professor could test the class on knowledge of this chapter asking a set of questions, and then give them another test a week later asking different questions, but still testing for the same knowledge. *Internal-consistency* is when the degree to which all the questions in a set are measuring the same thing. The advantage of this method over the other two is that the test is administered only once, thus saving time and money, and potentially speeding up the selection process. For example, assume that 30 questions were being asked about honesty. To determine internal-consistency, the test could be split into two, 15 questions in each set, and then a correlation over each person's average scores in the two question sets is used as the reliability estimate. A more detailed methodological discussion is beyond the scope of this text. Thus, reliability has to do with the consistency of predictors used in selection.

Validity
Extent to which a test actually measures what it says it measures. In selection, validity is the correlation between a predictor and job performance.

Validity **Validity** is simply the extent to which a test actually measures what it says it measures. The concept relates to inferences made from tests. For instance, it may be valid to assume that performance on a mechanical knowledge test may predict performance of a machinist in a manufacturing plant. However, it is probably invalid to assume that the same test scores indicate general intelligence or promotability for a manufacturing sales representative. For a general intelligence test to be valid, it must actually measure intelligence, not just a person's vocabulary. An employment test that is valid must measure the person's ability to perform the job for which she or he is being hired. Clearly, if a test is not valid, it should not be used. A test must be validated for use in a specific company's application, not "in general" by the test vendor.[4] Two approaches to validation are content and criterion-related validity. Even though these two strategies are different, they are interrelated.

Reliability is a *necessary* but not *sufficient* condition for validity. For instance, if the needle of the scale is two kilograms away from zero, I always over-report my weight by two kilograms. Is the measurement consistent? Yes, but it is consistently wrong! Is the measurement valid? No! If I wanted to test someone for the position of typist, and asked that person their weight, they would most likely be able to use the scale to weigh themselves and report the measurement. The weight measure would be reliable, but not valid for testing the ability of a typist. So the measure is reliable, but not valid and should not be used.

Content validity
Validity measured by a logical, non-statistical method to identify the KSAs and other characteristics necessary to perform a job.

Content Validity Content validity occurs when the tester *is* concerned with the type of behaviour involved in the test performance. A test has **content validity** if it reflects an actual sample of the work done on the job in question. For example, an arithmetic test for a retail cashier might contain problems about determining amounts for refunds, purchases, and merchandise exchanges. Content validity is especially useful if the workforce is not large enough to allow other, more statistical approaches.

A content validity study begins with a comprehensive job analysis to identify what is done in the job and what KSAs are used. Then managers, supervisors, and HR specialists must identify the most important KSAs needed for the job. Finally, a test is devised to determine if individuals have the necessary KSAs. The "test" may be an interview question about previous supervisory experience, or an ability test in which someone types a letter using a word-processing software program, or a knowledge test about programming.

Many practitioners and specialists see content validity as a commonsense standard for validating staffing requirements, and as more realistic than statistical standards. Consequently, content validity approaches are growing in use.

Criterion-related validity
Validity measured by a procedure that uses a test as the predictor of how well an individual will perform on the job.

Criterion-Related Validity Employment tests attempt to predict how well an individual will perform on the job. In measuring **criterion-related validity,** a test is the *predictor,* and the measures for job performance are the *criterion variables* (see Figure 6-3). Job analysis determines, as accurately as possible, what KSAs and behaviours are needed for each task in the job.

Correlation coefficient
Index number giving the relationship between a predictor and a criterion variable.

In the example in Figure 6-3, people who scored higher on the test also tended to do better on the job (a higher job performance score is better). The exact relationship between a test and performance is calculated by a correlation coefficient. A **correlation coefficient** is an index number giving the relationship between a predictor and a criterion variable. Correlation coefficients can range from −1.0 to +1.0. A correlation coefficient of +.80 (r^2) indicates that the test is a good predictor, whereas a correlation coefficient of −.25 (r^2) indicates that the test is a poor predictor. Thus, a high correlation (closest to −1.0 to +1.0) suggests that the test can differentiate between the better-performing employees and those with poor performance records.

Figure 6-3 *Test Scores and Job Performance*

Applicant	Predictor (test score) (0–100, with 100 high)	Criterion (job performance, on a 5-point scale) (1–5 scale, 5 high)
Joe	60	2
Rashad	75	3
Anne	88	4
Sarah	52	1
Fred	80	4
Sally	95	5
Juan	85	4
Linda	58	2
Jeff	78	3
A. J.	65	3

Note: Correlation looks at the relationships between the test scores and job performance of the whole group.

Figure 6-4 *Concurrent and Predictive Validity*

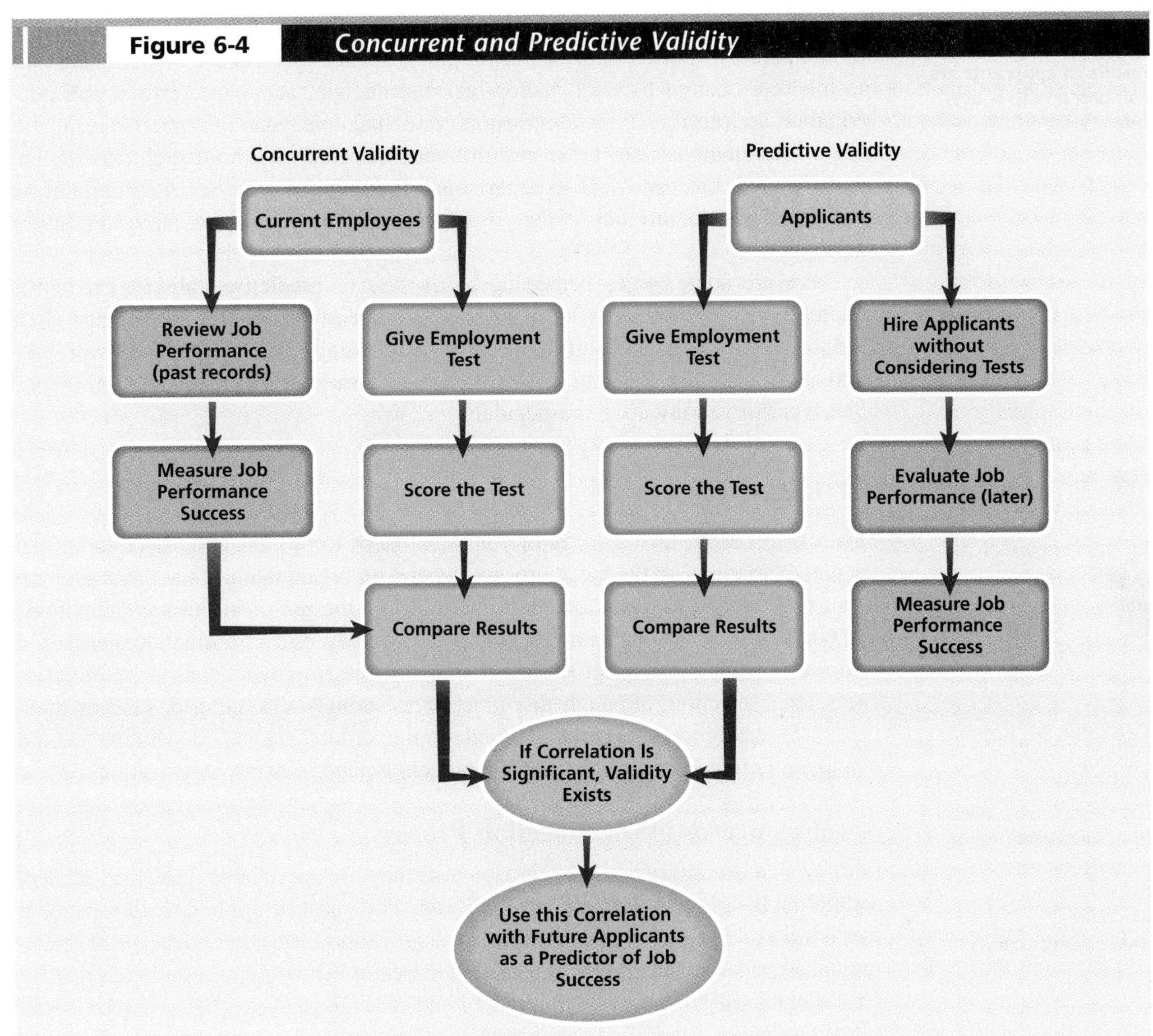

There are two approaches to criterion-related validity. *Concurrent validity* is an "at-the-same-time" approach, and *predictive validity* is a "before-the-fact" approach. Figure 6-4 depicts both approaches.

Concurrent validity Measured when an employer tests current employees and correlates the scores with their performance ratings.

Concurrent Validity *Concurrent* means "at the same time." As shown in Figure 6-4, **concurrent validity** is measured when an employer tests current employees and correlates the scores with their performance ratings on such measures as accident rates, absenteeism records, and supervisory performance appraisals. This type of validity is called *concurrent* because the job performance measures and the test scores are available at the same time (concurrently), rather than subject to a time lag as in the predictive validity approach.

A drawback of the concurrent validity approach is that employees who have not performed satisfactorily on the job are probably no longer with the firm and therefore cannot be tested, and extremely good employees may have been promoted or may have left the organization for better jobs. Also, any learning that has taken place on the job may influence test scores, presenting another problem.

Predictive validity Measured when test results of applicants are compared with subsequent job performance.

Predictive Validity To measure **predictive validity,** test results of applicants are compared with their subsequent job performance (see Figure 6-4). Success on the job is measured by such factors as absenteeism, accidents, errors, and performance appraisals. If the employees who had one year of experience at the time of hire demonstrates better performance than those without such experience, as calculated by statistical comparisons, then the experience requirement is considered a valid predictor of performance and may be used in hiring future employees.

There are some issues pertaining to the use of predictive validity. Predictive validity requires: (1) a fairly large number of people (usually at least 30), and (2) a time gap between the test and the performance (usually one year). As a result, predictive validity is not useful in many situations. Because of these and other problems, other types of validity are more popular.

The Selection Process

Canadian HR Reporter
This website offers a newsletter focusing on the recruitment, selection, and retention of human resources in today's changing workforce.
www.hrreporter.com

2 Most organizations take a series of consistent steps to process and select applicants for jobs. Variations on the basic process depend on organizational size, nature of the jobs to be filled, number of people to be selected, the use of electronic technology, and other factors. This process can take place in a day or over a much longer period of time. If the applicant is processed in one day, the employer usually checks references after selection, although this practice is strongly discouraged. One or more phases of the process may be omitted or the order changed, depending on the employer. Figure 6-5 shows a selection process typical in many organizations.

Legal Concerns in the Selection Process

Employers must ensure that the selection tests they use are reliable, valid, job-related, and do not discriminate against any applicant. This must be applied to all aspects of recruitment and selection measures such as application forms, interviews, tests, background interviews, and any other selection activities. The only exception to this may be for bona fide occupational requirements (BFORs). The goal must be about selecting the most qualified candidate for the position. An employer who discriminates in employment decisions could be faced with a charge of discrimination under their respective human rights act.

Applicant Job Interest

Individuals desiring employment can indicate interest in a number of ways. Traditionally, individuals have submitted résumés by mail or fax, or applied in person at an employer's location. But with the growth in Internet recruiting, many individuals complete applications online or submit résumés electronically.

Regardless of how individuals express interest in employment, the selection process has an important public relations dimension. Discriminatory hiring practices, impolite interviewers, unnecessarily long waits, unreturned telephone inquiries, inappropriate testing procedures, and lack of follow-up responses can produce unfavourable impressions of an employer. Job applicants' perceptions of the organization, and even of the products or services it offers, will be influenced by how they are treated.

Realistic Job Previews Most job seekers appear to know little about organizations before applying to them for jobs. Consequently, when deciding whether or

Figure 6-5 *Selection Process Flowchart*

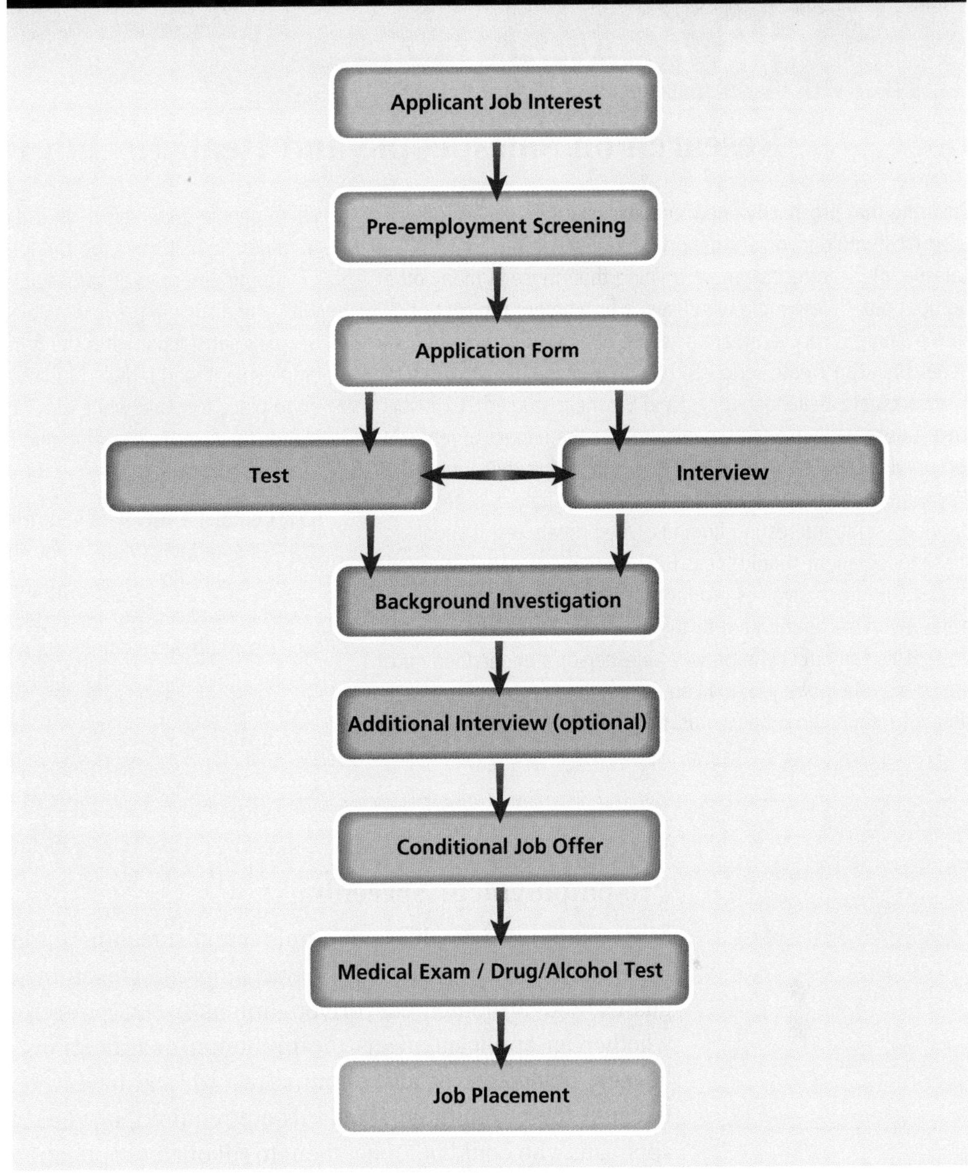

not to accept a job, they tend to give considerable weight to the information received from prospective employers in the recruiting/selection process. For applicants, information on pay, nature of the work, geographic location, and opportunity for promotion is useful. Unfortunately, some employers oversell their jobs in recruiting advertisements, making the jobs appear better than they really are in reality.

Realistic job preview (RJP) Process through which a job applicant receives an accurate picture of a job.

Through the process of a **realistic job preview (RJP),** applicants are provided with an accurate picture of a job, including the "organizational realities" surrounding it, so that they can better evaluate their own job expectations. With an RJP, the organization hopes to prevent unrealistic expectations, which helps reduce employee disenchantment and ultimately employee dissatisfaction and turnover. A review of research on RJPs found that they tend to be effective in that regard.[5] The HR Perspective reports on a research study involving salespeople and RJPs.

Research on Salespeople and Realistic Job Previews

Ensuring that prospective new employees are familiar with what their jobs would involve is important, but especially so with salespeople who receive more training than those in many other occupations. Salespeople who leave a firm before the cost of that training is recovered are a source of expense, and their departures can create serious problems for employers.

Barksdale, Bellenger, Boles, and Brashear studied 762 insurance salespeople in 54 companies to test the impact of realistic job previews (RJPs). The results were reported in the *Journal of Personal Selling and Sales Management.* Analysis of the data provided some interesting findings. One primary result suggests that management should focus RJPs on two separate but parallel tracks. One track involves productivity or performance, and the other involves commitment to the firm. In the area of performance, RJPs can directly improve a salesperson's understanding of her or his role in the job and can result in more positive perceptions of training. In other words, the need for training is clear when people understand what the job will entail and how training can help them do the job.

Commitment to or satisfaction with the firm can be enhanced with a realistic job preview as well. RJPs are related to the salespeople's satisfaction with the firm, commitment to continuing employment, and reduced turnover. Emphasizing why the firm is a good place to work, while making sure that an applicant understands the salesperson's job and role in the firm and industry, can increase commitment to stay if the individuals are hired.[6]

1. Conduct a survey of your friends and family and ask them if RJPs had any influence on their commitment and satisfaction with their organizations? What have you learned from the exercise?
2. Do you believe employers will actually be truthful about the negative aspects of a job in a tight labour market? Why or why not?

Pre-employment Screening

Many employers conduct pre-employment screening to determine if applicants meet the minimum qualifications for open jobs. For example, a firm that hires security guards and armoured-car drivers might use a pre-screening interview to verify whether an applicant meets the minimum qualifications of having a valid driver's licence, being free of any criminal record, and having been trained to use a pistol. Because these minimum standards are required, it would be a waste of time for any applicant who could not meet them to fill out an application form initially. Some areas typically covered by employers include types of available jobs, applicants' pay expectations, job location, and travel requirements.

Some employers have all job applicants fill out an application first. The completed application then becomes the basis for pre-screening information. But collecting, storing, and tracking all of these applications can create significant work for HR staff members. That is why pre-screening has grown to be more prevalent.

Electronic Screening Electronic pre-employment screening has increased dramatically in the past few years. One type of screening uses computer software to scan for keywords in résumés or applications submitted electronically. Hundreds of large companies use types of text-searching or artificial intelligence (AI) software to scan, score, and track résumés of applicants. For example, a large financial firm streamlined its application process so that individuals can complete applications electronically. The applicants' qualifications are then electronically compared with job profiles to determine which candidates are likely to be successful, and those candidates are contacted for interviews.

Pre-screening sorts the serious job contenders from the often hundreds of electronic applicants, by looking for keywords, key skills, or experience. Assessment evaluates skill level, experience, or even attitudes through an online test of some sort taken by the candidate.[7]

These and other features are often parts of "applicant tracking systems" that are used for screening, tracking, testing, assessing, and reporting on the people who apply for jobs. Such software systems are used most often when:[8]

- The volume of applicants is large
- The quality of hires needs to be increased
- Hiring cycles need to be shortened
- The cost of hiring needs to be reduced
- The firm needs to reach geographic areas not visited by recruiters

Applicant reactions to these technological innovations have been mixed. Company websites as part of the electronic screening process have been well received. Computer-based testing (online or simply on a computer) has had mixed reviews, perhaps depending on the design, administration, and feedback associated with the test. Satisfaction rates of applicants for online interviewing are lower than those for face-to-face interviewing. Computerized job simulations or situational judgment tests have also had mixed reviews.[9] Regardless of the electronic pre-employment systems used, the analyses must be job-related, without using age, gender, marital status, or other data as screening criteria. Otherwise, potential discrimination complaints could not be defended well.

Application Forms

Application forms are almost universally used and can take different formats. They must follow the same guidelines as are applied to the employment interview, where the solicitation of certain information is prohibited unless it is job-related. Illegal questions frequently found on application forms ask for the following information:

- Marital status
- Information on spouse
- Height/weight
- Date of high school graduation
- Number and ages of dependants
- Contact in case of emergency
- Age
- National/ethnic origin
- Sex
- Race or colour
- Religion
- Disability
- Medical information
- Criminal record or convictions

For example, questions about dependants can be used to identify "women with small children," who may not be hired because of a manager's perception that they will be absent more than "women without small children." The high school graduation date more closely identifies a person's age, which can be used to discriminate against individuals over 40. The question about emergency contact might reveal

Women with children are still productive employees despite the stereotypical views held by some employers.

Source: Galina Barskaya/ShutterStock

marital status or other protected personal information. Figure 6-6 provides an example of an application form that meets the requirements of the type of questions that can be asked.

Properly prepared, the application form serves several purposes:

- It is a record of the applicant's desire to obtain a position.
- It provides the interviewer with a profile of the applicant that can be used in the interview.
- It is a basic employee record for applicants who are hired.
- It can be used for research on the effectiveness of the selection process.

Figure 6-6 ***Sample Application Form***

HOCO
ENTERTAINMENT & RESORTS

APPLICATION FOR EMPLOYMENT

Comfort Inn • Quality Inn • Boston Pizza • Kelsey's • Rumours
Tim Hortons • Wendy's • Great Canadian Midway
Niagara SkyWheel • Canada Trading Company

FIRST NAME ____________ LAST NAME ____________

STREET ADDRESS ____________ APT. # ______

CITY ____________ POSTAL CODE ______ TELEPHONE ______

POSITIONS APPLIED FOR: 1. ______ 2. ______ 3. ______

CHECK YOUR AVAILABILITY STATUS: Full-time ☐ Part-time ☐ Seasonal ☐

HOURS AVAILABILITY – **Available Anytime (approx. 8am – 2am, all days) check ☐ or complete chart below:**

(am/pm)	Monday	Tuesday	Wednesday	Thursday	Friday	Saturday	Sunday
From							
To							

Are you available to work: Weekends: Yes ☐ No ☐ Late Nights: Yes ☐ No ☐ Shift Work: Yes ☐ No ☐

On which date are you available to start? ____________

RATE OF PAY EXPECTED______/HOUR HAVE YOU EVER WORKED FOR HOCO BEFORE? Yes ☐ No ☐

DO YOU HAVE FRIENDS OR RELATIVES CURRENTLY EMPLOYED BY HOCO? Yes ☐ No ☐
(If yes, please provide details).

EDUCATION

HIGHEST GRADE OR LEVEL COMPLETED ______ DIPLOMA/DEGREE OBTAINED ______

NAME OF PROGRAM ______ OTHER COURSES ______

WORKSHOPS, SEMINARS ____________

WORK EXPERIENCE

Please complete below, beginning with your MOST recent position or attach your résumé.

START DATE	END DATE	EMPLOYER	POSITION	JOB DUTIES	REASON FOR LEAVING

May we contact your most recent employer? Yes ☐ No ☐

PLEASE COMPLETE OTHER SIDE

Application Disclaimers and Notices Application forms need disclaimers and notices so that appropriate legal protections are stated by employers. The recommended disclosures and notices appearing on applications include:

- *Privacy Act:* Confirms to the applicant that the information collected is protected under the federal Provincial Freedom of Information and Protection of Privacy Act or relevant provincial privacy acts, and in accordance with the relevant Human Rights Acts.
- *Reference contacts:* Requests permission to contact previous employers listed by applicants as references.
- *Employment testing:* Notifies applicants of required drug tests, pencil and paper tests, physical exams, or other tests.
- *Application time limit:* Indicates how long applications are active (typically six months) and that individuals must reactivate their applications after that period.
- *Information falsification:* Conveys to an applicant signing the form that falsification of application information is grounds for immediate termination for cause.

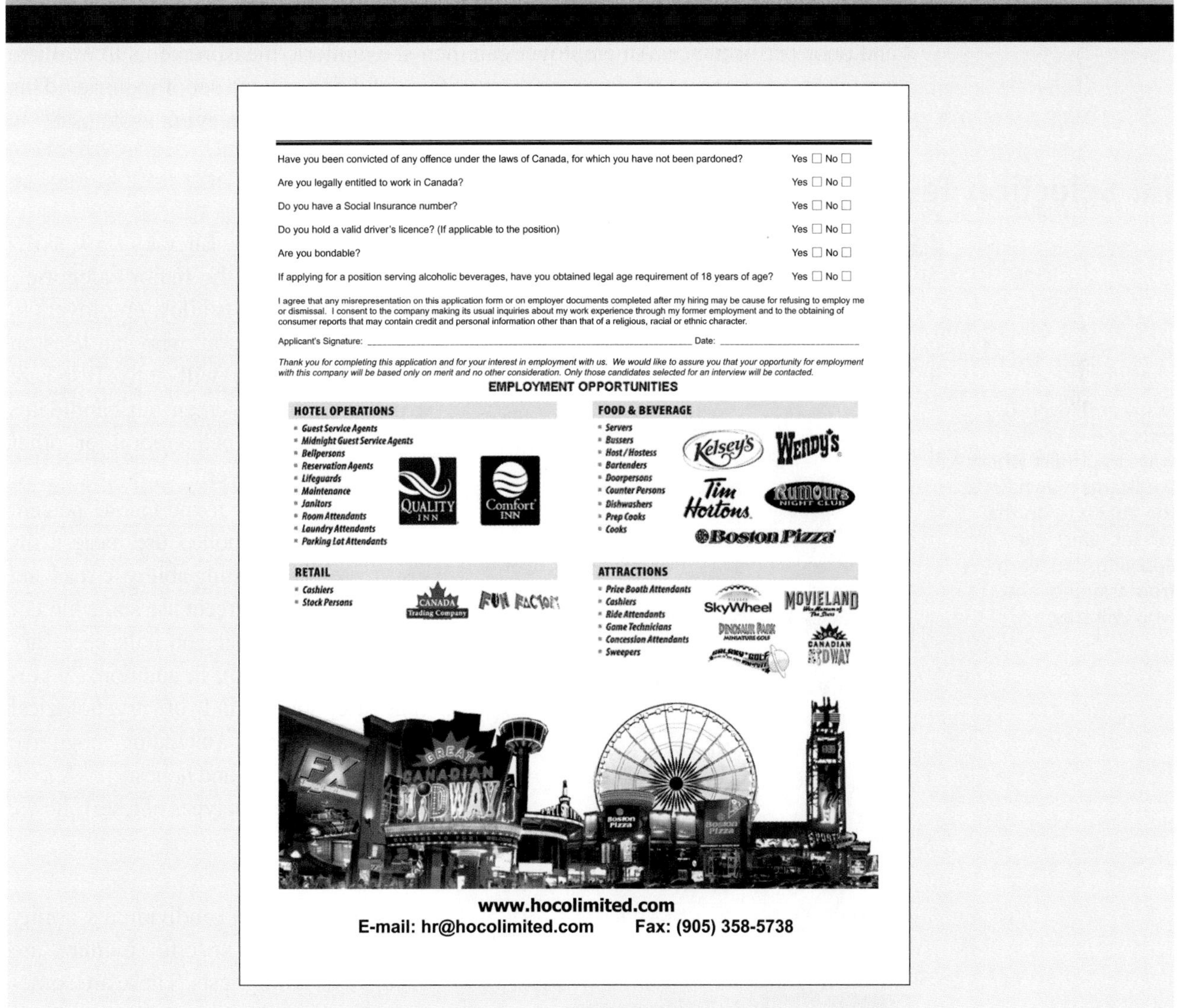

Have you been convicted of any offence under the laws of Canada, for which you have not been pardoned?	Yes ☐ No ☐
Are you legally entitled to work in Canada?	Yes ☐ No ☐
Do you have a Social Insurance number?	Yes ☐ No ☐
Do you hold a valid driver's licence? (If applicable to the position)	Yes ☐ No ☐
Are you bondable?	Yes ☐ No ☐
If applying for a position serving alcoholic beverages, have you obtained legal age requirement of 18 years of age?	Yes ☐ No ☐

I agree that any misrepresentation on this application form or on employer documents completed after my hiring may be cause for refusing to employ me or dismissal. I consent to the company making its usual inquiries about my work experience through my former employment and to the obtaining of consumer reports that may contain credit and personal information other than that of a religious, racial or ethnic character.

Applicant's Signature: ______________________ Date: ____________

Thank you for completing this application and for your interest in employment with us. We would like to assure you that your opportunity for employment with this company will be based only on merit and no other consideration. Only those candidates selected for an interview will be contacted.

EMPLOYMENT OPPORTUNITIES

HOTEL OPERATIONS

- Guest Service Agents
- Midnight Guest Service Agents
- Bellpersons
- Reservation Agents
- Lifeguards
- Maintenance
- Janitors
- Room Attendants
- Laundry Attendants
- Parking Lot Attendants

FOOD & BEVERAGE

- Servers
- Bussers
- Host/Hostess
- Bartenders
- Doorpersons
- Counter Persons
- Dishwashers
- Prep Cooks
- Cooks

RETAIL

- Cashiers
- Stock Persons

ATTRACTIONS

- Prize Booth Attendants
- Cashiers
- Ride Attendants
- Game Technicians
- Concession Attendants
- Sweepers

www.hocolimited.com
E-mail: hr@hocolimited.com Fax: (905) 358-5738

Source: HOCO Entertainment & Resorts, John Panici—H.R. Manager

- *Legality of the application form:* Notifies applicants if the form has been approved by the provincial Human Rights Commission. This is especially useful to smaller organizations that may not have the appropriate expertise in HR.

Résumés as Applications Applicants commonly provide background information through résumés. Consequently, if an applicant's résumé voluntarily furnishes some information that cannot be legally obtained, the employer should not use that information during the selection process. It is recommended that all who submit résumés complete an application form as well. Individuals who mail in résumés may be sent thank-you letters and application forms to be completed and returned.

Biodata and Weighted Application Forms Biographical data on an applicant can be gleaned from the application form, pencil-and-paper questionnaires, interviews, or communications with former employers. It is useful if there are large numbers of people doing the same job, or a large number of applicants for a small number of openings, as with online recruiting. In such cases, each data element will receive a score depending on the applicant's response. The scores for each applicant can be added, and the highest totals will indicate the applicants most likely to be satisfactory employees.

To develop biodata and weighted application forms, it is necessary to develop questions that can be asked legally and weights that differentiate between satisfactory and poor performance. An employer can then use numeric measurements to evaluate applicants' responses and compare them with a valid, job-related set of inquiries. This approach is at the heart of many electronic pre-employment screening systems.[10]

Selection Testing

3 Many kinds of tests may be used to help select good employees. Literacy tests, skills tests, psychological measurement tests, and honesty tests are the major categories. Carefully developed and properly administered employment tests allow employers to predict which applicants have the ability to do the job in question, who can learn in training, and who will stay. Tests are even available to screen out candidates who may create behavioural or other risks to the employer.[11]

Many employers use tests as one of the ways to predict which applicants may have the ability to do the job for which they are applying, can learn from training, and who will stay.

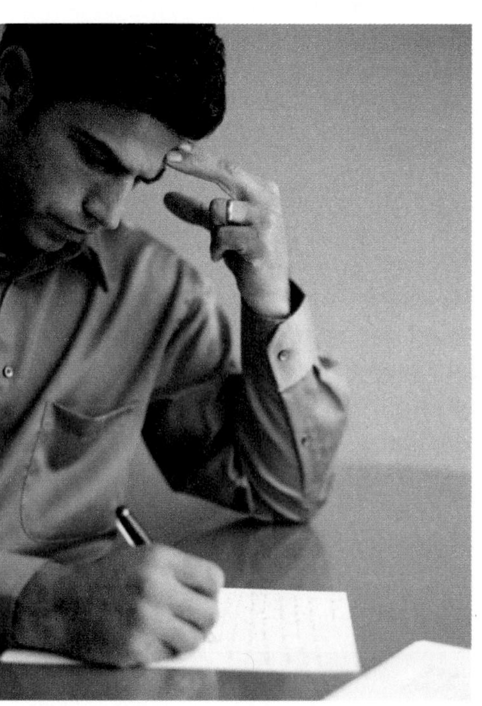

Source: Ryan McVay/Photodisc/Getty Images

A recent survey found that 41 percent of the employers polled use basic skills tests (essentially testing ability to read and do math) and 68 percent use some kind of job skills test (focusing on skills necessary to do a specific job). In addition, 29 percent use some kind of psychological measurement test (including cognitive ability, personality, and honesty).[12] A look at the most common types of tests follows.

Ability Tests

Tests that assess an individual's ability to perform in a specific manner are grouped as ability tests. These are sometimes further differentiated into *aptitude tests* and *achievement tests.*

Cognitive ability tests
Tests that measure an individual's thinking, memory, reasoning, verbal, and mathematical abilities.

Cognitive ability tests measure an individual's thinking, memory, reasoning, verbal, and mathematical abilities. Tests such as these can be used to determine applicants' basic knowledge of terminology and concepts, word fluency, spatial orientation, comprehension and retention span, general and mental ability, and conceptual reasoning. The Wonderlic Personnel Test and the General Aptitude Test Battery (GATB) are two widely used tests of this type. One consideration when using cognitive ability tests is to ensure that the cognitive concepts tested are clearly job related. An example of some Wonderlic questions would be as follows:

1. Look at the row of numbers below. What number comes next?
   8, 4, 2, 1, 1/2, 1/4 ?
   ◇ 4
   ◇ 1/2
   ◇ 1/8
   ◇ 1/4
   ◇ 1
2. A pen costs $0.80. How many pens can you purchase if you have $30.00?

General mental ability has been found to be a good predictor of job performance. The controversy in the use of general mental ability tests has to do with large differences in the scores of different racial groups.[13] Such tests cost less than personality tests and are highly reliable, and the verbal reasoning and numerical tests are valued for a wide range of jobs. However, certain visible minorities score one full standard deviation below non-minorities, and that discrepancy could result in adverse impact.[14] Adverse impact occurs when the selection rate for a designated group is lower than that for a relevant comparison group that has a higher selection rate.

Physical ability tests
Tests that measure an individual's abilities such as strength, endurance, and muscular movement.

Physical ability tests measure an individual's abilities such as strength, endurance, and muscular movement. At an electric utility, company line workers regularly must lift and carry equipment, climb ladders, and perform other physical tasks; testing of applicants' mobility, strength, and other physical attributes is job related. Some physical ability tests measure such areas as range of motion, strength and posture, and cardiovascular fitness. As noted later, care should be taken to limit physical ability testing until after a conditional job offer is made, in order to avoid violating human rights legislation.

Psychomotor tests
Tests that measure dexterity, hand-eye coordination, arm-hand steadiness, and other factors.

Different skill-based tests can be used, including **psychomotor tests,** which measure a person's dexterity, hand-eye coordination, arm-hand steadiness, and other factors. Such tests as the MacQuarrie Test for Mechanical Ability can measure manual dexterity for assembly-line workers and others by using psychomotor skills regularly.

Work sample tests
Tests that require an applicant to perform a simulated job task.

Many organizations use situational tests, or **work sample tests,** which require an applicant to perform a simulated task that is part of the target job. Having an applicant for a financial analyst's job prepare a computer spreadsheet is one such test. Requiring a person applying for a truck driver's job to back a truck to a loading dock is another. An "in-basket" test is a work sample test in which a job candidate is asked to respond to memos in a hypothetical in-basket that are typical of the problems faced by people holding that job. The key for any work sample test is the behavioural consistency between the criteria in the job and the requirements for the test.

Situational judgment tests
Tests that measure a person's judgment in work settings.

Situational judgment tests are designed to measure a person's judgment in work settings. The candidate is given a situation and a list of possible solutions to the problem. The candidate then has to make judgments about how to deal with the situation. Situational judgment tests are an additional form of job simulation.[15]

The following example demonstrates a typical situational judgment test for a salesperson:

> Your top performing salesperson is having personal problems. She is widely respected by the other employees. Recently, her performance has slipped badly and her attendance has become irregular. What are you most likely to do?
>
> a. Give her some time to work it out.
> b. Reduce her hours and have a newer person help with some of her customers.
> c. Counsel her about the importance of continued good performance.
> d. Ask the employee to come up with a performance improvement plan.
> e. Warn the employee that you will take disciplinary action if the problems continue.

Assessment Centres An assessment centre is not a place, but an assessment composed of a series of evaluative exercises and tests used for selection and development. Most often used in the selection process when filling managerial openings, assessment centres consist of multiple exercises and are evaluated by multiple raters. In one assessment centre, candidates go through a comprehensive interview, a pencil-and-paper test, individual and group simulations, and work exercises. The candidates' performances are then evaluated by a panel of trained raters. It is crucial that the tests and exercises in an assessment centre reflect the content of the job for which individuals are being screened, and the types of problems faced on that job.

Personality Tests

Personality is a unique blend of individual characteristics that affect interaction with a person's environment and help define a person. Many types of personality tests are available. One popular and widely used test is the Myers-Briggs Type Indicator (MBTI), however its validity has been called into question. It is much more useful in development of employees as opposed to selection, yet many organizations misuse the instrument.[16] There are many other personality tests such as the 16 Personality Factors, the Occupational Personality Questionnaire, and the California Psychological Inventory that are useful in selection.

The multitude of different personality traits has long frustrated psychologists, who have argued that there is a relatively small number of underlying *major* traits. The most widely accepted approach to studying these underlying personality traits (although not the only one) often refers to the "Big Five" personality traits. The Big Five that can be considered generally useful predictors of training success and job performance are shown in Figure 6-7.

Of the Big Five, conscientiousness has been found to be related to job success across most organizations and occupations. Extroversion has been found to predict success in jobs requiring social interaction, such as many sales jobs. The usefulness of the other three traits varies depending on the kind of job and organization.

Personality testing can be useful in identifying interpersonal traits needed in jobs and can reveal more information about abilities and interests. However, intrusive questions, lack of face validity, and the need to use them with other selection methods can present problems.[17] Such tests have been used to predict many factors including success in training, ability to develop new business, and performance on managerial jobs.[18] When used in selection, psychological or personality testing must be solidly related to the job.[19]

"Fakability" and Personality Tests "Faking" is a major concern for employers using personality tests. Most test publishers do not dispute that test profiles can be

Figure 6-7 *Big Five Personality Characteristics*

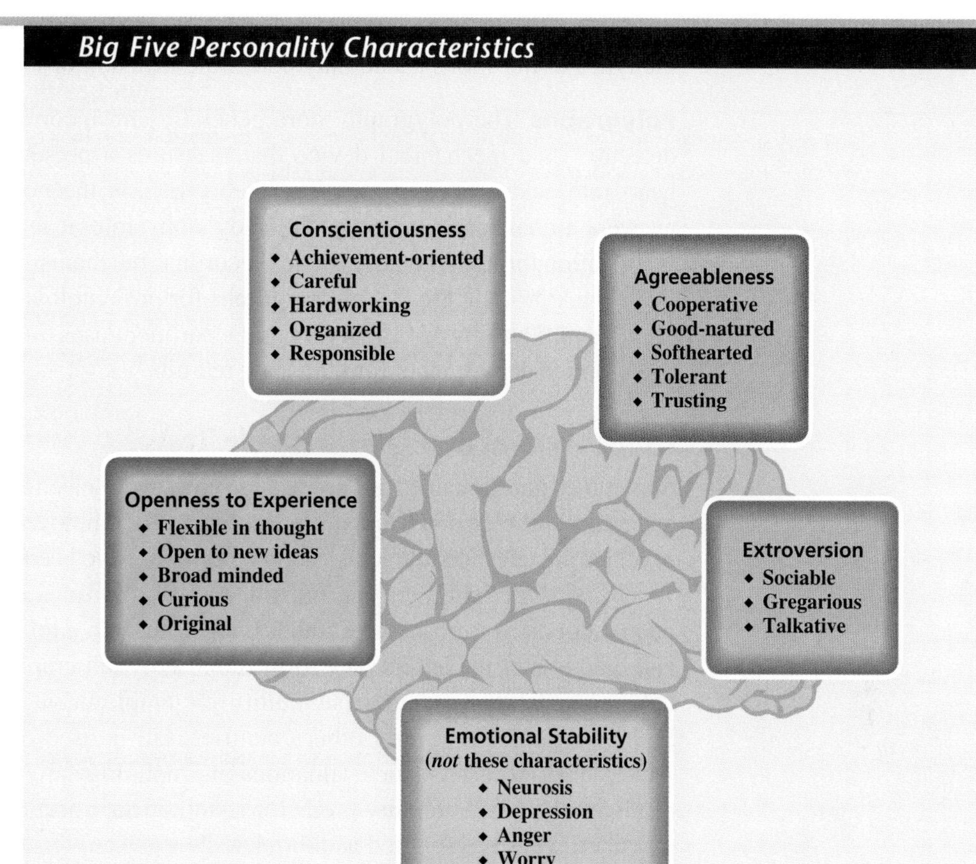

falsified, and they try to reduce faking by including questions that together constitute a social desirability or "lie" scale.[20] Researchers generally favour the use of "corrections" based on components of the test to account for faking—a preference that also constitutes an argument for professional scoring of personality tests.[21]

Honesty/Integrity Tests

Different types of tests are being used by employers to assess the honesty and integrity of applicants and employees. They include standardized honesty/integrity tests and polygraph tests. Both are controversial.

Employers use these tests for several reasons. Firms such as retailers use honesty tests to screen out potentially dishonest individuals and decrease the incidence of employee theft. These firms believe that giving honesty tests also sends a message to applicants and employees alike that dishonesty will not be tolerated.

Honesty/integrity tests may be valid as broad screening devices for organizations if used properly. However, it is important that the tests be chosen, used, and evaluated in ways that ensure that they are and remain valid and reliable. They should be used as one piece of the selection process, along with applications, interviews, and other data.[22] One documented concern about integrity tests, as well as for personality tests, is their "fakability." Research indicates that test takers are more able to fake honesty and pass integrity tests than to falsify profiles on personality tests.[23] Some questions that could be asked in an honesty test are: *"Have you ever stolen anything?" "Have you ever lied?" "Have you ever cheated on a test?"* The use of honesty/integrity tests can have a negative impact on public relations with applicants. A final concern is that the types of questions asked may constitute invasion of individual privacy.

Polygraphs The polygraph, more generally and incorrectly referred to as the "lie detector," is a mechanical device that measures a person's galvanic skin response, heart rate, and breathing rate. The theory behind the polygraph is that if a person answers a question incorrectly, the body's physiological responses will "reveal" the falsification through the polygraph's recording mechanisms.[24] Both Ontario and New Brunswick prohibit the use of polygraphs for pre-employment screening purposes by employers. The City of Calgary's Fire Department uses this type of test for applicants, as do police departments for their new recruits.

Controversial and Questionable Tests

Sometimes questionable tests are used in employee selection. Experts warn of the legal and ethical problems in using those techniques for employee selection. Graphology and psychics are questionable job selection tools that have been used by various employers.

Graphology "analyzes" an individual's handwriting. Such characteristics as how people dot an *i* or cross a *t,* whether they write with a left or right slant, and the size and boldness of the letters they form supposedly tell graphologists about the individuals' personalities and their suitability for employment. Graphology is popular in France, Israel, and several other countries, but is used on a limited basis in North America. Formal scientific evaluations of graphology are not easily found. The value of this tool as a personality predictor is somewhat questionable, and use of this tool may not be easily validated as job related.

Some firms use *psychics* to help them select managerial talent. The psychics are supposedly able to determine if a person is suited for a job intellectually and emotionally. However, most businesses probably would not want anyone to know that they used psychic advisers.

Legal Concerns and Selection Testing

Canadian Human Rights Commission
This website provides information about events and regulations within the mandate of the Canadian Human Rights commission.
www.chrc-ccdp.ca

Employers must make sure that the selection tests they use are valid, are job-related, and do not discriminate against designated group members, or other situations such as language. Several court cases have ruled that some tests used by employers may be discriminatory. The Supreme Court of Canada decision in *Meiorin* created a unified test to determine if a violation of the Canadian Human Rights Act can be justified as a *bona fide occupational requirement* (BFOR). This landmark case is also important because it set new legal standards for the use of tests in personnel selection. Tawney Meiorin was employed as a firefighter by the British Columbia Ministry of Forests. Three years after being hired, the government adopted a series of fitness tests that all employees were required to pass. At that time, her performance was deemed to be satisfactory. She passed all the tests except for one that required her to run 2.5 km in which she was 50 seconds over the time limit. She attempted the test four times, but without success. As a result she was fired. Though the fitness tests had a valid purpose of ensuring safety, the court found that the research that the tests were based on was incomplete and "impressionistic," and did not take into account the differences between men and women in establishing an aerobic standard. Even with proper training, most women could never achieve the same aerobic capacity as men. While the employer tried to justify the test as a bona fide occupational requirement, it was not reasonable considering that there was no credible evidence showing that the prescribed aerobic capacity was necessary for either men or women to perform their jobs. As well, at the time, Ms. Meiorin had completed her work well, without incident. The tribunal ruled that she was to be returned to her job, and that she be compensated for loss wages. In summary, the role of testing in the selection process must be kept in perspective because tests represent only one possible data source, and they must be used appropriately and legally.[25]

Selection Interviewing

4 Selection interviewing of job applicants is done both to obtain additional information and to clarify information gathered throughout the selection process. Typically, interviews are conducted at two levels: first, as an initial screening interview simply to see if the person has minimum qualifications, and then later, as an in-depth interview perhaps involving HR staff members and operating managers in the departments where the individuals will work. The more senior the position, the more interviews, that are longer in length, will be conducted.

Before the in-depth interview, information from all available sources is pulled together so that interviewers can identify and ask questions about conflicting information that may have emerged from tests, application forms, and references. In addition, interviewers must obtain as much pertinent information about the applicants as possible during the limited time of the interview itself, and evaluate this information against job standards. As Figure 6-8 shows, there are a number of types of interviews. They range from structured to unstructured and vary in terms of appropriateness for selection.

Reliability and Validity of Interviews

Inter-rater reliability
Inter-rater reliability is the degree of agreement between different observers, or between the same observer on two different occasions.

To be useful, interviews must be reliable, allowing interviewers to pick the same capabilities again and again in applicants. Some interviewers may be better than others at selecting individuals who will perform well. A high *intra*-rater reliability (within the same interviewer) can be demonstrated, but only moderate-to-low *inter*-rater reliability (across different interviewers) is generally shown. **Inter-rater reliability** becomes important when each of several interviewers is selecting employees from a pool of applicants, or if the employer uses team or panel interviews with multiple interviewers.

The interview is popular with employers because it has high "face validity," that is, it seems valid to employers, and they like it. It is often assumed that if someone interviews

Figure 6-8 *Types of Selection Interviews*

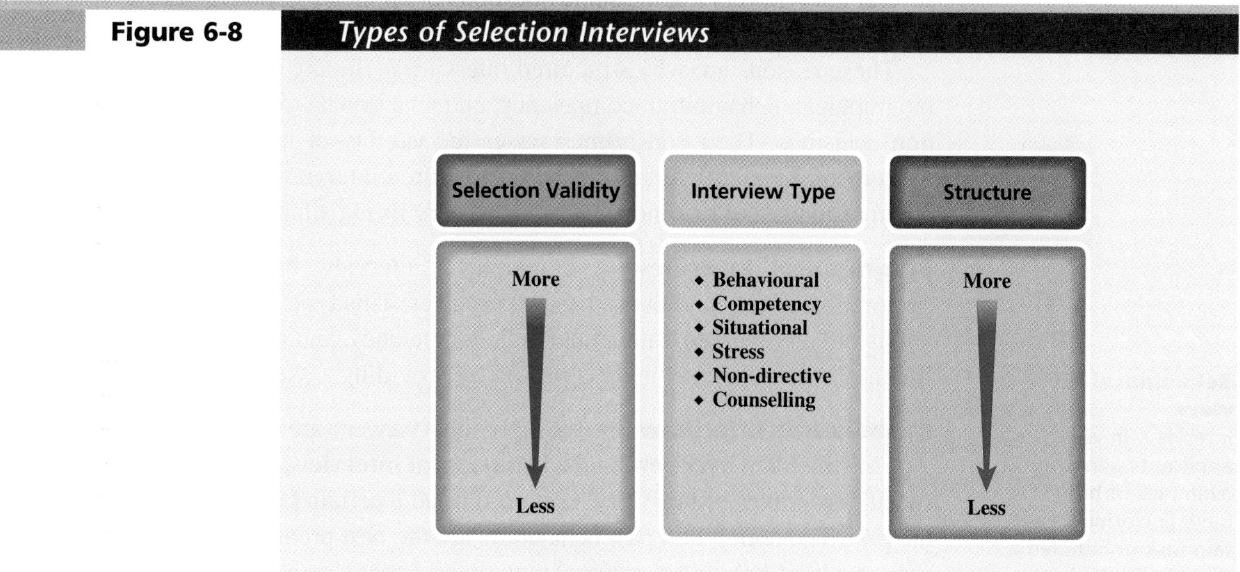

well and the information obtained in the interview is useful, then the individual will perform well on the job. However, research over several decades has consistently confirmed that an unstructured interview is not an especially valid predictor of job performance and success. Applicants are usually asked different questions, making comparison of applicants very difficult. That is why use of structured interviews has grown in popularity.

Structured Interviews

Structured interview
Interview that uses a set of standardized questions asked of all job applicants.

A **structured interview** uses a set of standardized questions asked of all applicants. The interviewer asks every applicant the same basic questions, so that comparisons among applicants can more easily be made. This type of interview allows an interviewer to prepare job-related questions in advance and then complete a standardized interviewee evaluation form that provides documentation indicating why one applicant was selected over another. The structured interview is especially useful in the initial screening phase because of the large number of applicants that may need to be considered in this step of the selection process. The structured interview does not have to be rigid. The pre-determined questions should be asked in a logical manner, but interviewers can avoid reading them word for word down the list. Also, the applicants should be allowed adequate opportunity to explain their answers, and each interviewer should probe with additional questions until she or he fully understands the responses. The questions should also be open ended, so that it allows the applicant to expand on the question, as opposed to using a closed ended question that would simply have the applicant respond with a yes or no answer. Sample questions that might be asked of all applicants for a retail sales clerk opening are as follows:

- "I noticed on your application that you were previously employed with __________. How did you get a job there?"
- "Tell me about your responsibilities and duties with __________."
- "Describe a time, when you, as a customer, were frustrated because of the way a store clerk treated you. What do you think should have been done?"
- "How did you handle an abusive and rude customer?"

Research on interviews consistently finds structured interviews to be more reliable and valid than other interview approaches. The structured format ensures that a given interviewer has similar information on each candidate. It also ensures that when several interviewers ask the same questions of applicants, there is greater consistency in the subsequent evaluation of those candidates.

These reasons are why structured interviews—in any of several forms, including biographical, behavioural, competency, and situational—are recommended for selection decisions. Their consistency raises the validity of the interview as a selection instrument. Less-structured or even unstructured interviews have their places as well but are usually not recommended for ordinary hiring situations.

Biographical Interview A biographical interview focuses on a chronological exploration of the candidate's past experiences. This type of interview is widely used and is often combined with situational, competency, and other forms of information. It contributes to the picture of a person by providing a sketch of past experiences.

Behavioural interview
Interview in which applicants give specific examples of how they have performed a certain task or handled a problem in the past.

Behavioural Interview Increasingly, interviewers are using an experience-based type of structured interview. In the **behavioural interview,** applicants are asked to give specific examples of how they have performed a certain task or handled a problem in the past. The notion that past behaviours are the best predictors of future actions provides the logic behind behavioural interviews. Learning about how candidates describe

Structured interviews are more reliable and valid than other types of interviews.

Source: Marcin Balcerzak/ShutterStock

their previous behaviours helps in determining which applicants may be best suited for current jobs. For example, applicants might be asked the following questions:

- "How did you handle a situation that had no rules or guidelines for employee discipline?"
- "Why did you choose that approach?"
- "How did your supervisor react?"
- "How was the situation finally resolved?"

Competency Interview The *competency interview* is similar to the behavioural interview except that the questions are designed specifically to provide the interviewer with something to measure the applicant's response against—that is, the "competency profile" for the position, which includes a list of competencies necessary to do that particular job.[26] Adler, a well-known selection expert, is credited with what he calls the one-question interview: "Describe your most significant accomplishment." The answers are expected to reveal the candidate's competencies in making that achievement.[27] A variation focuses on problems in the interviewing company and how the candidate would solve them. TD Bank Financial Group uses competency-based interviewing techniques. For example, if *relating to customers* is a competency for success on the job, the interviewer might ask: "Tell me about a situation when you had to build a relationship with a new customer? How did you develop the relationship? What feedback did you receive from the customer?" When you respond to questions such as these, the interviewer will be looking for the applicant to provide a brief description of the situation, your actions, and the results of your actions.[28]

Developing competency-based questions and behavioural-based questions is time-consuming. Further, competency and behavioural interviews may simply identify which candidate is the most articulate person or the best at creating a positive impression.

Situational interview
Structured interview composed of questions about how applicants might handle specific job situations.

Situational Interview The situational interview is a structured interview composed of questions about how applicants might handle specific job situations. Interview questions are based on job analysis and checked by experts in the job for content validity. For some situational interviews, job experts also rate responses to the questions in order to facilitate the ranking of candidates. The interviewer can code the suitability of the answer, assign point values, and add up the total number of points an interviewee received. The scoring guide is based on critical incident techniques of the job. Subject matter experts (SMEs) review the job to determine behaviours that have been shown to be either effective or ineffective in a given situation in the past. For example, being at work on time may be critical, how the incumbent is supposed to handle difficult situations, or how they lead their group. Some situational questions include:

- "You are a supervisor, and an employee consistently arrives late to work. What action do you take?"
- "One of your employees tells you in confidence that she has seen one of her co-workers steal. What do you do?"
- "You feel that your boss is discriminating against you because you are older than other employees. How do you handle this?"

Research on both behavioural and situational interviews shows that they can predict performance equally well.[29] However, when a descriptively anchored scale for rating answers was added, the behavioural or competency approach was found to have higher validity.[30] The following example demonstrates the use of an anchored scale that is scored, using a situational interview question:

> A customer brings in a car for repair on Monday and is asked to return on Wednesday. The repair isn't finished when the customer returns on Wednesday. How would you handle the situation as the service manager?
>
> 0 Points Tell the customer that the car isn't finished and to come back this afternoon.
>
> 3 Points Reassure the customer that their car will be ready shortly, apologizing for the customer having to wait, then go to the shop to get an accurate estimate of time needed to complete the repair.
>
> 5 Points Call the customer and let them know that their car will not be ready so that they don't make an unnecessary trip to the shop, extending your apologies for the situation, what has happened, and let them know when it will be ready.

Less-Structured Interviews

Some interviews are unplanned and have no structure. Often, these interviews are conducted by operating managers or supervisors who have had little training on interviewing do's and don'ts. An *unstructured interview* occurs when the interviewer "wings it," asking questions that have no identified direct purpose, such as, "Tell me about yourself."

A *semi-structured interview* is a guided conversation in which broad questions are asked and new questions arise as a result of the discussion. In the hands of a professional interviewer trained in the psychology of personality theory, semi-structured interviews have been found to be better than structured interviews for accurately predicting personality.[31] However, personality can also be predicted with a pencil-and-paper or Web-based test if necessary.

Non-directive interview
Interview that uses questions developed from the answers to previous questions.

A **non-directive interview** uses questions that are developed from the answers to previous questions. The interviewer asks general questions designed to prompt the applicant to discuss herself or himself. The interviewer then picks up on an idea in the applicant's response and uses it to shape the next question. For example, if the applicant says, "One reason that I enjoyed my last job was my supervisor," the interviewer might ask, "What type of supervisor do you most enjoy working with?"

With a non-directive interview, as with any less-structured interview, difficulties include keeping the conversation job related and obtaining comparable data on various applicants. Many non-directive interviews are only semi-organized; as a result, a combination of general and specific questions is asked in no set order, and different questions are asked of different applicants for the same job. Comparing and ranking candidates is more open to subjective judgments and legal challenges under this format. This is why it is best used only in very specific settings.

Stress Interview

Stress interview
Interview designed to create anxiety and put pressure on applicants to see how they respond.

A **stress interview** is a special type of interview designed to create anxiety and put pressure on applicants to see how they respond. In a stress interview, the interviewer assumes an extremely aggressive and insulting posture. Those who use this approach often justify doing so with individuals who will encounter high degrees of stress on the job, such as consumer-complaint clerks in a department store or air traffic controllers.

The stress interview is a high-risk approach for an employer. The typical applicant is already somewhat anxious in any interview, and the stress interview can easily generate a poor image of the interviewer and the employer. Consequently, an applicant that the organization wishes to hire might turn down the job offer. Even so, many interviewers deliberately put applicants under stress.

Who Conducts Interviews?

Interviews can be conducted individually, by several individuals in sequence, or by panels or teams of individuals. For some jobs, such as entry-level jobs requiring lesser skills, applicants often are interviewed by an HR representative alone. For other jobs, employers screen applicants by using multiple interviews, beginning with an HR representative and following up with interviews conducted by appropriate supervisors and managers. Then a selection decision is made based on discussions by those who have conducted the interviews. When an interviewee must see several people, often many of the interviews are redundant and therefore unnecessarily time-consuming.

Panel interview
Interview in which several interviewers meet with the candidate at the same time.

In a **panel interview,** several interviewers meet with the candidate at the same time. All the interviewers hear the same responses. Panel interviews may be combined with individual interviews. For example, to select a new marketing manager in a distribution firm, three vice-presidents interviewed the top two candidates after the vice-president of sales had conducted individual interviews to identify the two finalists. On the negative side, without planning by the panel of interviewers, an unstructured interview can result. Also, applicants are frequently uncomfortable with the group interview format.

Team interview
Interview in which applicants are interviewed by the team members with whom they will work.

The prevalence of work teams has increased the use of the team interview, in which applicants are interviewed by the team members with whom they will work. Involving team members in the selection of their co-workers can improve the success of the team. However, training is required to make sure that team members understand the selection process, interviewing, and legal constraints. A selection procedure in which the team votes for the top choice may be inappropriate; usually, the decision should be made by consensus, which may take longer. A test has been developed to help select employees for team-based organizations; when an employer uses the test in combination with a team interview its chances of picking a "team player" are increased.[32]

Video Interviewing A number of employers use video interviewing to augment or replace in-depth telephone interviews. Often, video interviews are used to narrow a pool of candidates down to two or three finalists, who are then interviewed in person. An applicant is asked to go to a video-conferencing facility scheduled by the employer. At the designated time, an applicant and those conducting the interview are video linked. Video technology using the Internet and digital cameras gives employers additional interviewing options.

Video interviewing is used most by large corporations; executive recruiting firms; and college and university placement offices, which offer the technology to aid both students and employers. Savings on time and travel costs are an advantage of video interviewing. A disadvantage is that applicants seem to be more skeptical of video interviews than face-to-face interviews.[33]

Effective Interviewing

Many people think that the ability to interview is an innate talent, but this contention is difficult to support. Just being personable and liking to talk is no guarantee that someone will be an effective interviewer. Interviewing skills are developed through training. A number of suggestions for making interviewing more effective have been developed. One thing that should always be done is to notify the candidate well in advance that they will have to complete employment tests, if you decide to use these, in addition to the interview. Four key points commonly cited are as follows:

- *Plan the interview:* Interviewers should review pre-employment screening information, the application or résumé, and the appropriate job description before beginning the interview, and then identify specific areas for questioning during the interview.
- *Control the interview:* This includes knowing in advance what information must be collected, systematically collecting it during the interview, and stopping when that information has been collected. Controlling the interview does not mean monopolizing the conversation; effective interviewers should talk no more than about 25 percent of the time in an in-depth interview.
- *Use effective questioning techniques:* The questioning techniques used by an interviewer can and do significantly affect the type and quality of information obtained.[34] *Describe, who, what, when, why, tell me, how,* and *which* are all good words and phrases for beginning questions that will produce longer and more informative answers. Figure 6-9 lists questions commonly used in selection interviews.
- *Take excessive notes during all stages of the interview process:* Due to problems that can arise out of applicants claiming that they were discriminated against during the selection process, it is imperative that interviewers write down all comments provided by the applicants, including comments made by the interviewer. In one instance, a former HR manager's notes were used ten years later in a wrongful dismissal case that brought allegations of promises made during an interview. The notes indicated what the applicant had asked, what was answered, and the applicant's comments to those responses. The case was dismissed because of the interviewer's notes.

Interview problems exist with both interviewers and applicants. The HR Perspective (on p. 230) relates stories illustrating some negative situations.

Questions to Avoid Certain kinds of questions should be avoided in selection interviews:

- *Closed-ended questions:* Unless verifying specific information, the interviewer should avoid closed-ended questions that can be answered "Yes" or "No." For

Figure 6-9 *Questions Commonly Used in Selection Interviews*

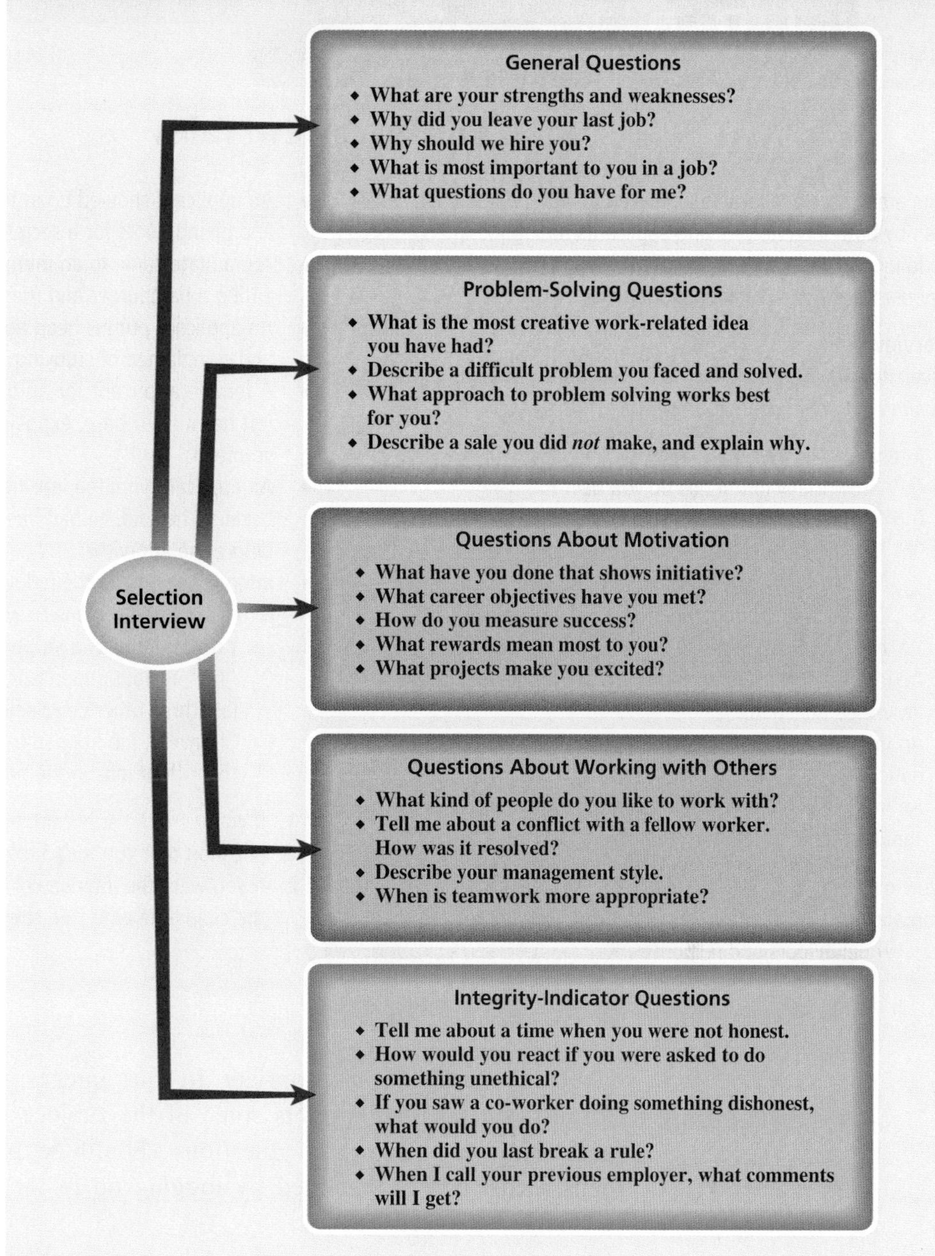

Selection Interview
General Questions
• What are your strengths and weaknesses?
• Why did you leave your last job?
• Why should we hire you?
• What is most important to you in a job?
• What questions do you have for me?
Problem-Solving Questions
• What is the most creative work-related idea you have had?
• Describe a difficult problem you faced and solved.
• What approach to problem solving works best for you?
• Describe a sale you did *not* make, and explain why.
Questions About Motivation
• What have you done that shows initiative?
• What career objectives have you met?
• How do you measure success?
• What rewards mean most to you?
• What projects make you excited?
Questions About Working with Others
• What kind of people do you like to work with?
• Tell me about a conflict with a fellow worker. How was it resolved?
• Describe your management style.
• When is teamwork more appropriate?
Integrity-Indicator Questions
• Tell me about a time when you were not honest.
• How would you react if you were asked to do something unethical?
• If you saw a co-worker doing something dishonest, what would you do?
• When did you last break a rule?
• When I call your previous employer, what comments will I get?

example, "Did you have good attendance on your last job?" will probably be answered simply, "Yes."

- *Obvious questions:* An obvious question is one for which the interviewer already has the answer and the applicant knows it.
- *Questions that rarely produce a true answer:* An example is, "How did you get along with your co-workers?" The likely answer is, "Just fine."
- *Leading questions:* A leading question is one to which the answer is obvious from the way that the question is asked. For example, "How do you like working with other people?" suggests the answer, "I like it."
- *Illegal questions:* Questions that involve information such as race, age, gender, ethnic origin, race, religion, marital status, and number of children are illegal.

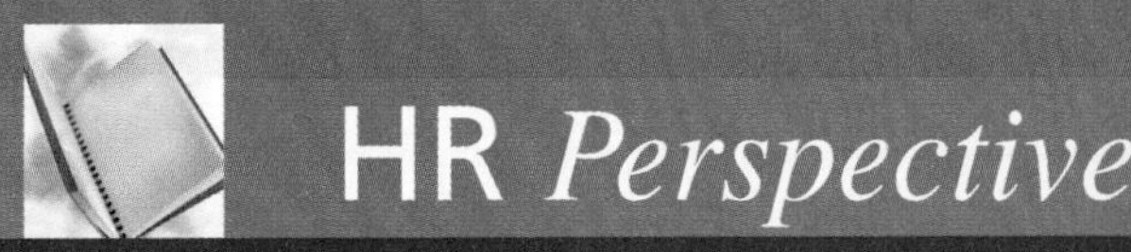

Job Interview Tales

Some amusing, unbelievable, and even inappropriate actions are taken by both interviewers and applicants during job interviews. The following examples of poor interviewing behaviours and responses *are not* recommended for use!

Interviewers
University and college students have encountered some interviewers who act in strange or inappropriate ways:

- Interviewers asked the following questions:
  - "How many girlfriends do you have?"
  - "What method of birth control do you use?"
  - "Would you like to see my appendectomy scar?"
  - "What do your mother and father do for a living?"
  - "What will your boyfriend think of you working long hours?"
- An interviewer talked on the phone while the applicant answered questions.
- An interviewer asked the applicant to guess what his nationality was.
- An interviewer watched television over the applicant's shoulder during the interview.

Interviewees
Some applicants also apparently do not provide acceptable interview behaviours and responses:

- An applicant showed up in torn camouflage pants, a T-shirt, and hiking boots for a secretarial job interview.
- A graduate came to an interview wearing sunglasses and eating a hamburger and fries.
- An applicant put his head down on the interviewer's desk and complained of studying all night.
- A female applicant for an office job wore a shirt that left her midriff bare, exposing multiple tattoos on her stomach.
- An applicant vomited into the interviewer's trash can because, he said, he had been drinking for several hours before the interview.
- Interviewees made the following statements:
  - "Do I have to come to work before 9:00 a.m., because I work nights as a stripper?"
  - "My previous supervisor didn't like me—just like at my last three other companies."
  - "I haven't job hopped because I was fired from all of them [four jobs in the past year]."

1. If you were the applicant, how would you deal with a question that you found offensive or discriminatory?
2. If you were the interviewer, how would you deal with the candidate who said she was a part-time stripper?

They are just as inappropriate in the interview as on the application form. Figure 6-10 highlights some of the subject areas to be avoided and a suggestion as to how the questions should be phrased. A more comprehensive list can be obtained by logging on to the Canadian Human Rights Commission's website.

- *Questions that are not job related:* All questions should be directly related to the job for which the interviewee has applied.

Listening Responses to Avoid Effective interviewers avoid listening responses such as nodding, pausing, making casual remarks, echoing, and mirroring. A friendly but neutral demeanour is appropriate. Listening responses are an essential part of everyday, normal conversation, but they may unintentionally provide feedback to the applicant. Applicants may try to please interviewers and look to the interviewers' listening responses for cues. Even though the listening responses may be subtle, they do provide information to applicants. However, giving no response to applicants' answers may imply boredom or inattention. Therefore, interviewers should make a neutral comment, acknowledge the answers, or use a reply such as, "That is interesting information" or just "thank you" and move on to the next question.

Figure 6-10 ***Subject Areas to be Treated Cautiously in Employment Questions***

Subject	Avoid Asking.....	Preferred Question	Comments
Name	About name change, whether through marriage, or even their maiden name	Ask after selection if needed to check on previously held jobs or education credentials	
Marital Status	Marital status, whether their spouse may be transferred or about spouse's employment	If transfer or travel is part of job, ask whether he or she can meet the requirements of the job	Information on dependants can be determined after selection if necessary for benefits
Family Status	Number of children or dependants or about child-care arrangements	Ask if the applicant would be able to work the required hours, and if applicable, overtime	Contacts for emergencies and/or details on dependants can be determined after selection if applicable
Religion	Whether applicant will work on a specific religious holiday, their religious affiliations, frequency of church attendance, or references from clergy	Explain the required work shift and ask whether such a schedule poses problems for the applicant	Accommodation of an employee's religious beliefs is the employer's duty
Disability	For a list of all disabilities, limitations or health problems, if the applicant drinks or uses drugs, ever received psychiatric care or been hospitalized for emotional problems and if they ever received worker's compensation	Ask whether the applicant has any condition that could affect ability to do the job or ask if the applicant has any condition that should be considered in selection.	A disability is only relevant to job ability if it threatens the safety of the applicant, co-workers or public, and prevents the applicant from a safe and adequate job performance even when reasonable efforts are made to accommodate the disability
Pardoned Conviction	If an applicant has ever been convicted, arrested, or has a criminal record	If bonding is a job requirement, ask whether the applicant is eligible	Inquiries about criminal record or convictions are discouraged unless related to job duties

Source: Adapted from *A Guide to Screening and Selection in Employment,* February 2001, pp. 3–5; www.chrc-ccdp.ca/pdf/screen.pdf. Canadian Human Rights Commission. Reproduced with the permission of the Ministry of Public Works and Government Services, 2006.

Problems in the Interview

Operating managers and supervisors are more likely to use poor interviewing techniques because they do not interview often or lack training. Several problems are commonly encountered in the interview.

Snap Judgments Unfortunately, many interviewers decide whether an applicant is suitable for the job within the first two to four minutes of the interview, and spend the balance of the interview looking for evidence to support their decision. This impression may be based on a review of the individual's application form or on more subjective factors such as dress or appearance. Ideally, the interviewer should collect all the information possible on an applicant before making a judgment.

Negative Emphasis As might be expected, unfavourable information about an applicant is the biggest factor considered in interviewers' decisions about overall suitability.

Unfavourable information is usually given more weight than favourable information. Often, a single negative characteristic may bar an individual from being accepted, whereas no amount of positive characteristics will guarantee a candidate's acceptance.

Halo Effect Interviewers should try to avoid the *halo effect,* which occurs when an interviewer allows a prominent characteristic to overshadow other evidence. For instance, the halo effect is present if an interviewer lets a candidate's athletic accomplishments overshadow other characteristics, and then hires the applicant because "athletes make good salespeople." *Devil's horns* is the reverse of the halo effect. It occurs when an interviewer allows a negative characteristic, such as inappropriate dress or a low grade point average, to overshadow other evidence.

Biases and Stereotyping Personal biases and stereotyping of applicants should be avoided in interviews.[35] One type of bias, the "similarity" bias, occurs because interviewers tend to favour or select people they perceive to be similar to themselves. The similarity can be in age, race, sex, previous work experiences, personal background, or other factors. As workforce demographics shift, interviewers should be aware of any personal tendencies to stereotype individuals because of demographic characteristics and differences, and be careful to avoid doing so.

Influence Tactics Interviewers must learn to recognize and handle influence tactics of the applicant. Influence can occur as either a soft approach where the applicant uses ingratiation or rational persuasion. Alternatively, an applicant can use a hard tactic such as using pressure.[36] An interviewer can handle influence tactics by not encouraging it. If the interviewer supports influence tactics, the applicant will take the cue and continue giving answers that reflect it. If the interviewer instead makes the applicant aware that he or she is not being taken in, the interviewer re-establishes control over the interview.

Background Investigation

5 Background investigations are very important in employment situations. As a recent study indicates, the number of applicants who lie is alarmingly high at over 35 percent. Background investigation may take place either before or after the in-depth interview. It costs the organization some time and money, but it generally proves beneficial when making selection decisions. Technology has played an increasing role in helping employers conduct background investigations, as the Technology Transforming HR illustrates.

A background screening has four goals: to show that the employer exercised due diligence in hiring; to provide factual information about a candidate; to discourage applicants with something to hide; to encourage applicants to be honest on applications and during interviews.[37]

A comprehensive background check costs about $200 per applicant.[38] Employers must ensure that they are abiding by the relevant privacy acts when conducting background checks. International background checks may present special challenges. Employers must ensure that they obtain written consent from individuals when they collect, use, or disclose personal information on that person.[39]

The value of background investigation is evident when the investigation reveals that applicants have misrepresented their qualifications and backgrounds. The most common pieces of false information given are length of prior employment, past salary, criminal record, and former job title. Additionally, many universities report that inquiries on former students often reveal that "graduates" never graduated, and sometimes reveal that

Background checks should be conducted on all applicants to ensure that candidates have not misrepresented themselves.

"students" did not even attend the university. Another type of credential fraud uses the mail-order "degree mill." To enhance their chances of employment, individuals purchase unaccredited degrees from organizations posing as "universities." These entities provide their "students" degrees for fees and require "no exams, no studying, no classes."

The only way for employers to protect themselves from résumé fraud and false credentials is to get verification on applicants either before or after hire. If hired, an employee can be terminated for falsifying employment information. It is unwise for employers to assume that "someone else has already checked." Too often, that assumption has been proved wrong. Two areas that have received special scrutiny since the 9/11 attacks are airline employees and truck drivers.[40]

Technology Transforming HR

The Future of Selection

A poor hiring decision can be expensive for organizations resulting in increased costs for lost time and recruiting and hiring a new employee. With increasing pressure to hire the right person the first time, many companies are striving to refine their selection process to weed out poor candidates before they become a costly mistake.

Piers Steel, assistant professor at the University of Calgary, has found what he believes is the formula for successful candidate selection. This selection model, dubbed synthetic validity, combines database technology with a complicated mathematical formula that can be used to predict job performance. Though the model is complex, Steel claims it can simplify the hiring process to one step. With the synthetic validity model, organizations need only to go online and describe the job to create a selection process that will chose better candidates than even the most experienced recruiters.

The process begins by using information gathered from supervisors, job analysts, and employees to measure every aspect of the job, breaking it down into the basic work behaviours such as leadership, decision making, and organization that are common characteristics for a position. Depending on the complexity of the position, this could involve as few as eight or as many as 40 different job related characteristics. These characteristics are then compared to the abilities of a pool of prospective candidates in order to determine those candidates who are the best match for the position. The system can then dictate what job specific testing should be administered and how to combine and score the test results in order to select the ideal candidate.

While synthetic validity can significantly decrease the time and costs associated with hiring, organizations shouldn't give up on their current selection process just yet. Although Steel expects to have a commercially workable system available within the year, creating a comprehensive database will require input from over 40 000 employees and a financial cost of between $500,000 to $3 million.[41]

1. What benefits or drawbacks do you see in using synthetic validity in the candidate selection process? For organizations? For candidates?
2. Do you foresee the synthetic validity model replacing traditional hiring practices? Why or why not?

Sources of Background Information

Background information, can be obtained from a number of sources. Some of these sources can be obtained during the interviewing stage, others only if job-related (criminal, credit, and motor vehicle records), and others can be obtained once a conditional offer for employment has been made (pre employment medical), and the others when the employee begins their employment (Social Insurance number). Some of these sources are:

- Previous employment records
- Pre employment medical
- Professional certifications/licences
- Credit history
- Social Insurance number
- Criminal records
- Education/degree documentation
- Motor vehicle records
- Honesty tests
- Sex offenders lists

Personal references, such as those from relatives, clergy, or friends, are of little value, and should not even be used. No applicant seeks a recommendation from somebody who would give a negative response. Instead, work-related references from previous employers and supervisors should be relied on.

Reference-Checking Methods

Several methods of obtaining information from references are available to an employer, with telephoning the reference the most commonly used. Many experts recommend that employers conducting a telephone reference check use a form focusing on factual verification of information given by the applicant, such as employment dates, salary history, type of job responsibilities, and attendance record. Other items often include reasons for leaving the previous job, the individual's manner of working with supervisors and other employees, and other more subjective information. Many firms that are called for references will provide only factual information. But the use of the form can provide evidence that a diligent effort was made.

Written methods of reference checking are also used. Some organizations send preprinted reference forms to individuals who are giving references for applicants. These forms often contain a release statement signed by the applicant, so that those providing references can see that they have been released from liability on the information they furnish. Specific or general letters of reference also are requested by some employers or provided by applicants. Employers can face conflicting thoughts when asked to give references for former employees, as the following discussion illustrates.

Giving References on Former Employees In a number of court cases, individuals have sued their former employers for slander, libel, or defamation of character as a result of what the employers said to other potential employers that prevented the individuals from obtaining jobs. Because of such problems, lawyers advise organizations that are asked about former employees to give out only name, employment date, and title; many organizations have adopted policies restricting the release of reference information. The problem in only confirming information, or providing vague information, may leave the impression that the employee may not be a good employee, thus impinging on their opportunity to secure gainful employment. Another difficulty that may arise occurs when an employee has been terminated and there is an outstanding settlement to be resolved. If a positive reference is supplied and the individual secures employment, then the settlement will be resolved probably at a lesser amount, and to the satisfaction of the terminating employer. It could backfire though if the individual does not get the job, and a positive reference justifies that the employer wrongfully terminated the employee.

However, employers are increasingly concerned that they could be found liable for *failing* to tell a prospective employer that the person about whom it is inquiring was fired for violent behaviour, theft, criminal behaviour, sexual harassment, etc.[42] The Treaty Group retained Drake International to recruit the best possible candidate for their bookkeeping position including all pre-screening functions such as evaluation and reference checking. Drake referred Beverly Simpson to Treaty and she was hired for the position. However, during the course of her employment with Treaty, Simpson proceeded to defraud the company of $263,000. In a subsequent investigation, it was found that Simpson had two criminal convictions for defrauding other employers, important information which Drake International failed or neglected to uncover during the course of its pre-employment screening. Treaty sued and obtained a judgment against Simpson but was unable to collect. They then sued Drake International which was ordered to compensate Treaty for half the amount. Treaty was also found partially liable because they had failed to adequately supervise and initiate internal controls to minimize their exposure to fraud. The courts felt that the company downloaded the responsibility to check references to a third party.[43]

Clearly, employers are in a difficult position. Because of threats of lawsuits, they must obtain information on potential employees but are unwilling to give out information in return. If a former employer supplies a reference that misrepresents important aspects of the employee's performance for issues such as theft or violence, it may be vulnerable to a claim for negligently misrepresenting the reference if in fact the employee goes on to commit a crime with the new employer. Employers can rely on a defence of "qualified privilege" if they told the truth and there was no malice intent if statements they provide are deemed to be untrue.[44] Still, if former employers will not cooperate, it is difficult. Changing the way that questions are asked may improve the chance for a response.[45] It is also recommended that the task for providing references be centralized in HR to ensure consistency.

Legal Constraints on Background Investigations

An employer's most important action when conducting a background investigation is to obtain from the applicant a signed release giving the employer permission to conduct the investigation. This applies equally when an employee leaves an organization. The recommendation is that during an exit interview, an employer obtains a signed release authorizing the employer to provide reference information on the former employee in the future.

Risks of Negligent Hiring and Negligent Retention The costs of failing to check references may be high. Some organizations have become targets of lawsuits that charge them with negligence in hiring workers who have committed violent acts on the job. Lawyers say that an employer's liability hinges on how well it investigates an applicant's background. Prior convictions and frequent moves or gaps in employment should be cues for further inquiry. Details provided on the application form by the applicant should be investigated to the greatest extent possible, so the employer can show that due diligence was exercised. Also, employers should document their efforts to check background information by noting who was contacted, when, and what information was or was not provided. This documentation can aid in countering negligent hiring claims.

Negligent hiring
Occurs when an employer fails to check an employee's background and the employee injures someone.

Negligent retention
Occurs when an employer becomes aware that an employee may be unfit for employment, continues to employ the person, and the person injures someone.

Negligent hiring occurs when an employer fails to check an employee's background and the employee injures someone. There is a potential negligent hiring problem when: the employer hired an unfit employee who injures others, the employer did an inadequate background check, or the employer failed to find facts that would have led to rejection because of potential risk.[46] A related situation, **negligent retention,** occurs when an employer becomes aware that an employee may be unfit for employment, but continues to employ the person, and the person injures someone.

Money is one reason why employers are concerned about obtaining proper reference checks, but it is not the only reason to check the background of employees. In services such as child care for example, employers have to be concerned with safety issues. The Quebec government conducted background checks on the province's 35 000 daycare workers after an investigation into 7030 daycare owners found that 20 had criminal records.[47]

Credit Checks Many employers check applicants' credit histories. The logic is that poor credit histories may signal irresponsibility, an assumption which may or may not be correct. Firms that check applicants' credit records must ensure that the request is job-related. To ensure that you comply with provincial or federal privacy legislation, written consent must be obtained from the person being checked, and furnishing the applicant with a copy of the report. Credit history should be checked on applicants for jobs in which use of, access to, or management of money is an essential job function. Commonly, financial institutions check credit histories on loan officers or tellers, and retailers conduct credit checks on cashiers and managerial staff.

Medical Examinations and Inquiries

Medical information on applicants may be used to determine their physical and mental capabilities for performing jobs. Physical standards for jobs should be realistic, justifiable, and geared to the job requirements. Workers with disabilities can perform satisfactorily in many jobs. However, in many places, they are rejected because of their disabilities, rather than being screened and placed in appropriate jobs.

Organizations cannot reject an individual because of a disability, nor can they ask job applicants any question related to their disability. Employers can ask if the applicant is able to perform the functions of the job, or if they need accommodation. Once a conditional offer of employment is made, the employer pays for a physical examination of the applicant. It should be made clear that the applicant who has been offered the job is not "hired" until successful completion of the physical inquiry. Once the physical examination has been completed, then the doctor will let the employer know if the individual is cleared for work, and if any accommodation is required. Employers are obligated under human rights legislation to make accommodation where it is reasonable, and will not put undue hardship on the employer.

Drug Testing The question of drug testing relates to the pre-employment testing of employees and during their employment. The use of drug testing as part of the selection process has increased in the past few years, however it is still a very controversial topic. Federal and provincial human rights legislation prohibit discrimination on the basis of a disability. Current or former dependence on drugs or alcohol is considered a disability under the federal act, and will likely be interpreted in the same manner at the provincial level. Issues around reasonable accommodation and establishing a *bona fide occupational requirement* (BFOR) for treating someone differently need to be addressed. Prevention initiatives including access to assessment, employee assistance programs (EAPs), treatment, and follow-up services, as well as modifying hours or duties in certain circumstances would all contribute to accommodation responsibilities.

Currently there are no provincial or federal laws that would specifically prohibit drug testing, and there have been no Supreme Court decisions in this area. However, a number of recent decisions provide some guidance on where the law may stand on this issue. Although each case has its own unique aspects, it appears the trend has been to find testing acceptable as part of an investigation in an unfit for duty (reasonable cause) or post accident/incident situation, as part of a monitoring program after treatment, as a condition of return to duty after a policy violation, and on an ongoing follow-up basis. Testing has also been upheld as a condition of certification to a higher safety-risk position, and on a random basis for alcohol only. And in all circumstances, it must be part of a comprehensive policy that includes accommodation measures for those who have an alcohol or drug dependency. Although testing on a pre-employment and random basis was recently upheld for safety-sensitive positions in the *Autocar Connaisseur* case before the federal human rights tribunal, a number of employers are facing union challenges against random testing in their own programs.[48]

Salvatore Milazzo had been a bus driver with Autocar Connaisseur Inc., a subsidiary of Coach Canada Inc., for several years. In August 1999, his employer ordered him to undergo a pre-employment drug test. Milazzo was not originally considered for testing, since he had not been required to drive to the U.S. when he was hired. Given the fact that his test results came back positive, Milazzo was terminated in accordance with Autocar's "zero tolerance" drug policy. Mr. Milazzo then filed a discrimination complaint with the Canadian Human Rights Commission, on the grounds of a perceived disability, namely drug dependency. The issue was therefore to determine whether pre-employment and random drug testing could be considered to be consistent with the Canadian Human Rights Act. In light of the *Entrop* case, which was decided by the Ontario Court of Appeal, Justice Laskin confirmed that such testing was discriminatory within the meaning of Ontario human rights legislation. Furthermore, the Canadian Human Rights Commission based its decision for this case on the new policy concerning the use of drug testing, adopted in 2002 as a result of the Entrop case. Therefore, Autocar Connaisseur's drug testing policy was found to be reasonably necessary to accomplish the company's legitimate work-related goal of promoting road safety. However, the tribunal upheld Milazzo's complaint and ordered Autocar Connaisseur "to immediately cease the discriminatory practice of failing to accommodate employees or prospective employees who test positive in company sponsored drug tests, in cases where the individual can establish that he suffers from a substance-related disability.[49]

A recent decision involving Weyerhaeuser in B.C. helps to regain the proper focus on the question of drug and alcohol testing. The focus should not be on the narrow question of whether there is a known substance abuse problem but on the broader question of principle: *whether the particular testing the employer seeks to carry out is reasonable in the particular circumstances of its workplace.* The analysis in the *Weyerhaeuser* case should help to support testing policies in inherently safety sensitive workplaces. It accepts the inherent safety risk—not actual harm or a near-miss—as the justification for testing that could take place before a person takes a safety sensitive position. This is a small step toward one form of random testing. However, Canadian law remains a long way short of approving truly random testing. Canadian arbitrators and courts remain concerned about invasion of personal privacy rights and of the limited ability of substance testing to establish current impairment or to predict the likelihood of future impairment.[50]

If drug testing is to be used during the interview process, because it is deemed to be job-related, then it cannot be administered until a conditional offer of employment has been made. Included in the conditional offer of employment is that random drug tests will take place during the course of employment. A number of organizations that administer such testing are Imperial Oil, Motor Coach Canada, and Weyerhaeuser Co.

Even though drug testing is controversial, pre-employment and random drug testing has become widespread in oil and gas industries, with employers putting the onus on employees and unions to challenge the policies. Random drug testing is being conducted, but to what extent remains to be seen. Pre-employment testing is far more common among employers such as Suncor and Petro-Canada. What seems to be clear is that if someone is caught abusing drugs, they have to be accommodated. For employees who test positive for drug abuse, once treated, they then can be randomly tested to ensure that they are complying with their treatment. The problem is that the extent of abuse cannot be determined by random testing. Currently there are mixed reasons for wanting pre-employment and random drug testing. Some groups are concerned about safety, others about absenteeism and tardiness, and yet others genuinely want to help those who have a problem. While the rules are clear that testing can only be done for safety-related reasons, others have opposing views.[51]

Genetic Testing Another controversial area of medical testing is genetic testing. The use of genetic testing for employment in Canada is strictly prohibited. Due to the high costs of health care, some employers may want to know what medical risks they are taking on when they hire an employee. What is most controversial is that the tests may be used to exclude individuals from certain jobs if they have genetic conditions that increase their health risks. Because people cannot change their genetic makeup, the potential for discrimination based on a particular genetic characteristic, such as the probability of getting breast cancer, is real.

Making the Final Decision

Now that the final applicants have completed their application forms, gone through a series of tests, and had their final interviews, it is time for the manager or supervisor to make the final selection decision. HR will assist in the final decision, but it is the manager or supervisor who has the final say in the choice. Decisions can be made in two ways: subjective or objective, or a combination of the two. When a decision is made using a subjective approach, the decision-maker is basing the selection of the candidate on a "gut feel" or on their intuition. There are interviewers who feel they can size up an individual in a matter of minutes. This approach may be used when there are few resources, little HR expertise, and the decision-maker wants a quick resolve. This is a very imprecise way of making such an important decision, and one that would be hard to justify if any complaints of discrimination were made against the organization. The more appropriate method would be to use a more objective, statistical approach. By quantifying the selection procedure, and using reliable and valid tests, the final decision should be more accurate, and easier to defend. The decision on what measures to include in the final analysis will depend on how comprehensive the selection program is in an organization.

If an employer chooses to use only one predictor (for example, a test) to select who will be hired, the decision is straightforward. If the test is valid and encompasses a major dimension of a job, and the applicant does well on the test, he or she can be hired. When an employer uses several predictors (for example, three years of experience, a university degree, and a certain score on an aptitude test), qualified candidates are those who possess sufficient amounts of each of those predictors. When more than one predictor is used, they must be combined in some way. Two approaches for combining predictors are:

- *Multiple hurdles:* A minimum cutoff is set on each predictor, and each minimum level must be "passed." For example, to be hired, a candidate for a sales representative job must achieve a minimum education level, a certain score on a sales aptitude test, and a minimum score on a structured interview.

- *Compensatory approach:* Scores from individual predictors are added together and combined into an overall score, thus allowing a higher score on one predictor to offset, or compensate for, a lower score on another. The combined index takes into consideration performance on all predictors. For example, when admitting students into graduate business programs, a higher score on the math portion of an admissions test may offset a lower score on the verbal part of the test.

The approaches that can be used in the final decision can be very basic, or much more comprehensive in nature. Whatever approach is used, it must be reliable and valid, to ensure that the most qualified candidate has been selected for the position. Once that decision has been made, a final offer can then be extended.

Making the Job Offer

The final step of the selection process is offering someone employment. HR usually handles this task. Job offers are often extended over the phone, and many are then formalized in letters and sent to applicants. It is important that the offer document be reviewed by legal counsel and that the terms and conditions of employment be clearly identified. Care should be taken to avoid vague, general statements and promises about bonuses, work schedules, or other matters that might change later. These documents also should provide for the individuals to sign an acceptance of the offer and return it to the employer, who should place it in the individual's personnel files.

Staffing Global Assignments

6 With the globalization of business, organizations are now sending employees all over the world to work on short or extended periods. Staffing global assignments involves selecting, placing, and locating employees in other countries. The need for individuals who can provide leadership in global organizations emphasizes the importance of global staffing.[52]

When staffing global assignments, cost is a major consideration. The cost of establishing a manager or professional in another country can run as high as $1 million for a three-year job assignment. The cost of placing a key manager outside of North America is often twice the manager's annual salary. If the manager is going to Japan, the cost may be even higher when housing expenses, schooling subsidies, and tax equalization payment are calculated. Further, if a manager, professional, or executive quits an international assignment prematurely or insists on a transfer home, associated costs can equal or exceed the annual salary. "Failure" rates for managers sent to other countries may run as high as 40–50 percent in some firms or countries.[53]

Types of Global Employees

Global organizations can be staffed in a number of different ways, including expatriates, host-country nationals, and third-country nationals. Each staffing option presents some unique HR management challenges. For instance, when staffing with citizens of different countries, different tax laws and other factors apply. HR professionals need to be knowledgeable about the laws and customs of each country represented in their workforce.

Expatriate
Citizen of one country who is working in a second country and employed by an organization headquartered in the first country.

Host-country national
Citizen of one country who is working in that country and employed by an organization headquartered in a second country.

Third-country national
Citizen of one country who is working in a second country and employed by an organization headquartered in a third country.

An **expatriate** is a citizen of one country who is working in a second country and employed by an organization headquartered in the first country. Experienced expatriates can provide a pool of talent that can be tapped as the organization expands its operations more broadly into even more countries.[54]

A **host-country national** is a citizen of one country who is working in that country and employed by an organization headquartered in a second country. Host-country nationals often know the culture, politics, laws, and business customs better than an outsider would.

A **third-country national** is a citizen of one country who is working in a second country and employed by an organization headquartered in a third country. For example, a Canadian citizen working for a British oil company as a manager in Norway is a third-country national. Staffing with third-country nationals shows a truly global approach.

Selection Process for Global Assignments

The selection process for an international assignment should provide a realistic picture of the life, work, and culture to which the employee may be sent. HR managers start by preparing a comprehensive description of the job to be done. This description notes responsibilities that would be unusual in the home nation, including negotiating with public officials; interpreting local work codes; and responding to ethical, moral, and personal issues such as religious prohibitions and personal freedoms.[55] Certain countries, such as Canada, the U.S., and Australia, also require work visas before the foreign employee enters the new country. This documentation should be arranged well in advance of the individual's arrival or they will be denied access. Figure 6-11

Figure 6-11 *Selection Factors for Global Employees*

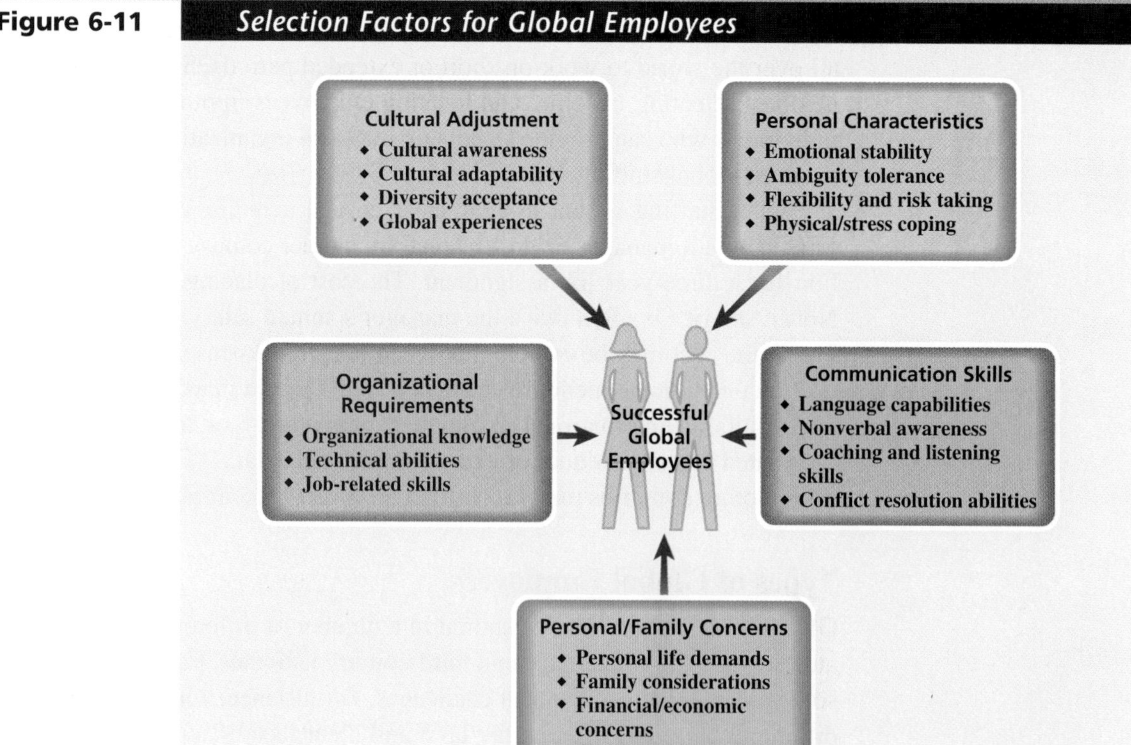

shows the most frequently cited key competencies for successful global employees. The five areas are as follows:

- **Cultural Adjustment** Crucial to global success for individuals is how they adjust to the cultural differences in their foreign assignments.[56] Awareness of cultural issues and differences, and acceptance of diverse cultural demands and customs are important areas to examine.
- **Organizational Requirements** Many global employers find that knowledge of the organization and how it operates is important.
- **Personal Characteristics** The experiences of many global firms demonstrate that the best employees in the home country may not be the best employees in a global assignment, primarily because of personal characteristics of individuals.
- **Communication Skills** One of the most basic skills needed by expatriate employees is the ability to communicate orally and in writing in the host-country language. Inability to communicate adequately in the language may significantly inhibit the success of an expatriate.
- **Personal/Family Concerns** The preferences and attitudes of spouses and other family members are major staffing concerns. Two of the most common reasons for turning down international assignments are family considerations and spouses' careers.

SUMMARY

1 Selection is the process that matches individuals and their qualifications to jobs in an organization. Placement of people should consider both person/job fit and person/organization fit. Predictors linked to criteria are used to identify the applicants who are most likely to perform jobs successfully. Job-related validation requires that tests measure what they are supposed to measure (validity) in a consistent manner (reliability). One type of validity is content validity, which uses a sample of the actual work to be performed. The two criterion-related validity strategies measure concurrent validity and predictive validity.

2 The selection process—from applicant interest through pre-employment screening, application, testing, interviewing, and background investigation—must be handled by trained, knowledgeable individuals. A growing number of employers use electronic pre-employment screening. Application forms must meet human rights guidelines and must ask only for job-related information.

3 Selection tests include ability tests, assessment centres, personality tests, honesty/integrity tests, and other more controversial types of tests. Polygraph tests continue to be controversial. Some jurisdictions allow these tests to be used in employment. Other controversial tests include drug and alcohol testing, which can only be used when there is a high-safety risk. The Supreme Court of Canada has set new legal standards for the use of tests in personnel selection.

4 Structured interviews, including behavioural and situational ones, are more effective and face fewer human rights complaints than do unstructured interviews and non-directive interviews. With more organizations focusing on competencies, there has been an increase in the use of competency interviews. Interviews can be conducted individually, by multiple individuals, or by video technology. Regardless of the method, effective interviewing questioning techniques should be used. Problems commonly found in interviews are snap judgments, negative emphasis, halo effect, biases and stereotyping, and influence tactics.

5 Background investigation can be conducted in a variety of areas. When either requesting or giving reference information, employers must take care to avoid potential legal concerns such as negligent hiring, libel, and slander. To comply with privacy acts and human rights acts, employees must sign a release form. Background information should be sought with respect to previous employment, credit, criminal, and medical checks if job-related.

6 Global organizations can be staffed by individuals who are expatriates, host-country nationals, or third-country nationals. Selection factors for global employees include cultural adjustment, personal characteristics, communication skills, personal/family concerns, and organizational requirements.

KEY TERMS

Behavioural interview, p. 224
Cognitive ability tests, p. 219
Concurrent validity, p. 211
Content validity, p. 209
Correlation coefficient, p. 210
Criterion-related validity, p. 210
Employment "test," p. 208
Expatriate, p. 240
Host-country national, p. 240
Inter-rater reliability, p. 223
Negligent hiring, p. 235
Negligent retention, p. 235
Non-directive interview, p. 226
Panel interview, p. 227
Person/job fit, p. 207
Person-organization fit, p. 207
Physical ability tests, p. 219
Placement, p. 206
Predictive validity, p. 212
Predictors, p. 207
Psychomotor tests, p. 219
Realistic job preview (RJP), p. 213
Reliability, p. 209
Selection, p. 206
Selection criterion, p. 207
Situational interview, p. 226
Situational judgment tests, p. 219
Stress interview, p. 227
Structured interview, p. 224
Team interview, p. 227
Third-country national, p. 240
Validity, p. 209
Work sample tests, p. 219

REVIEW AND APPLICATION QUESTIONS

1 Using the concepts of reliability and validity, describe what they mean and provide examples to demonstrate how they are useful in selection.

2 Describe the purposes that the application form serves.

3 Describe the various tests that can be utilized in selection, and provide examples of what those tests would be measuring.

4 Explain the different types of interviews that can be conducted, and provide examples for each of the types of questions that might be asked.

5 How would you do a complete background investigation on applicants to minimize concerns about negligent hiring?

6 Describe how global organizations can be staffed, and what unique challenges you may be faced with by these choices.

EXPERIENTIAL EXERCISES

1. Search the Internet for an example of three application forms for a Canadian organization and download the form. Alternatively pick up an application form from a local retailer, fast-food restaurant, or other type of business. Review the application form against the list provided in this chapter on what is considered illegal. Identify potential problems with the application form that you have downloaded.
2. Design three questions for an interview to be conducted for an assistant manager at a large retail store. The duties may include hiring staff,

conducting performance appraisals, handling discipline matters, handling cash, theft of merchandise from both staff and customers, and dealing with irate customers. You should design three questions for each of the following interviews, as well as design scoring guides to go with each of the questions:
   a. behavioural
   b. situational
   c. competency interviews (refer to this chapter for a list of competencies)
3. Search the Internet for relevant case law in Canada or search in your school library or other relevant source to locate a case related to the following topics:
   a. employee given a bad reference from a previous employer
   b. discrimination in hiring based on one of the prohibited grounds such as sex, age, etc.
   c. employee sues organization for discrimination in testing used in selection process.

   You are expected to summarize each of the awards in about a half page, indicating the relevance to selection, and how the decision of each of these awards has impacted on how we conduct the selection and retention of employees. Since the *Meiorin* decision has already been summarized in this chapter, you cannot use this particular case or any other case discussed in the chapter. Find new examples.
4. You are in the process of prescreening applicants for the position of sales assistant for your purchasing department. You learn through the grapevine that the individual had been charged with careless driving, which resulted in the death of an elderly gentleman, several years ago. This is upsetting for you because your best friend was killed the same way only months ago. The candidate appears to be well-suited to the job, but with this criminal past you just don't want to take a chance on hiring someone of this character. What should you do in this type of situation?

LEARNING REVIEW

To check your knowledge of the chapter, review the following. (Answers after the case.)

1 More than anything else, placement of human resources should be seen as:
   a. a public relations activity
   b. an operating management responsibility
   c. a matching process
   d. an HR unit responsibility

2 Properly prepared, the application form serves several purposes except?
   a. Record of the applicant's desire to obtain a postion.
   b. It is a basic employee record for applicants who are hired.
   c. It can be used for research on the effectiveness of the selection process.
   d. It can provide information on disabilities.

3 Instruments that assess an individual's ability to perform in a specific manner are __________ tests.
   a. aptitude
   b. knowledge
   c. ability
   d. behavioural

4 The interview is popular with employers because it has high:
   a. content validity
   b. face validity
   c. predictive validity
   d. contrast validity

5 Background screening has four goals except:
   a. to show that the employer exercised due diligence in hiring
   b. to discourage applicants with something to hide
   c. to encourage applicants to be honest on applications and during interviews
   d. to determine information related to illegal activities that may or may not pertain directly to the job

6 An expatriate is:
   a. A citizen of one country who is working in a second country and employed by an organization headquartered in a third country.
   b. A citizen of one country who is working in that country and employed by an organization headquartered in the second country.
   c. A citizen of one country who is working in a second country and employed by an organization.
   d. A citizen of one country working in that same country.

CASE

CANADIAN AIR FORCE

In 2005 a man who applied to be a Canadian Forces' pilot filed a complaint with the Canadian Human Rights Commission after he failed to meet the Air Force's anthropometric, or physical standards for pilots. He was considered too short by the standards that he believed were discriminatory because these standards were based on a survey of male pilots in the 1960s. Lt-Col. Donald Albert who is the director of personnel development for the Air Force acknowledged that the Air Force was, "rejecting a number of applicants that otherwise could have been good applicants."

The Canadian Forces' pilots were all male until the 1970s, which is when more women began to apply for positions. The standards that were developed from the 1960s surveys led to the rejection of 50 to 60 percent of female candidates. Although the Canadian Forces recognized this problem, it was not until the mid 1990s that a selection model that would attempt to alleviate this problem would begin to be developed. Pierre Meunier who is a defence scientist with Defence and Research in Development Canada in Toronto developed a computer program that takes into account the digital photographs of Forces' personnel to determine uniform size. He wondered whether this program could be used in the pilot selection process.

For four years, Meunier measured cockpits to determine the body dimensions needed to safely operate the Forces' 14 different aircrafts. From these measurements, Meunier developed a computer model that would accurately predict who would be able to fit into a particular cockpit. The model takes into account three occupational requirements which are vision (being able to see over the nose of the plane and being able to see all the instruments), reach (being able to reach all the instruments in the cockpit), and clearance (being able to fit in the cockpit and eject from the aircraft without hitting anything on the way out). The model is based on 14 physical measurements as opposed to the four that was used in the previous standards. Meunier found that the cockpits are more accommodating than originally thought and that, "The majority of candidates will have no problem qualifying. It's the people at the fringes, the very tall or the very short, who might still have problems." The Canadian Forces implemented the model in November 2005.

Until March 2006, the measurements had to be taken manually but the computer system has since been modified to take photos of a candidate in standing and seating positions. The computer is then able to generate the candidate's measurements, which are compared to Meunier's model in order to determine the aircrafts that the candidate will be physically suited to fly. The Air Force must still determine how many planes a candidate must be physically suited to, in order to pass the anthropometric standards of the selection process.[57]

Questions

1. The Canadian Forces have used the same anthropometric standards since the 1960s up until late 2005. Discuss the validity of these old standards in comparison to the new standards.
2. What should be taken into account by the Air Force when it makes a decision on how many planes a candidate should be able to fly in order to pass the anthropometric portion of the selection process.

Learning Review Answers: 1. c 2. d 3. c 4. b 5. d. 6. c

DEAD RECKONING

This segment from *The National* attempts to shed light on the allegations made against the Saskatoon police force. Saskatoon police were accused of giving "Starlight Tours" to several Aboriginals that involved driving the victims to the outskirts of the city and leaving them there to walk back to the city on their own. Several of the alleged cases took place in the frigid Saskatoon winter and involved fatalities.

The videoclip gives details about the cover-up involved in documented cases and the harassment of a witness and his family. When two police officers were convicted for their actions, the Saskatoon Police dismissed it as an isolated incident involving rogue police officers.

Both Saskatoon mayor and former police officer Jim Madden and the Chief of Police Russell Sabo spoke to the *The National* and acknowledged that there was wrongdoing and that an investigation should be conducted in order to help the Saskatoon Police Department move forward and correct its past mistakes.[1]

Questions

1. Do you believe it is possible for the Aboriginal community in Saskatoon to get over its mistrust of the police department? What actions should be taken by the Saskatoon Police to make their wrongdoings right?
2. What do you think about Mayor Jim Madden's decision to come forward and reveal his knowledge of an internal coverup within the police department?
3. What do you feel will be the reaction of Aboriginal police officers? Those wanting to be police officers? How can these issues be overcome?

HIRING WARS

This segment from *Venture* illustrates the intense competition between high tech companies to recruit qualified employees. The shortage of trained employees in the high tech sector has led to aggressive recruitment methods by both Canadian high tech firms such as Newbridge Networks and their American counterparts, most notably Cisco. These firms are not only focusing their efforts on new graduates but also on their competitors' employees.

The recruitment methods used by the firms have been developed to lure qualified candidates. The power of high tech employees over employers is so high that they can command a 10-percent increase in salary from a competitive firm who may also promise such benefits as stock options. The video clip highlights some of the creative ideas that high tech companies such as Cisco have used to recruit their competitors' employees. An aggressive company like Cisco does not mind if its recruitment methods are being copied because it is always looking to develop methods that can be used in the future.

The segment raises the important issue of American companies coming into Canada to recruit employees who are needed at home. A question that arises is whether Canadian companies can compete with a "pitch" that promises potential employees more money and more sun.[2]

Questions

1. What advantages in recruitment do Canadian high tech firms have over their American counterparts?
2. Discuss the pros and cons of employee referrals.
3. Would you rather work for Cisco or Newbridge Networks and why?

"TRUTH & CONSEQUENCES" OR "HONESTY TESTS"?

This segment from *The National* documents the dismissal of Trina Benedict from her job at a Sobey's grocery store. After Ms. Benedict took a leave of absence from her bakery position, she was required to take an honesty test before she reassumed her position. Ms. Benedict believed that answering the test truthfully would lead to successful results. However, the test predicted that Ms. Benedict would have the tendency to steal in the future based on her honest responses. All of this despite the fact that she had had a good record prior to her departure.

Many retail stores believe that honesty tests are justified due to the high rate of employee theft. Half of all shoplifting comes from store employees. Two questions that arise concern the validity of the tests as well as their administration. For example, will the question, "Do you blush?" predict whether a person has a tendency to steal or not? Also there is no legislation that makes sure that employers are using the test in a fair and systematic manner. There is no guarantee that a firm will not take other parts of the application process into account when screening out applicants who fail an honesty test.[3]

Questions

1. Discuss the validity of honesty tests.
2. Do you feel that Ms. Benedict was discriminated against? Why or why not?
3. Do you believe that the administration of such tests should be regulated?

PART 3

Training and Developing Human Resources

CHAPTER

Training Human Resources

Learning Objectives

After you have read this chapter, you should be able to:

1 Define orientation and discuss why employee orientation programs are vital to the acclimatization of new employees to the organization.

2 Define training and discuss why a strategic approach is important, and introduce the four phases of the training process.

3 Identify three types of analyses used to determine training needs.

4 Discuss training design, learner readiness, and ability to learn.

5 Explain internal, external, and e-learning as training delivery approaches.

6 Give an example for each of the four levels of training evaluation.

7 Describe the importance of intercultural competence training for global employers.

HR *Headline*

Does Training Get the Respect It Deserves?

Company trainers often complain that training does not get the respect it deserves as a major means for accomplishing goals set by management. One indication of this concern is that drastic cuts in training budgets often are seen when the economy slows or a company's profitability declines. Those cuts call into question how essential training is when times get tough. Trainers argue that deferring training in organizations is like deferring maintenance on an automobile—it can come back to haunt the person who puts it off. An HR professor at Northwestern University suggests, "What happens is you start mortgaging your future. Employees cannot be as productive if they are not adequately trained."

Isabel Roberts, director of business development for Brie Engineering Systems Ltd. in Oshawa, Ontario, an automation engineering firm with 40 employees, says training on Eric's robots, built into the product's cost, begins in the classroom. "We do all our own training, beginning with an overview of the equipment so people understand how all the different parts work together." The company reevaluated its training efforts and put training dollars to work more effectively on the specific problems of individual employees. Also, it used internal trainers instead of outside training consultants.

Few companies measure the long-term effectiveness of training. Also, few firms develop maps for individual employee training and follow up after the training. Another problem is that employers seldom put constraints on the kind of training that is allowed. For instance, if someone wants to get a law degree through the company tuition reimbursement plan, even though the company does not need another lawyer, that degree is frequently paid for anyway.

In summary, training must be both desired by the employee and beneficial for the organization. It is crucial that employers follow up to see that what was learned as part of the training produces value for the company. As training becomes more efficient and effective, it likely will not be cut as much during tight budget times.[1]

"Knowledge management is the art of creating value by using the organization's intellectual capital."

—John Lewison

The competitive pressures facing organizations today require employees whose knowledge and ideas are current, and whose skills and abilities can deliver results. As organizations compete and change, training becomes even more critical than before. Employees who must adapt to the many changes facing organizations must be trained continually in order to maintain and update their KSAs. Also, managers must have training and development to enhance their leadership skills and abilities. In a number of situations, employers have documented that effective training produces productivity gains that more than offset the cost of the training.

Nature of Training

1 As each of us who have started a new job knows, the first day can be fraught with anxiety and worry. We are entering a world of uncertainty—we don't know where things are, we are in unfamiliar surroundings, we are meeting endless new people, we are learning aspects of a job for which we may not be entirely familiar, and we want to make good first impressions. Employers can help ease this process by introducing **orientation** training, which is the planned introduction of new employees to their jobs, co-workers, and the organization. Orientation training is offered by most employers in some form or another.

Orientation
Planned introduction of new employees to their jobs, co-workers, and the organization.

Orientation requires cooperation between individuals in the HR unit and operating managers and supervisors. In a small organization without an HR department, the new employee's supervisor or manager usually assumes most of the responsibility for orientation.[2] In large organizations, managers and supervisors, as well as the HR department, generally work as a team to orient new employees.

Orientation exposes employees to the culture that is fostered throughout the organization by becoming aware of policies, procedures, practices, and organizational lingo. It also provides new employees the opportunity to make a smoother transition to the organization likely making employees feel more comfortable and welcome to the organization. Orientation is part of a long-term investment in an employee. Orientation usually is associated with a new employee starting with an organization, but it could also be applied to an employee transfer from a subsidiary or other part of an organization. Orientation training should be applied to help the organization reach strategic goals of the organization.

Advantages of Orientation

There are many advantages to be gained by incorporating orientation training to the organization. They include the following:[3]

- Reduces anxiety
- Leads to better performance on the job
- Leads to higher rates of retention
- Shortens time to be a more productive employee
- Lowers grievances likely as a result of the clear expectations that are outlined

Effective Orientation

Effective orientation efforts contribute to both short-term and long-term success for employees. The HR Practice contains some suggestions on how to make employee orientation more effective. In addition to the advantages discussed above, effective orientation also achieves several key purposes:

- Establishes a favourable employee impression of the organization and the job
- Provides organization and job information
- Enhances interpersonal acceptance by co-workers
- Accelerates socialization and integration of the new employee into the organization
- Ensures that employee performance and productivity begin more quickly

Socialization Some research studies and employer surveys report that the socialization of new employees and their initial commitment to the organization are positively affected by orientation.[4] This socialization enhances the "person/organization fit," which reinforces the employee's positive view of the job, co-workers, and the organization. Additionally, employers have found that higher employee retention rates result when new employees receive effective orientation. For example, one individual reported that her first day on the job was a disaster! The employee had been told that she would be the HR supervisor, but would have some additional clerical duties from the purchasing department. She was not even on the job more than an hour when she was told that purchase orders were backed up and she had to catch up on three weeks of typing. Instead of having a pleasant first day on the job, she started looking for a new job immediately, and subsequently left at the first opportunity that presented itself.

Orientation also contributes to overall organizational performance by helping employees to more quickly feel that they are a part of the organization and can begin contributing to organizational work efforts. For example, the Global Boot Camp is ThoughtWorks' way of introducing recent grads or new hires with little experience to the company. It's a crash course in corporate culture, programming, and getting along with others. After three weeks of classroom training, which includes lessons in object-oriented programming, consulting basics, and other technologies, recruits are put to work for 13 weeks of project experience. The secret sauce is how the culture of the company makes it all work without ruffling feathers.[5] Not all orientation programs last three weeks. Some may be as short as a half-day, or even just one or two days. The Public Service Commission offers two-day orientation training in Ottawa so that employees can learn about the context in which they perform their work in the nation's capital.[6] Other programs may be longer in scope as well lasting for up to six months. And unfortunately, some are seemingly non-existent, except for signing payroll forms for the first hour or so on the job.

Electronic Delivery One way of expanding the efficiency of orientation is to use electronic resources. A number of employers place general employee orientation information on company intranets or corporate websites. New employees log on and go through much of the general material on organizational history, structure, products and services, mission, and other background, instead of sitting in a classroom where the information is delivered in person or by videotape.[7] Specific questions and concerns can be addressed by HR staff and others after employees review the Web-based information. Unfortunately, many new employee orientation sessions come across as boring, irrelevant, and a waste of time to both new employees and their department supervisors and managers.[8]

The Canadian government provides an example of what an orientation should entail. Figure 7-1 demonstrates what they do. Typically a checklist is developed that lists who will be responsible for what aspect of the orientation, with agendas and timetables. This helps to ensure the employee knows what to expect at all steps of the orientation process.

HR *Practice*

Effective New Employee Orientation

Effective new employee orientation requires planning and preparation. Unfortunately, orientation is often conducted rather haphazardly. To make orientation more effective, the following suggestions may be useful:

- *Prepare for new employees:* New employees must feel that they belong and are important to the organization. Both the supervisor and the HR unit should be prepared to give each new employee this perception. Further, co-workers should be prepared for a new employee's arrival. The manager or supervisor should discuss the purpose of hiring the new worker with all current employees before the arrival of the new worker.
- *Consider using mentors:* Some organizations assign co-workers or peers to serve as buddies or mentors as part of the new employees' orientation. It is particularly useful to involve more experienced and higher-performing individuals who can serve as role models for new employees.
- *Use an orientation checklist:* An orientation checklist can be used by HR department representatives, the new employee's supervisor, or both, to cover what the new employee needs to know now. Many employers have new employees sign the checklist to verify that they have been told of pertinent rules and procedures.
- *Cover needed information:* It is important to give employees information on the policies, work rules, and benefits of the company. Policies about sick leave, tardiness, absenteeism, vacations, benefits, codes of conduct, dress code, parking, and safety rules must be made known to every new employee. Also, the employee's supervisor or manager should describe the routine of a normal workday for the employee the first morning.
- *Present orientation information effectively:* Managers and HR representatives should determine the most appropriate ways to present orientation information. Employees will retain more of the orientation information if it is presented in a manner that encourages them to learn. In addition to videotapes, movies, slides, and charts, self-paced electronic orientation can be used.
- *Avoid information overload:* One common failing of many orientation programs is information overload. New workers presented with too many facts may ignore important details or inaccurately recall much of the information.
- *Evaluate and follow up:* An HR representative or manager can evaluate the effectiveness of the orientation by conducting follow-up interviews with new employees a few weeks or months after the orientation. Employee questionnaires also can be used for follow-up. Unfortunately, it appears that most employers do limited or no evaluation of the effectiveness of orientation.

1. Why do you think organizations do such a poor job on orientation programs?
2. Working in small groups, discuss your experiences with orientation and determine what qualities the better orientation programs displayed, and what qualities the poorer orientation programs demonstrated.

Upon completion of the orientation program, employees should begin their jobs. Training on the job will likely continue for some time. Throughout an employee's work tenure, there will be other times in which training will be required. The following section discusses this next phase.

Training

Training
Process whereby people acquire the necessary knowledge, skills, and abilities (KSAs) to perform jobs.

2 **Training** is the process whereby people acquire the necessary knowledge, skills, and abilities (KSAs) to perform jobs. Poorly trained employees may perform poorly and make costly mistakes. Training provides employees with specific, identifiable knowledge and skills for use in their present jobs. Sometimes a distinction is drawn between *training* and *development,* with development being broader in scope and focusing on individuals' gaining new KSAs useful for both present and future jobs. Development is discussed in Chapter 8; training is the focus of this chapter.

Figure 7-1 ***Government of Canada Orientation Program***

Orientation

Employee orientation is part of a long-term investment in a new employee. It is an initial process that provides easy access to basic information, programs and services, gives clarification and allows new employees to take an active role in their organization.

- **Introduce new employees to their new environment**
- **Make new employees feel welcome and comfortable**
- **Retain a pool of new, capable employees**

Benefits:

- **Establish clear standards that help reduce disputes and limit liability**
- **Promote consistent management**
- **Inform new employees of the company's policies**
- **Demonstrate a commitment to equal treatment of personnel**
- **Provide protection from claims of discrimination and sexual harassment**

In some organizations an employee handbook is available to all employees. The content of the handbook covers the key topics covered in an orientation session for new employees.

What should employee orientation programs include?

An orientation program helps the employee understand their assigned duties, terms and conditions of employment as well as the organizational culture. It provides the following information:

welcome employee to company

orientation to business:

- **history**
- **mission statement**
- **goals and objectives**
- **organizational structure, e.g., own job description and relationship of position to other positions**
- **future plans**

company policies and procedures, for example:

- **dress code**
- **reporting procedures**
- **smoking restrictions**
- **expense claims**

legislation

safety procedures

emergency procedures

technical information:

- **operating telephone system**
- **who to call for repairs**

(continued)

Figure 7-1 *continued*

explanation of benefit package:

- **group insurance**
- **sick leave**
- **holidays**

tour facility and work areas:

- **introduce employees**
- **identify amenities, e.g., washrooms, shower**
- **explain emergency procedures**
- **identify safety equipment**

describe job responsibilities and performance expectations:

- **review job description**
- **review product standards**
- **discuss applicable legislation**
- **provide manuals for operating equipment**

finalize employment documentation

Source: HR for Employers—Orientation, http://hrmanagement.gc.ca/gol/hrmanagement/site.nsf/en/hr11563.html, Service Canada, 2006. Reprinted with the permission of the Minister of Public Works and Government Services Canada, 2006.

Training may include "hard" skills such as teaching a programmer how to use C++, an accountant how to make an income statement, or a machinist apprentice how to set up a drill press. "Soft" skills are critical in many instances and can be taught as well. They include communicating, mentoring, managing a meeting, and working as part of a team.[9]

New Context of Training

Contemporary training in organizations has evolved significantly over the past decade. Brought on by changes in the competitive environment and technology, this evolution is altering the way training is done. It has affected four areas in particular: organizational competitiveness, knowledge management, revenue, and performance.

Canadian Society for Training and Development
This website on training and development contains information on research, education seminars, and conferences.
www.cstd.ca

Organizational Competitiveness and Training More employers are recognizing that training their human resources is vital. Canadian organizations spent an average of $914 per employee in 2004, an increase from $824 in 2003. Most organizations make training available to full-time staff (92 percent) and part-time staff (88 percent). As a percentage of payroll training investment has stayed relatively constant, from 1.57 percent in 2001 to 1.55 percent in 2003.[10]

General Electric, Dell Computers, Motorola, Marriott, Cisco, FedEx, and Telus all emphasize the importance of training employees and managers. These companies and others recognize that training and HR development efforts are integral to competitive business success. In a sense, for these companies, training is similar to the "continuous improvement" practiced by some manufacturing firms. The nature of technological innovation and change is such that if employees are not trained all the time, they fall behind and the company becomes less competitive. For example, consider the telecommunications industry today compared with five years ago, with all the new technologies, wireless services, and competitive shifts. Without continual training, organizations may not have staff members with the KSAs needed to compete effectively.

Training also assists organizational competitiveness by aiding in the retention of employees. As emphasized in Chapter 6, a primary reason why many individuals stay or leave organizations is career training and development opportunities. Employers that invest in training and developing their employees enhance retention efforts. However, there are employers who do not invest in training and development since it is their belief that trained employees will seek out alternate employment once they have acquired the necessary skills. CRST Van Expedited made a sizable investment in training drivers at its facilities, only to have their trained drivers solicited away by another carrier, J.B. Hunt. Because CRST was losing many of its newly trained drivers to companies such as J.B. Hunt it asked that drivers undergoing commercial driver's licence and finishing training at CRST's expense sign employment agreements of up to one year. Litigation is ongoing between the two companies, as CRST attempts to protect its investment.[11]

Knowledge Management and Training For much of history, competitive advantage among organizations was measured in terms of physical capital. However, as the information age has evolved, "intelligence" became the raw material that many organizations make and sell through their "knowledge workers." **Knowledge management** is the way an organization identifies and leverages knowledge in order to be competitive. It is the art of creating value by using organizational intellectual capital, which is what the organization (or, more exactly, the people in the organization) knows, and it includes intellectual properties such as patents and copyrights.[12]

Knowledge management
The way an organization identifies and leverages knowledge in order to be competitive.

Multiple definitions of knowledge management exist, some referring to the technology used to transfer information. Technology can indeed help transmit knowledge, but having technology does not mean people will use it to manage knowledge effectively. Knowledge management is a conscious effort to get the right knowledge to the right people at the right time so that it can be shared and put into action. It involves more than simply a technological infrastructure.[13]

Training as a Revenue Source Some organizations have identified that training can be a source of business revenue. For instance, Microsoft, Ceridian, Cisco, Hewlett-Packard, and other technology firms bundle training with products and services sold to customers. Also, manufacturers of industrial equipment offer customers training on machine upgrades and new features. Customers of many of these firms pay for additional training either by course, by participant, or as part of equipment or software purchases. Not only are the costs of the trainers' salary, travel, and other expenses covered, but the suppliers make a profit on the training through the fees paid by customers. As a side benefit, customer satisfaction and loyalty increase if customers know how to use the products and services purchased. Thus, customer training aids customer retention and enhances future sales revenues.

Integration of Performance and Training Job performance, training, and employee learning must be integrated to be effective. First, as training progressively moves "closer to the job" in order to produce "real-time" learning, the linkage between training and job performance is vital. Consider the following example: many Canadian Air Force flight-line personnel must undergo regular safety training. The days of sending them to a conference room where they watch a one-hour videotape on safety are gone. Today, they are taken out on the flight line and trained with the actual equipment (i.e., in a real situation, with real tools and equipment and people), not moved to an artificial learning environment. Trainees can watch the trainer put on the necessary gear in the proper manner, attempt to replicate the actions themselves, and receive real-time feedback in an actual work setting.

Second, organizations are seeking more authentic (and hence more effective) training experiences for their trainees, using real business problems to advance employee learning. Rather than separating the training experience from the context of actual job performance, trainers incorporate everyday business issues as learning examples, thus increasing the realism of training exercises and scenarios. As part of management training at GE, managers are given actual business problems to solve, and they must present their solutions to organizational business leaders. Using real situations for practice is yet another way of merging the lines between training, learning, and job performance.

Performance Consulting

Performance consulting
Process in which a trainer and the organizational client work together to determine what needs to be done to improve results.

Training should result in improved organizational performance. Ensuring that it does may require a "performance consulting" approach. **Performance consulting** is a process in which a trainer (either internal or external to the organization) and the organizational client work together to decide what needs to be done to improve results. That may or may not include training.

As Figure 7-2 depicts, performance consulting compares desired and actual organizational results with desired and actual employee performance. Once these comparisons are made, then performance consulting takes a broad approach to performance issues. It does so by:

- Focusing on identifying and addressing root causes of performance problems
- Recognizing that the interaction of individual and organizational factors influences employee performance
- Documenting the actions and accomplishments of high performers and comparing them with actions of more typical performers.[14]

Figure 7-2 *Performance Consulting*

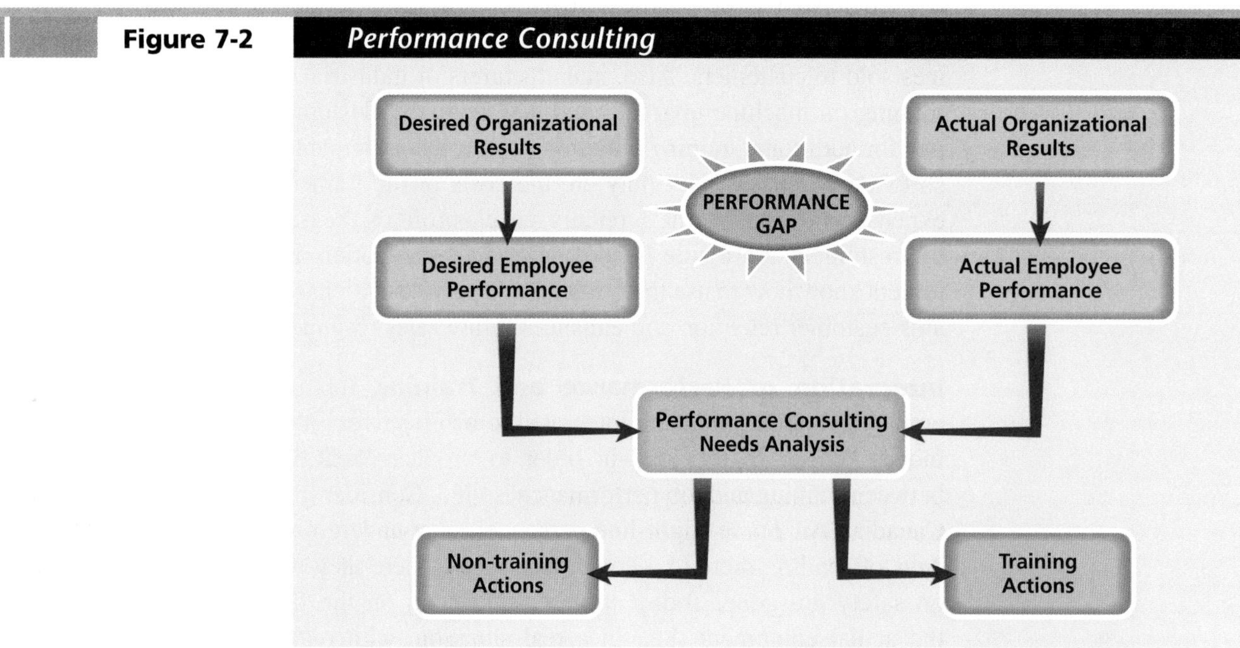

International Society for Performance Improvement
This professional organization focuses on improving productivity and performance in the workplace.
www.ispi.org

Regardless of whether the trainer is an internal employee or an outside consultant, a performance consulting approach recognizes that training alone cannot automatically solve every employee performance problem. Instead, training is one piece of a larger "bundled solution." For instance, some employee performance issues might be resolved by creating a training program for employees, and others might call for compensation or job design changes.

Managers are likely the best source of technical information used in employee skills training. They also are in a good position to decide when employees need training or re-training. Their close and continual interaction with employees puts managers in the most appropriate place to determine and discuss employee training possibilities and plans with individual employees. However, compared with individual operating managers, HR often operates with a more long-range view of employee training and development for the entire organization. This difference is especially true at lower levels in the organization. The performance consulting approach is most likely to come from HR or from a consultant that HR has hired. Therefore, a "training partnership" between the HR staff members and operating managers is important.

Chief Learning Officers (CLOs)

To emphasize the importance of training, some organizations have created a position entitled *Chief Learning Officer (CLO)* or *Chief Knowledge Officer (CKO)*. The CLO is not just a training director with an inflated new title. Instead, the CLO is a leader who designs knowledge through training for individual employees and the organization. CLOs must demonstrate a high level of comfort in working with boards of directors and the top management team, a track record of success in running some type of business unit, and an understanding of adult learning technologies and processes. If they possess these characteristics, then CLOs are more likely to take the lead in developing strategic training plans for their organizations.

Training and Organizational Strategy

Training represents a significant expenditure in most organizations. But it is too often viewed tactically rather than strategically, as upper management is often not clear what it wants from training and therefore fails to connect training with the strategy and goals of the organization.[15] Figure 7-3 shows how training might be used to help accomplish various strategies in an organization. Ideally, the upper management group understands that the training function can provide valuable intelligence about the necessary core skills. If the training unit understands the strategic direction of the organization, it can find creative ways to move people in the direction of the various strategies. For example, if a company plans to computerize their payroll system at the end of the current year—training for the new system needs to be an objective at the departmental level as well as at the operational level.

Training that is seen as being aligned with the direction that the organization is going gets higher usage; and providing support for people to get that training is viewed by employees as positive for the strategies of the organization.[16] If a company is trying to distinguish itself from its competition through the quality of its customer service, then significant customer service training is needed to support the strategic direction of the firm. If another firm differentiates itself from competitors with products or services that customers perceive as distinctive and unique, then training resources should be shifted to keeping employees abreast of the latest advertising and

Figure 7-3 Linking Organizational Strategies and Training

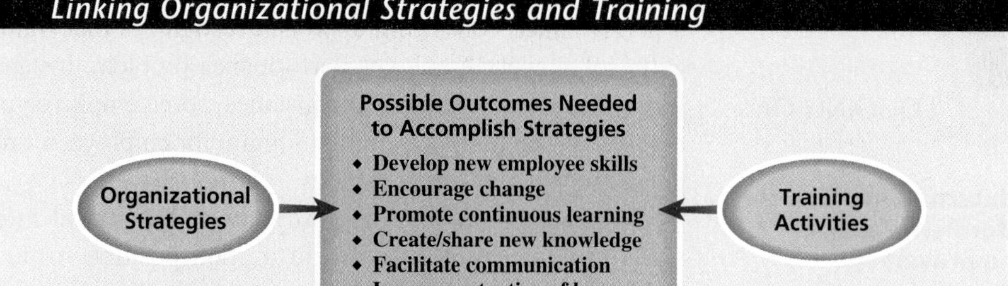

Source: Based on ideas from Lisa A. Burke and Joseph V. Wilson III.

marketing ideas. For instance, an exclusive jewellery store selling Rolex watches and expensive jewellery must ensure that its employees are trained on all the models, features, and operations of such items.

Benefits of Strategic Training

The benefits of strategic training are numerous. First, strategic training enables HR and training professionals to get intimately involved with the business, partner with operating managers to help solve their problems, and make significant contributions to organizational results. Strategic training also may prevent HR professionals and trainers from chasing fads or the hottest or latest type of training gimmick.[17] Additionally a strategic training mindset reduces the likelihood of thinking that training alone can solve most employee or organizational problems. It is not uncommon for operating managers and trainers to react to most important performance problems by saying, "I need a training program on X." With a strategic training focus, the organization is more likely to assess such requests to determine what training and/or non-training approaches might address the most important performance issues.

The value of strategic training can be seen at Walt Disney World where the company has established specific strategic training plans. Implementing strategic training plans results in a distinct and noted competitive advantage for the organization. For example at the Disney Institute, employees (called "cast members") gain critical experience from the perspective of their guests. As a part of their training, individuals taking hotel reservations stay at a resort as guests in order to gain greater understanding of what they are selling and to experience the services themselves.

Training and Global Strategies

For global firms the most brilliant strategies ever devised will not work unless there are well-trained employees throughout the world to carry them out. For example, the successful development of *global strategies* is inhibited primarily by training deficits such as these:[18]

- Workforces with disparate competencies
- A declining pool of Canadian employees willing to go overseas
- Slow, expensive, and inflexible "on campus" training options

Ernst & Young is recognized for its investment in the growth and development of its employees. For three years they have been placed in the Top 10 among *Training* magazine's Training Top 100, which recognized the scope and breadth of learning offerings—from Web-based modules and instructor-led training to mentoring and counselling systems. The company was ranked one of the global Top 10 e-learning companies by Brandon-Hall.com for the quantity, quality, and impact of their e-learning initiatives and our learning portal, which is helping professionals worldwide maintain their competitive edge, as the winner of a Smithsonian Technology Award.[19]

Developing Strategic Training Plans

Training plans allow organizations to identify what is needed for employee performance *before* training begins. It is at this stage that fit with strategic issues is ensured. A good training plan deals with the following questions:[20]

- Is there really a need for the training?
- Who needs to be trained?
- Who will do the training?
- What form will the training take?
- How will knowledge be transferred to the job?
- How will the training be evaluated?

Training Process

The way firms organize and structure the training affects the way employees experience the training, which in turn influences the effectiveness of the training.[21] Effective training requires the use of a systematic training process. Figure 7-4 shows the four phases of such a process: assessment, design, delivery, and evaluation. Using such a process reduces the likelihood that unplanned, uncoordinated, and haphazard training efforts will occur. A discussion of each phase of the training process follows.

Figure 7-4 *Systematic Training Process*

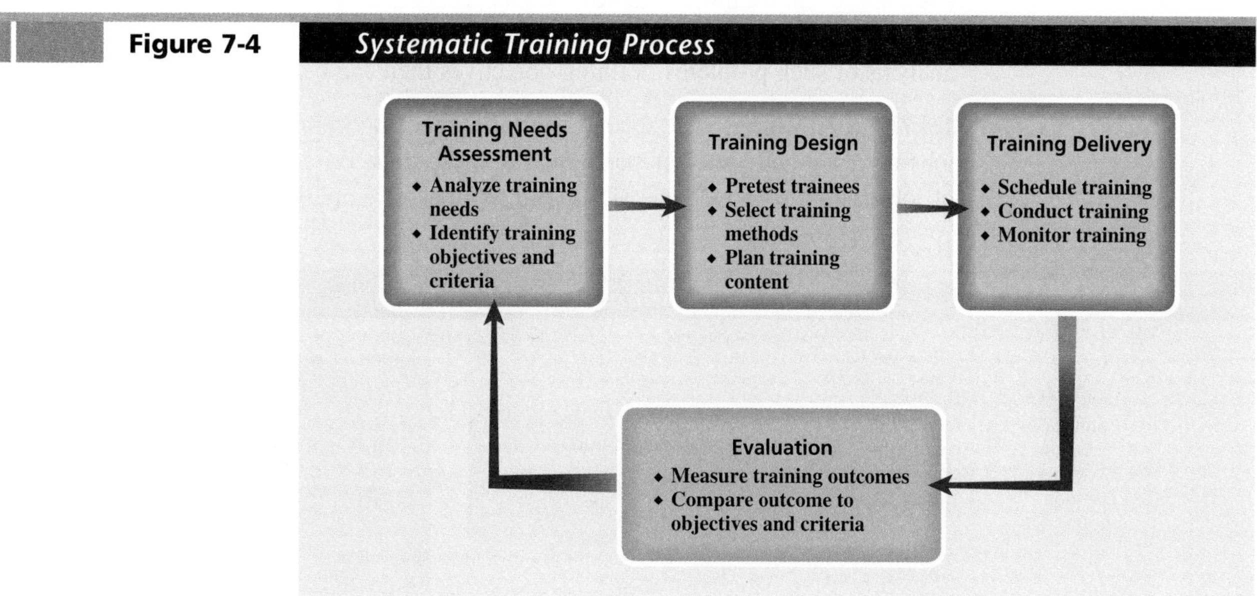

Training Needs Assessment

3 Assessing organizational training needs represents the diagnostic phase of a training plan. This assessment considers issues of employee and organizational performance to determine if training can help. Needs assessment measures the competencies of a company, a group, or an individual as they relate to what is required in the strategic plan. It is necessary to find out what is happening and what should be happening before deciding if training will help, and if it will help, what kind is needed.[22] For instance, suppose that in looking at the performance of clerks in a billing department, a manager identifies problems that employees have with their data-entry and keyboarding abilities, and she decides that they would benefit from instruction in these areas. As part of assessing the training needs, the manager has the clerks take a data-entry test to measure their current keyboarding skills. Then the manager establishes an objective of increasing the clerks' keyboarding speed to 60 words per minute without errors. The number of words per minute without errors is the criterion against which training success can be measured, and it represents the way in which the objective is made specific.

Analyzing Training Needs

The first step in training needs assessment is analyzing what training is needed. Figure 7-5 shows the three sources of analyzing training needs.

Organizational Analyses Training needs can be diagnosed through analyzing organizational outcomes. A part of HR planning is the identification of the knowledge, skills, and abilities that will be needed in the future as both jobs and the organization change. Both internal and external forces will influence training and must be considered when doing organizational analyses. For instance, the problems posed by the technical obsolescence of current employees and an insufficiently educated labour pool from which to draw new workers should be confronted before those training needs become critical.

One important source for organizational analyses comes from various operational measures of organizational performance. On a continuing basis, detailed analyses of HR data reveal training weaknesses. Departments or areas with high turnover, high absenteeism, low performance, or other deficiencies can be pinpointed. Following an analysis of such problems, training objectives then can be developed.

Job/Task Analyses The second way of diagnosing training needs is to analyze the jobs involved and the tasks performed in those jobs. By comparing the requirements of jobs with the knowledge, skills, and abilities of employees, training needs can be

Figure 7-5 *Sources of the Information Used in Training Needs Assessment*

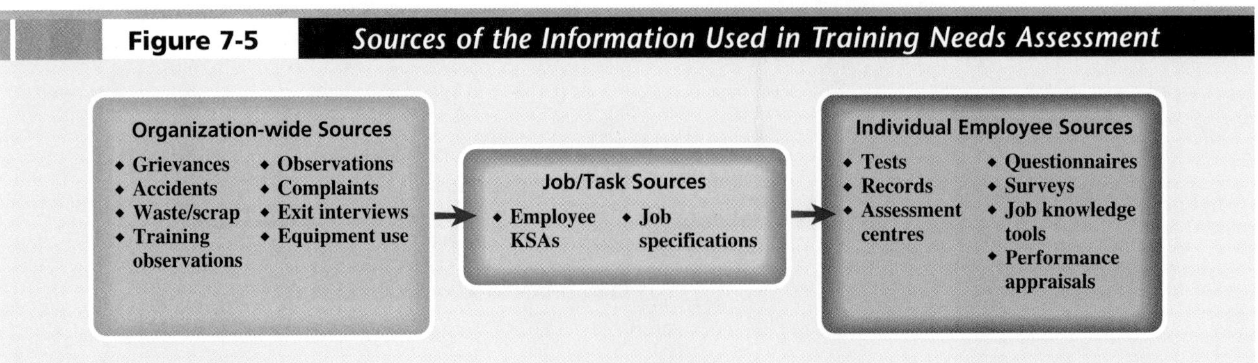

identified. Current job specifications can be a source for such an analysis. For example, at a manufacturing firm, analyses identified the tasks performed by engineers who served as technical instructors for other employees. By listing the tasks required of a technical instructor, management established a program to teach specific instructional skills; thus, the engineers were able to become more successful instructors.

Individual Analyses The third means of diagnosing training needs focuses on individuals and how they perform their jobs. The most common approach for making these individual analyses is to use performance appraisal data. In some instances, a good HR information system can be used to identify individuals who require training in specific areas in order to be eligible for promotion. To assess training needs through the performance appraisal process, the organization first determines an employee's performance inadequacies in a formal review. Then, it can design some type of training to help the employee overcome the weaknesses.

Another way of assessing individual training needs is to survey both managerial and non-managerial employees about what training is needed. Such surveys can also be useful in building support for training from those who will be trained, because the employees will have provided input for identifying their training needs. A training needs survey can take the form of questionnaires or interviews with supervisors and employees individually or in groups. The purpose is to gather information on problems perceived by the individuals involved. In addition to performance appraisals and training surveys, Figure 7-6 lists sources that are useful for individual analyses.

Establishing Training Objectives and Priorities

Once training needs have been identified using appropriate analyses, then training objectives and priorities can be established by a "gap analysis," which indicates the distance between where an organization is with its employee KSAs and where it needs to be. Training objectives and priorities are set to close the gap. Three types of training objectives can be set:

- *Knowledge:* Impart cognitive information and details to trainees.
- *Skill:* Develop behaviour changes in how jobs and various task requirements are performed.
- *Attitude:* Create interest in and awareness of the importance of training.

The success of training should be measured in terms of the objectives set. Useful objectives are measurable. For example, an objective for a new salesclerk might be to "demonstrate the ability to explain the function of each product in the department within two weeks." This objective checks on internalization, or whether the person really learned and is able to use the training.

Because training seldom is an unlimited budget item and because organizations have multiple training needs, prioritization is necessary. Ideally, management ranks

Figure 7-6 *Individual Analysis*

• Skills tests	• Questionnaires
• Individual assessment tests	• Attitude surveys
• Records of critical incidents	• Job knowledge tools
• Assessment centres	

training needs based on organizational objectives.[23] Conducting the training most needed to improve the performance of the organization will produce visible results more quickly.

Training Design

4 Once training objectives have been determined, training design can start. Whether job-specific or broader in nature, training must be designed to address the assessed specific needs. Effective training design considers learning concepts, different approaches to training, and legal issues.

Working in organizations should be a continual learning process, and learning is the focus of all training activities. Different approaches are possible, but learning is a complex psychological process.[24] As depicted in Figure 7-7, there are three primary considerations when designing training: (1) determining learner readiness, (2) understanding different learning styles, and (3) designing training for transfer. Each of these elements must be considered for the training design to mesh.

Learner Readiness

For training to be successful, learners must be ready to learn.[25] Learner readiness means having the basic skills necessary for learning, the motivation to learn, and self-efficacy.

Ability to Learn Learners must possess basic skills, such as fundamental reading and math proficiency, and sufficient cognitive abilities. Companies may discover that some workers lack the requisite skills to comprehend their training effectively. Various firms have found that a significant number of job applicants and current

Figure 7-7 *Elements of Training Design*

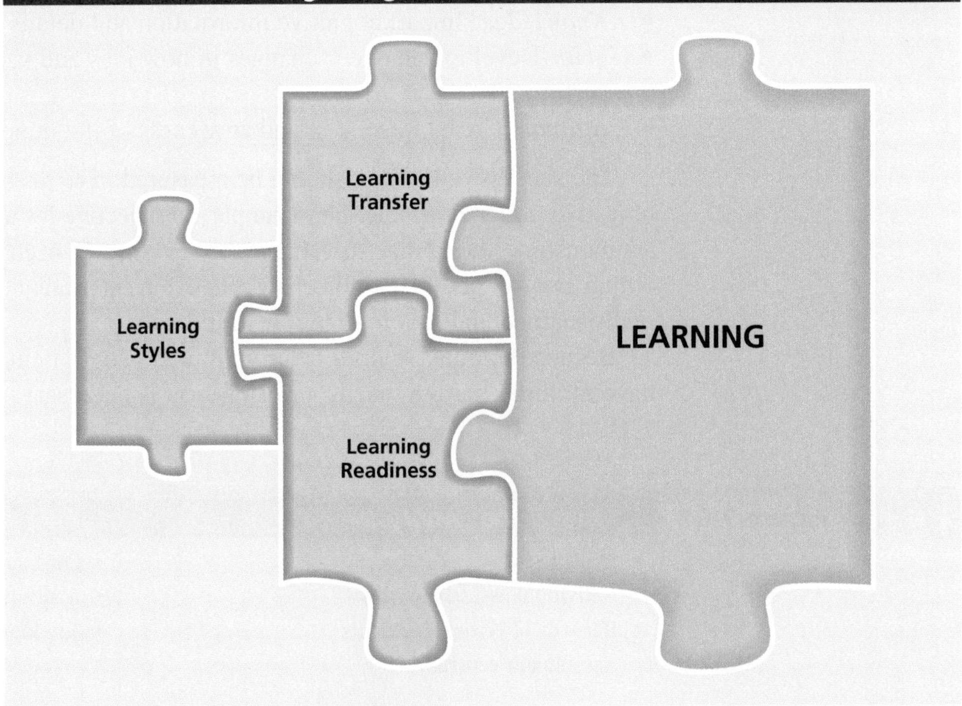

employees lack the reading, writing, and math skills needed to do the jobs. Employers might deal with the lack of basic employee skills in several ways:

- Offer remedial training to people in their current workforce who need it.
- Hire workers they know are deficient and then implement specific workplace training.
- Work with local schools to help better educate potential hires for jobs.

Motivation to Learn A person's desire to learn training content is referred to as "motivation to learn" and is influenced by multiple factors. For example, the extent to which a student taking a college or university course is motivated to learn the course content might be influenced by personal career interests and values, degree plan requirements and area of study, the positive value the student places on getting an A in the course, or simply personal expectations of doing well in school. The student's motivation level may also be influenced by the instructor's motivation and ability, friends' encouragement to do well, classmates' motivation levels, the physical classroom environment, and the training methods used. Regardless of what the motivation is, without it, the student will not learn the material.

Self-efficacy
Person's belief that he or she *can* successfully learn the training program content.

Self-Efficacy Learners must also possess **self-efficacy,** which refers to a person's belief that he or she *can* successfully learn the training program content. For learners to be ready for and receptive to the training content, they must feel that it is possible for them to learn it. As an example, some students' levels of self-efficacy diminish in math or statistics courses when they do not feel adequately able to grasp the material. These perceptions may have nothing to do with their actual ability to learn, but rather reflect the way they see themselves and their abilities. Instructors and trainers must find appropriate ways to boost the confidence of trainees who are unsure of their learning abilities. For instance, people with a low level of belief that they can learn certain content may benefit from one-on-one training.

Learning Styles

In designing training interventions, trainers also should consider individual learning styles. For example, *auditory* learners learn best by listening to someone else tell them about the training content. *Tactile* learners must "get their hands on" the training resources and use them. *Visual* learners think in pictures and figures and need to see the purpose and process of the training. Trainers who address all these styles by using multiple training methods can design more effective training.

Training many different people from diverse backgrounds poses a significant challenge in today's work organizations. Research reveals that in addition to considering cultural, gender, and race/ethnicity diversity, training design sometimes must address some special issues presented by adult learning. For instance, assume a firm is training a group of 30 customer service representatives, ten of whom are under age 25 and highly computer and Internet literate, and the remainder of whom are older and not as computer proficient. Certainly, the training design must consider that all the trainees are adults, but they come with widely varying learning styles, experiences, and anxieties.

Training older adults in technology may require greater attention to explaining the need for changes and to building the older trainees' confidence in their abilities to learn new technology. In contrast, younger adults are likely willing to try new technology because of their earlier exposure to computers and technology. As a consequence of differences such as these, a variety of training designs and delivery considerations must be assessed when developing training for adults of various ages.

Adult Learning Malcolm Knowles's classic work on adult learning suggests five principles for designing training for adults. That and subsequent work by others suggests that adults:

1. Have the need to know why they are learning something
2. Have a need to be self-directed
3. Bring more work-related experiences into the learning process
4. Enter into a learning experience with a problem-centred approach to learning
5. Are motivated to learn by both extrinsic and intrinsic factors

Adult learners in work organizations present different issues for training design based on Knowles's principles.[26] For instance, trainers cannot expect to do a "brain dump" of material without giving trainees the context or bigger picture of why participants need the training information. This concept is referred to as *whole learning* or *Gestalt learning*. As applied to job training, this means that instructions should be divided into small elements *after* employees have had the opportunity to see how all the elements fit together—that trainers should present the big picture first.

Active practice
Performance of job-related tasks and duties by trainees during training.

Spaced practice
Practice performed in several sessions spaced over a period of hours or days.

Massed practice
Practice performed all at once.

Adult learners should be encouraged to bring work-related problems to training as a way to make the material more relevant to them.[27] Effective training should involve participants in learning by actively engaging them in the learning and problem-solving process. **Active practice** occurs when trainees perform job-related tasks and duties during training. It is more effective than simply reading or passively listening. For instance, if a person is being trained as a customer service representative, after being given some basic selling instructions and product details, the trainee calls a customer and uses the knowledge received. Active practice can be structured in two ways. The first, **spaced practice,** occurs when several practice sessions are spaced over a period of hours or days. The second, **massed practice,** occurs when a person performs all the practice at once. Spaced practice works better for some types of skill or physical learning that requires muscle memory, whereas for other kinds of learning, such as memorizing tasks, massed practice is usually more effective.

Adult learners present different issues for training design.

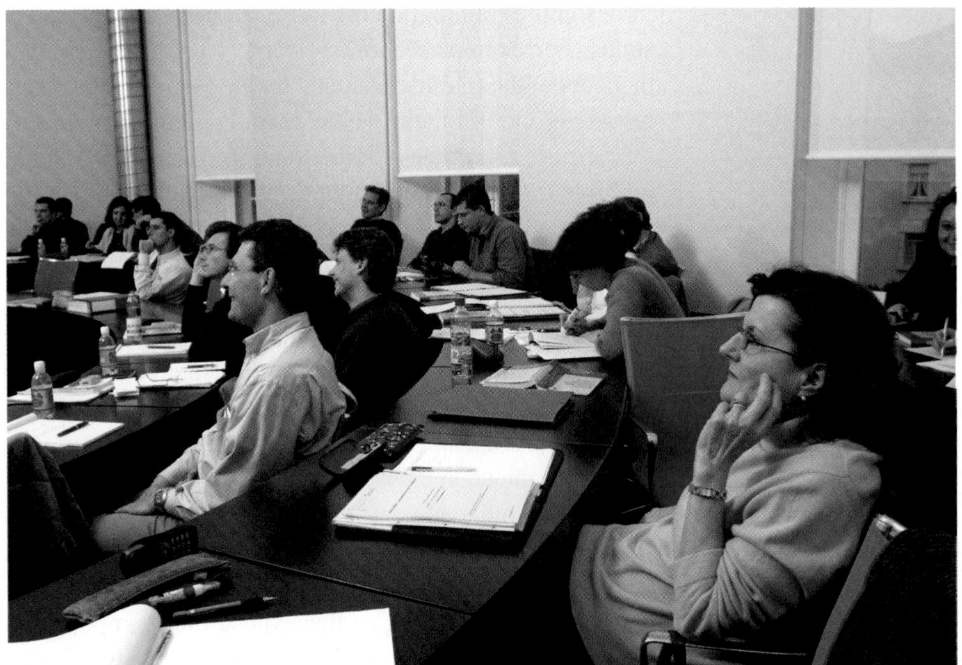

Source: Lancelot et Naelle/ShutterStock

Imagine the difficulty of trying to memorize the lists of options for 20 dishwasher models, one model a day for 20 days. By the time an appliance distribution salesperson learned the last option, the person likely would have forgotten the first one.

Behaviour modelling
Copying someone else's behaviour.

Behaviour Modelling The most elementary way in which people learn—and one of the best—is **behaviour modelling,** or copying someone else's behaviour. The use of behaviour modelling is particularly appropriate for skill training in which the trainees must use both knowledge and practice. For example, a new supervisor receives training and mentoring on how to handle disciplinary discussions with employees by observing as the HR director or department manager deals with such problems. Behaviour modelling is used extensively as the primary means for training supervisors and managers in interpersonal skills. It can aid in the transfer and usage of those skills by the trained supervisors. Fortunately or unfortunately, many supervisors and managers end up modelling the behaviour they see their bosses use. For that reason, effective training should include good examples of how to handle interpersonal and other issues and problems.

Reinforcement
Based on the idea that people tend to repeat responses that give them some type of positive reward and avoid actions associated with negative consequences.

Immediate confirmation
Based on the idea that people learn best if reinforcement and feedback are given after training.

Reinforcement and Immediate Confirmation The concept of **reinforcement** is based on the *law of effect,* which states that people tend to repeat responses that give them some type of positive reward and to avoid actions associated with negative consequences. Closely related is a learning concept called **immediate confirmation,** which is based on the idea that people learn best if reinforcement and feedback are given as soon as possible after training. Immediate confirmation corrects errors that, if made throughout the training, might establish an undesirable pattern that would need to be unlearned. It also aids with the transfer of training to the actual work done.

Transfer of Training

Finally, trainers should design training for the highest possible transfer from the class to the job. Transfer occurs when trainees actually use on the job what they learned in training. Estimates of how much training effectively gets transferred in corporate training are fairly dismal.[28] When training is transferred it is embedded in the employees who have participated in the training and are now putting it to use in their everyday responsibilities on the job. When this occurs it is important that everyone involved in the training or those who will be affected by the training ensure that the training is integrated into the work environment.

Effective transfer of training meets two conditions. First, the trainees can take the material learned in training and apply it to the job context in which they work. Second, employees maintain their use of the learned material over time.

A number of approaches can increase the transfer of training.[29] Offering trainees an overview of the training content and process before the actual training seems to help with both short-term and longer-term training transfer. Another specific way to aid transfer of training to job situations is to ensure that the training mirrors the job context as much as possible. For example, training managers to be better selection interviewers should include role-playing with "applicants" who respond in the same way that real applicants would. To support the more introverted individual it is important to offer other options such as problem solving using small group discussion or real-life case analysis. In addition, to increase the transfer of training key stakeholders need to be consulted to gain their support and that will likely provide for a better opportunity at transferring training.[30] Organizations might want to experiment with collaborative approaches to training that could result in a higher degree of transferred learning. Creating and establishing a peer mentoring program might be another way to approach the transfer of training challenge.

There are a number of barriers that could be associated with the transfer of training including

- Communication
- Type of training not effective
- E-training: person being trained
- Climate and culture of organization
- Lack of support from supervisors or managers
- Limited resources

Training Categories

Training can be designed to meet a number of objectives and can be classified in various ways. Some common groupings include the following:

- *Required and regular training:* Complies with various mandated legal requirements (e.g., OH&S, employment equity, pay equity) and is given to all employees (new employee orientation)
- *Job/technical training:* Enables employees to perform their jobs, tasks, and responsibilities well (e.g., product knowledge, technical processes and procedures, and customer relations)
- *Interpersonal and problem-solving training:* Addresses both operational and interpersonal problems and seeks to improve organizational working relationships (e.g., interpersonal communication, managerial/supervisory skills, and conflict resolution)
- *Developmental and innovative training:* Provides long-term focus to enhance individual and organizational KSAs for the future (e.g., business practices, executive development, and organizational change)

Cross training
Training people to do more than one job.

Cross Training **Cross training** occurs when people are trained to do more than one job—theirs and someone else's. For the employer, the advantages of cross training are flexibility and development. If an employee gets sick or quits, there is someone already trained to do the job. However, while cross training is attractive to the employer, it is not always appreciated by employees, who often feel that it requires them to do more work for the same pay.

In some organizations, the culture may be such that people seek cross-training assignments to grow or prepare for a promotion, but that is not the case in all organizations. Unions typically are not in support of cross training, as it threatens job jurisdiction and broadens jobs. Cross training may require scheduling work differently during training, and temporarily decreased productivity may result from it as people learn.

An effective cross-training program can overcome the concerns mentioned and has the potential to be good for both employer and employee. Learning "bonuses" can be awarded for successfully completing cross training, to make it more appealing to employees.

Legal Issues and Training

A number of legal issues must be considered when designing and delivering training. One concern centres on the criteria and practices used to select individuals for inclusion in training programs, making sure that those criteria are job related and do not unfairly restrict the participation of designated group members. Also, failure to accommodate the participation of individuals with disabilities in training exposes organizations to human rights charges of discrimination. The last concern pertains to Quebec's requirements that all companies operating in that province with a payroll of

$1 million or more, is required to invest a minimum amount of 1 percent of their payroll in training and development. The training must meet specific criteria and special circumstances that many organizations are unaware.

Another contemporary issue is employers' requiring trainees to sign contracts in order to protect the costs and time invested in specialized employee training. For instance, a telecommunications firm paid $77,000 to train four network technicians and certify them in specialized equipment. The firm required that the technicians sign training contracts whereby one-fourth of the cost would be forgiven each year the employee stayed with the organization following the training. A technician who left sooner would be liable to the firm for the unforgiven balance. Health-care organizations, IT firms, and some other employers use training contracts.

Training Delivery

5 Once training has been designed, then the actual delivery of training can begin. It is generally recommended that the training be pilot-tested or conducted on a trial basis to ensure that the training meets the needs identified and that the design is appropriate. Regardless of the type of training done, a number of approaches and methods can be used to deliver it. The growth of training technology continues to expand the available choices.

Whatever the approach used, a variety of considerations must be balanced when selecting training delivery methods. The common variables considered are:

- Nature of training
- Subject matter
- Number of trainees
- Individual vs. team
- Self-paced vs. guided
- Training resources/costs
- E-learning vs. traditional learning
- Geographic locations
- Time allotted
- Completion timeline

To illustrate, a large firm with many new hires may be able to conduct employee orientation using the Internet, videotapes, and specific HR staff members. However, a small firm with few new hires may have an HR staff member meet individually with the new hires for several hours. Or a medium-sized company with three locations in a geographic area may bring supervisors together for a two-day training workshop once a quarter. However, a large global firm may use Web-based courses to reach supervisors throughout the world, with content available in several languages. Frequently, training is conducted internally, but some types of training use external or technological training resources.

Internal Training

Internal training generally applies very specifically to a job. It is popular because it saves the cost of sending employees away for training and often avoids the cost of outside trainers. Frequently, skills-based, technical training is conducted inside organizations. Due to rapid changes in technology, the building and updating of technical skills have become crucial training needs. Basic technical skills training is also being mandated by federal regulations in areas where the Occupational Heath and Safety, the Transportation of Dangerous Goods, Workplace Hazardous Materials Information System (WHMIS), the Environmental Protection Agency (EPA), and other agencies have jurisdiction.

Informal training Training that occurs through interactions and feedback among employees.

Informal Training One internal source of training is **informal training,** which occurs through interactions and feedback among employees. Much of what the employees know about their jobs they learn informally from asking questions and getting advice from other employees and their supervisors, rather than from formal training programs.

Figure 7-8 **Stages for On-the-Job Training (OJT)**

Prepare the Trainees	Present the Information	Have the Trainees Practise	Do Follow-up
• Put them at ease • Find out what they know • Get them interested	• Tell, show, question • Present one point at a time • Make sure the trainees know	• Have the trainees perform the tasks • Ask questions • Observe and correct • Evaluate mastery	• Put the trainees on their own • Check frequently • Reduce follow-up as performance improves

On-the-Job Training (OJT) The most common type of training at all levels in an organization is *on-the-job training (OJT).* In contrast with informal training, which often occurs spontaneously, OJT should be planned. The supervisor or manager conducting the training must be able to both teach and show the employees what to do. Based on a guided form of training known as *job instruction training (JIT),* on-the-job training is most effective if a logical progression of stages is used, as shown in Figure 7-8.

On-the-job training (OJT) is the most common form of training utilized, and is most effective if planned appropriately.

On-the-job training is by far the most commonly used form of training because it is flexible and relevant to what employees do.[31] However, OJT has some problems. Often, those doing the training may have no experience in training, no time to do it, and no desire to participate in it. Under such conditions, learners essentially are on their own, and training likely will not be effective.[32] Another problem is that OJT can disrupt regular work. Unfortunately, OJT can amount to no training at all in some circumstances, especially if the trainers simply abandon the trainees to learn the job alone. Also, bad habits or incorrect information from the supervisor or manager can be transferred to the trainees. On the other hand, well-planned and well-executed OJT can be very effective.

Source: © 2006 JupiterImages and its Licensors. All Rights Reserved.

Off-the-Job Training

Off-the-job training, or external training, is training that takes place outside the employing organization, and is used extensively by organizations of all sizes. Large organizations use external training if they lack the capability to train people internally or when many people need to be trained quickly. External training may be the best option for training in smaller firms due to limitations in the size of their HR staffs and in the number of employees who may need various types of specialized training. Whatever the size of the organization, external training occurs for several reasons:

- It may be less expensive for an employer to have an outside trainer conduct training in areas where internal training resources are limited.
- The organization may have insufficient time to develop internal training materials.
- The HR staff may not have the necessary level of expertise for the subject matter in which training is needed.
- There are advantages to having employees interact with managers and peers in other companies in training programs held externally.

Outsourcing of Training Many employers of all sizes outsource training to external training firms, consultants, and other entities. However, the number of employers outsourcing training appears to be declining. According to data from the Conference Board of Canada's "Learning and Development Outlook 2005 Report" on training the outsourcing of training declined sharply because of cost concerns, a greater emphasis on internal linking of training to organizational strategies, and other issues.[33]

A popular route for some employers is to use vendors and suppliers to train employees. Several computer software vendors offer employees technical certifications on their software. For example, being a Microsoft Certified Product Specialist gives employees credentials that show their level of technical expertise. Such certifications provide employees with items to put on their résumés should they decide to change jobs. These certifications also benefit employers, who can use them as job specifications for hiring and promotion.

Many suppliers, including software providers, host users' conferences, where employees from a number of firms receive detailed training on using the product and new features being added. Some vendors will conduct the training inside an organization as well if sufficient numbers of employees are to be trained.

Government-Supported Job Training Federal and provincial governments provide a wide range of external training assistance. For example, in 2005, the federal government announced its commitment to ensuring Canada has skilled workers. It is investing on three main fronts: updating the skills of our existing workforce; addressing the needs of groups with special needs, such as youth and the Aboriginal population; and ensuring internationally trained workers can fully participate in the labour market and Canadian society. The federal government is working with provincial/territorial governments, licensing and regulatory bodies, sector councils, employers and many other groups to improve the integration of internationally trained workers into the workforce and society. The issues being addressed include: accelerating the assessment and recognition of foreign credentials; implementing Enhanced Language Training and Bridge to Work initiatives; and providing up-to-date and pertinent labour market information.[34]

Government programs sponsored through various provincial and municipal agencies provide training dollars to employers who hire new workers, particularly those who have been unemployed for a long time or have been receiving welfare benefits. Many of these *welfare to work programs* can be found throughout Canada.

Educational Assistance Programs Some employers pay for additional education for their employees. Typically, the employee pays for courses that apply to college diplomas or university degrees, or other relevant training that the employer deems important to the employee's work, and is reimbursed upon successful completion of a course. The amounts paid by the employer are considered taxable income for the employee.

Traditional forms of employee educational programs pose risks for the employer, because upon completion of the degree, the employee may choose to take the new skills and go elsewhere. PricewaterhouseCoopers (PWC) deals with that situation. PWC will repay an employee's loan for an MBA within three years—but only if the employee stays for three years after getting the degree. The company does not agree to provide the opportunity for everyone; it offers the arrangement only to those with several years of employment and potential to move up in the organization.[35]

E-learning: Online Training

E-learning
Use of the Internet or an organizational intranet to conduct training online.

E-learning is use of the Internet or an organizational intranet to conduct training online. An intranet is similar to the Internet, but it is a private organizational network behind "firewall" software that restricts access to authorized users, including employees participating in e-learning. Specific examples of how e-learning is being used in training are shown in the Technology Transforming HR.

E-learning caught on widely with employers because of its promise of cost savings and access to more employees. According to *Training* magazine's 2003 Industry Report, 50 percent of manufacturers often use the Internet or a company intranet or extranet for *training*. Web courses constituted 61 percent of all computer-delivered courses in 2003—a big increase from 13 percent in 2002. E-learning will account for more than $18 billion in sales in 2005.[36] Studies have shown that people who train on a simulation program retain about 75 percent of the material. In comparison, lectures yield a retention rate of only about 5 percent, audio-visual presentations 20 percent and discussion groups 50 percent.[37]

Technology Transforming HR

Examples of E-learning Programs

Technology has enabled e-learning to take place, and employers are using it in many different ways and for many different kinds of training. For example: W. R. Grace Co., a global company with offices in Ajax, Ontario, and Valleyfield Quebec, uses e-learning in its Grace Global Learning Centre, which is available 24/7 to its 6000 employees worldwide. Toronto's Mount Sinai Hospital, an internationally recognized 462-bed health-care centre affiliated with the University of Toronto, recognized that its increasingly busy clinical staff simply did not have the time for traditional training methods. Sinai e-Learning is used for training on electronic clinical documentation, electronic medication administration, and computerized physician order entry. This training method enables physicians, residents, and nurses to expedite the application learning process without interfering with their busy schedules, as well as ensure that clinical staff would be able to apply their knowledge in scenarios that accurately reflected real-world clinical situations.

In the transportation industry, e-learning has been used to ensure compliance with mandatory training regulations. Pilots-in-training can now log onto the Internet from a desktop in the training centre and go through the same exercises they would have gone through in a real cockpit. The simulation, which graphically depicts parts of the cockpit on a computer screen, allows the pilots to play online with the same controls and face the same situations they would normally have to deal with in the actual aircraft.

Other industries have also made effective use of e-learning. The Independent Grocers Association, through the IGA Institute, offers e-learning opportunities resulting in certification for three entry-level grocery store positions: stocker, courtesy clerk, and cashier. Rogers AT&T Wireless is currently in the process of developing new modules for the Interactive Training Tree, an online tool provided by Redwood eLearning Systems. Rogers develops custom modules to be used with Redwood's software, which offers an online role-playing experience for 12 000 sales representatives across Canada.[38]

1. What are the advantages of e-learning that are inherent in the examples discussed?
2. Do you feel that this type of training would be beneficial to everyone? Why or why not?

Even in information technology, where one would think that e-learning would be popular, it is not effective. Despite well-designed online courses with hands-on exercises, text-based peer interaction, and expert mentoring through e-mail discussions and telephone calls, e-learning is just not motivating voluntary, self-paced IT professionals to move beyond a few hours of training.[39] Research suggests that online courses are just as effective in delivering simple concepts such as basic economic ideas, but classroom instruction is more effective at delivering complex concepts such as advanced economic theories.[40] Further, if courses are optional or have little impact, low completion rates appear more likely. Also, in some situations, getting the necessary material might not require finishing the class. Finally, adults generally have positive attitudes about technology-based classes, but frustration and technology-related problems can change those attitudes.[41]

The solution seems to be "blended learning" programs that combine short, fast-paced, interactive computer-based lessons and teleconferencing with traditional classroom instruction and simulation. Deciding which training is best handled by which medium is important too.

Developing E-learning Rather than being adopted just for its efficiency, e-learning should meet strategic training needs. Certain criteria to consider before adopting e-learning include the following:

- Sufficient top management support and funding are committed to developing and implementing e-learning.
- Managers and HR professionals must be "retrained" to accept the idea that training is being decentralized and individualized.
- Current training methods (compared with e-learning) are not adequately meeting organizational training needs.
- Potential learners are adequately computer literate and have ready access to computers and the Internet.
- Trainees attending pre-scheduled training programs are geographically separated, and travel time and costs are concerns.
- Sufficient numbers of trainees exist, and many trainees are self-motivated enough to direct their own learning.

Taking existing training materials, putting them on the Internet, and cutting the training budget is not the way to success in e-learning. An important question is: Can this material be learned just as well online as through conventional methods? To create a traditional eight-hour course for use in the classroom requires about 25 percent of the time required to create the same course for use online. Savings come from reducing learner costs (travel, time, hotel, etc.) and spreading the cost of developing the e-course over many trainees. Making e-learning pay often may require ensuring that many people participate as learners.[42]

Some people (especially those with reading problems) do not learn as well online. Companies have found that making some kind of online "lab" where employees can go to get away from their desks to study works best. Simulations, including those incorporating virtual classrooms, and marketing the training inside the company also increase the success of e-learning.[43]

Advantages and Disadvantages of E-learning The rapid growth of e-learning makes the Internet or an intranet a viable means for delivering training content. E-learning has both advantages and disadvantages that must be considered. In addition to being concerned about employee access to e-learning and their desire to use it, some employers worry that trainees will use e-learning to complete courses quickly but will not retain and use much of their learning.

In sum, e-learning is the latest development in the evolution of training delivery. Some of the biggest obstacles to using it will continue to be keeping up with the rapid change in technological innovation, knowing when and how much to invest, and designing e-courses appropriately. Undoubtedly, e-learning will have a major impact on HR and training, but there are no "ten easy steps" to making e-learning successful. Figure 7-9 presents a listing of e-learning's most commonly cited advantages and disadvantages.

Training Approaches

Whether training is delivered internally, externally, or through e-learning, appropriate training approaches must be chosen. The following overview classifies common training approaches into several major groups. Some are used more for job-based training, while others are used more for development.

Cooperative Training Cooperative training approaches mix classroom training and on-the-job experiences. This training can take several forms. One form, generally referred to as *school-to-work transition,* helps individuals move into jobs while still in school or upon completion of formal schooling.[44] Such efforts may be arranged with high schools, community colleges, universities, or with specialized training courses such as hairdressing or massage therapy.

A form of cooperative training called *internship* usually combines job training with classroom instruction from schools, colleges, and universities. Internships benefit both employers and interns. Interns get "real-world" exposure, a line on their résumés, and a chance to closely examine a possible employer. Employers get a cost-effective source of labour and a chance to see an intern at work before making a final hiring decision.

Another form of cooperative training used by employers, trade unions, and government agencies is *apprentice training.* An apprenticeship program provides an employee with on-the-job experience under the guidance of a skilled and certified worker. Apprenticeships train people for jobs in skilled crafts, such as carpentry,

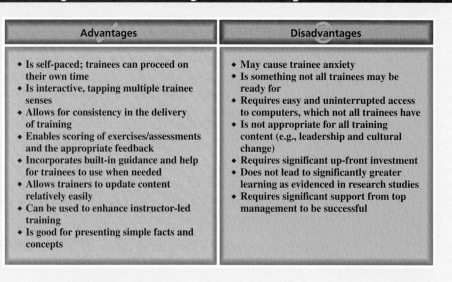

Figure 7-9 Advantages and Disadvantages of E-learning

Advantages	Disadvantages
• Is self-paced; trainees can proceed on their own time • Is interactive, tapping multiple trainee senses • Allows for consistency in the delivery of training • Enables scoring of exercises/assessments and the appropriate feedback • Incorporates built-in guidance and help for trainees to use when needed • Allows trainers to update content relatively easily • Can be used to enhance instructor-led training • Is good for presenting simple facts and concepts	• May cause trainee anxiety • Is something not all trainees may be ready for • Requires easy and uninterrupted access to computers, which not all trainees have • Is not appropriate for all training content (e.g., leadership and cultural change) • Requires significant up-front investment • Does not lead to significantly greater learning as evidenced in research studies • Requires significant support from top management to be successful

Source: Developed by Lisa A. Burke and Robert L. Mathis.

An apprenticeship program provides an employee on-the-job experience under the guidance of a skilled and certified worker.

Source: Marten Czamanske/ShutterStock

plumbing, photoengraving, typesetting, and welding. Apprenticeships usually last from two to five years depending on the occupation. During this time, the apprentice usually receives lower wages than the certified individual.

Instructor-Led Classroom and Conference Training Instructor-led training is still the most prevalent approach to training. Employer-conducted short courses, lectures, and meetings usually consist of classroom training, whereas numerous employee development courses offered by professional organizations, trade associations, and educational institutions are examples of conference training. A particularly important aspect of classroom training is the need to recognize that adults in a classroom setting have different expectations and learning styles from those of younger students. A number of large firms have established their own "universities" to offer classroom and other training as part of curricula for employees. Because these corporate universities generally offer both training and development courses, they are discussed in Chapter 8.

The Ellis Charts
The Ellis Charts provide a comparative overview of apprentice training programs across Canada. They are produced by Human Resources and Skills Development Canada (HRSDC) in partnership with the Canadian Council of Directors of Apprenticeship (CCDA).
www.ellischart.ca

Distance Training/Learning A growing number of college and university classes use some form of Internet-based course support. Blackboard and WebCT are two popular support packages that thousands of college and university professors use to make their lecture content available to students. These packages enable virtual chat and electronic file exchange among course participants, and also enhance instructor/student contact. Many large employers, as well as colleges and universities, use interactive two-way television to present classes. The medium allows an instructor in one place to see and respond to a "class" in any number of other locations. With a fully configured system, employees can take courses from anywhere in the world.

Simulations and Training The explosive growth in information technology in the past few years has revolutionized the way all individuals work, including how they are trained. Today, computer-based training involves a wide array of multimedia technologies—including sound, motion (video and animation), graphics, and hypertext—to tap multiple learner senses. Video streaming allows video clips of training materials to be stored on a firm's network server. Employees can then access the material using the firm's intranet.

Computer-supported simulations within organizational training can replicate the psychological and behavioural requirements of a task, often in addition to providing some amount of physical resemblance to the trainee's work environment. From highly complicated systems that replicate difficult landing scenarios for pilots, to programs that help medical trainees learn to sew sutures, simulations allow for safe training when the risks associated with failure are high. Virtual reality is also used to create an artificial environment for trainees so that they can participate in the training. For example, virtual reality is used in some military operations training and in the robotic manufacturing of electronic equipment.[45]

Blackboard
Blackboard is a website that offers a complete set of software products and services for e-education development.
www.blackboard.com

The new technologies incorporated into training delivery also affect the design, administration, and support of training. Some companies have invested in electronic registration and recordkeeping systems that allow trainers to register participants, record exam results, and monitor learning progress.

Generally, technology is moving from centre stage to becoming embedded in the learning and training processes. As learning and work merge even closer in the future, technology is likely to integrate seamlessly into the work environment of more employees. This integration will allow employees to spend less time in the future learning how to use technology, and more time on learning the desired content.

Training Evaluation

6 Evaluation of training compares the post-training results to the pre-training objectives of managers, trainers, and trainees. Too often, training is conducted with little thought of measuring and evaluating it later to see how well it worked. Because training is both time-consuming and costly, it should be evaluated.[46]

Levels of Evaluation

It is best to consider how training is to be evaluated before it begins. Donald L. Kirkpatrick identified four levels at which training can be evaluated. As Figure 7-10 shows, the evaluation of training becomes successively more difficult as it moves from measuring reaction to measuring learning to measuring behaviour and then to measuring results. But the training that affects behaviour and results versus reaction and learning provides greater value.[47]

Reaction Organizations evaluate the reaction levels of trainees by conducting interviews with or administering questionnaires to the trainees. Assume that 30 managers

Figure 7-10 *Levels of Training Evaluation*

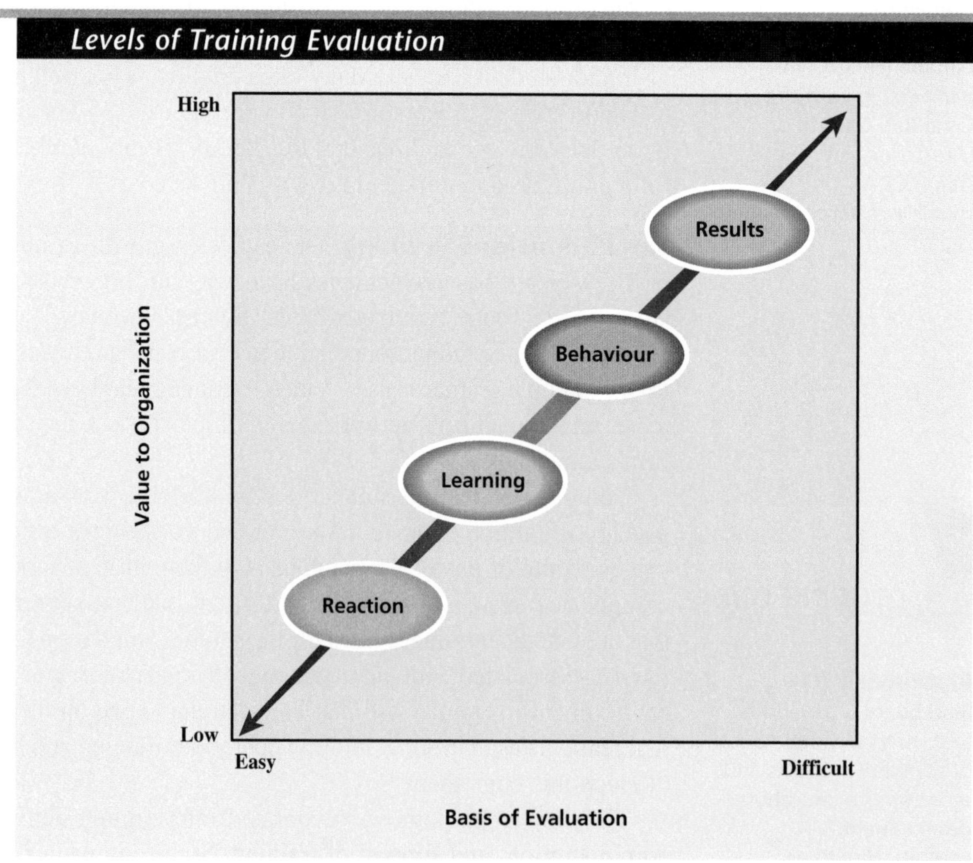

attend a two-day workshop on effective interviewing skills. A reaction-level measure could be gathered by having the managers complete a survey that asked them to rate the value of the training, the style of the instructors, and the usefulness of the training to them. If the survey were administered immediately after the workshop, it might measure only how much the managers liked the training rather than how the training benefited them or how it affected the way they conduct interviews.

Learning Learning levels can be evaluated by measuring how well trainees have learned facts, ideas, concepts, theories, and attitudes. Tests on the training material are commonly used for evaluating learning, and they can be given both before and after training to provide scores that can be compared. If test scores indicate learning problems, then instructors get feedback and courses can be redesigned so that the content can be delivered more effectively. Of course, learning enough to pass a test does not guarantee that trainees will remember the training content months later or will change job behaviours.[48]

Behaviour Evaluating training at the behavioural level means: (1) measuring the effect of training on job performance through interviews of trainees and their co-workers, and (2) observing job performance. For instance, the managers who participated in the interviewing workshop might be observed conducting actual interviews of applicants for jobs in their departments. If the managers asked questions as they had been trained and used appropriate follow-up questions, then behavioural indicators of the interviewing training exist. Behaviours are more difficult to measure than are reaction and learning. Even if behaviours do change after training, the results that management desires may not be obtained.

Results Employers evaluate results by measuring the effect of training on the achievement of organizational objectives. Because results such as productivity, turnover, quality, time, sales, and costs are relatively concrete, this type of evaluation can be done by comparing records before and after training. For the managers who attended the interviewing training, evaluators could gather records of the number of individuals hired compared with the number of employment offers made before and after the training.[49]

The difficulty with measuring results is pinpointing whether changes were actually the result of training or of other major factors. For example, managers who completed the interviewing training program can be measured on employee turnover before and after the training. But turnover also depends on the current economic situation, the demand for products, and many other variables.

Training Evaluation Designs

With or without benchmarking data, internal evaluations of training programs can be designed in a number of ways. The rigour of the three designs discussed next increases with each level.

Post-Measure The most obvious way to evaluate training effectiveness is to determine after the training whether the individuals can perform the way management wants them to perform. Assume that a customer service manager has 20 representatives who need to improve their data-entry speeds. After a one-day training session, they take a test to measure their speeds. If the representatives can all type the required speed after training, was the training beneficial? It is difficult to say; perhaps most of them could have done as well before training. Tests after training do not always clearly indicate whether a performance is a result of the training or could have been achieved without the training.

Pre-/Post-Measure By designing the evaluation differently, the issue of pre-test skill levels can be considered. If the manager had measured the data-entry speed before and after training, she could have known whether the training made any difference. However, a question would have remained: Was any increase in speed a response to the training, or did these employees simply work faster because they knew they were being tested? People often perform better when they know their efforts are being evaluated.

Pre-/Post-Measure with a Control Group Another evaluation design can address this problem. In addition to testing the 20 representatives who will be trained, the manager can test another group of representatives who will not be trained, to see if they do as well as those who are to be trained. This second group is called a control group. If the trained representatives work significantly faster after training than those who were not trained, the manager can then be reasonably sure that the training was effective.

Training Evaluation Metrics

As mentioned earlier, training is expensive, and therefore it is one HR function that requires measurement and monitoring. Cost-benefit analysis and ROI analysis are commonly used to do so, as are various benchmarking approaches.

Cost-benefit analysis Comparison of costs and benefits associated with training.

Cost-Benefit Analysis Training results can be examined through **cost-benefit analysis,** which is comparison of costs and benefits associated with training. Figure 7-11 shows some costs and benefits that may result from training. Even though some benefits (such as attitude changes) are hard to quantify, comparison of costs and benefits associated with training remains a way to determine whether or not training is cost-effective. For example, one firm evaluated a traditional safety training program and found that the program did not lead to a reduction in accidents. Therefore, the safety training was redesigned, and better safety practices resulted. However, measurement of both the costs and the benefits listed in Figure 7-11 may be difficult.

LOGGING ON...

Scorecard for Skills
This website is dedicated to measuring the effectiveness of workplace programs. Developed by the Conference Board of Canada, the site includes a tool to build your own balanced scorecard.
www.scorecardforskills.com

Return on Investment (ROI) Analysis In organizations, training is often expected to produce a return on investment (ROI). Still, in too many circumstances, training is justified because someone liked it, rather than on the basis of resource accountability. Firms that measure ROI on training include GE, Deloitte, LensCrafters, Sears, and Apple Computer.[50]

Benchmarking In addition to evaluating training internally, some organizations use benchmark measures to compare it with training done in other organizations. To do benchmarking, HR professionals gather data on training in their organization and compare them with data on training at other organizations in the same industry and of a similar size. Comparison data are available through the Canadian Society for

Figure 7-11 *Some Typical Costs and Benefits of Training*

Typical Costs	Typical Benefits
• Trainer's salary and time	• Increase in production
• Trainee's salaries and time	• Reduction in errors and accidents
• Materials for training	• Reduction in turnover
• Expenses for trainer and trainees	• Less supervision necessary
• Cost of facilities and equipment	• Ability to use new capabilities
• Lost productivity (opportunity cost)	• Attitude changes

Training and Development and its Benchmarking Service. This service has training-related data from more than 1000 participating employers who complete detailed questionnaires annually. Training also can be benchmarked against data from the Saratoga Institute or the Benchmarking Network.

Training for Global Assignments

7 The cultural sensitivity training that expatriates and their families receive before departure significantly affects the success of an overseas assignment. Unfortunately, various surveys have found that only 50–60 percent of global employers provide formal training programs for expatriates and their families. When such programs are offered, most expatriates participate in them, and the programs usually produce a positive effect on cross-cultural adjustment.[51]

The most common topics covered in pre-departure cultural sensitivity training are: daily living conditions, cultural customs, business issues, country history, climate, and transportation and communication systems. Individuals selected to work outside their home countries need answers to many specific questions about their host countries.[52] Training in various areas helps expatriates and their families adjust to and deal with host-country counterparts. Training in customs and practices can be especially valuable to individuals who will not live outside the home country but will travel to other countries on business.

A related issue is the promotion and transfer of foreign citizens to positions in Canada. As more global organizations start or expand Canadian operations, more cross-cultural training will be necessary for international employees relocated to Canada. For example, many Japanese firms operating in Canada conduct training programs to prepare Japanese for the food, customs, labour and HR practices, and other facets of working and living in Canada. Family issues continue to be a pressing matter for the success or failure of foreign assignments. One consultant tells the story of the wife of a French company executive who was "abandoned" in the Toronto-area, without access to any support. She couldn't speak a word of English and left saying it was the worse two years of her life. Helping Canadian workers accept a foreign boss is another concern. These issues all underscore the importance of training and development for international adjustment.[53]

Intercultural Competence Training

Growing numbers of global employers are providing intercultural competence training for their global employees. Intercultural competence incorporates a wide range of human social skills and personality characteristics. As noted in Figure 7-12, three components of intercultural competence require attention when training expatriates for global assignments. The key components are:

- *Cognitive:* What does the person know about other cultures?
- *Emotional:* How does the person view other cultures, and how sensitive is the person to cultural customs and issues?
- *Behavioural:* How does the person act in intercultural situations?

Increasingly, global employers are using cultural sensitivity training methods that allow individuals to behave in international situations and then receive feedback. One popular method is the Culture Assimilator. Used worldwide, especially by European-based firms, the Culture Assimilator is a programmed training and learning method consisting of short case studies and critical incidents. The case studies describe intercultural interactions and potential misunderstandings involving expatriates and host-country nationals.

Figure 7-12 *Intercultural Competence Training*

Component	Possible Training
Cognitive	◆ Culture-specific training (traditions, history, cultural customs, etc.) ◆ Language course
Emotional	◆ *Uneasiness:* Social skills training focusing on new/unclear and intercultural situations ◆ *Prejudices:* Coaching may be clarifying ◆ *Sensitivity:* Communication skills course (active listening, verbal/nonverbal cues, empathy)
Behavioural	◆ Culture assimilator ◆ International projects ◆ Social skills training focusing on intercultural situations

Source: Developed by Andrea Graf, Ph.D., Technical University of Braunschweig, Germany, and Robert L. Mathis, Ph.D., SPHR.

SUMMARY

1 To ensure the smooth transition of new employees and an exposure to an organization's culture, orientation training should be incorporated. Orientation requires cooperation between individuals in the HR department and operating managers and supervisors. Orientation should be viewed as a long-term investment in an employee. There are many advantages to orientation such as, but not limited to, reducing anxiety, leading to better job performance and higher rates of retention. Effective orientation provides organization and job information, accelerates socialization and integration of new employees to the organization, establishes favourable employee impressions and ensures employee performance and productivity begin more quickly. Socialization enhances "person/organization fit." Some orientation programs may be very basic, while others may be more elaborate and last over longer periods of time. The new employee will meet face-to-face with HR and managers, but the use of technology may also be used to introduce the new employee to the history, structure, products and services, mission, and other important information about the organization. Orientation should be planned with appropriate checklists and ample coordination.

2 Training is the process that provides people with the necessary KSAs they need to do their jobs. Training affects factors such as organizational competitiveness, knowledge management, revenue, and performance. Performance consulting compares desired and actual results in order to identify needed training and non-training actions. A strategic approach to training links organizational strategies and HR planning to various training efforts. The training process consists of four phases: assessment, design, delivery, and evaluation.

3 Training needs can be assessed using organizational, job/task, and individual analyses. Organizational analyses consider the internal and external forces that can impact on training. Job/task analyses involves an understanding of the knowledge, skills, and abilities of employees. At the individual analysis stage, information is gathered on the training specific individuals may require either based on performance issues, or new skills that may be required. Once needs analyses are finalized, then training objectives can be set to help the organization meet those needs.

4 Training design must consider learner readiness, learning styles, learning transfer, training categories, and legal issues. Learner readiness is concerned with an individual's ability or motivation to learn and their self-efficacy about learning. Various employee groups have different learning styles which need to be understood. Behaviour modelling

is the most elementary way in which people learn. Trainers should design training for the highest possible transfer from the class to the job. Orientation as a kind of training is designed to help new employees learn about their jobs.

5 Training can be delivered internally through classes, informally, and on the job. External training may be delivered by outside sources such as government training programs. E-learning is training conducted using the Internet or an intranet, and its development must consider both its advantages and its disadvantages. Common training approaches include cooperative training, classroom and conference training, and distance training/learning. Various organizations are taking advantage of training that uses technology such as multimedia, video streaming, simulation, and virtual reality.

6 Training can be evaluated at four levels: reaction, learning, behaviour, and results. Training evaluation metrics may include cost-benefit analysis, return-on-investment analysis, and benchmarking. A pre-/post-measure with a control group is the most rigorous design for training evaluation; other, less rigorous designs can be used as well.

7 Pre-departure orientation significantly affects the success of international assignments, but it is not universally offered. Intercultural competence training helps prepare employees to respond more appropriately to situations encountered during global assignments.

KEY TERMS

Active practice, p. 264
Behaviour modelling, p. 265
Cost-benefit analysis, p. 276
Cross training, p. 266
E-learning, p. 270
Immediate confirmation, p. 265
Informal training, p. 267
Knowledge management, p. 255
Massed practice, p. 264
Orientation, p. 250
Performance consulting, p. 256
Reinforcement, p. 265
Self-efficacy, p. 263
Spaced practice, p. 264
Training, p. 252

REVIEW AND APPLICATION QUESTIONS

1 What are five advantages of conducting new employee orientation training?

2 What steps can HR professionals take to overcome the organizational tendency to cut training when money is tight?

3 Assume that you want to identify training needs for a group of sales employees in a luxury-oriented jewellery store. What would you do?

4 Working in small groups, discuss the different learning styles that individuals might possess. What are the learning styles of the individuals in your group? Based on your understanding of each other's learning styles, what does that mean to each of you with regards to how you learn in the classroom? What will it mean in the workplace?

5 Discuss the advantages and disadvantages of on-the-job training.

6 Describe the four levels of training evaluation? What are the inherent problems with each of these levels?

7 You are a Canadian born manager who will be going to work in China on a work assignment for two years. Your spouse and 12-year-old twin daughters are going with you. The assignment is due to commence in six months. What type of training would be required for this assignment?

EXPERIENTIAL EXERCICES

1. Develop a briefing for division managers that shows the advantages and disadvantages of e-learning. Use Web sources, including the following website: www.conferenceboard.ca/education/pdf/e-learning_for_the_workplace.pdf.
2. You and your team work as trainers for J&J Toy Limited. You have been asked to prepare an orientation program for new employees in the manufacturing department. You are to develop a profile for J&J Toy Limited. Some questions to consider are: size of organization, how long in business, locations, type of toys (manufactured or distributed), sales per year, key individuals in your organization, type of benefits offered, union or non-union, what material is to be presented, how the material will be presented, who will conduct the orientation, and all other relevant information that you feel should be considered. Once you have the specifications developed, you are to design an orientation program. The students in your classroom will represent the new manufacturing employees. You are to deliver an orientation program to your new employees. Therefore you must develop relevant materials, along with an agenda of what the new employees can expect in their orientation program. A written report of your orientation program is required. Your presentation will be completed in ten minutes.
3. Finding employees who are in skilled trades is a major concern to Canadian organizations due to the shortage of these workers. Determine what skilled trades can be achieved using an apprenticeship program? What is the process required for these trades to learn their new craft? For example, how does someone become a plumber, an auto mechanic, an electrician, etc.? What is the minimum education required? What amount of time is required on the job, and how much is required in school before achieving their licence? How much do they get paid, and who pays for their wages during their training? Does it differ across the provinces?
4. You have been hired by the newly formed Provincial Services Heating Company to train a group of new recruits in the door-to-door selling of their services. The recruits are young individuals with minimal education. However, the requirements are not that demanding, except that these individuals will be working on commission and the more they can sell the more money the company will earn. As part of the training you are to provide a script for the new recruits to follow when they speak with potential customers. The script goes like this: "Hello, my name is __________ and I represent the Provincial Services Heating Company. We are here to ensure that you are not paying too much for your heating services. I would like to review a copy of your last heating bill so that I can determine if you are getting the best possible deal." (The name of your company sounds official enough that people should respond, even though you have nothing to do with any official government agency.) On review of the bill you can quickly point out the savings your company can offer. Once you have pointed out the savings you are then to present a contract for them to sign with the guaranteed savings over the next three years. The next part of the training will be to engage in role-playing. Upon review of the requirements you start to ponder the ethics of this format. What are the potential problems with this type of training, if any?

LEARNING REVIEW

To check your knowledge of the chapter, review the following. (Answers after the case.)

1 An orientation allows an employee to get a sense of the organization's:
   a. procedures
   b. culture
   c. rules
   d. all of the above

2 The performance consulting approach recognizes that it is important to consider:
   a. existing training methods
   b. the separation of training from development
   c. non-training factors such as compensation
   d. the cost of training programs

3 Once training needs have been identified using appropriate analyses, then training objectives and priorities can be established by a(n):
   a. needs analyses
   b. gap analyses

c. organizational analyses
d. job/task analyses

4 When they are ready to learn, people have the ability to learn, __________, and the belief that they can learn.
a. the right attitude
b. time
c. a desire to learn
d. organizational support

5 Once training has been designed, it is recommended that training be:
a. delivered to the employees identified as needing the training
b. computerized
c. pilot-tested
d. assessed for its cost-benefit to the organization

6 When a college or university asks students to complete an instructor-evaluation survey, it is evaluating training at the __________ level.
a. results
b. learning
c. reaction
d. behaviour

7 One of the more pressing issues for the success or failure of foreign assignments is:
a. cultural customs
b. family issues
c. prejudice of locals
d. human social skills

CASE

CISCO SYSTEMS AND E-LEARNING CENTRE OF EXCELLENCE

Cisco Systems has established itself as a worldwide leader in Internet networking through its deployment of Internet-based business solutions for enterprise organizations, service providers, and small/emerging businesses. In April 2001, Cisco Systems Canada Co. unveiled the first Cisco E-Learning Centre of Excellence in Canada. Pierre-Paul Allard who is the managing director of Cisco Systems Canada describes E-Learning Centre of Excellence as, "a one-stop e-learning facility to help Canada's business leaders recognize the power of Internet-enabled learning and implement solutions to maximize employee productivity, increase competitive advantage and lower costs." The centre which is located in Toronto, will give high-level executive teams the opportunity to participate in two to four-day learning workshops with Cisco e-learning experts.

E-learning gives organizations the tools to stay up-to-date with changes that are occurring in the knowledge-based Internet economy. E-learning can be incorporated into all areas of training including new product information, career development training, and employee orientation. The average Canadian firm invests about 11–25 hours of training per employee per year. The usage of e-learning can result in the elimination of the need for classroom time, reduced cost, and the improvement of real-time access to information.

The first enterprise participant at the Cisco E-Learning Centre of Excellence was the Trillium Health Centre, which is a two-site community hospital that serves patients from the City of Mississauga and southwest Etobicoke. Peter Dickens, vice president of Organizational Development at the Trillium Health Centre, believes that embracing e-learning at Trillium is a necessity: "At Trillium Health Centre, our goal is to be an innovation leader in the health-care industry. Our close association with Cisco Systems allows us to learn from the internationally recognized leader in e-learning—giving us access to the best practices and technological solutions necessary to reach our lofty goals." "With a fast-growing staff of more than 2500 full and part-time employees, and a hectic, 24/7 work environment, traditional educational concepts simply don't work."[54]

Questions

1. What are the advantages that classroom training has over e-learning? Do you believe that classroom training will one day be eliminated?
2. Why do you believe that traditional educational concepts will not work in a fast growing organization? How will e-learning eliminate these emerging problems?

Learning Review Answers: 1. d 2. c 3. b 4. c 5. c 6. c 7. b

CHAPTER

Careers and HR Development

Learning Objectives

After you have read this chapter, you should be able to:

1 Differentiate between organization-centred and individual-centred career planning.

2 Discuss several career issues that organizations and employees face.

3 Discuss the purpose of employee development and list options for development needs analyses.

4 Explain why succession planning has become more important.

5 Identify several management development methods.

HR *Headline*

Developing Leaders Is a Challenge

Developing the talent in a workforce is challenging, but perhaps most demanding of all is developing future leadership talent for the organization. Development is different from training because it is not a one-time event, it is an ongoing process. One consultant suggests a rule of thumb: If an organization is going outside for leaders more than 20 percent of the time, its leadership development efforts are not effective.

Leader development programs are effective when addressing questions such as, What exactly do people need to be successful leaders? And what skill sets and behaviours do they require? Then the issues of succession planning, classroom training, coaching, work experiences, and appropriate pay must be dealt with in turn.

To emphasize the importance of leadership development, some firms base rewards for managers partly on how well the managers develop their employees, particularly those with leadership potential. In some cases, 10 percent to 20 percent of an executive's annual bonus may be based on how well talent under that executive is being developed. Another approach used is to consider the number of leaders an executive has developed and willingly given up to other parts of the organization—a "net talent exporter" approach. Contrast this approach to executives who "hoard" talent in their divisions so that they do not face turnover of their key staff.

Development, especially for leadership, has to be customized for each person so that individual strengths and areas for improvement are identified. The goal is to identify strengths that employees may not realize and also reveal areas where their abilities need to be enhanced. Every employee's development plan and activities will be different because each person has different capabilities. For the development of executives, it even may entail an external coach to assist individuals using a one-on-one process. Regardless of the means used, career development is important to both the organization and the individual, and doing it well is in the best interests of both.[1]

"Nothing is more important than growing your 'A' players and promptly dealing with your 'C' players."

—Richard Brown

Traditionally, career development efforts targeted managerial personnel to help them look beyond their current jobs and to prepare them for a variety of future jobs in the organization. But development for all employees, not just managers, is necessary for organizations to have the needed **human resource capabilities** for future growth and change. Human resource capabilities is defined as the reliable access to the required people (quantity) with the skills, abilities, attributes and competencies (quality) that the organization needs to meet its purpose and deliver its outputs, in accordance with its strategic goals.[2]

Human resource capabilities
The human resource capability of an organization consists of reliable access to the required people (quantity) with the skills, abilities, attributes, and competencies (quality) that the organization needs to meet its purpose and deliver its outputs, in accordance with its strategic goals.

Mergers, acquisitions, re-structurings, and layoffs all have influenced the way people and organizations look at careers and development. In the "new career," the individual—not the organization—manages her or his own development. Such self-development consists of personal educational experiences, training, organizational experiences, projects, and even changes in occupational fields.[3] Under this system, the individual defines career success, and the result may or may not coincide with the organizational view of success.

Organizations promote this "self-reliance" in career development by telling employees they should focus on creating employability for themselves in the uncertain future. However, employability must also be defined in such a way that it provides value for the employing organization. It is a dilemma of sorts that if employers give employees unrestricted access to development opportunities, employers may not be able to retain talent in the highly competitive labour markets of today.

Careers and Career Planning

Career
Series of work-related positions a person occupies throughout life.

1 A **career** is the series of work-related positions a person occupies throughout life. People pursue careers to satisfy deeply individual needs. At one time, identifying with one employer seemed to fulfill many of those needs. Now, individuals and organizations view careers in distinctly different ways.

Indeed, in a few industries, changing jobs and companies every year or two is becoming more the norm than the exception. Canadian workers in high-demand fields often dictate their own circumstances to some extent. For instance, the average 30 to 35-year-old in North America typically has already worked for up to seven different firms. However, workers in other fields change jobs infrequently. Physicians, teachers, economists, electricians, and others do not change jobs as frequently. Valuable employees, deluged with job offers, switch jobs at a rate higher than in the past. Further, some individuals exhibit more loyalty to their careers than to an employer. Though organizations may use employment agreements containing non-compete clauses to put some restrictions on job hoppers, those clauses must be enforced in court, taking time and organizational resources. All these factors and more are changing how careers are defined and viewed.

Evolution of Careers

The old model of a career in which a person worked his or her way up the ladder in one organization is becoming rarer because smaller companies provide less room to move up. Also, various signs indicate that the patterns of individuals' work lives are changing in many areas: more freelancing, more working at home, more frequent job changes, more job opportunities but less security. Rather than letting jobs define their lives, more people set goals for the type of lives they want and then use jobs to meet those goals. However, for dual-career couples and working women, balancing work demands with personal and family responsibilities is a growing challenge.

For employers, career issues have changed too. The best people will not go to workplaces viewed as undesirable, because they do not have to do so. Employers must focus on retaining and developing talented workers by providing coaching, mentoring, and appropriate assignments.

Global Evolution of Careers Insecurity caused by layoffs and downsizings marks a trend that stands in sharp contrast to the trend toward personal control over career goals. A greater number of older male workers express fear of losing their jobs. This situation is not just a North American phenomenon. Many Japanese workers who have typically worked for one Japanese company their entire lives are experiencing similar job insecurity. In Europe, efforts to keep the traditional career system of job security are becoming more costly. Employers are pressuring European governments to dismantle outmoded labour rules that make eliminating employees difficult, while workers are pressuring the same governments to alleviate high unemployment rates. As a result, careers for many individuals contain both more flexibility and more insecurity.

Career Planning Perspectives

Careers are different and still evolving, and their evolution puts a premium on career development by both the employers and the employees. Employers that fail to help employees focus their careers in areas that benefit the organization may face shortages of employees who believe themselves to be ready to assume new jobs and responsibilities. Employees who fail to achieve psychological success, or a feeling of pride and accomplishment, in their careers may change careers, look outside work for "life success," or simply be unhappy. Effective career planning considers both organization-centred and individual-centred perspectives. Figure 8-1 summarizes the perspectives and interaction between the organizational and individual approaches to career planning.

Organization-centred career planning
Career planning that focuses on identifying career paths that provide for the logical progression of people between jobs in an organization.

Organization-Centred Career Planning

Organization-centred career planning focuses on identifying career paths that provide for the logical progression of people between jobs in an organization. Individuals follow these paths as they advance in organizational units. For example, a person might enter the sales department as a sales representative, then be promoted to account director, to sales manager, and finally to vice president of sales.

Figure 8-1 *Organizational and Individual Career Planning Perspectives*

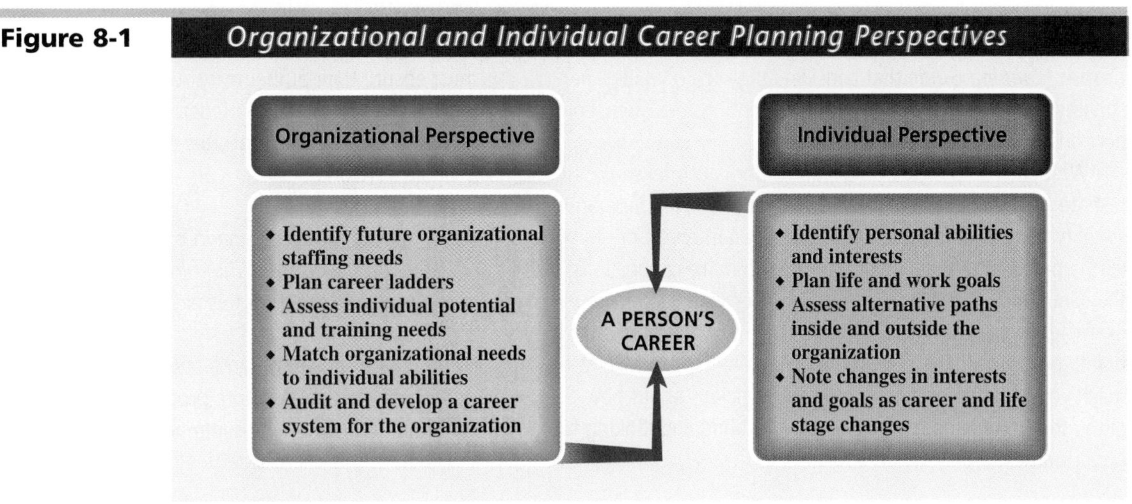

Organizational Perspective
Individual Perspective
• Identify future organizational staffing needs
• Plan career ladders
• Assess individual potential and training needs
• Match organizational needs to individual abilities
• Audit and develop a career system for the organization
A PERSON'S CAREER
• Identify personal abilities and interests
• Plan life and work goals
• Assess alternative paths inside and outside the organization
• Note changes in interests and goals as career and life stage changes

Career Planner
This website can assist individuals with career planning.
www.careerplanner.com

Top management is responsible for developing career planning programs. A good program identifies career paths and includes performance appraisal, development, opportunities for transfer and promotion, and some planning for succession. To communicate with employees about opportunities and to help with planning, employers frequently use career workshops, a career "centre" or newsletter, and career counselling. Individual managers must frequently play the role of coach and counsellor in their direct contact with individual employees and within an HR-designed career management system.

For example, at one firm, major changes in the organization led to significant career dislocations. Previous career paths were closed, and management emphasized that employees had to take greater responsibility for their own careers. Into this potential chaos came managers who had been trained as "career coaches" for their employees. The entire process has changed from one in which employees "received" career planning to one in which they developed their own careers—roles for both managers and employees were changed.

Yes-Canada B.C.
This website can assist individuals with career planning.
www.careerpathsonline.com/contents.cfm

The systems an employer uses to manage careers in the organization should be planned and managed in an integrated fashion to guide managers in developing employees' careers.[4] One such system is the career path, or "map," which is created and shared with the individual employee. Yes-Canada B.C. is a non-profit organization dedicated to increasing access to career and labour market information and assisting youth with their transition into the workforce or further education and training. It caters to individuals in B.C. and the Yukon, however access is available to anyone. The site provides numerous online tests to help an individual understand themselves, and their particular career choices. Technology Transforming HR illustrates the value of such sites, with the *10 Step Career Planning Guide* that can be found at Yes-Canada B.C.

Technology Transforming HR

Web-Based Career Planning Tools

Yes-Canada B.C. is a site that offers youth access to the *10 Step Career Planning Guide* that considers the area of values, personality, learning styles, skills, interests, options, research, connections, goals, and action.

With each step of the guide, participants can take specific tests to learn more about themselves. For example, there are personality tests to determine if a person is an introvert or an extrovert, a personal interest inventory, how to make connections in the community, as well as setting goals for your career. For example, if you stated that your short-term goal was to start a band, the site would give you the five main steps to take to reach your goal, from talking to local musicians about how they did it, to letting people know about your band and looking for opportunities to play for an audience.

Individuals can access numerous online sites, although they must ensure their authenticity. A site such as Yes-Canada B.C., which is sponsored by the federal government, and that has links to various other provincial sites to help youth looking for work, is a viable network.[5]

1. Connect with Yes-Canada B.C. and work your way through the *10 Step Career Planning Guide*. What did you find out about yourself from this exercise that you did not already know?
2. Prepare short-term and long-term career goals. Ensure you complete item 1 before proceeding to this step. You are to hand in a one-page summary to your instructor on completion of this exercise.

Career paths Represent employees' movements through opportunities over time.

Career Paths Employees need to know their strengths and weakness, and they often discover those with some company-sponsored assessments. Then, career paths to develop the weak areas and finetune the strengths are developed. **Career paths** represent employees' movements through opportunities over time. While most career paths are thought of as leading upward, good opportunities also exist in cross-functional or horizontal directions.[6]

An innovative use of career paths called "skill supply chains" allows employees to move to other companies as they succeed where they are. For example, in Philadelphia, more than 200 employers (banks, fast-food restaurants, supermarkets, retailers, hotels, etc.) participate in a skill supply chain in the form of a "tiered employment" system aimed at underemployed entry-level workers. People enter the paths at tier 1 after receiving four weeks of customer service training, and find themselves flipping burgers or cleaning hotel rooms. They have to be successful for six months, with counsellors checking attendance and performance. If they do well, they can apply for tier 2 positions either at their current employers or at another company in the system. After a year in tier 2, successful employees can apply for tier 3 jobs, which include entry-level store manager jobs. Viewing each job not as a dead end but as a rung on a ladder makes people stay and perform well. This kind of career path system is based on the same drivers as those that operate in a private employer's career path system.[7] In Canada various industries such as transportation and aerospace are seeking innovative ways to keep skilled workers in their own industry.

Organizational retrenchment and downsizing have changed career plans for many people. More and more individuals have had to face "career transitions"—in other words, they have had to find new jobs. These transitions have identified the importance of individual-centred career planning.

Individual-Centred Career Planning

Individual-centred career planning Career planning focusing on an individual's career rather than on organizational needs.

Individual-centred career planning focuses on an individual's career rather than on organizational needs. It is done by the employees themselves when they analyze their individual goals and capabilities. Such efforts might consider situations both inside and outside the organization that could expand a person's career.[8] Although individuals are the only ones who can know for certain what they consider a successful career, even they are not always able to figure that out. For example, few university or college students enrolled in business programs know exactly what they want to do upon graduation; many can eliminate some types of jobs but might be interested in any of several others. For individuals to manage their own careers, three activities must happen:

- *Self-assessment:* Individuals need to think about what interests them, what they do not like, what they do well, and their strengths and weaknesses. Career advisers use a number of tools to help people understand themselves. Common professional tests include the Strong Interest Inventory to determine preferences among vocational occupations, and the Allport-Vernon-Lindzey Study of Values to identify a person's dominant values. The Myers-Brigg Type Indicator (MBTI) is another tool used in career counselling. The Strong Interest Inventory and the MBTI can also be combined to provide more far-reaching results to aid in understanding yourself, and to explore career options,
- *Feedback on reality:* Employees need feedback on how well they are doing, how bosses see their capabilities, and where they fit in organizational plans for the future. One source of this information is through performance appraisal feedback.[9]

- *Setting of career goals:* Deciding on a desired path, setting some timetables, and writing down these items all set the stage for a person to pursue the career of choice. These career goals are supported by short-term plans for the individual to get the experience or training necessary to move toward the goals.

Because individual-centred career planning focuses on the individual, it may change depending on shifts in the individual's interests, abilities, circumstances, and family issues. A career based on such planning is referred to as "protean" because it is changeable. A successful "protean" career does not simply include *what* a person knows (although that knowledge keeps changing) but also includes *who* that person knows (through relationships and networking) and an understanding, based on experience, as to *why* activities are done the way they are done.[10] For individuals today, careers are rarely lived out in a single organizational setting. Instead, careers are "boundaryless" in that they might span several companies, industries, jobs, and projects.

How People Choose Careers Four general individual characteristics affect how people make career choices. They are as follows:

- *Interests:* People tend to pursue careers that they believe match their interests. But over time, interests change for many people, and career decisions eventually are made based on special skills, abilities, and career paths that are realistic for them.
- *Self-image:* A career is an extension of a person's self-image, as well as a moulder of it. People follow careers they can "see" themselves in and avoid those that do not fit with their perceptions of their talents, motives, and values.
- *Personality:* An employee's personality includes her or his personal orientation (for example, inclination to be realistic, enterprising, or artistic) and personal needs (including affiliation, power, and achievement needs). Individuals with certain personality types gravitate to different clusters of occupations.
- *Social backgrounds:* Socioeconomic status and the educational levels and occupations of a person's parents are included in that person's social background. Children of a physician or a welder know from a parent what that job is like and may either seek or reject it based on how they view the parent's job.

People often choose careers based on interests or personality and choose organizations to work for that fit with their own personal characteristics, interests, and needs.

Source: © Royalty-Free/Corbis

Less is known about how and why people choose specific organizations than about why they choose specific careers. One obvious factor is timing—the availability of a job when the person is looking for work. The amount of information available about alternatives is an important factor as well. Beyond these issues, people seem to pick an organization on the basis of a "fit" between the climate of the organization as they view it and their own personal characteristics, interests, and needs.

General Career Progression

The typical career of many individuals today probably includes different positions, transitions, and organizations—more so than in the past, when employees were less mobile and organizations were more stable as long-term employers. Therefore, it is useful to think about general patterns in people's lives and the effects on their careers.

Many theorists in adult development describe the first half of life as the young adult's quest for competence and for a way to make a mark in the world. According to this view, a person attains happiness during this time primarily through achievement and the acquisition of capabilities. The second half of life is different. Once the adult starts to measure time from the expected end of life rather than from the beginning the need for competence and acquisition changes to the need for integrity, values, and well-being. For many people, internal values take precedence over external scorecards or accomplishments such as wealth and job title status. In addition, mature adults already possess certain skills, so their focus may shift to interests other than skills acquisition. Career-ending concerns, such as life after retirement, reflect additional shifts. Figure 8-2 shows a model identifying general career and life periods.

Contained within this life pattern is the idea that careers and lives are not predictably linear but cyclical. Individuals experience periods of high stability, followed by transition periods of less stability, and by inevitable discoveries, disappointments, and triumphs. These cycles of structure and transition occur throughout individuals' lives and careers. This cyclical view may be an especially useful perspective for individuals affected by downsizing or early career plateaus in large organizations. Such a perspective argues for the importance of flexibility in an individual's career. It also emphasizes the importance of individuals' continuing to acquire more and diverse knowledge, skills, and abilities.

Career Transitions and HR

Three career transitions are of special interests to HR: organizational entry and socialization, transfers and promotions, and job loss. Starting as a new employee can be overwhelming. "Entry shock" is especially difficult for younger new hires who find the work world very different from school. Entry shock includes the following concerns:

- *Supervisors:* The boss/employee relationship is different from the student/teacher relationship.
- *Feedback:* In school, feedback is frequent and measurable, although it is not that way in most jobs.

Figure 8-2 *General Career Periods*

	CAREER STAGE			
Characteristics	**Early Career**	**Mid-Career**	**Late Career**	**Career End**
Age group	**+/− 20 years**	**30–40 years**	**+/− 50 years**	**60–70 years**
Needs	**Identifying interests, exploring several jobs**	**Advancing in career; lifestyle may limit options, growth, opportunities**	**Updating skills; individual is settled in; individual is a leader whose opinions are valued**	**Planning for retirement, examining non-work interests**
Concerns	**External rewards, acquiring more capabilities**	**Values, contribution, integrity, well-being**	**Mentoring, disengaging, organizational continuance**	**Retirement, part-time employment**

- *Time:* School has short (quarter/semester) time cycles, whereas time horizons are longer at work.
- *The work:* Problems are more tightly defined at school; at work, the logistical and political aspects of solving problems are less certain.

Job loss has been most associated with downsizing, mergers, and acquisitions. Losing a job is a stressful event in one's career, frequently causing depression, anxiety, and nervousness. The financial implications and the effects on family can be extreme as well. Yet the potential for job loss continues to increase and should be considered in career decision making.[11]

Transfers and promotions offer opportunities for employees to develop. However, unlike new hires, employees who have moved to new positions are often expected to perform well immediately, though that may not be realistic. International transfers cause even more difficulties than in-country transfers for many.

Being Abroad
This website, which is geared toward expatriate workers, contains useful information about working abroad and repatriation.
www.beingabroad.com

Global Career Development

Many expatriates experience anxiety about their continued career progression. Therefore, the international experiences of expatriates must offer benefits both to the employer and to the expatriate's career as well.[12] Firms sometimes address this issue by bringing expatriates back to the home country for development programs and interaction with other company managers and professionals. Another useful approach is to establish a mentoring system that matches an expatriate with a corporate executive at the headquarters.[13]

Repatriation
Planning, training, and reassignment of global employees to their home countries.

Repatriation Another global development is **repatriation,** which involves planning, training, and reassignment of global employees to their home countries. For example, after expatriates are brought home, they no longer receive special compensation packages available to them during their assignments, which means that they experience a net decrease in income, even if they receive promotions and pay increases. In addition to dealing with concerns about personal finances, returning expatriates must often re-acclimate to Canadian lifestyles, transportation services, and other cultural circumstances, especially if they have been living in less-developed countries.

Re-acclimatizing remains a substantial problem for the families, as well as for the employee. One Japanese manager who was working in Canada was faced with a difficult dilemma on his return to Japan. His children had been born in Canada, and had attended elementary school in Canada. Upon their return to Japan, the children faced ridicule from the other schoolchildren because their mannerisms were different, and culturally they were Canadian despite their Japanese heritage. The children were teased by other children as not being Japanese. This adds additional stress to families in these situations.

Back in the home organization, repatriated employees must readjust to closer working and reporting relationships with other corporate employees. Often, expatriates have had a greater degree of flexibility, autonomy, and independent decision making than their counterparts in Canada.

Another major concern focuses on the organizational status of expatriates upon return. Many expatriates wonder what jobs they will have, whether their international experiences will be valued, and how they will be accepted back into the organization. Unfortunately, many global employers do a poor job of repatriation.[14] To counter this problem, some companies provide career planning, the mentoring programs mentioned earlier, and even guarantees of employment upon completion of foreign assignments.

Development Issues Global managers are more expensive than home-country managers, and more problematic as well. Must global firms have learned that it is often a mistake to staff foreign operations with only personnel from headquarters, and they quickly hire nationals to work in a country. For this reason, global management development must focus on developing local managers as well as global executives. Development areas typically include: cultural issues, running a business, leading and managing, handling problematic people, personal qualities, self, and career.

Late-Career/Retirement Issues

Whether retirement comes at age 50 or age 70, it can require a major adjustment for many people. Some areas of emotional adjustment faced by many retirees include: self-direction, a need to belong, sources of achievement, personal space, and goals. To help address concerns over these issues, as well as anxieties about finances, some employers offer pre-retirement planning seminars for employees. Such seminars may make retirement less frightening for some and more possible for others.[15]

Canadian companies will face a severe shortage of badly needed skills in the coming decade unless they act now to convince top-performing older employees to delay or phase in their retirement.[16] In Canada only 30 percent of the workforce want to work past 65.[17] Currently the average Canadian retires at 57 in the public sector and 61 in others, while at least 18 percent of seniors won't ever retire because they can't afford to.[18] Obviously, organizations are going to have to offer programs that will appeal to older workers in order to increase the number of older workers in the workplace. Figure 8-3 highlights the proportion of employed workers over the age of 55 in 2002, and their respective industries. Some industries will be harder hit than others with respect to industries with excessive people retiring.

Career development for people toward the ends of their careers may be managed in a number of ways.[19] Phased-in retirement, consulting arrangements, and callback of some retirees as needed all act as means for gradual disengagement between the organization and the individual.

In an attempt to be mindful of the problems that retirement poses for some individuals, organizations are experimenting with phased-in retirement through gradually reduced workweeks and increased vacation time, accompanied by appropriate pay adjustments. These and other pre-retirement and post-retirement programs help individuals transition to a useful retirement and may keep experienced people available to the organization for a longer time.

However, phased-in retirement (which is widely seen as a good situation for all involved) faces a considerable obstacle in current pension law. Under many pension plans employees who are working may not receive pension benefits until they reach the normal retirement age. For example, a 54-year-old employee cannot cut back to 20 hours a week and collect a monthly retirement benefit. A phased-in retirement program allows an employee to work part-time and accrue benefits based on the hours he or she has actually worked, while at the same time collecting a partial pension for days not worked. The problem in Canada is that the Income Tax Act (ITA) prohibits phased-in retirement. Specifically, the ITA does not allow a member of a defined benefit (DB) plan to simultaneously collect and accrue a pension from the same organization. Quebec's pension legislation sidesteps the ITA restrictions and does provide for a type of "delayed" or "phased-in" retirement where plan members who work part-time beyond the normal retirement date can also continue to accrue a pension. In Quebec, plan members who take a phased-in retirement may receive regular lump

Figure 8-3 *Proportion of the Employed Population Aged 55 and Over, by Industry, 2002*

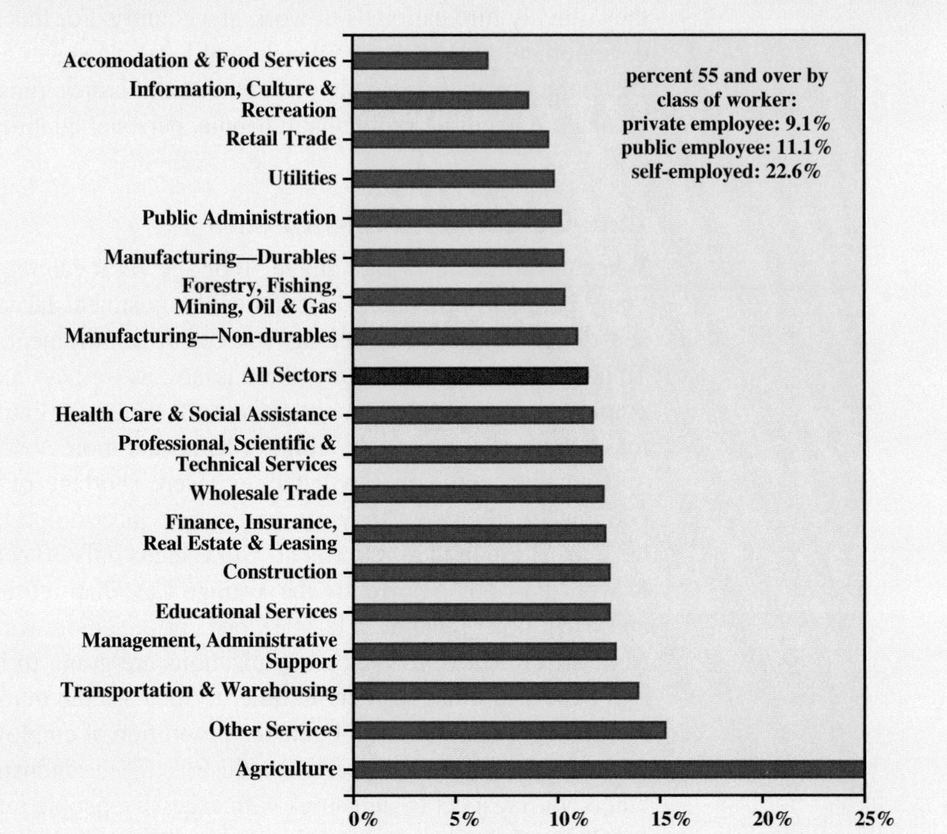

Source: Arlene Wortsman, Phased-In Retirement Options Needed for Skills Shortage Challenge: A CLBC Commentary, Canadian Labour and Business Centre Using Labour Force Survey Data, October 2003. Reprinted by permission.

sum benefits from the pension plan during the phased-in retirement to make up for lost income. The value of these lump sum payments are then deducted from the value of the pension available at full retirement.[20] With the imminent shortage of skilled workers, more phased-in approaches to retirement are required that allow for alternative work arrangements to keep skilled workers involved in the workforce.[21]

The phenomenon of "forced" early retirement often occurs as a result of downsizings and organizational restructurings. These events have required thousands of individuals, including many managers and professionals, to determine what is important to them while still active and healthy. As a result, some of the "younger retirees" begin second careers rather than focusing primarily on leisure activities or travel. To be successful with early retirement, management must avoid several legal issues such as forced early retirement and pressuring workers over age 55 to resign.[22]

Designated Group Member Career Issues

As previously discussed, discrimination in employment opportunities for the designated group members exists. Each faces difficulties in the workplace in terms of being accepted as equals, and being given equal opportunity to career advancement. Stereotypical attitudes exist for each of the designated groups, although each has their own unique set of issues to deal with when it comes to career opportunities. It is important that all groups be treated equally and be given the same opportunities based on their individual merit. Even though all groups should have the same access to career planning, and career advancement, the way each group is handled may differ.

Women and Careers A recent labour market trend in Canada shows an increased participation of women. Twenty-five years ago, 48.2 percent of women aged 45 to 54 and 31.9 percent of women aged 55 to 64, participated in the labour force. In 2001, this proportion had increased to 76.3 percent and 41.8 percent, respectively. The overall participation rate of Canadian women in 2002 was a record-high 60.7 percent. Women are found in all occupations and jobs, but their careers may have a different element than those of men. Women give birth to children, and in most societies women are also primarily responsible for taking care of the children. The effect of this biology and sociology is that women's careers are often interrupted for childbirth and childrearing.

The career approach for women frequently is to work hard before children arrive, step off the career track to be at home when the kids are young, and go back to work with a job that allows flexibility when the children are older. This approach is referred to as "sequencing." But some women who sequence are concerned that the job market will not welcome them when they return, or that the time away will hurt their advancement chances. For example, Jennifer Lee was torn between two loves—her career as a hardware designer and her 10-month-old baby girl. She chose to stay home. Two years later, she still wrestles with her decision. She vacillates between feeling that she is doing what is right for her two daughters and wondering how she ended up at home. Her experience as a stay-at-home mom has been "halfway horrible," leaving her feeling isolated and frustrated. "My children are growing and will have a life. And I'll have a life again one day," she says.[23] Women need to be concerned about how they are accepted on their return to work. The HR Perspective highlights what happened when a legendary adman spoke at an industry event to a group of men and women in 2005. Many believe he was espousing the typical belief about women who try to balance their work and family.

The interaction and conflicts among home, family, and a career affects the average woman differently than it does men.[24] By the time men and women have been out of school for six years, women have worked on average 30 percent less time than men. Sixteen years out of school, women average half as much work experience as men.[25] These and other career differences provide different circumstances for many females. Employers can tap into the female labour market to a greater extent with child care, flexible work policies, and a general willingness to be accommodative.

Aboriginal Peoples When it comes to career counselling for Aboriginal peoples, and as noted by one writer on this subject, "To be effective, counselling must fit with certain Native values."[26] The counselling process must include the importance of spirituality and the community and the use of the worker's extended family. McCormick and Amundson have developed a culturally relevant Career–Life Planning Model for First Nations People that takes into consideration components such as connectedness (respecting the belief that all things are interrelated), balance (acknowledging the interdependence of all things within an integrated whole), roles and responsibilities (incorporating integral linkages to family and community), gifts (identifying unique talents that contribute to the good of all), and values (identifying family, community and cultural sources of meaning). They propose including important family and community members in the counselling process with the counsellor taking the role of the facilitator. The talking/healing circle format of this approach starts with individual

Sexist Remarks Remain Alive and Oh Not So Well!!

WPP Group PLC is one of the world's largest marketing services and has over 1700 offices, in 104 different countries, and over 62 000 employees. They are a very diversified company, and includes advertising agencies J. Walter Thompson Company, Ogilvy & Mather Worldwide, Young & Rubicam, and Red Cell, to name but a few of their conglomerate affiliations. Some of their top clients include American Express, AT&T, Colgate-Palmolive, Ford, IBM, GlaxoSmithKline, Nestlé, Pfizer, Philip Morris, and Unilever. With a company this size, no one would have expected its legendary adman, Neil French, the worldwide creative director of WPP Group to say what he did to 300 men and women attending an industry event entitled "ihaveanidea," sponsored by FirstLight and Ogilvy, in Toronto, October 6, 2005.

At the event, French was interviewed by two advertising stars. The advertisements for the event stated that "No question will be spared and no topic will be taboo as we reveal the source of Neil's gift for advertising." The advertising was true to its word—when French was asked the question why women were underrepresented among the top ranks of creative directors, he replied "Because they're crap." He then elaborated by saying that "women are apt to wimp out and go suckle something." To add insult to injury, he also had a "French" barmaid serving him drinks on stage.

His disparaging remarks caused a number of people to leave the event and a barrage of e-mails from female executives in WPP companies. Nancy Vonk, a senior co-chief creative officer at WPP's Ogilvy agency in Toronto said she was stunned by the remarks, "I almost managed to blank out the idiocy of the French barmaid for a while . . . but by the time Neil let into the women—the slacker-breeders who he made clear really don't belong in this man's game—my jaded jaw hit the floor," she said. She further added, "What struck me so hard as he described a group that will inevitably wimp out and 'go suckle something' after their short stint in advertising, was that in his honest opinion he was voicing the inner thoughts of legions of men in the senior ranks of our business," she wrote on the ihaveanidea.org website.

According to a study released in November 2005 by Catalyst, men consider women to be less adept at problem solving. That sort of skill is necessary to be an effective leader. Since men continue to sit in most chief executive spots, any male-held stereotype will only continue to be in place. In this same study women were also found to be better at stereotypically feminine caretaking skills such as supporting and rewarding, while men were found to excel at more conventionally masculine taking-charge skills such as influencing superiors and delegating responsibility. What this means is that men run the organization and women support them.

Ilene Lang, president of Catalyst, suggests that French is a walking example of the kind of stereotyping we are talking about. "He is saying because women are mothers, they can't be good leaders. And we know from all our research, that's just not the case. Women are ambitious, just as ambitious as men."

Vonk on the other hand sees some good in all of this negative publicity. She said if this incident shines a spotlight on an "obvious problem" with the industry among many men, then "there is a good thing that can come from it." French resigned several weeks after the incident.[27]

1. Do you believe that Neil French is really telling us what some men feel about women in the workplace? Why or why not?
2. Do you feel that this is the sentiment felt throughout industry, or is this typical of the advertising industry only?

self-reflection on the components described earlier, as well as on labour market options, educational concerns, interests, and personality/spirit. Family and community members are also asked to contribute their reflections on each component. At the end of the process, which may require several sessions, McCormick and Amundson suggest a ceremony in which others identify their roles and responsibilities in facilitating the individual's career journey.[28] Therefore, career counselling may take on different attributes for each specific group.

Visible Minorities Visible minorities face particular barriers in employment opportunities unique onto themselves. In a recent study by the Conference Board of Canada, *The Voices of Visible Minorities: Speaking Out on Breaking Down Barriers* conducted in 2004, focus group participants spoke about being turned down for opportunities because of "lack of fit" for senior positions, because they speak with an accent, or because their credentials or work experience are not taken seriously. Focus group participants took charge of their careers by using networking and mentoring opportunities inside and outside their workplaces, fostering a "can-do" attitude and not turning down opportunities to demonstrate their skills, they made a conscious effort to take any job, while they continued to apply for work more in line with their credentials, and they also obtained credentials from Canadian educational institutions.[29] Some organizations are making concerted efforts to ensure that visible minorities are given ample career development opportunities. For example, the Manitoba provincial government has designed an internship, equity, and employee development program designed to increase the number of visible minority group members in working for the government. Successful candidates will be eligible for orientation, coaching, training, and development in support of career plans.[30] Family Service Association (FSA) of Toronto, a not-for-profit social service provider with 150 employees, has had hiring processes to recognize foreign credentials in place since the early 1990s. Instead of focusing on specific Canadian qualifications and experience, the association "looks at volunteer work that has important value to FSA." Additionally, job postings list only minimal qualifications to ensure that everyone has an equal opportunity. Ernst & Young invites newcomers to attend a one-day workshop called "Succeeding in Canada." The workshop focuses mostly on working in Canada, but also on living in Canada. The workshop provides specific information on ways to get paperwork in order and even such details as where to buy parkas. Newcomers are invited to bring their spouses or significant others to the workshop.[31]

Persons with Disabilities The issues for persons with disabilities is far more complicated than it is for other designated group members. Labour force participation rates are at 49 percent for people with disabilities, compared to 65 percent for the general population. Unemployment rates for people with disabilities are also close to 70 percent above the national average.[32] Career development for this group is hampered by the fact that the group is underemployed, and therefore employment of this group is by far the more serious concern. There is ample evidence that a substantial proportion of people with disabilities who are not currently in the labour force are capable of being employed in some way, given proper supports and removal of barriers. As for workplace barriers, they can largely be classified as either physical or attitudinal. With regards to physical barriers, job accommodations, usually of nominal cost, can enable many people with disabilities to be fully employed. Employers who have provided such accommodations say that the savings they have achieved average 27 times the cost of providing the accommodations. Accessibility continues to be problematic. In regard to attitudinal barriers, misperceptions and lack of information on the part of employers do play a role in keeping people with disabilities out of the workforce.[33] In a recent study conducted by the Canadian Abilities Foundation entitled *Neglected or Hidden,* it was determined that a disconnect exists between employers, people with disabilities, and the service providers who help these individuals enter the workforce. Employers do not know where to turn for help and, to their knowledge, had also never been contacted by a community organization that assists disabled jobseekers.[34] Successful employers who gainfully employ disabled employees know how to make these connections. Once a disabled employee is employed, they are then able to begin career development programs. Supervisors should discuss career expectations with each employee, including an evaluation of the employee's interests, talents, and skills in relation to the requirements of available jobs. If an employee's career goals seem unachievable, the supervisor should provide constructive feedback and try to reach an agreement with the employee on appropriate goals and paths to achieving them. However, the supervisor should not assume an employee's disability will be a barrier. Education, training, and transition programs need to become more flexible and accessible. This is key to ensuring better employment opportunities for persons with disabilities and securing a better economic future through employment.

Special Career Issues for Organizations and Individuals

2 The goals and perspectives in career planning may differ for organizations and individuals, but three issues can be problematic for both, although for different reasons. Those are career plateaus (or the lack of opportunity to move up), dealing with technical professionals who do not want to go into management, and dual-career couples.

Career Plateaus

Those who do not change jobs may face another problem: career plateaus. As the baby-boomer generation reaches mid-life and beyond, and as large employers cut back on their workforces, increasing numbers of employees find themselves "stuck" at a certain career level or "plateau." This plateauing may seem like a sign of failure to some people, and plateaued employees can cause problems for employers if their frustrations affect their job performance.

Many workers define career success in terms of upward mobility. As the opportunities to move up decrease, some employers try to convince employees they can find job satisfaction in lateral movement. Such moves can be reasonable if employees learn new skills that increase individual marketability in case of future layoffs, termination, or organizational re-structuring.[35]

One strategy for individuals to get off career plateaus is to take seminars and university courses. This approach may reveal new opportunities for plateaued employees. Rotating workers to other departments is another way to deal with career plateaus. A computer chip manufacturer instituted a formal "poaching" program that encouraged managers to recruit employees from other departments, thereby giving employees greater opportunities to experience new challenges without having to leave the employer. Some plateaued individuals change careers and go into other lines of work altogether.[36] Figure 8-4 shows a "portable" career path that can include major changes to deal with being plateaued. In summary, plateaued employees present a particular challenge for employers. They can affect morale if they become negative, but they may also represent valuable resources that are not being well used.

Figure 8-4 *"Portable" Career Path*

Beginning	Expanding	Changing	Sustaining	Concluding
Spend several years at large company to learn skills and build network	Use networking to develop broader skills and make contacts; establish good reputation	Change industries, or go to work for smaller companies; start a company	Refresh skills; take a sabbatical; go back to school; gain experience in non-profit organizations	Move to appealing projects as a temporary employee or subcontractor

Technical and Professional Workers

Technical and professional workers, such as engineers, scientists, physical therapists, and IT systems experts, present a special challenge for organizations.[37] Many of these individuals want to stay in their technical areas rather than enter management; yet advancement in many organizations frequently requires a move into management. Most of these people like the idea of the responsibility and opportunity associated with advancement, but they do not want to leave the professional and technical puzzles and problems at which they excel.

Dual-career ladder System that allows a person to advance up either a management ladder or a corresponding ladder on the technical/professional side of a career.

The dual-career ladder is an attempt to solve this problem. As shown in Figure 8-5, a **dual-career ladder** is a system that allows a person to advance up either a management ladder or a corresponding ladder on the technical/professional side of a career. Dual-career ladders are now used at IBM and many other firms. They are most common in technology-driven industries such as pharmaceuticals, chemicals, computers, and electronics. For instance, a telecommunications firm created a dual-career ladder in its data processing department to reward talented technical people who do not want to move into management. Different tracks, each with attractive job titles and pay opportunities, are provided.

Unfortunately, the technical/professional ladder is sometimes viewed as "second-class citizenship" within the organization. For a second or third career track to be taken seriously, the standards applied to technical/professional promotions must be just as rigorous as those applied to management promotions.

Dual-Career Couples

As the number of women in the workforce, particularly in professional careers, continues to increase, so does the number of dual-career couples. Marriages in which

Figure 8-5 *Dual-Career Ladder for Engineers*

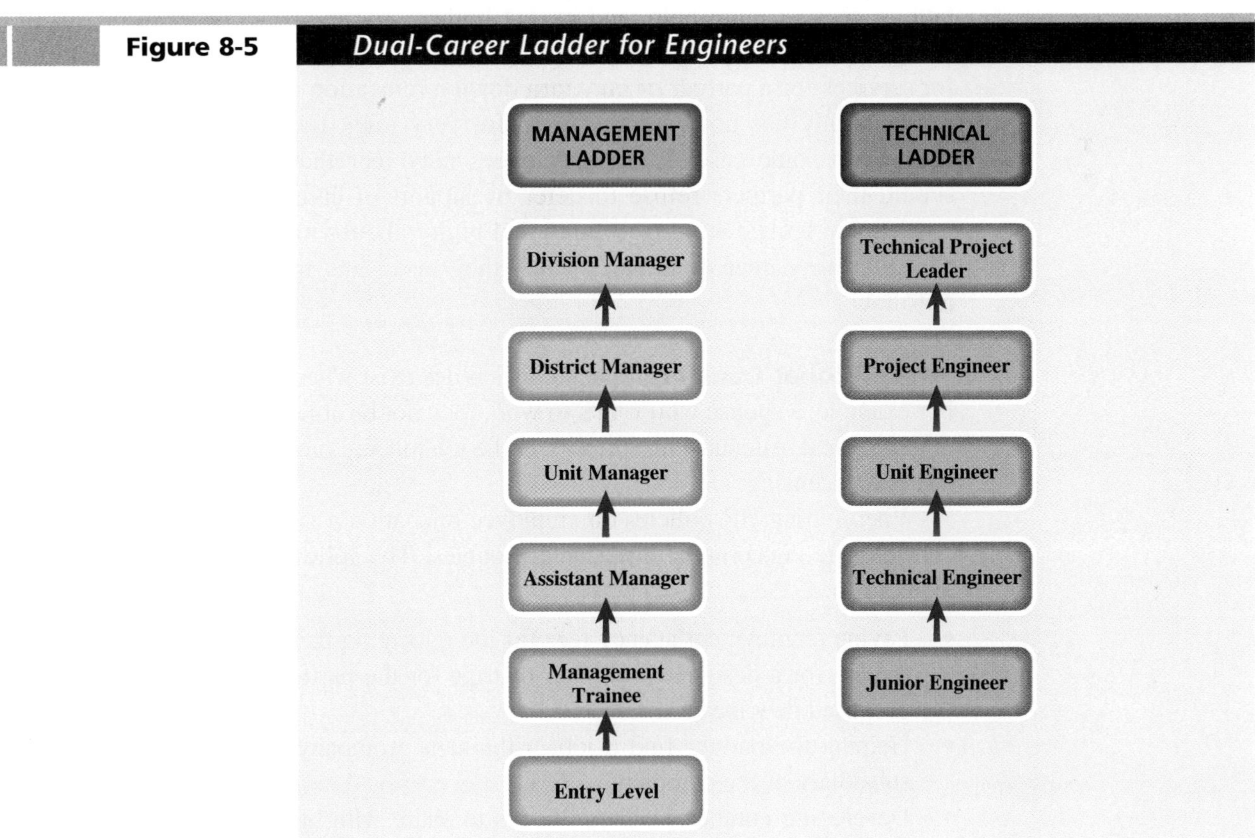

both mates are managers, professionals, or technicians doubled over the past two decades. Problem areas for dual-career couples include family issues and job transfers causing relocations.[38]

For dual-career couples with children, family issues may conflict with career progression. Thus, in job transfer situations, one partner's flexibility may depend on what is "best" for the family. Companies may consider part-time work, flextime, and work-at-home arrangements as possible options, especially for parents with younger children.

It is important that the career development problems of dual-career couples be recognized as early as possible, especially if they involve transfer of locations. Early planning by employees and their supervisors can prevent crises from occurring. Whenever possible, having both partners involved in planning, even when one is not employed by the company, has been found to enhance the success of such efforts.[39]

Relocation of Dual-Career Couples Traditionally, employees accepted transfers as part of upward mobility in organizations. However, for some dual-career couples, the mobility required because of one partner's transfer often interferes with the other's career. In addition to having two careers, dual-career couples often have established support networks of co-workers, friends, and business contacts to cope with both their careers and their personal lives. Relocating one partner in a dual-career couple may mean upsetting this carefully constructed network for the other person or creating a "commuting" relationship.

Recruiting a member of a dual-career couple may mean having an equally attractive job available for the candidate's partner at the new location. Dual-career couples may lose some income when relocating; thus, they often have higher expectations, request more help, and expect higher salaries when asked to do so. In a company without a partner-assistance program, an employee may be hesitant to ask for services for a partner or may turn down a relocation request. Because the dual-career family has not been the norm for very long, traditional role expectations remain. In some cases, male employees may fear they will appear "unmanly" should their partners refuse to defer in support of career changes. On the other hand, some female employees may feel guilty about violating the traditional concept of male career dominance when they move and males must quit their jobs to follow.

Global Transfers Special difficulties exist when the transfer is overseas.[40] For example, a spouse who wants to work may not be able to get a work permit, may find that local residents have priority in the job market, or may find incompatible certification/licensing.

When setting HR policies on employee relocation assistance, organizations must consider the concerns of dual-career couples. The following approaches can help them do so:

- Paying employment agency fees for the relocating partner
- Paying for a designated number of trips for the partner to look for a job in the proposed new location
- Helping the partner find a job in the same company or in another division or subsidiary of the company
- Developing computerized job banks to share with other companies in the area that list partners available for job openings

Developing Human Resources

Development Efforts to improve employees' abilities to handle a variety of assignments and to cultivate employees' capabilities beyond those required by the current job.

3 **Development** represents efforts to improve employees' abilities to handle a variety of assignments and to cultivate employees' capabilities beyond those required by the current job. Development benefits both organizations and individuals. Employees and managers with appropriate experiences and abilities may enhance organizational competitiveness and the ability to adapt to a changing environment. In the development process, individuals' careers also may evolve and gain new or different focuses.

Development differs from training. It is possible to train most people to run a copy machine, answer customer service questions, drive a truck, operate a computer, or assemble a radio. However, development in areas such as judgment, responsibility, decision making, and communication presents a bigger challenge. These areas may or may not develop through life experiences of individuals. A planned system of development experiences for all employees, not just managers, can help expand the overall level of capabilities in an organization. Figure 8-6 profiles development and compares it with training.

At the organizational level of analysis, executives craft the broader organizational strategies and should establish a system for developing the people to manage and achieve those identified strategies. Development must be tied to this strategic planning because the firm needs to develop appropriate talents to carry out the plans. Successful HR development focuses on employee and managerial succession on several levels and in several different pathways as part of that development.

Currently, more jobs take on the characteristics of *knowledge work.* Workers in these jobs combine mastery of technical expertise with the ability to work in teams, form relationships with customers, and analyze their own practices. Managing such jobs involves guiding and integrating increasingly autonomous, highly skilled people.

HR planning anticipates the movement of people in the organization due to retirements, promotions, and transfers. Also, it helps identify the capabilities that will be needed by the organization in the future and the development necessary for people to be available to meet those needs. Figure 8-7 illustrates the HR development process.

Figure 8-6 *Training vs. Development*

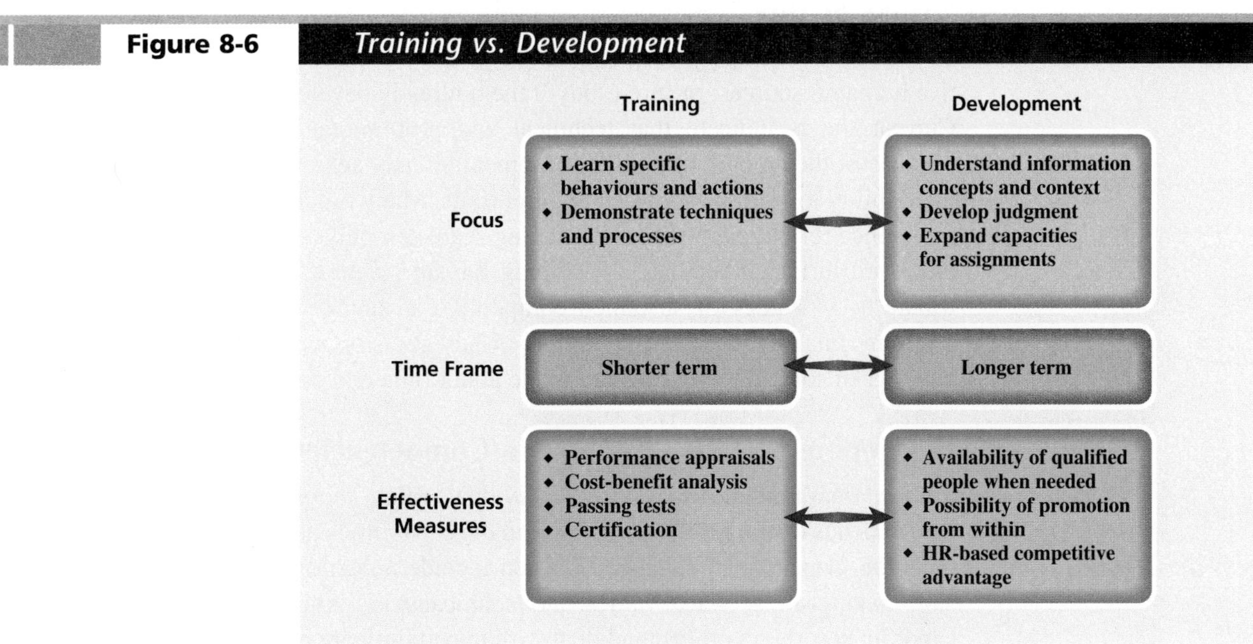

Figure 8-7 HR Development Process in an Organization

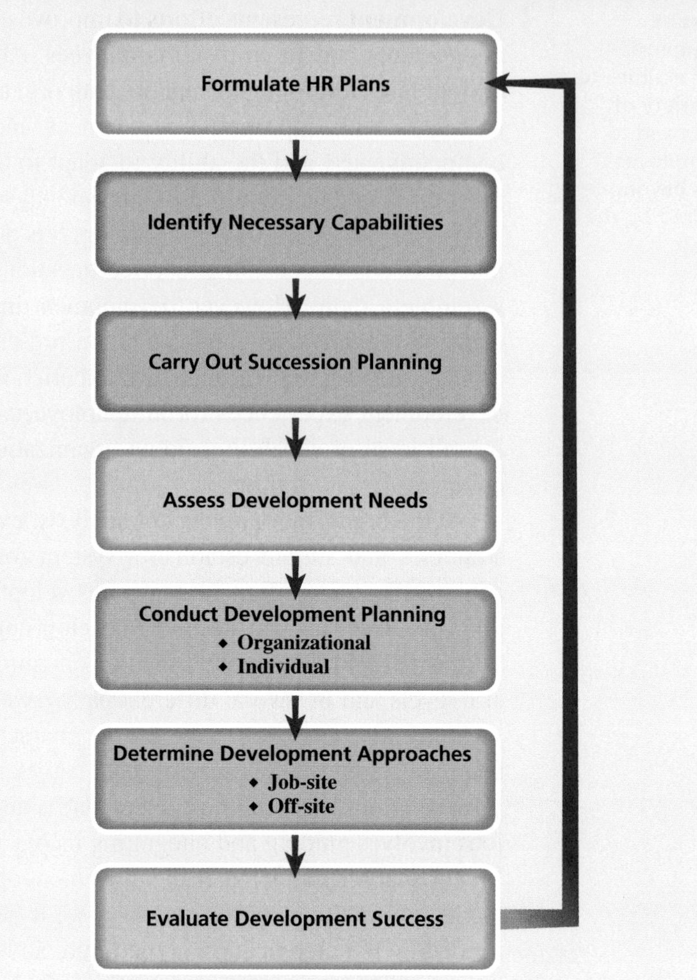

"Make or Buy"?

To some extent, employers face a "make-or-buy" choice: develop ("make") competitive human resources, or hire ("buy") them already developed from somewhere else. Current trends indicate that technical and professional people usually are hired because of the amount of skill development already achieved, rather than because of their ability to learn or their behavioural traits. Many organizations show an apparent preference for buying rather than making scarce employees in today's labour market. However, hiring rather than developing human resource capabilities may not contribute to a strategy of sustained competitive advantage through human resources. Like any financial decision, the make-or-buy decision can be quantified and calculated when some assumptions are made about time and costs.

Developing Specific Capabilities/Competencies

Exactly what kind of development individuals might require to expand their capabilities depends on both the individuals and the capabilities needed. Some important and common management capabilities often include an action orientation, quality decision-making skills, ethical values, and technical skills. Ability to build teams, develop subordinates, direct others, and deal with uncertainty are equally important but much less commonly developed capabilities for successful managers. For some tech specialties (tech support, database administration, network design, etc.), certain non-technical abilities must be developed as well: ability to work under pressure, work independently, solve problems quickly, and use past knowledge in a new situation.

Development frequently includes a focus on enhancing judgment and responsibility. How exactly to develop an "action orientation" or the "ability to work under pressure" must be addressed by organizations. These capabilities cannot successfully be taught in a course, and not everyone will develop them. As a result, development is more difficult in certain areas than in others.[41]

One point about development is clear: in studies that asked employees what they want out of their jobs, training and development ranked at or near the top. Because the assets individuals have to sell are their knowledge, skills, and abilities, many people view the development of their KSAs as an important part of their organizational package. This type of development works for many but not all.

Lifelong Learning

Learning and development are closely linked. For most people, lifelong learning and development are much more likely and desirable. For many professionals, lifelong learning may mean meeting continuing education requirements to keep certified. Several provinces have made it mandatory for teachers to be re-certified. A number of professional designation holders must also keep active in learning and giving back to their communities in order to keep their certification. For other employees, learning and development may involve training to expand existing skills and to prepare for different jobs, for promotions, or even for new jobs after retirement.[42]

Assistance from employers for needed lifelong development typically comes through programs at work, including tuition reimbursement programs. However, much of lifelong learning is voluntary, takes place outside work hours, and is not always formal.[43] Although it may have no immediate relevance to a person's current job, learning often can enhance the individual's confidence, ideas, or enthusiasm.[44]

Redevelopment

Whether due to a desire for career change or because the employer needs different capabilities, people may shift jobs in mid-life or mid-career. Redeveloping or retraining people in the capabilities they need is logical and important. In the last decade, the number of university and college enrollees over the age of 35 has increased dramatically. But helping employees go back to school is only one way of redeveloping them. Some companies offer redevelopment programs to recruit experienced workers from other fields. For example, different firms needing truck drivers, reporters, and IT workers have sponsored second-career programs. Public-sector employers have been using redevelopment opportunities as one recruiting tool as well.

Company Websites and Career Development

Many employers have websites, and on some of those websites is a section labelled "careers." The careers section can be used for many purposes, including listing open jobs for current employees looking to change jobs. The website is a link to the external world, but it can also be a link to existing employee development.

Sites also can be used for career assessment, information, and instruction.[45] One organization that uses their website to help employees chart career paths is TD. The

Career Advisor site is a comprehensive career management tool for employees to figure out how best to develop themselves, overcome career challenges, and find root causes to burnout and work/life imbalances.[46]

Development Needs Analyses

Like employee training, employee development begins with analyses of the needs of both the organization and the individuals. Either the company or the individual can analyze what a given person needs to develop. The goal, of course, is to identify strengths and weaknesses. Methods that organizations use to assess development needs include assessment centres, psychological testing, and performance appraisals.

Assessment Centres

Assessment centres Collections of instruments and exercises designed to diagnose individuals' development needs.

Assessment centres are collections of instruments and exercises designed to diagnose individuals' development needs.[47] An assessment centre is not a place. Organizational leadership uses assessment centres for both developing and selecting managers. Many types of employers use assessment centres.

In a typical assessment-centre experience, an individual spends two or three days away from the job performing many assessment activities. These activities might include role-playing, pencil-and-paper tests, cases, leaderless-group discussions, computer-based simulations, management games, and peer evaluations. Frequently, they also include in-basket exercises, in which the individual handles typical problems coming across a manager's desk. For the most part, the exercises represent situations that require the use of managerial skills and behaviours. During the exercises, several specially trained judges observe the participants.

Assessment centres provide an excellent means for determining management potential. Management and participants often praise them because they are likely to overcome many of the biases inherent in interview situations, supervisor ratings, and written tests. Experience shows that key variables such as leadership, initiative, and supervisory skills cannot be measured with paper-and-pencil tests alone. Assessment centres also offer the advantage of helping identify employees with potential in large organizations. Supervisors may nominate people for the assessment centre, or employees may volunteer. For talented people, the opportunity to volunteer is invaluable because supervisors may not recognize their potential interests and capabilities.

Assessment centres can also raise concerns.[48] Some managers may use the assessment centre to avoid making difficult promotion decisions. Suppose a plant supervisor has personally decided that an employee is not qualified for promotion. Rather than be straightforward and inform the employee, the supervisor sends the employee to the assessment centre, hoping the report will show that the employee is unqualified for promotion. Problems between the employee and the supervisor may worsen if the employee earns a positive report. Using the assessment centre for this purpose does not aid the development of the employee and is not recommended.

Psychological Testing

Psychological pencil-and-paper tests have been used for several years to determine employees' development potential and needs. Intelligence tests, verbal and mathematical reasoning tests, and personality tests are often given. Even a test that supposedly assesses commonsense is available. Psychological testing can furnish useful information on individuals about such factors as motivation, reasoning abilities, leadership style, interpersonal response traits, and job preferences.

The biggest problem with psychological testing lies in interpretation, because untrained managers, supervisors, and workers usually cannot accurately interpret test results. After a professional scores the tests and reports the scores to someone in the organization, untrained managers may attach their own meanings to the results. Also, some psychological tests are of limited validity, and test-takers can easily fake desirable responses. Thus, psychological testing is appropriate only when the testing and feedback process is closely supervised by a qualified professional.

Performance Appraisals

Well-done performance appraisals can be a source of development information. Performance data on productivity, employee relations, job knowledge, and other relevant dimensions can be gathered in such assessments. As noted in Chapter 9, appraisals designed for development purposes may be more useful in aiding individual employee development than appraisals designed strictly for administrative purposes.

Succession Planning

Succession planning
Process of identifying a longer-term plan for the orderly replacement of key employees.

4 Planning for the succession of key executives, managers, and other employees is an important part of HR development. **Succession planning** is the process of identifying a longer-term plan for the orderly replacement of key employees. The need to replace key employees results from promotions, transfers, retirements, deaths, disabilities, departures, and other events. Succession planning often focuses on top management, such as ensuring a CEO successor.[49] However, limiting succession planning just to top executive jobs is a mistake. For instance, in a health-care institution, identifying successors for accounting manager, marketing director, admissions supervisor, IT technician, physical therapist, and other key jobs is just as crucial as succession planning for the top executive jobs.

Succession in Small and Closely Held Organizations

Succession planning can be especially important in small and medium-sized firms, but studies show that few of these firms formalize succession plans. In fact, more than half of the respondents in one study named lack of succession planning as the biggest threat facing small businesses.[50] In closely held family firms (those that are not publicly traded on stock exchanges), many CEOs plan to pass the business on to a family member. Most of these firms would benefit from planning for orderly succession. Addressing development needs of the successor also helps to avoid a host of potential problems for both the organization and family member relationships.[51]

Succession Planning Process

Whether in small or large firms, succession planning is linked to strategic HR planning through the process shown in Figure 8-8. In that process, both the quantity and the capabilities of potential successors must be linked to organizational strategies and plans. For example, at Dole Food, with 61 000 workers in 90 countries, there is talent all over the world, but the company did not have comprehensive knowledge of who the managers were or what they could do. Dole is a highly decentralized company and

Figure 8-8 *Succession Planning Process*

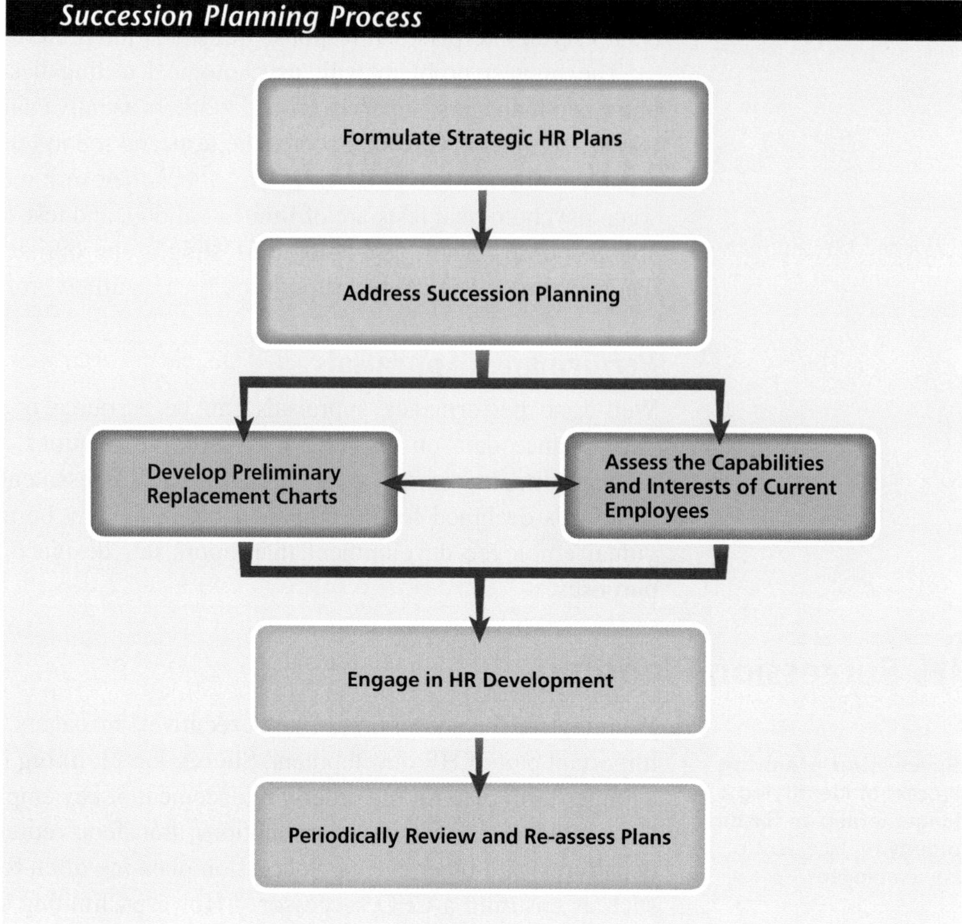

feels the need for a succession planning process to bring forward the best for advancement. Part of its solution includes Web-based software to support the process.[52]

Two coordinated activities begin the actual process of succession planning. First, the development of preliminary replacement charts ensures that the right individuals with sufficient capabilities and experience to perform the targeted jobs are available at the right time. Replacement charts (similar to depth charts used by football teams) both show the backup "players" at each position and identify positions without a current qualified backup player. The charts identify who could take over key jobs if someone leaves, retires, dies unexpectedly, or otherwise creates a vacancy. Second, assessment of the capabilities and interests of current employees provides information that can be placed into the preliminary replacement charts. The HR Perspective discusses the importance of successful planning.

Choosing a Development Approach

5 The most common development approaches can be categorized under two major headings: job-site development and off-site development. Both are appropriate in developing managers and other employees. Investing in human intellectual capital, whether on or off the job, becomes imperative for organizations as "knowledge work" aspects increase for almost all employers. Yet, identifying the right mix and approaches for development needs remains an art rather than a science.

Succession Planning Is Booming

Succession planning has become a greater concern in North American firms as the supply of executives and managers is becoming more scarce. A huge shortage is ahead as the baby-boomer generation begins to retire. The impact will be huge in Canada for all levels of employees. In 2011, the first wave of the baby-boomers—a cohort that comprises about one-third of the total Canadian population—is slated to reach the retirement age of 65 years. The critical concern in many firms is that departing managers and executives represent some of the most experienced leaders.

Often the employees in the firms tapped to take their places are currently in their 30s and 40s and have 10–15 years' work experience. But these employees often have work/family issues that impact their careers. In particular, some women in this group may have young children and may want to work part-time or shorter weeks. However, their jobs may not be compatible with such flexibility, which may affect succession planning and leadership development opportunities for them.

Succession planning is also important for the survival of a company; failing to plan for future leaders can leave a real gap. One firm that addressed this issue is Deloitte & Touche, a large accounting firm, where 17 percent of current partners and directors are women, up from 6.5 percent in 1993. "Succession planning is important for us because we feel strongly we need diversity in leadership," one director notes. That is why so many organizations want to plan rather than leave succession to chance.[53]

This traditional approach to succession planning does not always work for each employer. For example, at PepsiCo, a study showed that the succession planning process was taking too much time, so the company developed "acceleration pools." These pools focus on developing candidates for the executive level, rather than targeting one or two people for specific jobs. An executive resource board is responsible for placing pool members into situations where they can develop.[54] Other companies do succession planning as well. Eli Lilly, Dow Chemical, and Sonoco Products all use a system that identifies critical positions for development as part of the succession planning process.[55]

1. With the impending shortage of management by 2011, what can employers do to ensure people in their organizations acquire the management skills that will be desired?
2. What can you do to ensure that you are ready to take on a more senior position by 2011?

Job-Site Development Approaches

All too often, unplanned and perhaps useless activities pass as development on the job. To ensure that the desired development actually occurs, managers must plan and coordinate development efforts. A number of job-site development methods can be used.

Coaching
Training and feedback given to employees by immediate supervisors.

Coaching The oldest on-the-job development technique is **coaching,** which is the training and feedback given to employees by immediate supervisors. Coaching involves a continual process of learning by doing. For coaching to be effective, employees and their supervisors or managers must have a healthy and open relationship. Many firms conduct formal training courses to improve the coaching skills of their managers and supervisors.

Unfortunately, organizations may be tempted to implement coaching without any planning at all. Even someone who is good at a job or a particular part of a job will not necessarily be able to coach someone else to do it well. "Coaches" can easily fall short in guiding learners systematically, even if they know which experiences are best. Often the coach's job responsibilities take priority over learning and coaching of subordinates. Also, the intellectual component of many capabilities might be better learned from a book or a course before coaching occurs.

Sometimes "executive" coaches, hired by either individual executives or employers, work with individual managers and executives. These outside coaches

For coaching to be effective, employees and supervisors must have a healthy and open relationship.

Source: © 2006 JupiterImages and its Licensors. All Rights Reserved.

critique and advise the individuals. They are discussed along with management development, later in this chapter.

Committee Assignments Assigning promising employees to important committees may broaden their experiences and can help them understand the personalities, issues, and processes governing the organization. For instance, employees on a safety committee can gain a greater understanding of safety management, which would help them to become supervisors. They may also experience the problems involved in maintaining employee safety awareness. However, managers need to guard against committee assignments that turn into time-wasting activities.

Job rotation
Process of shifting a person from job to job.

Job Rotation The process of shifting a person from job to job is called **job rotation.** In some firms, job rotation is unplanned. In other organizations, managers follow elaborate charts and schedules, precisely planning a rotation program for each employee. Regardless of the approach, job rotation is widely used as a development technique. For example, a promising young manager may spend three months in the plant, three months in corporate planning, and three months in purchasing. When properly handled, such job rotation fosters a greater understanding of the organization.[56]

A disadvantage of job rotation is that it can be expensive because a substantial amount of time is taken when trainees change positions; the trainess must become acquainted with different people and techniques in each new unit.

When opportunities for promotion are scarce, job rotation through lateral transfers may help rekindle enthusiasm and develop employees' talents. The best lateral moves do one or more of the following: move the person into the core business, provide closer contact with customers, or teach new skills or perspectives.

"Assistant-to" Positions Some firms create "assistant-to" positions, which are staff positions immediately under a manager. Through such jobs, trainees can work with outstanding managers they might not otherwise have met. Some organizations set up "junior boards of directors" or "management cabinets" to which trainees may be appointed. These assignments provide useful experiences if they present challenging or interesting assignments to trainees.

Online Development Technology can provide an appropriate tool for development. Online development can take many forms, such as video conferencing, live chat rooms, document sharing, video and audio streaming, and Web-based courses. HR staff members can facilitate online development by providing a "learning portal," which is a centralized website for news, information, course listings, and materials.

Online development allows participation in courses previously out of reach due to geographic or cost considerations. It allows costs to be spread over a larger number of people, and it can be combined with virtual reality and other technological tools to make presentations more interesting. It can eliminate travel as well. However, because of the time needed to develop online materials or perhaps because those materials are not seen as clearly appropriate for development efforts, online development is not widely used.

Corporate Universities and Career Development Centres Large organizations may use "corporate universities" to develop managers or other employees. Corporate universities take various forms. Sometimes regarded as little more than fancy packaging for company training, they often do not provide a degree, accreditation, or graduation in the traditional sense. A related alternative, partnerships between companies and traditional universities, continues where the universities design and teach specific courses for employers.

Career development centres are often set up to coordinate inhouse programs and programs provided by suppliers. They may include assessment data for individuals, career goals and strategies, coaching, seminars, and online approaches.

Learning Organization Knowledge-based organizations, which deal primarily with ideas and information, must have employees who are experts at one or more conceptual tasks. These employees continuously learn and solve problems in their areas of expertise. Developing such employees requires an "organizational learning capacity" based on a culture of solving problems and learning new ways not previously used.[57] Figure 8-9 depicts some possible means for developing employees in a learning organization.

It is difficult to describe a "learning organization," except to say that it is an employer in which development occurs through shared information, culture, and leadership that values learning. It focuses on employees who want to learn to develop new capabilities. A learning mindset is probably difficult to introduce into

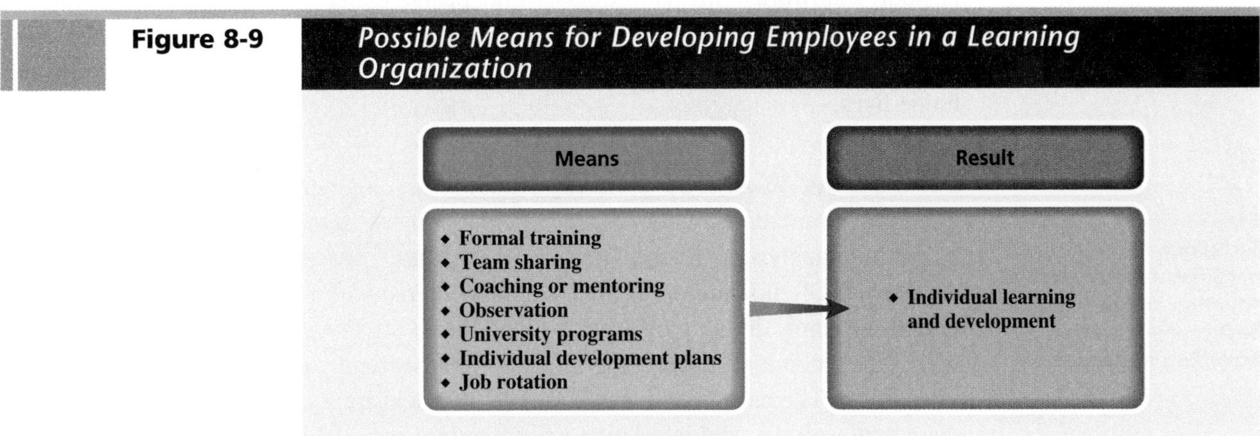

an organization where it does not exist. But where it does exist, it represents the ultimate potential for development. It remains a theoretical and somewhat idealistic model in HR development.

Off-Site Development Approaches

Off-the-job development techniques give individuals opportunities to get away from the job and concentrate solely on what is to be learned. Moreover, contact with others who are concerned with somewhat different problems and come from different organizations may provide employees with new and different perspectives. Various off-site methods are used.

Classroom Courses and Degrees Most off-the-job development programs include some classroom instruction. Most people are familiar with classroom training, which gives it the advantage of being widely accepted. But the lecture system sometimes used in classroom instruction encourages passive listening and reduced learner participation, which is a distinct disadvantage. Sometimes trainees have little opportunity to question, clarify, and discuss the lecture material. The effectiveness of classroom instruction depends on multiple factors: group size, trainees' abilities, instructors' capabilities and styles, and subject matter.

Organizations often send employees to externally sponsored seminars or professional courses, such as those offered by the Canadian Management Association. Many organizations also encourage continuing education by reimbursing employees for the costs of approved courses. Tuition reimbursement programs provide incentive for employees to study for advanced degrees, such as MBAs, through evening and weekend classes, outside their regular workdays.

Human Relations Training This type of training attempts to prepare supervisors to deal with "people problems" brought to them by their employees. The training focuses on the development of the human relations skills a person needs to work well with others. Most human relations programs typically are aimed at new or relatively inexperienced first-line supervisors and middle managers. They cover motivation, leadership, employee communication, and other behavioural topics.

The most common reason employees fail after being promoted to management is poor teamwork with subordinates and peers. Other common reasons for management failure include not understanding expectations, failure to meet goals, difficulty adjusting to management responsibilities, and inability to balance work and home lives.

Simulations (Business Games) Another development approach uses business games, or simulations, which are available commercially. A **simulation** requires participants to analyze a situation and decide the best course of action according to the data given. Often simulations are computer-interactive in nature. For example, individuals or teams draw up marketing plans for an organization to determine such factors as the amount of resources to allocate for advertising, product design, selling, and sales effort. The participants make a variety of decisions, and then the computer tells them how well they did in relation to competing individuals or teams. Managers have also used simulations to diagnose organizational problems.

Simulation
Technique that requires participants to analyze a situation and decide the best course of action according to data given.

When properly used, a simulation is a valuable management development tool. However, the lack of realism can diminish the learning experience. The focus must be learning, not just "playing the game."

Sabbatical
Paid time off the job to develop and rejuvenate oneself.

Sabbaticals and Leaves of Absence A **sabbatical** is paid time off the job to develop and rejuvenate oneself. Popular for many years in the academic world, sabbaticals have been adopted in the business community as well. About 19 percent of U.S. corporations offer sabbaticals.[58] That figure is unknown in Canada, as sabbaticals are a relatively new concept for Canadian organizations. Larger organizations are more apt to give such a benefit. For example, RBC Financial Group companies offer eight weeks of paid sabbatical as the need arises, and at the discretion of the manager; The Toronto Sun chain offers four weeks of paid sabbaticals after ten years of service, and Intel offers eight weeks of paid sabbatical on completion of seven years of service.[59] Some firms give employees three to six months off with pay to work on "socially desirable" projects. Such projects have included leading training programs in urban ghettos, providing technical assistance in foreign countries, and participating in corporate volunteer programs to aid non-profit organizations such as The United Way.

Companies that offer sabbaticals speak well of the results. Positive reasons for sabbaticals are to help prevent employee burnout, offer advantages in recruiting and retention, and boost individual employee morale. One obvious disadvantage of paid sabbaticals is the cost. Also, the nature of the learning experience generally falls outside the control of the organization, leaving it somewhat to chance.

Outdoor Training Many organizations send executives and managers off to adventures in the wilderness, called outdoor training. As development tools, the rationale for using these wilderness excursions, which can last seven days or longer, is that such experiences can increase self-confidence and help individuals re-evaluate personal goals and efforts.[60] For individuals in work groups or teams, shared risks and challenges outside the office environment can create a sense of teamwork. The challenges may include white-water rafting on a river, rock climbing and backpacking in the Rocky Mountains, or handling a longboat off the coast of Nova Scotia.

Wilderness excursions can increase self-confidence and help individuals re-evaluate personal goals and efforts as well as create a sense of teamwork.

Source: Matt Ragen/ShutterStock

Survival-type management development courses may have more impact than many other management seminars. But companies must consider the inherent perils. Some participants have been unable to handle the physical and emotional challenges associated with rappelling down a cliff or climbing a 12-metre tower. The decision to sponsor such programs should depend on the personalities of the employees involved.[61]

To be effective, a development approach must mesh with HR strategies. Figure 8-10 summarizes the major advantages and disadvantages of the various on-site and off-site approaches to development.

Figure 8-10 *Advantages and Disadvantages of Major Development Approaches*

JOB-SITE METHODS	ADVANTAGES	DISADVANTAGES
• Coaching	• Is natural and job related	• Can lack good coaches because they are difficult to find
• Committee assignments	• Involve participants in critical processes	• Can be time wasters
• Job rotation	• Gives excellent overview of the organization	• Has a long start-up time
• "Assistant-to" positions	• Provide exposure to an excellent manager	• May be difficult to set up because of possible shortage of good assignments
• Online development	• Is flexible	• Occupies a niche that is not yet well defined
• Corporate universities / career development centres	• Can combine academic and real world at work	• May be "universities" in name only
• Learning organizations	• Has perhaps the ideal mindset for development	• Has a mindset that is essentially a theoretical, idealistic notion for most organizations

OFF-SITE METHODS	ADVANTAGES	DISADVANTAGES
• Classroom courses and degrees	• Is familiar and accepted; has status	• Does not always improve performance
• Human relations training	• Deals with important management skills	• Is difficult to measure for effectiveness
• Simulations (business games)	• Offers realism and integration	• May involve inappropriate "game playing"
• Sabbaticals and leaves of absence	• Are rejuvenating as well as developmental	• Is expensive; employees may lose contact with job
• Outdoor training	• Increases self-confidence and teamwork through physical challenges	• Is not appropriate for all because of physical nature; may be dangerous

Management Development

Although development is important for all employees, it is essential for managers. Effective management development imparts the knowledge and judgment needed by managers. Without appropriate development, managers may lack the capabilities to best deploy and manage resources (including employees) throughout the organization.

Experience plays a central role in management development. Indeed, experience often contributes more to the development of senior managers than does classroom training, because much of it occurs in varying circumstances on the job over time. Yet, in many organizations it is difficult to find managers for middle-level jobs. Some individuals refuse to take middle-management jobs. As a middle manager, "you're a backstop, caught in the middle between upper management and the workforce," a cost accounting manager (who quit management) noted. "I was told 50 hours a week was not enough and that I had to work my people harder. . . . The few dollars more were not worth the pain." Similarly, not all companies seem to take the time to develop their own executive-level managers. Instead, executives often are hired from the outside. Figure 8-11 shows experience-based sources of managers' learning and lists some important lessons in effectively developing middle-managers and upper-level managers.

Management Resource Group
This website on management and leadership development contains free publications, which can be downloaded.
www.mrg.com

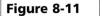

Figure 8-11 *Management Lessons Learned from Job Experience*

SOURCES OF MANAGERS' LEARNING
Job Transitions
• New jobs
• Problems
• New people
• Changes in responsibilities
Challenges
• Starting or changing some major organizational feature
• Having decision-making responsibility
• Influencing others without formal authority
Obstacles
• A bad job situation
• A difficult boss
• Demanding clients
• Unsupportive peers
• Negative economic circumstances
LESSONS MANAGERS NEED TO LEARN
• Setting agendas: Developing technical/business knowledge, taking responsibility, setting goals
• Handling relationships: Dealing successfully with people
• Management values: Understanding successful management behaviour
• Personality qualities: Having the temperament necessary to deal with the chaos and ambiguity of executive life
• Self-awareness: Understanding oneself and how one affects others

Management Development Methods

A number of approaches are used to mould and enhance the experience that managers need to be effective. The most widely used methods are leadership development, management modelling, management coaching, management mentoring, supervisory development, and executive education.

Leadership Development An effective leader creates positive change and is important for an organization. But like all developmental capacities, leadership cannot be taught to everyone.

Many companies have leadership development programs—but a recent survey found that only about 25 percent of those programs were rated high for quality.[62] In addition, the failure rate of new executives is around 50 percent in the first 18 months and two-thirds in five years.[63] Clearly, there is a need for better leadership development. However, what many people think of as leadership is really supervision and management—defining the job to be done and getting it done. Leadership is not only defining the job but also explaining why it must be done.

Management Modelling A common adage in management development says that managers tend to manage as they were managed. In other words, managers learn by behaviour modelling, or copying someone else's behaviour. This tendency is not surprising, because a great deal of human behaviour is learned by modelling. Children learn by modelling the behaviours of parents and older children. Management development efforts can take advantage of natural human behaviour by matching young or developing managers with appropriate models and then reinforcing the desirable behaviours exhibited by the learners. The modelling process involves more than straightforward imitation, or copying; it is considerably more complex. For example, one can learn what not to do by observing a model who does something wrong. Thus, exposure to both positive and negative models can benefit a new manager.

Management Coaching Coaching combines observation with suggestions. Like modelling, it complements the natural way humans learn. A brief outline of good coaching pointers often includes the following:

- Explaining appropriate behaviour
- Making clear why actions were taken
- Accurately stating observations
- Providing possible alternatives/suggestions
- Following up and reinforcing behaviours used

In the context of management development, coaching involves a relationship between two managers for a period of time as they perform their jobs. Effective coaching requires patience and good communication skills.

A specific application of coaching is use of "executive coaching." Companies use executive coaches to help rising stars improve interpersonal skills or decision-making skills. In some cases they are used to help deal with problematic management styles. Executive coaches are predominately female and come from a psychology or counselling background. Some come to the office, but about half do their coaching by phone. Some coaches work for individual executives, but about three-quarters are paid by the executive's firm.[64] Coaches can serve many roles for a client by providing key questions and general directions.[65] Research on the effectiveness of coaching is scarce. The research that is available suggests that sometimes coaching can be beneficial.[66]

Management mentoring
Relationship in which experienced managers aid individuals in the earlier stages of their careers.

Management Mentoring A method called **management mentoring** is a relationship in which experienced managers aid individuals in the earlier stages of their careers. Such a relationship provides an environment for conveying technical, interpersonal, and organizational skills from the more-experienced person to a designated less-experienced person. Not only does the inexperienced employee benefit, but the mentor may enjoy the challenge of sharing his or her wisdom.[67]

However, mentoring is not without its problems. Young minority managers frequently report difficulty finding mentors. Also, men generally show less willingness than women to be mentors. Further, mentors who are dissatisfied with their jobs and those who teach a narrow or distorted view of events may not help a young manager's development. Fortunately, many managers have a series of advisers or mentors during their careers and may find advantages in learning from the different mentors.[68] For example, the unique qualities of individual mentors may help less-experienced managers identify key behaviours in management success and failure. Further, those being mentored may find previous mentors to be useful sources for networking.[69] Figure 8-12 describes the four stages in most successful mentoring relationships.

Management Mentoring and the Glass Ceiling In virtually all countries in the world, the proportion of women holding management jobs is lower than the proportion of men holding such jobs. The term *glass ceiling* has been used to describe the situation in which women fail to progress into top management positions. In Canada women are making slow but steady strides into management and the executive suite. Nationally, women hold 34 percent of managerial/professional positions and 14.4 percent of corporate officer positions, and those figures are higher in certain geographic regions, and for certain industries.[70]

 **Figure 8-12** *Stages in Management Mentoring Relationships*

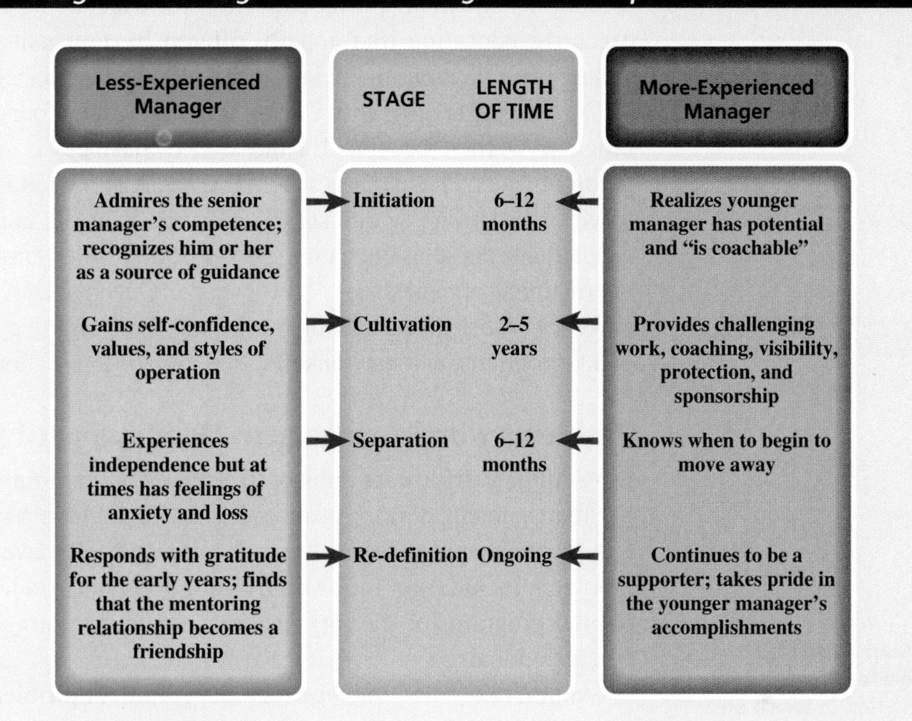

Less-Experienced Manager
STAGE
LENGTH OF TIME
More-Experienced Manager
Admires the senior manager's competence; recognizes him or her as a source of guidance
Initiation
6–12 months
Realizes younger manager has potential and "is coachable"
Gains self-confidence, values, and styles of operation
Cultivation
2–5 years
Provides challenging work, coaching, visibility, protection, and sponsorship
Experiences independence but at times has feelings of anxiety and loss
Separation
6–12 months
Knows when to begin to move away
Responds with gratitude for the early years; finds that the mentoring relationship becomes a friendship
Re-definition
Ongoing
Continues to be a supporter; takes pride in the younger manager's accomplishments

Canadian Association of Women Executives and Entrepreneurs (CAWEE)

CAWEE provides opportunities for all businesswomen at every stage of their career, to empower other women in the development and advancement of their business and professional lives, fostering financial independence, professional development, and personal satisfaction.

www.cawee.net

Women have typically been at a disadvantage because they have not been part of the inner circle, or what is referred to as "the old boys network." This network is defined as an informal group of senior men, who keep each other informed of available opportunities, and who may do things socially to keep the connection alive. Typically men will get together for sporting events such as going to baseball games, golfing, or going out for drinks. This usually excludes women, and therefore creates a glass ceiling that is difficult to break through. One approach to breaking through the glass ceiling is mentoring. For example, in some firms, women with mentors move up more often than those without mentors. Most of the literature on women and mentoring, based on various narratives of successful women executives, suggests that breaking the glass ceiling requires developing political sophistication, building credibility, refining a management style, and shouldering responsibilities. Women generally rate high in the skills needed for success where teamwork and partnering are important.

Supervisor Development At the beginning level for managerial development is the first-line supervisory job. It is often difficult to go from being one of the work group to being the boss. Further, the NYMs (new young managers), who are used to functioning as individual contributors, require new skills and mindsets to be successful supervisors.[71]

Development for supervisors may vary but usually contains common elements. The usual materials for supervisor training and development include several topics: basic management, performance evaluation, time management, conflict management, team building, and communication.

Executive Education Executives in an organization often face difficult jobs due to changing and unknown circumstances. "Churning" at the top of organizations and the stresses of executive jobs contribute to increased turnover in these positions. In an effort to decrease turnover, some organizations are experimenting with a relatively recent phenomenon: special education for executives. This type of training includes executive education traditionally offered by university business schools and adds strategy formulation, financial models, logistics, alliances, and global issues.

A female executive with Coca-Cola attended the four-day Harvard Business School program Women Leading Business. "My business is in a man's world—to have a group of peers, in one place, was very nice. And a good learning situation as well," she noted.[72] According to one survey, Harvard is in the number one place for executive education because of the nature and flexibility of its various programs for a number of international organizations.[73] In Canada, Queen's University School of Business is ranked as the leading school in Canada for Executive Development and Executive MBA programs, and has ranked in the Top 10 internationally as well.[74]

Problems with Management Development Efforts

Development efforts are subject to certain common mistakes and problems. Most of the management development problems in Canada have resulted from inadequate HR planning and a lack of coordination of HR development efforts.[75] Common problems include the following: failing to conduct adequate needs analysis, trying out fad programs or training methods, and substituting training for selecting qualified individuals.

Encapsulated development
Situation in which an individual learns new methods and ideas in a development course and returns to a work unit that is still bound by old attitudes and methods.

Another common management development problem is **encapsulated development,** which occurs when an individual learns new methods and ideas in a development course and returns to a work unit that is still bound by old attitudes and methods. Therefore, the trainee cannot apply new ways to handle certain situations because of resistance from those having an investment in the status quo. The development was "encapsulated" in the classroom and is essentially not used on the job.

SUMMARY

1 Career planning may focus on organizational needs, individual needs, or both. A person chooses a career according to interests, self-image, personality, social background, and other factors. A person's life is cyclical, as is his or her career. Looking at the two together offers a useful perspective for the future. Global career development has special challenges, including repatriation.

2 Organizations increasingly are dealing with individuals who have hit career plateaus, late career issues, and special issues with women employees. Technical employees sometimes may be able to follow dual-career ladders. Dual-career couples increasingly require relocation assistance for the partners of transferring employees.

3 Development differs from training because it focuses on less tangible aspects of performance, such as attitudes and values. Successful development requires the support of top management and an understanding of how development relates to other HR activities. Assessment centres provide valid methods of assessing needs for management talent and development.

4 Succession planning is the process that identifies how key employees are to be replaced. It is important not to limit succession planning to top executive jobs. Succession planning is critical to small and medium-sized firms, but studies show that few of these firms formalize such plans. Succession planning is linked to strategic HR planning. Two coordinated activities begin the actual succession planning process—development of preliminary replacement charts and the assessment of capabilities and interests of current employees.

5 On-the-job development methods include coaching, committee assignments, job rotation, assistant-to positions, online development, corporate universities/career development centres, and a learning

mindset. Off-the-job development methods include classroom courses and degrees, human relations training, simulations, sabbaticals and leaves of absence, and outdoor training. Through mentoring and modelling, younger managers can acquire the skills and know-how necessary to be successful. Mentoring follows a four-stage progression in most cases. Supervisory development requires employees to develop new capabilities and mindsets to be successful.

KEY TERMS

Assessment centres, p. 302
Career, p. 284
Career paths, p. 287
Coaching, p. 305
Development, p. 299
Dual-career ladder, p. 297
Encapsulated development, p. 314
Human resource capabilities, p. 284
Individual-centred career planning, p. 287
Job rotation, p. 306
Management mentoring, p. 312
Organization-centred career planning, p. 285
Repatriation, p. 290
Sabbatical, p. 309
Simulation, p. 308
Succession planning, p. 303

REVIEW AND APPLICATION QUESTIONS

1 What is the difference between organization-centred career planning and individual-centred career planning?

2 Identify problems that dual-career couples pose for employers and employees.

3 Describe the differences between development versus training.

4 Why is succession planning important in businesses of all sizes today?

5 Discuss the problems that exist with management development efforts.

EXPERIENTIAL EXERCISES

1. What two roles can be played by a company website with a careers section? Go to Hewlett-Packard's website, www.jobshp.com, as well as three other firms, for examples. Report your findings to your group and discuss your findings.
2. Working in small groups, each group member is to interview three people regarding their working careers, on the questions listed below. You need to interview people over 40, so you can speak with parents, grandparents, aunts, uncles, or other people you know. You are to ask them the following:
   a. At what age do you plan to retire? If already retired, what age did they retire?
   b. If they want to keep working past age 65, find out why they want to?
   c. If they retired early, why did they?
   d. How many careers have they had? What were they?
   e. Why did they choose the career(s) that they did?
   f. Were they satisfied with their career choices?

   Based on their responses, do they match what you have read in your textbook? If not, how do they differ? Discuss the responses with your group members to see if there are many differences. If there are many differences, what are they? Why might they be so different, or so similar?
3. Working in teams of males (Joe) and females (Cathy), assume the following. You are engaged to be married in the next three months. Cathy has been offered an opportunity to work in Jordan for the next two years beginning in about three months. Her new job will be vice president of administrative services, Telco Plus, earning a salary that is equivalent to about $250,000 Canadian plus other perks as a maid, butler, driver, cook, personal trainer, and a home valued at about

$1.2 million Canadian, which is owned by the company. Therefore, there will be no housing expenses. Cathy's current salary is presently $175,000 in her director's role. Joe is currently earning $130,000 plus commissions in his sales position at Microset Canada. Commissions for the year are expected to be in the $80,000 range, which is about the same as last year. Joe's manager is very pleased with his performance, and there is talk about him moving up in the company in about a year. If Joe decides to go with Cathy, Telco Plus cannot make any job offers to him and Microset has no opportunities for him in Jordan. Joe would be completely on his own. As a couple, what would you do?

4. While conducting an audit of your staff to determine who has been promoted in the last five years, you discover that in certain departments, there are an inordinate number of male managers versus female managers, even though the females have been there longer. You also find out that the other designated group members have not been progressing as well as they should have. Again, it appears to be occurring in the same departments where females have been disadvantaged. Upon further investigation you discover that career development opportunities have not been extended to many designated group members. The reason cited is that only those people at a certain level within the organization have been offered such opportunities. You decide to look further into the matter, and find that the departments where there is good progress made in developing all designated group members, development plans had been submitted for all staff with a concerted effort to ensure equal opportunity to all employees. Although all departments were told that only certain levels should be given career development opportunities, these departments decided it was fair to treat everyone the same, thus giving everyone the same opportunities. How should you go about rectifying this inequity among the departments without causing any hard feelings for all people involved?

LEARNING REVIEW

To check your knowledge of the chapter, review the following. (Answers after the case.)

1 In recent years, the way people look at careers has changed. Now, the individual, not the organization, manages her or his own development. This switch has been caused by:
   a. an increase in moonlighting
   b. challenges to traditional ethical values
   c. corporate growth and international expansion
   d. mergers, acquisitions, restructurings, and layoffs

2 A career plateau occurs when:
   a. a technical worker has no prospects for advancement
   b. a dual-career couple mutually agree to put their marriage ahead of their careers
   c. baby boomers reach mid-life and mid-career
   d. employees find themselves "stuck" at a career level

3 When setting HR policies on employee relocation assistance for dual-career couples, the following approaches can help them do so except:
   a. paying employment agency fees for the relocating partner
   b. paying for designated number of trips for the partner to look for a job in the new location
   c. helping the partner find a job in the same company or in another division or subsidiary of the company
   d. paying the partner's lost wages while they look for work

4 The need to replace employees results from:
   a. promotions
   b. demotions
   c. departures
   d. retirements

5 As a development technique, the best lateral transfers:
   a. provide a continual process of learning
   b. move the person into the core business
   c. ensure that trainees have an opportunity to deal with interesting assignments
   d. provide a monetary incentive for taking on new work

CASE

EMPLOYEES CHARTING THEIR CAREER PATHS AT TD

Headquartered in Toronto, Canada, with more than 51 000 employees in offices around the world, the Toronto-Dominion Bank and its subsidiaries are collectively known as TD Bank Financial Group (TDBFG). TD Bank Financial Group offers a full range of financial products and services to approximately 13 million customers worldwide. Several years ago employee career assistance became a "huge priority" for the bank because the bank wanted to be an employer of choice. They were concerned about the percentage of their workforce that would be retiring in the next five to ten years, so they wanted to begin their planning process earlier rather than later.

The need for better career management assistance started to emerge in 2002. Senior executives were receiving more and more anecdotal feedback that seemed to suggest employees wanted better career development opportunities and support. That suspicion was later backed up with some comprehensive research of employees' wants and needs. Employees stated that what interested them most about working at TD was skill development and career development.

The leadership group and HR team decided to put more time and money into employee career management. The bank believed that everyone has to be responsible for their own careers, and they wanted to find a way to help employees feel better about their career paths but without being overly intrusive. To allow employees the opportunity to self-manage their careers, they decided to use the Internet as the tool to help employees accomplish their goals.

TD partnered with BBM Human Resource Consultants Inc. and its head, Barbara Moses, to create a website that would help employees with all aspects of career management. The site was to respond to every issue a working person might have. It was also very important that the site not look like it was associated with the bank at all since employees were going online to share personal thoughts and feelings about their work. Through a combination of interactive diagnostic instruments, personal reports, advice, tools, and action planning exercises, the Career Advisor site is a comprehensive career management tool that enables employees to figure out how best to develop themselves, overcome career challenges, and diagnose the root causes of burnout and work/life imbalances. There are also modules for managers looking to improve their coaching skills. Employees can also produce reports on such things as work styles or preferred work environments to give to managers.

Employees should be able to figure out their motivations, work styles, and preferences. The site helps employees understand whether they work best in a fast-paced, multitasking environment or if they will thrive in a setting where they can do one thing at a time. In some cases, employees will be able to make changes in their current jobs and in others they may in fact decide the job they are in isn't the right one for them. The requests arising directly from employees using the site will be likely more intelligent and well thought out. Only 5 percent of the employees were reported as wanting to change their jobs.

At the onset of the system being launched, more than 5000 of the bank's 35 000 Canadian employees had tried it, with about 125 new users signing up every week. Based on how the site is being used and how the information is being accessed, about 81 percent of them are there because they want to develop themselves. Sixty-five percent said they are there looking for tips and strategies to manage their careers. Wanting to move ahead was cited by 52 percent and about half said they have some confusion about where they want to go or are thinking about changing direction. Thirty-six percent said they are in the midst of a career malady or burnout. The bank was surprised at the overwhelming success of the Career Advisor site since their announcement of the program had merely been an internal e-mail memo.

Managers love it because they are having completely different conversations with employees who are better able to articulate what they want and where they need to go to be happy and productive. "They understand themselves better and what satisfies them in their job."[76]

Questions

1. What potential advantages and disadvantages might exist with this type of tool?
2. How would you go about communicating this type of tool to your employees?

Learning Review Answers: 1. d 2. d 3. d 4. b 5. b

CHAPTER 9

Performance Management and Appraisal

Learning Objectives

After you have read this chapter, you should be able to:

1 Identify the components of performance management systems.

2 Discuss important employee performance measures including individual performance factors.

3 Explain the administrative and developmental uses of performance appraisal and the legal implications of performance management.

4 Describe the decisions concerning the performance appraisal process.

5 Introduce the methods of appraising performance and their advantages and disadvantages.

6 Discuss the importance of training managers and employees about performance appraisal, and give examples of several rater errors.

7 Identify several concerns about appraisal feedback and ways to make it more effective.

HR *Headline*

Performance Appraisals—Necessary but Not Popular

Many employees receive performance reviews from their managers and supervisors. Some of those reviews are very favourable, some are positive, and a few are negative. For managers and employees alike, the performance appraisal process, often done once a year, is not popular.

Various surveys have identified that a majority of employees view performance appraisals as "a joke," "an administrative game," "wasted time," "based on favouritism," and "not linked to pay." The most frequent criticisms include:

- With today's emphasis on teamwork, appraisals focus too much on the individual and do too little to develop employees to perform better.
- Many employees who receive reviews and supervisors who give reviews generally say that the appraisal process does not help improve workers' performance.
- Many appraisals are seen as inconsistent, focused on the short term, subjective, and valuable only for identifying employees who are performing extremely well or poorly.

However, employers must have some system for justifying the pay increases they give and the promotion or termination decisions they make. Also, most employees and managers want to communicate about how the employees are performing their jobs, and about additional training and development that would be beneficial. So, improvements in performance appraisals are needed to address the negative views held by many employees and managers.[1]

> *"Performance appraisal systems are like seat belts—most people believe they are necessary, but don't like to use them."*
>
> *—Dick Grote*

At the heart of organizational success is performance, which is driven by organizational and individual efforts leading to achieving goals and objectives. Performance management systems are a key means for HR management to contribute to organizational performance.

Nature of Performance Management

Performance management Composed of the processes used to identify, measure, communicate, develop, and reward employee performance.

1 **Performance management** is composed of the processes used to identify, measure, communicate, develop, and reward employee performance. As shown in Figure 9-1, performance management links organizational strategies to results.

All performance management efforts should be driven by business strategies. Firms such as Payless ShoeSource and PPG Canada Inc. have developed performance management systems by breaking their business plans into sub-plans for units and departments.[2] Those plans have then served as the foundation for accomplishing the following functions:

Figure 9-1 *Performance Management Linkage*

Organizational Strategies
Performance Management
• Identify expected performance levels
• Encourage high levels of performance
• Measure individual performance; then evaluate
• Provide feedback on individual performance
• Provide assistance as needed
• Reward or discipline depending on performance
Employee Performance
Performance Management Outcomes
• Pay increases
• Incentive rewards
• Promotions/advancement
• Training and development
• Career planning
• Disciplinary actions
Organizational Results
• Goals met or not met
• Employee satisfaction or dissatisfaction strong or weak
• Coordination between performance and pay

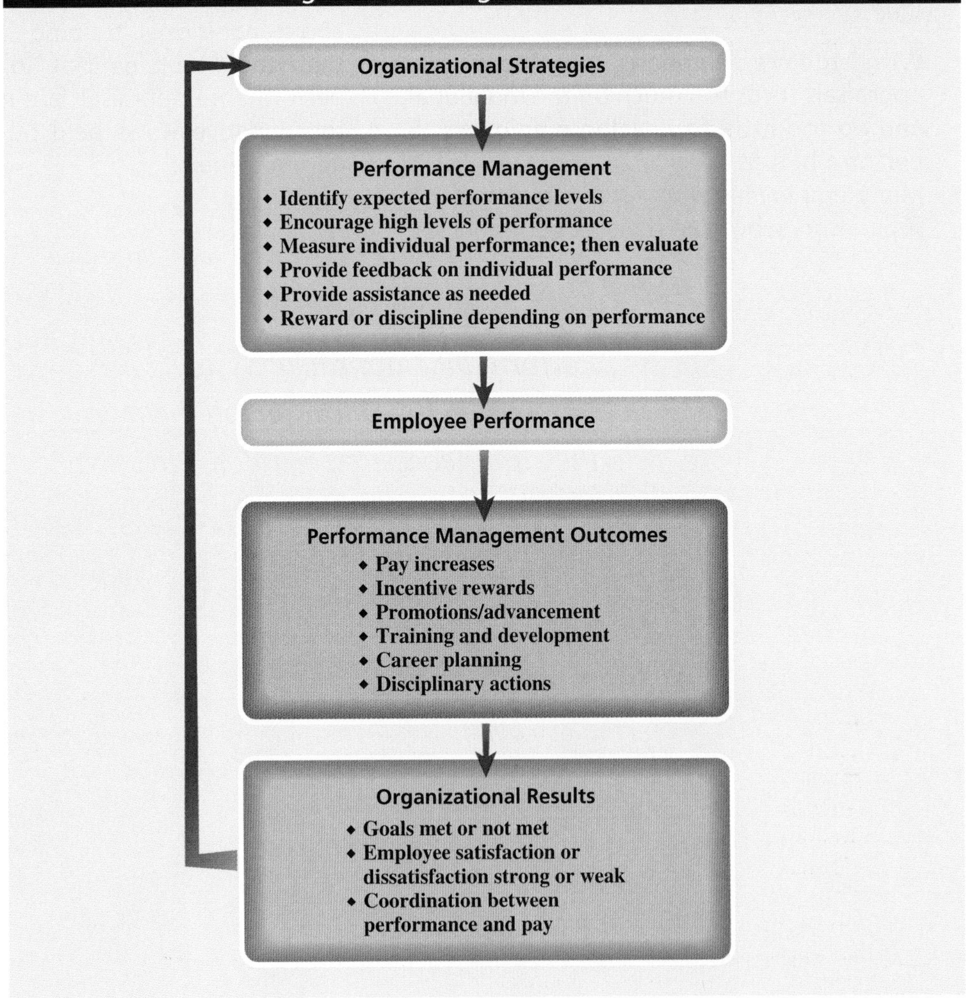

- Provide information to employees about their performance.
- Clarify the organizational performance expectations.
- Identify the development steps that are needed to enhance employee performance.
- Document performance for personnel actions.
- Provide rewards for achieving performance objectives.

Difference Between Performance Management and Performance Appraisals

Performance appraisal
Process of evaluating how well employees perform their jobs and then communicating that information to the employees.

In many organizations, managers and employees mistakenly equate performance appraisals with performance management. **Performance appraisal** is the process of evaluating how well employees perform their jobs and then communicating that information to the employees. Performance appraisal is also called *employee rating, employee evaluation, performance review,* and *performance evaluation.* It is easiest to think of performance appraisal as the way that performance management is implemented, as follows:

Performance Management	⇒	**Performance Appraisals**	⇒	**Performance Feedback**	⇒	**Performance Rewards and Development**

Performance management systems in organizations can be effective in countering the narrow and negative views of performance appraisals. For instance, at Windsor Family Credit Union, the CEO and other executives support performance management as part of the corporate culture. Involvement and training of managers and employees are part of performance management efforts. Also, all performance reviews are linked to key performance "drivers," such as teamwork.[3]

Performance-Focused Organizational Culture

Organizational cultures vary dramatically on many dimensions, one of which is the emphasis on performance management. Some corporate cultures are based on *entitlement,* meaning that adequate performance and stability dominate the organization. Employee rewards systems vary little from person to person and are not based on individual performance differences. As a result, the performance appraisal activities are seen as having little tie to performance and as being primarily a "bureaucratic exercise."

International Society for Performance Improvement
This association is dedicated to improving human performance in the workplace. The website includes links to many valuable articles.
www.ispi.org

At the other end of the spectrum is a *performance-driven* organizational culture focused on corporate values, results, information sharing, and performance appraisal systems that link results to employee compensation and development. The importance of a performance-focused culture is seen in the results of several studies. One longitudinal study of 207 companies in 22 industries found that firms with performance-focused cultures had significantly higher growth in company revenue, employment, net income, and stock prices than did companies with different cultures. Another study, by Becker, Huselid, and Ulrich, found that firms with strong performance cultures had dramatically better results as well.[4]

As the HR Globally indicates, wider cultural values affect performance management and organizational cultures. Those wider cultural values must be considered in a global workforce.

Cultural Differences in Performance Management

Performance management systems and performance appraisal processes are very common in Canada and in some other countries. When they are transported for use in other countries where multinational organizations have operations, or when they are used with employees having non-North American cultural backgrounds, problems can arise.

In some countries and cultures, it is uncommon for managers to rate employees or to give direct feedback, particularly if some points are negative. For instance, in several countries, including China and Japan, there is a high respect for authority and age. Consequently, expecting younger subordinates to engage in joint discussions with their managers through a performance appraisal process is uncommon. Use of such programs as multisource/360-degree feedback (discussed later in this chapter) would be culturally inappropriate.

In various other cultures, employees may view criticism from superiors as personally devastating rather than as useful feedback indicating training and development needs. Therefore, many managers do not provide feedback, nor do employees expect it.

Even in the physical settings for the appraisal discussions, "cultural customs" associated with formal meetings may need to be observed. In some Eastern European countries, it is common to have coffee and pastries or an alcoholic drink before beginning any formal discussion. These examples illustrate that the performance management processes may need to be adapted, or even not used in certain global settings.[5]

1. Considering Canada's multicultural makeup, what potential cultural barriers could arise with performance appraisals in organizations?
2. How do you feel managers should deal with negative feedback?

Executive Commitment to Performance Management

One crucial aspect of a performance-focused culture is executive involvement in continually reinforcing the performance message.[6] If top executives do performance reviews on employees who report directly to them, then they are supporting the performance culture. In many organizations, performance appraisals are supposed to be done by all managers, but senior executives never do them, nor are they held accountable for conducting feedback with their employees. Another indicator of a performance-focused culture is executive compensation plans that are clearly linked to company performance measures, rather than compensation systems that allow huge payouts for executives when results are mediocre and give employees small or no pay increases.

Identifying and Measuring Employee Performance

2 The second phase of an effective performance management system is that important performance measures are identified and used. Employee performance measures common to most jobs include the following elements:

- Quantity of output
- Quality of output
- Timeliness of output
- Presence at work

Job criteria
Important elements in a given job.

Other dimensions of performance beyond these general ones apply to various jobs. Specific **job criteria,** or dimensions of job performance, identify the most important elements in a given job. For example, a professor's job often includes the job criteria of teaching, research, and service. Job criteria are identified from well-written job descriptions that contain the most important factors of individual jobs. They define what the organization pays employees to do; therefore, the performance of individuals on job criteria should be measured and compared against standards, and then the results communicated to the employee.

Multiple job criteria are the rule rather than the exception in many jobs. Often, a given individual might demonstrate better performance on some job criteria than others. Also, some criteria might be more important than others to the organization. Weights can be used to show the relative importance of several job criteria in one job. For example, in a management job at a company that values revenue, cost control, and employee development, weights might be assigned as follows:

Management Job Criteria at Sample Firm	Weight
Revenue increase	**40%**
Cost control	**30%**
Employee development	**30%**
Total Management Performance	**100%**

Individual Performance Factors

The three major factors that affect how a given individual performs are (1) individual ability to do the work, (2) effort expended, and (3) organizational support. The relationship of those factors is widely acknowledged in management literature as follows:

$$\text{Performance } (P) = \text{Ability } (A) \times \text{Effort } (E) \times \text{Support } (S)$$

Individual performance is enhanced to the degree that all three components are present with an individual employee, and diminished if any of these factors is reduced or absent. For instance, assume that several production workers have the abilities to do their jobs and work hard, but the organization provides outmoded equipment or the management style of supervisors causes negative reactions by the workers. Or assume that a customer service representative in a call centre has the necessary abilities and the employer provides excellent support, but the individual hates "being tied to a telephone cord" all day and is frequently absent because of that dislike, even though the job pays well. In both cases, individual performance is likely to be lower than it would be if all three components were present. Individual motivation, one of the variables that affects effort, is often missing from the performance equation.

Types of Performance Information

Managers can use three types of information about how employees are performing their jobs, as Figure 9-2 shows. *Trait-based information* identifies a character trait of the employee—such as attitude, initiative, or creativity—and may or may not be job related. Because traits tend to be ambiguous, and favouritism of raters can affect how traits are viewed, trait-based performance appraisals are generally too vague to use when making performance-based HR decisions such as promotions or terminations.

Behaviour-based information focuses on specific behaviours that lead to job success. For a salesperson, the behaviour "verbal persuasion" can be observed and used as information on performance. Although more difficult to identify, behavioural

Figure 9-2 Types of Performance Information

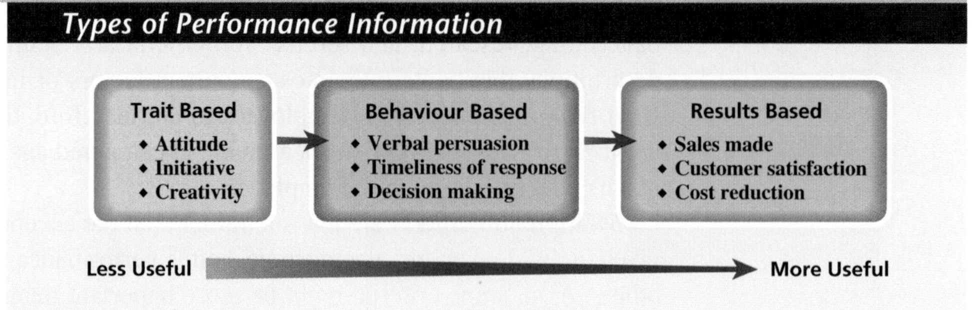

information clearly specifies the behaviours management wants to see. A potential problem arises when any of several behaviours can lead to successful performance in a given situation. For example, identifying successful use of verbal persuasion for a salesperson might be difficult because an approach that is successful when used by one salesperson may not be successful when used by another.

Results-based information considers employee accomplishments. For jobs in which measurement is easy and obvious, a results-based approach works well. However, that which is measured tends to be emphasized, and that emphasis may leave out equally important but unmeasurable parts of the job. For example, a car sales representative who gets paid *only* for sales may be unwilling to do paperwork or other work not directly related to selling cars. Further, ethical or even legal issues may arise when only results are emphasized and how the results were achieved is not considered.

Performance measures can also be viewed as objective or subjective. *Objective* measures can be observed directly—for example, the number of cars sold or the number of invoices processed can be counted. *Subjective* measures require judgment on the part of the evaluator and are more difficult to determine. One example of a subjective measure is a supervisor's ratings of an employee's "attitude," which cannot be seen directly. Consequently, both objective and subjective measures should be used carefully.

Criterion relevance
The extent to which the criterion measured represents behaviours that constitute job performance

Criterion deficiency
Describe job performance behaviours that are not measured by the criterion

Criterion contamination
The degree to which the criterion measure is influenced by measures or behaviours that are not part of the job performance

Relevance of Performance Criteria

Measuring performance requires the use of **relevant criteria** that focus on the most important aspects of employees' jobs. For example, measuring the initiative of customer service representatives in an insurance claims centre may be less relevant than measuring the number of calls they handle properly. This example stresses that the most important job criteria should be identified in the employees' job descriptions.

Performance measures that leave out some important job duties are considered to be **criterion deficient.** For example, measurement of an employment interviewer's performance is likely to be deficient if it evaluates only the number of applicants hired and not the quality of those hired or how long those hired stay at the company. On the other hand, including some irrelevant **criteria contaminates** the measure. For example, appearance might be a contaminating criterion in measuring the performance of a telemarketing sales representative whom customers never see. Managers need to guard against using deficient or contaminated performance measures.

Additionally, *overemphasis* on one or two criteria can lead to problems. For example, overstressing the number of traffic tickets written by a police officer, or the revenue generated by a sales representative, may lead to ignoring other performance areas. Ethical issues can arise because employees may falsify results in order to meet the one or two criteria that are overemphasized.[7] The corporate scandals involving Enron, the federal sponsorship scandal, Nortel, Bre-X, and others illustrate this concern.

Reliability

Reliability, in the context of performance, concerns the consistency of the raters when assessing the performance results of an employee using the same appraisal tools. Using the same tools should yield similar results when two or more managers rate the same employee. There should also be consistency throughout the organization when managers are appraising all employees. This becomes important with the increased use of multisourced appraisal formats such as with 360-degree feedback.

Practicality

For appraisals to be considered practical, an appraisal system and its outcome measures must be accepted by everyone involved in the appraisal. If one participant, such as the employee, does not feel that performance appraisal is adequately assessing their performance on measures that they feel are relevant, then the appraisal will not be viewed as useful to the employee. This is equally important to those who are designing and administering the appraisals. If a manager appraises an employee on criterion measures that do not adequately define the job, then the manager will feel the results are incompatible with the goals the employee should be achieving, and there will be no practical usefulness of the appraisal. Another important issue concerns the criterion selected. If, for example, the criterion was based on units produced per month, but machinery kept breaking down, then the measure would not be reliable, nor valid, and therefore of no practical relevance for job performance.

Fairness

The performance appraisal process must be perceived as fair by everyone involved. The results of performance appraisals will ultimately result in salary increases, promotions, transfers and even termination, so the concept of fairness cannot be taken for granted. The problem often arises from "rater errors" that occur when certain employees are rated more highly than another because a manager may like the other employee more or vice-versa. It only takes one incident of a perceived unfair appraisal transaction to draw concerns from employees about an appraisal process being administered unfairly for the performance program to come into question. Therefore, managers must ensure that they are duly diligent about administering the program fairly among the employees. Awareness of "rater errors" can help in this regard and will be discussed later in the chapter.

Performance Standards

Performance standards define the expected levels of performance, and are "benchmarks" or "goals" or "targets"—depending on the approach taken. Performance standards need to be written in a way that captures all important elements to achieve the expected goals. One approach to writing up performance standards uses the *"SMART"* approach: *S* = Specific, *M* = Measurable, *A* = Attainable, *R* = Relevant, *T* = Time-bound. Using this approach will benefit both organizations and employees. In a sense, performance standards define satisfactory job performance. It is recommended that performance standards be established *before* the work is performed. Well-defined standards ensure that everyone involved knows the levels of accomplishment expected.

Both numerical and non-numerical standards can be established. Sales quotas and production output standards are familiar numerical performance standards. A standard of performance can also be based on non-numerical criteria. The following performance standards illustrate both types:

Job Criterion: **Keep current on supplier technology.**
Performance Standards: **1. Every four months, invite suppliers to make presentation of newest technology. 2. Visit supplier plants twice a year. 3. Attend trade shows quarterly.**
Job Criterion: **Do price or cost analysis as appropriate.**
Performance Standard: **Performance is acceptable when employee follows all requirements of the procedure "Price and Cost Analysis."**

Performance standards can be set by managers, employees, or others such as quality control inspectors or financial analysts. Generally, it is recommended that managers and supervisors review and discuss the standards with employees and get their input. The joint involvement of employees and their supervisors is critical to how the performance standards are perceived and used. Standards can be identified effectively by employees and their supervisors because both usually know what constitutes satisfactory performance of the dimensions of the employees' jobs.

Job analysis is the basis on which performance standards are derived to evaluate and measure objectives developed. It is often used in performance appraisal programs

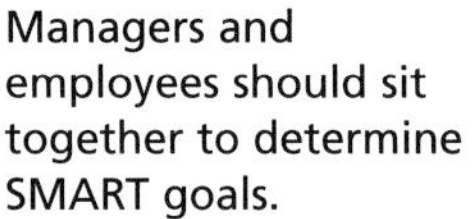

Managers and employees should sit together to determine SMART goals.

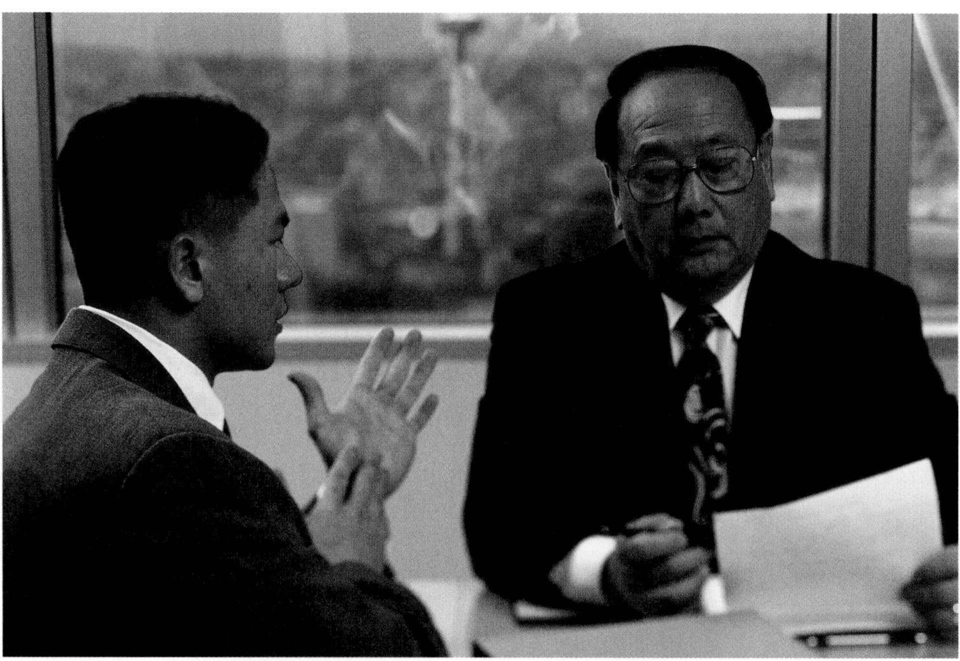

Source: Keith Brofsky/Photodisc/Getty Images

to help the manager and individual develop or identify particular standards that the performance will be evaluated against. Performance standards can also be built right into the job description which is another result of job analysis. The job description can be used as a guide to generate performance standards on which behaviour is evaluated.[8]

Legal and Effective Performance Appraisal Processes

3 To be an effective part of performance management, performance appraisals must accomplish three major purposes: legal compliance and documentation, administrative uses, and developmental uses. Because these three purposes may have conflicting effects, achieving them all is challenging in many organizations. The decisions made in designing the appraisal process can influence the degree to which appraisals serve those purposes.

Legal Concerns and Performance Appraisals

Because appraisals are supposed to measure how well employees are doing their jobs, it may seem unnecessary to emphasize that performance appraisals must be job related. Yet courts have ruled in numerous cases that performance appraisals were discriminatory and not job related. In June 2001, the British Columbia Supreme Court ruled in favour of a salesman who was dismissed due to an unwarranted poor performance appraisal. In the four years that Donald Marlowe worked for Ashland Canada Inc., he always managed to surpass his personal sales goals and he also increased sales in his region by 500 percent. Despite his outstanding performance, his new supervisor gave him the lowest possible rating on his performance appraisal, which also featured unsupported allegations of misconduct. A few months after the appraisal, Marlowe was dismissed by Ashland. The B.C court found that the actions of the man's supervisor were "harsh, vindictive, malicious and reprehensible" and the court believed that the appraisal was primarily used as a reason for not giving the salesman a bonus. The court also determined that the appraisal also led to his dismissal and a negative reference given to a prospective employer. The court gave punitive damages to Marlowe in the sum of $20,000. The court stated that "Employers are bound to deal with matters of employment fairly and in good faith."[9]

When it comes to poor performance, many employers view it as incompetence. The distinction between incompetence and other forms of employee misconduct that give rise to just cause was addressed by J. Ritter of the Alberta Court of Queen's Bench in the following passage from *Bogden v. Purolator Courier Ltd.*: "Here, to a large extent, the employer bases its dismissal of the plaintiff on the plaintiff's incompetence. In order to establish that an employee's incompetence is grounds for dismissal, an employer must show more than mere dissatisfaction with the employee's work, and it is not enough to show that the employee was careless or indifferent. To establish cause on the basis of incompetence the employer must show: 1) the level of job performance that it required and that the level required was communicated to the employee; 2) that it gave suitable instruction to the employee to enable him to meet the standard; 3) the employee was incapable of meeting the standard; and 4) there had been a warning to the employee that failure to meet the standard would result in his dismissal."[10]

CCH's Canadian Labour Law Reporter
This website offers valuable legal management information on performance appraisals and other HR topics.
www.cch.ca

The elements of a performance appraisal system that can survive court tests can be determined from existing case law. Various cases have identified the elements of a legally defensible performance appraisal to include the following:

- Objective performance appraisal criteria based on job analysis
- Absence of disparate impact and evidence of validity
- Formal evaluation criteria that limit managerial discretion
- A rating instrument linked to job duties and responsibilities
- Documentation of the appraisal activities
- Personal knowledge of and contact with the appraised individual
- Training of supervisors in conducting appraisals
- A review process that prevents one manager, acting alone, from controlling an employee's career
- Counselling to help poor performers improve

Uses of Performance Appraisals

Organizations generally use performance appraisals in two potentially conflicting ways. One use is to provide a measure of performance for consideration in making pay or other administrative decisions about employees. This administrative role often creates stress for managers doing the appraisals. The other use focuses on the development of individuals. In this role, the manager acts more as counsellor and coach than as judge, which may change the tone of the appraisal. The developmental performance appraisal emphasizes identifying current training and development needs, as well as planning employees' future opportunities and career directions. Figure 9-3 shows both uses for performance appraisal.

Administrative Uses of Appraisals Three administrative uses of appraisal affect managers and employees the most. They are: (1) determining pay adjustments; (2) making job placement decisions on promotions, transfers, and demotions; and (3) choosing employee disciplinary actions up to and including termination of employment.

A performance appraisal system is often the link between additional pay and other rewards that employees receive, and their job performance. Performance-based compensation affirms the idea that pay raises are given for performance accomplishments rather than based on length of service (seniority) or granted automatically to all employees at the same percentage levels. In pay-for-performance

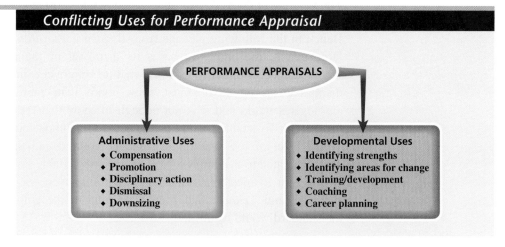

Figure 9-3 *Conflicting Uses for Performance Appraisal*

compensation systems, historically supervisors and managers have evaluated the performance of individual employees and also made compensation recommendations for the same employees. If any part of the appraisal process fails, better-performing employees may not receive larger pay increases, and the result is perceived inequity in compensation.

Many Canadian workers say that they see little connection between their performance and the size of their pay increases, due to flaws in the performance appraisal processes. However, the use of performance appraisals to determine pay is common. Consequently, many people argue that performance appraisals and pay discussions should be separated. Two major realities support this view. One is that employees often focus more on the pay amount received than on the appraisal feedback that identifies what they have done well or need to improve. The other is that managers sometimes manipulate performance appraisal ratings to justify the pay treatment they wish to give specific individuals. As a result of the second circumstance, many employees view the appraisal process as a "game," since compensation increases have already been determined before the appraisal decision.

To address these issues, numerous organizations have managers first conduct performance appraisals and discuss the results with employees, then several weeks later hold a shorter meeting in which pay is discussed. With this approach, the results of the performance appraisal can be considered before the amount of the pay adjustment is determined. Also, the performance appraisal discussions between managers/supervisors and employees can focus on the developmental uses of appraisals.

Employees are interested in the other administrative uses of performance appraisal as well, such as decisions about promotions, terminations, layoffs, and transfer assignments. Promotions and demotions based on performance must be documented through performance appraisals; otherwise, legal problems can result.

To improve the administrative processes of performance appraisals, many employers have implemented software so that managers can prepare appraisals electronically.[11] In Technology Transforming HR, Mount Sinai Hospital in Toronto has chosen to go online for performance management.

Developmental Uses of Appraisals For employees, performance appraisal can be a primary source of information and feedback, which are often important to their future development. In the process of identifying employee strengths, weaknesses, potentials, and training needs through performance appraisal feedback, supervisors can inform employees about their progress, discuss areas where additional training may be beneficial, and outline future development plans. The manager's role in such a situation parallels that of a coach, discussing good performance, explaining what improvement is necessary, and showing employees how to improve. After all, many employees do not always know where and how to improve, and managers should not expect improvement if they are unwilling to provide developmental feedback.

The purpose of such feedback is both to reinforce satisfactory employee performance and to address performance deficiencies. Positive reinforcement for desired behaviours contributes to both individual and organizational development. The development function of performance appraisal also can identify areas in which the employee might wish to grow. For example, in a performance appraisal interview targeted exclusively to development, an employee found out that the only factor keeping her from being

Technology Transforming HR

Mount Sinai Goes Online

Hospitals must go through an accreditation review every three years. HR development and management is an important component of the review. In 2003, Mount Sinai Hospital in Toronto received praise for recruitment, retention, human rights, workplace behaviour, and diversity programs. However, the hospital was advised to improve performance management in order for its employees to receive regular feedback. As a result, (with the support of employees) the hospital has implemented an automated performance management system. Before the implementation of the system, the hospital had been using a paper-based system that led to incomplete recordkeeping. Employees wanted a performance review process that was regular and fair.

The advantages of the system include giving managers the ability to access previous appraisals, as well as compare performance results by area of competency or by work group. The hospital has chosen the Halogen's eAppraisal Healthcare system because it is easy to use. It is "based on the cascading of goals from the high-level mission statement, through departmental goals to group goals and individual activities."

Appraisal can be reported as numerical or anecdotal or a combination of both. The system has the capacity to incorporate ratings from different sources that is beneficial when the manager does not work near the employee. This can also give Mount Sinai the ability to introduce a 360-degree appraisal system in the future. However, Debbie Fisher, senior vice president of organizational development and strategic projects at Mount Sinai, points out that, "The automated system is only a way to record information. It does not take away from the personal approach. I would prefer that people spend more time talking and less writing."[12]

1. Is there any guarantee that using a computerized performance appraisal system will lead to more fair appraisals and regular feedback? Why or why not?
2. Would a 360-degree rating process be useful for all staff at Mount Sinai? Why or why not?

considered for a management job in her firm was the lack of a working knowledge of cost accounting. Her supervisor suggested that she consider taking some night courses at the local college.

The use of teams provides a different set of circumstances for developmental appraisal. The manager may not see all of an employee's work, but the employee's team members do. Teams can provide developmental feedback. However, it is still an open question whether teams can handle administrative appraisals. When teams are allowed to design appraisal systems, they tend to "get rid of judgment" and avoid differential rewards. Thus, group appraisal may be best suited to developmental purposes, not administrative uses.

4 Decisions Concerning the Performance Appraisal Process

A number of decisions must be made when designing performance appraisal systems. Some important ones are identifying the appraisal responsibilities of the HR unit and of the operating managers, the type of appraisal system to use, the timing of appraisals, and who conducts appraisals.

Appraisal Responsibilities The appraisal process can benefit both the organization and the employees, if done properly. As Figure 9-4 shows, the HR unit typically designs a performance appraisal system. The operating managers then appraise employees using the appraisal system. During development of the formal appraisal system, managers usually offer input as to how the final system will work.

Figure 9-4 *Typical Division of HR Responsibilities: Performance Appraisal*

HR Unit	Managers
• Designs and maintains appraisal system • Trains raters • Tracks timely receipt of appraisals • Reviews completed appraisals for consistency	• Typically rate performance of employees • Prepare formal appraisal documents • Review appraisals with employees • Identify development areas

It is important for managers to understand appraisals as *their* responsibility. Through the appraisal process, good employee performance can be developed to be even better, and poor employee performance can be improved or poor performers may be removed from the organization. Performance appraisal is not simply an HR requirement; it must also be a management process, because guiding employees' performance is among the most important responsibilities of managers.

Informal vs. Systematic Appraisal Processes Performance appraisals can occur in two ways: informally and/or systematically. A supervisor conducts an *informal appraisal* whenever necessary. The day-to-day working relationship between a manager and an employee offers an opportunity for the employee's performance to be evaluated. A manager communicates this evaluation through conversation on the job, over coffee, or by an on-the-spot discussion of a specific occurrence.

Frequent informal feedback to employees can prevent "surprises" during a formal performance review. However, informal appraisal can become *too* informal. For example, a senior executive at a large firm so dreaded face-to-face evaluations that he recently delivered one manager's review while both sat in adjoining stalls in the men's room.

A *systematic appraisal* is used when the contact between manager and employee is formal, and a system is in place to report managerial impressions and observations on employee performance. One survey found that almost 90 percent of employers have a formal performance management system or process.[13] Although an informal appraisal is useful and necessary, it should not take the place of formal appraisal.

Systematic appraisals feature a regular time interval, which distinguishes them from informal appraisals. Both employees and managers know that performance will be reviewed on a regular basis, and they can plan for performance discussions.

Timing of Appraisals Employees commonly receive a "probationary" or "introductory" appraisal 60–90 days after hiring, again at six months, and annually thereafter. However, "probationary" or "introductory" employees, who are new and in a trial period, should be informally evaluated often—perhaps weekly for the first month, monthly thereafter until the end of the introductory period, and then annually, at a minimum. For high-demand employees, some employers use accelerated appraisals—every six months instead of every year. This is done to retain turnover-prone employees because more feedback has been given and pay raises have occurred more often.

To separate the administrative and developmental uses of appraisals, some employers implement the following appraisal schedule: First there is a performance review and discussion. Some time after that there is a separate training, development, and objective-setting session. Within two weeks of that there is a compensation adjustment discussion. Having three separate discussions provides both the employee and the employee's manager with opportunities to focus on the administrative, developmental, and compensation issues. Using this framework is generally better than addressing all three areas in one discussion of an hour or less, once a year.

Who Conducts Appraisals?

Performance appraisals can be conducted by anyone familiar with the performance of individual employees. Possible combinations include the following:

- Supervisors rating their employees
- Employees rating their superiors
- Team members rating each other
- Employees rating themselves
- Outside sources rating employees
- A variety of parties providing multisource/360-degree feedback

The most common method used is the rating of employees by their immediate supervisors or managers to whom supervisors report. The immediate superior has the main responsibility for appraisals in most organizations, although often the supervisor's boss may review and approve the appraisals. The growing use of teams and a concern with customer input contribute to two fast-growing sources of appraisal information: team members and parties outside the organization. Multisource (or 360-degree) feedback combines numerous methods and has recently grown in popularity.

Supervisory Rating of Subordinates The most widely used means of rating employees is based on the assumption that the immediate supervisor is the person most qualified to evaluate an employee's performance realistically and fairly. To help themselves provide accurate evaluations, some supervisors keep performance logs noting their employees' accomplishments and concerns. These logs provide specific examples to use when rating performance. Figure 9-5 highlights the traditional review process by which supervisors conduct performance appraisals on employees.

Employee Rating of Managers A number of organizations today ask employees or group members to rate the performance of supervisors and managers. A prime example of this type of rating takes place in colleges and universities, where students evaluate the performance of professors in the classroom. Performance appraisal ratings also are used for management development purposes.

Having employees rate managers provides three primary advantages. First, in critical manager/employee relationships, employee ratings can be quite useful for identifying competent managers, for example the rating of leaders by combat soldiers. Second, this type of rating program can help make a manager more responsive to employees. This advantage can quickly become a disadvantage if the manager focuses on being "nice" rather than on managing; people who are nice but have no other qualifications may not be good managers in many situations. Finally, employee appraisals can contribute to career development efforts for managers by identifying areas for growth.

Figure 9-5  *Traditional Performance Appraisal Process*

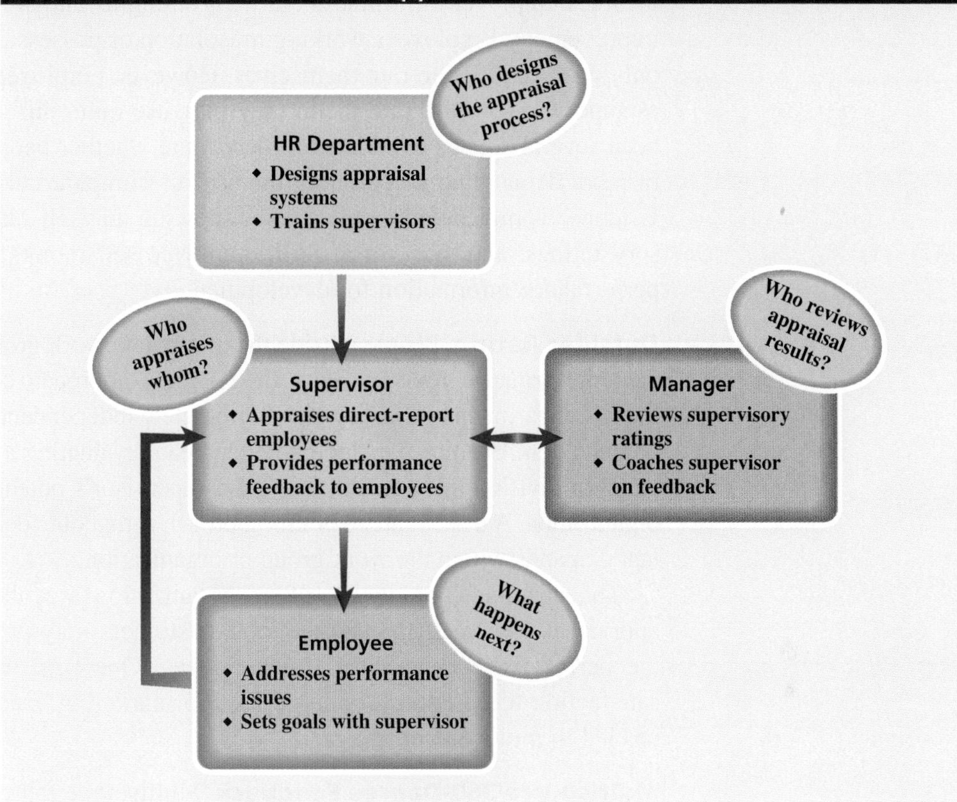

A major disadvantage of having employees rate managers is the negative reaction many superiors have to being evaluated by employees. Also, the fear of reprisals may be too great for employees to give realistic ratings. This fear may prompt workers to rate their managers only on the way the managers treat them, not on critical job requirements. The problems associated with this appraisal approach limit its usefulness to certain situations, including managerial development and improvement efforts.

Team/Peer Rating Having employees and team members rate each other is another type of appraisal with potential both to help and to hurt. Peer and team ratings are especially useful when supervisors do not have the opportunity to observe each employee's performance, but other work group members do. One challenge of this approach is how to obtain ratings with virtual or global teams, in which the individuals work primarily through technology, not in person. Another challenge is how to obtain ratings from and for individuals who are on different special project teams throughout the year.

Some contend that any performance appraisal, including team/peer ratings, can negatively affect teamwork and participative management efforts. Although team members have good information on one another's performance, they may not choose to share it. They may unfairly attack, or "go easy" to spare feelings. Some organizations attempt to overcome such problems by using anonymous appraisals and/or having a consultant or HR manager interpret team/peer ratings. Despite the problems, team/peer performance ratings are probably inevitable, especially where work teams are used extensively.[14]

Self-Rating Self-appraisal works in certain situations. As a self-development tool, it forces employees to think about their strengths and weaknesses and set goals for improvement. Employees working in isolation or possessing unique skills may be the only ones qualified to rate themselves. However, employees may not rate themselves as supervisors would rate them; they may use quite different standards. There have been several studies conducted to determine whether people tend to be more lenient or more demanding when rating themselves compared to the ratings of supervisors. Evidence is mixed with some studies showing that self-rating is higher than supervisory ratings, and vice versa. Still, employee self-ratings can be a useful source of performance information for development.

Outsider Rating People outside the immediate work group may be called in to conduct performance reviews. This field review approach can include someone from the HR department as a reviewer, or completely independent reviewers from outside the organization. Examples include a review team evaluating a university president, and a panel of division managers evaluating a supervisor's potential for advancement in the organization. A disadvantage of this approach is that outsiders may not know the important demands within the work group or organization.

The customers or clients of an organization are obvious sources for outside appraisals. For sales and service jobs, customers may provide very useful input on the performance behaviours of employees. One firm measures customer service satisfaction to determine bonuses for top marketing executives. Use of such input has led to multisource ratings.

Multisource/360-Degree Feedback Multisource rating, or 360-degree feedback, has grown in popularity. In 2002, a research team from the John Molson School of Business at Concordia University found that of 101 organizations surveyed, 43 percent used 360-degree feedback programs and out of those not using it, nine organizations were considering using it in the future.[15] Multisource/360-degree

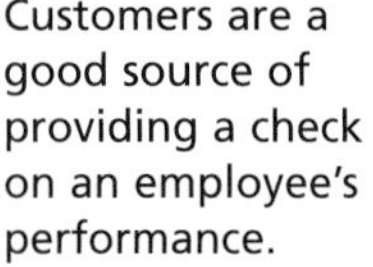
Customers are a good source of providing a check on an employee's performance.

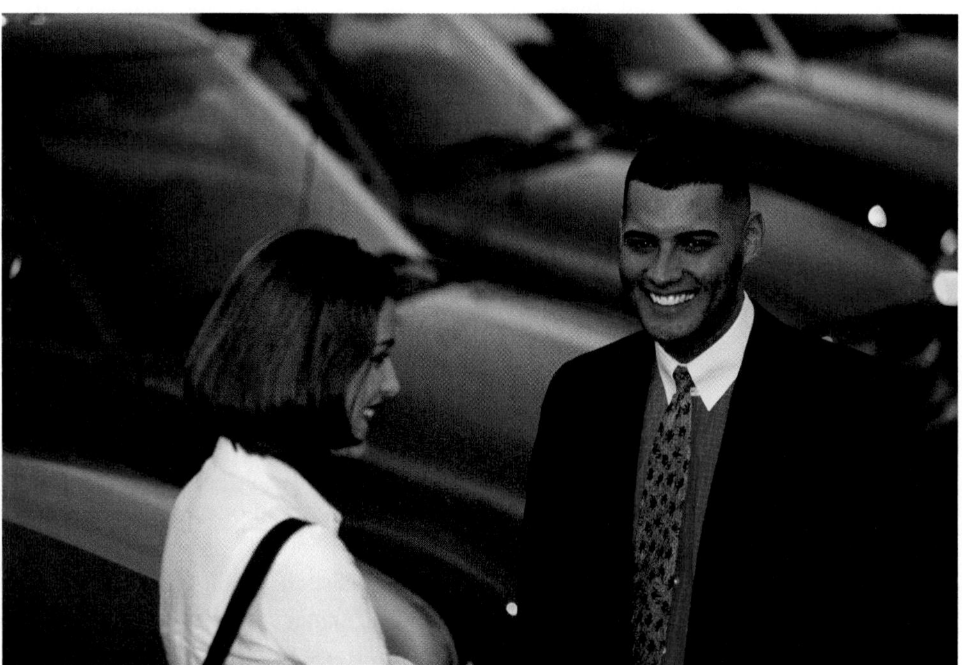

Source: Skip Nall/Photodisc/Getty Images

feedback recognizes that for a growing number of jobs, employee performance is multi-dimensional and crosses departmental, organizational, and even global boundaries. The major purpose of 360-degree feedback is *not* to increase uniformity by soliciting like-minded views. Instead, it is to capture evaluations of the individual employee's different roles. Figure 9-6 shows graphically some of the parties who may be involved in 360-degree feedback. For example, an HR manager for an insurance firm deals with seven regional sales managers, HR administrators in five claims centres, and various corporate executives in finance, legal, and information technology. The vice president of HR uses 360-degree feedback to gather data on all facets of the HR manager's job before completing a performance appraisal on the manager. Similar examples can be cited in numerous managerial, professional, technical, operational, and administrative jobs.

Significant administrative time and paperwork are required to request, obtain, and summarize feedback from multiple raters. Use of Web-based systems can significantly reduce the administrative demands of multisource ratings.

Developmental Use of Multisource Feedback As originally designed and used, multisource feedback focuses on the use of appraisals for future development of individuals. Conflict resolution skills, decision-making abilities, team effectiveness, communication skills, managerial styles, and technical capabilities are just some of the developmental areas that can be examined. Even in a multisource system, the manager remains a focal point, both to receive the feedback initially and to follow up with the employee appropriately.

Administrative Use of Multisource Feedback The popularity of 360-degree feedback systems has led to the results being used for making compensation, promotion, termination, and other administrative decisions. When using 360-degree feedback for administrative purposes, managers must anticipate potential problems.[16] Differences among raters can present a challenge, especially in the use of 360-degree ratings for discipline or pay decisions. Bias can just as easily be rooted in customers, subordinates, and peers as in a boss, and the lack of accountability of those sources can affect

Figure 9-6 *Multisource Appraisal*

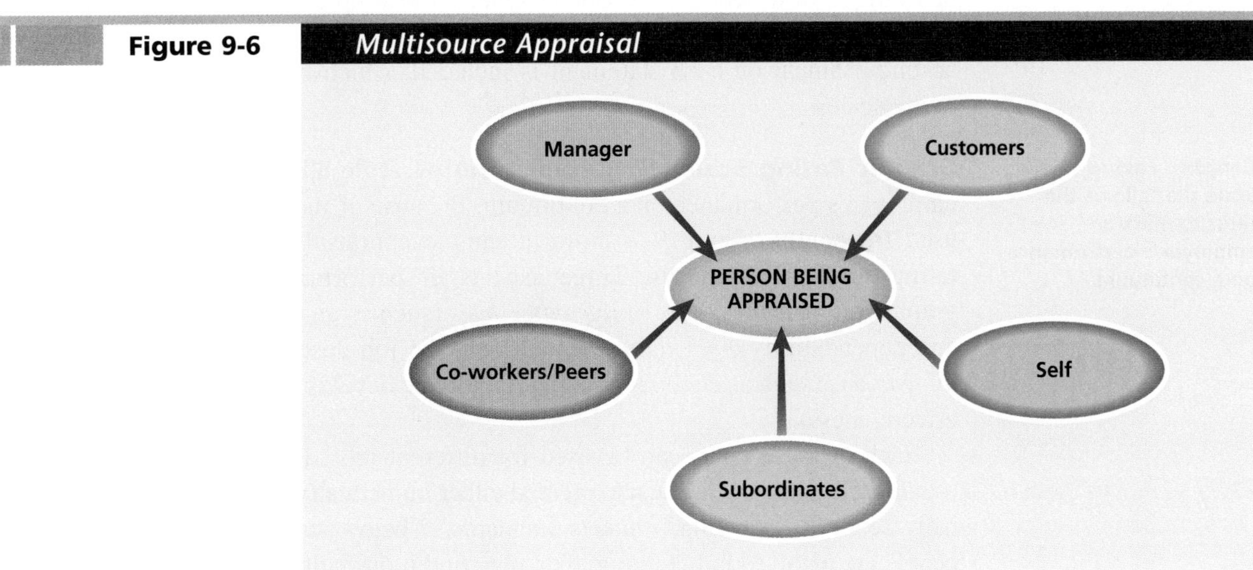

the ratings. "Inflation" of ratings is common when the sources know that their input will affect someone's pay or career. Also, issues of the confidentiality of the input and whether it is truly kept anonymous have led to lawsuits. Even though multisource approaches to performance appraisal offer possible solutions to the well-documented dissatisfaction with performance appraisal, a number of questions arise as multisource appraisals become more common.

Evaluating Multisource Feedback Research on multisource/360-degree feedback has revealed both positives and negatives. Studies have found that there can be more variability than expected in the ratings given by the different sources. Thus, supervisor ratings must carry more weight than peer or subordinate input to resolve the differences.[17] Other studies have found differences between employee self-ratings and multisource ratings. One concern is that those peers who rate poor-performing co-workers tend to inflate the ratings of those people so that the peers themselves can get higher overall evaluation results.[18]

One concern is whether 360-degree appraisals improve the process or simply multiply the number of problems by the total number of raters. Also, some wonder whether multisource appraisals really create better decisions that offset the additional time and investment required. These issues appear to be less threatening when the 360-degree feedback is used *only for development.* But they may effectively reduce the use of multisource appraisals as an administrative tool in many situations.

Methods for Appraising Performance

5 Performance can be appraised by a number of methods. Some employers use one method for all jobs and employees, some use different methods for different groups of employees, and others use a combination of methods. The following discussion highlights different methods and some of the pluses and minuses of each.

Category Scaling Methods

The simplest methods for appraising performance are category scaling methods, which require a manager to mark an employee's level of performance on a specific form divided into categories of performance. A *checklist* uses a list of statements or words from which raters check statements most representative of the characteristics and performance of employees. Often, a scale indicating perceived level of accomplishment on each statement is included, which becomes a type of graphic rating scale.

Graphic rating scale Scale that allows the rater to mark an employee's performance on a continuum.

Graphic Rating Scales The **graphic rating scale** allows the rater to mark an employee's performance on a continuum. Because of its simplicity, this method is used frequently. Figure 9-7 shows a sample appraisal form combining graphic rating scales with essays. Three aspects of performance are appraised using graphic rating scales: *descriptive categories* (such as quantity of work, attendance, and dependability), *job duties* (taken from the job description), and *behavioural dimensions* (such as decision making, employee development, and communication effectiveness).

Each of these types can be used for different jobs. How well employees meet established standards is often expressed either numerically (e.g., 5, 4, 3, 2, 1) or verbally (e.g., "outstanding," "meets standards," "below standards"). If two or more people are involved in the rating, they may find it difficult to agree on the exact level

Figure 9-7 *Sample Performance Appraisal Form*

Date sent: 4/19/07 | Return by: 5/01/07
Name: Joe Hernandez | Job title: Receiving Clerk
Department: Receiving | Supervisor: Marian Williams
Employment status (check one): Full-time _x_ Part-time ____ | Date of hire: 5/12/00
Rating period: From: 5/12/06 To: 5/12/07
Reason for appraisal (check one): Regular interval _x_ Introductory ___ Counselling only___ Discharge___

Using the following definitions, rate the performance as I, M, or E.

I—Performance is below job requirements and improvement is needed.

M—Performance meets job requirements and standards.

E—Performance exceeds job requirements and standards most of the time.

SPECIFIC JOB RESPONSIBILITIES: List the prinicipal activities from the job summary, rate the performance on each job duty by placing an X on the rating scale at the appropriate location, and make appropriate comments to explain the rating.

I ———————— M ———————— E

Job Duty #1: Inventory receiving and checking
Explanation: ____________________

I ———————— M ———————— E

Job Duty #2: Accurate recordkeeping
Explanation: ____________________

I ———————— M ———————— E

Attendance (including absences and tardies): Number of absences ___ Number of tardies ___
Explanation: ____________________

Overall rating: In the box provided, place the letter—I, M, or E—that best describes the employee's overall performance. [ ]

Explanation: ____________________

---

of performance achieved relative to the standard. Figure 9-8 defines the terms one company uses in evaluating employee performance. Notice that each level specifies performance standards or expectations in order to reduce variation in interpretations of the standards by different supervisors and employees.

Concerns with Graphic Rating Scales Graphic rating scales in many forms are widely used because they are easy to develop; however, they encourage errors on the

Figure 9-8 Terms Defining Standards at One Company

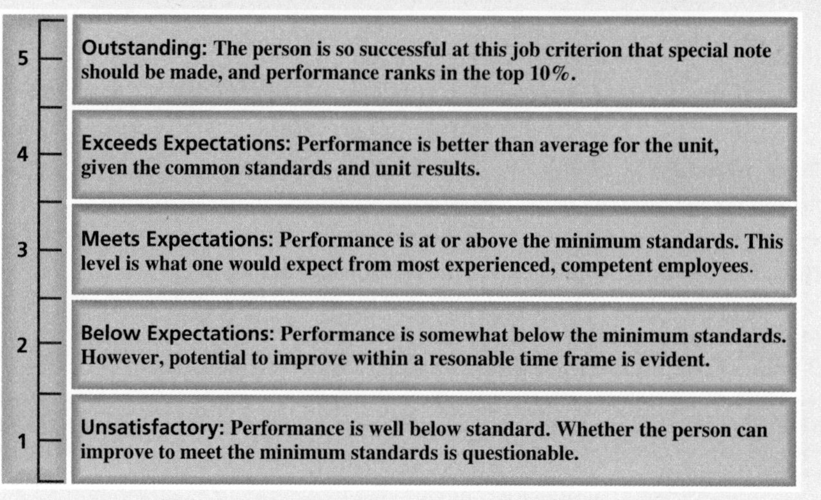

part of the raters, who may depend too heavily on the form to define performance. Also, graphic rating scales tend to emphasize the rating instrument itself and its limitations. If they fit the person and the job, the scales work well. However, if they fit poorly, managers and employees who must use them frequently complain about "the rating form."

A key point must be emphasized. Regardless of the scales used, the focus should be on the job duties and responsibilities identified in job descriptions. The closer the link between the scales and what people actually do, as identified in current and complete job descriptions, the stronger the relationship between the ratings and the job, as viewed by employees and managers. Also, should the performance appraisal results be challenged by legal actions, the more performance appraisals are tied to what people actually do, the more likely employers are to prevail in those legal situations.

An additional drawback to graphic rating scales is that often, separate traits or factors are grouped together, and the rater is given only one box to check. For example, "dependability" could refer to meeting deadlines for reports, or it could refer to attendance and tardiness. If a supervisor gives an employee a rating of 3, which aspect of "dependability" is being rated? One supervisor might rate her employees on meeting deadlines, while another supervisor rates his employees on attendance.

Another drawback is that the descriptive words sometimes used in scales may have different meanings to different raters. Terms such as *initiative* and *cooperation* are subject to many interpretations, especially if used in conjunction with words such as *outstanding, average,* and *poor.* Also, the number of scale points and how they are used can create problems, as the HR Perspective indicates.

Behavioural Rating Scales

In an attempt to overcome some of the concerns with graphic rating scales, employers may use behavioural rating scales, which are designed to assess an employee's *behaviour* instead of other characteristics. There are different approaches, but all describe specific examples of employee job behaviours.

HR Perspective

I'm Rated a 4; Why Not a 5?

One of the biggest areas of contention with appraisals is how many points to use on a graphic rating scale. Scales of 1–10, 1–7, 1–5, 1–4, and 1–3 are all used. In some firms, 1 is low; in others, 1 is high. Confusion is compounded if the meanings of the numbers are not identified.

Odd-numbered scales are used more frequently than even-numbered ones because they allow a mid-point to be identified. Probably the most widely used scale has 5 points, ranging from 1 ("low") to 5 ("high"), with 3 being labelled "satisfactory" or "meeting standards." However, in reality, many supervisors do not rate employees at either the highest or lowest levels. A comment often heard is, "If an employee is rated a 1, he or she will be terminated, and no one deserves a 5 because no one is a superstar." Couple this distorted thinking with the reaction of employees who receive a 4, which is a solid rating: often their first question is, "What do I have to do to be rated a 5?" The rating manager may reply "A 4 is a really good rating; no one gets a 5." Logically, the employee thinks, "If no one can get a 5, why is it on the form?"

Use of 9-point scales poses similar problems, with it well understood that "no one gets a 10" and "if someone gets lower than a 6, that person has a limited employment future." Similar problems exist with 7-point and 4-point scales.

The "numbers game" would not be a big concern, except that the ratings are often tied to pay increase amounts. For instance, a 3 rating may mean a 2 percent–3 percent raise, a 4 rating a 4 percent–5 percent raise, and a 5 rating a 6 percent–7 percent raise.

What is the solution? Research and the experiences of many organizations suggest that there has to be a good definition of what each level means, and then a clear description of the performance standards associated with each level for each job duty and responsibility. Without close links between the rating levels, the job duties and responsibilities, and the performance accomplishments, the appraisal number and "the form," not the performance, become the focus. Training supervisors and managers is the most significant way to improve the performance appraisal process.

1. Is it absolutely necessary to use these types of rating scales at all? Why or why not?
2. Provide specific examples of the key attributes of employees performing at 5 (highest level), 3 (middle level), and 1 (lowest level)?

Behaviourally anchored rating scales (BARS) Scales describe behaviours differentiating between effective and ineffective performers that can be observed and anchor them at points on a scale

Behaviourally Anchored Rating Scales (BARS) **Behaviourally anchored rating scales (BARS)** describe behaviours differentiating between effective and ineffective performers that can be observed and anchor them at points on a scale. The applicant's behaviour are compared against examples and rated accordingly. The content of the scale is developed from a job analysis and is based on responses to critical job incidents or situations. Anchor statements are usually developed by a group of people familiar with the job. These are typically employees and managers. Assignment to a dimension usually requires the agreement of 60 percent–70 percent of the group. The group then assigns each anchor a number that represents how good or bad the behaviour is, and the anchors are fitted to a scale. Figure 9-9 contains an example that rates customer service skills for individuals taking orders for a national catalogue retailer. Spelling out the behaviours associated with each level of performance helps minimize some of the problems noted for the graphic rating scale.

Advantages of BARS A distinct advantage of the BARS method is that the scales are often developed by the same people who will eventually use them. Therefore, there should be an understanding and awareness of the scale, which will contribute to more accurate assessment of performance. Also, BARS is helpful to raters by their usage of technical terms. The BARS method defines the dimensions and behavioural labels in the language and terminology of the rater. This helps to ensure that the dimensions and the labels are interpreted the same by all raters, thereby increasing interrater

Figure 9-9 *Behaviourally Anchored Rating Scale for Customer Service Skills*

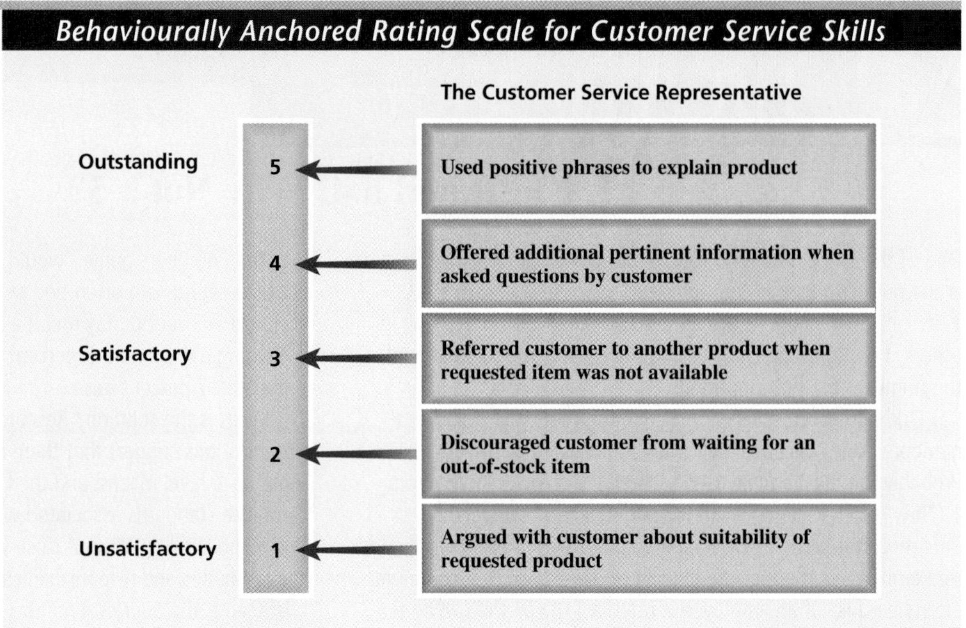

reliability. Perhaps one of the most appealing features of BARS is that it uses specific behavioural incidents as anchors. In addition, behaviourally based methods have been shown to lead to elevated levels of goal clarity, goal commitment, and goal acceptance compared to graphic rating scales. In summary, the BARS format not only corrects for errors in graphic rating scales, it provides many substantial advantages over other scale formats.

Concerns with Bars Despite the positive attributes of BARS, several problems do exist. First, developing and maintaining behaviourally anchored rating scales require extensive time and effort, and financial resources. In addition, various appraisal forms are needed to accommodate different types of jobs in an organization. For instance, because nurses, dietitians, and admissions clerks in a hospital all have distinct job descriptions, a separate BARS form needs to be developed for each job, and for each task and/or competency in each job. Another concern is that the rater may tend to measure behaviour and not performance, because the behaviour is so clearly defined. A BARS for one job does not translate to another job as it is hard to apply to managerial/professional jobs. Where job outputs can't be directly measured, BARS usually become general behavioural descriptions and the behaviours described are assumed to be relevant to performance. In spite of all the shortfalls, BARS is still considered to be the best rating procedure for performance.

Comparative Methods

Comparative methods require that managers directly compare the performance levels of their employees against one another. For example, the information systems supervisor would compare the performance of a programmer with that of other programmers. Comparative techniques include ranking and forced distribution.

Ranking
Performance appraisal method in which all employees are listed from highest to lowest in performance.

Ranking The **ranking** method lists all employees from highest to lowest in performance. The primary drawback of the ranking method is that the sizes of the differences between individuals are not well defined. For example, the performances of individuals ranked second and third may differ little, while the performances of those ranked third and fourth differ a great deal. This drawback can be overcome to some extent by assigning points to indicate the sizes of the gaps. Ranking also means someone must be last, which ignores the possibility that the last-ranked individual in one group might be equal to the top-ranked employee in a different group. Further, the ranking task becomes unwieldy if the group to be ranked is large.

Forced distribution Performance appraisal method in which ratings of employees' performance are distributed along a bell-shaped curve.

Forced Distribution Forced distribution is a technique for distributing ratings that are generated with any of the other appraisal methods, and comparing the ratings of people in a work group. With the **forced distribution** method, the ratings of employees' performance are distributed along a bell-shaped curve. For example, a medical clinic administrator ranking employees on a 5-point scale would have to rate 10 percent as a 1 ("unsatisfactory"), 20 percent as a 2 ("below expectations"), 40 percent as a 3 ("meets expectations"), 20 percent as a 4 ("above expectations"), and 10 percent as a 5 ("outstanding").

Forced distribution is used in some form by an estimated 30 percent of all firms with performance appraisal systems. At General Electric, in the "20-70-10" program, managers identify the top 20 percent and reward them richly so that few will leave. The bottom 10 percent are given a chance to improve or leave. The forced distribution system is controversial because of both its advantages and its disadvantages, which are discussed next.[19]

Advantages and Disadvantages of Forced Distribution One reason why firms have mandated the use of forced distributions for appraisal ratings is to deal with "rater inflation." If employers do not require a forced distribution, performance appraisal ratings often do not approximate the normal distribution of the bell-shaped curve (see Figure 9-10).

The use of a forced distribution system makes managers identify high, average, and low performers. Thus, high performers can be rewarded and developed, while low

Figure 9-10 *Forced Distribution on a Bell-Shaped Curve*

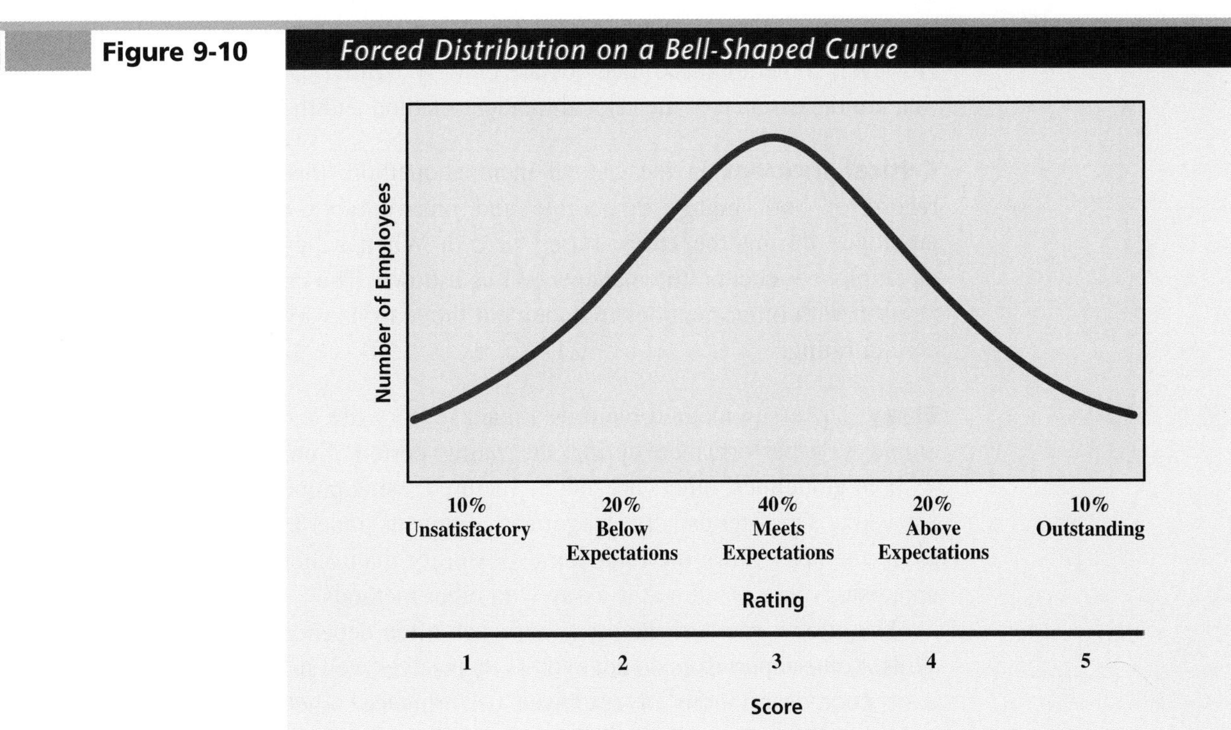

performers can be "encouraged" to improve or leave. At ATI Technologies, a Markham, Ontario-based chip manufacturer, vice president of human resources Michel Cadieux believes that his firm's use of the system helps identify top performers and that, "if someone is hired in a technical area, and they should have the technical skills but they don't, well, we would probably have to make a change. We would hire someone who does."[20] Advocates of forced ranking also state that forced distribution ensures that compensation increases truly are differentiated by performance rather than being spread somewhat equally among all employees.[21]

But the forced distribution method suffers from several drawbacks.[22] One problem is that a supervisor may resist placing any individual in the lowest (or the highest) group. Difficulties also arise when the rater must explain to an employee why she or he was placed in one group and others were placed in higher groups. Further, with small groups, the assumption that a bell-shaped or other distribution of performance occurs may be faulty. Finally, in some cases, the manager may make false distinctions between employees. By comparing people against each other, rather than against a standard of job performance, supervisors trying to fill the percentages may end up giving employees subjective ratings.

A number of actions are recommended to address these problems if a forced distribution system is to be used. They include many that are similar to those for making other methods of appraisals more legal and effective.[23]

- Use specific, objective criteria and standards.
- Involve employees in planning and designing the programs.
- Ensure that sufficient numbers of people are rated, so that statistical rankings are relevant.
- Train managers, and review their ratings to ensure that they are job related, not based on favouritism.

Narrative Methods

Managers and HR specialists are required to provide written appraisal information. However, some appraisal methods are entirely written. Documentation and description are the essence of the critical incident method and the essay method.

Critical Incident In the critical incident method, the manager keeps a written record of both highly favourable and unfavourable actions performed by an employee during the entire rating period. When a "critical incident" involving an employee occurs, the manager writes it down. The critical incident method can be used with other methods to document the reasons why an employee was given a certain rating.

Essay The essay method requires a manager to write a short essay describing each employee's performance during the rating period. Some "free-form" essays are without guidelines; others are more structured, using prepared questions that must be answered. The rater usually categorizes comments under a few general headings. The essay method allows the rater more flexibility than other methods do. As a result, appraisers often combine the essay with other methods.

The effectiveness of the essay approach often depends on a supervisor's writing skills. Some supervisors do not express themselves well in writing and as a result produce poor descriptions of employee performance, whereas others have excellent writing skills and can create highly positive impressions.

Results-Based Methods

A results-based performance appraisal system focuses on concrete standards of performance that employees are expected to achieve. Goals are often mutually set by the employee and the manager. For senior positions, employees will typically advise their manager of what they feel would be appropriate goals for their position, based on what is needed in the job and in meeting the overall strategies of the organization. Junior employees will typically need more assistance from their managers to set appropriate goals. Any goals that are established will need to be frequently assessed to ensure that the goals are being met. If there are problems, then these need to be addressed. Sometimes goals may need to be reestablished if goals are met prematurely, or if there are unforeseen issues that prevent the employee from reaching those goals. One problem that is common among results-based performance is that it does not take into consideration any deficiencies in why the employee did not reach a goal, or what they did to achieve it. The focus may be on obtaining the goal. Sometimes goals may be affected by factors that are external to employee's performance. The management by objectives approach is the most common form of results-based performance appraisal known, however, a newer model is the balanced scorecard.

Management by objectives (MBO)
Performance appraisal method that specifies the performance goals that an individual and manager mutually identify.

Management by Objectives (MBO) **Management by objectives (MBO)** specifies the performance goals that an individual and manager mutually identify. Each manager sets objectives derived from the overall goals and objectives of the organization; however, MBO should not be a disguised means for a superior to dictate the objectives of individual managers or employees. Other names for MBO include *appraisal by results, target coaching, work planning and review, performance objective setting,* and *mutual goal setting.*

MBO Process Implementing a guided self-appraisal system using MBO is a four-stage process. The stages are as follows:

1. *Job review and agreement:* The employee and the superior review the job description and the key activities that constitute the employee's job. The idea is to agree on the exact makeup of the job.
2. *Development of performance standards:* Together, the employee and his or her superior develop specific standards of performance and determine a satisfactory level of performance that is specific and measurable. For example, a quota of selling five cars a month may be an appropriate performance standard for a salesperson.
3. *Setting of objectives:* Together, the employee and the superior establish objectives that are realistically attainable.
4. *Continuing performance discussions:* The employee and the superior use the objectives as bases for continuing discussions about the employee's performance. Although a formal review session may be scheduled, the employee and the supervisor do not necessarily wait until the appointed time to discuss performance. Objectives can be mutually modified as warranted.

The MBO process seems to be most useful with managerial personnel and employees who have a fairly wide range of flexibility and control over their jobs. When imposed on a rigid and autocratic management system, MBO often has failed. Emphasizing penalties for not meeting objectives defeats the development and participative nature of MBO.

Balanced Scorecard As discussed at the beginning of the chapter, the measurement of an employee's performance must be linked to an organization's strategies. One remedy for this is to use a balanced scorecard approach as it links the strategy, resource allocation and performance appraisal systems (see Figure 9-11). The balanced scorecard was introduced in 1992 by professors from Harvard, Robert Kaplan and David Norton, and is used by a number of Fortune 500 companies. It is a tool that translates an organization's mission and strategy, into a comprehensive set of performance measures and targets. While conceptually similar to an MBO program it goes one step further in that it considers multiple segments of the organization from which to develop employee objectives. It provides feedback around both the internal business processes and external outcomes in order to continuously improve strategic performance and results. Four key perspectives of an organization are measured: [24]

- Financial
- Internal business processes
- Learning and growth
- Customer

Figure 9-11 *The Balanced Scorecard*

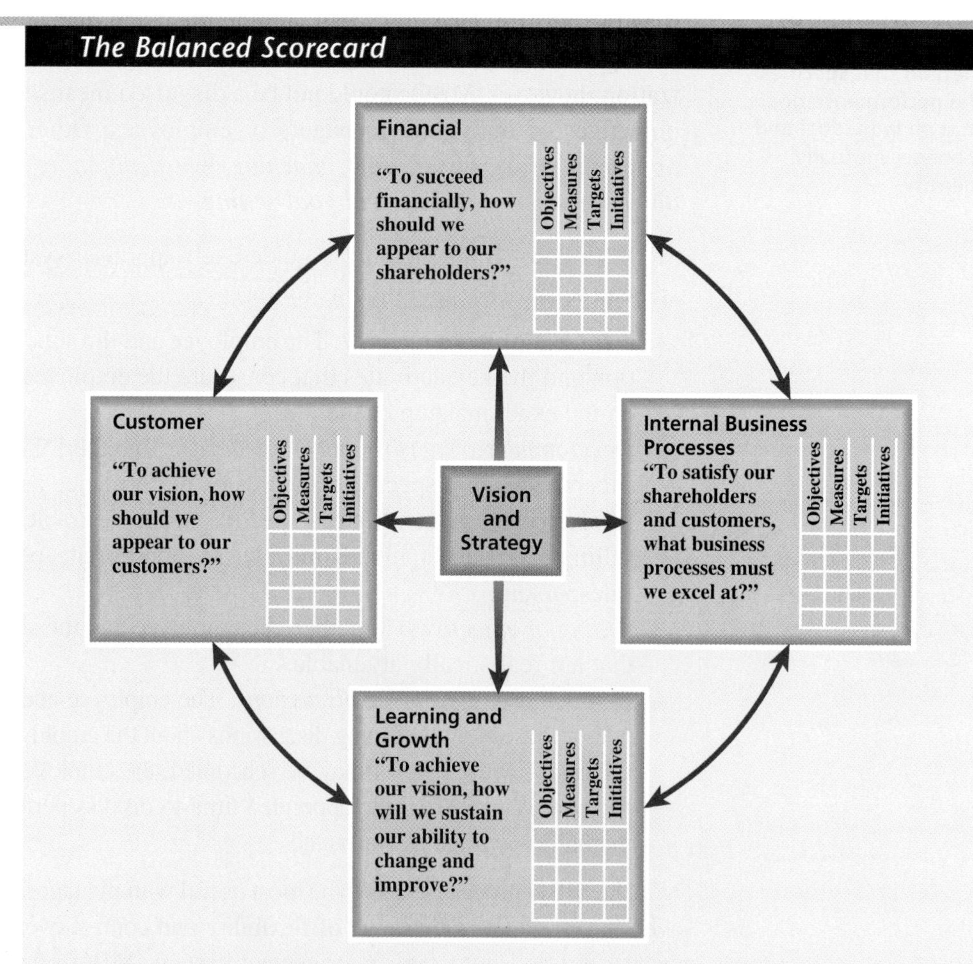

Source: Robert Kaplan and David Norton, "Strategic Learning and the Balanced Scorecard," *Strategy & Leadership* 24, no. 5, September/October 1996, 18–24.

Kaplan and Norton cite the following benefits of using the balanced scorecard:

- Focusing the whole organization on the few key things needed to create breakthrough performance.
- Helping to integrate various corporate programs, such as quality, re-engineering, and customer service initiatives.
- Breaking down strategic measures to local levels so that unit managers, operators, and employees can see what's required at their level to roll into excellent performance overall.

Potential Problems with Balanced Scorecard According to Paul Niven, author of *Balanced Scorecard Step by Step: Maximizing Performance and Maintaining Results,* the balanced scorecard approach can be successful if the following issues are avoided:[25]

Lack of cascading Organizations of any appreciable size, however, must cascade the scorecard from top to bottom if they hope to gain the advantages offered by this system. Employees can work to achieve goals based on those just above them that will make sense to them, and within reach and reason.

No new measures When moving towards a balanced scorecard approach, organizations may try and fit their old performance measures into the new approach. This is the time that everyone must reestablish their performance goals to fit with the new program.

Consistent management practices Many organizations fail when their policies are at odds with one another. A good example is attempting to manage by the balanced scorecard yet compensating executives solely on short-term financial performance, or insisting on teamwork, but rewarding individuals for their contributions.

Timing Some organizations want to wait until they have all of their measures in place, or they try and implement it too soon. Often the best results are achieved when organizations take the necessary time to let the ideas and discussions grow and develop, moving from concept to reality and in so doing producing innovative new measures and solutions.

No objectives for the balanced scorecard program A lack of guiding objectives often results from having the scorecard developed as an "add on" to another large-scale change project. With no clearly articulated goal for the program it can be easily misunderstood and ultimately ignored until it simply fades from view.

No strategy At the very core of the scorecard concept is the organization's strategy—guiding all actions, decisions, and ensuring alignment from top to bottom. A scorecard can be developed without the aid of a strategy but it then becomes a key performance indicator or stakeholder system, lacking in many of the attributes offered from a true balanced scorecard.

Lack of balanced scorecard education and training In their haste to build scorecards the vast majority of organizations will sacrifice the upfront effort of providing meaningful and detailed scorecard training to those expected to use the system. It is important to take the necessary time at the beginning of the project to develop a comprehensive scorecard curriculum that includes background on the concept, your objectives in implementing it, typical problems, success stories, and project details.

No executive sponsorship Many scorecard elements will take place in stages—first strategy is deciphered and translated, objectives, measures, targets, and initiatives are then developed, the scorecard is cascaded throughout the organization, and finally it becomes embedded in the organization's managerial processes. Executive support and sponsorship is the common thread that connects the entire end-to-end process. Without a strong and vocal leader present at each and every juncture the effort can quickly stall.

Combination of Methods

No single appraisal method is best for all situations. Therefore, a performance measurement system that uses a combination of methods may be sensible in certain circumstances. Using combinations may offset some of the advantages and disadvantages of individual methods. Category scaling methods sometimes are easy to develop, but they usually do little to measure strategic accomplishments. Further, they may make interrater reliability problems worse. Comparative approaches help reduce leniency and other errors, which makes them useful for administrative decisions such as determining pay raises. But comparative approaches do a poor job of linking performance to organizational goals, and they do not provide feedback for improvement as well as other methods do.

Narrative methods work well for development because they potentially generate more feedback information. However, without good definitions of criteria or standards, they can be so unstructured as to be of little value. Also, these methods work poorly for administrative uses. The management-by-objectives approach works well to link performance to organizational goals, but it can require much effort and time for defining expectations and explaining the process to employees. Narrative and results-based methods such as MBO approaches and balanced scorecard may not work as well for lower-level jobs as for jobs with more varied duties and responsibilities.

When managers can articulate what they want a performance appraisal system to accomplish, they can choose and mix methods to realize those advantages. For example, one combination might include a graphic rating scale of performance on major job criteria, a narrative of developmental needs, and an overall ranking of employees in a department. Different categories of employees (e.g., salaried, supervisory, and non-supervisory and hourly) might require different combinations of methods.

Training of Managers and Employees

6 Court decisions on the legality of performance appraisals and research on appraisal effectiveness both stress the importance of training managers and employees on performance management and conducting performance appraisals. As the HR Perspective describes, managers with positive views of the performance appraisal system are more likely to use the system effectively. Unfortunately, such training occurs only sporadically or not at all in many organizations. One survey found that over half of all employers provide employees with little or no performance management training and a third provide managers with little or no such training.[26]

For employees, performance appraisal training focuses on the purposes of appraisal, the appraisal process and timing, and how performance criteria and standards are linked to job duties and responsibilities. Some training also discusses how employees should rate their own performance and use that information in discussions with their supervisors and managers.

Most systems can be improved by training supervisors in doing performance appraisals.[27] Because conducting appraisals is critical, training should centre around minimizing rater errors and providing raters with details on documenting performance information.

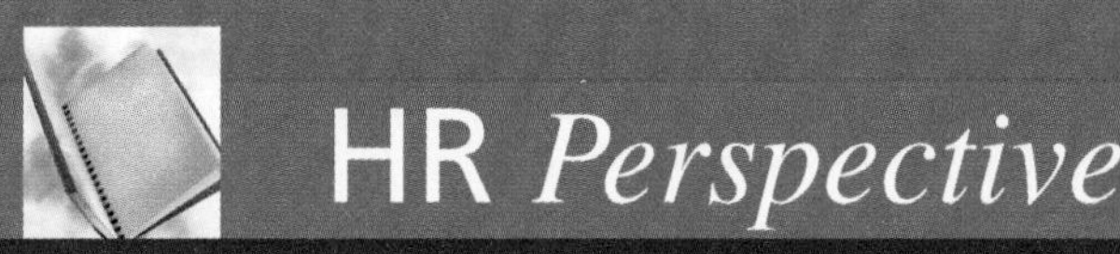

Research on Performance Raters and Performance Appraisals

How managers and supervisors complete performance appraisals on employees is affected by how the raters view the appraisal process. The impact of raters' attitudes and beliefs was examined by Tziner, Murphy, and Cleveland in a study published in the *International Journal of Selection and Assessment.*

The study was based on surveys of about 250 managers from different organizations, and all those managers had responsibilities for doing performance appraisals on employees. One area studied was the extent to which raters felt they had the information and skills needed to accurately rate their subordinates. Additionally, the researchers addressed rater attitudes and beliefs about the appraisal system, rater conscientiousness, and rating behaviours.

Results of the study found that raters who viewed the appraisal system more favourably tended to make greater distinctions when rating employees. Those raters also reported being more comfortable making performance rating distinctions among subordinates in comparison with managers with a more negative view of appraisal systems. The analyses also found that raters who were less confident and conscientious let their more negative views of the appraisal process affect their ratings.

From an HR perspective, this study emphasizes the importance of training in order to create a more positive view of performance appraisal systems. That training can help generate more realistic and objective appraisals.[28]

Training is especially essential for those who have recently been promoted to jobs in which conducting performance appraisals is a new experience for them. Without training, managers and supervisors often "repeat the past." This means they appraise others much as they have been appraised in the past, which often will have been done poorly. The list below is not comprehensive, but it does identify some topics frequently covered in appraisal training.

- Appraisal process and timing
- Performance criteria and job standards that should be considered
- How to communicate positive and negative feedback
- When and how to discuss training and development goals
- Conducting and discussing the compensation review
- How to avoid common rating errors

Rater Errors

There are many possible sources of error in the performance appraisal process. One of the major sources is mistakes made by raters. Although completely eliminating these errors is impossible, making raters aware of them through training is helpful. Figure 9-12 lists some common rater errors.

Varying Standards When appraising employees, a manager should avoid applying different standards and expectations for employees performing similar jobs. Such problems often result from the use of ambiguous criteria and subjective weightings by supervisors.

Recency effect
Occurs when a rater gives greater weight to recent events when appraising an individual's performance.

Recency and Primacy Effects The **recency effect** occurs when a rater gives greater weight to recent events when appraising an individual's performance. Giving a student a course grade based only on his performance in the last week of class, and giving a drill press operator a high rating even though she made the quota only in the

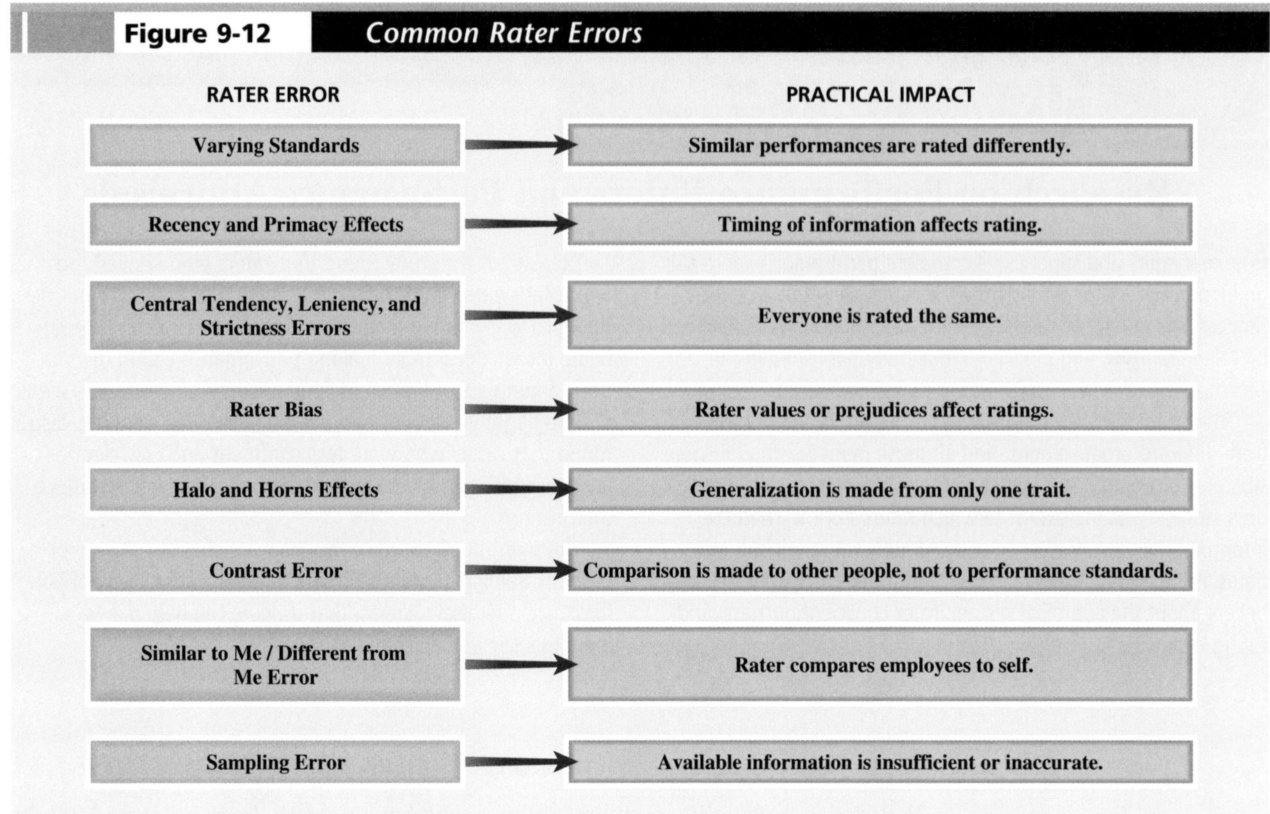

RATER ERROR
PRACTICAL IMPACT
Varying Standards
Similar performances are rated differently.
Recency and Primacy Effects
Timing of information affects rating.
Central Tendency, Leniency, and Strictness Errors
Everyone is rated the same.
Rater Bias
Rater values or prejudices affect ratings.
Halo and Horns Effects
Generalization is made from only one trait.
Contrast Error
Comparison is made to other people, not to performance standards.
Similar to Me / Different from Me Error
Rater compares employees to self.
Sampling Error
Available information is insufficient or inaccurate.

Figure 9-12 *Common Rater Errors*

Primacy effect
Occurs when a rater gives greater weight to information received first when appraising an individual's performance.

Central tendency error
Occurs when a rater gives all employees a score within a narrow range in the middle of the scale.

Leniency error
Occurs when ratings of all employees fall at the high end of the scale.

Strictness error
Occurs when ratings of all employees fall at the low end of the scale.

Rater bias
Occurs when a rater's values or prejudices distort the rating.

last two weeks of the rating period are examples. The opposite is the **primacy effect,** which occurs when a rater gives greater weight to information received first.

Central Tendency, Leniency, and Strictness Errors Ask students and they will tell you the names of professors who tend to grade easier or harder. A manager may develop a similar *rating pattern.* Appraisers who rate all employees within a narrow range in the middle of the scale (i.e., rate everyone as "average") commit a **central tendency error,** giving even outstanding and poor performers an "average" rating.

Rating patterns also may exhibit leniency or strictness. The **leniency error** occurs when ratings of all employees fall at the high end of the scale. The **strictness error** occurs when a manager uses only the lower part of the scale to rate employees. To avoid conflict, managers often rate employees higher than they should. This "ratings boost" is especially likely when no manager or HR representative reviews the completed appraisals.

Rater Bias Rater bias occurs when a rater's values or prejudices distort the rating. Such bias may be unconscious or quite intentional. For example, a manager's dislike of certain ethnic groups may cause distortion in appraisal information for some people. Use of age, religion, seniority, sex, appearance, or other "classifications" also may skew appraisal ratings if the appraisal process is not properly designed. A review of appraisal ratings by higher-level managers may help correct this problem.

Halo and Horns Effects The **halo effect** occurs when a rater scores an employee high on all job criteria because of performance in one area. For example,

Halo effect
Occurs when a rater scores an employee high on all job criteria because of performance in one area.

if a worker has few absences, her supervisor might give her a high rating in all other areas of work, including quantity and quality of output, without really thinking about the employee's other characteristics separately. The opposite is the *"horns" effect,* occurring when a low rating on one characteristic leads to an overall low rating.

Contrast error
Tendency to rate people relative to others rather than against performance standards.

Contrast Error Rating should be done using established standards. One problem is the **contrast error,** which is the tendency to rate people relative to others rather than against performance standards. For example, if everyone else in a group performs at a mediocre level, a person performing somewhat better may be rated as "excellent" because of the contrast effect. But in a group where many employees are performing well, the same person might receive a lower rating. Although it may be appropriate to compare people at times, the performance rating usually should reflect comparison against performance standards, not against other people.

Similar to Me/Different from Me Error Sometimes raters are influenced by whether people show characteristics that are the same as or different from their own. For example, if a manager has an MBA degree, he might give subordinates with MBAs higher appraisals than those with only bachelor's degrees. The error comes in measuring an individual against another person rather than measuring how well the individual fulfills the expectations of the job.

Sampling Error If the rater has seen only a small sample of the person's work, an appraisal may be subject to sampling error. For example, assume that 95 percent of the reports prepared by an employee have been satisfactory, but a manager sees only the 5 percent with errors. If the supervisor rates the person's performance as "poor," then a sampling error has occurred. Ideally, the work being rated should be a broad and representative sample of all the work done by the employee.

Appraisal Feedback

7 After completing appraisals, managers need to communicate the results in order to give employees a clear understanding of how they stand in the eyes of their immediate superiors and the organization. Organizations commonly require managers to discuss appraisals with employees. The appraisal feedback interview provides an opportunity to clear up any misunderstandings on both sides. In this interview, the manager should focus on coaching and development, and not just tell the employee, "Here is how you rate and why." Emphasizing development gives both parties an opportunity to consider the employee's performance as part of appraisal feedback.[29]

Appraisal Interview

The appraisal interview presents both an opportunity and a danger. It can be an emotional experience for the manager and the employee because the manager must communicate both praise and constructive criticism. A major concern for managers is how to emphasize the positive aspects of the employee's performance while still discussing ways to make needed improvements. If the interview is handled poorly, the employee may feel resentment, which could lead to conflict in future working relationships.

Employees usually approach an appraisal interview with some concern. They may feel that discussions about performance are both personal and important to their continued job success. At the same time, they want to know how their

Figure 9-13 Appraisal Interview Hints

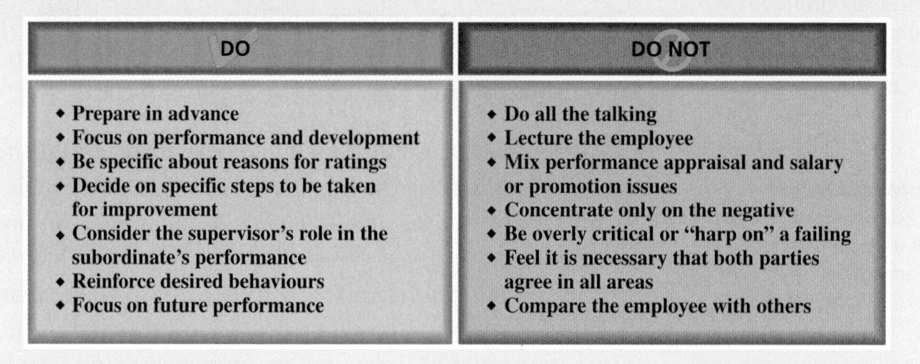

DO	DO NOT
• Prepare in advance • Focus on performance and development • Be specific about reasons for ratings • Decide on specific steps to be taken for improvement • Consider the supervisor's role in the subordinate's performance • Reinforce desired behaviours • Focus on future performance	• Do all the talking • Lecture the employee • Mix performance appraisal and salary or promotion issues • Concentrate only on the negative • Be overly critical or "harp on" a failing • Feel it is necessary that both parties agree in all areas • Compare the employee with others

managers feel about their performance. Figure 9-13 summarizes hints for an effective appraisal interview for supervisors and managers.

How to Conduct the Appraisal When conducting a performance appraisal interview it is stressed that the interview be focused on the individual whose performance is being appraised and therefore the appraisee should receive about 60 percent of the speaking time. By emphasizing two-way communication between the appraisee and the appraiser, a more effective performance management system will result. Lastly, the performance appraisal interview should focus on the future performance of the individual than on the past performance. The interview in the performance appraisal is one component of the performance management system in any organization, however, the outcomes should be focused on satisfying the training and development needs of the individual being appraised.[30]

The climate of the performance appraisal interview should take place in a private and neutral location and the atmosphere should be friendly and informal. It is critical for the appraiser to set aside a reasonable amount of time to conduct a thorough interview with the individual, usually in excess of an hour. It is also important for the appraiser to have all the necessary resources to ensure that the employee perceives the interview to be important to their further development. The appraiser should highlight the strengths of individuals' performance as well as performance deficiencies. An appraisee should not be exposed to any surprises. Their performance should be constantly monitored, and issues addressed immediately. The performance appraisal interview is meant to be a two-way discussion that emphasizes mutual goal-setting through a collaborative approach between the appraiser and appraisee.[31]

Feedback as a System

The three commonly recognized components of a feedback system are data, evaluation of that data, and some action based on the evaluation. *Data* are factual pieces of information regarding observed actions or consequences. Most often, data are facts that report what happened, such as "Charlie solved an engineering problem" or "Mary spoke harshly to an engineer." Data alone rarely tells the whole story. For instance, Mary's speaking harshly may have been an instance of poor communication and reflective of a lack of sensitivity, or it may have been a proper and necessary action. Someone must evaluate the meaning or value of the data.

Evaluation is the way the feedback system reacts to the facts, and it requires performance standards. Managers might evaluate the same factual information differently than would customers (for example, regarding merchandise exchange or credit decisions) or co-workers. Evaluation can be done by the person supplying the data, by a supervisor, or by a group.

For feedback to cause change, some decisions must be made regarding subsequent *action*. In traditional appraisal systems, the manager makes specific suggestions regarding future actions the employee might take. Employee input often is encouraged as well. In 360-degree feedback, people from whom information was solicited might also suggest actions that the individual may consider. It may be necessary to involve those providing information if the subsequent actions are highly interdependent and require coordination with the information providers. Regardless of the process used, the feedback components (data, evaluation, and action) are necessary parts of a successful performance appraisal feedback system.

Reactions of Managers

Managers and supervisors who must complete appraisals of their employees often resist the appraisal process. Many managers feel that their role calls on them to assist, encourage, coach, and counsel employees to improve their performance. However, being a judge on the one hand and a coach and a counsellor on the other hand may cause internal conflict and confusion for many managers.[32]

Knowing that appraisals may affect employees' future careers also may cause altered or biased ratings. This problem is even more likely when managers know that they will have to communicate and defend their ratings to the employees, their bosses, or HR specialists.[33] Managers can easily avoid providing negative feedback to an employee in an appraisal interview, and thus avoid unpleasantness in an interpersonal situation, by making the employee's ratings positive. But avoidance helps no one. A manager owes an employee a well-executed appraisal, as the HR Practice indicates.

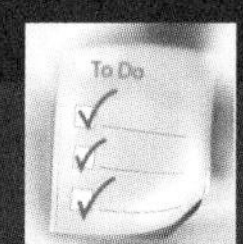

HR *Practice*

Lessons from Two Different Performances: A Supervisor's Story

My employees who do the best work are usually easy to get along with, but not always. I worked with one employee who alienated me and all his colleagues with his fierce competitiveness. He was quick to point out our mistakes, never spoke positively, and usually whined when someone else had a good project that he thought should have been his instead. I tried praising him and sought out his counsel to ease his obvious insecurities, but he was no fun to be around. However, he *was* productive. He got to work early and left late, was always eager to do more, and frequently worked overtime. He always did good work, could be counted on, and never missed a deadline. When he finally left, I realized I had come to rely on him, even though I did not miss his sour jealousy. He would not change.

Another employee and I shared common interests: some hobbies, the same work values and goals, and other interests. He was generous and willing to help, and his colleagues liked and appreciated him. Early on, he was a good producer, but later, he began procrastinating and often turned in incomplete work. I discussed it with him, and he promised to do better. But he did not. Project after project either flopped or was not done properly. Finally, I told him he would have to improve or find another job. The fact that I considered him a friend made that conversation painful, and I put it off longer than I should have. He told me he felt betrayed, and quit. Yet, when he got a new job, he called to say he had been unhappy but had been unable to move until I had pushed.[34]

1. What conclusions about performance management and performance appraisal can you draw from these two real-world examples?
2. Is just being a productive employee the most important attribute of an employee?

Reactions of Appraised Employees

Employees may well see the appraisal process as a threat and feel that the only way for them to get a higher rating is for someone else to receive a low rating. This win/lose perception is encouraged by comparative methods of rating. Emphasis on the self-improvement and developmental aspects of appraisal appears to be the most effective means to reduce these reactions from those participating in the appraisal process.[35]

Another common employee reaction resembles students' reactions to tests. A professor may prepare a test he or she feels is fair, but it does not necessarily follow that students will feel the test is fair; they simply may see it differently. Likewise, employees being appraised may not necessarily agree with the manager doing the appraising. However, in most cases, employees will view appraisals done well as what they are meant to be—constructive feedback.[36]

Effective Performance Management

Regardless of the approach used, managers must understand the intended outcome of performance management. When performance management is used to develop employees as resources, it usually works. When one key part of performance management, a performance appraisal, is used to punish employees, performance management is less effective. In its simplest form as part of performance management, performance appraisal is a manager's observation: "Here are your strengths and weaknesses, and here is a way to develop for the future." Done well, performance management can lead to higher employee motivation and satisfaction. To be effective, a performance management system, including the performance appraisal processes, should be:

- Consistent with the strategic mission of the organization
- Beneficial as a development tool
- Useful as an administrative tool
- Legal and job related
- Viewed as generally fair by employees
- Effective in documenting employee performance

SUMMARY

1 Performance management systems attempt to identify, measure, communicate, develop, and reward employee performance. All performance management efforts should be driven by business strategies. An effective performance management system clarifies and provides information to employees regarding performance expectations as well as an understandable process that identifies what is required to enhance the performance of individuals in the organization. It is critical that the performance management system support the documentation of performance for future actions taken by the organization. It is essential that a rewards system be created that supports the achievement of performance objectives of employees in the organization.

Performance appraisal and performance management must not be confused as being the same thing. Performance management has a broad organizational focus, whereas performance appraisals are the processes used to evaluate how employees perform their jobs and then communicate that information to employees.

2 Effective performance management has a number of components, beginning with a performance-focused organizational culture. Job criteria identify important elements of a job, and the relevance of job criteria affects the establishment of performance standards. Performance standards are measurable objectives of expected levels of performance and can be developed using the SMART approach (specific, measurable, attainable, relevant, and time bound).

3 Performance appraisal systems must satisfy legal compliance and documentation, administrative uses and developmental uses, which can be very challenging in a number of organizations. Numerous court decisions affect the design and use of the performance appraisal process and many have ruled that performance appraisal decisions were discriminatory and not job related. There are a number of elements that should be included to ensure that the performance appraisal is legally defensible including objective criteria used based on job analysis, documentation of appraisal activities, training of supervisors to conduct appraisal appropriately, and counselling poor performers to help improve performance to name a few. Often performance appraisals are used to determine pay adjustments, decisions on promotions, transfers, and demotions, or choosing disciplinary actions as well as for developmental purposes.

4 A number of decisions must be made when creating a performance appraisal system in organizations. The performance appraisal system is typically designed by HR and the responsibility of managing the process is carried out by unit managers. Performance appraisals can be done either informally or systematically. Informal appraisals occur when the supervisor feels that they are necessary. Systematic appraisals are formal contacts between the manager and the employee with a formal system in place to report impressions and observations on employee performance. Most organizations establish a "probationary" appraisal at some reasonable time after an employee has been hired and have an annual performance appraisal conducted from that point forward. Appraisals can be conducted by superiors, employees (rating superiors or themselves), teams, outsiders, or a variety of sources.

5 Appraisal methods include category scaling, comparative, narrative, and results-based methods. Category scaling methods, especially graphic rating scales and behavioural rating scales, are widely used and determine an employee's level of performance by answering a set of established questions. Comparative methods require that managers compare the performance levels of their employees against one another including ranking and forced distribution, which raise methodological concerns. Narrative methods are written documentation and description of employees' behaviour by managers and HR specialists and include the critical incident technique and the essay approach. Results-based methods of performance appraisal focus on performance results of employees and of the overall business as whole and include MBO and the balanced scorecard approach.

6 Training managers and employees on conducting performance appraisals can contribute to the effectiveness of a performance management system. Many performance appraisal problems are caused by a number of different rater errors that can be eliminated by providing training supervisors who are responsible for conducting performance appraisals. There are many topics that should be covered in appraisal training including specific details on the process and timing, the criteria on which performance is evaluated, conducting the review, and how to avoid rating errors to name a few. Rating errors include recency effect, primary effect, central tendency error, leniency error, strictness error, rater bias, halo effect, contrast error, similar to me/different from me error, and sampling error.

7 The appraisal feedback interview is a vital part of any appraisal system, and the reactions of both managers and employees must be considered. It often is an emotional experience for both the employee and the manager. It is critical to emphasize positive achievements in an employees performance. It is critical that the manager be prepared for the interview and make the employee feel that this is an essential component of the performance management system to support them to improve performance. Feedback components include data, evaluation of the data and some action based on the data.

KEY TERMS

Behaviourally anchored rating scales (BARS), p. 339
Central tendency error, p. 348
Contrast error, p. 349
Criterion contamination, p. 324
Criterion deficiency, p. 324
Criterion relevance, p. 324

Forced distribution, p. 341
Graphic rating scale, p. 336
Halo effect, p. 349
Job criteria, p. 322
Leniency error, p. 348
Management by objectives (MBO), p. 343
Performance appraisal, p. 321
Performance management, p. 320
Primacy effect, p. 348
Ranking, p. 340
Rater bias, p. 348
Recency effect, p. 347
Strictness error, p. 348

REVIEW AND APPLICATION QUESTIONS

1 Describe how an organizational culture and the use of performance criteria and standards affect the remaining components of a performance management system.

2 What are the three types of information managers can use about how employees are performing their jobs?

3 What are the administrative and developmental uses of appraisal?

4 Discuss the advantages and disadvantages of the different people and/or groups who can conduct performance appraisals.

5 Define the methods of appraising performance and their advantages and disadvantages.

6 Suppose you are a supervisor. What errors might you make when preparing a performance appraisal on a clerical employee? How might you avoid those errors?

7 Describe the three commonly recognized components of a feedback system?

EXPERIENTIAL EXERCISES

1. Review the performance appraisal process and appraisal form used by a current or former employer, and compare them with those provided by other students. Also review other appraisal forms by going to www.hr-guide.com/, performance appraisals, online forms, and looking at several examples of performance appraisals. Then, develop a report suggesting changes to make the performance appraisal form and process you reviewed more effective.
2. Working in groups, search articles related to performance management for the past two years in *Journal of Applied Psychology*, *Canadian Journal of Administrative Sciences*, *Academy of Management Journal*, *Journal of Organizational Behavior*, and *Personnel Review*, and report on what academics are reporting on performance appraisals. Select at least two articles from each of these journals, and prepare a two-page summary of your findings. Report on your findings to the class.
3. This is a three-part assignment. For the first part, you are to develop a performance appraisal form using a combination approach. Ensure that you appropriately define the performance standards. In part two of the assignment, identify important job dimensions and prepare six tasks for a position that you and your group members may be familiar with, e.g., professor, cleaner, server, or other similar job. Based on those dimensions, develop job criterion for each of the tasks, from which an individual's performance could be assessed. In part three, you are to prepare a policy that will outline how performances are to be conducted, who will be involved in the process, the feedback mechanism, including how to conduct the appraisals, and all other relevant information that should be included in a policy. Do you feel that the form you developed would work in conjunction with the job that you would be assessing and the policy you have developed? How can you improve upon what you have developed?

4. As the newly appointed HR director you have been advised by the CEO that the company must downsize and that the most recent performance appraisal ratings will be used to make the final decision. Upon reviewing the appraisals you determine that 20 of the 150 employees do not have rating scores, but rather a N/A beside the scores. When you approach the managers they indicate that these employees have been with the company since the beginning and that when the appraisal system was put in place, the CEO said that these workers were exempt from appraisals and would always be treated with the highest respect because they had been with the company since its startup 30 years ago. You approach the CEO about this dilemma and he indicates that he is aware of this and it is probably time that these employees be terminated because many of them are about to retire soon and they aren't productive anymore. You ask the CEO if he can really make that decision without really knowing about their performance. He responds that they have a lot of pension credits and that they will be provided with more than ample severance pay. He also believes that this would be good for the younger workforce with young families to support, and that they will work harder and have more energy because they are younger. What are the ethical issues with the decision that will be made? How can the HR director go against the desires of the CEO without hurting their own career?

LEARNING REVIEW

To check your knowledge of the chapter, review the following. (Answers after the case.)

1 All performance management efforts should be driven by:
a. profits
b. business strategies
c. management systems
d. vision of the organization.

2 Specific __________, or dimensions, of job performance identify the most important elements in a given job.
a. job criteria
b. essential functions
c. tasks
d. performance criteria

3 A legally defensible performance appraisal system should include:
a. appraisal criteria based on job analysis
b. opportunity for self-appraisals
c. informal evaluation criteria to permit managerial discretion
d. input from outsiders who can provide objective feedback

4 A __________ appraisal is used when the contact between manager and employee is formal.
a. preplanned
b. developmental
c. systematic
d. multi-purpose

5 A method frequently used by supervisors to rate the performance of subordinates on a continuum is:
a. critical incidents
b. graphic rating scales
c. essay
d. ranking

6 The tendency to rate people relative to others rather than against performance standards is referred to as:
a. contrast error
b. halo effect
c. rater bias
d. central tendency error

7 The three commonly recognized components of a feedback system are all the following except:
a. data
b. evaluation
c. specificity
d. action

CASE

PERFORMANCE MANAGEMENT IMPROVEMENTS FOR BRISTOL-MYERS SQUIBB

Bristol-Myers Squibb (BMS) is one of the world's largest pharmaceutical firms and is widely known for its innovative research. But the firm has not limited its innovations to products. Several years ago BMS leaders decided that the company's performance management system needed to be reinvented. Specifically, they determined that the existing performance appraisal process was not working. Managers were "form focused," meaning that they were so concentrated on filling out the performance review forms, that the content of the forms was not being used for employee coaching and development. Also, most of the attention of managers and employees was historical and what employees had done in the past. Little attention was being given to how employees could develop and improve in the future.

The most radical steps taken were to totally eliminate the appraisal forms and their rating scales and to request that managers not discuss pay increases during performance review sessions. Instead, a new "performance partnership" became the focus. At all levels of BMS, managers were trained to hold regular meetings with their employees. At these meetings managers and employees review performance goals expectations. Together they set expectations and timelines for accomplishing the goals. Rather than meeting just once a year, the performance partnership update occurs throughout the year.

The changes in the performance management system have led to several positive results. First, employees are more active participants, rather than just getting their ratings on forms and then passively listening to the managers. Also, a greater amount of time is spent on coaching because managers were trained on use of a guided feedback approach. This approach has led to more discussions in which employees and managers emphasize joint problem-solving and goal achievements. Although the system takes more managerial and employee time, the coaching and employee involvement have created a more positive relationship and improved individual and managerial performance.[37]

Questions

1. Discuss how this case illustrates the conflict between the administrative use and developmental use of appraisals.
2. What would be some of the advantages and disadvantages of eliminating the use of appraisal forms and ratings?

Learning Activity Answers: 1. b 2. a 3. a 4. c 5. b 6. a 7. c

COUNTRY KIDS

In "Country Kids," *The National* examines the state of daycare throughout the country. The need for Canadian families to have a dual-income household has led the federal government to continuously assess the feasibility of universal daycare throughout the country.

In the 1990s, Quebec became the first and only province to legislate universal daycare. Although the Canadian government would like to model a universal daycare program after the one in Quebec, not all parents are receiving the benefits of the system. Many young families in Quebec are still on waiting lists that are 900 names long and may have to resort to placing their children in private daycares. The Quebec government spends approximately $1.4 billion in its "underfunded" daycares.

The lack of daycare centres in many parts of the countries has led many Canadians to put off their careers until their children are able to attend school full time. As a result, many families are being forced to survive on a single income. In the segment, a mother in Manitoba was unable to be a substitute teacher because of her inability to find proper care for her young children. The competition for spaces in daycares is so intense, that some parents have placed their children on a daycare waiting list even before their child was born.[1]

Questions

1. Should employers address family planning issues with its employees in regards to career development? Why or why not?
2. Should employers actively help its employees to find proper daycare?
3. Do you think universal daycare will ever be legislated in Canada? Is it a good idea?

EXECUTIVE PAY

This segment from *Venture* highlights an "insurrection" organized by the shareholders of Vector Aerospace. In just four years, the company's stock price dropped from $9 a share to $2 a share. Although the company's profitability was diminishing, Vector's board of directors still made the decision to approve a $30-million golden handshake given to several of the company's executives. Vector's shareholders decided that it had had enough and staged a meeting to voice its disapproval of the actions taken by its board of directors.

The segment also provides other examples of company executives receiving generous payments and benefits while cuts are being made elsewhere within the company. If a company such as Air Canada or Vector is unprofitable then how is it possible to justify a $20-million bonus for the president?

The shareholders at Vector did not believe that the golden handshakes were fair and used their power to influence the company to dismiss its board of directors. Just as labourers in the industrial revolution used pickets to increase their share in the profits, common shareholders are using their proxy votes to increase corporate accountability.[2]

Questions

1. In the video clip the executives were referred to as "talent." Do you believe that any of the executives mentioned in the segment were being compensated based on their talent? Why or why not?
2. How should the performance of executives be appraised? Should it be based on company profitability or on other factors?

PART 4

Compensating Human Resources

CHAPTER 10

Compensation Strategies and Practices

Learning Objectives

After you have read this chapter, you should be able to:

1 Identify the two general types of compensation and the components of each.

2 Discuss four issues associated with strategic compensation design.

3 Describe the various pieces of legislation that impact on compensation strategies and practices.

4 Outline the process of developing a base pay system and describe the two means of valuing jobs using job evaluation (internal to the organization) and market pricing (external to the market).

5 Outline the process of developing pay structures.

6 Explain two ways individual pay increases are determined.

HR *Headline*

Compensation Strategies Differ at Costco and Wal-Mart

Different firms follow different compensation strategies due to varying business strategies. Those differences are evident at Costco Wholesale and Wal-Mart in the discount retail industry. Costco's business strategy stresses customer service and selling higher margin products to more affluent customers. This means that it needs to have lower employee turnover, higher productivity, and employees providing quality customer service. To retain and motivate its employees, Costco has adopted a compensation strategy that provides an average hourly wage of $15.97, and broad-based health and retirement benefits. Over 80 percent of all Costco employees participate in the Costco benefits plans. One payoff for Costco is that employee turnover rates average about 6 percent annually.

Wal-Mart, which has Sam's Club and Wal-Mart stores, uses a different compensation strategy that is consistent with its business strategy of keeping prices low and constantly reducing costs. This strategy has been successful in reducing prices of goods sold to Wal-Mart customers. The average wage for Wal-Mart employees is $9.47 an hour and for Sam's Club employees is $11.52 an hour (excluding 25 percent of the workers, who are part-timers and are paid lower rates). Wal-Mart also has required employees to pay more of their benefits costs in the past few years, and as a result has seen significantly less employee participation in the benefits plans. The turnover rate for first-year employees at Sam's Club averages over 20 percent, and the turnover rate for all employees at Wal-Mart has been about 50 percent a year. This overall rate means that Wal-Mart must hire 600 000 individuals a year just to keep the same size workforce. When staffing of new stores is included, over 1 million people must be hired annually.[1]

The differences between the compensation strategies of Costco and Wal-Mart do not mean that one strategy is better than the other. Instead, they illustrate how compensation strategies are aligned with business strategies, and the operational consequences of those strategies. It will be interesting to observe to what extent the compensation strategies shift in each firm as competitive pressures continue to grow.

> *"Money is power, freedom, a cushion, the root of all evil, the sum of blessings."*
>
> *—Carl Sandburg*

Compensation costs represent significant expenditures in most organizations. For instance, at one large health-care organization, employee payroll and benefits expenditures constitute almost 60 percent of all costs. Although actual compensation costs can be easily calculated, the value derived by employers and employees proves more difficult to identify. Compensation systems in organizations must be linked to organizational objectives and strategies. As the opening discussion illustrates, different firms have different strategies for compensation. Additionally, compensation systems must balance the interests and costs of the employers with the needs and expectations of employees.

Nature of Compensation

1 Compensation is an important factor affecting how and why people choose to work at one organization versus others. To attract and retain competent employees, employers must be reasonably competitive with several types of compensation.

Types of Compensation

Rewards can be both intrinsic and extrinsic. *Intrinsic rewards* are those rewards that are derived from the working environment such as: the opportunity for personal growth, quality of work life, job satisfaction, challenge, personal and professional development opportunities, belonging, freedom to act, visionary leadership, receiving praise for completing a project or meeting performance objectives. *Extrinsic rewards* are tangible and take both monetary and non-monetary forms. Tangible components of a compensation program are of two general types (see Figure 10-1). With *direct compensation,* the employer exchanges monetary rewards for work done. Employers provide *indirect compensation*—like health insurance—to everyone simply for being members of the organization. *Base pay* and *variable pay* are the most common forms of direct compensation. Indirect compensation commonly consists of employee *benefits.*

Base pay
Basic compensation that an employee receives, usually as a wage or a salary.

Base Pay The basic compensation that an employee receives, usually as a wage or a salary, is called **base pay.** Many organizations use two base pay categories, *hourly*

Figure 10-1 *Components of a Compensation System*

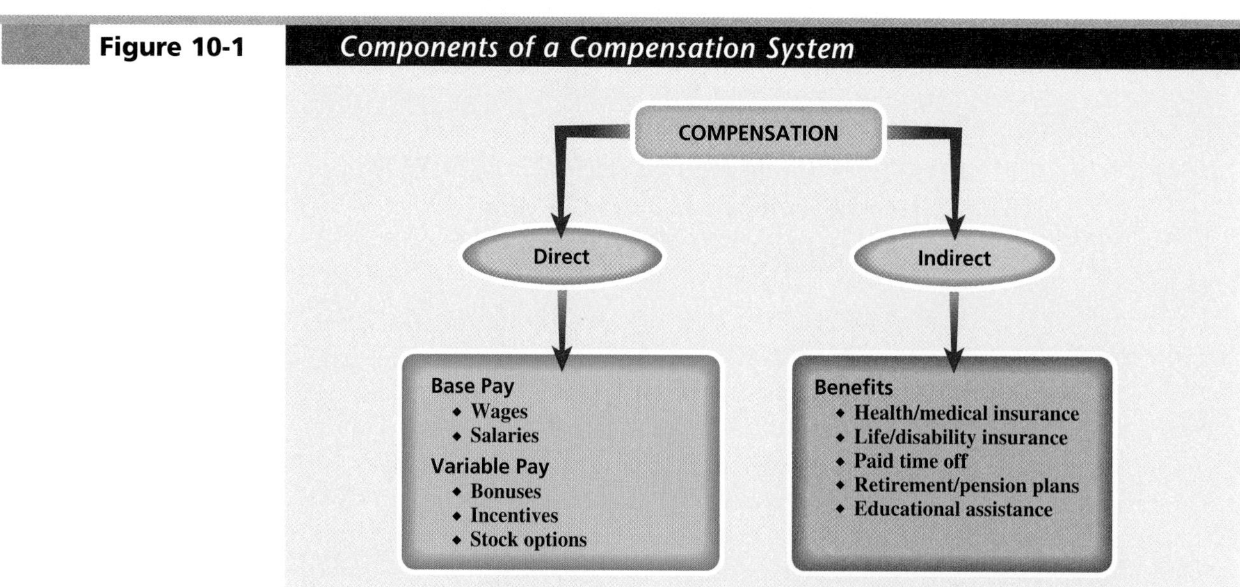

Wages
Payments directly calculated on the amount of time worked.

Salaries
Consistent payments made each period regardless of the number of hours worked.

and *salaried*, which are identified according to the way pay is distributed and the nature of the jobs. Hourly pay is the most common means and is based on time. Employees paid hourly receive **wages,** which are payments directly calculated on the amount of time worked. In contrast, people paid **salaries** receive consistent payments each period regardless of the number of hours worked. Being paid a salary has typically carried higher status for employees than has being paid a wage. Some organizations maintain an all-salaried approach with their manufacturing and clerical employees in order to create a greater sense of loyalty and organizational commitment. However, they still must pay overtime to certain employees as defined by federal, provincial, and territorial legislation.

Variable pay
Compensation linked directly to individual, team, or organizational performance.

Variable Pay Another type of direct pay is **variable pay,** which is compensation linked directly to individual, team, or organizational performance. The most common types of variable pay for most employees are bonuses and incentive program payments. Executives often receive longer-term rewards such as stock options. Variable pay, including executive compensation, is discussed in Chapter 11.

Benefit
Indirect reward given to an employee or a group of employees for organizational membership.

Benefits Many organizations provide numerous extrinsic rewards in an indirect manner. With indirect compensation, employees receive the tangible value of the rewards without receiving actual cash. A **benefit** is an indirect reward—for instance, health insurance, vacation pay, or a retirement pension—given to an employee or a group of employees for organizational membership, regardless of performance.

Compensation Responsibilities

To administer compensation expenditures wisely, HR specialists and operating managers must work together. A typical division of compensation responsibilities is illustrated in Figure 10-2. HR specialists guide the development and administration of an organizational compensation system and conduct job evaluations and wage surveys. Also, because of the technical complexity involved, HR specialists typically assume responsibility for developing base pay programs and salary structures and policies. Operating managers evaluate the performance of employees and consider their performance when deciding compensation increases within the policies and guidelines established by the HR unit and upper management. HR specialists may or may not process payroll. This labour-intensive responsibility is typically among the first to be outsourced. As the Technology Transforming HR discussion indicates, outsourcing payroll can be a difficult transition, unless you work with an experienced organization.

Figure 10-2 *Typical Division of HR Responsibilities: Compensation*

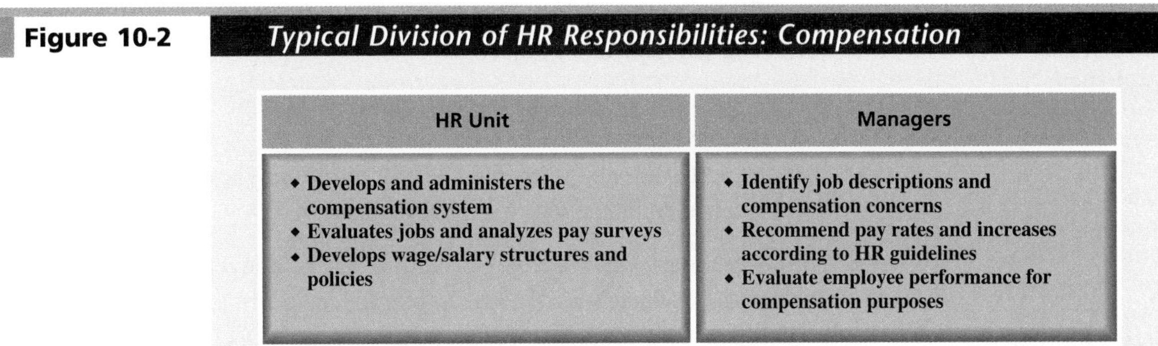

HR Unit	Managers
• Develops and administers the compensation system • Evaluates jobs and analyzes pay surveys • Develops wage/salary structures and policies	• Identify job descriptions and compensation concerns • Recommend pay rates and increases according to HR guidelines • Evaluate employee performance for compensation purposes

Technology Transforming HR

Making the Payroll Transition Smoothly

The implementation of a new payroll system is often dreaded by a company's payroll department because it can be a painful transitional process. When Andrés Wines made the decision to implement a new payroll system, the organization's payroll manager Debbie Adams found the implementation to be a "fun process from start to finish," rather than the dreaded process many anticipate. In 2001, the Grimsby, Ontario-based wine producer and marketer made the decision to switch vendors, selecting Ceridian, for its outsourced payroll function. Adams had previously used Ceridian and anticipated a high level of support from the firm.

Adams attributes her enjoyment to her high level of involvement in the process. In her previous experiences with implementations, Adams was kept at a distance from the process and would be contacted only when information was needed. Adams was so involved with Ceridian in this implementation that she had the confidence to go on vacation in the first week that the system was up and running.

Andrés payroll is not a simple matter because its employees are located throughout the country and in completely different businesses. Its winery operations can be found in Nova Scotia, Ontario, and British Columbia. The company is also involved in the home winemaking industry, runs a network of retail outlets, as well as two restaurants in Niagara-on-the-Lake: "Because of all the different business units, with the old payroll system the company was essentially running seven different systems. But Ceridian was able to mirror them and convert them all at the same time so that everything is now the same everywhere."

Ceridian is responsible for every aspect of Andrés' payroll including remittances, T4 preparation, and direct deposits. Adams is responsible for ensuring that everything she enters is correct. Andrés is also making use of the HR portion of Ceridian's software by using it to uncover job evaluation information, track injuries, and follow disciplinary issues. The only difficulty that Andrés has had with the new system is when the company purchased new computers and servers, but Ceridian provided strong customer support when confronted with such difficulties. Adams suggests that any company going through a payroll transition should enter the implementation with an open mind and be involved in the process by asking questions.[2]

1. What factor do you believe contributed most significantly to the successful implementation of the new payroll system at Andrés?
2. Do you believe that companies who outsource their payroll function would have more difficulty with implementing a new payroll system than a company who does not outsource?

Strategic Compensation

World at Work
Formerly the Canadian Compensation Association, WorldatWork is the world's leading not-for-profit professional association dedicated to knowledge leadership in compensation, benefits, and total rewards.
www.worldatwork.org/waw/canada/worldatwork-canada.jsp

An effective compensation system in an organization should be linked to the organizational strategies and objectives. Because so many organizational funds are spent on compensation-related activities, it is critical for top management and HR executives to match compensation systems and practices with what the organization is trying to accomplish.

According to the strategic view of compensation, organizations must make a number of important decisions about the nature of a compensation system to achieve the following compensation objectives:

- Legal compliance with all appropriate laws and regulations
- Cost effectiveness for the organization
- Internal, external, and individual equity for employees
- Performance enhancement for the organization

Employers must balance compensation costs at a level that both ensures organizational competitiveness and rewards employees sufficiently for their knowledge, skills, abilities, and performance accomplishments. Decisions about compensation systems should be guided by the compensation philosophy of the organization.

Compensation Philosophies

Two basic compensation philosophies lie on opposite ends of a continuum, as shown in Figure 10-3. At one end of the continuum is the *entitlement* philosophy; at the other end is the *performance* philosophy. Most compensation systems fall somewhere in between, although there is a growing emphasis being placed on performance.

Entitlement philosophy
Assumes that individuals who have worked another year are entitled to pay increases, with little regard for performance differences.

Entitlement Philosophy The **entitlement philosophy** assumes that individuals who have worked another year are entitled to pay increases, with little regard for performance differences. Many traditional organizations that give automatic increases to their employees every year practise the entitlement philosophy. Further, most of those employees receive the same or nearly the same percentage increase each year.

Commonly, in organizations with an entitlement philosophy, base pay increases are referred to as *cost-of-living* raises, even if they are not tied specifically to economic indicators. Following an entitlement philosophy some employers guarantee that pay scales will be raised each year, which ultimately means that employer costs increase, regardless of employee performance or organizational competitive pressures. Market comparisons of compensation tend to be made within an industry, rather than more broadly among firms of all types. Bonuses in many entitlement-oriented organizations are determined in a paternalistic manner that often fails to reflect operating results. Therefore, employees "expect" the bonuses, and the bonuses become another form of entitlement.

Pay-for-performance philosophy
Requires that compensation changes reflect individual performance differences.

Performance Philosophy The **pay-for-performance philosophy** requires that compensation changes reflect individual performance differences. Organizations operating under this philosophy do not guarantee additional or increased compensation simply for completing another year of organizational service. Instead, they structure pay and incentives to reflect performance differences among employees. Employees who perform well receive larger increases in compensation; those who do not perform satisfactorily see little or no increase in compensation.[3] Thus, employees who perform satisfactorily or better maintain or advance their positions in relation to market compensation levels, whereas poor or marginal performers may fall behind. Also, bonuses and incentives are based on individual, group, and/or organizational performance.

Few organizations totally follow performance-oriented compensation practices, but there is an overall trend to greater use of pay-for-performance systems. A survey of Fortune 1000 firms found that over 80 percent of the firms use some type of

Figure 10-3 *Continuum of Compensation Philosophies*

← Entitlement	Performance →
• Seniority basis • Across-the-board raises • Pay scales raised annually • Industry comparisons of compensation only • "Santa Claus" bonuses	• No raises for length of service • No raises for longer-service poor performers • Market-adjusted pay structures • Broader industy comparison • Bonuses tied to performance results

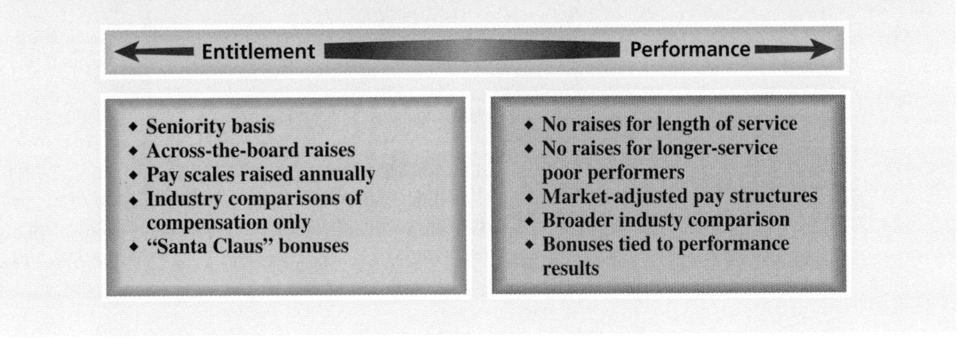

performance-based compensation plans. The study found that growth in the past decade had been greater in individual incentive plans and team/group reward systems than organization-wide gainsharing, profit sharing, and stock option plans.[4] Such plans may help reduce employee turnover and increase employee commitment and retention.[5] An outgrowth of different compensation philosophies is the use of varying approaches to implementing compensation systems.

Compensation Approaches

Compensation is an important tool for recruiting, motivating, and retaining good people. Indeed, although the goals of recruiting, motivating, and retaining good people has remained fairly constant, the ways in which some companies approach them have altered dramatically. Figure 10-4 presents some of the choices organizations must make between the traditional compensation approach and a total rewards approach.

Traditional Compensation Approach Traditional compensation systems have evolved over a period of time to reflect a logical and rational approach to compensating employees. Job descriptions identify tasks and responsibilities, and are then used to decide which jobs are more valuable. These systems use a job evaluation system to calculate the value that each job contributes to the organization. That value is then used to establish a pay range that reflects a person's progression as he or she grows and presumably gets better at the job.

For some organizations that are in relatively stable industries, a traditional compensation approach makes sense and offers certain advantages in specific competitive situations. This approach may be more legally defensible, less complex, and viewed as more "fair" by average and below-average employees. However, the total rewards approach helps retain top performers, can be more flexible when the economy goes up or down, and is favoured by top-performing companies.

Total Rewards Approach The total rewards approach tries to place a value on individuals rather than just on jobs. When determining compensation, managers

Figure 10-4 Compensation Approaches

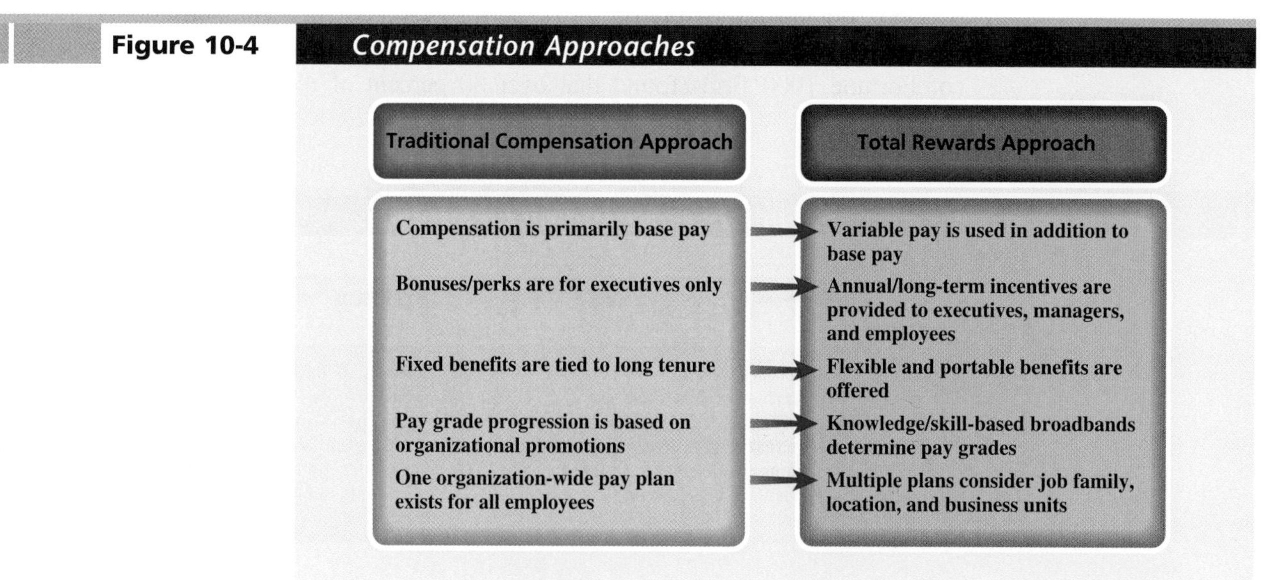
Traditional Compensation Approach
Total Rewards Approach
Compensation is primarily base pay
Variable pay is used in addition to base pay
Bonuses/perks are for executives only
Annual/long-term incentives are provided to executives, managers, and employees
Fixed benefits are tied to long tenure
Flexible and portable benefits are offered
Pay grade progression is based on organizational promotions
Knowledge/skill-based broadbands determine pay grades
One organization-wide pay plan exists for all employees
Multiple plans consider job family, location, and business units

factor in elements such as how much an employee knows or how competent an employee is. Currently, some organizations have variable pay programs as part of a total rewards approach for all levels of employees. Widespread use of various incentive plans, team bonuses, organizational gainsharing programs, and other designs links growth in compensation to results.[6] The positive effects of a total rewards approach have been identified by InSystems Inc., a software company located in Markham, Ontario. InSystems Inc. conducted a survey to find out how employees viewed their compensation package. Employees indicated that they didn't like their incentive plans, the way they were designed or structured, and that it was too complex. Employees also wanted high performance to be recognized, and they were unsure as to why some employees were getting incentives while others were not. In addition, employees wanted to ensure that people who were high performers could get more sizable rewards. Employees also felt that training and professional development was not being distributed equitably. To remedy the problems, a new job evaluation methodology was created, a retirement savings program was introduced for the first time, incentive programs were revised and new recognition programs introduced. The new program has contributed to increasing customer satisfaction and improving corporate performance.[7]

HR Metrics and Compensation

Employers spend huge amounts of money for employee compensation. Just like any other area of expenditures, compensation expenditures should be evaluated to determine their effectiveness. Many measures can be used for this evaluation. One survey of 1200 companies found that employee turnover/retention is widely used.[8] This usage assumes that how well compensation systems operate affects employees' decisions about staying or leaving the organization. Other more specific measures are used as well, such as the ones in Figure 10-5.[9]

The numbers for calculating these measures are readily available to most HR professionals and chief financial officers, but in a large number of firms, such calculations are not made. To be even more useful, these compensation metrics should be computed each year, and then compared with metrics from past years to show how the rate of compensation changes compares with the rate of changes in the organization overall (revenues, expenses, etc.).

Figure 10-5 *HR Metrics for Compensation*

HR Performance Area	Method of Calculation
1. Pay and benefits as percentage of operating expense	Total pay and benefits expenditures
2. Human value added	Revenue − Operating expense − Pay and benefits = Adjusted profit ÷ Full-time-equivalent employees (FTEs)
3. Return on human capital invested	Revenue − Operating expense − Pay and benefits = Adjusted profit ÷ Pay and benefits
4. Employee cost factor	Total compensation and benefits ÷ Full-time-equivalent employees (FTEs)

Compensation System Design Issues

2 Depending on the compensation philosophies, strategies, and approaches identified for an organization, a number of decisions are made that affect the design of the compensation system. Some important ones are highlighted next beginning with global issues.

Global Compensation Issues

Organizations with employees in different countries face some special design issues for compensation. Variations in laws, living costs, tax policies, and other factors all must be considered in establishing the compensation for local employees and managers, as well as for managers and professionals brought in from other countries. Even fluctuations in the values of various monetary currencies must be tracked and adjustments made as the currencies rise or fall in relation to currency rates in other countries. With these and numerous other concerns, developing and managing a global compensation system becomes extremely complex.

One significant global issue in compensation design is how to compensate the employees from different countries.

Compensating Host-Country Nationals In many countries, the local wage scales vary significantly. For instance, in some less-developed countries, pay levels for degreed professionals may range from $15,000 to $30,000 a year, whereas in Europe and North America, individuals with the same qualifications are paid $50,000 to $80,000 a year. Lower-skilled local workers may make as little as $300 a month in less-developed countries, whereas comparable employees make $1,500 to $2,000 a month in North America and Europe. These large compensation differences have led to significant "international outsourcing" of jobs to lower-wage countries. The movement of call centre and information technology jobs to India and manufacturing jobs to China, the Philippines, and Mexico are examples.

In designing a compensation system, an organization must decide whether local wages are to be paid to host-country nationals, or more global wage levels are to be considered. Many global employers pay local wages to most employees, except those in senior management and technical positions. Those employers get accused of paying "slave wages," even though the host-country employees have jobs in countries with high unemployment rates and are often paid significantly more than if they worked for local employers.

LOGGING ON...

Runzheimer International
This firm's international service provides information on expatriate compensation.
www.runzheimer.com

Balance-sheet approach
Compensation plan that equalizes cost differences between identical international and home-country assignments.

Compensating Third-Country Nationals Decisions about the compensation levels for third-country nationals are often a function of the originating country of the employees. For example, Indonesians who are working in Turkey may be paid wages that are similar to or lower than those of locals. However, a German engineering manager working in Thailand is likely to be paid about the same as or more than in Germany, much like an expatriate.

Compensating Expatriates The typical components of an international compensation package for expatriates are shown in Figure 10-6. Notice that a number of items are often included.

The two primary approaches to international compensation for expatriates are the **balance-sheet approach** and the global market approach. The balance-sheet approach is a compensation plan that equalizes cost differences between the international assignment and the same assignment in the home country of the individual or the corporation. It has been estimated that the aggregate employer costs for an expatriate,

Figure 10-6 *Typical Components of Expatriate Compensation*

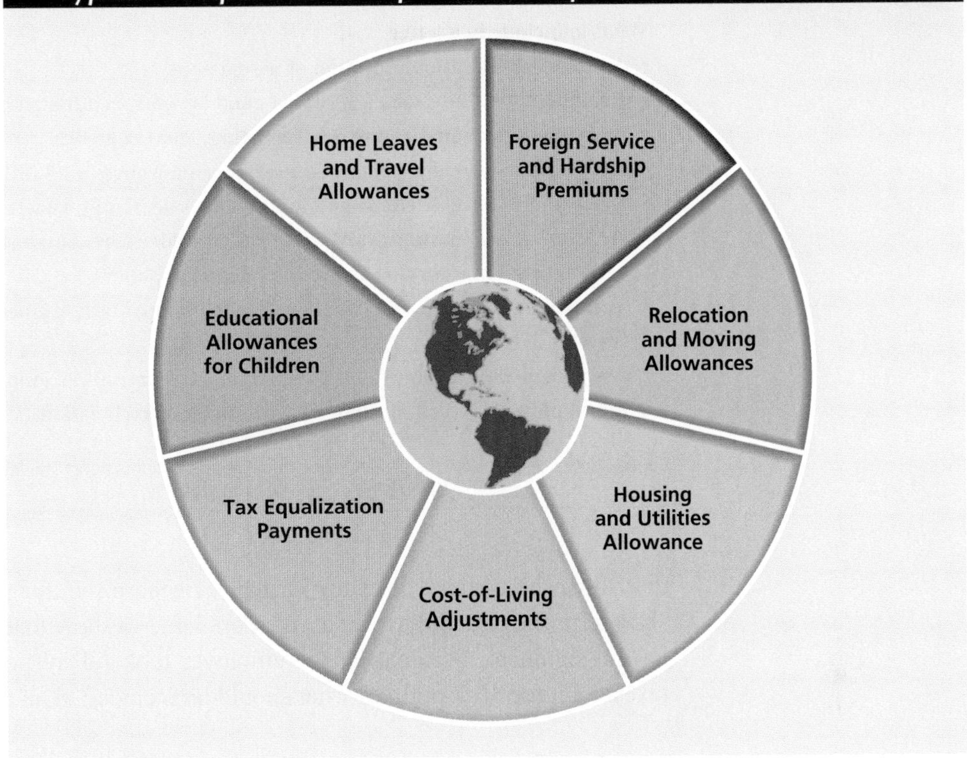

including all allowances, is three to four times the expatriate's salary.[10] Thus, if an expatriate's salary is $120,000, the actual cost of employing that person is likely to be $360,000 to $480,000.

Global market approach
Compensation plan that attempts to be more comprehensive in providing base pay, incentives, benefits, and relocation expenses regardless of the country to which the employee is assigned.

Tax equalization plan
Compensation plan used to protect expatriates from negative tax consequences.

Unlike the balance-sheet approach, the **global market approach** views international assignments as continual, not just temporary, if they may take employees to different countries for differing lengths of time. The global market approach attempts to be more comprehensive in providing base pay, incentives, benefits, and relocation expenses regardless of the country to which the employee is assigned. Further, the reactions of host-country nationals to the pay practices for expatriates must be considered.[11] Therefore, the global market approach to compensation requires greater flexibility, more detailed analyses, and significant administrative effort.

Many international compensation systems attempt to protect expatriates from negative tax consequences by using a **tax equalization plan.** Under such a plan, the company adjusts an employee's base income downward by the amount of estimated home-country tax to be paid for the year. Thus, the employee pays only the foreign-country tax. For instance, a tax equalization plan helps ensure that Canadian expatriates will not pay any more or less in taxes than if they were working in Canada. Because of the variation in tax laws and rates from country to country, tax equalization is very complex to determine. An employee should secure an "assignment letter" from their employer that verifies that the employee will not suffer any financial loss due to the assignment. In one instance, an IT specialist was sent on an assignment to Germany for a couple of days. The assignment stretched into months. Due to the extended stay, the employee became known as a "stealth pat"—someone whose temporary work assignment has become a de facto relocation. The employee did not mind the assignment since she was really enjoying her stay, but a problem arose when she went to pay her taxes and she found out

Figure 10-7 **International Assignment Letters**

What to include in a letter

- **Assignment: Location, duration of assignment.**
- **Remuneration: Base salary, incentives and benefits, pension plans, and currency of payment.**
- **Tax issues: Tax equalization, tax reporting, and tax advice.**
- **Host country: Housing, goods and services allowances, and differentials.**
- **Relocation program: Home and automobile sale, family allowances (if family doesn't relocate), house hunting, moving, schooling, elder care, language training, and cultural acclimatization programs as per the relocation policy.**
- **Vacation and home leave: Number of trips, compensation, emergency and compassionate travel provisions.**
- **Assignment conclusion: Items covered under repatriation, employment opportunities upon the employee's return, dealing with dismissal or resignation.**

Source: Joyce Head, "How Paper Can Protect International Relocations: The Importance of an International Assignment Letter," *Canadian HR Reporter,* March 13, 2006.

that she owed country taxes to Germany. Because the assignment was supposed to be short term she did not have an assignment letter to show that she was indeed on a short-term assignment. Fortunately, the employer took full responsibility for the additional taxes.[12] Figure 10-7 outlines what should be included in an assignment letter.

Market Competitiveness and Compensation

Providing competitive compensation to employees, whether globally, domestically, or locally, is a concern for all employers. Some organizations establish specific policies about where they wish to be positioned in the labour market. These policies use a *quartile strategy,* as illustrated in Figure 10-8. Data in pay surveys reveal that the dollar differential between quartiles is generally 15 percent–20 percent.

"Meet the Market" Strategy Most employers choose to position themselves in the *second quartile* (median), in the middle of the market, as identified by pay data

Figure 10-8 **Compensation Quartile Strategies**

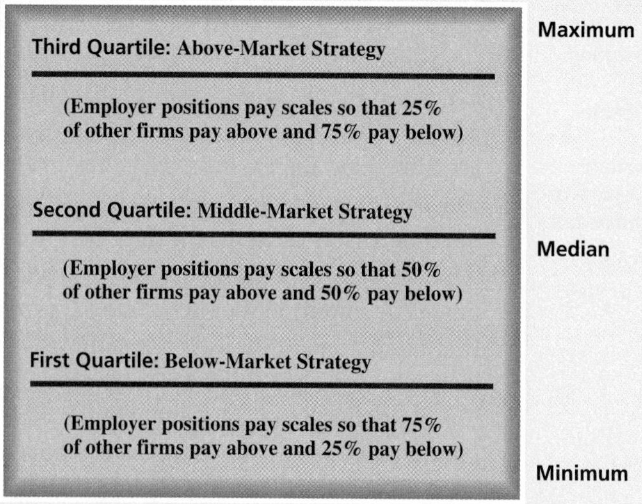

Third Quartile: Above-Market Strategy	Maximum
(Employer positions pay scales so that 25% of other firms pay above and 75% pay below)	
Second Quartile: Middle-Market Strategy	Median
(Employer positions pay scales so that 50% of other firms pay above and 50% pay below)	
First Quartile: Below-Market Strategy	
(Employer positions pay scales so that 75% of other firms pay above and 25% pay below)	Minimum

from surveys of other employers' compensation plans. Choosing this level attempts to balance employer cost pressures and the need to attract and retain employees, by providing mid-level compensation scales that "meet the market" for the employer's jobs.

"Lag the Market" Strategy An employer using a *first-quartile* strategy may choose to "lag the market" by paying below market levels, for several reasons. If the employer is experiencing a shortage of funds, it may be unable to pay more. Also, when an abundance of workers is available, particularly those with lower skills, a below-market approach can be used to attract sufficient workers at a lesser cost. Often a lag policy is associated with a low cost strategy. The downside of this strategy is that it increases the likelihood of higher worker turnover, thus increasing costs with lower productivity and potential quality issues. If the labour market supply tightens, then attracting and retaining workers becomes more difficult.

"Lead the Market" Strategy A *third-quartile* strategy uses an aggressive approach to "lead the market." This strategy generally enables a company to attract and retain sufficient workers with the required capabilities and to be more selective when hiring. Because it is a higher-cost approach, organizations often look for ways to increase the productivity of employees receiving above-market wages. Adopting a lead policy is more appropriate to companies who adopt a differentiation strategy. Figure 10-9 illustrates the respective market strategies.

Figure 10-9 *Market Strategies*

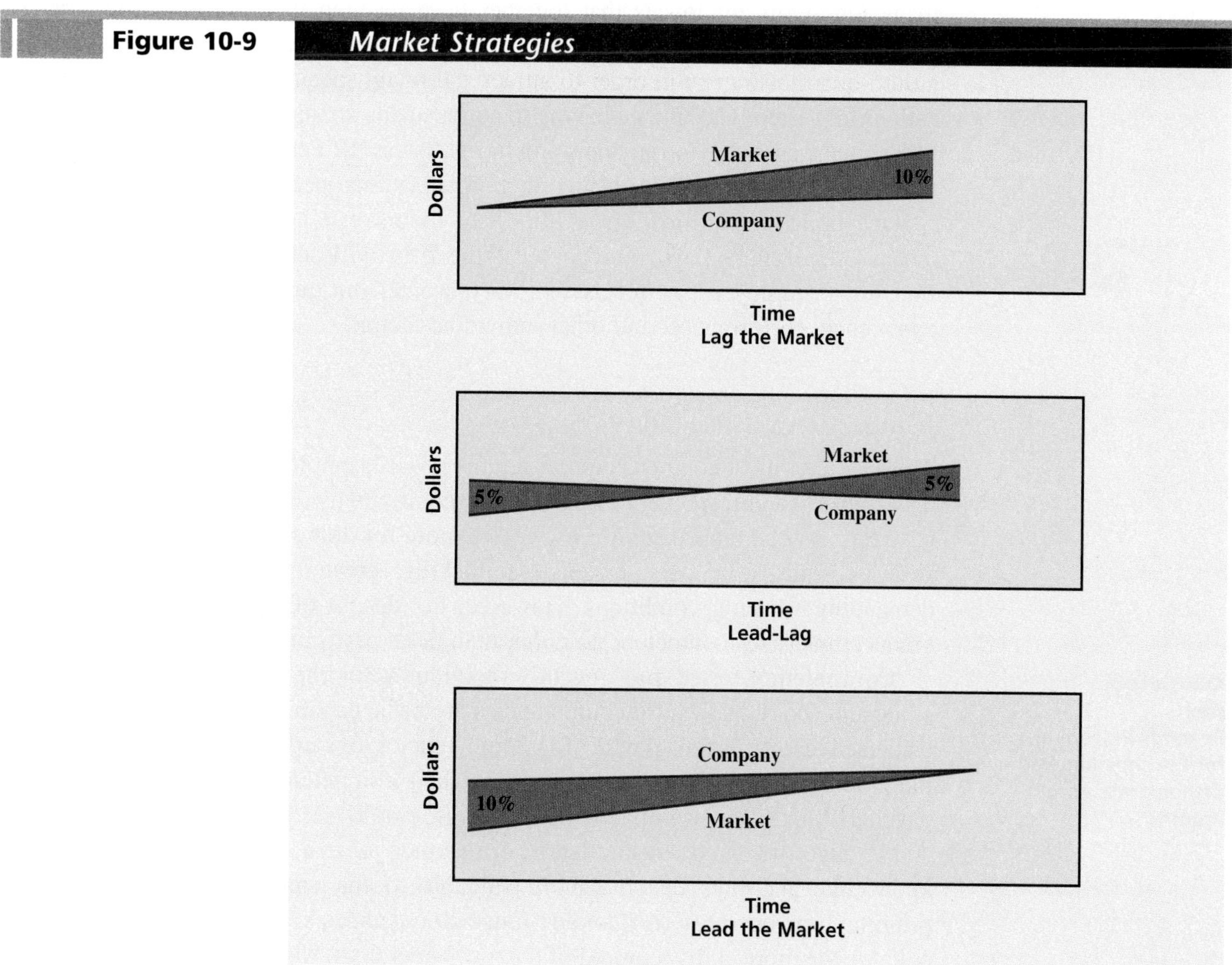

"Lead/Lag the Market" Strategy Another potential compensation policy is to "lead/lag" the market. Its goal is to balance salary costs with competitiveness. This strategy is favoured by many organizations because of its middle ground position. This middle ground position ensures that the company is still able to compete, while at the same time not generating higher costs. By employing this policy companies will lead market salaries for the first half of the year and lag the market for the remaining six months.

Mix of Strategies for Different Employees Even though it would be ideal to adopt one compensation strategy for an organization, companies generally will have to adopt different strategies for each of its respective employee groups. Market match or market lead policies, are generally required for attracting, retaining, and maintaining the talent of professional and managerial employees. A market match or market lag policy is more appropriately applied to clerical, administrative, and unskilled employees who may not require the same type of efforts to attract, retain, or maintain employees.

Selecting a Quartile Deciding which quartile to position pay structures in is a function of a number of considerations. The financial resources available, competitiveness pressures, and the market availability of employees with different capabilities are external factors. Some employers with extensive benefits programs or broad-based incentive programs may choose a first-quartile strategy, so that their overall compensation costs and levels are competitive. Other firms may have union contracts and many long-term employees that together have resulted in a third-quartile strategy. A firm in a highly competitive industry or in a remote rural location may choose to use a third-quartile strategy in order to attract and retain specialized talent. Many organizations in western Canada are having to adopt such a strategy to encourage workers to fill the many available jobs in their provinces. As the HR Perspective discusses, the pay levels and pay structures used can affect organizational performance.

One point of clarification is important to make: Choosing a quartile strategy means identifying at what broad level the firm will set its compensation levels. Individual employee pay levels will vary around the quartile level, depending on experience, performance, and other individual factors.

Competency-Based Pay

The design of most compensation programs rewards employees for carrying out their tasks, duties, and responsibilities. The job requirements determine which employees have higher base rates. Employees receive more for doing jobs that require a greater variety of tasks, more knowledge and skills, greater physical effort, or more demanding working conditions. However, the design of some compensation programs emphasizes competencies rather than tasks performed.

Competency-based pay
Rewards individuals for the capabilities they demonstrate and acquire.

Competency-based pay rewards individuals for the capabilities they demonstrate and acquire. Because competencies are basic capabilities that can be linked to enhanced performance, paying for competencies rewards employees who exhibit more versatility and continue to develop their competencies. In knowledge-based pay (KBP) or skill-based pay (SBP) systems, employees start at a base level of pay and receive increases as they learn to do other jobs or gain additional skills and knowledge and thus become more valuable to the employer.[13] For example, a printing firm operates two-colour, four-colour, and six-colour presses. The more colours, the more skills required of the press operators. Under a KBP or SBP system,

HR *Perspective*

Research on Pay Levels, Pay Structures, and Organizational Performance

The extent to which organizational compensation systems can affect organizational performance has been widely discussed. To gather specific insights, Brown, Sturman, and Simmering conducted a study on how organizational pay structures and pay levels were tied to organizational performance in over 300 hospitals in California. The results were discussed in the *Academy of Management Journal.*

The researchers examined how the market pay level strategies used in the hospitals were linked to organizational performance measures. Specifically, this study found that pay level and pay structure decisions were significantly related to financial return on assets, patient outcomes, and resource usage efficiencies. For example, having higher pay levels was related to greater efficiency in the use of resources and in patient outcome measures such as average length of stay.

The general message of this study reinforces the proposition that compensation decisions about pay structures and pay levels do influence organizational performance. For instance, compensation decisions may influence employee turnover or retention, which can contribute to higher or lower employee performance and productivity. Also, compensation decisions play a role in whether or not individuals accept employment, which may ultimately affect organizational performance.[14]

1. Do you feel that the results of this study can be generalized across other industries with the same results? Why or why not?
2. Would you turn down a job because the compensation was lower than your expectations? What other issues would be part of your overall decision to accept a position? How important is compensation compared to everything else?

press operators increase their pay as they learn how to operate the more complex presses, even though sometimes they may be running only two-colour jobs.

The success of competency plans requires managerial commitment to a philosophy different from the traditional one in organizations. Both the organization and employees can benefit from a properly designed and implemented competency-based system.

When an organization moves to a competency-based system, considerable time must be spent identifying the required competencies for various jobs. Reliance on items such as relevant college diplomas and university degrees may provide more emphasis on demonstrated knowledge and competencies.[15] *Progression* of employees must be possible, and employees must be paid appropriately for all their competencies. Any *limitations* on the numbers of people who can acquire more competencies should be clearly identified. *Training* in the appropriate competencies is particularly critical. Also, a competency-based system needs to acknowledge or certify employees as they acquire certain competencies, and then to verify the maintenance of those *competencies.* In summary, use of a competency-based system requires significant investment of management time and commitment.[16]

Many firms are now attempting to apply the concept of pay for knowledge to their professional and managerial personnel through the use of competency-based pay systems. These can vary greatly in format. For example, a defence electronics firm has a master list of more than 30 competencies that may apply to professional and managerial staff, and each department selects those most relevant to its operations. Pay raises are tied to the achievement of each competency. In another case, a manufacturing firm pays managers for their degree of progress in mastering four managerial competencies that are deemed to apply to all managerial jobs. In a third case, professional and managerial employees negotiate "learning contracts" with their supervisor, and pay increases are based on accomplishment of these objectives.[17]

Individual vs. Team Rewards

As some organizations have shifted to using work teams, they face the logical concern of how to develop compensation programs that build on the team concept. At issue is how to compensate the individual whose performance may also be evaluated on the basis of team achievement. Paying everyone on a team the same amount, even though they demonstrate differing competencies and levels of performance, obviously creates concerns for many employees.

Many organizations use team rewards as variable pay above base pay. For base pay, they compensate individuals on the basis of competencies. Variable pay rewards for teams are most frequently distributed annually as specified dollar amounts, not as percentages of base pay. Team-based rewards may not succeed. A machinery manufacturer found that team-based pay resulted in a number of dysfunctional consequences. Employees tried to get friends onto their teams and others off their teams. Also, some employees exerted influence to get team members to favour them when pay decisions were made. Competition and acrimony between teams created internal conflicts. Consequently, the firm dropped their team-based plan and shifted to a company-wide incentive program, which had been successful.[18]

The most successful uses of team-based compensation have been as variable pay on top of base pay. Rather than substituting for base pay, team-based rewards appear to be useful when compensating a team for performance beyond the satisfactory level. Discussion of team-based incentives is contained in Chapter 11.

Many compensation plans are starting to incorporate team-based rewards above base pay in recognition of goal achievement.

Compensation Fairness

Most people in organizations work in order to gain rewards for their efforts. Except in volunteer organizations, people expect to receive fair value, in the form of tangible compensation, for their efforts. Whether employees are considering base pay, variable pay, or benefits, the extent to which they perceive that compensation to be fair often affects their performance and how they view their jobs and employers.

Equity
Perceived fairness between what a person does and what the person receives.

Equity is the perceived fairness between what a person does (inputs) and what the person receives (outcomes). Individuals judge equity in compensation by comparing their input (effort and performance) against the effort and performance of others and against the outcomes (the rewards received). These comparisons are personal and are based on individual perceptions, not just facts. A sense of inequity occurs when the comparison suggests an imbalance between input and outcomes. Figure 10-10 indicates the individual, organizational, and external dimensions of equity related to compensation.

External Equity If an employer does not provide compensation that employees view as equitable in relation to the compensation provided to employees performing similar jobs in other organizations, that employer is likely to experience higher turnover. Other drawbacks include greater difficulty in recruiting qualified and high-demand individuals. Also, by not being competitive, the employer is more likely to attract and retain individuals with less knowledge and fewer skills and abilities, resulting in lower overall organizational performance. Organizations track external equity by using pay surveys, which are discussed later in this chapter, and by looking at the compensation policies of competing employers.

Internal Equity in Compensation Internal equity means that employees receive compensation in relation to the knowledge, skills, and abilities (KSAs) they use in their jobs as well as their responsibilities and accomplishments. More importantly, to address the wage disparities between males and females, pay equity legislation has been enacted in various jurisdictions throughout Canada. Under such legislation consideration for four factors, which may contribute to differences in male and female pay must be considered: skill, effort, responsibility, and working conditions. Pay equity is discussed in more detail in the next section pertaining to legal constraints. Two key issues—procedural justice and distributive justice—relate to internal equity.

Figure 10-10 *Equity Considerations in Compensation*

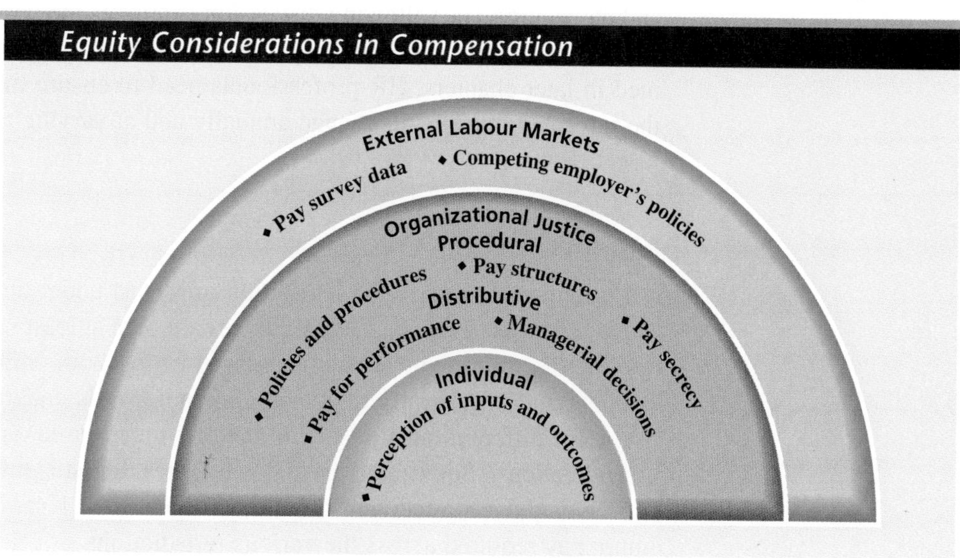

Procedural justice Perceived fairness of the process and procedures used to make decisions about employees.

Distributive justice Perceived fairness in the distribution of outcomes.

Procedural justice is the perceived fairness of the process and procedures used to make decisions about employees, including their pay. As it applies to compensation, the entire process of determining base pay for jobs, allocating pay increases, and measuring performance must be perceived as fair.

A related issue that must be considered is **distributive justice,** which is the perceived fairness in the distribution of outcomes. As one example, if a hardworking employee whose performance is outstanding receives the same across-the-board raise as an employee with attendance problems and mediocre performance, then inequity may be perceived. Likewise, if two employees have similar performance records but one receives a significantly greater pay raise, the other may perceive an inequity due to supervisory favouritism or other factors not related to the job.

To address concerns about both types of justice, some organizations establish compensation appeals procedures. Typically, employees are encouraged to contact the HR department after discussing their concerns with their immediate supervisors and managers.

Pay Secrecy vs. Openness Another equity issue concerns the degree of secrecy or openness that organizations have regarding their pay systems. Pay information kept secret in "closed" systems includes how much others make, what raises others have received, and even what pay grades and ranges exist in the organization. Some firms have policies that prohibit employees from discussing their pay with other employees, and violations of these policies can lead to disciplinary action.[19]

A number of organizations are opening up their pay systems to some degree by providing employees with more information on compensation policies, distributing a general description of the compensation system, and indicating where an individual's pay is within a pay grade. Such information allows employees to make more accurate equity comparisons.

Having a more open pay system has been found to have positive effects on employee retention and organizational effectiveness.[20]

Legal Constraints on Pay Systems

3 Compensation systems must comply with many government constraints. The important areas addressed by the laws include minimum-wage standards, hours of work, and pay equity. The following discussion examines the laws and regulations affecting base compensation; laws and regulations affecting incentives and benefits are examined in later chapters. HR professionals need to ensure that they keep up-to-date on the information as it can change annually and at varying times between the different jurisdictions.

Minimum Wage

All provinces have enacted legislation governed under their respective Employment Standards Acts to ensure that employees are paid at least minimum wage. These rates vary across the provinces. Legislation affecting both employees of the federal government and of federally regulated companies falls under the Canada Labour Code. There are different rates in each of the provinces based on regional and occupational considerations. Some also have lower rates for students, inexperienced workers, and/or employees receiving gratuities. Figure 10-11 shows the differences in minimum pay required across the various jurisdictions.

Figure 10-11 Minimum Wage Rates and Overtime Across Canada as of June 1, 2007

	Minimum Wage	Differential Minimum Wage Rate	Overtime Rate
Alberta	$7.00	n/a	1.5x after 8hrs/d or 44hrs/wk
British Columbia	$8.00	$6.00 for 1st 500 hours worked	1.5x after 8/d or 40/wk; 2x after 10/d, 48/wk
Manitoba	$7.60	n/a	1.5x after 8/d or 40/wk
New Brunswick	$6.50	n/a	1.5x after 44/wk
Newfoundland and Labrador	$7.00	n/a	1.5x min wage after 40/wk
Northwest Territories	$8.25	n/a	1.5x after 8/d or 40/wk
Nova Scotia	$7.15	$6.35 for inexperienced workers	1.5x min wage after 48/wk
Nunavut	$8.50	n/a	
Ontario	$8.00	$7.25 student; $6.75 liquor service	1.5x after 44hrs/wk
Prince Edward Island	$7.15	n/a	1.5x after 48/wk
Quebec	$7.75	$6.85 for worker receiving gratuity	1.5x after 40hrs/wk
Saskatchewan	$7.95	n/a	1.5x after 8hrs/d or 40 hrs/wk
Yukon	$8.25	n/a	
Federal	(provincial rates, adjusted to province)		1.5x after 8hrs/d or 40hrs/wk

Source: Various provincial employment standards websites; http://www.gov.mb.ca/labour/labmgt/resbr/wages/minwage.html.

Overtime

Certain employees are subject to receiving overtime. Each jurisdiction differs on the minimum amount of hours that must be worked before an employee is subject to overtime. Some companies will also offer more than the minimum to employees. For example, Company XYZ may agree that a normal workweek in their company is considered to be 37.5 hours per week, and that any hours worked after that time will be paid at 1.5x the regular rate of pay. It is their choice to pay better than what is stated by law. Usually larger companies offer more attractive pay options. There are numerous policies that organizations can adopt, however they cannot offer anything less than what is required by law. For example, the Canada Labour Code states that overtime at 1.5x of regular pay will be paid after eight hours/day or 40 hours per week, and then 2x after working ten hours/day or 48 hours/week. In British Columbia, 1.5x of regular pay will be paid after working eight hours/day or 40 hours/week. In Ontario, 1.5x of regular pay will be paid after working 44 hours/week.

Certain professions are exempt from earning overtime. The determination of who is exempt is spelled out in each applicable jurisdiction's legislative requirements. It is well known that managers generally fall under this category and are not reimbursed for any overtime. Employers must be careful about who they classify as managers because there are particular rules that specify who is a manager and who is not. Some employers will purposely give an employee a title of "manager" or "supervisor" for the purpose of avoiding overtime pay. Employers are cautioned against doing this since they could find themselves liable for reimbursing their employees for overtime hours, and any legislated deductions that were not remitted to the government.

In the United States employees who fall under this category of manager are referred to as an "exempt employee." Exempt employees are exempted from overtime. On the other hand, a non-exempt employee is entitled to overtime in the U.S. While these terms do not carry any legal standing in Canada, many organizations in Canada use these terms to denote who receives overtime and who does not. This is a result of many Canadian organizations with U.S.-based parent companies adopting the terminology of their American counterparts, and so the terms "exempt and non-exempt" have found their way into Canadian organizations. Even though a Canadian company may be American owned, the jurisdiction for pay must be based on Canadian legislation, as is the case with any foreign-owned subsidiary operating in Canada.

Hours of Work

As discussed above, while minimum wage rates apply, so do the hours of work required. Compensation professionals and managers must be aware of the hours of work required so that they can appropriately determine their compensation budgets. As you can see in Figure 10-11, overtime differs across the provinces. As previously mentioned, it is common that 1.5x the regular rate of pay is required after a certain minimum amount of hours has been worked.

Child Labour Provisions

Since the minimum rates of pay are much lower for students than they are for the general population, some employers may be tempted to hire as many students as possible to keep labour costs lower. While this can present a win-win for both parties, it can also be detrimental to the child in terms of not fulfilling their educational requirements, or working in industries that are deemed to be dangerous. Concerted efforts have been made globally to protect the young worker. Human resources professionals and others who are involved in the recruitment, selection, and payment of wages must ensure that they are adhering to the applicable laws. Figure 10-12 is an example of the requirements for child labour in Ontario. All jurisdictions have their own requirements.

Independent Contractor Regulations

The growing use of contingent workers by many organizations has focused attention on another group of legal regulations—those identifying the criteria that independent contractors must meet. The issue of whether an individual is an employee or is self-employed has been challenged a number of times in court cases over the years. Four factors, termed "tests" are used to determine the correct status of an individual: control test, integration test, economic reality test, and the specified result test. The control test considers how

Figure 10-12 *Minimum Age Requirements for Working in Ontario****

14 years old	**Establishments such as offices, stores, arenas, restaurant serving areas.**
15 years old	**Factories (other than logging operations), restaurant kitchens; and warehouses).**
16 years old	**Construction, surface mine (except the working face); logging operations; mining plants.**
18 years old	**Underground mining or a working face of a surface mine; window cleaning.**

Source: Protecting Yourself: Tips for Young Workers (2004), Ontario Ministry of Labour. © Queen's Printer for Ontario, 2004. Reproduced with permission.

much say the employer has over the individual's completion of work. The integration test is concerned with how integral the assignment is to the normal running of the business. The economic reality test looks at the risk of profit or loss to the individual. The specified result test determines how much control the individual has over completion of the task.[21]

Classifying someone as an independent contractor rather than an employee offers a major advantage. The employer does not have to pay employment insurance, Canada pension, or workers' compensation costs. These additional payroll levies may add 10 percent or more to the costs of hiring the individual as an employee.

Legislation on Equal Pay and Pay Equity

As discussed in Chapter 3 various legislative efforts have addressed the issue of wage discrimination on the basis of gender. Legislation to deal with equal pay can be found in human rights legislation, employment standards legislation, and pay equity legislation. The most overt forms of pay discrimination are generally handled by human rights legislation and employment standards laws. Canada's 13 jurisdictions provide for some type of equal pay in their human rights legislation although it may only refer generally to job discrimination rather than specifically to equity in wages. In six jurisdictions, there are equality of pay provisions under the employment standards law and six have pay equity laws. Pay equity legislation in Ontario and Quebec apply to both the private and public sectors, while in Manitoba, New Brunswick, Nova Scotia, and Prince Edward Island, it applies only to the public sector. Most jurisdictions have more than one law that deals with equal pay.

Pay equity
Right to equal pay for work of equal value. The value of the job is based on the levels of skill, effort, responsibility, and working conditions involved in doing the work.

Pay equity is the right to equal pay for work of equal value. When incorporating the concept of pay equity, the value of the job in question should be based on the levels of skill, effort, responsibility, and working conditions involved in doing the work. Skill measures things according to level of difficulty and things that require training or practice and includes mental and physical abilities required to perform the job. Effort measures the mental or physical drain on employees. Responsibility measures things that have varying degrees of impact or importance to the organization. Finally, working conditions refer to the context within which employees are required to perform their jobs, and the level of stress, or bothersome or dangerous work involved. By including these four factors, elements of the job that might be overlooked can be captured. When these aspects are not considered, the value of the job for the female can be underestimated. When discussing pay equity, there are three important, but different ideas to be considered:

LOGGING ON...

Ontario Pay Equity Commission
The Pay Equity Office (PEO) is responsible for implementing and enforcing the Pay Equity Act. The PEO investigates, mediates, and resolves complaints under the act. The PEO also provides programs and services to help employers, employees, and bargaining agents understand and comply with the Pay Equity Act.
www.payequity.gov.on.ca/index_pec.html

- Equal Pay for Equal Work—addresses the most overt form of discrimination in wages on the basis of gender. It involves direct comparison of jobs occupied by the opposite genders where the job is the same or basically the same. For example, two machinists, one male and one female doing the same work with the same qualifications, performance and seniority, but the female is paid less.
- Equal Pay for Work of Equal Value—provides for reducing the wage gap by comparing jobs of a different nature that are considered "male" or "female" dominated jobs.
- Pay Equity Laws—refers to legislated programs that aim to achieve equity in pay in an organized manner. Pay equity laws are most often proactive in that they don't require a complaint to be filed in order to achieve their goal. They use specific targets and deadlines and the collective bargaining process to achieve their goals.

Pay equity legislation was enacted in Canada in 1987 to address the historical wage gap that exists between men and women. Pay equity is governed by the Canadian Humans Rights Act and the Equal Wages Guideline. The Pay Equity Act requires that

Work that has traditionally been performed by women, such as child-care worker, librarian, or nurse, has not achieved fair and equal pay practices compared to positions traditionally performed by men such as mechanic, janitor, or firefighter.

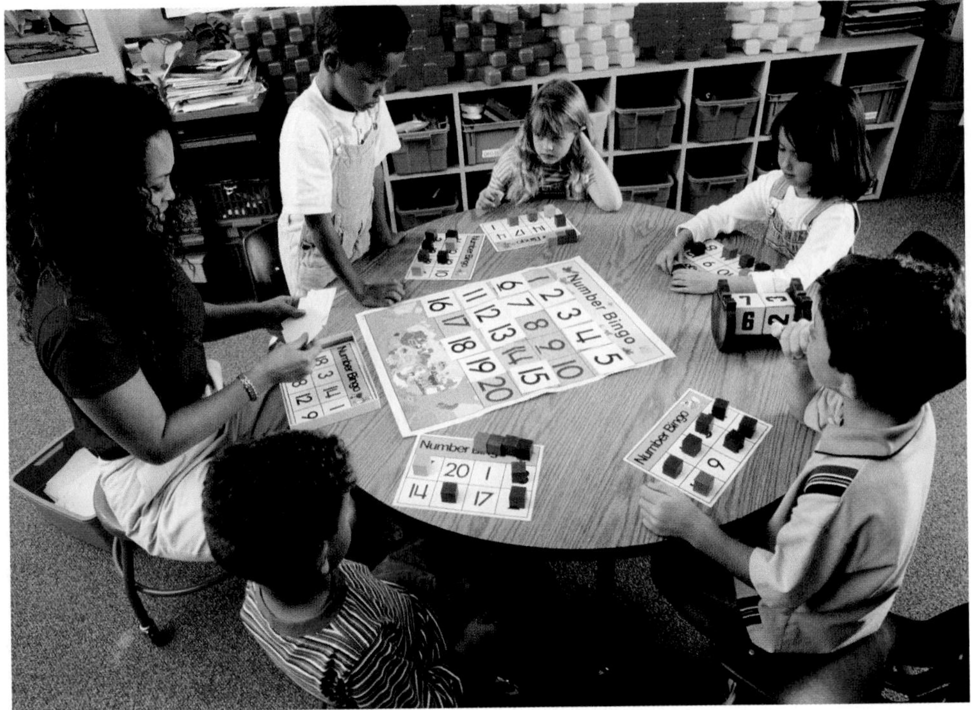

Source: © Royalty-Free/Corbis

jobs be evaluated and work mostly or traditionally performed by women be compared to work mostly or traditionally performed by men. If jobs are of comparable value, then female jobs must be paid at least the same as male jobs. Female jobs are jobs mostly or traditionally performed by women such as librarian, child-care worker, or administrative assistant. Male jobs are jobs mostly or traditionally performed by men such as truck driver, firefighter, or shipper/receiver.

In Ontario, all public sector employers and large employers in the private sector (those with 100 or more employees in 1987) were required to post pay equity plans. Smaller private sector employers (those with 10 to 99 employees in 1987) could opt to post pay equity plans, but must have done so by December 31, 1992. Employers who posted were able to phase in pay equity adjustments, spending a minimum of 1 percent of the company's total Ontario payroll for each year before each pay equity adjustment was due, beginning on the mandatory first adjustment date.

If pay inequity is found to exist in an organization, each January 1, pay equity adjustments are to be provided to the females whom jobs have been found to be undervalued. A minimum of 1 percent of the previous year's payroll is to be used for pay equity adjustments, and these are to be given on top of the female's normal pay increases, until pay equity is achieved. Pay equity adjustments can be distributed in a number of ways as long as the female job class with the lowest job rate receives more. For example, an employer could provide pay equity adjustments to all female job classes requiring adjustments the same amount, larger adjustments can be given to the female job classes that require the largest adjustment, or larger pay equity adjustments can be given to the job classes with small discrepancies so that the inequities can be eliminated quickly. Regardless of what choice an employer takes to eliminate the pay inequities, all of the 1 percent must be spent. Employers who do not post their plans on time need to calculate what they would have owed employees in each year of the phasing in period and make retroactive adjustments. Therefore, if employees who have since left the organization would have received these adjustments, then they are still entitled to be paid the amount owing, even though they are no longer with the organization.

Pay differences can be justified on the basis of merit (better performance), seniority (longer service), quantity or quality of work, or factors other than gender. Similar pay must be given for jobs requiring equal skills, equal effort, or equal responsibility or jobs performed under similar working conditions. If employees do not feel that pay differences are justified, or that the employer has not followed the pay equity guidelines, then they can file a complaint with the Pay Equity Commission. Each jurisdiction will have their own specific rules on how to handle pay equity complaints. Generally, an individual who files a complaint does not have to provide their name, or they can ask to ensure that their name is not disclosed to their employer. A Review Officer has the power to write an order to resolve all pay equity complaints. If either party is not satisfied with the Review Officer's resolution, then a request to hear the case can be made before the Pay Equity Hearings Tribunal.

Not all organizations have embraced pay equity legislation. Employers such as Air Canada, Canada Post, Bell Canada, and the federal government have continued to incur the expense of prolonged court cases and tribunal hearings that span decades rather than pay women fairly. In May 2006, Bell Canada was awaiting the ratification of a deal that would end a 14-year-long pay equity dispute with 5000 Bell Canada telephone operators (most of whom are women). The former and current employees who range in age from 35 to 70-years-old would each receive $25,000 to $30,000 if the deal is ratified. According to Communications, Energy and Paperworkers and Union of Canada president Brian Payne, the settlement, "will bring closure to one of the longest fought struggles in the labour movement."[22]

Development of a Base Pay System

4 As shown in Figure 10-13, a base compensation system is developed using current job descriptions and job specifications. These information sources are used when *valuing jobs* and analyzing *pay surveys.* These activities are designed to ensure that the pay system is both internally equitable and externally competitive. The data compiled in these two activities are used to design *pay structures,* including *pay grades* and minimum-to-maximum *pay ranges.* After pay structures are established, individual jobs must be placed in the appropriate pay grades and employees' pay must be adjusted according to length of service and performance. Finally, the pay system must be monitored and updated.

Employers want their employees to perceive their pay as appropriate in relation to pay for jobs performed by others inside the organization. Frequently, employees and managers make comments such as, "This job is more important than that job in another department, so why are the two jobs paid about the same?" To provide a systematic basis for determining the relative value of jobs within an organization, the employer evaluates every job in the organization on the basis of the four factors related to pay equity: skill, effort, responsibility, and working conditions.

Two general approaches for valuing jobs are available: job evaluation and market pricing. Both approaches are used to determine initial values of jobs in relation to other jobs in an organization.

job evaluation
Formal, systematic means to identify the relative worth of jobs within an organization.

Valuing Jobs with Job Evaluation Methods

Job evaluation is a formal, systematic means to identify the relative worth of jobs within an organization. Several job evaluation methods are available for use by employers of different sizes. Job evaluation committees are normally assigned and trained in the

Figure 10-13 Compensation Administration Process

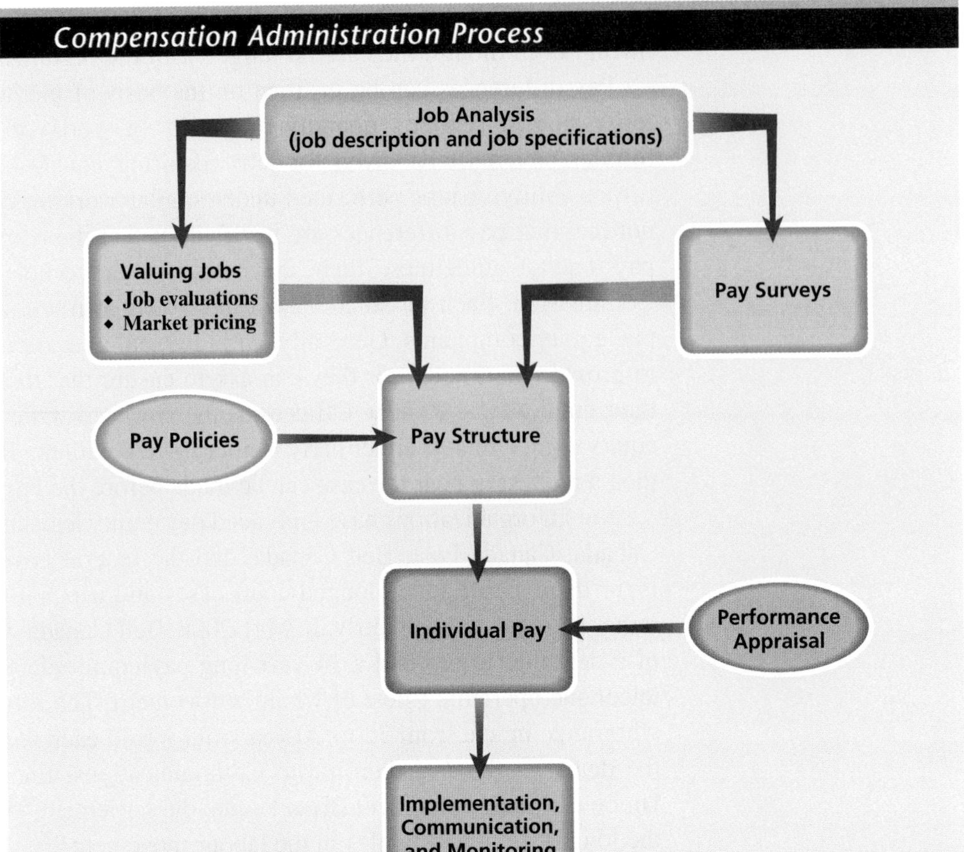

job evaluation system employed in their organization. Human resources, specifically key compensation professionals, will chair these committees. The committee should be as diverse as possible, ensuring enough male to female ratios and ethnic representation, with different levels of authority within the organization, and that enough of the key departments are represented on the committee. The task of the committee is to conduct job evaluations as may be required. They may even be charged with the task of determining the compensable factors. The size of the committee depends on the size of the organization, and the complexity of the evaluation system being employed. For example, the Job Evaluation Committee for the City of Saskatoon consists of three union representatives and three managers.[23] In a smaller organization, the department manager and the HR representative would probably handle the job evaluation.

Ranking Method

The ranking method is considered to be the simplest and most basic form of job evaluation and can be used for a small number of jobs. It is a whole job method because the entire job is considered rather than the individual components. *Straight ranking*, which is feasible for a limited number of jobs (20 or less), lists each job on a card with job titles and brief descriptions, and orders the job from highest to lowest. *Alternation ranking* lists the names of employees on the lefthand side of a sheet of paper—preferably in random order. If the rankings are for salary purposes, a supervisor is asked to choose the "most valuable" employee on the list, cross his or her name off, and put it at the top of the column on the righthand side of the sheet. Next, the supervisor selects the "least valuable" employee on the list, crosses his or her name off, and puts it at the bottom of the righthand column. The ranker then selects the "most valuable" person from the remaining list, crosses his or her name off and enters it below the top name on the righthand list, and so on. One other ranking method is *paired-comparison ranking*. This technique is probably just as accurate as alternation ranking and might be more so. But with large numbers of employees it becomes extremely time consuming and cumbersome. For example, if you have five employees, Sally, John, Danny, Cathy, and Mary and we list their names on the left-hand side of the sheet. We then compare Sally with John on whatever criterion we have chosen, say, present value to the organization. If we feel Sally is more valuable than John, we put a tally beside Sally's name. We then compare Sally with Danny, with Cathy, and with Mary. The process is repeated for each individual. The person with the most tallies is the most valuable person, at least in the eyes of the rater; the person with no tallies at all is regarded as the least valuable person. Figure 10-14 demonstrates a paired-comparison ranking process.

A problem with ranking is that it can be extremely subjective, leaving managers the difficult task of explaining why one job is ranked higher than another to employees whose pay is affected by the ranking, especially when the ranking involves a large number of jobs. Since there is no standard used for comparison, new jobs would have to be compared with the existing jobs to determine its appropriate rank. In essence, the ranking process would have to be repeated each time a new job is added to the organization. The ranking method generally is more appropriate in a small organization having relatively few jobs.

Job Classification Method

In the classification method of job evaluation, descriptions of each class of jobs are written, and then each job in the organization is put into a grade according to the class description it best matches. Like the ranking system, it too is a whole job method of evaluation. Classification standards define the scope of work associated with particular occupational groups. They are also measurement tools that serve as a common yardstick on which to assess the degree of difficulty of work (e.g., novice through to expert). They provide a standardized means of ensuring consistency in how similar work is evaluated across the organization.

This method of job evaluation is typically used in government pay systems such as in Canada and the United States, although other organizations such as the Mennonite Church in Canada have also adopted this method. In the Public Service of Canada classification system, the organization of work and employees is referred to as the

Figure 10-14 *Paired-Comparison Job Ranking Table*

Column over row	Sally	John	Danny	Cathy	Mary	Job Total
Sally		**2**	**0**	**2**	**2**	**6**
John	**0**		**0**	**1**	**2**	**3**
Danny	**2**	**2**		**2**	**2**	**8**
Cathy	**0**	**0**	**0**		**0**	**0**
Mary	**2**	**2**	**0**	**1**		**5**

2 = more important , 1 = the same, 0 = less important

occupational group structure. A two-letter code is used to describe the occupational group's title. For example, "AS" stands for the Administrative Services Group that contains employees primarily engaged in administrative work, the Foreign Service (FS) Group contains rotational employees primarily engaged in the political, economic, and immigration functions of the foreign service, and so on. The number assigned to the occupational group designator refers to the step or level within the group (e.g., the first level of the AS group is referred to as AS-1). The major difficulty with the classification method is that subjective judgments are needed to develop the class descriptions and to place jobs accurately in them. With a wide variety of jobs and generally written class descriptions, some jobs could easily fall into two or three different grades. One of the greatest advantages to using this type of system is its flexibility since it can be used in both small and large organizations.

Point Method

Compensable factor
Factor that identifies a job value commonly present throughout a group of jobs.

The most widely used job evaluation method, the point method or point-factor system, is more sophisticated than the ranking and classification methods. As a job-content valuation technique that uses quantitative methodology, it breaks jobs down into various **compensable factors.** A compensable factor identifies a job value commonly present throughout a group of jobs. The four factors of skill, effort, responsibility, and working conditions serve as a basis for the compensable factors of most job evaluation systems. Often organizations will adopt additional compensable factors that may be important to their organization. Under each of the factors, subfactors may also be derived. As a quantitative method, numerical values are assigned to compensable factors and their subfactors. These values are then summed to determine the overall value of the job. The higher the value of the job, the higher the relative worth of the job to the organization.

Compensable factors must be defined and assigned a range of points based on the factor's relative value to the organization. Compensable factors are then weighted to represent the relative importance of each factor to the job and then weightings are assigned to the subfactors. Factor weights must be distributed 100 percent among the factors, although the percentages will differ among the factors, depending on their level of importance to an organization. Consider the job of a miner working underground. One might assume that the most heavily weighted compensable factor would be working conditions. For example, two subfactors under working conditions might be environment and hazardous conditions. If working conditions were weighted at 40 percent, then environment and hazardous conditions could be assigned weights of 30 percent and 10 percent respectively if environment were more important than hazardous conditions. That means 60 percent is left to distribute amongst the other factors. All compensable factors are weighted, as are their subfactors. Each of the factors and subfactors must then be divided into degrees and duly defined. Once the compensable factors and subfactors have been weighted, defined, and each degree assigned a point value, then a job evaluation can take place.

The number of compensable factors an organization chooses to use, as well as any subfactors depends on what the organization values. Therefore, one organization cannot necessarily adopt another organizations' point method as they are generally reflective of an organization's values and are unique to their situation. At the University of British Columbia, a point factor system is used for some of its employees (including diverse positions as library staff, medical office assistants, and stage technicians) who are rated according to skills, responsibility, effort, and working conditions through the interpretation of 13 specific factors that include knowledge, learning experience, judgment, contacts, hazards, and dexterity. Each factor is divided into levels that each carry a point value that is based on the weight of the factor.[24]

Figure 10-15 provides an example of compensable factors and subfactors adopted by an organization for their point system and their assigned weightings. In this example, both skill and responsibility factors are most important to the organization since 35 percent of the available points has been assigned to each of these factors. The determination of how many points usually uses, as a rule of thumb, 250 points times the number of compensable factors. In the example shown in Figure 10-15 there are four compensable factors times 250 points equals 1000 points to be distributed as the organization feels is necessary. For example: skill is worth 350 points (e.g., 1000 points × 35 percent), effort 200 points, responsibility 350 points, and working conditions 100 points. These points are then divided by the subfactors according to their assigned value. Figure 10-16 provides an example of a defined subfactor for responsibility for financial resources with four degree levels.

A special type of point method used by the consulting firm, the Hay Group, has received widespread application, although it is most often used with professional,

Figure 10-15 *Compensable Factor Weights, Points, and Degrees*

Skill (35% divided between three subfactors)

Subfactors	*Weight*	*Points*	*Points for Levels (Degrees)*					
			1	2	3	4	5	6
Knowledge	15%	150	30	60	90	120	150	
Interpersonal Skills/Contacts	12%	120	24	48	72	96	120	
Problem Solving/Judgment	8%	80	16	32	48	64	80	

Effort (20% divided between two subfactors)

Subfactors	*Weight*	*Points*	*Points for Levels (Degrees)*					
			1	2	3	4	5	6
Mental Effort	12%	120	24	48	72	96	120	
Physical Effort	8%	80	16	32	48	64	80	

Responsibility (35% divided between four subfactors)

Subfactors	*Weight*	*Points*	*Points for Levels (Degrees)*					
			1	2	3	4	5	6
Personnel/Policies/Practices	12%	120	20	40	60	80	100	120
Information Resources	10%	100	20	40	60	80	100	
Financial Resources	8%	80	20	40	60	80		
Material Resources	5%	50	10	20	30	40	50	

Working Conditions (10% applied to one subfactor)

Subfactors	*Weight*	*Points*	*Points for Levels (Degrees)*					
			1	2	3	4	5	6
Environment	10%	100	20	40	60	80	100	

Note: Example point allocation between degree levels: Working Conditions 10% (1000) = 100 points/5 levels = 20. Therefore, each degree level will be worth 20 points, beginning with 20, and ending with 100 points. Therefore, degrees are equidistance apart from one another.

Figure 10-16 *Example of Defined Degrees of Subfactor: Responsibility for Financial Resources*

This subfactor measures the degree of accountability for money, financial data, financial records and related decisions, and the acquisition and/or expenditure of funds.

Level 1: **Infrequently is involved in financial matters, typically on a relief basis . . .**

Level 2: **Compiles information and data required for financial activity . . .**

Level 3: **Ensures recording of assets and liabilities, accounting, and financial transactions . . .**

Level 4: **Formulates budget of whole organization. Develops policy for financial control and cash management systems . . .**

managerial, and executive employees. The *Hay system* uses three factors and numerically measures the degree to which each of these factors is required in a job.[25] The three factors and their subfactors are as follows:

Know-How	Problem-Solving Ability	Accountability
• Functional expertise	• Environment	• Freedom to act
• Managerial skills	• Challenge	• Impact of end results
• Human relations		• Magnitude

The Hay system's compensable factors are directly related to the four compensable factors stipulated in pay equity legislation. For example, skill is equivalent to know-how, effort is associated with problem solving, responsibility is related to accountability, and working conditions considers physical effort, environmental factors, sensory attention, and mental stress. The University of New Brunswick has implemented the Hay system for its administrative, professional, and technical employees.

The point method has been widely used because it is relatively simple to use and it considers the components of a job rather than the total job. It is also easily understood by employees, and therefore much easier to communicate. A major advantage of the point system is the stability of the rating scales. Once the scales are developed, they may be used for a considerable amount of time without revision. However, point systems have been criticized for reinforcing traditional organizational structures and job rigidity. It also takes time to develop and install and can be quite costly, particularly if job descriptions must be developed. Some of the work can be cut down by purchasing a system already developed by a consultant, but the new plan must be adapted to fit with your organization. Although not perfect, the point method of job evaluation is generally better than the classification and ranking methods because it quantifies job elements.

Factor-Comparison Method

The factor-comparison method is a quantitative and quite complex combination of the ranking and point methods. It is not widely used, but many of its components are incorporated into many job evaluation plans, including the plan that is used the most, the Hay system. Factor comparison involves judging which jobs contain more of certain compensable factors. Jobs are compared with each other, but on one factor at a time. A job evaluation committee selects and rank-orders key jobs in an organization against a set of compensable factors. A dollar value is established against each compensable factor and a scale is developed based on the going rates of the jobs in the market. Figure 10-17 demonstrates the final outcome for this type of evaluation.

Figure 10-17 *Job Evaluation: Factor Comparison*

Wage Allocation	Mental Requirements	Physical Requirements	Skill Requirements	Responsibility	Working Conditions
.00					
.20					Truck Driver
.40			Truck Driver	Parts Attendant	Machine Operator
.60					Punch Press Operator
.80	Punch Press Operator	Punch Press Operator		Truck Driver	
1.00			Stocker		Stocker
1.20	Stocker		Parts Inspector	Punch Press Operator	Parts Inspector
1.40				Stocker	
1.60					
1.80			Machine Operator	Parts Inspector	
2.00		Parts Inspector	Parts Attendant		
2.20	Parts Attendant	Parts Attendant			
2.40					
2.60					
2.80		Stocker	Punch Press Operator		
3.00		Machine Operator			
3.20					Parts Attendant
3.40	Truck Driver	Truck Driver		Machine Operator	
3.60	Machine Operator				
3.80					
4.00					
4.20					
4.40					
4.60					
4.80	Parts Inspector				
5.00					

Five jobs have been evaluated on five compensable factors. The truck driver has been ranked as lowest in working conditions, and parts attendant the highest. In total, the truck driver earns $3.50 on mental requirements, $3.60 on physical requirements, $0.40 for skill requirements, $1.00 for responsibility, and $0.20 for working conditions for a total of $8.70 per hour.

A major advantage of the factor-comparison method is that it is tailored specifically to one organization. Each organization must develop its own key jobs and its own factors. As well, fewer compensable factors are usually involved, thus reducing any potential overlap. The major disadvantages of the factor-comparison method are that it is complex, difficult to use, and time-consuming to establish and develop.

Integrated and Computerized Systems

Some organizations are linking the components of wage and salary programs through computerized and statistical techniques. From a bank of compensable factors, employers can select those most relevant for the different job families in the organization, rate the jobs, and then analyze job evaluation and pay survey relationships.

These systems are less separate methods than they are applications of information technology and advanced statistics to the process of developing a wage and salary program.

Legal Issues and Job Evaluation Employers usually view the task of evaluating jobs to determine rates of pay as separate from the tasks of selecting individuals for those jobs and taking disciplinary action against employees. However, because job evaluation affects the employment relationship, specifically the pay of individuals, it involves several legal issues that may cross over into broader employment concerns and that must be addressed.

Critics have charged that traditional job evaluation programs place less weight on knowledge, skills, and working conditions for many female-dominated jobs in office and clerical areas than on the same factors for male-dominated jobs in craft and manufacturing areas. These critics have attacked typical job evaluations as being gender biased. Employers counter that because they base their pay rates heavily on external equity comparisons in the labour market, they are simply reflecting rates the "market economy" sets for jobs and workers, rather than discriminating. However, as previously discussed, implementing a pay equity system that considers the four compensatory factors of skill, effort, responsibility, and working conditions can help to alleviate these issues associated with pay inequities because it tends to capture commonly overlooked features of work.

Valuing Jobs Using Market Pricing

Market pricing
Use of pay survey data to identify the relative value of jobs based on what other employers pay for similar jobs.

Market pricing uses market pay data to identify the relative value of jobs based on what other employers pay for similar jobs. Jobs are arranged in groups tied directly to similar survey data amounts. Larger companies such as Marriott International and Dow Chemical are among employers who are relying on market pricing as a way to value their positions.[26] In Canada, smaller organizations and or those who do not use job evaluation systems rely mainly on market pricing to determine the value of their positions to their organizations.

Key to market pricing is identifying relevant market pay for jobs that are good "matches" with the employer's jobs, geographic considerations, and company strategies and philosophies about desired market competitiveness levels.[27] Obviously much of the accuracy of market pricing rests on the sources and quality of the pay surveys used.

Advantages of Market Pricing The primary advantage cited for the use of market pricing is that it closely ties organizational pay levels to what is actually occurring in the market, without being distorted by "internal" job evaluation.[28] For years, criticisms of job evaluation have focused on the subjectivity of traditional job evaluations caused by organizational "politics," or the biases of those doing the ranking, classifications, or pointing.

An additional advantage of market pricing is that it allows an employer to communicate to employees that the compensation system is truly "market linked," rather than sometimes being distorted by internal issues. Employees often see a compensation system that was developed using market pricing as having "face validity" and as being more objective than a compensation system that was developed using the traditional job evaluation methods.

Disadvantages of Market Pricing The foremost disadvantage of market pricing is that it relies on accurate and appropriate market survey data, yet, for numerous jobs, pay survey data is limited or may not be gathered in methodologically sound ways. A closely related problem is that the responsibilities of a specific job in a company may be somewhat different from those of the "matching" job identified in the survey.

The scope of market data is another concern. Some employers who are labour market "competitors" may not participate in surveys, and the absence of their data can distort the market values used. A practical concern is that market pricing requires a firm to obtain a wide range of sources, particularly if it is geographically and globally dispersed.

Finally, tying pay levels to market data can lead to wide fluctuations based on market conditions. One has only to look back at the extremes of the information technology job market from 1999 to today, when pay levels increased dramatically then fell back because of the "dot-com" boom and bust. For these and other types of jobs, the debate over the use of job evaluation versus market pricing is likely to continue because both approaches have pluses and minuses associated with them.[29]

Pay Surveys

Pay survey
Collection of data on compensation rates for workers performing similar jobs in other organizations.

Benchmark jobs
Jobs found in many organizations and performed by several individuals who have similar duties that are relatively stable and require similar KSAs.

A **pay survey** is a collection of data on compensation rates for workers performing similar jobs in other organizations. Both job evaluation and market pricing are tied to surveys of the pay that other organizations provide for similar jobs.

Because jobs may vary widely in an organization, it is particularly important to identify **benchmark jobs**—jobs that are found in many other organizations. Often these jobs are performed by individuals who have similar duties that require similar knowledge, skills, and abilities (KSAs). For example, benchmark jobs commonly used in clerical/office situations are accounts payable assistant, administrative assistant, and receptionist. Benchmark jobs are used because they provide "anchors" against which individual jobs can be compared.

An employer may obtain surveys conducted by other organizations, access Internet data, or conduct its own survey. Many different surveys are available from a variety of sources. National surveys on many jobs and industries come from Statistics Canada, Human Resources Development Canada (wage settlement), Department of Justice Canada; professional and national trade associations; and various management consulting companies. In many communities, employers participate in wage surveys sponsored by the local chamber of commerce or local HR associations, to provide information relevant to jobs in the community.

Internet-Based Pay Surveys HR professionals can access a wide range of pay survey data online. In many cases, pay survey questionnaires are distributed electronically rather than as printed copies, and HR staff members complete the questionnaires electronically. Entities that have moved partially or totally to Web-based questionnaires report increased member participation and satisfaction.

The move to electronic surveys has had several advantages.[30] First, HR or account specialists can complete the electronic surveys by linking company payroll databases to the survey data requested. Doing this requires significantly less time than would be spent filling out printed survey forms. Also, submitting the survey data electronically reduces the time needed to enter the data and prepare the final report to send back to participating firms.

It is anticipated that over the next five years, most pay surveys will be conducted using electronic, Web-based technology. Also, the Internet provides a large

LOGGING ON...

PayScale
This website is the premium provider of online compensation reports and salary surveys for consumers and businesses in Canada.
www.payscale.com/salary-survey/aid-6837/raname-SALARY/fid-7031

number of pay survey sources and data. However, use of these sources requires caution because their accuracy and completeness may not be verifiable or may not be applicable to individual firms and employees. The HR Practice discusses how to address employee questions regarding pay survey data that is accessible from the Internet.

Using Pay Surveys The proper use of pay surveys requires evaluating a number of factors to determine if the data is relevant and valid. Areas that should be examined for each survey include the following questions:

- *Participants:* Does the survey cover a realistic sample of the employers with whom the organization competes for employees?
- *Broad-based:* Does the survey include data from employers of different sizes, industries, and locales?
- *Timeliness:* How current are the data (determined by the date the survey was conducted)?
- *Methodology:* How established is the survey, and how qualified are those who conducted it?
- *Job matches:* Does the survey contain job summaries so that appropriate matches to job descriptions can be made?

HR *Practice*

Questions about Internet Pay Survey Data

One challenge facing HR professionals and managers is how to respond to employees who find salary information on Internet sources, such as www.Salary.com. Other pay data are available to individuals through e-newsletters from various professional and trade associations and through member-access Web pages. It is becoming common for employees who are dissatisfied with their pay to bring Internet data to HR professionals or their managers and ask why their current pay is different from the pay in that Internet data.

Responding to such questions from employees requires addressing a number of areas. Even Salary.com includes explanations on its website, under the links "my salary is lower" and "my salary is higher." Consider the following points when discussing employee concerns:[31]

- *Job titles and responsibilities:* Comparison should be made against the employee's full job description, not just job titles and the brief job summaries on the websites.
- *Experience, KSAs, and performance:* Individuals in different organizations may have jobs with similar descriptions but vary significantly in their experience levels, KSAs, and performance. Most pay survey data on the Internet is an average of multiple companies and of multiple employees in those companies.
- *Geographic differences:* Many pay survey sites on the Internet use geographic index numbers, not actual data from employers in a particular area. For certain jobs, surveys of actual employers and jobs from a specific local area may reflect different numbers than those index numbers.
- *Company size and industry:* Pay levels may vary significantly by company size, with smaller firms often having lower pay. Also, pay levels for comparable jobs are often lower in certain industries, such as retail and banking, than they are in utilities or highly unionized manufacturing firms.
- *Base pay vs. total compensation:* Employers vary in the use of benefits and incentive compensation programs. An employee may work in a firm with a benefits or incentive program that is significantly better or worse than the programs offered by firms whose data appear in Internet surveys. However, Internet data usually reflect only base pay amounts.

1. How would you deal with an employee who approaches you with Internet salary survey data that shows that their job may very well be underpaid?
2. What would you suggest should be done to avoid problems of employees bringing Internet salary surveys to you that may expose your organization as underpaying its employees?

Pay Structures

Job family
Group of jobs having common organizational characteristics.

5 Once job evaluations and pay survey data are gathered, pay structures can be developed using the process identified in Figure 10-18. Data from the evaluation of jobs and the pay surveys may lead to the establishment of several different pay structures for different job families, rather than just one structure for all jobs. A **job family** is a group of jobs having common organizational characteristics. In organizations there can be a number of different job families. Examples of some common pay structures based on different job families include: (1) hourly and salaried; (2) office, plant, technical, professional, and managerial; and (3) clerical, information technology, professional, supervisory, management, and executive. The nature, culture, and structure of the organization are considerations for determining how many and which pay structures to have.

Pay grades
Groupings of individual jobs having approximately the same job worth.

Pay Grades

In the process of establishing a pay structure, organizations use **pay grades** to group individual jobs having approximately the same job worth. Although no set rules govern establishing pay grades, some overall suggestions can be useful.

Figure 10-18 *Establishing Pay Structures*

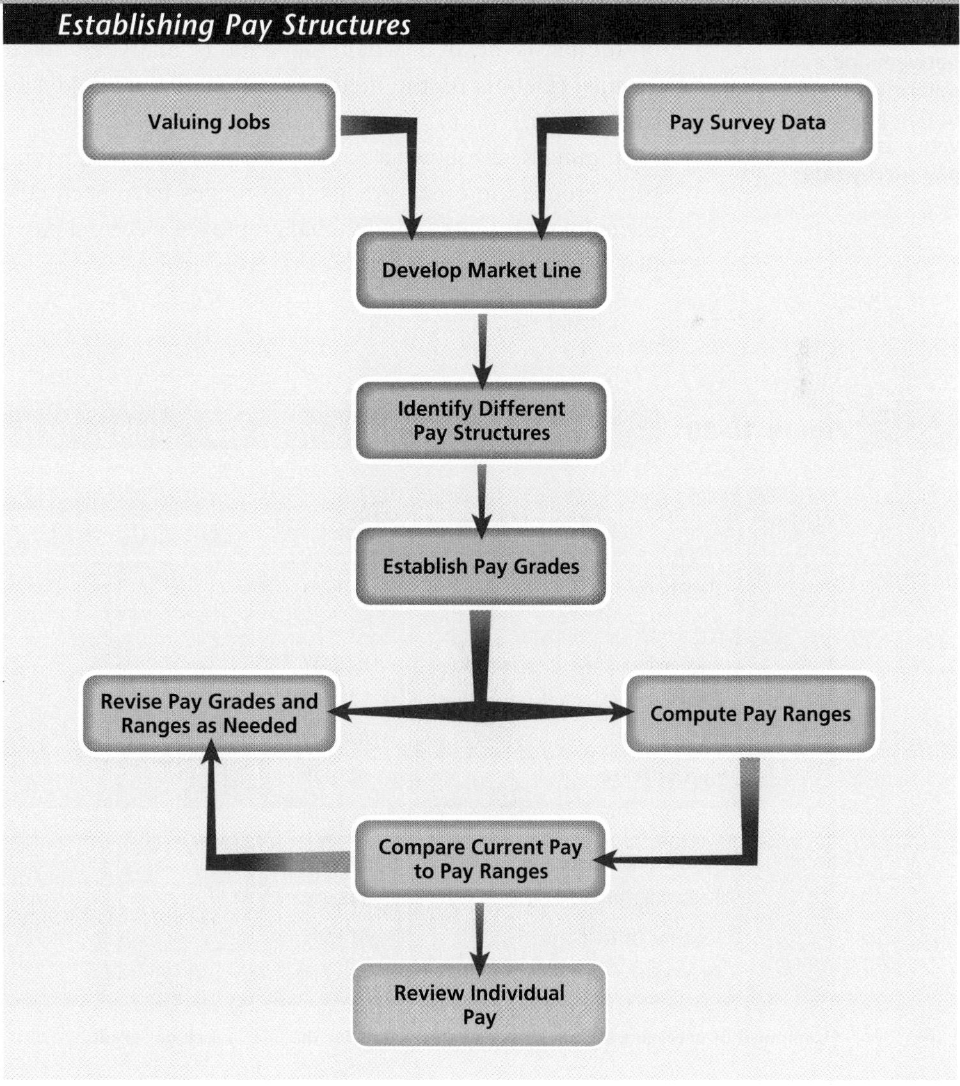

Generally, 11–17 grades are used in small and medium-sized companies, that is, companies with fewer than 500 employees. Two methods are commonly used to establish pay grades: market banding and use of job evaluation data.

Market banding
Grouping jobs into pay grades based on similar market survey amounts.

Setting Pay Grades Using Market Banding Closely linked to the use of market pricing to value jobs, **market banding** groups jobs into pay grades based on similar market survey amounts. Figure 10-19 shows two "bands" for jobs in a local bank. The midpoint of the survey average is used to develop pay range minimums and maximums, the methods of which are discussed later in this chapter.

Market line
Graph line that shows the relationship between job value as determined by job evaluation points and job value as determined by pay survey rates.

Setting Pay Grades Using Job Evaluation Points The second approach to determining pay grades uses job evaluation points or other data generated from the traditional job evaluation methods discussed earlier in the chapter. This process ties pay survey information to job evaluation data by plotting a *wage curve* and *scattergram.* This plotting involves first making a graph that charts job evaluation points and pay survey rates for all surveyed jobs. The graph shows the distribution of pay for the surveyed jobs, allowing a linear trend line to be developed by the *least-squares regression method.* Also, a curvilinear line can be developed by multiple regression and other statistical techniques. The end result is the development of a **market line** that shows the relationship between job value as determined by job evaluation points and pay survey rates. Generally, an r^2 of +.85 or higher is desired when the data is analyzed by different job families and groups. (Details on the methods and statistical analyses can be found in compensation texts.)[32]

Figure 10-20 shows a market line and how jobs having similar point values have been grouped into pay grades. Pay ranges have been computed for each pay grade. Each dot represents an individual employee's current pay in relation to the pay ranges that have been developed.

Figure 10-19 *Market-Banded Pay Grades for Community Bank*

Grade	Job	Pay Survey Summary	Pay Grade		
			Minimum	Midpoint*	Maximum
2	Bookkeeper Loan Clerk Customer Service Representative Data Entry/Computer Operator Head Teller Special Teller	$22,913 $22,705 $22,337 $22,309 $22,305 $22,179	$17,966	$22,458	$26,950
1	Mail Clerk/Messenger Proof Machine Operator General Office Clerk Receptionist	$19,167 $18,970 $18,594 $18,184	$14,962	$18,703	$22,444

***Computed by averaging the pay survey summary data for the jobs in each pay grade.**

Pay Ranges

The pay range for each pay grade also must be established. Using the market line as a starting point, the employer can determine minimum and maximum pay levels for each pay grade by making the market line the midpoint line of the new pay structure (see Figure 10-20). For example, in a particular pay grade, the maximum value may be 20 percent above the midpoint located on the market line, and the minimum value may be 20 percent below it.

Once pay grades and ranges have been computed, then the current pay of employees must be compared with the draft ranges. If the pay of a significant number of employees falls outside the ranges, then a revision of the pay grades and ranges may be needed. Also, once costing and budgeting scenarios are run to assess the financial impact of the new pay structures, then pay policy decisions about market positioning may have to be revised, by either lowering or raising the ranges. A growing number of employers are reducing the number of pay grades and expanding pay ranges by broadbanding.

Broadbanding
Practice of using fewer pay grades with much broader ranges than in traditional compensation systems.

Broadbanding **Broadbanding** is the practice of using fewer pay grades with much broader ranges than in traditional compensation systems. Combining many grades

Figure 10-20 *Example of Pay Grades and Pay Ranges*

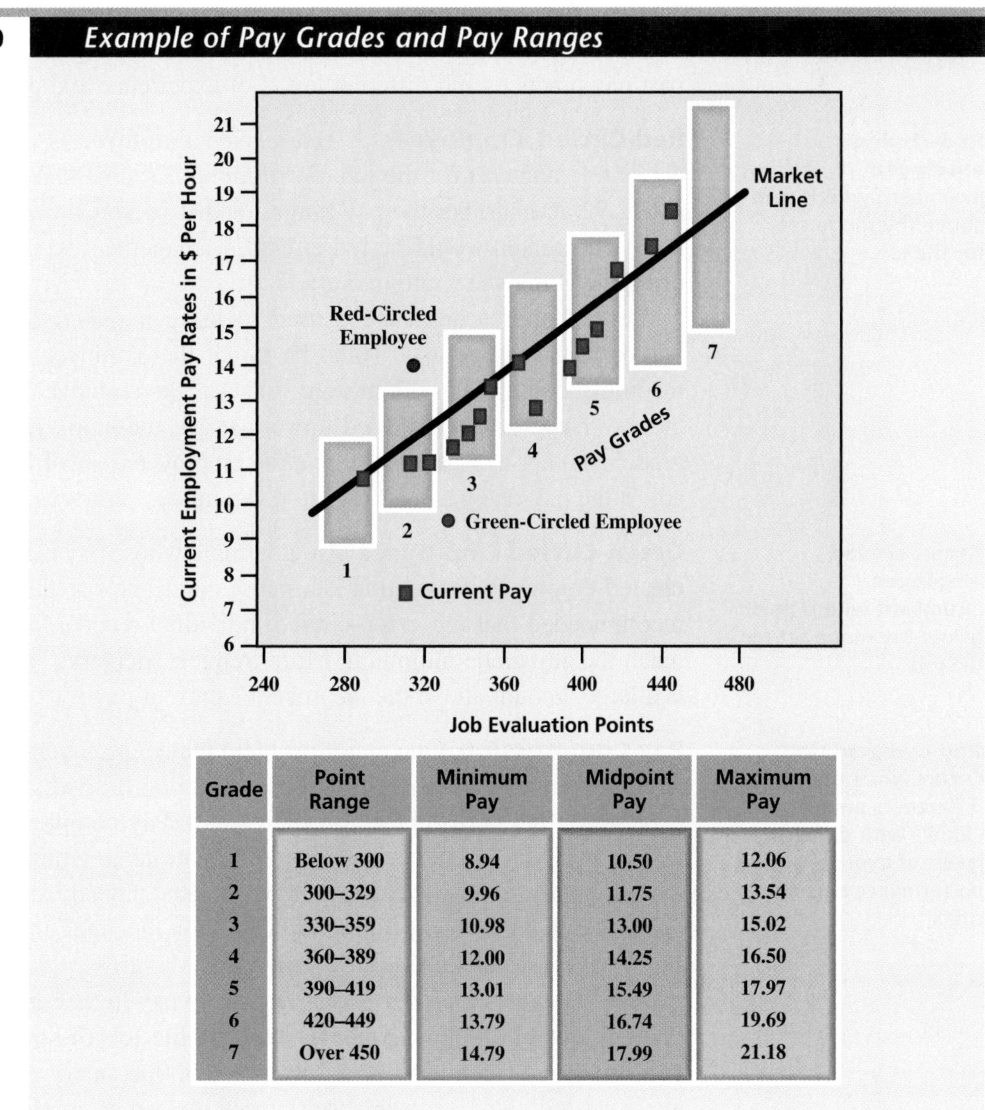

Grade	Point Range	Minimum Pay	Midpoint Pay	Maximum Pay
1	Below 300	8.94	10.50	12.06
2	300–329	9.96	11.75	13.54
3	330–359	10.98	13.00	15.02
4	360–389	12.00	14.25	16.50
5	390–419	13.01	15.49	17.97
6	420–449	13.79	16.74	19.69
7	Over 450	14.79	17.99	21.18

into these broadbands is designed to encourage horizontal movement and therefore more skill acquisition. The main advantage of broadbanding is that it is more consistent with the flattening of organizational levels and the growing use of jobs that are multidimensional.[33] The primary reasons for using broadbanding are: (1) to create more flexible organizations, (2) to encourage competency development, and (3) to emphasize career development.

A problem with broadbanding is that many employees have become "conditioned" to the idea that a promotion is accompanied by a pay raise and movement to a new pay grade. As a result of removing this grade progression, the organization may be seen as offering fewer upward promotion opportunities. Despite these and other problems, it is likely that broadbanding will continue to grow in usage.

Individual Pay

Once managers have determined pay ranges, they can set the pay for specific individuals. Setting a range for each pay grade gives flexibility by allowing individuals to progress within a grade instead of having to move to a new grade each time they receive a raise. A pay range also allows managers to reward the better-performing employees while maintaining the integrity of the pay system.

Regardless of how well a pay structure is constructed, there usually are a few individuals whose pay is lower than the minimum or higher than the maximum due to past pay practices and different levels of experience and performance.

Red-circled employee
Incumbent who is paid above the range set for the job.

Red-Circled Employees A **red-circled employee** is an incumbent who is paid above the range set for the job. For example, assume that an employee's current pay is $12.92 an hour, but the pay range for that person's pay grade is $8.94–$12.06 an hour. The person would be red circled. Management would try over a year or so to bring the employee's rate into grade.

Several approaches can be used to bring a red-circled person's pay into line. Although the fastest way would be to cut the employee's pay, that approach is not recommended and is seldom used. Instead, the employee's pay may be frozen until the pay range can be adjusted upward to get the employee's pay rate back into the grade. Another approach is to give the employee a small lump-sum payment but not adjust the pay rate when others are given raises.

Green-circled employee
Incumbent who is paid below the range set for the job.

Green-Circled Employees An individual whose pay is below the range is a **green-circled employee.** Promotion is a major contributor to this situation. Generally, it is recommended that the green-circled individual receive fairly rapid pay increases to reach the pay grade minimum. More frequent increases can be used if the minimum is a large amount above the incumbent's current pay.

Pay compression
Occurs when the pay differences among individuals with different levels of experience and performance become small.

Pay Compression One major problem many employers face is **pay compression,** which occurs when the pay differences among individuals with different levels of experience and performance become small. Pay compression occurs for a number of reasons, but the major one involves situations in which labour market pay levels increase more rapidly than current employees' pay adjustments. This is particularly difficult when the pay differential between a manager and their report is small.

In response to shortages of particular job skills in a highly competitive labour market, managers may occasionally have to pay higher amounts to hire people with those scarce skills. For example, suppose the job of specialized information systems analyst is identified as a $48,000–$68,000 salary range in one company, but qualified individuals are in short supply and other employers are paying $70,000.

To fill the job the firm likely will have to pay the higher rate. Suppose also that several analysts who have been with the firm for several years started at $55,000 and have received 4-percent increases each year. These current employees may still be making less than the $70,000 paid to attract and retain new analysts from outside with less experience. One partial solution to pay compression is to have employees follow a step progression based on length of service, assuming performance is satisfactory or better.[34]

Determining Pay Increases

6 Decisions about pay increases are often critical ones in the relationships between employees, their managers, and the organization. Individuals express expectations about their pay and about how much of an increase is "fair," especially in comparison with the increases received by other employees. There are several ways to determine pay increases, including: performance, seniority, cost-of-living adjustments, and lump-sum increases. These methods can be used separately or in combination.

Performance and Merit Increases

Merit pay
Merit pay programs reward employees with permanent increases to base pay according to differences in performance.

Just noticeable difference (JND)
Sometimes referred to as just-meaningful pay, is the minimum pay increase that employees will see as making a substantial change in compensation.

The most commonly used pay-for-performance system is **merit pay.** Compensation systems that provide merit increases should ensure that these increases reflect the performance level of the employees. There are many criticisms regarding merit pay, but the one most often noted has to do with the size of the increase.

Regardless of whatever pay increase is granted, the concept of **just noticeable difference (JND),** or just-meaningful pay as it is sometimes referred to, cannot be overlooked. If pay increases are not perceived to be large enough by employees, the benefits expected from a merit pay system may not surface. For example, if a pay increase is only slightly larger than the increase in cost of living, employees may not perceive it as an increase and see it as merely "staying even" with their current pay. As another example, if a superior performer receives a pay increase that he or she does not consider to be much larger than increases for average performers, the superior performer may experience dissatisfaction and a decrease in motivation, although the system was designed to provide the superior performer with a satisfying reward that would lead to continuing motivation and good performance. The difficulty for organizations is in deciding how much more the good performer's pay increase should be compared to the average employee's. Another concern stems from budget constraints which can adversely impact on JND.

How much is enough? Research continues on this issue, with no clear definition of the exact amount. However, one study reports that the increase should be between 6 and 8 percent of an employee's current salary to make enough difference to motivate employees. Merit guide charts are used, considering individual performance levels to allocate increases.[35]

Pay Adjustment Matrix

Compa-ratio
Pay level divided by the midpoint of the pay range.

Some system for integrating appraisals and pay changes must be developed and applied equally. Often, this integration is done through the development of a *pay adjustment matrix,* or *salary or merit guide chart.* Use of pay adjustment matrices bases adjustments in part on a person's **compa-ratio,** which is the pay level divided by the midpoint of the pay range. To illustrate, the compa-ratio for two employees would be:

$$\text{Employee } R = \frac{\$16.50 \text{ (current pay)}}{\$15.00 \text{ (midpoint)}} \times 100 = 110 \text{ (Compa-ratio)}$$

$$\text{Employee } J = \frac{\$13.05 \text{ (current pay)}}{\$15.00 \text{ (midpoint)}} \times 100 = 87 \text{ (Compa-ratio)}$$

Salary guide charts reflect a person's upward movement in an organization. That movement often depends on the person's performance, as rated in an appraisal, and on the person's position in the pay range, which has some relation to experience as well. A person's placement on the chart determines what pay raise the person should receive. For example, if employee *J* is rated as exceeding expectations (2) with a compa-ratio of 87, that person is eligible for a raise of 7 percent–9 percent, according to the chart in Figure 10-21.

Two interesting facets of the sample matrix illustrate the emphasis on paying for performance. First, individuals whose performance is below expectations receive small to no raises, not even a so-called cost-of-living raise. This approach sends a strong signal that poor performers will not continue to receive increases just by completing another year of service.

Second, as employees move up the pay range, they must exhibit higher performance to obtain the same percentage raise as those lower in the range performing at the "meets performance expectations" (2) level. This approach is taken because the firm is paying above the market midpoint but receiving only satisfactory performance rather than above-market performance. Charts can be constructed to reflect the specific pay-for-performance policy and philosophy in an organization. In addition to the

Figure 10-21 *Pay Adjustment Matrix*

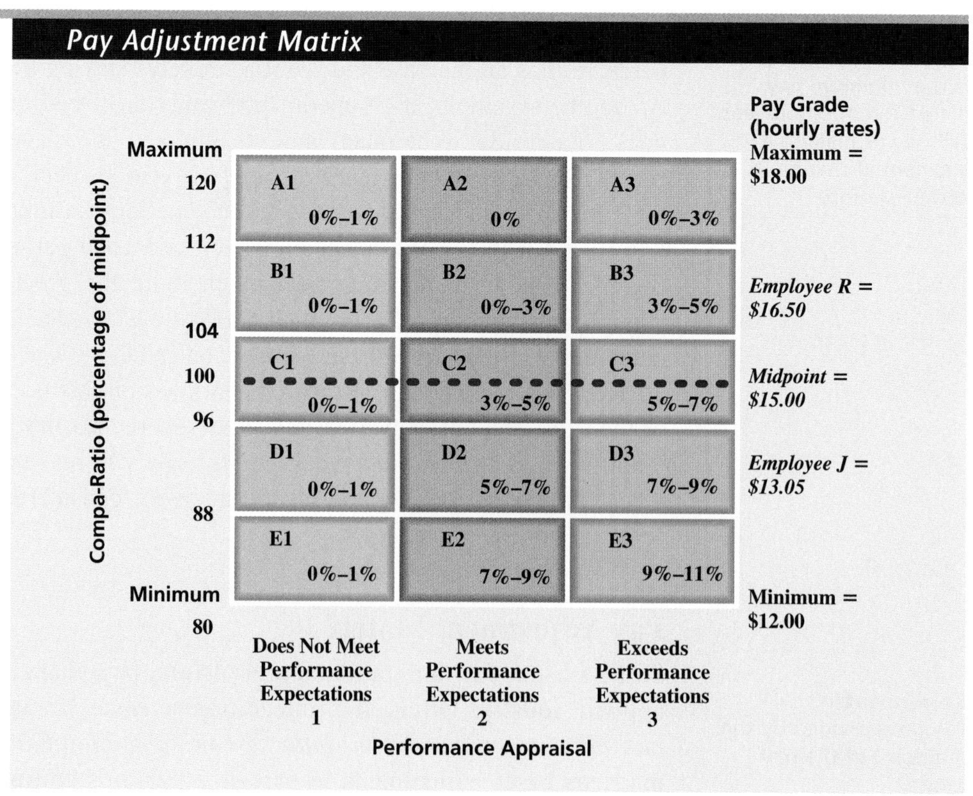

merit component that is used in the development of these salary matrices, an often overlooked component that must be built into annual salary increases and salary ranges is the cost of living.

Seniority

Seniority
Time spent in the organization or on a particular job.

Seniority, or time spent in the organization or on a particular job, can be used as the basis for pay increases. Many employers have policies that require a person to be employed for a certain length of time before being eligible for pay increases. Pay adjustments based on seniority often are set as automatic steps once a person has been employed the required length of time, although performance must be at least satisfactory in many non-union systems.

Cost-of-Living Adjustments (COLAs)

A common pay-raise practice is the use of a *cost-of-living adjustment (COLA).* Often, these adjustments are tied to changes in the Consumer Price Index (CPI) or some other general economic measure. The Consumer Price Index (CPI), which provides a broad measure of the cost of living in Canada, is based on the retail price of a representative shopping basket of about 600 goods and services from an average household's expenditure: food, housing, transportation, furniture, clothing, and recreation. However, numerous studies have revealed that the CPI overstates the actual cost of living.

Unfortunately, some employers give across-the-board raises and call them *merit raises,* which they are not. If all employees get a pay increase, it is legitimately viewed as a cost-of-living adjustment that has little to do with merit or good performance. For this reason, employers should reserve the term *merit* for any amount above the standard raise, and they should state clearly which amount is for performance and which is the "automatic" COLA.

A common pay-raise practice is the use of a cost-of-living adjustment (COLA). These adjustments are tied to the Consumer Price Index (CPI).

Source: TRBFoto/Photodisc/Getty Images

Lump-Sum Increases (LSIs)

Most employees who receive pay increases, either for merit or for seniority, first receive an increase in the amount of their regular monthly or weekly paycheque. For example, an employee who makes $2000 per month and then receives a 3-percent increase will move to $2060 per month.

Lump-sum increase (LSI)
One-time payment of all or part of a yearly pay increase.

In contrast, a **lump-sum increase (LSI)** is a one-time payment of all or part of a yearly pay increase. The pure LSI approach does not increase the base pay. Therefore, in the example of a person making $2000 per month, if an LSI of 3 percent is granted, then the person receives a lump sum of $720 ($2000 × 12 × .03 percent). However, the base rate remains at $2000 per month, which slows down the progression of the base wages. The firm can vary the amount of the "lump" from one year to the next, without having to continually raise the base rate. Some organizations place a limit on how much of a merit increase can be taken as a lump-sum payment. Other organizations split the lump sum into two cheques, each representing one-half of a year's pay raise.

An LSI plan offers advantages and disadvantages. The major advantage of an LSI plan is that it heightens employees' awareness of what their performance "merited." Another advantage is that the firm can use LSIs to slow down the increase of base pay, and thus reduce or avoid the compounding effect on succeeding raises. One disadvantage of LSI plans is that workers who take a lump-sum payment may become discouraged because their base pay has not changed. Unions generally resist LSI programs for this reason; unions also resist LSI programs because of their impact on pensions and benefits, unless the total amount paid including the LSI is used in pension computations.

SUMMARY

1 Compensation provided by an organization can come directly through base pay and variable pay and indirectly through benefits. For compensation expenditures to be administered effectively, compensation responsibilities of both HR specialists and managers must be performed well. Compensation practices are closely related to the strategies, objectives, culture, and philosophies of organizations. A continuum of compensation philosophies exists, ranging from an entitlement philosophy to a performance philosophy. A number of companies are using a total rewards approach to compensation. HR metrics can and should be used to measure the effectiveness of compensation.

2 Compensation practices for international employees are much more complex than those for domestic employees, because they are affected by many more factors. Decisions about compensation must always consider market competitiveness and positioning, use of competency-based pay, team rewards, and fairness. When designing and administering compensation programs, internal and external equity, organizational justice, and pay openness, must all be considered.

3 There are a number of legal constraints on pay systems that human resources professionals must be concerned about. Both the Canada Labour Code and Employment Standards Acts outline legislation to cover their designated employees. These legal constraints are related to minimum-wage standards, hours of work, including overtime requirements and pay equity. Each jurisdiction in Canada has their own specific rules with respect to each of these pieces of legislation. Child labour laws also must be adhered to. Due to the increase in contingent workers, the rules surrounding the employment of independent contractors is becoming more important in a determination of whether an employee is a contractor or an employee. Pay equity is a major concern for employers as the need to reduce the historical wage gap between men and women increases. The concepts of equal pay for equal work and equal pay for work of equal value are paramount to this understanding.

4 A base pay system is developed using information from valuations of jobs and pay surveys, both of which are designed to ensure that the pay system is internally equitable and externally competitive.

The values of jobs can be determined using either job evaluation or market pricing. One of the simplest job evaluation methods is ranking. Some ranking methods are either straight, alternation, or paired comparison. Job classification method is another system used mainly by governments. Both ranking and job classification are whole job methods. A point method or point-factor system is more sophisticated and is a job-content valuation technique that uses quantitative methodology with compensable factors. A special type of point system is the Hay system. The factor-comparison method is also quantitative, but is rather a complex combination of ranking and point methods. Computerized systems are gaining in popularity. Market pricing uses market pay data to identify the relative value of jobs based on what employers pay in similar jobs. Organizations should not rely solely on market pricing. Organizations should participate in pay surveys using benchmark jobs to collect pay data.

5 Once a firm has collected pay survey data, it can develop a pay structure, which is composed of pay grades and pay ranges. Broadbanding, which uses fewer pay grades with wider ranges, provides greater career movement possibilities for employees and has grown in popularity. Individual pay must take into account the placement of employees within pay grades. Problems involving "red-circled" jobs, whose rates are above pay range, and "green-circled" jobs, whose rates are below pay range, may be addressed in a number of ways.

6 Individual pay increases can be based on performance, seniority, cost-of-living adjustments, lump-sum increases, or a different combination of approaches. A pay adjustment matrix is important when considering pay for performance, merit increases, cost of living, compa-ratios and how the employee is moving through their respective salary ranges. The concept of just noticeable difference must be considered when granting pay increases.

KEY TERMS

Balance-sheet approach, p. 368
Base pay, p. 362
Benchmark jobs, p. 389
Benefit, p. 363
Broadbanding, p. 393
Compa-ratio, p. 395
Compensable factor, p. 384
Competency-based pay, p. 372
Distributive justice, p. 376
Entitlement philosophy, p. 365
Equity, p. 375
Global market approach, p. 369
Green-circled employee, p. 394
Job evaluation, p. 381
Job family, p. 391
Just noticeable difference (JND), p. 395
Lump-sum increase (LSI), p. 398
Market banding, p. 392
Market line, p. 392
Market pricing, p. 388
Merit pay, p. 395
Pay compression, p. 394
Pay equity, p. 379
Pay-for-performance philosophy, p. 365
Pay grades, p. 391
Pay survey, p. 389
Procedural justice, p. 376
Red-circled employee, p. 394
Salaries, p. 363
Seniority, p. 397
Tax equalization plan, p. 369
Variable pay, p. 363
Wages, p. 363

REVIEW AND APPLICATION QUESTIONS

1 You have been named human resources manager for a company that has 180 employees and no formal base pay system. What steps will you take to develop such a coordinated system?

2 If you had an employee who was going to be assigned to a job in another country for an extended period of time, what should you do with respect to their pay?

3 Discuss the various legal constraints that exist for pay systems.

4 Outline the process of developing a base pay system and describe the two means of valuing jobs using job evaluation and market pricing.

5 Outline the process of developing pay structures.

6 Discuss the different methods for determining pay increases. What method do you think is most appropriate and why? Does it depend on different situations? If so, what are they?

EXPERIENTIAL EXERCISES

1. You are the HR director for an insurance company with regional offices in several provinces. For each office, you want to be sure that the administrative assistants reporting to the regional manager are paid appropriately. Go to www.salaryexpert.com/index.cfm to find geographic pay survey data for this job in Montreal, Halifax, Vancouver, Winnipeg, Toronto, Ottawa, Windsor, Edmonton, and Charlottetown. Then, recommend pay ranges; identify the low, median, and high of each pay range. To present the data, list the offices in order from lowest median pay to highest median pay.
2. Develop pay adjustment matrices to address an organization who adopts a "lag the market" strategy, "lead the market" strategy, and "match the market" strategy. Assume that your research shows that annual increases being paid this year for your industry are 5 percent. Your organization's overall compa-ratio is 96 percent.
3. ABC Company, a manufacturer of plastic flower pots, has about 250 employees. The manufacturing population has 175 employees who are mainly assembly line workers and supervisory staff. The office has 75 administrative and supervisory employees. Working conditions are typical for an office, with air conditioning and ergonomically designed workstations. The building is only three years old and has all sorts of amenities such as a cafeteria, exercise room, relaxation room, and theatre room. There are very few accidents, and morale is good among the employees. The average tenure in the company is 12 years. You have been asked to conduct a job evaluation using a point evaluation method for the office staff. You have been presented with four job descriptions to begin the process. You are required to do the following:
   a. You may make assumptions on any information that may be missing.
   b. You may use the compensable factors described in Figure 10-15 as a starting point for this exercise.
   c. Based on the information you have been provided with determine how the compensable factors will be weighted and what subfactors you might choose?
   d. On what basis did you select the weightings and subfactors?
   e. Conducting the job evaluation, what position has the highest point? The lowest points? Discuss the differences and similarities.

   Receptionist—As the main contact for your organization, the individual sits at the main reception desk responding to telephone calls and inquiries from guests. There are some minor tasks involving the computer, in addition to sorting the mail. The individual must sit for prolonged periods of time, and deal with some customers who may be upset at times. A minimum of grade 12 education is required. There is no supervision required.

   Salesperson—The salesperson is responsible for the sale of products to retail stores such as The Bay, Home Depot, and Rona. Responsible for the Ontario market, the individual is expected to drive to locations as required, or to fly to the outer regions. A minimum of five years of working experience is required. There is no supervision of staff.

   Purchasing Supervisor—Managing three employees, the purchasing supervisor is responsible for securing material for production, office supplies, and for contracts for services such as the cafeteria vendor, cleaning staff, and other services such as photocopiers and computers. The supervisor may have to meet with vendors for the purposes of establishing contracts. A minimum of five years of working experience is required.

HR Assistant—The HR assistant will process paperwork for new employees, set up interviews for the HR manager, answer telephones for the department, assist the HR manager and the accounting manager with clerical duties and administrative duties such as typing correspondence, department filing, etc. This is an entry-level position, requiring a minimum of one year of working experience. There is no supervision of staff.

4. Your organization has offices throughout Canada and you are the corporate HR manager working out of the Vancouver head office. Payroll and human resources management is decentralized, meaning that each of the regions is responsible for their own hiring and termination of employees, and payment of wages. You have just received a telephone call from the Employment Insurance office indicating that an employee of yours has indicated to them that they have been laid off from your office in Winnipeg, but that they do not have a Record of Employment (ROE) severing their employment. Whenever an employee is terminated from employment, they must be provided with a Record of Employment stating what their last year of earnings has been, and why their employment has been severed. Upon further review of your master files, you determine that this is not an employee of yours, but indicate to the officer that you will get back to them. You immediately call the HR manager in the Winnipeg office inquiring about this individual. You are told that this person had worked for their office as an independent contractor over the past two years and that their services are no longer required and that they have been terminated. You also learn that the individual was advised that they reported to John Jackson, the operations manager in that region, and that they were required to work from 8:30 a.m. to 5:00 p.m. each day. Since they were classified as an independent contractor, no deductions for income tax, EI or CPP, or workers' compensation were ever taken or considered. Vacation pay was never paid out. Annual performance appraisals were conducted, and they were provided with an office with a computer. Do you consider them to be an employee or an independent contractor? Why or why not? What is your next step?

LEARNING REVIEW

To check your knowledge of the chapter, review the following. (Answers after the case.)

1 The entitlement philosophy of compensation is characterized by:
a. pay structures adjusted to market pressures
b. broad pay comparisons beyond specific industry practices
c. bonuses tied to performance
d. across-the-board raises

2 Most employers position their pay programs in the __________ quartile of their market as identified by data from surveys of other employers' compensation plans.
a. first
b. second
c. third
d. fourth

3 The control test for the independent contractor determination is:
a. employer determines if work is an integral part of their work
b. how much say the employer has over the individual's completion of work
c. the opportunity for profit (or loss)
d. the nature of the control

4 A factor that identifies a job value commonly present through a group of jobs is a(n):
a. factor comparison
b. internal structure
c. compensable factor
d. classification method

5 Pay compression occurs primarily because:
  a. employers fail to conduct performance appraisals
  b. organizations fail to conduct pay surveys
  c. labour market pay levels increase more than employers' pay adjustments
  d. employers pay below the minimum of their pay ranges

6 Use of pay adjustment matrices bases adjustments in part on a person's:
  a. performance
  b. seniority
  c. compa-ratio
  d. individual pay

CASE

"TO PAY OR NOT TO PAY"—IS THAT REALLY THE QUESTION?

Pay equity legislation, implemented over two decades ago, is a human right protected by the Canadian Human Rights Act. The current law prohibits differences in wages between female and male employees who work in the same establishment and perform work of "equal value." The law applies to employees in the federal public sector and businesses under the federal jurisdiction, such as banks, CN Rail, Bell, and Canada Post. Skill, effort, responsibility, and working conditions are the factors that are examined to determine the value of a particular type of work. Needless to say, this legislation has not been fully embraced by most of these organizations and court cases are usually the norm. One such example rests with Canada Post, which has been enthralled in a battle with its union, the Public Service Alliance of Canada (PSAC), since 1983. This battle has been touted as the "longest pay equity fight in Canada."

The union alleged that about 6000 current and former clerical and regulatory workers are owed back pay estimated to be about $150 million due to inequities in pay. Workers in the male-dominated postal operations group were earning almost 60 percent more than the group of clerical and regulatory workers, 80 percent of whom were women. Canada Post has maintained that they did not discriminate based on sex and that differences in collective bargaining and the power of different unions to negotiate on behalf of their members may have caused the disparity. The wage gap was eventually eliminated in June 2002 when a new job evaluation plan was agreed upon by both the union and Canada Post. However, this did not address the inequities that were the crux of the problem prior to this date.

In 2005, the Canadian human rights tribunal found that a wage gap caused by systemic sex discrimination had existed prior to 2002 and ordered Canada Post to pay the lost wages dating back to 1982, including interest and costs. However, due to uncertainty around job information and non-wage compensation issues, the tribunal ordered the amount to be reduced by half, much to the union's chagrin. The union estimates the final amount to be about $150 million and has reluctantly agreed to accept the judgment. Canada Post on the other hand has filed an appeal with Federal Court, which had not been resolved during the writing of this case.

A review of other longstanding pay equity disputes (Air Canada and Bell Telephone) indicates that problems with the legislation may be contributing to these long and drawn out issues. A task force to address pay equity issues began in 2001. Among the many concerns is the length of time it takes to hear cases. On average, lawsuits arising out of the federal pay equity provisions in the Canadian Human Rights Act take 176 days of hearings, more than ten times the typical length of other discrimination cases before the human rights tribunal. The Canada Post case took more than 400 days of hearings. More importantly, the task force recommended that a proactive pay equity system that would place the burden on employers, not complainants, to ensure the principle of equal pay for equal work is enacted. Because individuals wouldn't have access to information about others' pay and job descriptions, the system effectively shuts out all but unions from filing complaints. A problem exists for smaller employers that don't have the resources to hire compensation consultants to conduct job evaluations, so the creation of an independent body to help employers is needed.

Minister of Justice Irwin Cotler and Minister of Labour and Housing Joe Fontana said they would need further consultation to examine four key issues. These include the relationship between pay equity and collective bargaining, the obligations of employers and unions, the establishment of pay equity committees to manage the process and the authority vested in them, and the definition of establishment. The ministers added that they're working toward introducing a bill in late 2006 or early 2007.

Questions

1. What can an organization, such as Canada Post that has several unions, do to ensure that pay remains equitable among all of its employees?
2. What should Canada Post do at this point? Why?
3. Have the issues surrounding pay equity legislation mainly contributed to the Canada Post issue, or is the employer or union being selfish? Hint: You may need to review writings on the pay equity task force.[36]

Learning Review Answers: 1. d 2. b 3. b 4. c, 5. c, 6. b

CHAPTER

Variable Pay and Executive Compensation

Learning Objectives

After you have read this chapter, you should be able to:

1 Define variable pay and identify three elements of successful pay-for-performance plans.

2 Discuss three types of individual incentives.

3 Explain three ways that sales employees are typically compensated.

4 Identify key concerns that must be addressed when designing group/team variable pay plans.

5 Discuss why profit sharing and employee stock ownership are common organizational incentive plans.

6 Identify the components of executive compensation and discuss criticisms of executive compensation levels.

HR *Headline*

Pay-for-Performance Plans

Pay-for-performance incentive plans are growing in popularity. Over 80 percent of all firms report that they have some type of plan whereby employees receive additional compensation tied to performance. Sales, customer service, productivity, attendance, safety, and executive incentive plans are the common ones. The performance rewarded can be individual, group, or organizational, or a combination of these.

One firm that has successfully made use of pay-for-performance plans is Intuit Canada. Best known for Quicken, TurboTax, and QuickBooks software, Intuit Canada has used incentive plans to increase employee retention and customer response service at its call centres, which handle thousands of calls a day. Concerned by a past 30-percent annual turnover rate and too many errors and missed sales opportunities, Intuit Canada developed a pay-for-performance program that focuses on sales productivity, accuracy, and customer feedback analyses. Specific performance goals were set that trigger the payment of incentives. Under the new program, employees who perform better on those criteria receive greater rewards. Since the firm introduced the plan, turnover has dropped, and accuracy, sales, and customer service ratings all have improved. Follow-up evaluation of the program revealed that Intuit has received a significant return on its investment (ROI) in the incentive program.

It appears that other firms that use pay-for-performance plans need to learn from Intuit. Even though companies overall spend an average of 9 percent of payroll costs on such pay plans, almost half of them report that they use no formal means to assess the effectiveness of those plans. Just as disturbing, over 20 percent of companies that use incentive plans fail to communicate the performance goals to employees. Fortunately, over three-fourths of the firms that do communicate their plans and goals report that those efforts have contributed to better business results, which is the purpose of having such plans.[1]

"Some people make more money, others make less. More is better."

—Anonymous employee

Pay-for-performance is being utilized by a growing number of employers. In today's competitive global economy, many employers believe that people become more productive if compensation varies directly according to performance. A significant number of employers are adding to their traditional base pay programs by offering employees additional compensation. The amount of payment varies based on the degree to which individual, group/team, and organizational performance goals are attained.

Variable Pay: Incentives for Performance

Variable pay
Compensation linked directly to individual, group/team, and/or organizational performance.

1 **Variable pay** is compensation linked to individual, group/team, and/or organizational performance. It includes incentives, bonuses, gainsharing and goal plans and is any form of direct pay that is not folded into base pay. Variable pay plans attempt to provide tangible rewards to employees for performance beyond normal expectations. The philosophical foundation of variable pay rests on several basic assumptions:

- Some jobs contribute more to organizational success than others.
- Some people perform better and are more productive than others.
- Employees who perform better should receive more compensation.
- Some of employees' total compensation should be tied directly to performance.

Pay-for-performance has a different philosophical base than does the traditional compensation system based on seniority or length of service. In the traditional organization, length of service is a primary differentiating factor between people. Differences in job responsibilities are recognized through different amounts of base pay. However, giving additional rewards to some people and not others is seen as potentially divisive and as hampering employees' working together. These thoughts are why many labour unions oppose pay-for-performance programs. However, many individual workers expect to be rewarded for performance differences that increase organizational results. Unions have traditionally been opposed to variable pay because of the belief it will lead to a reduction in base pay. However according to a study conducted by the Conference Board of Canada, this is rarely the case. The study actually reported that 30 percent of unionized workplaces have variable pay plans that are used as a bonus to the employees' base salary.[2]

Developing Successful Pay-for-Performance Plans

Employers adopt variable pay or incentive plans for a number of reasons. The main ones include desires to do the following:

- Link more directly strategic business goals and employee performance.
- Enhance organizational results and reward employees financially for their contributions.
- Reward employees to recognize different levels of employee performance.
- Achieve HR objectives, such as increasing retention, reducing turnover, recognizing training, or rewarding safety and attendance.

Variable pay plans can be considered successful if they meet the objectives the organization had for them when they were initiated. Figure 11-1 shows three elements that can affect the success of a variable pay plan. These elements are discussed next.

Does the Plan Fit the Organization? In the case of pay-for-performance plans, one size does not fit all. A plan that has worked well for one company will not necessarily work well for another. Obviously, the plan must be linked to the objectives of the

Figure 11-1 *Effective Incentive Plans*

Does the plan fit with business strategies and culture?
Are the appropriate actions rewarded?
Is the plan administered properly?
INCENTIVE PLAN SUCCESS

organization. The sentiment that "one size does not fit all" is echoed by Hewitt Associates in Toronto, Ontario, "Organizations need to design and implement variable pay plans that will balance organizational goals and corporate culture. Variable pay plans must be customized to address the specific needs of the organization or even customized for specific groups within the organization? One size does not fit all."[3]

The success of any variable pay program relies on its consistency with the culture of the organization. For example, if an organization is autocratic and adheres to traditional rules and procedures, an incentive system that rewards flexibility and teamwork is likely to fail. The incentive plan is "planted" in the wrong growing environment.

When linking pay to performance organizations must make sure that what is being rewarded ties to meeting organizational objectives.

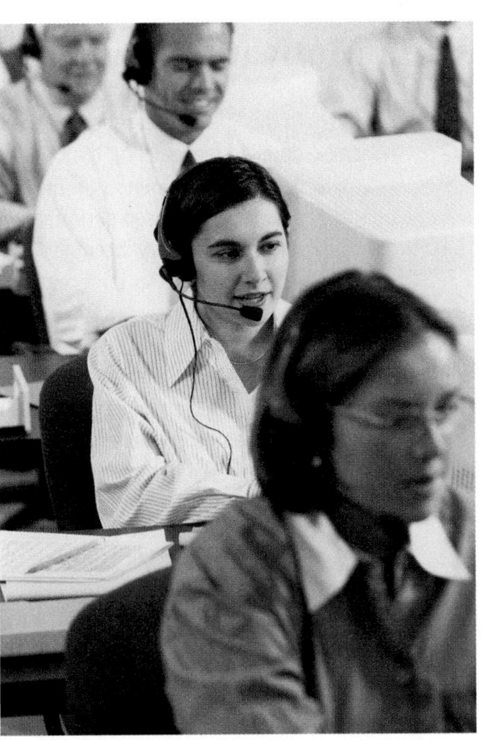

Source: Photodisc/Getty Images

Does the Plan Reward the Appropriate Actions? Variable pay systems should be tied as much as possible to desired performance. Employees must see a direct relationship between their efforts and their financial rewards.

Because people tend to produce what is measured and rewarded, organizations must make sure that what is being rewarded ties to meeting organizational objectives. Use of multiple measures helps ensure that various performance dimensions are not omitted. For example, assume a hotel reservation centre wants to set incentives for employees to increase productivity by lowering the time they spend on each call. If that reduction is the only measure, the quality of customer service and the number of reservations made might drop as employees rush callers in order to reduce talk time. Therefore, the centre should consider basing rewards on multiple measures, such as talk time, reservations booked, and the results of customer satisfaction surveys.

Linking pay to performance may not always be appropriate. For instance, if the output cannot be measured objectively, management may not be able to correctly reward the higher performers with more pay. Managers may not even be able to accurately identify the higher performers. Under those circumstances, individual variable pay is inappropriate.

Is the Plan Administered Properly? A variable pay plan may be complex or simple, but it will be successful only if employees understand what they have to do to be rewarded. The more complicated a plan is, the more difficult it will be to communicate it meaningfully to employees. Experts generally recommend that a variable pay plan include several performance criteria. However, having two or three areas of focus should not overly complicate the calculations necessary for employees to determine their own incentive amounts. Managers also need to be able to explain clearly what future performance targets need to be met and what the rewards will be.

Successful plans clearly identify how much is provided to employees separate from their base pay amounts. That separation makes a distinct connection between performance and pay. It also reinforces the notion that part of the employees' pay must be "re-earned" in the next performance period. The HR Perspective describes a study on incentives and motivation.

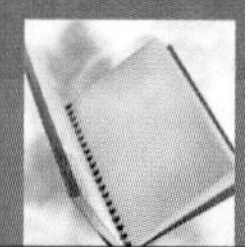

HR *Perspective*

Incentives and Motivation Research

Stajkovic and Luthans compared the effects on productivity of four incentive approaches. The approaches were:

(1) routine pay-for-performance,
(2) monetary incentives,
(3) social recognition, and
(4) performance feedback.

The study reported in the *Academy of Management Journal* took place in the operations division of a company with over 7000 employees. The organization spent significant time and effort objectively measuring the performance of employees. The study looked at employee performance and productivity in light of each of the four different types of incentives.

The "routine pay-for-performance" group simply earned extra pay for increased performance. The "monetary incentives" group also received pay-for-performance, but supervisors were trained to use the pay as a consequence when critical performance was exhibited. In the "social recognition" group, recognition and attention were used by trained supervisors as rewards. In the "performance feedback" group, individuals received detailed feedback on their performance results.

The study found that the routine pay-for-performance approach increased performance over the baseline by 11 percent, and the monetary incentives approach increased performance by 32 percent. The social recognition approach increased performance by 24 percent, and the performance feedback approach by 20 percent.

Overall, the results of the study indicate that pay can indeed improve performance. However, it apparently works best when it is presented contingently (that is, based on productivity and performance) and accompanied by social recognition and performance feedback.[4]

1. As an individual what have been the different incentive programs you have had experience with? Were the programs effective? Why or why not?
2. Is not having a job and being paid a fair wage appropriate without having to be rewarded with incentive programs? Why or why not?

Measuring the Success of Variable Pay Plans

The results of variable pay plans, like those in other areas of HR, should be measured to determine the success of the programs. Different measures of success can be used; depending on the nature of the plan and the goals set for it.[5] Figure 11-2 shows some examples of different measures that may be used to evaluate variable pay plans.

Regardless of the plan, the critical decision is to gather and evaluate data to determine if the expenditures on it are justified by increased performance and results. If the measures show positive analyses, then the plan is truly pay-for-performance in nature.

Successes and Failures of Variable Pay Plans

Even though variable pay has grown in popularity, some attempts to implement it have succeeded and others have not. Incentives *do* work, but they are not a panacea because their success depends on the circumstances.

The positive view that many employers have for variable pay is not shared universally by all employees. If individuals see incentives as desirable, they are more likely to put forth the extra effort to attain the performance objectives that trigger the incentive payouts. As one indicator, a survey of employees found that only 29 percent believe that they are rewarded when doing a good job. Discouragingly for firms with incentive plans, approximately the same low percentage of employees indicated that they were motivated by their employers' incentive plans.[6] One problem is that many employees prefer that performance rewards increase their base pay, rather than be given as a one-time, lump-sum payment. Further, many employees prefer individual rewards to group/team or organizational incentives.

Hewitt Associates
Hewitt surveys, research papers, and publications offer valuable news updates and HR information that will inspire you and help your business succeed.
http://was4.hewitt.com/hewitt/worldwide/canada/index.htm

Providing variable pay plans that are successful can be complex and requires significant, continuing efforts. Some suggestions that appear to contribute to successful incentive plans are as follows:

- Develop clear, understandable plans that are continually communicated.
- Use realistic performance measures.
- Keep the plans current and linked to organizational objectives.
- Clearly link performance results to payouts that truly recognize performance differences.
- Identify variable pay incentives separately from base pay.

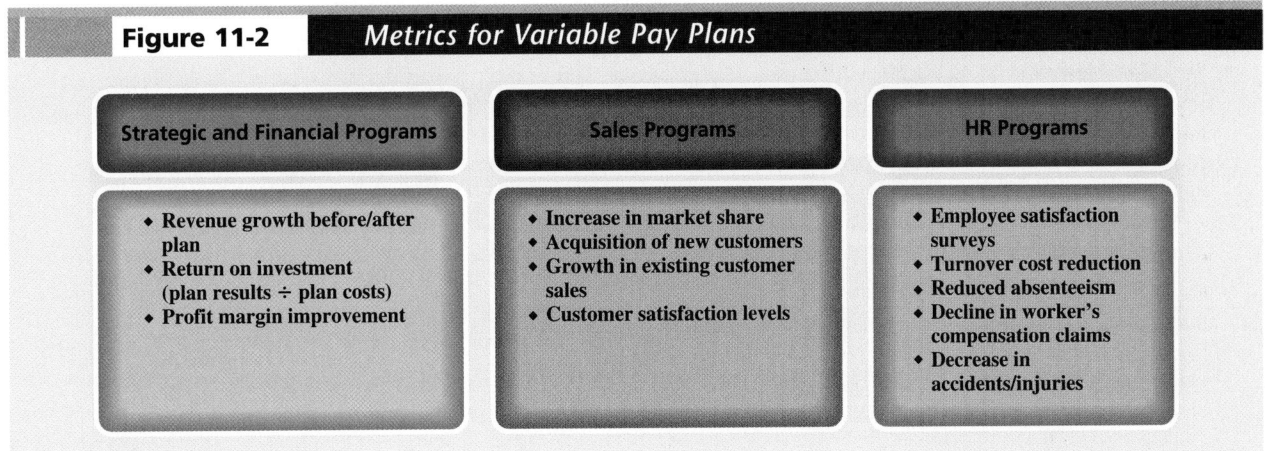

Figure 11-2
Metrics for Variable Pay Plans
Strategic and Financial Programs
• Revenue growth before/after plan
• Return on investment (plan results ÷ plan costs)
• Profit margin improvement
Sales Programs
• Increase in market share
• Acquisition of new customers
• Growth in existing customer sales
• Customer satisfaction levels
HR Programs
• Employee satisfaction surveys
• Turnover cost reduction
• Reduced absenteeism
• Decline in worker's compensation claims
• Decrease in accidents/injuries

Types of Variable Pay

Individual incentives are given to reward the effort and performance of individuals. Some common means of providing variable pay to individuals are piece-rate systems, sales commissions, and bonuses. Others include special recognition rewards such as trips or merchandise. With individual incentives, employees may focus on what is best for them personally and may block or inhibit the performance of other individuals with whom they are competing. That is why group/team incentives have been developed.

When an organization rewards an entire group/team for its performance, cooperation among the members may increase as well. The most common *group/team incentives* are gainsharing or goalsharing plans, in which employee teams that meet certain goals share in the gains measured against performance targets. Often, those programs focus on quality improvement, cost reduction, and other measurable results.

Organizational incentives reward people according to the performance results of the entire organization. This approach assumes that all employees working together can generate greater organizational results that lead to better financial performance. These programs often share some of the financial gains made by the firm with employees through payments calculated as a percentage of the employees' base pay. The most prevalent forms of organization-wide incentives are profit-sharing plans and employee stock plans. Figure 11-3 shows some of the programs under each type of incentive or variable pay plan.

Individual Incentives

2 Individual incentive systems try to tie individual effort to additional rewards. Conditions necessary for the use of individual incentive plans are as follows:

- *Individual performance must be identified:* The performance of each individual must be measured and identified because each employee has job responsibilities and tasks that can be separated from those of other employees.
- *Independent work must be performed:* Individual contributions result from independent work and effort given by individual employers.
- *Individual competitiveness must be desired:* Because individuals generally pursue the incentives for themselves, competition among employees often occurs. Therefore, independent competition in which some individuals "win" and others do not must be desired.

Figure 11-3 *Types of Variable Pay Plans*

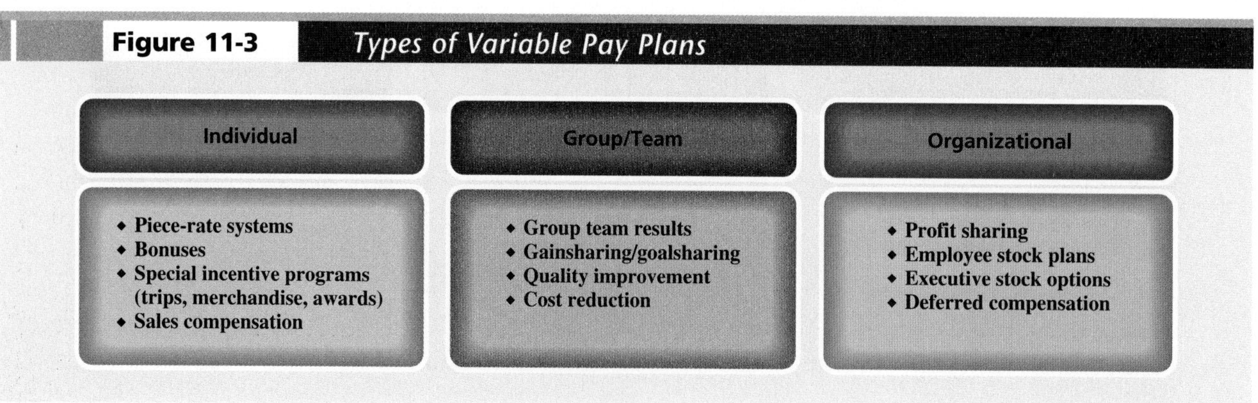

Individual
• Piece-rate systems
• Bonuses
• Special incentive programs (trips, merchandise, awards)
• Sales compensation
Group/Team
• Group team results
• Gainsharing/goalsharing
• Quality improvement
• Cost reduction
Organizational
• Profit sharing
• Employee stock plans
• Executive stock options
• Deferred compensation

- *Individualism must be stressed in the organizational culture:* The culture of the organization must be one that emphasizes individual growth, achievements, and rewards. If an organization emphasizes teamwork and cooperation, then individual incentives may be counterproductive.

Piece-Rate Systems

Straight piece-rate system
Pay system in which wages are determined by multiplying the number of units produced by the piece rate for one unit.

The most basic individual incentive systems are piece-rate systems, whether straight or differential. Under the **straight piece-rate system,** wages are determined by multiplying the number of units produced (such as garments sewn or service calls handled) by the piece rate for one unit. Because the cost is the same for each unit, the wage for each employee is easy to figure, and labour costs can be accurately predicted. A *differential piece-rate system* pays employees one piece-rate wage for units produced up to a standard output and a higher piece-rate wage for units produced over the standard. Many possible combinations of straight and differential piece-rate systems can be used, depending on situational factors.

Despite their incentive value, piece-rate systems are difficult to apply because determining standards is a complex and costly process for many types of jobs. In some instances, the cost of determining and maintaining the standards may be greater than the benefits derived. Also, jobs in which individuals have limited control over output or in which high standards of quality are necessary may be unsuited to piecework.

Another more pressing issue pertaining to piece-rate systems concerns the safety aspect. Piece-rate systems have been blamed for encouraging accidents and safety violations. Many miners do not use piece rates for fear that miners may sacrifice safety for productivity. Pizza delivery drivers have been known to try and make their delivery destination within a specified period, sometimes getting into accidents. Messenger services, or bicycle couriers are yet another industry that have continuous problems with safety. Lack of courier bicycle parking and easy access to buildings often leads to "short cuts" (e.g., riding the wrong way on one-way streets or riding on sidewalks). Conditions that encourage these short cuts must be addressed by not just the couriers, but also by courier companies and building managers. The piece-rate pay system means couriers must ride fast to make a decent wage and dealing with this situation must involve the cooperation of their employers.[7]

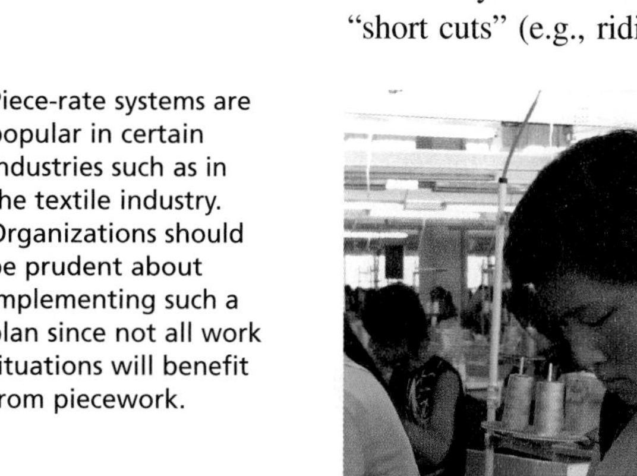

Piece-rate systems are popular in certain industries such as in the textile industry. Organizations should be prudent about implementing such a plan since not all work situations will benefit from piecework.

Source: Luisa Fernanda Gonzalez/ShutterStock

Bonuses

Bonus
One-time payment that does not become part of the employee's base pay.

Individual employees may receive additional compensation in the form of a **bonus,** which is a one-time payment that does not become part of the employee's base pay. Growing in popularity, individual bonuses are used at all levels in some firms.

A bonus can recognize performance by an employee, a team, or the organization as a whole. When performance results are good, bonuses go up. When performance results are not met, bonuses go down. Most employers base part of an employee's bonus on individual performance and part on company results, as appropriate.

Bonuses can also be used to reward employees for contributing new ideas, developing skills, or obtaining professional certifications. When the skills or certifications are acquired by an employee, a pay increase or a one-time bonus may follow. For example, a financial services firm provides the equivalent of two weeks' pay to employees who master job-relevant computer skills. Another firm gives one week's pay to members of the HR staff who obtain professional certifications such as their Certified Human Resources Professional (CHRP) or their Certified Compensation Professional (CCP) designations.

"Spot" Bonuses A special type of bonus used is a "spot" bonus, so called because it can be awarded at any time. Spot bonuses are given for a number of reasons. For instance, a spot bonus reward may be given to an information technology employee who installed a computer software upgrade, which required extensive time and effort. Other examples are to compensate a nurse who dealt successfully with a difficult patient and to pay a customer service employee who resolved the problems of a major client. A doctor at a clinic rewarded one of the receptionists with a dinner for both her and her husband because she was working extra hours, while a new employee was being recruited.

Often, spot bonuses are given in cash, although some firms provide managers with gift cards, travel vouchers, or other rewards. The keys to successful use of spot bonuses are to keep the amounts reasonable and to provide them for exceptional performance accomplishments.[8] The downside to their use is that it can create jealousy and resentment from other employees, who may feel that they were deserving but did not get a spot bonus.

Special Incentive Programs

Numerous special incentive programs have been used to reward individuals, ranging from one-time contests for meeting performance targets to awards for performance over time. For instance, safe-driving awards are given to truck drivers with no accidents or violations on their records during a year. Although special programs can be developed for groups and for entire organizations, they often focus on rewarding only high-performing individuals. Figure 11-4 shows purposes for special incentives.

Performance Awards Cash, merchandise, gift certificates, and travel are the most frequently used incentive rewards for significant performance. Cash is still highly

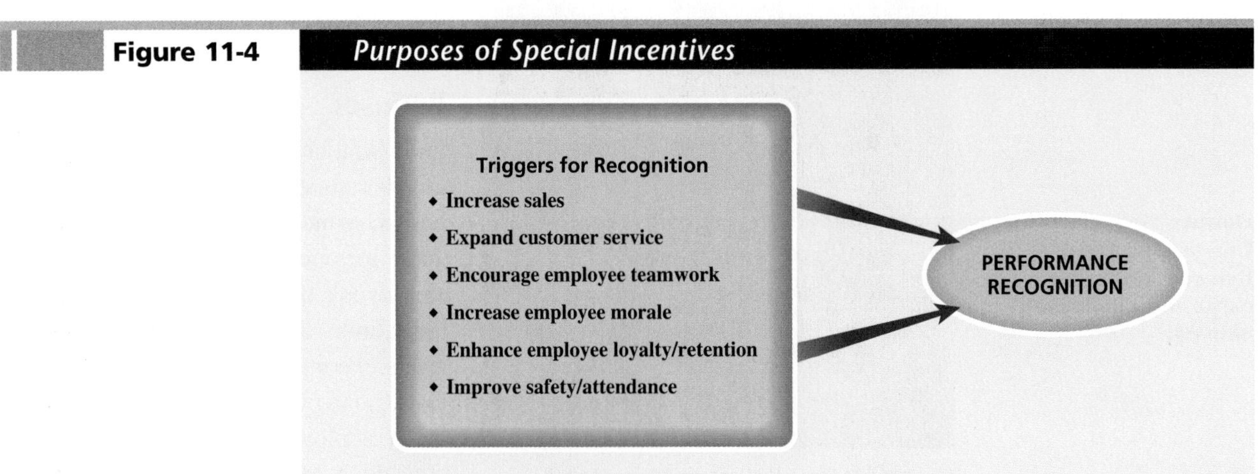

valued by many employees because they can decide how to spend it. However, travel awards, particularly to popular destinations such as Whistler, Banff, and international locations such as Hawaii, appeal to many employees.

According to a study by *Incentive* magazine, the most effective incentives for sales employees are travel, cash, merchandise, or a combination of these means.[9] Generally, employees appreciate the "trophy" value of such awards as much as the actual monetary value.[10]

Recognition Awards Another type of program recognizes individual employees for their performance or service. For instance, many organizations in industries, such as hotels, restaurants, and retailers, have established "employee of the month" and "employee of the year" awards. Hotels often use favourable guest comment cards as the basis for providing recognition awards to front desk representatives, housekeepers, and other hourly employees. Shell uses recognition awards at its gasoline stations, and it has seen an increase in the favourable ratings of customers at stations where those awards have been given.[11]

Recognition awards often work best when given to acknowledge specific efforts and activities that the organization has targeted as important. The criteria for selecting award winners may be determined subjectively in some situations; however, formally identified criteria provide greater objectivity and are more likely to be seen as rewarding performance rather than as favouritism. When giving recognition awards, organizations should use specific examples to describe clearly how those receiving the awards were selected.

Service Awards Another type of reward given to individual employees is the *service award.* Although service awards may often be portrayed as rewarding performance over a number of years, in reality, they recognize length of service and have little linkage to employees' actual performance.

Sales Compensation

3 The compensation paid to employees involved with sales and marketing is partly or entirely tied to individual sales performance. Salespeople who sell more receive more total compensation than those who sell less. Sales incentives are perhaps the most widely used individual incentives. With some sales compensation plans, ethical issues and conflicts can arise, as the HR Perspective describes.[12]

Types of Sales Compensation Plans

Sales compensation plans can be of several general types, depending on the degree which total compensation includes some variable pay tied to sales performance. A look at three general types of sales compensation and some challenges to sales compensation follows.

Salary-Only Some companies pay salespeople only a salary. The *salary-only approach* is useful when an organization emphasizes serving and retaining existing accounts, over generating new sales and accounts. This approach is frequently used to protect the income of new sales representatives for a period of time while they are building up their sales clientele. Generally, the employer extends the salary-only approach for new sales representatives to no more than six months, at which point it implements a salary-plus-commission or salary-plus-bonuses system (discussed later in this section). Salespeople who want extrinsic rewards function less effectively

HR *Perspective*

Ethical Concerns and Sales Compensation

Commission programs can effectively drive the behaviour of sales representatives, especially if the performance measures are based wholly or mostly on sales volume and revenues. However, certain employees may act unethically to obtain incentives.

A number of legal experts and academics express concerns that some sales incentives programs encourage unethical behaviour, particularly if compensation is based solely on commissions. For instance, there have been reports that individuals in other countries buying major industrial equipment have received bribes or kickbacks from sales representatives. The bribes are paid from the incentives received by the sales representatives. This criticism applies especially with major transactions such as large industrial machines, aircraft contracts, and even large insurance policies.

One way of addressing these ethical issues uses a mixture of guaranteed base salary and lowered commission rates. Other approaches use other sales-related dimensions, such as customer service, repeat business, and customer satisfaction. For instance, sales commissions for investment brokers might be linked to increasing a client's net portfolio value, rather than only to generating trades. How realistic such methods are in a variety of sales situations may be debated. But clearly, ethical issues must be considered when developing and managing sales incentive plans.[13]

1. Given that it takes the efforts of many employees to complete a sales transaction, does it make sense to reward only sales personnel with commissions? Why or why not? What do you suggest should be done about compensation, if anything?
2. How should an individual handle unethical sales issues when dealing in countries where kickbacks are standard practice? What factors would impact the decisions the salesperson would make?

in salary-only plans because they are less motivated to sell without additional performance-related compensation.

Commission
Compensation computed as a percentage of sales in units or dollars.

Straight Commission An individual incentive system that is widely used in sales jobs is the **commission**, which is compensation computed as a percentage of sales in units or dollars. Commissions are integrated into the pay given to sales workers in three common ways: straight commission, salary plus commission, and bonuses.

In the *straight commission system,* a sales representative receives a percentage of the value of the sales made. Consider a sales representative working for a consumer products company. She receives no compensation if no sales are made, but she receives a percentage of the total amount of all sales revenue made in her territory. The advantage of this system is that it requires sales representatives to sell in order to earn. The disadvantage is that it offers no security for the sales staff.[14]

What does happen if someone doesn't earn enough in commissions to be paid at least the minimum wage? According to various Employment Standards Acts such as Ontario and Alberta, if an employee's pay is based completely or partly on commission, it must amount to at least the minimum wage for each hour the employee has worked. This does not apply, however, to a salesperson who normally sells away from their employer's office or plant (except those who sell on a route). To ensure an employee is receiving the minimum wage, the total amount the employee earned in regular wages over a workweek is divided by the number of hours the employee worked in that week. Here's an example. (Note: Where overtime hours are worked, the calculation is more complicated.)[15]

Luba earned $150, working 25 hours during her workweek in March 2006:

$$\$150 \div 25 = \$6$$

The minimum wage is $7.75 an hour; 25 hours at $7.75 is $193.75. Therefore, Luba is owed the difference between her commission pay ($150) and what her employer would have paid for the same number of hours at the minimum wage ($193.75):

$193.75 − $150 = $43.75 (Luba's employer owes her $43.75.)

Draw
Amount advanced from and repaid to future commissions earned by the employee.

To offset this insecurity, some employers use a **draw** system, in which sales representatives can draw advance payments against future commissions. The amounts drawn are then deducted from future commission cheques. Arrangements must be made for repayment of drawn amounts if individuals leave the organization before earning their draws in commissions.

Salary-Plus-Commission or Bonuses The form of sales compensation used most frequently is the *salary-plus-commission,* which combines the stability of a salary with the performance aspect of a commission. A common split is 70 percent salary to 30 percent commission, although the split varies by industry and by numerous other factors. Many organizations also pay salespeople salaries and then offer bonuses that are a percentage of the base pay, tied to how well the employee meets various sales targets or other criteria.

Sales Compensation Challenges

Sales incentives work well, especially when they are tied to strategic initiatives of the organization.[16] However, they do present many challenges—from calculating total pay correctly, to dealing with sales in e-business, to causing competition among salespeople. Often, sales compensation plans become quite complex, and tracking individual incentives can be demanding. As the Technology Transforming

Technology Transforming HR

Enterprise Incentive Management Systems

To improve the administration of incentive plans, employers are turning to HR technology. Use of enterprise incentive management (EIM) software has become widespread. These systems are advantageous because they can track the performance of numerous employees worldwide who may be covered by different incentive plans. Consider a company that has different product lines, geographic locations, and company subsidiaries, and imagine tracking the performance of hundreds or thousands of sales representatives for a sales incentive program. Or imagine manually tracking attendance, safety, and training incentives for firms with many employees worldwide.

Such was the challenge facing Carl Zeiss, a manufacturer of optical and optoelectronic products that is headquartered in Germany and operates in over 30 countries. Carl Zeiss decided to cut administrative time and costs, as well as increase the accuracy and timeliness of incentive information, by switching to an EIM software system. After several years, the new system allows different business groups to administer their own sales incentive plans. The system also allows managers to identify the most productive sales representatives. With this information, managers can arrange for those high producers to provide "success stories" to other salespeople, who then can adapt their sales approaches. Overall, it is evident that the data provided by the EIM system are helping executives and managers worldwide at Carl Zeiss to support and manage their salesforces more effectively.[17]

1. Would a system of electronic monitoring as described above not be perceived as a lack of trust among employees? How could this affect the motivation of employees?
2. What could be done in your current position or any other positions you have held in the past to track incentives? If no incentives were used, describe how incentives could have been introduced and what could have been done to monitor achievement of results?

HR identifies, Internet-based software has helped companies to post results daily, weekly, or monthly and salespeople can use it to track their results.

The last few years have seen the growth of sales compensation plans with different design features. Many of them are multitiered and can be rather complex. Selling over the Internet brings challenges to incentive compensation as well. Some sales organizations combine individual and group sales bonus programs. In these programs, a portion of the sales incentive is linked to the attainment of group sales goals.[18] This approach is supposed to encourage cooperation and teamwork among the salespeople, but that may not always occur.

Sales Performance Metrics Successfully using variable sales compensation requires establishing clear performance criteria and measures. Generally, no more than three sales performance measures should be used in a sales compensation plan. Consultants criticize many sales commission plans as being too complex to motivate sales representatives. Other plans may be too simple, focusing only on the salesperson's pay, not on organizational objectives. Many companies measure performance primarily by comparing an individual's sales revenue against established quotas. The plans would be better if the organizations used a variety of criteria, including obtaining new accounts and selling high-value versus low-value items that reflect marketing plans. Figure 11-5 shows the criteria commonly used to determine incentive payments for salespeople and how they are part of determining sales effectiveness.

Effectiveness of Sales Incentive Plans There are so many organizations with sales incentive plans that it would be logical to think those plans are effective. However, many sales compensation plans are not seen as effective by either salespeople or managers and executives. One study found that sales productivity was not above targets in over half of all the surveyed firms and that the respondents were dissatisfied with their sales incentive plans. Consequently, almost 80 percent of the firms had made at least six changes in those plans in a two-year period.[19] Such frequent changes reduce the effectiveness of plans and create concerns and frustrations with the sales representatives and managers. HR professionals may be involved in designing, revising, and communicating sales incentive plans, as well as in responding to the complaints and concerns of sales representatives.

Figure 11-5 *Determining Sales Effectiveness*

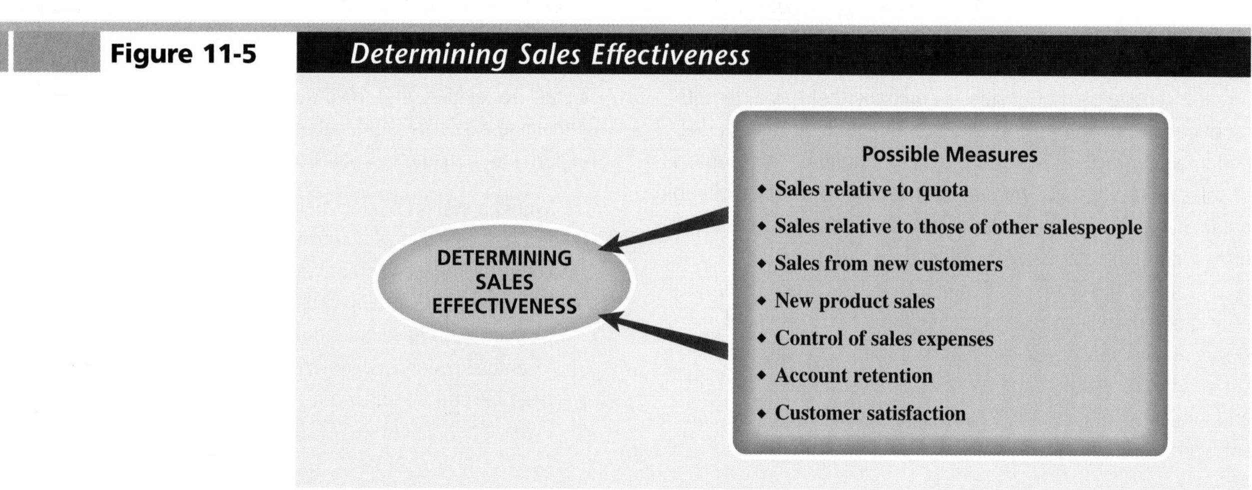

DETERMINING SALES EFFECTIVENESS
Possible Measures
• Sales relative to quota
• Sales relative to those of other salespeople
• Sales from new customers
• New product sales
• Control of sales expenses
• Account retention
• Customer satisfaction

Group/Team Incentives

4 The use of groups/teams in organizations has implications for compensation. Although the use of groups/teams has increased substantially in the past few years, the question of how to compensate their members equitably remains a significant challenge. As Figure 11-6 notes, a number of reasons prompt organizations to establish variable pay plans for groups/teams. According to several studies, about 80 percent of large firms provide rewards for work groups or teams in some way.[20]

Design of Group/Team Incentive Plans

In designing group/team incentive plans, organizations must consider a number of issues. The main concerns are how and when to distribute the incentives, and who will make decisions about the incentive amounts.

Distribution of Group/Team Incentives Several decisions about how to distribute and allocate group/team rewards must be made. The two primary ways for distributing those rewards are as follows:

1. *Same-size reward for each member:* With this approach, all members receive the same payout, regardless of job level, current pay, seniority, or individual performance differences.
2. *Different-size reward for each member:* With this approach, employers vary individual rewards depending on such factors as contribution to group/team results, current pay, years of experience, and skill levels of jobs performed.

Generally, more organizations use the first approach in addition to different levels of individual pay. The combination rewards performance by making the group/team incentive equal, while still recognizing that individual pay differences exist and are important to many employees. The size of the group/team incentive can be determined either by using a percentage of base pay for the individuals or the group/team as a whole, or by offering a specific dollar amount. For example, one firm pays members individual base rates that reflect years of experience and any additional training that they have. Additionally, the group/team reward is distributed to all as a flat dollar amount.

Timing of Group/Team Incentives How often group/team incentives are paid out is another important consideration. Some of the choices seen in firms with group/team incentives are monthly, quarterly, semiannually, and annually. The most common period used is annually. However, the shorter the time period, the greater the

Figure 11-6 *Why Organizations Establish Variable Pay Plans for Groups/Teams*

$
GROUP/TEAM VARIABLE PAY
• Enhances productivity
• Ties earnings to group or team performance
• Improves quality
• Aids recruiting and retention of employees
• Improves employee morale

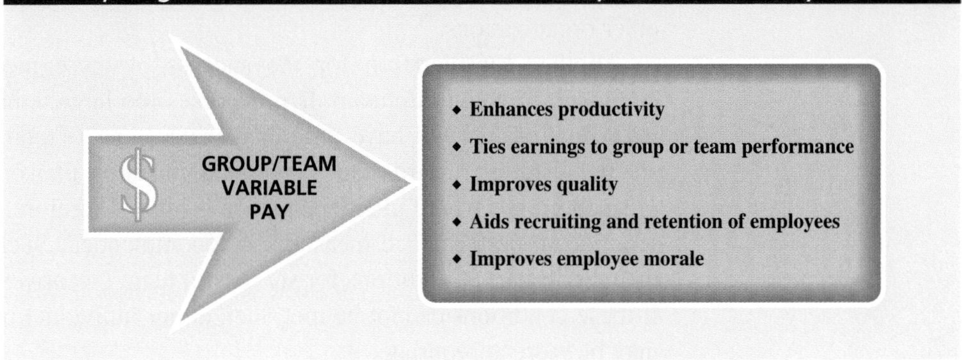

HRM Guide Canada—Compensation
This website discusses incentives in detail.
www.hrmguide.net/canada/

likelihood that employees will see a closer link between their efforts and the performance results that trigger the award payouts. Employers may limit the group/team rewards to $1,000 or less, allowing them to pay out rewards more frequently. The nature of the teamwork, measurement criteria, and organizational results must all be considered when determining the appropriate time period.

Decision Making About Group/Team Incentive Amounts To reinforce the effectiveness of working together, some group/team incentive programs allow members to make decisions about how to allocate the rewards to individuals. In some situations, members vote; in some, a group/team leader decides. In other situations, the incentive "pot" is divided equally, thus avoiding conflict and recognizing that all members contributed to the team results. For example, this type of system is sometimes used in restaurants where the tips received by the serving staff are shared among all staff. However, many companies have found group/team members unwilling to handle incentive decisions for co-workers.

Problems with Group/Team Incentives

The difference between rewarding team members *equally* and rewarding them *equitably* triggers many of the problems associated with group/team incentives. Rewards distributed in equal amounts to all members may be perceived as "unfair" by employees who work harder, have more capabilities, or perform more difficult jobs. This problem is compounded when an individual who is performing poorly prevents the group/team from meeting the goals needed to trigger the incentive payment. Also, employees working in groups/teams have shown a relatively low level of satisfaction with rewards that are the same for all, versus rewards based on performance, which often may be viewed as more equitable.

Generally, managers view the concept of people working in groups/teams as beneficial. But many employees still expect to be paid according to individual performance, to a large extent. Until this individualism is recognized and compensation programs that are viewed as more equitable by more "team members" are developed, caution should be used in creating and implementing group/team incentives.

Successes and Failures of Group/Team Incentives

The unique nature of each group/team and its members figures prominently in the success of establishing incentive rewards.[21] The employer must consider the history of the group and its past performance. The success of team incentives was demonstrated at a garment manufacturing plant where worker productivity increased 14 percent after a shift was made to a group compensation system from an individual piece-rate compensation system.[22] However, simultaneously introducing the teamwork concept and changing to group/team incentives has not been as successful in other organizations.[23]

Another consideration for the success of these incentives is the number of employees in the group/team. If it becomes too large, employees may feel that their individual efforts will have little or no effect on the total performance of the group and the resulting rewards. But group/team incentive plans may encourage cooperation in small groups where interdependence is high. Therefore, in those groups, the use of group/team performance measures is recommended. Such plans have been used in many industries. Conditions for successful team incentives are shown in Figure 11-7. If these conditions cannot be met, then either individual or organizational incentives may be more appropriate.

Figure 11-7 Conditions for Successful Group/Team Incentives

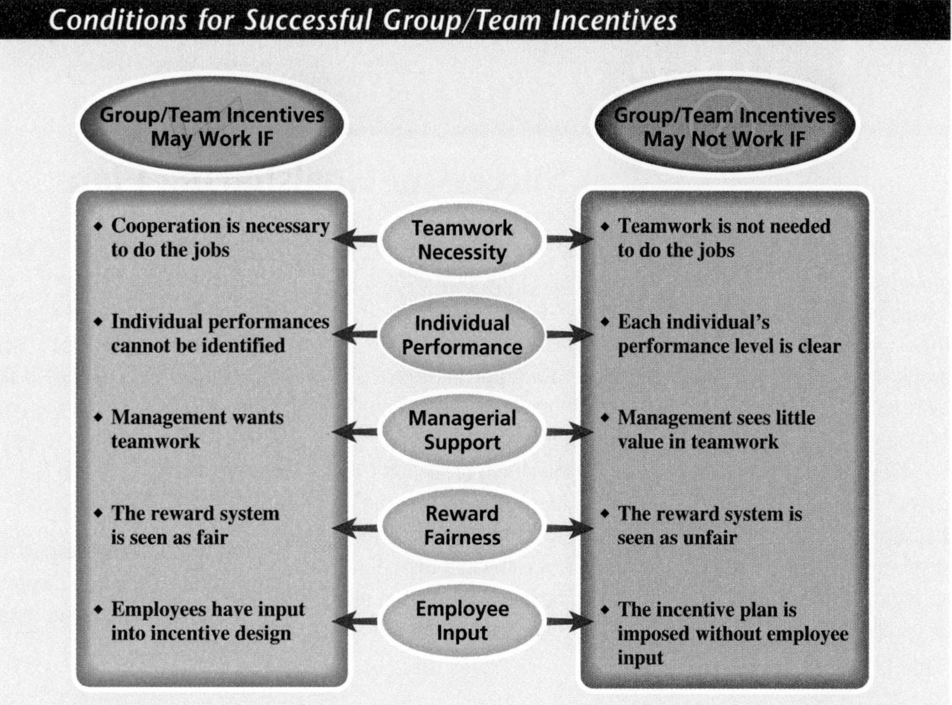

Types of Group/Team Incentives

Group/team reward systems use various ways of compensating individuals. The components include individual wages and salaries in addition to the additional rewards. Most organizations using group/team incentives continue to pay individuals based either on the jobs performed or the individuals' competencies and capabilities. The two most frequently used types of group/team incentives situations are work team results and gainsharing.

Group/Team Results Pay plans for groups/teams may reward all members equally on the basis of group output, cost savings, or quality improvement. The design of most group/team incentives is based on a "self-funding" principle, which means that the money to be used as incentive rewards is obtained through improvement of organizational results. A good example is gainsharing, which can be extended within a group or plantwide.

Gainsharing
System of sharing with employees greater-than-expected gains in profits and/or productivity according to a predetermined formula.

Gainsharing The system of sharing with employees greater-than-expected gains in profits and/or productivity according to a predetermined formula is **gainsharing.** Also called *teamsharing* or goalsharing, the focus is to increase "discretionary efforts," that is, the difference between the maximum amount of effort a person can exert and the minimum amount of effort that a person needs to exert to keep from being fired. Workers in many organizations are not paid for discretionary efforts, but are paid to meet the minimum acceptable level of effort required. When workers do demonstrate discretionary efforts, the organization can afford to pay them more than the going rate, because the extra efforts produce financial gains over and above the returns of minimal efforts. Some organizations have labelled their programs *goalsharing* to emphasize the attainment of results based on business strategy objectives. Two successful goalsharing programs are described in the HR Perspective.

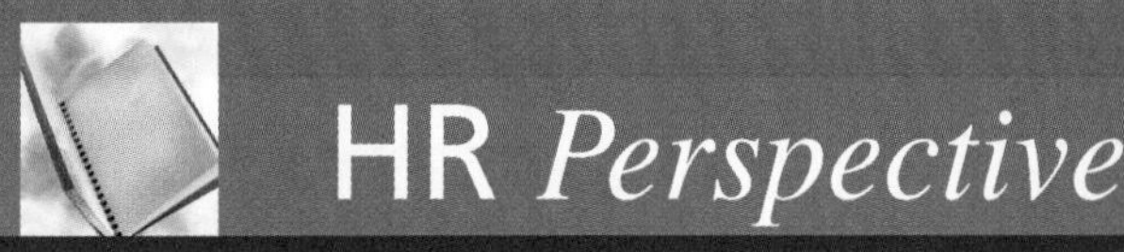

Successful Goalsharing Plans

In a 2005 study by Waterstone Human Capital Ltd. and *Canadian Business*, WestJet Airlines stood out as having the most admired Canadian corporate culture. The company receives more than 1000 unsolicited résumés every week and currently has 5000 employees. Don Bell who is the executive vice president from WestJet states that since WestJet's establishment in 1996 its goal has been to cultivate a company that people want to work for.

WestJet's managers believe that the alignment of the interests of its people (WestJet prefers to call its employees "people" because it dislikes conventional labels) with its business creates a strong corporate culture. The company has cultivated this culture through several measures including the empowerment of all of its people, open communication, and a successful employee stock program.

WestJet's employees receive profit-sharing cheques twice a year and have the option of receiving up to 20 percent of their salaries in shares (shares can be purchased as common shares or can be placed into RRSPs, which will be matched 100 percent by WestJet). The director of in-flight training and standards describes the benefits of the employee stock program: "All of us are owners here, and we're very passionate about what we do. When you have a stake in the company, you want to do whatever it takes to make it work."[24]

1. Is it reasonable to expect that all employees will buy into Westjet's employee ownership philosophy?
2. What are the inherent risks with this type of pay plan for employees?

To develop and implement a gainsharing or goalsharing plan, management must identify the ways in which increased productivity, quality, and financial performance can occur and decide that some of the gains should be shared with employees. Often, measures such as labour costs, overtime hours, and quality benchmarks are used. Both organizational measures and departmental measures may be used, with the weights for gainsharing split between the two categories. Plans frequently require that an individual must exhibit satisfactory performance to receive the gainsharing payments.

Several gainsharing plans exist. One, called Improshare, sets group piece-rate standards and pays bonuses when the standard is exceeded. The Scanlon plan, uses employee committees and passes on savings to the employees upon achieving cost savings based on employee efforts. The Rucker plan, while conceptually similar to the Scanlon plan, rewards employees by passing on savings achieved through reduction in production-related costs.

Improshare
A gainsharing program in which the gain is the decrease in the labour hours needed to produce one unit of product with the gains spent equally between the organization and its employees.

Improshare Improshare, or "improved productivity through sharing plan," is a type of gainsharing plan in which industrial engineers conduct time studies to determine how many hours it shoud take to produce a unit of product. When the actual productivity is greater than the baseline, a percentage of savings is shared with employees. Here the productivity improvement of employees is estimated from the number of workhours saved for a given number of units produced. The value of the savings is shared between company and employees. This plan is minimally affected by changes in sales volume, technology and capital equipment, product mix, or price and wage increases.

Improshare is the easiest of the gainsharing plans to understand and install. The disadvantage of this kind of system is that it is a one-factor system, and does not take into account changes in prices, revenue volume, client satisfaction, client loyalty, and a range of other issues which may be very important in a particular organization. More importantly, the focus is on quantity, not quality. When quality is sacrificed, there are obvious repercussions for profitability if customer service becomes compromised.

Scanlon plan
A gainsharing program in which the employees receive a bonus if the ratio of labour costs to the sales value of production is below a set standard.

Scanlon Plan The **Scanlon plan** was developed from the innovative work of Joseph Scanlon, a steelworker and union leader, during the 1930s. During the Depression he determined that a company's health and survival depended on a climate of cooperation rather than competition between labour and management. As a staff member of the United Steelworkers of America, he used his ideas to improve productivity thereby saving many organizations and jobs. The early "Scanlon plans," included a monthly cash bonus to all employees when labour costs were reduced below historical base periods. Today, each Scanlon plan is unique and created by a team of employees. Each plan includes how information is shared, how employees are involved in decision making, how gains are shared, and how training and development are practised. A Scanlon plan gives employees a bonus if the ratio of labour costs to the sales value of production is below a set standard. Workers need to keep labour costs low enough and produce as much as possible with that amount of labour. Employees share in pre-established cost savings, based upon employee effort. Formal employee participation is necessary with the Scanlon plan, as well as periodic progress reporting and an incentive formula. The payouts may differ in the organization, but the norm is to set some money aside for times when bonuses may not be able to be paid out. For example, the company might take 25 percent of the savings for itself, and give back 75 percent to the workers. The workers may agree to set aside 25 percent, and only take 50 percent, thus banking the 25 percent for another time.

Figure 11-8 provides an example of the basic elements of a Scanlon plan. In this example, the standard is a ratio of 25/100, or 25 percent, and the workers produced parts worth $1.6 million. To meet the standards, the labour costs should be less than 25 percent of $1.6 million, or $400,000. Since the actual labour costs were $300,000, the workers will get a gainsharing based on the $100,000 difference between the $400,000 target and the actual labour costs of $300,000.

Research results indicate that Scanlon plans consistently increase productivity, reduce costs, increase quality, reduce scrap, increase employee involvement, improve communications, and improve labour relations. A study conducted at Sears has shown that Scanlon units have statistically higher financial performance, customer satisfaction, and employee satisfaction compared to similar non Scanlon units. The University of Wisconsin has shown that the Scanlon implementation practices have the highest correlation with gainsharing success. Scanlon companies have been rated

Figure 11-8 *Scanlon Plan Gains Example*

Target Ratio **Total labour cost/sales value of production (SVP)**	**= 25/100**
Sales value of production (SVP)	**= $1,600,000**
Goal: 25/100 × $1,600,000	**= $400,000**
Actual: $300,000	
Gain: $400,000 – $300,000	**= $100,000**
Payout: 25%, or $25,000 to the organization	
50%, or $50,000 to the employees	
25%, or $25,000 banked for another time for the employees	

among the Top 100 Best Places to work in North America and have received numerous quality awards including the Baldridge Award, the Shingo Prize, and the GM/Ford/Chrysler supplier of the year.[25]

Rucker plan
A gainsharing program in which the ratio measuring the gain compares labour costs to the value added in production (output minus the cost of materials, supplies, and services).

Rucker Plan The **Rucker plan** came later than the Scanlon plan. It takes a much broader view of production expenses. The Rucker plan formula measures the ratio of labour costs to value added. The organization then shares gains in this ratio with employees. The ratio can be improved by reducing any production costs and by increasing output. This plan offers an incentive to reduce production related costs such as wasteful use of supplies. The payout scheme can be similar to the Scanlon plan, however the formulas used to arrive at the savings are much more complex. The organization keeps a share of the gain, places a portion in a reserve account for the employees to use at another time and distributes the rest to the employees in the group.

Figure 11-9 provides an example of a Rucker plan. In this example, a baseline calculation is determined so that the actual improvements can be derived. Normal monthly sales have been calculated as $1,000,000 and the cost of bought-in materials and services at $500,000 leaves a value added of $500,000 ($1,000,000 – $500,000). A ratio of wages to the value added is determined to be 40 percent ($200,000:$500,000). To determine the savings achieved by the employees, the monthly sales of $1.2 million is subtracted from the cost of the bought-in items of $600,000 to arrive at an added value of $600,000. The improvement is therefore calculated as the added value of $600,000 – the baseline value added of $500,000 = $100,000. Therefore, the $100,000 improvement is shared at 40 percent or $40,000 to be shared between the company and the employees according to a predetermined amount. In this example the payout is determined as 25 percent for the organization and 75 percent for the employees. The calculation could change, depending on the agreed upon amount between the company and the employees.

The Rucker plan and the Scanlon plan are quite similar in that any baseline calculations should be made on average achievements of an organization, not on a year that has been dismal or too successful as these would not be representative of the

Figure 11-9 *Rucker Plan Gains Example*

BASELINE ESTABLISHED:	
Normal Monthly Sales:	**$1,000,000**
***Cost of bought-in materials and services*:**	**$500,000**
***Added Value*: Normal Monthly Sales –**	
Cost of bought-in materials and services =	**$500,000**
***Wages*:**	**$200,000**
Ratio of Wages:Added Value:	***200,000:500,000 = 40%***
CALCULATION—FIRST MONTH OF OPERATIONS:	
Sales:	***$1,200,000***
Cost of bought-in materials and services:	***$600,000***
Added Value	***$600,000***
Improvement:	
Added value this month $600,000 – baseline added value $500,000 =	***$100,000***
improvement shared at 40 percent =	***$40,000 to be shared***
Payout: 25%, or $10,000 to the organization	
50%, or $20,000 to the employees	
25%, or $10,000 banked for another time for the employees	

organization's achievements. Inappropriate calculations could result in excessive payouts by the organization. Committees are also important to the success of these plans. Their task is to solicit suggestions from employees. Without new ideas for improvements in either plan's goals, the plans could lose momentum with no resulting bonuses, and eventual demise. Participation of all employees is absolutely essential for success.[26]

Earnings-at-Risk

Earnings-at-risk
Incentive plans designed to enhance performance, in part, by creating base wage dissatisfaction that, in turn, triggers greater effort directed toward performance behaviours rewarded with incentive pay.

Earnings-at-risk (EAR) incentive plans are designed to enhance performance, in part, by creating base wage dissatisfaction that, in turn, triggers greater effort directed toward performance behaviours rewarded with incentive pay. However, employee disatisfaction with EAR plans in general and base wages in particular may also produce unintended consequences that counteract any benefits these plans produce. In a study of 167 sales and customer-service employees working under an EAR plan, the findings suggest that managers who decide to adopt an EAR plan should be aware of the negative reactions employees may have to these plans, the level of personal control employees actually have over targeted performance behaviours, and the need for a level playing field that does not put newer employees at a disadvantage.[27]

Organizational Incentives

5 An organizational incentive system compensates all employees in the organization according to how well the organization as a whole performs during the year. The basic concept behind organizational incentive plans is that overall results may depend on organization-wide or plantwide cooperation. The purpose of these plans is to produce better results by rewarding cooperation throughout the organization. For example, conflict between marketing and production can be overcome if management uses an incentive system that emphasizes organization-wide profit and productivity. To be effective, an organizational incentive program should include everyone from nonexempt employees to managers and executives. Two common organizational incentive systems are profit sharing and employee stock plans.

Profit Sharing

Profit sharing
System to distribute a portion of the profits of the organization to employees.

As the name implies, **profit sharing** distributes some portion of organizational profits to employees. The primary objectives of profit-sharing plans include the following:

- Increase productivity and organizational performance.
- Attract or retain employees.
- Improve product/service quality.
- Enhance employee morale.

Typically, the percentage of the profits distributed to employees is set by the end of the year before distribution. In some profit-sharing plans, employees receive portions of the profits at the end of the year; in others, the profits are deferred, placed in a fund, and made available to employees on retirement or on their departure from the organization. Figure 11-10 shows how profit-sharing plans can be funded and allocated.

Unions sometimes are skeptical of profit-sharing plans. Often, the level of profits is influenced by factors not under the employees' control, such as accounting decisions, marketing efforts, competition, and elements of executive compensation.

Figure 11-10 ***Framework Choices for a Profit-Sharing Plan***

Funding Choices	Allocation Choices
• Fixed percentage of profits • Sliding percentage based on sales or return assests • Unit profits • Some other formula	• Equally to all employees • Based on employee earnings • Based on earnings or years of service • Based on contribution and performance

However, in recent years, some unions have supported profit-sharing plans that tie employees' pay increases to improvements against organizational performance measures, not just the "bottom-line" numbers.

Drawbacks of Profit-Sharing Plans When used throughout an organization, including lower-echelon workers, profit-sharing plans can have some drawbacks. First, employees must trust that management will disclose accurate financial and profit information. As many people know, both the definition and level of profit can depend on the accounting systems used and on decisions made. To be credible, management must be willing to disclose sufficient financial and profit information to alleviate the skepticism of employees, particularly if profit-sharing levels fall from those of previous years. Second, profits may vary a great deal from year to year, resulting in windfalls or losses beyond the employees' control. Third, payoffs are generally far removed from employees' efforts, and therefore, higher rewards may not be strongly linked to better performance.

Employee Stock Plans

Two types of organizational incentive plans use employer stock ownership to reward employees. The goal of these plans is to get employees to think and act like "owners."[28]

Stock option plan
Plan that gives employees the right to purchase a fixed number of shares of company stock at a specified price for a limited period of time.

A **stock option plan** gives employees the right to purchase a fixed number of shares of company stock at a specified exercise price for a limited period of time. If the market price of the stock exceeds the exercise price, employees can then exercise the option and buy the stock. The number of firms giving stock options to non-executives has declined some in recent years, primarily due to changing laws and accounting regulations.

Employee stock ownership plan (ESOP)
Plan whereby employees have significant stock ownership in their employers.

Employee Stock Ownership Plans (ESOPs) An **employee stock ownership plan (ESOP)** is designed to give employees significant stock ownership in their employers. According to the Canadian ESOP Survey Results, an estimated 24 percent of Canadian firms offer broad employee-ownership programs. Of the companies that did not have ESOPs (76 percent of respondents), 80 percent would consider implementing an ESOP. On average ESOP participation rates range from 25 percent to 50 percent.[29]

Establishing an ESOP creates several advantages. The major one is that the firm can receive favourable tax treatment on the earnings earmarked for use in the ESOP. Another is that an ESOP gives employees a "piece of the action" so that they can share in the growth and profitability of their firm. Employee ownership may motivate employees to be more productive and focused on organizational performance.[30]

Many people approve of the concept of employee ownership as a kind of "people's capitalism." However, the sharing can also be a disadvantage for employees because it makes both their wages/salaries and their retirement benefits dependent on the performance of their employers. This concentration poses even greater risk for retirees because the value of pension fund assets is also dependent on how well the company performs. The financial bankruptcy and travails of several airlines illustrate that an ESOP does not necessarily guarantee success for the employees who become investors.[31]

Executive Compensation

6 Many organizations, especially large ones, administer compensation for executives differently from compensation for lower-level employees. At the heart of most executive compensation plans is the idea that executives should be rewarded if the organization grows in profitability and value over a period of years. Therefore, variable pay distributed through different types of incentives is a significant part of executive compensation.

Global Executive Compensation

Executive compensation packages vary significantly from country to country. In multinational firms, the differences may be less pronounced because executives are often part of global corporate compensation plans. In comparable-sized firms in Europe and North America, total cash compensation for chief executive officers (CEOs) is similar, about $2.5 million a year. But long-term incentives are used more in French and German companies than in the United Kingdom. Scandinavian firms pay their CEOs about 30 percent less than do other European firms.[32] Also, Japanese CEOs are paid about one-third of what U.S. CEOs in comparable-sized firms are paid.[33] Critics of executive pay levels point out that in the U.S., many corporate CEOs make almost 200 times more than do average workers in their firms, up from 35 times more in the 1970s. In Japan, the ratio is 15:1, and in Europe, 20:1. Worldwide, the various elements of compensation shown in Figure 11-11 are used to different degrees.

Elements of Executive Compensation

Because high-salaried executives are in higher tax brackets, many executive compensation packages are designed to offer significant tax savings. These savings occur

Figure 11-11 *Components of Executive Compensation Packages*

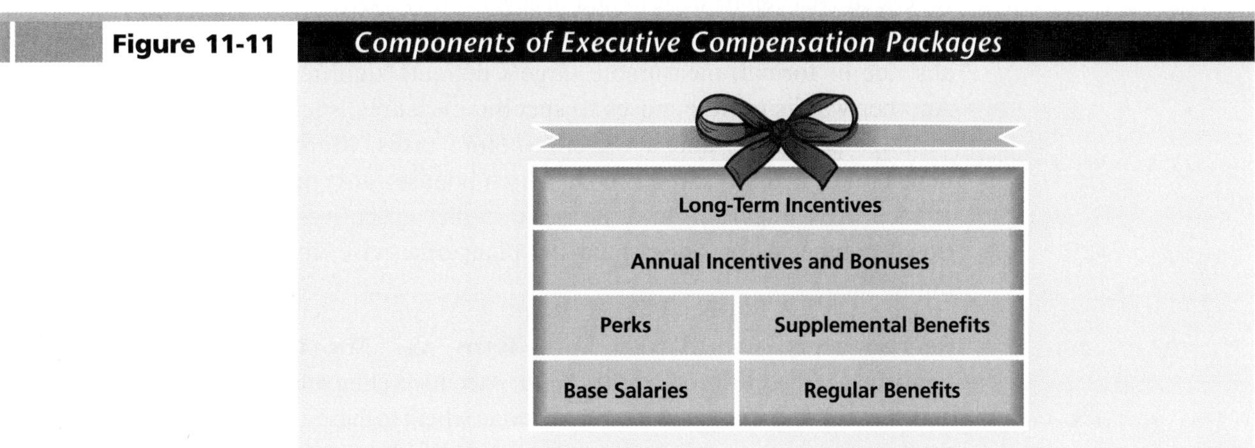

through use of deferred compensation methods whereby taxes are not due until after the executives leave the firm. According to a review of the compensation packages of CEOs of 350 large companies, long-term incentives constitute 68 percent of the total CEO compensation.[34]

Executive Salaries Salaries of executives vary by the type of job, size of organization, industry, and other factors. In some organizations, particularly non-profits, salaries often make up 90 percent or more of total compensation. In contrast, in large corporations, salaries may constitute 30 percent or less of the total package. Survey data on executive salaries are often reviewed by boards of directors to ensure that their organizations are competitive. Organizations such as Petro Canada and Telus Canada have their salaries reviewed by boards of directors.

Executive Benefits Many executives are covered by *regular benefits plans* that are also available to non-executive employees, including traditional retirement, health insurance, and vacations plans. In addition, executives may receive *supplemental benefits* that other employees do not receive. For example, executive health plans with no co-payments and with no limitations on deductibles or physician choice are popular among small and middle-size businesses. Corporate-owned insurance on the life of the executive is also popular; this insurance pays both the executive's estate and the company in the event of death. One supplemental benefit that has grown in popularity is company-paid financial planning for executives. Trusts of various kinds may be designed by the company to help the executives deal with estate-planning and tax issues. Deferred compensation is another possible means of helping executives with tax liabilities caused by incentive compensation plans.

Perquisites (perks)
Special benefits—usually non-cash items—for executives.

Executive Perquisites (Perks) In addition to the regular benefits received by all employees, executives often receive benefits called perquisites. **Perquisites (perks)** are special benefits—usually non-cash items—for executives. Many executives value the status enhancement of these visible symbols, which allow them to be seen as "very important people" both inside and outside their organizations. Perks can also offer substantial tax savings because some of them are not taxed as income. Some commonly used executive perks are company cars, health club and country club memberships, first-class air travel, use of private jets, stress counselling, and chauffer services.[35]

Annual Executive Incentives and Bonuses Annual incentives and bonuses for executives can be determined in several ways. One way is to use a discretionary system whereby the CEO and the board of directors decide on bonuses; the absence of formal, measurable targets detracts significantly from this approach. Another way is to tie bonuses to specific measures, such as return on investment, earnings per share, and net profits before taxes. More complex systems create bonus pools and thresholds above which bonuses are computed. Whatever method is used, it is important to describe it so that executives attempting to earn additional compensation understand the plan; otherwise, the incentive effect will be diminished.

Performance Incentives: Long-Term vs. Short-Term Use of executive performance-based incentives try to tie executive compensation to long-term growth and success of the organization. However, whether these incentives really emphasize the long term or merely represent a series of short-term rewards is controversial.

Certain executive perks, while offering substantial tax savings because some are not considered taxable income, also provide executives with the opportunity to relax in the midst of their demanding work schedules.

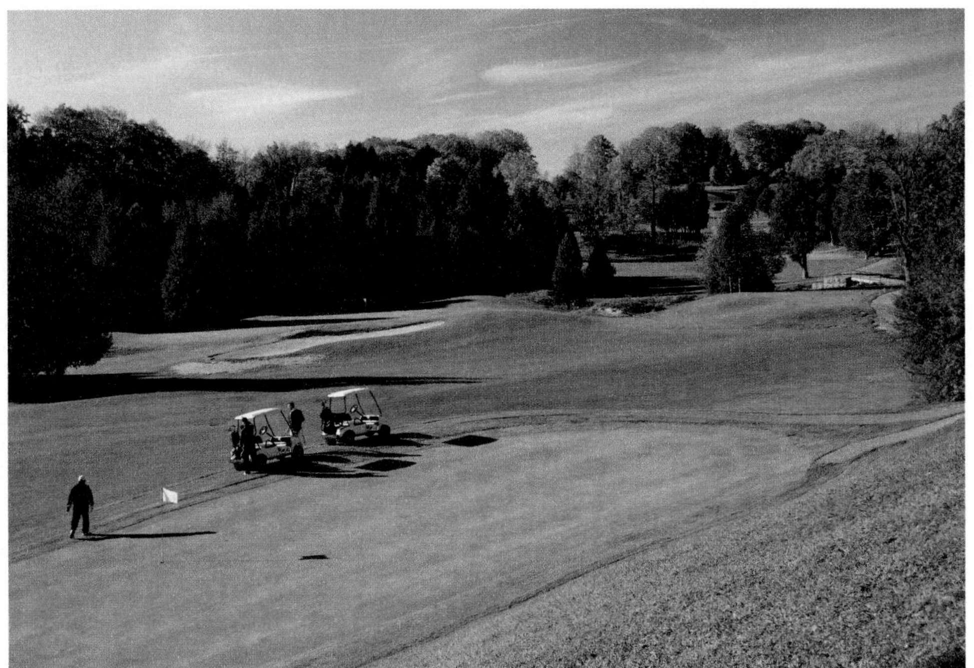

Source: Kondrachov Vladimir/ShutterStock

Short-term rewards based on quarterly or annual performance may not result in the kind of long-run-oriented decisions necessary for the company to perform well over multiple years.

As would be expected, the total amount of pay-for-performance incentives varies by management level, with CEOs receiving significantly more than subsidiary or other senior managers. One study found that the typical CEO gets about half of all the total incentives paid to all senior managers and executives.[36]

The most widely used long-term incentives are stock option plans. A stock option gives individuals the right to buy stock in a company, usually at an advantageous price. Despite the prevalence of such plans, research has found little relationship between providing CEOs with stock options and subsequent firm performance.[37] Because of the numerous corporate scandals involving executives at Enron, Nortel, WorldCom, Tyco, and others who received outrageously high compensation due to stock options, the use of stock options has declined.[38] Instead, more firms with publicly traded stock are using means such as *restricted stock, phantom stock, performance shares,* and other specialized technical forms, which are beyond the scope of this discussion.

Another outcome of the recent corporate abuses by executives was the passage of the Sarbanes-Oxley Act (SOX) of 2002 in the U.S. This act has numerous provisions that have affected the accounting and financial reporting requirements of different types of executive compensation. SOX mandates that CEOs and CFOs of companies listed on U.S. stock exchanges must certify and sign off on interim and annual statements as well as their corporate governance framework. If the CEOs cannot comply by the stipulated date(s), the penalties can be swift and severe: the company's stock could be de-listed, heavy fines imposed, and top executives could be prosecuted. SOX's influence extends to subsidiaries of American companies operating outside the U.S. such as GE Canada and foreign companies whose stock trades in the U.S. such as most of Canada's big banks. Bill C-198 is Canada's SOX equivalent. Any company complying with SOX will likely also comply with C-198.[39]

LOGGING ON...

Canadian Securities Administrators (CSA)
The Canadian Securities Administrators (CSA) is a forum for the 13 securities regulators of Canada's provinces and territories to coordinate and harmonize regulation of the Canadian capital markets. A key function includes the monitoring and enforcement of executive pay disclosure.
www.csa-acvm.ca/

"Reasonableness" of Executive Compensation

The notion that monetary incentives tied to performance result in improved performance makes sense to most people. However, there is an ongoing debate about whether executive compensation in Canada is truly linked to performance. This is particularly concerning given the astronomical amounts of some executive compensation packages, as highlighted in the HR Perspective.

The reasonableness of executive compensation is often justified by comparison to compensation market surveys, but these surveys usually provide a range of compensation data that requires interpretation. Various questions have been suggested for determining if executive pay is "reasonable," including the following useful ones:

- Would another company hire this person as an executive?
- How does the executive's compensation compare with that for executives in similar companies in the industry?
- Is the executive's pay consistent with pay for other employees within the company?
- What would an investor pay for the level of performance of the executive?

Linkage Between Executive Compensation and Corporate Performance

Of all the executive compensation issues that are debated, the one discussed most frequently is whether or not executive compensation levels are sufficiently linked

HR *Perspective*

Is Any Executive Worth Over $50 Million a Year?

The staggeringly large amounts of some annual compensation packages for executives have raised ethical questions. A primary question is if any single CEO is really deserving of compensation totalling over $50 million when stock option profits, retirement bonuses, and other payments are included.

To illustrate, the following corporate executives received huge sums: Ruben Mark (Colgate-Palmolive), $141.1 million; Steve Jobs (Apple Computer), $74.8 million; and George David (United Technologies), $70.5 million. Numerous other CEOs, such as Frank Stronach (Magna), received yearly compensation of over $20 million, including long-term stock option gains and other payments.

On top of these large annual amounts, executives have negotiated "departure agreements." Richard Grasso, former CEO of the New York Stock Exchange, was to receive over $180 million in the year he was asked to quit, as well as a "retirement agreement." Controversy over the package caused him to relinquish some of this amount.

"Departure-and-consulting agreements" for executives are another area of concern. These arrangements were provided for retiring CEOs such as Jack Welsh (GE), who received up to $3.4 million, and John Bryan (Sara Lee), who received $5 million. Major controversies arose at American Airlines and Delta Airlines when it was publicized that the departing CEOs at those companies were to receive $1.5 and $3 million respectively a year after resigning. That disclosure occurred at the same time that unionized airline employees were being asked to negotiate wage and benefits reductions.[40]

Of course, these figures, large as they are, provide little meaning unless put into context. If the company is doing well and performing above competitors and expectations, the huge packages might be justifiable to stockholders. Certainly, the opposite can be true as well.

1. The question that still must be addressed by boards of directors, stockholders, and executives is: How realistic and ethical is it to provide such huge amounts to one person, when many other executives have contributed to organizational performance and do not receive such lavish payouts? What do you think?
2. Should legislation be enacted to deal with this issue? If so, what should it entail?

to organizational performance.[41] One key aspect of evaluating all the studies on this topic is the performance measures used. Numerous studies have examined different facets of this topic.[42] In many settings, financial measures such as return on equity, return to shareholders, earnings per share, and net income before taxes are used to measure performance. However, a number of firms also incorporate nonfinancial organizational measures of performance when determining executive bonuses and incentives. Customer satisfaction, employee satisfaction, market share, productivity, and quality are other areas measured for executive performance rewards.

Measurement of executive performance varies from firm to firm. Some executive compensation packages use a short-term focus of one year, which may lead to large rewards for executive performance in a given year even though corporate performance over a multi-year period is mediocre. This difference is especially pronounced if the yearly measures are carefully chosen. Executives can even manipulate earnings per share by selling assets, liquidating inventories, or reducing research and development expenditures. All these actions may make organizational performance look better, but they may impair the long-term growth of the organization.

A number of other executive compensation issues and concerns are discussed. Figure 11-12 highlights the criticisms and counterarguments of some common points of contention.

One of the more controversial issues is that some executives seem to get large awards for negative actions. It seems contradictory from an employee's perspective to reward executives who often improve corporate results by cutting staff, laying off employees, changing pension plans, or increasing the deductible on the health insurance. But sometimes cost-cutting measures are necessary to keep a company afloat. However, a sense of reasonableness may be appropriate too; if rank and file employees suffer, giving bonuses and large payouts to executives appears counterproductive, and even hypocritical.

Figure 11-12 *Common Executive Compensation Issues*

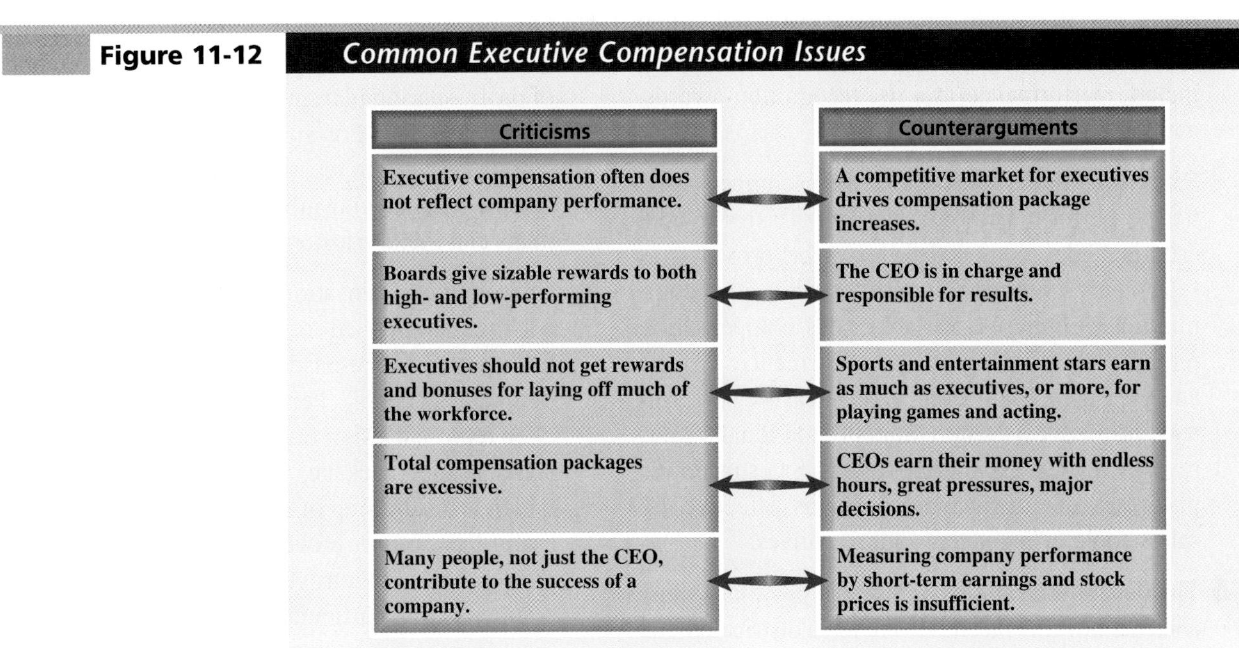

Criticisms
Counterarguments
Executive compensation often does not reflect company performance.
A competitive market for executives drives compensation package increases.
Boards give sizable rewards to both high- and low-performing executives.
The CEO is in charge and responsible for results.
Executives should not get rewards and bonuses for laying off much of the workforce.
Sports and entertainment stars earn as much as executives, or more, for playing games and acting.
Total compensation packages are excessive.
CEOs earn their money with endless hours, great pressures, major decisions.
Many people, not just the CEO, contribute to the success of a company.
Measuring company performance by short-term earnings and stock prices is insufficient.

Compensation committee Subgroup of the board of directors, composed of directors who are not officers of the firm.

Executive Compensation and Boards of Directors In most organizations, the board of directors is the major policy-setting entity and must approve executive compensation packages. The **compensation committee** usually is a subgroup of the board, composed of directors who are not officers of the firm. Compensation committees generally make recommendations to the board of directors on overall pay policies, salaries for top officers, supplemental compensation such as stock options and bonuses, and additional perquisites for executives.

Increasingly, the independence of these committees has been criticized.[43] One major concern voiced by many critics is that the base pay and bonuses of CEOs are often set by the members of board compensation committees, many of whom are CEOs of other companies with similar compensation packages. Also, the compensation advisers and consultants to the CEOs often collect large fees, and critics charge that those fees distort the objectivity of the advice given.

To counter criticism, some corporations have changed the composition of the compensation committees by taking actions such as prohibiting "insider" company officers from serving on them.[44] Also, some firms have empowered the compensation committees to hire and pay compensation consultants without involving executive management.

SUMMARY

1 Variable pay, also called incentives, is compensation that can be linked to individual, group/team, and/or organizational performance. Effective variable pay plans should fit both business strategies and organizational cultures, appropriately award actions, and be administered properly. The results of variable pay plans should be measured to determine their success.

2 There are many types of variable pay including individual incentives, group/team incentives, and organizational incentives. Piece-rate and bonus plans are the most commonly used individual incentives. Special incentives for individuals may include performance awards, recognition awards, and service awards.

3 Sales employees may have their compensation tied to performance on a number of sales-related criteria. Sales compensation can be provided as salary only, commission only, or salary plus commission or bonuses. Variable sales compensation requires establishing clear performance criteria and measures. Many companies measure performance primarily by comparing an individual's sales revenue against established quotas. Sales incentive plans are not always perceived as effective by salespeople or managers and executives.

4 The design of group/team variable pay plans must consider how the incentives are to be distributed, the timing of the incentive payments, and who will make decisions about the variable payout. Problems with group/team incentives exist, particularly how the incentives are distributed in relation to performance. The two most frequently used group/team incentives include work team results and gainsharing. The most common group/team incentives are gainsharing and goalsharing plans. The Scanlan plan, Rucker plan, and Improshare are examples of gainsharing plans. Earnings-at-risk is another type of plan that is sometimes viewed negatively by employees.

5 Organization-wide rewards include profit-sharing and stock ownership plans. Unions are very skeptical of profit-sharing plans, although they are becoming more receptive. For such plans to be successful, employees need to feel that management is honestly disclosing financial information. Employee stock plans can include a stock option plan, or an ESOP.

6 Executive compensation must be viewed as a total package composed of salaries, bonuses, long-term performance-based incentives, benefits, and perquisites (perks). Performance-based incentives often represent a significant portion of an executive's compensation package. A compensation committee, which is a subgroup of the board of directors, generally has authority over executive compensation plans. Much controversy surrounds executive compensation particularly because many executives seem to get large awards for negative actions.

KEY TERMS

Bonus, p. 411
Commission, p. 414
Compensation committee, p. 430
Draw, p. 415
Earnings-at-risk, p. 423
Employee stock ownership plan (ESOP), p. 424
Gainsharing, p. 419
Improshare, p. 420
Perquisites (perks), p. 426
Profit sharing, p. 423
Rucker plan, p. 422
Scanlon plan, p. 421
Stock option plan, p. 424
Straight piece-rate system, p. 411
Variable pay, p. 406

REVIEW AND APPLICATION QUESTIONS

1 Discuss why pay-for-performance plans have become more popular and what elements are needed to make them successful.

2 Give examples of individual incentives that an organization can implement. Describe the pros and cons of implementing each of these different plans.

3 Your CEO has asked your HR department to implement a sales incentive plan for your regional salespeople. Your salespeople are responsible for selling security systems to businesses. What type of program would be most appropriate? How did you arrive at this decision?

4 What is gainsharing and what types of plans exist? What are the pros and cons of each of these plans?

5 Describe the advantages and disadvantages of profit-sharing plans.

6 Discuss the negative issues surrounding executive pay. Do you feel that the negative issues are warranted or not? Explain why or why not?

EXPERIENTIAL EXERCISES

1. Assume you are an organization that sells a special software program to car dealerships to help them maintain their inventory of parts and vehicles. Your sales personnel are required to travel throughout the province, although they may be required to work at the office from time to time when they are trying to catch up on some paperwork. Develop what you feel would be an appropriate compensation package for them.
2. Your organization has decided to implement teams and to incorporate incentives conducive to a team environment. You are expected to develop a comprehensive plan, outlining what particular incentives would work. You need to send a report to your CEO outlining how you arrived at this plan, and why you feel it would be successful. You should also note any potential issues that could arise.
3. Working in groups of five, you are to conduct a survey to determine if individuals working in teams would prefer to be paid incentives based on the team's overall results, a combination of team-based results and individual results, or just based on their own individual efforts, regardless of the team's performance as a whole. Each member of your group is to ask ten family members and/or friends who are working full-time. You should then compile and analyze the results. What are your findings? Are the findings what you expected? Why or why not? What does this all mean? As an HR consultant what would you recommend to your CEO?
4. You have been hired as the HR manager for a Japanese electronics company, Mitzsisu Electronics, who is setting up business in your city. You are Mitzsisu's first employee, as they understand the importance of HR. Two days later the sales manager, Jim Stern, comes onboard. Jim used to act as a sales agent, selling the product on behalf of Mitzsisu in Canada. Mitzsisu realizes that it needs to be in Canada to directly support their customers. The two of you and the Japanese

managers form the executive for the Canadian operations. The Japanese executives meet with both of you to discuss the commission structure for the sales staff that will be starting soon. Jim has already made job offers to some ex-employees without having consulted you first. As the meeting gets underway Jim suggests a commission structure that you know is far too generous for the industry. You realize then that Jim is taking advantage of the Japanese because they do not know the North American market well. You are in a difficult situation because Jim has had a past relationship with these executives and you are new and do not want to come across as being difficult to work with. However, you have a sinking feeling that Jim is not the type of employee who can be trusted. What can you do to ensure that the Japanese are not being taken advantage of now or in the future by Jim? How can you maintain a good working relationship with Jim knowing that at some point you will have to challenge him head-on on some of these issues?

LEARNING REVIEW

To check your knowledge of the chapter, review the following. (Answers after the case.)

1 Which of the following is a philosophical foundation of variable pay?
   a. Some people perform better than others.
   b. Time spent each day is the primary measure of contributions.
   c. Length of service within the organization is the primary differentiating factor between people.
   d. Contributions to the organization are recognized through different amounts of base pay.

2 The most common group/team incentives are _______ and _____________.
   a. commissions, incentives
   b. commissions, gainsharing
   c. goalsharing, commissions
   d. gainsharing, goalsharing

3 The most frequently used form of sales compensation is the:
   a. straight commission
   b. draw against commission
   c. salary plus commission
   d. piece-rate system

4 The most prevalent form of organization-wide incentives is:
   a. individual incentives
   b. gainsharing
   c. bonuses
   d. profit-sharing plans

5 The purpose of organizational incentive plans is to:
   a. give back to employees for their efforts
   b. increase profitability
   c. produce better results by rewarding cooperation throughout the organization
   d. increase customer service initiatives

6 Which of the following executive incentive is used to emphasize the long-term growth and success of the organization?
   a. Executive perquisites
   b. Executive bonus plans
   c. Golden parachutes
   d. Stock options

CASE

COMPENSATION AND EMPLOYEE MOTIVATION AT DOFASCO

Established in 1912, Dofasco, Canada's largest steel producer believes their competitive advantage comes from building relationships with their employees based on trust, respect, and shared rewards. From their primary facility in Hamilton, Ontario, Dofasco's commitment to their over 7000 employees is illustrated not only by the company's recreation facilities, employee programs, and annual events but also through a compensation plan designed to motivate and reward employees for delivering superior performance.

Dofasco has a long tradition of encouraging employee productivity and loyalty through compensation. In 1938, Dofasco introduced a profit-sharing program making them the first company in Canada to motivate their employees through sharing the company's success. With this program, each Dofasco employee receives an equal bonus based on a percentage of the company's pre-tax income.

In 1996, Dofasco also successfully tied their compensation plan to corporate performance. All employees, from cafeteria cooks to senior managers, have a percentage of their salary based on variable pay. This plan enables employees to earn bonuses up to 20 percent, increasing to 30 percent to 60 percent for senior mangers, based on achieving organizational targets related to financial, health and safety, and customer service performance.

With less than 1-percent turnover, and a ten-year productivity gain twice that of Canada's manufacturing sector, Dofasco has proven that their competitive strength is their people. It's no wonder that Dofasco has been consistently listed as a top employer by *MacLeans Magazine's* Canada's Top 100 Employers and *The Globe and Mail's Report on Business Magazine's* 50 Best Companies to Work for in Canada.[45]

Questions

1. What issues do you think Dofasco considered when implementing their variable pay program?
2. What other compensation programs would you recommend Dofasco adopt to recognize and reward their employees?

Learning Review Answers: 1. a 2. d 3. c 4. d 5. c 6. d

CHAPTER

Managing Employee Benefits

Learning Objectives

After you have read this chapter, you should be able to:

1 Define a benefit and identify four strategic benefit considerations.

2 Distinguish between mandated and voluntary benefits.

3 Discuss the shift of retirement plans from defined-benefit to defined-contribution plans.

4 Explain the importance of managing the costs of health benefits and identify some methods of doing so.

5 Describe the growth of financial, family-oriented, and time-off benefits and their importance to many employees.

6 Summarize benefits communication and flexible benefits as considerations in benefits administration.

HR *Headline*

Employers and Employees Face Escalating Benefits Costs

A permeating concern in the Canadian workforce is anxiety about benefits. With good reasons, employees become anxious as employers try to reduce benefits in order to control costs. Statistics Canada reports that mandatory non-wage benefits (EI, CPP/QPP, and workers' compensation) was about 12 percent of payroll and the cost of discretionary non-wage benefits (e.g., paid leave, profit and stock option plans) have grown from 23 to 36 percent of payroll. The biggest cost increases have been in health benefits, anticipated to rise over 15 percent in the next few years. The largest component of the health benefit costs are prescription drugs where total drug spending in Canada increased to 8.8 percent in 2004.

To counter the cost increases, employers are taking steps to reduce or even eliminate benefits. Actions that companies are taking include increasing the amount that employees and retirees have to pay for health insurance, reducing employer contributions to pension programs, and implementing prescription drug management programs. These actions have reduced employee satisfaction with their benefits, especially in smaller companies. In a recent study conducted for a Canadian pharmaceutical company, only 58 percent of the 1500 respondents said their plan met their needs extremely or very well, down from 73 percent in 1999. Many employees voice concerns that their annual pay increases only cover the extra benefits charges they must pay. But, the pressures on benefits costs is likely to continue, and the employer/employee conflicts and anxieties over benefits costs will grow.[1]

> *"Despite rising costs, employers continue to offer a broad array of benefits to workers."*
>
> —*Bruce Josten*

Benefit
Indirect reward given to an employee or a group of employees for organizational membership.

Employers provide benefits to their workers for being part of the organization. A **benefit** is an indirect reward given to an employee or a group of employees for organizational membership. Benefits often include retirement plans, vacations with pay, extended health insurance, educational assistance, and many more programs.

Benefits are costly for the typical employer. They average over 40 percent of payroll expenses for employers, and in highly unionized manufacturing and utility industries, they may be as high as 80 percent of payroll. In fact, the costs related to employee health and wellness has emerged as one of the top business issues for Canadian chief executives.[2] Figure 12-1 shows the results of a CEO study on health and productivity in Canadian industry, and the CEOs' related concerns about the increasing costs of health care over the long term.

Strategic Perspectives on Benefits

1 Benefits should be looked at as a vital part of the overall compensation strategies of the organization.[3] For instance, an organization can choose to compete for employees by providing base compensation, variable pay, or benefits, or perhaps all three. Which approach is chosen depends on many factors, such as competition, organizational life cycle, and corporate strategy. For example, a new firm may choose to have lower base pay and use high variable incentives to attract new employees, but keep the cost of benefits as low as possible for a while. Or an organization that hires predominately younger female employees might choose a family-friendly set of benefits such as child-care assistance to attract and retain employees, but offer little variable pay and market-level base pay.

The reasons why employers offer benefits are multifaceted and tie into strategic considerations. As Figure 12-2 indicates, there are four aspects to looking at benefits strategically.

Figure 12-1 *Long-Term Issues for CEOs*

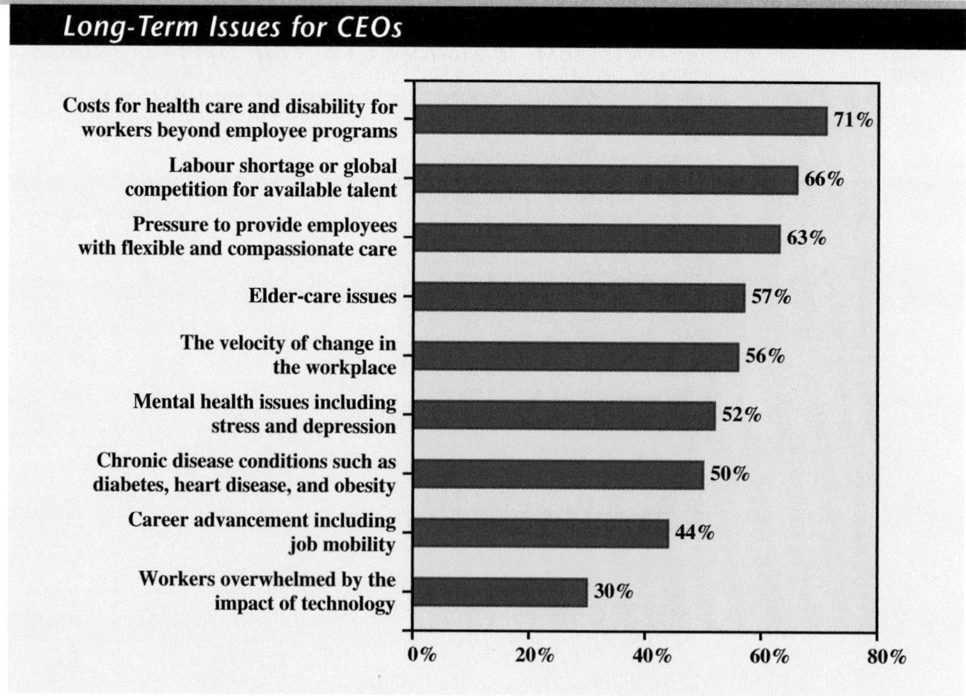

Source: FIGworld CEO Study on Health and Productivity in the Canadian Industry, based on responses of telephone interviews with 114 CEOs, 2005.

Figure 12-2 *Strategic Benefits Considerations*

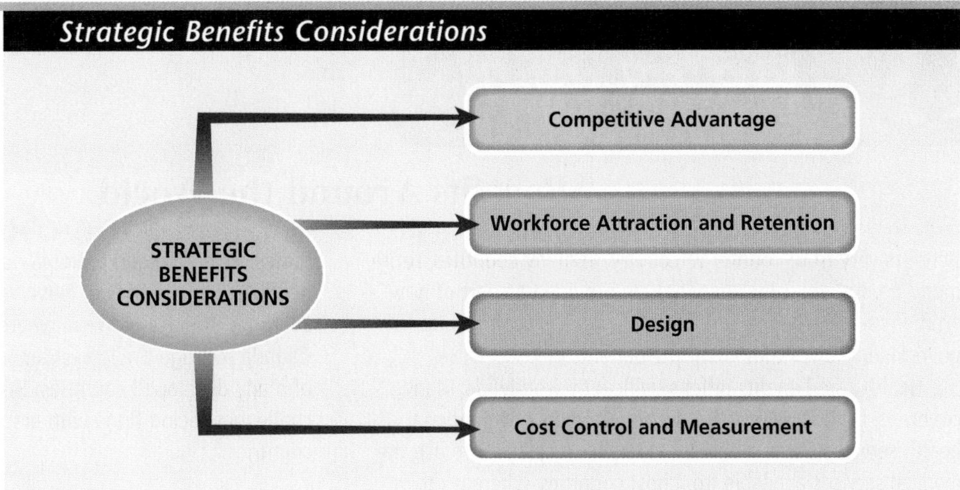

Benefits Canada
This website consists of surveys, archived articles, and the latest trends and information regarding pension investment and employee benefits.
www.benefitscanada.com

Benefits as Competitive Advantage

Employers offer some benefits to aid recruiting and retention, some because they are required to do so, and some simply because doing so reinforces the company philosophy of social and corporate citizenship. Employers with good benefits are viewed positively within a community and the industry by customers, current employees, and workers in other firms. Conversely, the employers who are seen as skimping on benefits, cutting benefits, or taking advantage of workers may be viewed negatively.

The benefits offered can aid in reducing employee absenteeism and turnover, which may boost organizational performance. Employee wellness benefits at both large and small employers have been shown to reduce absenteeism due to illness problems and employee turnover because of health concerns. Time-off leave programs aid in reducing absenteeism and turnover as well. An additional strategic challenge that can affect the competitive advantage of a firm is the differences in benefits worldwide, as the HR Globally discussion illustrates.

Benefits and Workforce Attraction/Retention

The composition of the Canadian workforce is changing, and expectations about benefits of different generations of employees are affecting benefit decisions. For instance, many "baby boomers" who are approaching retirement age are more concerned about retirement benefits and health care, where many younger workers are more interested in portable flexible benefits. However, all generations expect medical and dental insurance. Having benefit plans that appeal to the different groups is vital to attracting and retaining all employees.

It is well established that benefits influence employees' decisions about which particular employer to work for, whether to stay with or leave an employer, and when to retire. A major advantage of benefits is that they generally are not taxed as income to employees. For this reason, they represent a somewhat more valuable reward to employees than an equivalent cash payment. For example, assume that employee Clara Smith is in a 25-percent tax bracket. If Clara earns an extra $400, she must pay $100 in taxes on this amount (disregarding exemptions). But if her employer provides prescription drug coverage in a benefits plan, and she receives the $400 as payments for prescription drugs, she is not taxed on the amount, and she receives the value of the entire $400 not just $300. This feature makes benefits a desirable form of compensation to employees.

Benefits Around the World

Benefits vary from country to country. In many countries, retirement, health, and other benefits are provided as part of government services. Employers are taxed heavily to pay into government funds that cover the benefits.

Health-care benefits differ significantly worldwide. Many countries, including Great Britain and Canada, have national health services. Some global firms require employees to use the medical services available from host countries, whereas other global employers provide special coverage that allows expatriates to receive health care from private providers. Arranging quality private coverage becomes an especially important issue for global employees located in various underdeveloped countries where the availability and quality of medical facilities and treatment varies widely.

Retirement and pension systems are provided by the government in many countries as well. National pension programs in Germany, France, and Japan, among other countries, are facing significant financial pressures due to their aging workforces and populations. Such challenges also face the pension and health-care systems in Canada.

The amount of leave and vacation time also varies significantly around the globe. Of 130 countries, only the United States, Australia, and Ethiopia do not provide paid leave for new parents. The annual leave/vacation in European countries averages 36 days per year, whereas the United States and Canada average the lowest amounts of annual vacation leave of many developed countries. These examples illustrate the challenges facing firms with employees located in different countries.[4]

1. Working in groups, search the Web to determine what vacation time, maternity leave, pension plan, and health care are provided fo employees in Italy, Sweden, and Australia by their governments. How do these compare to what is offered in Canada (select a province of your choice)? What recommendations would you provide to any individual who is planning to work in any one of these countries who has a family with small children, and/or to single individuals?
2. Who do you feel should take responsibility for benefits? Should it be the employer, the government, the employee, or combination? Once students have selected their choice, debating teams can be established to defend each team's position as to why they feel their choice is most valid.

Benefits Design

Benefits plans can provide flexibility and choices for employees, or can be standardized for all employees. Increasingly, employers are finding that providing employees with some choices and flexibility allows individuals to tailor their benefits to their own situations. However, the more choices available, the more administrative demands are placed on organizations.

A number of decisions are part of benefits design. Some key ones are the following:

- How much total compensation, including benefits, should be provided?
- What part of the total compensation of individuals should benefits constitute?
- What expense levels are acceptable for each benefit offered?
- Why is each type of benefit offered?
- Which employees should be given or offered which benefits?
- What is being received by the organization in return for each benefit?
- How does having a comprehensive benefits package help minimize turnover or maximize recruiting and retention of employees?
- How flexible should the package of benefits be?

Total benefits costs can be funded by contributions from both the employer and the employee. If the employer fully subsidizes a benefit, the cost to the employee is zero. But if an employer chooses to pay $400 a month toward an employee's health insurance premium and the premium costs $550 a month, the cost to the employee is $150 a month.

Part-Time Employee Benefits Another key design issue is whether or not to provide benefits coverage to employees who are not regular full-time employees. Many employers do not provide part-time employee benefits, except some time-off leave benefits. According to a Conference Board of Canada study on part-time benefits, of the large employers surveyed, 20 percent provided part-timers with benefits.[5] Part-time employees who do receive benefits usually do so in proportion to the percentage of full-time work time they provide.

UPS, the package delivery firm, provides health benefits to most part-time employees. Starbucks and some qualifying employees of Canadian Tire also provide benefits to part-timers. These firms indicate that providing benefits positively affects their ability to attract and retain part-time workers in tight labour markets.[6] In Saskatchewan a business with ten or more full-time equivalent employees must provide benefits to eligible part-time employees if they are offering benefits to full-time employees. This ensures some level of equality among the employees.

Benefits Cost Control and Measurement

Many employees tend to take benefits for granted. So many organizations offer health insurance that employees expect it. Because benefits expenditures have risen significantly in the past few years, particularly for health care, employers are focusing more attention on measuring and controlling benefits costs, and even reducing or dropping benefits offered to employees. Employers are using metrics shown in Figure 12-3.[7]

Benefits Interface, Inc.
This website serves as a gateway for employers to access ideas on how to better manage their benefit plans.
http://benefits.org

Benefits Effectiveness Metrics The significant costs associated with benefits require that analyses be conducted to determine the payoffs for the benefits. With the wide range of benefits that are offered, numerous HR metrics can be used.

Other metrics are used to measure the return on the expenditures for various benefits programs provided by employers. Some common benefits that employers track using HR metrics are workers' compensation, wellness programs, prescription drug costs, leave time, tuition aid, and disability insurance. The overriding point is that both benefits expenditures generally and costs for individual benefits specifically need to be measured and evaluated as part of strategic benefits management.

Types of Benefits

2 A wide range of benefits are offered by employers. Some are mandated by government legislation, while others are offered voluntarily by employers as part of their HR strategies. Each of these is discussed in the following sections. Figure 12-4 shows the differences between government mandated and discretionary programs offered by employers.

Figure 12-3 *Common Measurements of Benefits Effectiveness*

- **Benefits as a percentage of payroll (pattern over a multi-year period)**
- **Benefits expenditures per full-time equivalent (FTE) employee**
- **Benefits costs by employee group (full-time vs. part-time, union vs. non-union, office, management, professional, technical, etc.)**
- **Benefits administration costs (including staff time multiplied by the staff pay and benefits costs per hour)**
- **Health-care benefits costs per participating employee**

Figure 12-4 *Types of Benefits*

Government-Mandated Programs	Discretionary Benefits Offered by Employers
Canada Pension Plan/Quebec Pension Plan—Federal jurisdiction • Disability Benefits • Survivor Benefits	**Retirement Plans** • Defined Benefits Plan • Defined Contribution Plan • Group RRSP • Deferred Profit Sharing Plan
Employment Insurance (EI)—Federal jurisdiction • Basic • Compassionate care benefits • Maternity • Parental (biological or adoptive parents) • Sickness	**Supplementary Unemployment Benefits—Coordinated with government plan**
Old Age Security—Federal jurisdiction	**Health Benefits—including extended health, dental, insurance** • Health Spending Accounts
Workers' Compensation—Provincial jurisdiction	**Financial** • Financial services (e.g., credit unions) • Relocation assistance • Life insurance • Disability insurance • Educational assistance
Provincial Medicare—Provincial/Federal—Federal government transfers subsidy payments to the provinces and then provinces fund the shortfalls	**Time off** • Military reserve time off • Election and jury leaves • Lunch and rest breaks • Holidays and vacations • Family leave

Government-Mandated Security Benefits

There are many mandated security benefits that employers in Canada must provide to employees under federal, provincial, and territorial laws. These include Canada Pension Plan/Quebec Pension Plan, Old Age Security, Employment Insurance, Workers' Compensation, and provincial health-care programs. Each of these is discussed below.

Canada/Quebec Pension Plan (CPP/QPP)
The CPP/QPP are Canada's major pension plans, providing regular payments to people in retirement who have contributed to either of these plans (or both) over the years.

Canada/Quebec Pension Plan (CPP/QPP) **Canada Pension Plan (CPP) and Quebec Pension Plan (QPP)** are Canada's major pension plans, providing regular payments to people in retirement who have contributed to either of these plans (or both) over the years. The CPP operates throughout Canada, except for Quebec, which has QPP, its own similar, but not identical, program. If you are between the ages of 18 and 70, you and your employer contribute to either of these plans every time you receive a paycheque. Self-employed workers must contribute both the employee and the employer portion of the payments.

Contributions are calculated using the amount of pensionable earnings less an exempt amount established by the government annually. In 2006, the maximum pensionable earnings were set at $42,100 with a basic exemption of $3,500. The employee and employer contribution rates for 2006 were calculated at 4.95 percent, and the self-employed contribution rate was 9.9 percent. The maximum employer and employee contribution to the plan for 2006 was $1,910.70, and the maximum self-employed contribution was $3,821.40. The maximums in 2005 were $1,861.20 and $3,722.40. These amounts change every year, however these examples are provided to give you an idea of how these are calculated.

For example, if you were earning $50,000 for the year, the maximum amount that would be used to determine your deduction for CPP would be based on:

$42,100 pensionable earnings – $3,500 basic exemption = $38,600 pensionable earnings × CPP contribution rate of 4.95% = $1,910.70 CPP deduction for the year

Your employer would also remit an equal amount of $1,910.70 to the government. If you are self-employed, then you would submit the employer portion plus your portion, which would equal $3,821.40.

Benefit payouts are based on the number of years you've worked and your earnings during that time, and are adjusted to keep pace with inflation. Your retirement pension is not started automatically. You must apply for it. CPP/QPP officially kicks in at age 65, but you can apply to receive it as early as your 60th birthday or as late as age 70. Even though it is the responsibility of the employee to make these applications, HR can assist the employee by letting them know well ahead of their retirement date to ensure they are aware of the rules regarding this application. There are other CPP/QPP benefits that you may be eligible to receive, such as disability payments and survivor benefits.

Disability Payments A CPP/QPP disability benefit is available to people who have made enough contributions to the CPP/QPP, and whose disability prevents them from working at any job on a regular basis. The disability must be long lasting or likely to result in death. People who qualify for disability benefits from other programs may not qualify for the CPP/QPP disability benefit. There are also benefits available to the children of a person who receives a CPP/QPP disability benefit.

The Canada Pension Plan Disability *Vocational Rehabilitation Program* is designed to help people who receive a CPP disability benefit to return to work. In the past, many people receiving benefits because of a severe and prolonged disability believed that they were permanently out of the workforce. Today, new technology, medical treatments, and skills training are making it possible for some people with severe disabilities to become part of and remain in the workforce.

A number of Canadians will be retiring in record numbers in the coming years. Many will draw upon the different forms of pension available to them.

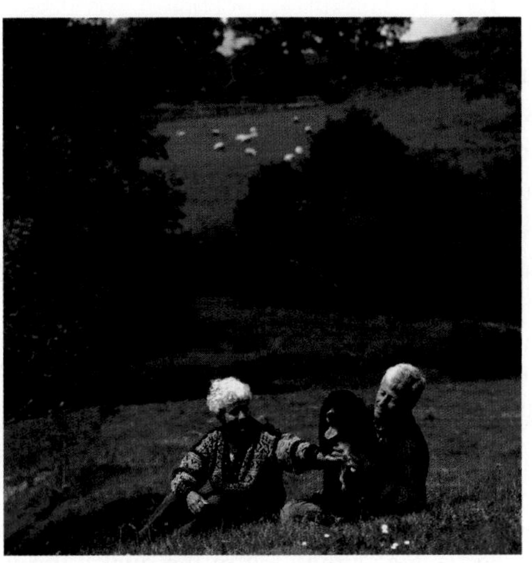

Source: Colin Paterson/Getty Images

Survivor Benefits CPP/QPP survivor benefits are paid to a deceased contributor's estate, surviving spouse or common-law partner, and dependent children. There are three types of benefits available:

- The *death benefit* is a one-time payment to, or on behalf of, the estate of a deceased CPP/QPP contributor;
- The *CPP/QPP survivor's pension* is paid to the person who, at the time of death, is the legal spouse or common-law partner of the deceased contributor. If you are a separated legal spouse and there is no cohabiting common-law partner, you may qualify for this benefit.
- The *CPP/QPP children's benefit* is paid to a dependent natural or adopted child of the deceased contributor, or a child in the care and control of the deceased contributor, at the time of death. The child must be either under age 18, or between the ages of 18 and 25 and in full-time attendance at a school or university.

Old Age Security (OAS)
The OAS pension program provides a monthly retirement benefit based on your age and the amount of time you have lived in Canada.

Old Age Security (OAS) Funded by the federal government with general tax revenues, the **Old Age Security (OAS)** program provides a monthly retirement benefit based on your age and the amount of time you have lived in Canada. Benefits include the basic OAS pension and the Guaranteed Income Supplement (GIS). The basic OAS pension is not based on income; it's a taxable, fully indexed benefit (adjusted quarterly to keep pace with inflation) available to all Canadian residents 65 and older. Your employment history is not a factor in determining eligibility, nor do you have to be "retired" (you can continue to work and still receive the benefit). To get the basic OAS benefit, you have to apply for it at least six months prior to reaching age 65. In recent years, OAS benefits have been "clawed back" meaning that higher-income pensioners have to pay back all or part of the benefit at tax time. HR can offer their assistance to pending retirees to make sure they are aware of the necessity to complete their applications well ahead of time.

Guaranteed Income Supplement (GIS) Guaranteed income supplement (GIS) is an additional monthly benefit paid to residents of Canada who receive a basic, full or partial OAS pension and who have little or no other income. If you are 65 or older and your retirement income is low enough, you may qualify for this tax-free income supplement offered by the federal government. Generally, how much you receive is calculated and pro-rated based on your income from the previous year.

Employment Insurance (EI)
Employment Insurance (EI) provides temporary financial assistance for unemployed Canadians while they look for work or upgrade their skills. Eligibility depends on the individuals previous work record.

Employment Insurance (EI) **Employment Insurance (EI)** provides temporary financial assistance for unemployed Canadians while they look for work or upgrade their skills. Canadians who are sick, pregnant, or caring for a newborn or adopted child, as well as those who must care for a family member who is seriously ill with a significant risk of death, may also be assisted by Employment Insurance. There is usually a two-week waiting period before any benefits can be received. Workers fired for misconduct, or who quit their job, are ineligible to collect EI.

The Basic Benefit As of 2006, the basic EI benefit rate was 55 percent of average insured earnings up to a maximum amount of $413 per week. The EI payment is a taxable income. Regular benefits can be paid from *14 to a maximum of 45 weeks.* The number of weeks of benefits that may be paid are determined at the start date of the benefit period, based on the unemployment rate in your region and the amount of insurable hours you have accumulated in the qualifying period. The insurable hours are calculated based on how many hours you have worked over the last 52 weeks. The allowable payment is the same for all EI benefits paid, however, the number of weeks the benefit is to be paid will differ.

Compassionate Care Benefits Compassionate care benefits are available if an employee has to be away from work temporarily to provide care or support to a family member who is gravely ill with a significant risk of death. Benefits may be paid up to a maximum of *six weeks.*

Maternity benefits are payable to the birth mother or surrogate mother for a maximum of *15 weeks. Parental benefits* are payable either to the biological or adoptive parents while they are caring for a newborn or an adopted child, up to a maximum of *35 weeks. Sickness benefits* may be paid up to *15 weeks* to a person who is unable to work because of sickness, injury, or quarantine. You may receive *up to 50 weeks* when regular EI benefits are combined with maternity, parental, and sickness benefits.

Employees pay premiums on all earnings up to the annual maximum salary of $39,000. In 2006, the deductions for employees were calculated as $1.87 for every $100 of salary until $39,000 was reached, for a maximum contribution of $729.30 for the year. The employer deduction was $2.62 per $100 of insurable earnings. The 2006 EI premium rate for *Quebec residents* is less at $1.53 for every $100 of salary for a maximum contribution amount of $596.70 per year, and for employers it was $2.14 per $100 of insurable earnings. The rates for Quebec are lower because their provincial government offers its own parental benefits, thus reducing the burden on the EI system.

Employers who provide employees with disability coverage for short-term illness or injury, are eligible for a reduction in their EI premium rate. This is because if an employee were to become ill, other sources of income would be available to them, and they would not need to use EI, thus reducing the financial load on EI.

Supplemental unemployment benefits (SUB) are closely related to EI, but they are not required by law. A provision in some union contracts requires organizations to contribute to a fund that supplements the EI available to employees. The purpose is to top up employees' employment insurance (EI) benefits during a period of unemployment because of training, sickness, accident or disability, maternity or parental leave, or a temporary stoppage of work. Organizations who implement such a plan need to register and coordinate their plan with the government. For example, the benefit payable by the organization under a SUB plan is a weekly amount, which combined with the EI benefit and any other earnings from employment, will equal 95 percent of the employee's normal authorized prorated annual salary at the commencement of the leave. The amount of top-up will depend on what the organization decides to offer, or whatever can be negotiated if there is a union involved.

Workers' compensation
Security benefits provided to persons injured on the job.

Workers' Compensation Workers' compensation provides benefits to persons injured on the job. A mandatory, no-fault, work injury insurance system, Workers' Compensation is managed by provincial Workers' Compensation Boards (WCB) and is funded entirely by employers who pay premiums that vary depending on the general risk of the industry. Figure 12-5 provides an example of some of the different industries and their respective rates determined by the Workplace Safety and Insurance Board (WSIB) of Ontario. Industries that are more dangerous tend to have higher premiums attached to them. Individual employers may not have to pay the premium rate posted. If an employer in a dangerous industry, such as logging, takes safety measures that result in a much reduced injury frequency compared to another organization that does not take safety seriously and who has multiple accidents, will see a reduction in the premium they have to pay.

Figure 12-5 *2006 Premium Rates Example—Ontario WSIB*

Rate Group	Description	2006 Premium Rate ($)	2005 Premium Rate ($)	Percent Change
030	Logging	11.43	11.16	2.4%
033	Mill Products and Forestry Services	8.22	7.67	7.2%
036	Veneers, Plywood, and Wood Preservation	4.41	4.58	–3.7%
110	Gold Mines	8.53	7.80	9.4%
134	Aggregates	6.11	5.48	11.5%
159	Livestock Farms	7.10	6.45	10.1%
184	Poultry Farms and Agricultural Services	2.45	2.19	11.9%
190	Landscaping and Related Services	4.77	4.69	1.7%
207	Meat and Fish Products	4.35	4.06	7.1%

The 2006 average premium rate for Schedule 1 employers is $2.26 for every $100 of insurable earnings, an increase of 3 percent over the average rate for 2005.

This 3-percent average rate increase does not mean rates will increase for all employers.

Premium rates for individual rate groups have been recalculated based primarily on injury frequency and claims costs for individual rate groups.

The annual maximum earnings ceiling for 2006 is $69,400. Earnings over the annual maximum are not insured.

Source: Workplace Safety and Insurance Board, 2006 Premium Rates, May 18, 2006.

WCBs exist to promote safe workplaces and to protect employers and injured workers through a sustainable accident insurance program. The workers' compensation system provides cash benefits, medical care, and rehabilitation services to employees for injuries or illnesses occurring within the scope of their employment. Employees who need to use this benefit will be paid according to the schedule in their respective jurisdiction. For example, in Saskatchewan, employees who need to use this benefit can expect to receive 90 percent of their probable take-home pay to a maximum that is set each year. If the maximum gross employment earnings allowed under the Workers' Compensation Act was $55,000 per year in Saskatchewan, then the maximum a recipient could receive would be $1,057.69 per week. Figure 12-6 demonstrates how such a calculation would be made.

Provincial medicare Canada's publicly funded health-care system provides essential and affordable health-care services for all Canadians, regardless of their income. It is administered on a provincial or territorial basis, within guidelines set by the federal government.

Provincial Medicare Canada's publicly funded health-care system provides essential and affordable health-care services for all Canadians, regardless of their income. **Medicare** is administered on a provincial or territorial basis, within guidelines set by the federal government. Certain provinces (British Columbia, Alberta, and Ontario) require health-care premiums for services. In these provinces either a health tax is levied, or a premium. Employers are expected to make such deductions from an employee's pay and remit the payment to the government. Larger employers typically cover such expenses as a benefit, or if there is a union, it can sometimes be negotiated as an additional benefit. Under the Canada Health Act, however, health services cannot be denied due to financial inability to pay premiums.

Figure 12-6 *Example of Benefit Payable Under Saskatchewan WCB Rules*

EFFECTIVE March 1, 2005

BASED ON CLAIMANT BIRTH DATE: 01/01/1960

CALCULATION FORMULA—Gross earnings less probable deductions (income tax payable, CPP, EI premiums) = net earnings or take-home pay

A married individual with two dependants and a weekly gross employment salary of $900.00

Weekly gross or before-tax salary	$900.00
Weekly after-tax salary	696.43
less Canadian Pension Plan	–35.79
less Employment Insurance	–14.63
equals probable net employment earnings	$646.01

WCB weekly wage-loss benefits = 90 percent of probable net employment earnings (0.9 × 646.01) = $581.41 weekly payment

Under the terms of the Canada Health Act, the provinces provide all residents with health insurance cards, which entitle the bearer to receive free medical care for almost all procedures. Patients are free to choose their own doctor, hospital, etc. Health institutions are either private and non-profit (such as university hospitals) or provincially run (such as Quebec's CLSC system).

Canada's health-care system provides diagnostic, treatment, and preventive services to every Canadian regardless of their income level. All provinces and territories

Canada's health-care system is among the best in the world, providing diagnostic, treatment, and preventive services to every Canadian regardless of their income level.

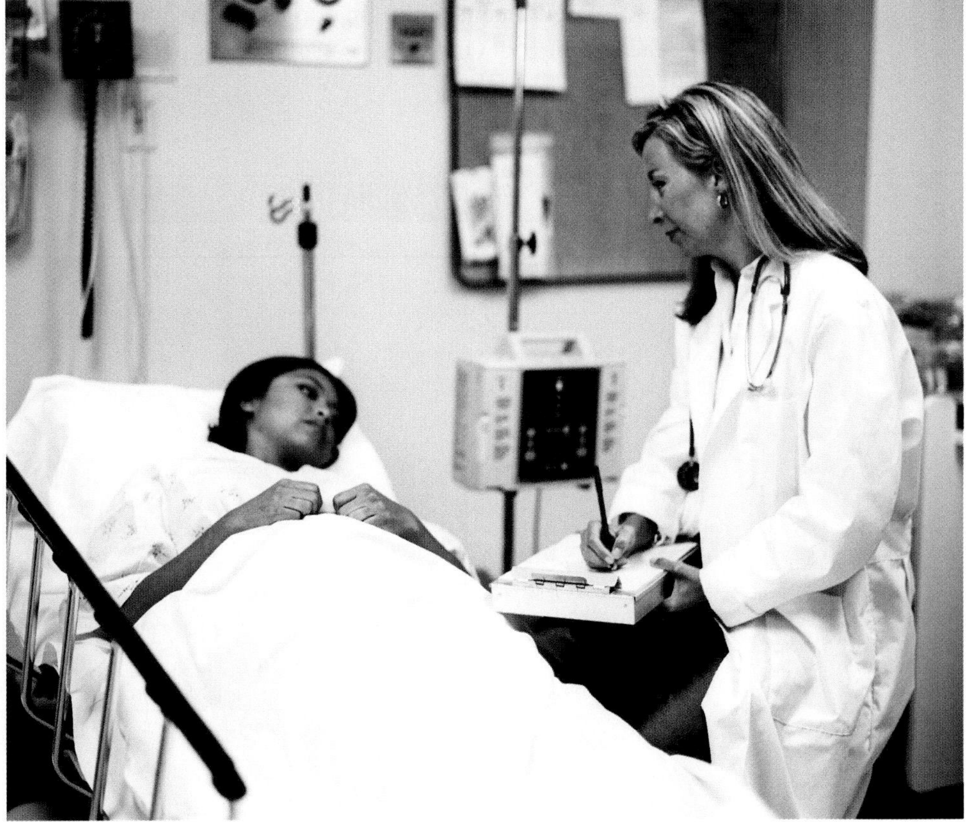

Source: © 2006 JupiterImages and its Licensors. All Rights Reserved.

provide some level of public drug benefit coverage to its constituents. For example, an individual who is in hospital will be provided with the necessary medications; vaccinations for children; cancer treatment. However, provinces do not cover over-the-counter medications and some employers may have an extended medical plan to cover for such expenses. Low income seniors in Canada, as well as those on social assistance, have drug coverage for certain out-of-pocket expenses. Dental care is not covered by any government insurance plans. Canadians rely on their employers, individual private insurance, or simply pay cash themselves for dental treatments. The range of services for vision care coverage is widely varied among the provinces. Generally, vision care is covered (cataract surgery, diabetic vision care, some laser eye surgeries required as a result of disease); the main exception is the standard vision test, which patients are required to pay 100 percent of the cost. Naturopathic services are covered in some cases, but homeopathic services are generally not covered. Chiropractic is partially covered in some provinces and cosmetic procedures are not typically covered.

Retirement Benefits

3 The aging of the workforce in many countries is affecting retirement planning for individuals and retirement plan costs for employers and governments. By 2030 seniors (Canadians over the age of 65), will form 20 percent of the population, up from 12 percent in 1990. Figure 12-7 shows the increase in the portion of Canadians age 65 and older for the period 1900–2030. The income security of future retirees is endangered by the shift to more precarious jobs, the greater fragility of workplace pension plans, and the limited scope of public pensions. Surprisingly, with the issues associated with financial support for retirees, there has been a steady decline in the age of retirement and a majority of Canadians do not plan on working beyond the age of 65.[8] Of retired Canadians, 38 percent of women and 27 percent of men

Figure 12-7 *Canada's Aging Population*

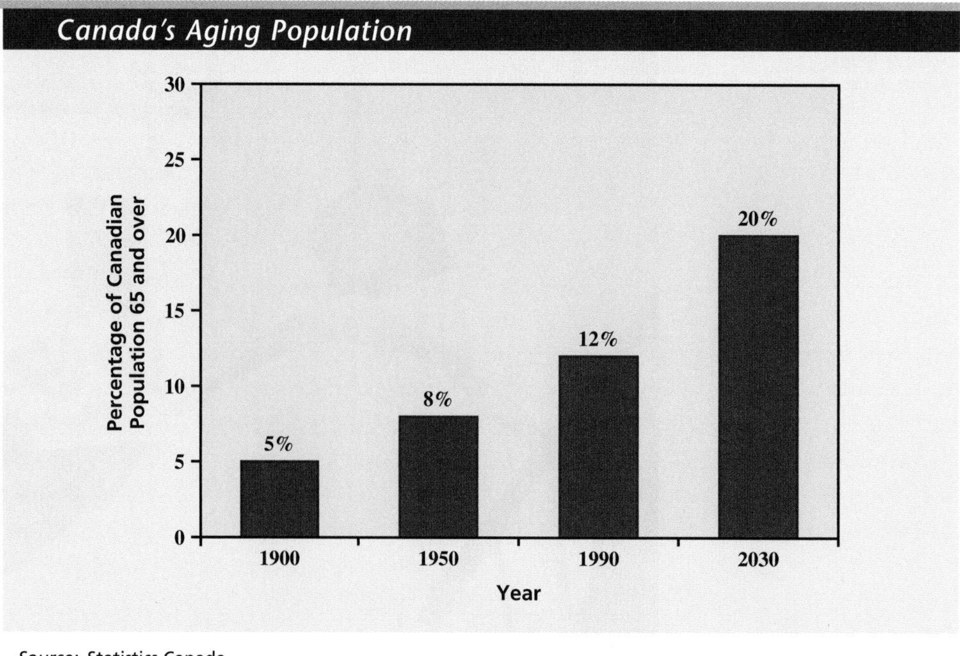

Source: Statistics Canada.

left the labour force before age 60. With more people retiring earlier and living longer, retirement benefits are becoming a greater concern for employers, employees, and retired employees.[9]

For unionized workers, participation in workplace pensions is widespread; about 80 percent of unionized workers belong to workplace pension plans. For non-unionized workers, participation is much more limited with only about 37 percent belonging to workplace pension programs.[10] Coverage ranges from almost 100 percent for public sector workers to about 30 percent for employees of private sector firms. Even though most unions negotiate pension plans for its members, company pension plans are also positively associated with size of employer and earnings and education level.[11] The importance of having a company pension plan cannot be underestimated, as it provides retirees with the income necessary to maintain a lifestyle that is comfortable when integrated with government-sponsored plans such as CPP/QPP and OAS benefits.

Retirement Benefits and Age Discrimination

Forcing an employee to retire by reason of age is considered to be a human rights issue and is legislated by human rights legislation. In Quebec, provisions dealing specifically with mandatory retirement are also contained in labour standards legislation. It is against the law to force Canadians to retire in Nunavut, Yukon, Northwest Territories, Alberta, Manitoba, Quebec, Prince Edward Island, New Brunswick, and Ontario. Under human rights legislation at the federal level, and in British Columbia, Nova Scotia, and Saskatchewan, older employees are protected against discrimination based on age until they reach age 65. This means that employees who are 65 or over cannot file a complaint for age discrimination if they are forced to retire. The discussion on abolishing mandatory retirement continues, and it is expected that Canada will abolish mandatory retirement across all jurisdictions in the future.

For jurisdictions that have abolished mandatory retirement, employers have had to develop policies to comply with retirement regulations. In many employer pension plans, "normal retirement" is the age at which employees can retire and collect full pension benefits. Employers must decide whether individuals who continue to work past normal retirement age (perhaps 65) should receive the full benefits package, especially pension credits. Future changes in pension legislation may increase the age for full benefits past 65. Modifications in policies are likely. Despite the removal of mandatory retirement provisions in many provinces and territories, the age at which individuals retire has continued to decline in Canada.

Early Retirement Many pension plans include provisions for early retirement to give workers voluntary opportunities to leave their jobs. After spending 25–30 years working for the same employer, individuals may wish to use their talents in other areas. Phased-in and part-time retirements offer alternatives that individuals and firms are using.

Some employers use early retirement buyout programs to cut back their workforces and reduce costs. Employers must take care to make these early retirement programs truly voluntary. Forcing workers to take advantage of an early retirement buyout program could result in wrongful dismissal or age discrimination cases.

Retiree Benefits Some employers choose to offer their retirees benefits, which may be paid for by the retirees, the company, or both. The costs of such coverage have risen dramatically. As a result, more than half of Canadian employers, faced with increasing health-care costs, plan to cut the level of benefits they provide to retired employees. A study conducted by Hewitt Associates found that most cuts will primarily affect future retirees. Retirees will be forced to dip into their pension income to help pay for their drug, dental, and vision care benefits.

One problem with retiree pension benefits that some firms in the private and public sectors are facing is unfunded pension liabilities. The Hospitals of Ontario Pension Plan had an unfunded liability of $227 million at the end of 2004. The Ontario Teachers' Pension Plan estimated a shortfall of $19.4 billion in 2005 and in British Columbia, the Public Sector Pension Plan covering 24 000 government employees reported an unfunded liability of $767 million in 2005.[12]

Unfortunately, most Canadians have inadequate savings and retirement benefits for funding their retirements. Over half (56 percent), say they are not saving enough money for retirement right now. According to a study by the Employee Benefit Research Institute, almost 70 percent of individuals over age 55 have less than $250,000 in savings and investments.[13] Therefore, they are heavily dependent on employer-provided retirement benefits. But many employers with fewer than 100 workers do not offer retirement benefits.

Employer-Sponsored Pension Plans

Retirement plans sponsored by your employer can help provide a source of income in retirement. The types of plans available include: defined-benefit plan, defined-contribution plan, group RRSP, and deferred profit-sharing plan. Organizations are not required to offer pension plans to employees, and fewer than half of Canadian workers are covered by them. Small firms offer **pension plans** less often than do large ones.

Pension plan
Retirement program established and funded by the employer and employees.

Defined-Benefit Pension Plans (DBPP) A "traditional" pension plan, in which the employer traditionally makes the contributions and the employees are guaranteed a fixed benefit upon retirement. Sometimes, employees are required to contribute to the plan. It all depends on how the employer has set up the plan. The employer is responsible for the funding of a **defined-benefit pension plan's** liabilities, or promised benefits. The benefit is based on years of service, age, and either final earnings or a benefit multiplier. For example, assume an organization chooses to calculate the benefit on the last five years of average earnings of $56,000, multiplied by 2 percent, multiplied by 15 years of service then the annual pension would be $56,000 × 2% × 15 years of service for an annual pension of $16,800, or a monthly pension of $1,400.

Defined-benefit pension plan (DBPP)
Retirement program in which an employee is promised a pension amount based on age and service.

The employees' contributions are based on actuarial calculations on the *benefits* to be received by the employees after retirement and the *methods* used to determine such benefits. A defined-benefit plan gives employees greater assurance of benefits and greater predictability in the amount of benefits that will be available for retirement. Defined-benefit plans are often preferred by workers with longer service, as well as by small-business owners, and are often negotiated by unions.[14]

If the funding in a defined-benefit plan is insufficient, the employer may have to make up the shortfall. Therefore, many employers have dropped defined-benefit plans in favour of defined-contribution plans so that their contribution liabilities are known.[15] As discussed previously a number of public-sector employers with defined-benefit plans are finding that there are significant shortfalls in funding. Air Canada is an example of an organization that has managed to keep its defined-benefit plan, but has had to make adjustments in order to ensure its viability. They were granted permission to amortize their existing deficiencies over ten years instead of the five years provided for by law. However, the strategy that Air Canada has adopted has not been well received by many, highlighting the need for better corporate governance and more transparent corporate bookkeeping.[16]

Defined-contribution pension plan (DCPP) Retirement program in which the employer makes an annual payment to an employee's pension account.

Defined-Contribution Pension Plans (DCPP) Also known as money purchase plans, **defined-contribution pension plans** allow both the employee and the employer to make specific annual contributions to an account based on the employee's earnings. The pension is determined by what has accumulated over the years through these contributions and the interest that has been generated. Unfortunately, the exact amount of the pension will not be known until retirement. At retirement, the accumulated value of the plan must be used to purchase either a life annuity or, with some pension plans, a Life Income Fund (LIF). Because these plans hinge on the investment returns on the previous contributions, which can vary according to profitability or other factors, employees' retirement benefits are somewhat less secure and predictable. But because of their structure, these plans are sometimes preferred by younger, shorter-service employees.

In a study conducted by Watson Wyatt and the Conference Board of Canada, 18 percent of the CFOs surveyed (n = 68) said they had terminated at least one of their plans or converted to a defined-contribution plan because of the shortfalls in funding for defined-benefit plans. Another 11 percent were in the process of making changes. A recent merger of Agricore and United Grain Growers resulted in a switch to a defined-contribution pension arrangement. Employees were unhappy with the previous defined-benefit plan, and the majority of the employees perceive the DCPP to be an advantage. Education and training programs have helped the employees to make sound retirement investment decisions.[17]

Many plan sponsors who established DCPPs in recent years believed that, in contrast to DB plans, these arrangements would simplify administration, control costs, and limit their liability. Evidence thus far suggests that these plans bring their own challenges and risks. As the DCPP environment matures further, it will be important for all DCPP stakeholders to monitor these and other emerging issues.

Group RRSPs A group RRSP is a collection of individual RRSPs administered by the employer for the employees of a company

Group RRSPs Employers may opt for a group RRSP over a pension plan. Employers sponsor a collection of individual RRSPs on behalf of their employees. The employees then contribute to the RRSP that is administered by the employer. Automatic payroll deductions are made. **Group RRSPs** are flexible because employees are typically offered a choice of how the funds are invested and how much to contribute. The biggest difference between contributing to a group RRSP or contributing to an individual RRSP is that with the group RRSP, the contributions are deducted at source and the employee is not taxed on these contributions. In other words, you get an immediate tax deduction. With some group plans, the employer may choose to encourage their employees to contribute to the group RRSP by matching contributions by a certain percentage. If the employer matches your contributions by 5 or 10 percent it's like earning an additional 5 or 10 percent on your investments.

If the employer contributes to the employee's RRSP, it assists in attracting and retaining employees. One of the biggest advantages is the fact that the employer is not liable for guaranteeing a specific amount of income when an employee retires.

Deferred profit-sharing plan (DPSP) A plan that gives employees a share in the profits of the company that is paid out as a pension at retirement

Deferred Profit-Sharing Plans (DPSP) Some employers use **deferred profit-sharing plans** to help build employee retirement funds. The funds are secured from company profits. With a DPSP, an employer makes contributions on behalf of an employee. Both the contributions and any investment income earned remains tax-sheltered until retirement. When the employee retires, the funds can either be transferred to an RRSP or they can select a suitable retirement income option. Employees can withdraw money prior to retiring, however they will have to pay income tax on it unless it is transferred into an RRSP, Registered Retirement Income Fund (RRIF), or other employer pension plan.

Many smaller employers do not offer pension plans for a number of reasons. The primary reason, in addition to their cost, is the administrative burdens imposed by government legislation.

Contributory plan
Pension plan in which the money for pension benefits is paid in by both employees and employers.

Non-contributory plan
Pension plan in which all the funds for pension benefits are provided by the employer.

Vesting
Right of employees to receive certain benefits from their pension plans.

Locked-in
Locked-in means that the contributions to the plan cannot be withdrawn by the employee.

Portability
A pension plan feature that allows employees to move their pension benefits from one employer to another.

Pension Terms and Concepts Pension plans can be either contributory or non-contributory. In a **contributory plan,** money for pension benefits is paid in by both employees and the employer. In a **non-contributory plan,** the employer provides all the funds for pension benefits. As expected, the non-contributory plans are generally preferred by employees and labour unions.

Certain rights are attached to employee pension plans. Various laws and provisions have been passed to address the rights of employees to receive benefits from their pension plans. Called **vesting,** this right assures employees of a certain pension, provided they work a minimum number of years. In Canada, the normal vesting period is two years. If employees resign or are terminated before they have been employed for the required time, no pension rights accrue to them except the funds they have contributed. If employees stay the allotted time, they retain their pension rights and receive the funds contributed by both the employer and themselves. Once the vesting period has been reached, the pension funds contributed by both the employer and themselves are then **locked-in,** meaning the contributions to the plan cannot be withdrawn by the employee and that the employee can receive the benefit of those contributions only in the form of a pension at retirement.

Another feature of employee pensions in Canada is **portability.** If an employee leaves their employer to which they have made pension contributions, and these funds are vested and locked-in, employees can move their pension benefits to either their new employer if they have a registered pension plan, a locked-in RRSP, or they can leave the funds with the employer until such time as they want to move them, or to draw on their pension. The danger with leaving a pension with an employer you have left is that you have little control over what is going on with your money, and you may forget about the employer years later.

Pension Plan Legislation Pension plan legislation is very complex, and a full discussion is beyond the scope of this text. The purpose of pension legislation is to regulate private pension plans so that employees who put money into them or depend on a pension for retirement funds actually receive the money when they retire. Legislation ensures that valuations be conducted by organization's actuaries to ensure the funding and the solvency of the pension plans.

When surpluses in pension plans exist, the question that is often asked is who do the surpluses belong to when a pension plan is in partial wind-up? A recent case heard before the Supreme Court of Canada makes it clear that surpluses belong to the plan members. The case involving the *Monsanto* pension plan came to an end on July 29, 2004, when the Supreme Court of Canada dismissed the appeal of Monsanto and the ACPM (Association of Canadian Pension Management) concerning the distribution of the surplus to plan members terminated during a partial wind-up of a defined-benefit pension plan. Monsanto and the ACPM sought to overturn an Ontario Court of Appeal ruling that held that terminated DBPP members have the right to a portion of the surplus that "relates" to them in a partial wind-up. The Supreme Court upheld that ruling in a decision that has enormous implications for DBPP sponsors. According to industry experts, the *Monsanto* decision has the potential to destabilize and reduce Canadian private-sector pension coverage.[18]

Every province continues to introduce various changes to pension legislation. For example, Manitoba and Alberta have introduced significant changes to their pension standards acts. Manitoba has allowed unlocking of pension funds, following Saskatchewan's lead in 2002. However, there are certain restrictions for each of these provisions.[19] There are numerous examples of other provinces that have introduced differing pieces of legislation. What is important is that human resources professionals need to ensure that they work with pension consultants who will help them navigate this very complicated and everchanging landscape of legislation.

Health-Care Benefits

4 Employers provide a variety of health-care and medical benefits, usually through insurance coverage. The most common plans cover extended health care including prescription drugs, vision care expenses, and dental for employees and their dependants. Basic health-care insurance to cover both normal and major medical expenses is desired by most employees. Ninety percent of Canadians have some form of drug plan coverage. However, most must pay a deductible or premium to ensure coverage. Dental insurance is also important to many employees. Some dental plans include orthodontic coverage, which is a major expense for some families. Some employers also offer vision insurance through their health benefits. A larger percentage of the vision care plans require employees to pay all or part of the coverage costs. Most firms do not cover the costs for Lasik and other elective surgeries to correct vision.

Many organizations offer a benefits plan to their employees, which usually includes reimbursement of prescription drugs. Unfortunately, health costs continue to climb forcing employers to revisit these plans and implement cuts by way of reduced reimbursement and increased costs to the employees.

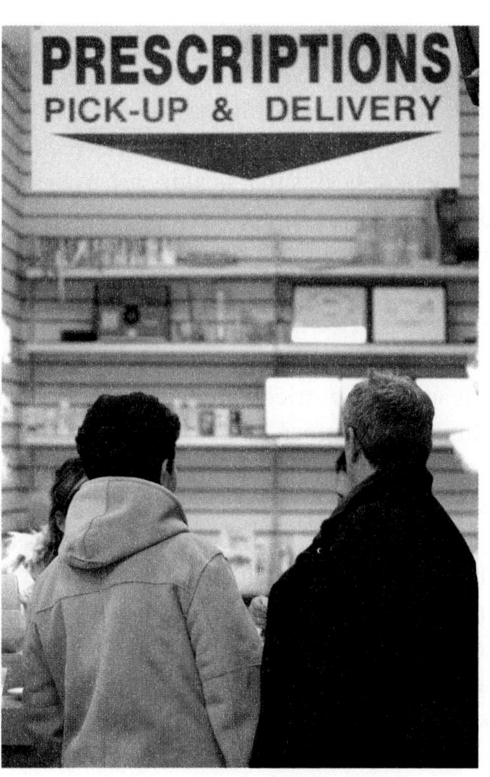

Source: Natalia Bratslavsky/ShutterStock

Increases in Health Benefits Costs

For several decades, the costs of health care have escalated at a rate well above the rates of inflation and changes in workers' earnings. Since the mid-1990s, employer health-care benefits costs have been increasing significantly faster than inflation or workers' earnings. In a compensation survey conducted by the Conference Board of Canada, more than two-thirds of respondents expected to spend more on health benefits. For 38 percent of unionized survey respondents, containing benefit costs ranked as one of their top three bargaining issues. Mercer Human Resource Consulting estimates that employers may spend up to 8 percent of their payroll on these benefits by 2007. Forty-eight percent of survey respondents identified drug expenditures as the primary factor for increasing costs and 63 percent ranked pharmaceuticals in the top three. Dental care ranked second, and hospital and medical services came in third as a contributing factor.[20]

There are a number of reasons for increases to employee health benefits. In general the trend factors provided for increases result from:[21]

- Double-digit inflation of drug plans
- Increased introduction of new drugs in the market with increased media attention educating the consumer on potential drug therapies
- Increased use of services
- New technology and services
- Changes in the mix of services
- Shifting costs from the public to private sector.
- Wellness programs that have not been embraced
- Aging population

As a result of the large increases, many employers find that dealing with health-care benefits is time-consuming and expensive. This is especially frustrating for employers who have found that many employees seem to take their health benefits for granted. Consequently, a growing number of firms, particularly smaller ones, have asked, "Why are we offering these benefits anyway?" and have answered the question by discontinuing or dramatically cutting health benefits.

In 2002, more than $85 billion was spent for health care in Canada with 70 percent of the costs paid for by the publicly funded system. Corporate Canada and individuals paid the remaining 30 percent. Over the last few years with the rapid growth of small offices and home offices there has been an increase in individuals purchasing their own medical and dental coverage. These individual plans, however, only account for 15 percent of the total of all private coverage, while Canadian employers are expected to pay the remaining 85 percent this year.[22]

Retirees Health Benefits Costs Another group whose benefits costs are rising is retirees whose former employers still provide health benefit coverage. For instance, at General Motors, there are 2.4 retired employees for every active employee. Increasing the problem at GM is that health-care usage rates for older retirees is significantly higher than it is for current employees. The shocking statistic is that GM has to add $1,400 per vehicle for employee and retiree health-care costs, which costs more than the steel used to build the cars.[23]

A study conducted by Hewitt Associates found that organizations plan to reduce retiree health-care benefits in the next three years plan. Some of the initiatives they plan to implement are to have stricter eligibility requirements meaning that employees will require a minimum number of years of service before they are qualified for post-retirement health-care benefits. There will also be reductions in medical coverage, including eliminating medical services, increasing deductibles/co-payments, and capping certain health-care services. Increased cost-sharing will be implemented and there will be an increase in flexible retiree benefit plans. As a way to control costs, many companies are now offering flexible retiree benefit programs. Rather than fund the benefits, monetary allowances are being made available to retirees. Hewitt Associates recommends that before making any changes to retiree plans, organizations must first assess their current retiree health-care program, analyze the impact any change would make on costs and on employees, and develop an integrated strategy that supports their overall benefit objectives.[24]

Making such drastic changes to retiree benefits raises troubling ethical concerns. Many of the retirees worked for their employers for 20, 30, 40, or more years. Yet the reward for their long and loyal service increasingly is a reduction in health-care benefits.

Controlling Health-Care Benefits Costs

Employers offering health-care benefits are taking a number of approaches to controlling their costs. The most prominent ones are changing co-payments and employee contributions, determining the source of medical conditions and offering health promotion strategies to address the problems when feasible. While the U.S. has adopted a strategy of managed health care, Canada has not fully accepted the notion of managed health care, and its potential for a two-tiered health-care system. This may not be the case for long, as Canadian governments continue to look for more innovative ways of controlling health-care benefit costs. Health spending accounts are also increasingly being used as a cost-control measure.

Co-payment
Strategy requiring employees to pay a portion of the cost of the benefit premiums.

Changing Co-Payments, Employee Contributions and Limiting Coverage As health insurance costs rise, employers have tried to shift some of those costs to employees. The **co-payment** strategy requires employees to pay a portion of the cost of the premiums towards their benefits. Other strategies have included reducing the amount of reimbursement provided on certain benefits, as well as introducing a limit on the amount of benefit to be received and implementing a deductible. Another way to control the rising costs of benefits is to limit the coverage to only the employee, excluding family members. If for example XYZ Inc. offers both health and dental benefits, the premium may be split 50–50: meaning that the company pays for one half of the monthly premium, and the other half is deducted from the employee's paycheque. Additionally there may be a deductible that must be satisfied before reimbursement is made on a claim, and the reimbursement might only be made at 80 percent, after a deductible of $100 per person has been satisfied. Finally coverage may only be for $1,500 per person per year for dental, and a maximum of $1,000 per person for prescriptions. Therefore, if Joe goes to the dentist and the bill is $400, after the deductible of $100, there is $300 left to be paid, but reimbursement is only at 80 percent, then Joe will be reimbursed $240 of the $400 bill ($400 – $100 = $300 × 80% = $240). After this visit, Joe only has $1,100 left in dental coverage for the year, and since the deductible is satisfied, all future bills, up to the maximum, will be reimbursed at 80 percent. Prescriptions would work the same.

Employers are continually looking at ways to cut costs, and often times may limit the use of certain benefits. Prescription drugs are one area where significant savings can be made by putting a cap on pharmacy dispensing fees, allowing only generic drugs to be dispensed, or not allowing certain drugs to be covered.

Health Promotion Strategies A more innovative approach to cutting benefit costs is to determine what particular medical conditions employees are being treated for, and then to develop targeted health promoting strategies. For example, Enbridge Gas Distribution worked with its benefits carrier to identify the prescription drugs its employees used most frequently. Enbridge then designed health and wellness activities in the workplace that addressed the conditions underlying the use of those drugs. Another organization, Delta Hotels, focuses on the philosophy that engaged and satisfied employees are also healthier, and on creating the right culture. The company's prescription drug costs are less than half that of the industry average.[25]

Managed Health Care A system used extensively in the U.S. is the concept of **managed health care.** Managed health care consists of approaches that monitor and reduce medical costs through restrictions and market system alternatives. Managed health-care plans emphasize primary and preventive care, the use of specific providers who will charge lower prices, restrictions on certain kinds of treatment, and prices negotiated with hospitals and physicians.

Managed health care Approaches that monitor and reduce medical costs through restrictions and market system alternatives.

One managed health-care approach in the U.S. is the **preferred provider organization (PPO),** a health-care provider that contracts with an employer or an employer group to supply health-care services to employees at a competitive rate. Employees have the freedom to go to other providers if they want to pay the differences in costs. *Point-of-service plans* are somewhat similar, offering financial incentives to encourage employees to use designated medical providers.

Preferred provider organization (PPO) A health-care provider that contracts with an employer group to supply health-care services to employees at a competitive rate.

Another prominent managed health-care approach in the U.S. is a **health maintenance organization (HMO),** which provides services for a fixed period on a prepaid basis. The HMO emphasizes both prevention and correction. An employer contracts with an HMO and its staff of physicians and medical personnel to furnish complete medical care, except for hospitalization. The employer pays a flat rate per enrolled employee or per enrolled family. The covered individuals may then go to the HMO for health care as often as they need to. Supplemental policies for hospitalization are also provided.

Health maintenance organization (HMO) Plan that provides services for a fixed period on a pre-paid basis.

The U.S. model of managed health care is not without its faults. Critics contend that competing HMOs spend millions of dollars on business matters such as conducting destructive price wars and acquiring other businesses instead of focusing on innovation in health care. Many employees do not like having to go through a "primary-care physician" before being able to see medical specialists.

The use of managed health care may continue to grow in Canada because of increasingly long waiting lists for surgery, increased government interference in the relationship between patients and doctors, tax increases, and general inferior medicine with less choice for patients, which stems from the shortage of doctors in Canada. In June 2005 the Supreme Court of Canada struck down a Quebec law banning private medical insurance. There are concerns that Canada's health-care system could eventually result in a two-tiered health-care system.[26] The concern with a two-tiered health-care system is that only those who can afford medical care will be able to enjoy such services, while others will not.

In a recent study conducted by the National Forum on Health in 2004, participants noted that Canada's health-care system was important to them and that the "universality of the system helped distinguish Canada from the United States in a way that showed us to be a more generous and compassionate society." Having said that they also feel Canada's health system is threatened and has the potential to be Americanized with user fees and a growing gap between the rich and the poor. [27] Figure 12-8 presents a reality of what a two-tiered system in Canada could mean.

Health Spending Account (HSA) A **health spending account (HSA)** or a defined-contribution health plan is a tax-effective feature that complements an employee's regular benefit plan by providing them with additional choice for managing health-related expenses. HSA plans are emerging as an important cost-control measure that addresses the needs of both plan sponsors and their employees.

Health spending account (HSA) One that provides employer financial contributions to employees to cover their own health-related expenses.

Essentially, an HSA works like a bank account. The employer and the participating employee group decide on an annual HSA amount per employee. The amount, in the form of credits, is calculated the same way for every employee—either as a percentage of salary, a flat amount per employee or a combination of both. Each

Figure 12-8 *Managed Health Care and a Two-Tiered Health System*

Two Tier Health Care Explained
NUMBER TEN IS NEXT
1
2
10
©Mike Constable 10 05 union-art.com

Source: Mike Constable/union-art.com

employee receives his or her own HSA account with HSA credits being allocated on a predetermined schedule by the employer. The employee then draws upon the credits to pay for health-related expenses incurred by themselves, their spouse, or eligible dependants. For instance, assume an employer sets aside $250 a month for each employee. One employee may choose orthodontics costing $230 a month, and use her remaining $20 for purchasing additional life insurance. Another employee may choose family dental plan coverage costing $480 a month, and have the additional $230 a month deducted from his paycheque.

In addition to the cost savings advantages, there are many other advantages achieved by HSAs. HSAs can also positively impact employee morale since employees have more control in making decisions that affect their own health. The employer is perceived as a facilitator by making a defined monetary contribution to the HSA. Since employees become more involved in making their own decisions on what to pay for, it will result in a better understanding of benefit costs. This type of benefit may also assist to attract and retain high-calibre employees, leading to low turnover rates and an overall positive view of the employer.

HSAs provide taxation advantages to both employees and employers. HSA benefits payments are not subject to federal income tax. Quebec taxes HSA benefits, which can be included in the medical expenses tax credit. The employer can deduct reimbursements for eligible medical expenses and applicable administration fees. However, taxation advantages are restricted by a number of factors: the employer's financial capacity to fund the plan and Canada Revenue Agency legislation, which states that the plan must qualify as a plan of insurance, meaning that unused credits are returned to the employer at the end of the plan year or carryforward period. Under this legislation, employees lose non-taxable dollars. As well, there is no real advantage to an employee using payroll deductions to contribute to an HSA, since the employee is taxed on the gross amount of salary paid, including the amount withheld through payroll deductions for employee-funded credits.[28]

Many employers offer programs to educate employees about health-care costs and how to reduce them. Newsletters, formal classes, and many other approaches are all designed to help employees understand why health-care costs are increasing and what they can do to control them. Some employers even have *wellness programs* offering financial incentives to improve health habits. These programs, discussed more in Chapter 13, reward employees who stop smoking, lose weight, and participate in exercise programs, among other activities.

The HR Perspective discusses a study on employee satisfaction with health benefits and retirement. It also highlights the educational aspects of their programs, as well as their feelings on cost cutting of programs.

HR *Perspective*

Research on Satisfaction with Health Benefits

A study of over 1200 employees across Canada entitled *2003 Pulse on Plan Members* sought to determine plan members satisfaction with their retirement savings plan and health benefits. The survey looked at what motivated plan members, their awareness and perceptions of the plans, their attitudes, preferences, and commitment level, as well as their behaviour and loyalty.

The survey reported the following with respect to pension plans:

- Eighty percent of respondents were satisfied with their employee retirement savings plan and the same number claimed to have a good understanding of the plan.
- Sixty-five percent said they would probably not take a job with a company that didn't have an employee retirement savings plan.
- Forty-seven percent said they would consider leaving their current employer if offered the same salary and a better plan.
- Seventy-five percent use benefits statements (75 percent) or plan brochures (71 percent) to improve their understanding of their plans. The least commonly used sources were union/association member sources (36 percent) and the Internet (29 percent).
- Forty-nine percent of Canadians are offered retirement planning educational seminars through their employers, but only 42 percent of those offered these seminars reported actually attending them.
- Sixty-six percent of plan members expect their employers to ante up should the plan be in a deficit position.
- Ninety percent of defined benefit plan members are very or somewhat confident that their plans would pay the promised benefit, even in the current climate of plan shortfalls.
- Twenty-one percent would expect to contribute more to the plan in an underfunded situation.
- Fifteen percent would expect to receive fewer benefits.

For employee health benefits, the following was reported:

- Eighty-four percent were satisfied with their health benefits
- Eighty-eight percent had a good understanding of the plan.
- Forty-seven percent of respondents said that employee health benefits plans were an important factor in influencing them to join their current employers.
- Seventy-one percent would be unlikely to take a job with a company that does not have such a plan.
- Forty-eight percent said that if another company offered them the same salary and a better employee health benefits plan, they would consider leaving their current company.
- Seventy-one percent consider their health benefits part of their total income.
- Ninety-three percent view their health benefits as insurance for themselves and their families.
- If they were to trade in their health benefits plans for money, 44 percent would expect to receive between $500 and $2000.
- Twenty percent of Canadians say they are offered additional credits and/or dollars that they can use to pay for benefits that are not covered under their plans.
- Plan members are happy with having the option to choose; of those who are given the option to select their benefits, 87 percent are pleased with it. Of those without this option, 62 percent think it would be a good idea.

- Eighty percent with employer-sponsored health benefits plans use brochures (80 percent) or benefits statements (64 percent) to improve their understanding of their plans. More than half (57 percent) also use human resource departments and 31 percent use union/associations as sources of information. Despite the current emphasis on electronic communication, only 26 percent reported using the Internet as a source of information about their health benefits plans.
- Programs that Canadians are most likely to make use of if covered by their health benefits plans include: fitness facility (80 percent), stress management workshop (68 percent), cholesterol/blood pressure assessment (67 percent), and healthy meal options (67 percent).
- Programs they would not make use of include: smoking cessation (62 percent), weight loss (52 percent), and motivational speaker (52 percent).
- Eighty-one percent feel that the quality of health and benefits-related information provided by their employer is sufficient.
- Sixty-one percent of Canadians said they were very or somewhat confident in Canada's health-care system.
- Seventy-four percent of respondents said they would help control costs by using generic drugs, 48 percent would pay pharmacy dispensing fees, and 48 percent would pay a deductible.

This study shows that there is room for improvement in a number of areas, although on the whole employees are generally satisfied with both their pension plans and their health-care benefits. Such surveys are required to ensure satisfaction with programs, and to gain an understanding of the employee's perceptions. By helping members to understand the true value of their retirement savings and health benefits plans, sponsors can boost their members' confidence, satisfaction, and continuance, which results in higher retention and greater morale among employees.[29]

1. Based on the results reported, what do you consider to be areas of concern? What would you do to increase the level of satisfaction for employees in the particular area of concern?
2. Working in your groups, determine what benefits are most important to each of you, and then compare your answers to those found in the survey? What is different? Why?

Employee Reactions to Cost-Control Efforts

As would be expected, many employees can be skeptical about or even hostile to employer efforts to control health benefits costs. Surveys of employees have found that they are more dissatisfied with changes to their health benefits than with the moderation of base pay increases. In a recent study, employees reported that given a choice between their current benefits plan and an annual payment of $8,000, 66 percent of the respondents said they would take their benefits, even though $8,000 would far exceed the value of the services an employee will likely use.[30]

For cost-control efforts to work for employers, the gap between employees' and employers' views on benefits must be bridged, which requires significant communication and education of employees to counter their negative reactions.[31] Yet, one survey found that over 60 percent of employees spend less than one hour selecting benefits plans, and half spend less than 30 minutes.[32] Key in communicating cost control of health benefits is sharing information and having a continuing communication plan. As indicated in HR Perspective, communication methods include a newsletter, wellness programs, employee workshops, and intranet. Another factor to be considered is the demographics of the workforce. At Dofasco in Hamilton, Ontario, they provide newer [younger] employees with electronic communication and the Internet, while the older workforce depends on hard copy.[33]

Financial Benefits

5 Employers may offer workers a wide range of special benefits that provide financial support to employees: financial services, relocation assistance, insurance benefits (in addition to health insurance), educational assistance, and others. Employers find that such benefits can be useful in attracting and retaining employees. Workers like receiving these benefits, which often are not taxed as income.

Financial Services

Financial benefits include a wide variety of items. A *credit union* sponsored by the employer provides saving and lending services for employees. *Purchase discounts* allow employees to buy goods or services from their employers at reduced rates. For example, a furniture manufacturer may allow employees to buy furniture at wholesale cost plus 10 percent, or an automotive company may sell vehicles to employees at cost plus 5 percent on payroll deduction.

Stock purchase plan
Plan in which the corporation provides matching funds equal to the amount invested by the employee for the purchase of stock in the company.

Employee *savings plans* or *stock investment plans* of different types may be available. To illustrate, in a **stock purchase plan,** the employer provides matching funds equal to the amount invested by the employee for the purchase of stock in the company. Often, employees may buy the stock at a discount. This type of plan allows employees to benefit from the future growth of the corporation. Also, the intent of such a plan is to develop greater employee loyalty and interest in the organization and its success.[34]

Financial planning and counselling are especially valuable services for executives, many of whom may need information on investments and tax shelters, as well as comprehensive financial counselling, because of their higher levels of compensation. The importance of these financial planning benefits likely will grow as a greater percentage of workers approach retirement age and need to plan financially for retirement.

Relocation Assistance

Relocation benefits of various types are offered by many firms. Some employers offer temporary relocation benefits, while others provide assistance in finding a job for the spouse of a transferred employee. Numerous other financial-related benefits may be offered as well, including the use of a company car, company expense accounts, and assistance in buying or selling a house.

Valued employees sometimes are asked to transfer to other company locations that will require employer financial assistance.

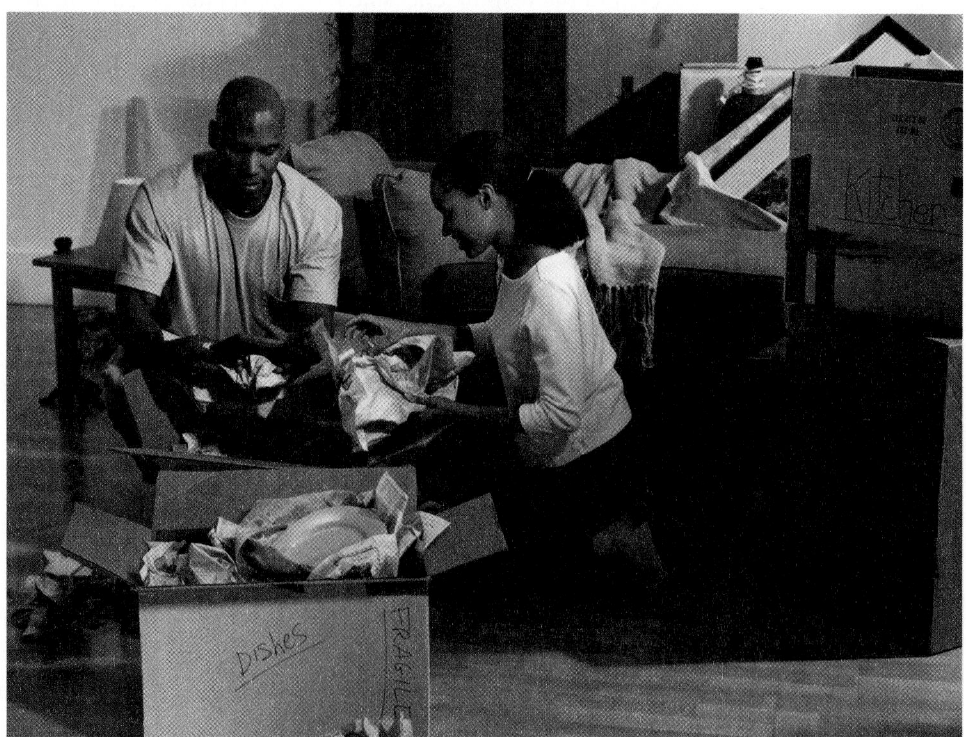

Source: Ryan McVay/Photodisc Green/Getty Images

Insurance Benefits

In addition to health-related insurance, some employers provide other types of insurance. These benefits offer major advantages for employees because many employers pay some or all of the costs. Even when employers do not pay any of the costs, employees still benefit because of the lower rates available through group programs. The most common types of insurance benefits are the following:

- *Life insurance:* Bought as a group policy, the employer pays all or some of the premiums. A typical level of coverage is one-and-a-half or two times an employee's annual salary.
- *Disability insurance: Short-term* and *long-term disability insurance* provides continuing income protection for employees who become disabled and unable to work. Long-term disability insurance is much more common because many employers cover short-term disability situations through sick leave programs. Employees normally pay the long-term disability premiums since any benefit they received will be non-taxable if the employee pays the premium.

Educational Assistance

Another benefit that saves financial resources of employees comes in the form of *educational assistance* and tuition aid, which pays some or all of the costs associated with formal education courses and degree programs, including the costs of books and laboratory materials. Some employers pay for schooling on a proportional schedule, depending on the grades received; others simply require a passing grade of C or above. Unless the education paid for by the employer meets certain conditions, the cost of educational aid must be counted as taxable income by employees.

ROI of Tuition Aid Providing educational benefits through tuition aid programs is a very popular benefit with employees. It has been estimated that in one year, U.S. employers spend over $10 billion for tuition aid, but only 2 percent of those firms conduct HR analyses to determine the return on their investment in tuition aid for those involved in these programs.[35] To make educational benefits programs more effective, the following factors could be measured: employee retention, internal promotions, increased employee satisfaction, and others.

Family-Oriented Benefits

The composition of families in Canada has changed significantly in the past few decades. The number of traditional families, in which the man goes to work and the woman stays home to raise children, has declined significantly, while the percentage of two-worker families has more than doubled. The growth in dual-career couples, single-parent households, and work demands on many workers have increased the emphasis some employers are placing on family-oriented benefits. As mentioned in earlier chapters, balancing family and work demands presents a major challenge to many workers at all levels of organizations. Therefore, employers have established a variety of family-oriented benefits.

Family-Care Benefits Family issues are growing in importance for many organizations and for many workers. One repercussion of this emphasis is that employees without families may feel some resentment against those who seem to get special privileges because they have families. Many employees do not have children under the age of 18 and are offered fewer opportunities to use personal days off, flexible scheduling, telecommuting, etc. Further, they are more frequently asked to travel or put in overtime because they "don't have a family."[36] Nevertheless, a variety of family benefits are available in many organizations.

Child-Care Assistance Balancing work and family responsibilities is a major challenge for many workers. Whether single parents or dual-career couples, these employees often experience difficulty obtaining high-quality, affordable child care. Employers are addressing the child-care issue in the following ways:

- Providing referral services to help parents locate child-care providers
- Establishing discounts at daycare centres, which may be subsidized by the employer
- Arranging with hospitals to offer sick-child programs partially paid for by the employer
- Developing after-school programs for older schoolage children, often in conjunction with local public and private school systems
- Offering onsite child-care centres

CIBC in Toronto launched a backup daycare centre in 2002. The program proved to be successful with a saving of 6800 employee days representing nearly $1.4 million in productivity savings when employees used the centre to look after their children on short notice. The plan is available to both full and part-time employees. Because of its success in Toronto, CIBC plans to launch more facilities across the country.[37] Husky Injection Molding Systems in Bolton, Ontario also provides temporary child care for emergency situations.[38]

Eldercare Canada
Eldercare Canada acts as a referral resource, strategic planner, and project manager to meet unique needs of family situations.
www.eldercarecanada.ca

Elder-Care Assistance Another family issue of importance is caring for elderly relatives.[39] Various organizations have surveyed their employees and found that as many as 25 percent–30 percent of them have had to miss work to care for aging relatives. The responsibilities associated with caring for elderly family members have resulted in reduced work performance, increased absenteeism, and more personal stress for the affected employees.[40] Lost productivity and absenteeism caused by workers caring for elders cost employers billions of dollars a year. Some responses by employers have included conducting needs surveys, providing resources, and giving referrals to elder-care providers.

The sandwich generation is having a more difficult time. Statistics Canada found that one in ten Canadians between the ages of 45 and 64 currently struggles with caring for young children, as well as elderly parents. Another 83 percent also hold down a job.[41]

Measuring the Effectiveness of Family Benefits Employers that have provided child-care and other family-friendly assistance have found the programs beneficial for several reasons. The greatest advantage is in aiding employee retention.[42] Employees are more likely to stay with employers who aid them with work/life balancing. One study of child-care benefits identified savings of $5.50 for every $1.00 spent.[43] The savings are primarily due to decreased employee absenteeism and turnover. Analyses of elder-care costs/benefits show similar results. To determine such metrics, costs for recruiting, training, turnover, and lost productivity are included.[44]

Time-Off Benefits

Time-off benefits represent an estimated 5 percent–13 percent of total compensation. Employers give employees paid time off in a variety of circumstances. Paid lunch breaks and rest periods, holidays, and vacations are common. But time off is given for a number of other purposes as well. Time-off benefits also include various leaves of absence such as for voting, jury duty, bereavement leave, or sick leave.

Holiday Pay Most employers provide pay for a variety of holidays. Canadian employers commonly offer 10–12 holidays annually. Employers in many other countries are required to provide a significantly higher number of holidays, approaching 20–30 days in some cases. In both Canada. and other countries, the number of holidays offered can vary depending on federal, provincial or territorial laws and union contracts. Figure 12-9 lists the statutory holidays by jurisdiction.

As an abuse-control measure, employers commonly require employees to work the last scheduled day before a holiday and the first scheduled workday after a holiday to be eligible for holiday pay. Some employers pay time-and-a-half to hourly employees who must work holidays. Also, some employers provide some company holiday parties and holiday bonus programs such as food gifts (turkeys at Thanksgiving) or holiday gift cards.

Vacation Pay Paid vacations are a common benefit. Employers often use graduated vacation-time scales based on employees' lengths of service. Some organizations have a "use it or lose it" policy whereby vacation time cannot be carried over from year to year.

Some employers have policies to "buy back" unused vacation time. Other employers, may have policies requiring employees to take a minimum number of vacation days off in a row. Regardless of the vacation policies used, employees are often required to work the day before and the day after vacation time off.

Leaves of Absence Employers grant *leaves of absence,* taken as time off with or without pay, for a variety of reasons. All the leaves discussed here add to employer costs even if unpaid, because the missing employee's work must be covered, either by other employees working additionally or by temporary employees working under contract.

Medical and Sick Leave Medical and sick leave are closely related. Many employers allow employees to miss a limited number of days because of illness without losing pay. Some employers allow employees to accumulate unused sick

Figure 12-9 *Statutory Holidays in Canada*

New Year's Day
Good Friday (or Easter Monday in Quebec)
Canada Day (Memorial Day in Newfoundland)
Labour Day
Christmas Day: all jurisdictions
Victoria Day (Dollard Day in Quebec)
Thanksgiving Day: all jurisdictions, except the Atlantic provinces (New Brunswick, Newfoundland, Nova Scotia, and Prince Edward Island)
First Monday in August: British Columbia (British Columbia Day), New Brunswick (New Brunswick Day), Saskatchewan (Saskatchewan Day), Northwest Territories, Nunavut
Remembrance Day: federal jurisdiction, Alberta, British Columbia, Northwest Territories, Nunavut, Saskatchewan, Yukon
Boxing Day: federal jurisdiction, Ontario
Other statutory holidays include Family Day in Alberta (third Monday of February); National Aboriginal Day in the Northwest Territories (June 21); St. John the Baptist's Day in Quebec (National Holiday, June 24); and Discovery Day in the Yukon (third Monday in August).

leave, which may be used in case of catastrophic illnesses. Others pay their employees for unused sick leave. Some organizations have shifted emphasis to reward people who do not use sick leave by giving them **well-pay**—extra pay for not taking sick leave.

Well-pay
Extra pay for not taking sick leave.

Other Leaves Other types of leaves are given for a variety of purposes. Some, such as military leave, election leave, and jury leave, are required by federal, provincial, and territorial laws. With heightened security and major emphasis on Canadian peacekeeping in other parts of the world, military leave policies (MLP) are becoming more common. Employers commonly pay the difference between the employee's regular pay and the military, election, or jury pay. As Reserve Force service is voluntary, there is no legislation in Canada that compels employers to provide time off for reservists, but because of this increased awareness of our military, many HR managers of small and mid-sized Canadian companies are now searching for a military leave model that will meet their organizational requirements. For HR managers who are considering developing a MLP, a pro-forma created by an HR specialist is available at www.cflc.forces.gc.ca.

Funeral leave or *bereavement leave* is another common type of leave offered. Absence of up to three days for the death of immediate family members is usually granted. Some policies also give unpaid time off for the death of more distant relatives or of friends. Proof of the death is usually requested. In one instance, an employee in an organization was found to have attended his mother's funeral on six different occasions. Only when the organization began asking for proof, could they stop the abuse as they then had a record in the employee's file.

Paid-time-off (PTO) plans
Plans that combine all sick leave, vacation time, and holidays into a total number of hours or days that employees can take off with pay.

Paid-Time-Off (PTO) Plans Other employers have made use of a **paid-time-off plan,** which combines sick leave, vacations, and holidays into a total number of hours or days that employees can take off with pay. Various studies have found that about two-thirds of all employers have PTO plans, up from one-third in the past several years. More importantly, about 60 percent of those employers have found PTO plans more effective than other means of reducing absenteeism and in having time off scheduled more efficiently.[45] Additionally, employee understanding and acceptance of leave policies may improve.[46]

Miscellaneous Benefits

Employers offer a wide variety of miscellaneous benefits. Some of the benefits are voluntary, meaning that employees can participate in them and pay for the costs themselves, often at group discount rates. Others are unique to employers and are provided at little or no cost to employees.

Social and Recreational Benefits Some benefits and services are social and recreational in nature, such as tennis courts, bowling leagues, picnics, parties, employer-sponsored athletic teams, organizationally owned recreational lodges, and other sponsored activities and interest groups. As interest in employee wellness has increased, more firms are providing recreational facilities and activities. The idea behind social and recreational programs is to promote employee happiness and team spirit. Employees may appreciate this type of benefit, but managers should not necessarily expect increased job productivity or job satisfaction as a result. Further, employers should retain control of all events associated with their organizations because of possible legal responsibility.

Severance pay Security benefit voluntarily offered by employers to employees who lose their jobs.

Severance Pay Severance pay is a security benefit voluntarily offered by employers to the employees who lose their jobs. The Canada Labour Code also provides for severance pay to employees who have 12 months' service or more. Ontario has a similar provision covering employees with five years' service or more. In both jurisdictions, severance pay is payable in cases of both group and individual termination of employment provided the eligibility requirements are met. Severed employees may receive lump-sum severance payments if their employment is terminated by the employer. For example, if a facility closes because it is outmoded and is no longer economically profitable to operate, the employees who lose their jobs may receive lump-sum payments based on their years of service. Severance pay provisions often provide higher severance payments corresponding to an employee's level within the organization and the person's years of employment. Severance pay is frequently offered for individuals whose jobs are eliminated or who leave by mutual agreement with their employers. The employment standards act in each of the respective jurisdictions and the Canada Labour Code require that employers provide advance notice if a mass layoff or facility closing is to occur. Prince Edward Island is the only jurisdiction in Canada that does not require a minimum notice period of at least four weeks prior to any permanent layoff of a group of employees.

Some employers have offered reduced amounts of cash severance and replaced some of the severance value with continued health insurance and outplacement assistance. Through *outplacement assistance,* ex-employees receive résumé writing instruction, interviewing skills workshops, and career counselling.

Unique Benefits Offered Employers provide a wide variety of unique benefits, ranging from transportation subsidies to self-defence training to company food services to health-club memberships. More unusual ones include pet insurance, which is offered by a number of employers, including the Weather Channel. In this program, employees get group rates on pet insurance that provides discounts when they pay for veterinarian services, pet food and supplies, and boarding/kennel services.[47]

Another unique benefit is provided through the Professional Association of Diving Instructors (PADI). In its corporate program, employees receive discounts when getting their scuba diving certifications. The PADI program is available at 4700 dive centres worldwide.[48] There are other unusual benefits, too many to mention, all designed to differentiate employers from others and to provide unique benefits to employees.

Benefits Administration

6 With the myriad of benefits and regulations, it is easy to see why many organizations must make coordinated efforts to administer benefits programs. Figure 12-10 shows how benefits administration responsibilities can be split between HR specialists and operating managers. HR specialists play the more significant role, but managers must assume responsibility for some of the communication aspects of benefits administration.

Benefits Communication

Employees generally do not know much about the values and costs associated with the benefits they receive from employers, so benefits communication and benefits satisfaction are linked. Consequently, many employers have instituted special benefits

Figure 12-10 *Typical Division of HR Responsibilities: Benefits Administration*

HR Unit	Managers
• Develops and administers benefits systems • Answers employees' technical questions on benefits • Monitors benefits usage • Suggests benefits cost-control approaches	• Answer simple questions on benefits • Maintain liaison with HR specialist on benefits • Maintain good communications with employees near retirement • Coordinate use of time-off benefits

communication systems to inform employees about the value of the benefits they provide. For instance, the retailer Pier 1 Imports uses various means, including videos, CDs, electronic alerts, newsletters, and employee meetings, to ensure that employees are knowledgeable about their benefits.[49]

Benefits Statements Some employers also give each employee a "personal statement of benefits" that translates benefits into dollar amounts. Pension legislation requires that employees receive an annual pension-reporting statement, which also can be included in the personal statement. Employers hope that by educating employees about their benefits and the costs, they can better manage expenditures and can give employees a better appreciation of the value of employers' payments.

HR Technology and Benefits

The spread of HR technology, particularly Internet-based systems, has significantly changed the benefits administration time and activities for HR staff members. Internet-based systems are being used to communicate benefits information, conduct employee benefits surveys, and facilitate other benefits communications. The Technology Transforming HR describes ways that companies are using technology to communicate health benefits information to employees.

Use of information technology also allows employees to change their benefits choices, track their benefits balances, and submit questions to HR staff members and external benefits providers. Use of the Internet for benefits enrollment has tripled in three years.[50] The greatest use has been to allow employees to sign up for, change, or update their benefits choices through Web-based systems. Previously, HR departments had to send out paper forms, hold numerous benefits meetings, and answer many phone calls from employees. The switch to online enrollment and communications has led to reductions in HR staff and benefits administration costs.

Flexible Benefits

Flexible benefits plan
Program that allows employees to select the benefits they prefer from groups of benefits established by the employer.

As part of both benefits design and administration many employers have flexible benefits plans that offer employees choices.

A **flexible benefits plan,** sometimes called a *flex plan* or *cafeteria plan,* allows employees to select the benefits they prefer from groups of benefits established by the employer. By having a variety of "dishes," or benefits, available, each employee can select an individual combination of benefits within some overall limits.

Technology Transforming HR

Online Benefits

Use of the Internet for a variety of benefits-related purposes is widespread. Many firms provide health-plan and wellness information to employees online. Communicating such information is especially important as firms try to hold down health benefits costs through consumer-driven health plans.

Cigna, a large health and retirement insurance firm, provides a website for 16 million members whose employers use Cigna as a vendor. On that Web portal, individuals can review health-plan options, track the status of their medical claims, and locate medical providers.

Other firms use Web sources for accessing health and wellness information. Xerox and Johnson & Johnson each make wellness information available to employees online. Employees can complete confidential personal health profiles and in return get health and wellness analyses. These analyses suggest various wellness activities and direct employees to online resources they can review. Xerox employees who participate enter a drawing for gift certificates. Participation of the 40 000 Johnson & Johnson employees has grown to 90 percent in two years, and provides the company with both healthier employees and savings of over $8.5 million a year. These examples illustrate that both employers and employees gain from online resources for employee benefits.[51]

1. How can an organization ensure that their communication program is leading to healthier employees?
2. Do an online search to find three companies (other than the ones mentioned in the above example) that have an online benefits communication program. What are the pros and cons of each of these programs you have located, and what could they do to improve their information? Explain your answers in detail.

As a result of the changing composition of the workforce, flexible benefits plans have grown in popularity. Flexible benefits systems recognize that individual employee situations differ because of age, family status, and lifestyle. For instance, dual-career couples may not want the same benefits from two different employers. Under a flex plan, one of them can forgo some benefits that are available in the partner's plan and take other benefits instead.[52]

Problems with Flexible Plans A problem with flexibility in benefits choice is that an inappropriate benefits package may be chosen by an employee. A young construction worker may not choose a disability benefit; however, if he or she is injured, the family may suffer financial hardship. Part of this problem can be overcome by requiring employees to select a core set of benefits (life, health, and disability insurance) and then offering options on other benefits.

Adverse selection Situation in which only higher-risk employees select and use certain benefits.

Another problem can be **adverse selection,** whereby only higher-risk employees select and use certain benefits. Because many insurance plans are based on a group rate, the employer may face higher rates if insufficient numbers of employees select an insurance option.

Finally, because many flexible plans have become so complex, they require more administrative time and information systems to track the different choices made by employees. Despite all these disadvantages, flex plans will likely continue to grow in popularity.

The ability to match all the various benefits available to differing employee needs, while also controlling some costs, will be a continuing challenge for employers of all sizes. But doing so is critical to effective HR management and may ultimately affect organizational success.

SUMMARY

1 Benefits provide additional compensation to some employees as a reward for organizational membership. Because benefits generally are not taxed, they are highly desired by employees. The average employee now receives an amount equal to about 40 percent of pay in benefit compensation. Strategic considerations for benefits include their value in creating a competitive advantage and aiding in attracting and retaining employees. Benefits design and cost-control actions are crucial to strategic benefits efforts.

2 Benefits can be viewed as mandatory or voluntary. Government-mandated security benefits include Canada Pension Plan/Quebec Pension Plan (CPP/QPP), Employment Insurance (EI), Workers' Compensation and provincial medicare. CPP/QPP are major pension plans and provide regular pension payments, disability payments when no other sick benefits exist, and survivor benefits for surviving spouse and dependent children. Old Age Security (OAS) is also available to retirees age 65 and above. EI is available to people who have lost their employment for valid reasons, compassionate care benefits, maternity, parental and sickness benefits. Supplemental unemployment benefits (SUB) are not provided by law, and are often provisions in union agreements, topping up an employee's EI premiums. Workers' Compensation provides benefits to persons injured on the job. Provincial medicare provides basic health-care for Canadians. Dental is not covered under provincial plans. Canada's health-care system remains in flux.

3 Organizations provide retirement benefits through defined-benefit (DB) and defined-contribution (DC) pension plans, group RRSPs, and deferred profit-sharing plans. Pension legislation is complex. Many organizations are trying to decrease the use of DB and many of the larger plans are in deficit. Use of DC plans and individual retirement accounts is growing. Some plans are contributory, and others are non-contributory. Pension legislation states that employees who contribute to pension plans, be locked-in and vested after two years of service. Pension plans are also portable.

4 Because health-care benefits costs have increased significantly, employers are managing their health benefits costs more aggressively. Efforts to control the costs of health benefits have included changing employee co-payments and employee contributions, determining the source of medical conditions and offering health promotion strategies to address the problems, using managed care, and using health-spending accounts.

5 Various types of financial services, relocation assistance, insurance benefits, educational assistance, and other benefits enhance the appeal of an organization to employees. Family-oriented benefits include offering adoption benefits, child-care assistance, and elder-care assistance. Holiday pay, vacation pay, and various leaves of absence are means of providing time-off benefits to employees.

6 Because of the variety of benefit options available and the costs involved, employers must develop effective systems to communicate those options and costs to their employees. Flexible benefits plans, which can be tailored to individual needs and situations, are increasing in popularity.

KEY TERMS

Adverse selection, p. 465
Benefit, p. 436
Canada/Quebec Pension Plan (CPP/QPP), p. 440
Contributory plan, p. 450
Co-payment, p. 453
Deferred profit-sharing plan (DPSP), p. 449
Defined-benefit pension plan (DBPP), p. 448
Defined-contribution pension plan (DCPP), p. 449
Employment Insurance (EI), p. 442
Flexible benefits plan, p. 464
Group RRSPs, p. 449
Health maintenance organization (HMO), p. 454
Health spending account (HSA), p. 454
Locked-in, p. 450
Managed health care, p. 454
Non-contributory plan, p. 450

Old age security (OAS), p. 442
Paid-time-off (PTO) plans, p. 462
Pension plan, p. 448
Portability, p. 450
Preferred provider organization (PPO), p. 454
Provincial medicare, p. 444
Severance pay, p. 463
Stock purchase plan, p. 458
Vesting, p. 450
Well-pay, p. 462
Workers' compensation, p. 443

REVIEW AND APPLICATION QUESTIONS

1 Why are benefits strategically important to employers and what are some key strategic considerations?

2 If an employee becomes ill, what are the potential programs, mandatory and/or employer, that are available to the employee. Consider both short and long term.

3 What are the pros and cons of both defined-benefit and defined-contribution plans? As an employee which plan would you prefer and why?

4 Discuss the following statement: "Health-care costs are out of control in Canada, and increasing conflicts between employers and employees are likely as employers try to reduce their health benefits costs."

5 Discuss the various financial programs that are available to employees.

6 Design a flexible benefits plan for a small and a large organization. What do you anticipate to be potential problems for both these types of organizations?

EXPERIENTIAL EXERCISES

1. Working in groups of five, you are to arrive at a new employee benefits plan for your employees. Your organization has 80 employees, with an average age of 35. Half of the staff are married with children. This is the first time your employer has implemented a benefits program. Recent surveys of the industry shows that your competitors are also putting in benefit plans, and the employees have indicated that they wish to have such benefits. What are some of the considerations you must make in determining the type of plan that you will implement? What type of plan do you think will be appropriate for your organization?

2. Your organization has decided to implement a defined-contribution plan and they have asked you to prepare a communication strategy for the organization. You need to determine the most effective way to communicate the strategy, as well as a presentation to the employees. Pretend your classmates are the employees for the organization, and prepare a five-minute presentation on a defined-contribution plan. You need to determine what should be included. As such, you may have to conduct some extra research in addition to the information provided in the text.

3. Search the Web, and find an organization's benefit plan that is posted. Using the information provided, determine ways to cut costs from the plan. How would you go about communicating the cuts to the employees? What would you say? Plan your communication to the employees.

4. The Textile Company has for years had a benefits plan for the employees only. Recently it has decided to include dependants and will pay part of the premium for their coverage. The employees have completed the necessary paperwork and while you are reviewing the paperwork, you notice that one of the managers has listed his girlfriend as his dependant. Usually this would be okay, because people living together are considered to be married under the law. The problem you are having is that you don't believe they are living together, and that would mean that she is not eligible for coverage. How do you go about asking the manager if she is living with him or not? Do you foresee any problems with this request? What are some of the issues associated with asking this type of question?

LEARNING REVIEW

To check your knowledge of the chapter, review the following. (Answers after the case.)

1 Countries that offer among the lowest amounts of annual vacation leave are:
a. Italy and France
b. Finland and Sweden
c. The United States and Canada
d. Japan and Korea

2 An insurable earning is associated with what benefit:
a. statutory holidays
b. Canada pension
c. severance
d. jury duty

3 An employee's right to receive benefits from a pension plan is called:
a. funding
b. contributory
c. portable
d. vesting

4 A(n) __________ is an employee's portion of the cost of both insurance premiums and extended health care.
a. pre-payment
b. co-payment
c. contribution
d. annual payment

5 Financial planning and counselling are especially valuable services for:
a. executives
b. hourly employees
c. salaried employees
d. all of the above

6 Legislation requires that employees be provided with an annual statement for:
a. Supplementary unemployment insurance
b. Employment insurance
c. OAS
d. Pension

CASE

TOTAL REWARDS—A UNIQUE SOLUTION

Total rewards are difficult to define because it can have different meanings for different companies. A successful total rewards program at one company may spell disaster at another company. Two companies that take a completely different approach from each other are the RBC Financial Group and TransAlta Corporation.

RBC made the decision to pursue a total rewards strategy in the summer of 2002 after its aggressive expansion in the United States. RBC's number of American employees grew from 1000 to 1500. RBC's development of the program began with asking 16 000 of its 65 000 employees what they wanted to see in the total rewards package. RBC's human resource department found that most of its employees wanted flexibility and choice. Zabeen Hirji who is the senior vice president of human resources at RBC, pointed out that, "What an employee wants today and what gets to the top of their list today may be different five years from now."

The total rewards program that was implemented at RBC included a new service recognition award (at the two-year mark). The award is presented to employees in front of their co-workers in the hopes that it will boost their morale and consequently reduce turnover. The cornerstone of the program is referred to as the four quadrants which are (1) pay, (2) benefits, (3) learning and career development, and (4) work environment. RBC has been promoting this program through an intranet site and its employee magazine. On the site "Me and RBC" employees are allowed to examine and use the quadrants to develop their own total rewards program.

In contrast to RBC, the Calgary-based power-generation firm TransAlta Corporation has linked its rewards and performance together as part of its total rewards strategy for its 2500 employees. Marc Lattoni who is TransAlta's total rewards director recognizes that flexible working hours and a good culture are important but they should not be part of rewards: "There's a bunch of stuff that goes on that we provide employees from the point of view of engagement and facilitating work-life, but we don't consider them rewards. Those are part of the package of the work environment and the work culture as opposed to a reward. All employees are eligible for flexible hours regardless of the nature of their work performance. TransAlta believes that superior performance is rewarded with superior pay." As Lattoni pointed out, "the value of your pensions, for example, is a function of your base pay and your base pay is a function of your competency. So there's a reward linkage." [53]

Questions

1. What are the unique features of each of these two different total rewards plans?
2. Working in groups, discuss what you would consider to be part of a total rewards package? What are the differing views among your group members? Why do you think they are different? If they are the same, why is this happening?

Learning Review Answers: 1. c 2. b 3. d 4. c 5. a 6. d

PART 4
VIDEO CASES

CARPENTER'S INVESTMENT CRUSADE

The United Brotherhood of Carpenters has invested $3 billion in Canadian companies to ensure that its members receive a healthy pension when they retire. Due to "shady corporate accounting practices" a company can deceive its shareholders into believing that it is more profitable than it really is. Many members of the union fear that when they retire their pension will be non-existent due to accounting practices such as not declaring stock options as an expense in the yearly income statement. As a result, the union has decided to become actively involved in shareholder meetings in order to get their concerns across.

This segment from *Venture* follows the group of carpenters to meetings with companies such as Celestica, INCO, Esso, and Fairmont Hotels. The carpenters did not have the same levels of success at the various meetings. However, companies with active shareholders do perform 2 to 3 points better than companies without active shareholders. Since many carpenters have opted to retire early due to the risky nature of the work it is important to the union that it is able to provide its members with a comfortable pension.[1]

Questions

1. From the various meetings, do you believe that the carpenters were making a difference and getting their points across?
2. What is the role of education in ensuring that carpenters have a healthy pension?
3. What are the risks involved in having a corporate pension plan?

PENSION PROMISE

When Cold Metal Products in Hamilton, Ontario, went bankrupt, its employees not only lost their jobs, but they also lost a large portion of their pension plans. *The National* examines how a couple of employees who were near retirement are coping with the loss of their hard-earned pensions. Unfortunately, these employees are unable to enjoy their retirement and have had to go back to work in order to survive.

In the 1990s, pension plans were attractive until the "The Perfect Storm" emerged—the stock market crash and companies unable to fully replenish their pension plans were all the ingredients needed to cause this downward trend in pension plans. The difficulties with pension plans have led 30 percent of companies to move to eliminate them altogether.

Canadian bankruptcy laws have placed employees at the bottom of the payment list behind secured creditors and banks. The video clip documents the lobbying efforts of Canadian Steelworkers to change these laws and place employees higher on that list. However, there is a strong argument coming out of corporate Canada that companies are more likely to declare bankruptcy because banks will be unwilling to give loans if they are least likely to be paid back.[2]

Questions

1. Do you believe that Canadian companies should eliminate pension plans? Why or why not?
2. Should the Canadian government place employees higher on the payment list after a company goes bankrupt?

PART 5

Employee Relations

CHAPTER 13

Health, Safety, and Security

Learning Objectives

After you have read this chapter, you should be able to:

1 Define health, safety, and security and the young workers program.

2 Identify the basic provisions of the occupational health and safety legislation, recordkeeping, and inspection requirements.

3 Discuss the issues surrounding hazard control including WHMIS and ergonomics.

4 Explain workplace violence as a security issue and describe some components of an effective security program.

5 Discuss the activities that constitute effective safety management.

6 Describe three workplace health issues and how employers are responding to them.

7 Specify several global health, safety, and security concerns.

HR *Headline*

The Lessons of Westray

On Saturday, May 9, 1992 a methane gas explosion rocked the Westray coal mine in Plymouth, Nova Scotia killing 26 miners. Shortly after, the company declared bankruptcy and as a result never made it to court to face 52 non-criminal counts associated with its operation of an unsafe mine. A Royal Commission of Inquiry conducted by the Nova Scotia government. found that the explosion was preventable. According to the report written by Nova Scotia Supreme Court Justice Peter Richard, the tragedy at Westray, "is a story of incompetence, of mismanagement, of bureaucratic bungling, of deceit, of ruthlessness, of cover-up, of apathy, of expediency and of cynical indifference."

The Nova Scotia government was ordered by a labour tribunal to pay $1,200,000 in severance to 117 miners who had lost their jobs as a result of the explosion. The company may have been able to avoid the explosion and its subsequent decline had it listened to the concerns voiced by miners who complained about their working conditions and lack of safety training. Two months before the explosion, a safety report surfaced in which a union official stated, "I feel there will be someone killed in the near future."

Although the story of Westray was covered by both national and international media outlets, there continues to be more devastating mining disasters in other parts of the world. In January 2006 there was an explosion at the Sago Mine in West Virginia that led to the deaths of 12 miners. According to *USA Today*, the mine "had been cited for hundreds of federal safety violations since it opened in 1999. Among the infractions were at least 16 related to failures to prevent or adequately monitor the buildup of explosive gases in the mine." In China, the death of miners on the job is not out of the ordinary because of the lax implementation of mine safety laws. In early 2005, the gas explosion at the Sunjiawan coal mine killed 210 people. The very next day there was another explosion at an illegal coal mine in Fuyyuan County, killing another five people.

Several years after the Westray mine disaster, Bill C-45 (also known as the Westray Bill) was enacted as law in March 2004 to address such tragedies in Canada. Under the criminal code, it established a legal duty for all persons directing the work of others to take reasonable steps to ensure the safety of workers and the public. As such, individuals and organizations could be criminally charged and sentenced to prison. Such legislation has helped to increase awareness among business owners and to properly focus the need to be responsible to the health and safety of organizations in Canada.

Unfortunately, other mining companies and governments around the world have not learned from the disaster at Westray. After more than a decade since the explosion, there continues to be mining disasters that could be prevented either through legislation or a pro-active stance from mining companies. The message is clear to employers in Canada that employees who are killed on the job due to blatant neglect will not be tolerated. Such legislation enacted on a global basis would certainly go a long way to make greedy owners heed to the health and safety obligations they have to their employees.[1]

"If only it weren't for the people always getting tangled up with the machinery . . . Earth would be an engineer's paradise."

—Kurt Vonnegut

Today employers are expected to provide work environments that are safe, secure, and healthy. At one time, employers viewed accidents and occupational diseases as unavoidable by-products of work. This idea may still be prevalent in some less-developed countries, and as noted in the opening HR Headline, in some industries more than others. Fortunately, in Canada and in most developed nations, the concept of using prevention and control to minimize or eliminate risks in workplaces is much more prevalent today. Legislation such as Bill C-45 that attempts to severely reprimand negligent people responsible for the safety of others should help to secure the health and safety of employees.

Employers in a variety of industries have found that emphasizing health and safety pays off in a number of ways. Lower employee benefits costs for health care, fewer work-related accidents, lower workers' compensation costs, and more productive employees are all results of employers' stressing health and safety.

Health, Safety, and Security

1 A number of federal, provincial, and territorial laws have established health and safety requirements for Canadian employers. In light of such legislation, employers still continue to cut corners at the expense of workers' lives as was noted in the opening case. Some industries are worse than others. Despite the poor safety attitudes of some employers, there are many others who go to great lengths to ensure the health and safety of their workers. For example, safety leaders such as Alcan, General Motors, and Brock University have recognized that addressing health, safety, and security issues is part of effective HR management.

Nature of Health, Safety, and Security

Health
General state of physical, mental, and emotional well-being.

Safety
Condition in which the physical well-being of people is protected.

Security
Protection of employees and organizational facilities.

The terms *health, safety,* and *security* are closely related. The broader and somewhat more nebulous term is **health,** which refers to a general state of physical, mental, and emotional well-being. A healthy person is free from illness, injury, or mental and emotional problems that impair normal human activity. Health management practices in organizations strive to maintain the overall well-being of individuals.

Typically, **safety** refers to a condition in which the physical well-being of people is protected. The main purpose of effective safety programs in organizations is to prevent work-related injuries and accidents. The purpose of **security** is protecting employees and organizational facilities. With the growth of workplace violence, security at work has become an even greater concern for employers and employees alike.

Health, Safety, and Security Responsibilities

The general goal of providing a safe, secure, and healthy workplace is reached by operating managers and HR working together. As Figure 13-1 indicates, the primary health, safety, and security responsibilities in an organization usually fall on supervisors and managers. An HR manager or safety specialist can help coordinate health and safety programs, investigate accidents, produce safety program materials, and conduct formal safety training. However, department supervisors and managers play key roles in maintaining safe working conditions and a healthy workforce. For example, a supervisor in a warehouse has several health and safety responsibilities: reminding employees to wear safety hats; checking on the cleanliness of the work

Figure 13-1 **Typical Division of HR Responsibilities: Health, Safety, and Security**

HR Unit	Managers
• Coordinates health and safety programs • Develops safety reporting system • Provides accident investigation expertise • Provides technical expertise on accident prevention • Develops restricted-access procedures and employee identification systems • Trains managers to recognize and handle difficult employee situations	• Monitor the health and safety of employees daily • Coach employees to be safety conscious • Investigate accidents • Observe the health and safety behaviour of employees • Monitor workplace for security problems • Communicate with employees to identify potentially difficult employees • Follow security procedures and recommend changes as needed

area; observing employees for any alcohol, drug, or emotional problems that may affect their work behaviour; and recommending equipment changes (such as screens, railings, or other safety devices) to engineering specialists in the organization.

A position that is becoming more common in many companies is that of safety, health, and environment officer. This combination may make sense where danger results from chemical or other sources of pollution that may be hazardous to both employees and the public or the environment. Because both safety and environmental responsibilities require working with different government agencies, a good choice is to fill this job with someone who has the skills to ensure compliance with a wide range of regulatory issues.[2]

Security affects everyone in an organization and is often an HR responsibility. Since 9/11 and the massive blackout in Canada and the U.S. in 2003, the security issues that an employer might worry about have grown in number and scope. Certainly, workplace violence, computer security, and theft at work have been and continue to be concerns. But now, for some employers, security issues include protecting employees from terrorist attacks, loss of electric service, bomb threats, and hostage situations. Perhaps more correctly labelled "crisis management planning" at its most extreme, dealing with such issues provides an opportunity for HR to create value in the organization and to help mitigate some risks to the company.[3]

Managing *risk* to the company can take the form of avoiding negligent hiring or negligent retention by keeping workers who should have been terminated. In either case, HR is well situated to be of assistance.[4]

Current State of Health, Safety, and Security

In 2004 approximately 340 000 non-fatal injuries and illnesses and 928 workplace fatalities occurred in Canadian workplaces. Average injury frequency based on 100 workers ranges from a low 1.3 (New Brunswick) to a high of 4.8 (Manitoba). The overall average for Canada is 2.6. The average cost of a workers' compensation claim is $13,610.[5]

The three major causes of injury (overextending, falling, and bodily reaction) were responsible for over half of the direct costs of injury. Accident *costs* have gone up faster than inflation because of the rapid increase in medical costs even though the number of accidents has been decreasing for some time.[6] A report last June by the International Labour Organization (ILO) noted that the economic costs of work-related

CanOSH—Young Workers Programs
This site provides links to a series of occupational safety and health (OSH) resources for young workers and/or individuals who are new to the workforce.
www.canoshweb.org/en/young_workers.html

occupational injuries and disease are rapidly increasing. Compensation figures indicate that approximately 4 percent of the world's gross domestic product disappears with the cost of diseases through absence from work, sickness treatment, disability, and survivor benefits. The biggest killer now is cancer, resulting in about 640 000 deaths a year, a figure that represents 32 percent of all work-related fatalities. Circulatory disease accounted for 23 percent of such deaths, followed by accidents that were responsible for 19 percent of fatalities. Surprisingly, asbestos is still a killer years after its fatal properties were widely reported.[7] April 28 has been proclaimed the annual Day of Mourning in Canada, which honours those who have died, been injured, or who have become sick because of their jobs. In 2000, the Day of Mourning specifically recognized young workers.[8] See the HR Perspective for a discussion on young workers.

Research on health and safety continues to show that poorly managed companies have higher losses from accidents, but well-managed companies have lower losses from accidents.[9] Jurisdictions throughout Canada have made a concerted effort to reduce accidents with great success. Figure 13-2 displays the decrease in loss-time

HR *Perspective*

The Disturbing Facts About Our Kids at Work!!

You will probably remember when you made your first visit to the local HRSDC office so that you could apply for your social insurance number. This number was your ticket to the employment line. What you might not have considered were the potentially life-threatening hazards present in the workplace that go with this honour.

Statistics show that one in seven young workers is injured on the job. There are approximately 60 000 workplace injuries in Canada involving 15 to 29-year-olds and approximately 60 deaths per year. After car accidents, the leading causes of death among young people are machine injuries and electrocutions. Many of these tragedies could easily have been avoided if a few basic safety rules had been followed, and if the employer had adequately trained the new employee to recognize potentially dangerous situations. Because of these issues, workers' compensation boards across Canada provide information to employers to help them train young workers. Also, many of these boards have made presentations at high schools to get the message out to young workers that they have rights when it comes to their health and safety.

Unfortunately, young workers are often too afraid to ask about workplace safety or job training because they want to make good first impressions. Also, young workers often say nothing because they may not want to be the centre of attention or they don't want to rock the boat. An organization that promotes good health and safety practices should encourage young workers to ask questions, particularly when their health and safety may be at risk. There are a number of questions that young workers should ask themselves so that they become more familiar with the situation:

- What are the dangers of my job?
- Are there any hazards (noise, chemicals, radiation) that I should know about?
- Will I receive job safety training? When?
- Is there any safety gear that I'll be expected to wear? Will I receive training in how to use it?
- Will I be trained in emergency procedures (fire, chemical spill?) When?
- Where are fire extinguishers, first aid kits, and other emergency equipment located?
- What are my health and safety responsibilities?
- Who do I ask if I have a safety question?
- Do you have safety meetings?
- What do I do if I get hurt? Who is the first aid person?

Three skills are necessary to achieve the highest levels of safety: you must possess knowledge about the hazards you encounter, practice skills to avoid them, and the motivation to apply your safety skills and knowledge.[10]

1. Working in groups, discuss the safety training each of you have received in your previous workplaces. What was the training and how could it have been improved upon?
2. Search the Web to determine what resources are available to young workers. Write a report discussing the elements of your findings and any recommendations you would have to improve the health and safety of young workers.

Figure 13-2 ***Loss-Time Injuries by Province and Territory***

	1994	1995	1996	1997	1998	1999	2000	2001	2002	2003	2004
NL	6646	6150	5272	5295	5879	6640	6609	6173	5517	5247	4834
PEI	2094	2443	2436	1794	2034	2099	2066	1779	1475	1241	1037
NS	13 223	10 463	7940	8199	8159	8547	9232	9082	8724	8849	9173
NB	4784	4310	3906	4212	4729	5170	5354	5162	4685	4604	4185
QC	135 482	129 926	119 633	117 407	116 060	116 797	119 135	112 887	110 244	107 160	104 209
ON	125 638	118 812	103 071	101 806	97 190	100 727	104 154	98 359	95 568	93 234	90 397
MB	17 740	17 405	17 255	17 738	18 658	18 979	19 721	18 544	17 919	17 586	17 260
SK	13 337	14 206	13 465	14 345	13 872	13 720	14 945	15 065	15 623	15 135	13 880
AB	30 801	30 285	31 835	35 234	36 104	35 393	39 393	38 755	38 426	37 335	35 969
BC	79 428	74 881	71 602	72 428	71 502	70 090	70 661	66 076	59 530	56 946	52 289
NT/NU	1120	1049	975	873	780	871	835	889	968	936	817
YT	463	534	495	520	393	417	397	445	495	442	452
Total	430 756	410 464	377 885	379 851	375 360	379 450	392 502	373 216	359 174	348 715	340 502

Source: Association of Workers' Compensation Boards of Canada, reprinted by permission.

injuries over ten years. The "time-loss injury" means an injury/disease where an employee is compensated for a loss of wages following a work-related injury, or exposure to a noxious substance, or receives compensation for a permanent disability with or without any time lost in his or her employment (for example, if an employee is compensated for a loss of hearing resulting from excessive noise in the workplace). Time-loss injuries have decreased over the past ten years for the country as a whole. Saskatchewan and Alberta are the only two provinces that have seen increases in the number of injury/disease occurrences. Quebec remains the province with the most incidents, while the Yukon is the smallest.

Unfortunately some jobs are more prone to accidents than others, however accidents can occur anytime employees and employers fail to follow safe work practices.

Source: Danny Zhan/ShutterStock

One group that has the highest rate of accidents is young workers. Worker compensation boards across Canada have each embarked on young worker programs to enhance the training and awareness of young workers rights in the workplace. These programs have proved successful with decreased accident rates for workers aged 15–24. However, young workers still experience higher accidents than other workers.

Occupational Health and Safety Legislation

2 In Canada, occupational health and safety is regulated through acts, regulations, guidelines, standards, and codes. Federally, health and safety is regulated through the Canada Labour Code. Each province and territory has its own Occupational Health and Safety Acts, which consists of the rights and duties of all parties involved. Although the provincial and territorial acts do differ marginally from each other, they all consist of: (1) an act, (2) powers of enforcement, (3) the right of workers to refuse to do unsafe work, (4) protection of workers from reprisals, and (5) duties and responsibilities for employers and others.

Occupational health and safety is based on an internal responsibility system (IRS) where the employee and the employer are jointly responsible for health and safety. All employees have three fundamental rights:

- *The right to know* about what hazards are present on the job, how these hazards affect the worker, and health and safety training.
- *The right to participate* in joint health and safety committees, and to report unsafe practices and conditions.
- *The right to refuse unsafe work* without fear of reprisal. These rights are limited when it comes to health-care workers, corrections officers, police officers, and firefighters, given the nature of their work. There are procedures to be followed in the event of a work refusal.

The right to refuse unsafe work is more complex than it may appear on the surface. There are procedures to be followed. If the worker feels the work he or she is performing is unsafe, the worker must raise his or her concern to the supervisor who will check the situation. The supervisor, union member, health and safety representative, or H&S committee member will review the situation and make a recommendation to the employee whether they feel the task is safe or not. If the group feels the work is safe, but the worker still does not, then the worker can still refuse without fear of reprisal. A government inspector will then be called in to make an assessment of the situation. In the meantime, the worker will be assigned another task, and the supervisor can call upon another worker to take over the task, but must advise the worker of the other worker's refusal and concern. If that worker decides to turn down the job they have a right to do so if they do not feel it is safe. If after inspection the government inspector feels the job is safe then the worker must return to work, or else face disciplinary reprisal.

With rights come responsibilities as well. There are many stakeholders responsible for health and safety within organizations. These stakeholders are the employer, the supervisor, the employee, and the joint health and safety committees.

Duties of Employers, Owners, and Contractors

It is imperative that employers fulfill their primary duty of providing their employees with a safe work environment. Commonly referred to as the "general duty clause," every province and territory in Canada has similar occupational health and safety legislation that describes the obligations of employers and workers. By including the words "reasonably practicable," legislators make the *Occupational Health and Safety Act (OH&S)* "strict liability" legislation and introduce the possibility of a "due diligence defence." Strict liability laws give you the opportunity to make rational decisions. You have the option of deciding if you do or do not proceed with a particular action depending upon the circumstances.

Due diligence
Employers shall take all reasonable precautions, under the particular circumstances, to prevent injuries or accidents in the workplace.

Due diligence thus means that employers shall take all reasonable precautions, under the particular circumstances, to prevent injuries or accidents in the workplace. This duty also applies to situations that are not addressed elsewhere in the occupational health and safety legislation. To exercise due diligence, an employer must implement a plan to identify possible workplace hazards and carry out the appropriate corrective action to prevent accidents or injuries arising from these hazards. It is not enough to correct the action after the fact, it is important that the effort was made to eliminate the potential for injuries or accidents in the workplace before they take place.[11] Figure 13-3 provides a checklist that employers should use to ensure that they are being duly diligent. By answering "yes" to all the questions on the checklist, the employer will demonstrate that they have been duly diligent and thus be able to provide a legal defence from criminal charges arising from health and safety incidents.

As discussed at the beginning of this chapter, Bill C-45 (the Westray Bill) was enacted under the Criminal Code. It imposes criminal liability on corporations and individuals, that fail to take reasonable measures to protect employee and public safety. Corporations cannot be imprisoned so the Criminal Code provides for fines when corporations are convicted of crimes. In the case of a summary conviction offence (less serious offences that are punishable for individuals by up to six

Figure 13-3 *Example of a Due Diligence Checklist*

Yes	No	
___	___	**Do you know and understand your safety and health responsibilities?**
___	___	**Do you have definite procedures in place to identify and control hazards?**
___	___	**Have you integrated safety into all aspects of your work?**
___	___	**Do you set objectives for safety and health just as you do for quality, production, and sales?**
___	___	**Have you committed appropriate resources to safety and health?**
___	___	**Have you explained safety and health responsibilities to all employees and made sure that they understand it?**
___	___	**Have employees been trained to work safely and use proper protective equipment?**
___	___	**Is there a hazard reporting procedure in place that encourages employees to report all unsafe conditions and unsafe practices to their supervisors?**
___	___	**Are managers, supervisors, and workers held accountable for safety and health just as they are held accountable for quality?**
___	___	**Is safety a factor when acquiring new equipment or changing a process?**
___	___	**Do you keep records of your program activities and improvements?**
___	___	**Do you keep records of the training each employee has received?**
___	___	**Do your records show that you take disciplinary action when an employee violates safety procedures?**
___	___	**Do you review your OHS program at least once a year and make improvements as needed?**

Source: Canadian Centre for Occupational Health and Safety (CCOHS): Occupational Health and Safety Legislation—Due Diligence, January 20, 1999. Reprinted by permission.

months in jail and/or a $2,000 fine), the Code provides for a fine of up to $25,000 for corporations. Bill C-45 would increase the maximum fine on an organization for a summary conviction offence to $100,000. For the more serious, indictable offences, the Code already provides no limit on the fine that can be imposed on an organization. Penalties for negligence include up to ten years in prison for injuries caused to an employee(s), or life imprisonment in the case of the death of an employee(s).

As part of the duties required under occupational health and safety legislation, *employers* are expected at a minimum to ensure the following are provided for in their organizations:

- Prepare, review, and maintain health and safety policy
- Establish a joint health and safety committee and to respond to any recommendations the committee may make
- Provide information, instruction, and supervision to ensure employee health and safety
- Meet prescribed standards
- Provide/maintain personal protection equipment (PPE)
- Investigate and report accidents and illnesses
- Control exposure to safety hazards and hazard substances
- Appoint competent person as supervisor
- Establish an occupational health service
- Post a copy of the OH&S Act in the workplace

Contractors (or constructors) have similar responsibilities as employers, however they have to notify authorities in a specified amount of time before a construction project is scheduled to begin. The notice usually involves approximate cost, scope, and start date of the project. They are responsible for ensuring that anyone who works for them on projects has had sufficient training. They too must exercise due diligence with their employees, or whomever they contract with to carry out business on their behalf.

Duties of Supervisors

A supervisor is defined as a person (with or without a title) who has charge of a workplace and authority over a worker. Under the Occupational Health and Safety Acts, a supervisor's duties include advising workers of possible hazards, providing training, providing written instruction when possible, ensuring that workers comply with the OH&S Act and regulations as well as use or wear safety equipment, devices, or clothing. A supervisor must take every reasonable precaution to ensure that his or her workers are protected. Therefore, they should also discipline for continuous safety infractions when necessary.

Duties of Workers

Workers have responsibilities as well. A worker is expected to comply with the OH&S Act and regulations, properly use safety equipment and clothes, follow all safety procedures, report hazards to the supervisor and report any contraventions of the act or regulations, as well as to report accidents. A worker is prohibited from making any safety device ineffective, using any hazardous equipment or machine in unsafe conditions and engaging in rough or boisterous conduct. National Wrecking Company, a demolition company based in Chicago, Illinois, with offices in Ontario, was fined $250,000, a supervisor was fined $15,000, and a worker was fined $10,000 for violations of the Ontario OH&S Act that resulted in the death of a worker. Each party was found responsible in some way for the individual's death. This provides an example of where employees must take caution to ensure the safety of their co-workers.[12]

Duties of Joint Health and Safety Committee

Joint Health and Safety Committees (JH&S) are required by nine jurisdictions in Canada and the minister responsible in the remaining four jurisdictions has the discretionary power to call for the formation of committees. The role of the JH&S committee is to provide a neutral environment where labour and management can work together to create a safe and healthy workplace. The committees must have equal employer/employee representation, and at least one management and one worker member must be trained and certified in topics such as legislation, general safety, hygiene, workers' rights and duties, and joint committees. JH&S committees are required to meet regularly (Ontario every three months, federal every month), deal with worker health and safety concerns, participate in identifying risks, perform routine workplace inspections, and resolve work refusals.

LOGGING ON...

Canadian Centre for Occupational Health and Safety
This website offers Canadian employees and employers information about legislation, and access to numerous educational resources.
www.ccohs.ca

Legislation in occupational health and safety has made employers and employees more aware of health and safety considerations. Legislation has also contributed to reductions in the number of accidents and injuries in some cases. But in other industries, and in some provinces, legislation has had varying results. Figure 13-4 indicates that most occupational injuries under federal jurisdiction occurred in the road transport and air transport sectors (26.2 percent and 19.7 percent of injuries,

Figure 13-4 *Proportion of all Occupational Injuries by Province, Territory 2000*

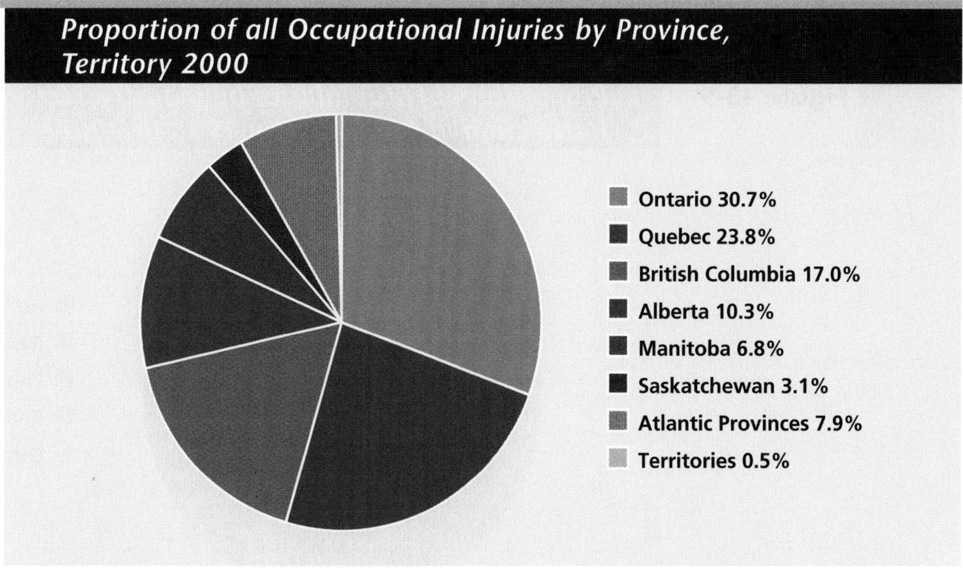

Source: Occupational Injuries Among Canadian Federal Jurisdiction Employers 1998–2002, Labour Program, Human Resources and Skills Development Canada. Reproduced with the permission of Her Majesty the Queen in Right of Canada 2006.

respectively). Fatal injuries occurred in large part in the road transport sector only, with 54.2 percent of all fatal injuries in the federal jurisdiction. These are denoted in Figure 13-5.

Workers' Compensation

Workers' compensation first came to Canada with parliament's passage of the Ontario Workmen's Compensation Act in 1914. Today, provincial and territorial workers' compensation acts are administered by workers' compensation boards (WCB). Under these laws, employers contribute to an insurance fund to compensate employees for injuries received while on the job. Premiums paid reflect the accident rates of the employers, with employers that have higher incident rates being assessed higher premiums. These laws usually provide payments to replace wages for injured workers, depending on the amount of lost time and the wage level. They also provide payments to cover medical bills, and for retraining if a worker cannot go back to the current job. Leading causes of worker injuries, which often result in workers' compensation claims, are overextension, falls, and losing balance.

Social Goals of Workers' Compensation Workers' compensation aims to achieve two social goals. The first is to prevent injuries or to reduce the psychological impact of an injury. The second is to rehabilitate any injured worker so that they can return to work as quickly as possible. However, claims for psychological trauma are not necessarily covered by workers' compensation since the legislation in some provinces covers only the psychological impact of a specific, unusual traumatic event. The cumulative impact of smaller traumas, even if clearly work-related and totally disabling, is not covered. Identifying valid trauma poses the same challenge as claims for toxic exposure.

A new twist on workers' compensation coverage relates to the increasing use of telecommuting by employees. In most situations, while working at home for employers, individuals are covered under workers' compensation laws. Therefore, if

Figure 13-5 *Proportion of Fatal Injuries by Industry Sectors Under Federal Jurisdiction in Canada from 1998 to 2002*

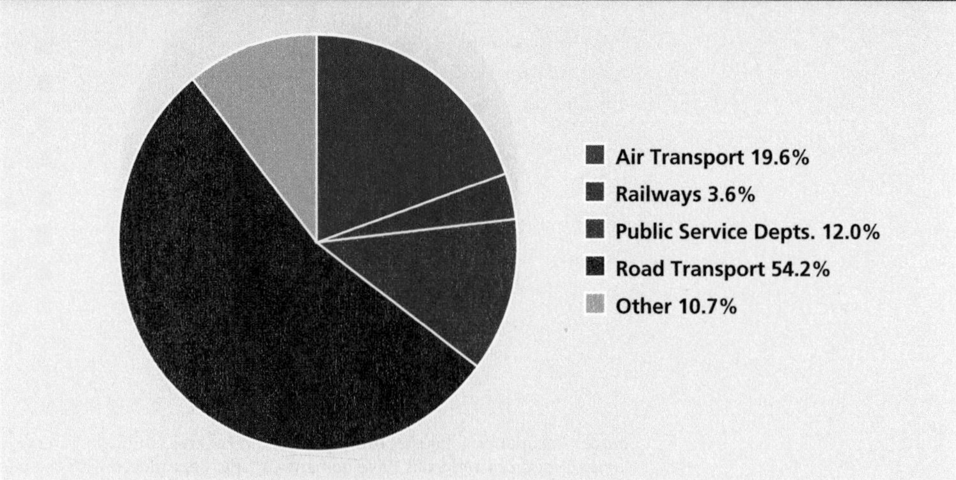

Source: Occupational Injuries Among Canadian Federal Jurisdiction Employers 1998–2002, Labour Program, Human Resources and Skills Development Canada. Reproduced with the permission of Her Majesty the Queen in Right of Canada 2006.

an employee is injured while doing employer-related work at home, the employer likely is liable for the injury. This aspect of workers' compensation liability is not widely known.

First Aid Requirements and Reporting to WCB Every jurisdiction in Canada has requirements for first aid in the workplace. In some provinces, such as in Ontario, all employers covered by the Workplace Safety and Insurance Act are required to have first aid equipment, facilities, and trained personnel in all workplaces. Regulation 1101, incorporated into the Workplace Safety and Insurance Act, states what each employer is obligated to provide. Employees are required to seek first aid attention no matter how small the injury may be. Employers are obligated to ensure medical treatment is provided and to provide transportation to either the hospital or the employee's home if required. Employers must complete a Form 7 and send it to the Workplace Safety and Insurance Board (WSIB) within three days of learning of a work-related injury or occupational disease that either causes a worker to be absent from their regular work; require modified duties at less than regular pay; earn less than regular pay at regular work; require modified duties at regular pay for more than seven calendar days; and/or obtain health care. When a death occurs on the job the appropriate ministry needs to be called immediately. Workplaces must also ensure that an individual who holds an up-to-date first aid certificate is available. They are usually responsible for keeping the supplies up-to-date in the first aid kits. Across most jurisdictions there must be at least one qualified first aid person for workplaces with less than five employees. In larger establishments, a more qualified first aid person, such as an occupational health nurse, must be employed.

Compensation Rates and Methods When an employee has a work related injury and are not able to work, they receive workers' compensation insurance. Payment is usually based on a percentage of net earnings, which is the salary amount determined after deductions have been made, or it might be based on average earnings. Every jurisdiction is different, and the rates can change from time to time. Workers' compensation is based on an individual's past earnings and not on the potential for future earnings.

There are two forms of compensation: (1) cash benefits or (2) wage or earnings loss. The first form is based on the severity or nature of the injuries. An injured worker will be paid until the disability is no longer in existence. Also, an injured worker can receive cash benefits for a non-economic loss. A non-economic loss will cover for activities that the individual used to be able to carry out, but is no longer able. For example, if the individual can no longer participate in activities such as golfing or camping with the family, etc., then an economic assessment is made and the employee is paid out an amount for the loss of the enjoyment. A wage or earnings loss occurs when an injured employee can no longer earn the same amount of money that they had made prior to the injury. This form of compensation is paid out until the employee is able to reach the wage he or she used to make.[13]

Controlling Workers' Compensation Costs Workers' compensation costs have increased for many employers and have become a major issue throughout all jurisdictions. These costs represent from 2 percent–10 percent of payroll for most employers. The major contributors to the increases have been higher medical costs and in some cases fraud. False and exaggerated claims make up the bulk of the fraud.[14] Employers must continually monitor their workers' compensation expenditures. Efforts to reduce workplace injuries, illnesses, and fraud can reduce workers' compensation premiums and claims costs. Many of the safety and health management suggestions discussed later in this chapter can contribute to reducing workers' compensation costs.

Discussions on fraud usually zero in on the employee. There are endless accounts of employees who have claimed to be too disabled to return to work to perform a function such as heavy lifting, but when put under surveillance have been seen lifting heavier items at home. But there are two sides to WCB systems: the workers who collect benefits and employers who pay into the system. A published British Columbia WCB assessment audit revealed that a significant percentage of employers "misreported their assessments" resulting in a conservative loss of $20 million to the WCB. Of the audited employers, the WCB found that: 36 percent misreported wages and salaries; 30 percent misreported subcontractors' earnings; 20 percent misreported shareholders earnings; and 14 percent were incorrectly classified. The audit found that 27 percent of the audited employers in the construction industry and 23 percent of those audited in the manufacturing industry misreported to the WCB. The report went on to say, "When employers misreport, they do so at the expense of other employers in their rate group, who end up subsidizing their assessment payments. Employers who don't pay their fair share of assessments gain a financial advantage over their competitors in the marketplace."[15]

Workplace Inspections by Inspection Officers

Workplace inspections are carried out to ensure compliance with the *Occupational Health and Safety Act* and regulations and to ensure that the internal responsibility system (IRS) is working. Inspections also provide the workplace parties with access to the special knowledge and expertise in occupational health and safety available from the government through inspectors. When inspections occur will depend on the type of workplace, its size, and its past record of health and safety. For example, construction projects may be inspected every three or four weeks; a factory may be inspected as problems arise; and a mine may be inspected about three times a year. Inspections may also be conducted in response to a specific complaint about a workplace. Such complaints are kept confidential. The inspection involves a thorough examination of the physical condition of the workplace by the inspector, who is usually accompanied by both employer and worker representatives.

The powers of the inspector are quite broad and employers are obligated under law to comply with any requests. They have the authority to enter any workplace without a warrant or notice. It is a contravention of the act to interfere in any way with an inspection. This includes giving false information, failing to give required information, or interfering with any monitoring equipment left in the workplace. One case occurred in Ontario when an owner of a body shop failed to allow an inspector to enter his premises. He was jailed for a month, and paid a fine.

Where there are contraventions of the act or the regulations, an inspector will issue written orders to the employer to comply with the law within a certain time period or, if the hazard is imminent to comply immediately. An inspector's order can require the employer to submit a plan to the ministry, specifying when and how he or she will comply with the order. When an inspector issues an order or a report of the inspection, a copy of the order or report must be posted in the workplace, where it is most likely to be seen by the workers. A copy must also be given to either the joint health and safety committee or the health and safety representative.

Child Labour and Health and Safety

Safety concerns are reflected in restrictions affecting younger workers, especially those under the age of 18. In Canada, the provinces, the territories, and the federal government regulate the employment of children and youths. Generally, children and youths under 18 may work as long as it does not hurt their health, welfare, or safety or interfere with school attendance. Most provinces do not allow children under the age of 14 to work except in special cases. In general, youths may start working in most industries and occupations at the age of 14 in New Brunswick, Newfoundland and Labrador, Ontario, and Quebec, at age 15 in Alberta and British Columbia, and at age 16 in Manitoba. In Nova Scotia, Prince Edward Island, and Saskatchewan, children younger than 14 may work in many jobs without a permit, but there are restrictions. Saskatchewan is one province that is considering reducing the age at which children can work as a means to address the skills shortage issue in that province.

The concern for the health and safety of young workers is real. A 24-year-old was killed shortly after midnight while trying to stop a young man from stealing $12 worth of gas in Maple Ridge, B.C. In August 2005, an 18-year-old female was killed walking home from her restaurant job at Wendy's at 12:30 a.m. in Ottawa. Her attacker was charged with murder in June 2006. In 2006, at least two more teenagers died on the job during night-time robberies—one at a gas station in Montreal, the other at a convenience store in Winnipeg. Workers are obviously more vulnerable in some settings compared to others.[16]

Most provinces prohibit minors from working on a variety of jobs that are dangerous, difficult, or likely to have a bad effect on a child's moral development. For example, in New Brunswick, minors under the age of 14 may not work in garages, dancehalls, or other places listed in the law. In Nova Scotia, minors under the age of 16 may not work in shooting galleries, pool rooms, or other places listed in the law. These incidents have heightened the issue about providing transportation to young workers who work after midnight. Currently some provinces have this mandated, but for the majority it does not apply, leaving young people vulnerable.

Penalties for Violation of OH&S Law

Under federal law, the maximum fine a person can receive is between $100,000 and $1,000,000 and/or two years' jail term on indictment. The provinces and territories will have different assessments. In Ontario, the maximum a person can receive is $25,000 fine and/or two months' jail time. A corporation can receive up to a $500,000 fine. With Bill C-45 now in force, there will be increased incidents of jail time.

Hazard Control

Hazard
Any activity, situation, or substance that can cause harm.

Safety hazard
Any force strong enough to cause injury in an accident. An injury caused by a safety hazard is usually obvious.

3 Employers have a legal and moral duty to protect the health and safety of workers by preventing workplace injuries and illness. Workers have a duty to help with prevention efforts. Workplace injuries and illnesses can be prevented if unsafe work practices are corrected and workplace hazards are identified and dealt with. Every workplace, large or small, should have a system in place to identify hazards, assess the risk of those hazards, and make the necessary changes to control risk.

Occupational hazards exist in all workplaces. A **hazard** is any activity, situation, or substance that can cause harm. Occupational hazards are divided into two broad categories: safety hazards and health hazards. **Safety hazards** cause physical harm such as cuts, broken bones, strains and sprains. Safety hazards cause harm when workplace controls are not adequate. Generally health hazards cause occupational illnesses (e.g., respiratory problems caused by exposure to chemical substances, noise-induced hearing loss, repetitive strain injuries). It may produce serious and immediate effects and/or long term problems. Someone with an occupational illness may not recognize the symptoms immediately.

Occupational health hazard
An occupational health hazard is any material or condition that may cause occupational injuries and/or illness.

Occupational health hazards include chemicals (e.g., battery acid, solvents), which is addressed through WHMIS training, biological hazards (e.g., bacteria, viruses, dusts, moulds), physical agents (e.g., energy sources strong enough to harm the body, such as electric currents, heat, light, vibration, noise, radiation), ergonomic hazards (e.g., poor work station design), and other stress agents (e.g., violence and harassment). There are three basic steps in controlling the risk from those hazards:

1. *eliminate hazards* posed by equipment and work processes at their source (e.g., redesign the work process, substitute a safer chemical for a hazardous chemical, use new equipment)
2. if it is not practical to eliminate hazards, *control the hazard* to reduce the risk to workers (e.g., machine guards, noise enclosures, ventilation to dilute the concentration of a hazardous substance)
3. if it is not practical to control the hazard, *protect workers from the hazard* by using tools such as administrative controls, safe work procedures, effective safety training, proper supervision, or personal protective equipment (PPE).

The following will focus on hazards related to chemicals and a discussion of WHMIS and ergonomics as well as some basic controls to protect workers from hazards. The last of the hazards, workplace security, will be addressed in the next section.

Employers must ensure that their employees are wearing the proper protective equipment (PPE) when performing their jobs, ensuring adherence to due diligence.

Source: Robert Pernell/ShutterStock

Workplace Hazardous Materials Information System (WHMIS)
A comprehensive plan for providing information on the safe handling of hazardous materials used in Canadian workplaces.

Workplace Hazardous Materials Information System (WHMIS)

The **Workplace Hazardous Materials Information System (WHMIS)** was enacted as Bill-70 on June 30, 1987. WHMIS is a comprehensive plan for providing information on the safe handling of hazardous materials used in Canadian workplaces. Under federal legislation it involves the sale and import of controlled products (hazardous materials). Under provincial legislation, once a controlled product enters a workplace, jurisdiction over the product shifts from federal to provincial governments (except for workplaces under federal jurisdiction, where the provisions of the amended Canada Labour Code apply). It addresses one of the workers' fundamental rights to know about the safety and health hazards that may be associated with the materials or chemicals they use at work. It is based on three elements:

1. *Labels.* There are two types of labels that are required in the labelling of dangerous material substances—*supplier and workplace labels. Supplier* labels contain six mandatory items: hatched border, written in English and French, product identifier, supplier identifier, hazard symbol(s), and MSDS reference. Containers with more than 100 ml must also include risk phrases, precautionary measures, and first aid measures. *Workplace* labels are used to identify the class of the material. They appear on all controlled products produced in a workplace or transferred to other containers by the employer. They must show the product identifier (product name), information for the safe handling of the product, and a statement that the MSDS is available. Figure 13-6 shows the hazard symbols that might appear on a supplier label.
2. *Material Safety Data Sheets (MSDSs).* A MSDS is a document that contains information on the potential hazards (health, fire, reactivity, and environmental) and how to work safely with the chemical product. It also contains information on the use, storage, handling, and emergency procedures all related to the hazards of the material. The MSDS contains much more information about the material than the label. MSDSs are prepared by the supplier or manufacturer of the material. There are nine categories of information that must be present on an MSDS in Canada: (1) product information including product identifier (name), manufacturer and supplier's names, addresses, and emergency phone numbers; (2) hazardous ingredients; (3) physical data; (4) fire or explosion hazard data; (5) reactivity data: information on the chemical instability of a product and the substances it may react with; (6) toxicological properties and health effects; (7) preventive measures; (8) first aid measures; (9) preparation information including who is responsible for preparation and date of preparation of the MSDS. Employees must know where the MSDSs are kept at all times. They must also be updated every three years, or sooner if information changes. MSDSs can be kept on computer, as long as everyone is trained on how to access the information.
3. *Training.* Employers must provide WHMIS training to all of their employees. Once trained, an employee should be able to identify the WHMIS hazard symbols, read both types of WHMIS labels, and have the ability to apply the information used on an MSDS.

Ergonomics
Study and design of the work environment to address physiological and physical demands on individuals.

Ergonomics

Ergonomics is the study and design of the work environment to address physiological and physical demands on individuals. In a work setting, ergonomic studies look at such factors as fatigue, lighting, tools, equipment layout, and placement of controls.

Figure 13-6 WHMIS Classes and Hazard Symbols

There are 8 WHMIS hazard symbols. Employers must train workers to recognize these symbols and to know what they mean.

Class A: Compressed Gas
This class includes compressed gases, dissolved gases, and gases liquefied by compression or refrigeration.

Class B: Flammable and Combustible Material
This class includes solids, liquids, and gases capable of catching fire in the presence of a spark or open flame under normal working conditions.

Class C: Oxidizing Material
These materials increase the risk of fire if they come in contact with flammable or combustible materials.

Class D: Poisonous and Infectious Material Division 1: Materials Causing Immediate and Serious Toxic Effects
These materials can cause death or injury when a person is exposed to small amounts. Examples: sodium cyanide, hydrogen sulphide.

Class D: Poisonous and Infectious Material Division 2: Materials Causing Other Toxic Effects
These materials can cause life-threatening and serious long-term health problems as well as less severe but immediate reactions in a person who is repeatedly exposed to small amounts.

Class D: Poisonous and Infectious Material Division 3: Biohazardous Infectious Material
These materials contain harmful micro-organisms that have been classified into Risk Groups 2, 3, and 4 as determined by the World Health Organization (WHO) or the Medical Research Council of Canada.

Class E: Corrosive Material
This class includes caustic and acid materials that can destroy the skin or eat through metals. Examples: sodium hydroxide, hydrochloric acid, nitric acid.

Class F: Dangerously Reactive Material
These products may self-react dangerously (for example, they may explode) upon standing or when exposed to physical shock or to increased pressure or temperature, or they emit toxic gases when exposed to water.

Source: WHMIS Classes, Divisions, and Subdivisions and Corresponding Hazard Symbols, Health Canada. Adapted and reproduced with the permission of the Minister of Public Works and Government Services Canada, 2006.

In Canada, British Columbia was the first province to pass ergonomic legislation due to the fact that over a five-year period, one third of compensation claims in British Columbia came from ergonomics-related injuries.[17] Saskatchewan followed suit not long after. According to the Workplace Safety and Insurance Board in Ontario, there were 41 670 musculoskeletal injuries resulting in lost time at work in 2003, which accounted for over 40 percent of all lost-time injuries in Ontario workplaces. Although legislation has not yet been enacted in Ontario with respect to ergonomics, Ontario established an Ergonomics Advisory Panel in February 2005 as part of its plan to reduce workplace injuries by 20 percent by 2008.[18] In 2006, Ontario Ministry of Labour inspectors began targeting high-risk workplaces in industrial and health sectors to raise awareness of pains and strains. Each organization's experience with these types of injuries are reviewed along with the preventive steps they have taken, and when necessary, issue orders. Employers have a duty under the Occupational Health and Safety Act to take every reasonable precaution to protect workers from injury; this includes protecting against ergonomic-related hazards.[19]

Workplace pains and strains are also known as musculoskeletal disorders or injury (MSDs or MSIs), repetitive strain injury (RSI), cumulative trauma disorder (CTD), and repetitive motion injury (RMI). These types of injuries affect the muscles, tendons, ligaments, and nerves. Figure 13-7 demonstrates some problems that may be encountered in the workplace when a workstation is not set up properly, as well as the proper way to set up a workstation.

Cumulative trauma disorders (CTDs) Muscle and skeletal injuries that occur when workers repetitively use the same muscles to perform tasks.

Cumulative trauma disorders (CTDs) are muscle and skeletal injuries that occur when workers repetitively use the same muscles to perform tasks. Carpal tunnel

Figure 13-7 *Workstation Design*

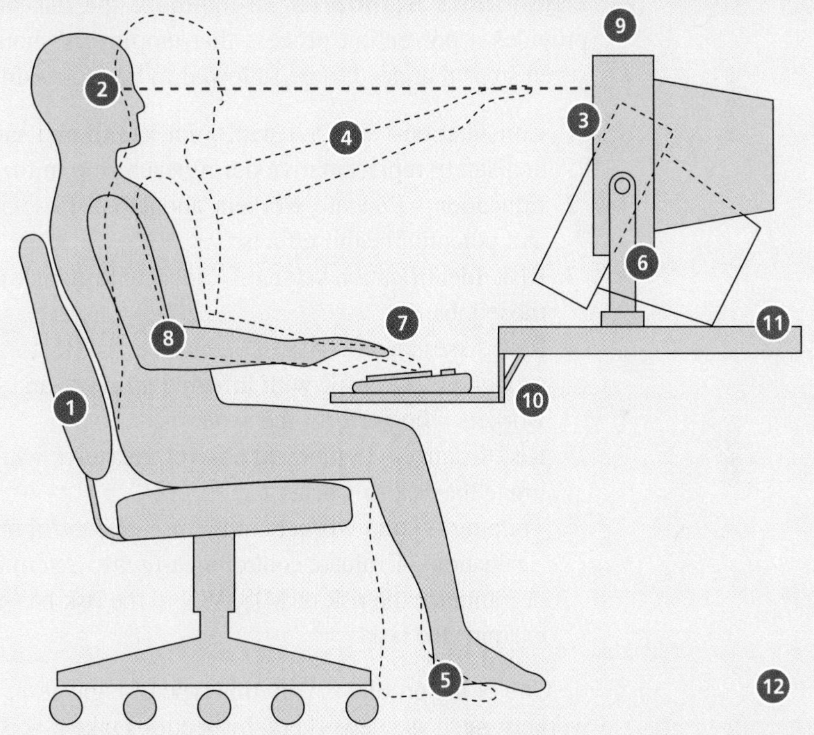

1. Use a good chair with a dynamic chair back and sit back.
2. Top of monitor casing 2–3" (5–8 cm) above eye level.
3. No glare on screen, use an optical glass anti-glare filter where needed.
4. Sit at arms' length from monitor.
5. Feet on floor or stable footrest.
6. Use a document holder, preferably in-line with the computer screen.
7. Wrists flat and straight in relation to forearms to use keyboard/mouse/input device.
8. Arms and elbows relaxed close to body.
9. Centre monitor and keyboard in front of you.
10. Use a negative tilt keyboard tray with an upper mouse platform or downward tiltable platform adjacent to keyboard.
11. Use a stable work surface and stable (no bounce) keyboard tray.
12. Take frequent short breaks (microbreaks).

Source: Information on this page was compiled by the DEA651 class of 2000—Bethany Johnson; Emily Kuperstein; Mari Mitchell; Heidi Tinnes; with Garrick Goh (TA) and Professor Alan Hedge, Cornell University Ergonomics Website, November 2, 2002. Reprinted by permission.

syndrome, a cumulative trauma disorder, is an injury common to people who put their hands through repetitive motions such as typing, playing certain musical instruments, cutting, and sewing. The motion irritates the tendons in the carpal tunnel area of the wrist. As the tendons swell, they squeeze the median nerve. The result is pain and numbness in the thumb, index finger, and middle finger. The hands of victims become clumsy and weak. Pain at night increases, and at advanced stages, not even surgery can cure the problem. Victims eventually lose feeling in their hands if they do not receive timely treatment.

Problems caused by repetitive and cumulative injuries occur in a variety of work settings. The meatpacking industry has the highest level of CTDs. Grocery cashiers experience CTDs from repetitively twisting their wrists when they scan bar codes on canned goods. Office workers experience CTDs too, primarily from doing extensive typing and data entry on computers and computer-related equipment. Most recently, attention has focused on the application of ergonomic principles to the design of workstations where computer operators work with personal computers and video display terminals for extended periods of time.

Ergonomics Standards To minimize the risk of MSD, the government of B.C. provides a prevention process that employers should follow. They have developed seven steps that need to be followed to be successful:[20]

1. Consultation—Consult with joint health and safety committee or worker health and safety representative during each step in the MSI prevention process.
2. Education—Educate workers about risk factors, signs and symptoms of injury, and potential health effects.
3. Risk Identification—Identify jobs with a risk of MSI. Identify risk factors on those jobs.
4. Risk Assessment—Assess identified risk factors to determine the degree of risk to workers. Consult with affected workers and a representative sample of other workers who perform the same risks.
5. Risk Control—Implement control measures where required, to eliminate or minimize the risk to workers.
6. Training—Train workers in the use of control measures.
7. Evaluation—Evaluate control measures to determine their effectiveness to eliminate or minimize the risk of MIS. Where the risk has not been effectively controlled, re-examine the task.

One of the problems with this type of legislation is that it does not address certain workers, such as teleworkers. Inspections take place at the workplace only, and not at an individual's home. The HR Perspective highlights the ergonomics issues associated with telework.

Successful Ergonomics Programs There are several components of a successful ergonomics program. First, management must commit to reducing injuries caused by repetition and cumulative trauma, including providing financial and other resources to support the efforts. Involvement of employees is key to getting employee support. Other actions should include reviewing jobs where CTD problems could exist and ensuring that proper equipment, seating, lighting, and other engineering solutions are utilized. Also, supervisors and managers should be trained to observe signs of CTD and how to respond to employee complaints about musculoskeletal and repetitive motion problems.

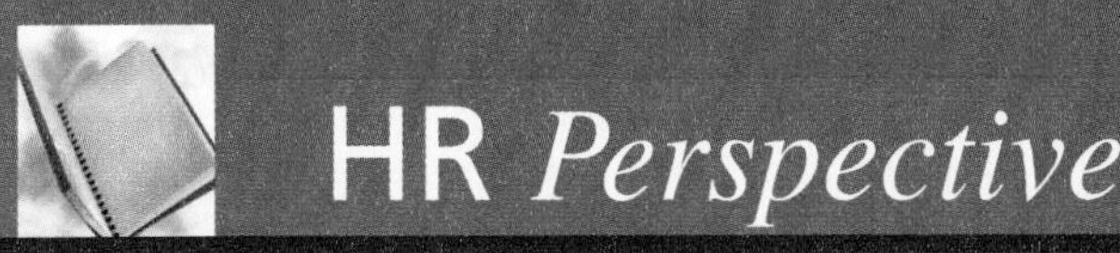

HR Perspective

Telework and Ergonomics

Flexible work arrangements, such as allowing workers to work away from their regular place of employment, have increased due to the rapid growth of information technology in recent years. It is estimated that more than 1.5 million Canadians use some form of telework (usually in the home). Unfortunately, ergonomics is often ignored by both employer and employees who use telework. This ignorance, plus a lack of training, leads to a greater risk of injuries or health problems: "The absence of information or training for teleworkers means they are most likely to suffer ergonomic injuries or problems. These can include eye-strain, back problems, repetitive stress and other injuries. In turn, these can lead to absenteeism and diminished productivity."

Employers have a duty to provide all of their workers with a safe work environment. When an employer has agreed to a flexible arrangement with an employee, both parties should consider using these ergonomic tips when setting up a home office:

- The desk, chair and other accessories are of comparable quality to those in the office. For example: the desk should be the appropriate height and be sturdy enough to handle the weight of any peripheral equipment placed on it such as computers, printers, fax machines, scanners;
- The workstation is adjusted properly: the keyboard is at the right height (wrists are in a neutral position). The kitchen table is not an ideal work surface as the table is too high and doesn't allow for proper positioning of the wrists in relation to the keyboard; and
- Lighting is properly arranged: there should not be reflections on or glare from the computer monitor.[21]

1. Working in groups, have each member contact an employer to determine if they have an ergonomics policy. Once all group members have secured a policy, compare them for similarities and differences? What did you find? What would you suggest to these companies?
2. Working with the policies secured for question 1, develop an ergonomics policy that students should use while attending school. Does it differ from the policies you solicited? What is different? Why is it different?

Lockout/Tagout

Lockout/tagout
Requirement that locks and tags be used to make equipment inoperative for repair or adjustment.

Lockout/tagout is a procedure used to control the flow of hazardous energy that could result in injury or death. To comply with legislation, firms must provide mechanics and tradespeople with locks and tags for use when they make equipment inoperative for repair or adjustment to prevent accidental startup of defective machinery. Only the person whose name is printed on the tag or engraved on the lock may remove the device.

Personal Protective Equipment (PPE)

Personal protective equipment (PPE)
Clothing or equipment worn to minimize a hazard.

A goal of legislation has been to develop standards for **personal protective equipment (PPE).** PPE is clothing or equipment worn to minimize a hazard. PPE does not remove a hazard and it does not guarantee protection. Legislative standards require that employers analyze job hazards, provide adequate PPE to employees in hazardous jobs, and train employees in the use of PPE items. Common PPE items include safety glasses, hard hats, and safety shoes. If the work environment presents hazards or if employees might have contact with hazardous chemicals and substances on the job, then employers are required to provide PPE to all those employees.

Security Concerns at Work

4 The last of the hazards are related to security concerns at work. Traditionally, when employers have addressed worker health, safety, and security, they have been concerned about reducing workplace accidents, improving workers' safety practices, and

reducing health hazards at work. Over the past decade, providing security for employees has grown in importance. Top security concerns at work are as follows:

- Workplace violence
- Internet/intranet security
- Business interruption/disaster recovery
- Fraud/white-collar crime
- Employee selection/screening concerns

Notice that virtually all of these areas have significant HR implications. Heading the list of security concerns is workplace violence.

Workplace Violence

Canadian Initiative on Workplace Violence (CIWV)
This initiative provides research, information, and training on workplace violence.
www.workplaceviolence.ca/

In 2002, the Ontario Workplace Safety and Insurance Board received 1747 claims for lost-time injuries—injuries that forced the employee to take at least a day off work—that resulted from assaults and violent acts in the workplace. That figure was between 10 and 15 percent higher than in each of the previous six years. Fatalities are quite rare in Canada, unlike that of the U.S. that reports 10–15 workplace homicides every year.[22] A July 1998 report on workplace violence by the International Labour Organization compiled from 130 000 interviews found that [23]

- Canada ranks 4th out of 32 countries for the number of women assaulted in the workplace
- Canada ranks 5th for the number of men assaulted in the workplace
- Canadian women report the 4th highest incidence of sexual harassment in the workplace

Almost 80 percent of workplace killings occur when a stranger comes on the premises. In the remaining 20 percent, the killer has some relationship with the workplace—as a former employee, customer, etc.[24] It is always a shock when a disgruntled employee or former employee resorts to workplace violence in the workplace to deal with their anger and grievances.

There are a number of warning signs and characteristics of a potentially violent person at work. Individuals who have committed the most violent acts have had the relatively common profile depicted in Figure 13-8. A person with some of these signs may cope for years until a trauma pushes the individual over the edge. A profound humiliation or rejection, the end of a marriage, the loss of a lawsuit, or termination from a job may make a difficult employee turn violent.

Figure 13-8 *Profile of a Potentially Violent Employee*

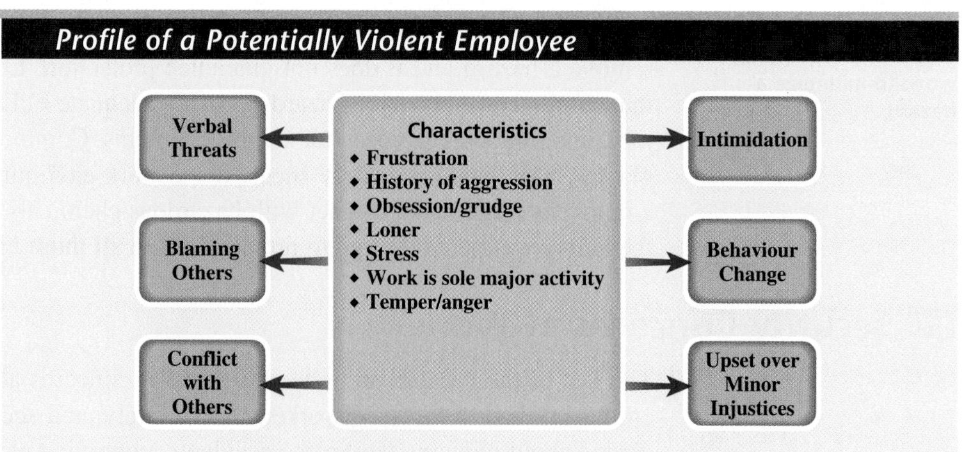

Employers need to ensure that they are providing workplaces that are free of workplace violence. If violence does occur, then employers must have plans to respond afterwards.

Source: Brand X Pictures/Alamy

Management of Workplace Violence The increase in workplace violence has led many employers to develop policies and practices for preventing and responding to workplace violence. As a first step, employers need to conduct a risk assessment of the organization and its employees. Unfortunately, few employers have conducted such a study. After completing a study, an organization can establish HR policies to identify how workplace violence is to be dealt with in conjunction with disciplinary actions and referrals to employee assistance programs.

One aspect of these policies is a violence response team. A violence response team, composed of security personnel, key managers, HR staff members, and selected employees, functions much like a safety committee but with a different focus. Such teams conduct analyses, respond to and investigate employee threats, and may even help calm angry, volatile employees.

Post-violence response is another part of managing workplace violence. Whether the violence results in physical injuries or deaths, or just intense interpersonal conflicts, it is important that employers have plans to respond afterward. Their response must reassure employees who may be fearful of returning to work or who experience anxiety and sleeplessness, among other reactions. Providing referrals to employee assistance programs (EAP) resources, allowing employees time to meet with HR staff, and arranging for trained counsellors onsite are all part of post-violence response efforts.

Domestic Causes of Workplace Violence Women are much more likely than men to experience violence committed as a result of a personal relationship. Too often, violence that begins at home with family or "friends" can spill over to the workplace. One in five homicides of women at work is perpetrated by current or former husbands or boyfriends. Also, many abused women report being harassed frequently at work, by telephone, or in person by abusing partners.

Workplace violence is a difficult concern, and guarantees for eliminating it do not exist. However, the following are suggestions that may help combat violence at work.

- Zero-tolerance policies (immediate termination for violent acts or threats)
- Referral of both violent employees and victims to EAPs
- Employee/supervisor training in conflict resolution and stress recognition
- Access to legal counselling
- Use of restraining orders against aggressors
- Training to identify potential victims, bullies, or aggressors
- Self-defence training for employees
- Careful screening for violent predictors in the employee selection process
- Limited access to the facility
- Profiling of potentially violent workers
- Formation of a violence response team

Bullying in the Workplace The CCOHS defines bullying as, "acts or verbal comments that could 'mentally' hurt or isolate a person in the workplace." It also involves repeated incidents that are intended to, "intimidate, offend, degrade, or humiliate a particular person or group of people." Examples of workplace bullying include:

- Spreading malicious rumours, gossip, or innuendo that is not true
- Excluding or isolating someone socially
- Intimidating a person
- Undermining or deliberately impeding a person's work
- Physically abusing or threatening abuse
- Removing areas of responsibilities without cause
- Constantly changing work guidelines
- Establishing impossible deadlines that will set up the individual to fail
- Withholding necessary information or purposefully giving the wrong information

A victim of bullying can develop feelings of shock, anger, frustration, vulnerability, and physical symptoms such as loss of sleep and/or appetite. These symptoms can result in an increase in absenteeism, turnover, and stress for the victims involved.[25] Automatically they can react violently if pushed too far.

On April 6, 1999, a former employee of OC Transpo in Ottawa went on a shooting rampage that left four employees dead and then took his own life. The killer had himself been the victim of workplace harassment. Among the recommendations of a coroner's inquest was that the definition of workplace violence should include not only physical violence but also psychological violence such as bullying, mobbing, teasing, ridicule, or any other act or words that could psychologically hurt or isolate a person in the workplace. At that time no bullying legislation existed.[26] As a result of this incident, the first anti-bullying law in North America came into effect on June 1, 2004 in Quebec. More recently, a B.C. male employee was charged with second-degree murder in an altercation that resulted in the death of another male co-worker.[27]

Quebec has amended its Labour Standards Act to deal with psychological harassment in the workplace. The new Quebec law defines psychological harassment as "any vexatious behaviour in the form of repeated and hostile or unwanted conduct, verbal comments, actions or gestures that affect an employee's dignity or psychological or physical integrity and that results in a harmful work environment for the employee." According to the Commission des normes du travail, surveys show that up to 1 in 10 Quebec workers has been the subject of harmful bullying, intimidation, or belittlement by a boss or co-worker. Officials emphasize that they want to prevent rather than prosecute. Systems are in place to settle most claims by negotiation. A similar amendment has been proposed to the Canada Labour Code, which applies to all federal government employees. The Workplace Psychological Harassment Prevention Act would impose fines of up to $10,000 for "hostile, inappropriate and unwanted conduct, verbal comments or gestures . . ." as well as "any abuse of authority, including intimidation, threats, blackmail or coercion." Bullying legislation will also be enacted in Ontario in the near future.[28]

Training on Dealing with Workplace Violence Managers, HR staff members, supervisors, and employees should be trained on how to recognize the signs of a potentially violent employee and what to do when violence occurs. During training at many firms, participants learn the typical profile of potentially violent employees and are trained to notify the HR department and to refer employees to outside counselling professionals. Specific suggestions addressed in training for dealing with potentially violent employees include the following:

- Notice verbal and non-verbal reactions by individuals that may indicate anger or hostility.

- Listen to individuals exhibiting such reactions, and pay attention to the words, actions, and unspoken "messages."
- Ask questions requiring explanations and longer answers that allow individuals to "vent."
- Respond calmly and non-threateningly to individuals' emotions, and acknowledge concerns and understanding about how the individuals feel.
- Get assistance from others, particularly HR staff members or another manager not directly affected by the situation being discussed.
- Indicate the need for time to respond to the concerns voiced, and then set up another time for follow-up.
- Notify security personnel and HR staff members whenever employees' behaviours change dramatically or when job disciplinary action may provoke significant reactions by employees.

Security Management

An overall approach to security management is needed to address a wide range of issues, including workplace violence. Often, HR managers have responsibility for security programs, or they work closely with security managers or consultants to address employee security issues.

Security audit
Comprehensive review of organizational security.

Security Audit In a security audit, HR staff conduct a comprehensive review of organizational security. Sometimes called a *vulnerability analysis,* such an audit uses managers inside the organization (such as the HR manager and the facilities manager) and outsiders (such as security consultants, police officers, fire officials, and computer security experts) to assess security issues.

Typically, a security audit begins with a survey of the area around the facility. Such factors as lighting in parking lots, traffic flow, location of emergency response services, crime in the surrounding neighbourhood, and the layout of the buildings and grounds are evaluated.[29] The audit also may include a review of the security available within the firm, including the capabilities of guards. Another part of the security audit reviews disaster plans, which address how to deal with events such as earthquakes, floods, tornados, hurricanes, and fires. Efforts to prepare for catastrophes like these have become even more prominent since 9/11.

Controlled Access A key part of security involves controlling access to the physical facilities of the organization. As mentioned earlier, many workplace homicides occur during robberies. Therefore, employees who are most vulnerable, such as taxi drivers and convenience store clerks, often are provided bulletproof partitions and restricted access areas.

Many organizations limit access to facilities and work areas by using electronic access or keycard systems. Although not foolproof, these systems can make it more difficult for an unauthorized person, such as an estranged husband or a disgruntled ex-employee, to enter the premises. Access controls can also be used in elevators and stairwells to prevent unauthorized persons from entering designated areas within a facility.[30]

Computer Security Yet another part of security centres on controlling access to computer systems. With so many transactions and records being handled by computers, adequate security provisions are crucial to prevent unauthorized access to computer information systems. Growth of the Internet and of e-mail systems has made computer security issues an even greater concern. This concern is magnified when individuals are terminated or leave an organization. HR staff must coordinate with information technology staff to change passwords, delete access codes, and otherwise protect company information systems.[31]

Security Personnel

Providing adequately trained security personnel in sufficient numbers is a critical part of security management. Many employers contract for these personnel with firms specializing in security. If security is handled inhouse, security personnel must be selected and trained to handle a variety of workplace security problems, ranging from dealing with violent behaviour by an employee to taking charge in natural disasters.

Safety Management

5 Well-designed and well-managed safety programs can pay dividends in reduced accidents and associated costs, such as workers' compensation and possible fines. Further, accidents and other safety concerns usually decline as a result of management efforts emphasizing safety. Often, the difference between firms with good safety performance and firms that are well below the industry average is that the former have effective safety management programs.

Successful safety management is not a mystery. The topic has been researched extensively.[32] A summary of what is known about managing to minimize accidents includes discussion of these issues:

- Organizational commitment
- Policies, discipline, and recordkeeping
- Training and communication
- Participation (safety committees)
- Inspection, investigation, and evaluation

Organizational Commitment and a Safety Culture

Three approaches are used by employers in managing safety. Figure 13-9 shows the organizational, engineering, and individual approaches and their components. Successful programs may use all three in dealing with safety issues.

At the heart of safety management is an organizational commitment to a comprehensive safety effort. This effort should be coordinated from the top level of management to include all members of the organization. It should also be reflected in managerial actions. If the president of a small electrical manufacturing firm does not wear a hard hat in the manufacturing shop, he can hardly expect to enforce a requirement that all employees wear hard hats in the shop. Unfortunately, sincere support by top management often is missing from safety programs.

One result of a strong commitment to safety is that a "safety culture" pervades the organization. Firms such as 3M, DuPont Chemical, and Dofasco are well known for emphasizing safety as part of their organizational cultures.

Safety and Engineering Employers can prevent some accidents by having machines, equipment, and work areas designed so that workers who daydream periodically or who perform potentially dangerous jobs cannot injure themselves and others. Providing safety equipment and guards on machinery, installing emergency switches, installing safety rails, keeping aisles clear, and installing adequate ventilation, lighting, heating, and air conditioning can all help make work environments safer.

Figure 13-9 Approaches to Effective Safety Management

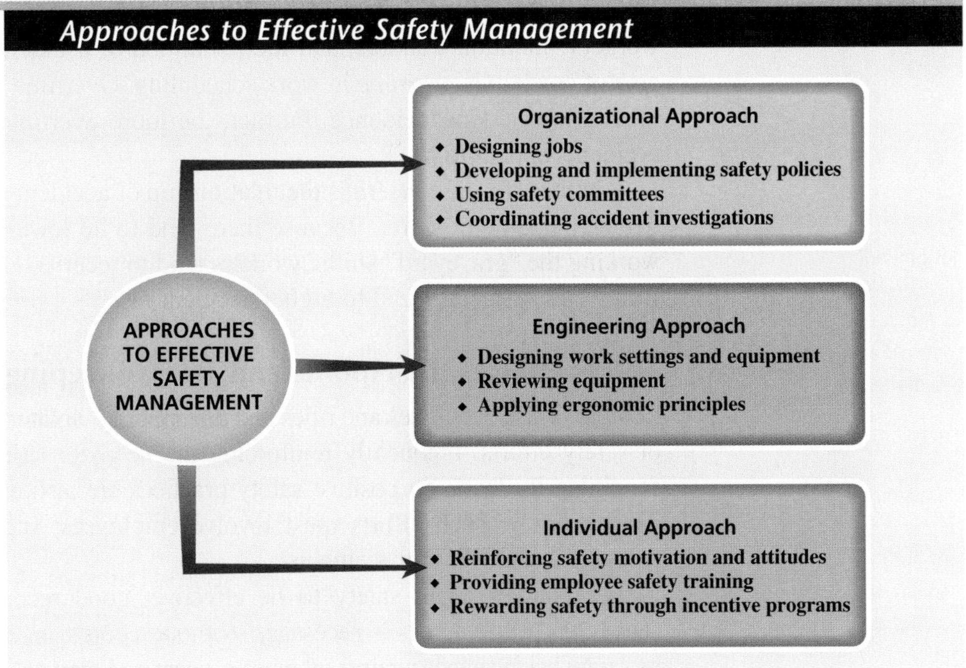

Designing a job properly requires consideration of the physical setting of the job. The way the workspace surrounding a job is utilized can influence the worker's performance of the job itself. Several factors that affect safety have been identified, including size of work area, kinds of materials used, sensory conditions, distance between work areas, and interference from noise and traffic flow.

Individual Considerations and Safety Engineers approach safety from the perspective of redesigning the machinery or the work area. Industrial psychologists and "human factors" experts see safety differently. They address the proper match of individuals to jobs and emphasize employee training in safety methods, fatigue reduction, and health awareness. Numerous field studies with thousands of employees, conducted by experts, have looked at the human factors in accidents. The results have shown a definite relationship between *emotional factors,* such as stress, and accidents. Other studies point to the importance of *individual differences, motivation, attitudes,* and *learning* as key factors in controlling the human element in safety.

Behaviour-based safety (BBS) approaches are efforts to reduce *risky behaviour* and increase safe behaviour by defining unsafe behaviour and attempting to change it.[33] BBS provides companies with a new-data gathering process that both complements and supports other safety programs already in place, e.g., inspections, audits, etc. Dow Chemical's Sarnia site started using BBS in late 1994 with their site contractors and achieved significant results. On average, a reduction of 30 percent in recordable injuries in the first year and up to 90 percent over a three-year period was achieved at Dow Chemical.[34] A successful BBS program is dependent on it being a "fact-finding" program vs. a "fault-finding" program. While BBS is beneficial, it does not constitute a complete approach to dealing with safety.

Work schedules can be another cause for accidents. The relationship between work schedules and accidents can be explained as follows: Fatigue based on physical exertion sometimes exists in the industrial workplace of today. Boredom, which occurs when a person is required to do the same tasks for a long period of time, is rather common. As fatigue increases, motivation decreases; when motivation decreases, workers' attention wanders, and the likelihood of accidents increases.[35] A particular area of concern is *overtime* in work scheduling. Overtime work has been consistently related to accident incidence. Further, the more overtime worked, the more severe accidents appear to be.[36]

Another area of concern is the relationship of accident rates to *different shifts,* particularly late-night shifts. Because there tend to be fewer supervisors and managers working the "graveyard" shifts, workers tend to receive less training and supervision. Both of these factors lead to higher accident rates.

Safety Policies, Discipline, and Recordkeeping

Designing safety policies and rules and disciplining violators are important components of safety efforts. Frequently reinforcing the need for safe behaviour and frequently supplying feedback on positive safety practices are also effective ways of improving worker safety. Such efforts must involve employees, supervisors, managers, safety specialists, and HR staff members.

For policies about safety to be effective, good recordkeeping about accidents, causes, and other details is necessary. Without records, an employer cannot benchmark its safety performance against other employers and may not realize there is a problem.[37] More importantly, employers are required by law to keep up-to-date information on all aspects of health and safety. The following are examples of what kinds of information should be tracked:

- Work related injuries, illnesses, and fatalities
- Record of all first aid treatment
- Record of compensation records
- Summary of work related injuries, illnesses, and fatalities
- Number of employees and total hours worked
- Training received on specific pieces of equipment or other related training with a signature acknowledging the specifics of the training with accurate dates
- Discipline including all verbal discussions documented and written
- Accident investigation reports
- Workplace inspections
- WHMIS information

Safety Training and Communication

Good safety training reduces accidents. Supervisors should receive the training first, and then employees should receive it as well, because untrained workers are more likely to have accidents. Safety training can be done in various ways. Regular sessions with supervisors, managers, and employees are often coordinated by HR staff members.

Communication of safety procedures, reasons why accidents occurred, and what to do in an emergency is critical. Without effective communication about safety, training is insufficient. To reinforce safety training, continuous communication to develop safety consciousness is necessary. Merely sending safety memos is not enough. Producing newsletters, changing safety posters, continually updating bulletin boards, and posting safety information in visible areas are also recommended.

Employers may need to communicate in a variety of media and languages to address the special needs of workers who have vision, speech, or hearing impairments; who are not proficient in English; or who are challenged in other ways.[38]

Inspection, Investigation, and Evaluation

Workplace inspections are conducted on a regular basis by a safety committee. Problem areas should be addressed immediately, to keep productivity at the highest possible levels. The goal of the committee is to identify potentially hazardous conditions, and to notify senior management in writing of their findings. A check-off list is used to ensure that all areas inspected in the workplace are reviewed and addressed. It is up to senior management to address the concerns.

Another type of inspection that may occur is an accident investigation. An accident investigation is beneficial because it can determine direct causes, identify contributing causes, prevent similar accidents, create a permanent record, determine costs, and promote safety awareness among employees.[39] An accident investigation can be influenced by the timing of the investigation, the severity of the accident, and legal requirements (in terms of reporting requirements).

When accidents occur, they must be investigated by the employer's safety committee or safety coordinator. The phases of accident investigation are depicted in Figure 13-10. In investigating the scene of an accident, the inspector needs to:

1. Determine which physical and environmental conditions contributed to the accident. Investigation at the scene should be done as soon as possible after an accident to ensure that the conditions under which the accident occurred have not changed significantly.
2. Interview the injured employee, his or her supervisor, and witnesses to the accident. The interviewer attempts to determine what happened and what caused the accident. These interviews may also generate some suggestions on how to prevent similar accidents in the future.
3. Using observations of the scene and interviews, the investigator completes an accident investigation report.
4. The investigator makes recommendations on how the accident could have been prevented, and on what changes are needed to avoid similar accidents. Identifying why an accident occurred is useful; taking steps to prevent similar accidents from occurring is also important.

Closely related to accident investigation is research to determine ways of preventing accidents. Employing safety engineers or having outside experts evaluate the safety of working conditions is useful. If many similar accidents seem to occur in an organizational unit, a safety training program may be necessary to emphasize safe working practices. As an example, a printing company reported a greater-than-average number of back injuries among employees who lifted heavy boxes. Safety training on the proper way to lift heavy objects was initiated to reduce the number of back injuries.

Organizations should monitor and evaluate their safety efforts. Just as organizational accounting records are audited, a firm's safety efforts should be audited periodically as well. Accident and injury statistics should be compared with previous

Figure 13-10 *Phases of Accident Investigation*

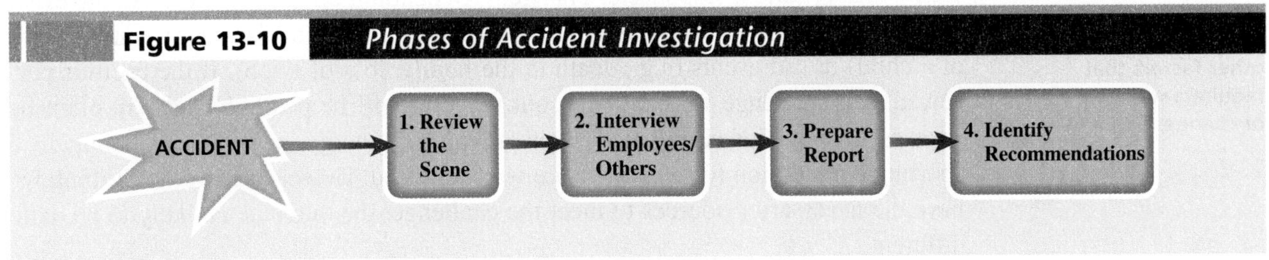

accident patterns to identify any significant changes. This analysis should be designed to measure progress in safety management.

Employee Health and Wellness

Warren Shepell
Warren Shepell assists organizations in optimizing their potential success by developing and delivering effective services and solutions that focus on the emotional and psychological well-being of their employees.
www.warrenshepell.com/

6 Employee health problems are varied—and somewhat inevitable. They can range from minor illnesses such as colds to serious illnesses related to the jobs performed. Some employees have emotional health problems that can lead to alcohol or drug problems. Some problems are chronic; others are transitory. All may affect organizational operations and individual employee productivity.

Employers face a variety of workplace health issues. Previously in this chapter, cumulative trauma injuries and exposure to hazardous chemicals have been discussed because OH&S acts have addressed these concerns through regulations or standards. There are other concerns associated with emotional/mental health, which can lead to stress that could result in such things as depression, employee substance abuse, and obesity.

Emotional/Mental Health

Mental health is defined as a state of emotional and psychological well-being in which an individual is able to use his or her cognitive and emotional capabilities, function in society, and meet the ordinary demands of everyday life. Mental health affects every part of our daily lives. How well we feel plays a major role in our health and how we get along with others or react to events.

Canadian Mental Health Association
The Canadian Mental Health Association is a nationwide, charitable organization that promotes the mental health of all and supports the resilience and recovery of people experiencing mental illness.
www.cmha.ca/

Many individuals today are facing work, family, and personal life pressures. Although most people manage these pressures successfully, some individuals have difficulties handling the demands. Also, specific events, such as the death of a spouse, divorce, or medical problems, can affect individuals who otherwise have been coping successfully with life pressures. A variety of emotional/mental health issues arise at work that must be addressed by employers. Employers should be cautious when using disciplinary policies if employees diagnosed with such illnesses have work-related problems.

Mental health claims are the fastest growing category of disability costs in Canada. They account for an estimated 30 to 40 percent of the disability claims recorded by Canada's major insurers and employers. Three-quarters of employers say mental health issues are the leading cause of short and long-term disability claims in their organization. Additionally, it is estimated that one in five Canadians experiences a mental health problem at some point during their life.[40] Stress that keeps individuals from successfully handling the multiple demands they face is one concern of mental health issues.

Stress

Stress
Stress is the result of any emotional, physical, social, economic, or other factors that require a response or change.

Everyday individuals experience some amount of stress. It is a normal part of life. Defined, **stress** is the result of any emotional, physical, social, economic, or other factors that require a response or change.[41] Depending on how we perceive the event in question, stress can arise from either joyous (e.g., planning for your wedding, birth of a child) or sad events (e.g., death in the family, loss of a job). If the event is perceived as a challenge we can meet, our reaction will be positive, and will often be seen as a source of stimulation, motivation, and energy, such as competing in a sporting competition for which we are well prepared. However, if we don't think we have the necessary resources to meet the challenge, the outcome is likely to be quite different.

All people encounter stress; when "stress overload" hits, work-related consequences can result. HR professionals, managers, and supervisors all must be prepared to handle employee stress; otherwise, employees may "burn out" or exhibit unhealthy behaviours, such as drinking too much alcohol, misusing prescription drugs, and bursting out in anger.[42] "Workplace stress" can be harmful physical and emotional responses that can happen when there is a conflict between job demands on the employee and the amount of control an employee has over meeting these demands. In general, the combination of high demands in a job and a low amount of control over the situation can lead to stress.[43] Stress can be positive, negative, or extremely debilitating.

Types of Stress When anyone mentions the word stress it congers up negative notions. However, not all stress is bad and stress that is positive can lead to better performance. However, negative stress is of great concern because it can be detrimental to an individual's health and well-being. The types of stress that might exist are explained below.

Eustress
Positive stress that is usually short-term that arises when motivation and inspiration are needed.

Eustress **Eustress** is positive stress that is usually short-term that arises when motivation and inspiration are needed. As such it is a beneficial stress that enhances performance, and leads to a positive outcome. For example, an athlete experiences eustress before a competition.

Distress
A negative and harmful stress that, when prolonged, can lead to disease, poor performance, and impaired interpersonal relationships.

Distress Negative stress, or **distress,** can also arise. The body adapts to negative stress with disease, poor performance, and impaired interpersonal relationships. This is a harmful stress that may have a noticeable short-term or long-term effect on individuals if they fail to cope with or adapt to the effect of stress. Someone who is constantly relocating or changing jobs may experience distress.

The line between stress and distress varies from person to person. Distress is created when stress builds up and becomes overwhelming and unbearable, causing us to choose more escape activities than healthy, coping behaviours. The danger signals, or indicators, of distress in the workplace include withdrawal, serious illness, and increased absenteeism.

Burnout
The most severe type of stress; A syndrome of complete physical and emotional exhaustion with psychological, psychophysiological, and behavioural components.

Burnout The most severe type of stress is **burnout.** It is a syndrome of complete physical and emotional exhaustion with psychological, psychophysiological, and behavioural components. It is characterized by pessimism, paranoia, rigidity, diminished sense of humour, increased physical complaints, self-medication, and social withdrawal. Burnout is a chronic condition that occurs in the helping professions such as doctors, nurses, teachers, lawyers, social workers, and police officers.[44] There is a certain consensus around the idea that factors such as role ambiguity, the feeling of lack of control of one's work environment, and the lack of cohesion between work expectations and its reality set the stage for burnout.

Job Stressors

Stressors
The external situations that lead to stress

Stressors **Stressors** are the external situations that lead to stress. The stressor may lead either to distress or to eustress but many researchers refer to stressor as only the negative stressor.[45] Figure 13-11 provides categories and example of stressors that can affect employees in their jobs and personal life. Beyond trying to communicate with the employee and relieving some workload pressures, it is generally recommended that supervisors and managers contact the HR staff, who may intervene and may refer affected employees to outside resources through employee assistance programs.

Figure 13-11 *Categories and Examples of Job Stressors*

Categories of Job Stressors	Examples
Factors unique to the job	• **workload (overload and underload)** • **pace/variety/meaningfulness of work** • **autonomy (e.g., the ability to make your own decisions about your own job or about specific tasks)** • **shiftwork/hours of work** • **physical environment (noise, air quality, etc.)** • **isolation at the workplace (emotional or working alone)**
Role in the organization	• **role conflict (conflicting job demands, multiple supervisors/managers)** • **role ambiguity (lack of clarity about responsibilities, expectations, etc.)** • **level of responsibility**
Career development	• **under/over-promotion** • **job security (fear of redundancy either from economy, or a lack of tasks or work to do)** • **career development opportunities** • **overall job satisfaction**
Relationships at work (interpersonal)	• **supervisors** • **co-workers** • **subordinates** • **threat of violence, harassment, etc. (threats to personal safety)**
Organizational structure/climate	• **participation (or non-participation) in decision making** • **management style** • **communication patterns**

Source: Adapted from Murphy, L.R., "Occupational Stress Management: Current Status and Future Direction," in *Trends in Organizational Behavior,* 1995, Vol. 2, © John Wiley & Sons Limited. Reproduced with permission.

Reactions to Stress

As discussed above, occupational stress occurs when the demands of work exceed the individual's capacity and resources to adequately cope with them. Stress can be acute, such as the stress that occurs in the face of immediate danger, or it can be chronic when a person is dealing with a long-term stressful situation. Originally described by Hans Selye in the 1920s, the body's reaction to stress is referred to as General Adaptation Syndrome (GAS). The principle of GAS states that when the body detects an external stress it will begin to adapt to accommodate the stress until the point that adaptation and support of the stress becomes impossible. A model of GAS is presented in Figure 13-12. There are three stages to GAS: alarm, resistance, and exhaustion.[46]

Alarm During the alarm stage: the body responds with panic—a "fight or flight" reaction. The hormones flow, the heart beats faster, we breathe harder, we sweat, our senses are more alert, we are ready for protective action—running or attacking. As we experience this defence today in the form of fear, anxiety, panic, anger, sadness, etc., we lose some of our mental alertness and organization. Frightened speakers might end up rushing through their talks, lose their trains of thought, or stumble over their words. Nervous workers being watched by their supervisors fumble with their tools.

Resistance If the stress continues, the body enters the second stage, called resistance. The body must stop being in a state of alarm; the body can't take it. So, the body attempts to adjust to the stress. The individual calms down a little, but the body is still

Figure 13-12 Selye's General Adaptation Syndrome (GAS)

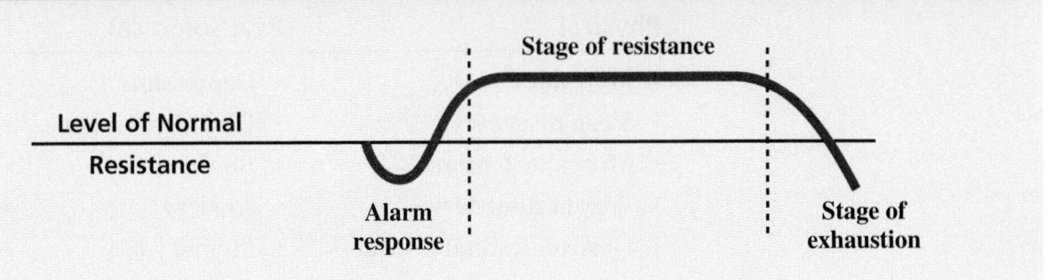

Source: Adapted from Hans Selye, *The Stress of Life*, McGraw-Hill, 1976. © The McGraw-Hill Companies, Inc. Reprinted by permission.

working overtime; the individual may become more accustomed to being stressed but their concentration and decisions continue to be poor. The person feels run down. As the pressure mounts they may struggle to meet the various demands expected. The individual starts getting bouts of irritation, there is over-reaction to minor issues, their sleep pattern starts getting altered and they start getting weaker both mentally and physically. Very clear physical, psychological, and behavioural changes are observed by others.

Exhaustion When the stressful condition is prolonged, and even after observing distinct symptoms of resistance phase, appropriate measures are not resorted to, then the exhaustion phase takes over. This may result in having no enthusiasm to work or even to live and psychosomatic diseases emerge. There is emotional breakdown, insomnia, heart and blood pressure complications, and a host of other very painful symptoms associated with burnout. The burnout has started.

Other Reactions to Stress

If stress is not handled appropriately, it can result in physical, psychological, or behavioural problems as mentioned through the phases of the GAS. *Physical* stress refers to a physiological reaction of the body to various triggers. For example, an employee could suffer migraines, suffer weight gain or loss, or sleep poorly. *Psychologically,* the employee may feel frustrated, impatient, anxious, or irritable. If the situation is not addressed, the individual may become unmotivated, depressed, and apathetic. *Behaviourally,* workers may increasingly be absent from their jobs, consume more alcohol, or take more drugs, and their productivity may diminish. Some may even consider quitting their jobs. Figure 13-13 highlights the many reactions that can occur. Only substance abuse, depression, and obesity are discussed in this chapter, however, as the list indicates, stress can lead to many different concerns for employees.

Substance abuse
Use of illicit substances or misuse of controlled substances, alcohol, or other drugs.

Substance Abuse Use of illicit substances or misuse of controlled substances, alcohol, or other drugs is called **substance abuse.** Substance abuse indicates that you cannot handle the pressures in your life and are willing to jeopardize your health, safety, and security. A person who suffers from substance abuse can often relapse when they have been exposed to excessive stress. The millions of substance abusers in the workforce cost global employers billions of dollars annually. The Canadian Centre on Substance Abuse (CCSA) reported that in 2002 substance abuse cost the Canadian economy more than $40 billion (an increase of about $25 billion since 1992). This figure includes the costs for alcohol (about $14.6 billion), tobacco (over $17 billion), and illegal drugs ($8.2 billion). The largest economic costs of substance abuse include absenteeism from work.[47]

Figure 13-13 *Physical, Physiological, and Psychological Reactions to Stress*

Physical	Psychological	Behavioural
• Migraines	• Depression	• Absenteeism
• Sleep disorders	• Discouragement	• Drug abuse and dependency
• Muscular tension	• Boredom	• Excessive consumption of medicine
• Weight disorders	• Anxiety	• Sexual disorders
• Gastrointestinal disorders	• Memory loss	• Impatience
• Increased blood pressure	• Dissatisfaction	• Aggressiveness
• Allergies	• Frustration	• Eating disorders
• Increased cholesterol rate	• Irritability	• Diminished creativity and initiative
• Dermatological disorders	• Discouragement	• Problems with interpersonal relationships
	• Pessimism	• Frequent mood swings
		• Superficial relationships
		• Lower tolerance of frustrations
		• Disinterest
		• Isolation

Employers' concerns about substance abuse stem from the ways it alters work behaviours, causing increased tardiness, increased absenteeism, a slower workpace, a higher rate of mistakes, and less time spent at the workstation. It can also cause an increase in withdrawal (physical and psychological) and antagonistic behaviours, which may lead to workplace violence.

According to CCSA, workplaces should encourage the establishment of a procedure or policy so that workers with a substance abuse problem can receive help in a "professional and consistent manner." A workplace should preplan policies and procedures to ease the difficulties faced by its employees. Managers and supervisors should be trained to recognize and deal with substance abuse issues.[48]

People abuse drugs and alcohol for many reasons; employers prefer that employees *not* use drugs for an equally large number of reasons.[49] But it is expensive, and there are enough difficulties with it that some management teams wonder what a cost-benefit analysis might reveal.[50]

Figure 13-14 shows common signs of substance abuse. However, not all signs are present in any one case. A pattern that includes some of these behaviours should be a reason to pay closer attention.

Substance Abuse Testing and Legislation In Canada there are no federal or provincial regulations regarding employment-related alcohol and drug testing. Instead,

Figure 13-14 *Common Signs of Substance Abuse*

- Fatigue
- Slurred speech
- Flushed cheeks
- Difficulty walking
- Inconsistency
- Difficulty remembering details
- Argumentative behaviour
- Missed deadlines

- Many unscheduled absences (especially on Mondays and Fridays)
- Depression
- Irritability
- Emotionalism
- Overreacting
- Violence
- Frequently borrowing money

guidelines have been developed based on recent court decisions such as *Entrop v. Imperial Oil Limited*. Random and pre-employment drug testing of public employees is a human rights violation and not allowed under the Canadian Human Rights Act. Employers can test for impairment for workers in safety-sensitive jobs, but only with "strong reasonable cause," such as the occurrence of an accident. Even then, if a test comes back positive, the employer must "accommodate the needs" of the worker, including providing counselling, medical testing, or even reassignment to a less safety-sensitive position. Positive drug tests simply confirm an individual's previous exposure to drugs, not whether the person is capable of performing the essential requirements of their job. Any tests that are conducted must be reliable and valid. For alcohol, testing is normally done using a breathalyzer device, saliva (mouth swab) or taking a blood sample. For drugs, the most widespread practice is urinalysis. The *Entrop* decision clarifies two key issues. With respect to drug and alcohol testing, the decision clarifies that random alcohol testing can be justified in certain circumstances. By contrast, random drug testing will likely not be permissible until there is a method of testing for present impairment by drugs.[51]

Depression Depression is another common emotional/mental health concern. Estimates are that 20 percent of individuals in workplaces suffer from depression. One indicator of the extent of clinical depression is that sales of prescription drugs covered by employee benefits plans to treat depression, such as Prozac and Zoloft, have risen significantly in the past several years.[52]

The effects of depression are seen at all organizational levels, from warehouses and accounting offices to executive suites. Carried to the extreme, depression can result in an employee suicide. The subsequent guilt and sorrow felt by those who worked with the deceased becomes an issue for HR staff, who may be aided by crisis counsellors. To deal with depression, it is recommended that HR professionals, managers, and supervisors be trained in the symptoms of depression and what to do when symptoms are noticed. Often, employees who appear to be depressed are then guided to employee assistance programs and helped with obtaining medical treatment.

Obesity A study that began in 1994 found that almost one-quarter of Canadians who had been overweight in 1994–995 had become obese by 2002–2003. Only half as many Canadians, (about 10 percent) who had been overweight were in the normal weight range eight years later.[53]

Obesity is a fact of modern life and a concern to employers, and a movement to involve employers in employee weight management is apparently gaining momentum. The reason employers are concerned is cost. The total direct cost of obesity in Canada in 2004 was estimated to be about $3.4 billion. The three largest contributors were hypertension ($684 million), coronary artery disease ($541 million), and type 2 diabetes ($310 million).[54]

Direct and Indirect Costs of Stress

Work-related mental health problems may be caused by events stemming from the private life of the employee, the employee's workplace, or the society in which the employee evolves. Apart from having serious consequences for mental and physical health, the impact of stress is obvious in organizations. Among other things, stress is responsible for higher rates of absenteeism, staff turnover, and lower productivity, and the direct and indirect costs of this can be considerable.

According to a survey of 281 Canadian organizations (700 000 employees) by Watson Wyatt Worldwide in 2001, the direct costs of absenteeism have increased since 1997 and currently represent 7.1 percent of the wage bill. If the indirect costs (overtime, replacements, decreased productivity, etc.) are added to the direct costs, the total cost of mental health problems comes to 17 percent of the wage bill. In Canada, the economic impact of work-related mental health problems is estimated to be $14.4 billion annually.[55]

In a recent corporate opinion poll conducted in 2000, 1056 people said they participated in private group insurance programs, and 62 percent of respondents said that they were very stressed at work. This poll also examined the effect of stress on the respondents and found that 64 percent claimed to be irritable or worried. Some also noted that they suffered from insomnia (42 percent) and 21 percent reported that they were sick more often.[56] Stress-related absenteeism is estimated to cost Canadian employers approximately $3.5 billion every year.[57] Figure 13-15 highlights the variables that make up the direct and indirect costs to business as a result of stress.[58]

Stress Management

Stress management encompasses techniques intended to equip a person with effective coping mechanisms for dealing with psychological stress. The key to managing stress is to make it work for you instead of against you. The following is a list of techniques that you should do in order to ensure that you maintain your mental health and well-being.[59]

- Look at your lifestyle and try to avoid, alter, or accept the stressful situation;
- Use relaxation techniques, like deep breathing;
- Take a stress break—see a movie or read a book;
- Patience! Do one thing at a time;
- Don't try to be perfect;
- Learn to say "no";
- Put a little fun into your day;
- Share your problems with others.

Workplace Air Quality

Another health concern for employers is air quality. A number of employees work in settings where air quality is a health issue. Poor air quality may occur in "sealed" buildings (where windows cannot be opened) and when airflow is reduced to save energy and cut operating costs. Also, inadequate ventilation, as well as airborne contamination from carpets, moulds, copy machines, adhesives, and fungi, can cause poor air quality and employee illnesses. In industrial settings, the presence of various chemicals and substances also can lead to poor air quality. In recent years, there has been legislation in provinces including Ontario and Newfoundland that bans smoking in all public places, including workspaces.

Figure 13-15 *Direct and Indirect Costs as a Result of Stress*

Indirect	Direct
• Occasional absence	• Salaries for replacement staff
• Short-term disability	• Training costs for replacement staff
• Long-term disability	• Reduced productivity
• Medication	• Increased turnover of staff
• Paramedical costs	• Presenteeism (come to work despite being ill)
	• Deterioration of the atmosphere at work
	• Unhappy workers
	• Overtime

Health Promotion

Health promotion Supportive approach of facilitating and encouraging healthy actions and lifestyles among employees.

Employers concerned about maintaining a healthy workforce must move beyond simply providing healthy working conditions and begin promoting employee health and wellness in other ways. **Health promotion** is a supportive approach of facilitating and encouraging healthy actions and lifestyles among employees. Health promotion efforts can range from providing information and increasing employee awareness of health issues, to creating an organizational culture supportive of employee health enhancements, as Figure 13-16 indicates. Going beyond just compliance with workplace safety and health regulations, organizations engage in health promotion by encouraging employees to make physiological, mental, and social choices that improve their health.

The first level of health promotion leaves much to individual initiatives for following through and making changes in actions and behaviours. Employers provide information on such topics as weight control, stress management, nutrition, exercise, and smoking cessation. Even though such efforts may be beneficial for some employees, employers who wish to impact employees' health must offer second-level efforts, such as more comprehensive programs and actions that focus on the lifestyle "wellness" of employees. The third level requires a commitment to wellness that is seldom seen in employers.

Wellness programs Programs designed to maintain or improve employee health before problems arise.

Wellness Programs Employers' desires to improve productivity, decrease absenteeism, and control health-care costs have come together in the "wellness" movement. **Wellness programs** are designed to maintain or improve employee health before problems arise, by encouraging self-directed lifestyle changes. Early wellness programs were aimed primarily at reducing the cost and risk of disease. Newer programs emphasize healthy lifestyles and environment, including reduced cholesterol and heart disease risks and individualized exercise programs and follow-up. Employer-sponsored support groups have been established for individuals dealing with health issues such as weight loss, nutrition, and smoking cessation.

The top-rated topics for wellness programs are stress management, exercise/fitness, screenings/checkups, health insurance education, disease management (heart disease, diabetes, etc.), nutrition and diet, and smoking cessation. The Technology Transforming HR deals with a recent innovation in this area—online wellness programs.

Organizations can assess the effectiveness of their wellness programs in a number of ways. Looking at participation rates by employees is one way. Studies have found that participation rates vary by age and type of activity, but generally, over half of employees participate in the different activities in a wellness program.[60] Although

Figure 13-16 *Health Promotion Levels*

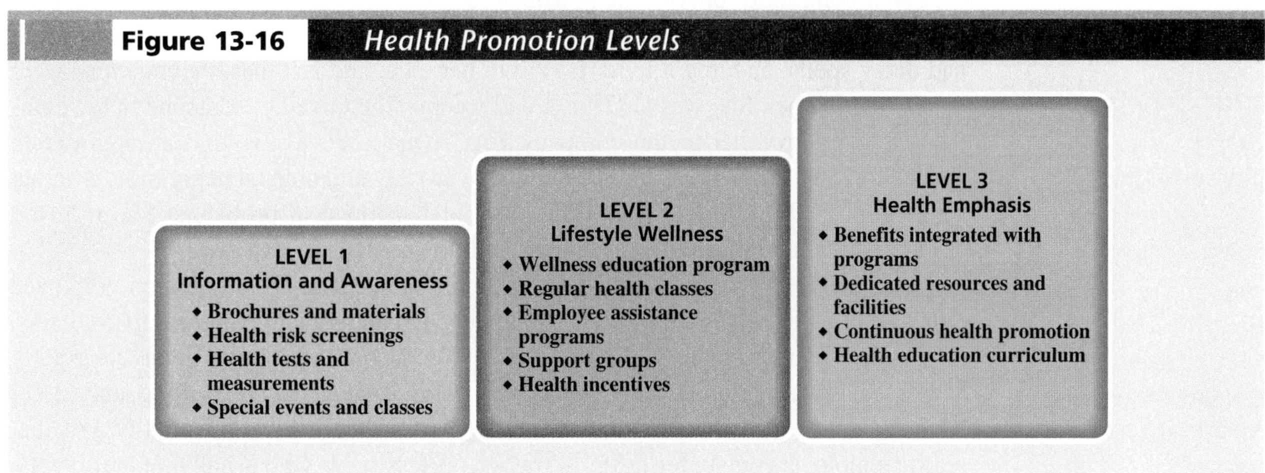

LEVEL 1
Information and Awareness
• Brochures and materials
• Health risk screenings
• Health tests and measurements
• Special events and classes
LEVEL 2
Lifestyle Wellness
• Wellness education program
• Regular health classes
• Employee assistance programs
• Support groups
• Health incentives
LEVEL 3
Health Emphasis
• Benefits integrated with programs
• Dedicated resources and facilities
• Continuous health promotion
• Health education curriculum

Technology Transforming HR

Online Health?

Web-based wellness programs seem almost impossible. Doesn't a physician need to examine a patient in order to prescribe a wellness plan? Employees can't exercise online, can they? But compared with traditional wellness programs, online wellness programs do a good job of providing information at a reasonable cost. Administrative, printing, and mailing expenses are not nearly as high with online programs as with typical onsite programs.

Ford, Microsoft, Chevron, and Watson Wyatt Worldwide, are just a few of the companies that offer online wellness programs. These programs use information and subtle psychology to motivate people to live healthier lifestyles. They typically focus on exercise, nutrition, sleep, and stress and life balance.

In one online wellness program, each day participants answer a series of questions about their behaviour in the last 24 hours: How much food and water did you consume? How much exercise and sleep did you get? and so on. The program then computes life practice indexes from the information, to show the participants how well they are doing. A key to the program is an "online coach" who monitors each participant and sends e-mails of praise or nudges the person to follow healthier behaviours.

Such services can be delivered for $5–$15 per employee, compared with $25–$50 per employee for a more conventional service. Employees seem to like it—a study revealed that 92 percent found the service helpful, and 48 percent went online rather than calling or meeting face-to-face, because the online program offers immediate access and information. Most individuals logged on to get information on specific subjects of interest.[61]

1. What do you perceive as the advantages and disadvantages to this type of system?
2. What would be included in such a system? Conduct an online search to determine what companies are including this type of program? Do you think it is as effective as meeting with someone such as a personal trainer on a day-to-day basis? Why or why not?

more participation would be beneficial, the programs have resulted in healthier lifestyles for more employees. Cost-benefit analyses by organizations also tend to support the continuation of wellness programs.

Employee assistance program (EAP) Program that provides counselling and other help to employees having emotional, physical, or other personal problems.

Employee Assistance Programs (EAPs) One method organizations use as a broad-based response to health issues is an **employee assistance program (EAP),** which provides counselling and other help to employees having emotional, physical, or other personal problems. In such a program, an employer contracts with a counselling agency. Employees who have problems may then contact the agency, either voluntarily or by employer referral, for assistance with a broad range of problems. Counselling costs are paid for by the employer, either in total or up to a pre-established limit.

EAPs commonly provide help with troubled employees, problem identification, short-term intervention, and referral services. For example, an administrative assistant had dizzy spells, endured a loud ringing in her ears, and felt that life and work were overwhelming her. She was also upset and weepy. She talked to someone in the company who referred her to the company EAP, which helped her find an appropriate counsellor. She learned that she suffered from anxiety and clinical depression, and that her mental health problems were the basis of her physical problems. She received appropriate treatment and her employer paid for most of the expenses.[62]

EAPs help employees with a variety of problems. The most common employee issues dealt with are: (1) depression and anxiety, (2) marital and relationship problems, (3) legal difficulties, and (4) family and children concerns. Other areas commonly addressed as part of an EAP include substance abuse, financial counselling, and career advice. Critical to employee usage of an EAP is preserving confidentiality. For that reason, employers outsource EAPs to trained professionals who usually report only the numbers of employees and services provided, rather than details on individuals using an EAP. The effectiveness of EAPs depends on how well employers integrate and support them in the workplace.[63]

Global Health, Safety, and Security

7 Health and safety laws and regulations vary from country to country, ranging from virtually non-existent to more stringent than those in Canada. The importance placed on workplace safety relates somewhat to the level of regulation in each country.

International Emergency Health Services

With more and more expatriates working internationally, especially in some less-developed countries, significant health and safety issues require attention. Addressing these issues is part of the HR role. One consideration is provision of emergency evacuation services. For instance, how to evacuate and care for an expatriate employee who sustains internal injuries in a car accident in the Ukraine or Sierra Leone may be a major issue. Many global firms purchase coverage for their international employees from an organization that provides emergency services, such as International SOS, Global Assistance & Healthcare, or MEDEX Global Group. If an emergency arises, the emergency services company dispatches physicians or even transports employees by chartered aircraft. If adequate medical assistance can be obtained locally, the emergency services company maintains a referral list and arranges for the expatriate to receive treatment. Emergency services firms may also provide legal counsel in foreign countries, emergency cash for medical expenses, and assistance in reissuing lost documents. Some large multinationals have begun to expand their EAP coverage to include international employees as well.[64]

International Security and Terrorism

Travel Warnings
Current travel warnings and consular advisories by country are available from Foreign Affairs Canada.
www.voyage.gc.ca/dest/sos/warnings-en.asp

As more Canadian firms operate internationally, the threat of terrorist actions against those firms, and the employees working for them, increases. The extent to which employees are likely to experience security problems and violence depends on the country. It is crucial that the HR staff regularly check the security conditions in countries where expatriates are travelling and working.

Global firms take a variety of actions to address security concerns.[65] For example, one U.S. firm removed signs identifying its offices and facilities in a Latin American country in order to reduce the visibility of the firm and thus reduce its potential as a target for terrorist acts. Many international firms screen entry by all employees, and many use metal detectors to scan all packages, briefcases, and other items. Firms commonly use physical barriers such as iron security fences, concrete barricades, bulletproof glass, and electronic surveillance devices in offices as part of their security efforts.

Kidnapping

Not all violence occurs at work. Kidnapping, murder, home invasion, robberies, and carjackings happen relatively frequently in some cities, such as Mexico City. In a number of countries throughout the world, U.S. citizens are especially vulnerable to extortion, kidnapping, bombing, physical harassment, and other terrorist activities. Canadian citizens are not immune either as the number of innocent Canadians being kidnapped in Iraq continues to climb. Today many of these kidnappings are politically motivated because of the war in the middle east.

To counter such threats, many global firms have *kidnap and ransom insurance*. This insurance covers the costs of paying ransoms to obtain releases of kidnapped employees and family members, pay for the bodily injuries suffered by kidnap victims, and deal with negotiation and other expenses.

Individual employees and their family members working and living abroad must constantly be aware of security concerns. Both pre-departure and ongoing security training should be given to all expatriates, their dependants, and employees of global firms working internationally, especially if located in high-risk areas.

LOGGING ON...

Pandemic Influenza Portal
This portal provides one-stop access to online information from several Government of Canada departments and agencies about pandemic influenza, avian flu, seasonal flu, and related matters.
www.influenza.gc.ca

Pandemics

The last decade has seen new issues for the health and safety of all global citizens. For most Canadians, and especially Ontarians, the memory of the 2003 severe acute respiratory syndrome (SARS) outbreak is fresh. Close to 400 health-care workers and ordinary people were infected, and in all, 44 people died in Toronto before SARS was under control. Other issues of concern continue to be HIV, anthrax, West Nile virus, smallpox outbreaks, and now the avian flu, among many others. This list will continue to grow. Canadian governments learned many lessons from the SARS outbreak, and have been working diligently to coordinate emergency response for many of these ensuing concerns nationally. Human resources management should have an emergency response plan in place to cover catastrophic events and be prepared to put the plan in action.

SUMMARY

1 Health is a general state of physical, mental, and emotional well-being. Safety is a condition in which the physical well-being of people is protected. Security is the protection of employees and organizational facilities. Poorly managed companies have higher losses from accidents. Young workers have the highest rate of accidents.

2 Federal, provincial, and territorial governments have occupational health and safety acts that state that employers have a general duty to provide safe and healthy working conditions. Workers' compensation coverage is provided by employers to protect employees who suffer job-related injuries and illnesses. All employees have three fundamental rights: Right to know, right to participate, and right to refuse unsafe work. Managers must be duly diligent to ensure safe working environment for employees. Bill C-45, enacted under the Criminal Code, imposes criminal liability on corporations and individuals that fail to take reasonable measures to protect employee and public safety. Managers, supervisors, employees, health and safety committees, contractors, all have responsibilities and duties to health and safety. Workers compensation boards have been established under each of the jurisdictions. Employers contribute to an insurance fund to compensate employees for injuries on the job. The premium rates paid by the employer reflects the accident rates of the employers. There are cash benefits or wage or earnings loss paid to employees in the form of compensation. Workplace inspectors can enter the organization at any time to ensure a safe working environment. Each of the provinces has specific rules with respect to the age of the workers. Penalties exist for employers who fail to comply with OH&S legislation in their respective jurisdictions.

3 Hazard control and assessment is important to ensuring the health and safety of all employees. There are safety hazards and health hazards. Safety hazards cause physical harm such as cuts or broken bones. Health hazards cause occupational illnesses such as respiratory problems that may produce serious and immediate effects and/or long-term problems. WHMIS addresses exposure to hazardous materials. WHMIS is based on three elements: labels, MSDSs, and training. Ergonomics looks at the physiological and physical demands of work. Controls include lockout/tag out procedures and PPE programs.

4 Another hazard control is associated with workplace violence and bullying. Security of workplaces has grown in importance, particularly as the frequency of workplace violence increases. Employers can enhance security by conducting a security audit,

controlling access to workplaces and computer systems, screening employees adequately during the selection process, providing security personnel, ensuring there is a policy in place, and by providing training to all employees. Quebec has amended its Labour Standards Act to deal with psychological harassment in the workplace.

5 OH&S addresses employee work assignments, requires employers to keep records on occupational illnesses and injuries, inspects workplaces, and can issue citations for several levels of violations. Effective safety management requires integrating three approaches: organizational, engineering, and individual. Developing safety policies, disciplining violators, keeping safety records, conducting safety training, communicating on safety issues, establishing safety committees, inspecting work areas for safety concerns, investigating accidents, and evaluating safety efforts are all part of comprehensive safety management.

6 Emotional/mental health concerns can lead to stress that could result in such things as depression, substance abuse, obesity, and violence in the workplace. Mental health issues are the leading cause of short and long-term disability claims in organizations. Stress is a part of normal life that everyone experiences on a regular basis. Everyone handles stress differently and there are different types of stress. Eustress is positive stress that arises when motivation and inspiration are needed. Distress is negative stress that can be harmful. Employers promote employee health at several levels to improve organizational operations and individual employee productivity. Burnout is the most severe type of stress. Stress is caused by different external situations such as factors unique to the job, the role in the organization, career development, interpersonal relationships, and organizational structure and climate. People react to stress in different ways that can be explained through general adaptation syndrome (GAS). The individual can react to stress either physically, psychologically, or behaviourally. Other effects of stress can be substance abuse, depression, and obesity. Employers have responded to health problems by establishing and supporting wellness programs and employee assistance programs (EAPs). Establishing and maintaining an organizational culture of health continues to pay off for a number of employers.

7 Global security relates somewhat to the varying levels of regulation in different countries. Security problems around the world are well documented but do not always get enough attention. Employers need to be concerned about employees' risk of being kidnapped in certain countries, therefore extra care needs to be taken. With globalization, there is much concern about pandemics such as the avian flu and SARS.

KEY TERMS

Burnout, p. 501
Cumulative trauma disorders (CTDs), p. 489
Distress, p. 501
Due diligence, p. 479
Employee assistance program (EAP), p. 508
Ergonomics, p. 487
Eustress, p. 501
Hazard, p. 485
Health, p. 474
Health promotion, p. 507
Lockout/tagout, p. 491
Occupational health hazard, p. 486
Personal protective equipment (PPE), p. 491
Safety, p. 474
Safety hazard, p. 485
Security, p. 474
Security audit, p. 495
Stress, p. 500
Stressors, p. 501
Substance abuse, p. 503
Wellness programs, p. 507
Workplace Hazardous Materials Information System (WHMIS), p. 487

REVIEW AND APPLICATION QUESTIONS

1 Using the chart presented in Figure 13-2, Loss-Time Injuries by Province and Territory, analyze the results and prepare a presentation on your findings.

2 How does one go about controlling workers' compensation costs, and why is that important?

3 What are the elements that make up a WHMIS program?

4 Discuss the top security concerns at work? What are you most concerned about and why? What can an organization do to help with this concern?

5 What is necessary to ensure successful safety management in an organization?

6 Should drug and alcohol testing be randomly used in the workplace? Why or why not?

7 What are the concerns that an organization may have with respect to sending employees on international assignments? Why do you feel these are valid concerns?

EXPERIENTIAL EXERCISES

1. As the HR manager of a distribution and warehouse firm with 600 employees, you plan to discuss the merits of a company wellness program at an executive staff meeting next week. The topics to cover include what a wellness program is, how it can benefit the company and employees, and the process for establishing it. Prepare a 5-minute presentation considering the topics to be discussed. The class will represent the executives of your organization.
2. As the health and safety coordinator, you have been asked to prepare a health and safety presentation for a group of young workers who will be joining your organization for the summer. You are asked to research what is available and to prepare a ten-minute presentation using your class as the "summer students" you will be training.
3. Determine how much each jurisdiction paid out in workers' compensation claims over the past three years (each jurisdiction may have different years posted—just use what they have), report on what the rate of reimbursement was in each jurisdiction (e.g., 75 percent, 85 percent, 90 percent). Conducting an analysis, what province is paying the highest and the lowest compensation claims? What are the reasons for the differences in each jurisdiction? Prepare a written report outlining your findings.
4. Your mother owns a small construction firm. Since you've taken this class you now have become aware of the various issues associated with health and safety. Your mother tells you that she will be hiring underaged summer students so that she can save costs. Business has not been doing well and she needs to watch her overhead. You tell her about child labour laws and workers' compensation concerns. She indicates that it doesn't matter because she will be paying them under the table so she'll save money in wages, government remittances, and workers' compensation. You've told her your concerns and she doesn't want to listen to you. You're concerned for the safety of the kids, and for your mother if she were to have a serious claim against her firm. What should you do?

LEARNING REVIEW

To check your knowledge of the chapter, review the following. (Answers after the case.)

1 The biggest killer in work-related fatalities is:
a. circulatory
b. cancer
c. electrocution
d. falls

2 Who is responsible for workers' compensation costs?
a. Employers
b. Employees
c. Employees and employers jointly
d. Provincial, territorial, and federal governments

3 Every workplace, large or small, should have a system in place to:
a. control risk
b. assess the risk
c. identify hazards
d. all of the above

4 The most common cause of homicides at work are:
a. attacks by disgruntled employees
b. armed robbery attempts
c. attacks by former employees
d. confrontations resulting from abusive domestic relationships

5 Three approaches managers use to manage safety include all except:
a. organizational
b. individual
c. engineering
d. group

6 The largest economic costs of substance abuse includes:

a. absenteeism
b. fatigue
c. obesity
d. emotional health

7 Global concerns for health, safety, and security include all except for:

a. terrorism
b. kidnapping
c. emergency health
d. health promotion

CASE

THE FINE LINE BETWEEN BULLYING AND LEADERSHIP

In November 2002, Louise Landry decided that she could no longer work as an HR coordinater at Boise Alljoist Ltd.'s St. Jacques, New Brunswick plant (a subsidiary of an American company with headquarters in Boise, Idaho). Landry resigned from the position because of the harassing behaviour displayed by her plant manager Scott Hall. Landry first joined the company in 2000 as a health and safety coordinater and was promoted by Hall to HR coordinater, a few months after his arrival to the plant in August 2001. Landry did receive several complaints from other employees concerning Hall's behaviour but was hesitant to report him due to a fear that she would lose her job. Since Hall was a high-performing manager who was able to reach company targets, complaints made about Hall's behaviour either went unnoticed or resulted in lenient disciplinary action.

In the fall of 2001, a team of auditors went to the plant with the purpose of conducting a financial and inventory audit. The auditors experienced first hand Hall's harassing and uncomfortable behaviour towards his subordinates. Hall (who is married) openly commented to a group of workers that he wanted to sleep with Landry. One auditor noted that Hall did not have a problem with publicly condemning his employees to the point that they were afraid to speak out against him. The team of auditors took their concerns to the head office in Idaho. When Hall's supervisor contacted him about the complaints, Hall claimed that he did not believe at the time that he was doing anything inappropriate. Hall said that he would not do anything like this again. However, Hall's behaviour was brought to the attention of Boise's corporate office on two subsequent occasions (by another auditing team and a company executive). He was further disciplined but not dismissed.

Landry was often the subject of Hall's inappropriate behaviour. When a large group went out for dinner, Hall commented (in front of a group that included Landry and her boyfriend) that he would like to see Landry in a mini-skirt with fishnet stockings riding a motorcycle. Landry's boyfriend became very angry with Hall but was told by Landry to leave it alone because she did not want to lose her job. On another occasion, Hall told Landry that he believed that people in their positions should have affairs. He also told her that he had only had sex with one woman and inquired about her own sexual experiences. After Hall received disciplinary action in 2002, Landry began to experience abusive behaviour from Hall who accused her of being late as well as not completing her assignments. The abuse became unbearable for Landry who decided to give up the job that she once feared she would lose if she stood up to Landry.

Landry resigned eight months before head office finally made the decision to dismiss Hall. After he was fired, Hall filed a wrongful dismissal suit against the company. In 2005, the court found that head office was justified in firing Hall because, "In many instances Hall's conduct was a gross and gratuitous abuse of his power. He controlled the men under his supervision by screaming, swearing and threatening them, and he controlled the women by embarrassing and humiliating them. He confused bullying with leadership."[66]

Questions

1. What do you perceive as the difference between sexual harassment and bullying? Do you feel this is really about sexual harassment or is it bullying? Explain your answer.
2. What responsibility should the organization take for this incident? How could it have been handled differently?

Learning Review Answers: 1. b. 2. a 3. d 4. b 5. d 6. a 7. d

CHAPTER

Employee Rights and Discipline

Learning Objectives

After you have read this chapter, you should be able to:

1 Explain the difference between statutory rights and contractual rights.

2 Discuss how wrongful discharge, just cause, and due process are interrelated.

3 Identify employee rights associated with access to employee records and free speech, and the issues associated with workplace monitoring, employer investigations, and drug testing.

4 List elements to consider when developing an employee handbook.

5 Differentiate between the positive approach and progressive approach to discipline.

HR *Headline*

Tracking Employees with Technology

The use of technology has expanded the extent of conflicts over employer and employee rights. Technology has blurred the line between company time and private time. For instance, many employees feel that it is acceptable to use their company computers for personal matters. So when the company monitors e-mail, voice mail, and Internet use by employees, conflicts arise. Employers have disciplined or fired employees who used company computers to access pornographic websites, or who wasted worktime by browsing eBay, downloading music files, or playing games.

The battle over the use of technology is also expanding in other areas. Police officers can be tracked using GPS systems, and their logbooks can be compared against what the tracking system shows. In a number of cities, officers have been disciplined or fired for falsifying logbooks to show them as being on duty, when they really were parked, sleeping, or in a local coffee shop or bar. Trucking firms use GPS systems to track locations, schedules, and routes of drivers. Other firms track the keystrokes of data-entry processors or length of call time of customer service representatives. A computer was stolen from the vehicle of a B.C. Rail employee, but was recovered due to a special tracking system. Ontario-based Air IIQ track their fleet of trucks so that drivers don't go into restricted areas such as crossing the U.S. border, where insurance rates are different. Fleet companies in Calgary track staff during business hours, as do taxi companies in Toronto.

Generally, court decisions have supported employers' rights to track and monitor employees when the employees are using company facilities, company computer systems, and on-the-job time. But employers must inform employees that monitoring can occur and get signed permissions from them. Undoubtedly, these efforts help clarify employer and employee rights, but despite them, conflicts are likely to grow as employers use more advanced technology to track the employees' performance.[1]

"The right to be left alone—the most comprehensive of rights and the most valued by civilized men."

—Louis Brandeis

This chapter considers three related and important issues in managing human resources: employee rights, HR policies and rules, and discipline. These areas may seem separate, but they definitely are not. The policies and rules that an organization enacts help to define employees' rights at that employer, as well as constrain those rights (sometimes inappropriately or illegally). Similarly, discipline for those who fail to follow policies and rules is often seen as a fundamental right of employers. Employees who feel that their employers have taken inappropriate action can challenge that action—both inside and outside the organization—using an internal dispute resolution process or through a variety of external legal means.

Rights and Responsibilities Issues

Rights
Powers, privileges, or interests that belong to a person by law, nature, or tradition.

1 Rights generally do not exist in the abstract. Instead, they exist only when someone is successful in demanding their application. **Rights** are powers, privileges, or interests that belong to a person by law, nature, or tradition. Of course, defining a right presents considerable potential for disagreement. For example, does an employee have a right to privacy of communication in personal matters when using the employer's computer on company time? Moreover, *legal rights* may or may not correspond to certain *moral rights,* and the reverse is true as well—a situation that opens "rights" up to controversy and lawsuits.

Responsibilities
Obligations to perform certain tasks and duties.

Rights are offset by **responsibilities,** which are obligations to perform certain tasks and duties. Employment is a reciprocal relationship (both sides have rights and obligations). For example, if an employee has the right to a safe working environment, then the employer must have an obligation to provide a safe workplace. If the employer has a right to expect uninterrupted, high-quality work from the employee, then the worker has the responsibility to be on the job and to meet job performance standards. The reciprocal nature of rights and responsibilities suggests that both parties to an employment relationship should regard the other as having rights and should treat the other with respect.

Statutory Rights

Statutory rights
Rights based on laws or statutes.

Employees' **statutory rights** are the result of specific laws or statutes passed by federal, provincial, or territorial governments. Various federal, provincial, or territorial laws have granted employees certain rights at work, such as equal employment opportunity, collective bargaining, and workplace safety. These laws and their interpretations also have been the subject of a considerable number of court cases.

Contractual Rights

Contractual rights
Rights based on a specific contract between an employer and an employee.

An employee's **contractual rights** are based on a specific contract with an employer. For instance, a union and an employer may agree on a labour contract that specifies certain terms, conditions, and rights that employees represented by the union have with the employer.

Contracts formalize the employment relationship. For instance, when hiring an independent contractor or a consultant, an employer should use a contract to spell out the work to be performed, expected time lines, parameters, and costs and fees to be incurred. Contractual rights can be spelled out formally in written employment contracts or implied in employer handbooks and policies disseminated to employees.

Employment contract
Agreement that formally outlines the details of employment.

Employment Contracts A formal **employment contract** is an agreement that outlines the details of employment. Written employment contracts are often very detailed. Traditionally, employment contracts have been used mostly for executives and senior managers, but the use of employment contracts is filtering down the organization to include highly specialized professional and technical employees who have scarce skills.

Depending on the organization and individuals involved, employment agreements may contain a number of provisions, as Figure 14-1 depicts. Some key provisions are highlighted next.

Typically, an *identification section* lists the parties to the contract, and the general nature of the employee's job duties. The level of compensation and types of benefits are often addressed, including any special compensation, benefits, incentives, or perquisites ("perks") to be provided by the employer. The employment contract may also note whether the employment relationship is to be for an indeterminate time, or whether it can be renewed automatically after a specified period of time. The contract may spell out a severance agreement, continuation of benefits, and other factors related to the employee's leaving the employer.[2]

Restrictive Covenants

Restrictive covenants are often used to protect a business against exploitation by employees, ex-employees, shareholders, or previous owners. Confidential information about the business, trade secrets, or familiarity and/or relations with suppliers or clients can give these individuals a tremendous competitive advantage. For this reason restrictive covenants are often included in the employment contracts of senior managers,

Figure 14-1 *Typical Provisions in Employment Contracts*

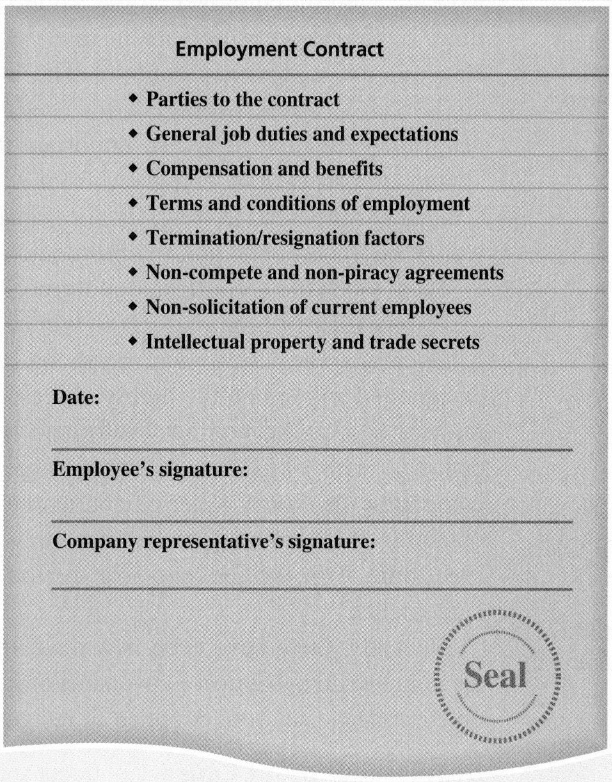
Employment Contract

- Parties to the contract
- General job duties and expectations
- Compensation and benefits
- Terms and conditions of employment
- Termination/resignation factors
- Non-compete and non-piracy agreements
- Non-solicitation of current employees
- Intellectual property and trade secrets

Date:

Employee's signature:

Company representative's signature:

Seal

professionals, or technical and sales employees. The basic goal of these restrictive covenants is to prevent the employee from using customer lists or trade secrets. They should not be used to prevent an employee from using his or her skills and knowledge or to prevent competition generally. The three main types of restrictive covenants are non-disclosure, non-solicitation, and non-competition.

Non-Disclosure Non-disclosure clauses are intended to protect what is essentially a property right. Your business plans, trade secrets, customer lists, and other confidential information are the "property" of your business. Clauses that protect this "property" are usually enforceable unless they attempt to protect information that is really in the public domain. Therefore, you cannot stop employees from using the skills they have acquired while they worked for you, but you can stop them from disclosing customer lists or other confidential business information that is your property. Concerned about the need to protect intellectual property and trade secrets as well as wasted activity using the Internet, a poll of 100 senior executives of large Canadian companies found 70 percent of the organizations monitor employee computer activity.[3]

Non-Solicitation Agreement A non-solicitation clause is used to ensure the employee won't solicit customers for the purpose of selling any products or services which are substantially similar to those you currently sell. This clause can be drafted to be enforceable during the employment relationship and for a certain period of time thereafter. What is more difficult to control is when former customers seek out the departed employees. Therefore, non-complete clauses can help to control this situation.

Non-compete agreements Agreements that prohibit individuals who leave the organization from competing with an employer in the same line of business for a specified period of time.

Non-Compete Agreement Commonly, employment contracts include **non-compete agreements,** which prohibit individuals who leave the organization from working with an employer in the same line of business for a specified period of time. A non-compete agreement may be presented as a separate contract or as a clause in an employment contract. These are used primarily when new employees are hired. Non-competition clauses need to be reasonable in terms of duration and geographic location. It is also important to ensure they are not too broad in scope. Trying to restrict your employee from starting a competing business anywhere in Canada for the next 15 years is not going to be found to be reasonable.[4] In other words, courts are reluctant to enforce non-compete agreements.

Sometimes these clauses are enforceable. In 2003, five employees of Ubisoft, a game publisher in Montreal left to work for a competitor, Electronic Arts. The five game creators held a range of positions including artistic, programming, and game design, and worked on the highly successful computer game, Splinter Cell. Four of the five had signed non-disclosure and non-compete clauses in their employment contracts with Ubisoft. In the non-compete clause, they agreed not to work for a competitor in North America for a one-year period. Ubisoft was successful in obtaining a restraining order that prevented the employees from working for Electronic Arts for the one-year period in compliance with their non-compete agreements.[5]

Recently, there have been new developments in restrictive covenants. Contracts are being written to enforce covenants on dismissal without cause, shorter restrictions on convenants, and longer notice of resignations.[6]

LOGGING ON...

HRM Guide Canada
This website features Canadian human resource management articles, features, and links.
www.hrmguide.net/canada/

Dismissal Without Cause Contracts are starting to use language that indicates the covenants will apply regardless of the manner of dismissal. So even if the employee is dismissed without notice or in an unfair or bad-faith manner, the covenant clearly states it applies regardless of how the dismissal is handled.

Shorter Restrictions In the past, longer time periods, such as three to five years, were put into restrictive covenants. Courts often take a dim view of long restrictions, so employers are going to a shorter period, often 12 months, and narrowing the geographic scope of the restrictions. As well, since so much work can now be done over the Internet, the geographic restriction can be problematic.

Notice of Resignation Some contracts are requiring employees to give a specified amount of notice during resignation, and that during the notice period the employee can't engage in competitive activities. An employer has to be reasonable about the amount of notice time they require. It likely won't be able to require two years' notice of resignation, but three months might be enforceable.

Implied Contracts

The idea that a contract (even an implied or unwritten one) exists between individuals and their employers affects the employment relationship. The rights and responsibilities of the employee may be spelled out in a job description, in an employment contract, in HR policies, or in a handbook, but often are not. The rights and responsibilities of the employee may also exist *only* as unwritten employer expectations about what is acceptable behaviour or performance on the part of the employee. For instance, a number of court decisions have held that if an employer hires someone for an indefinite period or promises job security, the employer has created an implied contract. Such promises establish employee expectations.[7] When the employer fails to follow up on the implied promises, the employee may pursue remedies in court. Numerous court decisions have held that such implied promises, especially when contained in an employee handbook constitute a contract between an employer and its employees, even without a signed document.

Rights Affecting the Employment Relationship

2 As employees increasingly regard themselves as free agents in the workplace—and as the power of unions declines—the struggle between individual employee and employer "rights" is heightening. Employers frequently do not fare well in court. Further, employers are not the only ones liable in many cases. Individual managers and supervisors have also been found liable when hiring or promotion decisions have been based on discriminatory factors, or when they have had knowledge of such conduct and have not taken steps to stop it. Several concepts from law and psychology influence the employment relationship: just cause, due process, and distributive and procedural justice.

Wrongful Dismissal

Wrongful dismissal Termination of an individual's employment for reasons that are unfair, unreasonable, or without sufficient cause.

Wrongful dismissal refers to situations where an employee has been fired (dismissed) unfairly, unreasonably, or without sufficient cause. A 1989 case defined it as follows: "In wrongful dismissal cases, the wrong suffered by the employee is the breach by the employer of the implied contract term to give reasonable notice before terminating the contract of employment. Damages are awarded to place the employee in the same position as he/she would have been had reasonable notice been

Employees are sometimes terminated either with or without cause. In any case, employees should in most cases be treated with dignity and respect as this is a difficult time for them, as well as difficult for the employees at work.

Source: © John Henley/CORBIS

given."[8] Additionally, courts generally have held that unionized workers cannot pursue wrongful dismissal because they are covered by the grievance arbitration process.

A landmark decision handed down by the Supreme Court in 1997 changed the wrongful dismissal landscape. In *Wallace v. United Grain Growers*, the case established that employees will receive additional notice if the employer acts in a callous manner during termination. Wallace was hired away from a competitor he had worked at for 25 years. Due to his length of service and security, he negotiated for a guarantee of job security, fair treatment, and remuneration. He was told that if he performed as expected he would have a job until he retired. He turned out to be a top performer and was the top salesperson every year from 1972 to 1986, when his employment was abruptly terminated by his sales manager with no explanation. Days earlier this same manager had praised Wallace on doing such a good job. A week later a written explanation explained that Wallace was terminated for inability to perform his duties satisfactorily. Wallace filed a wrongful dismissal suit. United Grain Growers alleged that Wallace was dismissed for cause. Wallace did not fare well because of the allegation of cause and sought psychiatric help and was unable to find another job. Word leaked out to others in the industry that Wallace had been fired for cause and assumed that he had done something wrong. After several appeals at lower courts, the Supreme Court of Canada awarded Wallace 24 months' notice. The court felt that United Grain Growers had "made a conscious decision to 'play hardball' with Wallace and maintained unfounded allegations against him until the day the trial began. As a result of the unfounded allegations, word got out about the dismissal and it was rumoured in the industry that Wallace had been involved in some wrongdoing." The judge said to ensure that employees receive adequate protection, employers ought to be held to an obligation of good faith and fair dealings in the manner of dismissal. If that obligation is broken, then there should be consequences such as lengthening the notice period.[9]

Employers should take several precautions to reduce wrongful dismissal liabilities. Having a well-written employee handbook, that is well communicated, training managers, and maintaining adequate documentation are key.[10] Figure 14-2 offers suggestions for preparing a defence against wrongful-dismissal lawsuits.

Constructive dismissal
Occurs when an employer did not directly dismiss the employee but the employer changed the job so completely that the employment contract was effectively at an end.

Closely related to wrongful discharge is constructive dismissal, which occurs when an employer did not directly dismiss the employee but the employer changed the job so completely that the employment contract was effectively at an end.[11] Under normal circumstances, an employee who resigns rather than being dismissed cannot later collect damages for violation of legal rights. In a leading case in 1997, the Supreme Court of Canada defined constructive dismissal as follows: "To reach the conclusion that an employee has been constructively dismissed, the Court must

Figure 14-2 *Keys for Preparing a Defence Against Wrongful Dismissal: The "Paper Trail"*

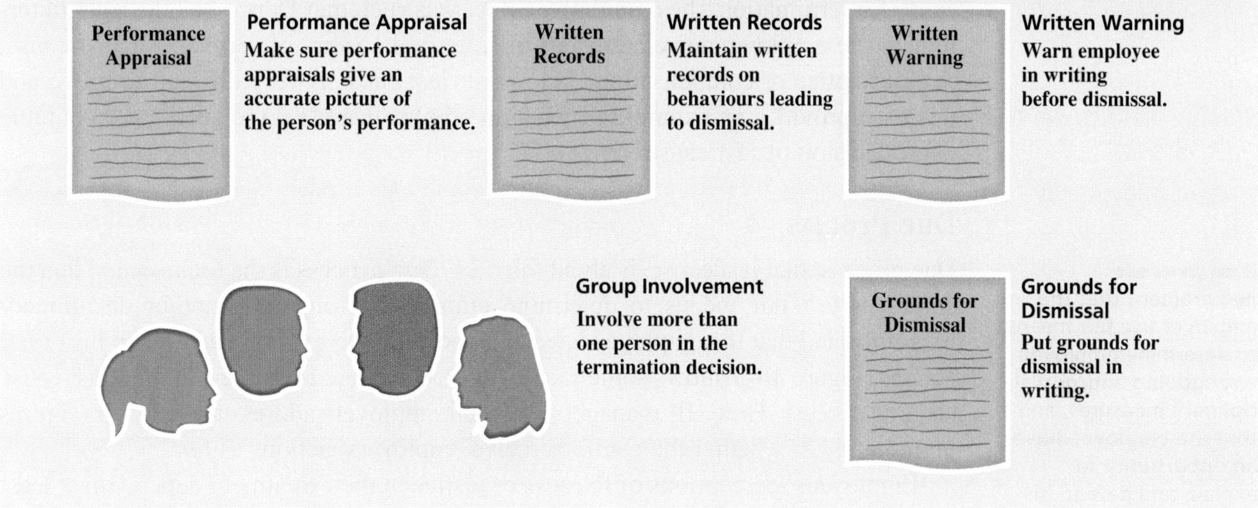

Performance Appraisal

Performance Appraisal
Make sure performance appraisals give an accurate picture of the person's performance.

Written Records

Written Records
Maintain written records on behaviours leading to dismissal.

Written Warning

Written Warning
Warn employee in writing before dismissal.

Group Involvement
Involve more than one person in the termination decision.

Grounds for Dismissal

Grounds for Dismissal
Put grounds for dismissal in writing.

determine whether the unilateral changes imposed by the employee substantially altered the essential terms of the employer's contract of employment. Generally, if the employee clearly indicates non-acceptance of the new conditions of employment to the employer, there has been a constructive dismissal only if the employee leaves within a reasonable period of time (usually short period). By not resigning, the employee indicates his/her acceptance of the new employment conditions."[12]

Just Cause

Just cause
Reasonable justification for taking employment-related action.

Just cause is reasonable justification for taking employment-related action. Even though definitions of *just cause* vary, the overall concern is fairness. To be viewed by others as *just,* any disciplinary action must be based on facts in the individual case. Some examples of just cause dismissal include the following:[13]

- sexual harassment
- breach of duty or fidelity
- conflict of interest
- misrepresenting qualifications
- willful disobedience
- theft
- fraud and dishonesty
- excessive absenteeism or lateness
- intoxication
- breach of rules or company policies

In *Daley v. Depco International Inc.*, Daley had worked for nearly 13 years in the production group, earning approximately $50,000. He was 58 years old when Depco terminated his employment. Over a 28-month period, Depco utilized its policy of progressive discipline to document nine separate incidences of misconduct related to safety infractions or production problems that adversely affected Depco's operations, often requiring production line stoppages. Daley had been counselled, verbally warned, warned in writing, and suspended prior to the ultimate penalty of dismissal for cause having been implemented. The court felt that Daley's continued carelessness amounted to a repudiation of the employment contract. The court concluded that Daley failed to carry out his responsibilities properly and was warned repeatedly. As a result, while no individual incident was sufficient to constitute just cause for termination, the cumulative effect was such that Depco had the right to terminate the employment relationship in spite of 13 years of service, for just cause, without notice or compensation.[14] However just cause is very difficult to prove and this case provides an example of what an employer must do to secure a favourable court decision of just cause.

Due Process

Due process
Requirement that the employer use fair means to determine employee wrongdoing and/or disciplinary measures, and that the employee have an opportunity to explain and defend his or her actions.

Due process, like just cause, is about fairness. **Due process** is the requirement that the employer use fair means to determine employee wrongdoing and/or disciplinary measures, and that the employee have an opportunity to explain and defend his or her actions. Figure 14-3 shows some factors to be considered when evaluating just cause and due process. How HR managers and their employers address these factors figures prominently in whether the courts perceive employers' actions as fair.

Distributive justice
Perceived fairness in the distribution of outcomes.

Employees' perceptions of fairness or justice in their treatment depend on at least two other factors. First, people obviously prefer *favourable outcomes* for themselves. They decide the favourability of their outcomes by comparing them with the outcomes of others, given their relative situations. This decision involves the concept of **distributive justice,** which deals with the question, Were outcomes distributed fairly? Fairness would not include disciplinary action based on favouritism when some are punished and others are not. Therefore, often fairness is dependent on employee perceptions.[15]

Procedural justice
Perceived fairness of the processes used to make decisions about employees.

The second factor, procedural justice, focuses on whether the *procedures* that led to an action were appropriate, were clear, and provided an opportunity for employee input. **Procedural justice** deals with the question, Was the decision-making process fair? Due process is a key part of procedural justice when making promotion, pay, discipline, and other HR decisions.[16] If organizations provide procedural justice, employees tend to respond with positive behaviours that benefit the organization in return. For instance, one study found that procedural justice was a key factor in the level of trust subordinates had in their managers.[17]

Figure 14-3 *Criteria for Evaluating Just Cause and Due Process*

Just-Cause Determinants
- Was the employee warned of the consequences of the conduct?
- Was the employer's rule reasonable?
- Did management investigate before disciplining?
- Was the investigation fair and impartial?
- Was there evidence of guilt?
- Were the rules and penalties applied evenhandedly?
- Was the penalty reasonable, given the offence?

Due Process Considerations
- How have precedents been handled?
- Is a complaint process available?
- Was the complaint process used?
- Was retaliation used against the employee?
- Was the decision based on facts?
- Were the actions and processes viewed as fair by outside entities?

Complaint Procedures and Due Process In most cases, the complaint procedures used to provide due process for unionized employees differ from those for non-union employees. For unionized employees, due process usually refers to the right to use the grievance procedure specified in the union contract. Due process may involve including specific steps in the grievance process, imposing time limits, following arbitration procedures, and providing knowledge of disciplinary penalties. More discussion of the grievance process and procedures in unions can be found in Chapter 15.

Many organizations, especially smaller ones, use an "open door" policy. This policy means that anyone with a complaint can talk with a manager, an HR representative, or an executive. Often, however, the door is not really open, especially if criticisms or conflicts are part of the complaint. Therefore, non-union organizations generally benefit from having formal complaint procedures that provide due process for their employees.[18] Just the presence of such a formal complaint mechanism provides one indicator that an employee has been given due process. Further, if employees view a due process procedure as fair and available for use, they may be less likely to sue their employers or quit their jobs. The HR Perspective discusses research that supports this view.

Alternative Dispute Resolution (ADR) as Due Process

Disputes between management and employees over different work issues are normal and inevitable. How the parties resolve their disputes becomes important. Formal grievance procedures and lawsuits provide two resolution methods. However, more and more companies look to alternative means of ensuring that due process occurs in cases involving employee rights. Employers that handle disputes effectively have lower legal costs and faster resolution times.[19] Dissatisfaction with the expenses and

HR *Perspective*

Workplace Effects of Employees' Perceived Mistreatment

The effects of employee perceptions of workplace treatment have been widely discussed. A study by Boswell and Olson-Buchanan published in the *Academy of Management Journal* provided some interesting insights.

The researchers received over 400 surveys from staff employees at a university. Those surveyed were asked if they had experienced unfair treatment at work in the previous year, and if so, they were asked how they had responded. Information about their lengths of service, supervisory relationships, and loyalty was assessed.

Analyses revealed that the filing of grievances was related to both perceived and actual workplace mistreatment. It was found that individuals who felt mistreated were more likely to leave the university than those who had not been treated unfairly. Those with longer tenure, more loyalty, and greater supervisory support were less likely to leave. Those who had filed grievances were no more likely to leave than those who felt mistreated but had not filed a grievance. However, those who perceived personal mistreatment who said things such as, "The supervisor did not like me," "Everything I did was wrong," "She would embarrass me," or "I was told I was not sick when I took sick leave," were much more likely to withdraw from work.

The authors of the study concluded that grievance systems are supposed to provide an outlet for voicing concerns about mistreatment. However, filing a grievance does not seem to change the rate at which people who perceive that they were mistreated choose to leave the organization. If a grievance system is supposed to help an organization retain workers, it is not as effective as expected.[20]

1. Based on the findings of this study why do you feel the grievance system was not effective in retaining workers?
2. Based on your own experiences, what else can an organization do to ensure that employees feel they are treated well at work?

delays that are common in the court system when lawsuits are filed explains the growth in alternative dispute resolution (ADR) methods such as arbitration, peer review panels, and ombuds.

Arbitration

Disagreements between employers and employees often mean lawsuits and large legal bills for settlement. In some jurisdictions, there is statutory arbitration available to some non-union employees. Non-unionized employees with the necessary length of service in Quebec (two years of service), Nova Scotia (ten years of service), and federally (one year of service) can request arbitration of their dismissals by government-appointed adjudicators. These arbitrations are conducted in much the same informal manner as under collective agreements. Quebec and federal legislation and case law exclude senior managerial employees from this scheme. Adjudicators have the power to order the reinstatement of discharged employees, as well as to grant damages based on reasonable notice principles. Case law under these statutes requires employees to use progressive discipline in much the same way as for unionized employees. Use of these recourses has become increasingly popular federally and in Quebec because adjudicators often grant more generous notice periods than the courts when they do not order reinstatement. The adjudication process is also less costly for an employee than litigation before a court.[21]

Arbitration
Process that uses a neutral third party to make a decision.

Arbitration is a process that uses a neutral third party to make a decision, thereby eliminating the necessity of using the court system. Arbitration has been a common feature in union contracts. However, it must be set up carefully if the employers want to use it in non-union situations.[22]

Studies suggest that only one third of Canadian workplaces offer internal grievance mechanisms that are quite simple.[23] The most common procedure used by Canadian employers is the "open door policy," whereby employees are merely encouraged to discuss any problems with their immediate supervisors or other management personnel. Other measures used by employers in Canada include: senior management review; peer review, where a panel usually composed of both employee and management members hears and resolves complaints; and the use of an ombuds.[24] The use of formal processes, such as arbitration, is quite rare in non-unionized settings in Canada. Even when offered, internal grievance procedures are not used very often in non-unionized workplaces in Canada. In one recent survey, 47 percent of Canadian employers reported that their grievance procedures had not been used at all during the previous year.[25]

Peer Review Panels

Some employers allow their employees to appeal disciplinary actions to an internal committee of employees. This panel reviews the actions and makes recommendations or decisions. Panel members are specially trained volunteers who sign confidentiality agreements, after which the company empowers them to hear appeals. Eastman Kodak uses peer review panels as part of its resolution support services program. Employees from all parts of the company serve as panel members.[26]

Peer review panels can serve as the last stage of a formal complaint process for non-union employees, and their use has reduced the likelihood of unhappy employees' filing lawsuits. If an employee does file a lawsuit, the employer presents a stronger case if a group of the employee's peers previously reviewed the employer's decision and found it to be appropriate. In general, these panels reverse management decisions much less often than might be expected.

Some organizations use peer reviews, which are groups of employees, specially trained, to handle disciplinary appeals.

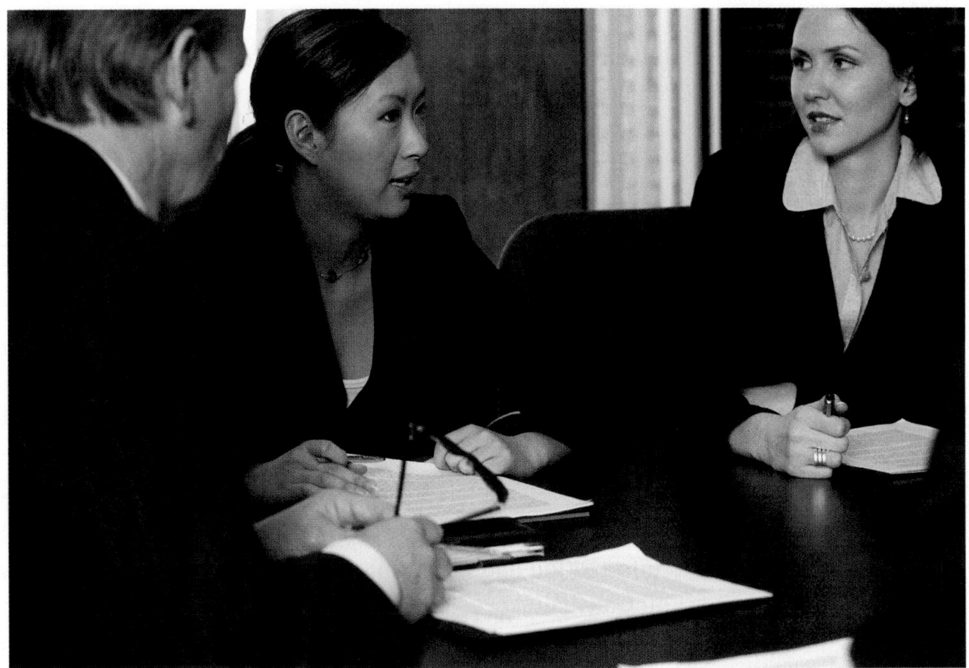

Source: © 2006 JupiterImages and its Licensors. All Rights Reserved.

Ombuds

Some organizations ensure process fairness through ombuds, who are individuals outside the normal chain of command that act as problem solvers for both management and employees. At Brock University, Scotiabank, and other firms, ombuds have effectively addressed complaints about unfair treatment, employee/supervisor conflicts, and other workplace behaviour issues.[27] Ombuds address employees' complaints and operate with a high degree of confidentiality. Any follow-up to resolve problems is often handled informally, except when situations include unusual or significant illegal actions.

Balancing Employer Security Concerns and Employee Rights

3 The issues of privacy are becoming more prevalent in North American workplaces. Employees expect to have some privacy at work, even if they are on their employer's premises and using the employer's equipment. At the same time, it's normal that working for someone will mean giving up some privacy. Employers need basic information about their employees for things like pay and benefits, and they have to be able to ensure that work is being done efficiently and safely.

The possibilities for infringing on privacy are greater than ever before. Psychological tests, Web-browsing records, video surveillance, keystroke monitoring, genetic testing: the information an employer can have about employees is limitless. Employers can balance their "need to know" with their employees' right to privacy, if they ensure that they collect, use, and disclose personal information about their employees for appropriate purposes only.

But balancing employer and employee rights is becoming more difficult. On one side, employers have a legitimate need to ensure that employees are performing their jobs properly in a secure environment. On the other side, employees expect the rights that they have both at work and away from work to be protected.

LOGGING ON...

Office of the Privacy Commissioner of Canada

The Commissioner is an advocate for the privacy rights of Canadians and works independently of the government to investigate complaints from individuals with respect to the federal public sector and the private sector.

www.privcom.gc.ca/

Right to privacy
An individual's freedom from unauthorized and unreasonable intrusion into their personal affairs.

The **right to privacy** is defined in legal terms as an individual's freedom from unauthorized and unreasonable intrusion into personal affairs. There is no explicit right to privacy in Canada's Constitution and Charter of Rights and Freedoms. However, in interpreting section 8 of the Charter, which grants the right to be secure against unreasonable search or seizure, Canada's courts have recognized an individual's right to a reasonable expectation of privacy.[28] Several provinces have also enacted right-to-privacy statutes. A scope of privacy concerns exists in other countries as well, as the HR Globally discussion explains. HR policies and priorities in organizations are specifically affected by such issues as access to employee records, employees' freedom of expression, workplace monitoring, employer investigations, and substance abuse and drug testing.

Privacy Rights and Employee Records

Privacy is regulated at both the federal and provincial level. At the federal level, privacy is protected by two acts: the 1982 federal Privacy Act and the 2001 Personal Information and Electronic Documents Act (PIPEDA). Every province and territory in Canada (except for Newfoundland) has guidelines to protect personal information held by government departments and agencies. The provincial and territorial privacy acts guarantee individuals' rights to view and correct their personal information. The acts are administered and overseen by an independent commissioner or ombuds, with the authority to investigate complaints.

The federal Privacy Act of 1982 regulates the collection, use, and disclosure of personal information held by federal public agencies and provides individuals a right of access to personal information held by those agencies, subject to some exceptions, including an exemption for court records.

HR *Globally*

European Union Data-Protection Directive

The European Union (EU) has been a leader in addressing privacy concerns of its citizens. In 1998, the EU Data-Protection Directive was enacted to require organizations to protect personal data. The directive has wide-ranging consequences for government entities, Internet providers, health-care providers, and employers. The directive goes so far as to forbid the transfer of personal data to countries outside the EU if data-privacy safeguards and guarantees do not exist. The directive is affecting multinational firms in both business and employee matters. The EU has investigated and/or filed complaints against United Airlines, Microsoft, Ford, Marriott, and numerous other global firms for violating the provisions of the directive. As it affects employee data and records, the directive states the following:

- Personal data can be gathered only for identified reasons.
- Individuals must receive information about who receives and processes their data and why the data are being gathered.
- Persons have the right to access the data collected about them and to change, delete, or correct these details.
- Legal actions may be taken by individuals for misuse of their personal data.

These four provisions have significant implications for employer recordkeeping processes, including who accesses data, what data is collected, and how it is used. As the directive is implemented in all EU countries, including the ten new members admitted in 2004, HR recordkeeping systems and procedures in many companies worldwide will be affected.[29]

1. What can employers do to be proactive to protect employees' privacy rights?
2. Do you think it is reasonable for the EU to expect that all information will remain confidential in light of multinationals working in their countries? Why or why not?

PIPEDA was approved by Parliament in April 2000 to address the private sector. The act adopts the CSA International Privacy Code into law for private sector organizations that process personal information "in the course of a commercial activity," and for federally regulated employers with respect to their employees. It does not apply to information collected for personal, journalistic, artistic, literary, or non-commercial purposes.

The purpose of the Personal Information Protection and Electronic Documents Act is to provide Canadians with a right of privacy with respect to their personal information that is collected, used, or disclosed by an organization in the private sector in an era in which technology increasingly facilitates the collection and free flow of information. British Columbia, Alberta, and Quebec are exempt from PIPEDA since they have their own privacy legislation that has been deemed to be substantially similar to PIPEDA.[30]

Respecting Employees' Privacy An employer's need for information should be balanced with an employee's right to privacy. For almost all personal information—including pay and benefit records, formal and informal personnel files, video or audio tapes, and records of Web-browsing, electronic mail, and keystrokes—the following basic rules help to establish and maintain that balance:[31]

- The employer should say what personal information it collects from employees, why it collects it, and what it does with it.
- Collection, use, or disclosure of personal information should normally be done only with an employee's knowledge and consent.
- The employer should only collect personal information that's necessary for its stated purpose, and collect it by fair and lawful means.
- The employer should normally use or disclose personal information only for the purposes that it collected it for, and keep it only as long as it's needed for those purposes, unless it has the employee's consent to do something else with it, or is legally required to use or disclose it for other purposes.
- Employees' personal information needs to be accurate, complete, and up-to-date.
- Employees should be able to access their personal information, and be able to challenge the accuracy and completeness of it.

Employee Medical Records Patients have a right to expect that their personal health information will not be collected unless it is necessary for their care and that it will not be used in any way that could do them harm. Organizations and health information custodians must obtain a separate and express consent for collecting, using, or disclosing genetic information. Genetic information must also be stored separately from other personal health information. Express consent is required for the collection of personal health information by an organization that is not a health information custodian.

Employee Personnel Records Section 24 of the Canada Labour Standards Regulations identifies the required records to be kept on file for inspection by an inspector under the Canada Labour Code. Employers must keep payroll and other employment records for at least 36 months. Every jurisdiction has different requirements. For example, in Ontario, employers are required to retain the name, address, and date of hire for three years after the employee ceases to be employed. Records as to the number of hours worked, the pay records, vacation, and all documents relating to pregnancy leave, parental leave, and emergency leave must also be retained for three years. In Manitoba, employee records must be retained for five years after termination. As illustrated in Figure 14-4, there are specific rules under various pieces of legislation as to how long records should be maintained.

Figure 14-4 Employee Record Files

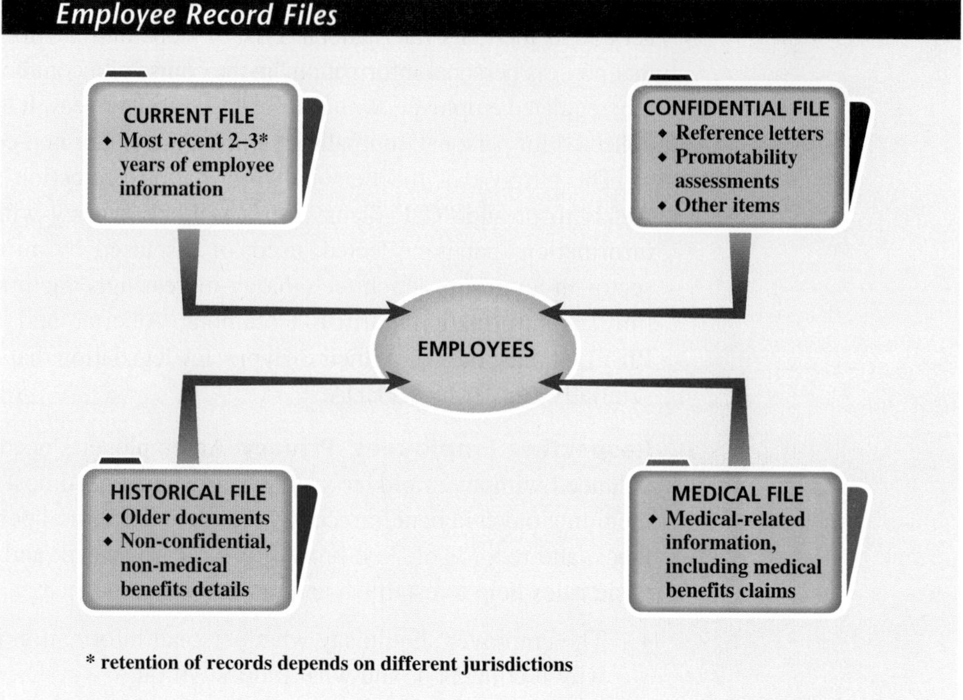

Essential personnel files and records should usually be maintained for three to five years. However, different types of records should be maintained for shorter or longer periods of time because of various legal and regulatory standards.[32]

Security of Employee Records It is important that specific access restrictions and security procedures for employee records be established. These restrictions and procedures are designed to protect the privacy of employees and to protect employers from potential liability for improper disclosure of personal information. The following guidelines are offered regarding employer access and storage of employee records:

- Restrict access to records to a limited number of individuals.
- Use confidential passwords for accessing employee records in various HRIS databases.
- Set up separate files and restricted databases for especially sensitive employee information.
- Inform employees what types of data are retained.
- Purge employee records of outdated data.

Employees' Freedom of Expression

The right of individuals to freedom of expression, or freedom of speech as it is often referred, is protected by the Charter of Rights and Freedom. However, that freedom is *not* an unrestricted one in the workplace. Three areas in which employees' freedom of expression have collided with employers' restrictions are controversial views, whistleblowing, and monitoring of e-mail and voice mail.

Employee Advocacy of Controversial Views Questions of freedom of expression arise over the right of employees to advocate controversial viewpoints at work. Numerous examples can be cited. For instance: Can an employee of a tobacco company join in anti-smoking demonstrations outside of work? and Can a disgruntled employee at a non-union employer wear a union badge on his cap at work? In the fall of 2005 controversy sparked around the world in condemnation of a dozen cartoons depicting Muslim's Prophet Muhammad published by a Danish newspaper. Several other newswires in Europe followed suit and published them as well. The reaction to the cartoons resulted in numerous riots around the world, and a number of deaths as Muslims around the world retaliated over the display of disrespect towards their Prophet. The controversy eventually reached Canada. In February 2006, a professor from St. Mary's put the cartoons on his office door to make a statement about academic freedom and to promote debate on campus. The university took a dim view of the professor's statement and asked him to take the cartoons down. Because the school owns the outside of the door, he did. He threatened to bring the cartoons to class the next day, but instead chose to make comment only. In retaliation he threatened to launch a union grievance because it impacted on his job description. The union did find support for his cause. Student protests took place the next day angered over his actions.[33]

Whistleblowers
Individuals who report real or perceived wrongs committed by their employers.

Whistleblowing Individuals who report real or perceived wrongs committed by their employers are called **whistleblowers.** The reasons why people report actions that they question vary, and are often individual in nature.[34] Many well-known whistleblowing incidents have occurred in the past several years in Canada. Three respected scientists were terminated from Health Canada because they exposed Monsanto's plan to have Bovine Growth Hormone approved in Canada; Dr. Nancy Oliveri was threatened with dismissal from the Hospital for Sick Children for raising concerns about a problematic drug Apotex was developing; and Myriam Bédard, was fired from her job at VIA Rail in 2001 over her concerns about the federal sponsorship program.[35] Unfortunately, it is common for whistleblowers to experience demotion, dismissal, and negative treatment from their employers after they disclose the unlawful act and corruption. For example, Myriam Bédard, a former Olympic athlete, said in February 2004 that she had been fired from her marketing job at Via Rail after questioning invoices for advertising work by Groupaction, the main company wrapped up in the sponsorship scandal. Bédard said she wrote to Prime Minister Paul Martin when she saw him on TV urging Canadians to come forward with whatever information they had about the sponsorship program. Via Rail chair Jean Pelletier was later fired for calling Bédard a "pitiful, single woman," saying she was trying to draw attention to herself with the allegations.[36]

New whistleblower protection legislation came into force in Canada on September 15, 2004. Bill C-25 covers all public sector and Crown corporation employees. Whistleblower legislation does not extend to the Canadian Security Intelligence Service, the Communications Security establishment, and uniformed members of the RCMP or the Armed Forces. Employers who use employment-related intimidation or retaliation against whistleblowers now risk criminal liability as a result of the addition of section 425.1 to the Criminal Code of Canada.[37]

Saskatchewan is the only province in Canada to have whistleblower legislation similar to federal legislation. However, the Supreme Court of Canada recently made a decision regarding section 74 of the Labour Standards Act of Saskatchewan. In *Merk v. International Association of Bridge, Structural, Ornamental and Reinforcing Iron Workers, Local 77,* Merk was fired as a bookkeeper and office manager of Local 77 because she blew the whistle on alleged financial abuses by her immediate supervisor, the local president, and the business manager. The court ruled that she had been discharged because she reported the financial misconduct. The Criminal Code and the Supreme Court of Canada decision make it clear that Canadian employers should be aware that they cannot discipline or dismiss employees for blowing the whistle on unlawful corporate conduct.[38] Employers should therefore create internal whistle-blower programs to address employee complaints and maintain better control over information concerning alleged unlawful corporate conduct.

The culture of the organization often affects the degree to which employees report inappropriate or illegal actions internally or resort to using outside contacts.[39] Employers need to address two key questions in regard to whistleblowing: (1) When do employees have the right to speak out with protection from retribution? and (2) When do employees violate the confidentiality of their jobs by speaking out? Even though the answers may be difficult to determine, retaliation against whistleblowers clearly is not allowed.

Monitoring of E-mail and Voice Mail Advances in information and telecommunications technology have become a major issue for employers regarding employee privacy.[40] Many employers provide employees with computers and telephones for work-related purposes. But as with any other form of communication, such as telephones and faxes, employees are quick to discover personal uses for this "business" equipment. Such personal use may create legitimate concerns for an employer, which covers a wide range from the loss of productivity of the equipment or employees while engaged in personal use through to potential civil or criminal liability in respect of an employee's transmission of unlawful materials. Many employers have specialized software that can retrieve deleted e-mail, voicemail, and even record each keystroke made on their computers.

An employer can restrict the use of e-mail by employees. However, an employer may be on shaky legal ground if it attempts to monitor an employee's use of e-mails or voicemails or to discipline for such use, because its legal ability to do so may be compromised by an employee's reasonable expectation of privacy. For these reasons, employers should implement a policy that outlines the boundaries of permissible use and also clearly stipulates that the access is provided for business purposes, with no expectation of privacy. The policy should be communicated and signed by the employee.

One problem with both e-mail and voice mail is that most people express themselves more casually than they would in formal memos. This tendency can create sloppy, racist, sexist, or otherwise defamatory messages. In *Di Vito and Mathers v. Macdonald Dettwiler & Associates*, a 1996 B.C. Supreme Court case, the court upheld the dismissal of two employees for their role in circulating an e-mail containing derogatory comments about an overweight employee. Influencing the court's decision was the fact that the employees' actions had negatively impacted their co-worker and the work environment.[41] Other cases have been brought over jokes that were forwarded that had profanity or racial undertones. Another problem is that e-mail messages can be sent rapidly to multiple (sometimes unintended) recipients.

Also, both e-mail and voice mail can be stored, and often legal cases hinge on retrieval of those messages. CIBC turned employee's e-mails into a "potent legal weapon." Six executives left the bank to start up a competing investment firm, Genuity Capital Markets. The Bank alleged that the six employees took confidential information and recruited bank employees. Such cases are common, in light of non-compete clauses discussed earlier in the chapter, but this was one of the first cases where a Canadian employer actually went through the employees' e-mails and presented it as evidence in court. CIBC was able to tap into messages sent by BlackBerrys, which the former executives apparently believed were protected by a private system of e-mail communications known as PINning (personal identification numbers or PINs). The bank was also able to secure communications from e-mail and instant messaging.[42] Figure 14-5 depicts recommended actions.

To address the various concerns regarding monitoring of e-mail and voice mail, many employers have established policies with four elements. Those elements are as follows:

- Voice mail, e-mail, and computer files are provided by the employer and are for business use only.
- Use of these media for personal reasons is restricted and subject to employer review.
- All computer passwords and codes must be available to the employer.
- The employer reserves the right to monitor or search any of the media, without notice, for business purposes.
- Discipline procedures should be included for breach of policy.
- All employees will be treated fairly.

Workplace Monitoring

The monitoring of e-mail and voice mail is only one illustration of how employers watch the workplace. Several forces have led to a growth in workplace monitoring, both in Canada and in the U.S. One major force is the expansion in available technology, ranging from the Internet to global tracking devices to enhanced video capabilities and improved information systems software. Second, the events of 9/11 in 2001 led to passage of the USA Patriot Act, which expanded legislation to allow government investigators to engage in broader monitoring of individuals, including workplaces, in order to protect national security.[43] For Canada, the Patriot Act could impinge on Canadian privacy rights. In B.C., a public-sector union raised alarm over the government's intention to outsource the management of health information and some employee records to a

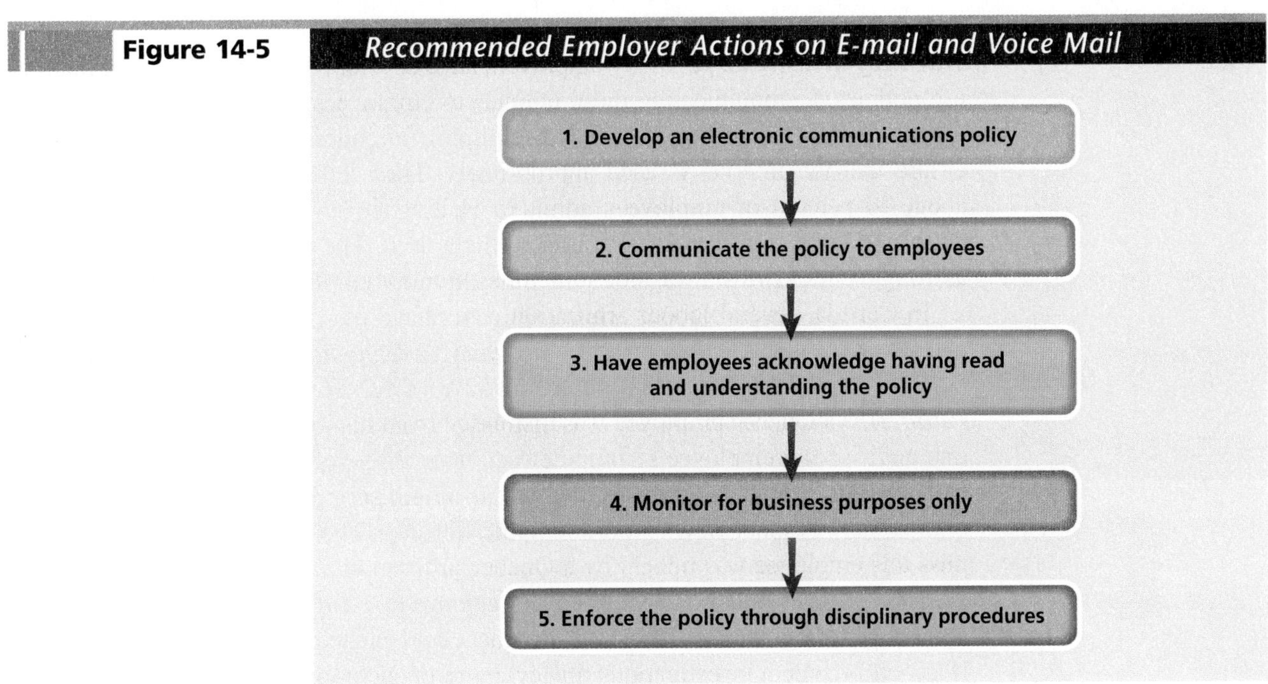

1. Develop an electronic communications policy
2. Communicate the policy to employees
3. Have employees acknowledge having read and understanding the policy
4. Monitor for business purposes only
5. Enforce the policy through disciplinary procedures

Figure 14-5 *Recommended Employer Actions on E-mail and Voice Mail*

U.S.-based firm. At issue is concern that the USA Patriot Act allows federal authorities investigating terrorist activities to access records on more relaxed grounds than are usual. Canadian records in the U.S. would then be subjected to this law.[44]

The growing use of technology in organizations is making it more difficult to balance employer security rights with employee privacy concerns.[45] While computers, cameras, and telecommunications systems are transforming many workplaces, the use of these items by employers to monitor employee actions is amplifying concerns that the privacy rights of employees are being threatened.[46] Despite the privacy conflicts, many employers are checking on employees by tracking Internet use, monitoring performance, conducting video surveillance, checking keystrokes, etc.

Monitoring should always be the last resort—reserved for cases where an unsafe practice needs to be stopped immediately or if the activity causes harm to people or to the organization. If an organization chooses to engage in electronic monitoring, it's very important that employees are informed in advance that their activities will be monitored and they are given adequate explanations for this monitoring. Most companies claim that although they monitor everyone, they only use this information if they have reason to suspect an employee is engaging in negative behaviours.

A recent case in Canada demonstrates the need to be prudent about monitoring employees. Parkland Regional Library in Lacombe, Alberta, violated the privacy of an information technology worker by installing software on his computer to monitor his productivity without his knowledge. The worker discovered the equipment and removed it. The question raised by the courts was whether the information that was being collected was "personal" as defined by the Act. The privacy commissioner felt that the content of the transcription was not personal information, but that the errors or the speed of performance of the task may have a personal aspect. "If most or even all of the information that was collected was (the complainant's) work-related activity, all of it had a personal component in this case, because it was to be used to determine how much work he did, or his style or manner of doing it or his own choices as to how to prioritize it." Therefore, the library was collecting personal information as defined in the act. The library was unable to justify why monitoring the specific employee was warranted, particularly when other employees were not being monitored.[47]

Tracking Internet Use Many employers have developed and disseminated Internet use policies. Communicating these policies to employees, enforcing them by monitoring employee Internet use, and disciplining offenders are the ways employers ensure that the Internet is used appropriately. These efforts are necessary because about 90 percent of employees admit to visiting non-work websites during work hours and many companies are watching them do it. The numbers vary, but as many as 70 percent of firms always or sometimes monitor employees' Internet use.[48]

In Canada, several labour arbitration cases have focused on employee dismissal due to inappropriate computer use. In *Syndicat Canadien Des Communication de l'Energie et du Papier, section locale 552 c. CAE Electronique Lteè. (Grief du Petruzzi)*,[49] a Quebec employee was dismissed from his job after his employer's routine audit of the employee's computer activities discovered that he had spent more than 50 percent of his work hours over a four-month period surfing the Internet. Much of the time was spent viewing pornographic websites. The employer's decision to dismiss this employee was upheld by a Quebec arbitration panel.[50]

Through such monitoring, employers attempt to guard against some employees' accessing pornographic or other websites that could create problems for the employers. If law enforcement investigations find evidence of such access, the employer could be accused of aiding and abetting illegal behaviour. Therefore, many employers have purchased software that tracks the websites accessed by employees. Also, some employers use software programs for blocking certain categories and websites that are inappropriate for business use.

Monitoring Employee Performance Employee activity may be monitored to measure performance, ensure performance quality and customer service, check for theft, or enforce company rules or laws. The common concerns in a monitored workplace usually centre not on whether or not monitoring should be used, but on how it should be conducted, how the information should be used, and how feedback should be communicated to employees.[51]

At a minimum, employers should obtain a signed employee consent form that indicates that performance will be monitored regularly and phone calls will be taped regularly. Also, it is recommended that employers provide employees with feedback on monitoring results to help employees improve their performance and to commend them for good performance. For example, one major hotel reservation centre allows employees to listen to their customer service calls and rate their own performance. Then, the employees meet with their supervisors to discuss both positive and negative performance issues.

Conducting Video Surveillance at Work Numerous employers have installed video surveillance systems in workplaces. Some employers use these systems to ensure employee security, such as in parking lots, garages, and dimly lit exterior areas. Other employers have installed them on retail sales floors and in production areas, parts and inventory rooms, and lobbies. When video surveillance is extended into employee restrooms, changing rooms, and other more private areas, employer rights and employee privacy collide. Video surveillance in private areas is considered to be intrusive and generally not allowed. As a general principle, employers have to use the least intrusive methods to meet objectives. In some cases, the use of cameras is acceptable, as illustrated by one Quebec ruling. The case dealt with the issue of privacy and the admissibility of videotaped evidence. A company was having problems

Many employers are installing video surveillance to monitor workplace against theft and for security issues. The use of these systems must be disclosed to employees.

Source: Steve Krongard/The Image Bank/Getty Images

with vandalism in the washrooms. Somebody was intentionally blocking toilets with toilet paper. "They couldn't find out who was doing it, so they put cameras in the stalls, but only focused on the toilet paper dispenser." The employer showed it had tried everything else, so the court said the cameras in the stalls, though seemingly extreme, were not abusive under the circumstances.[52]

As with other forms of monitoring, it is important that employers develop a video surveillance policy, inform employees about the policy, perform the surveillance only for legitimate business purposes, and strictly limit those who view the surveillance results.

Employer Investigations

Another area of concern regarding employee rights involves workplace investigations. Whether on or off the job, unethical or illegal employee behaviour can be a serious problem for organizations. Employee misconduct may include illegal drug use, falsification of documents, misuse of company funds, disclosure of organizational secrets, workplace violence, employment harassment, and theft.

Another problem faced by employers is *employee theft* of property and vital company secrets. Retailers are estimated to lose over $1.2 billion a year to employee theft. White-collar theft through embezzlement, accepting bribes, and stealing company property is a growing concern.[53] If the organizational culture encourages or allows questionable behaviour, then employees are more likely to see theft as acceptable.[54]

Employee theft and other workplace misconduct can be addressed using a number of methods, as Figure 14-6 indicates. Besides watching current employees through the various types of surveillance and monitoring, firms may screen applicants through means such as honesty testing and background checks, in order to avoid hiring individuals who are more likely to violate workplace standards of conduct.

Honesty and Polygraph Tests Pencil-and-paper honesty tests are alternatives to polygraph testing. Honesty tests are widely used, particularly in the retail industry and in other selected industries, and more than two dozen variations of them are available. Polygraph tests are not admissible in court, due their low reliability and validity. They are also not legal in most jurisdictions in Canada.

Reviewing Unusual Behaviour Another method of addressing workplace conduct is to review unusual behaviour on and off the job. For instance, if an employee is suddenly wearing many new clothes and spending lavishly, inquiries as to the reasons why and the resources used might be warranted. In one case, inquiries at a government office revealed that a clerk had "borrowed" over $50,000 to purchase numerous items and take several trips to gambling destinations. In such situations, care should be taken during the review.

Conducting Work-Related Investigations Workplace investigations are frequently conducted using technology. Technological advances allow employers to review e-mails, access computer logs, conduct video surveillance, and use other

Figure 14-6 *Means Used to Reduce Employee Theft and Misconduct*

Before Hire	After Hire
• Applicant screening • Honesty testing • Background investigation	• Workplace monitoring • Review of unusual behaviour changes

investigative tactics. When using audiotaping, wiretapping, and other electronic methods, care should be taken to avoid violating privacy and legal regulations.[55]

Workplace investigations can be conducted internally or externally. Often, HR staff and company security personnel lead internal investigations. Employers can hire outside investigators and as long as surveillance takes place in a public place, there should be no problems with respect to privacy.

Canadian Centre on Substance Abuse (CCSA)
The Canadian Centre on Substance Abuse (CCSA) is Canada's national addictions agency. Their mission is to provide objective, evidence-based information and advice that will help reduce the health, social, and economic harm associated with substance abuse and addictions.
www.ccsa.ca/ccsa/

Substance Abuse and Drug Testing

Employee substance abuse and drug testing have received a great deal of attention. Concern about substance abuse at work is appropriate given that absenteeism, accident/damage rates, health-care expenses, and theft/fraud are higher for workers using illegal substances or misusing legal substances such as drugs and alcohol. Figure 14-7 identifies some of the financial effects of substance abuse. Ways to address substance abuse problems were discussed in Chapter 13; employee rights concerning those means are discussed in the following sections.

Drug Testing and Employee Rights Random and pre-employment drug testing of public employees are human rights violation and not allowed under the Canadian Human Rights Act. Post-accident testing, workplace drug testing for "reasonable" cause, and random alcohol testing for safety-sensitive employees are generally acceptable under the law. Employers can test for impairment for workers in safety-sensitive jobs, but only with "strong reasonable cause," such as the occurrence of an accident. These rules apply to workers in all of Canada's federally regulated industries and could also serve as guidelines for small companies not covered by federal regulations.

Employee Rights and Personal Behaviour

An additional area in which employer and employee rights may conflict concerns personal behaviour off the job. Employers encounter special difficulty in establishing "just cause" for disciplining employees for their off-the-job behaviour. Most people believe an employer should not control the lives of its employees off the job except in the case of clear job-related consequences. For example, what should an employer do if an employee

Figure 14-7 How Substance Abuse Affects Employers Financially

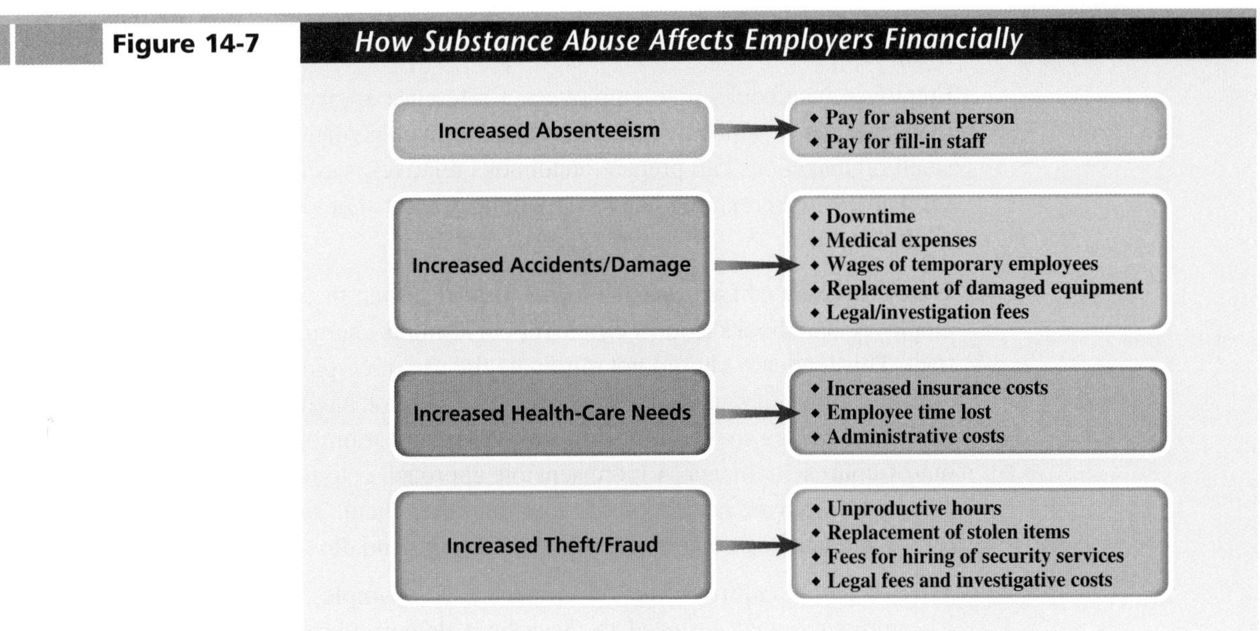

is an acknowledged transvestite, a member of an activist environmental group, a leader in a racist group, or an exotic dancer on weekends? These are just a few cases in which employee rights and personal behaviours can conflict with employer expectations.

To appropriately deal with employee rights, certain policies, procedures, and rules are required in order to provide guidelines for expected behaviour in the workplace. The following section presents these provisions, as well as how to incorporate them effectively in the workplace.

HR Policies, Procedures, and Rules

Policies
General guidelines that focus organizational actions.

Procedures
Customary methods of handling activities.

Rules
Specific guidelines that regulate and restrict the behaviour of individuals.

4 HR policies, procedures, and rules greatly affect employee rights (just discussed) and discipline (discussed next). Where there is a choice among actions, policies act as general guidelines that focus organizational actions. **Policies** are general in nature, whereas procedures and rules are specific to the situation. The important role of policies requires that they be reviewed regularly.

Procedures provide customary methods of handling activities and are more specific than policies. For example, a policy may state that employees will be given vacation according to years of service, and a procedure establishes a specific method for authorizing vacation time without disrupting work.

Rules are specific guidelines that regulate and restrict the behaviour of individuals. They are similar to procedures in that they guide action and typically allow no discretion in their application. Rules reflect a management decision that action be taken—or not taken—in a given situation, and they provide more specific behavioural guidelines than do policies.

Responsibilities for HR Policies, Procedures, and Rules

For HR policies, procedures, and rules to be effective, coordination between the HR unit and operating managers is vital. As Figure 14-8 shows, managers are the main users and enforcers of rules, procedures, and policies, and they should receive some training and explanation in how to carry them out. The HR unit supports managers, reviews policies and disciplinary rules, and trains managers to use them. Often policies, procedures, and rules are provided in employee handbooks.

Employee Handbooks

Employee handbooks give employees a reference source for company policies and rules and can be a positive tool for effective management of human resources. Even small organizations can prepare handbooks relatively easily using available computer software. When preparing handbooks, management should consider legal issues, readability, and use.

Legal Review of Language As mentioned earlier, there is a current trend of using employee handbooks against employers in lawsuits charging a broken "implied" contract. This tendency should not eliminate the use of employee handbooks as a way of communicating policies to employees. In fact, not having an employee handbook with HR policies spelled out can leave an organization open to costly litigation and out-of-court settlements. A more sensible approach is to first develop sound HR policies and employee handbooks to communicate them, and then have legal counsel review the language contained in them. Recommendations include the following:

- *Eliminate controversial phrases.* For example, the phrase "permanent employee" may be used to describe a person who has passed a probationary

Figure 14-8 *Typical Division of HR Responsibilities: Policies, Procedures, and Rules*

HR Unit	Managers
• Designs formal mechanisms for coordinating HR policies • Assists in development of organization-wide HR policies, procedures, and rules • Provides information on application of HR policies, procedures, and rules • Trains managers to administer policies, procedures, and rules	• Help in developing HR policies and rules • Review policies and rules with all employees • Apply HR policies, procedures, and rules • Explain rules and policies to all employees • Give feedback on effectiveness of policies and rules

period. This wording can lead to disagreement over what the parties meant by "permanent." A more appropriate phrase is "regular employee."

- *Use disclaimers.* Courts generally uphold disclaimers, but only if they are prominently shown in the handbook. To ensure that disclaimers do not negate the positive image presented by the handbook, they should not be overused. A disclaimer in the handbook can read as follows:

  > This employee handbook is not intended to be a contract or any part of a contractual agreement between the employer and the employee. The employer reserves the right to modify, delete, or add to any policies set forth herein without notice.

- *Keep the handbook current.* Many employers simply add new material to handbooks rather than deleting old, inapplicable rules. Those old rules can become the basis for new lawsuits. Consequently, handbooks and HR policies should be reviewed periodically and revised every few years.

Readability The HR specialists who prepare employee handbooks sometimes fail to write at an appropriate reading level. One review of some company handbooks revealed that on average, they were written at the third-year college level, which is much higher than the typical reading level of employees in most organizations. One solution is to test the readability of the handbook on a sample of employees before publishing it.

Use Another important factor to be considered in preparing an employee handbook is how it will be used. In addition to distributing policies and rules in an employee handbook, employers must communicate freely about HR issues, policies, and rules, and disseminate organizational information widely.[56]

To communicate and discuss HR information, a growing number of firms are distributing employee handbooks electronically using an intranet, which enables employees to access policies in employee handbooks at any time. It also allows changes in policies to be made electronically rather than distributed as paper copies.

Communicating HR Information

HR communication focuses on the receipt and dissemination of HR data and information throughout the organization. *Downward communication* flows from top management to the rest of the organization, informing employees about what is and will be happening in the organization, and what are the expectations and goals of top management. *Upward communication* enables managers to know about the ideas, concerns, and information needs of employees. Various methods are used to facilitate both types of communication.

Organizations communicate with employees through internal publications and media, including newspapers, company magazines, organizational newsletters, videotapes, Internet postings, and e-mail announcements. Whatever the formal means used, managers should make an honest attempt to communicate information employees need to know. The spread of electronic communications allows for more timely and widespread dissemination of HR information, as the Technology Transforming HR discussion indicates.

Employee Discipline

Discipline
Form of training that enforces organizational rules.

5 The earlier discussion about employee rights provides an appropriate introduction to the topic of employee discipline, because employee rights often are a key issue in disciplinary cases. Discipline is a form of training that enforces organizational rules. Those most often affected by the discipline systems are problem employees. Fortunately, problem employees comprise a small number of employees, but they often are the ones who cause the most disciplinary situations. If employers fail to deal with problem employees, negative effects on other employees and work groups often result. Common disciplinary issues caused by problem employees include absenteeism, tardiness, productivity deficiencies, alcoholism, and insubordination.

Figure 14-9 shows a possible division of responsibilities for discipline between the HR unit and operating managers. Notice that managers and supervisors are the ones to make disciplinary decisions and administer the discipline. HR specialists are often consulted before disciplinary action is instituted, and they may assist managers in administering the disciplinary action.

Technology Transforming HR

Electronic HR Communications

As electronic and telecommunications systems have developed, many employers have added more technological methods of communicating with employees. With the growth of information systems in organizations and more use of e-mail systems, communications through organizations can be immediate. These operate worldwide through networks. For example, Musicland, a national retailer, provides its store managers with weekly newsletters that are printed out for distribution to store employees. Additional news and store project tasks also are sent electronically on a regular basis to store managers and employees.

These systems often result in the bypassing of the formal organizational structure and channels to communicate with employees. The retailer Ikea uses its intranet to disseminate new product details, review company policies, identify job postings, and provide online training materials. In break rooms and training rooms at Ikea, there are intranet terminals for employees to use.

Some organizations also communicate using Web-based communication, which links facilities and groups in various locations. This way, technology allows the same message to be delivered simultaneously to various audiences. One retailing company using electronic communications is Limited Brands, whose stores include Victoria's Secret, The Limited, and Bath & Body Works. The Limited's regional and district managers all have laptops and wireless equipment for receiving operational and policy updates. The Limited's system even allows text messages to be sent directly to stores through its cash register system.

Another aspect of HR technology is expanded use of electronic "message boards" on company websites. Message boards allow communication among management, employees, and others on issues of concern. They can be useful, but are sometimes problematic if the communication becomes negative, insulting, or even filled with profanity. Thus, technology provides many advantages for HR communications, but some drawbacks as well.[57]

1. With so much communication being thrown at employees on a daily basis, either through work, or at home, do you think you actually pay attention to constant communication? That is, do you think communication can be too much of a good thing? Explain your answer.
2. What do you see as the advantages and disadvantages to multiple sources of electronic communication?

Figure 14-9 Typical Division of HR Responsibilities: Discipline

HR Unit	Managers
• Designs HR procedures that consider employees' rights • Designs a progressive discipline process in non-union organizations • Trains managers to use the discipline process • Helps managers administer discipline	• Are knowledgeable about organizational policies and rules • Make disciplinary decisions • Notify employees who violate policies and rules • Discuss discipline follow-up with employees

Approaches to Discipline

The disciplinary system can be viewed as an application of behaviour modification to problem or unproductive employees. The best discipline is clearly self-discipline. Most people can usually be counted on to do their jobs effectively when they understand what is required at work. Yet some find that the prospect of external discipline helps their self-discipline. One approach is the use of positive discipline.

Positive Discipline Approach

The positive discipline approach builds on the philosophy that violations are actions that can usually be corrected constructively without penalty. In this approach, managers focus on using fact-finding and guidance to encourage desirable behaviours, rather than using penalties to discourage undesirable behaviours. The four steps to positive discipline are as follows:

1. *Counselling:* The goal of this phase is to heighten employee awareness of organizational policies and rules. Often, people simply need to be made aware of rules, and knowledge of possible disciplinary actions may prevent violations.
2. *Written documentation:* If the employee fails to correct her or his behaviour, then a second conference becomes necessary. Whereas the first stage took place as a conversation between supervisor and employee, this stage is documented in written form, and written solutions are identified to prevent further problems from occurring.
3. *Final warning:* If the employee does not follow the written solutions noted in the second step, a final warning conference is held. In that conference, the supervisor emphasizes to the employee the importance of correcting the inappropriate actions. Some firms incorporate a decision day off, in which the employee is given a day off with pay to develop a firm, written action plan to remedy the problem behaviours. The decision day off is used to emphasize the seriousness of the problem and the manager's determination to see that the behaviour is changed.
4. *Discharge:* If the employee fails to follow the action plan that was developed, and further problems exist, then the supervisor can discharge the employee.

The advantage of this positive approach to discipline is that it focuses on problem solving. The greatest difficulty with the positive approach to discipline is the extensive amount of training required for supervisors and managers to become effective counsellors, and the need for more supervisory time with this approach than with the progressive discipline, which is discussed next.

Progressive Discipline Approach Progressive discipline incorporates steps that become progressively more stringent and are designed to change the employee's inappropriate behaviour. Figure 14-10 shows a typical progressive discipline process; most progressive discipline procedures use verbal and written reprimands and suspension before resorting to dismissal. At one manufacturing firm, an employee's failure to call in when he or she will be absent from work may lead to a suspension after the third offence in a year. Suspension sends the employees a strong message that undesirable job behaviours must change, or termination is likely to follow.

While appearing similar to positive discipline, progressive discipline is more administrative and process-oriented. Following the progressive sequence ensures that both the nature and the seriousness of the problem are clearly communicated to the employee. Not all steps in the progressive discipline procedure are followed in every case. Certain serious offences are exempted from the progressive procedure and may result in immediate termination. Typical offences leading to immediate termination include intoxication at work, alcohol or drug use at work, fighting, and theft. However, if a firm has a progressive discipline policy, it should be followed. Failure to follow written policies for progressive discipline, in a consistent manner, could potentially invalidate an employee's dismissal.[58]

Reasons Why Discipline Might Not Be Used

For a number of reasons, managers may be reluctant to use discipline. Some of the main ones include the following:

- *Organizational culture of avoiding discipline:* If the organizational "norm" is to avoid penalizing problem employees, then managers are less likely to use discipline or to dismiss problem employees.
- *Lack of support:* Many managers do not want to use discipline because they fear that their decisions will not be supported by higher management. The degree of support is also a function of the organizational culture.
- *Guilt:* Some managers realize that before they became managers, they committed the same violations as their employees, and feel that they cannot discipline others for doing something they used to do.

Figure 14-10 *Progressive Discipline Process*

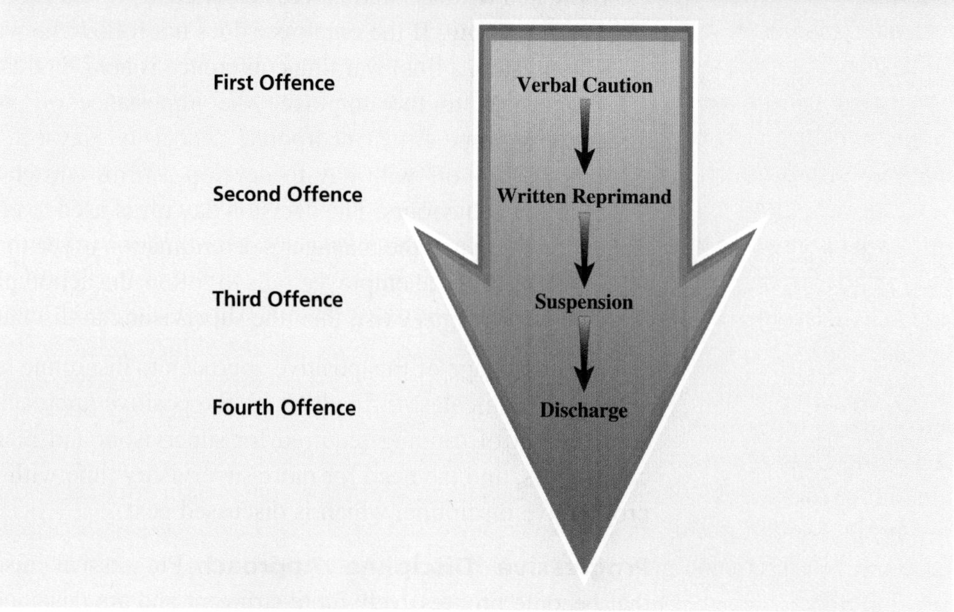

- *Fear of loss of friendship:* Managers may fear losing friendships or damaging personal relationships if they discipline employees.
- *Avoidance of time loss:* When applied properly, discipline requires considerable time and effort. Sometimes, it is easier for managers to avoid taking the time required for disciplining, especially if their actions may be overturned on review by higher management.
- *Fear of lawsuits:* Managers are increasingly concerned about being sued for disciplining someone, particularly for taking the ultimate disciplinary step of termination.

Effective Discipline

Because of legal concerns, managers must understand discipline and know how to administer it properly. Effective discipline should be aimed at the problem behaviours, not at the employee personally, because the reason for discipline is to improve performance. Distributive and procedural justice suggests that if a manager tolerates unacceptable behaviour, other employees may resent the unfairness of that tolerance. The HR Practice relates an old management analogy about effective discipline, and offers a helpful way to remember the essentials.

Training of Supervisors Training supervisors and managers in when and how discipline should be used is crucial. Employees see disciplinary action given by trained supervisors who base their responses on procedural justice as more fair than discipline done by untrained supervisors. Regardless of the disciplinary approach used, training in counselling and in communications skills provides supervisors and managers with the tools necessary to deal with employee performance problems.

Discharge: The Final Disciplinary Step

The final stage in the disciplinary process is termination. Both the positive and the progressive approaches to discipline clearly provide employees with warnings about the seriousness of their performance problems before dismissal occurs. Terminating workers because they do not keep their own promises is more likely to appear equitable and defensible to a jury.

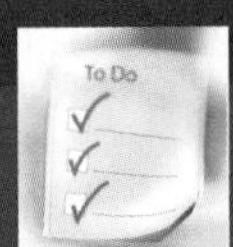

HR *Practice*

Hot-Stove Rule

For many years, the hot-stove rule has been a part of successful training programs designed to teach supervisors about discipline. Good discipline is like a hot stove in these ways:

- *It provides a warning.* A hot stove sends a warning in the form of heat that you can feel, and you know that if you touch it, you will be burned. Employees need a warning too before discipline occurs.
- *It is consistent.* A hot stove burns every time. Good discipline addresses the same offence under the same circumstances every time it occurs.
- *It is immediate.* A hot stove burns immediately if it is touched. The longer after an offence the discipline occurs, the less effective it is in changing behaviour.
- *It is impersonal.* A hot stove burns anyone who touches it. Good discipline is not emotional or random, and it affects each violator the same.

1. Do you feel the "hot-stove rule" is appropriate? Why or why not?
2. Working in groups, devise a discipline policy that incorporates the hot-stove rule concept.

Termination Process When terminating an employee, it is important to use a well-defined process. The following process, used by one large firm, is typical:[59]

1. *Coordinate manager and HR review:* The disciplining manager, that manager's superior, and an HR representative should review the documentation and make the final determination that the employee will be terminated. To protect the organization against costly and embarrassing litigation, strong supporting documentation validating the termination should be secured before proceeding with this action.
2. *Select a neutral location:* It is generally recommended that termination occur in the HR department or a conference room, not the supervisor/manager's office. This location is not in the department where other employees can observe and is where needed HR documentation is available.
3. *When "not" to conduct termination:* Never terminate on a Monday, or a Friday, special dates such as birthdays, or anniversary dates, or other events such as writing exams, or at Christmas, or as the employee heads off for vacation, etc. Terminating on Friday cuts off access to health professionals if the individual needs to speak to someone. They could be very distraught over the action. Noon is usually a good time to conduct the termination, since many employees will be away from the office. It is less embarrassing for the employee when they have to walk out the building, usually escorted.
4. *Conduct the termination meeting:* The manager arranges for the employee to go to the termination location, where the HR representative and the manager are. The manager informs the employee of the reason for the termination. The HR representative acts as an observer, and takes notes of the proceedings. Any discussion with the employee should be based on facts and is not subject to change. Throughout the termination discussion, the supervisor and the HR representative should remain professional and calm, rather than becoming emotional or apologetic or making demeaning remarks. This meeting should take no more than five minutes. Prolonging the meeting only allows the employee to become angry and agitated, so it is best to make it as quick as possible, ensuring that the information has been adequately relayed.
5. *Briefly discuss termination benefits:* The HR representative briefly explains the employee's benefits rights, answers any payroll-related questions, and advises on the Record of Employment for Employment Insurance. It is not advisable to disclose all terms of the final settlement at this time. The individual will be quite devastated and much of the information relayed will not be absorbed. HR should advise the individual to review the settlement offer at home with family members and/or legal counsel, and to call if there are any questions. On termination without cause the employee will have to sign off on acceptance of the final termination offer at a later date. Do not allow them to sign their acceptance of the offer at this meeting, or it could be deemed to be signed under duress. If there is a subsequent court case against the organization, this will not be viewed positively by the courts.
6. *Retreive company property:* At the same time, the HR representative should retrieve the security badge, credit cards, and other company property. Many employers provide a specific letter or memo, which can serve as evidence that the employee was notified of the termination decision and details of benefits rights.
7. *Escort the employee from the building:* This phase is controversial, as the HR Perspective describes. The goal is to ensure that the employee, who is likely to be upset, angry, or emotional, is removed from the premises quickly without obvious conflicts and to prevent any possible concerns about computer or physical security. Depending on the individual, they may return to their office or workspace to retrieve their personal belongings. In many cases, someone should retrieve their

coat and/or purse, ensuring that another person acts as a witness when those things are retrieved. The rest of their belongings should be couriered to their home within the next 24 hours.

8. *Arrange for safe transportation home:* Never let the person drive home alone as they may be too upset to drive. Either have someone drive them home in their vehicle, and have someone follow so they can return the driver to work. If they don't have transportation, arrange a taxi for them.
9. *Notify the department staff:* The supervisor or manager returns to the department and notifies the department staff that the individual is no longer employed. No details or explanations should be provided, to avoid any long discussions and possible legal ramifications. Also, employees should be informed that if the ex-employee contacts them at work, the person should be referred to the HR department. However, the company cannot control contacts outside of work hours or locations.

In some cases an outplacement person will be part of the process. They can either sit in on the termination meeting, or they can be waiting nearby to help walk the employee out and drive them home. Often they will take the individual out for a coffee so that they can discuss the termination and what will be the next steps for the employee with the outplacement process.

Separation agreement
Agreement in which a terminated employee agrees not to sue the employer, in exchange for specified benefits.

Separation Agreements In most termination situations, formal contracts may be used. One type is a **separation agreement,** in which an employee who is being

HR *Perspective*

"You're Fired—Get Out"

One difficult phase of employee termination is removal of ex-employees and their personal possessions from the company facilities. Both ethical and fairness issues arise in this action.

The standard advice from legal experts is to physically remove the employee as quickly as possible. This is often done by having the employee escorted by security guards out of the building. Some firms allow terminated employees to return to their desks, offices, or lockers to retrieve personal items under the observation of security personnel and the department supervisor/manager. But this means the ex-employee may be seen by and may talk with co-workers while still upset or angry.

Another approach used is that after the HR representative has explained the termination to the employee, the HR representative asks the employee if there is anything immediately needed from a desk or a locker—such as keys, a wallet, a purse, or a coat. The employee is not allowed back into the department; instead, at the same time, their supervisor/manager is excused to go and get the personal effects requested by the employee. The remaining items will be inventoried by the department manager and some witnesses within 24 hours and boxed up, and then may be picked up from security by the employee or sent directly to the employee's home address.

These methods sound prudent. But what happens if employees are being terminated, not for cause but because jobs are being cut? At one university, employees with 15–20 years' service were told they had to be escorted by security officers back to their offices, get their personal possessions, and be off-campus in one hour. At a large company, employees were given a box and told that they had 30 minutes to get their personal items under the view of security personnel, and that their computer access had been eliminated while they were in the termination meeting. In both situations, the reactions of the ex-employees and the remaining employees were very negative. To them, the removal process showed a lack of trust in long-time employees with satisfactory performance records, who, as one remaining employee said, "were treated like criminals."

1. How do you view the need to balance legal rights, security, employee morale, and HR policies when removing terminated employees?
2. What would you do if an employee who you allowed to return to their office to collect their personal belongings became agitated while you were escorting them, and they refused to go directly to their office? Assume there are a lot of employees around? Assume there are no employees around?

terminated agrees not to sue the employer, in exchange for specified benefits, such as additional severance pay or other "considerations."

For such agreements to be legally enforceable, the considerations usually should be additional items not part of normal termination benefits. For international employees, different legal requirements may exist in various countries, including certain requirements for severance pay and benefits. When using separation agreements, care must be taken to avoid the appearance of constructive discharge of employees. Use of such agreements should be reviewed by legal counsel to ensure that you are meeting the minimum requirements stated under employment standards acts or the Canada Labour Code.[60] Figure 14-11 demonstrates what would be entailed in a termination letter and subsequent separation agreement.[61]

Figure 14-11 *Sample Termination Letter*

NOTE: This is a sample letter only and should not be used without being reviewed by a lawyer.

January 20, 2007

Mr. Simon Grant
1700 Sackville Rd.
Halifax, Nova Scotia

Dear Mr. Grant:

This letter will confirm that your services with Hunters Iron Works (HIW) are no longer required, effective today. After ongoing discussions regarding your declining performance over the last year, and the revenue losses totalling $75,000, we are no longer able to accept your diminishing performance. Over the past year we have met on 23 separate occasions, but we have not been able to help you improve, despite the many hours spent trying to help you.

In accordance with Nova Scotia's Labour Standards Code, HIW will pay you eight weeks of pay in lieu of notice. We will also be paying you four weeks of outstanding vacation pay. In addition to your pay in lieu of notice and your vacation pay, we are also offering you the following severance package:

(1) Six (6) months of continuous salary, or until you commence employment elsewhere, whichever period is the shortest.

(2) In the event that you commence employment within the six (6) month period, HIW will pay you a lump sum equal to fifty percent (50%) of the remainder of the salary you otherwise would have collected over the six (6) month period.

(3) Your benefits, with the exception of out of country medical coverage and long term disability, will continue during the six (6) month period or until you commence employment elsewhere, whichever occurs first. Your entitlement to long term disability benefits shall cease at the end of the month on the 31st. I have enclosed a form with the insurance companies contact numbers where you will have an opportunity to purchase insurance directly from them if you wish.

(4) In addition we will continue to make pension plan contributions, subject to the salary continuation payments provided for above. When the salary continuance ends, there will be no further contributions made to the pension. On completion of these contributions you will need to decide whether you wish to leave your pension with HIW, transfer the funds to your new employer, or transfer the funds into a locked-in RRSP.

(5) To assist you with your search, we have employed the outplacement services of Jones Mitchell & Associates who will assist you in your re-employment strategies for the next three months commencing today.

(6) You will be paid your accrued vacation pay on your next paycheque. Your record of employment (ROE) will be provided to you at the end of the period of salary continuation. Your cheque will continue to be deposited during the payment period, or until you commence new employment.

The payments provided in this letter are conditional upon you accepting the following terms:

(1) Your prompt reporting to HIW of any employment which you might commence in the next six (6) months.

(2) Your maintaining strict confidentiality with respect to the terms of this arrangement, except discussion with your financial or legal advisers.

(3) **You further agree to keep confidential all information received or to which you had access during your employment with HIW as per our confidentiality agreement.**

(4) **Your agreement to sign and return an original copy of the attached release agreement on or before the end of business one week from today.** ***[Note: Ensure the employee releases all relevant or possible claims against the employer]***

All payments referred to in this proposal are subject to the usual statutory deductions. Please feel free to contact Morely Tate, our Employment Relations Manager, should you have questions regarding this termination offer.

Sincerely,

Madeline Darling, BSc., P.Eng.
General Manager

SUMMARY

1 The employment relationship is a reciprocal one in which both employers and employees have statutory and contractual rights, as well as responsibilities. Both parties have rights and should treat each other with respect. Statutory rights include such things as equal employment opportunity, collective bargaining, and workplace safety. Contractual rights can be spelled out in an employment contract or be implied as a result of employer promises. Restrictive covenants are often used to protect a business against exploitation by others. The three main types of restrictive covenants are non-disclosure, non-solicitation, and non-competition agreements. Non-competition clauses are often difficult to enforce, however, there have been some successful cases. Implied promises, especially when contained in employee handbooks, constitute a contract between an employer and its employees, even without a signed document.

2 Wrongful discharge occurs when an employer improperly or illegally terminates an individual's employment. Just cause for employment-related actions should exist. When just cause is absent, constructive dismissal may occur, in which the terms of the employee's job change so completely that the employment contract is ended. The courts expect to see evidence of due process in employment-related cases. Due process is important for both unionized and non-union employees. In non-union situations, alternative dispute resolution (ADR) means may be used such as arbitration, peer review panels, and an ombuds.

3 Balancing employer security concerns and employee rights becomes an issue when dealing with access to employee records, free speech, workplace monitoring, employer investigations, and substance abuse and drug testing. Employers increasingly are facing privacy and free speech issues in areas such as whistleblowing and monitoring of e-mail and voice mail. Employer investigations must be done to protect both employer and employee rights. Courts have recognized an individual's right to a reasonable expectation of privacy. Every province (except for Newfoundland) has guidelines to protect personal information held by government departments and agencies. The employer must protect the information it collects from its employees, and must be done only with the employee's knowledge and consent. Whistleblowing legislation has been enacted to protect employees who expose illegal activities of their employer. An employer must notify employees that they are monitoring e-mail and voice mail. These modes of communication have been used against employees in court cases, where employees have been terminated, or have misused the devices for work unassociated with their employer. Monitoring must be implemented consistently throughout the organization. Drug testing provides a widely used and legal method for employers to deal with increasing drug problems at work. However, testing must be associated in safety-sensitive areas, as well as applied consistently throughout the workplace.

4 To be effective, HR policies, procedures, and rules should be consistent, necessary, applicable, understandable, reasonable, and communicated. Courts sometimes view employee handbooks as implied contracts. However, these can be used against an

employer so controversial phrases should be avoided and disclaimers included, and be kept up-to-date,

5 Although employee self-discipline is the goal, positive or progressive discipline is sometimes necessary to encourage self-discipline. Managers may fail to discipline for a variety of reasons. However, effective discipline can have positive effects on the productivity of employees. Supervisors must be trained in when and how discipline should be used. If termination is required, it is important to use a well-defined process. Separation agreements are typically drawn up outlining the terms and conditions of the termination.

KEY TERMS

Arbitration, p. 524
Constructive dismissal, p. 520
Contractual rights, p. 516
Discipline, p. 538
Distributive justice, p. 522
Due process, p. 522
Employment contract, p. 516
Just cause, p. 521
Non-compete agreements, p. 518
Policies, p. 536
Procedural justice, p. 522
Procedures, p. 536
Responsibilities, p. 516
Right to privacy, p. 526
Rights, p. 516
Rules, p. 536
Separation agreement, p. 543
Statutory rights, p. 516
Whistleblowers, p. 529
Wrongful dismissal, p. 519

REVIEW AND APPLICATION QUESTIONS

1 Explain the difference between statutory rights and contractual rights.

2 Identify how the issues of due process and just cause are linked to employer disciplinary actions.

3 Discuss the following statement: "Even though efforts to restrict employees' freedom of expression at work may be permissible, such efforts raise troubling questions affecting individual rights."

4 What are the elements involved in putting together an effective policy? Provide an example of how a policy should be set up.

5 Explain the four steps to positive discipline.

EXPERIENTIAL EXERCISES

1. You have been asked by the HR director to develop a policy on workplace surveillance. Prepare half page policies as if you were creating a real policy. You should write a report outlining the issues involved in performing this task. You should also prepare a five-minute Powerpoint presentation to make before the class.

2. Working in groups, each member should review company websites to learn about their privacy policies. Alternatively, you should call HR departments to find out what policies exist, and how they are handling these matters. What did you learn from this exercise?

3. Assume that as the HR manager, you have decided to prepare some guidelines for supervisors to use when they have to discipline employees. Gather the information needed using Internet resources and prepare a guide for supervisors on both positive and progressive discipline.

4. You are hired under the guise of a "technology specialist" in charge of special projects. At least that is what everyone thinks. Your real job is to set up surveillance on all employees throughout the organization. The organization suspects that someone may be stealing sensitive and confidential information, and so you are to set up traps in order to catch the culprit(s). No one in your department, or even human resources, is to know what you do exactly. You are a little uncomfortable with this because you are well aware of the laws, and you don't really like the idea of spying on people. But you need a job badly and

there is nothing else for you to do. The job pays an excessive amount of money that you would never be able to earn in the next five years. What are you going to do? List the pros and cons of your decision. What are the specific pieces of legislation that you will be affected by?

LEARNING REVIEW

To check your knowledge of the chapter, review the following. (Answers after the case.)

1 Rights are offset by:
   a. specific laws
   b. reciprocal relationships
   c. responsibilities
   d. standards

2 _________ is deliberately making conditions intolerable to get an employee to quit.
   a. Involuntary quit
   b. Mandatory termination
   c. Voluntary resignation
   d. Constructive dismissal

3 The concept of _________ focuses on the perceived fairness of the process used to make decisions about employees.
   a. arbitration
   b. distributive justice
   c. procedural justice
   d. constructive discharge

4 A _________ is composed of employees who hear appeals from disciplined employees and make recommendations or decisions.
   a. co-worker resolution panel
   b. discipline committee
   c. employee arbitration jury
   d. peer review panel

5 The following are all reasons why discipline might not be used except for:
   a. fear of losing friendship
   b. fear of lawsuits
   c. corporate support
   d. lack of support

CASE

MANAGER ON CAMERA

A retail store was losing cash, but *only* when the surveillance system was turned off. The surveillance system could be turned off only from the manager's office. When the manager went on vacation, a video camera with no audio pickup was placed in his office to see how the system was being deactivated. When he returned from vacation, he noticed the camera and discussed it with the HR department but made no effort to have it removed.

The employer decided to transfer the manager to the same position at a nearby store because he had risen quickly through the ranks at the current store and was experiencing difficulty managing his former co-workers. The employer explained to the manager that the transfer decision was made to give him an opportunity to develop further with the company. The employer offered to give the manager its standard relocation package, or a raise to offset the increased commuting costs.

The manager rejected the transfer and resigned. Then he sued the employer, claiming it had wrongfully monitored his communications and that the transfer was in retaliation for his having raised the issue of his right to privacy. The employer argued that the firm's surveillance practices were legal and that the transfer was in no way an adverse employment action against the manager.[63] You be the judge.

Questions

1. Do you believe that the company was guilty of an illegal surveillance?
2. Was the company guilty of violating the manager's rights? Why or why not?

Learning Review Answers: 1. d 2. d 3. c 4. c 5. c

CHAPTER

Union/Management Relations

Learning Objectives

After you have read this chapter, you should be able to:

1 Describe what a union is and explain why employees join unions.

2 Discuss decline in union membership in Canada.

3 Explain the roles of the federal and provincial governments in labour relations.

4 Discuss the stages of the unionization process.

5 Describe the issues involved in preparing for contract negotiation.

6 Describe the typical collective bargaining process.

7 Explain the grievance procedure and why it is important for employers.

HR *Headline*

Is Wal-Mart Losing The Union Fight In Canada?

The fight to keep Wal-Mart union free continues, but are they starting to lose their battle? In March 2006, the second Wal-Mart Tire and Lube Express (TLE) shop in British Columbia won their battle for union certification. The majority of workers at the store (located in Surrey) had voted seven months earlier in favour of joining the United Food and Commercial Workers (UFCW) Local 1518. However, Wal-Mart challenged the vote. On March 3, the British Columbia Labour Relations Board gave the authorization to count votes cast by workers from two separate TLE shops. Employees at one location voted 5–7 for unionization while the employees at the TLE shop on 88th Street voted 7–2 in favour of unionization. The local's president Brooke Sundin commented, "Despite the delays forced upon these Wal-Mart workers, they are now members of our union and we couldn't be happier about that. We will be approaching the company shortly to begin negotiations for a contract."

The movement to unionize various Wal-Mart stores in Canada has not been an easy process for either side. The most notable case of unionization involves a Wal-Mart store located in Jonquière, Québec. In the summer of 2004, Québec's labour board certified the union. Earlier in the year the workers narrowly rejected a unionization bid, however, the UFCW managed to get a majority of employees to sign union cards, which led to the labour board's decision to grant certification. Michael J. Fraser, UFCW Canada's national director believed that it was a "great victory" for all Wal-Mart employees and he emphasized the comments made by Wal-Mart that it would not close the store and would work with the union, "Wal-Mart is on the record stating they support work-place democracy. The majority of workers in Jonquière have spoken, so we expect Wal-Mart to listen and get down to negotiating a contract without delay . . . So Wal-Mart workers should stop believing the rumours that their store will close if they exercise the right to form a union." However, in February 2005 Wal-Mart announced the closure of the newly unionized store. Although, Wal-Mart claimed that the store was not "meeting profit targets," UFCW saw the closure as a direct result of the unionization. In September 2005, the Labour Relations Board found that the closure of the store was "anti-union" and that it did violate the labour code.

Employees at a Wal-Mart in Windsor, Ontario, rejected an attempt to unionize the store just a month after the announcement of the closure of the Jonquière store. UFCW was "not surprised" by the results because of the fear tactics used by the company including posting a notice about the store closing in Québec. Before the vote, the UFCW filed allegations of unfair labour practices against Wal-Mart with the Ontario Labour Relations Board relating to an attempt to unionize the same Windsor store between 1996 and 1997. The UFCW claims that a company representative unlawfully coached two employees to oppose the union drive. The campaign did result in the first ever union certification of a Wal-Mart because it was automatically certified due to unfair labour practices. However, the provincial Conservative government at the time passed a bill that would strip the board of its remedial certification powers. Within a year, amidst a string of lawsuits and counter-suits the store was decertified.

Allegations of an anti-union stance were also made during the first attempt to unionize a store in Saskatchewan. In 2004, the UFCW was attempting to organize a union drive at a Wal-Mart in Weyburn, Saskatchewan. A group of employees at the store filed a reply with a petition that opposed the union's application. Some of the employees filed unfair labour practices claiming that the union used intimidating conduct to coerce them into joining the union. The UFCW requested that the company hand over internal documents that outlined anti-union strategies. The labour board in Saskatchewan ordered the company to hand the documents over. However, Wal-Mart took the case to the Saskatchewan Court of Queen's Bench. On July 23, 2004, the court ruled that the board should have never asked for the documents without determining the relevance of the documents to the hearing. The case eventually made its way to the Supreme Court of Canada and on April 7, 2005 Wal-Mart was finally ordered to hand over the documents to the board who would determine its relevance to the proceedings that would take place in the fall of 2005. In July 2006, a Saskatchewan court quashed Wal-Mart Canada's demand that the Saskatchewan Labour Relations Board (SLRB) be prohibited from ruling on any application to unionize Wal-Mart locations in Saskatchewan. In addition to the application for Weyburn, Moose Jaw and North Battleford, Saskatchewan, Wal-Marts are also awaiting certification decisions. Despite all of the UFCW's efforts, the stores that have been organized in Canada have yet to reach a collective agreement, although under Canadian law some of those will be resolved soon.[1]

"Unions have a place, and as long as management doesn't manage well, you are going to have unions."

—Steve Darien

Union
Formal association of workers that promotes the interests of its members through collective action.

A **union** is a formal association of workers that promotes the interests of its members through collective action. The state and nature of union/management relations vary among countries. In Canada labour laws have clearly stated that workers may join unions when they wish to do so. Although fewer workers choose to do so today than before, the mechanisms remain for a union resurgence if employees feel that they need formal representation to deal with management.

Nature of Unions

1 Employers usually would rather not have to deal with unions because unions constrain what managers can and cannot do in a number of areas. Generally, union workers receive higher wages and benefits than do non-union workers.[2] In turn unions *can* be associated with higher productivity, although management must find labour-saving ways of doing work to offset the higher labour costs.[3]

Some employers pursue a strategy of good relations with unions. Others may choose an aggressive, adversarial approach. Regardless of the type of employer, several common factors explain why employees unionize.

Why Employees Unionize

As Figure 15-1 shows, the major factors that can trigger unionization are issues of compensation, working environment, management style, and employee treatment. Whether a union targets a group of employees or the employees request union assistance, the union must win support from the employees to become their legal representative. Research over the years has consistently shown that employees join unions for two primary reasons: (1) they are dissatisfied with how they are treated by their employers and (2) they believe that unions can improve their work situations. If employees do not receive what they perceive as fair from their employers, they may turn to unions for help obtaining what they believe is equitable.

Figure 15-1 *Factors Leading to Employee Unionization*

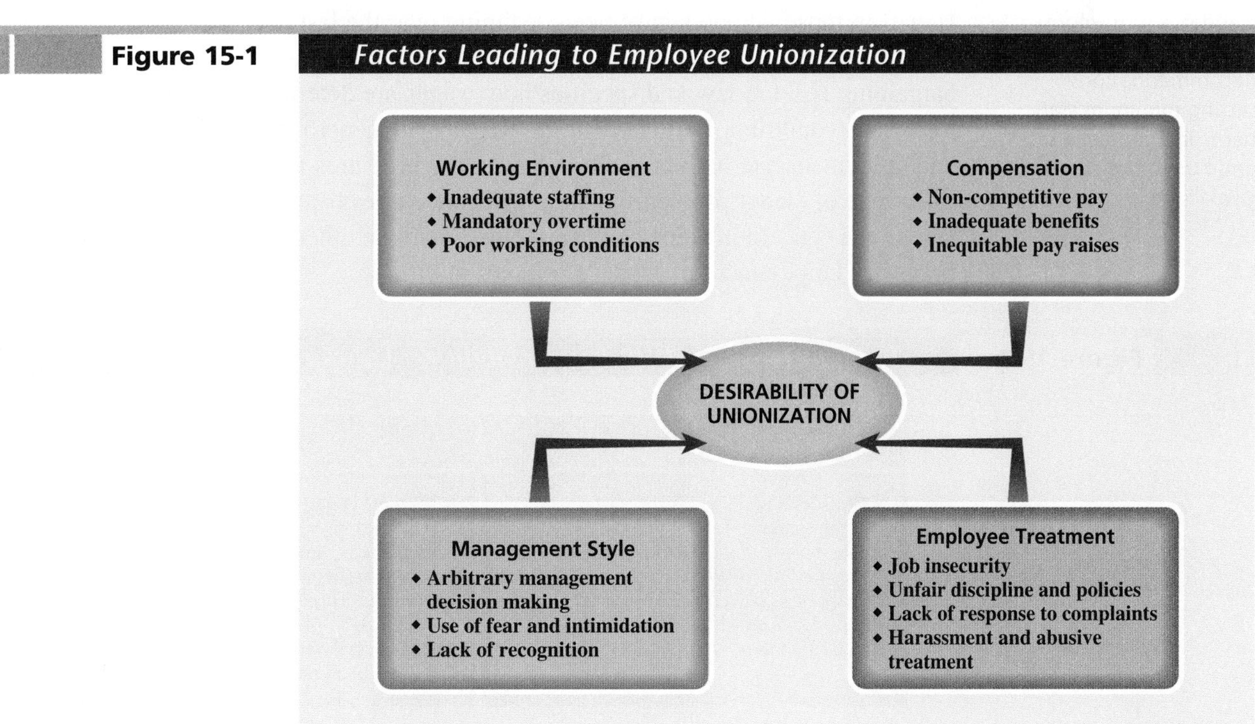

When union leaders are asked by non-union workers, "Why should I join a union?" they respond with a list of reasons. Unions offer employees respect, effective complaint procedures, better wages and benefits, job stability, and security.

The primary determinant of whether employees unionize is management. Reasonably competitive compensation, a good working environment, effective management and supervision, and fair and responsive treatment of workers all act as antidotes to unionization efforts. Unionization results when employees feel disrespected, unsafe, underpaid, and unappreciated, and see a union as a viable option. Once unionization occurs, the union's ability to foster commitment from members and to remain as their bargaining agent depends on how well the union succeeds in providing services that its members want. To prevent unionization, as well as to work effectively with unions already representing employees, both HR professionals and operating managers must be attentive and responsive to employees.

HR Responsibilities with Unions

The pattern of dealing with unionized employees varies among organizations. In some organizations, operating management handles labour relations and HR is minimally involved. In other organizations, the HR unit takes primary responsibility for labour relations. A typical division of responsibilities between the HR unit and operating managers in dealing with unions falls somewhere between these extremes, as shown in Figure 15-2.

LOGGING ON...

International Labour Organization
The ILO formulates international labour standards in the form of Conventions and Recommendations setting minimum standards in employment and human rights.
www.ilo.org

Global Labour Union Issues

In some countries, unions either do not exist at all or are relatively weak. Such is the case in China and a number of African countries. In other countries, unions are extremely strong and are closely tied to political parties. For instance, in Italy and France, national strikes occur regularly to protest proposed changes in government policy on retirement, pension programs, and regulations regarding dismissal of employees. The strength of unions in several countries is illustrated in Figure 15-3. However, those numbers have been declining over the last decade.[4]

Even though union membership is falling in many advanced countries, collective bargaining is set in law and specifies how wages are determined in Europe. In many European countries, artificially high wages and generous benefits have kept the unemployment rate high as well; however, the pressures for change are increasing.[5] The range of labour problems is quite wide and varies from country to country. Child labour is a concern in some countries, outsourcing in others, whereas changes in participatory employment practices are issues in others.[6]

Figure 15-2 *Typical Division of HR Responsibilities: Labour Relations*

HR Unit	Managers
• Deals with union organizing attempts at the company level • Monitors "climate" for unionization and union relationships • Helps negotiate labour agreements • Provides detailed knowledge of labour legislation as needed	• Promote conditions conducive to positive relationships with employees • Avoid unfair labour practices during organizing efforts • Administer the labour agreement on a daily basis • Resolve grievances and problems between management and employees

Figure 15-3 **Union Membership as a Percentage of the Workforce for Selected Countries**

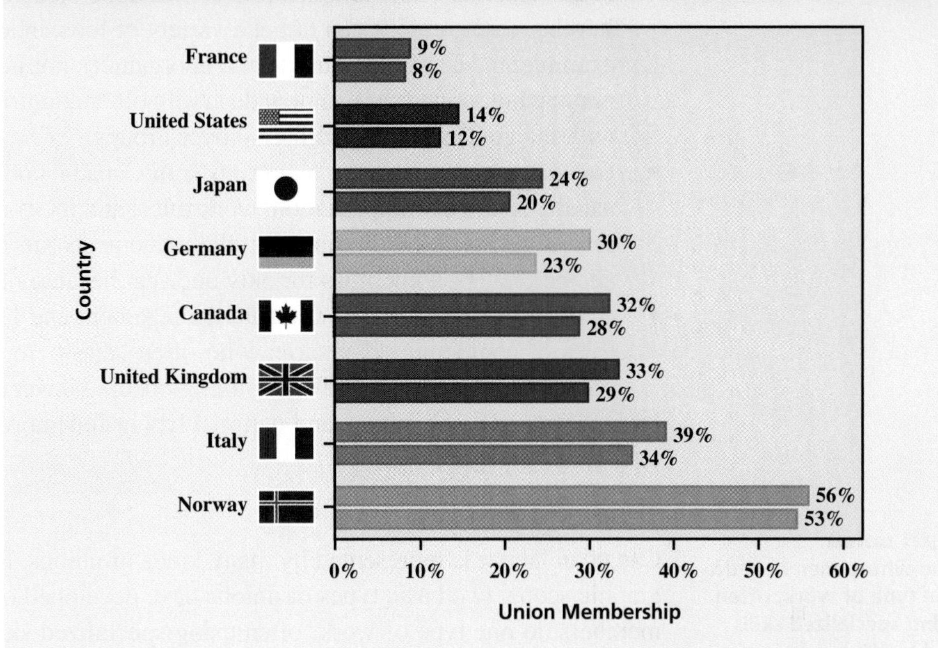

Note: Bars represent the decline in union density since 1995 to 2003. As you look at Canada, you will note that in 1995 union density sat at 32%, compared to 28% in 2003. The most noticeable drop in union density has occurred in Germany. Since 1995 their union density has declined from 30% to a low of 23% in 2003.

Co-determination Practice whereby union or worker representatives are given positions on a company's board of directors.

Some countries require that firms have union or worker representatives on their boards of directors. This practice, called **co-determination,** is common in European countries. Differences from country to country in how collective bargaining occurs also are quite noticeable. In Canada, local unions bargain with individual employers to set wages and working conditions. In Australia, unions argue their cases before arbitration tribunals. In Scandinavia, national agreements with associations of employers are the norm. In France and Germany, industry-wide or regional agreements are common. In Japan, local unions bargain but combine at some point to determine national wage patterns.

Global labour relations standards are being addressed by several organizations. The International Labour Organization, based in Switzerland, coordinates the efforts of labour unions worldwide and has issued some principles and rights at work. Such coordination is increasingly occurring as unions deal with multinational firms having operations in multiple countries.

Unions in Canada

The union movement in Canada has been characterized by some approaches different from those used in other countries. In Canada, the key emphases have been the following:

- *Economic issues:* In Canada, unions have typically focused on improving the "bread-and-butter" issues for their members—wages, benefits, job security, and working conditions. In some other countries, political power and activism are equal concerns along with economic issues.

- *Organization by kind of job and employer:* In Canada, carpenters often belong to the carpenters' union, truck drivers to the Teamsters, nurses and teachers belong to associations. Also, unionization can be done on a company-by-company basis. In other cases, unions can target a variety of jobs, industries, and employers. For example, the Canadian Auto Workers organizes not just automotive workers, but nursing homes and the airline industry. In other countries, national unions bargain with the government or with employer groups.
- *Collective agreements as "contracts":* In Canada, collective bargaining contracts usually spell out compensation, work rules, and the conditions of employment for several years. In other countries, the agreements are made with the government and employers, sometimes for only one year because of political and social issues.
- *Competitive relations:* In Canada, management and labour traditionally take the roles of competing adversaries who often "clash" to reach agreement. In many other countries, "tripartite" bargaining occurs between the national government, employers' associations, and national labour federations.

Union Structures

Craft union
One whose members do one type of work, often using specialized skills and training.

Industrial union
One that includes many persons working in the same industry or company, regardless of jobs held.

Canadian labour is represented by many kinds of unions. Regardless of size and geographic scope, two basic types of unions have developed over time. In a **craft union,** members do one type of work, often using specialized skills and training. Members of a craft union usually engage in manual occupation that requires extensive training and a high degree of skill, such as carpentry, plumbing, linotype operation, although craft unions are diversifying more these days. Examples of craft unions are the International Union of Bricklayers and Allied Craft Workers (BAC) and International Brotherhood of Electrical Union (IBEW). An **industrial union** includes many persons working in the same industry or company, regardless of jobs held. The United

The Canadian Auto Workers (CAW) union represents workers in the automotive industry.

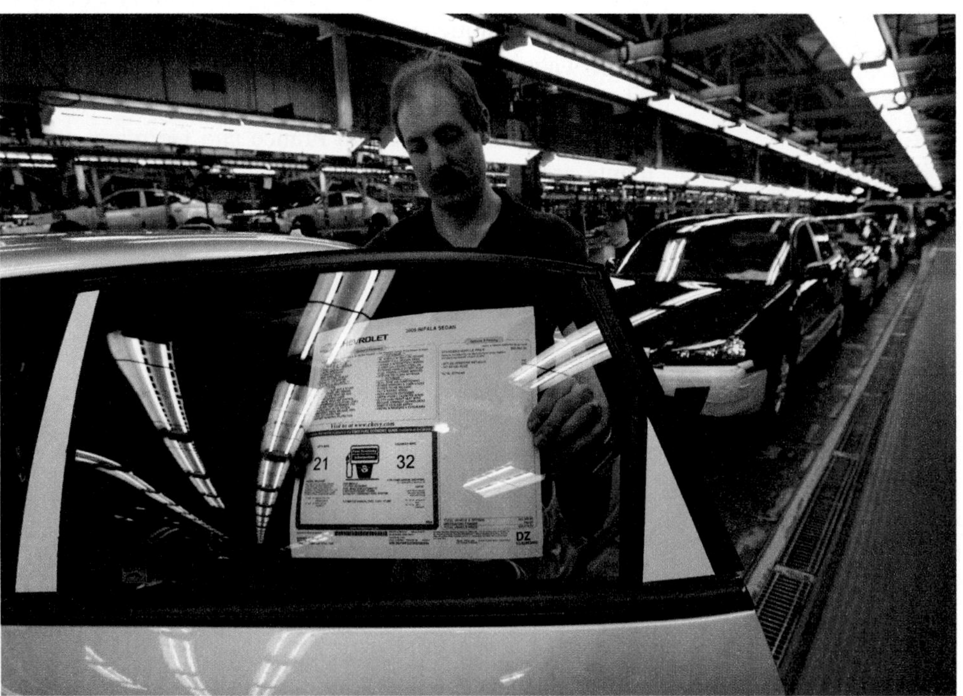

Source: Reuters/Landov

Food and Commercial Workers (UFCW), the Canadian Auto Workers (CAW), the United Steelworkers of America (USWA), and Communications, Energy & Paperworkers Union of Canada (CEP), are examples of industrial unions.

Federation
Group of autonomous national and international unions.

Labour organizations have developed complex organizational structures with multiple levels. The broadest level is the **federation,** which is a group of autonomous national and international unions. A federation allows individual unions to work together and present a more unified front to the public, legislators, and members. The Canadian Labour Congress (CLC) is the central labour body in Canada to which most Canadian labor unions are affiliated. The CLC brings together Canada's national and international unions, the provincial and territorial federations of labour, and 137 district labour councils. The most prominent federation in the United States is the AFL-CIO, which is a confederation of national and international unions.

LOGGING ON...

Canadian Labour Congress (CLC)
The CLC's homepage provides union movement information.
www.clc-ctc.ca

National and International Unions National and international unions are not governed by a federation even if they are affiliated with it. They collect dues and have their own boards, specialized publications, and separate constitutions and bylaws. Such national-international unions as the United Steelworkers of America (USWA), the Canadian Auto Workers (CAW), and the Canadian Union of Public Employees (CUPE) determine broad union policy and offer services to local union units. They also help maintain financial records and provide a base from which additional organizing drives may take place. Political infighting and corruption sometimes pose problems for national unions and international unions. A prime example is when the Canadian arm of the United Auto Workers (UAW) broke away from its American parent to form the Canadian Auto Workers (CAW). Canadian workers were not happy with the concessions their American brothers and sisters were giving into, and adamantly opposed the American union-executive's calls for concessions throughout North America. The CAW have continued to fight against concessions in most of their negotiations, although they have had to concede in critical situations.

Local Unions Local unions may be centred around a particular employer organization or geographic location. The membership of local unions elect officers who are subject to removal if they do not perform satisfactorily. For this reason, local union officers tend to be concerned with how they are perceived by the union members. They often react to situations as politicians do because their positions depend on obtaining votes. The local unions are the focus and the heart of labour/management relations in most Canadian companies. Functions of a local union include such activities as negotiation and administration of the collective agreement, collection and processing of union dues, educating members, organizing members, community service, and involvement in political action.

Business agent
Full-time union official who operates the union office and assists union members.

Union steward
Employee elected to serve as the first-line representative of unionized workers.

A **business agent** is a full-time, paid union official who is assigned by the national or international union to assist the local unions in his or her assigned jurisdiction. The agent assists the local union to which they are assigned, to negotiate contracts with management, attend grievances or arbitration hearings, and becomes involved in attempts to unionize employees in other organizations. A **union steward** is an employee who is elected to serve as the first-line representative of unionized workers. Union stewards are the lowest-level union official. A union steward addresses grievances with supervisors and generally represents employees at the worksite. As a volunteer, they often devote much of their own time, for which they are not paid, to attend to union business. Other elected positions in the union may include a president, vice president, treasurer, and a secretary. Unions will often have committees such as executive, communications, education, grievance, membership, negotiating, and women's committees. What type of committee the union decides to incorporate into the workplace will depend on the national or local union mandate, the type of employee's they represent, or other special circumstances associated with the employer.

Alternative Employee Representation Model The presumption by many is that workers are either in a union or they are not. There are several other ways in which workers can achieve non-union representation without having to go through the formal unionization process. These arrangements do not have any legal status in that they cannot obtain any of the rights granted under labour relations domains, but they can arrive at group employment contracts that are meant to replicate a union agreement that establish how the work relationship will be handled. One study that was conducted a number of years ago, indicated that almost 20 percent of Canadian workers participated in non-union forms of employee representation.[7] Slightly more than one third of blue-collar workers in the petroleum industry belong to these types of arrangements.[8]

Daphne Taras, a leading researcher on this topic, points out the following alternative arrangements available to employees: [9]

- complex non-union systems that are either complements to unions (e.g., the National Joint Council within the federal civil service) or substitutes to unions (e.g., the Imperial Oil joint industrial council, or Dofasco's "people" policies and practices, or other companies' use of staff associations in preference to unions). These company-based representation plans are quite popular among managers who wish to deal directly with their employees and avoid unions.[10]
- professional organizations such as those that represent doctors, lawyers, and engineers.
- non-union staff associations that provide some representation rights to managers.

Union Mergers

Like companies, unions find strength in size. As such, there has been a trend in Canada since the 1990s to merge with other unions. Union mergers have occurred because of the increasing mergers of Canadian corporations and as a result of members demand for more efficient delivery of bargaining and administrative services.[11] For smaller unions, these mergers provide financial and union-organizing resources. Larger unions can add new members to cover managerial and administrative costs without spending funds to organize non-union workers to become members.[12]

Union Membership in Canada

Union density
The proportion of paid workers who are union members and who have signed union membership cards.

2 **Union density,** the proportion of paid workers who are union members who have signed membership cards, is a commonly used indicator of the strength and potential influence of the labour movement in a country. For Canada, union density sat at a high of about 39 percent in the mid-1980s, but since that time, those figures have started to decline at a much faster pace than what would be desired by union organizers. Over the past five years, union density has been fairly stable in Canada. Although union density has dropped marginally in some provinces, it has increased slightly in others. Alberta remains the province with the lowest density at 24 percent, while Quebec sits at 41 percent. Figure 15-4 highlights the rate of union coverage across Canada.

In 2004, unions in Canada represented 75.5 percent of all public-sector workers and only 19 percent of the private-sector workforce. By comparison, the U.S. story is much lower with only 13.8% of the workforce unionized. Private-sector unionization

Figure 15-4 Rate of Union Coverage: Canada and Provinces 1999–2003

Province	1999	2000	2001	2002	2003
Newfoundland	40.03%	39.13%	40.01%	39.07%	39.63%
P.E.I.	29.44%	29.38%	30.18%	30.95%	29.83%
Nova Scotia	30.02%	30.19%	29.31%	28.04%	28.61%
New Brunswick	27.94%	29.44%	28.80%	28.11%	27.80%
Quebec	39.51%	39.93%	40.42%	40.40%	41.18%
Ontario	28.06%	28.24%	27.82%	28.12%	28.53%
Manitoba	36.92%	36.52%	36.69%	36.14%	37.26%
Saskatchewan	35.18%	35.14%	36.15%	35.83%	35.69%
Alberta	25.30%	23.75%	24.63%	24.48%	24.17%
BC	35.39%	35.81%	35.13%	34.65%	33.80%
Canada	32.17%	32.23%	32.18%	32.15%	32.39%

Source: "Rate of Union Coverage: Canada and Provinces 1999–2003," data is adapted from Statistics Canada, Labour Force Survey.

sits at 8.6 percent, and public-sector unionization at 40.7 percent.[13] Despite the fact that unionization in Canada is much more healthy than in the U.S., the decline in unionization is still of mounting concern to Canadian union organizers. There are a multitude of reasons for the difference between the two countries, but among the most viable is the growth in public sector unions in Canada supported by legislation that tends to offer more right to unions that they do in the U.S.

Despite declining union membership, unions continue to persist in their quest to increase union membership. In the past several years, a few unions have organized in a variety of industries including finance, insurance, real estate and leasing, nursing, support staff, university teachers, graduate students, retail, child care and homecare, as well as construction. What is distinct about the majority of these occupations is that many are female-dominated occupations in the service sector. To offset the declining numbers in manufacturing, unions are beginning to target groups that have been traditionally non-union. Older industrial unions that have been most successful in unionizing the service sector are the United Steelworkers of America (USWA) and the Canadian Auto Workers (CAW).[14] For example, the CAW was recently certified to represent employees of the upscale Terminal City Club in Vancouver; the Hotel Employees & Restaurant Employees Union (HERE) has successfully organized young Kentucky Fried Chicken employees in Regina; and the Communications, Energy and Paperworkers of Canada Union (CEP) has been approached by Bell Canada's middle managers for protection. The CAW continues to work on an organizing drive to certify United Church ministers. Middle managers, service sector employees, young people, women, immigrants: these are labour's new frontiers as the trade union movement strives to reinvent itself in the 21st century.[15]

Reasons for Union Membership Decline

It is speculated that several issues have contributed to the decline of unions: deregulation, foreign competition, a larger number of people looking for jobs, and a general perception by firms that dealing with unions is expensive compared with non-union alternatives. Also, management at many employers has taken a much more activist stance against unions than during the previous years of union growth.

To some extent, unions may be a victim of their own successes. Unions have emphasized helping workers obtain higher wages, shorter working hours, job security, and safe working conditions from their employers. Some experts and union leaders believe that one cause for the decline of unions has been their success in getting those important issues passed into law for everyone. Therefore, unions are not as necessary for many workers, even though those workers enjoy the results of past union efforts to influence legislation.

Geographic Changes Over the past decade, job growth in Canada has been the greatest in Western Canada, particularly in Alberta. Alberta also has the lowest percentage of unionized workers, at only 24% (public service sector 72.6 percent and private service sector 12.6 percent), followed by Ontario at 29 percent, with the largest workforce and the highest decline in union density. Alberta is also considered Canada's most business-friendly province. This stands out even more when one considers that Alberta's western neighbours—B.C., Saskatchewan, and Manitoba—all have much higher unionization rates of 34 percent–37 percent. The Alberta Federation of Labour (AFL) has stated that "Alberta labour laws discourage unions" and that there are "loopholes" in the Labour Code that make it harder to certify unions in Alberta than in other places in Canada. The AFL's concerns do raise an interesting question, How is it possible for Alberta, with its large industrialized sector, to have a unionization rate behind that even of unindustrialized PEI?[16]

Another issue involves the movement of many low-skill jobs outside Canada. Primarily to take advantage of cheaper labour, many manufacturers with heavily unionized Canadian workforces have moved a significant number of low-skill jobs to the Philippines, China, Thailand, and Mexico. The passage of the North American Free Trade Agreement (NAFTA) provided a major impetus for moving low-skill, low-wage jobs to Mexico. It removed tariffs and restrictions affecting the flow of goods and services among the United States, Canada, and Mexico. Because of significantly lower wage rates in Mexico, a number of jobs previously susceptible to unionization in Canada have been moved there.[17]

Industrial Changes Another cause for the decline of unions is the shift in Canadian jobs from industries such as manufacturing, construction, and mining to service industries. There is a small percentage of union members in the financial services and wholesale/retail industries, the sectors in which many new jobs have been added, whereas the number of industrial jobs continues to shrink. In summary, union membership is primarily concentrated in the shrinking part of the economy, and unions are making only modest inroads into the fastest-growing segments in the Canadian economy. A look at Figure 15-5 reveals that non-governmental union members are heavily concentrated in transportation, utilities, and other "industrial" jobs.

Workforce Changes Many of the workforce and economic changes discussed in Chapter 1 have contributed to the decline in union representation of the labour force.[18] The primary growth in jobs in the Canadian economy has been in technology, financial, and other service industries. There are growing numbers of white-collar employees including clerical workers, insurance claims representatives, data input processors, nurses, teachers, computer technicians, and retail sales workers. Unions have increased efforts to organize white-collar workers as advances in technology have boosted their numbers in the workforce. However, unions face a major difficulty in organizing these workers.

Figure 15-5 Union Membership by Industry

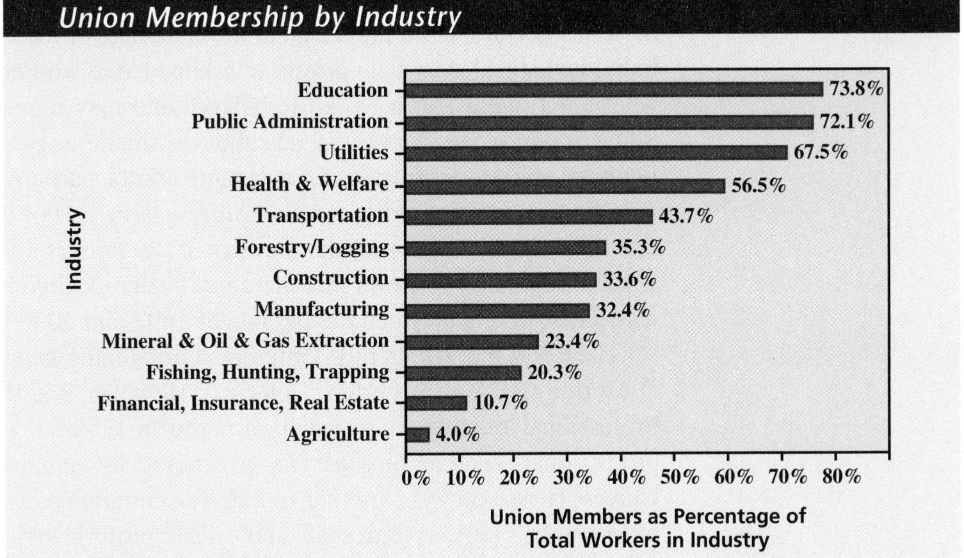

Source: Based on Statistics Canada Labour Force Survey, 1997 and 2002.

The growing percentage of women in the Canadian workforce presents another challenge to unions. In the past, unions have not been as successful in organizing women workers as they have been in organizing men workers. Some unions are trying to focus more on recruiting women members, and unions have been in the forefront in the push for legislation on such family-related goals as child care, maternity and paternity leave, pay equity, and flexible work arrangements. Women in "pink-collar" low-skill service jobs have been somewhat more likely to join unions than women working in white-collar jobs.

Union Targets for Membership Growth

In an attempt to counteract the overall decline in union membership, unions are focusing on a number of industries and types of workers. Some frequently targeted groups are professionals, contingent and part-time workers, and low-skill workers. Canadian labour strategists are avidly following a number of potential breakthroughs in the United States, where organizers have targeted the U.S. operations of IBM and the Seattle-based customer service workforce at high-tech Amazon.com Inc.[19] Even though there are potential growth opportunities in technology, the bankruptcies of many dot-coms has made unionization more difficult. The unionization of some Wal-Mart stores in Canada has captured worldwide attention, as unions target part-time workers.

Professionals Traditionally professionals in many occupations have been skeptical of the advantages of unionization.[20] However, professionals who have turned to unionization include engineers, nurses, teachers, and professors. Unions are making concerted efforts to try and unionize these types of workers, however it continues to be difficult to achieve this outside of public-sector unions.

Knowledge workers present a particular problem for unions. There are a number of reasons that unions may meet with resistance in organizing professionals. Managers of knowledge workers tend to make a concerted effort to praise their employees, provide ample monetary reward, and recognition in exchange for their employees' creativity and innovation that make their businesses successful. This is particularly true for engineering and technical staff. Another reason is that many of these workers are more interested in the challenge of the work, and therefore are very individualistic. The typical profile of a knowledge worker tends to be a young male, who is not interested in work/life balance and may move from contract to contract. Some of the contract work may take them to smaller organizations, which is more difficult for unions to infiltrate. Knowledge workers, particularly in the gaming industry, blur the line between work and play, since a large part of their job is to play games so that they can stay on top of the industry. Extra hours on the job is seen as play—not work.[21] Figure 15-6 shows that there has been a decline in the union density of professional workers between the periods of 1997 and 2002.[22]

The CAW met with a failed attempt at organizing knowledge workers at Research in Motion (RIM) in Waterloo, Ontario.[23] However, not all attempts have failed. The Professional Employees Association based in Victoria, B.C. represents about 2500 professionals such as pharmacists, psychologists, engineers, and IT workers at the University of Victoria. Another union, Telecommunications Employees Association of Manitoba (TEAM) represents about 1200 professionals, including some managers from Manitoba Telecom Services.[24]

Non-Standard and Contingent Work Non-standard and contingent work, defined as part-time work, temporary work including term or contract, seasonal, casual, own-account self-employment, or multiple jobholding grew in the early 1990s but has since stabilized.[25] As many employers have added workers performing non-standard or contingent work, instead of full-time employees, unions have tried to unionize part-time, temporary, and other employees. Time will tell if the efforts to unionize part-time workers and other groups will halt the decline of union membership in Canada. When unions are present, collective bargaining agreements frequently limit the amount of non-standard or contingent labour that may be used.

One of the major concerns for unions is the notion of precarious employment. Precarious employment is defined as forms of employment involving atypical employment contracts, limited social benefits and statutory entitlements, job insecurity, low job tenure, low earnings, poor working conditions, and high risks of ill health.[26]

Figure 15-6 *Changes in Union Coverage Between 1997 and 2002*

Overall Union Coverage	1997	2002
In private sector	21.5%	19.6%
In public sector	75.8%	75.8%
In business services		
Professional/scientific/technical	5.85	5.7%
Management/administrative	15.1%	15.0%
In "white-collar" occupations		
Professionals in business and finance	8.3%	7.9%
Finance/insurance/administrative	6.0%	4.8%
Secretaries	9.1%	8.2%
Administrative and regulatory occupations	7.3%	5.9%
Clerical	17.6%	14.6%
Professionals in natural and applied sciences	10.6%	7.4%
Technical occupations in natural and applied sciences	23.6%	20.2%

Source: "Changes in Union Coverage Between 1997 and 2002" data is adapted in part from Statistics Canada's Labour Force Survey.

Unions are trying to organize lower-skilled workers such as nurses aids, cooks, and launderers who have traditionally not been unionized.

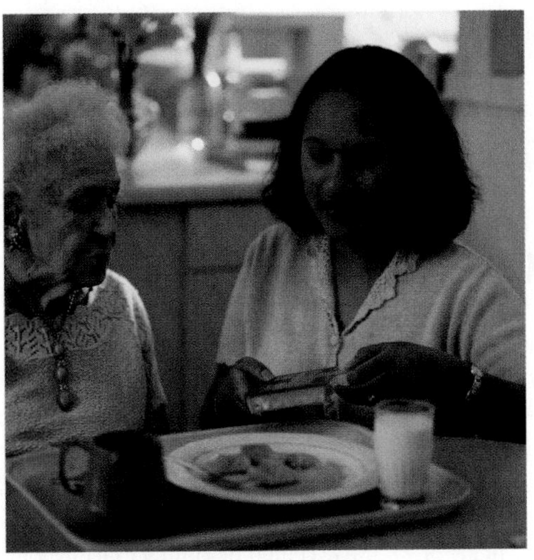

Source: Keith Brofsky/Photodisc Green/Getty Images

Therefore, non-standard work arrangements bring with them other concerns that unions also try to address. One such group that exemplifies this type of work arrangement are graduate student workers who are vulnerable to being employed for short periods, taking on extra workload while trying to complete their studies, at the expense of completing their own work. Because of the nature of this type of work, with the lack of security that is associated with it, the unionization of these students is a source of potential growth for unions. However, unionizing this particular group of workers is proving difficult for unions since the nature of the student's work allows them to work off campus, and reaching them is very difficult. In addition, they are only employed in this type of role for short durations.[27] The HR Perspective demonstrates the power that such workers have when they are unionized and how workers can react when they feel disadvantaged in the workplace.

Low-Skill Workers On the other end of the labour scale, unions have targeted low-skill workers, many of whom have lower-paying, less desirable jobs. Janitors, building cleaners, and nursing home aides are examples of groups targeted by unions. For instance, in the health-care industry, workers in nursing homes dealing with the elderly are a fast-growing segment of the workforce. Many employees in this industry are relatively dissatisfied. The industry is often noted for its low pay and hard work, and many employees are women who work as nurse's aides, cooks, and launderers and in other low-wage jobs. Many of these individuals are also immigrants, and unions are targeting immigrant workers in low-skill jobs. Although these efforts are not always successful, unions are likely to continue pursuing industries and employers with numerous low-skill jobs and workers. The advantages of unionization are especially strong for these employees.[28]

Public-Sector Unionism

Unions have had tremendous success with public-sector employees, particularly with federal, provincial, and municipal government workers. The government sector is the most highly unionized segment of the Canadian workforce as previously discussed. The three largest unions in Canada represent all public sector workers. Federal employees joined the Public Service Alliance of Canada (PSCA). As provincial governments passed similar legislation, workers joined the National Union of Provincial Government Employees (NUPGE) and the Canadian Union of Public Employees (CUPE). Teachers, nurses, social workers, professors, and others involved in government-related jobs are also increasingly unionized.

Unionization of government employees presents some unique problems and challenges. As a result, public sector employees do not enjoy the same freedoms to negotiate as compared to the private sector. First, some employees work in critical service areas. Allowing police officers, firefighters, and sanitation workers to strike endangers public health and safety. Consequently, labour law prohibits work stoppages by certain

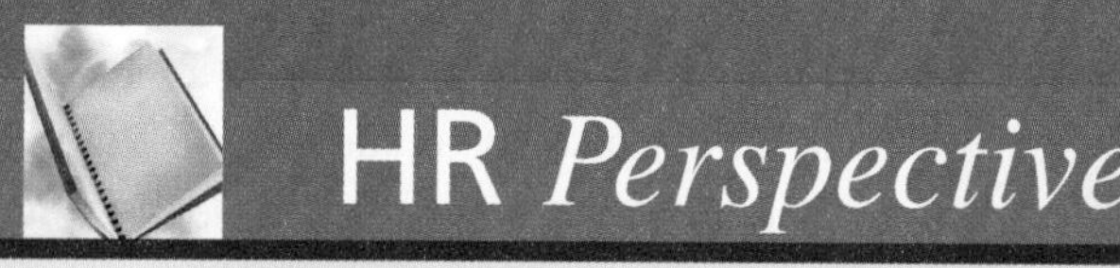

Precarious Workers Launch the Longest Strike in Canadian University History

On October 26, 2000, CUPE Local 3903, representing approximately 2100 teaching assistants, contract faculty, and newly certified graduate assistants, went on strike at York University. This strike was recorded as one of the longest running strikes in Canadian university history, lasting 78 days. Not only did it severely cripple the university system, but it threatened to cancel the school term, ultimately affecting 40 000 students, many of whom were planning to graduate.

The university's objective was to limit cost increases and remove any direct connection between tuition fees, wages, or other benefits. The union's objectives were to gain tuition indexing, gain uniform wages across department, a small amount of summer funding, and some minimal health benefits—at complete odds with the university's objectives. All three groups had common concerns that added to the strength of the union's resolve. Despite the concern by students that they might lose their year, the strikers received an unprecedented amount of support from York University Faculty Association (YUFA), CAW workers, and the students.

The university brought the deadlock to the forefront when they requested that an offer they made to the union be brought to the membership. The union declined as they felt the offer was not the mandate they were sent to negotiate. At the request of the university, the Ministry of Labour ordered a ratification vote—something that had not been done in a number of years. The offer was voted down by both teaching and graduate assistants by 69 percent and 78 percent respectively, but was accepted by contract faculty with a vote of only 53 percent. However, this victory was short lived since contract faculty refused to cross the picket line. The parties immediately resumed bargaining, and four days later the strike was settled and everyone returned to work and school. For the 400 graduate assistants this was their first contract. They successfully negotiated increased wages, health benefit increases, discrimination and harassment language, and a grievance procedure.[29]

1. Why do you think the workers were successful in this particular strike?
2. Do you feel that precarious workers, such as graduate students, should be able to join unions? Why or why not?

public employees who provide essential services. These laws also identify a variety of ways to resolve negotiation impasses, including interest arbitration, an unrestricted right-to-strike model, a designated or controlled strike model, and legislation.

No-Strike, Interest Arbitration Model In this particular model, both sides submit evidence to an arbitrator who determines the terms of the collective agreement. Arbitrators consider the compensation and working conditions of employees doing similar work in other workplaces. Evidence suggests that interest arbitration leads to higher wage increases as opposed to the use of strike. This is also known as *final offer arbitration.*

Unrestricted Right-to-Strike Model Employees who conduct work in nonessential services, such as administrative employees, are allowed to strike. However, even when these employees go on strike, it can cause problems for citizens who may need to have documents prepared. For example, the issuing of passports or birth certificates can be problematic in emergency situations.

Designated or Controlled Strike Model In the designated or controlled strike model employees are given the right to strike, but some employees must ensure that essential services are still maintained. If no agreement on who can strike is reached, then the respective labour relations board will hear the dispute. Compulsory binding arbitration is used for workers who perform essential services.

Legislation Back-to-work legislation is generally used to end a strike or a lockout in an industry that the government decides is essential to the operating of the economy. It can also be used to end an illegal strike, either by a group that is deemed essential and is therefore prevented by law from going on strike, or by workers who have gone out in violation of an existing contract. Typically, back-to-work legislation is imposed only after some time has passed, further efforts at reaching a settlement have failed, and there is considerable public pressure to end the dispute. Interest arbitration is usually used to settle such issues. The use of such legislation has been used to order back nurses, transit workers, and air traffic controllers. Since 1950, the federal government has only passed this legislation about 30 times.[30]

Industrial Relations Legislation In Canada

3 The fight for union recognition in Canada has been fraught with adversity dating back to the end of the 18th century. Employers were vehemently opposed to unions, and a number of questionable anti-union tactics were used to suppress any union advancement. Some of those tactics that employers used included the yellow dog contract whereby employees had to promise not to join unions, banned public union meetings, hired strikebreakers or goons, blacklisted anyone who showed a penchant towards unions, fired anyone with indicated union loyalty, and put union activists in jail.

Legislation enacted over the years has changed much of the earlier anti-union tactics to a situation where there is much more consultation between the parties. There still remains a faction though of employers and union activists who engage in adversarial relations, making unionization a difficult process in many cases. Labour legislation enacted at both the provincial and federal levels has specific rules that guide the labour relations process in Canada.

Union Strategies

As unions have evolved, they have adopted one of two strategies—business unionism or social unionism strategy. These strategies guide the way unions will frame their activities and what they will try to achieve for their workers. A focus on **business unionism,** which is based on an American tradition, is concerned about improving the terms of employment such as compensation and working conditions in negotiations. A Canadian perspective focuses on a **social unionism strategy,** which is not only concerned with the terms of employment, but also on the broader economic and social changes that benefit all of society. A number of Canadian unions have tried to address social issues pertaining to gender-specific patterns of discrimination, immigrant workers, gay and lesbian workers, workers from the First Nations, and those with disabilities.

Business unionism Based on American tradition, a strategy concerned about improving the terms of employment such as compensation.

Social unionism Based on a Canadian perspective, a strategy concerned with the terms of employment and the broader economic and social changes that benefit all of society.

Provincial and Federal Industrial Relations Legislation

Under the Canadian constitution, labour legislation is primarily a provincial responsibility since the provinces have jurisdiction over labour relations for approximately 90 percent of the Canadian workforce. Each of the provinces has its own labour relations boards that act as independent, quasi-judicial tribunal mandated to mediate and adjudicate a variety of employment and labour relations-related matters under a number of statutes in each respective provincial jurisdiction. What makes it difficult for human resources and labour relations specialists is the familiarization with the different labour laws that exist across Canada. An organization that has unionized workforces in Quebec, P.E.I., and Manitoba, for example, must be familiar with the labour legislation that exists within each of those respective jurisdictions. The following are the types of applications that provincial boards may respond to:[31]

- certification (establishing bargaining rights) and decertification of trade unions (also called terminating bargaining rights) in a workplace
- direction that a first collective agreement be settled by arbitration where the workplace parties have been unable to sign their first agreement
- declaration concerning the status of a successor trade union
- status of an employer (in the context of a sale of a business or one employer's relatedness to one or more other employers)
- trade union's duty of fair representation of its members
- trade union's duty of fair referral of its members
- unfair labour practices by any workplace party
- religious exemption from having to pay dues to a trade union
- work assignment disputes (also known as jurisdictional disputes)
- illegal strikes or lockouts
- early termination of collective agreements
- referrals of grievances to arbitration in the construction industry
- accreditation in the construction industry
- requests for reconsideration of board decisions

Under federal jurisdiction, the Canadian Industrial Relations Board (CIRB) has jurisdiction for employees engaged in industries that include interprovincial transportation (air, land, and water), broadcasting, banking, longshoring and grain handling, and to private sector employees in Nunavut, the Yukon, and the Northwest Territories. The CIRB is an independent, representational, quasi-judicial tribunal responsible for the interpretation and administration of Part I (Industrial Relations) and certain provisions of Part II (Occupational Health and Safety) of the Canada Labour Code. The board's expertise and composition allow it to deal effectively with the complexities of labour relations issues, to determine the underlying causes of disputes, and to facilitate agreement among the parties.

Similar to the provincial labour relations boards, the CIRB is responsible for certifying trade unions, investigating complaints of unfair labour practice, issuing cease and desist orders in cases of unlawful strikes and lockouts, rendering decisions on jurisdictional issues, and dealing with complex situations arising from a sale of business. It will process, hear, and determine applications and complaints fairly, expeditiously, and economically. Before adjudication, it plays an active role in helping parties to resolve their disputes through mediation and alternative dispute resolution approaches. It also protects the rights of employees and employers, and in constructively resolving conflicts.[32]

Unionization Process

4 The typical union organizing process is outlined in Figure 15-7. The process of unionizing an employer may begin in one of two primary ways: (1) a union targeting an industry or a company, or (2) employees requesting union representation. In the first case, the local or national union identifies a firm or an industry in which it believes unionization can succeed. The logic for targeting is that if the union succeeds in one firm or a portion of the industry, then many other workers in the industry will be more willing to consider unionizing.

Figure 15-7 *Typical Unionization Process*

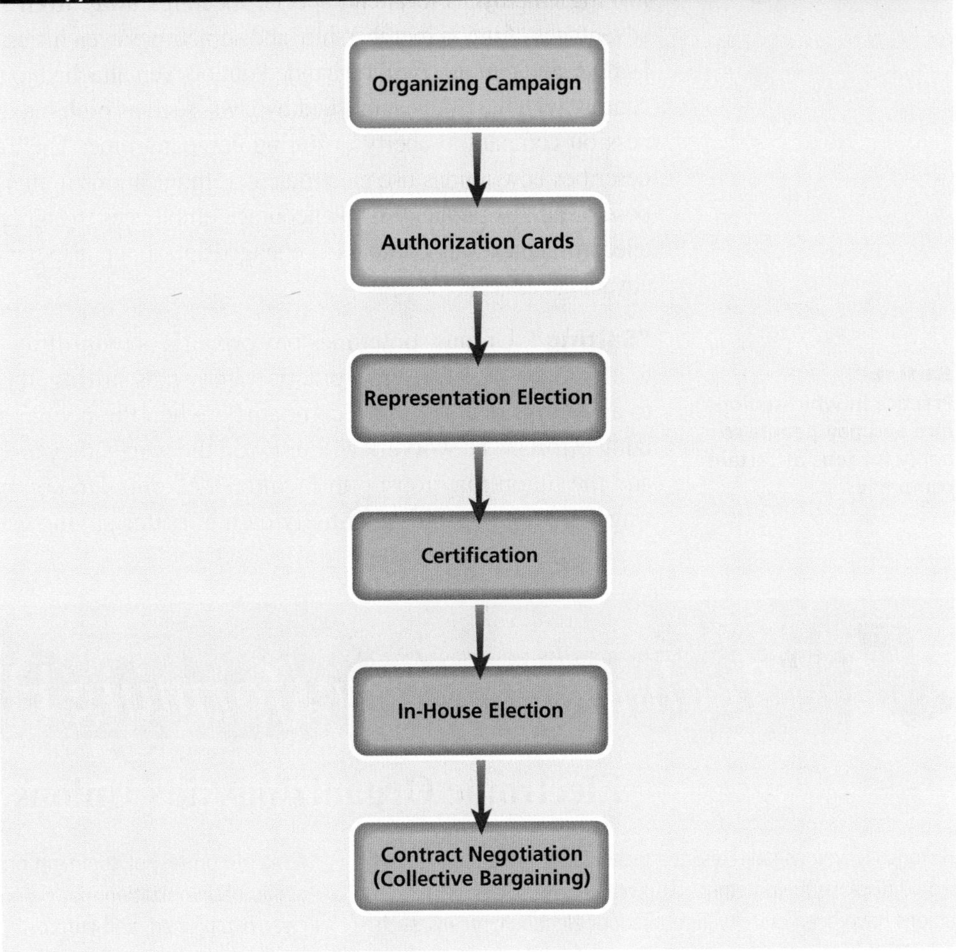

In the second case, the impetus for union organizing occurs when individual workers in an employer contact a union and express a desire to unionize. The employees themselves—or the union—may then begin to campaign to win support among the other employees.

Employers may make strategic decisions and take aggressive steps to remain non-union. Such a choice to remain non-union may require some specific HR policies and philosophies. For example, "preventive" employee relations may emphasize good morale and loyalty based on concern for employees, competitive wages and benefits, a fair system for dealing with employee complaints, and safe working conditions. Other issues may also play a part in employees' decisions to stay non-union, but if employers adequately address the points just listed, fewer workers are likely to feel the need for a union to represent them.

Once unionizing efforts begin, all activities must conform to the requirements established by applicable labour laws. Both management and the union must adhere to those requirements, or the results of the effort can be appealed to the respective labour relations boards and overturned.

Organizing Campaign

Like other entities seeking members, a union usually mounts an organizing campaign to persuade individuals to support its efforts. The persuasion takes many forms, including personally contacting employees outside work, mailing materials to employees' homes, inviting employees to attend special meetings away from the company, publicizing the advantages of union membership, and sometimes even hiring union infiltrators. Brochures, leaflets, and circulars will be handed out or even attached to their vehicles, as long as they comply with the rules established by laws, such as prohibited from conducting union business on company property or during company time. The Technology Transforming HR describes how unions use electronic communications in their organizing efforts. The purpose of all this publicity is to encourage employees to sign authorization cards. However, telecommunications companies engaged in labour disputes can use technology to their advantage as well.

Salting
Practice in which unions hire and pay people to apply for jobs at certain companies.

"Salting" Unions sometimes pay organizers to infiltrate a targeted employer and try to organize workers. In this practice, known as **salting,** the unions hire and pay people to apply for jobs at certain companies; when the people are hired, they begin organizing efforts. The workers will draw on the wages they are earning from the employer, and the union may top-up the "salters" earnings to compensate them for the loss of wages that they could potentially earn at better paying establishments.

Technology Transforming HR

Electronic Organizing Aids Unions

Historically, unions have resisted technology innovations that would displace their members. However, for organizing attempts unions have been quite willing to adopt electronic means, such as establishing websites where interested workers can read about benefits of unionization. For instance, the Canadian Auto Workers has websites for all their major union campaigns and the United Steelworkers of America maintains an online database of Canadian collective agreements. This collection is considered to be the most comprehensive online data collection of agreements in Canada.

Broadband, another technology, makes it easier to provide and access sound clips and video clips of conference speeches or training sessions or demonstrations. Trade unions around the world are starting to use this technology more regularly. For instance, the Canadian Auto Workers union has had a regular weekly video news show online for several years now.

E-mail has also changed union organizing efforts. The United Food and Commercial Workers union receives over 100 e-mails in a typical day from workers wanting information on unionization and their rights to union representation. Other unions have gathered the home e-mail addresses of workers who are targets for unionization and sent those workers union solicitation information.

Employers with e-mail restrictions may enforce them when union solicitation e-mails are received, sent, or forwarded using employer-provided systems. Under a recent ruling by the National Labour Relations Board in the U.S., e-mail is protected as a "concerted activity." This ruling means that employees using e-mail to protest or comment on employers' actions or the desirability of unionization may be protected unless employers have clear, established, and enforced policies to the contrary. The importance of this ruling is that it may have an impact on Canadian labour legislation as this issue begins to evolve.

Organizations may use their power to control the technology used by the unions. Such is the case of Telus, a large telephone company, engaged in a long dispute with its union, the Telecommunications Workers of Canada Union (TWU). Telus blocked access to several pro-union websites from any Telus customer Internet connections. The company felt they were justified in blocking the site because it contained confidential "proprietary information" about Telus, encouraged people to tie up call centre phone lines, and endangered non-union staff by posting pictures of them crossing picket lines. Inadvertently, Telus's filtering also blocked 766 additional, unrelated sites with domain names hosted on the same server as the blocked site. Telus later restored access to the website after obtaining an injunction that prohibited the posting of photos that might intimidate or threaten anyone connected with the dispute.[33]

1. Should private organizations that are providing Internet services be allowed to arbitrarily decide what type of sites their customers can or cannot access?"
2. Do you agree that e-mail should be restricted or unrestricted when it comes to receiving or sending e-mail messages related to union matters? Why or why not?

Authorization Cards

Union authorization card
Card signed by an employee to designate a union as her or his collective bargaining agent.

A **union authorization card** is signed by an employee to designate a union as her or his collective bargaining agent. In Canada, there is minimum card sign-up threshold before a union may apply for certification. If the threshold is met, then a certification vote takes place. However, six Canadian jurisdictions have provision for automatic card certification, without a vote, with the percentage of workers required to have signed cards ranging from 50 percent plus one (the federal jurisdiction) to as high as 65 percent (the Manitoba jurisdiction). Unions must do everything possible to sign up enough members and avoid a ballot. Under a system of mandatory representation votes, a secret ballot is conducted to determine if the union has enough support from the bargaining unit to be certified.

In reality, the fact that an employee signs an authorization card does not mean that the employee is in favour of a union; it means only that the employee would like the opportunity to vote on having a union. Employees who do not want a union might sign authorization cards because they want management to know they are disgruntled.

Once the union feels enough authorization cards have been signed they will approach the labour board to have the union certified. The labour board will notify the organization and the application will be posted in the workplace.

Determining an Appropriate Bargaining Unit

Bargaining unit
Employees eligible to select a single union to represent and bargain collectively for them.

Before any election, the appropriate **bargaining unit** must be determined. A bargaining unit is composed of all employees eligible to select a single union to represent and bargain collectively for them. Probably no other determination is as central to the mandate of labour relations boards as determining the appropriate bargaining unit. Labour boards generally describe bargaining units in terms of jobs, not individuals. The type of jobs that would not be unionized would be owners, managerial staff, or anyone handling confidential labour relations matters. Other jobs may be included in this determination, but it will depend on the jurisdiction covered. In Ontario for example, blue and white collar employees will be put in different bargaining units. B.C. allows all employees in a bargaining unit. Some jurisdictions will also separate out part-time and full-time workers, putting them in separate bargaining units, while others will not.

The union will obviously make the first determination of what they consider to be an appropriate bargaining unit. The workers they select to represent will be the ones who will vote in favour of a union. Unions will select workers who have common skills, needs, and work experiences trying to ensure a bargaining unit that cannot be challenged by management or the labour board. Management's interests will of course be opposite to the union, seeking to add workers who will swing the vote in favour of no union. Therefore, the labour board will make the final determination of the appropriate bargaining unit. The employer will often challenge the bargaining unit as a means to avoid unionization.

In determining an appropriate bargaining unit, the labour board will consider a number of factors including the following:

- Wages, hours, and working conditions
- Traditional industry groupings for bargaining purposes
- Physical location and amount of interaction and working relationships between employee groups
- Desire not to split one employer's workforce into too many bargaining units

Representation Election

With a determination that the bargaining unit is appropriate, the labour board will supervise the election. In most jurisdictions requiring a ballot, there is a formal requirement for the board to normally hold a vote within five days (in three jurisdictions) to ten days (in one jurisdiction) of an application for certification.

If an election is held, the union need receive only a *majority of the votes*. For example, if a group of 200 employees is the identified bargaining unit, and only 50 people vote, only 26 (50 percent of those voting plus 1) need to vote yes for the union to be named as the representative of all 200 employees. Typically, the smaller the number of employees in the bargaining unit, the higher the likelihood that the union will win.

Unfair Labour Practices An unfair labour practice is any employer or union practice that is considered to be illegal either during or subsequent to the union organizing process. Because every employee is entitled to join a trade union and participate in its lawful activities, labour relations acts prohibit any conduct that might interfere with this right. Unfair labour practices vary in each of the jurisdictions, but all share some commonalities. The following represent some examples of unfair labour practices prohibited by employers:[34]

- Cannot engage in threats, coercion, or intimidation.
- Cannot require one-on-one meetings.
- Cannot engage in any form of interrogation of employees about their voting intentions.
- Cannot hire spies, detectives, or infiltrators in order to acquire information about or influence union activities.
- Cannot unilaterally alter the terms and conditions of employment during an organizing drive, unless this change would normally have occurred as a matter of tradition or established policy.
- Cannot promise to alter the terms of employment in response to the results of a union drive.
- Cannot shut down any establishment in order to avoid or eliminate a union, or discharge individuals on the grounds of "redundancy" if this discharge involves only union activists.
- Cannot dismiss an employee for misbehaviour that they have already been disciplined or forgiven for prior to the employer's knowledge of the organizing drive.

Employers do possess a number of rights. For example, they have the right to:

- Discharge, suspend, transfer, lay off, or otherwise discipline an employee for proper cause;
- Make a change in the employer's operation that is reasonably necessary for the proper conduct of business; and
- Express its views on any matter, including matters relating to an employer, a trade union or the representation of employees by a trade union, provided that it does not use intimidation or coercion.

The right for an organization to express its views, however, does have certain limitations. A recent decision handed down by the B.C. Labour Relations Board in *RMH Teleservices v. BCGEU* discusses the limits to an employer's "free speech" rights during a union organizing campaign. Employees were "forced to listen" to a slide show the employer played at the workplace. Five projectors were used to convey messages on the walls and on a screen in the middle of the call centre. The messages changed every few minutes and continued through the entire workday. Prior to the slide show, gifts were handed out. The gifts were frisbees, sand pails, chocolate bars, and water bottles containing messages from the employer in response to the union organizing campaign. The employees were asked if they wanted them and they were free to refuse. If the employee was not there, the gifts were left at the employee's workstation. The messages in the slide show and on the gifts dealt with issues such as job security, what a union may promise and what it can deliver, questions to ask the union and having a voice in the union. According to the B.C. Labour Relations Board, "The slide shows were so prominent, persistent, and impossible to miss that employees, while at work, would inevitably have been forced to view them or forced to consciously turn away from them. This is the type of communication where otherwise permissible views become coercive or intimidating. . . . while the gifts were of marginal value, viewed contextually in light of the overall communications by the employer, they were improperly intrusive and persistent."[35]

Unions also must ensure that they do not engage in unfair labour practices. Listed below are some examples of what unions cannot do during union organizing drives:

- Bargaining collectively or signing a collective agreement where another union is known to be the bargaining agent.
- Interfering with or participating in the formation of an employers' organization.
- Attempting to organize on the employer's premises during an employee's working hours without the consent of the employer.
- Using coercion, intimidation, threats, promises, or undue influence to encourage trade union membership.

Even though unions are prohibited from organizing during working hours without the employers consent, this does not mean that employees are prevented from discussing the merits of unionization and distributing union literature during the lunch hour or other work breaks.

Allegations of unfair labour practices are regarded as very serious matters. Frivolous submissions can be dealt harshly by a board, therefore, employers and unions should ensure that only blatant violations be brought before the respective boards. If an employer engages in unfair labour practice during certification, then the labour board can order anyone or any combination of remedies. Each jurisdiction will have its own remedy that may consist of the following:

- Cease and desist orders, which mean that the employer must stop violating the legislation. This could also extend to future unlawful conduct.
- Compensating the union or individual for financial losses that could result out of organizing costs for the union, or if an individual had been terminated, a reimbursement of their lost wages. Interest may also be attached.
- Reinstating employees who were unlawfully terminated.
- Ordering a new representation vote.
- Automatic certification.
- Posting or mailing a notice to employees.
- Prosecution, although this is rarely exercised.

Despite the rules of unfair labour practices and potential remedies, allegations continue to be made against employers who blatantly oppose union certification. Figure 15-8 shows the requirements for each of the jurisdictions with respect to signing authorization cards, certification votes, and power to certify in cases of unfair labour practices.

Figure 15-8 *Trade Union Application for Certification*

Jurisdictions	Proof of Support for Trade Union in Bargaining Unit	Minimum Support Required for Representation Vote[1] or Certification Without a Vote	Power to Certify if Unfair Labour Practice by Employer
Federal	Signing an application for membership and paying at least $5 to the union for or within the six months preceding the application	Representation vote: 35 percent. A representation vote is void if less than 35 percent of eligible employees actually vote. Certification without a vote: more than 50 percent.	The Board[2] may certify if it considers that, in the absence of the unfair labour practice, the union could reasonably have been expected to have had the support of a majority of employees in the bargaining unit.
Alberta	Maintaining membership and/or applying for it, and paying on one's own behalf at least $2 within 90 days preceding the application, or signing a petition supporting the union within that same period.	Representation vote: 40 percent.	No certification without a vote.
British Columbia	Signing and dating a membership card (effective January 18, 1993, the card must contain a specific statement) or maintaining active membership by paying dues, within 90 days preceding the application.	Representation vote: 45 percent (a majority in the case of an application to displace another union). No certification without a vote (see also last column).	The Board[2] may certify if it believes that it is likely the union would otherwise have obtained the required support. The union may be required to fulfill certain conditions to remain certified.
Manitoba	Being a member of the union six months before the application for certification or joining the union during those six months, and maintaining membership prior to the date of application.	Representation vote: 40 percent (45 percent in the case of an application to displace another union). Certification without a vote: 65 percent or more.	The Board[2] may certify if it believes that the employees' true wishes are not likely to be ascertained and the union has adequate membership support.
New Brunswick	Paying to the trade union on the employee's own behalf an amount of at least $1 in respect of initiation fees or periodic dues.	Representation vote: 40 percent. Certification without a vote: the Board[2] may certify if more than 50 percent, and must certify if more than 60 percent	The Board[2] may certify if it believes that the employees' true wishes are not likely to be ascertained and the union has adequate membership support.

Newfoundland and Labrador	**Signing an application for membership in the union within 90 days before the application for certification.**	**Representation vote: 40 percent.** **No certification without a vote, unless the parties jointly request the Board[2] not to proceed with the vote (if so, it may certify if satisfied that the trade union has the support of a majority of employees).**	
Nova Scotia	**Joining the union or signing an application for membership, and paying on the employee's own behalf at least $2 in union dues during the three months before the month in which the application is made, up to the date of application.**	**Representation vote: 40 percent.** **No certification without a vote (see also last column).**	**The Board[2] may certify if it believes that the vote does not reflect the true wishes of the employees and the union represents at least 40 percent of those in the unit.**
Ontario	**Employees in the unit who are members of the union on the application date.**	**Representation vote: 40 percent.** **No certification without a vote.**	**When a trade union was not able to demonstrate support from at least 40 percent of the employees in the proposed bargaining unit, or a representation vote did not likely reflect the employees' true wishes, the Board[2] may certify the union if no other remedy would be sufficient to counter the effects of an unfair labour practice.**
Prince Edward Island	**Being a member of the union or signing a document stating support for certification, and paying at least $2 in union dues within the three months preceding the application.**	**Representation vote: no percentage specified.** **Certification without a vote: more than 50 percent.**	
Quebec	**Signing an application for membership, duly dated and not revoked, and personally paying at least $2 in union dues within the 12 months preceding the application.**	**Representation vote: 35 percent.** **Certification without a vote: more than 50 percent.**	

(continued)

Figure 15-8 *Trade Union Application for Certification (continued)*

Saskatchewan	**Signing a card stating that the employee wishes to be represented by the union.**	**Representation vote: no percentage specified (25 percent in the case of an application to displace a certified union). Certification without a vote: more than 50 percent.**	**The Board[2] must order a vote if it considers that majority support would otherwise have been obtained.**

[1]The result of a representation vote is determined by a majority of the employees in a bargaining unit who exercise their right to vote. In Newfoundland and Labrador, if at least 70 percent of eligible employees have voted, the union will be certified if a majority of those who cast ballots support it; if less than 70 percent of the eligible employees have voted, the union will be certified if it has the support of a majority of those included in the bargaining unit. In New Brunswick and Quebec, the result of a representation vote is determined by a majority of those who are eligible to vote (i.e., the employees comprised in the bargaining unit).

[2]Board means the Labour Relations Board or, in Manitoba, the Labour Board, in New Brunswick, the Labour and Employment Board, and, in the federal jurisdiction, the Canada Industrial Relations Board.

Source: Labour Law Analysis, International and Intergovernmental Labour Affairs, Labour Branch, Human Resources and Skills Development Canada, January 1, 2006. Human Resources and Skills Development Canada. Reproduced with the permission of Her Majesty the Queen in Right of Canada 2006.

Certification and Decertification

Union certification
Occurs when a union becomes the legal representative for designated employees as granted by the labour relations board.

First contract arbitration
Once a newly formed union has been certified, the employer and the union must negotiate a first contract within a specified period of time.

Decertification
Process whereby a union is removed as the representative of a group of employees.

Official **certification** of a union as the legal representative for designated private-sector employees is given by the respective labour relations board. Once certified, the union attempts to negotiate a contract with the employer. The employer *must* bargain; refusing to bargain with a certified union constitutes an unfair labour practice.

Most provinces in Canada have laws that give an independent third party the power to step in and settle disputes with respect to the negotiation of the first contract. This process is known as **first contract arbitration** and either party can file an application with the labour board. Labour laws in Manitoba, British Columbia, Ontario, Quebec, Newfoundland, Saskatchewan, and the federal jurisdiction all provide for first contract mediation and binding arbitration. In provinces such as Alberta, if no contract has been reached ten months after the date of certification, an application to decertify can be filed. First contract arbitration has been an incentive for management and labour to bargain productively, and has improved labour-management relationships.

When members no longer wish to be represented by the union, they can use the election process to sever the relationship between themselves and the union. Similar to the unionization process, **decertification** is a process whereby a union is removed as the representative of a group of employees. Employees attempting to oust a union must obtain decertification authorization cards signed by at least 40 percent of the employees in the bargaining unit before an election may be called. If a majority of those voting in the election want to remove the union, the decertification effort succeeds. A decertification application may only be filed during an "open period," which begins after the start of the last three months of every collective agreement. A decertification application can always be filed during this three-month period. If an agreement lasts longer than three years, then there will be different "open periods."

Some reasons that employees decide to vote out a union are that the treatment provided by employers has improved, the union has been unable to address the changing needs of the organizational workforce, or the image of the union has declined. Most jurisdictions prohibit employers from initiating or supporting decertification because it is a matter between employees and unions, and employers must stay out of the process. Alberta is one exception where an employer can apply for decertification of the union only when it has not bargained collectively with a trade union for at least three years after certification.

In-House Election

Once the union is certified, the bargaining unit must elect the union officials. Those interested in key positions will campaign and then the national union will oversee a vote to elect the local president, vice president, secretary, and union stewards. The number of stewards to be elected will depend on the size of the organization, as will the key positions to be elected. Once the union executive is elected, various committees will be established.

In a first contract, the bargaining committee will need to be chosen rather quickly so that contract talks can begin. An existing union would already have the committees in place, and they would have been working on issues well before the contract talks would take place. The bargaining committee will be made up of the local president, the business agent at a minimum, and possibly other key individuals in the unit. When any one of the big three automotive companies are involved in negotiations, the highlights are televised nationally, with as many as 50 people representing the bargaining team for the union, and 50 for the company. Lawyers would also be involved, as would economists.

Collective Bargaining

Collective bargaining
Process whereby representatives of management and workers negotiate over wages, hours, and other terms and conditions of employment.

5 **Collective bargaining,** the last step in unionization, is the process whereby representatives of management and workers negotiate over wages, hours, and other terms and conditions of employment. This give-and-take process between representatives of the two organizations attempts to establish conditions beneficial to both. It is also a relationship based on relative power.

Six provinces (British Columbia, Manitoba, Ontario, Newfoundland, Alberta, and Saskatchewan) and the federal government provide a statutory "duty of fair representation." Each jurisdiction has its own practices and procedures. This statute requires unions to fairly represent all members of the bargaining unit on matters in the collective agreement. Unions may not act arbitrarily, discriminatorily, or in bad faith when processing grievances or in matters related to the employee's rights under a collective agreement.

The power relationship in collective bargaining involves conflict. The most significant aspect of collective bargaining is that it is a continuing relationship that does not end immediately after an agreement is reached. Instead, it continues for the life of the labour agreement and beyond. Therefore, the more cooperative management is the less hostility and conflict with unionized employees carries over to the workplace. However, this cooperation does not mean that the employer should give in to all union demands.

Management/union relations in collective bargaining can follow one of several patterns. Figure 15-9 depicts them as a continuum, ranging from conflict to collusion. On the left side of the continuum, management and the union see each other as enemies. On the right side, the two entities join together in collusion, which is relatively rare in Canadian labour history and is illegal. Most positions fall between these two

Figure 15-9 *Continuum of Collective Bargaining Relations*

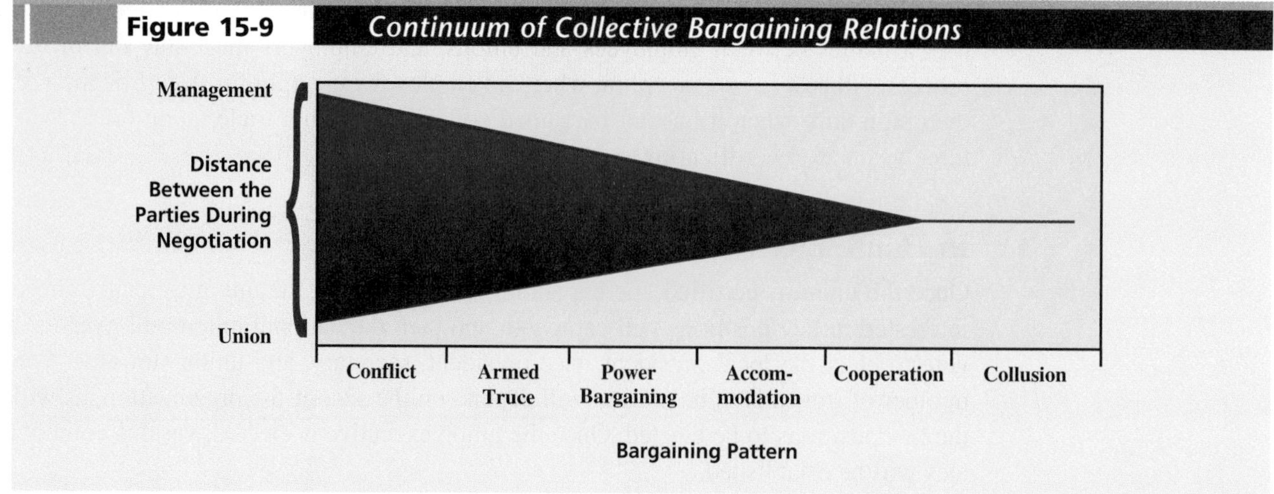

extremes. How union and management chose to deal with each other will set the tone for the collective bargaining process. The bargaining process might be based on distributive, integrative, attitudinal structuring, and intraorganizational bargaining.

Distributive Bargaining When parties engage in distributive bargaining, someone wins at the expense of the other. This is one of the more adversarial approaches, and usually denotes poor relations between the negotiating parties. It is sometimes referred to as *positional bargaining.*

Integrative Bargaining Integrative bargaining is more ideal since both parties gain from the experience, thus creating a win-win situation. The parties focus on working

During collective bargaining, management meets with union representatives to arrive at an agreement.

Source: © Reuters/CORBIS

together to problem-solve, and to ensure the interests of the parties. An outcome of this type of bargaining is *interest-based bargaining.*

Interest-based bargaining (IBB) The foremost difference between interest-based and traditional approaches to negotiations is the underlying assumption each party brings to the process. Interest-based bargaining is rooted in the idea that the fundamental interests (or concerns) of labour and management typically complement one another. For example, both parties want the employer to excel at what it does. This differs sharply from the traditional view that assumes that the parties' fundamental interests conflict with one another despite their ability to find some common ground.

Interest-based bargaining goes by a host of names such as consensus bargaining, problem-solving negotiations, win-win, mutual gains, collaborative bargaining, principled negotiations, and others. Five characteristics of interest-based negotiations: [36]

1. Bargaining over positions is avoided.
2. People are separated from the problem.
3. Focus is placed on interests, not positions.
4. Options for mutual gain are invented.
5. Objective criteria are used to select the appropriate resolution to an issue.

Attitudinal Structuring With attitudinal structuring both parties realize a need to change their relationship in order to achieve a successful outcome. If there are poor relations between the parties, then reaching a successful agreement could be difficult. As well, if collective bargaining does not go well, it could affect future relationships. It is in both parties' interests to strengthen the relationship before negotiations begin.

Intraorganizational Bargaining When parties enter into negotiations each are representing the needs and desires of their respective constituents, as well as the demands that each place on the other in order to satisfy their goals at the bargaining table. The members of the bargaining unit may also have different demands. For example, older employees may be concerned about pensions, while younger employees may be more concerned with job security and pay raises. Therefore, the activities of the negotiators in intraorganizational bargaining are to build internal consensus. During the process, it may become evident to the union negotiator that an employer may not have the funds to provide the wage increases the workers are expecting. The difficult task will be to convey the message to the workers that the information is valid, and that they should accept the contract that has been negotiated.

Buzz Hargrove, leader of the CAW found himself in a similar situation several years ago. When Air Canada filed for bankruptcy protection workers were skeptical because they realized concessions were going to be needed and everyone was wondering how much. Hargrove was well aware that major concessions would be required, but knew that the union needed to be assured that the company who would take over Air Canada would be someone the union could work with. Hargrove felt that Gerry Schwartz, founder and head of Onex Corporation, who had submitted a takeover bid, would be the answer. Hargrove therefore wholeheartedly endorsed the Onex takeover bid. CAW officials at Air Canada denounced Hargrove for making a deal with Onex without any discussion with union members and organized noisy demonstrations outside CAW offices in many cities across Canada. Hargrove had to balance the needs of the workers, the union executive, the company, and the new owners, something that proved difficult in this situation.[37]

Bargaining Structure

Employers sometimes have to deal with many different certified locals represented by various unions. For example, Air Canada negotiates with Canadian Union of Public Employees (CUPE), the International Association of Machinists, (IAM), Canadian Auto Workers union (CAW), and the pilots associations. One union may cover an entire industry, or there could be many unions involved. The CAW handles all the major automotive companies and CUPE handles most of the graduate student unions. Bargaining structure therefore refers to the number of unions, employers, and locations or establishments involved in contract negotiations.[38] Some of these structures may be single employer, single establishment, single union; or single employer, multiple establishments, single union.

Centralized vs. Decentralized Bargaining

Canada operates under a decentralized bargaining system that means most of the certified bargaining units are confined to the provincial level. Where industries cross borders, separate certified bargaining units may be established. Industrial unions generally try to negotiate on a broad basis to cover for degrees of differences across the country. The CAW tries to negotiate similar contracts for the auto workers. Craft unions operate in the construction industry. In both situations, unions are trying to take labour "out of competition" in order to require companies to compete on a basis other than wages.

In a centralized process, unions will try to negotiate for company-wide negotiations, even when the employer operates autonomous establishments. Without this tactic, unions may strike at one location, but may not be able to shut down operations entirely because the employer can easily have another one of their establishments produce the necessary goods and services. Therefore, there is an advantage for a union to negotiate multiple locations, with multiple bargaining units, on a company-wide basis. Employers may not always be opposed to this type of negotiation though, since it keeps wages and benefits, and administration the same, thus making the task much easier to manage. With different wage structures for example, employees could become disgruntled, adding to further complexity for the employer in administering the different contracts.

Pattern Bargaining Although Canada does not have a centralized system of bargaining in Canada, pattern bargaining comes closest to achieving the goal, even if only informally. Pattern bargaining occurs when negotiations in one industry or in one local serve as the basis for negotiations in other industries, companies, or localities. In Canada, the most notable set of pattern bargaining involves the auto industry. One of the big three is targeted, since negotiations happen about the same time, and whatever contract is achieved will be the one the other two will use as a pattern. Other industries where this occurs is in mining and steel. Inco and Falconbridge Nickel Mines operate in the same geographic area, and when one company achieves a contract, the end result will be similar for the other. Employers who are non-union often use this tactic to avoid unionism. If one unionized organization arrives at a contract, the other non-unionized company will offer similar wages and benefits to their workers. An example of this is Stelco and Dofasco.

Concession Bargaining In recent years, concessionary bargaining has gained momentum due to instability in the marketplace marked by recessions, deregulation, and foreign competition. To remain competitive, employers have been increasingly asking for unions to concede to reductions in wages, benefits, work rules, or to forego future benefits, in order to ensure longevity of their organizations. In the wake of 9/11, which caused a massive downturn in the airline industry, Air Canada filed for bankruptcy protection in 2003. Workers eventually agreed to over $1.3 billion in wage and benefits cuts, and a loss of 4000 jobs.[39]

Collective Bargaining Issues

The negotiation of a collective agreement must ensure that the minimum legal standards are maintained and that they comply with employment standards, human rights, and labour relations legislation. Under labour relations legislation, there are mandatory terms that must be included in the collective agreement. In addition there are voluntary terms that can be included that are unique to an organization, or could be based on the strategies of the organization and/or of the union.

Mandatory terms
Also known as articles or clauses, which must be included in a contract agreement in order to comply with labour relations legislation

Mandatory terms, also known as articles or clauses, that must be included in a contract agreement in order to comply with labour relations legislation include the following:[40]

- A prohibition against strikes and lockouts during the term of the agreement.
- A provision recognizing the union as the exclusive bargaining agent for the group of workers it represents.
- Several jurisdictions require that the agreement contain a compulsory dues check-off clause if the bargaining agent requests.
- A provision concerning technological investment and change by the employer.
- A provision for the arbitration of disputes relating to the administration of the agreement.
- A provision regarding successor rights in the case of a sale, transfer, consolidation, or other disposal of a business.
- A minimum term of one year.

Voluntary terms
The unique issues that come from the employer and the union.

Voluntary terms are the unique issues that come from the employer and the union. These must also comply with legislation. In other words, no one is allowed to negotiate anything less than what is offered by law. Some examples of voluntary terms may be benefits for retired employees, product prices for employees, or performance bonds are just a few examples of unique issues to be discussed. Figure 15-10 lists some of the most common articles found in collective agreements.

Although all clauses negotiated into a collective agreement are important, two clauses that are particularly important are management rights and union security.

Figure 15-10 *Collective Agreement Terms*

1. Union recognition	8. Term of agreement	15. Technological change
2. Management rights	9. Arbitration	16. Discrimination
3. No strike or lockout	10. Seniority	17. Severance pay
4. Union security	11. Probationary period	18. Successor rights
5. Union representation	12. Layoff	19. Salary
6. Grievance procedure	13. Hours of work and overtime	20. Benefits
7. Discharge and discipline	14. Restrictions contracting out	21. Holidays

Management Rights

Management rights
Rights reserved so that the employer can manage, direct, and control its business.

Virtually all labour contracts include **management rights,** which are rights reserved so that the employer can manage, direct, and control its business. Such a provision might read as follows:

> The employer retains all rights to manage, direct, and control its business in all particulars, except as such rights are expressly and specifically modified by the terms of this or any subsequent agreement.

By including such a provision, management attempts to preserve its unilateral right to make changes in areas not identified in a labour contract. Unions will always try to gain some control over this clause during negotiations.

Union Security

Union security provisions
Contract clauses to help the union obtain and retain members.

A major concern of union representatives when bargaining is the negotiation of **union security provisions,** which are contract clauses to help the union obtain and retain members. One union security provision is the *dues check-off,* which provides for the automatic deduction of union dues from the payroll cheques of union members. The dues check-off makes it much easier for the union to collect its funds; without it, the union must collect dues by billing each member separately.

Some employees, because of their religious convictions or beliefs, may object in general to joining unions or paying union dues and fees. Where a collective agreement requires union membership, those employees may apply to their respective board for an exemption. To receive an exemption, the employee's conviction must be based on an objection to trade unions in general and not simply an objection to the policies of a specific trade union. Exempt employees are required to pay the equivalent of union dues and fees to a charitable organization. An employee granted a religious conscience exemption is not entitled to participate in any votes held by the union or directed by a board or by the minister under the Code. They are, however, still eligible for all benefits derived from the union such as pay increases and better working conditions. They are also eligible to be treated as other employees under the "duty of fair representation."

Closed shop
Firm that requires individuals to join a union before they can be hired.

Open shop
Workers are not required to join or pay dues to a union.

Union shop
Workers who must join the union after a specified period of time and pay union dues at that time.

Maintenance-of-membership shop
Workers remain members of the union for the period of the labour contract.

Agency shop
Employee does not have to join the union, but must pay union dues.

Workers in unionized organizations have various degrees of freedom to join or not join the union. They are as follows:

- A **closed shop** is a business or industrial establishment whose employees are required to be union members as a precondition to employment. Usually this applies to the construction industry where hiring of card carrying union members is performed by the union.
- In an **open shop** union membership is not required in order to obtain a job or to continue employment.
- A **union shop** does not require employees to be union members as a condition of employment, but does require that they join the union or pay the equivalent of union dues within a set period of time following their hire. The timeframe is usually 30–60 days after being hired.
- A **maintenance-of-membership shop** does not require employees to join the union as a condition of employment, but all workers who voluntarily join must maintain their membership for the duration of the collective agreement as a condition of employment.
- Under an **agency shop** a union represents all employees regardless of union membership but requires that nonmembers pay union dues or fees. This mandatory

payment is known as the Rand formula. The dues are mandatory even if the worker is not a member of the union, because the worker benefits from the union's accomplishments within the workplace, such as ensuring higher wages or better job security. The name comes from Supreme Court of Canada Justice Ivan Rand, who introduced this formula in 1946 as an arbitration decision ending the strike of Ford Motor Company's employees in Windsor, Ontario.[41]

In the U.S., several states have "right-to-work" laws that makes union membership completely voluntary.[42] The right-to-work laws are in effect in 22 U.S. states. Legislation based on the 1947 Taft-Hartley Act makes it illegal to demand union membership and mandatory dues payment as a condition of employment. In right-to-work states, individual workers can revoke their membership at anytime and still receive the same union-negotiated benefits as their dues-paying co-workers, including the right to union representation. Organizations in the U.S. who are trying to avoid unions try to establish operations in one of the right-to-work states. In Canada, employers generally would prefer similar legislation. One employer, in first contract negotiations in New Brunswick tested the waters, and refused to accept inclusion of a union security clause and dues check-off. The employer soon learned that they could not negotiate without such a clause. There are concerns that anti-union provinces will enact similar legislation to that in the U.S since unionization in those particular states is very low.[43]

A growing type of union security in labour contracts is the *no-layoff policy,* or *job security guarantee.* Such a provision is especially important to many union workers because of the mergers, downsizings, and job reductions taking place in many industries.

Collective Bargaining Process

6 The collective bargaining process consists of a number of stages: preparation and initial demands, negotiations, settlement or impasse, and strikes and lockouts. Throughout the process, management and labour deal with the terms of their relationship. Figure 15-11 outlines the steps of the process.

Figure 15-11 *Collective Bargaining Process*

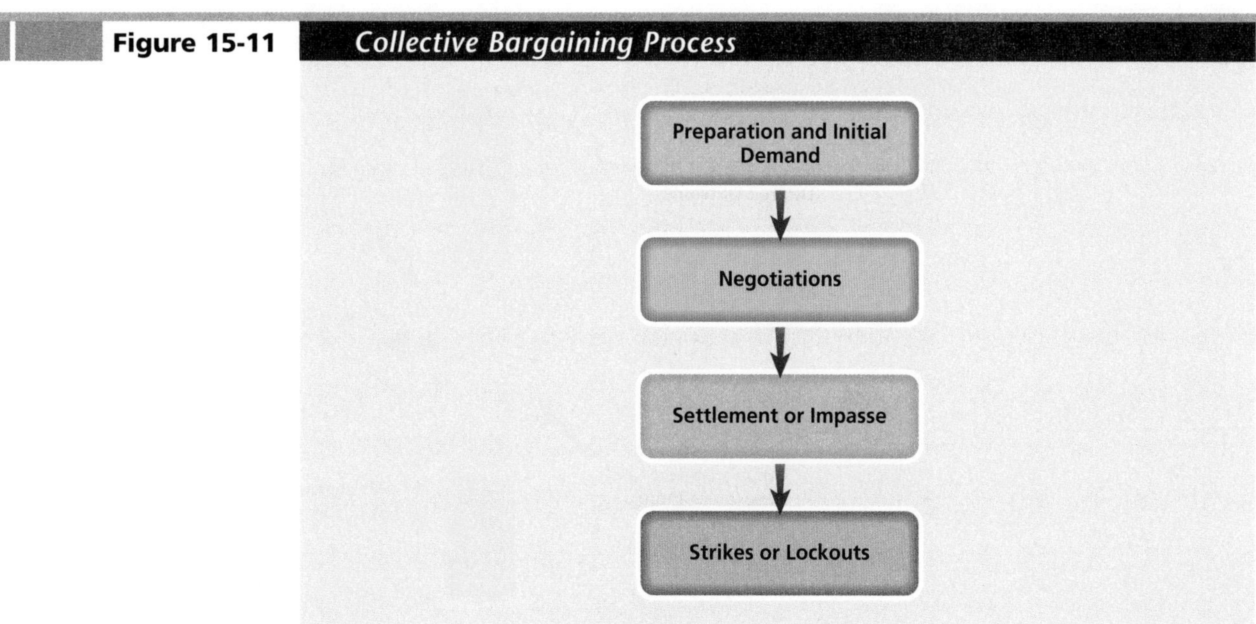

Preparation and Initial Demands

Both labour and management representatives spend much time preparing for negotiations. Employer and industry data concerning wages, benefits, working conditions, management and union rights, productivity, and absenteeism are gathered. If the organization argues that it cannot afford to pay what the union is asking, the employer's financial situation and accompanying data become all the more relevant. However, the union must request such information before the employer is obligated to provide it. Typical bargaining includes initial proposals of expectations by both sides. The initial list of demands is presented by the chief spokespersons for each side. The amount of rancor or calmness exhibited may set the tone for future negotiations between the parties.

Continuing Negotiations

After taking initial positions, each side attempts to determine what the other side values highly so that the best bargain can be struck. For example, the union may be asking the employer to pay for dental benefits as part of a package that also includes wage increases and retirement benefits. However, the union may be most interested in the retirement benefits, and may be willing to trade the dental payments for better retirement benefits. Management must determine what the union has as a priority and what exactly they would give up.

Through the negotiation process, the number of demands will gradually be narrowed down as each party gains a better understanding of what the other party really wants. This will lead to an understanding of the bargaining zone. It begins with an initial offer that is usually set high by the union, and a low offer from management. Each subsequent pass at negotiating items should get the parties closer to the middle, or the bargaining zone, where a final settlement can be achieved. Each party will have a bottom line, or resistance point, that they will not go above (management) or below (union). If this middle ground is not achieved, then the parties will reach a deadlock where a settlement will not be reached, and ultimately a lockout or a strike could ensue. Figure 15-12 demonstrates the "bargaining zone" with the expectations of each of the negotiating parties.

Figure 15-12 *The Bargaining Zone*

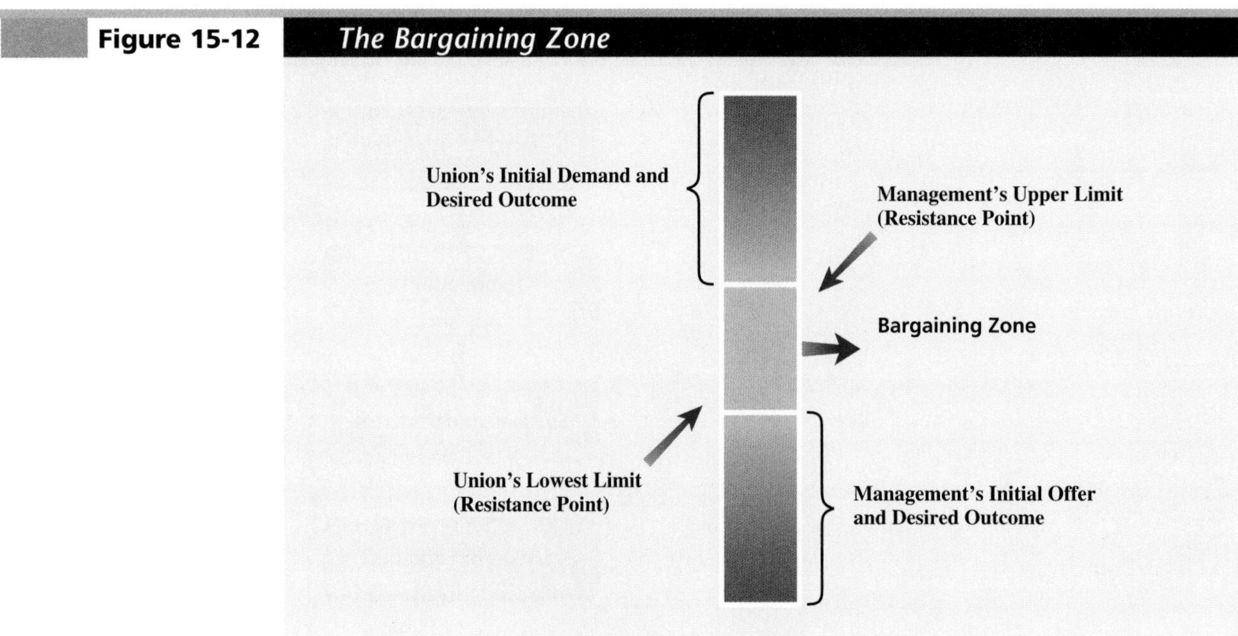

The very last items to be negotiated are benefits and then wages. Both sides need to take stock during negotiations to determine the costs and gains of what has been achieved at various points in time. If not enough money has been left on the table then the union may be in a vulnerable position when it comes time to negotiate this clause. The costs of wages and benefits are a concern in many industries, as well as for full- and part-time workers, and gender. For example: In the unionized American car-building companies (the GM, Ford, and Chrysler group), labour costs average $7,655 per car. In the non-unionized Japanese car-building companies in the U.S. (Toyota, Nissan, and Honda), labour costs average $6,052 per vehicle.[44] A study conducted in 2001 by Charlotte Yates of McMaster University found that part-time women who were unionized earned 40.2 percent more than non-unionized part-time women workers, and for part-time unionized men, the differential over non-unionized was 39.2 percent. For full-time unionized women, they earned 24 percent more than non-unionized women, and for men, they earned 13 percent more than non-unionized.[45] This example illustrates that it is common for wages and benefits to be higher in unionized firms.[46]

Good Faith Provisions in labour relations acts require that both employers and union bargaining representatives negotiate in good faith. In good-faith negotiations, the parties agree to engage in some give-and-take discussions for the purpose of reaching a collective agreement. If either party feels that the other has engaged in bad-faith bargaining, the complaint should be brought to the labour relations board. The following are a list of what might constitute bad-faith bargaining strategies:

- refusing to meet to bargain
- engaging in surface bargaining (no intention of reaching a collective agreement)
- scheduling times and places that would be considered unreasonable
- presenting an initial offer as a final offer without justification or rationale and refusing to negotiate further—known as Boulwarism
- refusing to bargain unless certain procedural conditions are met
- sending representatives to bargain who do not hold the authority to negotiate
- providing misleading or incomplete information
- not informing the other party of important decisions that may have a major impact on a sector
- seeking agreement to an illegal provision
- bargaining to impasse regarding the scope of an association's certification
- firing or disciplining union members or negotiators for reasons unrelated to their work, for no reason, during the negotiation process
- the employer bargaining directly with employees
- refusing to provide the rationale for a bargaining position
- attempting to reopen negotiation of terms that have already been settled

Settlement and Contract Agreement

After reaching an initial agreement, the bargaining parties usually return to their respective constituencies to determine if the informal agreement is acceptable. A particularly crucial stage is **ratification** of the labour agreement, which occurs when union members vote to accept the terms of a negotiated agreement. Before ratification, the union negotiating team explains the agreement to the union members and presents it for a vote. If the members approve the agreement, it is then formalized into a contract. If an agreement cannot be reached, then the negotiating teams need to find a way to reach an agreement. There are many remedies available to negotiating parties.

Ratification
Process by which union members vote to accept the terms of a negotiated labour agreement.

Bargaining Impasse

Regardless of the structure of the bargaining process, labour and management do not always reach agreement on the issues. If they reach an impasse, then the disputes can be taken to conciliation, mediation, or arbitration.

Conciliation
Process by which a third party attempts to keep union and management negotiators talking so that they can reach a voluntary settlement.

Conciliation When an impasse occurs, either party will contact the Labour Relations Board who will assign a conciliation officer. A **conciliation** officer, the third party, attempts to keep union and management negotiators talking so that they can reach a voluntary settlement, but makes no proposals for solutions. Their task is to act as a facilitator.

Some jurisdictions require the appointment of a conciliation board. The board will consist of a union and management representative, and a neutral third party. Evidence is provided by the parties and recommendations are made. The final recommendations are not binding, however some jurisdictions will enforce the recommendations if the parties agree to this, such as with firefighters or police services. If no progress is made with the board, then either party can request a "no board report" to the Minister of Labour. It means that a conciliation board will not be appointed and a strike or lock can commence within a specified time period.

Mediation
Process by which a third party helps the negotiators reach a settlement.

Mediation, the third party helps the negotiators reach a settlement once conciliation efforts have been exhausted. They also cannot impose a solution. The mediator may be a Ministry of Labour official or a private mediator that has been agreed upon by the parties. There is a fee for the use of a private mediator. A mediator plays a more active role in negotiations. They will speak privately with each of the parties pointing out various compromises and possible solutions that might be attempted, or to get them to see other perspectives on the issues. They help each side to understand the other's position. Particularly when the parties are adversarial, the mediator will try to get the parties to focus on the issues.

Fact-finding Fact-finding is a process found in some public sector labour relations statutes. A fact-finder is an individual who helps to clarify the issues of disagreement as an intermediate step between mediation and arbitration. They will investigate issues and report to the Minister of Labour. The report may contain recommendations and is usually made public. It is also not binding.

Arbitration
Process that uses a neutral third party to hear evidence from both parties and who makes a final and binding decision.

Arbitration In **arbitration,** a neutral third party hears evidence from both parties and who makes a final and binding decision. Arbitration can be conducted by an individual or a panel of individuals. "Interest" arbitration attempts to solve bargaining impasses, and is used primarily in the public sector. It is provided as an alternative to a strike or lockout for some employees. This type of arbitration is not frequently used in the private sector because companies generally do not want an outside party making decisions about their rights, wages, benefits, and other issues. Interest arbitration is different from grievance or "right" arbitration. Grievance, or "rights," arbitration is used extensively in the private sector. Fortunately, in many situations, agreements are reached through negotiations without the need for arbitration.[47] When disagreements continue, strikes or lockouts may occur.

Bargaining Power

Throughout the process both the union and management can rely on certain mechanisms to leverage their position towards a contract settlement. Bargaining power is the ability to obtain objectives despite the resistance to others. What helps gain power is the ability to impose sanctions on the other power. The union and management have many tactics at their disposal. The more common tactics are the strike and lockout, but there are many other opportunities for unions and management to exert power on each other. All of these may be used on their own or in combination with one another.

Union Bargaining Power

Unions have four primary ways in which it can apply influence over the employer and three secondary methods. The primary methods include the strike vote, the strike, picketing, (primary and secondary) and boycotting. The secondary methods include the solvency of the union, the timing of the strike, and the strike effectiveness.

The Strike Vote Before a union can go on strike, it must conduct a strike vote in advance. Each jurisdiction has different requirements as to when this must occur. Having a strike vote well in advance of a legal strike deadline can send a strong message to an organization that employees may want to strike. Even though employees may overwhelmingly vote to strike, does not mean that they actually will. It is used as leverage to try and gain position at negotiations.

Strikes

Strike
Work stoppage in which union members refuse to work in order to put pressure on an employer.

If a deadlock cannot be resolved through mediation or conciliation, then the union may revert to a strike. During a **strike,** union members refuse to work in order to put pressure on an employer. Often, the striking union members picket or demonstrate against the employer outside the place of business by carrying placards and signs. Once an employee goes on strike, then they cease to earn their regular income, so there is added pressure to the union and the workforce when this occurs. Strikers who serve on a picket line are entitled to strike pay, although this amount is usually much less than a striker's normal take-home pay. One union announced that full-time strikers would receive $350 a week for strike pay, and part-timers would receive $250 a week.[48] Strike pay will always be much less than the worker's normal take-home pay. The amount received will be dependent on the union's financial capabilities and the number of dependants in the worker's family.

Types of Strikes Five types of strikes can occur. They are as follows:

- *Economic strikes* happen when the parties fail to reach agreement during collective bargaining.
- *Unfair labour practices strikes* occur when union members walk away from their jobs over what they feel are illegal employer actions, such as refusal to bargain.
- *Wildcat strikes* occur during the life of the collective bargaining agreement without approval of union leadership and violate a no-strike clause in a labour contract. Strikers can be discharged or disciplined.
- *Jurisdictional strikes* exist when members of one union walk out to force the employer to assign work to them instead of to members of another union.
- *Sympathy strikes* take place when one union chooses to express support for another union involved in a dispute, even though the first union has no disagreement with the employer.

Many unions are reluctant to go on strike because of the financial losses their members would incur, or the fear that a strike would cause the employer to go bankrupt. Fortunately, the incident of strikes is low. In 1993, there were 381 strikes, compared to 379 in 2001. The highest incident of strikes occurs in the manufacturing industry. By comparison the U.S. only had 33 strikes in 1993, and only 29 in 2001.[49] This is related to the right-to-work legislation throughout most of the U.S.

Picketing
A form of non-violent resistance in which people congregate outside a place of work or location where an event is taking place to attempt to dissuade others from going in.

Picketing **Picketing** is a form of non-violent resistance in which people congregate outside a place of work or location where an event is taking place and attempt to dissuade others from going in ("crossing the picket line"). It is only lawful to picket when there is no collective agreement in place. A union which meets the legal requirements has the right to picket in a peaceful and orderly fashion on the public property at or near an employer's place of business. Most provinces, except British Columbia, do not extensively regulate picketing. Picketers may not trespass on private property, nor may they engage in intimidation, violence, or other illegal acts on the picket line. When illegal acts occur on the picket line, courts may grant an injunction to stop such activity. Picketing can become violent when those wishing to cross the picket line decide that they are going to get in. A recent strike by the colleges in Ontario ended in tragedy when an accounting faculty member was critically injured after being struck by a car while on picket duty.

Secondary picketing occurs when economic pressures are put on another employer or other person to try and induce them to use their influence to settle the contract dispute. Secondary picketing typically targets stores or distributors in the hope of persuading them and their customers to cease dealing with the company involved in the labour dispute. Under a 2002 ruling by the Supreme Court of Canada, secondary picketing is allowed as long as no illegal action or "wrongful action" occurs.[50] Secondary picketing does not extend to the personal homes of managers, which is considered to be illegal.

Boycotting
Union tactic to encourage others to refuse to patronize an employer.

Boycotting **Boycotting** is a union tactic to encourage others to refuse to patronize an employer. The CEP union asked the CLC to sanction a boycott of newspapers run by Torstar in the Hamilton area operations. The union was also successful in gaining support from the Hamilton and District Labour Council, which asked its affiliates to refuse to patronize advertisers in Torstar's Hamilton papers.

Other Tactics Another tactic used by unions is to boast the *solvency* of the union. If the union has substantial financial backing behind them, then it will prove to man-

During a strike unionized workers will picket their employer and receive strike pay.

Source: Norm Betts/Bloomberg News/Landov

agement that the union can stand its ground for as long as is needed. Other unions will often speak up and offer financial support to further add to the strength of the action. Another useful tool is the *timing of the strike,* which can be an advantage to either the union or the company. The recent strike by the colleges in Ontario is a case in point. Their strike started close to the end of the school term, threatening to interfere with the completion of classes and subsequent graduation. Much pressure was put on the colleges in this case. Finally, another tactic is the *effectiveness of the strike.* In a large organization with many skilled workers, it is difficult for an employer to recruit enough replacement workers to complete the necessary tasks. A smaller organization may not have this problem. This tactic could also work in the employer's favour.

Management Bargaining Power

Employers have at their disposal a number of ways in which they can apply pressure to reach a collective agreement. These include imposing lockouts, bringing in replacement workers, subcontracting out work, stockpiling inventories, and transferring work to other entities.

Lockout
Shutdown of company operations undertaken by management to prevent union members from working.

Lockout If a deadlock cannot be resolved, then an employer may revert to a lockout. In a **lockout,** management shuts down company operations to prevent union members from working. This action may avert possible damage or sabotage to company facilities or injury to employees who continue to work. It also gives management leverage as in the NHL lockout in 2004. The CBC locked out its workers in 2005 as it continued to change the job security clauses of the contract, opting for more contracting-out of work and more private-public partnerships.

Replacement of Workers on Strike The use of replacement workers, or "striker replacements," can put a union at a complete disadvantage. In Canada, there are a number of provinces that allow striker replacements. The use of striker replacement continues to be an emotional issue for unions, and a source of controversy between unions, governments, and workers.

Under federal legislation, the use of permanent or replacement workers is prohibited. Provincial legislation differs across the ten provinces. Both Quebec and British Columbia prohibit the use of both temporary and permanent replacements on lawful strikes or lockouts. Both provinces prohibit the use of new hires or employees from other locations or from other employers to do struck work. B.C. permits the use of managerial staff, but Quebec does not.

Professional strike breakers are prohibited in Ontario, Manitoba, Alberta, in addition to Quebec and British Columbia. Further, in these aforementioned provinces, and in Prince Edward Island and Nova Scotia (which vary to some degree by the province), labour statutes ensure that the striker retains his or her job at the end of the strike. For example, in Ontario, strikers may be reinstated anytime within six months of the strike once an unconditional application for work is made. The practice of hiring permanent replacement workers is rare across Canada. Striker replacement legislation in Canada is highlighted in Figure 15-13.

When an organization decides to exercise their right to use replacement workers, they must also be aware of the potential for violence. Consider that a striking worker who is picketing only receives a small amount of income from their union for picket-line duty. As they watch bus loads of replacement workers cross the picket lines (usually in buses for the safety of the replacement workers) to perform their jobs and receive payment, they will undoubtedly become very angry. Such was

Figure 15-13 ***Striker Replacement Legislation in Canada***

	Total Ban on All Replacements	Reinstatement Rights Provision	Professional Strikebreakers Banned	Provisions Protecting Those Who Refuse to Do Struck Work
Federal	**s. 94 (1998–present)**			
Alberta		**s. 88 (1988–present)**	**s. 152(1) (1988–present)**	**s. 147(f) (1988–present)**
British Columbia	**s. 68 (1993–present)**		**s. 3(3) (1973–present)**	**s. 68(3) (1993–present)**
Manitoba		**ss. 11, 12, 13 (1976–present)**	**ss. 14(1) (1973–present)**	**ss. 15, 16 (1973–present)**
New Brunswick				
Newfoundland		**s. 53(3)(a) (1989–present)**		**s. 53(3)(c)**
Nova Scotia				
Ontario	**s. 73 (1993–1995)**	**s. 80 (1995–present) s. 75(1) (1970–1993)**	**s. 78 (1983–present) s. 73(1) (1993–1995)**	
P.E.I.		**s. 9 (1987–present)**		
Quebec	**s. 109 (1978–present)**	**s. 98(a) (1978–present)**		
Saskatchewan		**s. 46 (1994–present)**		

Source: Singh and Jain, 2001; Survey of Canadian Ministries of Labour/Labour Departments/Labour Boards, 2004 and Singh, Zinni and Jain, "The Effects of the Use of Striker Replacement Workers in Canada: An Analysis of Four Cases," *Labor Studies Journal*, Volume 30, Number 2, Summer 2005, pp. 61–85, West Virginia University Press.

the case at the Yellowknife Giant Mines in the Northwest Territories in 1990. The owner, Peggy Witte, an American, decided that she would lock out the workers a day before the legal strike day, and that replacement workers would be brought in to perform mining duties. This angered the workers immensely. Tragedy struck on September 18, 1992, when three replacement workers and six union members who crossed the picket line were killed when their mining car hit a bomb that was taped to one of the rails inside the mine. Roger Warren, a miner who had worked for Giant mine for 12 years, was convicted for this crime in 1995 and was later sentenced to 20 years in prison.[51]

Another aspect of replacement workers is that managers will often take over the roles of the workers. Even though most legislation allows management workers to do this (except Quebec), management cannot completely fulfill the mandate as there are just not enough workers. Some workers will choose to cross the picket lines to continue their jobs. However, workers who choose to cross the picket line may be subject to ridicule and harassment from striking colleagues who will not look kindly on workers exercising this right. One of the authors of this text witnessed one professor being shunned by her colleagues for not having crossed the picket line when the entire faculty returned to work. She held her resolve about what she believed in, but her colleagues and administration treated her poorly for many years.

Subcontracting Out Work When a strike occurs and operations are shut down, employers run the risk of losing customers because they will find other sources for their needs. By subcontracting the work, the product or service continues to be offered. Unions often respond by trying to use boycotts or secondary picketing on the organization or persons taking on the work.

Stockpile of Inventories When an organization is aware that a strike might be pending, they will begin to stockpile inventories to ensure that they are able to provide supplies to their customers. This is typical in the mining industry where huge stockpiles are produced, since these strikes can be more lengthy compared to other industries. This also helps management avoid having to use replacement workers who may not be able to learn the job and to produce the amounts required.

Transfer of Work Often when an organization has other facilities they may chose to transfer production to the other location. The ease of doing this will depend on the industry. For example, a manufacturer of pens in Mississauga can easily have production increased at another facility in Northern Ontario, or even out of province.

Union/Management Cooperation

The adversarial relationship that naturally exists between unions and management may lead to strikes and lockouts. With increased uncertainty in the marketplace, there is growing recognition on the part of union leaders and employer representatives that cooperation between management and labour unions offers the most sensible route if organizations are to compete effectively in a global economy.[52]

Over the past decade, numerous firms have engaged in organizational and workplace restructuring in response to competitive pressures in their industries. Restructurings have had significant effects, such as lost jobs, changed work rules, and altered job responsibilities. When restructurings occur, unions can take different approaches, ranging from resistance to cooperation. Specifically, when unions have been able to obtain information and share that information with their members in order to work constructively with the company management at various levels, then organizational restructurings have been handled more successfully.

Cooperation and Joint Efforts

There are a number of notable examples of successful union/management cooperation. One frequently cited example is at GM-Suzuki in Ingersol, Ontario. There, union/management cooperation was established when management did not oppose the unionization of the CAMI plant. As a way to cope with this new relationship, the CAW national office released its *Statement on the Organization of Work* (CAW 1989) that would serve as a union guidepost to implementing the CAMI system and its attendant values of teamwork and labour-management collaboration.[53] Other firms with successful union/management cooperation include Ford and Boeing, despite occasional conflicts that arise.

Unions and Employee Ownership

Unions in some situations have encouraged workers to become partial or complete owners of the companies that employ them. These efforts were spurred by concerns that firms were preparing to shut down, merge, or be bought out, resulting in a cut in the number of union jobs and workers.[54]

Unions have been active in helping members put together employee stock ownership plans to purchase all or part of some firms. Such programs have been successful in some situations, but have caused problems in others. Some in the labour movement fear that such programs may undermine union support by creating a closer identification with the concerns and goals of employers, instead of "union solidarity."

Grievance Management

Complaint
Indication of employee dissatisfaction.

Grievance
Complaint formally stated in writing.

7 Unions know that employee dissatisfaction is a potential source of trouble for employers, whether it is expressed or not. Hidden dissatisfaction grows and creates reactions that may be completely out of proportion to the original concerns. Therefore, it is important that dissatisfaction be given an outlet. A **complaint,** which is merely an indication of employee dissatisfaction, is one outlet. Complaints often are made by employees who are not represented by unions.

If an employee is represented by a union, and the employee says, "I should have received the job transfer because I have more seniority, which is what the union contract states," and she submits it in writing, then that complaint becomes a grievance. A **grievance** is a complaint formally stated in writing.

Management should be concerned with both complaints and grievances, because both indicate potential problems within the workforce. Without a grievance procedure, management may be unable to respond to employee concerns because managers are unaware of them. Therefore, a formal grievance procedure provides a valuable communication tool for the organization, which also is beneficial for maintaining and improving employee relations.

Grievance Responsibilities

The typical division of responsibilities between the HR unit and operating managers for handling grievances is shown in Figure 15-14. These responsibilities vary considerably from one organization to another, even between unionized firms. But the HR unit usually has more general responsibilities. Managers must accept the grievance procedure as a possible constraint on some of their decisions.

Grievance Procedures

Grievance procedures
Formal channels of communication used to resolve grievances.

Grievance procedures are formal channels of communication designed to settle grievances as soon as possible after problems arise. First-line supervisors are usually closest to a problem. However, these supervisors are concerned with many other

Figure 15-14 *Typical Division of HR Responsibilities: Grievance Management*

HR Unit	Managers
• Assists in designing the grievance procedure • Monitors trends in grievance rates for the organization • May assist in preparing grievance cases for arbitration • May have responsibility for settling grievances	• Operate within provisions of the grievance procedure • Attempt to resolve grievances where possible • Document grievance cases for the grievance procedure • Engage in grievance prevention efforts

matters besides one employee's grievance, and may even be the subject of an employee's grievance. To receive the appropriate attention, grievances go through a specific process for resolution.

Union Representation in Grievance Procedures A unionized employee generally has a right to union representation if he or she is being questioned by management and if discipline may result. These rights must be spelled out in the collective agreement. If these *rights* are violated and the employee is dismissed, he or she usually will be reinstated with back pay.

Steps in a Grievance Procedure

Grievance procedures can vary in the number of steps they include. Figure 15-15 shows a typical grievance procedure, which consists of the following steps:

1. The employee discusses the grievance with the union steward (the representative of the union on the job) and the supervisor.
2. The union steward discusses the grievance with the supervisor's manager and/or the HR manager.
3. A committee of union officers discusses the grievance with appropriate company managers.
4. The business agent discusses the grievance with designated company executives or the corporate industrial relations officer.
5. If the grievance is not solved at this stage, it goes to arbitration.[55] An impartial third party may ultimately dispose of the grievance.

Grievance arbitration
Means by which a third party settles disputes arising from different interpretations of a labour contract.

Grievance arbitration is a means by which a third party settles disputes arising from different interpretations of a labour contract. Grievance arbitration decisions issued under labour contract provisions are enforceable. Grievance arbitration includes more than 50 topic areas, with discipline and discharge, safety and health, and security issues being most prevalent.

Figure 15-15 *Steps in a Typical Grievance Procedure*

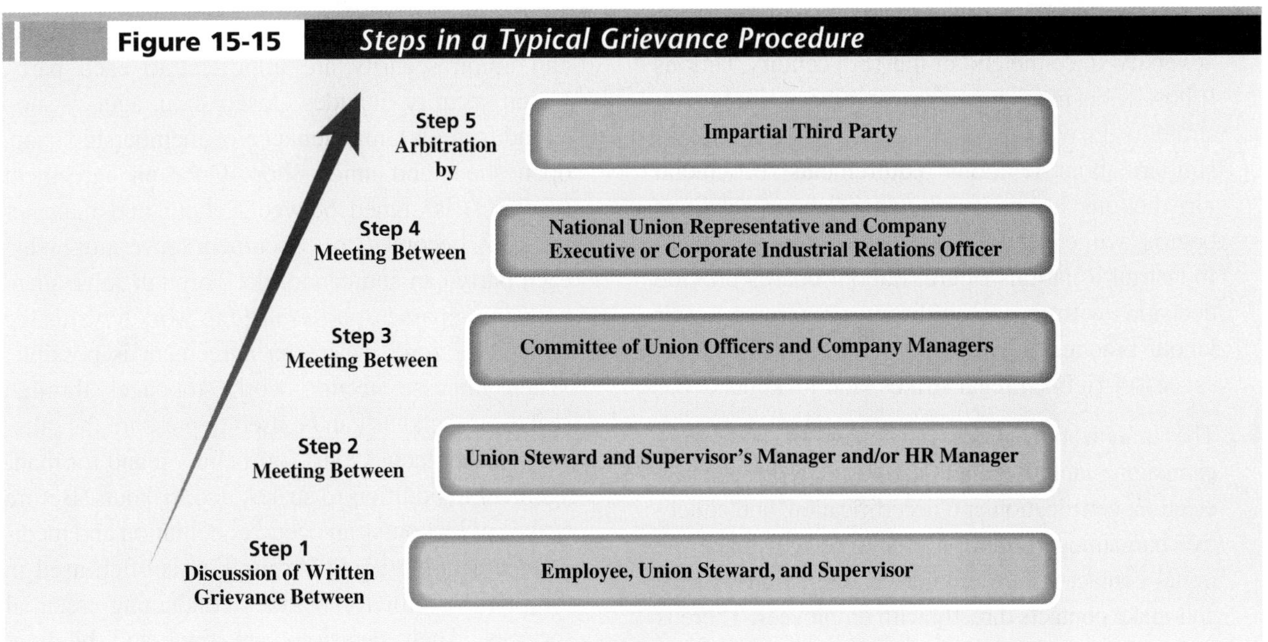

SUMMARY

1 A union is a formal association of workers that promotes the interests of its members through collective action. Workers join unions primarily because of management's failure to address organizational and job-related concerns. The structural levels of Canadian unions include federations, national and international unions, and local unions. Business agents and union stewards work at local levels. There are other alternative forms of union-management arrangements such as employer associations that are not covered under labour relations, but that have agreements that mimic union contracts.

2 In Canada, current union membership as a percentage of the workforce is down dramatically, to compose less than 19 percent of the private sector workforce. While public-sector unions have grown, unions in general have experienced a decline in membership due to geographic, workforce, industrial changes, deregulation, foreign competition, and a larger number of people looking for work. The public sector sits at 75.5-percent membership. In attempts to grow, unions are targeting professionals, non-standard and contingent work with part-time workers, and low-skill workers. Labour law in Canada prohibits work stoppages by certain workers. Back-to-work legislation is used for public-sector workers conducting essential services. The history of unions in the Canada indicates that they primarily focus on wages, hours, and working conditions.

3 Union recognition in Canada has been fraught with adversity since the end of the 18th century. Unions follow a business unionism or a social unionism strategy. Provincial and federal legislation have similar labour relations requirements. Provincial jurisdictions are covered under labour relations boards, while federal is covered by the Canadian Industrial Relations Board. Labour boards provide decisions with respect to disputes regarding unfair labour practices, certification and decertifications, successor rights, illegal strikes, and lockouts.

4 The unionization process includes an organizing campaign, authorization cards, a representation election, certification and decertification, and collective bargaining. Either an employee will make the initial contact with the union, or the union will try and make contacts directly with employees. There is increasing use of technology to reach workers. Some jurisdictions have automatic certification of a union if a minimum number of authorization cards are signed by employees. In other jurisdictions in addition to the authorization cards being signed, representation vote is conducted. Appropriate bargaining unit needs to be determined. Management will usually challenge the bargaining unit. During the organizing process both the union and management must not engage in unfair labour practices such as coercing, intimidating, or threatening workers. Employers have a right to express their views. If an unfair labour practice occurs, then the union can automatically be certified. Once a bargaining unit is determined, a first contract must be negotiated with one year of certification.

5 Collective bargaining occurs when management negotiates with representatives of workers over wages, hours, and working conditions. Bargaining relationship can be based on distributive (adversarial), integrative using interest-based bargaining approach toward win-win, attitudinal, or intraorganizational where the needs of workers, union, and employer must be balanced. The bargaining structure is decentralized in Canada. Patterned bargaining makes process more centralized. Concessionary bargaining is increasing. The issues subject to collective bargaining fall into two categories: mandatory and voluntary.

6 The collective bargaining process includes preparation and initial demands, negotiations, and settlement and contract agreement. Management rights and union security are important to each party. Union security includes closed shop, agency shop (Rand formula), maintenance-of-membership shop, open shop, and union shop. Once an agreement (contract) is signed between labour and management, it becomes the document governing what each party can and cannot do. Through subsequent bargaining passes, parties need to work towards the bargaining zone, where an agreement is possible. When impasse occurs, work stoppages through strikes or lockouts can be used to pressure the other party. Other tactics exist for the union and for management in addition to strikes and lockouts. Before strikes or lockouts can occur, conciliation and mediation must be utilized. Arbitration is often used in the public sector for workers conducting essential services. Their decisions are final and binding.

Union-management cooperation has been beneficial in a number of situations, although care must be taken to avoid violations of labour legislation.

7 Grievances express workers' written dissatisfactions or differences in contract interpretations. Grievances usually follow a formal process to resolution. A grievance procedure begins with the first-level supervisor and may end—if the grievance is not resolved along the way—with arbitration. There are typically five steps in the grievance process.

KEY TERMS

Agency shop, p. 578
Arbitration, p. 582
Bargaining unit, p. 567
Boycotting, p. 584
Business agent, p. 555
Business unionism, p. 563
Closed shop, p. 578
Co-determination, p. 553
Collective bargaining, p. 573
Complaint, p. 588
Conciliation, p. 582
Craft union, p. 554
Decertification, p. 572
Federation, p. 555
First contract arbitration, p. 572
Grievance, p. 588
Grievance arbitration, p. 589
Grievance procedures, p. 588
Industrial union, p. 554
Lockout, p. 585
Maintenance-of-membership shop, p. 578
Management rights, p. 578
Mandatory terms, p. 577
Mediation, p. 582
Open shop, p. 578
Picketing, p. 584
Ratification, p. 581
Salting, p. 566
Social unionism, p. 563
Strike, p. 583
Union, p. 551
Union authorization card, p. 567
Union certification, p. 572
Union density, p. 556
Union security provisions, p. 578
Union shop, p. 578
Union steward, p. 555
Voluntary terms, p. 577

REVIEW AND APPLICATION QUESTIONS

1 Discuss the following statement: "If management gets a union, it deserves one."

2 Why are unions declining in Canada?

3 Explain the roles of the various labour relations jurisdictions in Canada.

4 Suppose a co-worker just brought you a union leaflet urging employees to sign an authorization card. What do you expect to happen from this point on?

5 Describe the various bargaining relationships that might exist in union negotiating? Search the Internet to find examples of when these relationships have occurred in the past.

6 Explain the collective bargaining process in Canada.

7 Describe the grievance procedure. Would this procedure be appropriate for non-union organizations? Why or why not?

EXPERIENTIAL EXERCISES

1. As the HR manager, you have heard rumours about potential efforts to unionize your warehouse employees. Develop a policy that will outline what managers can say to employees regarding this process. Be sure to review relevant labour legislation in your jurisdiction.
2. Search the Internet for three different companies' grievance procedure. What are the similarities and differences between them? Which of the procedures is the best/worst and why?

3. You are to contact a labour union head office in your area and plan to meet with a union official from that office. Develop a set of questions to ask them about organizing attempts. For example: What are some of the problems they encounter when an organizing drive takes place? What are some of the more difficult cases they have had to handle? Find out as much about union organizing as you can. Prepare a written report on your findings, and prepare a five-minute Powerpoint presentation for class.

4. As an organization you have an unwritten policy of "no unions allowed." Therefore, all screening for new employees makes attempts to uncover anything about potential union desires the individual may have. You have thus hired the services of a consultant to devise a psychological test that will let you know whether a potential employee is a union advocate or not. You plan to use this test as a screening tool, meaning that if the individual shows a desire to unionize then you will not hire them. You've pointed out to your manager that this may not be legal but she has indicated that she doesn't believe this is a problem. What should you do if this policy is put in place? Is it a problem? Is it legal?

LEARNING REVIEW

To check your knowledge of the chapter, review the following. (Answers after the case.)

1 What is the primary determinant of whether or not employees unionize?
   a. Management
   b. Government
   c. Co-workers
   d. Union organizers

2 Unions have attempted to counteract the overall decline in membership by:
   a. reducing membership dues and initiation fees
   b. organizing manufacturing workers in less-developed countries
   c. organizing professionals
   d. attempting to unionize contingent and part-time workers

3 A yellow dog contract is a(n):
   a. Dues check-off
   b. Good faith bargaining agreement
   c. Employment agreement
   d. Union clause

4 In determining an appropriate bargaining unit, what will the labour board not consider?
   a. Wages
   b. Physical location
   c. Number of owners in the group
   d. Industry groupings

5 What is the most significant aspect of collective bargaining?
   a. To reach a first contract within two years of gaining union recognition.
   b. It is a continuing process that does not end immediately upon achieving a contract agreement.
   c. To require that employers bargain in good faith with union representatives.
   d. Ensures that strike mandates are fulfilled.

6 Which of the following bargaining issues would require either party to take illegal action?
   a. Requiring employees to take annual physical exams.
   b. Giving preference to union members when hiring employees.
   c. Management and unions negotiating before setting product prices.
   d. Requiring management to deduct union dues from employee payroll cheques.

7 "I should be given the opportunity for a transfer because I'm higher in seniority" is an example of:
   a. a complaint
   b. a grievance
   c. Both a and b
   d. neither a nor b

CASE

MANAGEMENT AND UNION WORKING TOGETHER

The British Columbia Association (BCAA) is an affiliate of the Canadian Automobile Association that primarily operates an emergency roadside service to its members. BCAA also employs travel agents and sales agents who specialize in a variety of insurance products. In 1997, a group of employees at various locations signed union cards with the possible fear of outsourcing due to recent business changes. After 90 years of operations, this was the first attempt to unionize employees at BCAA. According to Vern Oster, manager of employee relations, the certification process "was a brutal period in BCAA's life: months of legal battles and public bloodletting that resulted in upset and confused customers, as well as increased staff stress." In November 1997, the Labour Relations Board certified Local 378 of the Office and Professional Employees International Union as the bargaining agent for ten of BCAA's 21 sales centres, and later for a group of staff members at the emergency roadside offices.

The negotiations that took place after the certification were an even more painful process for both sides. The months of meetings, negotiations, and hearings before the Labour Relations Board led to a year-long strike. When the strike ended, the two sides continued to distrust each other. However, as Oster points out, "this approach was not only exceedingly unproductive it was also very costly for both sides to maintain."

The first step to building a better relationship between the two sides was the appointment of new representatives as key contacts. These individuals all had successful experiences with collaborative conflict resolution and decided that it would be best if the two sides try to trust each other slowly. Communication was improved by implementing regular meetings (on a bi-weekly basis) that would defuse any growing concerns before they became grievances. Also, a commitment was made to give a "heads-up" on any significant issues such as a planned change to the workforce. In two years, the number of formal grievances dropped by 70 percent.

The two sides have continued down this path of cooperation and trust though the establishment of various programs. With the assistance of the union, BCAA introduced an attendance management program that presumes an employee absence is legitimate unless there is evidence that proves its illegitimacy. In its first year of implementation, absenteeism dropped by 20 percent. After the attacks on the World Trade Centre in 2001, the travel industry experienced a slump. Instead of laying off a large portion of staff (which many travel agencies did), BCAA worked with the union to cut back on discretionary spending all across the business and asked for voluntary reductions in the employees' workweek. These actions resulted in staff and union support as well as a minimization in the need for layoffs that were only on a temporary basis.

The development in trust and communication has led to few formal grievances (four in 12 months). In contrast to the first set of negotiations that took two years to complete, the renegotiation of two collective agreements took only ten weeks to complete. The BCAA and the union (which is now the Canadian Office and Professional Employees Union) have built a solid working relationship.[56]

Questions

1. Why do you feel this arrangement is working so well?
2. If the organization is working out its differences, why is a union needed at all? Be prepared to debate this in class. The class will break up into two groups: One group will represent the union view, and the other will represent the company view.

Learning Review Answers: 1. a 2. d 3. c 4. c 5. b. 6. b 7. c

THE AIR UP THERE

This video clip about the Weyerhaeuser Pulp and Paper Mill in Dryden, Ontario, illustrates how the implementation of the proper safety measures is not always enough to protect workers. The Air Emissions Project (which began in 2002) correlated with a rise in employee illness. In 2003, a Dryden hospital reported that 140 workers were taken to emergency with the same symptoms that included headaches, dizziness, and nausea. Many employees were reluctant to report their symptoms because they believed that they would be perceived as "troublemakers."

Glen Drews worked as a contract electrician on the Air Emissions Project and was a health and safety representative at Weyerhaeuser. He felt he had the responsibility to protect his fellow workers and as a result he assembled a logbook of all the incidents that took place in the mill. He believed that a "collective voice" was needed in order for the company to take further measures to protect its employees.

The video clip follows Drews's efforts as well as describing both the emotional and physical trauma suffered by the mill's employees. Although there have been 400 Weyerhaeuser employees who have registered with the Occupational Health Clinic for Ontario Workers (OHCOW), there is still no factual link between their illness and the conditions at the mill during the Air Emissions Project.[1]

Questions

1. The employees at Weyerhaeuser were reluctant to report their illnesses due to a fear that they would be perceived negatively throughout the industry. How can a company like Weyerhaeuser encourage its employees to speak up and use their rights in the workplace?
2. Do you believe that a workplace fatality would have made Weyerhaeuser re-evaluate its safety measures? Why or why not?
3. Discuss the emotional impact on the employees at Weyerhaeuser. Do you believe that the emotional trauma has been more detrimental than the physical trauma? Discuss.

YOUNG BLOOD

This video highlights the move for unions to target young workers in order to ensure their future survival. Since the average age of a union member is 47, there is the strong possibility that the number of unionized employees will begin to diminish as the baby boom generation retires.

Only 15 percent of workers who are 15–24 years of age have joined a union. Many young workers are employed in traditionally non-unionized employment sectors (such as retail). It is believed that unions should move into employment sectors where young workers are prevalent in order to continue to protect employees throughout Canada.[2]

Questions

1. In what ways will unionization benefit young workers across Canada?
2. What do you think are the reasons that unions have traditionally been uninviting to young workers?

Notes

Chapter 1

1. Survey of Employment and Payrolls and Hours, Industry Canada 2004, www.statscan.ca.
2. Canadian Federation of Independent Business, "Building on Canada's Strength: Small Business Outlook & Budget Priorities for 2003," January 9, 2003, 1–24.
3. Lisa M. Aldisent, *Valuing People! How Human Capital Can Be Your Strongest Asset,* (Chicago: Dearborn Trade Publishing, 2002).
4. For a useful overview of human capital, see Leslie A. Weatherly, "Human Capital—The Elusive Asset," *SHRM Research Quarterly,* March 2003.
5. Bassi, "Human Capital Advantage: Developing Metrics for the Knowledge Era," Spring 2001 www.linezine.com; and Ramona D'Zinkowski, "The Measurement and Management of Intellectual Capital," *Management Accounting,* 78 (2000), 32–36.
6. Robert S. Kaplan and David P. Norton, "Measuring the Strategic Readiness of Intangible Assets," *Harvard Business Review,* February 2004, 52–60.
7. Alan P. Brache, "Managing Human Capabilities," *Journal of Organizational Excellence,* 22 (2003), 61.
8. *Human Capital Management: The CFO's Perspective* (New York: Mercer Human Resource Consulting, 2003).
9. Richard Finn, "Human-Capital Management (HCM)," *Human Resource Management International Digest,* 11 (2003), 2.
10. Christopher J. Collins and Kevin D. Clark, "Strategic Human Resource Practices, Top Management Team Social Networks, and Firm Performance," *Academy of Management Journal,* 46 (2003), 740–751.
11. Craig Alexander and Eric Lascelles, "Canadian Business Goes Global for Growth: Globalization: Peril or Panacea for Canadian Business?" TD Bank Financial Group, June 14, 2004, 1–23.
12. Bombardier, www.bombardier.com/index.jsp.
13. Anthony Goerzen and Paul W. Beamish, "The Changing Characteristics of Japanese Direct Investment in Canada: Japanese Investment in Canada in a Global Context," Asia Pacific Foundation of Canada, March 2005, 1–20.
14. IDC Presentation: Translating Outsourcing Success into Business Value, February 18, 2003.
15. David Ticoll and PWC, "A Fine Balance: The Impact of Offshore IT Services on Canada's IT Outsourcing," PricewaterhouseCoopers LLP Canada, 2004; Robert Scott, David Ticoll and Madhav Murti, "A Fine Balance: The Buying and Selling of Canada," PricewaterhouseCoopers LLP Canada, 2005, www.pwc.com/ca,
16. *Competitive Alternatives: KPMG's Guide to International Costs,* 2006 Edition, www.CompetitveAnalysis.com
17. *Competitive Alternatives: KPMG's Guide to International Costs,* 2004 Edition, www.CompetitveAnalysis.com.
18. "Trends in the Offshoring of IT Jobs," Prism Economics and Analyses, Software Human Resource Council (SHRC), April 2004, 1–30.
19. Ibid., p. 6.
20. "The Bombing of Air India Flight 182," *CBC News Online,* May 1, 2006, www.cbc.ca/news/background/airindia.
21. Statistics Canada, www.statscan.ca.
22. Association of Universities and Colleges of Canada, "Advanced Skills for the Knowledge Economy," 2002, 1–3, www.aucc.ca.
23. The Changing Profile of Canada's Labour Force 2001 Census: Analysis Series, Statistics Canada, www.statscan.ca.
24. Education at a Glance (Paris: Organization for Economic Cooperation and Development, 2003); Government of Canada, "Knowledge Matters: Skills and Learning for Canadians," September 23, 2005, 1–8, www11.sdc.gc.ca/sl-ca/doc/summary.shtml.
25. "Multiculturalism," *Canadian Heritage,* January 20, 2004, www.pch.gc.ca/progs/multi/what-multi_e.cfm
26. Martin Collacott, Canada's Immigration Policy: The Need for Major Reform, The Fraser Institute, September 2002.
27. The Changing Profile of Canada's Labour Force 2001 Census: Analysis Series, Statistics Canada, www.statscan.ca.
28. Government of Canada—Canadian Heritage, "Canadian Diversity: Respecting our Differences," January 20, 2004, 1–8, www.pch.gc.ca/progs/multi/respect_e.cfm?nav=2.
29. "Europe Looking to Women for Declining Work Force," *Omaha World-Herald,* December 22, 2003, D1; Statistics Canada, www.statscan.ca.
30. Jean-Phillipe Cotis, "Population Aging, Facing the Challenge," *OECD Observer,* September, 2003.
31. Judy Orr, "Job Rotations Give Future Leaders the Depth They Need," *Canadian HR Reporter,* January 30 2006, p. 17.
32. Charles Fishman, "The Wal-Mart You Don't Know," *Fast Company,* December 2003, 68.
33. *Tough Times, Tougher HR* (New York: Towers-Perrin, 2003).
34. "Internal HR: Outsourcing Growth," *Workforce Management,* December 2003, 89; and Beth McConnell, "Small Majority of Companies Outsource Some HR Duties," *HR News,* August 14, 2003, www.shrm.org/hrnews.
35. Uyen Vu, "HR's Future in Outsourcing Era," *Canadian HR Reporter,* April 10, 2006.
36. Brieger Peter, "HR Joins Outsourcing Trend: Communication Crucial: Keep Core Human Resources Work Inhouse: CEO," *National Post,* May 7, 2003, FP16.
37. Beth Rosenthal, "WestJet Lands top Talent by Outsourcing Recruiting Software," OutsourcingCanada.Com, August 2005, 1–4, www.outsourcing-canada.com/westjet.html.
38. Allen Halcrow, "A 360-Degree View of HR," *Workforce,* June 2002, 28–34.
39. Dina M. Cox and Channing H. Cox, "At the Table," *Workspan,* November 2003, 21–23.
40. *The National Post,* "We Want to be the Best," April 18, 2005, JV6-JV7.
41. Theresa Minton-Eversole, "HR Must Forge Partnerships . . .," *HR News,* October 10, 2003, www.shrm.org/hrnews.
42. Vera N. Held, "Huskey's Andree Briere on Productivity and Stress-Free Employees," *HR Professional,* August/September, 2003, 19–25.

43. Based on Edward E. Lawler III and Susan A. Mohrman, "HR as a Strategic Partner: What Does It Take to Make It Happen?" *Human Resource Planning,* 26 (2003), 15–28.
44. "BC Retailer Team up to Reduce Workplace Accidents," *Canadian HR Reporter,* October 27, 2003, www.hrreporter.com.
45. The authors acknowledge the assistance of Tim Kitely, Christine Lange, and Sanjeev Tina in providing research and content suggestions on HR technology.
46. *HR on the Web: The Investment Is Paying Off* (New York: Towers-Perrin, 2003).
47. "The Evolution of Workforce Technologies," Trend Watcher, January 23, 2004.
48. Based on "Detailed Business Case for Implementing a Human Resource Management System Strategy," compiled and presented by EIMS Project Core Team. April 2002.
49. Kristen B. Frasch, "Coca-Cola Talent Leader Shares Story of a Self-Service 'Soft Sell'," October 13, 2003, www.workindex.com.
50. "Cedar Workforce Technologies Survey," December 1, 2003, www.thecedargroup.com.
51. "Managing with Soul: Combining Corporate Integrity with the Bottom Line," November 14, 2003, www.workindex.com.
52. Department of Justice, Bill S-21, "The Corruption of Foreign Public Officials Act: A Guide," April 24, 2003, http://canada.justice.gc.ca/en/dept/pub/cfpoa/guide5.html
53. Jakob Svensson, "Who Must Pay Bribes and How Much? Evidence from a Cross-Section of Firms," *Quarterly Journal of Economics,* 118 (2003), 207.
54. Claire D'Souza, "An Inference of Gift-Giving Within Asian Business Culture," *Asia Pacific Journal of Marketing and Logistics,* 15 (2003), 27–39.
55. For a more in-depth discussion of HR ethical issues, see Linda Gravett, *HRM Ethics: Perspectives for a New Millennium* (Cincinnati: Atomic Dog Publishing, 2003).
56. Michelle R. Greenwood, "Ethics and HRM: A Review and Conceptual Analysis," *Journal of Business Ethics,* March 2002, 261–279.
57. "Survey Examines Relationship Between HR and Ethics," *HR News,* www.shrm.org/hrnews; other surveys; and personal interviews with selected HR professionals.
58. Adapted from Richard Stolz, "What HR Will Stand For," *Human Resource Executive,* January 2003, 20–28.
59. *National Business Ethics Survey* (Washington, DC: Ethics Resource Center, 2003).
60. Margaret M. Clark, "Corporate Ethics Programs Make a Difference, but Not the Only Difference," *HR Magazine,* July 2003, 36.
61. The summarization of the five competencies is based on Wayne Brockbank and Dave Ulrich, *Competencies for the New HR Guidebook* (Alexandria, VA: Society for Human Resource Management, 2003).
62. Shari Cauldron, "HR Is Dead, Long Live HR," *Workforce,* January 2003, 26–30.
63. Canadian Council of Human Resources Associations (CCHRA), www.cchra-cchra.ca/en3/standards/programme_normes.asp.
64. Susan J. Wells, "The Path Taken," *HR Magazine,* July 2003, 50–54.
65. Annually, SHRM and Mercer Human Resource Consultants do a compensation survey of HR jobs. For details see Human Resource Management Positions, part of the Mercer Benchmark Database at www.shrm.org or www.mercer.com.
66. Canadian Council of Human Resources Associations (CCHRA), www.cchra-cchra.ca/en3/standards/programme_normes.asp.
67. Based on Patrick J. Kiger, "HR Proves Its Value," *Workforce,* March 2002, 28–33.

Chapter 2

1. "CEOs Talk about HR Strategies: Gauging HR's Contribution," *Canadian HR Reporter*, May 23, 2005. Used by permission of Thomson Carswell.
2. Patrick M. Wright and Gary C. McMahan, "Theoretical Perspectives for Strategic Human Resource Management," *Journal of Management,* June 1992, Vol. 18, No. 2, 295–320.
3. HRSDC, www.hrsdc.gc.ca/en/lp/spila/wlb/awlbc/04canadian_response.shtml.
4. Eric Andrew, "Most Canadian Companies Are Still Not Treating HR as a Serious Strategy," *Workspan*, February 2006 p. 14.
5. "CEOs Talk about HR Strategies: Gauging HR's Contribution," *Canadian HR Reporter*, May 23, 2005.
6. Michael Porter, "What is Strategy," *Harvard Business Review*, November-December 1996, 68; Michael Porter, "Competitive Advantage: Creating a Sustaining Superior Performance," Chapter 2, "The Value Chain and Competitive Advantage," *New York Free Press*, 1985, 33–61.
7. Raymond E. Miles, Charles C. Snow, Alan D. Meyer and Henry L. Coleman Jr., "Organizational Strategy, Structure and Process," *Academy of Management Review,* 3 (1978), 546–562.
8. Kenneth R. Andrews, "The Concept of Corporate Strategy," Homewood, Illinois, *Irving Publishing,* (1987), 13.
9. Michael Porter, "What is Strategy," *Harvard Business Review*, November-December 1996, 68.
10. J. Barney, "Firm Resources and Sustained Competitive Advantage," *Journal of Management*, 17 (1991) 19–120.
11. Raymond E. Miles, Charles C. Snow, Alan D. Meyer and Henry L. Coleman Jr., "Organizational Strategy, Structure and Process," *Academy of Management Review,* 3 (1978), 546–562.
12. Charles W. L. Hill and Gareth R. Jones, Strategic Management Theory: An Integrated Approach, Second Edition, Boston, *Houghton Mifflin Company*, (1992).
13. Anil K. Gupta and Vijay Govindarajan, "Cultivating a Global Mindset," *Academy of Management Executive,* February 2002, 116–126.
14. Canadian Labour and Business Centre: Canadian Policy Research Networks for Task Force Two, "A Physician's Human Resource Strategy for Canada: Task Force Two," February 2005, 1–258.
15. K. S. Lee, G. H. Lim, and W. S. Lim, "Family Business Succession: Appropriation Risk and Choice of Successor," *Academy of Management Review,* 28 (2003), 657–666.
16. Elini T. Stavrou, "Leadership Succession in Owner-Managed Firms Through the Lens of Extraversion," *International Small Business Journal,* 21 (2003), 331.
17. Pramodita Sharma, James J. Chrisman, and Jess H. Chua, "Predictions of Satisfaction with the Succession Process in Family Firms," *Journal of Business Venturing,* 18 (2003), 667.
18. EKOS Research Associates, "2002 National Survey of Engineers," p. 1–14, June 23, 2003.
19. Public Service Commission of Canada, *"Executive Succession Reconsidered: Planning for Public Service Renewal,"* Labour Market and Research Unit Research Directorate, Cat. No. SC3-94/2002, October 2002, 1–61; Paul Waldie, "RCMP Hikes Pensions to Boost Recruitment," Workopolis.com, July 7, 2003; Canadian Association of Police Boards, "Recruitment and Retention Strategies," 2002 Conference; Doug Bruce and Derek Picard, "Succession Can Breed Success: SME Succession and Canada's Economic Prosperity," CFIB Research, June 2005.
20. Terence Mitchell et al., "How to Keep Your Best Employees: Developing an

Effective Retention Policy," *Academy of Management Executive,* 15, (2001), 96–107.
21. Aventis Pastuer, "Sustaining Retention, BHRC document, p. 12.
22. Maryann Hammers, "Starbucks Is Pleasing Employees and Pouring Profits," *Workforce Management,* October 2003, 58–59; and Maryann Hammers, "Babies Deliver a Loyal Workforce," *Workforce,* April 2003, 52; Robert Levering and Milton Moskowitz, "100 Best Companies to Work For," *Fortune,* January 20, 2003, 127–150.
23. Eiren Esen, "Job Security Survey," *SHRM Research,* June 2003, 22.
24. Steve Bates, "Getting Engaged," *HR Magazine,* February 2004, 44–51.
25. Hewitt Survey, www.hewitt.com/bestemployerws/caanda_p._4_pdf.
26. Ibid, p. 4.
27. "Hello Mr. Mom: 44 Per Cent of Working Dads Would Give Up Breadwinner Role to Spend More Time With Kids," *Canadian HR Reporter*, June 20, 2006.
28. Hewitt Survey, www.hewitt.com/bestemployerws/caanda_p._4_pdf
29. Karen Lee, "Overworked Employees More Likely to Fall Ill and Leave," *Benefits News,* June 15, 2001, 1.
30. Janice Cooney, "Mentoring Finding a Perfect Match for People Development," Conference Board of Canada.
31. "New Solution to Improving Employee Retention by as Much as 25%," *HR.Com,* March, 2003, 1, www.hr.com.
32. Ishak Saporta and Moshe Farjoun, "The Relationship Between Actual Promotions and Turnover Among Professional and Managerial-Administrative Occupational Groups," *Work and Occupations,* 30 (2003), 255–280.
33. Mary Elizabeth Burke et al., "SHRM 2003 Benefits Survey," *SHRM Research,* June 2003, 1–56.
34. Hewitt Survey, www.hewitt.com/bestemployerws/caanda_p._4_pdf.
35. David Jones and Daniel Skarlicki, "The Relationship Between Perceptions of Fairness and Voluntary Turnover Among Retail Employees," *Journal of Applied Social Psychology,* 33 (2003), 1226–1243.
36. Sue Shellenbarger, "Work and Family," *The Wall Street Journal,* February 20, 2002, B1.
37. Marcie Levine and Peter Tobia, "Take Stock Then Take Action," *HR.Com,* January 6, 2004, 1–5, *www.hr.com.*
38. Jean Fulton, "Canadian Workers are Third Most Motivated and Committed: Major Global Study, ISR, www.isrinsight.com; ISR, "Engaged Employees Drive the Bottom Line," ISR, www.isrsurveys.com.
39. Fay Hansen, "Weighing the Truth of Exit Interviews," *Workforce,* December 2002, 37; and Theresa Sweeney, "Exit Interviews," *Credit Union Management,* November 2002, 38–39.
40. Gary Burkett, "Employee Engagement," *Canadian HR Reporter*, September 12, 2005, 7–11.
41. Wayne F. Cascio, "Strategies for Responsible Restructuring," *Academy of Management Executive,* August 2002, 80–91.
42. *"Ford Extends Buyout,"* The Windsor Star, Thursday, April 13, 2006.
43. Susan R. Silvano, "The HR Executive's Strategic Role in Outplacement," *Human Resource Executive,* January 26, 2004, http://workindex.com.
44. *Corporate Social Responsibility Report,* Aviva Canada, www.aviva.com/csr05/index.asp?pageid=380, 2005
45. David Henry, "Mergers: Why Most Big Deals Don't Pay Off," *Business Week,* October 14, 2002, 60–70.
46. Jane Bryson, "Managing HRM Risk in a Merger," *Employee Relations,* 25 (2003), 14.
47. Teresa A. Daniel and Gary S. Metcalf, *The Management of People in Mergers and Acquisitions* (Westport, CT: Quorum, 2001).
48. Elissa D. Giffords and Richard P. Dina, "Changing Organizational Cultures," *Administration in Social Work,* 27 (2003), 69.
49. Steven H. Applebaum and Joy Gandell, "A Cross-Method Analyses of the Impact of Culture and Communications upon a Health-Care Merger," *Journal of Management,* 22 (2003), 370.
50. Christopher Cornell, "The Perfect Blend," *Human Resource Executive,* January 2004, 44–49.
51. *"Corporate Information Executive Speeches,"* Toronto Dominion Bank, June 12, 2002, www.td.com/communicate/speeches/12june02.jsp.
52. René Morissette, *"Are Good Jobs Disappearing in Canada?"* Cat. No. 11F0019MIE2005239, Business and Labour Market Analysis Division, Statistics Canada, January 26, 2005.
53. "Alberta Labour Shortage Draining Civil Service," New Briefs, *Canadian HR Reporter*, January 30, 2006.
54. How to measure HR activities by areas is described in detail in Jac Fitz-Enz and Barbara Davidson, *How to Measure Human Resources* (New York: McGraw-Hill, 2002).
55. Cindy Waxes, "Inside Jobs," *Human Resource Executive,* March 2, 2003, 36–37. Used by permission.
56. Jay Jamrog and Miles Overholt, "Building a Strategic HR Function: Continuing the Evaluation," (unpublished paper, Tampa, FL, 2004).
57. For details on these stages, see Brian E. Becher, Mark A. Huselid, and Dave Ulrich, *The HR Scorecard: Linking People, Strategy, and Performance* (Boston: Harvard Business School Press, 2001).
58. Robert S. Kaplan and David P. Norton, *The Strategy-Focused Organization: How Balanced Scorecard Companies Thrive in the New Business Environment* (Boston: Harvard Business School Press, 2001).
59. Steven Salterio and Allan Webb, "The Balanced Scorecard," *CA Magazine,* August 2003, 39–41.
60. The Balanced Scorecard Institute, www.balancedscorecard.org.
61. Christopher D. Itner, David F. Lancher, and Marshell W. Meyer, "Subjectivity and the Weighting of Performance Measures: Evidence from a Balanced Scorecard," *The Accounting Review,* 78 (2003), 725–758.
62. Brian E. Becker and Mark A. Huselid, "Measuring HR? Benchmarking is Not the Answer," *HR Magazine,* December 2003, 57–61.
63. Wayne Cascio, *Costing Human Resources,* 4th ed. (Cincinnati: South-Western College Publishing, 2003), 62–70.
64. Adapted from Clarence Lochhead and Alex Stephens, "Employee Retention, Labour Turnover and Knowledge Transfer: Case Studies from the Canadian Plastics Sector," April 2004, pp. 45–49. Used by permission of the Canadian Plastics Sector Conucil.

Part 1 Video Cases

1."Keeping Them," *Venture,* March 24, 1998, 6:30.

Chapter 3

1. Linda Bramble, "A Voice of Compassion Suzanne Rochon Burnett," *Niagara Magazine*, April/May 2005; The Métis Nation of Ontario, April 4, 2006, www.metisnation.org/news/06_apr_Suzanne_Rochon.html, Canadian Council for Aboriginal Business, February 2006, www.ccab.com/inductees.htm; and www.niagaramagazine.ca/articles/May2005/Niagara%20People/niagara_people_May_2005.htm.
2. Constitution Act, 1982(1), Schedule B, Part I, *Canadian Charter of Rights and Freedoms.*
3. "Unions Challenge Bill 29 Before the Supreme Court of Canada," International Union of Operating Engineers, February 10, 2006.
4. "Unions Challenge Bill 29, B.C.'s Contract-Busting Law," NUPGE, May 29, 2002; "Unions Challenge Bill 29 Before the Supreme Court of Canada,"

International Union of Operating Engineers, February 10, 2006.
5. "Equality Rights Definitions," New *Brunswick Human Rights Commission*, January 31, 2005.
6. "Guideline on BFOQ's, BFQ's and the Duty to Accommodate," *New Brunswick Human Rights Commission*, January 31, 2005.
7. "Policy on Height and Weight Requirements," Ontario Human Rights Commission, March 10, 2006.
8. Frank Schmidt, "The Problem of Group Differences in Ability Test Scores in Employment Selection," *Journal of Vocational Behaviour,* 1988, *V33,* 272–292.
9. Gangaram Singh and Frank Reid, "Are Seniority-Based Layoffs Discriminatory? The Adverse Impact of Layoffs on Designated Groups," *Relations Industrielles,* 1998, Vol. 53, No. 4.
10. Annual Report 2004–2005, "Table 2: Settlements by Ground in Cases Mediated and Conciliated in 2004/2005," *Ontario Human Rights Commission,* 2005.
11. "Canada's Action Plan Against Racism," *Canadian Heritage Multiculturalism,* http://patrimoinecanadien.gc.ca/multi/plan_action_plan/tous_all/index_e.cfm.
12. "Ethnic Diversity Survey: Portrait of a Multicultural Society," *The Daily:* Statistics Canada, Monday, September 29, 2003; "A Canada for All: Canada's Action Plan Against Racism—An Overview," *Department of Canadian Heritage*, 2005.
13. "Case Studies," Alberta Human Rights and Citizenship Commission, 2006.
14. *Central Okanagan School District No. 23 v. Renaud (1992),* 16 C.H.R.R. D/425 (S.C.C.) [Eng./Fr. 17 pp.].
15. "Supreme Court of Canada Reaffirms Commission Position on Religious Rights for Khalsa Sikhs to Wear Ceremonial Kirpans," *Ontario Human Rights Commission*, March 2, 2006.
16. "Understanding Ageism and Age Discrimination," *Ontario Human Rights Commission*, March 11, 2006.
17. "Collective Agreements and Older Workers in Canada," *Government of Canada*, Chapter 5: (Anti)-Discrimination Clauses and Practices, January 12, 2005.
18. "SHRM 2002 Workplace Demographic Trends Survey," *SHRM Research,* September 2002, 6.
19. Jessica Collison, "Older Workers Survey," *SHRM Research,* June 2003, 1–34.
20. "As Bill Gates Hits 50, Amicus Survey Reveals Ageism Rife in IT," *Labour Research Department,* October 28, 2005, www.amicustheunion.org.
21. C. Loughlin and J. Barling, "Young Workers Work Values, Attitudes and Behaviours," *Journal of Occupational and Organizational Psychology,* 2001, Vol. 74, No. 543–558.
22. M.J. (Peggy) O'Brien and Deborah Cushing, "Mandatory Retirement," BC HRMA Conference, Vancouver B.C., October 5, 2005; *McKinney v. University of Guelph*, [1990] 3 S.C.R. 229 [*McKinney*]; *Harrison v. University of British Columbia*, [1990] 3 S.C.R. 451 [*Harrison*].
23. *"Nearing the End of Mandatory Retirement in Canada?"* Fasken Martineau, n.d.
24. *Janzen v. Platy Enterprises Ltd.* (1989), 10 C.H.R.R. D/6205 (S.C.C.) [Eng./Fr. 31 pp.].
25. *Brooks v. Canada Safeway Ltd.* (1989) 59 D.L.R. 321.
26. *Vancouver Rape Relief Society v. British Columbia (Human Rights Commission),* [2000] B.C.J. No. 1143 (QL).
27. Guide to Human Rights Code, *Ontario Human Rights Commission,* May 26, 1999, p. 24; Nancy A. Eber, "Same-Sex Benefits Update: Ontario Government Reacts to Supreme Court of Canada Decision by Passing," November 1, 1999.
28. Gregory F. McGinnis, " Courts Say: Don't Fire the Wife for the Sins of her Husband," Stringer, Brisbin, Humphrey Management Lawyers, February 10, 2003.
29. "Family Status and the Ontario Human Rights Code," *Ontario Human Rights Commission,* n.d.
30. Paul Moloney and Vanessa Lu, "New Rules Urged to Curb Nepotism: T.O. Integrity Chief Gets Tough on Hiring – Wants Relatives Excluded from top Jobs," The Toronto Star, A1:A19.
31. *Brossard (Ville) v. Québec (Comm. des droits de la personne)* (1988), 10 C.H.R.R. D/5515 (S.C.C.) [Eng./Fr. 45 pp.].
32. *Entrop v. Imperial Oil* (1996), O.H.R.B.I.D. No. 30; Imperial Oil v. Entrop (2002) 37. C.H.R.R. D/481 (Ont. C.A.).
33. *Canada (Canadian Human Rights Commission) v. Toronto Dominion Bank* (1998), F.C.J. No. 1036; *Heather French,* "Canadian Federal Court of Appeal Rules Against Workplace Drug Testing," *Institute for a Drug-Free Workplace,* September 11, 1998.
34. "Complaint Process," *Alberta Human Rights and Citizenship Commission*, 2006.
35. "Complaints," *Canadian Human Rights Commission,* December 5, 2005.
36. "Discrimination and Harassment;" http://www.chrc=ccdp.ca/discrimination/what_is_it-en.asp. *Canadian Human Rights Commission.* Reproduced with the permission of the Ministry of Public Works and Government Services, 2006.
37. Louie Rosella, "Five Officers Disciplined for Passing Racist Email," *The Mississauga News*, Friday, May 5, 2006, p. 3.
38. "Sexual Harassment," *Alberta Human Rights Commission*, October 2002.
39. Jana Ritter, "A Corporate Affair: Ruling Love Out of Business," *The Galt Global Review*, February 11, 2003.
40. David Spears, "Can an Office Roman Get You Canned?" *Ottawa Business Journal*, May 27, 2005.
41. "Sexual Orientation Irrelevant in Sex Harassment Claims," *HR News,* November 2002, 6.
42. Excerpted from "Female Firefighters Walk Off Job in B.C. City, Alleging Harassment," CBC News. Used by permission, CBC.ca.
43. Karyn-Siobhan Robinson, *"*Cyber-Sex Permeates the Workplace,*" HR News,* April 2001, 10; *University of British Columbia v. C.U.P.E., Local 2950, 2005,* Carswell, BC 2569, 138 L.A.C. (4th) 358 (B.C. Arb. Bd.).
44. "Unwanted Sexual Attention and Sexual Harassment: Results of A Survey of Canadians," *Canadian Human Rights Commission*, Ottawa: Minister of Supply and Services Canada, 1983, p. 5.
45. "Sexual Assault: Dispelling the Myths," November 25, 2001; "Sexual Harassment in the Workplace," (1992) 7:1 The Reid Report 32.
46. *Shaw* v. *Levac Supply Ltd.* (1990), 14 C.H.R.R. D/36 (Ont. Bd.Inq.) [Eng. 32 pp.].
47. Judge Rosalie S. Abella, Commissioner, *"Equality in Employment: A Royal Commission Report,"* Ottawa: Supply and Services Canada, 1984.
48. Kamil Dib, "Diversity Works," Canadian Business, March 29–April 11, 2004, Vol. 77, Issue 2, 53–55.
49. "Guidelines for the Employment Equity Act and Regulations," *HRSDC*, March 3, 2003.
50. Section 2, Employment Equity Act, 1995.
51. "Federal Contractor's Program," *HRSDC*, May 7, 2003.
52. Abigail B. Bakan and Audrey Kobayashi, "Employment Equity Policy in Canada: An Interprovincial Comparison," *Status of Women Canada,* March 2000.
53. Government of Ontario, "An Act to Repeal Jobs Quotas and to Restore Merit-based Employment Practices in Ontario," *Statutes of Ontario*, Chapter 4: 1499–1503. December 14, 1995.
54. Kimberley Bachmann, Kamal Dib and Janice Cooney, "The Impact of Employment Equity on Corporate

Success in Canada," *The Conference Board of Canada*, March 2003.
55. "Guidelines for the Employment Equity Act and Regulations," *HRSDC*, March 3, 2003.
56. Based on *2001 Employment Equity Act Annual Report*, Human Resources and Skills Development Canada. Reproduced with the permission of Her Majesty the Queen in Right of Canada 2006.
57. "Guidelines for the Employment Equity Act and Regulations," *HRSDC*, March 3, 2003.
58. Harish Jain, Anil Verma, and Deborah Zinni, "Union Consultation by Employers and Employment Equity," *Human Resources and Skill Development Canada,* April 2003.
59. Tom Blackwell, "White Males Need not Apply: Internal E-mail Reveals Hiring Ban at Public Works," *National Post*, Saturday, November 19, 2005.
60. "Diversity and Employment Equity Fact Sheet: Removing Employment Barriers," *Manitoba Civil Service Commission,* n.d.
61. "2005 Annual Employment Equity Report," *Canadian Human Rights Commission*, May 3, 2006.
62. "*Women in Canada: A Gender-based Statistical Report*, 2005," *Statistics Canada, The Daily,* March 7, 2006.
63. "2005 Catalyst Census of Women Board Directors of the Fortune 500 Shows 10-Year Trend of Slow Progress and Persistent Challenges," *Catalyst,* March 29, 2006.
64. "Glass Ceiling to Boardroom in Place for Women at Global 200 Companies," *Corporate Women Directors Int.*, New York, October 8, 2004.
65. Linda Babcock et al., "Nice Girls Don't Ask," *Harvard Business Review,* October 2003, 14.
66. Kristi Arellano, "Undoing the Glass Ceiling," *The Denver Post,* December 22, 2003, 1E.
67. "Visible Minorities to Top 50% in Toronto, Vancouver by 2017," *CBC News*, June 2005.
68. Canadian Heritage, Canada 2017-Serving Canada's Multicultural Population for the Future- Policy Forum, 2005; "Canada's Performance 2005: The Government of Canada's Contribution," *Treasury Board of Canada Secretariat*, November 23, 2005.
69. "HR's Next Recruiting Challenge: No Diversity Plan; No Workers," *Human Resource Department Management Report,* January 2003, 1–2.
70. "Turn Diversity to Your Advantage," *Research Technology Management,* July 2003, 1–8.
71. "Hours of Diversity Training Has a Positive Bottom Line Impact," *SHRM/Fortune Survey of Diversity Initiatives on the Bottom Line,* in *Managing Training and Development,* July 2001, 1–6; Sheila Cschimpf, "Bottom Line Successes with Diversity Have Turned Employers into Advocates," *Bulletin to Management BNA Inc.,* May 15, 2003, 153–160; and "Nextel Diversity Training Produces an ROI of 163%," *Manager's Training and Development,* February 2003, 1–3.
72. Fay Manson, "Diversity's Business Case: Doesn't Add Up," *Workforce,* April 2003, 28–33.
73. C. W. Von Bergen et al., "Unintended Negative Effects of Diversity Management," *Public Personnel Management,* 31 (2002), 1–12.
74. Martha Frase-Blunt, "Thwarting the Diversity Backlash," *HR Magazine,* June 2003, 137–144.
75. "Brock Raises Awareness of Accessibility for all *P*eople," March 1, 2006. Used by permission.

Chapter 4

1. Lynn A Karoly and Constantin W. A. Panis, *The 21st Century at Work: Forces Shaping the Future Workforce and Workplace in the United States* (Santa Monica, CA: RAND Corporation, 2004).
2. "Special Report: Where Are the Jobs?" *Business Week,* March 22, 2004, 36–53.
3. "Study: Self-Service Is Finally Delivering," *Human Resource Executive,* January 2004, 52.
4. For details, see the International Association of Administrative Professionals, www.iaap-hq.org, and the International Association of Virtual Office Assistants, www.iavoa.com.
5. Figen Calzar, Umit S. Bitici, and Jillian McBryde, "A Business Process Approach to Human Resource Management," *Business Process Management,* 9 (2003), 190.
6. Martin Smith, "Business Process Design: Correlates of Success and Failure," *Quality Management Journal,* 10 (2003), 38–50.
7. Linda Arnison and Peter Miller, "Virtual Teams: A Virtue for the Conventional Team," *Journal of Workplace Learning,* 14 (2002), 166–174.
8. Carla Joinson, "Managing Virtual Teams," *HR Magazine,* June 2002, 69–73.
9. IPM Management Training and Development Corporation, www.work-place.ca.
10. "Put Down That Tool," *The Economist,* January 10, 2004, 55–56.
11. "Canadians Working Longer Hours," *Canadian Press,* Tuesday, May 9, 2006.
12. Acacia Aguirre, Health in Extended Hours Operations: Understanding the Challenges, Implementing Solutions, 2003, www.circadian.com.
13. "Part-Time Work and Family Friendly Practice in Canadian Workplaces" www.statscan.ca.
14. "Sample Job-Sharing Policy and Request Form," www.workforce.com.
15. "Telecommuting Advances Make Snow Days Less Unproductive," *Newsline,* January 28, 2004, www.sunspot.com.
16. Gartner Group Paper: Teleworking: The Quiet Revolution (2005 Update).
17. Keri E. Pearlson and Coral S. Saunders, "There's No Place Like Home: Managing Telecommuting Paradoxes," *Academy of Management Executive,* 14 (2001), 117–128.
18. Jane W. Gibson et al., "Telecommuting in the 21st Century," *Journal of Leadership and Organizational Studies,* 8 (2002), 75–87.
19. Anne Freedman, "Remote Control," *Human Resource Executive,* October 6, 2002, 41–45.
20. Anonymous, "Case Studies on Telework, etc," InnoVisions Canada, www.ivc.ca/studies/canadianstudies.htm; Gerry Blackwell, "Telework," *IT Business Edge,* May 25, 2006, www.itbusiness.ca/it/client/en/EDGE/News.asp?id=39531&bSearch=True.
21. Thiagarajan Srivinivasan and Brian Kleiner, "How to Hire Employees Effectively," *Management Research News,* 25 (2002), 65.
22. W. M. Keyserling et al., "Using Multiple Information Sources to Identify Opportunities for Ergonomic Interventions in Automotive Parts Distribution: A Case Study," *AIHA Journal,* 64 (2003), 690–702.
23. Donna Rodriguez et al., "Developing Competency Models to Promote Integrated Human Resource Practices," *Human Resource Management,* 41 (2002), 309.
24. Marcel R. Vander Klink and Jo Boon, "Competencies: The Triumph of a Fuzzy Concept," *International Journal of Human Resources Development and Management,* 3 (2003), 125.
25. Adapted from Monica Brophy and Tony Kiely, "Competencies: A New Sector," *Journal of European Industrial Training,* 26 (2002), 165–177.
26. For an illustration, see Francesa Sgobbi, "Web Design Skills and Competencies: An Empirical Analysis," *Human Systems Management,* 21 (2002), 115.
27. For a detailed discussion of the job analysis process and methods, see Michael T. Brannick and Edward Levine, *Job Analysis: Methods, Research, and Applications for Human Resource Management in the New Millennium* (Thousand Oaks, CA: Sage Publishing, 2002).

28. Kristen O. Prien, Erich P. Prien, and William Wooten, "Interrater Reliability in Job Analysis," *Public Personnel Management,* 32 (2003), 125–141.
29. I-Wei Chang and Brian H. Kleiner, "How to Conduct Job Analysis Effectively," *Management Research News,* 25 (2003), 73–82.
30. Dana C. Simmons, "Job Analysis, the Missing Ingredient in the Total Rewards Recipe," *Workspan,* September, 2002, 52–55.
31. David H. Jonassen, Wallace H. Hannum and Martin Tessmer, *Handbook of Task Analysis Procedures,* New York: Praeger: 1989.
32. S. A. Fine and W. W. Wiley, *An Introduction to Functional Analysis,* Kalamazoo, MI:W.E. Upjohn Institute for Employment Research, 1991.
33. Jeanne D. Mackiney et al., "Examining the Measurement Equivalence of Paper and Computerized Job Analysis Scales," (paper presented at the 18th annual conference of the Society for Industrial and Organizational Psychology, 2003).
34. Patrick Shannon and Bob Miller, "What's in a Title?" *WorldatWork Journal,* Fourth Quarter, 2003, 26–34.
35. Based on "Japanese Workplaces Drop Formalities to Enhance Output," *Omaha World-Herald,* November 16, 2003, 14A.
36. Merrie Spath, "Expanding Your Job Description," *Risk Management,* October 2002, 56.
37. Kenneth H. Pritchard, "Non-Prejudicial Language for ADA-Compliant Job Descriptions," SHRM Forum, November, 2002, www.shrm.org.
38. Purolator, "Corporate Information," www.purolator.com/media/corporate/faq.html; Uyen Vu, "How Purolator Dealt With Skyrocketing Costs" *Canadian HR Reporter,* March 13, 2006; 19, 5.

Chapter 5

1. John Sullivan, "How to Figure Out if You Are an Employer of Choice," *Workforce Online,* April 2003 www.workforce.com; Eilene Zimmerman, "Hospital President Sparks Groundbreaking Recruiting Campaign," *Workforce Online,* May 2003, www.workforce.com; Frank Jossi, "HR Is Turning into Brands," *Workforce Online,* July 2002, www.workforce.com; Jeff Dahlthorp, "Public Relations and Recruiting," IIRC Article, www.iirc.com/; "Five Great Recruiting Brands," *Workforce Online,* July 2003; "Global Execs Confirm Branding as Key Success Factor," *Right Communique,* Second Quarter 2002, 1; Gene C. George et al., "Building the Brand through People," *Worldatwork Journal,* First Quarter 2004, 39–45; Eva Innes, Jim Lyons and Jim Harris, "The Financial Post 100 Best Companies to Work for in Canada," 2005; and www.ellisdon.com/ed/careers/benefits/.
2. Adapted from John Sumser, "Roses in the Thorn Bush," *Hire.com,* 2003, 4, www.interbiznet.com.
3. John Sumser, "What Is Recruiting?" www.interbiznet.com.
4. Lacey Sheppy, "Recruitment at 35000 ft.," V14N5, CapitalNewsOnline/Carleton School of Journalism, April 2, 2005.
5. Lou Adler, "Why Your Hiring Strategy Must Map Your Business Strategy," February 20, 2004, www.erexchange.com.
6. Jeff Garton, "Strategy Strong Enough to Beat the Competition," *Employment Management Today,* Spring 2002, 2.
7. William McCready, "The First 25 years of the Northwestern Ontario Medical Programme," *Canadian Journal of Rural Medicine,* 2004, 9(2).
8. Industry Canada, "Technology Roadmaps: Competitiveness," stategis.gc.ca, June 1, 2005, http://strategis.ic.gc.ca.
9. Bruce McCracker, *"Canada, The High Touch/High Quality Call Center Outsourcing Option,"* www.outsourcing-Canada.com, 2003; Gary N. Bowen, "Nearshore? Farshore? Which Shore for CRM," www.outsourcing-Canada.com, 2003.
10. Dene Yeaman, "New Opportunities Old Shackles," *China Staff,* nd 7, 51–53, no. 02856020.
11. Martha Frase-Blunt, "Candidate Glut," *HR Magazine,* August 2003, 1.
12. Todd Hunter, "A Mountain of a Recruitment Problem," *Canadian HR Reporter*, December 6, 2004.
13. Rachel King, "The Messy Challenge and Big Payoff of Outsourced Recruiting," *Workforce Management Online,* October 2003, 1.
14. Michelle Martinez, "Recruiting Here and There," *HR Magazine,* September 2002, 96–97.
15. Sara Fister Gold, "Permanent-Hire Program Reduces Turnover," *Workforce,* July 2002, 74–77.
16. "Leased Workers Ask: Who Is the Boss," *Omaha World-Herald,* May 13, 2002, 2D.
17. Harold F. Krieger Jr., "Is There a Professional Employer Organization in Your Future?" *National Public Accountant,* May 5, 2003.
18. John M. Polson, "The PEO Phenomenon," *Employment Law Journal,* Spring 2002, 7–25.
19. Debra Williams, "Temporary Benefits," *Area Development,* October 2002, 36–37.
20. Melynda, Layton, "Are you Hiring an Employee or an Independent Contractor?" Nelligan O'Brien Payne, LLP, September 2005.
21. Adapted from: www.hrtools.com/HREssentials/P05_0683.asp.
22. Ann Macaulay, "IS Awards Celebrate 'Best Employer' of Immigrants," *Canadian HR Reporter,* May 26, 2006.
23. Ruth E. Thaler-Carter, "Diversify Your Recruitment Advertising," *HR Magazine,* June 2001, 1–5.
24. Susan Black and Claire M. Tallarico, "Latest Count of Top Women in Business Shows Little Progress Since Last Catalyst Census," News Release Catalyst Canada, April 27, 2005.
25. Carolyn J. Emerson, Hiromi Matsui and Lorraine Michael, "Women in SETT (Science, Engineering, Trades and Technology)—Building Communities," 10th CCWESTT National Conference, Brock University, St. Catharines, Ontario, June 12, 2004.
26. Lynne Sullivan, "Delivering a Solution for Skills Shortages," *Canadian HR Reporter*, July 12, 2004, 15.
27. Innovative Consulting Group & Insightrix, *Saskatoon Labour Market Assessment Study and Key Implementation Strategies,* March 2002, 1–155.
28. Moira Potter, "A Golden Opportunity for Older Workers to Energize Firms," *Canadian HR Reporter*, April 25, 2005, 13–16.
29. Doug Bruce, "Help Wanted: Results of CFIB Surveys on the Shortage of Qualified Labour," *CFIB Research Results,* February 2001, 1–8.
30. Terry Wager and Lynn Langrock, "Small Firms Offline on Internet Recruitment," *Canadian HR Reporter*, July 14, 2003, 5. Used by permission of Thomson Carswell.
31. Leslie Klaff, "New Internal Hiring Systems Reduce Cost and Boost Morale," *Workforce Management,* March 2004, 76–79; Cindy Waxer, "Inside Jobs," *Human Resource Executive,* June 10, 2003, 1; D. J. Chhabra, "Turbo Hiring," *Human Resource Executive,* March 2, 2004, 56–59.
32. Lin Grensing-Pophal, "Transferring Employees Smoothly Takes Time," *HR Magazine,* September 2001, 1 and Lin Grensing-Pophal, "Rules for Hitting the Road," *HR Magazine,* May 2002, 1.
33. Carroll Lachnit, "Employee Referral Saves Times, Saves Money, Delivers Quantity," *Workforce,* June 2001, 67–72.
34. "Referral Programs that Result in Great Hiring and Retention," *SHRM Forum Employment Management Association,* 2002, www.shrm.org/ema/library.
35. Todd Raphael, "Think Twice: Why Stars Switch Galaxies," *Workforce,* April 2002, 89; and "Re-recruiting Employees," *Practical Accountant,* September 2003, 23–25.

36. Arlise P. McKinney et al., "Recruiters' Use of GPA in Initial Screening Decisions," *Personnel Psychology,* 56 (2003), 823–845.
37. Joe Mullich, "College Recruiting Goes for Niches," *Workforce Management,* February 2004, 1.
38. Carla Joinson, "Red Hot College Recruiting," *Employment Management Today,* Fall 2001, 1–5.
39. Ibid.
40. Phyllis G. Hartman, "Strategic Recruiting by Partnering with Suppliers," *SHRM Forum Employment Management Association,* June 2002, www.shrm.org.
41. Kristine McGhee, *"Career Exposure Project 2005/2006,"* Aboriginal Employment Initiative (AEI), Presentation at Aboriginals and the Canadian Military: Past, Present, Future, June 21-22, 2006, Royal Military College, Canadian Forces Base, Kingston, Ontario.
42. Egon Zehnder, "A Simpler Way to Pay," *Harvard Business Review,* April 2001, 53–60.
43. "The Adoption of Quality Standards in Human-Asset-Intensive Service Organizations: The Case of Executive Search," *Global Competitiveness,* January 2002.
44. Martha Frase-Blunt, "Job Fair Challenges for HR," *HR Magazine,* April 2002, 1–5.
45. Statistics Canada, CANSIM, Table 358-0006, Catalogue no. 56F0004MIE, November 16, 2004; Anne Freedman, "The Web World-Wide," *Human Resource Executive,* March 6, 2002, 44–46.
46. Karen Frankola, "Better Recruiting on Corporate Web Sites," *Workforce Online,* May 2002, www.workforce .com.
47. P. Singh and D. Finn, "The Effects of Information Technology on Recruitment," *Journal of Labour Research,* 24 (2003), 395–408.
48. Gillian Flynn, "E-Recruiting Ushers in Legal Dangers," *Workforce,* April 2002, 70–72.
49. Based on Alison Stein Wellnar, "The Pickup Artists," July 2004, *Workforce Management Online,* www.workforce .com.

Chapter 6

1. Nancy Larin, "Something Can Be Done about Call Centre Turnover," *Canadian HR Reporter*, December 31, 2004. Used by permission of Thomson Carswell.
2. Todd Humber, "Offbeat Interviews," *Canadian HR Reporter*, May 17, 2004.
3. U.S. Department of Labor Employment and Training Administration, "Chapter 3: Understanding the Concepts of Reliability and Validity," 1999.
4. A. Wendell Williams, "'I'm in the Mood for Validity' or 'A Rose by any Other Name,'" *SHRM Forum,* June 2002, 1–2.
5. Richard Buda and Bruce Charnov, "Message Processing in Realistic Recruitment Practices," *Journal of Management Issues,* 25 (2003), 302–316.
6. Hiram C. Barksdale Jr. et al., "The Impact of Realistic Job Previews and Perceptions of Training on Salesforce Performance and Continuance Commitment: A Longitudinal Test," *Journal of Personal Selling and Sales Management,* 23 (2003), 125–138.
7. Bob Calandra, "Boosting Better Hues," *HR Executive,* March 2, 2004, 47–50.
8. Derek Chapman and Jane Webster, "Technology Use in Screening and Selection," *SHRM Forum,* June 2003, 1–5.
9. Neil Anderson, "Applicant and Recruiter Reactions to New Technology in Selection," *International Journal of Selection and Assessment,* 2 (2003), 121–136.
10. Michelle Martinez, "Screening for Quality on the Web," *Employment Management Today,* Winter 2004, 1; and John Mooney, "Pre-employment Testing on the Internet," *Public Personnel Management,* 31 (2002), 41–52.
11. David Arnold and John Jones, "Who the Devil's Applying Now? Companies Can Use Tests to Screen Out Dangerous Job Candidates," *Security Management,* March 2002, 85.
12. "2001 AMA Survey on Workplace Testing," *AMA Research,* www.amanet .org/research.
13. James L. Outtz, "The Role of Cognitive Ability Tests in Employment Selection," *Human Performance,* 15 (2002), 161–171; Nathan R. Kuncel et al., "Academic Performance, Career Potential, Creativity and Job Performance: Can One Construct Predict All?" *Journal of Personality and Social Psychology,* 86 (2004), 148–161; Jesús F. Salgado et al., "International Validity Generalization of GMA and Cognitive Abilities," *Personnel Psychology,* 56 (2003), 573–605; Kevin R. Murphy, "Can Conflicting Perspectives on the Role of g in Personnel Selection Be Resolved?" *Human Performance,* 15 (2002), 173–186.
14. Leaetta M. Hough et al., "Determinants, Detection and Amelioration of Adverse Impact in Personnel Selection Procedures," *International Journal of Selection and Assessment,* 9 (2001), 152–193; Patrick McKay and Dennis Doverspike, "African-Americans' Test Taking Attitudes and Their Effect on Cognitive Ability Test Performance," *Public Personnel Management,* 20 (2001), 67-75; and Dening S. Ones and Neil Anderson, "Gender and Ethnic Group Differences on Personality Scales in Selection: Some British Data," *Journal of Occupational and Organizational Psychology,* 75 (2002), 255–276.
15. Michael A. McDaniel and Nhung T. Nguyen, "Situational Judgment Tests: A Review of Practice and Constraints Assessed," *International Journal of Selection and Assessment,* 9 (2001), 103–113.
16. Todd Humber, "Psychometric Testing Often Misused in Recruitment," *Canadian HR Reporter*, May 17, 2004.
17. David W. Oakes et al., "Cognitive Ability and Personality Predictors of Training Program Skill Acquisition and Job Performance," *Journal of Business and Psychology,* 15 (2001), 523–548; Jay E. Janovics and Neil D. Christiansen, "Profiling New Business Development: Personality Correlates of Successful Ideation and Implementation, *Social Behaviour and Personality,* 31 (2003) 71–80; and C. Viswegvarn et al., "Do Impression Management Scales in Personality Inventories Predict Managerial Job Performance Ratings" *International Journal of Selection and Assessment,* 9 (2001), 277–289.
18. Joyce Hogan and Brent Holland, "Using Theory to Evaluate Personality and Job Performance Relations," *Journal of Applied Psychology,* 88 (2003), 100–112.
19. "Store Chain Settles Lawsuit over Testing," *Omaha World-Herald,* July 11, 2003, 7-M.
20. Lynn A. McFarland, "Warning Against Faking on a Personality Tests for Faking," *International Journal of Selection and Assessment,* 11 (2003), 265–276.
21. Richard D. Goffin and Neil D. Christiansen, "Correcting Personality Tests for Faking," *International Journal of Selection and Assessment,* 11 (2003), 340–344.
22. Gregory M. Hurtz and George M. Alliger, "Influence of Coaching on Integrity Test Performance and Unlikely Virtues Scale Scores," *Human Performance,* 15 (2002), 255–273; Dening S. Ones et al., "Personality and Absenteeism: A Meta Analysis of Integrity Tests," *European Journal of Personality,* 17 (2003), s19–s38.
23. Reagan D. Brown and Christopher M. Cothern, "Individual Differences in Faking Integrity Tests," *Psychological Reports,* 19 (2002), 691–702.

24. Ken Alder, "A Social History of Untruth: Lie Detection and Trust in Twentieth Century America," *Representations,* (Fall 2002), 11–33.
25. *British Columbia (Public Service Employee Relations Commission) v. BCGSEU (1999)*; Victor M. Catano, Willi H. Wiesner, Rick D. Hackett and Laura L. Methot, *Recruitment and Selection in Canada*, Third Edition, Thomson Nelson Publishing, Toronto, Ontario, 2005, p. 22–23.
26. Michael A. Warech, "Competency Based Interviewing at the Buckhead Beef Company," *Cornell Hotel and Restaurant Administration Quarterly,* February 2002, 70–78.
27. "Interviews That Cut to the Chase," *SHRM Forum,* May 2002, www.shrm.org.
28. TD Bank Financial Group, "Job Opportunities: Interviewing Tips," www.td.com/hr/interview_tips.jsp.
29. Arla L. Day and Sarah A. Carroll, "Situational and Patterned Behavioural Description Interviews," *Human Performance,* 16 (2003), 25–47.
30. Paul J. Taylor and Bruce Small, "Asking Applicants What They Would Do Versus What They Did Do," *Journal of Occupational and Organizational Psychology,* 75 (2002), 277–294.
31. Melinda C. Blackman, "Personality Judgment and the Utility of the Unstructured Employment Interview," *Basic and Applied Social Psychology,* 24 (2002), 241–250; Melinda C. Blackman and David C. Funder, "Effective Interview Practices for Accurately Assessing Counter Productive Traits," *International Journal of Selection and Assessment,* 10 (2002), 109–116.
32. Anita C. McClough and Steven G. Rogelberg, "Selection in Teams: An Exploration of the Teamwork Knowledge, Skills, and Ability Test," *International Journal of Selection and Assessment,* 11 (2003), 56–65.
33. Susan G. Strauss et al., "The Effects of Video Conference, Telephone, and Face-to-Face Media on Interviewer and Applicant Judgments in Employment Interviews," *Journal of Management,* 27 (2001), 363–381.
34. Nora Cate Shaeffer and Stanley Presser, "The Science of Asking Questions," *Annual Review of Sociology,* 29, (2003), 65–88.
35. D. S. Chapman and P. M. Rowe, "The Impact of Videoconference Technology, Interview Structure, and Interviewer Gender on Interviewer Evaluations," *Journal of Occupational and Organizational Psychology,* 74 (2001), 279–298.
36. Lynn A. McFarland et al., "Field Study Investigation of Applicant Use of Influence Tactics in a Selection Interview," *Journal of Psychology,* 136 (2002), 383–398.
37. Les Rosen, "Effective Pre-Employment Background Screening," *Protective Operations,* Spring 2002, 1–5.
38. Laura Cassiani, "Upfront Checking Means Fewer Fraud Investigations after the Fact," *Canadian HR Reporter,* November 20, 2000.
39. Office of the Privacy Commissioner of Canada, Fact Sheet, "Complying with the Personal Information Protection and Electronic Documents Act," www.privcom.gc.ca/fs-fi/02_05_d_16_e.asp, June 20, 2005.
40. Rick Barrett, "Employers Run Background Check on Driver Applicants to Curb Liability Costs," *Knight-Ridder Tribune Business News,* March 10, 2004; and "U.S. to Start Airline Background Checks," *Information Management Journal,* March 2004, 1–2.
41. "The Science of Hiring," *Canadian HR Reporter, HRReporter.com,* March 14, 2006; Derek Sankey, "Hire by the Numbers with Professor's Mathematical Formula," *Edmonton Journal,* March 29, 2006, G5; Patrick Brethour, "Sorry, Your Co-efficients Aren't Right for the Job," *The Globe and Mail,* March 7, 2006, pg B1; Piers Steel, Allen Huffcutt, & John Kammeyer-Muller. "From The Work One Knows The Worker: A Systematic Review Of The Challenges, Solutions, and Steps To Creating Synthetic Validity," *International Journal of Selection and Assessment*, Volume 14 Number 1 March 2006; and Paul Stanley, "Formula for Work and Love," *Star-Phoenix*. March 11, 2006, F18.
42. Rebecca Dean, "Are Employers Obligated to Reveal Information about a Former Employee's Misconduct to a Prospective Employer?" www.elinfonet.com/fedarticles.
43. Norman Grossman. "Reference Checks on Hiring," Workopolis.com, March 22, 2006.
44. Peter Israel, "Providing References to Employers: Should You or Shouldn't You?" *Canadian HR Reporter*, March 24, 2003.
45. Joe Mullich, "Cracking the Ex-Files," *Workforce Management,* September 2003, 51–54.
46. Pamela Babcock, "Spotting Lies," *HR Magazine,* October 2003, 1.
47. Cassiani, "Upfront Checking Means Fewer Fraud Investigations After the Fact," *Canadian HR Reporter*, November 20, 2000.
48. Barbara Butler & Associates Inc., 'Who is Responsible—Employer Perspective Dealing with Alcohol and Drug Issues Through a Comprehensive Approach," *Canadian Centre on Substance Abuse*, August 2005.
49. Milazzo and Canadian Human Rights Commission and Autocar Connaisseur Inc. and Motor Coach, 2003 CHRT 37, November 6, 2003, www.chrt-tcdp.gc.ca/search/view_html.asp?doid=502&lg=_e&isruling=0.
50. Earl G. Phillips, "Western Report: Drug Testing in Canada—A Random Step?" McCarthy Tétrault LLP, December 1, 2004; *Weyerhaeuser Co.,* [2004] B.C.C.A.A.A. No. 71 (Taylor).
51. Uyen Vu, "Alta. Employers Push Drug Testing Limits," Canadian HR Reporter, March 28, 2005.
52. Andrea C. Poe, "Selection Savvy," *HR Magazine,* April 2002, 1–4.
53. "Employers Opt for Shorter-Term Expatriate Assignments," *Newsline,* November 17, 2003, *www.mercerhr.com.*
54. Yaping Gong, "Subsidiary Staffing in Multinational Enterprises: Agency Resources, and Performance," *Academy of Management Journal,* 46 (2003), 728–739.
55. Brett Clegg and Sidney J. Gray, "Australian Expatriates in Thailand: Some Insights for Expatriate Management Policies," *International Journal of Human Resource Management,* 13 (2002), 598–623.
56. Joel Millman, "Repats Help Payless Shoes Branch Out in Latin America," *Wall Street Journal,* December 24, 2003, B1.
57. Based on "Sizing up the Candidate Pool" by Shannon Kile, *Canadian HR Reporter*, April 24, 2006. Used by permission of Thomson Carswell.

Part 2 Video Cases

1. "Dead Reckoning," *The National*, June 9, 2003, 13:48 minutes.
2. "Hiring Wars," *Venture*, September 23, 1997, 6:02.
3. "Truth & Consequences" or "Honesty Tests"? *The National*, CBC, September 28, 1998, 21:00.

Chapter 7

1. *Mike Ouellette,* "Training maximizes automation benefits Plant," *Willowdale*: July 11, 2005, 12; "Training for Efficiency," *Omaha World-Herald,* October 14, 2002, D1–D2.
2. "How 3 Companies Make New-Hire Training Mean Business," *Managing Training and Development,* September 2002, 1–3.
3. Service Canada: HR for Managers, www.hrmanagement.gc.ca/gol/

hrmanagement/site.nsf/en/hr11563.html; IAPA, "A Health and Safety Guide for Your Workplace: Orientation Training," May 2006.

4. Charlotte Garvey, "The Whirlwind of a New Job," *HR Magazine,* (June 2001), 1–5.
5. Andy Holloway, "Camp Bangalore," *Canadian Business*, June 29, 2005, 69-7226.
6. "Orientation to the Public Service," *Canada School of Public Service*, www.csps-efpc.gc.ca/ops-ofp/index_e.asp?lang=e&loid=507.
7. Betty Sosnin, "Is a Video in Your Vision?" *HR Magazine,* February 2001, 1–5.
8. Tom Sarner, "Welcome E-Board," *Human Resource Executive,* March 6, 2002, 38–39.
9. Kathryn A. Estrada, "In House Training for Soft Skills," www.shrm.org/hrresources.
10. Uyen Vu, "$824 to Train Isn't Enough, Conference Board Says," *Canadian HR Reporter,* July 18, 2005, 2.
11. "Court Blocks Certain J.B. Hunt Recruiting Tactics," *CCJ Journal*, March 2006.
12. John Lewison, "Knowledge Management," *SHRM White Paper,* October 2001, www.shrm.org/hrresources.
13. Chan Veng Seng et al., "The Contributions of Knowledge Management to Workplace Learning," *Journal of Workplace Learning,* 14 (2002), 138–147.
14. "Action Learning as a Strategy for Enhancing Market Competitiveness," *Global Competitiveness,* January 2002, 1–7.
15. Sharon Daniels, "Employee Training: A Strategic Approach to Better Return on Investment," *Journal of Business Strategy,* 24 (2003), 1–4.
16. Max Montesino, "Strategic Alignment of Training, Transfer-Enhancing Behaviors, and Training Usage," *Human Resource Development,* Spring 2002, 89–108.
17. Anastasios G. Karamono, "Complexity, Identity and the Value of Knowledge Intensive Exchanges," *Journal of Management Studies,* 40 (2003), 1871–1890; and Shari Caudron, "Just Say No to Training Fads," *T1D,* June 2002, 39–43.
18. Richard W. Oliver, "The Return on Human Capital," *Journal of Business Strategy,* 22 (2001), 7–10.
19. "Our Accomplishments," www.ey.com/GLOBAL/content.nsf/Canada/About EY.
20. Daniels, "Employee Training."
21. Amalia Santos and Mark Stuart, "Employee Perceptions and Their Influences on Training Effectiveness," *Human Resource Management Journal,* 13 (2003), 27–44; David N. Ashton, "The Impact of Organizational Structure and Practices on Learning in the Workplace," *International Journal of Training and Development,* 8 (2004), 43–53; and Paul M. Muchinsky, "When the Psychometrics of Test Development Meets Organizational Reality," *Personnel Psychology,* 57 (2004), 175–209.
22. Agnita D. Korsten, "Developing a Training Plan to Ensure Employees Keep Up with the Dynamics of Facility Management," *Journal of Facilities Management,* 1 (2003), 365–380.
23. Nicholas Clarke, "The Politics of Training Needs Assessment," *Journal of Workplace Learning,* 15 (2003), 141–153.
24. David C. Forman, "Eleven Common-Sense Learning Principles," *T1D,* September 2003, 39–46.
25. Ed Welsch, "Cautious Steps Ahead: A Slow Economy Means Readiness Assessments Are Back," *Online Learning,* January 2002, 20–24.
26. Paul Hager, "Lifelong Learning in the Workplace? Challenges and Issues," *Journal of Workplace Learning,* 16 (2004), 22–32.
27. Karen Evans et al., "Recognition of Tacit Skills: Sustained Learning Outcomes in Adult Learning," *International Journal of Training and Development,* 8 (2004), 54–72.
28. Jathan w. Janove, "Use It or Lose It," *HR Magazine*, April 2002, 1–3.
29. Chrysanthos Dellacros: Learning Negotiation Skills: Four Models of Knowledge Creation and Transfer," *Management Science,* April 2003, 1–13.
30. "Transfer of Learning: A Guide for Strengthening the Performance of Health Care Workers," *The Prime II Project*, JHPIEGO Corporation, March 2002.
31. Svernung Skule, "Learning Conditions at Work: A Framework to Understand and Assess Informal Learning in the Workplace," *International Journal of Training and Development,* 8 (2004), 8–20.
32. Jin Hyuk Kim and Chan Lee, "Implications of Near and Far Transfer of Training on Structured On-the-Job Training," *Advances in Developing Human Resources,* 3 (2001), 442–451.
33. R. Owen Parker and Janice Cooney, "Learning and Development Outlook 2005: Moving Beyond the Plateau—Time to Leverage Learning Investment," *Conference Board of Canada*, 2005, 1–56, ISBN 0-88763-687-X.
34. Government of Canada provides over $1.6 million to help integrate immigrants and foreign-trained Canadians into the workforce, *HRSDC, Government of Canada,* November 8, 2005.
35. Kevin Sweeney, "Education Benefits Adds ROI to MBA," *Employee Benefit News,* September 1, 2001, 1–3.
36. Joe Mullich, "A Second Act for E-Learning," *Workforce Management*, February 2004, 51–55.
37. Allison Rosset and Lisa Schafer, "What to Do About E-Dropouts," *T+D*, June 2003, 1–6; and Steve Alexander, "Do Not Pass Go: Why Do Learners Leave Online Courses Before Finishing Them?" *Online Learning*, March 2002, 1–3.
38. K. Boxer and B. Johnson, "How to Build an Online Training Center," *T1D* August 2002, 1–6; "Chains Upgrade to Online Training," *Nation's Restaurant News,* March 10, 2003, 1–4; "All Aboard E-Learning at Air, Rail Companies," *Information Week,* November 8, 2002, 1; "Transfers of Knowledge," *Progressive Grocer,* February 15, 2004; Marilyn Sani, "Masterung Healthvare Applications," *Health Management Technology*, May 2005, 40–42; *Marjo Johne*, "Virtual environments," *CMA Management*, February 2003, 27–32 *Shane Schick*, "Rogers animates staff with e-learning," *Computing Canada*, March 26, 2004, 24.
39. Leslie Laine, "Is E-Learning E-ffective for IT Training?" *T1D,* 57, June 2003, 1–5.
40. "Online Lessons," *American City and County,* March 1, 2003, 1–4.
41. Elizabeth T. Welsh et al., "E-Learning: Emerging Uses, Empirical Results and Future Directions," *International Journal of Training and Development,* 7 (2003), 245–251.
42. Frank Diekmann, "Everything You Wanted to Know About E-Learning," *Credit Union Journal,* July 23, 2001, 1–3.
43. Holly Dolezalek, "Pretending to Learn," *Training,* July/August 2003, 20–26; and Wendy Webb, "Who Moved My Training?" *Training,* January 2003, 1–4.
44. "Survey: School-to-Work Lacks Sponsors," *HR News,* February 2002, 4.
45. Henry Simpson and Randall Oser, "Evaluating Large-Scale Training Simulations," *Military Psychology,* 15 (2003), 25–40.
46. Eduardo Salas et al., "Training Evaluations in the Military," *Military Psychology,* 15 (2003), 3–46.
47. Kathryn Tyler, "Evaluating Evaluations," *HR Magazine,* June 2002, 1–4.
48. Mark A. Davis, "Evaluating Cognitive Training Outcomes," *Journal of Business and Psychology,* 18 (2003), 191–206.

49. Linda Bjornberg, "Training and Development: Best Practices," *Public Personnel Management,* 31 (2002), 507–516.
50. "How to Compute ROI for Online vs. Traditional Training," *HR Focus,* April 2002, 10–11.
51. Andy Meisler, "Companies Weigh the Cost of Prepping Expats," *Workforce Management,* February 2004, 60–63.
52. Stephen Cryne, "Foreign Assignments Increasing, Along with Employee Resistance," *Canadian HR Reporter*, September 27, 2004.
53. Jill Turbin, "Policy Borrowing: Lessons from European Transfer Training Practices," *International Journal of Training and Development,* 5 (2001), 96–111.
54. Based on "Cisco Systems Canada Co. Gives Boost to E-Learning in Canada," April 9, 2001, www.cisco.com/ca/newsroom/releases/elearn.shtml. Reprinted by permission.

Chapter 8

1. Christopher Cornell, "Follow the Leader," *Human Resource Executive,* February 2003, 28–32.
2. State Services Commission, Report on the Capability Project, Paper Prepared for the Minister of State Services, New Zealand, 1999.
3. "The Top 25 Managers," *Business Week,* January 14, 2002, 65–68.
4. Yehuda Baruch, "Career Systems in Transition," *Personnel Review,* 32 (2003), 231–251.
5. Yes-Canada BC, The 10 Step Career Planning Guide, access at http://10steps.careerpathsonline.com/guide/
6. Angela Karr, "Four Questions About Career Pathing," *Customer Interface,* June 2002, 38–43.
7. Eric Raimy, "Ladders of Success," *Human Resource Executive,* January 2002, 36–41.
8. "New and Emerging Occupations," *Occupational Outlook Quarterly,* September 2002, 1–13.
9. Steve H. Applebaum et al., "Career Management in Information Technology: A Case Study," *Career Development International,* 7 (2002), 142–159.
10. Roger D. Wessel et al., "Enhancing Career Development Through the Career Success Club," *Journal of Career Development,* 29 (2003), 265–276.
11. Julie Demers, "Keys to a Successful Career Transition," *CMA Management,* June 2002, 11–12.
12. Aldan Kelly et al., "Linking Organizational Training and Development Practices with New Forms of Career Structures," *Journal of European Industrial Training,* 27 (2003), 160.
13. Stephenie Overman, "Mentors Without Borders," *HR Magazine,* March 2004, 83–86; and George P. Hollenbeck and Morgan W. McCall Jr., "What Makes a Successful Global Executive?" *Business Society Review,* 12 (2001), 49–56.
14. Leslie Gross Klaff, "The Right Way to Bring Expats Home," *Workforce,* July 2002, 40–44.
15. Wilma G. Anderson, "Pre-retirees Offer Planning Opportunities," *National Underwriter Life and Health,* October 27, 2003, 40.
16. Statistics Canada, "General Social Survey: Social Support and Aging, 2002. Released September 2, 2003, Ottawa.
17. Virginia Galt, "Valued Workers Could Stay After 65," The Globe and Mail, Friday, May 2, 2003; Diane Moore, "Baby Boomers Redefining Their 'Golden Years', *Workopolis.com,* November 4, 2003, access at www.workopolis.com/servlet/Content/printer/20031104/goldenyears.
18. Rob Ferguson, "Blame it on Bismarck," Toronto Star, Saturday, August 24, 2004, AO4.
19. Martin M. Greller and Linda K. Stroh, "Extending Work Lives: Are Current Approaches Tools or Talismans?" in G. Adams and T. Beehr, eds., *Retirement: Reasons, Processes and Results* (New York: Springer Publishing, 2003), 115–135.
20. Hewitt Research Advisory, "Ontario Proposes Elimination of Mandatory Retirement," www.hewitt.com, July 18, 2003.
21. "Phased-In Retirement Options Needed for Skill Shortage Challenge," *Canadian Labour and Business Centre*, October 20, 2003.
22. Todd J. Maurer and Nancy E. Rafuse, "Learning Not Litigating: Managing Employee Development and Avoiding Claims of Age Discrimination," *Academy of Management Executive,* November 2001, 110–121.
23. Michelle Quinn, "A New Generation of Women Is 'Sequencing,'" *Denver Post,* May 10, 2004, 6C.
24. L. B. Hammer et al., "Work-Family Conflict and Work-Related Withdrawal Behaviours," *Journal of Business and Psychology,* 17 (2003), 419–436; Linda M. Hite and Kimberly S. McDonald, "Career Aspirations of Non-Managerial Women: Adjustment and Adaptation," *Journal of Career Development,* 29 (2003), 221–235; M. Ferber and G. Green, "Career or Family: What Choices Do College Women Have?" *Journal of Labour Research,* 24 (2003), 145–161; and Toni Schindler et al., "Intimate Partnership: Foundation to the Successful Balance of Family and Work," *American Journal of Family Therapy,* 31 (2003), 107–124.
25. Anne M. Alexander et al., "A Study of the Disparity in Wages and Benefits Between Men and Women in Wyoming" Research Paper, (University of Wyoming, College of Business, 2003), 10.
26. W. G. Darou, Counselling and the Northern Native. *Canadian Journal of Counselling.* Vol. 21:1, 33–41, 1987.
27. Sam Matthews, "Neil French Offers to Quit WPP after Sexist Comments," *BrandRepublic Daily NewsBulletin,* October 20, 2005, www.brandrepublic.com/; "WPP Comments on French Controversy," *Adweek.com*, October 21, 2005; Rob Davis, "Neil French Ousted From WPP After Sexist Remarks Calling Women "Crap"," *viploan.co.uk*, October 22, 2005, "Office Stereotyping and How it Stifles," *Rockford Register Star*, Business: Economy, Times-Post News Service, rrstar.com, November 7, 2005.
28. R. M. McCormick and N. R. Amundson, "A Career-Life Planning Model for First Nations People." *Journal of Employment Counselling.* 34, 1997.
29. "Visible Minorities Face Subtle Impediments to Career Advancement," *Conference Board of Canada*, September 9, 2004.
30. Internship, Equity and & Employee Development Programs, Career Gateway Program for Members of Visible Minorities, Manitoba Civil Service Commission, www.gov.mb.ca/csc/equity/cgpvm.html.
31. Ann Macaulay, IS Awards Celebrate 'Best Employers' of Immigrants: Winners Excel in Recruiting, Retaining and Promoting Skilled Immigrants, *Canadian HR Reporter,* May 22, 2006.
32. Alar Prost and David Redmond, "Employers Need Help with Integration," *Canadian HR Reporter*, December 19, 2005.
33. *"Lessons Learned Series,"* Disability Policies and Programs, Human Resources Development Canada, March 20, 2003.
34. Alar Prost, "Successful Recruiting From an Untapped Resource," *Canadian HR Reporter,* January 16, 2006.
35. Patrick Chang Boon Lee, "Going Beyond Career Plateaus," *Journal of Management Development,* 22 (2003), 538–551.
36. William D. Young, "Career Ladders," *SHRM White Paper,* November 2003, 1–5.
37. Keith Orndoff, "Developing Strategic Competencies," *Information Management Journal,* 36 (2002), 57–62.

38. Cenita Kupperbusch et al., "Predicting Husbands' and Wives' Retirement Satisfaction," *Journal of Social and Personal Relationships,* 20 (2003), 335–354; and Phyllis Moen, "Couples Work/Retirement Transitions," *Social Psychology Quarterly,* 64 (2001), 55–71.
39. Jeff D. Opdyke, "The Cost of a Mobile Marriage," *Wall Street Journal,* January 7, 2004, D1.
40. Julie Cook, "The Dual-Income Dilemma," *Human Resource Executive,* June 6, 2002, 22–26; and Julie Cook, "Gender Gap," *Human Resource Executive,* August 2002, 24–29.
41. "Competitive Intelligence Education: Competencies, Sources, and Trends," *Information Management Journal,* 38 (2004), 56–64.
42. Kelly A. Chillaregen et al., "Learning from Our Mistakes: Error Management Training for Mature Learners," *Journal of Business and Psychology,* 17 (2003), 369–385.
43. Richard Dealtry, "The Savvy Learner," *Journal of Workplace Learning,* 16 (2004), 101–109.
44. Neal E. Thornberry, "Corporate Entrepreneurship: Teaching Managers to Be Entrepreneurs," *Journal of Management Development,* 22 (2003), 329–344.
45. JoAnn Harris-Bowlsby and James P. Sampson Jr., "Computer-Based Career Planning Systems: Dreams and Reality," *Career Development Quarterly,* 49 (2001), 250–260.
46. David Brown, "TD Gives Employees Tool to Chart Career Paths," *Canadian HR Reporter*, June 20, 2005.
47. Joel Schettler, "Building Bench Strength: Assessment Centers Methodology for Developing Talent," *Training,* June 2002, 55–60.
48. Cam Caldwell et al., "Ten Classic Assessment Center Errors," *Public Personnel Management,* 32 (2003), 73–88.
49. Errol L. Biggs, "CEO Succession Planning: An Emerging Challenge for Boards of Directors," *Academy of Management Executive,* February 2004, 105–107.
50. Khai Sheang Lee et al., "Family Business Succession: Appropriate Risk and Choice of Successor," *Academy of Management Review,* 28 (2003), 657–666.
51. James Hutchison, "Succession Planning: Can a Family Member Cut It?" *Practical Accountant,* May 2003, 38–42.
52. Bill Roberts, "Matching Talents with Tasks," *HR Magazine,* November 2002, 1–4.
53. Stephanie Armour, "Playing the Succession Game," *USA Today,* November 24, 2003, 3B.
54. William C. Byham, "A New Look at Succession Management," *Ivey Business Journal,* May 2002, 10–13.
55. Jay A. Conger and Robert M. Fulmer, "Developing Your Leadership Pipeline," *Harvard Business Review,* December 2003, 76.
56. Martha Frase-Blunt, "Ready, Set, Rotate!" *HR Magazine,* October 2001, 1–5.
57. David Boud and Heather Middleton, "Learning from Others at Work: Communities of Practice and Informal Learning," *Journal of Workplace Learning,* 15 (2003), 194–202; and Jan Betts and Rick Holden, "Organizational Learning in a Public Sector Organization: A Case Study of Muddled Thinking," *Journal of Workplace Learning,* 15 (2003), 280–287.
58. Toddi Garner, "The Pause That Refreshes," *Business Week,* November 19, 2001, 138.
59. Ross Fattori, "Sabbatical Surefire Cure for Burnout," *Toronto Sun.Jobboom.ca*, accessed at www.canoe.ca/careerconnection
60. Douglas P. Shuit, "Sound the Retreat," *Workforce Management,* September 2003, 39–48.
61. John P. Meyer, "Four Territories of Experience," *Academy of Management Learning and Education,* 2 (2003), 352–263.
62. Christopher Cornell, "Confidence Rating," *Human Resource Executive,* November 2003, 78–83.
63. Christopher Cornell, "Fail Safe," www.workindex.com.
64. "Corporate Therapy," *The Economist,* November 15, 2003, 61.
65. Juan J. Colombo and W. B. Weither Jr., "Strategic Career Coaching for an Uncertain World," *Business Horizons,* July/August 2003, 33–38.
66. Joy McGovern et al., "Maximizing the Impact of Executive Coaching," *Manchester Review,* 6 (2001), 1–9; and Suzy Wales, "Why Coaching?" *Journal of Change Management,* 3 (2002), 275–282.
67. Kathryn Tyler, "Find Your Mentor," *HR Magazine,* March 2004, 89–93.
68. Stephen Billett, "Workplace Mentors: Demands and Benefits," *Journal of Workplace Learning,* 15 (2003), 105–113.
69. Suzanne C. de Janasz et al., "Mentor Networks and Career Success," *Academy of Management Executive,* November 2003, 78–89.
70. Claire M. Tallarico, "Latest Count of Top Women in Canadian Business Shows Little Progress Since Last Catalyst Census," *Catalyst News Release,* April 27, 2005; "Labour Force and Earnings, Quick Takes—Canadian Women," *Catalyst Information Center*, www.catalystwomen.org.
71. Lynda McDermott, "Developing the New Young Managers," *T&D,* October 2001, 42–48.
72. Tom Starner, "Woman's Day," *HR Executive,* December 2003, 33–38.
73. Jennifer Merritt, "The Education Edge," *Business Week,* October 20, 2003, 86; and Paul Farris et al., "Executive Education Programs Go Back to School," *Journal of Management Development,* 22 (2003), 784–795.
74. E. Joy Mighty and William Ashton, "Management Development: Hoax or Hero," *Journal of Management Development,* 22 (2003), 14–31.
75. "2005 EMBA Rankings," *BusinessWeek OnLine,* Monday, November 14, 2005.
76. David Brown, "TD Gives Employees Tool to Chart Career Paths," *Canadian HR Reporter*, June 20, 2005. Used by permission of Thomson Carswell.

Chapter 9

1. "U.S. Workers Give Performance Management Programs a Failing Grade," *Newsline,* April 19, 2004, *www.worldatwork.org*; and Susan R. Hobbs, "If Everyone Hates Performance Evaluations, Why Do Them?" *Bulletin to Management,* February 7, 2002, 47.
2. Kathy Goagne, "One Day at a Time: Using Performance Management to Translate Strategy into Results," *Workspan,* February 2002, 20–25.
3. Ann Macaulay, Joyce Grant and Uyen Vu, "CEO's Talk about HR Strategies: Gauging HR's Contribution," *Canadian HR Reporter*, May 23, 2005.
4. Brian E. Becker, Mark A. Huselid, and Dave Ulrich, *The HR Scorecard: Linking People, Strategy, and Performance* (Boston, MA: Harvard Business School Press, 2001).
5. Stefan Groeschl, "Cultural Implications for the Appraisal Process," *Cross-Cultural Management* 10 (2003), 67–80; and Kelly Woodford and Jeanne D. Maes, "Employee Performance Evaluations: Administering and Writing Them Correctly in the Multinational Setting," *Equal Opportunities International,* July 2002, 1–9.
6. Edward E. Lawler III and Michael McDermatt, "Current Performance Management Practices," *WorldatWork Journal,* Second Quarter 2003, 49–60.
7. Inge C. Kerssens–von Dronghen and Olaf Fisscher, "Ethical Dilemmas in Performance Management," *Journal of Business Ethics,* June 2003, 51.
8. HR Guide, www.hr-guide.com/data/G000.htm.
9. Marcia McDougall and Laura Cassiani. "HR Cited in Unfair Performance

Review" *Canadian HR Reporter,* September 10, 2001.
10. Abdul-Basit Khan and Robin Reinertson, "Canada: Incompetence or Poor Performance—Just Cause for Dismissal?" *Mondaq Labour and Employment,* September 28, 2005, accessed at www.mondaq.com/article.asp?articleid=35018&hotopic=1.
11. France Lampron and Linda Koski, "Implementing Web-Enabled Performance Management," *Workspan,* January 2004, 35–38.
12. Susan Singh, "Mount Sinai Goes Online for Performance Management," *Canadian HR Reporter,* June 21, 2005. Used by permission of Thomson Carswell.
13. "Performance Management Practices," www.ddi.com.
14. Susanne G. Scott and Walter O. Einstein, "Strategic Performance Appraisal in Team-Based Organizations: One Size Does Not Fit All," *Academy of Management Executive,* May 2001, 107–116.
15. Mehrdad Derayeh and Stephane Brutus "Learning From Others' 360-degree Experiences" *Canadian HR* Reporter, February 10, 2003.
16. Ginka Toegel and Jay A. Conger, "360-Degree Assessment: Time for Reinvention," *Academy of Management Learning and Education,* 2 (2003), 297–311.
17. Gary J. Greguras, John M. Ford, and Stepane Brutus, "Manager Attention to Multisource Feedback," *Journal of Management Development,* 22 (2003), 345.
18. Paul Atkins and Robert E. Wood, "Self- Versus Others' Ratings as Predictors of Assessment Center Ratings: Validation Evidence for 360-Degree Feedback Programs," *Personnel Psychology,* 55 (2002), 871–904.
19. Mark Lowrey, "Forcing the Issue," *Human Resource Executive,* October 16, 2003, 26–29.
20. Uyen Vu, "Marking Staff on a Bell Curve," *Canadian HR* Reporter, July 14, 2003.
21. Camille A. Olson and Gregory M. Davis, "Pro's and Con's of Forced Ranking and Other Relative Performance Ranking Systems," *SHRM Legal Report,* March 2003, 1–7.
22. Michael O'Malley, "Forced Ranking," *WorldatWork Journal,* First Quarter 2003, 31–39.
23. Orna Guralnik and Lori Anne Wordi, "Forced Distribution: A Controversy," *SHRM White Paper,* August 2003.
24. Robert Kaplan and David Norton, "Strategic Learning and the Balanced Scorecard," *Strategy & Leadership,* 24(5), September/October 1996, 18–24.
25. Paul Niven, *Balanced Scorecard Step by Step: Maximizing Performance and Maintaining Results,* March 2002, John Wiley & Sons, Inc., New York.
26. Colleen O'Neill and Lori Holsinger, "Effective Performance Management Systems," *WorldatWork Journal,* Second Quarter 2003, 61–67.
27. Eileen Piggot-Irvine, "Appraisal Training Focused on What Really Matters," *International Journal of Education Management,* 17 (2003), 254.
28. Based on Alron Tziner, Kevin R. Murphy, and Jeanette N. Cleveland, "Does Conscientiousness Moderate the Relationship Between Attitudes and Beliefs Regarding Performance Appraisal and Rating Behaviour?" *International Journal of Selection and Assessment,* 10 (2002), 218–224.
29. Gary E. Roberts, "Employee Performance Appraisal System Participation," *Public Personnel Management,* 31 (2002), 333–334.
30. Sarah Cook, "Appraisal Interviews," *Training Journal,* November 2005; 50.
31. Bob Losyk, "How to Conduct a Performance Appraisal," Public Management, Washington, April 2002, Vol. 84, Iss. 3, pg. 8, 4 pgs.; The Appraisal Interview, slides 22-25, www.busi.mun.ca/jaya/4320/s04/dessler_hrm_9ce_ch10.ppt#446,22.
32. Jonathan R. Anderson, "Measuring Human Capital: Performance Appraisal Effectiveness," (presentation, Indianapolis, IN Midwest Academy of Management, October 2002).
33. Bob Losyk, "How to Conduct a Performance Appraisal," *Public Management,* April 2002, 8–11.
34. Excerpted from "IN THE LEAD: What to Do When Your Favorite Workers Don't Make the Grade," by Carol Hymowitz, *Wall Street Journal,* Tuesday, April 11, 2000. Reprinted by permission of Wall Street Journal, copyright © 2000 Dow Jones & Company, Inc. All Rights Reserved Worldwide. License number 1530870124138.
35. Annette Simmons, "When Performance Reviews Fail," *T1D,* September 2003, 47–52.
36. Jay M. Jackman and Myra H. Strober, "Fear of Feedback," *Harvard Business Review,* April 2003, 101–107.
37. Based on "Adding New Life to Performance Reviews Keeps Employees, Managers Rejuvenated," *Bulletin to Management,* February 7, 2002, 41–42.

Part 3 Video Cases

1. "Country Kids," *The National*, CBC, February 9, 2005, 4:08 minutes.
2. "Executive Pay," *Venture*, December 7, 2003, 6:48.

Chapter 10

1. Based on Stanley Holmes and Wendy Zeller, "The Costco Way," *Business Week,* April 12, 2004, 76–77; "How Big Can IT Grow?" *The Economist,* April 17, 2004, 67–69; and "People Problems on Every Aisle," *Workforce Management,* February 2004, 26–34.
2. Based on Todd Humber, "A Taste For Payroll," *Canadian HR Reporter,* September 12, 2005. Used by permission of Thomson Carswell.
3. Steve Bates, "Top Pay for Best Performance," *HR Magazine,* January 2003, 31–38.
4. Edward E. Lawler III, "Pay Practices in Fortune 1000 Corporations," *WorldatWork Journal,* Fourth Quarter 2003, 45–54.
5. Michael C. Sturman et al., "Is It Worth It to Win the Talent War? Evaluating the Utility of Performance-Based Pay," *Personnel Psychology,* 56 (2003), 997–1035.
6. Frank H. Lyons and Dan Ben-Ora, "Total Rewards Strategy," *Compensation & Benefits Review,* March/April 2002, 34–40.
7. "Soft Side of Rewards Has Hard Impact," *Canadian HR Reporter*, April 5, 2004, 5-7.
8. DowScott et al., "Linking Compensation Policies and Programs to Organizational Effectiveness, *WorldatWork Journal,* Fourth Quarter 2003, 35–44.
9. Jac Fitz-Enz and Barbara Davison, *How to Measure Human Resources Management,* 3rd ed. (New York: McGraw-Hill, 2002); and www.shrm.org/hrtools.
10. Julie Cook, "Local Living," *Human Resource Executive,* November 11, 2003, www.workindex.com.
11. Soo Min Toh and Angelo S. Denisi, "Host Country National Reactions to Expatriate Pay Policies," *Academy of Management Review,* 28 (2003), 606–621.
12. Joyce Head, "How Paper Can Protection International Relocations: The Importance of an International Assignment Letter," *Canadian HR Reporter*, March 13, 2006.
13. Sofiane Sahraoui, "How to Pay for Knowledge," *Human Systems Management,* 21 (2002), 159.
14. Based on Mark P. Brown, Michael C. Sturman, and Marcia J. Simmering, "Compensation Policy and Organizational Performance: The Efficiency, Operational, and Financial Implications of Pay Levels and Pay Structures," *Academy of Management Journal,* 46 (2003), 752–762.
15. R. Eugene Hughes, "Skill or Diploma? The Potential Influence of Skill-Based

Pay Programs on Sources of Skills Acquisition and Degree Programs," *WorkStudy,* 45 (2003), 179.

16. Patricia K. Zingheim and Jay R. Schuster, "Reassessing the Value of Skill-Based Pay," *WorldatWork Journal,* Third Quarter 2002, 72–77.
17. Richard Long, "Pay for Knowledge for Managers to Complex to Put to Use," *Canadian HR Reporter,* HRReporter.com, March 11, 2005.
18. Charlotte Garvey, "Steer Teams with the Right Pay," *HR Magazine,* May 2002, 71–78.
19. Jonathan A. Segal, "Labour Pains for Union-Free Employers," *HR Magazine,* March 2004, 113–118.
20. Paul W. Mulvey et al., "Study Finds that Knowledge of Pay Processes Can Beat Out Amount of Pay in Employee Retention, Organizational Effectiveness," *Journal of Organizational Excellence,* Autumn 2002, 29; and Robert L. Heneman, Paul W. Mulvey, and Peter V. LeBlanc, "Improve Base Pay ROI by Increasing Employee Knowledge," *WorldatWork Journal,* Fourth Quarter 2002, 21–27.
21. Calgary Business Information Centre, Contractor vs Employee, www.calgary-smallbusiness.com/contractor.html.
22. "Bell Settles 14 Year-Long Pay Equity Battle," *Canadian HR Reporter.com,* May 16, 2006.
23. City of Saskatoon, http://city.saskatoon.sk.ca/org/employment_compensation/job_evaluation/index.asp.
24. University of British Columbia, http://hr.ubc.ca/comp/job_evaluation/2950.html.
25. Craig Skenes and Brian H. Kleiner, "The HAY System of Compensation," *Management Research News,* 26 (2003), 109–116.
26. Fay Hansen, "Power to the Line People," *Workforce,* June 2003, 71–75.
27. For details on how to conduct market pricing, see *Market Pricing: Unraveling the Mystery* (Scottsdale, AZ: WorldatWork, 2002).
28. Howard Risher, "Planning a 'Next Generation' Salary System," *Compensation & Benefits Review,* November/December 2002, 13–24.
29. Robert L. Heneman, "Job and Work Evaluation: A Literature Review," *Public Personnel Management,* 32 (2003), 47–72.
30. Nona Tobin, "Can Technology Ease the Pain of Salary Surveys?" *Public Personnel Management,* 31 (2002), 65–78.
31. For further details and discussion, see www.Salary.com.
32. For example, see Richard I. Henderson, *Compensation Management in a Knowledge-Based World,* 9th ed. (Upper Saddle River, NJ: Prentice Hall, 2003).
33. Andrew S. Rosen and David Turetsky, "Broadbanding: The Construction of a Career Management Framework," *WorldatWork Journal,* Fourth Quarter 2002, 45–55.
34. Andrew L. Klein, Kimberly M. Keating, and Lisa M. Ruggerio, "The Perils of Pay Inequity: Addressing the Problems of Compression," *WorldatWork Journal,* Fourth Quarter 2002, 56–62.
35. David A. Katkowski, Gina J. Medsker, Kenneth H. Pritchard, Literature Review of "Acceptable" or "Just Noticeably Different" Pay Increases, Metropolitan Washington Airports Authority, April 5, 2002.
36. "Canada Post Workers Win 20-year Pay Equity Fight," Saturday, October 8, 2005, *CTV.ca News Staff*; Uyen Vu, "22 Years and Counting: Canada Post Pay Equity Dispute Calls System into Question," *Canadian HR Reporter,* November 7, 2005; "Pay Equity Commitment Needs Legislative Action Now," Canadian Labour Congress, June 5, 2005.

Chapter 11

1. Adapted from Julie Cook, "Getting Intuit," *Human Resource Executive,* June 20, 2002, 28–34; and Kathleen H. Van Neck and Jessica Smilko, "Variable Pay Plans: Creating a Financial Partnership with the Workforce," *WorldatWork Journal,* Fourth Quarter 2002, 74–79.
2. Derrick Hynes, *"Variable Pay in Unionized Environments,"* Conference Board of Canada, September 12, 2002.
3. *"Pay-for-Performance Grows Popular,"* www.incentivemag.com, January 25, 2006.
4. Alexander D. Stajkovic and Fred Luthans, "Differential Effects of Incentive Motivators on Work Performance," *Academy of Management Journal,* 43 (2001), 580–590.
5. For details, see Leo Jakobson, "ROI: Show Me the Money," *Incentive,* March 2004, 26–29; Donna Oldenburg, "ROI Incentives: Tools for Measuring Excellence," *HR Magazine,* October 2002, 71–79; and Ravin Jesuthasan, "Business Performance Management: Improving Return on Rewards Investments," *WorldatWork Journal,* Fourth Quarter 2003, 55–64.
6. Tom Wilson and Harold N. Altmansberger, "Taking Variable Pay to a New Level," *Workspan,* December 2003, 44–47.
7. "Licensing of Cyclists and Couriers," The Toronto City Cycling Committee's (TCCC) 1992 Report, June 19, 1992, www.messmedia.org/messville/TCCC92.htm.
8. Chris Taylor, "On-the-Spot Incentives," *HR Magazine,* May 2004, 80–84.
9. "2004 Sales Facts Reports," *Incentive,* February 2004, 34–37.
10. Carol Patton, "Creative Motivation," *Human Resource Executive,* March 16, 2004, 23–25.
11. Leo Jakobson, "Shell Goes Further," *Incentive,* May 2004, 20.
12. Jill Harrington, "Look Who's Creeping," *Incentive,* March 2004, 16.
13. Charles H. Schwepker Jr., "An Exploratory Investigation of the Relationship Between Ethical Conflict and Salesperson Performance," *Journal of Business & Industrial Marketing,* 18 (2003), 45.
14. Jeff Bailey, "Market Spurs More Commission-Only Sales," *Wall Street Journal,* July 22, 2003, B4.
15. "How Are You Covered by the ESA?" *Employment Standards Act,* Ministry of Labour, www.labour.gov.on.ca/english/es/factsheets/fs_covered.html, June 12, 2006.
16. David H. Johnston, "Strategic Initiatives in Sales Compensation," *WorldatWork Journal,* Second Quarter 2003, 75–83.
17. Peter Kurlander and Scott Barton, "Improving Your Odds: Successful Incentive Compensation Automation," *Workspan,* January 2004, 30–33; and "Offers They Can't Refuse," February 17, 2003, www.fortune.com/sections.
18. John M. Bremen and Jan Blackburn, "Where Is Sales Compensation Heading?" *Workspan,* January 2003, 47–60.
19. "Pay-for-Performance Sales Comp Not Living Up to Expectations," *Newsline,* September 24, 2003, available at www.deloite.com.
20. Edward E. Lawler III, "Pay Practices in *Fortune* 1000 Corporations," *WorldatWork Journal,* Fourth Quarter 2003, 45–54.
21. Bianca Beersma et al., "Cooperation, Competition, and Team Rewards: Toward a Contingency Approach," *Academy of Management Journal,* 46 (2003), 572–590.
22. Barton H. Hamilton, Jack A. Nickerson, and Hideo Owen, "Team Incentives and Worker Heterogeneity," *Journal of Political Economy,* 111 (2003), 465.
23. Jerry McAdams and Elizabeth J. Hawk, "Making Group Incentive Plans Work," *WorldatWork Journal,* Third Quarter 2000, 28–34.
24. Andrew Wahl, "Culture Shock: A Survey of Canadian Executives Reveals that Corporate Culture Is in Need of Improvement," *Canadian Business,*

October 10–23, 2005; Michelle Magnan, "People Power," *Canadian Business Magazine,* October 2005.

25. Scanlon Leadership Network, www.scanlonleader.org/.
26. B. Graham-Moore and T. Ross, "*Productivity Gainsharing,*" Englewood Cliffs, NJ: Prentice-Hall, (1983).
27. Robert W. Renn, James R. van Scotter and W. Kevin Barksdale, "Earnings-at-Risk Incentive Plans: A Performance, Satisfaction and Turnover Dilemma," *Compensation & Benefits Review,"* Vol. 33, No. 4, 68-73, 2001.
28. Stephen H. Wagner, Christopher P. Parker, and Neil D. Christiansen, "Employees that Think and Act Like Owners," *Personnel Psychology,* 56 (2003), 847–871.
29. ESOP Builders Inc., "October 2001 Canadian ESOP Survey Results," www.esopbuilders.com/march99news .html
30. Corey Rosen, "To Grant or Not to Grant," *Workspan,* March 2004, 40–44.
31. "A Capital Idea," *Economist,* March 29, 2003, 70.
32. "Pay Packages of European Execs Reach U.S. Levels," January 21, 2004, www.haygroup.com.
33. Louis Aguilar, "Exec-Worker Pay Gap Widens to Gulf," *The Denver Post,* July 8, 2001, 16A.
34. "The WSJ/Mercer 2003 CEO Compensation Survey," *Wall Street Journal,* April 12, 2004, R6; and *The Mercer Report,* May 2004.
35. Anne Freedman, "Executive Bounty," *Human Resource Executive,* May 2, 2004, 44–47; and Alex Frangos, "Perks, Minus the Pizzazz," *Wall Street Journal,* April 14, 2003, R4.
36. R. K. Aggarwal and A. A. Samwick, "Performance Incentives Within Firms: The Effect of Managerial Responsibility," *Journal of Finance,* 58 (2003), 1613–1650.
37. Jean McGuire and Elie Matta, "CEO Stock Options: The Silent Dimension of Ownership," *Academy of Management Journal,* 46 (2003), 255–265.
38. Seymour Burchman and Blair Jones, "The Future of Stock Options," *WorldatWork Journal,* First Quarter 2004, 29–38.
39. Rodney K. Platt, "Sarbanes-Oxley Bane or Boon?" *Workspan,* March 2004, 22–27; and Bill Smiley and Wes Helms, "Corporate Accountability: A Sarbanes-Oxley Primer," *Toronto Users Group for Midrange Systems, March 2004.*
40. "Executive Compensation," *Business Week,* April 19, 2004, 106–120; and Gary Strauss, "CEOs Cash in After Tenure," *USA Today,* April 5, 2002, 1B–2B.37; Charles Elson, "What's Wrong with Executive Compensation?" *Harvard Business Review,* January 2003, 68.
41. Charles Elson, "What's Wrong with Executive Compensation?" *Harvard Business Review,* January 2003, 68.
42. For example, see James J. Corderio and Rajaram Viliyath, "Beyond Pay for Performance: A Panel Study of the Determinants of CEO Compensation," *American Business Review,* 21 (2003), 57–67; and Dan Dalton et al., "Meta-Analyses of Financial Performance and Equity: Fusion or Confusion?" *Academy of Management Journal,* 46 (2003), 13–26.
43. Jane T. Romweber, "The Effects of Good Compensation Committee Governance," *Workspan,* May 2003, 40–43; and Amy Hillman and Thomas Dalziel, "Boards of Directors and Firm Performance," *Academy of Management Review,* 28 (2003), 383–396.
44. Sydney Finkelstein and Ann C. Mooney, "Not the Usual Suspects: How to Use Board Process to Make Boards Better," *Academy of Management Executive,* May 2003, 101–113.
45. Dofasco, "Our Strength Is People," www.dofasco.ca/bins/content_page.asp?cid=339-342-347; "The Best Environmental, International, Community Corporate Citizens and Best Employer for 2004," *Corporate Knights,* June 10, 2004, www.corporateknights.ca/content/page.asp?name=2004_category_winners; Cheryl Dahle, "A Steelmarker's Heart of Gold," *Fast Company,* June 2003, 7; and Dofasco, "Rewards," www.dofasco.ca/bins/content_page.asp?cid=2366-2384.

Chapter 12

1. Jacqueline Taggart, "Benefits: Employers Struggle to Fund Current Health Benefits, Never Mind Making up for Public System Shortfalls," *Canadian HR Reporter*, April 19, 2004, pg. 11*;* David Brown, "Employees Willing to Help Defray Costs of Benefits: Study," *Canadian HR Reporter*, June 14, 2004, 1–2.
2. Mark Cox, "Employer-Sponsored Health Care Costs in Canada to Rise More than 15 Per Cent," *ConnectIT,* February 23, 2005.
3. Joseph J. Martocchio, *Employee Benefits: A Primer for Human Resource Professionals,* (New York: McGraw-Hill/Irwin, 2003), Chap. 1.
4. Kevin Sweeney, "Around the Benefits World," *Employee Benefit News,* October 2003, 35–36.
5. "Benefits for Part Timers and Contract Employees," *Benefits Canada*, June 25, 2003.
6. Elayne Robertson Demby, "Nothing Partial About These Benefits," *HR Magazine,* August 2003, 72–81; and Clarence Lochhead and Alex Stephens, "Employee Retention, Labour Turnover and Knowledge Transfer: Case Studies from the Plastics Sector," Canadian Plastics Sector Council, April 2004, www.cpsc-ccsp.ca/.
7. Examples of metrics for benefits can be found in Jim Simon, "Weighing the Cost of Employee Benefits," *Workspan,* March 2003, 56–57; and Jac Fitz-Enz and Barbara Davidson, *How to Measure Human Resources Management,* 3rd ed. (New York: McGraw-Hill, 2002), 141–156.
8. Don Kerr, Peter Ibbott and Roderic Beaujot, "Probing the Future of Mandatory Retirement in Canada," Discussion Paper No. 04-05, May 2004, Population Studies Centre, University of Western Ontario, London, Canada.
9. Akyeampong, Ernest, "Unionization and Fringe Benefits" in *Perspectives on Labour and Income*. Statistics Canada, Autumn, 2002.
10. Lipsett, Brenda and Mark Reesor, *Employer Sponsored Pension Plans—Who Benefits?* Ottawa: Human Resources Development Canada, 1997.
11. Grant Schellenberg, *Road to Retirement: Demographic and Economic Changes in the 90s*, Canadian Council on Social Development, 1994, 1–132.
12. Uyen Vu, "Cracks Appear in Public-Sector Pension Plans: Bumpy Road Ahead for Some of the Biggest DB Plans in Canada," *Canadian HR Reporter*, February 27, 2006, 1:4.
13. *EBRI 2004 Retirement Confidence Study,* www.ebri.org.
14. George B. Kozol, "Defined-Benefit Plans Emerge as Better Choice for Held Businesses," *Journal of Financial Service Professionals,* March 2003, 41–48.
15. Maureen Minehan, "Employer-Sponsored Pensions," *Workplace Visions,* 1 (2003).
16. Uyen Vu, "DB Shortfall Could Hit $190 Billion," *Canadian HR Reporter*, December 5, 2005, 1:6.
17. David Brown, "Pension Crisis has CFOs Reviewing Plan Design," *Canadian HR Reporter*, May 17, 2004, 1:3.
18. Caroline Helbronner, "The Monsanto Decision in Canada—Partial Wind-up of a DB Pension Plan," *Blakes Bulletin on Pension & Employee Benefits*, September 2005.
19. Greg Hurst and Dorn Smith. *"The Road West,"* Benefits Canada, October 2005.
20. "Health Benefits Costs Have Doubled Since 1990," *The Conference Board of Canada,* News Release, May 21, 2004, Ottawa.
21. "Costs of Health Plans Increases by 13%," Employee Benefits News

Canada, http://benefitnews.com/data/ebncanada.cfm, September 2005; Joanne Sica and Shawn O'Brien, "Challenges and Solutions in Drug Plan Management—Managing Rising Costs on a Global Scale," Cross Border Summit, AON Consulting, October 27, 2005.
22. Peter Merrick, "Rising Healthcare Costs Called a National Corporate Dilemma," Merrick Wealth Management Inc., V8N4, July 2004.
23. "Retiree Health-Care Costs Climb to $63.4 Billion at GM," *Omaha World-Herald*, March 12, 2004, B1.
24. "Postretirement Health Care Benefits in Canada 2006," *Hewitt Associates*, March 7, 2006.
25. "Canada Health Action: Building on the Legacy," Volume II, Synthesis Reports and Issues papers, Health Values Working Group Synthesis Report, May 28, 2004.
26. "Health Benefit Costs Have Doubled Since 1990," *Conference Board of Canada*, May 21, 2004.
27. "Canadians Warned They Will Pay for Medicare Ruling," *Canadian Press*, Saturday, September 17, 2005.
28. Camille Isaacs-Morell, *"The HSA Impact," Benefits Canada*, March 2005, p 53–55.
29. Sonya Felix, "The 2003 Pulse on Plan Members," *Benefits Canada*, October 2003, p 28–55.
30. David Brown, "Employees Willing to Help Defray Costs of Benefits: Study," *Canadian HR Reporter*, June 24, 2004, 1:3
31. Shari Caudron, "Delivering the Tough Benefit News," *Workforce*, September 2002, 32–36.
32. "Gap Emerges Between Employer/Employee Views on Workplace Satisfaction," December 9, 2003, www.metlife.com/researchcenter.
33. Sonya Felix, *"The 2003 Pulse on Plan Members,"* Benefits Canada, October 2003, p 28–55.
34. Andrea Kagan, "Can You Hear Me Now? The Importance of Communicating Employee Share Plans," *Workspan*, February 2004, 36–39.
35. "CIBC Expands Child Care Program for Employees," *Canadian HR Reporter*, February 23, 2005.
36. John Marvin and Nora Spinks, "Backup Child Care: Canada's New Employee Benefit," *Canadian HR Reporter*, November 8, 2004.
37. Andy Meister, "A Matter of Degrees," *Workforce Management*, May 2004, 32–38.
38. Maryann Hammers, "Family-Friendly Benefits Prompt Non-Parent Backlash," *Workforce Management*, August 2003, 77–79.
39. Uyen Vu, "'Sandwich Generation' Challenges big, and Getting Bigger," *Canadian HR Reporter*, October 25, 2004.
40. Nancy R. Lockwood, "The Aging Workforce: The Reality of the Impact of Older Workers and Eldercare in the Workplace," *SHRM Research Quarterly*, December 2003, www.shrm.org/research.
41. Barbara Parus, "Who's Watching Grandma?" *Workspan*, January, 20, 2004, 40–43.
42. Reagan Baughman, Daniela DiNardi, and Douglas Holtz-Eakin, "Productivity and Wage Effects of 'Family Friendly' Fringe Benefits," *International Journal of Manpower* 24 (2003), 247.
43. Patrick J. Kiger, "A Case for Child Care," *Workforce Management*, April 2004, 34–40.
44. Elayne Robertson Demby, "Do Your Family-Friendly Programs Make Cents?" *HR Magazine*, January 2004, 75–78.
45. Jackie Reinberg, "It's About Time: PTOs Gain Popularity," *Workspan*, February 2002, 53–56.
46. Lucky R. Ford and Karen Locke, "Paid Time Off as a Vehicle for Self-Definition and Sensemaking," *Journal of Organizational Behavior*, 23 (2002), 489.
47. Lynn Gresham, "Pet-Insurance Posts Ready Gain in Benefit Offering," *Employee Benefit News*, September 15, 2003, 63–64.
48. For information see Professional Association of Diving Instructors, *www.padi.com*.
49. Kelly M. Blassingame, "The Ship's Come In," *Employee Benefit News*, March 2004, 11.
50. Based on Laura Landro, "Online Data for Health Plans," *Wall Street Journal*, June 20, 2002, D4; and Jennifer L. Gatewood, "Luring the Liabilities," *Human Resource Executive*, March 20, 2002, 23–28.
51. "Employees Prefer to Enroll for Benefits Online," *SHRM Online*, February 27, 2003, www.shrm.org/hrnews.
52. Martin Levy, "C's of Cafeteria Plans," *Workspan*, June 2002, 43–46.
53. Based on "TransAlta Corporation Keeps Pay, Performance the Focus of Total Rewards" and "Banking on a Benefits Redesign" by Todd Humber, *Canadian HR Reporter*, February 23, 2004.

Part 4 Video Cases

1. "Carpenter's Investment Crusade," *Venture*, May 11, 2003, 14:26.
2. "Pension Promise," *The National*, CBC, November 15, 2004, 13:59.

Chapter 13

1. Based on Graeme Hamilton "Westray "Deceit," Deadly Mine Blast Preventable: Probe," *The Gazette*, December 2, 1997, Rachel Boomer and David Rodenhiser "Pay up, Westray Miners Say," *The Daily News*, December 31, 1997, Scott Lilly "How Many Brownies are there in this Administration," *Center for American Progress*, January 6, 2006 and Sara Davis and Mickey Spiegel "Take Tough Action to End China's Mining Tragedies" *The Wall Street Journal*, February 18, 2005.
2. Allan Rickmann and Andrew Ellis, "Must SHE Be Obeyed?" *Safety and Health Practitioner*, September 2003, 42–50.
3. Philip S. Deming, "Crisis Management Planning: A Human Resource Challenge," *SHRM White Paper*, April 2002, 1–5.
4. "Finding the Good Egg: Risk Management Begins with Hiring the Right People," *Commercial Carrier Journal*, June 2003, 41–47.
5. "National Work Injuries Statistics Program," *Association of Workers' Compensation Boards of Canada*, www.awbc.org/English/NWISP_Stats.htm.
6. "Injury Costs Skyrocket Study Finds," *National Underwriter Property and Casualty*, May 12, 2003, 30–33.
7. Wilfred List, "When a Worker Gets Hurt, So Does the Global Economy," *Canadian Occupational Safety*, www.industrialsourcebook,com, August 2002.
8. "Remembering the Sacrifice," *Canadian HR Reporter*, April 28, 2006.
9. "Delivering a One-Two Combination to Fatten the Cost of L.O.S.S.," *Occupational Hazards*, October 2003, 46–51; Paul D. Allison et al., "Corporate Health Revisited: Illness and Organizational Dynamics," *Journal of Applied Behavioural Science*, 38 (2002), 177–190; and Amparo Oliver et al., "The Effects of Organizational and Individual Factors on Occupational Accidents," *Journal of Occupational and Organizational Psychology*, 75 (2002), 473–488.
10. "Tips for Young Workers," Canadian Centre for Occupational Health and Safety. Used by permission.
11. *Due Diligence*, Workplace Health and Safety Bulletin, Government of Alberta, Human Resources and Employment, November 2005.
12. "National Wrecking Company, Supervisor and Worker Fined for Health and Safety Violations," Ontario Ministry of Labour, February 8, 2006.
13. WSIB Claims, Workers Safety Insurance Board, www.wsib.on.ca/

wsib/wsibsite.nsf/public/WSIBBenefits, March 15, 2006.
14. Jerry Landsma, "Red Flags to Spot Possible Comp Fraud," *Business Insurance*, November 24, 2003, 11–14.
15. Pat Byrne, "Compensation Watch—Fast Facts on Compensation Fraud; There's More to it than People Think," *Canadian Occupational Health,* March 2005.
16. Shannon Klie, "How Young is Too Young?: Saskatchewan Reviews Minimum Working Age," *Canadian HR Reporter*, March 13, 2006.
17. "Preventing Musculoskeletal Injury (MSI): A Guide for Employers and Joint Committees," *Workers Compensation Board of B.C.,* BK77.
18. "Prevent Workplace Pains & Strains! It's time to take action!" Ontario Ministry of Labour, January 28, 2006.
19. Todd Humber, "Ontario Grappling with Ergonomics," *Canadian HR Reporter*, April 11, 2005.
20. "Preventing Musculoskeletal Injury (MSI): A Guide for Employers and Joint Committees," *Workers Compensation Board of B.C.,* BK77.
21. "Ergonomics of Teleworkers Often Overlooked," by Bob Fortier, *Canadian HR Reporter,* June 6, 2005. Used by permission of Thomson Carswell.
22. Ann Perry, "Canada Has a High Rate of Office Violence," *The Toronto Star*, December 2, 2003; and Marlene Piturro, "Workplace Violence," *Strategic Finance,* May 2001, 35–38.
23. "Violence on the Job—A Global Problem: Taxi Drivers, Health Care Workers, Teachers Among Those at Highest Risk," *International Labour Organization,* July 20, 1998.
24. Robert Grossman, "Bulletproof Practices," *HR Magazine,* November 2002, 7–11.
25. Workplace Bullying Harms both Employees and Employers, *Canadian Center for Occupational Health and Safety,* V2N8, August 2004. www.ccohs.ca.
26. "Targeting Workplace Bullies," *Canadian Safety Council*, Vol. XLVIII, No. 3, July 2004, www.safety-council.org/info/OSH/bully-law.html.
27. "Workplace Fights Ends in Murder: RCMP Charges B.C. Worker with Second-Degree Murder," *Canadian HR Reporter,* May 26, 2006.
28. Wallace Immen, "Quebec Squares Off Against Bullies," *Commission des normes du travail*, www.cnt.gouv.qc.ca.
29. "Workplace Security," *Wall Street Journal Reports,* September 29, 2003, R1–R8.
30. "On Guard," *Wall Street Journal Reports,* March 11, 2002, R1–R16.
31. Will Strother, "A Security Primer," *SHRM White Paper,* www.shrm.org/hrtx.
32. J. Craig Wallace, "Can Accidents and Industrial Mishaps Be Predicted?" *Journal of Business and Psychology,* 17 (2003), 503–514; and Lovisa Olafsdottir, "Prevention Health and Safety Programs in Companies Provide a More Successful and Healthier Workplace," *Work,* 22 (2004), 27–30.
33. Don J. Eckenfelder, "Why We Need an Antidote for Behaviour-Based Safety," *Occupational Hazards,* September 2003, 98–105; and Steve Roberts, "How to Play It Safe," *Safety Management,* July 2003, 57–62.
34. "Observation Based Safety," Sarnia-Lambton Industrial Educational Cooperative, www.sarniasafety.com/aboutbbs.htm, n.d.
35. Denny Holland and Joe Luetzinger, "Fatigue Management: A Literature Review," *Journal of Employee Assistance*, 33 (2003), 24–35.
36. Philip Tucker, "The Impact of Rest Breaks upon Accident Risk, Fatigue and Performance," *Work and Stress,* 17 (2003), 123–137.
37. "Use This Information to Show Management Why You Need an OTS Injury Prevention Plan," *Safety Director's Report,* November 2003, 1–2.
38. Justin Pritchard, "Immigrants Dying to Work," *The Denver Post,* March 14, 2004, 4A.
39. "What is an Accident and Why Should it be Investigated?" The Canadian Centre for Occupational Health and Safety www.ccohs.ca, March 10, 2006.
40. Health Canada, *Canadian Health Network*, www.canadian-health-network.ca.
41. Canadian Mental Health Association, "Source of Workplace Stress," Richmond, British Columbia, n.d,, www.vcn.bc.ca/rmdcmha/credits.html.
42. Samuel B. Bacharach et al., "Driven to Drink," *Academy of Management Journal,* 45 (2002), 637–658.
43. "Mental Health and the Workplace," *Canada Safety Counci*l, 2005, www.safety-council.org/info/OSH/mentalhealth.html.
44. "CMA Study on Physician Burnout," Canadian Medical Association, November 2003; and "New Nurses Facing Burnout: Study," CBC News, www.cbc.ca, February 28, 2006.
45. George F. Grant, Elvis A. Ali and Elizabeth J. Thorsen, "Occupational Stress Among Canadian College Educators: A Review of the Literature," *College Quarterly*, Winter 1995, Vol. 3, No. 2, Winter 1995.
46. Hans Selve, "The General Adaptation Syndrome and the Diseases of Adaptation," *Journal of Clinical Endocrinology*, 6, p. 117–230; and Hans Selve, "*The Story of the Adaptation Syndrome*," Montreal, Quebec, Canada: Acta Inc., 1952.
47. J. Rehm et al., "The Costs of Substance Abuse in Canada 2002," *Canadian Centre on Substance Abuse (CCSA),* March 2006.
48. Ibid., 2006.
49. Samuel B. Bacharach et al., "Driven to Drink," *Academy of Management Journal,* 45 (2002), 637–658.
50. Matthew E. Paronto et al., "Drug Testing, Drug Treatment and Marijuana Use: A Fairness Perspective," *Journal of Applied Psychology,* 87 (2002), 1159–1166.
51. Ray C. Filion, "Court of Appeal Finally Issues Long Awaited Drug Testing Decision," *What's New in HR Law*, www.filion.on.ca/pdf/caselaws/hr007.pdf.
52. Barbara Morris, "Stress Test 2004," *Human Resource Executive,* January 2004, 38–43; and Cora Daniels, "The Last Taboo," *Fortune,* October 28, 2002, 137.
53. P. T. Katzmarzyk and I. Janssen, "The Economic Costs of Physical Inactivity and Obesity in Canada: An Update," *Canadian Journal of Applied Physiology*, 2004, 29:90–115.
54. T. Stephens and N. Joubert, "The Economic Burden of Mental Health Problems in Canada," *Chronic Diseases in Canada*, 22(12), 18–23, 2001.
55. J. Rehm et al., "The Costs of Substance Abuse in Canada 2002," *Canadian Centre on Substance Abuse (CCSA),* March 2006.
56. Aventis Pharma and Ipsos-Reid, "Aventis Poll on Health Care in 2001," *Report of the Pan Canadian Study*," Montreal, May 2001.
57. Aon, "From the Control of Absenteeism to the Management of Presence at Work, *Forum,* May–June, 1998.
58. "Mental Health at Work…From Defining to Solving the Problem," A Series: Booklet 1, Chair in Occupational Health and Safety, Université Laval, Quebec, Canada, 2005.
59. "Tips on Managing Your Stress," *Canadian Heart and Stroke Foundation*, n.d.
60. "How to Transform a Wellness Program into a Retention Tool," *Safety Director's Report,* September 2003, 5–10.
61. Traci Purdim, "Healthy, Wealthy, Wise and Web Based," *Industry Week,* May 2004, 52–53; and Michael Prince, "Altering Lifestyles Through Internet Fitness Monitoring," *Business Insurance,* April 8, 2002 1G; and "Ceridian Makes Online EAPS and Work Life Services a Real Possibility," *Managing Benefit Plans,* September 2002, 1–2.
62. "National Population Health Survey-Obesity: A Growing Issue" *The Daily.* April 7, 2005. www.statscan.ca/daily.

63. Kathryn Tyler, "Mind Matters," *HR Magazine,* August 2003, 1–4.
64. Linda Sutton, "Setting a Two-Year Plan," *Journal of Employee Assistance,* April 2003, 16–19.
65. John Pompe et al., "EAP Type Services for International Employees and Families," *WorldatWork Journal,* Second Quarter 2004, 69–78.
66. "Manager Confused Bullying with Leadership" by Todd Humber, *Canadian HR Reporter*, December 13, 2005. Used by permission of Thomson Carswell.

Chapter 14

1. Chris Wood, Brenda Branswell and Amy Cameron, "Who's Watching You," *MacLeans*, February 19, 2001; David Zweig and Virginia Galt, "Stop Snooping on Your Employees," *Globe and Mail*, Monday, April 16, 2001; Anne Sharratt, "Lost and found: New Tracking Devices are Helping in Recovery Stolen Goods from Cars to Computers," *Canadian Insurance Magazine*, March 2002; Javad Heydary, "Companies Step Up Electronic Monitoring of Employees," *E-Commerce Times*, July 2005, www.heydary.com/publications/employee-monitoring.html.
2. Yale D. Tauber and Carol S. Silverman, "Employment Contracts Get the Employers in the Game," *Workspan,* August 2002, 38–42.
3. Wallace Immen, "Canadian Executives Target On-line Activity," *The Globe and Mail*, Friday, August 19, 2005.
4. Peter Israel, "Preventing Former Employees from Competing," *Canadian Employment Law Today*, March 17, 2004.
5. Curt Feldman, "EA, Ubisoft Trade Fire Over Hire," *CNET Networks Entertainment: GameSpot*, January 31, 2006, www.gamespot.com/news/6143439.html.
6. Todd Humber, "Protecting the Most Valuable Asset: Covenants Can Protect Employers from Department Staff," *Canadian HR Reporter*, June 20, 2005.
7. Robin M. Kersey, ""An Ounce of Prevention…," Employment Agreements as Preventive Medicine," *Thompson, Dorfman and Sweatman LLP, Publications*, March 1999.
8. David Harris, "Wrongful Dismissal Law in Canada," *Duhaime's Employment & Labour Law Center,* May 2003.
9. Todd Humber, "The Wallace Factor: Landmark 1997 Supreme Court Decision Changed the Wrongful Dismissal Landscape. Here's How to Avoid Being 'Wallaced'," *Canadian HR Reporter*, January 31, 2005, R2.
10. Carrie Brodzinski, "Avoiding Wrongful Termination Suits," *National Underwriter,* October 13, 2003, 38–39.
11. Karen Zvulony, "What is Constructive Dismissal?" *Zvulony & Co. Publications*, n.d.
12. "Canada Labour Codes, Part III, Division X, XI and XIV, Definition of Constructive Dismissal," Government of Canada, No. 815-1-1PG-033, September 25, 2000.
13. Courtesy of Jeffrey S. Lowe, LLB—www.lawyers-bc.com 1999.
14. Norman Grosman, "Court Says Substandard Performance May Constitute Cause," Workopolis.com, April 4, 2005.
15. Kelly Mollica, "Perceptions of Fairness," *HR Magazine,* June 2004, 169–170.
16. Richard A. Posthuma, "Procedural Due Process and Procedural Justice in the Workplace," *Public Personnel Management,* 32 (2003), 181–195.
17. Julia Connell, Natalie Ferrs, and Tony Travaglione, "Engendering Trust in Manager-Subordinate Relationships: Predictors and Outcomes," *Personnel Review,* 32 (2003), 569–580.
18. Corinne Bendersky, "Organizational Dispute Resolute Systems," *Academy of Management Review,* 28 (2003), 643–656.
19. Richard Nimark, "Getting Dispute-Wise," *Dispute Resolution Journal,* February/April 2004, 56–57.
20. Based on Wendy R. Boswell and Julie B. Olson-Buchanan, "Experiencing Mistreatment at Work," *Academy of Management Journal,* 47 (2004), 129–139.
21. "Labour & Employment Law in Canada," Heenan Blaikie, www.heenanblaikie.com, September 2004.
22. Stella M. Swift, Catherine Jones-Riker, and James Sanford, "Legal and Procedural Strategies for Employees Utilizing Arbitration for Statutory Disputes," *Employee Responsibilities and Rights Journal,* March 2004, 37–47.
23. For example, see D.M. McCabe, "Grievance Processing: Non-Union Setting Peer Review Systems and Internal Corporate Tribunals: A Procedural Analysis," *Labor Law Journal* (August 1988) 496; T. Wagar, "Grievance Procedures in the Non-Union Environment" (1999–2000) vol. II *Labour Arbitration Yearbook* 127 at 128.
24. G. Furlong, "Dispute Resolution: Moving Beyond the Open Door," 24 *Canadian HR Reporter*, February 23, 1998, www.agreeinc.com/press10.htm.
25. T.Wagar, *supra* note 23.
26. Margaret M. Clark, "A Jury of Your Peers," *HR Magazine,* January 2004, 54–59.
27. Uyen Vu, "The Lonely Job of an Organization's Silent Referee," *Canadian HR Reporter,* February 23, 2004.
28. Cedric Laurant, "Privacy and Human Rights 2003," www.privacyinternational.org/survey/phr2003/index.htm.
29. For details, see John D. Woodward Jr. and Gary Roethenbaugh, "Fact Sheet on the European Union Privacy Directive," www.dss.state.ct.us/digital/eupriv.html; and Drew Robb, "Restricting Data Flow," *HR Magazine,* April 2003, 97–99.
30. "B.C., Alberta Privacy Legislation Pass PIPEDA Test," *Canadian HR Reporter,* November 3, 2004.
31. Fact Sheet, "Privacy in the Workplace," *Office of the Privacy Commissioner of Canada,* 2004. Reproduced with the permission of the Minister of Public Works and Government Services Canada, 2006.
32. Jonathan A. Segal, "Is It Shredding Time Yet?" *HR Magazine,* February 2003, 109–113.
33. "P.E.I. Student Paper Publishes Cartoons of Prophet," *CBC News*, February 8, 2006; "March Against Inflammatory Professor," *IMC Reporters,* February 9, 2006.
34. Michael J. Gundlach, Scott C. Douglas, and Mark J. Mantinko, "The Decision to Blow the Whistle: A Social Information Processing Framework," *Academy of Management Review,* 28 (2003), 107–123.
35. Steve Miach, "What's A Whistle-blower?, *MacLeans*, June 22, 2005; Mark Swartz, "The Importance of Encouraging Openness," *Workopolis*, February 22, 2006; and "Whistleblower Legislation Bill C-25, Disclosure Protection, *CBC News Online*, April 28, 2004.
36. "Whistleblower Legislation Bill C-25, Discloser Protection," *CBC News Online,* April 28, 2004.
37. "New Whistleblower Legislation Provides Criminal Sanctions Against Employers," *Labour and Employment Law Group,* October 2004.
38. Christina Catenacci, "Supreme Court of Canada Clarifies Provincial Whistleblower Legislation," *Canadian Payroll and Employment Law News,* February 2006.
39. Benisa Berry, "Organizational Culture: A Framework and Strategies for Facilitating Employee Whistle-blowing," *Employee Responsibilities and Rights Journal,* March 2004, 1.
40. Joan T. A. Gabel and Nancy R. Mansfield, "The Information Revolution and Its Impact on the Employment Relationship," *American Business Law Journal,* 40 (2003), 301–353.
41. 21 C.C.E.L. (2d) 137 (B.C.S.C. 1996).

42. Jacquie McNish, "E-Mail Used as Weapon in Court Case," *The Globe and Mail,* Thursday, January 6, 2005.
43. Nancy J. King, "Electronic Monitoring to Promote National Security Impacts Workplace Privacy," *Employee Responsibilities and Rights Journal,* September 2003, 127.
44. "The Year in HR: A Look Back at 2004 Through the Eyes of Canadian HR Reporter," *Canadian HR Reporter*, January 17, 2005.
45. Anthony M. Townsend and James T. Bennett, "Privacy, Technology, and Conflict: Emerging Issues and Action in Workplace Privacy," *Journal of Labour Research,* 24 (2003), 195–205.
46. Kirsten Martin and R. Edward Freeman, "Some Problems with Employee Monitoring," *Journal of Business Ethics,* April 2003, 353.
47. Todd Humber, "Keystroke Logging Violates Privacy," *Canadian HR Reporter*, November 3, 2005.
48. "HR Professionals and Privacy Issues," *Workplace Visions,* 1 (2001), 2; and Wallace Immen, "Canadian Executives Target On-line Activity," *The Globe and Mail*, Friday, August 19, 2005.
49. [2000] D.A.T.C. No. 15.
50. Michael Geist, "Computer and E-Mail Workplace Surveillance in Canada: The Shift from Reasonable Expectation of Privacy to Reasonable Surveillance, March 2002, Prepared for Canadian Judicial Council.
51. Robert H. Moorman and Deborah L. Wells, "Can Electronic Performance Monitoring Be Fair?" *Journal of Leadership and Organizational Studies,* 10 (2003), 2.
52. David Brown, "No-Cameras-at-Work Ruling Not Binding but Typical of Privacy Trend, *Canadian HR Reporter,* November 22, 2004.
53. John M. Ivancevich et al., "Deterring White-Collar Crime," *Academy of Management Executive,* May 2003, 114–127; "Retail Council of Canada 2003 Canadian Retail Security Report: Executive Summary," *Resources Protection Network*, September 23, 2003.
54. Robert B. Cialdini, Peta K. Petrova, and Noah J. Goldstein, "The Hidden Costs of Organizational Dishonesty," *MIT Sloan Management Review,* Spring 2004, 67.
55. Louis K. Obdyke, "Investigating Security Breaches, Workplace Theft, and Employee Fraud," *SHRM Legal Report,* www.shrm.org.
56. Ronni M. Travers, "By the Book: The Whys and Hows of Employee Handbooks," *Government Finance Review,* December 2003, 50.
57. Based on Pamela Babcock, "Sending the Message," *HR Magazine,* November 2003, 66–70.
58. Leanne E. Standryk, "How to Deal with Employee Misconduct," Lancaster, Brooks & Welch, Publications, www.lbwlawyers.com/publications/employeemisconduct.asp. n.d.
59. Adapted from Nicholas Dayan, SPHR, and Saralee Ryan.
60. Miguel A. Malo and Joaquin Perez, "Individual Dismissals in Europe and the United States: A Model on the Influence of the Legal Framework on Firing Costs," *European Journal of Law and Economics,* 14 (2003), 47; Jonathan A. Segal, "Get Quid Pro Quo When They Go," *HR Magazine,* December 2003, 121–125.
61. Adapted from Jorge Talbott, LLB, "Sample Termination Letter," *Labour Organizations.Org,* Ottawa, Canada, April 8, 2004, http://eworklaw.labourrelations.org/stories/2003/08/19/sampleTerminationLetter.html.
62. Based on "Life in Front of Camera Does Not Suit Manager," *Bulletin to Management,* July 6, 2000, 216.

Chapter 15

1. "Quebec Wal-Mart Could Be Unionized," *Canadian HR Reporter,* August 3, 2004; "Second B.C Wal-Mart Unionizes," *Canadian HR Reporter,* March 9, 2006; "Wal-Mart Workers Reject Union Again," *Canadian HR Reporter,* March 9, 2005; "UFCW Wants Quebec's Labour Board to Block Closing of Wal-Mart Store," *Canadian HR Reporter,* March 28, 2005; "Supreme Court Refuses to Hear Wal-Mart Appeal," *Canadian HR Reporter,* April 7, 2005; Roy J. Adams, "Organizing Wal-Mart: The Canadian Campaign," *Just Labour,* Volumes 6 & 7, Fall 2005; "Wal-Mart Attempt to Scuttle Labour Board Quashed by Saskatchewan Appeal Court," July 25, 2006, UFCW Canada, Your Voice at Work, www.ufcw.ca; *Wal-Mart Canada v. Saskatchewan Labour Relations Board,* July 20, 2006, 2006–SKQB–335, Saskatoon.
2. Thomas C. Buckmuller et al., "Union Effects on Health Insurance Provision and Coverage in the United States," *Industrial and Labour Relations Review,* 55 (2002), 610-628; and Daniel B. Klaff and Ronald G. Ehrenberg, "Collective Bargaining and Staff Salaries in American Colleges and Universities," *Industrial and Labor Relations Review,* 57 (2003), 92–104.
3. Barry T. Hirsch, "What Do Unions Do for Economic Performance"? *Discussion Paper Series IZA DP No. 892,* Institute for the Study of Labor, October 2003.
4. International Labour Organization, www.ilo.org, 1995; Jelle Visser, "Union Membership Statistics in 24 Countries," *Monthly Labor Review,* January 2006, 1–49.
5. Neal E. Boudette, "Strategic Shift," *Wall Street Journal,* March 11, 2004, A1; "A Plan to Put Germans Back into Jobs," *The Economist,* August 24, 2002, 41; and "Déjà Vu?" *The Economist,* June 7, 2003, 59.
6. Thomas Palley, "The Child Labor Problem," *Journal of Economic Issues,* 36 (2002), 601–615; Takao Kato and Motohiro Morishima, "The Productivity Effects of Participatory Employment Practices," *Industrial Relations,* 41 (2002), 487–519.
7. Noah Meltz and Seymour Martin Lipset, "Unpublished Survey of on Canadian and American Attitudes Towards Unions," 1997.
8. Daphne G. Taras and Allen Ponak, "Petro-Canada: A Model of Union Acceptance Strategy Within the Canadian Petroleum Industry". In Richard Chaykowski and Anil Verma, eds. *Firm Level IR/HR in Canada.* Kingston Ontario: Queens University IRC Press.
9. Daphen G. Taras, "Alternative Forms of Employee Representation and Labour Policy," *Human Resources Development Canada: Labour Program,* March 6, 2003.
10. Harshaw, M. 2000. "Nonunion Employee Representation at Dofasco," in *Nonunion Employee Representation: History, Contemporary Practice, and Policy*, ed. B.E. Kaufman and D.G. Taras, Armonk, NY: M.E. Sharpe and R.P. Chaykowski, "Advancing Public-Sector Labor-Management Relations through Consultation: The Role of the National Joint Council of the Public Service of Canada," in *Nonunion Employee Representation: History, Contemporary Practice, and Policy*, ed. B.E. Kaufman and D.G. Taras. Armonk, NY: M.E. Sharpe, 2000; D.J. Boone, "Operation of the Production District Joint Industrial Council, Imperial Oil," in *Nonunion Employee Representation: History, Contemporary Practice, and Policy*, ed. B.E. Kaufman and D.G. Taras. Armonk, NY: M.E. Sharpe, 2000.
11. Michael Lynk, "Union Democracy and the Law in Canada," *Just Labour,* Vol. 1, 2002, 15–30.
12. "Here, Unite Latest Duo to Tie Knot," *Nation's Restaurant News,* March 22, 2004, 30.
13. Charlotte A. B. Yates, "Expanding Labour's Horizons: Union Organizing and Strategic Change in Canada," *Just Labour*, Vol. 1, 2001, 31–40.
14. Jason Clemens, Niels Veldhuis, and Amela Karabegovic, "Explaining Canada's High Unionization Rates," *The Fraser Institute: Labour Market Survey,* August 2005.

15. "United Church Clergy Supporting Union," *Canadian Auto Workers,* Winter 2006, Vol. 2, Issue 2; and Virginia Galt, "Labour Movement Searches for New Frontier," *The Globe and Mail,* December 23, 2000.
16. "Alberta: Labour Market," *Social Inclusion Project/Campaign 2000*, 2005.
17. Huberto J. Nunez, "Maquila Workers in Mexico," *Labor History,* 43 (2002), 440–449.
18. Susan N. Houseman, "Why Employers Use Flexible Staffing Arrangements," *Industrial and Labor Relations Review,* 55 (October 2001), 149.
19. Virginia Galt, "Labour Movement Searches for New Frontier," *The Globe and Mail*, December 23, 2000.
20. Maureen Hannay, "The Unionization of Professionals," *Journal of Labor Research,* 23 (2002), 487–499.
21. Uyen Vu, "Targeting Knowledge Workers," *Canadian HR Reporter*, June 14, 2004, p. 7.
22. Ibid. p. 6.
23. Ibid. p. 7.
24. Ibid. p. 7.
25. Leah F. Vosko, Nancy Zukewich and Cynthia J. Cranford, "Precarious Jobs: A New Typology of Employment," *Perspective*, Statistics Canada, Catalogue Number 75-001-XIE, October 2003.
26. Cynthia J. Cranford, Leah F. Vosko, Nancy Zukewich, "The Gender of Precarious Employment in Canada," *Relations Industrielles,* 2003, Vol. 58 N3, 454–482.
27. Deborah M. Zinni, Parbudyal Singh, and Anne F. McLennan, "An Exploratory Study of Graduate Student Unions in Canada," *Relations Industrielles*, Vol. 60, No. 1, 2005, 145–176.
28. Roderick D. Iverson and D.B. Currwan, "Union Participation, Job Satisfaction and Employee Turnover," *Industrial Relations,* 42 (2003), 101–105; and Rosemary Batt et al., "Employee Voice, Human Resource Practices and Quit Rates," *Industrial and Labor Relations Review,* 55 (2002), 573–595.
29. Adapted from Deborah M. Zinni, Parbudyal Singh, and Anne F. MacLennan, "An Exploratory Study of Graduate Student Unions in Canada," *Relations Industrielles*, Vol. 60, No. 1, 2005, 145–176.
30. "Back to Work Legislation: When Negotiations Fail," *CBC News,* October 13, 2005.
31. "Does Your Concern Fall Under the Board," *Ontario Labour Relations Board*, September 2004, © Queen's Printer for Ontario, 2004. Reproduced with permission.
32. "About CIRB: The Board's Role," *Canadian Industrial Relations Board*, March 9, 2006, www.cirb-ccri.gc.ca/about/index_e.asp.
33. Jack Fiorito and William Bass, "The Use of Information Technology by National Unions: An Exploratory Analysis," *Industrial Relations,* 41 (2002), 34–47; Jack Darlington, "Casting the Net Wider; Twelve Tips for Taking the E-Union to the Next Level," Unions 21 Conference, London, March 8, 2003; "Telus Cuts Subscriber Access to Pro-Union Website," *CBC News*, July 24, 2005.
34. John Goddard, "Trade Union Recognition: Statutory Unfair Labour Practice Regimes in the U.S. and Canada," *Department of Trade and Industry*, Employment Relations Research Series No. 29, March 2004.
35. Earl G. Phillips, "Important New Decision on Unfair Labour Practices in British Columbia," *McCarthy Tétrault,* July 19, 2005.
36. Roger Fisher, William L. Ury, Bruce Patton, *Getting to Yes: Negotiating Agreement Without Giving In,* Penguin Books, 1991, 2nd Edition.
37. Guy Leblanc, "The Onex-Air Canada Struggle: Unions Pit Worker Against Worker," *International Committee of the Fourth International,* November 10, 1999.
38. Robert Rogow, "The Structure of Collective Bargaining," *Collective Bargaining in Canada,* ed. Amarjit Sethi (Toronto): Nelson Canada, 1989, p. 132.
39. "Air Canada Granted Bankruptcy Protection," *CBC News*, Thursday, December 4, 2003.
40. Thomas H. Stone and Noah M. Meltz, "Labour Relations," in *Human Resource Management in Canada*, 3rd Edition, Dryden: Toronto, Ontario, 1993.
41. Sebastian Lamb, "The Rand Formula: Heart and Soul of the Labour Movement?" *New Socialist,* n.d.
42. Amela Karabegović, Keith Godin,Jason Clemens, and Niels Veldhuis, "Measuring the Flexibility of Labour Relations Laws in Canada and the United States," *Fraser Institute Digital Publication,* September 2004.
43. Carole Pearson, "Could BC be Canada's Right-To-Work," *Beachhead*; "Wages Lower Whenever Open-Shop Laws Introduced in US," *Labor Notes,* May 2002.
44. David Kiley, "Foreign Companies Cast Long Shadows on Van Negotiations," *USA Today,* August 6, 2003, B1.
45. Charlotte A. B. Yates, ""Making it Your Economy: Economic Justice," *Ontario Federation of Labour,* The CSJ Foundation for Research and Education, 2001, pp. 1–20.
46. Bruce E. Kaufman, "Models of Union Wage Determination," *Industrial Relations,* 41 (2002), 110–157.
47. Corinne Bendersky, "Organizational Dispute Resolution Systems: A Complementaries Model," *Academy of Management Review,* 28 (2003), 643–656.
48. "87-M Strike Pay Boosted," *Canadian Energy and Paper Workers*, 2005.
49. International Labour Office, "Strikes and Lockouts, Workers involved and Workdays not Worked, by Selected Countries," *Yearbook of Labour Statistics*, 2003.
50. Robert Cooper, "Supreme Court of Canada Overturns Law Regarding Secondary Picketing," *Fasken Martineau*, May 2002, www.fasken.com.
51. Parbudyal Singh, Deborah Zinni and Harish Jain, "The Effects of the Use of Striker Replacement Workers in Canada: An Analysis of Four Cases," *Labor Studies Journal*, Volume 30, Number 2, Summer 2005, pp. 61–85, West Virginia University Press; P. Simao, "Statement from Reuters News Service," June 13, 2005, p.1; Lee Selleck, "Royal Oak Mines Didn't Bargain in Good Faith," Rules CLRB, *Labour Times*, December 1993, p. 3; Adrienne Tanner, "Union Reeling Over Mine Blast Murder Charges," *Toronto Star*, October 18, 1993, p. A3.
52. Sarah Oxenbridge and William Brown, "The Two Faces of Partnership?" *Employee Relations,* 24 (2002), 262–276.
53. Ann C. Frost, "Creating and Sustaining Local Union Capabilities: The Role of the National Union," *Relations Industrielles*, 2001, Vol. 56, No. 2.
54. Douglas M. McCabe, "Administering the Employment Relationship: The Ethics of Conflict Resolution in Relation to Justice in the Workplace," *Journal of Business Ethics,* 36 (2002), 33–48.
55. G. Roger King, "New Guidelines from the NLRB on Participative Management Initiatives and Employee Committees," *SHRM Legal Report,* November/December 2001, 1–4.
56. Adapted from "Surviving Union Certification," by Vern Oster, *HR Reporter*, September 12, 2005. Used by permission of Thomson Carswell.

Part 5 Video Cases

1. "The Air Up There," *The National*, February 3, 2003, 16:12.
2. "Young Blood," *Venture*, January 25, 2004, 2:13.

Glossary

A

Aboriginal peoples Defined by the Employment Equity Act as a North American Indian or a member of a First Nation, Métis or Inuit. North American Indians or members of a First Nation include status, treaty, or registered Indians, as well as non-status and non-registered Indians.

Acceptance rate Percent of applicants hired divided by total number of applicants.

Active practice Performance of job-related tasks and duties by trainees during training.

Adverse selection Situation in which only higher-risk employees select and use certain benefits.

Agency shop Employee does not have to join the union, but must pay union dues.

Applicant pool All persons who are actually evaluated for selection.

Applicant population A subset of the labour force population that is available for selection using a particular recruiting approach.

Arbitration Process that uses a neutral third party to hear evidence from both parties and who make final and binding decisions.

Assessment centres Collections of instruments and exercises designed to diagnose individuals' development needs.

Attitude survey A survey that focuses on employees' feelings and beliefs about their jobs and the organization.

Autonomy Extent of individual freedom and discretion in the work and its scheduling.

B

Balance-sheet approach Compensation plan that equalizes cost differences between identical international and home-country assignments.

Bargaining unit Employees eligible to select a single union to represent and bargain collectively for them.

Base pay Basic compensation that an employee receives, usually as a wage or a salary.

Behaviour modelling Copying someone else's behaviour.

Behavioural interview Interview in which applicants give specific examples of how they have performed a certain task or handled a problem in the past.

Behaviourally anchored rating scales (BARS) Scales describe behaviours differentiating between effective and ineffective performers that can be observed and anchor them at points on a scale

Benchmark jobs Jobs found in many organizations and performed by several individuals who have similar duties that are relatively stable and require similar KSAs.

Benchmarking Comparing specific measures of performance against data on those measures in other organizations.

Benefit Indirect reward given to an employee or a group of employees for organizational membership.

Bona fide occupational requirement (BFOR) A justifiable reason for discriminating against a member of a designated group.

Bonus One-time payment that does not become part of the employee's base pay.

Boycotting Union tactic to encourage others to refuse to patronize an employer.

Broadbanding Practice of using fewer pay grades with much broader ranges than in traditional compensation systems.

Burnout The most severe type of stress; a syndrome of complete physical and emotional exhaustion with psychological, psychophysiological, and behavioural components.

Business agent Full-time union official who operates the union office and assists union members.

Business process re-engineering (BPR) Measures for improving such activities as product development, customer service, and service delivery.

Business unionism Based on American tradition, a strategy concerned about improving the terms of employment such as compensation.

C

Canada/Quebec Pension Plan (CPP/QPP) The CPP/QPP are Canada's major pension plans, providing regular payments to people in retirement who have contributed to either of these plans (or both) over the years.

Canadian Charter of Rights and Freedoms Federal law enacted in 1982, guaranteeing fundamental rights and freedoms to all Canadians.

Canadian Human Rights Act A federal law prohibiting discrimination in employment under various prohibited grounds.

Career Series of work-related positions a person occupies throughout life.

Career paths Represents employee's movements through opportunities over time.

Central tendency error Occurs when a rater gives all employees a score within a narrow range in the middle of the scale.

Closed shop Firms that require individuals to join a union before they can be hired.

Coaching Training and feedback given to employees by immediate supervisors.

Co-determination Practice whereby union or worker representatives are given positions on a company's board of directors.

Cognitive ability tests Tests that measure an individual's thinking, memory, reasoning, verbal, and mathematical abilities.

Collaborative HR The process whereby HR professionals from several different organizations work jointly to address shared business problems.

Collective bargaining Process whereby representatives of management and workers negotiate over wages, hours, and other terms and conditions of employment.

Commission Compensation computed as a percentage of sales in units or dollars.

Compa-ratio Pay level divided by the midpoint of the pay range.

Compensable factor Factor that identifies a job value commonly present throughout a group of jobs.

Compensation committee Subgroup of the board of directors, composed of directors who are not officers of the firm.

Competencies Individual capabilities that can be linked to enhanced performance by individuals or teams.

Competency-based pay Rewards individuals for the capabilities they demonstrate and acquire.

Complaint Indication of employee dissatisfaction.

Compressed workweek Schedule in which a full week's work is accomplished in fewer than five 8-hour days.

Conciliation Process by which a third party attempts to keep union and management negotiators talking so that they can reach a voluntary settlement.

Concurrent validity Measured when an employer tests current employees and correlates the scores with their performance ratings.

Constructive dismissal Occurs when an employer did not directly dismiss the employee but the employer changed the job so completely that the employment contract was effectively at an end.

Content validity Validity measured by a logical, non-statistical method to identify the KSAs and other characteristics necessary to perform a job.

Contractual rights Rights based on a specific contract between an employer and an employee.

Contrast error Tendency to rate people relative to others rather than against performance standards.

Contributory plan Pension plan in which the money for pension benefits is paid in by both employees and employers.

Co-payment Strategy requiring employees to pay a portion of the cost of the benefit premiums.

Core competency A unique capability that creates high value and differentiates an organization from its competition.

Correlation coefficient Index number giving the relationship between a predictor and a criterion variable.

Cost-leadership strategy Strategy that approaches competition on the basis of low price and high quality of product or service.

Cost-benefit analysis Comparison of costs and benefits associated with training.

Craft union One whose members do one type of work, often using specialized skills and training.

Criterion contamination The degree to which the criterion measure is influenced by measures or behaviours that are not part of the job performance

Criterion deficiency Describes job performance behaviours that are not measured by the criterion

Criterion relevance The extent to which the criterion measured represents behaviours that constitute job performance.

Criterion-related validity Validity measured by a procedure that uses a test as the predictor of how well an individual will perform on the job.

Cross training Training people to do more than one job.

Cumulative trauma disorders (CTDs) Muscle and skeletal injuries that occur when workers repetitively use the same muscles to perform tasks.

D

Decertification Process whereby a union is removed as the representative of a group of employees.

Deferred profit-sharing plan (DPSP) A plan that gives employees a share in the profits of the company that is paid out as a pension at retirement.

Defined-benefit pension plan (DBPP) Retirement program in which an employee is promised a pension amount based on age and service.

Defined-contribution pension plan (DCPP) Retirement program in which the employers makes an annual payment to an employee's pension account.

Designated group members Those who are most disadvantaged in employment opportunities: women, Aboriginal peoples, visible minorities, and persons with disabilities.

Development Efforts to improve employees' abilities to handle a variety of assignments and to cultivate employees' capabilities beyond those required by the current job.

Differentiation strategy Strategy that is more appropriate in a dynamic environment characterized by rapid change, and requires continually finding new products and new markets.

Direct discrimination An adverse distinction based on a prohibited ground.

Discipline Form of training that enforces organizational rules.

Disparate impact Occurs when designated group members are substantially underrepresented in employment decisions

Distress A negative and harmful stress that, when prolonged, can lead to disease, poor performance, and impaired interpersonal relationships.

Distributive justice Perceived fairness in the distribution of outcomes.

Draw Amount advanced from and repaid to future commissions earned by the employee.

Dual-career ladder System that allows a person to advance up either a management ladder or a corresponding ladder on the technical/professional side of a career.

Due diligence Employers shall take all reasonable precautions, under the particular circumstances, to prevent injuries or accidents in the workplace.

Due process Requirement that the employer use fair means to determine employee wrongdoing and/or disciplinary measures, and that the employee have an opportunity to explain and defend his or her actions.

Duty Larger work segment composed of several tasks that are performed by an individual.

Duty to accommodate An employer's legal duty to take reasonable steps, in policies or conditions of work, to accommodate an employee's individual needs.

E

Earnings-at-risk Incentive plans designed to enhance performance, in part, by creating base wage dissatisfaction that, in turn, triggers greater effort directed toward performance behaviours rewarded with incentive pay.

Economic value added (EVA) Net operating profit of a firm after the cost of capital is deducted.

E-learning Use of the Internet or an organizational Intranet to conduct training online.

Employee assistance program (EAP) Program that provides counselling and other help to employees having emotional, physical, or other personal problems.

Employee stock ownership plan (ESOP) Plan whereby employees have significant stock ownership in their employers.

Employment contract Agreement that formally outlines the details of employment.

Employment "test" Any employment procedure used as the basis for making an employment-related decision.

Employment Insurance (EI) Provides temporary financial assistance for unemployed Canadians while they look for work or upgrade their skills. Eligibility depends on the individuals previous work record.

Encapsulated development Situation in which an individual learns new methods and ideas in a development course and returns to a work unit that is still bound by old attitudes and methods.

Engagement survey Engagement is defined as the degree to which workers identify with, are motivated by, and are willing to expend extra effort for their employer.

Entitlement philosophy Assumes that individuals who have worked another year are entitled to pay increases, with little regard for performance differences.

Environmental scanning Process of studying the environment of the organization to pinpoint opportunities and threats.

Equity Perceived fairness between what a person does and what the person receives.

E-recruiting methods Electronic method for recruiting, including internet job boards, professional/career websites, and employer websites.

Ergonomics Study and design of the work environment to address physiological and physical demands on individuals.

Eustress Positive stress that is usually short-term that arises when motivation and inspiration are needed.

Exit interview An interview in which individuals are asked to give their reasons for leaving the organization.

Expatriate Citizen of one country who is working in a second country and employed by an organization headquartered in the first country.

F

Federation Group of autonomous national and international unions.

Feedback Amount of information employees receive about how well or how poorly they have performed.

First contract arbitration Once a newly formed union has been certified, the employer and the union must negotiate a first contract within a specified period of time.

Flexible benefits plan Program that allows employees to select the benefits they prefer from groups of benefits established by the employer.

Flexible staffing Use of workers who are not traditional employees.

Flextime Scheduling arrangement in which employees work a set number of hours a day but vary starting and ending times.

Focused strategy Occurs when a firm concentrates its efforts on serving a distinctively defined market segment, which may include some combination of a portion of a product line, particular customer segment, limited geographic area or particularly distribution channel.

Forced distribution Performance appraisal method in which ratings of employees' performance are distributed along a bell-shaped curve.

Forecasting Using information from the past and the present to identify expected future conditions.

G

Gainsharing System of sharing with employees greater-than-expected gains in profits and/or productivity according to a predetermined formula.

Glass ceiling Discriminatory practices that have prevented women and other protected-class members from advancing to executive-level jobs.

Glass walls/glass elevators Practice of advancing women to senior management in positions that pay less than compared to other jobs.

Global market approach Compensation plan that attempts to be more comprehensive in providing base pay, incentives, benefits, and relocation expenses regardless of the country to which the employee is assigned.

Graphic rating scale Scale that allows the rater to mark an employee's performance on a continuum.

Green-circled employee Incumbent who is paid below the range set for the job.

Grievance Complaint formally stated in writing.

Grievance arbitration Means by which a third party settles disputes arising from different interpretations of a labour contract.

Grievance procedures Formal channels of communication used to resolve grievances.

Group RRSPs A collection of individual RRSPs administered by the employer for the employees of a company.

H

Halo effect Occurs when a rater scores an employee high on all job criteria because of performance in one area.

Hazard Any activity, situation, or substance that can cause harm.

Health General state of physical, mental, and emotional well-being.

Health maintenance organization (HMO) Plan that provides services for a fixed period on a pre-paid basis.

Health promotion Supportive approach of facilitating and encouraging health actions and lifestyles among employees.

Health spending account (HSA) One that provides employer financial contributions to employees to cover their own health-related expenses.

Host-country national Citizen of one country who is working in that country and employed by an organization headquartered in a second country.

Hostile environment Sexual harassment in which an individual's work performance or psychological well-being is unreasonably affected by intimidating or offensive working conditions.

HR audit Formal research effort that evaluates the current state of HR management in an organization.

HR generalist A person who has responsibility for performing a variety of HR activities.

HR metrics Specific measure tied to HR performance indicators.

HR specialist A person who has in-depth knowledge and expertise in a limited area of HR.

HR strategies Means used to anticipate and manage the supply of and demand for human resources.

Human capital The collective value of the capabilities, knowledge, skills, life experiences, and motivation of an organizational workforce.

Human resource (HR) management The policies, practices, and systems that influence employee's behaviour, attitude, and performance in the attainment of organizational goals.

Human resource capabilities Consists of reliable access to the required people (quantity) with the skills, abilities, attributes, and competencies (quality) that the organization needs to meet its purpose and deliver its outputs, in accordance with its strategic goals.

Human resource planning (HRP) The process of analyzing and identifying the need for and availability of human resources so that the organization can meet its objectives.

Human resource management system (HRMS) An integrated system providing information used by HR management, in conjunction with other managers in decision making; a system that lets you keep track of all your employees and information about them, usually done in a database or, more often, in a series of inter-related databases.

I

Immediate confirmation Based on the idea that people learn best if reinforcement and feedback are given after training.

Improshare A gainsharing program in which the gain is the decrease in the labour hours needed to produce one unit of product with the gains spent equally between the organization and its employees.

Independent contractors Workers who perform specific service on a contract basis.

Individual-centred career planning Career planning that focuses on an individual career rather than on organizational needs.

Industrial union One that includes many persons working in the same industry or company, regardless of jobs held.

Informal training Training that occurs through interactions and feedback among employees.

Inter-rater reliability Inter-rater reliability is the degree of agreement between different observers, or between the same observer on two different occasions.

J

Job Grouping of tasks, duties, and responsibilities that constitutes the total work assignment for employees.

Job analysis Systematic way of gathering and analyzing information about the content, context, and human requirements of jobs.

Job criteria Important elements in a given job.

Job description Indentification of the task, duties, and responsibilities of a job.

Job design Organizing tasks, duties, and responsibilities into a productive unit of work.

Job enlargement Broadening the scope of a job by expanding the number of different tasks to be performed.

Job enrichment Increasing the depth of a job by adding responsibility for planning, organizing, controlling, or evaluating the job.

Job evaluation Formal, systematic means to identify the relative worth of jobs within an organization.

Job family Group of jobs having common organizational characteristics.

Job posting System in which the employer provides notices of job openings and employees respond by applying.

Job rotation Process of shifting a person from job to job.

Job sharing Scheduling arrangement in which two employees perform the work of one full-time job.

Job specifications The knowledge, skills, and abilities (KSAs) an individual needs to perform a job satisfactorily.

Just cause Reasonable justification for taking employment-related action.

Just noticeable difference (JND) Sometimes referred to as just-meaningful pay, is the minimum pay increase that employees will see as making a substantial change in compensation.

K

Knowledge management The way an organization identifies and leverages knowledge in order to be competitive.

L

Labour force population All individuals who are available for selection if all possible recruitment strategies are used.

Labour markets External supply pool from which organizations attract employees.

Leniency error Occurs when ratings of all employees fall at the high end of the scale.

Locked-in The contributions to the plan that cannot be withdrawn by the employee.

Lockout Shutdown of company operations undertaken by management to prevent union members from working.

Lockout/tagout Requirement that locks and tags be used to make equipment inoperative for repair or adjustment.

Lump-sum increase (LSI) One-time payment of all or part of a yearly pay increase.

M

Maintenance-of-membership shop Workers remain members of the union for the period of the labour contract.

Managed health care Approaches that monitor and reduce medical costs through restrictions and market system alternatives.

Management by objectives (MBO) Performance appraisal method that specifies the performance goals that an individual and manager mutually identify.

Management mentoring Relationship in which experienced managers aid individuals in the earlier stages of their careers.

Management rights Rights reserved so that the employer can manage, direct, and control its business.

Mandatory issues Collective bargaining issues identified specifically by labour laws or court decisions as subject to bargaining.

Mandatory terms Also known as articles or clauses, which must be included in a contract agreement in order to comply with labour relations legislation.

Marginal job functions Duties that are part of a job but are incidental or ancillary to the purpose and nature of the job.

Market banding Grouping jobs into pay grades based on similar market survey amounts.

Market line Graph line that shows the relationship between job value as determined by job evaluation points and job value as determined by pay survey rates.

Market pricing Use of pay survey data to identify the relative value of jobs based on what other employers pay for similar jobs.

Massed practice Practice performed all at once.

Mediation Process by which a third party helps the negotiators reach a settlement

Mentoring Relationship in which experienced managers aid individuals in the earlier stages of their careers.

Merit pay Merit pay programs reward employees with permanent increases to base pay according to differences in performance.

Multiculturalism Ensures that all citizens can keep their identities, can take pride in their ancestry, and have a sense of belonging.

N

Negligent hiring Occurs when an employer fails to check an employee's background and the employee injures someone.

Negligent retention Occurs when an employer becomes aware that an employee may be unfit for employment, continues to employ the person, and the person injures someone.

Nepotism Practice of allowing relatives to work for the same employer.

Non-compete agreements Agreements that prohibit individuals who leave the organization from competing with an employer in the same line of business for a specified period of time.

Non-contributory plan Pension plan in which all the funds for pension benefits are provided by the employer.

Non-directive interview Interview that uses questions developed from the answers to previous questions.

O

Occupational health hazard An occupational health hazard is any material or condition that may cause occupational injuries and/or illness.

Offshoring Moving of work that would typically have been done domestically, to another country.

Old age security (OAS) The OAS pension program provides a monthly retirement benefit based on your age and the amount of time you have lived in Canada.

Open shop Workers are not required to join or pay dues to a union.

Organizational culture The shared values and beliefs in an organization; of a workforce.

Organizational strategy The pattern of decisions in a company that determines and reveals its objectives, purposes or goals, produces the principle policies and plans for achieving those goals.

Organization-centred career planning Career planning that focuses on jobs and on identifying career paths that provide for the logical progression of people between jobs in an organization.

Orientation Planned introduction of new employees to their jobs, co-workers, and the organization.

Outsourcing Business strategy that companies implement to focus on core functions in order to reduce costs.

P

Paid-time-off (PTO) plans Plans that combine all sick leave, vacation time, and holidays into a total number of hours or days that employees can take off with pay.

Panel interview Interview in which several interviewers meet with the candidate at the same time.

Pay compression Occurs when the differences among individuals with different levels of experience and performance become small.

Pay equity Right to equal pay for work of equal value. The value of the job is based on the levels of skill, effort, responsibility, and working conditions involved in doing the work. .

Pay-for-performance philosophy Requires that compensation changes reflect individual performance differences.

Pay grades Groupings of individual jobs having approximately the same job worth.

Pay survey Collection of data on compensation rates for workers performing similar jobs in other organizations.

Pension plan Retirement program established and funded by the employer and employees.

Performance appraisal Process of evaluating how well employees perform their jobs and then communicating that information to the employees.

Performance consulting Process in which a trainer and the organizational client work together to determine what needs to be done to improve results.

Performance management Composed of the processes used to identify, measure, communicate, develop, and reward employee performance.

Performance standards Indicators of what the job accomplishes and how performance is measured in key areas of the job description.

Perquisites (perks) Special benefits—usually non-cash items—for executives.

Person/job fit Matching characteristics of people with characteristics of jobs; match between individual KSAs and demands of the job or the needs/desires of an individual and what is provided by the job.

Person-organization fit The congruence between individuals and organizational factors.

Persons with disabilities Defined by the Employment Equity Act as persons who have a long-term or recurring physical, mental, sensory, psychiatric, or learning implement.

Personal protective equipment (PPE) Clothing or equipment worn to minimize a hazard.

Physical ability tests Tests that measure an individual's abilities such as strength, endurance, and muscular movement.

Picketing A form of non-violent resistance in which people congregate outside a place of work or location where an event is taking place to attempt to dissuade others from going in.

Placement Fitting a person to the right job.

Policies General guidelines that focus organizational actions.

Portability A pension plan feature that allows employees to move their pension benefits from one employer to another.

Position The group of tasks, duties, and responsibilities performed by an individual employee.

Predictive validity Measured when test results of applicants are compared with subsequent job performance.

Predictors Measurable or visible indicators of a selection criterion.

Preferred provider organization (PPO) A health-care provider that contracts with an employer group to supply health-care services to employees at a competitive rate.

Primacy effect Occurs when a rater gives greater weight to information received first when appraising an individual's performance.

Procedural justice Perceived fairness of the processes used to make decisions about employees.

Procedures Customary methods of handling activities.

Profit sharing System to distribute a portion of the profits of the organization to employees.

Provincial and territorial human rights legislation All provinces and territories have their own human rights laws and commissions prohibiting discrimination in employment.

Provincial medicare Canada's publicly funded health-care system provides essential and affordable health-care services for all Canadians, regardless of their income. It is administered on a provincial or territorial basis, within guidelines set by the federal government.

Psychometric practices Concerned with the design, administration, and interpretation of quantitative tests for the measurement of psychological variables such as intelligence, aptitude, and personality traits.

Psychomotor tests Tests that measure dexterity, hand-eye coordination, arm-hand steadiness, and other factors.

Q

Quid pro quo Sexual harassment in which employment outcomes are linked to the individual granting sexual favours.

R

Ranking Performance appraisal method in which all employees are listed from highest to lowest in performance.

Rater bias Occurs when a rater's values or prejudices distort the rating.

Ratification Process by which union members vote to accept the terms of a negotiated labour agreement.

Rating scale Effective and ineffective performers that can be observed and anchors them at points on a scale.

Realistic job preview (RJP) Process through which a job applicant receives an accurate picture of a job.

Recency effect Occurs when a rater gives greater weight to recent events when appraising an individual's performance.

Recruiting Process of generating a pool of qualified applicants for organizational jobs.

Red-circled employee Incumbent who is paid above the range set for the job.

Reinforcement Based on the idea that people tend to repeat responses that give them some type of positive reward and avoid actions associated with negative consequences.

Reliability Consistency of your measurement, or the degree to which an instrument measures the same way each time it is used under the same condition with the same subjects

Repatriation Planning, training, and reassignment of global employees to their home countries.

Responsibilities Obligations to perform certain tasks and duties.

Return on investment (ROI) Calculation showing the value of expenditures for HR activities.

Reverse discrimination When a person is denied an opportunity because of preferences given to designated group members who may be less qualified.

Right to privacy An individual's freedom from unauthorized and unreasonable intrusion into their personal affairs.

Rights Powers, privileges, or interests that belong to a person by law, nature, or tradition.

Rucker plan A gainsharing program in which the ratio measuring the gain compares labour costs to the value added in production (output minus the cost of materials, supplies, and services).

Rules Specific guidelines that regulate and restrict the behaviour of individuals.

S

Sabbatical Paid time off the job to develop and rejuvenate oneself.

Safety Condition in which the physical well-being of people is protected.

Safety hazard Any force strong enough to cause injury in an accident. An injury caused by a safety hazard is usually obvious.

Salaries Consistent payments made each period regardless of the number of hours worked.

Salting Practice in which unions hire and pay people to apply for jobs at certain companies.

Scanlan plan A gainsharing program in which the employees receive a bonus if the ratio of labour costs to the sales value of production is below a set standard.

Security Protection of employees and organizational facilities.

Security audit Comprehensive review of organizational security.

Selection Process of choosing individuals with qualifications needed to fill jobs in an organization.

Selection criterion Characteristic that a person must have to do a job successfully.

Selection rate Percentage hired from a given group of candidates.

Self-efficacy Person's belief that he or she *can* successfully learn the training program content.

Seniority Time spent in the organization or on a particular job.

Separation agreement Agreement in which a terminated employee agrees not to sue the employer, in exchange for specified benefits.

Severance pay Security benefit voluntarily offered by employers to employees who lose their jobs.

Sexual harassment Sexual harassment is unwanted, often coercive, sexual behaviour directed by one person towards another.

Simulation Technique that requires participants to analyze a situation and decide the best course of action according to the data given.

Situational interview Structured interview composed of questions about how applicants might handle specific job situations.

Situational judgment tests Tests that measure a person's judgment in work settings.

Skill variety Extent to which the work requires several different activities for successful completion.

Social unionism Based on a Canadian perspective, a strategy concerned with the terms of employment and the broader economic and social changes that benefit all of society.

Spaced practice Practice performed in several sessions spaced over a period of hours or days.

Statutory rights Rights based on laws or statutes.

Stock option plan Plan that gives the right to purchase a fixed number of shares of company stock at a specific price for a limited period of time.

Stock purchase plan Plan in which the corporation provides matching funds equal to the amount invested by the employee for the purchase of stock in the company.

Straight piece-rate system Pay system in which wages are determined by multiplying the number of units produced by the piece rate for one unit.

Strategic HR management (SHRM) Process of linking the HR function with the strategic objectives of the organization in order to improve performance.

Stress The result of any emotional, physical, social, economic, or other factors that require a response or change.

Stress interview Interview designed to create anxiety and put pressure on applicants to see how they respond.

Stressors The external situations that lead to stress.

Strictness error Occurs when ratings of all employees fall at the low end of the scale.

Strike Work stoppage in which union members refuse to work in order to put pressure on an employer.

Structured interview Interview that uses a set of standardized questions asked of all job applicants.

Substance abuse Use of illicit substances or misuse of controlled substances, alcohol, or other drugs.

Succession planning Process of identifying a longer-term plan for the orderly replacement of key employees.

Systemic (or constructive) discrimination Systemic discrimination occurs when a seemingly neutral policy or practice results in unintentional discrimination.

T

Task Distinct, identifiable work activity composed of motions.

Task identity Extent to which the job includes a "whole" identifiable unit of work that is carried out from start to finish and that results in a visible outcome.

Task significance Impact the job has on other people.

Tax equalization plan Compensation plan used to protect expatriates from negative tax consequences.

Team interview Interview in which applicants are interviewed by the team members with whom they will work.

Tax equalization plan Compensation plan used to protect expatriates from negative tax consequences.

Third-country national Citizen of one country who is working in a second country and employed by an organization headquartered in a third country.

Training Process whereby people acquire the necessary knowledge, skills, and abilities (KSAs) to perform jobs.

U

Undue hardship Significant difficulty or expense imposed on an employer in making an accommodation for individuals with disabilities.

Union Formal association of workers that promotes the interests of its members through collective action.

Union authorization card Card signed by an employee to designate a union as her or his collective bargaining agent.

Union certification Occurs when a union becomes the legal representative for designated employees as granted by the labour relations board.

Union density The proportion of paid workers who are union members and who have signed union membership cards.

Union security provisions Contract clauses to help the union obtain and retain members.

Union shop Workers who must join the union after a specified period of time and pay union dues at that time.

Union steward Employee selected to serve as the first-line representation of unionized workers.

V

Validity Extent to which a test actually measures what it says it measures. In selection, validity is the correlation between a predictor and job performance.

Variable pay Compensation linked directly to individual, group/team, and/or organizational performance.

Vesting Right of employees to receive certain benefits from their pension plans.

Visible minorities Persons (other than Aboriginal peoples) who are non-Caucasian in race or non-White in colour.

Voluntary terms The unique issues that come from the employer and the union.

W

Wages Payments directly calculated on the amount of time worked.

Wellness programs Programs designed to maintain or improve employee health before problems arise.

Well-pay Extra pay for not taking sick leave.

Whistleblowers Individuals who report real or perceived wrongs committed by their employers.

Work Effort directed toward accomplishing results.

Work sample tests Tests that require an applicant to perform a simulated job task.

Workers' compensation Security benefits provided to persons injured on the job.

Workflow analysis Study of the way work (inputs, activities, and outputs) moves through an organization.

Workplace hazardous materials information system (WHMIS) A comprehensive plan for providing information on the safe handling of hazardous materials used in Canadian workplaces.

Wrongful dismissal Termination of an individual's employment for reasons that are unfair, unreasonable, or without sufficient cause.

Y

Yield ratios Comparisons of the number of applicants at one stage of the recruiting process with the number at the next stage.

Name Index

Subject Index